PEÑÍNGUIDE TO SPANISH WINE

2013

www.guiapenin.com

Team:

Director: Carlos González
Editor in Chief: Javier Luengo
Tasting team: Carlos González, Javier Luengo and Pablo Vecilla
Texts: Javier Luengo, Carlos González and José Peñín
Database manager: Erika Laymuns
Advertising: Luna Castañeda
Cover design, layout and desktop publishing: Javier Herrán
Supervising editor: José Peñín

PUBLISHED BY: PI&ERRE
Santa Leonor, 65 - Edificio A - Bajo A
28037 – MADRID
SPAIN
Tel.: 0034 914 119 464 - Fax: 0034 915 159 499
comunicacion@guiapenin.com
www.guiapenin.com

ISBN: 978-84-95203-88-5
Copyright library: M-39030-2012
Printed by: Gamacolor

DISTRIBUTED BY: GRUPO COMERCIAL ANAYA
Juan Ignacio Luca de Tena, 15
Tel: 0034 913 938 800
28027 MADRID
SPAIN

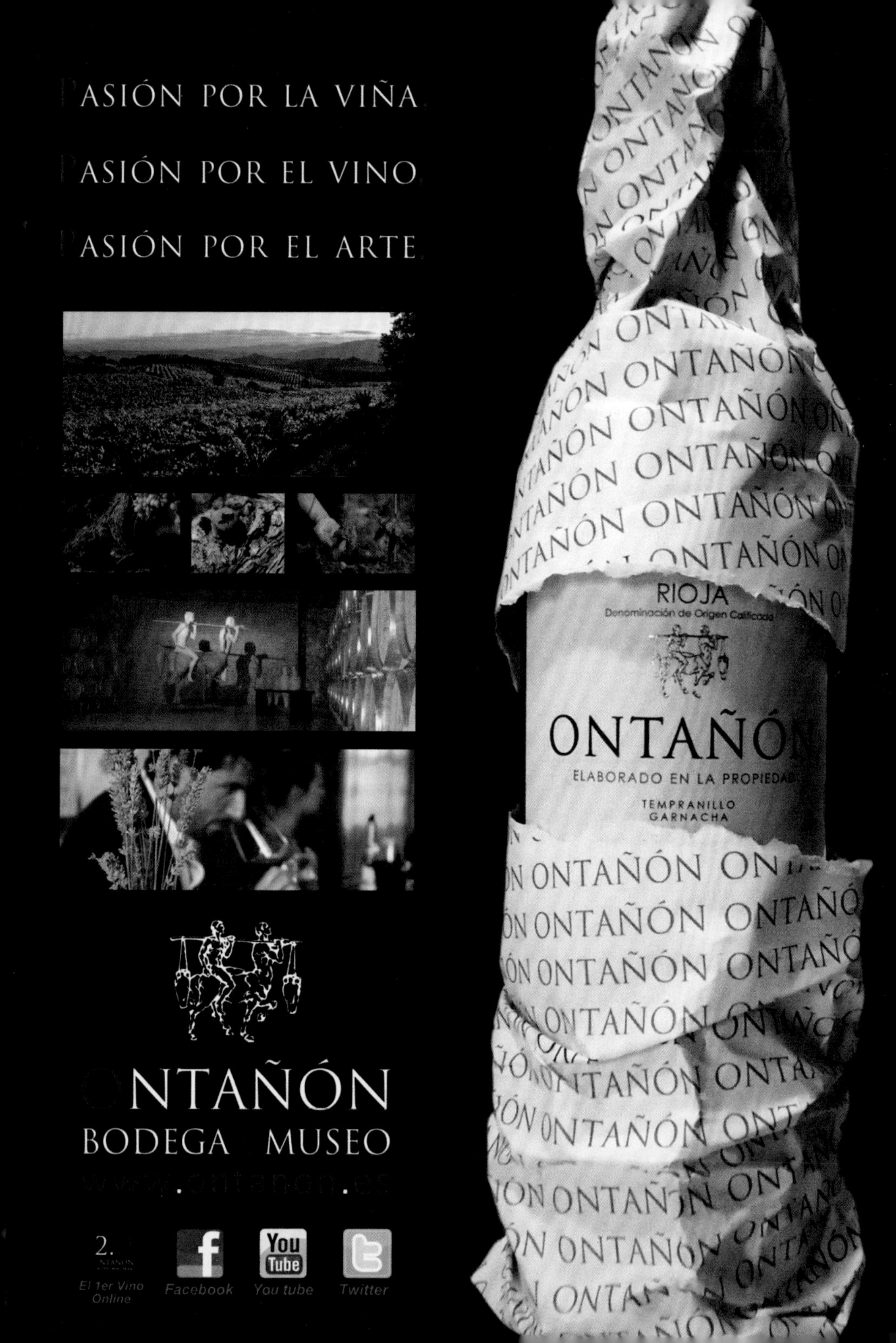
PASIÓN POR LA VIÑA
PASIÓN POR EL VINO
PASIÓN POR EL ARTE
ONTAÑÓN
BODEGA MUSEO
www.ontanon.es
El 1er Vino Online
Facebook
You Tube
You tube
Twitter
RIOJA
Denominación de Origen Calificada
ONTAÑÓN
ELABORADO EN LA PROPIEDAD
TEMPRANILLO
GARNACHA

GUÍA PEÑÍN; THE YEAR´S NEWS

As occurs every year, an increasing number of wineries are relying on the Guide to showcase their product to the final consumer. The number of wines tasted and assessed increases too, which of course leads to new ideas and methods of examining and understanding wine, not only in the Guide, but also from the www.guiapenin.com web page and mobile applications.

The conclusions obtained from this year s tastings seem to affirm a recent trend, which is that the overall average score continues on an unstoppable upward curve, rising from last year s figure of 87.3 to a score of 87.8 this year around; confirmation, if any were needed, of the ever-increasing quality of Spanish wine.

Another noteworthy aspect is the current trend to disclose the recommended retail price of each wine, reflected in 95% of the evaluated wines providing relevant price information, a variable that allows us to cross reference the tasting score of each wine with the pricing data facilitated by its producer, thereby permitting us to determine which wines have the best price-quality factor. A total of 2,301 wines, an unprecedented amount to date, have achieved the Guide s symbolic five-stars, which means that 25% of the wines rated this year boast a significant and persuasive selling point: value-for-money.

At tasting level, the main novelty of the year is the consolidation and expansion of the new trend in the development of red wines, reflected in the fashion for lighter, more expressive wines with pronounced fruit and balsamic characteristics, which are possible when the producer rejects the need for complete phenolic ripening (which can result in over-ripe, alcoholic wines with little personality), in favour of primary flavours . Fortunately this shift in wine-making philosophy is currently occurring not only in regions that suffer from the handicap of extreme heat, but also in cooler areas with delayed harvests, resulting in fragrant reds with elegant and subtle undertones. The trend is already in evidence on a national scale, and evident throughout regions as geographically distant and climatically distinct as Navarra, Rioja, Madrid and Murcia. Obviously there are cooler, moister regions where the climate naturally favours the production of this forward style of red wine, hence the great potential of northwestern Spanish reds.

Another notable development has been the slow but steady emergence of the trend for prolonged bottle-aged sparkling wine in the Cava denomination. It was only a few years ago that well-known Cava houses such as Gramona and Recaredo tentatively started marketing wines with up to 8 years ageing; today this tendency is catching on and is being implemented by firms such as Raventos i Blanc. All these Cava producers are now represented by wines with a podium score of at least 95 points.

Finally, it should be pointed out that 20 more wines made it to the podium this time around compared to last year, all scoring the requisite 95 points, thus making a total of 164 wines that we can classify as "of exceptional quality". A the top of the podium, as always, is the "Botas" range of sherry from Equipo Navazos, while the new release from Artadi, El Carretil 2010, tops the red wine category, outpointing even their flagship Viña El Pisón. The singular Mártires 2010 (made from white viura grapes) produced by Finca Allende scores 97 points, and Gramona s Celler Batlle 2000 achieves a remarkable 98 points, the highest score a cava has ever attained.

Carlos González

TASTING TEAM
AND WINE RAITING

A year has passed since the editorial in the 2012 edition which made clear that the work involved in tasting wines for this guide is a result of coordinated team-effort. Though there may still be those who think the Peñin Guide is a one-man-show and the ratings are purely subjective observations based on my personal opinion, nothing could be further from the truth.

In the past, when this handbook contained two thousand entries, this may have been the case. But since the mid-90 s, as the project expanded, I have always worked with a team; colleagues and collaborators that today are no longer with us but who now occupy senior positions in commerce and communication or write for various wine and drink publications, or are involved on a professional level in the viticulture industry. People whose skills and background were honed at this publication; experienced wine professionals trained and attuned to a model of tasting established by this author which is one based on objective assessment and the avoidance of emotions, whims and apprehensions when it comes to making a professional judgment, leaving aside personal preferences and partialities – traits usually associated with inexperienced or novice tasters.

There are always those who for one reason or another continue to remain skeptical and consider that what is done outside our borders by others is always better. They should be aware that the legendary Robert Parker is supported by a team of six tasters worldwide; Parker points are not only awarded by Bob, but also by the Wine Advocate. Other publications and experts, such as Bettane & Desseauve and the Wine Spectator also count on groups of tasting experts.

Today that responsibility lies with the group listed in the credits. A young team led by Carlos Gonzalez, who in addition to possessing an academic degree in oenology and viticulture also has considerable experience in the world of commercial tasting. Javier Luengo, a qualified journalist, who has from the beginning been a disciple of our innovative tasting system, and finally the young Pablo Vecilla, an expert instructor in showing people how to taste wine. All three of the above have come steadily through the ranks at the Guia Peñin.

They systematically examine different wines using the same criteria, supported by a computer-generated program, a method of tasting which we consider both rational and logical. My comments and evaluations are the same as those of the tasting team; those of the tasting team as if they were my own; invariably we find we are in agreement, give or take, so any discrepancies are negligible.

So what is my current role in the Guide? Obviously one which is appropriate for age and experience; to be the overseer of the formula and chief advocate for the carefully developed method of tasting and evaluation that has been established over the last twenty years, to safeguard the principles and concepts that were inherent from the very beginning, to work on new ideas for improving not only the Guide but also the Website, and finally to be on hand for consultation when the need arises – even expert tasters can sometimes have doubts. And finally, it hardly needs saying – to continue to taste and assess on a regular basis.

So in conclusion, the Peñin Guide really is greater than the sum of its parts.

Unfortunately, there are still wineries that seem reluctant to send us samples of wines that they feel might not score well, which is understandable if the product in question is excessively expensive. For wines in the more accessible price ranges, there exists an excellent system of assessment to rate these wines; the 5 star evaluation. This method of appraisal is based on the value-for-money premise, which forms the principle motive for purchase in the first place, not only for readers and consumers, but also for the commercial sector (distributors and retailers).

In addition, the value-for-money factor would seem to be the key element of interest among importers of Spanish wines, overshadowing even their activities in the premium-wine sector, a category which has expanded considerably in recent times. It should also be noted that the Guide is often used as the primary source of reference for foreign importers with regard to purchasing, its information and viewpoint proving indispensable in commercial transactions, thus highlighting the focus on the value sector. An offshoot of this is the growing importance attached to wines singled out by the Guide as "recommended value-for-money purchases", in itself a form of ranking, information which is relayed to us in feedback obtained from importers at the various international trade fairs we organize.

José Peñin

TEAM

From left to right Carlos González, Pablo Vecilla and Javier Luengo.

Carlos González (technical director Penin Guide)
cgonzalez@guiapenin.com

Born in Avila in 1979, Carlos Gonzalez is an Agricultural Engineer (University of Salamanca), with Masters in Enology and Viticulture (Torras and Associates) and a Masters in Wine Business Management (IE Business School). After practicing as a winemaker and vineyard technician, he undertook work as technical director for The Vintages of Spain. For the last six years he has headed the Technical Department of the Peñin Guide, responsible for the coordination of staff assignments and development of wine tastings that appear in the various guides under the Peñin group.

Javier Luengo (editorial and tasting)
jluengo@guiapenin.com

Born in Castellón de la Plana in 1976, Javier Luengo graduated with a degree in Journalism from the Universidad Complutense of Madrid and is also qualified in Integral Communications, University Francisco de Vitoria. After working as a journalist in different media agencies and publications, he joined the communication department of IP & ERRE as account director. Javier has been a professional taster for the Peñin team for four years, both wines and distillates. He is currently responsible for the different editorial publishing products covered by the Peñin Guide.

Pablo Vecilla (taster)
pvecilla@guiapenin.com

Born in Madrid in 1985, Pablo studies agricultural technical engineering at the Polytechnic University of Madrid. He has been head of the Cultural Association of La Carrasca, an entity that promotes wine culture in the university, which was also under his responsibility during 2008 and 2009. Pablo joined the Peñin tasting team in 2010. He currently operates the tasting courses organized by the Peñin Tasting School.

ACKNOWLEDGMENTS

To all the **Consejos Reguladores** that have so readily collaborated with the Guide, providing their buildings and professional staff to make the tastings possible. In other cases it was not their fault but problems on our part that did not make them happen in the end. We have to thank also –and very especially– **José Matás** from **Enoteca Casa Bernal**, in El Palmar (Murcia); **Juan Luis Pérez de Eulate** from **La Vinoteca**, a wine shop in Palma de Mallorca; Quim Vila from **Vila Viniteca**, a wine shop in Barcelona; **Casa del Vino La Baranda** from El Sauzal, and particularly **José Alfonso González Lorente**, as well as the **Casa del Vino of Gran Canaria; the Parque Tecnológico del Vino (VITEC)**, in Falset (Tarragona), and **Vinatería Pámpano** in Almendralejo (Badajoz).

SUMMARY

EXCEPTIONAL WINES

In each new edition of the Guide, a small and exclusive group of wines stand out from among the nearly ten thousand reviewed, special wines achieving near-sensory perfection, expressing perfectly their soils, climate and the origin of their caste.

This list of "wines of outstanding quality" could be described figuratively as a private members club with a long waiting list and it´s no surprise to see the same wines dominating the podium; it could not be otherwise. However, in this new edition, there seem to be exceptions, and turn-ups too, one of which was the usurping of the habitually highest scoring red, Contador, by El Carretil 2010 from Bodegas Artadi. And in the white wine category few could have imagined the highest rating would go to a viura based wine from Rioja, Finca Allende´s Martires 2010.

In Andalusia, the Navazos team continues to hog the limelight of the Jerez denomination, producing a fino and two manzanillas that border on perfection. Meanwhile, Gramona, once again, stands out as the exemplary representative of Cava with its enduring Celler Batlle 2000 Brut Gran Reserva, taking the sparkling-wine concept to a level approaching the typology of Grand Cru Champagne in terms of finesse, while staying true to its Catalan essence.

In addition to the highest-rated wines, there appear in the Guide some unfamiliar but innovative expressions of the winemaker´s craft that illustrate the different interpretations of varietal and terroir which are possible even in firmly established areas such as Rioja and Ribera del Duero. The podium has seen a considerable influx of new wines from the latter, the 2009 and 2010 harvests among two to be strongly represented. Gradually breaking into the premium quality level in recent years are wines such as Don Miguel Comenge 2009, Celia Vizcarra 2010, Prado Rey Elite 2010 and the new release from Pago de Carraovejas, El Anejón de la Cuesta de Liebres 2010. In the hands of great winemakers these wines are masterful examples of the best vintages; the French oenologist Olivier Rivière has crafted a 2010 garnacha of exceptional quality called Alto Redondo that proves Rioja does not lag behind in terms of quality or innovation, while Bodegas Pujanza hit the heights with their Pujanza Norte 2009. In Valdeorras Telmo Rodriguez and Pablo Eguzkiza have surprised us with a new creation, As Caborcas 2010.

The vitality of the Montsant region is rejuvenated on a yearly basis with exotic examples such as the Teixar 2010, made from a strain of garnacha by Vinyes Domenech, and the cariñena (known locally as samsó) made by Celler Vermunver, Genesi Varietal 2009. Even experienced winemakers from neighbouring Priorat, including Joan Asens (former oenologist at Alvaro Palacios), have beat a direct path to the potential of Monsant, as evidenced by the offerings from Alfredo Arribas, Trossos Tros Magnum Blanc y Negre, one a red garnacha, the other a white. Priorat is not exactly resting on its laurels either, and the standout Terroir al Limit winery, with its ability to interpret all that the region has to offer, has made a vibrant and balsamic wine: Torroja Vi de Vila 2009.

Raul Bobet, winemaker for both Ferret-Bobet and Castell D'Encus in Lleida, captivates us this year by placing two Priorat wines on the podium, Vinyes Velles 2010 and Seleccion Especial 2009, and at the same time introducing a new varietal from Costers del Segre, Thalarn 2010. In the Ribeira Sacra denomination of origin, Fernando Alqueira and Raul Perez surprise us with their interpretation of the almost unknown merenzao grape, Alquerira Merenzao 2010, a young red rounded off with a short stint in oak.

An interesting development in Rueda has been the launch of a new white from Bodegas Ordoñez, Nisia 2011, in which the first harvest made a sensation by scoring no less than 95 points.

EXCEPTIONAL WINES (SWEET WINES AND GENEROSOS)

WINE	WINERY
La Bota de Fino (Bota nº 35) FI	Equipo Navazos
La Bota de Manzanilla Pasada (Bota NO) Nº39 MZ	Equipo Navazos
La Bota de Manzanilla Pasada (Bota NO) Nº40 MZ	Equipo Navazos
Alvear PX 1830 PX Reserva	Alvear
Casta Diva Esencial "A Lucrecia Bori" B	Bodegas Gutiérrez de la Vega
Osborne Rare Sherry Solera BC 200 OL	Bodegas Osborne
Venerable VORS PX	Bodegas Osborne
Malvasía Dulce Carballo 1997 B	Bodegas Carballo
Casta Diva Fondillón Solera 1987 Fondillón	Bodegas Gutiérrez de la Vega
Reliquia AM	Bodegas Barbadillo
Osborne Rare Sherry AOS AM	Bodegas Osborne
La Bota de Cream nº 38 CR	Equipo Navazos
La Ina FI	Emilio Lustau
Manzanilla en Rama Saca de Invierno MZ	Bodegas Barbadillo
Don Gonzalo VOS OL	Valdespino
Solera Su Majestad VORS OL	Valdespino
Colección Roberto Amillo Palo Cortado PC	Espíritus de Jerez
Reliquia PX	Bodegas Barbadillo
Ordóñez & Co. Nº3 Viñas Viejas 2008 B	Bodegas Jorge Ordóñez & Co
Molino Real 2008 B	Compañía de Vinos Telmo Rodríguez
La Cañada PX	Pérez Barquero S.A.
La Bota de Pedro Ximenez nº36 Bota NO PX	Equipo Navazos
Casta Diva Reserva Real 2002 B Reserva	Bodegas Gutiérrez de la Vega
Barbadillo Amontillado VORS AM	Bodegas Barbadillo
La Bota de Amontillado (Bota nº 37) AM	Equipo Navazos
Amontillado Zoilo Ruiz Mateos AM	Zoilo Ruiz-Mateos
Colección Roberto Amillo Amontillado AM	Espíritus de Jerez
Del Príncipe AM	Real Tesoro
Ynocente FI	Valdespino
La Panesa Especial Fino FI	Hidalgo
San León Reserva de Familia MZ	Herederos de Argüeso S.A.
Manzanilla en Rama Saca de Primavera 2012 MZ	Bodegas Barbadillo
Sacristía AB MZ	Sacristía AB
Sibarita V.O.R.S. OL	Bodegas Osborne
Colección Roberto Amillo Oloroso OL	Espíritus de Jerez
Gonzalez Byass Añada 1982 PC	González Byass Jerez
Gran Orden PX	Bodegas Garvey Jerez
Pedro Ximenez Zoilo Ruiz Mateos PX	Bodegas Garvey Jerez
Colección Roberto Amillo Pedro Ximénez PX	Espíritus de Jerez
La Bota de Dulce Nº33 Color Solera	Equipo Navazos
Teneguía Malvasía Dulce 1996 B Reserva	Bodegas Teneguía
El Grifo Canari Dulce de Licor s/c B	El Grifo
Casa del Inca 2010 PX	Equipo Navazos
Humboldt 2001 Tinto dulce	Bodegas Insulares Tenerife
Humboldt 1997 Blanco dulce	Bodegas Insulares Tenerife
Pricum Aldebarán Vendimia Tardía 2008 B	Bodegas Margón

EXCEPTIONAL WINES (SWEET WINES AND GENEROSOS)

POINTS	TYPE	DO
99	Fino	Jerez
99	Manzanilla	Jerez
99	Manzanilla	Jerez
98	Pedro Ximénez	Montilla-Moriles
97	Blanco Dulce	Alicante
97	Oloroso	Jerez
97	Pedro Ximénez	Jerez
97	Blanco	La Palma
96	Fondillón	Alicante
96	Amontillado	Jerez
96	Amontillado	Jerez
96	Cream	Jerez
96	Fino	Jerez
96	Manzanilla	Jerez
96	Oloroso	Jerez
96	Oloroso	Jerez
96	Palo Cortado	Jerez
96	Pedro ximénez	Jerez
96	Blanco Dulce	Málaga y Sierras de Málaga
96	Blanco	Málaga y Sierras de Málaga
96	Pedro ximénez	Montilla-Moriles
96	Pedro Ximénez	Jerez
95	Blanco Dulce	Alicante
95	Amontillado	Jerez
95	Amontillado	Jerez
95	Amontillado	Jerez
95	Amontillado	Jerez
95	Amontillado	Jerez
95	Fino	Jerez
95	Fino	Jerez
95	Manzanilla	Jerez
95	Manzanilla	Jerez
95	Manzanilla	Jerez
95	Oloroso	Jerez
95	Oloroso	Jerez
95	Palo Cortado	Jerez
95	Pedro Ximénez	Jerez
95	Pedro Ximénez	Jerez
95	Pedro Ximénez	Jerez
95	Solera Dulce	Jerez
95	Blanco	La Palma
95	Blanco	Lanzarote
95	Pedro Ximénez	Montilla-Moriles
95	Tinto Dulce	Tacoronte-Acentejo
95	Blanco Dulce	Tacoronte-Acentejo
95	Blanco Dulce	Tierra de León

EXCEPTIONAL WINES (RED WINES)

WINE	WINERY
Artadi El Carretil 2010 T	Bodegas y Viñedos Artadi
L'Ermita 2010 TC	Alvaro Palacios
Regina Vides 2009 T	Bodegas Hermanos Sastre
Vega Sicilia Reserva Especial 94/99/00 T	Bodegas Vega Sicilia
Pingus 2010 T	Dominio de Pingus S.L.
Contador 2010 T	Bodega Contador
Dalmau 2007 TR	Marqués de Murrieta
Castillo Ygay 2001 TGR	Marqués de Murrieta
Victorino 2009 T	Teso la Monja
Termanthia 2010 T	Bodega Numanthia
Teso La Monja 2008 T	Teso la Monja
Moncerbal 2009 T	Descendientes de J. Palacios
La Faraona 2009 T	Descendientes de J. Palacios
Aquilón 2009 T	Bodegas Alto Moncayo
Thalarn 2010 T	Castell D'Encus
El Nido 2009 T	Bodegas El Nido
Ataulfos 2010 T	Bodegas Jiménez Landi
Espectacle 2009 T	Espectacle Vins
Sot Lefriec 2007 T	Alemany I Corrio
Torroja Vi de la Vila 2009 T	Terroir al Limit
Ferrer Bobet Selecció Especial 2009 T	Ferrer Bobet
Dominio do Bibei B 2008 T	Dominio do Bibei
Viña Sastre Pesus 2009 T	Bodegas Hermanos Sastre
Vega Sicilia Único 2003 T	Bodegas Vega Sicilia
Dominio de Atauta Llanos del Almendro 2009 T	Dominio de Atauta
Don Miguel Comenge 2009 T	Comenge Bodegas y Viñedos
Inés Vizcarra 2010 T	Bodegas Vizcarra
Pago de Carraovejas El Anejón de la Cuesta de las Liebres 2009 T	Pago de Carraovejas
Los Balancines Finca de Matanegra 2009 TC	Pago los Balancines
Viña El Pisón 2010 T	Bodegas y Viñedos Artadi
Pujanza Norte 2009 T	Bodegas y Viñedos Pujanza
Avrvs 2009 T	Finca Allende
San Vicente 2008 T	Señorío de San Vicente
La Viña de Andrés Romeo 2010 T	Bodega Contador
Amancio 2008 T	Sierra Cantabria
Malpuesto 2010 T	Bodegas Orben
La Nieta 2010 T	Viñedos de Páganos
Artuke K4 2010 T	Artuke Bodegas y Viñedos
Sierra Cantabria Colección Privada 2010 T	Sierra Cantabria
Finca El Bosque 2010 T	Sierra Cantabria
Dalmau 2009 TR	Marqués de Murrieta
Artadi La Poza de Ballesteros 2010 T	Bodegas y Viñedos Artadi
Cirsion 2009 T	Bodegas Roda
Irius Premium 2008 T	Bodegas Irius
Victorino 2010 T	Teso la Monja
Alabaster 2010 T	Teso la Monja
Numanthia 2010 T	Bodega Numanthia
El Reventón 2010 T	Daniel El Travieso S.L.

POINTS	TYPE	DO
98	Red	Rioja
97	Red	Priorat
97	Red	Ribera del Duero
97	Red	Ribera del Duero
97	Red	Ribera del Duero
97	Red	Rioja
97	Red	Rioja
97	Red	Rioja
97	Red	Toro
97	Red	Toro
97	Red	Toro
96	Red	Bierzo
96	Red	Bierzo
96	Red	Campo de Borja
96	Red	Costers del Segre
96	Red	Jumilla
96	Red	Méntrida
96	Red	Montsant
96	Red	Penedès
96	Red	Priorat
96	Red	Priorat
96	Red	Ribeira Sacra
96	Red	Ribera del Duero
96	Red	Ribera del Duero
96	Red	Ribera del Duero
96	Red	Ribera del Duero
96	Red	Ribera del Duero
96	Red	Ribera del Duero
96	Red	Ribera del Guadiana
96	Red	Rioja
96	Red	Rioja
96	Red	Rioja
96	Red	Rioja
96	Red	Rioja
96	Red	Rioja
96	Red	Rioja
96	Red	Rioja
96	Red	Rioja
96	Red	Rioja
96	Red	Rioja
96	Red	Rioja
96	Red	Rioja
96	Red	Rioja
96	Red	Somontano
96	Red	Toro
96	Red	Toro
96	Red	Toro
96	Red	VT CastyLe

EXCEPTIONAL WINES (RED WINES)

WINE	WINERY
Casa Cisca 2010 T	Bodegas Castaño
Curro 2010 T	Bodegas Bernabé Navarro
Villa de Corullón 2009 T	Descendientes de J. Palacios
Alto Moncayo 2009 T	Bodegas Alto Moncayo
Casa Castillo Pie Franco 2008 T	Propiedad Vitícola Casa Castillo
Las Gravas 2009 T	Propiedad Vitícola Casa Castillo
Finca Sandoval Cuvee TNS Magnum 2008 T	Finca Sandoval
The End 2010 T	Bodegas Jiménez Landi
Trossos Tros Negre Magnum 2008 T	Alfredo Arribas
Trossos Tros Negre 2009 T	Alfredo Arribas
Teixar 2010 T	Vinyes Domènech
Gènesi Varietal 2009 T	Celler Vermunver
Santa Cruz de Artazu 2010 T	Bodegas y Viñedos Artazu
Arínzano 2004 T	Señorío de Arínzano
Finca Dofí 2010 TC	Alvaro Palacios
Ferrer Bobet Vinyes Velles 2010 T	Ferrer Bobet
Arbossar 2009 T	Terroir al Limit
Ferrer Bobet Vinyes Velles 2009 T	Ferrer Bobet
Algueira Merenzao 2010 T Roble	Algueira
Viña Sastre Pago de Santa Cruz 2009 T	Bodegas Hermanos Sastre
Alión 2009 T	Bodegas y Viñedos Alión
Flor de Pingus 2010 T	Dominio de Pingus S.L.
Celia Vizcarra 2010 T	Bodegas Vizcarra
"María" Alonso del Yerro 2009 T	Viñedos Alonso del Yerro
Viña Pedrosa La Navilla 2009 T	Bodegas Hermanos Pérez Pascuas
Protos Selección Finca el Grajo Viejo 2009 T	Protos Bodegas Ribera Duero de Peñafiel
PradoRey Élite 2010 T	Real Sitio de Ventosilla
Cirsion 2010 T	Bodegas Roda
Castillo Ygay 2004 TGR	Marqués de Murrieta
Remírez de Ganuza 2006 TR	Bodegas Remírez de Ganuza
Artadi Pagos Viejos 2010 T	Bodegas y Viñedos Artadi
Sierra Cantabria Colección Privada 2009 T	Sierra Cantabria
La Cueva del Contador 2010 T	Bodega Contador
La Nieta 2009 T	Viñedos de Páganos
Finca El Bosque 2009 T	Sierra Cantabria
El Puntido 2009 T	Viñedos de Páganos
San Vicente 2009 T	Señorío de San Vicente
Artuke Finca de los Locos 2010 T	Artuke Bodegas y Viñedos
Artadi Valdeginés 2010 T	Bodegas y Viñedos Artadi
Macán Clásico 2009 T	Bodegas Benjamín de Rothschild & Vega Sicilia
Alto Redondo 2010 T	Olivier Rivière Vinos
Blecua 2007 TR	Blecua
Cenit 2008 T	Viñas del Cénit
Pintia 2009 T	Bodegas y Viñedos Pintia
Alabaster 2009 T	Teso la Monja
As Caborcas 2010 T	Compañía de Vinos Telmo Rodríguez
Finca Terrerazo 2010 T	Mustiguillo Viñedos y Bodega
Señorío de Otazu Altar 2006 T	Bodega Otazu
Abadía Retuerta Pago Negralada 2009 T Barrica	Abadía Retuerta
Abadía Retuerta Pago Valdebellón 2009 T Barrica	Abadía Retuerta

POINTS	TYPE	DO
96	Red	Yecla
95	Red	Alicante
95	Red	Bierzo
95	Red	Campo de Borja
95	Red	Jumilla
95	Red	Jumilla
95	Red	Manchuela
95	Red	Méntrida
95	Red	Montsant
95	Red	Montsant
95	Red	Montsant
95	Red	Montsant
95	Red	Navarra
95	Red	Pago Señorío de Arinzano
95	Red	Priorat
95	Red	Priorat
95	Red	Priorat
95	Red	Priorat
95	Red	Ribeira Sacra
95	Red	Ribera del Duero
95	Red	Ribera del Duero
95	Red	Ribera del Duero
95	Red	Ribera del Duero
95	Red	Ribera del Duero
95	Red	Ribera del Duero
95	Red	Ribera del Duero
95	Red	Ribera del Duero
95	Red	Rioja
95	Red	Rioja
95	Red	Rioja
95	Red	Rioja
95	Red	Rioja
95	Red	Rioja
95	Red	Rioja
95	Red	Rioja
95	Red	Rioja
95	Red	Rioja
95	Red	Rioja
95	Red	Rioja
95	Red	Rioja
95	Red	Rioja
95	Red	Somontano
95	Red	Tierra del Vino de Zamora
95	Red	Toro
95	Red	Toro
95	Red	Valdeorras
95	Red	Vino de Pago El Terrerazo
95	Red	Vinos de Pago de Otazu
95	Red	VT CastyLe
95	Red	VT CastyLe

EXCEPTIONAL WINES (WHITE WINES)

WINE	WINERY
Mártires 2010 B	Finca Allende
Trossos Tros Blanc Magnum 2009 B	Alfredo Arribas
Pazo Señorans Selección de Añada 2005 B	Pazo de Señorans
Pedrouzos Magnum 2010 B	Bodegas Valdesil
Mengoba Godello sobre lías 2010 B	Bodegas y Viñedo Mengoba
Chivite Colección 125 2009 BFB	J. Chivite Pagos & Estates
Chivite Colección 125 Vendimia Tardía B	J. Chivite Pagos & Estates
Nora da Neve 2009 BFB	Viña Nora
Albariño de Fefiñanes III año 2009 B	Bodegas del Palacio de Fefiñanes
Pazo de Piñeiro 2010 B	A. Pazos de Lusco
Belondrade y Lurton 2010 BFB	Belondrade
Nisia 2011 B	Bodegas Ordóñez
As Sortes 2011 B	Rafael Palacios

EXCEPTIONAL WINES (SPARKLING WINES)

WINE	WINERY
Gramona Celler Batlle 2000 BR Gran Reserva	Gramona
Gramona Celler Batlle 2001 BR Gran Reserva	Gramona
Recaredo Reserva Particular 2002 BN Gran Reserva	Recaredo
Raventós i Blanc Gran Reserva Personal M.R.N. 1998 BN	Josep Mª Raventós i Blanc
Gramona Colección de Arte 2000 BR Gran Reserva	Gramona
Raventós i Blanc Gran Reserva Personal M.R.N. 1999 BN Gran Reserva	Josep Mª Raventós i Blanc
Raventós i Blanc Gran Reserva Personal M.R.N. 2000 BN Gran Reserva	Josep Mª Raventós i Blanc

EXCEPTIONAL WINES (WHITE WINES)

POINTS	TYPE	DO
97	White	Rioja
96	White	Montsant
96	White	Rias Baixas
96	White	Valdeorras
95	White	Bierzo
95	White	Navarra
95	White	Navarra
95	White	Rias Baixas
95	White	Rias Baixas
95	White	Rias Baixas
95	White	Rueda
95	White	Rueda
95	White	Valdeorras

EXCEPTIONAL WINES (SPARKLING WINES)

POINTS	TYPE	DO
98	Brut	Cava
96	Brut	Cava
96	Brut Nature	Cava
96	Brut Nature	Cava
95	Brut	Cava
95	Brut Nature	Cava
95	Brut Nature	Cava

WINERIES and the TASTING of the WINES by DESIGNATION of ORIGIN

SCORING SYSTEM

95-100 EXCEPTIONAL
The wine excels among those of the same type, vintage and origin. It is in every sense extraordinary. It is full of complexity, with abundant sensory elements both on the nose and on the palate that arise from the combination of soil, grape variety, winemaking and ageing methods; elegant and utterly outstanding, it exceeds average commercial standards and in some cases it may still be unknown to the general public.

90-94 EXCELLENT
A wine with the same attributes as those indicated above but with less exceptional or significant characteristics.

85-89 VERY GOOD
The wine stands out thanks to features acquired through great winemaking and/or ageing standards, or an exceptional varietal character. It is a wine with unique features, although it may lack soil or terroir expression.

80-84 GOOD
Although not as distinctive, the wine expresses the basic characteristics of both its type and region of origin.

70-79 AVERAGE
The wine has no defects, but no virtues either.

60-69 NOT RECOMMENDED
It is a non-acceptable wine in which some faults are evident, although they may not spoil the overall flavour.

50-59 FAULTY
A non-acceptable wine from a sensory point of view that may be oxidised or have defects due to bad ageing or late racking; it may be an old wine past its best or a young wine with unfavourable fermentation off-odours.

ABBREVIATIONS

B	WHITE
BC	AGED WHITE
BFB	BARREL-FERMENTED WHITE
RD	ROSÉ
T	RED
TC	AGED (CRIANZA) RED
TR	AGED (RESERVA) RED
TGR	AGED (GRAN RESERVA) RED
FI	FINO
MZ	MANZANILLA
OL	OLOROSO
OLV	OLOROSO VIEJO (OLD OLOROSO)
AM	AMONTILLADO
PX	PEDRO XIMÉNEZ (SWEET)
PC	PALO CORTADO
CR	CREAM
PCR	PALE CREAM
GE	GENEROSO (FORTIFIED)
ESP	SPARKLING
BR	BRUT
BN	BRUT NATURE
SC	DRY
SS	SEMI-DRY
S/C	SIN COSECHA (NON-VINTAGE)

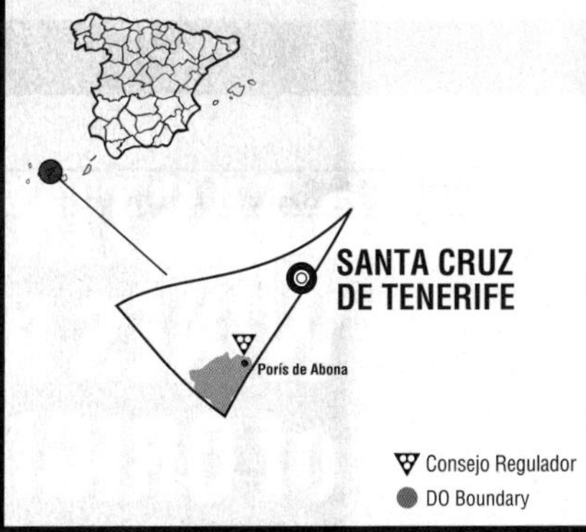

LOCATION:

In the southern area of the island of Tenerife, with vineyards which occupy the slopes of the Teide down to the coast. It covers the municipal districts of Adeje, Arona, Vilaflor, San Miguel de Abona, Granadilla de Abona, Arico and Fasnia.

CLIMATE:

Mediterranean on the coastal belt, and gradually cools down inland as a result of the trade winds. Rainfall varies between 350 mm per year on the coast and 550 mm inland. In the highest region, Vilaflor, the vineyards do not benefit from these winds as they face slightly west. Nevertheless, the more than 200 Ha of this small plateau produce wines with an acidity of 8 g/l due to the altitude, but with an alcohol content of 13%, as this area of the island has the longest hours of sunshine.

SOIL:

Distinction can be made between the sandy and calcareous soil inland and the more clayey, well drained soil of the higher regions, seeing as they are volcanic. The so-called 'Jable' soil is very typical, and is simply a very fine whitish volcanic sand, used by the local winegrower to cover the vineyards in order to retain humidity in the ground and to prevent weeds from growing. The vineyards are located at altitudes which range between 300 and 1,750 m (the better quality grapes are grown in the higher regions), which determines different grape harvesting dates in a period spanning the beginning of August up to October.

GRAPE VARIETIES:

WHITE: *Bastardo Blanco, Bermejuela, Forastera Blanca, Güal, Listán Blanca* (majority with 1,869 Ha), *Malvasía, Moscatel, Pedro Ximénez, Sabro, Torrontés, Verdello, Vijariego.* The white varieties make up the majority of the vineyards.
RED: *Bastardo Negro, Cabernet Sauvignon, Castellana Negra, Listán Negro, Listán Prieto, Malvasía Rosada, Moscatel Negro, Negramoll, Pinot Noir, Rubí Cabernet, Syrah, Tempranillo, Tintilla, Vijariego Negro.*

FIGURES:

Vineyard surface: 995 – **Wine-Growers:** 1,228 – **Wineries:** 17 – **2011 Harvest rating:** Good – **Production:** 620,000 litres – **Market percentages:** 100% domestic

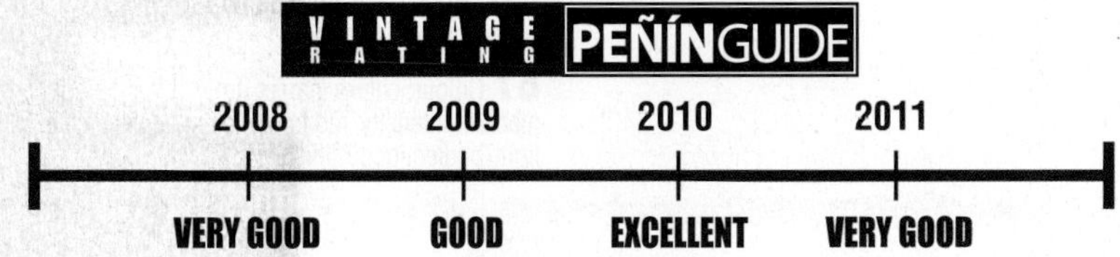

CONSEJO REGULADOR
Martín Rodríguez, 9 - 38588 Porís de Abona - Arico (Santa Cruz de Tenerife) - ☎: +34 922 164 241 - Fax: +34 922 164 135
@ vinosdeabona@vinosdeabona.com - www.vinosdeabona.com

BODEGA REVERÓN

Ctra. Gral. Vilaflor, Los Quemados, 8
38620 Vilaflor (Santa Cruz de Tenerife)
☎: +34 922 725 044 - Fax: +34 922 725 044
bodegasreveron@bodegasreveron.com
www.bodegasreveron.com

LOS QUEMADOS 2011 BFB
albillo.

88 Colour: bright straw. Nose: medium intensity, spicy, creamy oak, floral. Palate: flavourful, fruity, spicy, good acidity.

PAGOS REVERÓN AFRUTADO 2011 B
listán blanco.

86 Colour: bright straw. Nose: white flowers, jasmine, expressive. Palate: correct, flavourful, sweetness, fresh.

LOS QUEMADOS 2011 B
albillo.

85 Colour: bright straw. Nose: white flowers, citrus fruit. Palate: correct, fresh, fruity, easy to drink.

PAGOS REVERÓN 2011 B
listán blanco.

83

LOS QUEMADOS 2011 T
tempranillo, syrah, merlot.

87 Colour: bright cherry, purple rim. Nose: balanced, fruit expression, medium intensity, wild herbs. Palate: fruity, flavourful.

PAGOS REVERÓN 2010 T BARRICA
listán negro, ruby, tempranillo, castellana.

86 Colour: cherry, garnet rim. Nose: medium intensity, spicy, ripe fruit. Palate: fruity, flavourful.

PAGO REVERÓN 2010 T
listán negro, ruby, tempranillo, castellana.

84

BODEGA SAN BORONDON

San Benito, 24 Los Blanquitos
Granadilla de Abona (Santa Cruz de Tenerife)
☎: +34 922 773 303 - Fax: +34 922 773 303
estudio@medanoingenieros.com
www.sanborondon.com

SAN BORONDÓN 2010 B BARRICA
albillo, malvasía, listán blanco.

88 Colour: bright straw. Nose: medium intensity, white flowers, citrus fruit, sweet spices. Palate: fruity, flavourful, balanced, spicy.

SAN BORONDÓN 2010 T ROBLE
80% listán negro, 10% listán prieto, 10% otras.

86 Colour: deep cherry, garnet rim. Nose: toasty, sweet spices, balsamic herbs, ripe fruit. Palate: fruity, flavourful, easy to drink, fine bitter notes.

BODEGA SAN MIGUEL

Ctra. General del Sur, 5
38620 San Miguel de Abona (Santa Cruz de Tenerife)
☎: +34 922 700 300 - Fax: +34 922 700 301
bodega@casanmiguel.com
www.sanmiguelappis.com

MARQUÉS DE FUENTE AFRUTADO 2011 B

86 Colour: bright straw. Nose: medium intensity, fresh fruit, wild herbs, citrus fruit. Palate: fruity, easy to drink.

CHASNERO ACACIA 2011 B

86 Colour: bright straw. Nose: wild herbs, fragrant herbs, spicy. Palate: correct, good finish, good acidity.

MARQUÉS DE FUENTE 2011 B

85 Colour: bright straw. Nose: ripe fruit, citrus fruit, white flowers. Palate: correct, sweetness, easy to drink.

CHASNERO NEGREMOLL 2011 B

84

MARQUÉS DE FUENTE 2011 T
baboso negro, vijariego negro.

87 Colour: cherry, garnet rim. Nose: fragrant herbs, medium intensity, red berry notes, spicy. Palate: fruity, light-bodied, good finish.

CHASNERO 2011 T

85 Colour: cherry, purple rim. Nose: medium intensity, ripe fruit, scrubland. Palate: flavourful, fruity, correct.

MARQUÉS DE FUENTE 2010 T BARRICA
merlot.

88 Colour: cherry, garnet rim. Nose: balanced, sweet spices, ripe fruit, neat. Palate: fruity, good structure, flavourful, full.

CUMBRES DE ABONA

Bajada El Vizo, s/n
38580 Arico (Santa Cruz de Tenerife)
☎: +34 922 768 604 - Fax: +34 922 768 234
bodega@cumbresdeabona.es
www.cumbresabona.com

TESTAMENTO MALVASÍA DRY 2011 B

87 Colour: bright straw. Nose: medium intensity, dried flowers, fresh fruit. Palate: fresh, good acidity, easy to drink.

FLOR DE CHASNA 2011 B

86 Colour: bright straw. Nose: fresh, fragrant herbs, floral, citrus fruit. Palate: flavourful, fruity, good acidity, balanced.

TESTAMENTO MALVASÍA ESENCIA 2008 B

90 Colour: old gold. Nose: candied fruit, honeyed notes, faded flowers, complex. Palate: flavourful, fruity, good acidity.

FLOR DE CHASNA 2011 T BARRICA

91 Colour: bright cherry, purple rim. Nose: balanced, red berry notes, ripe fruit, spicy, creamy oak. Palate: good structure, fruity, fresh.

FLOR DE CHASNA VARIETAL 2011 T

86 Colour: bright cherry, purple rim. Nose: wild herbs, powerfull, fresh. Palate: light-bodied, easy to drink.

FLOR DE CHASNA NATURALMENTE DULCE 2009 T

85 Colour: cherry, garnet rim. Nose: sweet spices, powerfull, overripe fruit. Palate: sweet, rich, flavourful.

FRONTOS

Lomo Grande, 1- Los Blanquitos
38616 Granadilla de Abona (Santa Cruz de Tenerife)
☎: +34 922 777 253 - Fax: +34 922 777 246
bodega@tierradefrontos.com
www.tierradefrontos.com

FRONTOS 2011 B
verdejo, malvasía, marmajuelo, albillo.

87 Colour: bright straw, greenish rim. Nose: balanced, fresh, medium intensity, wild herbs. Palate: balanced, fine bitter notes, good acidity.

FRONTOS BLANCO SECO ECOLÓGICO 2011 B
100% listán blanco.

86 Colour: bright straw. Nose: fresh, ripe fruit, fragrant herbs. Palate: flavourful, fruity, correct, easy to drink.

FRONTOS SEMISECO 2011 B
100% listán blanco.

86 Colour: bright straw. Nose: medium intensity, balanced, white flowers. Palate: fruity, easy to drink, good finish.

FRONTOS 2011 RD
70% syrah, 30% listán prieto.

83

FRONTOS TINTO TIERRA 2011 T
70% syrah, 30% listán prieto.

87 Colour: bright cherry, purple rim. Nose: fresh, balsamic herbs, grassy, fresh fruit. Palate: light-bodied, good finish.

FRONTOS 2010 T
100% baboso negro.

88 Colour: cherry, garnet rim. Nose: spicy, medium intensity, ripe fruit, balanced. Palate: flavourful, balanced, balsamic.

JOTTOCAR

Marta, 3 Chimiche
38594 Granadilla de Abona (Santa Cruz de Tenerife)
☎: +34 922 777 285 - Fax: +34 922 777 259
ventas@menceychasna.com
www.menceychasna.es

MENCEY DE CHASNA 2011 B
100% listán blanco.

86 Colour: bright straw. Nose: fresh fruit, citrus fruit. Palate: fresh, flavourful, long, balsamic.

LOS TABLEROS 2010 B
listán blanco.

85 Colour: bright straw. Nose: medium intensity, balanced, jasmine. Palate: balanced, correct.

MENCEY DE CHASNA 2011 T
listán negro, ruby, cabernet sauvignon, syrah, tempranillo.

86 Colour: bright cherry, garnet rim. Nose: balanced, medium intensity, fresh, red berry notes. Palate: fruity, flavourful, easy to drink.

LOS TABLEROS 2011 T BARRICA
listán negro, castellana, ruby, cabernet sauvignon, tempranillo.

84

PEDRO HERNÁNDEZ TEJERA

Ctra. Archifira, s/n
38570 Fasnia (Santa Cruz de Tenerife)
☎: +34 616 920 832

VIÑA ARESE 2011 B

86 Colour: bright straw. Nose: medium intensity, fresh, citrus fruit, wild herbs. Palate: correct, easy to drink.

VIÑA ARESE AFRUTADO B

84

VIÑA ARESE 2011 T BARRICA

87 Colour: cherry, garnet rim. Nose: sweet spices, creamy oak, red berry notes, ripe fruit, wild herbs. Palate: balanced, fruity, easy to drink.

VIÑA ARESE 2011 T

83

RAFAEL YUSEF DELGADO

Ctra. General, 21
38595 Charco del Pino - Granadilla de Abona
(Santa Cruz de Tenerife)
☎: +34 616 509 104

CHIÑAMA 2011 T

85 Colour: bright cherry, purple rim. Nose: balanced, red berry notes, medium intensity. Palate: fruity, good finish, easy to drink.

TOMÁS FRÍAS GONZÁLEZ

Los Cazadores, s/n
38570 Fasnia (Santa Cruz de Tenerife)
☎: +34 922 164 301
ivanfriasperez@hotmail.com

VIJARIEGO NEGRO 2009 T

85 Colour: bright cherry. Nose: ripe fruit, toasty, spicy, fruit preserve, balanced, balsamic herbs. Palate: correct, ripe fruit, fine bitter notes.

VERA DE LA FUENTE BABOSO T
baboso negro.

83

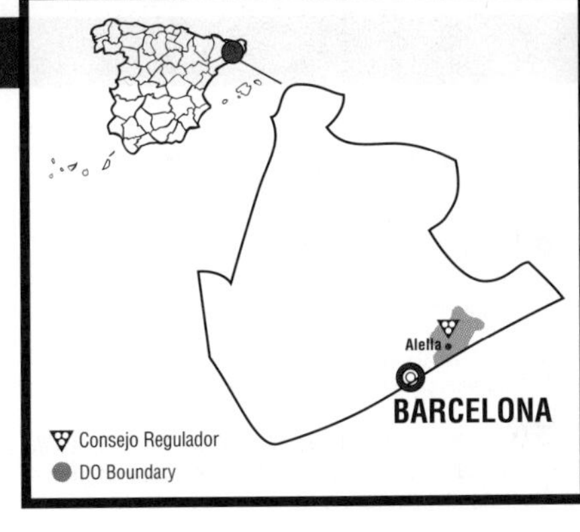

LOCATION:

It extends over the regions of El Maresme and el Vallès in Barcelona. It covers the municipal districts of Alella, Argentona, Cabrils, El Masnou, La Roca del Vallès, Martorelles, Montornès del Vallès, Montgat, Orrius, Premià de Dalt, Premià de Mar, Santa Mª de Martorelles, Sant Fost de Campsentelles, Teià, Tiana, Vallromanes, Vilanova del Vallès and Vilasar de Salt. The main feature of this region is the urban environment which surrounds this small stretch of vineyards; in fact, one of the smallest DO's in Spain.

CLIMATE:

A typically Mediterranean microclimate with mild winters and hot dry summers. The coastal hills play an important role, as they protect the vines from cold winds and condense the humidity from the sea.

SOIL:

Distinction can be made between the clayey soils of the interior slope of the coastal mountain range and the soil situated along the coastline. The latter, known as Sauló, is the most typical. Almost white in colour, it is renowned for it high permeability and great capacity to retain sunlight, which makes for a better ripening of the grapes.

GRAPE VARIETIES:

WHITE: *Pansa Blanca* (similar to the *Xarel·lo* from other regions in Catalonia), *Garnatxa Blanca, Pansa Rosada, Picapoll, Malvasía, Macabeo, Parellada, Chardonnay, Sauvignon Blanc* and *Chenin Blanc.*
RED (MINORITY): *Garnatxa Negra, Ull de Llebre* (*Tempranillo*), *Merlot, Pinot Noir, Syrah, Monastrell, Cabernet Sauvignon, Sumoll and Mataró.*

FIGURES:

Vineyard surface: 320 – **Wine-Growers:** 97 – **Wineries:** 8 – **2011 Harvest rating:** Very Good – **Production:** 569,200 litres – **Market percentages:** 85% domestic. 15% export

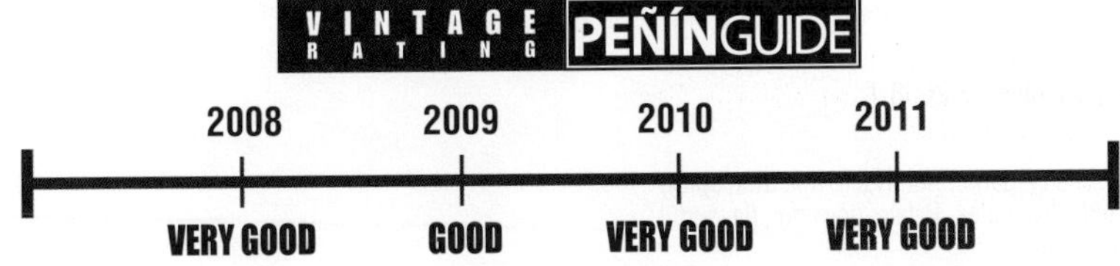

CONSEJO REGULADOR
Masía Can Magarola, s/n - 08328 Alella (Barcelona) - ☎: +34 935 559 153 - Fax: +34 935 405 249
@ doalella@doalella.org - www.doalella.org

ALELLA VINÍCOLA

Angel Guimerà, 62
08328 Alella (Barcelona)
☎: +34 935 403 842 - Fax: +34 935 401 648
xavi@alellavinicola.com
www.alellavinicola.com

MARFIL CLÀSSIC 2011 B
100% pansa blanca.

86 Colour: bright straw. Nose: fresh, white flowers, ripe fruit. Palate: flavourful, fruity, good acidity, balanced.

MARFIL BLANCO SECO 2011 B
100% pansa blanca.

85 Colour: bright golden. Nose: fruit liqueur notes, faded flowers, dried herbs. Palate: light-bodied, fresh, flavourful.

MARFIL MOLT DOLÇ 2003 B
100% pansa blanca.

93 Colour: old gold, amber rim. Nose: floral, honeyed notes, caramel. Palate: rich, spirituous, toasty, balanced, sweetness.

MARFIL GENEROSO SEMI 1976 B
100% pansa blanca.

91 Colour: old gold, amber rim. Nose: powerfull, varnish, sweet spices, candied fruit. Palate: balanced, flavourful, spicy, long, good acidity.

MARFIL GENEROSO SEC 1976 B
100% pansa blanca.

90 Colour: light mahogany. Nose: acetaldehyde, dry nuts, spicy, pattiserie. Palate: good finish, flavourful, toasty.

MARFIL ROSAT 2011 RD
50% garnacha, 50% syrah.

85 Colour: raspberry rose. Nose: floral, candied fruit, ripe fruit. Palate: light-bodied, fresh, fruity, flavourful.

MARFIL 2009 TC
30% garnacha, 40% cabernet sauvignon, 20% syrah, 10% merlot.

84

COSTA DEL MARESME 2008 T
garnacha.

88 Colour: cherry, garnet rim. Nose: ripe fruit, spicy, toasty, fine reductive notes. Palate: powerful, flavourful, toasty, round tannins.

VALLMORA MAGNUM 2008 T
100% garnacha.

87 Colour: cherry, garnet rim. Nose: ripe fruit, spicy, creamy oak, earthy notes, expressive. Palate: powerful, flavourful, toasty, balanced.

MARFIL MAGNUM 2008 TC
40% cabernet sauvignon, 40% garnacha, 20% syrah.

86 Colour: cherry, garnet rim. Nose: ripe fruit, spicy, creamy oak, toasty, balsamic herbs. Palate: powerful, flavourful, toasty, balanced.

MARFIL VIOLETA 2003 T
100% garnacha.

91 Colour: bright cherry, garnet rim. Nose: balsamic herbs, fruit preserve, spicy, dark chocolate. Palate: powerful, flavourful, fruity, toasty.

MARFIL BLANC DE NOIRS 2009 BR
100% garnacha.

89 Colour: bright straw. Nose: medium intensity, fresh fruit, dried herbs, fine lees, floral, elegant. Palate: fresh, fruity, flavourful, good acidity.

MARFIL ROSADO 2009 BR
100% garnacha.

88 Colour: raspberry rose. Nose: white flowers, red berry notes, balsamic herbs, elegant. Palate: fresh, fruity, light-bodied, flavourful, easy to drink.

MARFIL 2008 BN
80% pansa blanca, 20% chardonnay.

87 Colour: bright yellow. Nose: fine lees, dried flowers, fragrant herbs, fresh. Palate: powerful, flavourful, balanced, fine bead.

MARFIL MOSCATEL 2009 ESP
100% moscatel.

90 Colour: bright straw. Nose: candied fruit, white flowers, grapey, fresh. Palate: fresh, fruity, flavourful, good acidity, sweet.

ALTA ALELLA

Camí Baix de Tiana - Finca Can Genis
08391 Tiana (Barcelona)
☎: +34 934 693 720 - Fax: +34 934 691 343
altaalella@altaalella.cat
www.altaalella.cat

ALTA ALELLA LANIUS 2011 BFB
pansa blanca, chardonnay, sauvignon blanc, viognier, moscatel.

90 Colour: bright yellow. Nose: ripe fruit, honeyed notes, fragrant herbs, sweet spices. Palate: flavourful, complex, long, spicy.

ALTA ALELLA PARVUS CHARDONNAY 2011 B
chardonnay, pansa blanca.

89 Colour: bright yellow. Nose: citrus fruit, tropical fruit, floral. Palate: powerful, flavourful, full, easy to drink.

ALTA ALELLA EXEO 2011 BFB
chardonnay, viognier.

89 Colour: bright straw. Nose: white flowers, fresh fruit, sweet spices, citrus fruit. Palate: flavourful, long, creamy, good acidity, balanced.

ALTA ALELLA PANSA BLANCA 2011 B
pansa blanca.

88 Colour: bright straw. Nose: fresh, fresh fruit, white flowers, expressive, fragrant herbs. Palate: flavourful, fruity, fresh.

ALTA ALELLA BLANC DE NEU 2009 BFB
chardonnay, pansa blanca, viognier.

90 Colour: bright golden. Nose: acetaldehyde, ripe fruit, citrus fruit, honeyed notes, sweet spices. Palate: long, full, flavourful, complex.

ALTA ALELLA PARVUS ROSÉ 2011 RD
cabernet sauvignon.

85 Colour: raspberry rose. Nose: floral, ripe fruit, balsamic herbs, medium intensity. Palate: light-bodied, fresh, fruity, flavourful, easy to drink.

ALTA ALELLA PARVUS SYRAH 2010 T
syrah.

87 Colour: bright cherry. Nose: ripe fruit, sweet spices, creamy oak. Palate: flavourful, fruity, toasty, round tannins.

ALTA ALELLA PS XTREM 2010 TC
syrah.

85 Colour: cherry, garnet rim. Nose: ripe fruit, spicy, creamy oak, toasty. Palate: powerful, flavourful, toasty.

ALTA ALELLA ORBUS 2007 TC
syrah.

90 Colour: cherry, garnet rim. Nose: ripe fruit, spicy, creamy oak, toasty, complex. Taste powerful, flavourful, toasty, round tannins.

ALTA ALELLA S XTREM 2007 TC
syrah.

89 Colour: cherry, garnet rim. Nose: ripe fruit, toasty, sweet spices. Palate: flavourful, toasty, balanced.

ALTA ALELLA SYRAH DOLÇ 2006 T
syrah.

90 Colour: cherry, garnet rim. Nose: ripe fruit, fruit liqueur notes, aromatic coffee, sweet spices, toasty. Palate: powerful, flavourful, complex, long.

ALTA ALELLA DOLÇ MATARÓ 2010 TINTO DULCE
monastrell.

91 Colour: cherry, garnet rim. Nose: acetaldehyde, ripe fruit, fruit liqueur notes, dark chocolate, spicy. Palate: powerful, flavourful, rich, balanced.

BODEGAS CASTILLO DE SAJAZARRA

Del Río, s/n
26212 Sajazarra (La Rioja)
☎: +34 941 320 066 - Fax: +34 941 320 251
bodega@castillodesajazarra.com
www.castillodesajazarra.com

IN VITA ELVIWINES KOSHER 2011 B
60% pansa blanca, 40% sauvignon blanc.

90 Colour: bright straw. Nose: fresh, fresh fruit, white flowers, fragrant herbs. Palate: flavourful, fruity, good acidity, balanced.

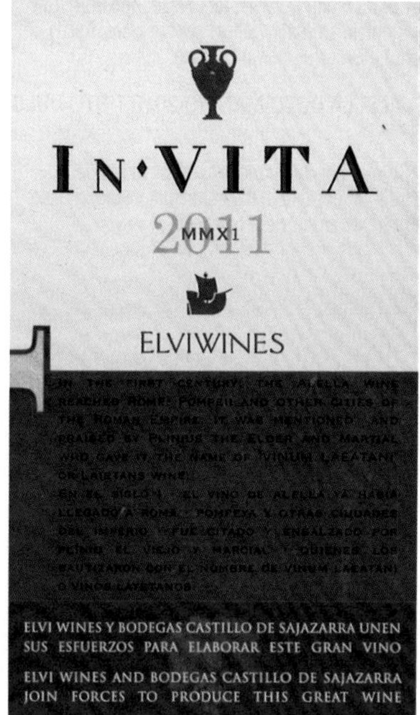

IN VITA 2010 B
60% pansa blanca, 40% sauvignon blanc.

91 Colour: bright straw. Nose: floral, balanced, fresh fruit, fragrant herbs. Palate: flavourful, fruity, good acidity.

BODEGAS ROURA - JUAN ANTONIO PÉREZ ROURA

Valls de Rials
08328 Alella (Barcelona)
☎: +34 933 527 456 - Fax: +34 933 524 339
roura@roura.es
www.roura.es

ROURA XAREL.LO 2011 B
100% xarel.lo.

86 Colour: bright straw. Nose: dried flowers, ripe fruit, fragrant herbs. Palate: light-bodied, fresh, fruity.

ROURA SAUVIGNON BLANC 2011 B
100% sauvignon blanc.

85 Colour: bright straw. Nose: fresh, fresh fruit, white flowers, expressive. Palate: flavourful, fruity, good acidity.

ROURA 2011 RD
100% merlot.

83

ROURA CRIANZA TRES CEPS 2009 TC
50% cabernet sauvignon, 30% merlot, 20% syrah.

88 Colour: cherry, garnet rim. Nose: earthy notes, ripe fruit, scrubland, balanced, creamy oak. Palate: powerful, flavourful, spicy.

ROURA COUPAGE 2009 T
50% merlot, 30% garnacha, 20% cabernet sauvignon.

87 Colour: cherry, garnet rim. Nose: ripe fruit, earthy notes, balsamic herbs, creamy oak. Palate: powerful, flavourful, spicy, long.

ROURA MERLOT 2007 TR
100% merlot.

86 Colour: cherry, garnet rim. Nose: ripe fruit, candied fruit, creamy oak, sweet spices. Palate: powerful, flavourful, spicy.

CELLER JOAQUIM BATLLE

Masía La Sentiu, s/n
08391 Tiana (Barcelona)
☎: +34 933 954 527 - Fax: +34 933 954 534
celler@joaquimbatlle.com
www.vinosdealella.com

FORANELL PICAPOLL 2010 B
picapoll.

86 Colour: bright golden. Nose: white flowers, jasmine, fragrant herbs, ripe fruit. Palate: powerful, flavourful, rich, fine bitter notes.

FORANELL 2009 B
picapoll, garnacha, pansa blanca.

84

FORANELL GARNATXA 2008 B
garnacha blanca.

87 Colour: bright yellow. Nose: powerfull, ripe fruit, sweet spices, creamy oak, fragrant herbs. Palate: rich, flavourful, fresh, good acidity.

FORANELL PANSA BLANCA 2008 B
pansa blanca.

86 Colour: bright golden. Nose: ripe fruit, powerfull, toasty, aged wood nuances, sweet spices. Palate: flavourful, fruity, spicy, toasty, long.

MARQUÉS DE ALELLA

Torrente, 38
08391 Tiana (Barcelona)
☎: +34 933 950 811 - Fax: +34 933 955 500
info@parxet.es
www.parxet.es

MARQUÉS DE ALELLA 2011 B
100% pansa blanca.

89 Colour: bright straw. Nose: fresh fruit, white flowers, expressive, dried herbs. Palate: flavourful, fruity, balanced, round.

MARQUÉS DE ALELLA VIOGNIER 2010 B
100% viognier.

89 Colour: bright yellow. Nose: floral, jasmine, ripe fruit, sweet spices, expressive. Palate: flavourful, rich, spicy, long.

MARQUÉS DE ALELLA PANSA BLANCA 2010 B
100% pansa blanca.

88 Colour: bright straw. Nose: white flowers, dried herbs, ripe fruit, fine lees. Palate: fruity, rich, flavourful, balanced.

MARQUÉS DE ALELLA ALLIER 2009 BFB
100% chardonnay.

90 Colour: bright golden. Nose: ripe fruit, dry nuts, powerfull, toasty, sweet spices. Palate: flavourful, fruity, spicy, toasty, long.

ACOT 2010 RD
100% syrah.

87 Colour: coppery red. Nose: dried flowers, red berry notes, ripe fruit, fragrant herbs. Palate: powerful, flavourful, easy to drink.

SAPIENS THE GAME SCP

Carrer dels Roures, 3
08348 Cabrils (Barcelona)
☎: +34 679 448 722
info@testuan.com
www.testuan.com

TESTUAN 2011 B
100% pansa blanca.

88 Colour: bright straw. Nose: white flowers, fragrant herbs, tropical fruit. Palate: fresh, fruity, light-bodied, flavourful.

DO ALICANTE

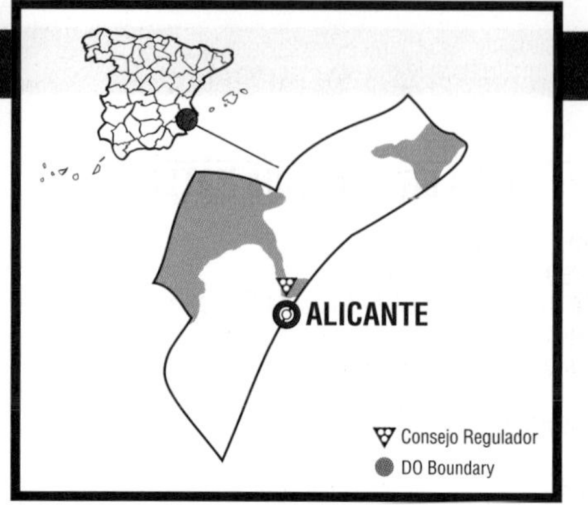

LOCATION:

In the province of Alicante (covering 51 municipal districts), and a small part of the province of Murcia. The vineyards extend over areas close to the coast (in the surroundings of the capital city of Alicante, and especially in the area of La Marina, a traditional producer of Moscatel), as well as in the interior of the province.

CLIMATE:

Distinction must be made between the vineyards situated closer to the coastline, where the climate is clearly Mediterranean and somewhat more humid, and those inland, which receive continental influences and have a lower level of rainfall.

SOIL:

In general, the majority of the soils in the region are of a dun limestone type, with little clay and hardly any organic matter.

GRAPE VARIETIES:

WHITE: *Merseguera, Moscatel de Alejandría, Macabeo, Planta Fina, Verdil, Airén, Chardonnay* and *Sauvignon Blanc.*
RED: *Monastrell, Garnacha Tinta* (*Alicante* or *Giró*), *Garnacha Tintorera, Bobal, Tempranillo, Cabernet Sauvignon, Merlot, Pinot Noir*, *Syrah* and *Petit Verdot.*

FIGURES:

Vineyard surface: 8,785 – **Wine-Growers:** 2,500 – **Wineries:** 54 – **2011 Harvest rating:** Very Good – **Production:** 12,780,129 litres – **Market percentages:** 78% domestic. 22% export

CONSEJO REGULADOR
Orense, 3, Entlo. Dcha. - 03003 Alicante - ☎: +34 965 984 478 - Fax: +34 965 229 295
@ crdo.alicante@crdo-alicante.org - www.crdo-alicante.org

BODEGA COOP. DE ALGUEÑA COOP. V.

Ctra. Rodriguillo, s/n
03668 Algueña (Alicante)
☎: +34 965 476 113 - Fax: +34 965 476 229
bodega@vinosdealguenya.es
www.vinosdealguenya.com

FONDONET 2010 T
100% monastrell.

87 Colour: cherry, garnet rim. Nose: fruit liqueur notes, red berry notes, spicy, faded flowers. Palate: good acidity, sweetness, powerful, flavourful.

TORREVIÑAS DOBLE PASTA 2010 T
100% monastrell.

85 Colour: cherry, garnet rim. Nose: ripe fruit, fruit expression, spicy, warm, toasty. Palate: spirituous, concentrated, fine bitter notes.

ALHENIA 2009 T
100% monastrell.

85 Colour: cherry, garnet rim. Nose: medium intensity, fragrant herbs, scrubland, ripe fruit, sweet spices. Palate: flavourful, spicy, ripe fruit.

CASA JIMÉNEZ 2008 TC
100% monastrell.

84

FONDILLÓN 1980 FONDILLÓN
100% monastrell.

87 Colour: dark mahogany. Nose: acetaldehyde, sweet spices, candied fruit, fruit liqueur notes. Palate: powerful, sweetness, fine bitter notes.

BODEGA COOPERATIVA SANT VICENTE FERRER

Avda. Las Palmas, 32
03725 Teulada (Alicante)
☎: +34 965 740 051 - Fax: +34 965 740 489
bodega@coop-santvicent.com
www.coop-santvicent.com

VIÑA TEULADA 2011 B JOVEN
100% moscatel.

86 Colour: bright straw. Nose: fresh, fresh fruit, white flowers. Palate: flavourful, fruity, good acidity, balanced.

PITÁGORA ESP
100% moscatel.

86 Colour: bright straw. Nose: expressive, varietal, citrus fruit, white flowers. Palate: flavourful, sweetness, fine bead.

TEULADA MOSCATEL RESERVA B RESERVA
moscatel.

90 Colour: light mahogany. Nose: powerfull, characterful, overripe fruit, dried fruit, acetaldehyde, pattiserie. Palate: powerful, sweet, fine bitter notes.

MISTELA SELECTA DE TEULADA VINO DE LICOR
moscatel.

85 Colour: bright straw. Nose: powerfull, characterful, varietal, honeyed notes. Palate: fine bitter notes, sweet, powerful.

BODEGA LA ENCINA

Pedro Más. 23
03407 La Encina (Alicante)
☎: +34 610 410 945 - Fax: +34 962 387 808
info@bodegasoldelaencina.com
www.bodegalaencina.com

ALBALAT 2010 T
monastrell.

88 Colour: cherry, garnet rim. Nose: powerfull, overripe fruit, warm, characterful, toasty, spicy. Palate: powerful, spicy, ripe fruit.

ROJOYDULCE 2010 T
100% monastrell.

78

ALBALAT 2009 TC
monastrell.

87 Colour: cherry, garnet rim. Nose: powerfull, overripe fruit, characterful, scrubland, toasty. Palate: powerful, concentrated, fine bitter notes.

BODEGA NUESTRA SEÑORA DE LAS VIRTUDES COOP. V.

Ctra. de Yecla, 9
03400 Villena (Alicante)
☎: +34 965 802 187
coopvillena@coopvillena.com
www.coopvillena.com

VINALOPÓ ESENCIA DEL MEDITERRÁNEO 2011 B
50% moscatel, 50% sauvignon blanc.

87 Colour: bright straw. Nose: fresh, fresh fruit, white flowers, expressive, fragrant herbs. Palate: flavourful, fruity, easy to drink.

VINALOPÓ MACABEO 2011 B
100% macabeo.

86 Colour: bright yellow. Nose: floral, ripe fruit, citrus fruit, fragrant herbs. Palate: light-bodied, fresh, fruity, easy to drink.

VINALOPÓ SAUVIGNON BLANC 2011 B
100% sauvignon blanc.

84

VINALOPÓ 2011 T
50% monastrell, 50% merlot.

87 Colour: cherry, purple rim. Nose: expressive, fresh fruit, red berry notes, floral. Palate: flavourful, fruity, good acidity, round tannins.

VINALOPÓ PETIT VERDOT 2010 T
100% petit verdot.

87 Colour: cherry, garnet rim. Nose: characterful, ripe fruit, scrubland, spicy. Palate: flavourful, spicy, fine bitter notes, good acidity.

VINALOPÓ MONASTRELL 2010 T
100% monastrell.

84

VINALOPÓ 2008 TC
50% monastrell, 50% cabernet sauvignon.

88 Colour: pale ruby, brick rim edge. Nose: overripe fruit, scrubland, old leather, creamy oak. Palate: powerful, flavourful, spicy, toasty.

VINALOPÓ 2005 TR
50% monastrell, 50% cabernet sauvignon.

82

TESORO DE VILLENA RESERVA ESPECIAL FONDILLÓN FONDILLÓN SOLERA
100% monastrell.

90 Colour: light mahogany. Nose: fruit liqueur notes, acetaldehyde, dried fruit, aromatic coffee, roasted almonds, caramel. Palate: powerful, spirituous, fine bitter notes, spirituous.

BODEGA SANTA CATALINA DEL MAÑÁN

Ctra. Monóvar-Pinoso, Km. 10,5
03649 Mañán Monóvar (Alicante)
☎: +34 966 960 096 - Fax: +34 966 960 096
bodegamanan@terra.es

MAÑÁ MARISQUERO 2011 B
50% moscatel, 50% macabeo.

86 Colour: bright straw. Nose: fresh, fresh fruit, white flowers. Palate: flavourful, fruity, good acidity, balanced.

MAÑÁ CHARDONNAY 2011 B
100% chardonnay.

85 Colour: bright straw. Nose: ripe fruit, tropical fruit, floral. Palate: fresh, fruity, light-bodied.

TORRENT DEL MAÑÁ 2011 B
50% airén, 50% merseguera.

82

TORRENT DEL MAÑÁ 2011 RD
monastrell.

88 Colour: rose, purple rim. Nose: powerfull, ripe fruit, red berry notes, floral, expressive. Palate: fleshy, powerful, fruity, fresh.

MAÑÁ SYRAH 2011 RD
100% syrah.

84

TERRA DEL MAÑÁ 2010 T
100% monastrell.

88 Colour: cherry, purple rim. Nose: floral, red berry notes, raspberry, expressive. Palate: powerful, flavourful, fruity, long.

MAÑA RUSTIC 2007 TC
100% cabernet sauvignon.

85 Colour: cherry, garnet rim. Nose: ripe fruit, toasty, grassy. Palate: powerful, flavourful, toasty.

TORRENT DEL MAÑÁ 2007 TC
70% monastrell, 15% merlot, 15% syrah.

84

TERRA DEL MAÑÁ 2007 TC
40% monastrell, 30% cabernet sauvignon, 30% tempranillo.

82

TORRENT DEL MAÑÁ 2006 TR
85% monastrell, 15% cabernet sauvignon.

82

GRAN MAÑÁN 1982 FONDILLÓN
100% monastrell.

87 Colour: light mahogany. Nose: spicy, aged wood nuances, aromatic coffee, acetaldehyde. Palate: powerful, sweet, fine bitter notes, spirituous.

GRAN MAÑÁN MOSCATEL
100% moscatel.

87 Colour: bright straw. Nose: powerfull, varietal, faded flowers, candied fruit. Palate: powerful, sweet, fine bitter notes, good acidity.

BODEGA VINESSENS

Ctra. de Caudete, Km. 1
03400 Villena (Alicante)
☎: +34 965 800 265
comercial@vinessens.es
www.vinessens.es

ESSENS 2011 BFB
chardonnay.

92 Colour: bright yellow. Nose: powerfull, ripe fruit, sweet spices, creamy oak, fragrant herbs. Palate: rich, smoky aftertaste, flavourful, fresh, good acidity.

SEIN 2010 TC
60% monastrell, 40% syrah.

92 Colour: cherry, garnet rim. Nose: spicy, creamy oak, toasty, complex, mineral, overripe fruit. Palate: powerful, flavourful, toasty, round tannins.

SEIN 2009 TC
monastrell, syrah.

92 Colour: cherry, garnet rim. Nose: spicy, creamy oak, toasty, characterful, ripe fruit, mineral. Palate: powerful, flavourful, toasty, round tannins.

EL TELAR 2009 TC
100% monastrell.

92 Colour: cherry, garnet rim. Nose: spicy, creamy oak, toasty, complex, varietal, warm. Palate: powerful, flavourful, toasty, round tannins.

BODEGAS ALEJANDRO PÉREZ MARTÍNEZ

El Mañán, HJ10
03640 Monóvar (Alicante)
☎: +34 966 960 291
bodegasalejandro@gmail.com

VEGA CUYAR 2011 B

85 Colour: bright straw. Nose: medium intensity, citrus fruit, white flowers. Palate: flavourful, fruity.

VEGA CUYAR 2011 T
100% monastrell.

86 Colour: cherry, purple rim. Nose: red berry notes, floral, wild herbs. Palate: flavourful, fruity, round tannins.

BODEGAS BERNABÉ NAVARRO

Ctra. Villena-Cañada, Km. 3
03400 Villena (Alicante)
☎: +34 966 770 353 - Fax: +34 966 770 353
info@bodegasbernabenavarro.com
www.bodegasbernabenavarro.com

BERYNA 2010 T
monastrell, otras.

92 Colour: cherry, garnet rim. Nose: mineral, powerfull, characterful, candied fruit, ripe fruit, toasty. Palate: powerful, concentrated, sweetness, fine bitter notes.

CASA BALAGUER 2008 T
monastrell, otras.

92 Colour: bright cherry. Nose: sweet spices, creamy oak, expressive, overripe fruit. Palate: flavourful, fruity, toasty, round tannins.

CURRO 2010 T
60% cabernet sauvignon, 40% monastrell.

95 Colour: cherry, garnet rim. Nose: ripe fruit, spicy, creamy oak, toasty, complex, earthy notes, powerfull. Palate: powerful, flavourful, toasty, round tannins.

BODEGAS BOCOPA

Paraje Les Pedreres, Autovía A-31, km. 200 - 201
03610 Petrer (Alicante)
☎: +34 966 950 489 - Fax: +34 966 950 406
info@bocopa.com
www.bocopa.com

MARINA ESPUMANTE RD
100% monastrell.

85 Colour: rose. Nose: powerfull, red berry notes, floral, fragrant herbs. Palate: flavourful, fruity, fresh.

ALCANTA MONASTRELL 2011 T
100% monastrell.

87 Colour: cherry, purple rim. Nose: red berry notes, floral, faded flowers, ripe fruit. Palate: flavourful, fruity, good acidity, round tannins.

TERRETA ROSÉ 2011 RD
100% monastrell.

89 Colour: raspberry rose. Nose: rose petals, fresh fruit, red berry notes, lactic notes. Palate: good acidity, powerful, flavourful, fresh, fruity, easy to drink.

LAUDUM CHARDONNAY 2010 BFB
100% chardonnay.

87 Colour: bright yellow. Nose: powerfull, ripe fruit, sweet spices, creamy oak. Palate: rich, smoky aftertaste, flavourful, fresh, good acidity.

LAUDUM 2007 TC
monastrell, merlot, cabernet sauvignon.

84

MARINA ALTA 2011 B
100% moscatel.

88 Colour: bright straw. Nose: fresh, fresh fruit, white flowers, varietal. Palate: flavourful, fruity, good acidity, balanced.

ALCANTA 2008 TC
monastrell, tempranillo.

88 Colour: cherry, garnet rim. Nose: ripe fruit, spicy, creamy oak, toasty, expressive. Palate: powerful, flavourful, toasty, round tannins.

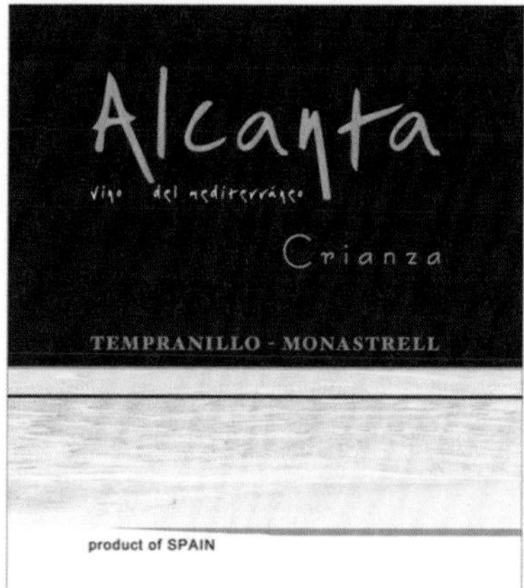

LAUDUM PETIT VERDOT 2008 T
100% petit verdot.

85 Colour: bright cherry. Nose: ripe fruit, sweet spices, creamy oak, scrubland. Palate: flavourful, fruity, toasty.

LAUDUM CABERNET SAUVIGNON 2008 T
100% cabernet sauvignon.

84

MARINA ESPUMANTE B
100% moscatel de alejandría.

87 Colour: bright straw. Nose: characterful, ripe fruit, citrus fruit, white flowers. Palate: flavourful, fruity, sweetness, good acidity, fine bead.

BODEGAS E. MENDOZA

Partida El Romeral, s/n
03580 Alfaz del Pi (Alicante)
☎: +34 965 888 639 - Fax: +34 965 889 232
bodegas-mendoza@bodegasmendoza.com
www.bodegasmendoza.com

ENRIQUE MENDOZA MOSCATEL DE MENDOZA 2009 B
100% moscatel.

94 Colour: bright straw. Nose: powerfull, varietal, characterful, complex, ripe fruit, citrus fruit, honeyed notes. Palate: flavourful, powerful, sweet, good acidity.

LAS QUEBRADAS 2010 T
100% monastrell.

94 Colour: cherry, garnet rim. Nose: ripe fruit, spicy, creamy oak, toasty, complex, earthy notes. Palate: powerful, flavourful, toasty, balanced.

ENRIQUE MENDOZA PETIT VERDOT 2010 TC
petit verdot.

93 Colour: cherry, garnet rim. Nose: ripe fruit, spicy, creamy oak, toasty, balsamic herbs, earthy notes. Palate: flavourful, toasty, round tannins, balanced.

ENRIQUE MENDOZA SHIRAZ 2009 TC
100% syrah.

92 Colour: cherry, garnet rim. Nose: fruit expression, red berry notes, toasty, sweet spices, new oak. Palate: powerful, flavourful, harsh oak tannins.

LA TREMENDA 2009 T
100% monastrell.

92 Colour: bright cherry. Nose: ripe fruit, sweet spices, creamy oak, mineral, smoky. Palate: flavourful, fruity, toasty, round tannins.

ENRIQUE MENDOZA SANTA ROSA 2008 TR
cabernet sauvignon, merlot, syrah.

93 Colour: cherry, garnet rim. Nose: ripe fruit, spicy, creamy oak, balsamic herbs, earthy notes. Palate: powerful, flavourful, toasty, round tannins, balanced, elegant.

ENRIQUE MENDOZA CABERNET - SHIRAZ 2008 TR
50% cabernet sauvignon, 50% syrah.

91 Colour: bright cherry. Nose: ripe fruit, sweet spices, creamy oak. Palate: flavourful, fruity, toasty, round tannins.

ENRIQUE MENDOZA MERLOT MONASTRELL 2008 T
50% merlot, 50% monastrell.

89 Colour: cherry, garnet rim. Nose: ripe fruit, spicy, creamy oak, toasty. Palate: powerful, flavourful, toasty, round tannins.

ENRIQUE MENDOZA CABERNET MONASTRELL 2008 T
50% cabernet sauvignon, 50% monastrell.

88 Colour: cherry, garnet rim. Nose: powerfull, toasty, sweet spices. Palate: flavourful, powerful, fine bitter notes.

ENRIQUE MENDOZA SANTA ROSA 2007 TR
70% cabernet sauvignon, 15% merlot, 15% syrah.

93 Colour: cherry, garnet rim. Nose: fruit expression, sweet spices, creamy oak, toasty, dark chocolate. Palate: powerful, spicy, ripe fruit, fine bitter notes.

ESTRECHO MONASTRELL 2007 T
100% monastrell.

92 Colour: cherry, garnet rim. Nose: spicy, creamy oak, toasty, characterful, warm, ripe fruit. Palate: powerful, flavourful, toasty, round tannins.

BODEGAS FAELO

Poeta Miguel Hernández, 60
03201 Elche (Alicante)
☎: +34 655 856 898
info@vinosladama.com
www.vinosladama.com

PALMA BLANCA 2011 B
100% moscatel.

88 Colour: bright golden. Nose: powerfull, varietal, candied fruit, citrus fruit, fruit liqueur notes. Palate: flavourful, sweet, good acidity.

L'ALBA 2011 RD
100% syrah.

87 Colour: rose, purple rim. Nose: powerfull, ripe fruit, floral, expressive. Palate: , powerful, fruity, fresh.

LA DAMA 2007 TC
60% cabernet sauvignon, 30% monastrell, 10% petit verdot.

88 Colour: very deep cherry. Nose: toasty, fruit liqueur notes, spicy, cocoa bean. Palate: spicy, ripe fruit, fine bitter notes.

BODEGAS FONDARIUM

Avda. de Alicante, s/n
03760 Ondara (Alicante)
☎: +34 619 172 487
info@bodegasfondarium.es
www.bodegasfondarium.es

FONDARIUM 2011 B
100% moscatel de alejandría.

87 Colour: bright yellow. Nose: white flowers, tropical fruit, ripe fruit, saline. Palate: light-bodied, fresh, fruity, easy to drink.

FONDARIUM 2006 TC

84

BODEGAS FRANCISCO GÓMEZ

Ctra. Villena - Pinoso, Km. 8,8
03400 Villena (Alicante)
☎: +34 965 979 195 - Fax: +34 965 979 196
info@bodegasfranciscogomez.es
www.bodegasfranciscogomez.es

BOCA NEGRA 2007 TC
monastrell.

90 Colour: bright cherry, garnet rim. Nose: powerfull, ripe fruit, spicy, mineral, balanced. Palate: warm, powerful, flavourful, round tannins.

SERRATA 2006 TR
monastrell, merlot, petit verdot, cabernet sauvignon.

88 Colour: cherry, garnet rim. Nose: ripe fruit, scrubland, spicy, mineral. Palate: powerful, flavourful, round tannins, toasty.

BOCA NEGRA DULCE T
monastrell.

87 Colour: deep cherry, orangey edge. Nose: overripe fruit, spicy, aromatic coffee, toasty. Palate: sweetness, rich, good finish.

BODEGAS GUTIÉRREZ DE LA VEGA

Les Quintanes, 1
03792 Parcent (Alicante)
☎: +34 966 403 871 - Fax: +34 966 405 257
info@castadiva.es
www.castadiva.es

CASTA DIVA COSECHA DORADA 2011 B
moscatel.

89 Colour: bright straw. Nose: white flowers, fresh fruit, citrus fruit. Palate: flavourful, fruity, fresh.

FURTIVA LÁGRIMA 2010 B

93 Colour: golden. Nose: candied fruit, white flowers, citrus fruit, honeyed notes. Palate: flavourful, sweet, fresh, fruity, long.

LA DIVA 2010 BC
moscatel.

92 Colour: golden. Aroma powerfull, floral, honeyed notes, candied fruit, fragrant herbs. Taste flavourful, sweet, fresh, fruity, good acidity, long.

CASTA DIVA RESERVA REAL 2002 B RESERVA
100% moscatel de alejandría.

95 Colour: bright golden. Nose: ripe fruit, faded flowers, mineral, acetaldehyde, sweet spices, cocoa bean, toasty. Palate: powerful, flavourful, balanced, long, toasty.

CASTA DIVA ESENCIAL "A LUCRECIA BORI" B
100% moscatel de alejandría.

97 Colour: iodine, amber rim. Nose: citrus fruit, floral, fragrant herbs, sweet spices, creamy oak, pattiserie. Palate: powerful, flavourful, creamy, long, ripe fruit, balanced.

CASTA DIVA RECÓNDITA ARMONÍA 2009 T

93 Colour: cherry, garnet rim. Nose: overripe fruit, ripe fruit, scrubland, mineral, spicy, creamy oak. Palate: powerful, flavourful, complex, long, balsamic.

PRÍNCIPE DE SALINAS 2009 TC
monastrell.

90 Colour: cherry, garnet rim. Nose: ripe fruit, medium intensity, earthy notes, complex, varietal. Palate: good structure, fruity, full.

ROJO Y NEGRO 2009 T
garnacha.

87 Colour: cherry, garnet rim. Nose: balanced, scrubland, spicy, ripe fruit. Palate: flavourful, correct.

VIÑA ULISES 2006 TR
garnacha, monastrell.

89 Colour: cherry, garnet rim. Nose: ripe fruit, spicy, creamy oak, toasty, warm. Palate: powerful, flavourful, toasty, round tannins.

CASTA DIVA 2001 FONDILLÓN

93 Colour: pale ruby, brick rim edge. Nose: acetaldehyde, varnish, aged wood nuances, dried fruit, expressive, toasty. Palate: long, ripe fruit, sweetness, spicy, toasty.

CASTA DIVA FONDILLÓN SOLERA 1987 FONDILLÓN
100% monastrell.

96 Colour: dark-red cherry. Nose: dry nuts, dried fruit, dark chocolate, sweet spices, creamy oak, toasty, acetaldehyde. Palate: fine bitter notes, flavourful, long, toasty, balanced, elegant.

BODEGAS MURVIEDRO

Ampliación Pol. El Romeral, s/n
46340 Requena (Valencia)
☎: +34 962 329 003 - Fax: +34 962 329 002
murviedro@murviedro.es
www.murviedro.es

DULCE DE MURVIEDRO 2011 B
moscatel de alejandría.

85 Colour: bright straw. Nose: powerfull, candied fruit, overripe fruit, citrus fruit. Palate: pruney, long, flavourful, sweet.

CUEVA DEL PERDÓN 2009 T
60% monastrell, 40% syrah.

90 Colour: bright cherry. Nose: sweet spices, creamy oak, expressive, ripe fruit. Palate: flavourful, fruity, toasty, round tannins.

BODEGAS PARCENT

Avda. Denia, 15 (Ctra. Parcent Alcalali)
03792 Parcent (Alicante)
☎: +34 636 536 693 - Fax: +34 966 405 467
armando@bodegasparcent.com
www.bodegasparcent.com

AURO 2011 B
chardonnay, moscatel.

88 Colour: bright straw. Nose: white flowers, tropical fruit, wild herbs. Palate: fine bitter notes, powerful, flavourful, fruity.

GRÀ D'OR BLANCO SECO 2011 B
moscatel.

83

DOLÇ D'ART B

87 Colour: bright straw. Nose: citrus fruit, fresh fruit, white flowers. Palate: flavourful, fruity, fresh.

ROSAT 2011 RD
syrah.

86 Colour: brilliant rose. Nose: floral, wild herbs, fruit expression. Palate: light-bodied, fresh, fruity, easy to drink.

BODEGAS SIERRA DE CABRERAS

Mollenta, 27
03638 Salinas (Alicante)
☎: +34 647 515 590
info@carabibas.com
www.carabibas.com

CARABIBAS VS 2010 T
65% cabernet sauvignon, 30% merlot, 5% monastrell.

91 Colour: bright cherry. Nose: sweet spices, creamy oak, expressive, overripe fruit, mineral. Palate: flavourful, fruity, toasty, round tannins.

BODEGAS SIERRA SALINAS

Paraje del Puerto, s/n (Ctra. Villena-Pinoso, km. 16)
30400 Villena (Alicante)
☎: +34 968 791 271 - Fax: +34 968 791 900
office@sierrasalinas.com
www.sierrasalinas.com

MO SALINAS MOSCATEL CHARDONNAY 2011 B
50% moscatel, 50% chardonnay.

88 Colour: bright straw. Nose: fresh, fresh fruit, white flowers. Palate: flavourful, fruity, good acidity, balanced.

MO SALINAS MONASTRELL 2011 RD
90% monastrell, 5% cabernet sauvignon, 5% garnacha tintorera.

87 Colour: bright cherry. Nose: medium intensity, fresh, red berry notes. Palate: easy to drink, light-bodied, fruity.

MO SALINAS MONASTRELL 2010 T
85% monastrell, 10% cabernet sauvignon, 5% garnacha tintorera.

90 Colour: bright cherry. Nose: ripe fruit, sweet spices, creamy oak, expressive, dark chocolate. Palate: flavourful, fruity, toasty, round tannins.

MIRA SALINAS 2009 T
50% monastrell, 20% cabernet sauvignon, 20% garnacha tintorera, 10% petit verdot.

93 Colour: cherry, garnet rim. Nose: spicy, creamy oak, toasty, complex, earthy notes, dry stone, fruit expression. Palate: powerful, flavourful, toasty, round tannins.

PUERTO SALINAS 2008 T
65% monastrell, 20% cabernet sauvignon, 15% garnacha tintorera.

90 Colour: cherry, garnet rim. Nose: dark chocolate, creamy oak, toasty, overripe fruit. Palate: spirituous, powerful, fine bitter notes.

SALINAS 1237 2007 T
20% monastrell, 40% cabernet sauvignon, 40% garnacha tintorera.

93 Colour: black cherry. Nose: powerfull, characterful, complex, creamy oak, toasty, new oak, ripe fruit. Palate: powerful, concentrated, good structure, harsh oak tannins.

BODEGAS TERRA NATURA

Pintor Juan Gris, 26
03400 Villena (Alicante)
☎: +34 965 801 486 - Fax: +34 965 800 978
comercial@aymnavarro.com
www.bodegasterranatura.com

TERRA NATURA 2011 B
macabeo.

86 Colour: bright straw. Nose: dried flowers, ripe fruit, fragrant herbs. Palate: thin, light-bodied, fresh, fruity.

TERRA NATURA 2011 T
100% monastrell.

89 Colour: cherry, purple rim. Nose: expressive, fresh fruit, red berry notes, floral. Palate: flavourful, fruity, good acidity, balanced.

MIGUEL NAVARRO MONASTRELL TEMPRANILLO 2010 T BARRICA
tempranillo, monastrell.

89 Colour: bright cherry. Nose: ripe fruit, sweet spices, creamy oak, warm. Palate: flavourful, toasty, round tannins.

MIGUEL NAVARRO 2007 TC
monastrell, syrah.

89 Colour: black cherry. Nose: red berry notes, dried flowers, scrubland, creamy oak. Palate: powerful, flavourful, balanced.

TERRA NATURA CLÁSICO 2006 TC
merlot.

87 Colour: deep cherry, garnet rim. Nose: spicy, pattiserie, aromatic coffee, wet leather, fruit liqueur notes. Palate: fine bitter notes, spirituous, spicy.

BODEGAS VICENTE GANDÍA

Ctra. Cheste a Godelleta, s/n
46370 Chiva (Valencia)
☎: +34 962 524 242 - Fax: +34 962 524 243
vuboldi@vicentegandia.com
www.vicentegandia.es

PUERTO ALICANTE CHARDONNAY 2011 B
100% chardonnay.

87 Colour: bright straw. Nose: candied fruit, citrus fruit, medium intensity. Palate: fine bitter notes, balanced, good acidity.

EL MIRACLE FUSIÓN 2011 B
70% chardonnay, 20% sauvignon blanc, 10% moscatel.

86 Colour: bright straw. Nose: white flowers, citrus fruit, fragrant herbs. Palate: flavourful, fruity, easy to drink.

EL MIRACLE MUSIC 2011 RD
syrah, garnacha.

86 Colour: rose, purple rim. Nose: powerfull, ripe fruit, red berry notes, floral. Palate: , powerful, fruity, fresh, easy to drink.

EL MIRACLE PLANET ORGANIC WINE 2011 T
100% monastrell.

84

PUERTO ALICANTE SYRAH 2010 T
100% syrah.

88 Colour: cherry, garnet rim. Nose: powerfull, ripe fruit, sweet spices, creamy oak. Palate: powerful, fine bitter notes, ripe fruit.

EL MIRACLE ART 2009 T
25% monastrell, 20% pinot noir, 20% syrah, 20% merlot, 15% tempranillo.

87 Colour: bright cherry. Nose: sweet spices, expressive, candied fruit, spicy. Palate: flavourful, fruity, toasty, round tannins.

BODEGAS VIVANZA

Ctra. Jumilla Pinoso , Km. 13
30520 Jumilla (Murcia)
☎: +34 965 980 144 - Fax: +34 965 215 651
agomez@domka.es
www.vivanza.es

VIVANZA 2011 B
verdil, sauvignon blanc.

85 Colour: bright straw. Nose: fresh, fresh fruit, white flowers, grassy. Palate: flavourful, fruity, good acidity.

VIVANZA 2009 T
monastrell, syrah, pinot noir.

85 Colour: cherry, purple rim. Nose: red berry notes, earthy notes, scrubland. Palate: flavourful, fruity, toasty.

LASCALA 2009 T
monastrell, cabernet sauvignon.

80

BODEGAS VOLVER

Pza. de Grecia, 1 Local 1B
45005 Toledo (Toledo)
☎: +34 925 167 493 - Fax: +34 925 167 059
export@bodegasvolver.com
www.bodegasvolver.com

TARIMA 2011 B
macabeo, merseguera, moscatel.

86 Colour: bright straw. Nose: fresh, fresh fruit, white flowers, balanced. Palate: flavourful, fruity, good acidity, balanced.

TARIMA MONASTREL 2011 T
monastrell.

88 Colour: deep cherry. Nose: fresh fruit, red berry notes, varietal, spicy. Palate: flavourful, fruity, good acidity, round tannins.

TARIMA MONASTREL 2010 T
100% monastrell.

88 Colour: cherry, garnet rim. Nose: expressive, varietal, sweet spices, aromatic coffee. Palate: flavourful, spicy, ripe fruit.

TARIMA HILL 2009 T
100% monastrell.

90 Colour: cherry, garnet rim. Nose: spicy, creamy oak, toasty, complex, overripe fruit. Palate: powerful, flavourful, toasty, round tannins.

BODEGAS XALÓ

Ctra. Xaló Alcalali, s/n
03727 Xaló (Alicante)
☎: +34 966 480 034 - Fax: +34 966 480 808
comercial@bodegasxalo.com
www.bodegasxalo.com

BAHÍA DE DENIA 2011 B JOVEN
100% moscatel.

90 Colour: bright straw. Nose: fresh, white flowers, varietal, ripe fruit. Palate: flavourful, fruity, good acidity, balanced.

VALL DE XALÓ 2011 B JOVEN
100% moscatel.

85 Colour: pale. Nose: fresh, fresh fruit, citrus fruit. Palate: flavourful, light-bodied, easy to drink.

VALL DE XALÓ 2011 T
100% garnacha.

86 Colour: cherry, purple rim. Nose: red berry notes, floral, ripe fruit. Palate: flavourful, fruity, good acidity, round tannins.

SERRA DE BERNIA 2010 T ROBLE
garnacha, syrah.

87 Colour: bright cherry. Nose: ripe fruit, sweet spices, creamy oak, expressive. Palate: flavourful, fruity, toasty, round tannins.

VALL DE XALÓ GIRÓ 2011
100% garnacha.

85 Colour: ruby red, brick rim edge. Nose: dried fruit, sweet spices, toasty. Palate: correct, unctuous, powerful, flavourful.

VALL DE XALÓ 2011 MISTELA
100% moscatel.

87 Colour: bright straw. Nose: powerfull, varietal, characterful, fruit expression, citrus fruit. Palate: powerful, sweetness, fine bitter notes, good acidity.

RIU RAU 2010 MISTELA
100% moscatel.

90 Colour: light mahogany. Nose: dried fruit, toasty, caramel, sweet spices. Palate: powerful, flavourful, sweetness, toasty.

BODEGAS Y VIÑEDOS EL SEQUÉ

El Sequé, 59
03650 Pinoso (Alicante)
☎: +34 945 600 119 - Fax: +34 945 600 850
elseque@artadi.com

EL SEQUÉ 2010 T
100% monastrell.

94 Colour: bright cherry. Nose: sweet spices, creamy oak, expressive, scrubland, red berry notes, toasty. Palate: flavourful, fruity, toasty, round tannins.

COMERCIAL GRUPO FREIXENET

Joan Sala, 2
08770 Sant Sadurní D'Anoia (Barcelona)
☎: +34 938 917 000 - Fax: +34 938 183 095
freixenet@freixenet.es
www.freixenet.es

NAUTA 2006 TC
100% monastrell.

90 Colour: light cherry, garnet rim. Nose: ripe fruit, creamy oak, sweet spices. Palate: powerful, flavourful, toasty, long.

FINCA COLLADO

Ctra. Villena Salinas, s/n
03638 Salinas (Alicante)
☎: +34 607 510 710 - Fax: +34 962 878 818
info@fincacollado.com
www.fincacollado.com

FINCA COLLADO 2010 BFB
chardonnay, moscatel.

84

FINCA COLLADO MERLOT 2009 T BARRICA
merlot.

87 Colour: bright cherry. Nose: sweet spices, creamy oak, ripe fruit. Palate: flavourful, fruity, toasty, round tannins.

FINCA COLLADO 2008 T
cabernet sauvignon, merlot.

88 Colour: cherry, garnet rim. Nose: ripe fruit, spicy, creamy oak, toasty. Palate: powerful, flavourful, toasty, long.

IBERICA BRUNO PRATS

Ctra. Monovar - Salinas CV 830, km. 3,2
03640 Monovar (Alicante)
☎: +34 645 963 122
stephanepoint@hotmail.com
www.fideliswines.com

MOSYCA 2009 T
30% syrah, 25% monastrell, 25% cabernet sauvignon, 20% petit verdot.

91 Colour: cherry, garnet rim. Nose: ripe fruit, spicy, creamy oak, toasty, varietal. Palate: powerful, flavourful, toasty, round tannins.

ALFYNAL 2009 T
100% monastrell.

90 Colour: black cherry. Nose: powerfull, varietal, characterful, overripe fruit, creamy oak, toasty. Palate: powerful, flavourful, concentrated, good acidity.

LA BODEGA DE PINOSO

Paseo de la Constitución, 82
03650 Pinoso (Alicante)
☎: +34 965 477 040 - Fax: +34 966 970 149
dptocomercial@labodegadepinoso.com
www.labodegadepinoso.com

VERMADOR 2011 B
50% macabeo, 50% airén.

87 Colour: bright straw. Nose: fresh, fresh fruit, white flowers, expressive, fragrant herbs. Palate: flavourful, fruity, good acidity.

TORRE DEL RELOJ 2011 B
50% macabeo, 50% airén.

83

VERMADOR 2011 RD
100% monastrell.

88 Colour: light cherry. Nose: ripe fruit, red berry notes, floral, expressive. Palate: , powerful, fruity, fresh.

TORRE DEL RELOJ 2011 RD
100% monastrell.

86 Colour: rose, purple rim. Nose: powerfull, red berry notes, floral. Palate: , powerful, fruity, fresh, easy to drink.

VERGEL SELECCIÓN BARRICAS 2010 T
70% monastrell, 20% syrah, 10% merlot.

90 Colour: cherry, garnet rim. Nose: ripe fruit, fruit expression, creamy oak, sweet spices. Palate: powerful, good structure, fine bitter notes.

VERGEL 2010 T
75% alicante bouschet, 20% merlot, 5% monastrell.

89 Colour: cherry, garnet rim. Nose: powerfull, characterful, ripe fruit, toasty, dark chocolate. Palate: powerful, spicy, good acidity.

PONTOS CEPA 50 2010 T
100% monastrell.

88 Colour: cherry, garnet rim. Nose: powerfull, characterful, spicy, dark chocolate. Palate: flavourful, concentrated, good acidity.

TORRE DEL RELOJ MONASTRELL 2010 T
100% monastrell.

87 Colour: cherry, garnet rim. Nose: powerfull, varietal, warm, scrubland. Palate: powerful, spicy, fine bitter notes.

VERMADOR 2010 T BARRICA
85% monastrell, 15% syrah.

86 Colour: cherry, garnet rim. Nose: red berry notes, ripe fruit, sweet spices. Palate: fruity, flavourful, toasty.

VERMADOR 2010 T
100% monastrell.

85 Colour: cherry, garnet rim. Nose: scrubland, spicy, ripe fruit. Palate: flavourful, powerful, fine bitter notes.

PONTOS 1932 2008 TC
100% monastrell.

88 Colour: pale ruby, brick rim edge. Nose: acetaldehyde, toasty, cocoa bean, fruit liqueur notes. Palate: powerful, flavourful, long, spicy, balanced.

PONTOS CLASIC 06 2006 TC
85% monastrell, 10% merlot, 5% cabernet sauvignon.

86 Colour: black cherry, orangey edge. Nose: overripe fruit, tobacco, old leather, toasty. Palate: good acidity, powerful, flavourful.

PRIMITIVO QUILES

Mayor, 4
03640 Monóvar (Alicante)
☎: +34 965 470 099 - Fax: +34 966 960 235
info@primitivoquiles.com
www.primitivoquiles.com

PRIMITIVO QUILES MONASTRELL-MERLOT 2010 T ROBLE
60% monastrell, 40% merlot.

84

PRIMITIVO QUILES MONASTRELL 2007 TC
100% monastrell.

83

RASPAY 2005 T RESERVA ESPECIAL
100% monastrell.

83

GRAN IMPERIAL GE
100% moscatel.

92 Colour: dark mahogany. Nose: powerfull, warm, fruit liqueur notes, fruit liqueur notes, sweet spices, aromatic coffee, dark chocolate. Palate: powerful, sweet, good acidity, fine bitter notes, spirituous.

PRIMITIVO QUILES FONDILLÓN 1948 GE
100% monastrell.

91 Colour: light mahogany. Nose: acetaldehyde, fruit liqueur notes, fruit liqueur notes, aromatic coffee, caramel. Palate: flavourful, powerful, spirituous, spicy, long.

PRIMITIVO QUILES MOSCATEL EXTRA VINO DE LICOR
100% moscatel.

88 Colour: light mahogany. Nose: acetaldehyde, dried fruit, caramel, dark chocolate, sweet spices. Palate: powerful, flavourful, rich, complex.

SALVADOR POVEDA

CV 830 Ctra. Salinas, Km. 3
03640 Monóvar (Alicante)
☎: +34 966 960 180 - Fax: +34 965 473 389
salvadorpoveda@salvadorpoveda.com
www.salvadorpoveda.com

TOSCAR MONASTRELL 2010 T
100% monastrell.

88 Colour: garnet rim. Nose: red berry notes, wild herbs, mineral, creamy oak. Palate: easy to drink, flavourful, powerful.

TOSCAR SYRAH 2009 T
100% syrah.

86 Colour: cherry, purple rim. Nose: floral, jasmine, wild herbs, ripe fruit. Palate: powerful, flavourful, toasty.

TOSCAR CABERNET SAUVIGNON 2008 TC
cabernet sauvignon.

86 Colour: cherry, garnet rim. Nose: fruit liqueur notes, dried fruit, creamy oak, dark chocolate. Palate: powerful, sweetness, powerful tannins.

TOSCAR MERLOT 2008 TC
merlot.

84

VIÑA VERMETA 2006 TR
monastrell.

86 Colour: bright cherry. Aroma ripe fruit, sweet spices, creamy oak, expressive. Taste flavourful, fruity, toasty, round tannins.

BORRASCA 2006 T
monastrell.

85 Colour: light cherry, orangey edge. Nose: scrubland, fruit preserve. Palate: flavourful, ripe fruit.

VINS DEL COMTAT

Turballos, 1 - 3
03820 Cocentaina (Alicante)
☎: +34 965 593 194 - Fax: +34 965 593 590
info@vinsdelcomtat.com
www.vinsdelcomtat.com

CRISTAL.LI B
100% moscatel de alejandría.

91 Colour: bright straw. Nose: fresh, fresh fruit, white flowers. Palate: flavourful, fruity, good acidity, balanced.

SANTA BÁRBARA 2009 T
50% monastrell, 50% cabernet sauvignon.

84

PEÑA CADIELLA 2008 T ROBLE
monastrell, merlot, cabernet sauvignon, tempranillo, giró.

87 Colour: cherry, garnet rim. Nose: powerfull, ripe fruit, sweet spices, toasty, dark chocolate. Palate: powerful, good acidity, fine bitter notes.

SERRELLA 2007 T
pinot noir, monastrell, petit verdot.

85 Colour: pale ruby, brick rim edge. Nose: slightly evolved, toasty, spicy, aromatic coffee, wet leather. Palate: sweetness, spirituous.

PENYA CADIELLA SELECCIÓ 2006 T
merlot, cabernet sauvignon, syrah, monastrell, giró, tempranillo.

89 Colour: cherry, garnet rim. Nose: creamy oak, aromatic coffee, dark chocolate, sweet spices, fruit liqueur notes. Palate: spicy, ripe fruit, fine bitter notes.

MONTCABRER 2006 T BARRICA
cabernet sauvignon.

87 Colour: cherry, garnet rim. Nose: overripe fruit, toasty, dark chocolate. Palate: powerful, concentrated, sweetness.

MAIGMÓ T
100% monastrell.

85 Colour: cherry, purple rim. Nose: expressive, red berry notes, ripe fruit. Palate: flavourful, fruity, good acidity, sweetness.

VIÑEDO Y BODEGA HERETAT DE CESILIA

Paraje Alcaydias, 4
03660 Novelda (Alicante)
☎: +34 965 605 385 - Fax: +34 965 604 763
administracion@heretatdecesilia.com
www.heretatdecesilia.com

CESILIA BLANC 2011 B
50% moscatel, 50% malvasía.

90 Colour: bright straw. Nose: fresh, fresh fruit, white flowers, dried herbs, citrus fruit. Palate: flavourful, fruity, good acidity, balanced.

CESILIA ROSÉ 2011 RD
85% merlot, 15% monastrell.

86 Colour: onion pink. Nose: candied fruit, dried flowers, fragrant herbs, sweet spices. Palate: light-bodied, flavourful, good acidity, long.

VIÑEDOS CULTURALES

Plaza Constitución, 8 - 1°
03380 Bigastro (Alicante)
☎: +34 966 770 353 - Fax: +34 966 770 353
vinedosculturales@gmail.com
http://vinedosculturales.blogspot.com.es/

LOS CIPRESES DE USALDÓN 2011 T
100% garnacha peluda.

93 Colour: cherry, purple rim. Nose: expressive, fresh fruit, floral, fragrant herbs. Palate: flavourful, fruity, good acidity, round tannins.

RAMBLIS DULCE 2010 T
monastrell.

91 Colour: black cherry. Nose: powerfull, characterful, overripe fruit, candied fruit. Palate: powerful, sweet, concentrated, complex.

DO ALMANSA

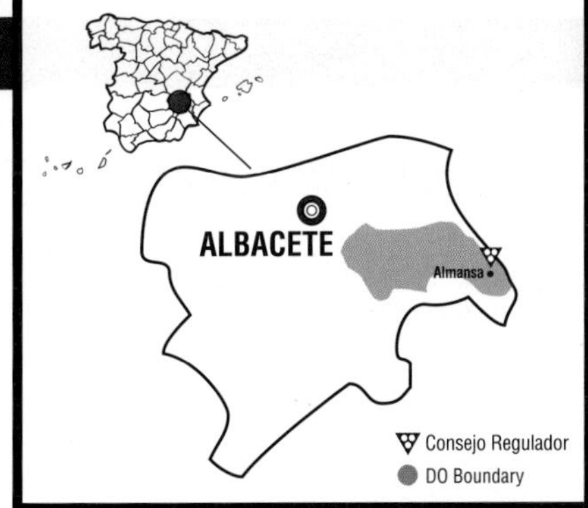

LOCATION:

In the eastern region of the province of Albacete. It covers the municipal areas of Almansa, Alpera, Bonete, Corral Rubio, Higueruela, Hoya Gonzalo, Pétrola and the municipal district of El Villar de Chinchilla.

CLIMATE:

Of a continental type, somewhat less extreme than the climate of La Mancha, although the summers are very hot, with temperatures which easily reach 40 °C. Rainfall, on the other hand, is scant, an average of about 350 mm a year. The majority of the vineyards are situated on the plains, although there are a few situated on the slopes.

SOIL:

The soil is limy, poor in organic matter and with some clayey areas. The vineyards are situated at an altitude of about 700 m.

GRAPE VARIETIES:

WHITE: *Airén, Verdejo* and *Sauvignon Blanc.*
RED: *Garnacha Tintorera* (most popular), *Cencibel* (*Tempranillo*), *Monastrell* (second most popular), *Syrah.*

FIGURES:

Vineyard surface: 7,400 – **Wine-Growers:** 760 – **Wineries:** 12 – **2011 Harvest rating:** Very Good – **Production:** 6,831,000 litres – **Market percentages:** 20% domestic. 80% export

CONSEJO REGULADOR
Avda. Carlos III, 4 (Hermita de San Blas) 02640 Almansa (Albacete) - ☎: +34 967 340 258. Fax: +34 967 310 842
@ info@vinosdealmansa.com - www.vinosdealmansa.com

BODEGA SANTA CRUZ DE ALPERA

Cooperativa, s/n
02690 Alpera (Albacete)
☎: +34 967 330 108 - Fax: +34 967 330 903
comercial@bodegasantacruz.com
www.bodegasantacruz.com

SANTA CRUZ DE ALPERA 2011 B
100% verdejo.

87 Colour: bright straw. Nose: white flowers, expressive, ripe fruit, fragrant herbs. Palate: flavourful, fruity, good acidity.

SANTA CRUZ DE ALPERA 2011 BFB
verdejo.

86 Colour: bright yellow. Nose: dried flowers, ripe fruit, fragrant herbs, spicy. Palate: powerful, flavourful, long.

SANTA CRUZ DE ALPERA 2011 RD
100% syrah.

86 Colour: rose, purple rim. Nose: powerfull, ripe fruit, red berry notes, floral. Palate: , powerful, fruity, fresh.

SANTA CRUZ DE ALPERA 2011 T
100% garnacha tintorera.

90 Colour: bright cherry, purple rim. Nose: fresh, red berry notes, balanced, violets. Palate: flavourful, fruity, good acidity.

RUPESTRE DE ALPERA 2009 T ROBLE
100% garnacha tintorera.

89 Colour: bright cherry. Nose: ripe fruit, sweet spices, creamy oak, expressive. Palate: flavourful, fruity, toasty, long.

ALBARROBLE 2009 TC
garnacha tintorera, monastrell.

87 Colour: deep cherry, purple rim. Nose: powerfull, balanced, scrubland, ripe fruit. Palate: fruity, balanced.

BODEGAS ALMANSEÑAS

Ctra. de Alpera, CM 3201 Km. 98,6
(Apdo. de Correos 324)
02640 Almansa (Albacete)
☎: +34 967 098 116 - Fax: +34 967 098 121
adaras@ventalavega.com
www.ventalavega.com

LA HUELLA DE ADARAS 2009 T
garnacha tintorera, monastrell, syrah.

90 Colour: cherry, garnet rim. Nose: damp earth, dry stone, ripe fruit, floral, scrubland. Palate: powerful, flavourful, long, balanced.

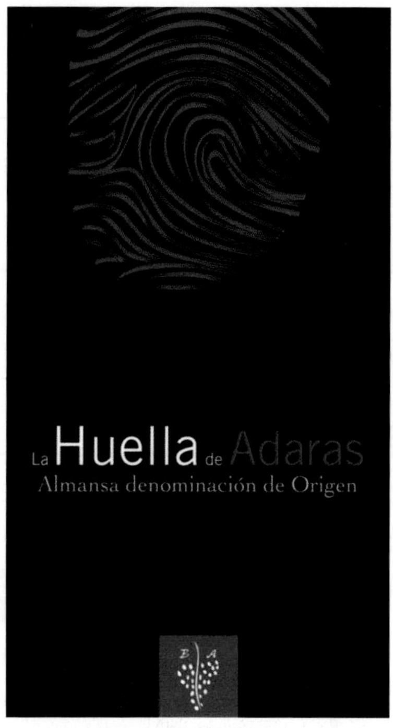

LA HUELLA DE ADARAS 2011 B
sauvignon blanc, verdejo.

85 Colour: bright straw. Nose: expressive, ripe fruit, dried flowers, fragrant herbs. Palate: flavourful, fruity, good acidity.

ADARAS SELECCIÓN 2010 BFB
sauvignon blanc.

86 Colour: bright straw. Nose: dried herbs, fragrant herbs, spicy. Palate: correct, light-bodied, good finish.

CALIZO DE ADARAS 2011 T
garnacha tintorera, monastrell, petit verdot, syrah.

89 Colour: cherry, purple rim. Nose: expressive, red berry notes, floral, dry stone, warm. Palate: flavourful, fruity, correct, balanced.

ALDEA DE ADARAS 2011 T
monastrell.

87 Colour: cherry, purple rim. Nose: ripe fruit, fruit preserve, wild herbs, warm. Palate: powerful, flavourful, full, ripe fruit.

LA VEGA DE ADARAS 2008 T
garnacha tintorera, monastrell.

88 Colour: cherry, garnet rim. Nose: powerfull, cocoa bean, fruit preserve, creamy oak. Palate: balanced, ripe fruit, round tannins.

ADARAS 2007 T
garnacha tintorera.

92 Colour: black cherry, garnet rim. Nose: ripe fruit, sweet spices, cocoa bean, dark chocolate. Palate: powerful, flavourful, toasty, balanced.

BODEGAS ATALAYA

Ctra. Almansa - Ayora, Km. 1
02640 Almansa (Albacete)
☎: +34 968 435 022 - Fax: +34 968 716 051
info@orowines.com
www.orowines.com

LAYA 2010 T
70% garnacha tintorera, 30% monastrell.

91 Colour: bright cherry. Nose: ripe fruit, sweet spices, creamy oak, expressive, red berry notes, fruit expression. Palate: flavourful, fruity, toasty, round tannins.

ALAYA 2010 T
100% garnacha tintorera.

91 Colour: black cherry. Nose: powerfull, fruit liqueur notes, raspberry, sweet spices, dark chocolate, toasty, varietal. Palate: powerful, flavourful, sweetness, fine bitter notes, fine bitter notes.

LA ATALAYA 2010 T
85% garnacha tintorera, 15% monastrell.

90 Colour: black cherry. Nose: roasted coffee, dark chocolate, ripe fruit. Palate: spicy, ripe fruit, fine bitter notes, round tannins.

SOC. COOP. AGRARIA SANTA QUITERIA, BODEGA TINTORALBA

Baltasar González Sáez, 34
02694 Higueruela (Albacete)
☎: +34 967 287 012 - Fax: +34 967 287 031
direccion@tintoralba.com
www.tintoralba.com

TINTORALBA 2011 T
100% garnacha tintorera.

89 Colour: cherry, purple rim. Nose: expressive, red berry notes, floral, lactic notes. Palate: flavourful, fruity, good acidity, easy to drink.

ALTITUD 1100 2011 T
100% garnacha tintorera.

88 Colour: cherry, purple rim. Nose: fresh fruit, red berry notes, floral, lactic notes. Palate: flavourful, fruity, good acidity, light-bodied, easy to drink.

DULCE TINTORALBA 2011 T
100% garnacha tintorera.

85 Colour: cherry, garnet rim. Nose: ripe fruit, floral, fragrant herbs, spicy, toasty. Palate: powerful, flavourful, fruity, sweet, balanced.

TINTORALBA 2010 T ROBLE
65% garnacha tintorera, 35% syrah.

86 Colour: bright cherry. Nose: ripe fruit, sweet spices, balsamic herbs, creamy oak. Palate: flavourful, fruity, toasty, round tannins, long.

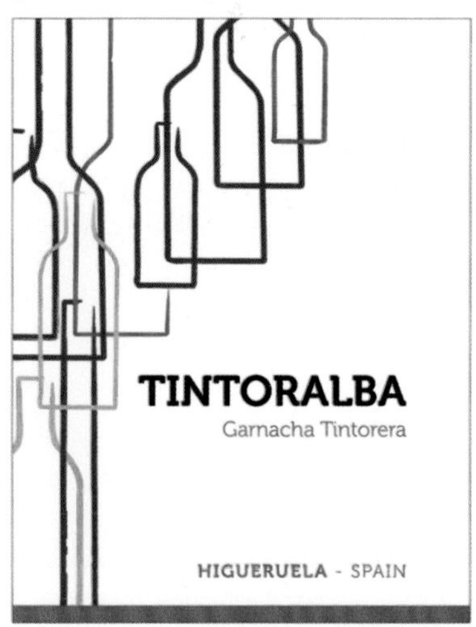

TINTORALBA SELECCIÓN 2008 T
70% garnacha tintorera, 30% syrah.

89 Colour: cherry, garnet rim. Nose: ripe fruit, spicy, creamy oak, toasty. Palate: powerful, flavourful, toasty, round tannins.

VENTA LA VEGA

San Francisco de Borga, 2 2º
46007 (Valencia)
☎: +34 618 544 397 - Fax: +34 967 098 121
dveiga@edicovalsa.com

VENTA LA VEGA VINTAGE 2011 T
garnacha tintorera, monastrell, syrah.

85 Colour: cherry, garnet rim. Nose: fruit preserve, scrubland, spicy. Palate: light-bodied, fresh, fruity.

VENTA LA VEGA OLD VINE 2009 T
garnacha tintorera, monastrell.

89 Colour: cherry, garnet rim. Nose: ripe fruit, spicy, creamy oak, complex. Palate: powerful, flavourful, toasty, round tannins.

DO ARABAKO TXAKOLINA

LOCATION:

It covers the region of Aiara (Ayala), situated in the north west of the province of Alava on the banks of the Nervion river basin. Specifically, it is made up of the municipalities of Amurrio, Artziniega, Aiara (Ayala), Laudio (Llodio) and Okondo.

CLIMATE:

Similar to that of the DO Bizkaiko Txakolina, determined by the influence of the Bay of Biscay, although somewhat less humid and slightly drier and fresher. In fact, the greatest risk in the region stems from frost in the spring. However, it should not be forgotten that part of its vineyards borders on the innermost plantations of the DO Bizkaiko Txakolina.

SOIL:

A great variety of formations are found, ranging from clayey to fundamentally stony, precisely those which to date are producing the best results and where fairly stable grape ripening is achieved.

GRAPE VARIETIES:

MAIN: *Hondarrabi Zuri* (80%).
AUTHORIZED: *Petit Manseng, Petit Corbu* and *Gross Manseng.*

FIGURES:

Vineyard surface: 100 – **Wine-Growers:** 45 – **Wineries:** 7 – **2011 Harvest rating:** Excellent – **Production:** 263,000 litres – **Market percentages:** 80% domestic. 20% export

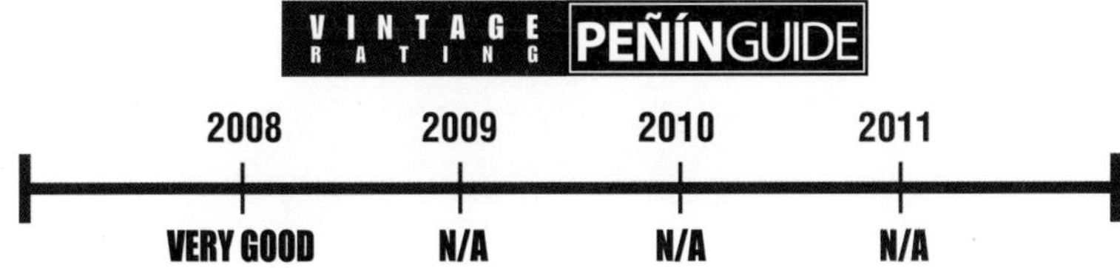

CONSEJO REGULADOR
Dionisio Aldama, 7- 1ºD Apdo. 36 - 01470 Amurrio (Álava) - ☎: +34 945 393 786 / 656 789 372 - Fax: +34 945 891 211
@ merino@txakolidealava.com - www.txakolidealava.com

OKENDO TXAKOLINA BODEGA SEÑORÍO DE ASTOBIZA

Barrio Jandiola, 16 (Caserío Aretxabala)
01409 Okondo (Álava)
☎: +34 945 898 516 - Fax: +34 945 898 447
comercial@senoriodeastobiza.com
www.senoriodeastobiza.com

MALKOA TXAKOLI 2011 B
100% hondarrabi zuri.

90 Colour: bright straw. Nose: medium intensity, fresh fruit, citrus fruit, white flowers. Palate: rich, flavourful, fruity.

SEÑORÍO DE ASTOBIZA 2011 B
70% hondarrabi zuri, 15% petit corbu, 15% gros manseng.

88 Colour: bright straw. Nose: medium intensity, wild herbs, citrus fruit, fresh. Palate: fresh, fruity, easy to drink.

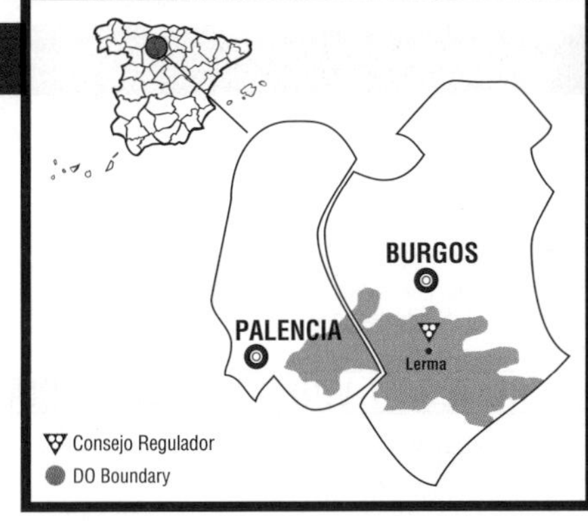

LOCATION:

With the medieval city of Lerma at the core of the region, Arlanza occupies the central and southern part of the province of Burgos, on the river valleys of the Arlanza and its subsidiaries, all the way westwards through 13 municipal districts of the province of Palencia until the Pisuerga River is reached.

CLIMATE:

The climate of this wine region is said to be one of the harshest within Castilla y León, with lower temperatures towards the western areas and rainfall higher on the eastern parts, in the highlands of the province of Soria.

SOIL:

Soil in the region is not particularly deep, with soft rocks underneath and good humidity levels. The landscape is one of rolling hills where vines are planted on varied soils, from limestone to calcareous, with abundant granite on certain areas.

GRAPE VARIETIES:

RED: *Tempranillo, Garnacha* and *Mencía.*
WHITE: *Albillo* and *Viura.*

FIGURES:

Vineyard surface: 465 – **Wine-Growers:** 278 – **Wineries:** 16 – **2011 Harvest rating:** Very Good – **Production:** 850,000 litres – **Market percentages:** 88% domestic. 12% export

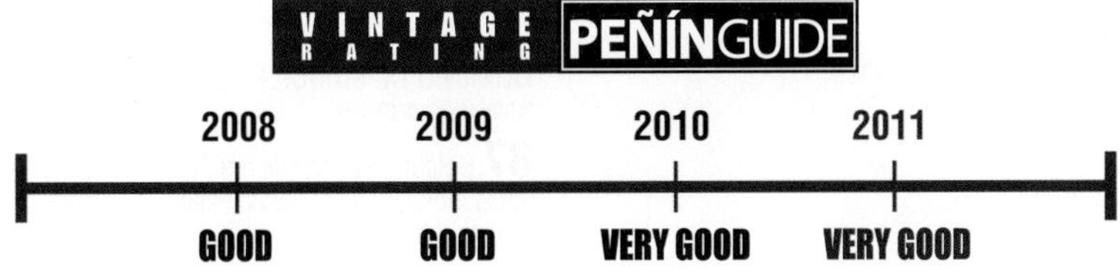

CONSEJO REGULADOR
Ronda de la Cárcel, 4 - 09340 Lerma (Burgos) - ☎: +34 947 171 046 - Fax: +34 947 171 046
@ info@arlanza.org - www.arlanza.org

ARLESE BODEGAS Y VIÑEDOS

Pol. Ind. de Villamanzo Parcela 109
09390 Villalmanzo (Burgos)
☎: +34 947 172 866 - Fax: +34 947 172 866
info@bodegasarlese.com
www.bodegasarlese.com

ALMANAQUE 2011 RD
100% tempranillo.

86 Colour: rose, purple rim. Nose: powerfull, ripe fruit, red berry notes, floral, lactic notes. Palate: , powerful, fruity, fresh.

ALMANAQUE 2011 T
100% tempranillo.

89 Colour: bright cherry, purple rim. Nose: expressive, red berry notes, violets. Palate: balanced, fine bitter notes, fruity, flavourful.

ALMANAQUE 2010 T ROBLE
100% tempranillo.

86 Colour: bright cherry. Nose: ripe fruit, sweet spices, creamy oak. Palate: flavourful, fruity, toasty.

ALMANAQUE 2007 TC
100% tempranillo.

86 Colour: cherry, purple rim. Nose: ripe fruit, spicy. Palate: flavourful, fruity, good finish.

BODEGA LA COLEGIADA

Ctra. Madrid-Irún, Km. 202,5
09340 Lerma (Burgos)
☎: +34 947 177 030 - Fax: +34 947 177 004
info@tintolerma.com
www.tintolerma.com

RISCO 2011 RD
70% tempranillo, 10% garnacha, 20% albillo.

84

GRAN LERMA 2009 TC
tempranillo.

91 Colour: cherry, garnet rim. Nose: ripe fruit, spicy, creamy oak, toasty, complex. Palate: powerful, flavourful, toasty, round tannins.

NABAL 2009 TC
tempranillo.

90 Colour: bright cherry. Nose: ripe fruit, sweet spices, creamy oak. Palate: flavourful, fruity, toasty, round tannins.

LERMA SELECCIÓN 2008 TR
tempranillo.

89 Colour: cherry, garnet rim. Nose: ripe fruit, spicy, creamy oak, fine reductive notes. Palate: powerful, flavourful, toasty, balanced.

BODEGA Y VIÑEDOS GARMENDIA

Finca Santa Rosalia, s/n
34260 Vizmalo (Burgos)
☎: +34 947 166 171 - Fax: +34 947 166 147
maria@bodegasgarmendia.com
www.bodegasgarmendia.com

GARMENDIA 2011 RD
tempranillo, garnacha.

88 Colour: rose, purple rim. Nose: powerfull, ripe fruit, red berry notes, floral, lactic notes. Palate: , powerful, fruity, fresh, easy to drink.

GARMENDIA 2010 T ROBLE
tempranillo.

89 Colour: bright cherry. Nose: ripe fruit, sweet spices, creamy oak, toasty. Palate: flavourful, fruity, spicy.

BODEGAS ARLANZA

Ctra. Madrid-Irún km 203,800
09390 Villalmanzo (Burgos)
☎: +34 947 172 070 - Fax: +34 947 170 259
comercial@bodegasarlanza.com
www.bodegasarlanza.com

DOMINIO DE MANCILES 2011 RD BARRICA
tempranillo, garnacha.

90 Colour: rose, purple rim. Nose: red berry notes, ripe fruit, balsamic herbs, floral, fresh, sweet spices, creamy oak. Palate: rich, powerful, flavourful, fruity.

DOMINIO DE MANCILES 2011 RD
tempranillo, garnacha.

87 Colour: rose, purple rim. Nose: ripe fruit, red berry notes, floral, fragrant herbs. Palate: , fruity, fresh, correct, easy to drink.

DOMINIO DE MANCILES 2011 T
tempranillo, cabernet sauvignon, mencía.

87 Colour: cherry, purple rim. Nose: fresh fruit, red berry notes, floral, lactic notes, powerfull. Palate: flavourful, fruity, good acidity.

DOMINIO DE MANCILES 2011 T BARRICA
tempranillo, cabernet sauvignon, mencía.

82

DOMINIO DE MANCILES SELECCIÓN 2007 TC
tempranillo.

87 Colour: cherry, garnet rim. Nose: ripe fruit, aromatic coffee, creamy oak, toasty, fine reductive notes. Palate: flavourful, long, balanced.

DOMINIO DE MANCILES 2004 T
tempranillo.

87 Colour: ruby red, orangey edge. Nose: cocoa bean, sweet spices, creamy oak, ripe fruit. Palate: powerful, flavourful, long, spicy.

BODEGAS MONTE AMÁN

Ctra. Santo Domingo de Silos, s/n
09348 Castrillo de Solarana (Burgos)
☎: +34 947 173 304 - Fax: +34 947 173 308
bodegas@monteaman.com
www.monteaman.com

MONTE AMÁN 2011 RD
100% tempranillo.

84

MONTE AMÁN 2011 T
100% tempranillo.

90 Colour: cherry, purple rim. Nose: fresh fruit, red berry notes, floral, balsamic herbs. Palate: flavourful, fruity, good acidity, round tannins.

MONTE AMÁN 5 MESES DE BARRICA 2011 T ROBLE
100% tempranillo.

87 Colour: bright cherry. Nose: ripe fruit, sweet spices, creamy oak, roasted coffee. Palate: flavourful, fruity, toasty, long.

MONTE AMÁN 2007 TC
100% tempranillo.

86 Colour: cherry, garnet rim. Nose: ripe fruit, spicy, creamy oak, aromatic coffee. Palate: flavourful, toasty, round tannins.

MONTE AMÁN 2004 TR
100% tempranillo.

86 Colour: dark-red cherry, orangey edge. Nose: ripe fruit, spicy, wet leather, cigar, toasty. Palate: long, spicy, flavourful.

BUEZO

Paraje Valdeazadón, s/n
09342 Mahamud (Burgos)
☎: +34 947 616 899 - Fax: +34 947 616 885
rfranco@buezo.com
www.buezo.com

BUEZO PETIT VERDOT TEMPRANILLO 2005 TR
50% petit verdot, 50% tempranillo.

91 Colour: cherry, garnet rim. Nose: ripe fruit, spicy, fine reductive notes, mineral. Palate: powerful, flavourful, toasty, round tannins, balanced.

BUEZO VARIETALES 2006 TC
50% tempranillo, 25% merlot, 25% cabernet sauvignon.

88 Colour: cherry, garnet rim. Nose: ripe fruit, wild herbs, balsamic herbs, spicy. Palate: balanced, flavourful, long, balsamic, spicy.

BUEZO NATTAN 2005 TR

91 Colour: cherry, garnet rim. Nose: balanced, toasty, spicy, ripe fruit. Palate: flavourful, good structure, round tannins.

BUEZO VARIETALES 2005 TR
50% tempranillo, 25% merlot, 25% cabernet sauvignon.

88 Colour: cherry, garnet rim. Nose: ripe fruit, spicy, toasty, balsamic herbs. Palate: powerful, flavourful, toasty, round tannins.

BUEZO TEMPRANILLO 2005 TR
100% tempranillo.

87 Colour: ruby red, orangey edge. Nose: fruit preserve, scrubland, sweet spices. Palate: flavourful, spicy, long, correct.

BUEZO PETIT VERDOT 2005 TR
50% petit verdot, 50% tempranillo.

87 Colour: cherry, garnet rim. Nose: ripe fruit, spicy, toasty, scrubland. Palate: powerful, flavourful, toasty, round tannins.

BUEZO NATTAN 2004 TR

90 Colour: cherry, garnet rim. Nose: ripe fruit, creamy oak, toasty, expressive, sweet spices, fine reductive notes. Palate: flavourful, toasty, round tannins, balanced.

BUEZO TEMPRANILLO 2004 TR
100% tempranillo.

89 Colour: pale ruby, brick rim edge. Nose: spicy, creamy oak, ripe fruit, balsamic herbs. Palate: balanced, flavourful, balsamic, spicy, long.

BUEZO PETIT VERDOT 2004 T
50% petit verdot, 50% tempranillo.

88 Colour: pale ruby, brick rim edge. Nose: spicy, fine reductive notes, wet leather, aged wood nuances, fruit liqueur notes. Palate: spicy, fine tannins, long.

PAGOS DE NEGREDO VIÑEDOS

Avda. Casado del Alisal, 26
34001 Palencia (Palencia)
☎: +34 979 700 450 - Fax: +34 979 702 171
administracion@pagosdenegredo.com
www.pagosdenegredo.com

PAGOS DE NEGREDO 2008 TC
tinto fino.

87 Colour: cherry, garnet rim. Nose: ripe fruit, spicy, creamy oak, toasty, scrubland. Palate: powerful, flavourful, toasty.

SEÑORÍO DE VALDESNEROS

Avda. La Paz, 4
34230 Torquemada (Palencia)
☎: +34 979 800 545 - Fax: +34 979 800 545
sv@bodegasvaldesneros.com
www.bodegasvaldesneros.com

SEÑORÍO DE VALDESNEROS 2011 RD
tempranillo.

87 Colour: rose, purple rim. Nose: powerfull, ripe fruit, red berry notes, floral, lactic notes. Palate: , powerful, fruity, fresh.

SEÑORÍO DE VALDESNEROS 2008 T ROBLE
tempranillo.

84

SEÑORÍO DE VALDESNEROS 2007 TC
tempranillo.

85 Colour: cherry, garnet rim. Nose: ripe fruit, spicy, old leather, cigar. Palate: powerful, flavourful, toasty.

ERUELO 2007 TC
tempranillo.

84

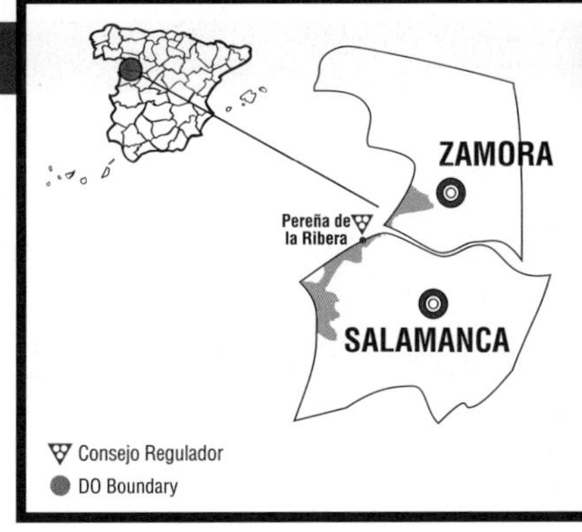

LOCATION:

In Las Arribes National Park, it comprises a narrow stretch of land along the southwest of Zamora and northeast of Salamanca. The vineyards occupy the valleys and steep terraces along the river Duero. Just a single municipal district, Fermoselle, has up to 90% of the total vineyard surface.

CLIMATE:

This wine region has a strong Mediterranean influence, given the prominent decrease in altitude that the territory features from the flat lands of the Sáyago area along the Duero valley until the river reaches Fermoselle, still in the province of Zamora. Rainfall is low all through the year, even during the averagely hot summer.

SOIL:

The region has shallow sandy soils with abundant quartz and stones, even some granite found in the area of Fermoselle. In the territory which is part of the province of Salamanca it is quite noticeable the presence of slate, the kind of rock also featured on the Portuguese part along the Duero, called Douro the other side of the border. The slate subsoil works a splendid thermal regulator capable of accumulating the heat from the sunshine during the day and to slowly release it during the night time.

GRAPE VARIETIES:

WHITE: *Malvasía, Verdejo* and *Albillo.*
RED: *Juan García, Rufete, Tempranillo* (preferential); *Mencía, Garnacha* (authorized).

FIGURES:

Vineyard surface: 452 – **Wine-Growers:** 362 – **Wineries:** 13 – **2011 Harvest rating:** Excellent – **Production:** 800,000 litres – **Market percentages:** 80% domestic. 20% export

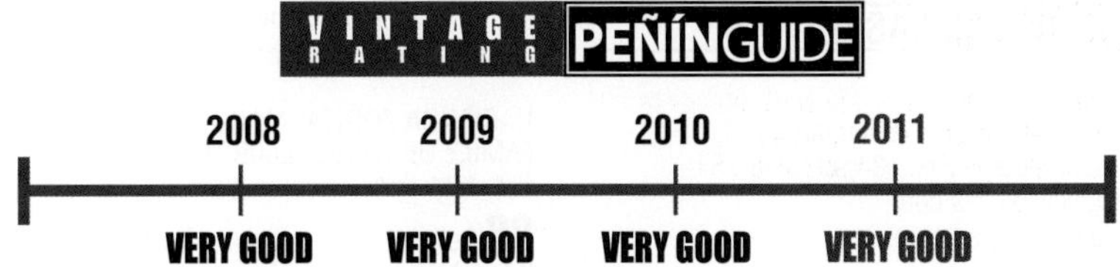

CONSEJO REGULADOR
La Almofea, 95 - 37175 Pereña de la Ribera (Salamanca) - ☎: +34 923 573 413 - Fax: +34 923 573 209
@ info@doarribes.com - www.vinoarribesduero.com

BODEGAS ARRIBES DEL DUERO

Ctra. Masueco, s/n
37251 Corporario - Aldeadavila (Salamanca)
☎: +34 923 169 195 - Fax: +34 923 169 195
secretaria@bodegasarribesdelduero.com
www.bodegasarribesdelduero.com

ARRIBES DE VETTONIA 2011 B
malvasía.

84

ARRIBES DE VETTONIA 2007 BFB
malvasía.

85 Colour: bright golden. Nose: ripe fruit, citrus fruit, grassy, faded flowers, warm, roasted coffee. Palate: spicy, powerful, flavourful.

ARRIBES DE VETTONIA 2011 RD
juan garcía.

85 Colour: brilliant rose. Nose: powerfull, ripe fruit, red berry notes, floral, balsamic herbs. Palate: , powerful, fruity, fresh, easy to drink.

ARRIBES DE VETTONIA 2010 T
juan garcía.

84

ARRIBES DE VETTONIA 2009 TC
juan garcía.

88 Colour: cherry, garnet rim. Nose: ripe fruit, spicy, creamy oak, sweet spices, expressive. Palate: flavourful, toasty, round tannins.

SECRETO DEL VETTON 2006 T
juan garcía.

90 Colour: cherry, garnet rim. Nose: ripe fruit, spicy, creamy oak, toasty, expressive. Palate: powerful, flavourful, balanced, long, spicy.

BODEGAS LAS GAVIAS

Avda. Constitución, 2
37175 Pereña de la Ribera (Salamanca)
☎: +34 902 108 031 - Fax: +34 987 218 751
info@bodegaslasgavias.com
www.bodegaslasgavias.com

POZO DE LOS HUMOS 2010 T
juan garcía.

86 Colour: light cherry. Nose: ripe fruit, dried flowers, scrubland, spicy, mineral. Palate: fresh, fruity, flavourful.

ALDANA 2009 T ROBLE
100% juan garcía.

85 Colour: cherry, garnet rim. Nose: ripe fruit, scrubland, spicy, creamy oak. Palate: light-bodied, fresh, fruity.

BODEGAS RIBERA DE PELAZAS

Camino de la Ermita, s/n
37175 Pereña de la Ribera (Salamanca)
☎: +34 902 108 031 - Fax: +34 987 218 751
bodega@bodegasriberadepelazas.com
www.bodegasriberadepelazas.com

ABADENGO 2011 B
malvasía.

87 Colour: bright yellow. Nose: ripe fruit, white flowers. Palate: flavourful, rich, fruity, correct.

ABADENGO 2008 TC
100% juan garcía.

88 Colour: cherry, garnet rim. Nose: balanced, ripe fruit, medium intensity. Palate: flavourful, good structure, fruity.

BRUÑAL 2007 T
100% bruñal.

90 Colour: cherry, garnet rim. Nose: ripe fruit, spicy, creamy oak, scrubland, earthy notes. Palate: powerful, flavourful, toasty, round tannins, elegant.

GRAN ABADENGO 2005 TR
juan garcía.

90 Colour: pale ruby, brick rim edge. Nose: spicy, wet leather, aged wood nuances, fruit liqueur notes, scrubland, earthy notes. Palate: spicy, long, round tannins, flavourful.

HACIENDAS DE ESPAÑA

Hacienda Zorita, Ctra. Ledesma, Km. 12
37115 Valverdón (Salamanca)
☎: +34 914 365 924
comunicacion@arcoinvest-group.com
www.haciendas-espana.com

HACIENDA ZORITA (MARQUÉS DE LA CONCORDIA FAMILY OF WINES) 2009 TC
100% tempranillo.

88 Colour: cherry, garnet rim. Nose: ripe fruit, spicy, toasty, balsamic herbs. Palate: powerful, flavourful, long, good acidity.

LA SETERA

Calzada, 7
49232 Fornillos de Fermoselle (Zamora)
☎: +34 980 612 925 - Fax: +34 980 612 925
lasetera@lasetera.com
www.lasetera.com

LA SETERA 2011 B
malvasía.

84

LA SETERA ROSADO DE LÁGRIMA 2011 RD
verdejo colorado.

85 Colour: raspberry rose. Nose: faded flowers, dried herbs, ripe fruit. Palate: flavourful, fresh, rich.

LA SETERA 2011 T
juan garcía.

84

LA SETERA 2010 T ROBLE
mencía.

89 Colour: bright cherry. Nose: ripe fruit, sweet spices, creamy oak, expressive, mineral. Palate: flavourful, fruity, toasty.

LA SETERA SELECCIÓN ESPECIAL 2009 T ROBLE
touriga.

92 Colour: bright cherry. Nose: ripe fruit, sweet spices, creamy oak, fragrant herbs. Palate: flavourful, fruity, toasty, round tannins, balanced.

LA SETERA 2009 TC
juan garcía.

86 Colour: cherry, garnet rim. Nose: ripe fruit, fruit liqueur notes, wild herbs, sweet spices. Palate: powerful, flavourful, toasty.

OCELLUM DURII

San Juan 56 - 57
49220 Fermoselle (Zamora)
☎: +34 983 390 606
ocellumdurii@hotmail.com

CONDADO DE FERMOSEL 2011 T
juan garcía, tempranillo, bruñal, rufete.

92 Colour: bright cherry. Nose: ripe fruit, sweet spices, creamy oak, balsamic herbs. Palate: flavourful, fruity, toasty, round tannins.

CONDADO DE FERMOSEL 2010 T
juan garcía, tempranillo, garnacha.

84

TRANSITIUM DURII 2008 T
juan garcía, tempranillo, bruñal.

91 Colour: bright cherry. Nose: ripe fruit, sweet spices, creamy oak, dark chocolate, cocoa bean, expressive. Palate: flavourful, fruity, toasty, round tannins.

TRANSITIUM DURII 2007 T
juan garcía, tempranillo, bruñal.

90 Colour: cherry, garnet rim. Nose: ripe fruit, spicy, creamy oak, toasty, balsamic herbs. Palate: flavourful, toasty, balanced, long.

TRANSITIUM DURII 2006 T
juan garcía, tempranillo, bruñal.

90 Colour: cherry, garnet rim. Nose: mineral, red berry notes, ripe fruit, fragrant herbs, spicy. Palate: flavourful, fresh, long, spicy, good finish.

DO BIERZO

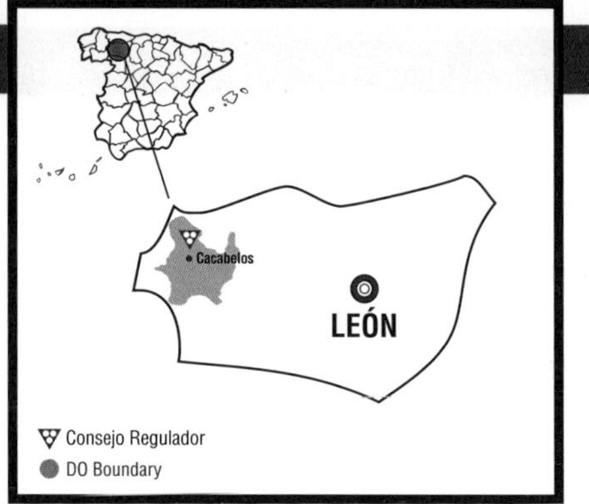

LOCATION:

In the north west of the province of León. It covers 23 municipal areas and occupies several valleys in mountainous terrain and a flat plain at a lower altitude than the plateau of León, with higher temperatures accompanied by more rainfall. It may be considered an area of transition between Galicia, León and Asturias.

CLIMATE:

Quite mild and benign, with a certain degree of humidity due to Galician influence, although somewhat dry like Castilla. Thanks to the low altitude, late frost is avoided quite successfully and the grapes are usually harvested one month before the rest of Castilla. The average rainfall per year is 721 mm.

SOIL:

In the mountain regions, it is made up of a mixture of fine elements, quartzite and slate. In general, the soil of the DO is humid, dun and slightly acidic. The greater quality indices are associated with the slightly sloped terraces close to the rivers, the half - terraced or steep slopes situated at an altitude of between 450 and 1,000 m.

GRAPE VARIETIES:

WHITE: *Godello, Palomino, Dona Blanca* and *Malvasia.*
RED: *Mencía* or *Negra* and *Garnacha Tintorera.*

FIGURES:

Vineyard surface: 3,045 – **Wine-Growers:** 2,634 – **Wineries:** 68 – **2011 Harvest rating:** S/C – **Production:** 12,275,897 litres – **Market percentages:** 83% domestic. 17% export

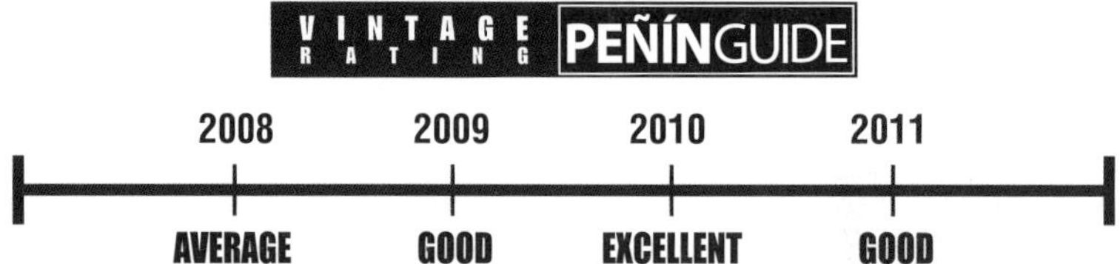

CONSEJO REGULADOR
Mencía, 1 - 24540 Cacabelos (León) - ☎: +34 987 549 408 - Fax: +34 987 547 077
@ info@crdobierzo.es @ comunicacion@crdobierzo.es - www.crdobierzo.es

AKILIA

Nicolás de Brujas, 27
24400 Ponferrada (León)
☎: +34 902 848 127
info@akiliawines.com
www.akiliawines.com

AKILIA 2011 T
mencía.

92 Colour: dark-red cherry. Nose: fine lees, smoky, cocoa bean, spicy, fruit expression. Palate: good structure, powerful, flavourful, rich, creamy, balsamic.

ÁLVAREZ DE TOLEDO VIÑEDOS Y GRUPO BODEGAS

Río Selmo, 8
24560 Toral de los Vados (León)
☎: +34 981 563 551
admon@bodegasalvarezdetoledo.com
www.bodegasalvarezdetoledo.com

ÁLVAREZ DE TOLEDO GODELLO 2011 B
godello, dona blanca.

87 Colour: bright straw. Nose: fresh fruit, white flowers, wild herbs. Palate: flavourful, fruity, good acidity.

ÁLVAREZ DE TOLEDO 2009 T ROBLE
mencía.

88 Colour: cherry, garnet rim. Nose: ripe fruit, spicy, creamy oak, dark chocolate, toasty. Palate: powerful, flavourful, toasty.

ÁLVAREZ DE TOLEDO 2008 T ROBLE
mencía.

88 Colour: bright cherry. Nose: ripe fruit, sweet spices, creamy oak, toasty. Palate: flavourful, toasty, round tannins.

BERNARDO ÁLVAREZ

San Pedro, 75
24530 Villadecanes (León)
☎: +34 987 562 129 - Fax: +34 987 562 129
migarron@bodegasbernardoalvarez.e.telefonica.net

CAMPO REDONDO GODELLO 2011 B
100% godello.

90 Colour: bright straw. Nose: fruit expression, ripe fruit, fragrant herbs. Palate: rich, full, powerful, flavourful, sweetness.

VIÑA MIGARRÓN 2011 B
dona blanca, jerez, godello.

88 Colour: straw. Nose: fragrant herbs, fresh fruit. Palate: fresh, fruity, light-bodied, flavourful.

VIÑA MIGARRÓN 2011 RD
100% mencía.

86 Colour: raspberry rose. Nose: floral, red berry notes, ripe fruit, dried herbs. Palate: fresh, fruity, flavourful.

CAMPO REDONDO 2010 T ROBLE
100% mencía.

89 Colour: bright cherry. Nose: ripe fruit, sweet spices, creamy oak, expressive. Palate: flavourful, fruity, toasty, balanced.

VIÑA MIGARRÓN 2010 T
100% mencía.

85 Colour: cherry, purple rim. Nose: floral, wild herbs, ripe fruit. Palate: flavourful, fruity, correct.

VIÑA MIGARRÓN 2008 TC
100% mencía.

86 Colour: cherry, garnet rim. Aroma ripe fruit, spicy, creamy oak, toasty, complex. Taste powerful, flavourful, toasty, round tannins.

BODEGA ALBERTO LEDO

Estación, 6
24500 Villafranca del Bierzo (León)
☎: +34 636 023 676
aallrs@msn.com
www.albertoledo.com

LEDO GODELLO 2011 B
godello.

87 Colour: bright golden. Nose: wild herbs, fresh fruit. Palate: fresh, dry, flavourful.

LEDO. 8 2008 T
mencía.

89 Colour: light cherry. Nose: spicy, aged wood nuances, ripe fruit, slightly evolved. Palate: spirituous, powerful, fruity, spicy, ripe fruit, toasty.

LEDO CLUB DE BARRICAS 2007 T
mencía.

90 Colour: cherry, garnet rim. Nose: ripe fruit, spicy, creamy oak, toasty, mineral. Palate: powerful, flavourful, toasty, round tannins, balanced.

LEDO SELECCIÓN 2007 T
mencía.

89 Colour: cherry, garnet rim. Nose: fruit preserve, spicy, old leather, creamy oak. Palate: powerful, flavourful, correct, balanced.

BODEGA DEL ABAD

Ctra. N-VI, km. 396
24549 Carracedelo (León)
☎: +34 987 562 417 - Fax: +34 987 562 428
vinos@bodegadelabad.com
www.bodegadelabad.com

ABAD DOM BUENO GODELLO 2011 B
100% godello.

89 Colour: bright straw. Nose: white flowers, ripe fruit. Palate: fresh, fruity, rich, flavourful.

GOTÍN DEL RISC GODELLO LÍAS 2008 B
100% godello.

91 Colour: bright golden. Nose: macerated fruit, faded flowers, varietal, powerfull, complex, ripe fruit. Palate: slightly acidic, powerful, complex, reductive nuances.

CARRACEDO 2008 TC
100% mencía.

91 Colour: very deep cherry. Nose: dark chocolate, spicy, ripe fruit, fruit preserve. Palate: sweetness, spirituous, powerful, flavourful, ripe fruit, creamy, balsamic.

GOTÍN DEL RISC ESSENCIA 2007 TC
100% mencía.

90 Colour: cherry, garnet rim. Nose: ripe fruit, spicy, creamy oak, roasted coffee. Palate: powerful, flavourful, toasty, round tannins.

BODEGA LA CAVA DEL BIERZO

Las Flores, s/n
24530 Valtuille de Abajo (León)
☎: +34 987 562 156 - Fax: +34 987 414 498
bodega@lacavadelbierzo.com
www.lacavadelbierzo.com

VAL TODIL 2011 T
mencía.

89 Colour: cherry, purple rim. Nose: red berry notes, ripe fruit, scrubland. Palate: flavourful, good acidity, long.

VAL TODIL 2011 T MACERACIÓN CARBÓNICA
mencía.

89 Colour: cherry, purple rim. Nose: expressive, fresh fruit, red berry notes, floral, violet drops, maceration notes. Palate: flavourful, fruity, good acidity.

BODEGA LUZDIVINA AMIGO

Ctra. Villafranca, 10
24516 Parandones (León)
☎: +34 987 544 826 - Fax: +34 987 544 826
info@bodegaluz.com
www.bodegaluz.com

BALOIRO 2011 B
godello, dona blanca, palomino.

88 Colour: bright yellow. Nose: grassy, macerated fruit, dry stone. Palate: spicy, ripe fruit, mineral, powerful, flavourful.

BALOIRO 2011 BFB
100% godello.

87 Colour: bright yellow. Nose: smoky, ripe fruit, scrubland. Palate: flavourful, fruity, fresh.

BALOIRO 2011 RD FERMENTADO EN BARRICA
mencía, garnacha tintorera.

86 Colour: brilliant rose. Nose: fresh fruit, balanced, varietal. Palate: fruity, flavourful, easy to drink, warm.

VIÑADEMOYA 2011 T
100% mencía.

87 Colour: deep cherry. Nose: balsamic herbs, ripe fruit, powerfull, caramel. Palate: sweetness, spirituous, powerful, flavourful.

BALOIRO 2009 TC
100% mencía.

89 Colour: very deep cherry. Nose: smoky, spicy, cedar wood, fruit preserve, fruit liqueur notes. Palate: creamy, pruney, ripe fruit.

VIÑADEMOYA LEIROS 2008 T
100% mencía.

84

BODEGA Y VIÑEDOS LUNA BEBERIDE

Ant. Ctra. Madrid - Coruña, Km. 402
24540 Cacabelos (León)
☎: +34 987 549 002 - Fax: +34 987 549 214
info@lunabeberide.es
www.lunabeberide.es

LB LUNA BEBERIDE 2010 B

87 Colour: bright straw. Nose: medium intensity, characterful, ripe fruit, dry nuts. Palate: correct, fine bitter notes, good acidity.

FINCA LA CUESTA LUNA BEBERIDE 2010 T ROBLE
mencía.

91 Colour: dark-red cherry, garnet rim. Nose: complex, expressive, varietal, red clay notes, red berry notes, ripe fruit, aromatic coffee, spicy, toasty. Palate: flavourful, powerful, mineral, toasty, ripe fruit.

ART LUNA BEBERIDE 2010 T
mencía.

90 Colour: very deep cherry. Nose: fruit preserve, smoky, cedar wood. Palate: spirituous, sweetness, powerful, flavourful, creamy, ripe fruit.

MENCÍA LUNA BEBERIDE 2010 T
mencía.

86 Colour: cherry, garnet rim. Nose: ripe fruit, scrubland, medium intensity. Palate: powerful, flavourful, long.

BODEGA Y VIÑEDOS MAS ASTURIAS

Fueros de Leon nº 1
24400 Ponferrada (León)
☎: +34 650 654 492
jose_mas_asturias@hotmail.com
www.bodegamasasturias.com

MASSURIA 2008 T
100% mencía.

91 Colour: deep cherry. Nose: complex, varietal, elegant, fresh fruit, fruit expression, spicy. Palate: flavourful, powerful, full, spirituous, complex.

BODEGAS ABANICO

Pol. Ind Ca l'Avellanet - Susany, 6
08553 Seva (Barcelona)
☎: +34 938 125 676 - Fax: +34 938 123 213
info@exportiberia.com
www.bodegasabanico.com

MANIUM 2008 T
100% mencía.

89 Colour: cherry, garnet rim. Nose: ripe fruit, spicy, creamy oak, toasty. Palate: powerful, flavourful, toasty, good acidity, balanced.

BODEGAS ADRIÁ

Antigua Ctra. Madrid - Coruña, Km. 408
24500 Villafranca del Bierzo (León)
☎: +34 987 540 907 - Fax: +34 987 540 347
info@bodegasadria.com
www.bodegasadria.com

VEGA MONTÁN GODELLO 2011 B
godello.

88 Colour: bright straw. Nose: fragrant herbs, ripe fruit, citrus fruit. Palate: flavourful, powerful, spicy.

VEGA MONTÁN MENCÍA 2010 T
mencía.

86 Colour: cherry, garnet rim. Nose: ripe fruit, scrubland, floral, mineral. Palate: powerful, flavourful, ripe fruit.

VEGA MONTÁN ADRIÁ 2010 T
mencía.

84

VIÑA BARROCA 2010 T
mencía.

82

VEGA MONTÁN SILK 2009 T
mencía.

87 Colour: cherry, garnet rim. Nose: ripe fruit, wild herbs, spicy, expressive, toasty. Palate: flavourful, long, spicy, balanced.

VEGA MONTÁN VELVET 2008 T
mencía.

88 Colour: cherry, garnet rim. Nose: ripe fruit, spicy, creamy oak, toasty, mineral. Palate: powerful, flavourful, toasty, round tannins.

VEGA MONTÁN ECLIPSE 2005 T
mencía.

93 Colour: pale ruby, brick rim edge. Nose: earthy notes, fine reductive notes, ripe fruit, spicy, creamy oak. Palate: correct, flavourful, long, fine tannins.

BODEGAS ALMÁZCARA MAJARA

Las Eras, 5
24398 Almázcara (León)
☎: +34 609 322 194 - Fax: +34 937 952 859
javier.alvarez@es.coimgroup.com
www.almazcaramajara.com

DEMASIADO CORAZÓN 2010 B
godello.

90 Colour: bright yellow. Nose: smoky, ripe fruit, wild herbs. Palate: flavourful, rich, fruity.

JARABE DE ALMÁZCARA MAJARA 2009 T
mencía.

90 Colour: cherry, garnet rim. Nose: ripe fruit, spicy, creamy oak, toasty, complex. Palate: powerful, flavourful, toasty, balanced.

ALMÁZCARA MAJARA 2007 T
mencía.

84

BODEGAS CUATRO PASOS

Santa María, 43
24540 Cacabelos (León)
☎: +34 987 548 089 - Fax: +34 986 526 901
bierzo@martincodax.com
www.cuatropasos.es

CUATRO PASOS 2011 RD
100% mencía.

87 Colour: brilliant rose. Nose: varietal, powerfull, fresh, fruit expression, earthy notes. Palate: fresh, fruity, powerful, easy to drink.

PIZARRAS DE OTERO 2011 T
100% mencía.

88 Colour: dark-red cherry. Nose: fruit preserve, violet drops, fruit expression. Palate: sweetness, spirituous, powerful, flavourful.

MARTÍN SARMIENTO 2010 T
100% mencía.

92 Colour: deep cherry, garnet rim. Nose: complex, varietal, fruit expression, cocoa bean, creamy oak. Palate: spirituous, round, warm, powerful, flavourful.

CUATRO PASOS 2010 T
100% mencía.

87 Colour: dark-red cherry. Nose: spicy, aged wood nuances, dark chocolate, toasty. Palate: powerful, spirituous, grainy tannins, spicy.

BODEGAS GODELIA

Antigua Ctra. N-VI, Km. 403,5
24547 Pieros (Cacabelos) (León)
☎: +34 987 546 279 - Fax: +34 987 548 026
info@godelia.es
www.godelia.es

GODELIA BLANCO SOBRE LÍAS 2011 B
80% godello, 20% dona blanca.

88 Colour: bright straw. Nose: white flowers, expressive, ripe fruit, dried herbs. Palate: flavourful, fruity, good acidity, balanced.

GODELIA BLANCO SELECCIÓN 2010 B
100% godello.

90 Colour: bright golden. Nose: fine lees, floral, fragrant herbs, citrus fruit, balanced. Palate: powerful, flavourful, spicy, long, fresh, fruity.

VIERNES 2011 T
100% mencía.

88 Colour: cherry, purple rim. Nose: fresh fruit, red berry notes, floral, balsamic herbs. Palate: flavourful, fruity, good acidity, balanced.

GODELIA 12 MESES 2010 T ROBLE
100% mencía.

93 Colour: bright cherry. Nose: ripe fruit, sweet spices, creamy oak, cocoa bean, dark chocolate, expressive. Palate: flavourful, fruity, toasty, complex, balanced, elegant.

GODELIA TINTO SELECCIÓN 2009 T
100% mencía.

94 Colour: cherry, garnet rim. Nose: ripe fruit, spicy, creamy oak, toasty, fragrant herbs, complex. Palate: powerful, flavourful, toasty, complex, round, long, spicy, balanced, elegant.

BODEGAS PEIQUE

El Bierzo, s/n
24530 Valtuille de Abajo (León)
☎: +34 987 562 044 - Fax: +34 987 562 044
bodega@bodegaspeique.com
www.bodegaspeique.com

PEIQUE GODELLO 2011 B
godello.

88 Colour: bright straw. Nose: fresh fruit, fragrant herbs, undergrowth. Palate: fresh, fruity, flavourful.

PEIQUE 2011 RD
mencía.

88 Colour: rose, purple rim. Nose: floral, fruit expression, powerfull, fresh. Palate: fruity, fresh, flavourful, complex.

PEIQUE TINTO MENCÍA 2011 T
mencía.

88 Colour: deep cherry. Nose: fruit expression, ripe fruit. Palate: fruity, spirituous, powerful, flavourful, sweetness.

RAMÓN VALLE 2009 T
mencía.

89 Colour: dark-red cherry. Nose: ripe fruit, dark chocolate, smoky, toasty, creamy oak. Palate: fruity, powerful, flavourful, spicy, ripe fruit.

PEIQUE VIÑEDOS VIEJOS 2008 T ROBLE
mencía.

92 Colour: dark-red cherry. Nose: undergrowth, varietal, closed, fruit liqueur notes, ripe fruit, creamy oak, toasty. Palate: balsamic, creamy, mineral, powerful, flavourful, fruity, spirituous.

PEIQUE SELECCIÓN FAMILIAR 2006 T
mencía.

93 Colour: deep cherry. Nose: damp earth, fruit expression, fine reductive notes, spicy, cedar wood. Palate: spirituous, powerful, flavourful, full, round, soft tannins.

BODEGAS Y VIÑEDO MENGOBA

Ctra. de Cacabelos, 11
24540 Sorribas (León)
☎: +34 649 940 800
gregory@mengoba.com
www.mengoba.com

BREZO GODELLO Y DOÑA BLANCA 2011 B
godello, dona blanca.

94 Colour: bright straw. Nose: ripe fruit, wild herbs, smoky, complex. Palate: spirituous, sweetness, powerful, flavourful, full.

MENGOBA GODELLO SOBRE LÍAS 2010 B
godello.

95 Colour: bright straw. Nose: spicy, candied fruit, smoky, complex, expressive, varietal. Palate: elegant, round, full, rich, complex.

BREZO MENCÍA 2011 T
mencía, alicante bouchet.

90 Colour: dark-red cherry. Nose: smoky, ripe fruit, fruit expression, maceration notes. Palate: spirituous, powerful, flavourful, sweetness, balsamic.

MENGOBA MENCÍA DE ESPANILLO 2009 T
mencía, alicante bouchet.

92 Colour: deep cherry. Nose: balsamic herbs, powerfull, varietal, complex, ripe fruit. Palate: creamy, balsamic, powerful, flavourful, spirituous, sweetness.

BODEGAS Y VIÑEDOS BERGIDENSES

Antigua N-VI Km. 400. Apdo. Correos, 62
24540 Cacabelos (León)
☎: +34 987 546 725 - Fax: +34 987 546 725
bergidenses@tegula.e.telefonica.net

VIÑA GARNELO 2011 B

88 Colour: straw. Nose: powerfull, varietal, neat, balanced, expressive. Palate: flavourful, powerful, rich, fresh.

VEGA DEL CÚA 2011 RD
mencía.

83

TÉGULA 2010 TC

87 Colour: deep cherry. Nose: toasty, spicy, aromatic coffee. Palate: flavourful, powerful, ripe fruit, fine bitter notes.

VEGA DEL CÚA 2010 T
mencía.

82

TÉGULA 2007 TR

93 Colour: cherry, garnet rim. Nose: spicy, creamy oak, toasty, complex, earthy notes, mineral. Palate: powerful, flavourful, toasty, round tannins.

BODEGAS Y VIÑEDOS CASTRO VENTOSA

Finca El Barredo, s/n
24530 Valtuille de Abajo (León)
☎: +34 987 562 148 - Fax: +34 987 562 191
info@castroventosa.com
www.castroventosa.com

EL CASTRO DE VALTUILLE JOVEN 2011 T
mencía.

89 Colour: cherry, garnet rim. Nose: balanced, ripe fruit, scrubland. Palate: flavourful, fruity, fine bitter notes.

CASTRO VENTOSA 2011 T
mencía.

88 Colour: cherry, purple rim. Nose: red berry notes, floral. Palate: flavourful, fruity, good acidity, round tannins, balsamic.

VALTUILLE CEPAS CENTENARIAS 2008 T ROBLE
mencía.

94 Colour: deep cherry. Nose: damp earth, truffle notes, ripe fruit, smoky, spicy, creamy oak. Palate: powerful, flavourful, spirituous, sweetness.

EL CASTRO DE VALTUILLE 2008 T
mencía.

92 Colour: deep cherry. Nose: macerated fruit, ripe fruit, spicy, creamy oak, toasty. Palate: powerful, flavourful, spirituous, spicy.

CASTRO VENTOSA"VINTAGE" 2008 T
100% mencía.

90 Colour: cherry, garnet rim. Nose: ripe fruit, spicy, creamy oak, earthy notes. Palate: powerful, flavourful, round tannins.

BODEGAS Y VIÑEDOS GANCEDO

Vistalegre, s/n
24548 Quilós (León)
☎: +34 987 134 980 - Fax: +34 987 563 278
info@bodegasgancedo.com
www.bodegasgancedo.com

VAL DE PAXARIÑAS "CAPRICHO" 2011 B
85% godello, 15% dona blanca.

92 Colour: bright straw. Nose: white flowers, fresh fruit, varietal, powerfull, fresh, expressive. Palate: rich, powerful, sweetness, spirituous.

HERENCIA DEL CAPRICHO 2009 BFB
90% godello, 10% dona blanca.

94 Colour: bright yellow. Nose: complex, characterful, elegant, fruit expression, candied fruit. Palate: fresh, full, powerful, rich.

HERENCIA DEL CAPRICHO 2008 BFB
90% godello, 10% dona blanca.

93 Colour: bright yellow. Nose: candied fruit, honeyed notes, fruit liqueur notes. Palate: creamy, spicy, ripe fruit, reductive nuances.

GANCEDO 2011 T
mencía.

90 Colour: very deep cherry. Nose: fruit preserve, violet drops, fruit liqueur notes, powerfull, caramel. Palate: powerful, flavourful, fruity, spirituous, sweetness, sweet tannins.

GANCEDO 2010 T
mencía.

91 Colour: dark-red cherry. Nose: wild herbs, red berry notes, complex, characterful. Palate: round, powerful, flavourful, varietal.

XESTAL 2008 T
mencía.

91 Colour: very deep cherry. Nose: mineral, undergrowth, fruit expression, fruit liqueur notes, ripe fruit. Palate: sweet tannins, powerful, flavourful, fruity, sweetness.

BODEGAS Y VIÑEDOS PAIXAR

Ribadeo, 56
24500 Villafranca del Bierzo (León)
☎: +34 987 549 002 - Fax: +34 987 549 214
info@lunabeberide.es

PAIXAR MENCÍA T
mencía.

91 Colour: deep cherry. Nose: spicy, aromatic coffee, creamy oak. Palate: fruity, spirituous, sweetness, powerful, flavourful, balsamic.

CASAR DE BURBIA

Travesía la Constitución s/n
24459 Carracedelo (León)
☎: +34 987 562 910 - Fax: +34 987 562 850
info@casardeburbia.com
www.casardeburbia.com

CASAR GODELLO 2011 B
100% godello.

91 Colour: bright yellow. Nose: white flowers, fragrant herbs, citrus fruit, fresh fruit, mineral. Palate: fresh, fruity, light-bodied, flavourful, balanced.

TEBAIDA 2010 T
100% mencía.

94 Colour: cherry, garnet rim. Nose: ripe fruit, spicy, balsamic herbs, creamy oak, earthy notes. Palate: long, spicy, powerful, flavourful.

CASAR DE BURBIA 2010 T
97% mencía, 3% garnacha.

91 Colour: cherry, garnet rim. Nose: red berry notes, ripe fruit, earthy notes, dry stone, sweet spices, creamy oak. Palate: flavourful, fresh, fruity.

TEBAIDA NEMESIO MAGNUM 2009 T
100% mencía.

94 Colour: cherry, garnet rim. Nose: ripe fruit, spicy, creamy oak, toasty, mineral, balanced. Palate: powerful, flavourful, toasty, round tannins, long, spicy, elegant.

HOMBROS 2009 T
100% mencía.

93 Colour: cherry, garnet rim. Nose: dry stone, balsamic herbs, ripe fruit, complex, toasty, creamy oak. Palate: powerful, flavourful, fruity, spicy, long, balanced.

TEBAIDA NEMESIO 2009 T
100% mencía.

92 Colour: cherry, garnet rim. Nose: ripe fruit, fragrant herbs, mineral, complex, spicy, creamy oak. Palate: good acidity, flavourful, fresh, fruity, balanced, elegant.

CEPAS DEL BIERZO

Ctra. de Sanabria, 111
24401 Ponferrada (León)
☎: +34 987 412 333 - Fax: +34 987 412 912
coocebier@coocebier.e.telefonica.net

FANEIRO 2011 T
mencía.

84

DON OSMUNDO 2008 T BARRICA
mencía.

87 Colour: cherry, garnet rim. Nose: ripe fruit, spicy, creamy oak, toasty. Palate: powerful, flavourful, toasty, round tannins.

COBERTIZO DE VIÑA RAMIRO

Promadelo Pol. 33 Parcela 407
24530 Valtuille de Abajo (León)
☎: +34 987 562 157 - Fax: +34 987 562 157
vinos@bodegacobertizo.com
www.bodegacobertizo.com

COBERTIZO 2011 T
mencía.

86 Colour: cherry, garnet rim. Nose: red berry notes, ripe fruit, balsamic herbs, balanced. Palate: powerful, flavourful, fruity, easy to drink.

COBERTIZO SELECCIÓN 2008 T ROBLE
mencía.

84

COBERTIZO 2008 T ROBLE
mencía.

82

COMPAÑÍA SANTA TRINIDAD XXI

24530 Villadecanes (León)
☎: +34 987 418 595
asesores@asofi.es

CORRO DAS XANAS 2011 T

89 Colour: deep cherry. Nose: complex, macerated fruit, ripe fruit, spicy, aromatic coffee. Palate: flavourful, powerful, spirituous, fruity.

DESCENDIENTES DE J. PALACIOS

Avda. Calvo Sotelo, 6
24500 Villafranca del Bierzo (León)
☎: +34 987 540 821 - Fax: +34 987 540 851
info@djpalacios.com

PÉTALOS DEL BIERZO 2010 T
mencía.

94 Colour: deep cherry. Nose: fresh fruit, balsamic herbs, scrubland, creamy oak. Palate: spicy, ripe fruit, fine bitter notes, good acidity.

MONCERBAL 2009 T
mencía.

96 Colour: very deep cherry. Nose: ripe fruit, sweet spices, scrubland, balsamic herbs. Palate: long, spicy, ripe fruit, balsamic, fine tannins.

LA FARAONA 2009 T
mencía.

96 Colour: very deep cherry. Nose: expressive, complex, elegant, ripe fruit, creamy oak, mineral, scrubland. Palate: flavourful, round, fine bitter notes.

VILLA DE CORULLÓN 2009 T
mencía.

95 Colour: deep cherry. Nose: fruit expression, ripe fruit, floral, mineral, toasty. Palate: spicy, fine bitter notes, good acidity.

LAS LAMAS 2009 T
mencía.

94 Colour: cherry, garnet rim. Nose: ripe fruit, earthy notes, toasty. Palate: flavourful, powerful, fine bitter notes, good acidity, spicy, ripe fruit.

DOMINIO DE LOS CEREZOS

Cno. de las Salgueras, s/n
24413 Molinaseca (León)
☎: +34 639 202 403
vangusvana@gmail.com

VAN GUS VANA 2009
mencía.

90 Colour: cherry, garnet rim. Nose: fruit expression, cocoa bean, new oak, complex. Palate: fruity, fresh, powerful, flavourful, elegant.

ESTEFANÍA

Ctra. Dehesas - Posada, s/n
24390 Ponferrada (León)
☎: +34 987 420 015 - Fax: +34 987 420 015
info@tilenus.com
www.tilenus.com

TILENUS 2011 T
100% mencía.

87 Colour: deep cherry. Nose: fruit liqueur notes, ripe fruit, dry stone, powerfull, warm. Palate: sweetness, spirituous, powerful, flavourful, fruity.

CASTILLO DE ULVER 2011 T
100% mencía.

87 Colour: dark-red cherry. Nose: varietal, expressive, powerfull, fruit preserve. Palate: balsamic, powerful, flavourful, fruity, pruney.

TILENUS 2008 T ROBLE
100% mencía.

89 Colour: dark-red cherry. Nose: spicy, ripe fruit, fruit liqueur notes, damp earth. Palate: balsamic, spicy.

TILENUS 2006 TC
100% mencía.

92 Colour: dark-red cherry, orangey edge. Nose: fine reductive notes, old leather, fruit preserve, sweet spices, cedar wood. Palate: elegant, round, good acidity.

TILENUS PAGOS DE POSADA 2004 T
100% mencía.

90 Colour: dark-red cherry, orangey edge. Nose: spicy, cocoa bean, creamy oak, toasty, tobacco, fine reductive notes. Palate: flavourful, powerful, creamy, spicy, toasty, smoky aftertaste, reductive nuances.

TILENUS PIEROS 2003 T
100% mencía.

90 Colour: dark-red cherry, orangey edge. Nose: fine reductive notes, tobacco, old leather, powerfull, complex. Palate: ripe fruit, spicy, reductive nuances, roasted-coffee aftertaste.

LOSADA VINOS DE FINCA

Ctra. a Villafranca LE-713, Km. 12
24540 Cacabelos (León)
☎: +34 987 548 053 - Fax: +34 987 548 069
bodega@losadavinosdefinca.com
www.losadavinosdefinca.com

LOSADA 2009 T
100% mencía.

91 Colour: dark-red cherry. Nose: fresh fruit, wild herbs, varietal, powerfull, expressive. Palate: fruity, full, powerful, flavourful.

LA BIENQUERIDA 2008 T
95% mencía, 5% otras.

93 Colour: very deep cherry. Nose: complex, candied fruit, smoky, spicy, cedar wood. Palate: creamy, ripe fruit, mineral, flavourful, powerful, spirituous, spicy.

ALTOS DE LOSADA 2008 T
100% mencía.

92 Colour: very deep cherry. Nose: ripe fruit, smoky, sweet spices, aged wood nuances, dark chocolate. Palate: sweetness, spirituous, powerful, flavourful.

MARTÍNEZ YEBRA

San Pedro, 96
24530 Villadecanes (León)
☎: +34 987 562 120 - Fax: +34 987 562 082
info@bodegamartinezyebra.es
www.bodegamartinezyebra.es

CANES 2010 T
mencía.

84

VIÑADECANES 2009 TC
mencía.

86 Colour: cherry, garnet rim. Nose: ripe fruit, fragrant herbs, dried flowers, spicy. Palate: flavourful, spicy, long.

VIÑADECANES TRES RACIMOS 2007 T
mencía.

86 Colour: dark-red cherry, orangey edge. Nose: ripe fruit, spicy, old leather, cigar. Palate: flavourful, spicy, long.

MENCÍAS DE DOS

Cuatro Calles, s/n
47491 La Seca (Valladolid)
☎: +34 983 103 223 - Fax: +34 983 816 561
info@sitiosdebodega.com
www.sitiosdebodega.com

DE 2 2011 T
100% mencía.

87 Colour: dark-red cherry. Nose: fresh, neat, varietal, ripe fruit. Palate: balsamic, ripe fruit, mineral, flavourful, fruity.

OTERO SANTÍN

Ortega y Gasset, 10
24402 Ponferrada (León)
☎: +34 987 410 101 - Fax: +34 987 418 544
oterobenito@gmail.com

OTERO SANTÍN 2011 B
godello.

90 Colour: bright straw. Nose: fresh, fresh fruit, white flowers. Palate: flavourful, fruity, good acidity, balanced.

OTERO SANTÍN 2011 RD
mencía.

88 Colour: rose, purple rim. Aroma powerfull, ripe fruit, red berry notes, floral, expressive. Taste fleshy, powerful, fruity, fresh.

OTERO SANTÍN 2011 T
mencía.

84

VALDECAMPO 2010 T
mencía.

86 Colour: cherry, garnet rim. Nose: red berry notes, ripe fruit, floral, balsamic herbs. Palate: light-bodied, flavourful, easy to drink.

PÉREZ CARAMÉS

Peña Picón, s/n
24500 Villafranca del Bierzo (León)
☎: +34 987 540 197 - Fax: +34 987 540 314
enoturismo@perezcarames.com
www.perezcarames.com

EL VINO DE LOS CÓNSULES DE ROMA 2011 T
100% mencía.

90 Colour: very deep cherry. Nose: fruit preserve, fruit liqueur notes, fruit expression, varietal, powerfull, warm. Palate: balsamic, powerful, flavourful, spirituous, sweetness, pruney.

VALDAIGA X 2011 T
100% mencía.

90 Colour: very deep cherry. Nose: earthy notes, damp earth, ripe fruit, fruit liqueur notes, fruit expression. Palate: fruity, flavourful, complex, sweetness, balsamic.

PRADA A TOPE

La Iglesia, s/n
24546 Canedo (León)
☎: +34 987 563 366 - Fax: +34 987 567 000
info@pradaatope.es
www.pradaatope.es

PRADA GODELLO 2011 B
godello.

91 Colour: bright straw. Nose: white flowers, jasmine, fragrant herbs. Palate: flavourful, powerful, full, rich, fruity, varietal.

PRADA 2011 RD
mencía, godello.

87 Colour: rose, purple rim. Nose: powerfull, complex, ripe fruit, red berry notes. Palate: flavourful, fine bitter notes, good acidity.

PALACIO DE CANEDO 2011 T MACERACIÓN CARBÓNICA
mencía.

89 Colour: bright cherry. Nose: powerfull, varietal, expressive, complex, fruit expression, ripe fruit, damp undergrowth. Palate: sweetness, fruity, powerful, flavourful.

VALENTÍN 2009 T ROBLE
mencía.

88 Colour: dark-red cherry. Nose: varietal, ripe fruit, fruit expression, cocoa bean, creamy oak. Palate: powerful, flavourful, aged character, toasty.

PICANTAL 2008 T
mencía.

90 Colour: dark-red cherry. Nose: ripe fruit, fruit liqueur notes, powerfull, warm, smoky, spicy, cedar wood, creamy oak. Palate: creamy, flavourful, powerful, spirituous, sweetness, round tannins, spicy.

LEGADO DE CANEDO 2007 T
mencía.

88 Colour: deep cherry. Nose: aged wood nuances, sweet spices, ripe fruit. Palate: powerful, flavourful, spirituous, spicy, toasty, harsh oak tannins.

PRADA A TOPE 2006 TR
mencía.

92 Colour: pale ruby, brick rim edge. Nose: spicy, fine reductive notes, wet leather, aged wood nuances, toasty. Palate: spicy, long, round tannins.

REAL MERUELO

Alto de Patricia
24400 Ponferrada (León)
☎: +34 616 429 253 - Fax: +34 987 425 616
donmeruelo@hotmail.com

DON MERUELO 2009 B
godello.

86 Colour: bright yellow. Nose: faded flowers, wild herbs, closed. Palate: rich, flavourful, balsamic.

DON MERUELO 2006 T
mencía.

85 Colour: cherry, garnet rim. Nose: ripe fruit, spicy, creamy oak. Palate: powerful, flavourful, toasty, round tannins.

RIBAS DEL CÚA

Finca Robledo, s/n
24540 Cacabelos (León)
☎: +34 987 471 017 - Fax: +34 987 971 016
bodega@ribasdelcua.com
www.ribasdelcua.com

RIBAS DEL CÚA 2011 T JOVEN
100% mencía.

87 Colour: cherry, purple rim. Nose: expressive, fresh fruit, red berry notes, floral. Palate: flavourful, fruity, good acidity, round tannins.

RIBAS DEL CÚA PRIVILEGIO 2006 T
100% mencía.

88 Colour: pale ruby, brick rim edge. Nose: spicy, fine reductive notes, wet leather, scrubland, earthy notes. Palate: spicy, long, ripe fruit, balsamic.

RODRÍGUEZ SANZO

Manuel Azaña, 9
47014 (Valladolid)
☎: +34 983 150 150 - Fax: +34 983 150 151
comunicacion@valsanzo.com
www.rodriguezsanzo.com

TERRAS DE JAVIER RODRÍGUEZ 2009 T
100% mencía.

93 Colour: cherry, garnet rim. Nose: powerfull, varietal, complex, expressive, red berry notes, lactic notes, fragrant herbs. Palate: flavourful, spicy, ripe fruit, long, round tannins.

SILVA BROCO

Bodega Silva Broco
24516 Lg. Parandones - Toral Vados (León)
☎: +34 987 553 043 - Fax: +34 987 553 043
antoniosilvabroco@hotmail.com

VIÑA BROCO 2011 T
mencía.

88 Colour: very deep cherry. Nose: powerfull, characterful, ripe fruit, spicy. Palate: powerful, fine bitter notes, good acidity.

LAGAR DE CAXÁN 2011 T
mencía.

84

SOTO DEL VICARIO

Ctra. Cacabelos- San Clemente, Pol. Ind. 908
Parcela 155
24547 San Clemente (León)
☎: +34 670 983 534 - Fax: +34 926 666 029
sandra.luque@pagodelvicario.com
www.sotodelvicario.com

GO DE GODELLO 2009 BFB
100% godello.

92 Colour: bright golden. Nose: ripe fruit, dry nuts, scrubland. Palate: elegant, round, spirituous, powerful, flavourful, complex, spicy.

SOTO DEL VICARIO MEN 2009 T
100% mencía.

91 Colour: deep cherry. Nose: toasty, creamy oak, fruit expression, complex. Palate: mineral, fruity, powerful, flavourful, sweetness, spirituous.

SOTO DEL VICARIO MEN SELECCIÓN 2008 T
100% mencía.

90 Colour: deep cherry. Nose: creamy oak, roasted coffee, ripe fruit. Palate: powerful, flavourful, sweetness, grainy tannins.

VINOS DE ARGANZA

Río Ancares, 2
24560 Toral de los Vados (León)
☎: +34 987 544 831 - Fax: +34 987 563 532
admon@vinosdearganza.com
www.vinosdearganza.com

SÉCULO 2011 B
godello, dona blanca.

85 Colour: bright straw. Nose: ripe fruit, citrus fruit, floral, dried herbs. Palate: powerful, flavourful, correct, easy to drink.

SÉCULO 2011 T
mencía.

88 Colour: cherry, purple rim. Nose: scrubland, balsamic herbs, ripe fruit. Palate: flavourful, fruity, fine bitter notes.

FLAVIUM 2011 T
mencía.

86 Colour: deep cherry. Nose: powerfull, ripe fruit, red berry notes. Palate: flavourful, fine bitter notes, good acidity.

CANEIROS 2011 T
mencía.

86 Colour: dark-red cherry. Nose: powerfull, varietal, complex, ripe fruit, fruit liqueur notes. Palate: fruity, fresh, balsamic.

FLAVIUM 2009 TC
mencía.

89 Colour: deep cherry. Nose: candied fruit, powerfull, expressive, varietal, smoky, spicy, aged wood nuances. Palate: powerful, flavourful, concentrated, ripe fruit.

SÉCULO 2009 TC
mencía.

87 Colour: cherry, garnet rim. Nose: ripe fruit, sweet spices, toasty. Palate: flavourful, powerful.

FLAVIUM SELECCIÓN 2008 T

87 Colour: bright cherry. Nose: ripe fruit, sweet spices, creamy oak, red berry notes. Palate: flavourful, fruity, toasty, round tannins.

FLAVIUM PREMIUM 2008 T
mencía.

86 Colour: deep cherry. Nose: aged wood nuances, roasted coffee, ripe fruit. Palate: spirituous, powerful, spicy, toasty.

SÉCULO 2006 TR
mencía.

88 Colour: deep cherry. Nose: creamy oak, dark chocolate, ripe fruit. Palate: powerful, fine bitter notes.

VINOS DEL BIERZO S. COOP.

Avda. Constitución, 106
24540 Cacabelos (León)
☎: +34 987 546 150 - Fax: +34 987 549 236
info@vinosdelbierzo.com
www.vinosdelbierzo.com

VINICIO GODELLO 2011 B
godello.

89 Colour: bright straw. Nose: fresh, neat, varietal. Palate: powerful, flavourful, fruity, rich.

VIÑA ORO 2011 B
dona blanca.

84

VIÑA ORO 2011 RD
mencía.

79

VIÑA ORO 2011 T
mencía.

83

GUERRA 2011 T
mencía.

79

GUERRA SELECCIÓN 2009 T
mencía.

81

VINICIO 2006 TC
mencía.

82

GUERRA 2005 TC
mencía.

83

VINOS VALTUILLE

La Fragua, s/n
24530 Valtuille de Abajo (León)
☎: +34 987 562 165 - Fax: +34 987 549 425
pagodevaldoneje@yahoo.es

PAGO DE VALDONEJE 2011 T
mencía.

89 Colour: cherry, purple rim. Nose: expressive, fresh fruit, red berry notes, floral. Palate: flavourful, fruity, good acidity.

PAGO DE VALDONEJE VIÑAS VIEJAS 2008 T
mencía.

92 Colour: cherry, garnet rim. Nose: ripe fruit, mineral, earthy notes, spicy, creamy oak. Palate: powerful, flavourful, long, balanced.

VIÑA ALBARES

Camino Real, s/n
24310 Albares de la Ribera (León)
☎: +34 987 519 147 - Fax: +34 987 519 152
info@vinaalbareswine.com
www.vinaalbareswine.com

TIERRAS DE ALBARES 2011 T
mencía.

86 Colour: dark-red cherry. Nose: fruit liqueur notes, ripe fruit, balsamic herbs. Palate: powerful, flavourful, ripe fruit, balsamic.

TIERRAS DE ALBARES 2008 TC
mencía.

88 Colour: cherry, garnet rim. Nose: spicy, creamy oak, toasty. Palate: powerful, flavourful, toasty, round tannins.

VIÑAS DEL BIERZO

Ctra. Ponferrada a Cacabelos, s/n
24410 Camponaraya (León)
☎: +34 987 463 009 - Fax: +34 987 450 323
vdelbierzo@granbierzo.com
www.granbierzo.com

MARQUÉS DE CORNATEL 2011 B
godello.

84

MARQUÉS DE CORNATEL 2011 RD
mencía.

86 Colour: rose, purple rim. Nose: powerfull, ripe fruit, red berry notes, floral, lactic notes. Palate: , powerful, fruity, fresh, easy to drink.

VALMAGAZ MENCÍA 2011 T
mencía.

80

MARQUÉS DE CORNATEL 2010 T ROBLE
mencía.

87 Colour: bright cherry. Nose: sweet spices, creamy oak, red berry notes. Palate: flavourful, fruity, toasty, round tannins.

GRAN BIERZO 2004 TR
mencía.

83

VIÑEDOS SINGULARES

Cuzco, 26 - 28, Nave 8
08030 (Barcelona)
☎: +34 609 168 191 - Fax: +34 934 807 076
info@vinedossingulares.com
www.vinedossingulares.com

CORRAL DEL OBISPO 2010 T
mencía.

88 Colour: bright cherry, garnet rim. Nose: wild herbs, balanced. Palate: balanced, fine bitter notes, long.

VIÑEDOS Y BODEGAS DOMINIO DE TARES

P.I. Bierzo Alto, Los Barredos, 4
24318 San Román de Bembibre (León)
☎: +34 987 514 550 - Fax: +34 987 514 570
info@dominiodetares.com
www.dominiodetares.com

DOMINIO DE TARES GODELLO 2011 BFB
100% godello.

92 Colour: pale. Nose: fruit expression, fragrant herbs, creamy oak. Palate: powerful, flavourful, full, fruity, smoky aftertaste.

BALTOS 2010 T
100% mencía.

87 Colour: dark-red cherry. Nose: ripe fruit, medium intensity, sweet spices, aged wood nuances. Palate: correct, warm, roasted-coffee aftertaste, ripe fruit, spicy.

DOMINIO DE TARES CEPAS VIEJAS 2009 TC
100% mencía.

91 Colour: deep cherry. Nose: spicy, toasty, new oak, ripe fruit. Palate: fruity, powerful, spicy, toasty.

TARES P. 3 2008 T ROBLE
100% mencía.

93 Colour: very deep cherry. Nose: damp earth, cocoa bean, spicy, sweet spices. Palate: powerful, flavourful, fruity, spirituous, sweetness, spicy, roasted-coffee aftertaste.

BEMBIBRE 2008 T
100% mencía.

90 Colour: very deep cherry. Nose: fruit liqueur notes, fruit liqueur notes, ripe fruit. Palate: creamy, spicy, mineral, flavourful, powerful, full.

VIÑEDOS Y BODEGAS PITTACUM

De la Iglesia, 11
24546 Arganza (León)
☎: +34 987 548 054 - Fax: +34 987 548 028
pittacum@pittacum.com
www.pittacum.com

TRES OBISPOS 2011 RD
mencía.

84

PITTACUM 2008 T BARRICA
mencía.

92 Colour: deep cherry. Nose: smoky, cocoa bean, sweet spices, fruit expression, ripe fruit, damp earth. Palate: complex, spirituous, good structure, powerful, flavourful, spicy, ripe fruit.

PITTACUM

PITTACUM AUREA 2008 TC
mencía.

93 Colour: very deep cherry. Nose: smoky, aged wood nuances, cocoa bean, fruit expression, ripe fruit. Palate: powerful, flavourful, fruity, sweetness, creamy, spicy, toasty.

LA PROHIBICIÓN 2008 T
garnacha tintorera.

93 Colour: bright cherry. Nose: ripe fruit, sweet spices, creamy oak, expressive. Palate: flavourful, fruity, toasty, round tannins, balanced.

DO BINISSALEM MALLORCA

LOCATION:

In the central region on the island of Majorca. It covers the municipal areas of Santa María del Camí, Binissalem, Sencelles, Consell and Santa Eugenia.

CLIMATE:

Mild Mediterranean, with dry, hot summers and short winters. The average rainfall per year is around 450 mm. The production region is protected from the northerly winds by the Sierra de Tramuntana and the Sierra de Alfabia mountain ranges.

SOIL:

The soil is of a brownish - grey or dun limey type, with limestone crusts on occasions. The slopes are quite gentle, and the vineyards are situated at an altitude ranging from 75 to 200 m.

GRAPE VARIETIES:

WHITE: *Moll* or *Prensal Blanc* (46 Ha), *Macabeo, Parellada, Moscatel* and *Chardonnay*.
RED: *Manto Negro* (majority 229 Ha), *Callet, Tempranillo, Syrah, Monastrell, Cabernet Sauvignon* (second red variety 56 Ha) and *Merlot*.

FIGURES:

Vineyard surface: 601 – **Wine-Growers:** 132 – **Wineries:** 14 – **2011 Harvest rating:** Very Good – **Production:** 1,700,140 litres – **Market percentages:** 84% domestic. 16% export

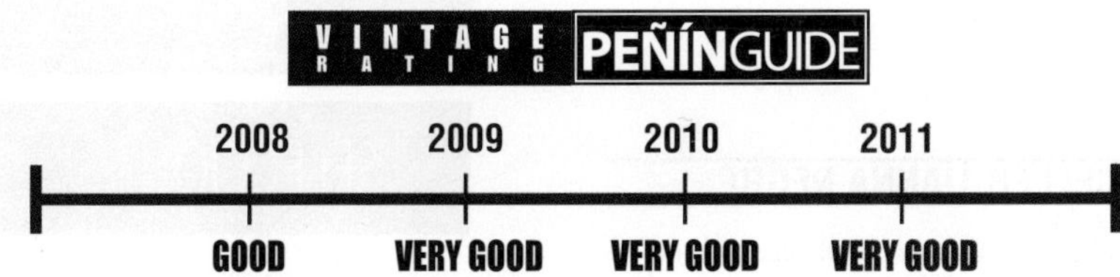

CONSEJO REGULADOR
Concepció, 7 - 07350 Binissalem (Illes Balears) - ☎: +34 971 512 191 - Fax: +34 971 886 522
@ info@binissalemdo.com - www.binissalemdo.com

BODEGUES MACIÀ BATLE

Camí Coanegra, s/n
07320 Santa María del Camí (Illes Balears)
☎: +34 971 140 014 - Fax: +34 971 140 086
correo@maciabatle.com
www.maciabatle.com

LLUM S/C B

89 Colour: bright yellow, greenish rim. Nose: floral, fresh fruit, citrus fruit. Palate: flavourful, good acidity, easy to drink.

MACIÀ BATLE BLANC DE BLANCS 2011 B
prensal, chardonnay.

88 Colour: bright yellow. Nose: wild herbs, fresh fruit, faded flowers. Palate: flavourful, fruity, balanced.

DOS MARIAS 2010 T ROBLE

88 Colour: cherry, garnet rim. Nose: ripe fruit, powerfull, sweet spices. Palate: fruity, easy to drink, round tannins.

P. DE MARÌA 2009 T

93 Colour: bright cherry. Nose: complex, powerfull, ripe fruit, scrubland, dark chocolate. Palate: flavourful, good acidity, round tannins.

MACIÀ BATLE 2009 TC
manto negro, syrah, cabernet sauvignon, merlot.

89 Colour: bright cherry, garnet rim. Nose: scrubland, ripe fruit, balanced, expressive. Palate: spicy, round tannins.

MACIÀ BATLE RESERVA PRIVADA 2008 TR
manto negro, merlot, cabernet sauvignon, syrah.

90 Colour: bright cherry. Nose: balsamic herbs, scrubland, ripe fruit, spicy. Palate: balanced, good acidity, round tannins.

CELLER TIANNA NEGRE

Camí des Mitjans. Desvio a la izquierda en el km. 1,5 de la Ctra. Binissalem-Inca
07350 Binissalem (Illes Balears)
☎: +34 971 886 826 - Fax: +34 971 226 201
info@tiannanegre.com
www.tiannanegre.com

TIANNA BOCCHORIS BLANC 2011 B
prensal, sauvignon blanc.

89 Colour: bright straw. Nose: balanced, medium intensity, dried herbs, fresh. Palate: fruity, rich, creamy, spicy.

RANDEMAR BLANC 2011 B
prensal, chardonnay, moscatel de frontignan.

84

SES NINES BLANC 2011 B
prensal, chardonnay, moscatel de frontignan.

83

VÉLOROSÉ 2011 RD
manto negro.

88 Colour: raspberry rose. Nose: citrus fruit, scrubland, expressive. Palate: powerful, ripe fruit, balanced.

SES NINES SELECCIO 2010 T
manto negro, cabernet sauvignon, syrah, merlot, callet, monastrell.

90 Colour: bright cherry, purple rim. Nose: expressive, fruit expression, balsamic herbs. Palate: flavourful, fruity, fresh, balanced.

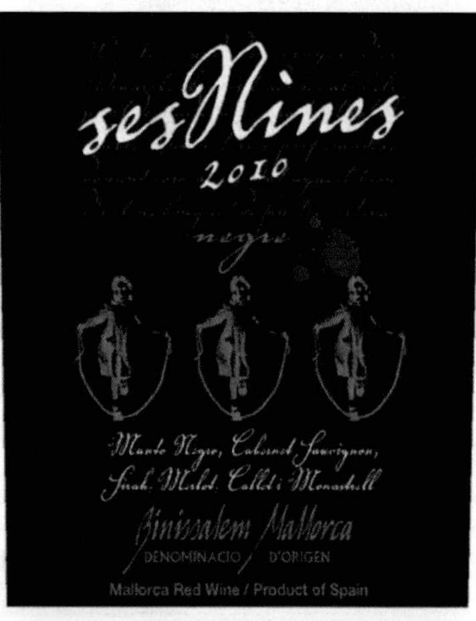

SES NINES ROSAT 2011 RD
manto negro, cabernet sauvignon.

86 Colour: light cherry, bright. Nose: red berry notes, ripe fruit, fragrant herbs. Palate: ripe fruit, flavourful.

RANDEMAR ROSAT 2011 RD
syrah, manto negro.

85 Colour: rose, purple rim. Nose: powerfull, ripe fruit, rose petals. Palate: fruity, flavourful, correct.

SES NINES NEGRE 2011 T
manto negro, cabernet sauvignon, callet, syrah, monastrell.

89 Colour: bright cherry. Nose: medium intensity, red berry notes, ripe fruit, floral. Palate: full, fruity, good acidity, fruity aftestaste.

RANDEMAR NEGRE 2011 T
manto negro, cabernet sauvignon, merlot, syrah.

87 Colour: bright cherry, purple rim. Nose: red berry notes, ripe fruit, scrubland. Palate: balanced, flavourful, fruity.

TIANNA NEGRE BOCCHORIS 2010 T
manto negro, cabernet sauvignon, syrah, merlot, callet, monastrell.

93 Colour: bright cherry, garnet rim. Nose: elegant, expressive, red berry notes, sweet spices. Palate: fruity, flavourful, balanced, round tannins.

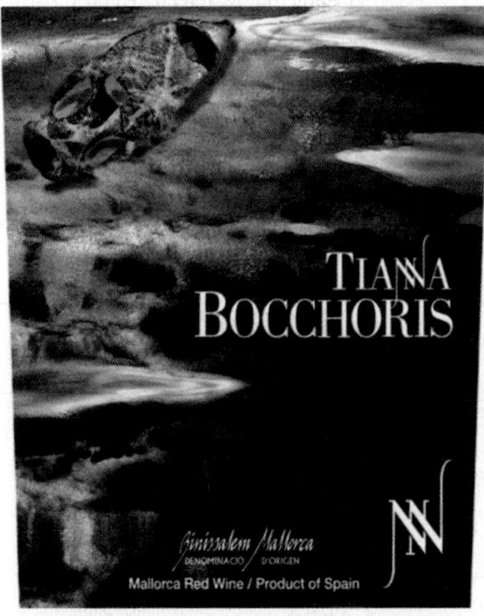

JAUME DE PUNTIRÓ

Pza. Nova, 23
07320 Santa María del Camí (Illes Balears)
☎: +34 971 620 023 - Fax: +34 971 620 023
pere@vinsjaumedepuntiro.com
www.vinsjaumedepuntiro.com

DAURAT 2011 BFB
prensal.

90 Colour: bright yellow. Nose: sweet spices, creamy oak, fresh fruit. Palate: fruity, flavourful, balanced, fine bitter notes.

JAUME DE PUNTIRÓ BLANC 2011 B
prensal.

86 Colour: bright straw. Nose: dried herbs, medium intensity, balanced. Palate: correct, balanced, easy to drink.

JAUME DE PUNTIRÓ MOSCATEL DOLÇ 2011 B
100% moscatel.

85 Colour: bright yellow. Nose: white flowers, jasmine, sweet spices. Palate: flavourful, fruity.

JAUME DE PUNTIRÓ CARMESÍ 2009 T
manto negro, callet.

90 Colour: cherry, garnet rim. Nose: spicy, balsamic herbs, ripe fruit, expressive. Palate: full, fruity, good acidity.

BUC 2008 TC
manto negro, cabernet sauvignon.

88 Colour: bright cherry, orangey edge. Nose: powerfull, spicy, scrubland. Palate: flavourful, balanced, fruity aftestaste.

J.P. 2006 TR
manto negro, cabernet sauvignon.

89 Colour: cherry, garnet rim. Nose: powerfull, creamy oak, cocoa bean, candied fruit. Palate: flavourful, rich, spicy.

JOSÉ L. FERRER

Conquistador, 103
07350 Binissalem (Illes Balears)
☎: +34 971 511 050 - Fax: +34 971 870 084
info@vinosferrer.com
www.vinosferrer.com

JOSÉ L. FERRER VERITAS 2011 BFB
60% moll, 40% chardonnay.

87 Colour: bright yellow. Nose: toasty, ripe fruit, white flowers, varietal. Palate: rich, easy to drink, ripe fruit.

JOSÉ L. FERRER BLANC DE BLANCS 2011 B
moll, chardonnay, moscatel.

83

JOSÉ L. FERRER 2011 RD
manto negro, callet, tempranillo, cabernet sauvignon, syrah.

86 Colour: rose, bright. Nose: medium intensity, scrubland, citrus fruit, red berry notes. Palate: fruity, easy to drink.

JOSÉ L. FERRER PEDRA DE BINISSALEM ROSAT 2011 RD
manto negro, cabernet sauvignon.

82

JOSÉ L. FERRER 2009 TC
manto negro, tempranillo, cabernet sauvignon, callet.

90 Colour: cherry, garnet rim. Nose: powerfull, dark chocolate, sweet spices, candied fruit. Palate: flavourful, rich, sweet tannins.

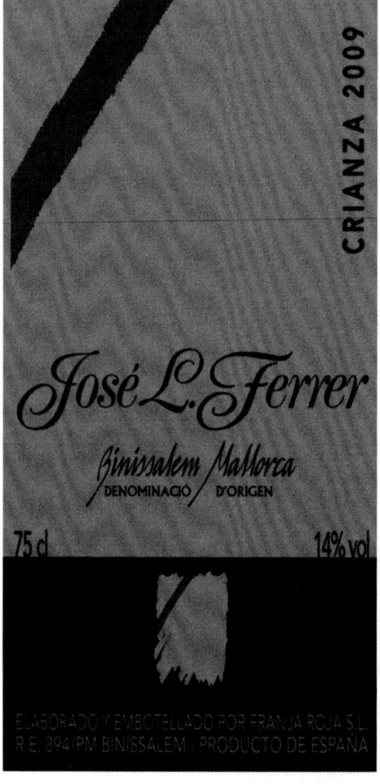

JOSÉ L. FERRER PEDRA DE BINISSALEM 2009 T
manto negro, cabernet sauvignon.

88 Colour: bright cherry, orangey edge. Nose: candied fruit, scrubland, cocoa bean. Palate: good structure, balanced, ripe fruit.

JOSÉ L. FERRER 2008 TR
manto negro, callet, cabernet sauvignon.

89 Colour: bright cherry, orangey edge. Nose: candied fruit, tobacco, spicy, powerfull, balsamic herbs. Palate: flavourful, fruity, balanced.

JOSÉ L. FERRER RESERVA FAMILIA 2007 TR
manto negro, callet.

89 Colour: bright cherry, orangey edge. Nose: fruit preserve, dark chocolate, sweet spices, powerfull. Palate: flavourful, ripe fruit, round tannins, spicy.

JOSÉ L. FERRER BRUT VERITAS 2009 ESP
moll, parellada, moscatel.

85 Colour: bright straw. Nose: medium intensity, fresh fruit, floral, spicy. Palate: fruity, flavourful, good acidity.

JOSÉ L. FERRER BRUT ROSADO VERITAS 2009 ESP

83

JOSÉ L. FERRER VERITAS DOLÇ 2010 MOSCATEL
100% moscatel.

87 Colour: bright yellow. Nose: balanced, varietal, white flowers, honeyed notes. Palate: flavourful, rich, correct.

VINS NADAL

Ramón Llull, 2
07350 Binissalem (Illes Balears)
☎: +34 971 511 058 - Fax: +34 971 870 150
albaflor@vinsnadal.com
www.vinsnadal.com

ALBAFLOR 2011 RD
36% manto negro, 36% merlot, 28% cabernet sauvignon.

87 Colour: rose. Nose: powerfull, red berry notes, ripe fruit, rose petals, wild herbs. Palate: flavourful, ripe fruit, long.

ALBAFLOR 2011 T
58% manto negro, 27,4% cabernet sauvignon, 14,6% merlot.

88 Colour: bright cherry, purple rim. Nose: earthy notes, red berry notes, ripe fruit. Palate: good structure, fruity, sweet tannins.

ALBAFLOR 2008 TC
55% manto negro, 27% cabernet sauvignon, 14% merlot, 4% syrah.

86 Colour: bright cherry, orangey edge. Nose: fruit preserve, spicy, old leather. Palate: correct, fruity, spicy.

ALBAFLOR 2007 TR
71% manto negro, 22% cabernet sauvignon, 7% merlot.

87 Colour: cherry, garnet rim. Nose: ripe fruit, spicy, creamy oak, toasty, balsamic herbs. Palate: powerful, flavourful, toasty, round tannins.

VINYA TAUJANA

Balanguera, 40
07142 Santa Eugenia (Illes Balears)
☎: +34 971 144 494 - Fax: +34 971 144 494
vinyataujana@gmail.com

VINYA TAUJANA BLANC DE BLANC 2011 B
prensal.

88 Colour: bright straw, greenish rim. Nose: medium intensity, wild herbs. Palate: correct, good acidity, easy to drink.

VINYA TAUJANA ROSAT 2011 RD
manto negro.

83

TORRENT FALS 2009 TC
manto negro, syrah.

89 Colour: bright cherry. Nose: balanced, red berry notes, scrubland. Palate: fruity, easy to drink, good acidity.

VINYES I VINS CA SA PADRINA

Camí dels Horts, s/n
07140 Sencelles (Illes Balears)
☎: +34 660 211 939 - Fax: +34 971 874 370
cellermantonegro@gmail.com

MOLLET SUÑER BIBILONI 2011 B JOVEN
prensal, chardonnay.

91 Colour: bright straw. Nose: expressive, ripe fruit, fruit expression, citrus fruit, floral. Palate: flavourful, fruity, good acidity, fine bitter notes.

MONTENEGRO SUÑER BIBILONI 2010 T ROBLE
manto negro, cabernet sauvignon, merlot, callet.

91 Colour: ruby red, garnet rim. Nose: mineral, ripe fruit, sweet spices, creamy oak. Palate: long, powerful, flavourful.

DO BIZKAIKO TXAKOLINA

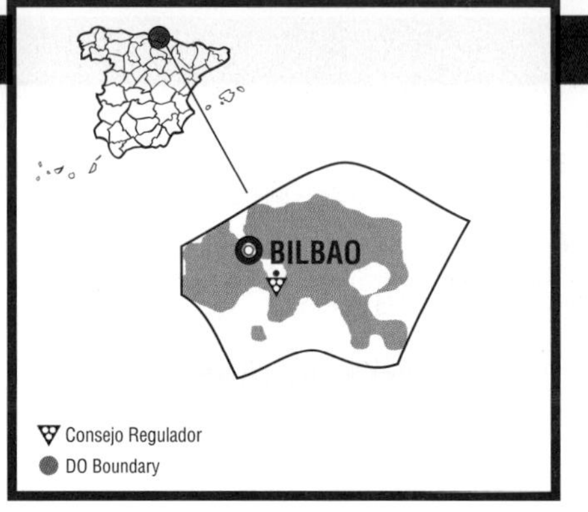

LOCATION:

In the province of Vizcaya. The production region covers both coastal areas and other areas inland.

CLIMATE:

Quite humid and mild due to the influence of the Bay of Biscay which tempers the temperatures. Fairly abundant rainfall, with an average of 1,000 to 1,300 mm per year.

SOIL:

Mainly clayey, although slightly acidic on occasions, with a fairly high organic matter content.

GRAPE VARIETIES:

WHITE: *Hondarrabi Zuri, Folle Blanche.*
RED: *Hondarrabi Beltza.*

FIGURES:

Vineyard surface: 358 – **Wine-Growers:** 238 – **Wineries:** 50 – **2011 Harvest rating:** Very Good – **Production:** 1,642,907 litres – **Market percentages:** 96% domestic. 4% export

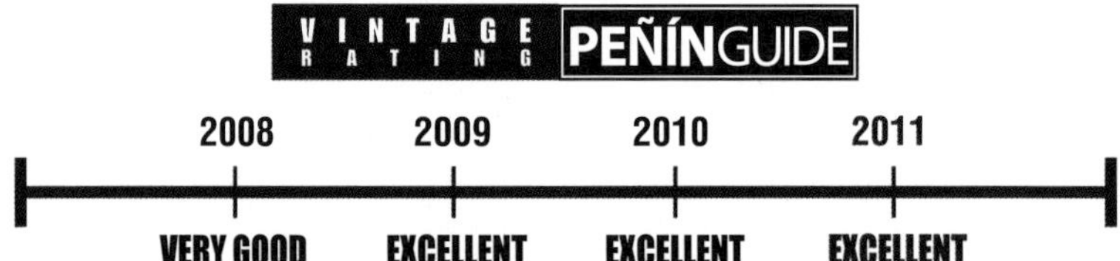

CONSEJO REGULADOR
Bº Mendibile, 42 - 48940 Leioa (Bizkaia) - ☎: +34 946 076 071 - Fax: +34 946 076 072
@ info@bizkaikotxacolina.org - www.bizkaikotxakolina.org

ABIO TXAKOLINA

Barrio Elexalde, 5 Caserío Basigo
48130 Bakio ()
☎: +34 946 194 345

ABIO TXACOLINA 2011 B

90 Colour: bright straw. Nose: fresh, white flowers, fresh fruit. Palate: flavourful, fruity, good acidity, balanced.

BASARTE

Urkitzaurrealde, 4
48130 Bakio (Bizkaia)
☎: +34 605 026 115
basarte@basarte.net
www.basarte.net

ADOS 2011 B

88 Colour: bright straw. Nose: fresh, white flowers, grassy, citrus fruit. Palate: flavourful, fruity, balanced.

BIKANDI TXAKOLINA

Eguzkitza, 6A
48200 Durango (Bizkaia)
☎: +34 616 292 436 - Fax: +34 946 816 519
miren@bikanditxakolina.com
www.bikanditxakolina.com

BIKANDI TXAKOLINA 2011 B

89 Colour: bright straw. Nose: white flowers, ripe fruit. Palate: flavourful, fruity, good acidity, balanced.

MIKELDI TXAKOLINA 2011 B

88 Colour: bright straw. Nose: fresh, fresh fruit, white flowers, varietal. Palate: flavourful, fruity, good acidity, balanced.

BODEGA AMUNATEGI

San Bartolomé, 57
48350 Busturia (Bizkaia)
☎: +34 685 737 398
info@amunategi.eu
www.amunategi.eu

AMUNATEGI 2011 B
60% hondarrabi zuri, 35% hondarrabi zuri zerratia, 5% hondarrabi beltza.

88 Colour: bright straw. Nose: fresh fruit, white flowers, tropical fruit. Palate: flavourful, good acidity, balanced.

BODEGA BERROJA

Ctra. de Zugastieta al Balcón de Bizkaia. Ajuria Barrio Berroja
48392 Muxika (Bizkaia)
☎: +34 944 106 254 - Fax: +34 946 309 390
txakoli@bodegaberroja.com
www.bodegaberroja.com

AGUIRREBEKO 2011 B
80% hondarrabi zuri, 15% folle blanch, 5% riesling.

88 Colour: bright straw. Nose: fresh, white flowers, ripe fruit. Palate: flavourful, fruity, balanced.

BERROJA 2010 B
80% hondarrabi zuri, 20% riesling.

88 Colour: bright straw. Nose: white flowers, expressive, ripe fruit, fine lees. Palate: flavourful, fruity, good acidity.

BODEGA ELIZALDE

Barrio Mendraka, 1
48230 Elorrio (Bizkaia)
☎: +34 946 820 000 - Fax: +34 946 820 000
kerixa@gmail.com

MENDRAKA 2011 B

87 Colour: bright straw. Nose: white flowers, ripe fruit. Palate: flavourful, fruity, good acidity.

BODEGA HARIZPE

Goimendia s/n
48700 Ondarroa (Bizkaia)
☎: +34 615 730 615 - Fax: +34 946 832 367
agroturismoharizpe@gmail.com
www.harizpe.com

HARIZPE 2011 B

88 Colour: bright straw. Nose: fresh, white flowers, ripe fruit. Palate: flavourful, fruity, good acidity, balanced.

BODEGA JON ANDER REKALDE

San Roke Bekoa, 11 (Artxanda)
48150 Sondika (Bizkaia)
☎: +34 944 458 631

ARTXANDA 2011 B

88 Colour: bright straw. Nose: fresh, white flowers, ripe fruit. Palate: flavourful, fruity, good acidity, balanced.

BODEGA VIÑA SULIBARRIA

El Bentorro, 4
48191 Galdames (Bizkaia)
☎: +34 946 100 107 - Fax: +34 946 100 107
info@vinasulibarria.com
www.viñasulibarria.com

TORRE DE LOIZAGA BIGARREN 2011 B

87 Colour: bright straw. Nose: powerfull, varietal, ripe fruit, scrubland. Palate: flavourful, good acidity.

TORRE DE LOIZAGA BIGARREN SELECCIÓN 2011 B

85 Colour: bright straw. Nose: ripe fruit, fine lees, grassy. Palate: flavourful, ripe fruit, good acidity.

DONIENE GORRONDONA TXAKOLINA

Gibelorratzagako San Pelaio, 1
48130 Bakio (Bizkaia)
☎: +34 946 194 795 - Fax: +34 946 195 831
gorrondona@donienegorrondona.com
www.donienegorrondona.com

GORRONDONA 2011 B
hondarrabi zuri, hondarrabi beltza, mune mahatsa.

89 Colour: bright straw. Nose: fresh, fresh fruit, white flowers, grassy, varietal. Palate: flavourful, fruity, good acidity, balanced.

DONIENE 2010 BFB
hondarrabi zuri.

91 Colour: bright yellow. Nose: powerfull, ripe fruit, sweet spices, creamy oak. Palate: rich, smoky aftertaste, flavourful, fresh, good acidity.

DONIENE 2010 B
hondarrabi zuri.

90 Colour: bright straw. Nose: scrubland, balsamic herbs, ripe fruit, citrus fruit. Palate: flavourful, good acidity.

GORRONDONA 2011 T
hondarrabi beltza.

85 Colour: cherry, purple rim. Nose: ripe fruit, balsamic herbs, grassy, green pepper. Palate: flavourful, varietal, grainy tannins.

ERDIKOETXE LANDETXEA

Goitioltza, 38
48196 Lezama (Bizkaia)
☎: +34 944 573 285 - Fax: +34 944 573 285
erdikoetxelandetxea@hotmail.com
www.nekatur.net

ERDIKOETXE 2011 B

86 Colour: bright straw. Nose: fresh, white flowers, ripe fruit, citrus fruit. Palatc: flavourful, fruity, good acidity, balanced.

ERDIKOETXE 2011 T

83

ITSASMENDI

Barrio Arane, 3
48300 Gernika (Bizkaia)
☎: +34 946 270 316 - Fax: +34 946 251 032
info@bodegasitsasmendi.com
www.bodegasitsasmendi.com

ITSAS MENDI 2011 B
hondarrabi zuri.

90 Colour: bright straw. Nose: fresh, white flowers, ripe fruit, grassy. Palate: flavourful, fruity, good acidity, balanced.

ITSASMENDI Nº 7 2010 B
hondarrabi zuri, riesling.

88 Colour: bright straw. Nose: white flowers, expressive, ripe fruit. Palate: flavourful, fruity, good acidity, balanced.

ITSAS ARTIZAR 2010 B

86 Colour: bright straw. Nose: ripe fruit, citrus fruit, fine lees, sweet spices. Palate: flavourful, sweetness, fine bitter notes.

ITSAS MENDI UREZTI 2008 B
hondarrabi zuri.

93 Colour: golden. Nose: powerfull, floral, honeyed notes, fragrant herbs, lactic notes. Palate: fresh, fruity, good acidity, long, sweetness.

ITURRIALDE

Barrio Legina, s/n
48195 Larrabetzu (Bizkaia)
☎: +34 946 742 706 - Fax: +34 946 741 221
txakoli@gorkaizagirre.com
www.gorkaizagirre.com

MARKO 2011 B

92 Colour: bright straw. Nose: fresh, fresh fruit, white flowers, expressive, balsamic herbs, scrubland. Palate: flavourful, fruity, good acidity, balanced.

GORKA IZAGIRRE 2011 B
50% hondarrabi zuri, hondarrabi zerratia.

90 Colour: bright straw. Nose: fresh, white flowers, expressive, scrubland, ripe fruit. Palate: flavourful, fruity, good acidity, balanced.

UIXAR 2011 B
100% hondarrabi zerratia.

90 Colour: bright straw. Nose: fresh, white flowers, mineral, varietal. Palate: flavourful, fruity, good acidity, balanced.

ARETXONDO 2011 B
50% hondarrabi zuri, 45% hondarrabi zerratia, 5% mune mahatsa.

89 Colour: bright straw. Nose: fresh, fresh fruit, expressive, floral, grassy. Palate: flavourful, fruity, good acidity, balanced.

NEKESOLO 2011 B
80% hondarrabi zerratia, 20% mune mahatsa.

89 Colour: bright straw. Nose: fresh, white flowers, expressive, ripe fruit, grassy. Palate: flavourful, fruity, balanced.

TORREKO 2011 B
40% hondarrabi zuri, 40% hondarrabi zerratia, 20% mune mahatsa.

88 Colour: bright straw. Nose: fresh, white flowers, varietal, ripe fruit. Palate: flavourful, fruity, good acidity.

E-GALA 2011 B
60% hondarrabi zerratia, 40% hondarrabi zuri.

88 Colour: bright straw. Nose: fresh, white flowers, expressive, ripe fruit, grassy. Palate: flavourful, fruity, good acidity, balanced.

42 2011 B

88 Colour: bright straw. Nose: fresh, white flowers, ripe fruit, citrus fruit. Palate: fruity, good acidity, balanced.

GORKA IZAGIRRE ARIMA 2010 B
100% hondarrabi zerratia.

90 Colour: golden. Nose: powerfull, floral, candied fruit, fragrant herbs. Palate: flavourful, sweet, fresh, fruity, good acidity, long.

JOSÉ ETXEBARRÍA URRUTIA

Txonebarri-C. Igartua, s/n
48110 Gatika (Bizkaia)
☎: +34 946 742 010

TXAKOLI ETXEBARRÍA 2011 B

84

LA ANTIGUA TXAKOLINA

Ctra. a Burgos, 9
48460 Orduña (Bizkaia)
☎: +34 696 198 194 - Fax: +34 945 383 509
peskayoli@euskalnet.net

TXAKOLI VINO DEL AÑO ANTIGUAKO AMA 2011 B
100% hondarrabi zuri.

83

MAGALARTE LEZAMA

B. Garaioltza, 92 B
48196 Lezama (Bizkaia)
☎: +34 944 556 508 - Fax: +34 944 556 508
magalarteinaki@yahoo.es

MAGALARTE IÑAKI ARETXABALETA 2011 B
hondarrabi zuri.

89 Colour: bright straw. Nose: fresh, white flowers, expressive, ripe fruit. Palate: flavourful, fruity, good acidity.

MAGALARTE IÑAKI ARETXABALETA 2011 BFB

89 Colour: bright straw. Nose: ripe fruit, cocoa bean, creamy oak. Palate: flavourful, powerful, complex.

SAGASTIBELTZA KARRANTZA 2011 B
hondarrabi zuri.

88 Colour: bright straw. Nose: fresh, white flowers. Palate: flavourful, fruity, good acidity.

MAGALARTE ZAMUDIO

Arteaga Auzoa, 107
48170 Zamudio (Bizkaia)
☎: +34 944 521 431 - Fax: +34 944 521 431
magalarte@hotmail.com

ARTEBAKARRA 2011 B
hondarrabi zuri, munemahatsa.

89 Colour: bright straw. Nose: fresh, expressive, floral, ripe fruit. Palate: good acidity, balanced.

MAGALARTE 2011 B
hondarrabi zuri, hondarrabi zarratia, petit manseng, riesling.

89 Colour: bright straw. Nose: fresh, white flowers, ripe fruit. Palate: flavourful, fruity, balanced.

ZABALONDO 2011 B
hondarrabi zuri, hondarrabi zarratia, mune mahatsa.

87 Colour: bright straw. Nose: fresh, fresh fruit, white flowers, varietal, floral. Palate: flavourful, fruity, good acidity, balanced.

MAISU C.B.

Barrio Ibazurra, 1
48460 Urduña/Orduña (Bizkaia)
☎: +34 945 384 126 - Fax: +34 945 384 126
maitedurana@gureahaleginak.com
www.gureahaleginak.com

GURE AHALEGINAK 2011 B
hondarrabi zuri.

86 Colour: bright straw. Nose: powerfull, varietal, ripe fruit, citrus fruit. Palate: flavourful, powerful, fine bitter notes.

FILOXERA 2010 T
hondarrabi beltza.

81

MERRUTXU UPELTEGIA

Caserío Merrutxu, Arboliz 23
48311 Ibarrangelu (Bizkaia)
☎: +34 946 276 435
info@merrutxu.com
www.txakolibizkaia.com

MERRUTXU 2011 B
hondarrabi zuri, chardonnay, folle blanch.

87 Colour: bright straw. Nose: fresh, fresh fruit, jasmine. Palate: flavourful, fruity, good acidity, balanced.

OTXANDURI TXAKOLINA

Otxanduri, 41
48498 Arrankudiaga (Bizkaia)
☎: +34 946 481 769
otxanduri@euskalnet.net

OTXANDURI 2011 B

90 Colour: bright straw. Nose: white flowers, ripe fruit. Palate: flavourful, fruity, good acidity, balanced.

ARTZAI 2010 B

88 Colour: bright straw. Nose: toasty, fruit liqueur notes, faded flowers. Palate: fine bitter notes, sweetness.

ARTZAI 2009 B

90 Colour: bright straw. Nose: cocoa bean, ripe fruit, toasty. Palate: fine bitter notes, sweetness, spicy.

TALLERI

Barrio Erroteta s/n
48115 Morga (Bizkaia)
☎: +34 944 651 689 - Fax: +34 944 651 689
www.bodegatalleri.com

BITXIA 2011 B
hondarrabi zuri.

85 Colour: bright straw. Nose: white flowers, fresh fruit. Palate: flavourful, fruity, good acidity, balanced.

TXAKOLI OXINBALTZA

Olleria 7 5ºA
48200 Durango (Bizkaia)
☎: +34 686 345 131
oxinbaltza@oxinbaltza.com
www.oxinbaltza.com

MAIORA 2011 B

89 Colour: bright straw. Nose: ripe fruit, fruit expression, citrus fruit, grassy. Palate: flavourful, fine bitter notes, fresh.

TXAKOLI SASINES

Barrio Bersonaga, 33 - Caserio Sasines
48195 Larrabetzu (Bizkaia)
☎: +34 944 558 196

SASINES 2011 B

88 Colour: bright straw. Nose: powerfull, balsamic herbs, grassy. Palate: flavourful, powerful, good acidity.

TXAKOLI TXABARRI

Muñeron, 17
48850 Zalla (Bizkaia)
☎: +34 946 390 947 - Fax: +34 946 390 947
itxasa@yahoo.es

TXABARRI 2011 B
80% hondarrabi zuri, 10% riesling, 10% sauvignon blanc.

87 Colour: bright straw. Nose: fresh, fresh fruit, white flowers. Palate: flavourful, fruity, good acidity, easy to drink.

TXABARRI 2011 RD
100% hondarrabi beltza.

80

TXABARRI 2011 T
100% hondarrabi beltza.

83

URIONDO

Barrio Urriondo, 2
48480 Zaratamo (Bizkaia)
☎: +34 946 711 870
uriondo.txakoli@gmail.com

URIONDO 2011 B
hondarrabi zuri, munemahatsa, txorimahatsa.

88 Colour: bright straw. Nose: fresh, white flowers, ripe fruit. Palate: fruity, good acidity, balanced.

URIONDO CUVÉE 2010 BFB
hondarrabi zuri, mune mahatsa, txorimahatsa.

86 Colour: bright straw. Nose: ripe fruit, sweet spices, white flowers. Palate: flavourful, powerful, spicy.

VIRGEN DE LOREA

Barrio de Lorea
48860 Otxaran-Zalla (Bizkaia)
☎: +34 944 242 680 - Fax: +34 946 670 521
virgendelorea@spankor.com
www.bodegasvirgendelorea.com

SEÑORÍO DE OTXARAN 2011 B
80% hondarrabi zuri, 20% folle blanch.

91 Colour: bright straw. Nose: fresh, white flowers, ripe fruit, grassy. Palate: flavourful, fruity, good acidity, balanced.

ARETXAGA 2011 B
80% hondarrabi zuri, 20% folle blanch.

88 Colour: bright straw. Nose: fresh, white flowers, fresh fruit, ripe fruit. Palate: flavourful, fruity, good acidity, balanced.

DO BULLAS

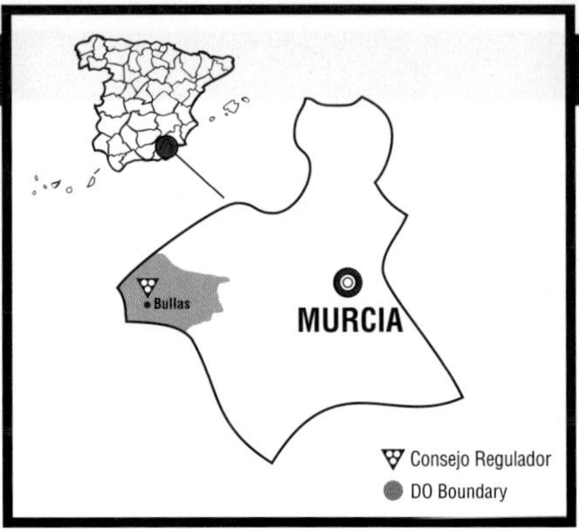

LOCATION:

In the province of Murcia. It covers the municipal areas of Bullas, Cehegín, Mula and Ricote, and several vineyards in the vicinity of Calasparra, Moratalla and Lorca.

CLIMATE:

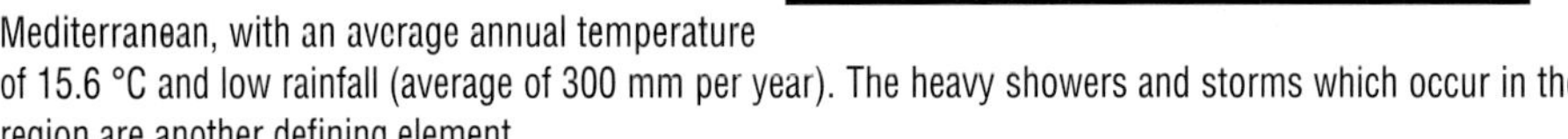

Mediterranean, with an average annual temperature of 15.6 °C and low rainfall (average of 300 mm per year). The heavy showers and storms which occur in the region are another defining element.

SOIL:

Brownish - grey limey soil, with limestone crusts, and alluvial. The terrain is rugged and determined by the layout of the little valleys, each with their own microclimate. Distinction can be made between 3 areas: one to the north north - east with an altitude of 400 – 500 m; another in the central region, situated at an altitude of 500 – 600 m; and the third in the western and north - western region, with the highest altitude (500 – 810 m), the highest concentration of vineyards and the best potential for quality.

GRAPE VARIETIES:

WHITE: *Macabeo* (main), *Airén, Chardonnay, Malvasía, Moscatel de Grano Menudo* and *Sauvignon Blanc.*
RED: *Monastrell* (main), *Petit Verdot, Tempranillo, Cabernet Sauvignon, Syrah, Merlot* and *Garnacha.*

FIGURES:

Vineyard surface: 2,300 – **Wine-Growers:** 640 – **Wineries:** 12 – **2011 Harvest rating:** Very Good – **Production:** 3,142,600 litres – **Market percentages:** 74% domestic. 26% export

VINTAGE RATING PEÑINGUIDE

2008	2009	2010	2011
VERY GOOD	VERY GOOD	VERY GOOD	N/A

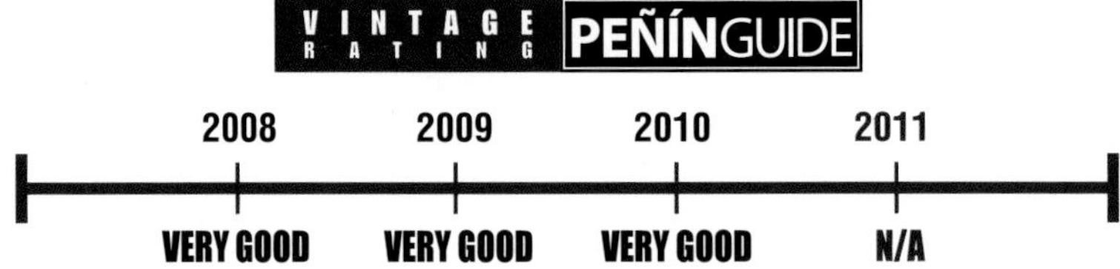

CONSEJO REGULADOR
Avda. de Murcia, 4 - 30180 Bullas (Murcia) - ☎: +34 968 652 601 - Fax: +34 968 652 601
@ consejoregulador@vinosdebullas.es - www.vinosdebullas.es

BODEGA BALCONA

Ctra. Bullas-Avilés, Km. 10 Valle del Aceniche
30180 Bullas (Murcia)
☎: +34 968 652 891
info@partal-vinos.com
www.partal-vinos.com

PARTAL 2004 T
60% monastrell, 17% syrah, 17% tempranillo, 10% cabernet sauvignon, 4% merlot.

88 Colour: pale ruby, brick rim edge. Nose: elegant, spicy, fine reductive notes, wet leather, aged wood nuances, fruit liqueur notes. Palate: spicy, fine tannins, elegant, long.

BODEGA MONASTRELL

Paraje El Aceniche
30150 Bullas (Murcia)
☎: +34 968 653 708 - Fax: +34 968 653 708
info@bodegamonastrell.com
www.bodegamonastrell.com

ALMUDÍ 2010 T
monastrell.

89 Colour: cherry, garnet rim. Nose: ripe fruit, earthy notes, balsamic herbs, spicy, toasty. Palate: powerful, flavourful, fresh, varietal.

CHAVEO 2007 TC
100% monastrell.

88 Colour: cherry, garnet rim. Nose: ripe fruit, earthy notes, sweet spices, fine reductive notes. Palate: long, flavourful, complex, spicy.

VALCHE 2006 TC
100% monastrell.

92 Colour: cherry, garnet rim. Nose: ripe fruit, mineral, aromatic coffee, sweet spices. Palate: long, flavourful, toasty, balanced.

BODEGA TERCIA DE ULEA

Tercia de Ulea, s/n
30440 Moratalla (Murcia)
☎: +34 968 433 213 - Fax: +34 968 433 965
info@terciadeulea.com
www.terciadeulea.com

REBELDÍA 2010 RD
80% monastrell, 15% syrah, 5% tempranillo.

79

ADIVINA 2010 RD
64% monastrell, 18% syrah, 18% cabernet sauvignon.

76

VIÑA BOTIAL 2010 T ROBLE
50% monastrell, 50% syrah.

87 Colour: deep cherry. Nose: red berry notes, overripe fruit, fragrant herbs, toasty. Palate: powerful, flavourful, fine bitter notes.

RAMBLA DE ULEA 2010 T
74% monastrell, 16% tempranillo, 10% cabernet sauvignon.

87 Colour: bright cherry. Nose: ripe fruit, sweet spices, creamy oak. Palate: flavourful, fruity, toasty, round tannins.

TERCIA DE ULEA TC
76% monastrell, 24% tempranillo.

90 Colour: cherry, garnet rim. Nose: spicy, toasty, red berry notes, floral. Palate: powerful, flavourful, toasty, round tannins.

BODEGAS DEL ROSARIO

Avda. de la Libertad, s/n
30180 Bullas (Murcia)
☎: +34 968 652 075 - Fax: +34 968 653 765
info@bodegasdelrosario.com
www.bodegasdelrosario.com

3000 AÑOS 2009 T
50% monastrell, 50% syrah.

92 Colour: bright cherry. Nose: sweet spices, creamy oak, overripe fruit. Palate: flavourful, fruity, toasty, round tannins.

LAS REÑAS MONASTRELL SHIRAZ SELECCIÓN 2009 T
70% monastrell, 30% syrah.

85 Colour: cherry, garnet rim. Nose: spicy, creamy oak, toasty, characterful, ripe fruit. Palate: powerful, flavourful, toasty, round tannins.

BODEGAS MERCADER-QUESADA

Herrera, 22
30180 Bullas (Murcia)
☎: +34 968 654 205 - Fax: +34 968 654 205
pilarquesadagil@yahoo.es
www.mundoenologico.com

MERCADER QUESADA VENDIMIA 2011 T

86 Colour: cherry, purple rim. Nose: fresh fruit, red berry notes, floral. Palate: flavourful, fruity, good acidity, round tannins.

MERCADER QUESADA SELECCIÓN MONASTRELL ECOLÓGICO 2008 T
monastrell.

85 Colour: bright cherry. Nose: sweet spices, creamy oak, ripe fruit. Palate: flavourful, fruity, toasty, round tannins.

CARRASCALEJO

Finca El Carrascalejo, s/n
30180 Bullas (Murcia)
☎: +34 968 652 003 - Fax: +34 968 652 003
carrascalejo@carrascalejo.com
www.carrascalejo.com

CARRASCALEJO 2011 RD
100% monastrell.

86 Colour: brilliant rose. Nose: lactic notes, dried flowers, red berry notes, expressive. Palate: fresh, fruity, easy to drink.

CARRASCALEJO 2011 T
100% monastrell.

87 Colour: cherry, purple rim. Nose: floral, red berry notes, balanced, powerfull. Palate: flavourful, fresh, fruity, easy to drink.

CARRASCALEJO 2009 TC
60% monastrell, 30% syrah, 10% cabernet sauvignon.

86 Colour: cherry, garnet rim. Nose: ripe fruit, roasted coffee, fine reductive notes. Palate: powerful, flavourful, complex.

COOPERATIVA VINÍCOLA AGRARIA SAN ISIDRO

Pol. Ind. Marimingo- Altiplano, s/n
30180 Bullas (Murcia)
☎: +34 968 654 991 - Fax: +34 968 652 160
bodegasanisidro@terra.es

CEPAS DEL ZORRO MACABEO 2011 B
100% macabeo.

83

CEPAS DEL ZORRO 2011 RD
80% monastrell, 20% garnacha.

88 Colour: rose, purple rim. Nose: ripe fruit, red berry notes, floral, powerfull. Palate: , powerful, fruity, fresh.

CEPAS DEL ZORRO 2011 T
90% monastrell, 10% syrah.

85 Colour: cherry, purple rim. Nose: expressive, fresh fruit, red berry notes, floral. Palate: flavourful, fruity, round tannins.

FERNANDO CARREÑO PEÑALVER

Andalucía, 40
30430 Cehegín (Murcia)
☎: +34 968 740 004 - Fax: +34 968 740 004
carrenobodegas@terra.es

MARMALLEJO 2009 TC
60% monastrell, 40% petit verdot.

85 Colour: bright cherry. Nose: sweet spices, creamy oak, ripe fruit. Palate: flavourful, fruity, toasty, round tannins.

MOLINO Y LAGARES DE BULLAS

Paraje Venta del Pino, s/n Parcela 38
30430 Cehegin (Murcia)
☎: +34 638 046 694 - Fax: +34 968 654 494
lavia@bodegaslavia.com
www.bodegaslavia.com

LAVIA MONASTRELL SYRAH 2008 TC
70% monastrell, 30% syrah.

94 Colour: bright cherry. Nose: ripe fruit, lactic notes, scrubland, balsamic herbs, spicy. Palate: flavourful, fruity, fine bitter notes, good acidity.

LAVIA+ 2007 TC
100% monastrell.

92 Colour: cherry, garnet rim. Nose: spicy, creamy oak, toasty, warm, overripe fruit. Palate: powerful, flavourful, toasty, round tannins.

LOCATION:

It is situated in the western region of the province of Zaragoza, along the foothills of the Sistema Ibérico, outlined by the network of rivers woven by the different tributaries of the Ebro: Jalón, Jiloca, Manubles, Mesa, Piedra and Ribota, and covers 46 municipal areas of the Ebro Valley.

CLIMATE:

Semi - arid and dry, although somewhat cooler than Cariñena and Borja, with cold winters, an average annual temperature which ranges between 12 and 14 °C, and a period of frost of between 5 and 7 months which greatly affects the production. The average rainfall ranges between 300 – 550 mm per year, with great day/night temperature contrasts during the ripening season.

SOIL:

In general, the soil has a high limestone content. It is formed by rugged stony materials from the nearby mountain ranges and is on many occasions accompanied by reddish clay. The region is the most rugged in Aragón, and the vineyards are situated at an altitude of between 550 and 880 m.

GRAPE VARIETIES:

WHITE: PREFERRED: *Macabeo* (25%) and *Malvasía.*
AUTHORIZED: *Moscatel de Alejandría, Garnacha Blanca, Sauvignon Blanc, Gewurztraiminer* and *Chardonnay.*
RED: PREFERRED: *Garnacha Tinta* (61.9%), *Tempranillo* (10%) and *Mazuela.*
AUTHORIZED: *Monastrell, Cabernet Sauvignon, Merlot, Bobal* and *Syrah.*

FIGURES:

Vineyard surface: 3,200 – **Wine-Growers:** 1,008 – **Wineries:** 16 – **2011 Harvest rating:** Excellent – **Production:** 61,260,140 litres – **Market percentages:** 15% domestic. 85% export

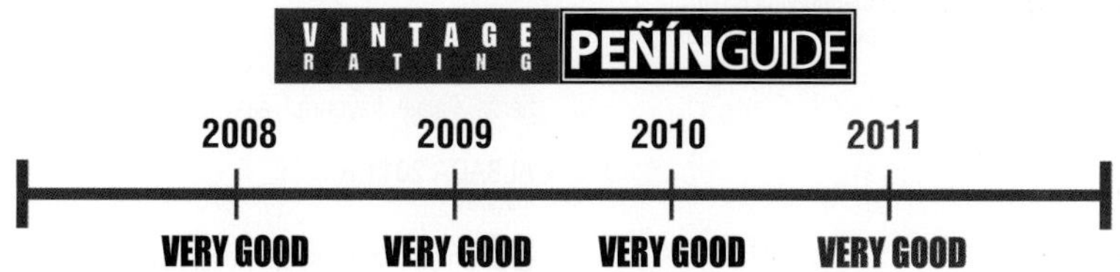

CONSEJO REGULADOR
Ctra. de Valencia, 8 - 50300 Calatayud (Zaragoza) - ☎: +34 976 884 260 - Fax: +34 976 885 912
@ administracion@docalatayud.com - www.docalatayud.com

AGUSTÍN CUBERO

La Charluca, s/n
50300 Calatayud (Zaragoza)
☎: +34 976 882 332 - Fax: +34 976 887 512
calatayud@bodegascubero.com
www.bodegascubero.com

UNUS 2011 B
macabeo.

86 Colour: bright straw. Nose: fragrant herbs, fresh, balanced, citrus fruit. Palate: correct, good acidity, fresh, fine bitter notes.

STYLO 2011 T
100% garnacha.

90 Colour: cherry, purple rim. Nose: ripe fruit, sweet spices, dry stone, complex. Palate: balanced, ripe fruit, long.

STYLO 2010 T
100% garnacha.

91 Colour: cherry, garnet rim. Nose: powerfull, sweet spices, toasty, ripe fruit, fragrant herbs. Palate: spicy, ripe fruit, long.

UNUS 2010 T
100% syrah.

89 Colour: cherry, purple rim. Nose: balanced, fruit expression, cocoa bean. Palate: flavourful, fruity, balanced.

ALIANZA DE GARAPITEROS

Plaza España, 6 Planta 1ª Oficina B
50001 (Zaragoza)
☎: +34 976 094 033 - Fax: +34 976 094 033
info@alianzadegarapiteros.es
www.alianzadegarapiteros.es

NIETRO MACABEO VIÑAS VIEJAS 2011 B
100% macabeo.

87 Colour: bright straw. Nose: citrus fruit, fruit expression, ripe fruit. Palate: flavourful, fruity, fresh.

NIETRO GARNACHA VIÑAS VIEJAS 2011 T
garnacha.

90 Colour: cherry, garnet rim. Nose: ripe fruit, scrubland, spicy, earthy notes. Palate: powerful, complex, flavourful, balanced.

ALQUÉZ GARNACHA VIÑAS VIEJAS 2010 T
100% garnacha.

89 Colour: bright cherry. Aroma ripe fruit, sweet spices, creamy oak, expressive. Taste flavourful, fruity, toasty, round tannins.

LAMIN GARNACHA VIÑAS VIEJAS 2009 T
100% garnacha.

89 Colour: cherry, garnet rim. Nose: ripe fruit, scrubland, spicy, dark chocolate, toasty. Palate: powerful, flavourful, long, toasty.

BODEGA COOPERATIVA VIRGEN DE LA SIERRA

Avda. de la Cooperativa, 21-23
50310 Villarroya de la Sierra (Zaragoza)
☎: +34 976 899 015 - Fax: +34 976 899 032
oficina@bodegavirgendelasierra.com
www.bodegavirgendelasierra.com

CRUZ DE PIEDRA 2011 B
macabeo.

86 Colour: bright straw. Nose: balanced, dry nuts, wild herbs. Palate: flavourful, easy to drink.

ALBADA 2011 B
macabeo.

85 Colour: bright straw. Nose: scrubland, fresh, medium intensity. Palate: fruity, good acidity.

CRUZ DE PIEDRA 2011 RD
garnacha.

87 Colour: rose, purple rim. Nose: powerfull, ripe fruit, red berry notes, floral. Palate: , powerful, fruity, fresh, easy to drink.

CRUZ DE PIEDRA 2011 T
garnacha.

87 Colour: deep cherry, purple rim. Nose: medium intensity, balsamic herbs, spicy. Palate: ripe fruit, balanced, long.

CRUZ DE PIEDRA SELECCIÓN ESPECIAL 2010 T
garnacha.

92 Colour: cherry, garnet rim. Nose: mineral, balsamic herbs, complex, red berry notes, sweet spices. Palate: good structure, flavourful, complex, round tannins.

ALBADA 2010 T
garnacha.

88 Colour: cherry, garnet rim. Nose: ripe fruit, spicy, toasty, warm. Palate: powerful, flavourful, toasty, round tannins.

CRUZ DE PIEDRA CAPRICHO 2008 T
garnacha.

89 Colour: cherry, garnet rim. Nose: ripe fruit, spicy, creamy oak, mineral, balsamic herbs. Palate: powerful, flavourful, toasty, round tannins, balanced.

ALBADA 2007 TR
garnacha.

86 Colour: cherry, garnet rim. Nose: powerfull, sweet spices, warm, ripe fruit. Palate: fruity, correct, good finish.

BODEGA SAN GREGORIO

Ctra. Villalengua, s/n
50312 Cervera de la Cañada (Zaragoza)
☎: +34 976 899 206 - Fax: +34 976 896 240
tresojos@bodegasangregorio.com
www.bodegasangregorio.com

ARMANTES 2011 B
macabeo.

85 Colour: bright straw. Nose: fresh, fresh fruit, white flowers, wild herbs. Palate: flavourful, fruity, good acidity.

ARMANTES 2011 T
50% garnacha, 50% tempranillo.

88 Colour: deep cherry, purple rim. Nose: red berry notes, ripe fruit, medium intensity, fruit expression. Palate: fruity, flavourful, easy to drink.

TRES OJOS GARNACHA 2011 T
garnacha.

87 Colour: deep cherry, purple rim. Nose: powerfull, ripe fruit, dried herbs. Palate: balanced, flavourful, good acidity.

TRES OJOS TEMPRANILLO 2011 T
tempranillo.

87 Colour: cherry, purple rim. Nose: ripe fruit, raspberry, balsamic herbs. Palate: powerful, flavourful, fruity.

ARMANTES SELECCIÓN ESPECIAL 2010 T
60% garnacha, 22% tempranillo, 6% merlot, 6% syrah, 6% cabernet sauvignon.

88 Colour: cherry, garnet rim. Nose: red berry notes, ripe fruit, varietal, creamy oak, toasty. Palate: spicy, powerful, flavourful, long.

TRES OJOS TEMPRANILLO 2010 T
tempranillo.

88 Colour: cherry, garnet rim. Nose: ripe fruit, scrubland, spicy. Palate: powerful, flavourful, harsh oak tannins.

TRES OJOS GARNACHA 2010 T
garnacha.

86 Colour: cherry, purple rim. Nose: floral, ripe fruit, balsamic herbs, mineral. Palate: flavourful, long, ripe fruit.

ARMANTES SELECCIÓN ESPECIAL 2009 T
60% garnacha, 22% tempranillo, 6% syrah, 6% merlot, 6% cabernet sauvignon.

90 Colour: bright cherry, garnet rim. Nose: complex, balanced, ripe fruit, dry stone. Palate: flavourful, fruity, round tannins.

MONTE ARMANTES CARMESÍ 2009 T
50% garnacha, 50% tempranillo.

88 Colour: cherry, garnet rim. Nose: ripe fruit, spicy, toasty, earthy notes. Palate: powerful, flavourful, toasty, harsh oak tannins.

ARMANTES 2008 TR
70% garnacha, 22% tempranillo, 8% syrah, merlot, cabernet sauvignon.

88 Colour: cherry, garnet rim. Nose: ripe fruit, spicy, creamy oak, toasty, complex. Palate: powerful, flavourful, toasty, round tannins.

ARMANTES 2007 TR
70% garnacha, 22% tempranillo, 8% syrah, merlot, cabernet sauvignon.

88 Colour: cherry, garnet rim. Nose: ripe fruit, fine reductive notes, dark chocolate, cocoa bean. Palate: correct, flavourful, spicy.

ARMANTES 2007 TC
85% tempranillo, 15% garnacha.

87 Colour: cherry, garnet rim. Nose: ripe fruit, spicy, fine reductive notes. Palate: powerful, flavourful, toasty, round tannins.

BODEGA VIRGEN DEL MAR Y DE LA CUESTA

Ctra. Monasterio de la Piedra, s/n
50219 Munebrega (Zaragoza)
☎: +34 976 895 071 - Fax: +34 976 895 171
bodegamunebrega@hotmail.com

MUZARES 2011 B
100% macabeo.

80

MUZARES 2011 RD
100% garnacha.

86 Colour: brilliant rose. Nose: fresh, red berry notes, balanced, dried herbs. Palate: balanced, good acidity.

MUZARES 2011 T
85% garnacha, 15% tempranillo.

88 Colour: cherry, purple rim. Nose: red berry notes, fruit liqueur notes, wild herbs, mineral. Palate: flavourful, good structure, long.

BODEGAS ATECA

Ctra. N-II, s/n
50200 Ateca (Zaragoza)
☎: +34 968 435 022 - Fax: +34 968 716 051
info@orowines.com
www.orowines.com

HONORO VERA GARNACHA 2011 T
100% garnacha.

90 Colour: cherry, purple rim. Nose: red berry notes, ripe fruit, mineral, spicy. Palate: powerful, flavourful, fruity, balanced.

ATTECA 2010 T
100% garnacha.

91 Colour: bright cherry. Nose: sweet spices, creamy oak, expressive, powerfull. Palate: flavourful, fruity, toasty, round tannins.

ATTECA ARMAS 2009 T
100% garnacha.

93 Colour: black cherry. Nose: mineral, earthy notes, powerfull, ripe fruit, fruit expression. Palate: flavourful, powerful, concentrated, toasty, harsh oak tannins.

BODEGAS AUGUSTA BILBILIS

Carramiedes, s/n
50331 Mara (Zaragoza)
☎: +34 677 547 127
bodegasaugustabilbilis@hotmail.com
www.bodegasaugustabilbilis.com

SAMITIER 2009 T
100% garnacha.

87 Colour: bright cherry. Nose: ripe fruit, sweet spices, creamy oak, mineral. Palate: fruity, toasty, flavourful.

SAMITIER 2008 T
100% garnacha.

90 Colour: cherry, garnet rim. Nose: ripe fruit, spicy, creamy oak, toasty, complex, dry stone. Palate: powerful, flavourful, toasty, balanced.

BODEGAS BRECA

Ctra. Monasterio de Piedra
502196 Munebrega (Zaragoza)
☎: +34 952 504 706
office@jorge-ordonez.es
www.grupojorgeordonez.com

GARNACHA DE FUEGO 2011 T
garnacha.

88 Colour: cherry, garnet rim. Nose: ripe fruit, red berry notes, sweet spices. Palate: flavourful, ripe fruit, spicy, fine bitter notes.

BODEGAS LANGA

Ctra. Nacional II, Km. 241,700
50300 Calatayud (Zaragoza)
☎: +34 976 881 818 - Fax: +34 976 884 463
info@bodegas-langa.com
www.bodegas-langa.com

LANGA CHARDONNAY 2011 B
100% chardonnay.

85 Colour: bright straw. Nose: fresh, fresh fruit, white flowers, ripe fruit. Palate: flavourful, fruity, good acidity, balanced.

LANGA EMOCIÓN 2010 T
50% cabernet sauvignon, 50% syrah.

90 Colour: cherry, garnet rim. Nose: ripe fruit, creamy oak, sweet spices. Palate: rich, flavourful, balanced, mineral, long.

LANGA TRADICIÓN 2010 T
100% garnacha.

90 Colour: cherry, garnet rim. Nose: medium intensity, ripe fruit, varnish, sweet spices, earthy notes. Palate: complex, good structure, powerful, flavourful, good acidity.

REYES DE ARAGÓN MERLOT SYRAH ECOLÓGICO 2010 T
merlot, syrah.

89 Colour: cherry, garnet rim. Nose: ripe fruit, raspberry, balsamic herbs, violets, toasty. Palate: balanced, powerful, flavourful, toasty.

LANGA MERLOT 2010 T
merlot.

89 Colour: cherry, garnet rim. Nose: ripe fruit, fragrant herbs, mineral, roasted coffee. Palate: full, flavourful, correct, long.

REAL DE ARAGÓN 2009 T
garnacha.

92 Colour: cherry, garnet rim. Nose: toasty, creamy oak, sweet spices. Palate: good structure, balanced, round, round tannins.

REYES DE ARAGÓN GARNACHA CABERNET 2009 TC
garnacha, cabernet sauvignon.

88 Colour: cherry, garnet rim. Nose: ripe fruit, creamy oak, toasty, mineral, balsamic herbs. Palate: powerful, flavourful, toasty, round tannins.

REYES DE ARAGÓN 2008 TR
garnacha, merlot.

88 Colour: cherry, garnet rim. Nose: ripe fruit, spicy, complex, mineral. Palate: powerful, flavourful, toasty, round tannins.

BODEGAS SAN ALEJANDRO

Ctra. Calatayud - Cariñena, Km. 16
50330 Miedes de Aragón (Zaragoza)
☎: +34 976 892 205 - Fax: +34 976 890 540
contacto@san-alejandro.com
www.san-alejandro.com

BALTASAR GRACIÁN MACABEO 2011 B
100% macabeo.

86 Colour: bright straw. Nose: white flowers, dry nuts, fragrant herbs, ripe fruit. Palate: correct, fresh, fruity.

BALTASAR GRACIÁN GARNACHA 2011 RD
100% garnacha.

88 Colour: rose, purple rim. Nose: expressive, lactic notes, red berry notes, ripe fruit, floral. Palate: powerful, flavourful, full, fruity.

BALTASAR GRACIÁN GARNACHA 2011 T
100% garnacha.

89 Colour: dark-red cherry, purple rim. Nose: expressive, red berry notes, mineral, balsamic herbs. Palate: flavourful, fruity, powerful, concentrated.

EVODIA 2011 T
100% garnacha.

87 Colour: cherry, purple rim. Nose: ripe fruit, balanced, neat, dried herbs. Palate: good structure, mineral, round tannins.

LAS ROCAS GARNACHA VIÑAS VIEJAS 2010 T
100% garnacha.

93 Colour: cherry, garnet rim. Nose: complex, elegant, red berry notes, ripe fruit. Palate: spicy, balsamic, balanced, round tannins.

LAS ROCAS GARNACHA 2010 T
100% garnacha.

92 Colour: bright cherry, garnet rim. Nose: ripe fruit, sweet spices, creamy oak, mineral. Palate: flavourful, toasty, round tannins, balanced.

BALTASAR GRACIÁN GARNACHA VIÑAS VIEJAS 2010 T
100% garnacha.

90 Colour: cherry, purple rim. Nose: ripe fruit, sweet spices, creamy oak, earthy notes. Palate: flavourful, fruity, toasty, round tannins.

BALTASAR GRACIÁN 2009 TC
70% garnacha, 20% tempranillo, 10% syrah.

92 Colour: cherry, garnet rim. Nose: ripe fruit, spicy, creamy oak, toasty, complex. Palate: powerful, flavourful, toasty, round tannins, long.

BALTASAR GRACIÁN GARNACHA VIÑAS VIEJAS 2009 T
100% garnacha.

92 Colour: cherry, garnet rim. Nose: balanced, complex, mineral, ripe fruit. Palate: spicy, balanced, good acidity, round tannins.

BALTASAR GRACIÁN TEMPRANILLO VIÑAS VIEJAS 2009 T
100% tempranillo.

89 Colour: cherry, garnet rim. Nose: ripe fruit, powerfull, sweet spices, dried herbs. Palate: flavourful, ripe fruit, good acidity.

BALTASAR GRACIÁN 2008 TR
70% garnacha, 20% tempranillo, 10% cabernet sauvignon.

92 Colour: cherry, garnet rim. Nose: ripe fruit, spicy, toasty, complex, dark chocolate, cocoa bean. Palate: powerful, flavourful, toasty, round tannins.

BODEGAS Y VIÑEDOS DEL JALÓN

Avda. José Antonio, 61
50340 Maluenda (Zaragoza)
☎: +34 976 893 017 - Fax: +34 976 546 969
info@castillodemaluenda.com
www.castillodemaluenda.com

ALTO LAS PIZARRAS 2010 T
garnacha.

90 Colour: cherry, garnet rim. Nose: medium intensity, balanced, sweet spices, ripe fruit, mineral, warm. Palate: flavourful, good structure, spicy.

TEOREMA 2010 T
garnacha.

90 Colour: cherry, garnet rim. Nose: balanced, expressive, dry stone. Palate: flavourful, ripe fruit, balanced.

LAS PIZARRAS 2010 T
garnacha.

89 Colour: cherry, garnet rim. Nose: ripe fruit, mineral, wild herbs, toasty. Palate: spicy, powerful, flavourful, long.

FABLA GARNACHA ESPECIAL 2010 T
garnacha.

89 Colour: cherry, garnet rim. Nose: ripe fruit, fruit liqueur notes, wild herbs, mineral. Palate: correct, powerful, flavourful, toasty.

CLARAVAL 2010 T
garnacha.

88 Colour: bright cherry. Nose: ripe fruit, sweet spices, fruit preserve. Palate: flavourful, fruity, toasty, round tannins.

SIOSY 2010 T
100% syrah.

87 Colour: cherry, purple rim. Nose: powerfull, ripe fruit, warm. Palate: flavourful, fruity, long.

EL ESCOCÉS VOLANTE

Barrio La Rosa Bajo, 16
50300 Calatayud (Zaragoza)
☎: +34 637 511 133
norrelrobertson@hotmail.com
www.escocesvolante.es

EL PUÑO BLANCO 2010 BFB
100% viognier.

93 Colour: bright yellow. Nose: dried flowers, citrus fruit, ripe fruit, dried herbs, scrubland, mineral, earthy notes, creamy oak. Palate: powerful, flavourful, spicy, balanced.

MANGA DEL BRUJO 2010 T
65% garnacha, 15% syrah, 15% tempranillo, 2,5% mazuelo, 2,5% monastrell.

94 Colour: bright cherry. Nose: ripe fruit, creamy oak, dry stone, dark chocolate, balsamic herbs. Palate: flavourful, fruity, good structure, good acidity, long, spicy.

DOS DEDOS DE FRENTE 2010 T
96% syrah, 4% viognier.

93 Colour: cherry, garnet rim. Nose: ripe fruit, sweet spices, cocoa bean, mineral, expressive. Palate: powerful, flavourful, fresh, fruity, spicy.

LA MULTA GARNACHA VIÑAS VIEJAS 2010 T
100% garnacha.

89 Colour: cherry, garnet rim. Nose: ripe fruit, fragrant herbs, mineral, balanced. Palate: good acidity, powerful, flavourful, balsamic, balanced.

EL PUÑO GARNACHA 2009 T
100% garnacha.

92 Colour: cherry, garnet rim. Aroma ripe fruit, spicy, creamy oak, toasty, complex. Taste powerful, flavourful, toasty, round tannins.

ESPIAGO-ALONSO VINEYARDS

Avda. Cooperativa, 7
50310 Villarroya De La Sierra (Zaragoza)
☎: +34 676 929 994
manuelespiago@yahoo.es
www.espiagoalonso.com

ALDA V 2010 B
100% viognier.

90 Colour: bright yellow. Nose: powerfull, ripe fruit, sweet spices, fragrant herbs, mineral. Palate: rich, flavourful, good acidity, elegant. Personality.

ALDA SYRAH & V 2009 T
syrah.

89 Colour: cherry, garnet rim. Nose: ripe fruit, spicy, creamy oak, toasty, mineral. Palate: powerful, flavourful, toasty, balanced.

ALDA GARNACHA 2009 T
garnacha.

89 Colour: cherry, garnet rim. Nose: ripe fruit, dry stone, dark chocolate, sweet spices, toasty. Palate: balanced, powerful, flavourful, toasty.

ESPIAGO 2009 T
garnacha, merlot, syrah.

88 Colour: cherry, garnet rim. Nose: ripe fruit, spicy, creamy oak, toasty. Palate: powerful, flavourful, toasty, round tannins.

ALDA MERLOT & V 2009 T
merlot.

87 Colour: cherry, garnet rim. Nose: powerfull, warm, fruit liqueur notes, candied fruit, spicy. Palate: correct, balanced.

LOBBAN WINES

Creueta, 24
08784 St. Jaume Sesoliveres (Barcelona)
☎: +34 667 551 695
info@lapamelita.com
www.lapamelita.com

EL GORDITO 2007 T
50% garnacha, 50% syrah.

87 Colour: cherry, garnet rim. Nose: medium intensity, ripe fruit, sweet spices. Palate: correct, ripe fruit.

NIÑO JESÚS

Las Tablas, s/n
50313 Aniñón (Zaragoza)
☎: +34 976 899 150 - Fax: +34 976 896 160
administracion@satninojesus.com
www.satninojesus.com

ESTECILLO 2011 B
100% macabeo.

86 Colour: bright straw. Nose: fresh fruit, white flowers, balsamic herbs. Palate: flavourful, fruity, good acidity.

ESTECILLO 2010 BFB
100% macabeo.

87 Colour: bright golden. Nose: ripe fruit, sweet spices, white flowers, spicy. Palate: flavourful, fruity, spicy.

ESTECILLO LEGADO GARNACHA & SYRAH 2010 T
50% garnacha, 50% syrah.

86 Colour: cherry, purple rim. Nose: fruit preserve, sweet spices, characterful. Palate: flavourful, correct.

ESTECILLO 2010 T
85% garnacha, 15% tempranillo.

85 Colour: cherry, garnet rim. Nose: ripe fruit, scrubland, spicy. Palate: correct, powerful, flavourful, long.

PAGOS ALTOS DE ACERED

Avda. Río Jalón, 62
50300 Calatayud (Zaragoza)
☎: +34 976 887 496 - Fax: +34 976 885 912
secretario@docalatayud.com
www.lajas.es

LAJAS 2009 T
garnacha.

94 Colour: cherry, garnet rim. Nose: closed, mineral, complex, sweet spices. Palate: balanced, long, round tannins.

LAJAS 2008 T
garnacha.

92 Colour: cherry, garnet rim. Nose: fruit preserve, warm, mineral, dark chocolate. Palate: balanced, spicy, ripe fruit, long.

LAJAS 2007 T
garnacha.

92 Colour: cherry, garnet rim. Nose: expressive, complex, sweet spices, ripe fruit, mineral. Palate: flavourful, good structure, good acidity.

DO CAMPO DE BORJA

LOCATION:

The DO Campo de Borja is made up of 16 municipal areas, situated in the north west of the province of Zaragoza and 60 km from the capital city, in an area of transition between the mountains of the Sistema Ibérico (at the foot of the Moncayo) and the Ebro Valley: Agón, Ainzón, Alberite, Albeta, Ambel, Bisimbre, Borja, Bulbuente, Burueta, El Buste, Fuendejalón, Magallón, Malejan, Pozuelo de Aragón, Tabuenca and Vera del Moncayo.

CLIMATE:

A rather extreme continental climate, with cold winters and dry, hot summers. One of its main characteristics is the influence of the 'Cierzo', a cold and dry north - westerly wind. Rainfall is rather scarce, with an average of between 350 and 450 mm per year.

SOIL:

The most abundant are brownish - grey limey soils, terrace soils and clayey ferrous soils. The vineyards are situated at an altitude of between 350 and 700 m on small slightly rolling hillsides, on terraces of the Huecha river and the Llanos de Plasencia, making up the Somontano del Moncayo.

GRAPE VARIETIES:

WHITE: *Macabeo, Garnacha Blanca, Moscatel, Chardonnay*, *Sauvignon Blanc* and *Verdejo.*
RED: *Garnacha* (majority with 75%), *Tempranillo, Mazuela, Cabernet Sauvignon, Merlot* and *Syrah.*

FIGURES:

Vineyard surface: 6,923 – **Wine-Growers:** 1,650 – **Wineries:** 17 – **2011 Harvest rating:** Very Good – **Production:** 19,243,307 litres – **Market percentages:** 37% domestic. 63% export

CONSEJO REGULADOR
Subida de San Andrés, 6 - 50570 Ainzón (Zaragoza) - ☎: +34 976 852 122 - Fax: +34 976 868 806
@ vinos@docampodeborja.com - www.docampodeborja.com

BODEGAS ALTO MONCAYO

Ctra. CV-606 Borja - El Buste, Km. 1,700
50540 Borja (Zaragoza)
☎: +34 976 867 116 - Fax: +34 976 867 752
info@bodegasaltomoncayo.com
www.bodegasaltomoncayo.com

AQUILÓN 2009 T
100% garnacha.

96 Colour: black cherry. Nose: cocoa bean, dark chocolate, sweet spices, ripe fruit, characterful, powerfull. Palate: round tannins, long, mineral, good finish, fruity, powerful, flavourful.

ALTO MONCAYO 2009 T
100% garnacha.

95 Colour: very deep cherry. Nose: ripe fruit, fruit preserve, sweet spices, cocoa bean, dark chocolate, mineral. Palate: powerful, flavourful, concentrated, complex.

ALTO MONCAYO VERATÓN 2009 T
100% garnacha.

93 Colour: cherry, garnet rim. Nose: ripe fruit, spicy, creamy oak, toasty, characterful, powerfull. Palate: powerful, flavourful, toasty, round tannins.

BODEGAS ARAGONESAS

Ctra. Magallón, s/n
50529 Fuendejalón (Zaragoza)
☎: +34 976 862 153 - Fax: +34 976 862 363
info@bodegasaragonesas.com
www.bodegasaragonesas.com

COTO DE HAYAS CHARDONNAY 2011 B
100% chardonnay.

86 Colour: bright yellow. Nose: powerfull, white flowers, ripe fruit. Palate: flavourful, fruity.

COTO DE HAYAS 2010 BFB
80% chardonnay, 17% macabeo, 3% moscatel.

88 Colour: bright yellow. Nose: medium intensity, white flowers, citrus fruit, spicy, wild herbs. Palate: fruity, flavourful, rich.

COTO DE HAYAS 2011 RD
90% garnacha, 10% cabernet sauvignon.

86 Colour: rose, bright. Nose: medium intensity, ripe fruit, faded flowers. Palate: fruity, flavourful.

COTO DE HAYAS GARNACHA CENTENARIA 2011 T
100% garnacha.

92 Colour: cherry, purple rim. Nose: red berry notes, ripe fruit, sweet spices, creamy oak, dark chocolate. Palate: powerful, flavourful, complex, long, toasty.

COTO DE HAYAS SOLO 10 2011 T
100% syrah.

90 Colour: cherry, purple rim. Nose: expressive, red berry notes, ripe fruit. Palate: flavourful, fruity, balanced, complex.

ARAGUS ECOLÓGICO 2011 T
90% garnacha, 10% syrah.

90 Colour: cherry, garnet rim. Nose: red berry notes, ripe fruit, floral, spicy, mineral. Palate: flavourful, complex, spicy, long.

ARAGUS 2011 T
85% garnacha, 15% cabernet sauvignon.

90 Colour: cherry, purple rim. Nose: red berry notes, ripe fruit, balsamic herbs. Palate: flavourful, good acidity, round tannins, correct, long.

COTO DE HAYAS GARNACHA SYRAH 2011 T
85% garnacha, 15% syrah.

89 Colour: cherry, purple rim. Nose: expressive, red berry notes, ripe fruit, mineral. Palate: flavourful, good acidity, full, balanced.

COTO DE HAYAS TEMPRANILLO CABERNET 2011 T
70% tempranillo, 30% cabernet sauvignon.

89 Colour: deep cherry, purple rim. Nose: cocoa bean, ripe fruit, balanced. Palate: flavourful, spicy, round tannins.

FAGUS DE COTO DE HAYAS 2010 T
100% garnacha.

93 Colour: deep cherry, garnet rim. Nose: powerfull, expressive, ripe fruit, cocoa bean, creamy oak. Palate: good structure, round tannins, full.

DON RAMÓN 2010 T BARRICA
75% garnacha, 25% tempranillo.

89 Colour: cherry, garnet rim. Nose: ripe fruit, aromatic coffee, dark chocolate, toasty, creamy oak. Palate: balanced, flavourful, toasty.

FAGUS 10º ANIVERSARIO 2009 T
100% garnacha.

94 Colour: bright cherry. Nose: ripe fruit, sweet spices, creamy oak, expressive, mineral. Palate: flavourful, fruity, toasty, round tannins. Personality.

ARAGONIA SELECCIÓN ESPECIAL 2009 T
100% garnacha.

90 Colour: bright cherry. Nose: ripe fruit, sweet spices, creamy oak, expressive, elegant. Palate: flavourful, fruity, toasty, round tannins.

COTO DE HAYAS 2009 TC
60% garnacha, 40% tempranillo.

88 Colour: cherry, garnet rim. Nose: ripe fruit, creamy oak, sweet spices. Palate: powerful, flavourful, toasty.

OXIA 2008 T
100% garnacha.

93 Colour: cherry, garnet rim. Nose: complex, mineral, ripe fruit, dark chocolate. Palate: full, fruity, round tannins, spicy.

COTO DE HAYAS 2008 TR
100% garnacha.

90 Colour: cherry, garnet rim. Nose: complex, balanced, dark chocolate, spicy, ripe fruit. Palate: balanced, long, flavourful.

OXIA 2006 TC
100% garnacha.

93 Colour: cherry, garnet rim. Nose: candied fruit, expressive, dark chocolate, tobacco, aromatic coffee, mineral. Palate: long, balanced, spicy.

COTO DE HAYAS MISTELA 2011 VINO DULCE NATURAL
100% garnacha.

90 Colour: pale ruby, brick rim edge. Nose: ripe fruit, sweet spices, aromatic coffee, dark chocolate, toasty. Palate: powerful, flavourful, toasty, balanced.

COTO DE HAYAS MOSCATEL 2011 VINO DULCE NATURAL
100% moscatel grano menudo.

86 Colour: bright yellow. Nose: balanced, medium intensity, white flowers, candied fruit. Palate: sweet, light-bodied, good finish.

BODEGAS BORDEJÉ

Ctra. Borja a Rueda, Km. 3
50570 Ainzón (Zaragoza)
☎: +34 976 868 080 - Fax: +34 976 868 989
ainzon@bodegasbordeje.com
www.bodegasbordeje.com

LIDIA 2008 B

86 Colour: bright yellow. Nose: candied fruit, dry nuts, spicy, smoky. Palate: flavourful, rich, ripe fruit.

MARI DULCIS VINO DE LICOR B
moscatel grano menudo.

88 Colour: golden. Aroma powerfull, floral, honeyed notes, candied fruit, fragrant herbs. Taste flavourful, sweet, fresh, fruity, good acidity, long.

ABUELO NICOLÁS 2010 T
merlot.

83

PAGO DE ROMEROSO 2007 TR

88 Colour: cherry, garnet rim. Nose: ripe fruit, scrubland, spicy, creamy oak. Palate: powerful, flavourful, spicy.

LELES DE BORDEJE 2007 TR
garnacha.

86 Colour: cherry, garnet rim. Nose: ripe fruit, fruit preserve, balsamic herbs, creamy oak. Palate: balanced, powerful, flavourful.

BORDEJÉ DON PABLO 2006 TR

85 Colour: cherry, garnet rim. Nose: spicy, creamy oak, toasty, fruit preserve. Palate: powerful, flavourful, toasty.

BORDEJÉ 2005 TR

87 Colour: pale ruby, brick rim edge. Nose: ripe fruit, scrubland, spicy, creamy oak, fine reductive notes. Palate: flavourful, long, correct.

PAGO DE HUECHASECA 2005 TR
tempranillo, merlot, cabernet sauvignon.

87 Colour: cherry, garnet rim. Nose: ripe fruit, spicy, creamy oak, toasty, complex. Palate: powerful, flavourful, toasty, round tannins.

CRISTINA VINO DE LICOR T
garnacha.

87 Colour: cherry, garnet rim. Nose: candied fruit, fruit preserve, dark chocolate, sweet spices, toasty. Palate: light-bodied, fresh, fruity, easy to drink.

BODEGAS BORSAO

Ctra. N- 122, Km. 63
50540 Borja (Zaragoza)
☎: +34 976 867 116 - Fax: +34 976 867 752
info@bodegasborsao.com
www.bodegasborsao.com

BORSAO SELECCIÓN 2011 B
100% macabeo.

85 Colour: bright straw. Nose: tropical fruit, white flowers, candied fruit. Palate: fresh, fruity, easy to drink.

BORSAO SELECCIÓN 2011 RD
100% garnacha.

88 Colour: brilliant rose, bright. Nose: ripe fruit, red berry notes, floral, balsamic herbs, fresh, lactic notes. Palate: , powerful, fruity, fresh, easy to drink.

BORSAO SELECCIÓN 2011 T
70% garnacha, 20% syrah, 10% tempranillo.

90 Colour: deep cherry, purple rim. Nose: red berry notes, ripe fruit, scrubland, varietal. Palate: fresh, fruity, flavourful, easy to drink.

BORSAO TRES PICOS 2010 T
100% garnacha.

92 Colour: cherry, garnet rim. Nose: fruit liqueur notes, floral, fragrant herbs, mineral, sweet spices, creamy oak. Palate: flavourful, fruity, spicy, balanced.

BORSAO BOLE 2009 T
70% garnacha, 30% syrah.

88 Colour: cherry, purple rim. Nose: ripe fruit, wild herbs, sweet spices, new oak, toasty. Palate: powerful, flavourful, spicy.

BORSAO BEROLA 2008 T
80% garnacha, 20% syrah.

90 Colour: cherry, garnet rim. Nose: ripe fruit, spicy, creamy oak, toasty, balsamic herbs, mineral. Palate: powerful, flavourful, toasty, balanced.

BORSAO SELECCIÓN 2008 TC
60% garnacha, 20% tempranillo, 20% merlot.

89 Colour: bright cherry. Nose: ripe fruit, sweet spices, creamy oak, mineral. Palate: flavourful, fruity, round tannins, spicy.

CRIANZAS Y VIÑEDOS SANTO CRISTO

Ctra. Tabuenca, s/n
50570 Ainzón (Zaragoza)
☎: +34 976 869 696 - Fax: +34 976 868 097
info@bodegas-santo-cristo.com
www.bodegas-santo-cristo.com

VIÑA COLLADO 2011 B
100% macabeo.

84

MOSCATEL AINZÓN 90 DÍAS 2010 B BARRICA
100% moscatel.

92 Colour: bright yellow. Nose: expressive, varietal, honeyed notes, sweet spices, candied fruit. Palate: rich, flavourful, balanced.

VIÑA COLLADO 2011 RD
100% garnacha.

85 Colour: light cherry. Nose: medium intensity, dried flowers, rose petals. Palate: light-bodied, easy to drink, correct.

VIÑA COLLADO 2011 T
100% garnacha.

88 Colour: cherry, purple rim. Nose: raspberry, red berry notes, floral, powerfull, expressive. Palate: powerful, flavourful, fruity, balanced.

SANTO CRISTO 2011 T ROBLE
70% tempranillo, 20% cabernet sauvignon, 10% garnacha.

87 Colour: bright cherry. Nose: ripe fruit, sweet spices, creamy oak. Palate: flavourful, fruity, toasty.

CAYUS SELECCIÓN 2010 T ROBLE
100% garnacha.

92 Colour: deep cherry, garnet rim. Nose: complex, expressive, cocoa bean, sweet spices, creamy oak, ripe fruit. Palate: flavourful, round tannins.

TERRAZAS DEL MONCAYO GARNACHA 2009 T ROBLE
100% garnacha.

90 Colour: cherry, garnet rim. Nose: spicy, creamy oak, toasty, complex, candied fruit. Palate: powerful, flavourful, toasty, round tannins.

PEÑAZUELA SELECCIÓN 2009 T ROBLE
100% garnacha.

87 Colour: cherry, garnet rim. Nose: ripe fruit, mineral, dark chocolate, sweet spices. Palate: powerful, flavourful, long, toasty.

VIÑA AINZÓN 2009 TC
garnacha, tempranillo, cabernet sauvignon.

87 Colour: deep cherry, garnet rim. Nose: powerfull, warm, ripe fruit, dark chocolate. Palate: balanced, round tannins.

VIÑA AINZÓN PREMIUM 2006 TR
90% garnacha, 10% tempranillo.

88 Colour: very deep cherry. Nose: powerfull, fruit preserve, dark chocolate, creamy oak. Palate: round tannins, long, flavourful.

MOSCATEL AINZÓN 2011 VINO DE LICOR
100% moscatel.

87 Colour: bright yellow. Nose: citrus fruit, honeyed notes, ripe fruit. Palate: powerful, flavourful, sweet, balanced.

FINCA VALDETALÓN

Subida San Andrés, 5
50570 Ainzón (Zaragoza)
☎: +34 976 910 611
info@valdetalon.com
www.valdetalon.com

VALDETALÓN MERLOT 2010 T
85% merlot, 15% cabernet sauvignon.

87 Colour: cherry, purple rim. Nose: red berry notes, ripe fruit, scrubland, spicy. Palate: powerful, flavourful, long.

VALDETALÓN CABERNET SAUVIGNON 2010 T
85% cabernet sauvignon, 15% merlot.

85 Colour: cherry, garnet rim. Nose: medium intensity, fruit preserve, fragrant herbs. Palate: flavourful, ripe fruit.

PAGOS DEL MONCAYO

Ctra. Z-372, Km. 1,6
50580 Vera de Moncayo (Zaragoza)
☎: +34 976 229 222
info@pagosdelmoncayo.com
www.pagosdelmoncayo.com

PAGOS DEL MONCAYO GARNACHA SYRAH 2011 T
65% garnacha, 35% syrah.

90 Colour: bright cherry, purple rim. Nose: balanced, red berry notes, ripe fruit, violets. Palate: flavourful, fruity, round tannins.

PAGOS DEL MONCAYO GARNACHA 2010 T
100% garnacha.

92 Colour: bright cherry, purple rim. Nose: complex, balanced, ripe fruit, mineral. Palate: good structure, round tannins, long.

PAGOS DEL MONCAYO SYRAH 2010 T
100% syrah.

92 Colour: very deep cherry, purple rim. Nose: complex, balanced, sweet spices, aromatic coffee. Palate: flavourful, spicy, fine bitter notes.

RUBERTE HERMANOS

Tenor Fleta, s/n
50520 Magallón (Zaragoza)
☎: +34 976 858 106 - Fax: +34 976 858 475
info@bodegasruberte.com
www.bodegasruberte.com

RUBERTE 2011 RD
garnacha.

85 Colour: rose, bright. Nose: floral, red berry notes, ripe fruit, balanced. Palate: fruity, correct, easy to drink.

RUBERTE 2008 TC
garnacha.

87 Colour: cherry, garnet rim. Nose: earthy notes, ripe fruit, spicy, creamy oak, toasty. Palate: powerful, flavourful, harsh oak tannins.

RUBERTE 2004 TR

89 Colour: pale ruby, brick rim edge. Nose: elegant, spicy, fine reductive notes, wet leather, aged wood nuances. Palate: spicy, fine tannins, long.

LOCATION:

In the province of Zaragoza, and occupies the Ebro valley covering 14 municipal areas: Aguarón, Aladrén, Alfamén, Almonacid de la Sierra, Alpartir, Cariñena, Cosuenda, Encinacorba, Longares, Mezalocha, Muel, Paniza, Tosos and Villanueva de Huerva.

CLIMATE:

A continental climate, with cold winters, hot summers and low rainfall. The viticulture is also influenced by the effect of the 'Cierzo'.

SOIL:

Mainly poor; either brownish - grey limey soil, or reddish dun soil settled on rocky deposits, or brownish - grey soil settled on alluvial deposits. The vineyards are situated at an altitude of between 400 and 800 m.

GRAPE VARIETIES:

WHITE: PREFERRED: *Macabeo* (majority 20%).
AUTHORIZED: *Garnacha Blanca, Moscatel Romano, Parellada* and *Chardonnay.*
RED: PREFERRED: *Garnacha Tinta* (majority 55%), *Tempranillo, Mazuela* (or *Cariñena*).
AUTHORIZED: *Juan Ibáñez, Cabernet Sauvignon, Syrah, Monastrell, Vidadillo* and *Merlot.*

FIGURES:

Vineyard surface: 14,447 – **Wine-Growers:** 1,520 – **Wineries:** 35 – **2011 Harvest rating:** Excellent – **Production:** 54,576,115 litres – **Market percentages:** 36% domestic. 64% export

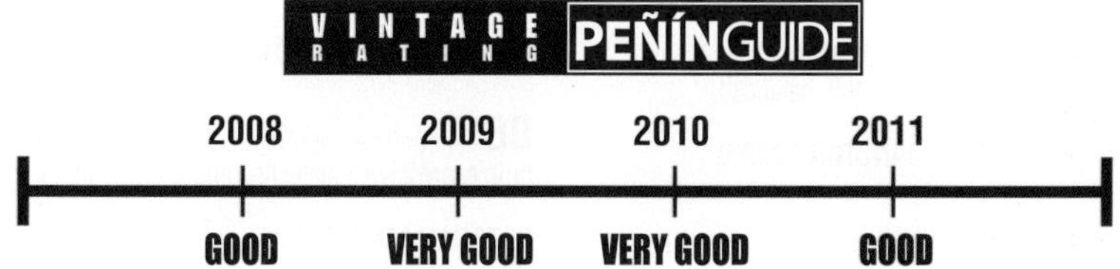

CONSEJO REGULADOR
Camino de la Platera, 7 - 50400 Cariñena (Zaragoza) - ☎: +34 902 190 713 /+34 976 793 031 - Fax: +34 976 621 107
@ consejoregulador@docarinena.com @ promocion@docarinena.com - www.docarinena.com

BIOENOS

Mayor, 88 Bajos
50400 Cariñena (Zaragoza)
☎: +34 976 620 045 - Fax: +34 976 622 082
bioenos@bioenos.com
www.bioenos.com

GORYS CRESPIELLO 2007 T
95% vidadilo, 5% garnacha.

93 Colour: cherry, garnet rim. Nose: ripe fruit, spicy, creamy oak, toasty, complex, mineral. Palate: powerful, flavourful, toasty, balanced.

PULCHRUM CRESPIELLO 2006 T
95% vidadillo, 5% garnacha.

91 Colour: cherry, purple rim. Nose: candied fruit, sweet spices, ripe fruit, balanced. Palate: complex, good structure, round tannins.

PULCHRUM CRESPIELLO 2004 T
95% vidadilo, 5% garnacha.

89 Colour: cherry, garnet rim. Nose: ripe fruit, candied fruit, earthy notes, creamy oak, toasty. Palate: powerful, flavourful, spicy.

BODEGAS AÑADAS

Ctra. Aguarón, km 47,100
50400 Cariñena (Zaragoza)
☎: +34 976 793 016 - Fax: +34 976 620 448
bodega@carewines.com
www.carewines.com

CARE CHARDONNAY 2011 B
100% chardonnay.

89 Colour: bright yellow. Nose: medium intensity, ripe fruit, floral. Palate: flavourful, rich, full, balanced.

CARE MOSCATEL DE ALEJANDRIA 2009 B
100% moscatel de alejandría.

88 Colour: bright yellow. Nose: citrus fruit, ripe fruit, white flowers. Palate: easy to drink, fruity, rich.

CARE 2011 RD
50% tempranillo, 50% cabernet sauvignon.

87 Colour: rose, purple rim. Nose: red berry notes, ripe fruit, floral, medium intensity. Palate: powerful, flavourful, balanced.

CARE 2011 T ROBLE
50% garnacha, 50% syrah.

90 Colour: cherry, purple rim. Nose: red berry notes, sweet spices, creamy oak, cocoa bean. Palate: powerful, flavourful, long, toasty.

CARE 2009 TC
70% tempranillo, 30% merlot.

88 Colour: bright cherry. Nose: ripe fruit, sweet spices, creamy oak, roasted coffee. Palate: flavourful, fruity, toasty.

CARE FINCA BANCALES 2008 TR
100% garnacha.

92 Colour: cherry, garnet rim. Nose: ripe fruit, scrubland, earthy notes, expressive. Palate: powerful, complex, flavourful, long, toasty.

CARE XCLNT 2008 T
20% syrah, 40% garnacha, 40% cabernet sauvignon.

89 Colour: cherry, garnet rim. Nose: ripe fruit, spicy, toasty, complex, fragrant herbs. Palate: powerful, flavourful, toasty, round tannins.

BODEGAS ESTEBAN MARTÍN

Camino Virgen de Lagunas, s/n
50461 Alfamén (Zaragoza)
☎: +34 976 628 490 - Fax: +34 976 628 488
info@estebanmartin.es
www.estebanmartin.com

ESTEBAN MARTÍN 2011 B
60% chardonnay, 40% macabeo.

85 Colour: bright yellow. Nose: medium intensity, floral, ripe fruit, citrus fruit. Palate: flavourful, fruity, good acidity.

ESTEBAN MARTÍN 2011 RD
50% garnacha, 50% syrah.

86 Colour: rose, purple rim. Nose: red berry notes, ripe fruit, expressive. Palate: flavourful, ripe fruit, long.

ESTEBAN MARTÍN 2011 T
60% garnacha, 40% syrah.

85 Colour: cherry, purple rim. Nose: medium intensity, fruit preserve, powerfull. Palate: flavourful, correct.

ESTEBAN MARTÍN 2007 TR
50% garnacha, 50% cabernet sauvignon.

85 Colour: cherry, garnet rim. Nose: fruit preserve, spicy, creamy oak, toasty. Palate: powerful, flavourful, spicy.

ESTEBAN MARTÍN 2008 TC
60% garnacha, 40% syrah.

88 Colour: cherry, garnet rim. Nose: ripe fruit, floral, fine reductive notes, creamy oak. Palate: powerful, flavourful, balanced.

BODEGAS IGNACIO MARÍN

San Valero, 1
50400 Cariñena (Zaragoza)
☎: +34 976 621 129 - Fax: +34 976 621 031
comercial@ignaciomarin.com
www.ignaciomarin.com

DUQUE DE MEDINA 2010 T
garnacha.

85 Colour: cherry, purple rim. Nose: warm, red berry notes, ripe fruit, spicy. Palate: flavourful, fruity, good acidity, correct.

MARÍN GARNACHA 2008 T
garnacha.

86 Colour: bright cherry. Nose: ripe fruit, sweet spices, toasty. Palate: flavourful, fruity, toasty, powerful.

MARÍN MERLOT 2008 T
merlot.

84

CAMPO MARÍN 2005 TR
tempranillo, garnacha, cariñena.

88 Colour: cherry, garnet rim, garnet rim. Nose: creamy oak, cocoa bean, sweet spices, powerfull. Palate: flavourful, ripe fruit, spicy.

BARÓN DE LAJOYOSA 2005 TGR
50% garnacha, 30% tempranillo, 20% cariñena.

82

BODEGAS LALAGUNA

Ctra. A-1304 de Longares a Alfamés, Km. 1,28
50460 Longares (Zaragoza)
☎: +34 657 804 783 - Fax: +34 976 369 980
bodegaslalaguna@bodegaslalaguna.com
www.bodegaslalaguna.com

LALAGUNA 2011 B
100% macabeo.

83

LALAGUNA 2011 RD
100% garnacha.

84

LALAGUNA 2011 T
100% garnacha.

82

LALAGUNA 2008 TC
70% garnacha, 20% mazuelo, 10% tempranillo.

85 Colour: cherry, garnet rim. Nose: ripe fruit, spicy, creamy oak. Palate: powerful, flavourful, long.

BODEGAS MANUEL MONEVA E HIJOS

Avda. Zaragoza, 10
50108 Almonacid de la Sierra (Zaragoza)
☎: +34 976 627 020 - Fax: +34 976 627 334
monevahijos@terra.es
www.bodegasmanuelmonevaehijos.com

VIÑA VADINA 2011 B
macabeo.

82

VIÑA VADINA 2011 RD
garnacha.

85 Colour: rose, bright. Nose: powerfull, ripe fruit. Palate: flavourful, rich, full, ripe fruit.

VIÑA VADINA TEMPRANILLO GARNACHA 2011 T
tempranillo, garnacha.

86 Colour: cherry, purple rim. Nose: ripe fruit, candied fruit, balsamic herbs. Palate: powerful, flavourful, fruity, easy to drink.

VIÑA VADINA GARNACHA 2010 T
garnacha.

83

VIÑA VADINA VENDIMIA SELECCIONADA 2009 T
100% garnacha.

89 Colour: black cherry, garnet rim. Nose: ripe fruit, mineral, balanced, spicy, toasty. Palate: flavourful, long, spicy.

VIÑA VADINA SELECCIÓN ESPECIAL 2008 T
garnacha.

88 Colour: bright cherry. Nose: ripe fruit, sweet spices, smoky. Palate: flavourful, fruity, toasty, round tannins.

BODEGAS PANIZA

Ctra. Valencia, Km. 53
50480 Paniza (Zaragoza)
☎: +34 976 622 515 - Fax: +34 976 622 958
info@bodegaspaniza.com
www.bodegasvirgenaguila.com

VAL DE PANIZA 2011 B
macabeo, chardonnay.

86 Colour: bright straw. Nose: tropical fruit, white flowers, fragrant herbs. Palate: powerful, flavourful, fresh, fruity.

JABALÍ VIURA & CHARDONNAY 2011 B
viura, chardonnay.

85 Colour: bright straw. Nose: medium intensity, ripe fruit, tropical fruit. Palate: rich, flavourful.

VAL DE PANIZA 2011 RD
garnacha.

86 Colour: raspberry rose. Nose: floral, red berry notes, ripe fruit, medium intensity. Palate: light-bodied, fresh, fruity.

JABALÍ GARNACHA-CABERNET 2011 RD
garnacha, cabernet sauvignon.

84

JABALÍ GARNACHA-SYRAH 2011 T
garnacha, syrah.

90 Colour: bright cherry, purple rim. Nose: ripe fruit, violets, powerfull, balanced. Palate: fruity, good structure, flavourful.

VAL DE PANIZA 2011 T
tempranillo, garnacha, syrah.

88 Colour: cherry, purple rim. Nose: expressive, fresh fruit, red berry notes, floral. Palate: flavourful, fruity, good acidity, round tannins.

JABALÍ TEMPRANILLO - CABERNET 2011 T
tempranillo, cabernet sauvignon.

88 Colour: cherry, purple rim. Nose: candied fruit, red berry notes, floral, balsamic herbs. Palate: powerful, flavourful, fruity, easy to drink.

SEÑORÍO DEL ÁGUILA 2009 TC
tempranillo, garnacha, cabernet sauvignon.

86 Colour: cherry, garnet rim. Nose: ripe fruit, dark chocolate, roasted coffee. Palate: powerful, flavourful, toasty.

SEÑORÍO DEL ÁGUILA 2008 TR
tempranillo, garnacha, cabernet sauvignon.

86 Colour: cherry, garnet rim. Nose: ripe fruit, spicy, creamy oak, toasty, complex. Palate: powerful, flavourful, toasty, round tannins.

ARTIGAZO 2007 T
garnacha, cabernet sauvignon, syrah.

88 Colour: cherry, garnet rim. Nose: ripe fruit, sweet spices, creamy oak, toasty. Palate: balanced, powerful, flavourful, long.

SEÑORÍO DEL ÁGUILA 2006 TGR
tempranillo, garnacha, cabernet sauvignon.

88 Colour: dark-red cherry, orangey edge. Nose: ripe fruit, powerfull, dark chocolate, cocoa bean. Palate: powerful, flavourful, spicy, fine tannins.

BODEGAS PRINUR

Ctra. N-330, Km. 449,150
50400 Cariñena (Zaragoza)
☎: +34 976 621 039 - Fax: +34 976 620 714
antonio@grupoprinur.com
www.bodegasprinur.com

PRINUR MACABEO 2011 B
macabeo.

84

PRINUR CHARDONNAY 2011 B
chardonnay.

82

PRINUR RED PASSION 2011 RD
merlot, garnacha.

85 Colour: rose. Nose: ripe fruit, medium intensity, floral. Palate: powerful, flavourful, fresh, fruity.

PRINUR BLUE JEANS 2007 T
tempranillo, syrah, garnacha, vidadilo, cabernet sauvignon.

87 Colour: cherry, garnet rim. Nose: spicy, creamy oak, toasty, complex, macerated fruit. Palate: powerful, flavourful, toasty.

PRINUR VIÑAS VIEJAS 2006 T
tempranillo, cabernet sauvignon, syrah, cariñena.

92 Colour: cherry, garnet rim. Nose: complex, spicy, ripe fruit, toasty, mineral. Palate: good structure, flavourful, long, full.

PRINUR SELECCIÓN CALAR 2005 T
tempranillo, cabernet sauvignon, garnacha.

91 Colour: cherry, garnet rim. Nose: ripe fruit, spicy, creamy oak, complex, earthy notes. Palate: powerful, flavourful, toasty, long, mineral.

BODEGAS SAN VALERO

Ctra. Nacional 330, Km. 450
50400 Cariñena (Zaragoza)
☎: +34 976 620 400 - Fax: +34 976 620 398
bsv@sanvalero.com
www.sanvalero.com

CARINVS MUSCAT 2011 B
moscatel de alejandría.

87 Colour: bright straw. Nose: white flowers, varietal, balanced, neat. Palate: flavourful, ripe fruit, fine bitter notes.

CARINVS CHARDONNAY 2011 B
chardonnay.

86 Colour: bright yellow. Nose: powerfull, ripe fruit, white flowers, mineral. Palate: powerful, flavourful, fine bitter notes.

CASTILLO DUCAY 2011 B
viura, chardonnay.

84

SIERRA DE VIENTO MOSCATEL VENDIMIA TARDÍA B
moscatel de alejandría.

92 Colour: old gold, amber rim. Nose: honeyed notes, dry nuts, candied fruit, sweet spices. Palate: rich, flavourful, complex, elegant, long.

CARINVS 2011 RD
cabernet sauvignon, syrah.

87 Colour: rose, purple rim. Nose: powerfull, red berry notes, floral, expressive. Palate: , powerful, fruity, fresh, easy to drink.

MONTE DUCAY 2011 RD

86 Colour: rose, purple rim. Nose: lactic notes, red berry notes, fresh fruit, floral. Palate: powerful, flavourful, fruity, easy to drink.

CASTILLO DUCAY 2011 RD
garnacha, cabernet sauvignon.

84

CASTILLO DUCAY 2011 T
garnacha, tempranillo, cabernet sauvignon.

87 Colour: cherry, purple rim. Nose: fresh fruit, red berry notes, floral, balsamic herbs. Palate: flavourful, fruity, good acidity.

CARINVS 2009 T ROBLE
garnacha, tempranillo, cabernet sauvignon, merlot, syrah.

86 Colour: cherry, purple rim. Nose: ripe fruit, balanced, powerfull, sweet spices. Palate: toasty, powerful, flavourful.

MONTE DUCAY 2008 TC
tempranillo, garnacha, syrah.

85 Colour: deep cherry, garnet rim. Nose: fruit preserve, spicy, warm. Palate: flavourful, fruity, easy to drink.

MONTE DUCAY PERGAMINO 2008 TR
tempranillo, garnacha, cabernet sauvignon.

84

SIERRA DE VIENTO GARNACHA GRAN SELECCIÓN 2006 T
garnacha.

91 Colour: deep cherry, garnet rim. Nose: powerfull, dark chocolate, sweet spices, creamy oak, fruit preserve. Palate: rich, powerful, round tannins.

MARQUÉS DE TOSOS 2005 TR
garnacha, tempranillo, cabernet sauvignon.

86 Colour: cherry, garnet rim. Nose: medium intensity, sweet spices, ripe fruit. Palate: fruity, balanced.

MONTE DUCAY 2004 TGR
tempranillo, garnacha, cabernet sauvignon.

87 Colour: pale ruby, brick rim edge. Nose: fruit liqueur notes, fruit liqueur notes, wet leather, tobacco, spicy. Palate: long, powerful, flavourful, spicy.

SIERRA DE VIENTO TEMPRANILLO 2011 T
tempranillo.

89 Colour: cherry, purple rim. Nose: powerfull, grassy, ripe fruit, red berry notes. Palate: correct, flavourful, long.

SIERRA DE VIENTO OLD VINES GARNACHA 2009 T
garnacha.

90 Colour: cherry, garnet rim. Nose: ripe fruit, balsamic herbs, mineral, spicy, creamy oak. Palate: full, powerful, flavourful, spicy.

BODEGAS VICTORIA

Camino Virgen de Lagunas, s/n Apdo. Correos 47
50400 Cariñena (Zaragoza)
☎: +34 976 621 007 - Fax: +34 976 621 106
comercial@bodegasvictoria.com
www.bodegasvictoria.com

DOMINIO DE LONGAZ PARCELA 79 2008 T
50% tempranillo, 50% syrah.

86 Colour: cherry, garnet rim. Nose: ripe fruit, spicy, fine reductive notes, creamy oak. Palate: flavourful, long, ripe fruit.

FINCA PARDINA 2008 T
10% merlot, 60% tempranillo, 20% cabernet sauvignon, 10% syrah.

84

LONGUS 2007 T
40% syrah, 30% merlot, 30% cabernet sauvignon.

91 Colour: cherry, garnet rim. Nose: sweet spices, cocoa bean, creamy oak, candied fruit. Palate: flavourful, balanced, ripe fruit, spicy.

DOMINIO DE LONGAZ PREMIUM 2006 T
syrah, merlot, cabernet sauvignon.

90 Colour: ruby red, orangey edge. Nose: mineral, earthy notes, ripe fruit, spicy, creamy oak, fine reductive notes. Palate: powerful, flavourful, long, spicy, balanced.

LONGUS 2006 T

90 Colour: cherry, garnet rim. Nose: ripe fruit, spicy, creamy oak, toasty, waxy notes, cigar, old leather. Palate: powerful, flavourful, toasty, round tannins.

CAMPOS DE LUZ

Avda. Diagonal, 590, 5º - 1
08021 (Barcelona)
☎: +34 660 445 464
info@vinergia.com
www.vinergia.com

CAMPOS DE LUZ 2011 B
viura, chardonnay, moscatel.

80

CAMPOS DE LUZ 2011 RD
100% garnacha.

84

CAMPOS DE LUZ GARNACHA 2011 T
100% garnacha.

87 Colour: cherry, purple rim. Nose: floral, red berry notes, lactic notes, expressive. Palate: powerful, flavourful, fruity, easy to drink.

CAMPOS DE LUZ 2008 TC
100% garnacha.

88 Colour: cherry, garnet rim. Nose: ripe fruit, spicy, creamy oak, toasty, complex. Palate: powerful, flavourful, toasty, round tannins.

CAMPOS DE LUZ GARNACHA 2006 TR
100% garnacha.

88 Colour: cherry, garnet rim. Nose: ripe fruit, spicy, creamy oak, toasty, fine reductive notes. Palate: powerful, flavourful, toasty.

COVINCA S. COOP.

Ctra, Valencia, s/n
50460 Longares (Zaragoza)
☎: +34 976 142 653 - Fax: +34 976 142 402
info@covinca.es
www.covinca.es

TORRELONGARES MACABEO 2011 B
macabeo.

84

TORRELONGARES 2011 RD
50% garnacha, 50% tempranillo.

83

TORRELONGARES GARNACHA 2011 T
garnacha.

85 Colour: cherry, purple rim. Nose: medium intensity, ripe fruit, balsamic herbs. Palate: powerful, flavourful.

TORRELONGARES EDICIÓN ESPECIAL MICRORRELATO 2011 T

85 Colour: cherry, purple rim. Nose: floral, ripe fruit, balsamic herbs. Palate: powerful, flavourful, balanced.

TERRAI S10 2010 T
100% syrah.

90 Colour: bright cherry. Nose: ripe fruit, sweet spices, creamy oak, expressive, toasty. Palate: flavourful, fruity, toasty, round tannins.

TORRELONGARES VARIETALES SYRAH 2010 T
syrah.

86 Colour: deep cherry, purple rim. Nose: powerfull, warm, ripe fruit, faded flowers. Palate: flavourful, spicy, ripe fruit.

TORRELONGARES LICOR DE GARNACHA S/C VINO DE LICOR
garnacha.

91 Colour: cherry, garnet rim. Nose: powerfull, dried fruit, fruit liqueur notes, sweet spices. Palate: flavourful, rich.

FINCA AYLÉS

Finca Aylés. Ctra. A-1101, Km. 24
50152 Mezalocha (Zaragoza)
☎: +34 976 140 473 - Fax: +34 976 140 268
info@pagoayles.com
www.pagoayles.com

DORONDÓN CHARDONNAY DE AYLÉS 2011 B
chardonnay.

88 Colour: bright straw. Nose: fresh, fresh fruit, white flowers, expressive. Palate: flavourful, fruity, good acidity, balanced, easy to drink.

ALDEYA DE AYLÉS MACABEO 2011 B
macabeo.

82

ALDEYA DE AYLÉS ROSADO 2011 RD
garnacha, syrah.

85 Colour: rose, purple rim. Nose: powerfull, ripe fruit, red berry notes, dried flowers. Palate: , powerful, fruity, fresh.

ALDEYA DE AYLÉS GARNACHA 2011 T
garnacha.

90 Colour: cherry, purple rim. Nose: expressive, ripe fruit, balsamic herbs, sweet spices, creamy oak. Palate: flavourful, fruity, good acidity, toasty, smoky aftertaste.

ALDEYA DE AYLÉS TINTO 2011 T
syrah, merlot, tempranillo, cabernet sauvignon.

86 Colour: cherry, purple rim. Nose: floral, ripe fruit. Palate: flavourful, fruity, round tannins, powerful.

SERENDIPIA MERLOT DE AYLÉS 2009 T
merlot.

93 Colour: cherry, garnet rim. Nose: ripe fruit, spicy, creamy oak, toasty, complex. Palate: powerful, flavourful, toasty, round tannins.

SERENDIPIA GARNACHA DE AYLÉS 2009 T
garnacha.

90 Colour: cherry, garnet rim. Nose: medium intensity, candied fruit. Palate: powerful, flavourful, toasty.

AYLÉS "TRES DE 3000" 2008 T
garnacha, merlot, cabernet sauvignon.

93 Colour: black cherry, garnet rim. Nose: ripe fruit, mineral, earthy notes, spicy, creamy oak, complex. Palate: powerful, flavourful, round, spicy, mineral.

ALDEYA DE AYLÉS TINTO BARRICA 2008 T BARRICA
tempranillo, merlot, cabernet sauvignon.

87 Colour: cherry, garnet rim. Nose: ripe fruit, spicy, old leather, tobacco. Palate: flavourful, long, spicy, balanced.

GRANDES VINOS Y VIÑEDOS

Ctra. Valencia Km 45,700
50400 Cariñena (Zaragoza)
☎: +34 976 621 261 - Fax: +34 976 621 253
info@grandesvinos.com
www.grandesvinos.com

MONASTERIO DE LAS VIÑAS 2011 B
macabeo.

85 Colour: bright straw. Nose: dried flowers, fragrant herbs, ripe fruit. Palate: fine bitter notes, light-bodied, flavourful.

CORONA DE ARAGÓN 2011 B
macabeo, chardonnay.

84

BESO DE VINO 2011 B
macabeo.

82

CORONA DE ARAGÓN DISPARATES MACABEO 2010 BFB
macabeo.

89 Colour: bright yellow. Nose: ripe fruit, sweet spices, creamy oak, fragrant herbs. Palate: rich, smoky aftertaste, fresh.

ANAYÓN CHARDONNAY 2009 B BARRICA
chardonnay.

90 Colour: bright golden. Nose: ripe fruit, dry nuts, powerfull, toasty. Palate: flavourful, fruity, spicy, toasty, long.

MONASTERIO DE LAS VIÑAS 2011 RD
garnacha.

87 Colour: rose, purple rim. Nose: red berry notes, ripe fruit, floral. Palate: powerful, flavourful, ripe fruit, easy to drink.

CORONA DE ARAGÓN 2011 RD
garnacha, syrah.

85 Colour: rose, purple rim. Nose: red berry notes, ripe fruit, floral, medium intensity. Palate: light-bodied, fresh, fruity.

BESO DE VINO 2011 RD
garnacha.

85 Colour: light cherry. Nose: faded flowers, medium intensity. Palate: flavourful, fine bitter notes, correct.

MONASTERIO DE LAS VIÑAS 2011 T
garnacha, tempranillo.

87 Colour: cherry, purple rim. Nose: expressive, fresh fruit, red berry notes, floral. Palate: flavourful, fruity, good acidity.

CORONA DE ARAGÓN GARNACHA 2011 T
garnacha.

85 Colour: bright cherry, purple rim. Nose: fruit preserve, powerfull. Palate: flavourful, easy to drink, correct.

CORONA DE ARAGÓN DISPARATES CARIÑENA 2010 T
cariñena.

90 Colour: black cherry, purple rim. Nose: balanced, ripe fruit, medium intensity, sweet spices. Palate: correct, spicy, ripe fruit.

BESO DE VINO SELECCIÓN 2010 T
syrah, garnacha.

89 Colour: cherry, purple rim. Nose: expressive, ripe fruit. Palate: flavourful, fruity, good acidity, round tannins.

CORONA DE ARAGÓN SPECIAL SELECTION 2010 T
garnacha, cariñena.

88 Colour: cherry, purple rim. Nose: candied fruit, sweet spices, cocoa bean. Palate: powerful, flavourful, long, spicy.

BESO DE VINO OLD VINE GARNACHA 2010 T
garnacha.

88 Colour: bright cherry. Nose: ripe fruit, expressive, scrubland, spicy. Palate: flavourful, fruity, toasty, round tannins.

CORONA DE ARAGÓN DISPARATES TEMPRANILLO 2010 T
tempranillo.

85 Colour: very deep cherry, purple rim. Nose: powerfull, balsamic herbs, fruit preserve. Palate: flavourful, fruity, easy to drink.

ANAYÓN 2009 T BARRICA
tempranillo, cabernet sauvignon, syrah.

90 Colour: cherry, garnet rim. Nose: ripe fruit, spicy, creamy oak, toasty, complex. Palate: powerful, flavourful, toasty, round tannins.

CORONA DE ARAGÓN 2009 TC
tempranillo, cabernet sauvignon, garnacha, cariñena.

89 Colour: cherry, garnet rim. Nose: ripe fruit, spicy, toasty, medium intensity, wild herbs. Palate: powerful, flavourful, toasty, round tannins.

CORONA DE ARAGÓN OLD VINE GARNACHA 2009 T
garnacha.

88 Colour: bright cherry. Aroma ripe fruit, sweet spices, creamy oak, expressive. Taste flavourful, fruity, toasty, round tannins.

ANAYÓN GARNACHA SELECCIÓN 2008 T
garnacha.

92 Colour: very deep cherry. Nose: creamy oak, dark chocolate, ripe fruit, spicy, mineral. Palate: good structure, rich, flavourful.

MONASTERIO DE LAS VIÑAS 2008 TC
garnacha, tempranillo, cariñena.

85 Colour: deep cherry, garnet rim. Nose: toasty, spicy, candied fruit, fruit preserve. Palate: powerful, flavourful.

CORONA DE ARAGÓN 2006 TR
tempranillo, cabernet sauvignon, cariñena, garnacha.

88 Colour: deep cherry, garnet rim. Nose: balanced, dark chocolate, creamy oak, fruit preserve. Palate: good structure, spicy.

MONASTERIO DE LAS VIÑAS 2006 TR
garnacha, tempranillo, cariñena.

86 Colour: cherry, purple rim. Nose: ripe fruit, spicy. Palate: correct, easy to drink.

MONASTERIO DE LAS VIÑAS 2005 TGR
garnacha, tempranillo, cariñena.

85 Colour: bright cherry, garnet rim. Nose: medium intensity, old leather, tobacco. Palate: flavourful, correct.

CORONA DE ARAGÓN 2004 TGR
tempranillo, cabernet sauvignon, cariñena, garnacha.

86 Colour: pale ruby, brick rim edge. Nose: spicy, wet leather, fruit liqueur notes. Palate: spicy, elegant, long, harsh oak tannins.

HACIENDA MOLLEDA

Ctra. Belchite, km 29,3
50154 Tosos (Zaragoza)
☎: +34 976 620 702 - Fax: +34 976 620 102
hm@haciendamolleda.com
www.haciendamolleda.com

HACIENDA MOLLEDA 2011 T
50% garnacha, 50% tempranillo.

87 Colour: cherry, purple rim. Nose: red berry notes, raspberry, candied fruit, fresh. Palate: powerful, fresh, fruity, flavourful, easy to drink.

GHM GRAN HACIENDA MOLLEDA 2009 T ROBLE
100% mazuelo.

90 Colour: cherry, garnet rim. Nose: ripe fruit, spicy, toasty, creamy oak. Palate: fine bitter notes, powerful, flavourful, balanced.

GHM GARNACHA HACIENDA MOLLEDA 2008 T
100% garnacha.

92 Colour: cherry, garnet rim. Nose: ripe fruit, spicy, creamy oak, toasty, complex. Palate: powerful, flavourful, toasty, round tannins.

HACIENDA MOLLEDA 2008 T ROBLE
45% tempranillo, 40% garnacha, 5% cariñena, 5% cabernet sauvignon, 5% syrah.

87 Colour: cherry, garnet rim. Nose: spicy, tobacco, ripe fruit. Palate: fruity, balanced, easy to drink, good acidity.

HACIENDA MOLLEDA GARNACHA 2007 T ROBLE
100% garnacha.

90 Colour: bright cherry, purple rim. Nose: balsamic herbs, ripe fruit, spicy. Palate: balanced, spicy, long, round tannins.

HEREDAD ANSÓN

Camino Eras Altas, s/n
50450 Muel (Zaragoza)
☎: +34 976 141 133 - Fax: +34 976 141 133
info@bodegasheredadanson.com
www.bodegasheredadanson.com

HEREDAD DE ANSÓN 2011 B
100% macabeo.

80

HEREDAD DE ANSÓN 2011 RD
100% garnacha.

85 Colour: rose, purple rim. Nose: medium intensity, fragrant herbs, dried flowers. Palate: fruity, flavourful.

HEREDAD DE ANSÓN MERLOT SYRAH S/C T
50% merlot, 50% syrah.

85 Colour: cherry, purple rim. Nose: fruit preserve, powerfull, warm. Palate: ripe fruit, fine bitter notes.

LIASON GARNACHA 2011 T
100% garnacha.

82

HEREDAD DE ANSÓN VENDIMIA SELECCIONADA 2009 T
85% garnacha, 15% syrah.

81

LEGUM 2007 T ROBLE
100% garnacha.

88 Colour: pale ruby, brick rim edge. Nose: elegant, spicy, fine reductive notes, fruit liqueur notes. Palate: spicy, fine tannins, elegant, long.

HEREDAD DE ANSÓN 2007 TC
80% garnacha, 10% tempranillo, 10% syrah.

84

LONG WINES

Avda. del Monte, 46
28120 Algete (Madrid)
☎: +34 916 221 305 - Fax: +34 916 220 029
www.longwines.com

PLEYADES GARNACHA 2011 T
100% garnacha.

84

PLEYADES SYRAH 2011 T
100% syrah.

83

PLEYADES 2007 TR
65% tempranillo, 20% syrah, 15% garnacha.

87 Colour: cherry, garnet rim. Aroma ripe fruit, spicy, creamy oak, toasty, complex. Taste powerful, flavourful, toasty, round tannins.

SOLAR DE URBEZO

San Valero, 14
50400 Cariñena (Zaragoza)
☎: +34 976 621 968 - Fax: +34 976 620 549
info@solardeurbezo.es
www.solardeurbezo.es

URBEZO CHARDONNAY 2011 B
100% chardonnay.

89 Colour: bright straw. Nose: balanced, medium intensity, white flowers, ripe fruit. Palate: full, fruity, long, balanced.

ALTIUS MERLOT 2011 RD
merlot.

88 Colour: rose. Nose: ripe fruit, floral, lactic notes, fragrant herbs. Palate: flavourful, fruity, rich.

URBEZO MERLOT 2011 RD
100% merlot.

87 Colour: rose, purple rim. Nose: red berry notes, ripe fruit, floral. Palate: flavourful, fresh, fruity, easy to drink.

ALTIUS GARNACHA 2011 T
garnacha.

90 Colour: cherry, purple rim. Nose: expressive, fresh fruit, red berry notes, floral, lactic notes. Palate: flavourful, fruity, good acidity, easy to drink.

URBEZO GARNACHA 2011 T
garnacha.

89 Colour: bright cherry, purple rim. Nose: medium intensity, ripe fruit, fragrant herbs. Palate: fruity, easy to drink.

ALTIUS SYRAH CABERNET 2011 T
syrah, cabernet sauvignon.

89 Colour: cherry, purple rim. Nose: balsamic herbs, scrubland, red berry notes, ripe fruit. Palate: powerful, flavourful, fruity, balsamic.

DANCE DEL MAR 2011 T
tempranillo, merlot.

87 Colour: cherry, purple rim. Nose: red berry notes, fresh fruit, lactic notes, expressive. Palate: light-bodied, fresh, fruity, easy to drink.

URBEZO 2009 TC
syrah, merlot, cabernet sauvignon.

90 Colour: deep cherry, garnet rim. Nose: complex, ripe fruit, sweet spices, cocoa bean, balsamic herbs. Palate: good structure, fruity.

VIÑA URBEZO 2011 T MACERACIÓN CARBÓNICA
garnacha, tempranillo.

90 Colour: cherry, purple rim. Nose: expressive, fresh fruit, red berry notes, floral. Palate: flavourful, fruity, good acidity.

ALTIUS 2009 TC

89 Colour: cherry, garnet rim. Nose: ripe fruit, spicy, toasty, herbaceous. Palate: powerful, flavourful, spicy.

URBEZO VENDIMIA SELECCIONADA 2007 T
garnacha, cariñena, syrah, cabernet sauvignon.

87 Colour: pale ruby, brick rim edge. Nose: fruit liqueur notes, fruit liqueur notes, balsamic herbs, old leather, tobacco. Palate: flavourful, long, spicy, round tannins.

URBEZO 2006 TR
cabernet sauvignon, merlot, syrah.

85 Colour: pale ruby, brick rim edge. Nose: spicy, wet leather, aged wood nuances, fruit liqueur notes. Palate: spicy, fine tannins, long.

TIERRA DE CUBAS

Ctra. A-220, Km. 24
50400 Cariñena (Zaragoza)
☎: +34 976 621 300 - Fax: +34 976 622 153
proveedores@tierradecubas.es

TIERRA DE CUBAS 2007 TC
syrah, cabernet sauvignon.

85 Colour: cherry, garnet rim. Nose: ripe fruit, spicy, creamy oak, balsamic herbs. Palate: good acidity, toasty, correct.

TIERRA DE CUBAS 2007 T ROBLE
tempranillo, syrah, cabernet sauvignon.

83

MONT D'SIR GARNACHA MERLOT 2007 T
garnacha, merlot.

83

VINNICO EXPORT

Muela, 16
03730 Jávea (Alicante)
☎: +34 965 791 967 - Fax: +34 966 461 471
info@vinnico.com
www.vinnico.com

FLOR DEL MONTGÓ OLD VINES GARNACHA 2010 T
100% garnacha.

83

VIÑEDOS Y BODEGAS PABLO

Avda. Zaragoza, 16
50108 Almonacid de la Sierra (Zaragoza)
☎: +34 976 627 037 - Fax: +34 976 627 102
granviu@granviu.com
www.granviu.com

MENGUANTE GARNACHA BLANCA 2011 B
garnacha blanca.

90 Colour: bright yellow. Nose: medium intensity, balanced, fragrant herbs, expressive. Palate: balanced, fruity, good acidity.

MENGUANTE TEMPRANILLO 2011 T ROBLE
tempranillo.

86 Colour: cherry, purple rim. Nose: powerfull, red berry notes, ripe fruit, sweet spices. Palate: flavourful, fruity.

MENGUANTE GARNACHA 2011 T
garnacha.

83

MENGUANTE SELECCIÓN GARNACHA 2010 T
garnacha.

88 Colour: bright cherry. Nose: ripe fruit, sweet spices, creamy oak, expressive. Palate: flavourful, fruity, toasty, round tannins.

GRAN VÍU SELECCIÓN 2009 T
garnacha, cabernet sauvignon, tempranillo, syrah.

89 Colour: cherry, garnet rim. Nose: ripe fruit, spicy, toasty, creamy oak. Palate: powerful, flavourful, good structure, toasty.

MENGUANTE VIDADILLO 2009 T
vidadilo.

89 Colour: cherry, garnet rim. Nose: ripe fruit, floral, spicy, toasty. Palate: powerful, flavourful, balanced, spicy.

GRAN VÍU GARNACHA DEL TERRENO 2006 T
garnacha.

91 Colour: cherry, garnet rim. Nose: ripe fruit, spicy, creamy oak, complex, scrubland. Palate: powerful, flavourful, toasty, round tannins.

DO CATALUNYA

LOCATION:

The production area covers the traditional vine - growing Catalonian regions, and practically coincides with the current DOs present in Catalonia plus a few municipal areas with vine - growing vocation.

CLIMATE AND SOIL:

Depending on the location of the vineyard, the same as those of the Catalonian DO's, whose characteristics are defined in this guide. See Alella, Empordà, Conca de Barberà, Costers del Segre, Montsant, Penedès, Pla de Bages, Priorat, Tarragona and Terra Alta.

GRAPE VARIETIES:

WHITE:
RECOMMENDED: *Chardonnay, Garnacha Blanca, Macabeo, Muscat, Parellada, Riesling, Sauvignon Blanc* and *Xarel·lo.*
AUTHORIZED: *Gewürztraminer, Subirat Parent* (*Malvasía*), *Malvasía de Sitges, Picapoll, Pedro Ximénez*, *Chenin*, *Riesling* and *Sauvignon Blanc*
RED:
RECOMMENDED: *Cabernet Franc, Cabernet Sauvignon, Garnacha, Garnacha Peluda, Merlot, Monastrell, Pinot Noir, Samsó* (*Cariñena*), *Trepat, Sumoll* and *Ull de Llebre* (*Tempranillo*).
AUTHORIZED: *Garnacha Tintorera* and *Syrah.*

FIGURES:

Vineyard surface: 51,881 – **Wine-Growers:** 9,561 – **Wineries:** 203 – **2011 Harvest rating:** Very Good – **Production:** 50,207,638 litres – **Market percentages:** 42% domestic. 58% export

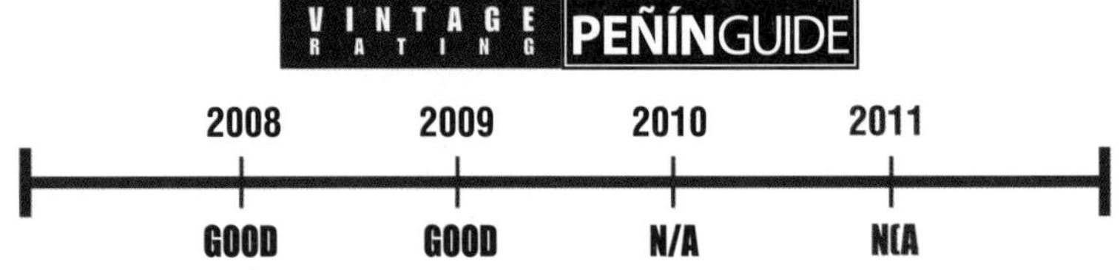

CONSEJO REGULADOR
Passeig Sunyer 4-6 - 1º - 43202 Reus - ☎: +34 977 328 103 - Fax: +34 977 321 357
@ info@do-catalunya.com - www.do-catalunya.com

ALBET I NOYA

Can Vendrell de la Codina, s/n
08739 Sant Pau D'Ordal (Barcelona)
☎: +34 938 994 812 - Fax: +34 938 994 930
albetinoya@albetinoya.cat
www.albetinoya.cat

ALBET I NOYA VINYA LAIA 2011 B
macabeo, xarel.lo, garnacha blanca.

88 Colour: bright straw. Nose: fresh, fresh fruit, white flowers, expressive. Palate: flavourful, fruity, good acidity, balanced.

ALBET I NOYA PETIT ALBET NEGRE 2011 T
ull de llebre, garnacha, cabernet sauvignon, merlot.

88 Colour: cherry, purple rim. Nose: expressive, red berry notes, floral, fragrant herbs. Palate: flavourful, fruity, good acidity, easy to drink.

ALBET I NOYA VINYA LAIA 2009 T
garnacha, tempranillo, cabernet sauvignon, merlot.

88 Colour: cherry, garnet rim. Nose: ripe fruit, spicy, creamy oak, toasty, complex. Palate: powerful, flavourful, toasty, round tannins.

BODEGAS 1898

Ctra. de Vic, 81
08241 Manresa (Barcelona)
☎: +34 938 743 511 - Fax: +34 938 737 204
info@bodegas1898.com
www.bodegas1898.com

SYNERA 2011 B
85% macabeo, 15% moscatel.

84

SYNERA 2011 RD
50% tempranillo, 50% garnacha.

86 Colour: rose, bright. Nose: balanced, red berry notes, rose petals. Palate: fruity, flavourful, balanced.

RAMÓN ROQUETA CABERNET SAUVIGNON 2011 T
100% cabernet sauvignon.

86 Colour: deep cherry. Nose: ripe fruit, scrubland, spicy. Palate: fruity, easy to drink, balanced, spicy.

RAMÓN ROQUETA TEMPRANILLO 2011 T
100% tempranillo.

86 Colour: cherry, purple rim. Nose: floral, ripe fruit, sweet spices. Palate: flavourful, fruity, good acidity, round tannins.

SYNERA 2011 T BARRICA
75% tempranillo, 25% cabernet sauvignon.

86 Colour: deep cherry, purple rim. Nose: powerfull, ripe fruit, scrubland. Palate: good structure, fruity, spicy.

BODEGAS PUIGGRÒS

Ctra. de Manresa, Km. 13
08711 Odena (Barcelona)
☎: +34 629 853 587
bodegaspuiggros@telefonica.net
www.bodegaspuiggros.com

SENTITS BLANCS 2011 B
garnacha blanca.

92 Colour: bright straw. Nose: powerfull, fine lees, ripe fruit, citrus fruit, lactic notes. Palate: flavourful, sweetness, good acidity.

SENTITS NEGRES 2010 T
garnacha.

93 Colour: deep cherry. Nose: ripe fruit, earthy notes, mineral, toasty, spicy. Palate: flavourful, fine bitter notes, good acidity, long.

SIGNES 2010 T
80% sumoll, 20% garnacha.

91 Colour: bright cherry. Nose: ripe fruit, sweet spices, creamy oak, red berry notes. Palate: flavourful, fruity, toasty, round tannins.

MESTRE VILA VELL VINYES VELLES 2009 T
sumoll.

88 Colour: cherry, garnet rim. Nose: characterful, fruit liqueur notes, grassy. Palate: flavourful, spicy, good acidity, grainy tannins.

BODEGAS TORRES

Miguel Torres i Carbó, 6
08720 Vilafranca del Penedès (Barcelona)
☎: +34 938 177 400 - Fax: +34 938 177 444
mailadmin@torres.es
www.torres.es

VIÑA ESMERALDA 2011 B
85% moscatel, 15% gewürztraminer.

87 Colour: bright straw. Nose: jasmine, white flowers, varietal. Palate: fruity, balanced.

CORONAS 2009 TC
86% tempranillo, 14% cabernet sauvignon.

87 Colour: cherry, garnet rim. Nose: medium intensity, spicy, tobacco. Palate: fruity, balanced, easy to drink.

VIÑA SOL 2011 B
100% parellada.

87 Colour: bright straw. Nose: medium intensity, fresh fruit, citrus fruit, wild herbs. Palate: correct, fine bitter notes, good acidity.

SAN VALENTÍN 2011 B
100% parellada.

84

DECASTA 2011 RD
65% garnacha, 35% cariñena.

87 Colour: rose, bright. Nose: fruit expression, fragrant herbs. Palate: balanced, ripe fruit, flavourful.

SANGRE DE TORO 2010 T
65% garnacha, 35% cariñena.

87 Colour: cherry, garnet rim. Nose: ripe fruit, spicy, candied fruit. Palate: balanced, ripe fruit, good acidity.

GRAN SANGRE DE TORO 2007 TR
60% garnacha, 25% cariñena, 15% syrah.

86 Colour: deep cherry, garnet rim. Nose: medium intensity, dark chocolate, spicy, ripe fruit. Palate: light-bodied, ripe fruit.

CA N'ESTRUC

Ctra. C-1414, Km. 1,05
08292 Esparreguera (Barcelona)
☎: +34 937 777 017 - Fax: +34 937 771 108
canestruc@vilaviniteca.es
www.canestruc.com

L'EQUILIBRISTA 2011 B
xarel.lo.

93 Colour: bright straw. Nose: candied fruit, ripe fruit, white flowers, mineral. Palate: ripe fruit, fine bitter notes, good acidity.

CA N'ESTRUC BLANC 2011 B
chardonnay, macabeo, moscatel.

89 Colour: bright straw. Nose: fresh, fresh fruit, white flowers, expressive. Palate: flavourful, fruity, good acidity, balanced.

IDOIA BLANC 2010 BFB
xarel.lo, macabeo, chardonnay, garnacha.

93 Colour: bright yellow. Nose: sweet spices, fruit expression, fresh fruit. Palate: flavourful, ripe fruit, fine bitter notes.

CA N'ESTRUC 2011 RD
syrah, merlot, garnacha.

83

CA N'ESTRUC 2011 T

89 Colour: deep cherry. Nose: toasty, spicy, ripe fruit, fruit expression. Palate: ripe fruit, good acidity, fine bitter notes.

L'EQUILIBRISTA GARNATXA 2010 T
100% garnacha.

93 Colour: bright cherry. Nose: sweet spices, creamy oak, expressive, fruit expression, lactic notes. Palate: flavourful, fruity, toasty, round tannins.

L'EQUILIBRISTA 2010 T
syrah, garnacha, cariñena.

92 Colour: bright cherry. Nose: sweet spices, creamy oak, fruit expression, red berry notes, earthy notes. Palate: flavourful, fruity, toasty, round tannins.

IDOIA 2010 T

89 Colour: cherry, garnet rim. Nose: toasty, spicy, creamy oak. Palate: flavourful, spicy, round tannins.

CAN BONASTRE WINE RESORT

Finca Can Bonastre de Sta Magdalena
Ctra. B 224 Km 13.2
08783 Masquefa (Barcelona)
☎: +34 937 726 167 - Fax: +34 937 727 929
bodega@canbonastre.com
www.canbonastre.com

ERUMIR 2011 B
sauvignon blanc, macabeo, riesling.

87 Colour: bright straw. Nose: fragrant herbs, white flowers, ripe fruit. Palate: flavourful, good acidity, long.

CAN BONASTRE PINOT NOIR 2009 T
pinot noir.

88 Colour: light cherry, garnet rim. Nose: elegant, balanced, floral, ripe fruit, sweet spices. Palate: fruity, correct, balanced.

CASTELL D'OR

Mare Rafols, 3- 1º 4º
08720 Vilafranca del Penedès (Barcelona)
☎: +34 938 905 446 - Fax: +34 938 905 446
castelldor@castelldor.com
www.castelldor.com

FLAMA D'OR 2011 B
60% macabeo, 40% xarel.lo.

84

PUIG DE SOLIVELLA 2011 B
80% macabeo, 20% parellada.

83

FLAMA D'OR 2011 RD
100% tempranillo.

85 Colour: rose, purple rim. Nose: medium intensity, red berry notes, ripe fruit. Palate: fruity, easy to drink.

PUIG DE SOLIVELLA 2011 RD
100% trepat.

85 Colour: rose, purple rim. Nose: ripe fruit, red berry notes, floral, expressive. Palate: , powerful, fruity, fresh.

FLAMA D'OR 2010 T
100% tempranillo.

83

PUIG DE SOLIVELLA 2009 T
75% ull de llebre, 25% garnacha.

84

FLAMA D'OR 2006 TR
40% cabernet sauvignon, 60% tempranillo.

86 Colour: cherry, garnet rim. Nose: ripe fruit, cocoa bean, sweet spices. Palate: flavourful, round tannins, spicy.

FLAMA D'OR 2004 TGR
100% cabernet sauvignon.

86 Colour: cherry, garnet rim. Nose: fruit preserve, tobacco, spicy, dark chocolate, balsamic herbs. Palate: fruity, spicy, balanced.

FLAMA D'OR 2011 SS
40% macabeo, 35% xarel.lo, 25% parellada.

84

FLAMA D'OR TINTO 2011 SS
80% tempranillo, 20% garnacha.

83

CAVAS BOHIGAS

Finca Can Maciá s/n
08711 Ódena (Barcelona)
☎: +34 938 048 100 - Fax: +34 938 032 366
comercial@bohigas.es
www.bohigas.es

BOHIGAS BLANC DE BLANCS 2011 B
xarel.lo.

90 Colour: bright straw. Nose: fresh fruit, white flowers, mineral, dried herbs. Palate: flavourful, fruity, good acidity, balanced.

UDINA DE FERMÍ BOHIGAS 2011 B
garnacha blanca, chenin blanc, xarel.lo.

88 Colour: bright straw. Nose: fresh, white flowers, expressive, ripe fruit. Palate: flavourful, fruity, good acidity, balanced.

BOHIGAS CABERNET SAUVIGNON 2009 TC
cabernet sauvignon, garnacha.

88 Colour: cherry, garnet rim. Nose: ripe fruit, wild herbs, earthy notes, varietal. Palate: spicy, flavourful, ripe fruit.

FERMÍ DE FERMÍ BOHIGAS 2008 TR
syrah.

90 Colour: cherry, garnet rim. Nose: balanced, ripe fruit, sweet spices, toasty. Palate: powerful, flavourful, long, spicy, round tannins, balsamic.

CAVES CONDE DE CARALT

Ctra. Sant Sadurní-Sant Pere de Riudebitlles, Km. 5
08775 Torrelavit (Barcelona)
☎: +34 938 917 070 - Fax: +34 938 996 006
condedecaralt@condedecaralt.com
www.condedecaralt.com

CONDE DE CARALT BLANC DE BLANCS 2011 B
macabeo, xarel.lo, parellada.

84

CONDE DE CARALT 2011 RD
tempranillo, merlot, monastrell.

84

CONDE DE CARALT 2007 TC
tempranillo, cabernet sauvignon, merlot.

87 Colour: cherry, garnet rim. Nose: ripe fruit, spicy, creamy oak, toasty. Palate: powerful, flavourful, toasty, round tannins.

CLOS D'AGON

Afores, s/n
17251 Calonge (Girona)
☎: +34 972 661 486 - Fax: +34 972 661 462
info@closdagon.com
www.closdagon.com

CLOS D'AGON 2011 B
39% viognier, 39% roussanne, 22% marsanne.

92 Colour: bright yellow. Nose: candied fruit, faded flowers, citrus fruit, spicy. Palate: flavourful, ripe fruit, good structure, long.

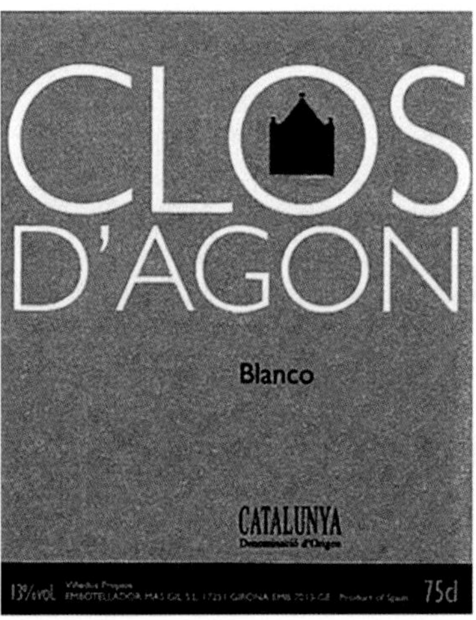

CLOS D'AGON 2010 T
45% cabernet franc, 30% syrah, 10% merlot, 10% petit verdot, 5% cabernet sauvignon.

93 Colour: black cherry, purple rim. Nose: fruit preserve, creamy oak, dark chocolate, expressive. Palate: good structure, powerful, round tannins.

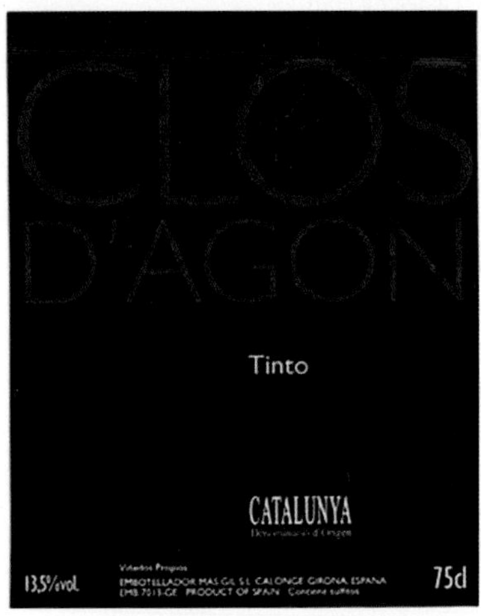

CLOS MONTBLANC

Ctra. Montblanc-Barbera, s/n
43422 Barberà de la Conca (Tarragona)
☎: +34 977 887 030 - Fax: +34 977 887 032
club@closmontblanc.com
www.closmontblanc.com

CLOS MONTBLANC CASTELL MACABEO/CHARDONNAY 2011 B
60% macabeo, 40% chardonnay.

87 Colour: bright straw. Nose: balanced, complex, white flowers, fragrant herbs. Palate: flavourful, fine bitter notes, ripe fruit.

CLOS MONTBLANC CASTELL TEMPRANILLO 2011 T
85% tempranillo, 15% cabernet sauvignon.

87 Colour: deep cherry, purple rim. Nose: balanced, ripe fruit, sweet spices. Palate: good structure, fruity, long.

CLOS MONTBLANC XIPELLA PREMIUM 2009 T
44% garnacha, 44% monastrell, 10% samsó, 2% syrah.

89 Colour: cherry, garnet rim. Nose: balanced, ripe fruit, dried flowers, scrubland, sweet spices, candied fruit. Palate: good structure, round tannins.

GRAU VELL

Can Grau Vell, s/n
08784 Hostalets de Pierola (Barcelona)
☎: +34 676 586 933 - Fax: +34 932 684 965
info@grauvell.cat

QUIKE 2011 RD

88 Colour: brilliant rose. Nose: white flowers, ripe fruit, scrubland. Palate: flavourful, fine bitter notes, good acidity.

ALCOR 2010 T
40% syrah, 25% garnacha, 15% monastrell, 10% marselan, 10% cabernet sauvignon.

93 Colour: bright cherry. Nose: ripe fruit, sweet spices, expressive, earthy notes, roasted coffee. Palate: flavourful, fruity, toasty, round tannins.

ALCOR 2008 T
syrah, cabernet sauvignon, garnacha.

93 Colour: cherry, garnet rim. Nose: ripe fruit, spicy, creamy oak, toasty, characterful. Palate: powerful, flavourful, toasty, round tannins.

ALCOR 2009

93 Colour: cherry, garnet rim. Nose: red berry notes, ripe fruit, dry stone, balsamic herbs, balanced, sweet spices, creamy oak. Palate: flavourful, fresh, long, round tannins.

JAUME GRAU - VINS GRAU

Ctra. C-37 de Igualada a Manresa, Km. 75,5
08255 Maians (Barcelona)
☎: +34 938 356 002 - Fax: +34 938 356 812
info@vinsgrau.com
www.vinsgrau.com

CLOS DEL RECÓ 2011 B
macabeo, xarel.lo, parellada.

85 Colour: bright straw. Nose: medium intensity, white flowers, wild herbs. Palate: fresh, fruity, correct.

CLOS DEL RECÓ 2011 RD
merlot.

84

CLOS DEL RECÓ 2011 T
tempranillo, merlot.

84

JAUME SERRA (J. GARCÍA CARRIÓN)

Ctra. de Vilanova, Km. 2,5
08800 Vilanova i la Geltru (Barcelona)
☎: +34 938 936 404 - Fax: +34 938 147 482
jaumeserra@jgc.es
www.garciacarrion.es

VIÑA DEL MAR SECO 2011 B

80

VIÑA DEL MAR SEMIDULCE 2011 B
xarel.lo, macabeo.

80

VIÑA DEL MAR 2011 RD

82

VIÑA DEL MAR 2010 T

80

VIÑA DEL MAR 2008 TC

81

LA XARMADA

Hisenda Casa Llivi, s/n
08796 Pacs del Penedès (Barcelona)
☎: +34 938 171 237 - Fax: +34 938 171 546
laxarmada@laxarmada.com
www.laxarmada.com

LA XARMADA BLANC DE BLANCS 2011 B

84

LA XARMADA 2011 RD
merlot, cabernet sauvignon.

84

LA XARMADA 2010 T
merlot, syrah.

81

LONG WINES

Avda. del Monte, 46
28120 Algete (Madrid)
☎: +34 916 221 305 - Fax: +34 916 220 029
www.longwines.com

ALTOS D'OLIVA 2004 TGR

87 Colour: deep cherry, orangey edge. Nose: fine reductive notes, tobacco, spicy. Palate: fruity, flavourful, balanced, good acidity.

MASET DEL LLEÓ

C-244, Km. 32,5
08792 La Granada del Penedès (Barcelona)
☎: +34 902 200 250 - Fax: +34 938 921 333
info@maset.com
www.maset.com

VIÑA SELENA S/C B

84

VIÑA SELENA S/C RD

83

MASET DEL LLEÓ SYRAH 2008 TR

92 Colour: cherry, garnet rim. Nose: ripe fruit, spicy, creamy oak, complex, dark chocolate. Palate: powerful, flavourful, toasty, round tannins.

MASET DEL LLEÓ GRAN ROBLE 2006 TR
tempranillo.

90 Colour: cherry, garnet rim. Aroma ripe fruit, spicy, creamy oak, toasty, complex. Taste powerful, flavourful, toasty, round tannins.

PORTAL DEL MONTSANT

Carrer de Dalt, s/n
43775 Marça (Tarragona)
☎: +34 933 950 811 - Fax: +34 933 955 500
info@parxet.es
www.parxet.es

SANTES 2010 B
macabeo.

89 Colour: bright straw. Nose: fresh, fresh fruit, white flowers, citrus fruit, fragrant herbs. Palate: flavourful, fruity, good acidity, balanced.

SANTES ROSÉ 2010 RD
merlot, cabernet sauvignon.

90 Colour: onion pink. Nose: elegant, candied fruit, dried flowers, fragrant herbs, red berry notes, mineral. Palate: light-bodied, flavourful, long, spicy, elegant. Personality.

RENÉ BARBIER

Ctra. Sant Sadurní a St. Pere Riudebitlles, km. 5
08775 Torrelavit (Barcelona)
☎: +34 938 917 070 - Fax: +34 938 996 006
renebarbier@renebarbier.es
www.renebarbier.com

RENÉ BARBIER KRALINER 2011 B
macabeo, xarel.lo, parellada.

85 Colour: bright straw. Nose: fresh, fresh fruit, white flowers. Palate: flavourful, fruity, good acidity, balanced, light-bodied, easy to drink.

RENÉ BARBIER VIÑA AUGUSTA 2011 B
macabeo, xarel.lo, parellada, moscatel.

85 Colour: bright straw. Nose: floral, balanced, jasmine. Palate: flavourful, fruity, correct, easy to drink.

RENÉ BARBIER ROSADO TRADICIÓN 2011 RD
tempranillo, merlot, monastrell.

86 Colour: rose, bright. Nose: red berry notes, ripe fruit, balanced, neat. Palate: flavourful, fruity, long.

ROCAMAR

Major, 80
08755 Castellbisbal (Barcelona)
☎: +34 937 720 900 - Fax: +34 937 721 495
info@rocamar.net
www.rocamar.net

MASIA RIBOT 2011 B
macabeo, parellada.

81 Colour: bright straw. Nose: medium intensity, dried herbs. Palate: correct, good finish.

BLANC DE PALANGRE B
macabeo, parellada.

78

ROSAT DE PALANGRE S/C RD
trepat.

78

MASIA RIBOT 2011 RD
tempranillo, garnacha.

83

MASIA RIBOT 2010 T
tempranillo, garnacha.

80

VALLFORMOSA

La Sala, 45
08735 Vilobi del Penedès (Barcelona)
☎: +34 938 978 286 - Fax: +34 938 978 355
vallformosa@vallformosa.es
www.vallformosa.com

LAVIÑA SEMI DULCE 2011 B
macabeo, garnacha.

83

VALLPLATA SEMI DULCE 2011 B
macabeo, garnacha.

82

VALLPLATA 2011 B
macabeo, garnacha.

82

LAVIÑA 2011 B
macabeo, garnacha.

81

LAVIÑA 2011 RD
tempranillo.

85 Colour: light cherry. Nose: medium intensity, red berry notes, floral. Palate: fruity, flavourful, correct.

VALLPLATA 2011 RD
tempranillo.

83

LAVIÑA 2011 T
merlot, tempranillo.

85 Colour: deep cherry, purple rim. Nose: powerfull, ripe fruit, violets. Palate: flavourful, correct, easy to drink, fruity.

VALLPLATA 2011 T
merlot, tempranillo.

84

DO CAVA

LOCATION:

The defined Cava region covers the sparkling wines produced according to the traditional method of a second fermentation in the bottle of 63 municipalities in the province of Barcelona, 52 in Tarragona, 12 in Lleida and 5 in Girona, as well as those of the municipal areas of Laguardia, Moreda de Álava and Oyón in Álava, Almendralejo in Badajoz, Mendavia and Viana in Navarra, Requena in Valencia, Ainzón and Cariñena in Zaragoza, and a further 18 municipalities of La Rioja.

CLIMATE:

That of each producing region stated in the previous epigraph. Nevertheless, the region in which the largest part of the production is concentrated (Penedès) has a Mediterranean climate, with some production areas being cooler and situated at a higher altitude.

SOIL:

This also depends on each producing region.

GRAPE VARIETIES:

WHITE: *Macabeo* (*Viura*), *Xarel.lo, Parellada, Subirat* (*Malvasía Riojana*) and *Chardonnay.*
RED: *Garnacha Tinta, Monastrell, Trepat* and *Pinot Noir.*

FIGURES:

Vineyard surface: 31,766 – **Wine-Growers:** 6,497 – **Wineries:** 252 – **2011 Harvest rating:** Very Good – **Production:** 174,813,000 litres – **Market percentages:** 36% domestic. 64% export

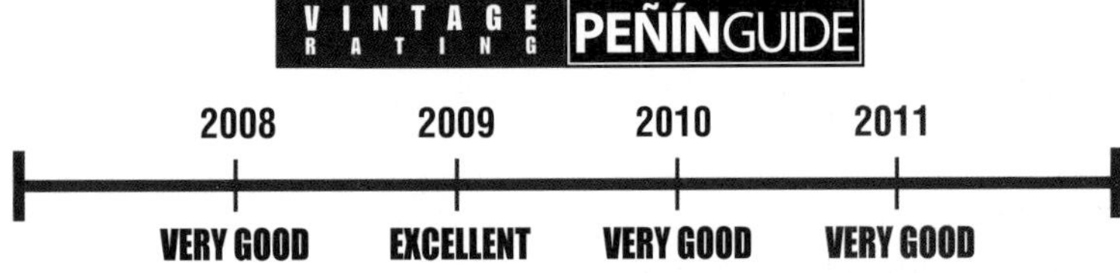

This denomination of origin, due to the wine-making process, does not make available single-year wines indicated by vintage, so the following evaluation refers to the overall quality of the wines that were palate:d this year.

CONSEJO REGULADOR
Avinguda Tarragona, 24 - 08720 Vilafranca del Penedès (Barcelona) - ☎: +34 938 903 104 - Fax: +34 938 901 567
@ consejo@crcava.es - www.crcava.es

1 + 1 = 3

Masía Navinés
08736 Guardiola de Font-Rubí (Barcelona)
☎: +34 938 974 069 - Fax: +34 938 974 724
umesu@umesufan3.com
www.umesufan3.com

CYGNUS 1 + 1 = 3 2009 BR
macabeo, xarel.lo, parellada.

90 Colour: bright yellow. Nose: white flowers, fragrant herbs, fruit expression. Palate: good acidity, fine bead, flavourful.

1 + 1 = 3 GRAN RESERVA ESPECIAL 2006 BN GRAN RESERVA
pinot noir, xarel.lo.

91 Colour: bright yellow, greenish rim. Nose: ripe fruit, dried herbs, complex. Palate: flavourful, good structure, fine bitter notes, good acidity.

1 + 1 = 3 2009 BR
macabeo, xarel.lo, parellada.

86 Colour: bright straw. Nose: medium intensity, fresh fruit, dried herbs, fine lees, floral. Palate: fresh, fruity, flavourful, good acidity.

1 + 1 = 3 SELECCIÓ ROSÉ 2009 BR
pinot noir, garnacha, trepat.

85 Colour: rose. Nose: red berry notes, ripe fruit, floral, expressive. Palate: flavourful, light-bodied, fresh.

CYGNUS 1 + 1 = 3 2008 BN RESERVA
macabeo, xarel.lo, parellada.

90 Colour: bright straw. Nose: fresh fruit, dried herbs, fine lees, floral. Palate: fresh, fruity, flavourful.

1 + 1 = 3 2008 BN
macabeo, xarel.lo, parellada.

88 Colour: bright yellow. Nose: fruit expression, white flowers, fragrant herbs, balanced. Palate: powerful, fresh, flavourful.

1 + 1 = 3 PINOT NOIR 2007 BN
pinot noir.

88 Colour: raspberry rose. Nose: raspberry, red berry notes, fresh, floral. Palate: long, balanced, good acidity, correct.

AGRÍCOLA DE BARBERÀ

Comercio, 40
43422 Barberà de la Conca (Tarragona)
☎: +34 977 887 035 - Fax: +34 977 887 035
cobarbera@doconcadebarbera.com

CASTELL DE LA COMANDA 2007 BR GRAN RESERVA
50% macabeo, 50% parellada.

86 Colour: bright golden. Nose: dry nuts, fragrant herbs. Palate: powerful, flavourful, good acidity, fine bitter notes.

CASTELL DE LA COMANDA 2007 BN GRAN RESERVA
50% macabeo, 50% parellada.

88 Colour: bright golden. Nose: fine lees, dry nuts, fragrant herbs, complex, sweet spices. Palate: powerful, flavourful, fine bead, fine bitter notes, long.

AGUSTÍ TORELLÓ MATA

La Serra, s/n PO Box 35
08770 Sant Sadurní D'Anoia (Barcelona)
☎: +34 938 911 173 - Fax: +34 938 912 616
comunicacio@agustitorellomata.com
www.agustitorellomata.com

AGUSTÍ TORELLÓ MATA ROSAT TREPAT 2010 BR RESERVA
100% trepat.

90 Colour: light cherry. Nose: medium intensity, red berry notes, rose petals, elegant. Palate: good acidity, balanced, fine bitter notes, fine bead.

BAYANUS ROSAT 375 2010 BR RESERVA
100% trepat.

87 Colour: raspberry rose. Nose: medium intensity, dried flowers, neat, rose petals. Palate: fruity, balanced, ripe fruit.

AGUSTÍ TORELLÓ MATA 2009 BR RESERVA
39% macabeo, 35% parellada, 26% xarel.lo.

88 Colour: yellow, greenish rim. Nose: medium intensity, dried flowers, dried herbs. Palate: flavourful, good acidity, balanced.

AGUSTÍ TORELLÓ MATA GRAN RESERVA BARRICA 2008 BN
100% macabeo.

92 Colour: bright straw. Nose: elegant, balanced, dry nuts, dried flowers, spicy. Palate: fine bitter notes, good acidity, ripe fruit.

AGUSTÍ TORELLÓ MATA 2008 BN GRAN RESERVA
38% macabeo, 28% xarel.lo, 34% parellada.

90 Colour: bright yellow. Nose: expressive, dry nuts, fine lees, dried flowers, medium intensity. Palate: long, ripe fruit, good acidity.

BAYANUS 375ML 2008 BN GRAN RESERVA
40% macabeo, 30% xarel.lo, 30% parellada.

90 Colour: bright straw. Nose: complex, expressive, fine lees, ripe fruit, dry nuts. Palate: flavourful, good structure, spicy.

KRIPTA 2006 BN GRAN RESERVA
45% macabeo, 35% parellada, 20% xarel.lo.

92 Colour: bright golden. Nose: fine lees, dry nuts, fragrant herbs, complex. Palate: powerful, flavourful, good acidity, fine bead, fine bitter notes.

AGUSTÍ TORELLÓ MATA MAGNUM 2006 BN GRAN RESERVA
45% macabeo, 25% xarel.lo, 30% parellada.

92 Colour: bright straw. Nose: dried herbs, fine lees, floral, ripe fruit, citrus fruit. Palate: fresh, fruity, flavourful, good acidity.

ALBET I NOYA

Can Vendrell de la Codina, s/n
08739 Sant Pau D'Ordal (Barcelona)
☎: +34 938 994 812 - Fax: +34 938 994 930
albetinoya@albetinoya.cat
www.albetinoya.cat

ALBET I NOYA DOLÇ DE POSTRES RESERVA
chardonnay, macabeo, parellada, xarel.lo.

88 Colour: bright straw, greenish rim. Nose: dry nuts, wild herbs, faded flowers, dried flowers. Palate: fruity, flavourful.

ALBET I NOYA BRUT 21 BARRICA BR
chardonnay, pinot noir.

91 Colour: bright yellow. Nose: complex, balanced, sweet spices, expressive, faded flowers. Palate: balanced, fine bitter notes, full.

ALBET I NOYA BRUT 21 BR
57% chardonnay, 43% parellada.

90 Colour: bright yellow, greenish rim. Nose: dried herbs, faded flowers, fine lees, fresh fruit. Palate: fine bitter notes, good acidity.

ALBET I NOYA BRUT ROSAT PINOT NOIR BR
100% pinot noir.

88 Colour: raspberry rose. Nose: dried flowers, red berry notes, ripe fruit, powerfull, dried herbs. Palate: flavourful, fruity, easy to drink.

ALBET I NOYA BR RESERVA
macabeo, xarel.lo, parellada, chardonnay.

88 Colour: bright straw. Nose: medium intensity, fresh fruit, dried herbs, fine lees. Palate: fresh, fruity, flavourful, good acidity.

ALBET I NOYA PETIT ALBET BRUT BR
xarel.lo, macabeo, parellada.

87 Colour: bright yellow. Nose: balanced, medium intensity, faded flowers, dried herbs. Palate: balanced, good acidity.

ALBET I NOYA 2008 BN GRAN RESERVA
macabeo, xarel.lo, parellada, chardonnay.

90 Colour: bright yellow, greenish rim. Nose: fine lees, dry nuts, fragrant herbs. Palate: powerful, flavourful, good acidity, fine bead, fine bitter notes.

ALSINA SARDÁ

Barrio Les Tarumbas, s/n
08733 Pla del Penedès (Barcelona)
☎: +34 938 988 132 - Fax: +34 938 988 671
alsina@alsinasarda.com
www.alsinasarda.com

ALSINA & SARDÁ BR RESERVA
40% macabeo, 40% xarel.lo, 20% parellada.

88 Colour: bright yellow. Nose: white flowers, fruit expression, fragrant herbs. Palate: fresh, light-bodied, flavourful.

ALSINA & SARDÁ 2009 BN RESERVA
40% macabeo, 40% xarel.lo, 20% parellada.

87 Colour: bright straw. Nose: white flowers, fresh fruit, pattiserie. Palate: fresh, balanced, flavourful.

ALSINA & SARDÁ SELLO 2008 BN GRAN RESERVA
55% xarel.lo, 30% macabeo, 15% parellada.

87 Colour: bright yellow. Nose: medium intensity, faded flowers, dried herbs, ripe fruit. Palate: correct, fine bitter notes, flavourful.

ALSINA & SARDÁ GRAN CUVÉE VESTIGIS 2006 BN GRAN RESERVA
20% macabeo, 20% xarel.lo, 20% parellada, 20% chardonnay, 20% pinot noir.

90 Colour: bright yellow. Nose: fine lees, dry nuts, fragrant herbs, complex. Palate: flavourful, fine bead, fine bitter notes.

ALSINA & SARDÁ MAS D'ALSINA BN RESERVA
65% chardonnay, 10% macabeo, 10% xarel.lo, 15% parellada.

90 Colour: bright straw. Nose: medium intensity, fresh fruit, dried herbs, fine lees, floral. Palate: fresh, fruity, flavourful, good acidity.

ALSINA & SARDÁ GRAN RESERVA ESPECIAL BN
50% xarel.lo, 50% chardonnay.

87 Colour: bright yellow. Nose: complex, faded flowers, ripe fruit, fragrant herbs. Palate: powerful, flavourful, long.

PINOT NOIR ROSAT DE ALSINA & SARDA BN
100% pinot noir.

87 Colour: raspberry rose. Nose: powerfull, dried flowers, ripe fruit, red berry notes. Palate: correct, powerful, fruity.

ALTA ALELLA

Camí Baix de Tiana - Finca Can Genis
08391 Tiana (Barcelona)
☎: +34 934 693 720 - Fax: +34 934 691 343
altaalella@altaalella.cat
www.altaalella.cat

PRIVAT LAIETÀ ILURO 2010 BN
mataró.

87 Colour: light cherry. Nose: medium intensity, floral, red berry notes, rose petals. Palate: flavourful, good acidity, fine bitter notes.

PRIVAT NU 2010 BN
pansa blanca.

87 Colour: bright straw. Nose: medium intensity, fresh fruit, fine lees, floral. Palate: fresh, fruity, flavourful, easy to drink.

PRIVAT ROSÉ 2010 BN
pinot noir, mataró.

82

PRIVAT 2009 BN
macabeo, xarel.lo, parellada, chardonnay.

87 Colour: bright straw. Nose: medium intensity, fresh fruit, fine lees, floral. Palate: fresh, fruity, flavourful, good acidity.

PRIVAT LAIETÀ 2008 BN RESERVA
chardonnay, pinot noir.

88 Colour: bright golden. Nose: complex, fine lees, dried flowers, fresh. Palate: flavourful, long, good acidity.

PRIVAT EVOLUCIÓ CHARDONNAY 2008 BN RESERVA
chardonnay.

88 Colour: bright straw. Nose: medium intensity, fresh fruit, dried herbs, fine lees, floral. Palate: fresh, fruity, flavourful, good acidity.

PRIVAT OPUS EVOLUTIUM 2007 BN GRAN RESERVA
chardonnay, pinot noir.

92 Colour: bright golden. Nose: fine lees, dry nuts, candied fruit, jasmine. Palate: powerful, flavourful, good acidity, fine bead, fine bitter notes.

ALTA ALELLA MIRGIN 2007 BN GRAN RESERVA
chardonnay, pinot noir, pansa blanca.

90 Colour: bright yellow. Nose: balanced, complex, fine lees, ripe fruit. Palate: balanced, fine bitter notes, spicy, long, toasty.

ALTA ALELLA MATARÓ ROSÉ 2007 BN
mataró.

88 Colour: salmon. Nose: elegant, fine lees, dried herbs, faded flowers, spicy. Palate: long, elegant, good acidity, fine bitter notes.

ALTA ALELLA MIRGIN ROSÉ 2007 BN
pinot noir.

85 Colour: coppery red. Nose: ripe fruit, faded flowers, lees reduction notes, scrubland. Palate: correct, easy to drink.

AVINYÓ CAVAS

Masia Can Fontanals
08793 Avinyonet del Penedès (Barcelona)
☎: +34 938 970 055 - Fax: +34 938 970 691
avinyo@avinyo.com
www.avinyo.com

AVINYÓ ROSÉ SUBLIM RD RESERVA
100% pinot noir.

83

AVINYÓ BR RESERVA
60% macabeo, 25% xarel.lo, 15% parellada.

88 Colour: bright yellow. Nose: white flowers, fragrant herbs, fresh. Palate: correct, fine bitter notes, flavourful, light-bodied.

AVINYÓ SELECCIÓ LA TICOTA 2006 BN GRAN RESERVA
65% xarel.lo, 35% macabeo.

90 Colour: yellow, greenish rim. Nose: balanced, lees reduction notes, faded flowers, dry nuts. Palate: balanced, fine bitter notes, good acidity.

AVINYÓ BLANC DE NOIRS BN RESERVA
100% pinot noir.

88 Colour: bright yellow. Nose: fine lees, dried flowers, dry nuts, balanced. Palate: flavourful, fresh, good acidity.

AVINYÓ BN RESERVA
55% macabeo, 35% xarel.lo, 10% parellada.

87 Colour: bright yellow. Nose: medium intensity, scrubland. Palate: flavourful, correct, good acidity.

BLANCHER-CAPDEVILA PUJOL

Plaça Pont Romà, Edificio Blancher
08770 Sant Sadurní D'Anoia (Barcelona)
☎: +34 938 183 286 - Fax: +34 938 911 961
blancher@blancher.es
www.blancher.es

BLANCHER 2008 BR RESERVA ESPECIAL
xarel.lo, macabeo, parellada.

84

BLANCHER OBRAC 2007 BR GRAN RESERVA
xarel.lo, macabeo, parellada.

87 Colour: bright golden. Nose: fragrant herbs, complex, lees reduction notes, spicy. Palate: powerful, flavourful, good acidity, fine bead.

BLANCHER ROSAT 2007 BR RESERVA
trepat, pinot noir.

84

CAPDEVILA PUJOL 2008 BN RESERVA
xarel.lo, macabeo, parellada.

87 Colour: bright straw. Nose: white flowers, fragrant herbs, medium intensity. Palate: balanced, good acidity, correct.

TERESA BLANCHER DE LA TIETA 2007 BN GRAN RESERVA
xarel.lo, macabeo, parellada.

89 Colour: bright straw. Nose: balanced, fresh, dried flowers, dried herbs. Palate: fruity, dry, good acidity, fine bitter notes.

MAGNUM CAPDEVILA PUJOL 2007 BN RESERVA
xarel.lo, macabeo, parellada.

87 Colour: bright straw. Nose: medium intensity, balanced. Palate: correct, fine bitter notes, easy to drink.

BLANCHER 2007 BN RESERVA
xarel.lo, macabeo, parellada.

87 Colour: bright straw. Nose: white flowers, fruit expression, fresh, expressive. Palate: fine bitter notes, light-bodied, flavourful, correct.

BLANCHER 2007 BN GRAN RESERVA
xarel.lo, macabeo, parellada.

84

BODEGA SANSTRAVÉ

De la Conca, 10
43412 Solivella (Tarragona)
☎: +34 977 892 165 - Fax: +34 977 892 073
bodega@sanstrave.com
www.sanstrave.com

SANSTRAVÉ 2007 BN GRAN RESERVA
macabeo, xarel.lo, parellada, chardonnay.

87 Colour: bright yellow. Nose: fine lees, dry nuts, fragrant herbs, complex. Palate: powerful, flavourful, good acidity, fine bead.

BODEGA SEBIRAN

Pérez Galdos, 1
46352 Campo Arcis - Requena (Valencia)
☎: +34 962 301 326 - Fax: +34 962 303 966
info@bodegasebiran.com
www.bodegasebiran.com

COTO D ARCIS ESPECIAL BR

90 Colour: bright straw. Nose: medium intensity, fresh fruit, dried herbs, fine lees, floral. Palate: fresh, fruity, flavourful, good acidity.

COTO D'ARCIS BR
macabeo.

86 Colour: bright straw. Nose: medium intensity, dried herbs, floral. Palate: fresh, fruity, flavourful, good acidity.

COTO D'ARCIS BN
macabeo.

87 Colour: bright golden. Nose: white flowers, fragrant herbs, sweet spices. Palate: correct, fine bitter notes, powerful, flavourful.

BODEGAS ABANICO

Pol. Ind Ca l'Avellanet - Susany, 6
08553 Seva (Barcelona)
☎: +34 938 125 676 - Fax: +34 938 123 213
info@exportiberia.com
www.bodegasabanico.com

RENAIXENÇA DELUXE CUVÉE
macabeo, parellada, xarel.lo.

88 Colour: bright yellow. Nose: dried flowers, ripe fruit, dry nuts, fragrant herbs. Palate: correct, flavourful, good acidity, fine bead.

RENAIXENÇA BR
macabeo, parellada, xarel.lo.

87 Colour: bright straw. Nose: medium intensity, fresh fruit, dried herbs, fine lees, floral. Palate: fresh, fruity, flavourful, good acidity.

RENAIXENÇA BN
macabeo, parellada, xarel.lo.

86 Colour: bright golden. Nose: dry nuts, fragrant herbs, complex, fine lees. Palate: powerful, flavourful, good acidity, fine bead, fine bitter notes.

BODEGAS BORDEJÉ

Ctra. Borja a Rueda, Km. 3
50570 Ainzón (Zaragoza)
☎: +34 976 868 080 - Fax: +34 976 868 989
ainzon@bodegasbordeje.com
www.bodegasbordeje.com

CAVA BORDEJÉ ROSADO DE GARNACHA 2010 BN
100% garnacha.

84

CAVA BORDEJÉ CHARDONNAY 2010 BN
100% chardonnay.

82

CAVA BORDEJÉ MACABEO 2008 ESP
100% macabeo.

80

BODEGAS CA N'ESTELLA

Masia Ca N'Estella, s/n
08635 Sant Esteve Sesrovires (Barcelona)
☎: +34 934 161 387 - Fax: +34 934 161 620
j.rodriguez@fincacanestella.com
www.fincacanestella.com

RABETLLAT I VIDAL BRUT CA N'ESTELLA 2010 BR
60% macabeo, 40% xarel.lo.

87 Colour: bright straw. Nose: medium intensity, fresh fruit, dried herbs, fine lees, floral. Palate: fresh, fruity, flavourful, good acidity.

RABETLLAT I VIDAL 2010 BN
80% chardonnay, 20% macabeo.

88 Colour: bright yellow. Nose: fine lees, white flowers, citrus fruit, fresh fruit, dried herbs. Palate: fresh, fruity, flavourful.

RABETLLAT I VIDAL GRAN RESERVA DE LA FINCA 2007 BN
80% chardonnay, 20% macabeo.

87 Colour: bright yellow. Nose: lees reduction notes, dry nuts, sweet spices, pattiserie. Palate: long, rich, flavourful.

RABETLLAT I VIDAL 2010 BRUT ROSADO
trepat.

85 Colour: raspberry rose. Nose: rose petals, fruit liqueur notes, raspberry, candied fruit. Palate: fresh, fruity, easy to drink.

BODEGAS CAPITÀ VIDAL

Ctra. Villafranca-Igualada, Km. 21
08733 Pla del Penedès (Barcelona)
☎: +34 938 988 630 - Fax: +34 938 988 625
capitavidal@capitavidal.com
www.capitavidal.com

FUCHS DE VIDAL BR
40% xarel.lo, 35% macabeo, 25% parellada.

84

FUCHS DE VIDAL 2008 BN GRAN RESERVA
50% xarel.lo, 30% macabeo, 20% parellada.

89 Colour: bright straw, greenish rim. Nose: balanced, dried herbs, floral, spicy. Palate: ripe fruit, long, good acidity, fine bitter notes.

FUCHS DE VIDAL CUVÉE BN RESERVA
40% xarel.lo, 35% macabeo, 25% parellada.

90 Colour: bright yellow. Nose: petrol notes, fine lees, dried flowers, dry nuts. Palate: powerful, flavourful, complex, long.

FUCHS DE VIDAL UNIC BN
50% chardonnay, 35% pinot noir, 15% macabeo, xarel.lo, parellada.

86 Colour: bright straw. Nose: fresh fruit, dried herbs, fine lees, floral. Palate: fresh, fruity, flavourful, good acidity.

PALAU SOLÁ BN
40% xarel.lo, 35% macabeo, 25% parellada.

85 Colour: bright yellow. Nose: white flowers, dried herbs, ripe fruit. Palate: fine bitter notes, flavourful, fruity.

FUCHS DE VIDAL ROSÉ PINOT NOIR BN
100% pinot noir.

84

QUATRE BARRES BN
40% xarel.lo, 35% macabeo, 25% parellada.

83

BODEGAS COVIÑAS

Avda. Rafael Duyos, s/n
46340 Requena (Valencia)
☎: +34 962 300 680 - Fax: +34 962 302 651
covinas@covinas.com
www.covinas.com

MARQUÉS DE PLATA BR
75% macabeo, 12,5% xarel.lo, 12,5% parellada.

82

MARQUÉS DE PLATA BN
75% macabeo, 12,5% xarel.lo, 12,5% parellada.

85 Colour: bright yellow. Nose: medium intensity, dried flowers, dried herbs. Palate: fresh, easy to drink.

BODEGAS FAUSTINO

Ctra. de Logroño, s/n
01320 Oyón (Álava)
☎: +34 945 622 500 - Fax: +34 945 622 511
info@bodegasfaustino.es
www.bodegasfaustino.es

CAVA FAUSTINO BR RESERVA
viura, chardonnay.

84

CAVA FAUSTINO ROSADO BR
100% garnacha.

82

BODEGAS HISPANO SUIZAS

Ctra. N-322, Km. 451,7 El Pontón
46357 Requena (Valencia)
☎: +34 661 894 200
info@bodegashispanosuizas.com
www.bodegashispanosuizas.com

TANTUM ERGO VINTAGE 2007
chardonnay, pinot noir.

93 Colour: bright yellow. Nose: ripe fruit, jasmine, complex, expressive, powerfull, fine lees. Palate: good structure, flavourful, long, fine bitter notes.

TANTUM ERGO PINOT NOIR ROSÉ 2010 BN
pinot noir.

93 Colour: salmon. Nose: candied fruit, faded flowers, fine lees, balanced. Palate: good acidity, balanced, fine bitter notes, fine bead.

TANTUM ERGO CHARDONNAY PINOT NOIR 2009 BN
chardonnay, pinot noir.

92 Colour: bright yellow. Nose: ripe fruit, spicy. Palate: balanced, fruity, flavourful, good acidity, fine bitter notes.

BODEGAS LA ESPERANZA

Brisol, 16 bis
28230 Las Rozas (Madrid)
☎: +34 917 104 880 - Fax: +34 917 104 881
anap@swd.es
www.swd.es

NOCHE Y DÍA ROSÉ (PINK LABEL) BR
100% trepat.

87 Colour: coppery red. Nose: floral, red berry notes, lactic notes, medium intensity. Palate: powerful, flavourful, fruity.

NOCHE Y DÍA (GREEN LABEL) BR
40% macabeo, 40% xarel.lo, 20% parellada.

86 Colour: bright straw. Nose: medium intensity, fresh fruit, floral, grassy. Palate: fresh, fruity, flavourful, good acidity.

NOCHE Y DÍA (YELLOW LABEL) BN
40% macabeo, 40% xarel.lo, 20% parellada.

83

NOCHE Y DÍA (BLUE LABEL) SS
40% macabeo, 40% xarel.lo, 20% parellada.

86 Colour: bright straw. Nose: medium intensity, dried flowers. Palate: fruity, sweet, good acidity, easy to drink.

BODEGAS LANGA

Ctra. Nacional II, Km. 241,700
50300 Calatayud (Zaragoza)
☎: +34 976 881 818 - Fax: +34 976 884 463
info@bodegas-langa.com
www.bodegas-langa.com

REYES DE ARAGÓN BR RESERVA
75% macabeo, 25% chardonnay.

85 Colour: bright yellow, greenish rim. Nose: scrubland, medium intensity. Palate: correct, good acidity.

REYES DE ARAGÓN BN RESERVA
75% chardonnay, 30% macabeo.

85 Colour: bright golden. Nose: pungent, pattiserie, ripe fruit.

REYES DE ARAGÓN BN GRAN RESERVA
70% chardonnay, 30% macabeo.

82

REYES DE ARAGÓN SELECCIÓN FAMILIAR BN
70% chardonnay, 30% macabeo.

82

BODEGAS MARQUÉS DE MONISTROL

Monistrol d'Anoia
08770 Sant Sadurní D'Anoia (Barcelona)
☎: +34 914 365 900
www.haciendas-espana.com

MAS DE MONISTROL BRUT VINTAGE 2009
macabeo, parraleta, xarel.lo, chardonnay.

87 Colour: bright yellow. Nose: white flowers, pattiserie, fresh fruit, fragrant herbs. Palate: light-bodied, fresh, fruity, easy to drink.

MAS DE MONISTROL PREMIUM CUVÉE MILLÉSIME 2008 BR

87 Colour: light cherry. Nose: floral, fine lees, fragrant herbs, red berry notes. Palate: correct, rich, powerful, flavourful, fruity.

MARQUÉS DE MONISTROL S/C BN
25% chardonnay, 30% macabeo, 15% xarel.lo, 30% parellada.

87 Colour: bright straw. Nose: medium intensity, fresh fruit, fine lees, floral, citrus fruit. Palate: fruity, flavourful, fresh, easy to drink.

MARQUÉS DE MONISTROL PREMIUM CUVÉE MILLÉSIME 2008 BN
macabeo, parellada, xarel.lo, chardonnay.

87 Colour: bright straw. Nose: faded flowers, ripe fruit, dried herbs, fine lees. Palate: light-bodied, fresh, fruity, flavourful.

MARQUÉS DE MONISTROL PREMIUM CUVÉE 2008 BN
25% chardonnay, 30% macabeo, 15% xarel.lo, 30% parellada.

84

MARQUÉS DE MONISTROL PREMIUM CUVÉE 2009 BRUT ROSÉ
70% pinot noir, 30% monastrell.

86 Colour: brilliant rose. Nose: balanced, medium intensity, fresh, red berry notes, dried herbs. Palate: fruity, fresh, good acidity.

CLOS MONISTROL 2009 EXTRA BRUT
25% chardonnay, 20% macabeo, 35% xarel.lo, 20% parellada.

86 Colour: bright straw. Nose: medium intensity, dried herbs, floral, pattiserie. Palate: fruity, flavourful, good acidity.

BODEGAS MUGA

Barrio de la Estación, s/n
26200 Haro (La Rioja)
☎: +34 941 311 825 - Fax: +34 941 312 867
info@bodegasmuga.com
www.bodegasmuga.com

CONDE DE HARO BR
95% viura, 5% malvasía.

88 Colour: bright straw. Nose: medium intensity, fresh fruit, fine lees, floral. Palate: fresh, fruity, good acidity.

BODEGAS MUR BARCELONA

Rambla de la Generalitat, 1-9
08770 Sant Sadurni D'Anoia (Barcelona)
☎: +34 938 183 641 - Fax: +34 938 914 366
info@mur-barcelona.com
www.mur-barcelona.com

ROBERT J. MUR ESPECIAL TRADICIÓ ROSÉ 2009 RD RESERVA
40% trepat, 30% monastrell, 20% garnacha, 10% pinot noir.

87 Colour: brilliant rose. Nose: floral, ripe fruit, fine lees, dried herbs. Palate: correct, easy to drink, good acidity, flavourful.

ROBERT J. MUR ESPECIAL TRADICIÓ 2009 BN RESERVA
xarel.lo, parellada, macabeo.

86 Colour: bright straw. Nose: fine lees, floral, tropical fruit, citrus fruit. Palate: fresh, good acidity, good finish.

GRAN MONTESQUIUS 2009 BN RESERVA
xarel.lo, parellada, macabeo.

85 Colour: bright straw. Nose: medium intensity, fresh fruit, dried herbs, fine lees, floral. Palate: fresh, fruity, thin.

GRAN MONTESQUIUS MAGNUM 2005 BN RESERVA
xarel.lo, parellada, macabeo.

88 Colour: bright yellow. Nose: citrus fruit, sweet spices, cocoa bean. Palate: flavourful, fine bitter notes, spicy.

BODEGAS MURVIEDRO

Ampliación Pol. El Romeral, s/n
46340 Requena (Valencia)
☎: +34 962 329 003 - Fax: +34 962 329 002
murviedro@murviedro.es
www.murviedro.es

LUNA DE MURVIEDRO BR
100% macabeo.

87 Colour: bright straw. Nose: white flowers, fresh, medium intensity. Palate: easy to drink, correct, good acidity.

LUNA DE MURVIEDRO ROSÉ BR
100% garnacha.

86 Colour: salmon. Nose: fresh fruit, floral, rose petals, balanced. Palate: fruity, fresh, easy to drink.

COROLILLA CHARDONNAY BR
100% chardonnay.

85 Colour: bright yellow. Nose: fine lees, white flowers, ripe fruit, fragrant herbs. Palate: rich, flavourful, long, balanced.

EXPRESIÓN SOLIDARITY CUVÉE CHARDONNAY BN
100% chardonnay.

87 Colour: bright yellow. Nose: powerfull, ripe fruit, wild herbs, lees reduction notes, candied fruit. Palate: flavourful, powerful, long.

BODEGAS OLARRA

Avda. de Mendavia, 30
26009 Logroño (La Rioja)
☎: +34 941 235 299 - Fax: +34 941 253 703
bodegasolarra@bodegasolarra.es
www.bodegasolarra.es

AÑARES BR
100% viura.

85 Colour: bright straw. Nose: medium intensity, fresh fruit, fine lees, floral. Palate: fresh, fruity, flavourful.

AÑARES BN
100% viura.

85 Colour: bright yellow. Nose: ripe fruit, tropical fruit, white flowers. Palate: light-bodied, fresh, flavourful.

BODEGAS ONDARRE

Ctra. de Aras, s/n
31230 Viana (Navarra)
☎: +34 948 645 300 - Fax: +34 948 646 002
bodegasondarre@bodegasondarre.es
www.bodegasondarre.es

ONDARRE BR
100% viura.

87 Colour: bright yellow. Nose: fragrant herbs, floral, expressive. Palate: flavourful, fresh, fruity.

ONDARRE BN
100% viura.

83

BODEGAS ROMALE

Pol. Ind. Parc. 6, Manz. D
06200 Almendralejo (Badajoz)
☎: +34 924 667 255 - Fax: +34 924 665 877
romale@romale.com
www.romale.com

VIÑA ROMALE 2010 BN
60% macabeo, 40% parellada.

83

BODEGAS ROURA - JUAN ANTONIO PÉREZ ROURA

Valls de Rials
08328 Alella (Barcelona)
☎: +34 933 527 456 - Fax: +34 933 524 339
roura@roura.es
www.roura.es

ROURA BR
75% xarel.lo, 25% chardonnay.

85 Colour: yellow, greenish rim. Nose: fresh fruit, dry nuts, dried herbs, white flowers. Palate: fruity, easy to drink.

ROURA BN
70% xarel.lo, 30% chardonnay.

86 Colour: bright straw. Nose: medium intensity, fresh fruit, dried herbs, fine lees. Palate: fresh, fruity, good acidity.

ROURA ROSAT BN
100% trepat.

83

BODEGAS SIGNAT

Escultor Llimona, s/n
08328 Alella (Barcelona)
☎: +34 935 403 400 - Fax: +34 935 401 471
signat@signat.es
www.signat.es

SIGNAT 5 ESTRELLAS BR RESERVA

91 Colour: bright straw. Nose: candied fruit, dry nuts, fine lees. Palate: flavourful, fine bitter notes, good acidity.

SIGNAT BR

85 Colour: bright yellow. Nose: candied fruit, citrus fruit, spicy. Palate: flavourful, fresh.

SIGNAT BN

88 Colour: bright straw. Nose: fresh fruit, dried herbs, fine lees, floral, neat, fresh. Palate: fresh, fruity, flavourful, good acidity.

BODEGAS TORROJA

Nogueral, 3
46357 Azagador (Valencia)
☎: +34 962 304 232 - Fax: +34 962 303 833
bodegastorroja@gmail.com
www.bodegastorroja.com

SYBARUS BR
80% macabeo, 20% chardonnay.

89 Colour: bright straw. Nose: fresh fruit, dried herbs, fine lees, floral. Palate: fresh, fruity, flavourful, good acidity.

SYBARUS BN
80% macabeo, 20% chardonnay.

87 Colour: bright straw. Nose: medium intensity, dried herbs, fine lees. Palate: fresh, fruity, flavourful, good acidity.

BODEGAS TRIAS BATLLE

Comerç, 6
08720 Vilafranca del Penedès (Barcelona)
☎: +34 938 902 627 - Fax: +34 938 901 724
bodegas@jtrias.com
www.jtrias.com

TRIAS BATLLE ROSADO BR
100% trepat.

87 Colour: light cherry, bright. Nose: red berry notes, dried herbs. Palate: flavourful, easy to drink, good acidity.

TRIAS BR RESERVA
45% macabeo, 30% xarel.lo, 25% parellada.

87 Colour: bright yellow. Nose: medium intensity, fresh fruit, fine lees, floral. Palate: flavourful, fine bitter notes, balanced, good acidity.

TRIAS BATLLE 2006 BN GRAN RESERVA
40% xarel.lo, 30% macabeo, 20% parellada, 10% chardonnay.

88 Colour: bright golden. Nose: fine lees, fragrant herbs. Palate: flavourful, good acidity, fine bead, fine bitter notes.

TRIAS BN RESERVA
45% macabeo, 30% xarel.lo, 25% parellada.

88 Colour: bright straw. Nose: white flowers, balanced. Palate: flavourful, good acidity, fresh, fruity.

BODEGAS TROBAT

Castelló, 10
17780 Garriguella (Girona)
☎: +34 972 530 092 - Fax: +34 972 552 530
bodegas.trobat@bmark.es
www.bodegastrobat.com

CELLER TROBAT 2011 BR
macabeo, xarel.lo, parellada.

88 Colour: bright straw. Nose: dried flowers, fragrant herbs, fine lees, citrus fruit. Palate: good acidity, flavourful, fresh.

CELLER TROBAT ROSAT 2010 BR
garnacha, monastrell.

85 Colour: light cherry. Nose: floral, red berry notes, ripe fruit, fresh. Palate: fruity, flavourful, easy to drink, light-bodied.

GRAN AMAT 2011 BN
macabeo, xarel.lo, parellada.

83

CELLER TROBAT 2009 BN RESERVA
macabeo, xarel.lo, parellada, chardonnay.

88 Colour: bright yellow. Nose: floral, fine lees, balanced. Palate: good acidity, fine bitter notes, fine bead, fruity.

CELLER TROBAT 2008 BN GRAN RESERVA
macabeo, xarel.lo, parellada, chardonnay.

87 Colour: bright golden. Nose: pattiserie, lees reduction notes, floral, ripe fruit, dried herbs. Palate: fine bitter notes, powerful, flavourful.

BODEGAS VEGAMAR

Garcesa, s/n
46175 Calles (Valencia)
☎: +34 962 109 813
info@bodegasvegamar.com
www.bodegasvegamar.com

DOMINIO DE CALLES 2010 BN
macabeo, chardonnay.

84

DOMINIO DE CALLES ROSADO 2010 BN
garnacha.

84

PRIVÉE 18 2009 BN RESERVA
macabeo, chardonnay.

86 Colour: bright yellow, . Nose: dried flowers, fine lees, fresh fruit. Palate: fresh, correct, fine bitter notes, good acidity.

DOMINIO DE CALLES EDICIÓN ESPECIAL 2007 BN RESERVA
macabeo, chardonnay.

86 Colour: bright straw. Nose: medium intensity, fresh fruit, dried herbs, fine lees, floral. Palate: fresh, fruity, flavourful.

BODEGAS VICENTE GANDÍA

Ctra. Cheste a Godelleta, s/n
46370 Chiva (Valencia)
☎: +34 962 524 242 - Fax: +34 962 524 243
vuboldi@vicentegandia.com
www.vicentegandia.es

HOYA DE CADENAS BR
macabeo.

88 Colour: bright yellow. Nose: dry nuts, dried flowers, fresh, balanced. Palate: good structure, flavourful, easy to drink.

EL MIRACLE BR
macabeo, chardonnay.

86 Colour: bright straw. Nose: medium intensity, dry nuts, fresh. Palate: light-bodied, fresh, easy to drink, good finish.

VICENTE GANDÍA ROSADO BR
garnacha.

86 Colour: coppery red. Nose: fruit expression, balanced, white flowers. Palate: fresh, fruity, easy to drink.

VICENTE GANDÍA BR
macabeo, chardonnay.

85 Colour: bright straw, greenish rim. Nose: medium intensity, candied fruit. Palate: light-bodied, easy to drink.

HOYA DE CADENAS ROSADO BR
garnacha.

84

HOYA DE CADENAS BN
macabeo.

87 Colour: bright yellow, greenish rim. Nose: medium intensity, balanced, dry nuts, dried flowers. Palate: flavourful, easy to drink, fine bitter notes.

VICENTE GANDÍA BN
macabeo.

86 Colour: bright straw. Nose: fresh, medium intensity, dry nuts, balanced, dried flowers. Palate: flavourful, good acidity.

BODEGUES SUMARROCA

Barrio El Rebato, s/n
08739 Subirats (Barcelona)
☎: +34 938 911 092 - Fax: +34 938 911 778
info@sumarroca.com
www.sumarroca.com

SUMARROCA ROSAT GRAN BRUT 2009 RD
100% pinot noir.

89 Colour: raspberry rose. Nose: faded flowers, red berry notes, ripe fruit, expressive. Palate: powerful, flavourful, fruity, long.

SUMARROCA GRAN BRUT ALLIER 2009 BR GRAN RESERVA
chardonnay, pinot noir, parellada.

93 Colour: bright yellow. Nose: toasty, dried flowers, fragrant herbs, spicy, nose:tic coffee. Palate: complex, flavourful, fine bitter notes, balanced, long. Personality.

SUMARROCA 2009 BR RESERVA
parellada, macabeo, xarel.lo, chardonnay.

90 Colour: bright straw. Nose: fresh fruit, fine lees, floral, fragrant herbs. Palate: fresh, fruity, flavourful, good acidity, balanced.

NÚRIA CLAVEROL 2008 BR
xarel.lo, chardonnay, parellada.

93 Colour: bright straw. Nose: fresh fruit, dried herbs, fine lees, floral, medium intensity, complex, fresh. Palate: fresh, fruity, flavourful, good acidity.

SUMARROCA GRAN BRUT BR GRAN RESERVA

91 Colour: bright yellow. Nose: white flowers, fresh fruit, fragrant herbs, expressive. Palate: balanced, powerful, flavourful, long.

SUMARROCA 2008 BN GRAN RESERVA
parellada, macabeo, xarel.lo, chardonnay.

91 Colour: bright golden. Nose: lees reduction notes, pattiserie, dried flowers, ripe fruit, elegant. Palate: powerful, flavourful, balanced, long.

SUMARROCA CUVÉE 2008 BN GRAN RESERVA
chardonnay, parellada.

90 Colour: bright golden. Nose: faded flowers, ripe fruit, dry nuts, pattiserie. Palate: good acidity, fine bitter notes, powerful, flavourful.

CAVA SUMARROCA BRUT ROSADO

88 Colour: light cherry. Nose: red berry notes, candied fruit, floral. Palate: powerful, flavourful, fruity, correct, fine bitter notes.

CAN FEIXES (HUGUET)

Finca Can Feixes, s/n
08718 Cabrera D'Anoia (Barcelona)
☎: +34 937 718 227 - Fax: +34 937 718 031
canfeixes@canfeixes.com
www.canfeixes.com

HUGUET 2007 BR GRAN RESERVA
parellada, macabeo, pinot noir.

88 Colour: bright golden. Nose: faded flowers, ripe fruit, dried herbs. Palate: correct, fine bitter notes, powerful, flavourful.

HUGUET 2007 BN GRAN RESERVA
parellada, macabeo, pinot noir.

88 Colour: bright straw. Nose: fresh fruit, floral, medium intensity. Palate: flavourful, fruity, good acidity, fine bitter notes.

CANALS & MUNNÉ

Ctra. de Sant Sadurni a Vilafranca, km. 0,5
08770 Sant Sadurní D'Anoia (Barcelona)
☎: +34 938 910 318 - Fax: +34 938 911 945
info@canalsimunne.com
www.canalsimunne.com

CANALS & MUNNÉ ROSÉ 2008 BR RESERVA
100% pinot noir.

84

CANALS & MUNNÉ INSUPERABLE 2006 BR GRAN RESERVA
40% macabeo, 30% xarel.lo, 30% parellada.

88 Colour: bright yellow. Nose: fresh fruit, floral, wild herbs. Palate: balanced, fine bitter notes, good acidity, spicy.

DIONYSUS ECO 2009 BN RESERVA
40% xarel.lo, 20% macabeo, 20% parellada, 20% chardonnay.

87 Colour: bright straw. Nose: dried herbs, fine lees, floral, citrus fruit. Palate: fresh, fruity, flavourful, good acidity, easy to drink.

CANALS & MUNNÉ 2008 BN GRAN RESERVA
40% xarel.lo, 20% parellada, 20% macabeo, 20% chardonnay.

87 Colour: bright straw, greenish rim. Nose: medium intensity, dried flowers, fresh. Palate: fresh, good acidity, fine bitter notes.

CANALS & MUNNÉ "1915 BY C Y M" 2008 BN GRAN RESERVA
40% pinot noir, 30% chardonnay, 30% xarel.lo.

87 Colour: bright straw, greenish rim. Nose: medium intensity, fresh, dried flowers, dried herbs. Palate: flavourful, fresh, easy to drink.

CANALS & MUNNÉ GRAN DUC 2007 BN GRAN RESERVA
40% pinot noir, 30% chardonnay, 30% xarel.lo.

90 Colour: bright golden. Nose: roasted almonds, toasty, faded flowers, dry nuts. Palate: long, spicy, fine bead, fine bitter notes.

CANALS & MUNNÉ MAGNUM 2006 BN GRAN RESERVA
40% xarel.lo, 20% macabeo, 20% chardonnay, 20% parellada.

91 Colour: bright golden. Nose: fine lees, dry nuts, fragrant herbs. Palate: powerful, flavourful, good acidity, fine bead, fine bitter notes.

CANALS & MUNNÉ (37,5 CL.) 2006 BN GRAN RESERVA
40% xarel.lo, 20% macabeo, 20% parellada, 20% chardonnay.

87 Colour: bright golden. Nose: fine lees, dry nuts, complex. Palate: powerful, flavourful, good acidity, fine bead, fine bitter notes.

CANALS & NUBIOLA

Avda. Casetes Mir, 2
08770 Sant Sadurní D'Anoia (Barcelona)
☎: +34 938 917 025 - Fax: +34 938 910 126
canalsnubiola@canalsnubiola.es
www.canalsnubiola.es

CANALS & NUBIOLA GRAPA BRUT 2010 BR
40% xarel.lo, 30% parellada, 30% macabeo.

86 Colour: bright straw. Nose: medium intensity, fresh fruit, dried herbs, fine lees, floral. Palate: fresh, fruity, flavourful, good acidity.

CANALS & NUBIOLA PLATA BRUT 2010 BR
40% parellada, 50% macabeo, 10% xarel.lo.

84

CANALS & NUBIOLA GRAPA NATURE 2009 BN RESERVA
33% parellada, 33% macabeo, 33% xarel.lo.

87 Colour: bright yellow. Nose: dried flowers, fine lees, fragrant herbs, medium intensity. Palate: powerful, flavourful, balanced.

CANALS NADAL

Ponent, 2
08733 El Pla del Penedès (Barcelona)
☎: +34 938 988 081 - Fax: +34 938 989 050
cava@canalsnadal.com
www.canalsnadal.com

CANALS NADAL ROSÉ 2010 BR RESERVA
100% trepat.

90 Colour: raspberry rose. Nose: red berry notes, fine lees, floral, fresh, expressive. Palate: fresh, fruity, powerful, flavourful, easy to drink.

CANALS NADAL 2010 BR
40% macabeo, 40% xarel.lo, 20% parellada.

87 Colour: bright yellow. Nose: fresh fruit, fine lees, white flowers. Palate: fruity, flavourful, light-bodied, fresh.

CANALS NADAL GRAN VINTAGE 2009 BR RESERVA
40% chardonnay, 30% macabeo, 20% xarel.lo, 10% parellada.

90 Colour: bright yellow. Nose: fine lees, dry nuts, fragrant herbs, complex. Palate: powerful, flavourful, good acidity, fine bead, fine bitter notes.

CANALS NADAL 2009 BR RESERVA
45% macabeo, 40% xarel.lo, 15% parellada.

89 Colour: bright yellow. Nose: white flowers, fresh fruit, spicy. Palate: good acidity, flavourful, easy to drink.

ANTONI CANALS NADAL CUPADA SELECCIÓ 2009 BR RESERVA
50% macabeo, 40% xarel.lo, 10% parellada.

86 Colour: bright straw. Nose: fine lees, ripe fruit, faded flowers. Palate: good acidity, slightly evolved, spicy.

ANTONI CANALS NADAL CUPADA SELECCIÓ MAGNUM 2008 BN FERMENTADO EN BARRICA
50% macabeo, 40% xarel.lo, 10% parellada.

89 Colour: bright yellow. Nose: white flowers, candied fruit, sweet spices, fragrant herbs. Palate: flavourful, sweetness, spicy, long.

CANALS NADAL 2008 BN RESERVA
45% macabeo, 40% xarel.lo, 15% parellada.

88 Colour: bright straw. Nose: fresh fruit, dried herbs, fine lees, floral. Palate: fresh, fruity, flavourful, good acidity.

CANALS NADAL 2007 BN GRAN RESERVA
50% macabeo, 40% xarel.lo, 10% parellada.

89 Colour: bright yellow. Nose: white flowers, fruit expression, fragrant herbs, fine lees. Palate: correct, flavourful, balanced.

CANALS NADAL MAGNUM 2007 BN GRAN RESERVA
45% macabeo, 40% xarel.lo, 15% parellada.

88 Colour: bright golden. Nose: dry nuts, fragrant herbs, lees reduction notes. Palate: powerful, flavourful, good acidity, fine bitter notes.

CASA ROJO

Sánchez Picazo, 53
30332 Balsapintada (Murcia)
☎: +34 968 151 520 - Fax: +34 968 151 690
marketing@casarojo.com
www.casarojo.com

1919 GARNACHA ROSÉ BR
100% garnacha.

86 Colour: coppery red. Nose: fine lees, floral, fresh fruit, fragrant herbs, medium intensity. Palate: light-bodied, fresh, fruity, easy to drink.

1919 MACABEO 2010 BN
100% macabeo.

84

1919 CHARDONNAY 2009 BN RESERVA
100% chardonnay.

87 Colour: bright golden. Nose: fine lees, dry nuts, fragrant herbs. Palate: powerful, flavourful, fine bead, fine bitter notes.

CASTELL D'AGE

Ctra.de Martorell a Capellades, 6-8
08782 La Beguda Baixa (Barcelona)
☎: +34 937 725 181 - Fax: +34 937 727 061
info@castelldage.com
www.castelldage.com

POCULUM BONI GENI 2006 GRAN RESERVA
50% chardonnay, 50% pinot noir.

84

CASTELL D'AGE ROSAT 2009 BR RESERVA
100% pinot noir.

84

CASTELL D'AGE ECOLÒGIC 2009 BN RESERVA
40% xarel.lo, 40% macabeo, 10% parellada, 10% chardonnay.

86 Colour: bright yellow. Nose: candied fruit, white flowers, pattiserie. Palate: fruity, powerful, flavourful.

ANNE MARIE COMTESSE 2009 BN RESERVA
40% xarel.lo, 40% macabeo, 20% parellada.

85 Colour: bright golden. Nose: faded flowers, dried herbs, dry nuts. Palate: powerful, flavourful, balanced.

CASTELL D'AGE CHARDONNAY 2008 BN RESERVA
100% chardonnay.

85 Colour: bright yellow. Nose: balanced, ripe fruit, dry nuts, dried flowers. Palate: flavourful, fine bitter notes.

CASTELL D'OR

Mare Rafols, 3- 1º 4º
08720 Vilafranca del Penedès (Barcelona)
☎: +34 938 905 446 - Fax: +34 938 905 446
castelldor@castelldor.com
www.castelldor.com

COSSETÀNIA BR RESERVA
50% xarel.lo, 30% macabeo, 20% parellada.

88 Colour: bright straw. Nose: medium intensity, fresh fruit, dried herbs, fine lees, floral. Palate: fresh, fruity, flavourful, good acidity.

FLAMA D'OR BRUT ROSAT BR
100% trepat.

88 Colour: light cherry. Nose: floral, red berry notes, raspberry, balanced. Palate: powerful, flavourful, fresh, fruity.

FRANCOLÍ BR RESERVA
50% macabeo, 50% parellada.

87 Colour: bright straw. Nose: medium intensity, fresh fruit, dried herbs. Palate: fresh, fruity, flavourful, good acidity.

COSSETÀNIA ROSADO BR
100% trepat.

85 Colour: salmon. Nose: floral, dried herbs, red berry notes, ripe fruit. Palate: light-bodied, fresh, easy to drink.

PUPITRE BR
40% xarel.lo, 40% macabeo, 20% parellada.

85 Colour: bright straw. Nose: fine lees, faded flowers, ripe fruit. Palate: fresh, fruity, flavourful, good acidity.

FRANCOLI ROSAT BR
100% trepat.

84

PUIG SOLIVELLA BR
60% macabeo, 40% parellada.

84

FRANCOLI BN
50% macabeo, 50% parellada.

86 Colour: bright yellow. Nose: fine lees, fragrant herbs, spicy, floral. Palate: powerful, rich, flavourful, long.

COSSETÀNIA BN
50% xarel.lo, 30% macabeo, 20% parellada.

86 Colour: bright straw, greenish rim. Nose: fresh, medium intensity, fine lees, floral. Palate: flavourful, fresh, good acidity.

FLAMA D'OR BN
40% xarel.lo, 35% macabeo, 25% parellada.

86 Colour: bright yellow. Nose: medium intensity, fresh fruit, fine lees, floral. Palate: fresh, fruity, flavourful.

PUPITRE BN
40% xarel.lo, 35% macabeo, 25% parellada.

86 Colour: bright straw. Nose: fresh fruit, dried herbs, fine lees, floral. Palate: fresh, fruity, flavourful, good acidity.

PUIG SOLIVELLA BN
60% macabeo, 40% parellada.

85 Colour: bright straw. Nose: fine lees, white flowers, candied fruit. Palate: light-bodied, fresh, flavourful.

FLAMA D'OR SS
50% macabeo, 30% xarel.lo, 20% parellada.

85 Colour: bright yellow. Nose: white flowers, candied fruit, fragrant herbs. Palate: sweetness, fresh, light-bodied.

CASTELL SANT ANTONI

Passeig del Parc, 13
08770 Sant Sadurní D'Anoia (Barcelona)
☎: +34 938 183 099 - Fax: +34 938 184 451
cava@castellsantantoni.com
www.castellsantantoni.com

CASTELL SANT ANTONI GRAN BRUT BR GRAN RESERVA

92 Colour: bright golden. Nose: fine lees, dry nuts, fragrant herbs, complex. Palate: powerful, flavourful, good acidity, fine bead, fine bitter notes.

CASTELL SANT ANTONI GRAN BRUT MAGNUM BR RESERVA

91 Colour: bright yellow. Nose: candied fruit, fruit liqueur notes, lees reduction notes, sweet spices. Palate: flavourful, powerful, fine bitter notes.

CASTELL SANT ANTONI 37.5 BRUT BR

90 Colour: bright straw. Nose: medium intensity, dried herbs, fine lees, floral, candied fruit, dry nuts. Palate: fresh, fruity, flavourful, good acidity.

CASTELL SANT ANTONI BRUT DE POSTRE BR

88 Colour: bright straw. Nose: candied fruit, ripe fruit, lees reduction notes, floral, sweet spices. Palate: powerful, flavourful, creamy, easy to drink.

CASTELL SANT ANTONI PRIMVS PRIMVM BR

85 Colour: coppery red. Nose: raspberry, powerfull, fine lees, floral. Palate: good acidity, powerful, flavourful, fruity, easy to drink.

CASTELL SANT ANTONI GRAN RESERVA MAGNUM 2005 BN

93 Colour: bright straw. Nose: expressive, elegant, fine lees, dry nuts. Palate: balanced, fine bitter notes, good acidity, fine bead.

CASTELL SANT ANTONI GRAN RESERVA 2005 BN

91 Colour: bright yellow. Nose: dry nuts, lees reduction notes, fragrant herbs, pattiserie. Palate: powerful, flavourful, spicy, long.

CASTELL SANT ANTONI TORRE DE L'HOMENATGE 2003 BN

93 Colour: bright golden. Nose: fine lees, dry nuts, fragrant herbs, complex, ripe fruit. Palate: powerful, flavourful, good acidity, fine bead, fine bitter notes.

CASTELL SANT ANTONI TORRE DE L'HOMENATGE 1999 BN GRAN RESERVA

94 Colour: bright golden. Nose: dry nuts, fragrant herbs, complex, lees reduction notes, candied fruit. Palate: powerful, flavourful, good acidity, fine bead, fine bitter notes.

CASTELL SANT ANTONI GRAN BARRICA BN GRAN RESERVA

91 Colour: bright golden. Nose: fine lees, dry nuts, fragrant herbs, complex, spicy. Palate: powerful, flavourful, good acidity, fine bead, fine bitter notes.

CASTELL SANT ANTONI 37.5 BRUT NATURE BN

91 Colour: bright straw. Nose: medium intensity, dried herbs, fine lees, floral, candied fruit, sweet spices, toasty. Palate: fresh, good acidity, flavourful, long.

CASTELL SANT ANTONI CAMÍ DEL SOT MAGNUM BN RESERVA

91 Colour: bright straw. Nose: fresh fruit, dried herbs, fine lees, floral, characterful. Palate: fresh, fruity, flavourful, good acidity.

CASTELL SANT ANTONI CAMÍ DEL SOT BN RESERVA

91 Colour: bright straw. Nose: dried herbs, fine lees, floral, candied fruit. Palate: fresh, fruity, flavourful, good acidity.

CASTELL SANT ANTONI PRIMVS PRIMVM BN RESERVA

87 Colour: bright straw. Nose: medium intensity, fresh fruit, dried herbs, fine lees, floral. Palate: fresh, fruity, flavourful, good acidity.

CASTELL SANT ANTONI GRAN ROSAT PINOT NOIR BN

87 Colour: raspberry rose. Nose: ripe fruit, fine lees, floral, red berry notes. Palate: good acidity, powerful, flavourful, fresh.

CASTELL SANT ANTONI CAMÍ DEL SOT 37.5 BN

87 Colour: bright straw. Nose: medium intensity, ripe fruit, lees reduction notes, dry nuts. Palate: fine bitter notes, good acidity, fine bead.

CASTELLBLANCH

Avda. Casetes Mir, 2
08770 Sant Sadurní D'Anoia (Barcelona)
☎: +34 938 917 025 - Fax: +34 938 910 126
castellblanch@castellblanch.es
www.castellblanch.es

CASTELLBLANCH DUO MACABEO XAREL-LO 2010 BR
50% macabeo, 50% xarel.lo.

87 Colour: bright straw. Nose: medium intensity, dried herbs, fine lees, floral, candied fruit. Palate: fresh, fruity, flavourful.

CASTELLBLANCH BRUT ZERO 2008 BR RESERVA
60% parellada, 30% macabeo, 10% xarel.lo.

89 Colour: bright straw. Nose: powerfull, ripe fruit, sweet spices. Palate: flavourful, powerful, fine bitter notes.

CASTELLBLANCH GRAN CUVEÉ 2008 BN RESERVA
40% parellada, 30% macabeo, 30% xarel.lo.

90 Colour: bright straw. Nose: medium intensity, dried herbs, fine lees, floral, toasty. Palate: fresh, fruity, flavourful, good acidity.

CASTELLBLANCH DOS LUSTROS 2008 BN RESERVA
40% parellada, 40% macabeo, 20% xarel.lo.

88 Colour: bright straw. Nose: medium intensity, fresh fruit, dried herbs, fine lees, ripe fruit. Palate: fresh, fruity, flavourful, good acidity.

CASTELLROIG - FINCA SABATÉ I COCA

Ctra. Sant Sadurní d'Anoia a Vilafranca del Penedès, Km. 1
08739 Subirats (Barcelona)
☎: +34 938 911 927 - Fax: +34 938 914 055
info@castellroig.com
www.castellroig.com

CASTELLROIG ROSAT 2010 BR
trepat.

86 Colour: light cherry, bright. Nose: floral, fragrant herbs, fine lees. Palate: flavourful, fruity, good acidity, correct.

CASTELLROIG 2010 BN
xarel.lo, macabeo, parellada.

87 Colour: yellow, greenish rim. Nose: balanced, dried flowers, fragrant herbs. Palate: good acidity, correct.

CASTELLROIG 2009 BN RESERVA
xarel.lo, macabeo, parellada.

89 Colour: bright yellow. Nose: fresh fruit, dried herbs, fine lees, floral. Palate: fresh, fruity, flavourful, fine bead, fine bitter notes.

CASTELLROIG 2008 BN GRAN RESERVA
xarel.lo, macabeo.

87 Colour: bright yellow. Nose: fresh fruit, balanced, fine lees, floral. Palate: flavourful, fruity, good acidity.

CASTILLO PERELADA VINOS Y CAVAS

Avda. Barcelona, 78
08720 Vilafranca del Penedès (Barcelona)
☎: +34 938 180 676 - Fax: +34 938 180 926
perelada@castilloperalada.com
www.castilloperelada.com

CASTILLO PERELADA CUVÉE ESPECIAL ROSADO 2009 BR
trepat.

87 Colour: salmon. Nose: red berry notes, ripe fruit, dried flowers, fine lees, fresh. Palate: good acidity, fine bitter notes, powerful, flavourful.

CASTILLO PERELADA BR RESERVA
macabeo, xarel.lo, parellada.

87 Colour: bright straw. Nose: dried herbs, fine lees, floral, citrus fruit. Palate: flavourful, good acidity, fine bead, easy to drink.

TORRE GALATEA BR
pinot noir, trepat, monastrell.

87 Colour: rose. Nose: floral, rose petals, red berry notes, raspberry, powerfull. Palate: good acidity, powerful, flavourful, fruity.

CASTILLO PERELADA CUVÉE ESPECIAL 2009 BN
macabeo, parellada, xarel.lo, chardonnay.

90 Colour: bright yellow. Nose: white flowers, fresh fruit, fragrant herbs. Palate: correct, fine bitter notes, flavourful, easy to drink.

GRAN CLAUSTRO DE CASTILLO PERELADA 2009 BN RESERVA
chardonnay, pinot noir, parellada.

89 Colour: bright yellow. Nose: ripe fruit, lees reduction notes, fragrant herbs, pattiserie. Palate: powerful, flavourful, balanced.

CASTILLO PERELADA 2009 BN
parellada, xarel.lo, macabeo.

87 Colour: bright yellow. Nose: ripe fruit, fine lees, dried herbs, fresh. Palate: light-bodied, flavourful, fresh, easy to drink.

CASTILLO PERELADA CHARDONNAY 2009 BN
chardonnay.

86 Colour: bright straw. Nose: medium intensity, fresh fruit, dried herbs, fine lees, floral. Palate: fresh, fruity, flavourful.

GRAN CLAUSTRO CUVÉE ESPECIAL DE CASTILLO PERELADA 2007 BN GRAN RESERVA
chardonnay, pinot noir, parellada.

90 Colour: bright golden. Nose: white flowers, ripe fruit, dry nuts, fragrant herbs, pattiserie. Palate: fine bitter notes, powerful, flavourful.

CASTILLO PERELADA BRUT ROSADO
trepat, monastrell, pinot noir.

85 Colour: rose. Nose: red berry notes, ripe fruit, floral, powerfull. Palate: fine bitter notes, fruity, flavourful, easy to drink.

CAVA BERDIÉ

Les Conilleres (La Conillera Gran)
08732 Castellví de la Marca (Barcelona)
☎: +34 902 800 229 - Fax: +34 938 919 735
info@cavaberdie.com
www.cavaberdie.com

BERDIÉ GRAN ANYADA 2004
macabeo, xarel.lo, parellada.

87 Colour: bright golden. Nose: candied fruit, balanced, faded flowers, fine lees. Palate: good structure, ripe fruit, toasty.

BERDIÉ AMOR 2009 BR RESERVA
macabeo, xarel.lo, parellada, garnacha.

90 Colour: onion pink. Nose: floral, fruit expression, fragrant herbs. Palate: good acidity, balanced, flavourful, long.

BERDIÉ RUPESTRE 2009 BR RESERVA
macabeo, xarel.lo, parellada.

88 Colour: bright straw. Nose: medium intensity, fresh fruit, dried herbs, fine lees. Palate: fresh, fruity, good acidity.

BERDIÉ ROSA 2009 BR RESERVA
monastrell, garnacha.

86 Colour: rose. Nose: red berry notes, balanced, rose petals. Palate: fresh, fruity, easy to drink.

BERDIÉ NATURE 2009 BN RESERVA
macabeo, xarel.lo, parellada.

87 Colour: bright yellow. Nose: balanced, white flowers, fresh fruit. Palate: fruity, flavourful, good acidity.

BERDIÉ 2007 BN GRAN RESERVA
macabeo, xarel.lo, parellada.

89 Colour: bright straw. Nose: fine lees, fragrant herbs, ripe fruit. Palate: fine bead, fine bitter notes, correct, complex.

BERDIÉ GRAN RUPESTRE 2006 EXTRA BRUT GRAN RESERVA
macabeo, xarel.lo, parellada.

87 Colour: bright golden. Nose: dry nuts, fragrant herbs, complex, toasty. Palate: powerful, flavourful, fine bead, fine bitter notes.

BERDIÉ GRAN ANYADA 2005 EXTRA BRUT GRAN RESERVA
macabeo, xarel.lo, parellada.

89 Colour: bright golden. Nose: fine lees, dry nuts, fragrant herbs, complex. Palate: powerful, flavourful, good acidity, fine bead, fine bitter notes.

CAVA CONDE DE VALICOURT

Sant Antoni, 33-35
08770 Sant Sadurní D'Anoia (Barcelona)
☎: +34 938 910 036
cavas@condedevalicourt.com
www.condedevalicourt.com

ROSÉ DE VALICOURT 2010 BR RESERVA
100% garnacha.

80

COUPAGE DE ALICIA 2009 BR RESERVA
40% parellada, 30% macabeo, 30% xarel.lo.

87 Colour: bright straw. Nose: medium intensity, dried herbs, fine lees, floral, dry nuts. Palate: fresh, fruity, flavourful, good acidity.

PERMONT'S 2010 BN
40% macabeo, 40% xarel.lo, 20% parellada.

85 Colour: bright straw. Nose: medium intensity, dried herbs, fine lees, floral, candied fruit. Palate: fresh, fruity, flavourful, good acidity.

COUPAGE DE ALICIA 2008 BN GRAN RESERVA
40% parellada, 30% macabeo, 30% xarel.lo.

85 Colour: bright yellow. Nose: medium intensity, dried herbs, faded flowers. Palate: flavourful, powerful, correct.

GRAND PAS DE SUCRE MAGNUM 2007 BN GRAN RESERVA
40% parellada, 30% macabeo, 30% xarel.lo.

88 Colour: bright straw. Nose: balanced, fresh, dried flowers, neat. Palate: correct, good acidity, fine bitter notes.

MAJESTUOSO 2007 BN GRAN RESERVA
40% macabeo, 40% xarel.lo, 20% parellada.

87 Colour: bright yellow. Nosc: floral, dried herbs, fine lees, expressive. Palate: fine bitter notes, correct, flavourful.

PAS DE SUCRE 2007 BN GRAN RESERVA
40% parellada, 30% macabeo, 30% xarel.lo.

86 Colour: bright golden. Nose: ripe fruit, dried herbs, dry nuts. Palate: flavourful, long, fine bitter notes.

CAVA CRISTINA COLOMER BERNAT

Diputació, 58-60
08770 Sant Sadurní D'Anoia (Barcelona)
☎: +34 938 910 804 - Fax: +34 938 913 034
ccolomer@cavescolomer.com
www.cavescolomer.com

COLOMER HOMENATGE A GAUDÍ PINOT NOIR ROSÉ 2010 BR RESERVA
100% pinot noir.

86 Colour: brilliant rose. Nose: ripe fruit, red berry notes, powerfull. Palate: flavourful, good structure, full, long, good acidity.

COLOMER GRAN RESERVA D'AUTOR 2008 BR
xarel.lo, chardonnay, macabeo, pinot noir, parellada.

88 Colour: bright golden. Nose: fine lees, dry nuts, fragrant herbs, complex. Palate: powerful, flavourful, good acidity, fine bead, fine bitter notes.

COLOMER COSTA 2010 BN RESERVA
xarel.lo, macabeo, parellada.

90 Colour: bright straw. Nose: medium intensity, fresh fruit, dried herbs, fine lees. Palate: fresh, fruity, flavourful, good acidity.

COLOMER COSTA MAGNUM 2009 BN RESERVA
xarel.lo, macabeo, parellada.

88 Colour: bright straw. Nose: neat, dry nuts, balanced. Palate: flavourful, fresh, good acidity, fine bitter notes.

COLOMER PRESTIGE 2008 BN GRAN RESERVA
xarel.lo, chardonnay, macabeo, pinot noir, parellada.

91 Colour: bright yellow. Nose: dry nuts, white flowers, dried herbs, expressive. Palate: complex, powerful, flavourful.

COLOMER "ER" MAGNUM 2008 BN GRAN RESERVA
xarel.lo, chardonnay, macabeo, pinot noir, parellada.

89 Colour: bright yellow. Nose: fresh fruit, citrus fruit, dry nuts, balanced, fresh. Palate: balanced, good acidity, fine bitter notes.

CAVA JOSEP M. FERRET GUASCH

Barri L'Alzinar, 68
08739 Font-Rubí (Barcelona)
☎: +34 938 979 037 - Fax: +34 938 979 414
ferretguasch@ferretguasch.com
www.ferretguasch.com

JOSEP M. FERRET GUASCH 2008 BN RESERVA
10% macabeo, 60% xarel.lo, 30% parellada.

88 Colour: bright yellow. Nose: ripe fruit, white flowers, balanced. Palate: flavourful, fruity, good acidity.

FERRET GUASCH COUPAGE SARA 2004 BN GRAN RESERVA
10% macabeo, 50% xarel.lo, 20% parellada, 20% chardonnay.

90 Colour: bright yellow. Nose: fine lees, dry nuts, fragrant herbs. Palate: powerful, flavourful, good acidity, fine bead, fine bitter notes.

JOSEP M. FERRET GUASCH 2004 BN GRAN RESERVA
20% macabeo, 60% xarel.lo, 20% parellada.

89 Colour: bright yellow. Nose: fine lees, dry nuts, fragrant herbs, complex. Palate: powerful, flavourful, good acidity, fine bead, fine bitter notes.

CAVA M. BOSCH

Ctra. San Martí Sarroca s/n
08737 Torroella de Foix (Barcelona)
☎: +34 938 405 488 - Fax: +34 938 403 026
info@grupombosch.com
www.cavesmbosch.com

M. BOSCH RESERVA FAMILIAR BN RESERVA
macabeo, xarel.lo, parellada.

84

CAVA MARÍA CASANOVAS

Montserrat, 117
08770 Sant Sadurní D'Anoia (Barcelona)
☎: +34 938 910 812 - Fax: +34 938 911 572
mariacasanovas@brutnature.com
www.mariacasanovas.com

MARÍA CASANOVAS GLAÇ 2010 BN
pinot noir, xarel.lo, macabeo, parellada.

87 Colour: bright straw. Nose: citrus fruit, candied fruit, dried herbs, faded flowers. Palate: fresh, fruity, balsamic.

MARÍA CASANOVAS 2009 BN GRAN RESERVA
chardonnay, pinot noir, xarel.lo, macabeo, parellada.

91 Colour: bright golden. Nose: fine lees, dry nuts, fragrant herbs, complex. Palate: powerful, flavourful, good acidity, fine bead, fine bitter notes.

CAVA OLIVÉ BATLLORI

Barri Els Casots
08739 Subirats (Barcelona)
☎: +34 938 993 103
info@olivebatllori.com
www.olivebatllori.com

OLIVE BATLLORI 2009 BR
macabeo, xarel.lo, parellada.

83

GRAN BRUT OLIVE BATLLORI 2009 BN
xarel.lo, macabeo, parellada, pinot noir, chardonnay.

88 Colour: bright straw. Nose: white flowers, fine lees, citrus fruit, ripe fruit. Palate: balanced, fresh, fruity, flavourful.

OLIVE BATLLORI 2009 BN
macabeo, xarel.lo, parellada.

84

CAVA REVERTÉ

Paseo Tomás García Rebull, 4
43885 Salomó (Tarragona)
☎: +34 630 929 380 - Fax: +34 977 629 246
enricreverte@terra.es
www.cavareverte.com

CAVA REVERTÉ 2009 BN
60% xarel.lo, 20% macabeo, 20% parellada.

87 Colour: bright straw. Nose: fresh fruit, dried herbs, fine lees, floral. Palate: fresh, fruity, flavourful, good acidity.

CAVA REVERTÉ "ELECTE" 2008 BN
40% xarel.lo, 20% macabeo, 20% parellada, 20% chardonnay.

90 Colour: bright yellow. Nose: fine lees, floral, citrus fruit, dried herbs, expressive. Palate: good acidity, fine bead, fine bitter notes, flavourful.

CAVA VIDAL I FERRÉ

Nou, 2
43815 Les Pobles (Tarragona)
☎: +34 977 638 554 - Fax: +34 977 638 554
vidaliferre@vidaliferre.com
www.vidaliferre.com

VIDAL I FERRÉ BR RESERVA
macabeo, xarel.lo, parellada.

89 Colour: bright straw, greenish rim. Nose: balanced, medium intensity, fine lees, dried flowers. Palate: flavourful, good acidity, fine bitter notes.

VIDAL I FERRÉ BN GRAN RESERVA
xarel.lo, parellada, macabeo.

91 Colour: bright golden. Nose: dried flowers, dry nuts, fragrant herbs, fine lees. Palate: powerful, flavourful, balanced, fine bitter notes.

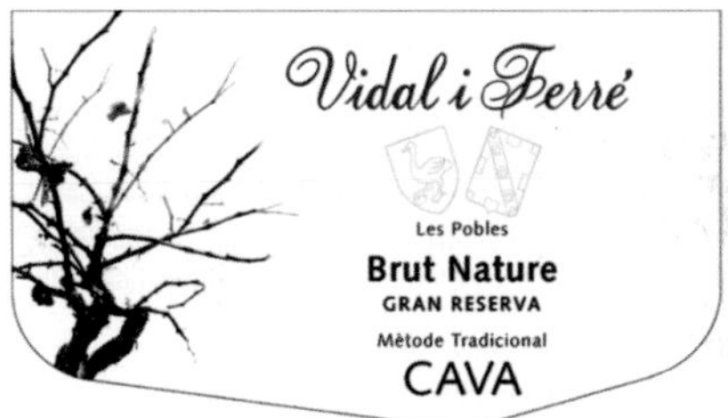

VIDAL I FERRÉ BN RESERVA
macabeo, xarel.lo, parellada.

85 Colour: bright yellow. Nose: powerfull, ripe fruit, dried herbs. Palate: good acidity, fine bitter notes, flavourful.

VIDAL I FERRÉ SS
macabeo, xarel.lo, parellada.

87 Colour: bright straw. Nose: white flowers, fresh fruit, neat, fresh. Palate: powerful, flavourful, fresh, easy to drink.

CAVA XAMÓS

Can Tutusaus, 51
08738 Pontons (Barcelona)
☎: +34 932 451 842
xamos@xamos.net
www.xamos.net

CAVA XAMÓS ELEGANT 2007 BN RESERVA
parellada, macabeo, xarel.lo, chardonnay.

86 Colour: bright straw. Nose: medium intensity, fresh fruit, dried herbs, fine lees, floral. Palate: fresh, fruity, flavourful, good acidity.

CAVAS BERTHA

Lavernó, 14
08770 Sant Sadurní D'Anoia (Barcelona)
☎: +34 938 911 091
cavabertha@cavabertha.com
www.cavabertha.com

BERTHA MAX GRAN RESERVA
macabeo, xarel.lo, parellada, chardonnay, pinot noir.

88 Colour: bright golden. Nose: lees reduction notes, faded flowers, dry nuts, sweet spices. Palate: good acidity, fine bitter notes.

BERTHA BRUT 1989 BR
macabeo, xarel.lo, parellada.

87 Colour: bright straw. Nose: fresh fruit, dried herbs, fine lees, floral, citrus fruit. Palate: fresh, fruity, flavourful, good acidity.

BERTHA LOUNGE BR
macabeo, xarel.lo, parellada.

84

BERTHA 2009 BN RESERVA
macabeo, xarel.lo, parellada.

84

BERTHA 2007 BN GRAN RESERVA
macabeo, xarel.lo, parellada.

84

BERTHA SEGLE XXI BN GRAN RESERVA
macabeo, xarel.lo, parellada, chardonnay.

90 Colour: bright yellow. Nose: fine lees, dry nuts, fragrant herbs, complex. Palate: powerful, flavourful, good acidity, fine bead, fine bitter notes.

BERTHA BRUT ROSADO RESERVA
pinot noir.

89 Colour: coppery red. Nose: lees reduction notes, faded flowers, candied fruit, expressive. Palate: powerful, flavourful, complex, fresh, fruity.

CAVAS BOHIGAS

Finca Can Maciá s/n
08711 Ódena (Barcelona)
☎: +34 938 048 100 - Fax: +34 938 032 366
comercial@bohigas.es
www.bohigas.es

BOHIGAS BR RESERVA
macabeo, xarel.lo, parellada.

87 Colour: bright straw. Nose: medium intensity, fresh fruit, dried herbs, fine lees, floral. Palate: fresh, fruity, flavourful, good acidity.

MAS MACIÀ BR
macabeo, xarel.lo, parellada.

80

NOA BN
pinot noir, xarel.lo.

90 Colour: bright yellow. Nose: fragrant herbs, fine lees, fresh fruit, expressive. Palate: fine bead, powerful, flavourful.

CAVAS BOLET

Finca Mas Lluet, s/n
08732 Castellvi de la Marca (Barcelona)
☎: +34 938 918 153
cavasbolet@cavasbolet.com
www.cavasbolet.com

BOLET PINOT NOIR 2007 RD RESERVA
pinot noir.

84

BOLET ECO 2008 BR RESERVA
macabeo, xarel.lo, parellada.

85 Colour: bright straw. Nose: medium intensity, fresh fruit, fine lees, floral. Palate: fresh, fruity, flavourful.

CAN PLANES D'EN PERULL 2008 BN RESERVA
macabeo, xarel.lo, parellada.

87 Colour: bright golden. Nose: dry nuts, fragrant herbs, lees reduction notes, pattiserie. Palate: powerful, flavourful, fine bitter notes.

BOLET ECO 2008 BN RESERVA
macabeo, xarel.lo, parellada.

85 Colour: bright golden. Nose: ripe fruit, lees reduction notes, powerfull, sweet spices. Palate: good acidity, fine bitter notes, flavourful.

BOLET SELECCIÓN FAMILIAR 2002 BN RESERVA
macabeo, xarel.lo, parellada.

79

BOLET ECO BN GRAN RESERVA
macabeo, xarel.lo, parellada.

84

CAVAS EL MAS FERRER

S. Sebastia, 25 C'al Avi
08739 Subirats (Barcelona)
☎: +34 938 988 292 - Fax: +34 938 988 545
info@elmasferrer.com
www.elmasferrer.com

EL MAS FERRER SEGLE XXI 2006 B GRAN RESERVA
32,5% macabeo, 35% xarel.lo, 32,5% parellada.

89 Colour: bright yellow. Nose: balanced, white flowers, elegant. Palate: balanced, correct, good acidity, fine bitter notes.

EL MAS FERRER 2010 BR
34% macabeo, 28% xarel.lo, 38% parellada.

89 Colour: bright straw. Nose: fresh fruit, white flowers, expressive. Palate: correct, fresh, good acidity, balanced.

EL MAS FERRER 2009 BR RESERVA
35% macabeo, 36% xarel.lo, 29% parellada.

88 Colour: bright yellow. Nose: candied fruit, white flowers, fragrant herbs. Palate: light-bodied, fresh, flavourful.

EL MAS FERRER 2008 BN RESERVA
34% macabeo, 35% xarel.lo, 31% parellada.

87 Colour: bright straw. Nose: medium intensity, fresh fruit, dried herbs, fine lees, faded flowers. Palate: fruity, flavourful, good acidity.

EL MAS FERRER FAMILIAR 2007 BN GRAN RESERVA
32% macabeo, 35% xarel.lo, 33% parellada.

89 Colour: bright yellow. Nose: ripe fruit, faded flowers, dried herbs. Palate: complex, powerful, flavourful, balanced.

CAVAS FERRET

Avda. de Catalunya, 36
08736 Guardiola de Font-Rubí (Barcelona)
☎: +34 938 979 148 - Fax: +34 938 979 285
ferret@cavasferret.com
www.cavasferret.com

FERRET BR RESERVA
40% macabeo, 40% parellada, 20% xarel.lo.

90 Colour: bright straw. Nose: fresh fruit, dried herbs, fine lees, floral. Palate: fresh, fruity, flavourful, good acidity, fine bead.

FERRET ROSADO BR RESERVA
60% trepat, 20% garnacha, 20% monastrell.

89 Colour: light cherry. Nose: red berry notes, floral, balanced, medium intensity. Palate: good acidity, balanced.

FERRET 2007 BN GRAN RESERVA
macabeo, xarel.lo, parellada.

90 Colour: bright yellow. Nose: candied fruit, white flowers, fragrant herbs. Palate: fine bitter notes, powerful, flavourful.

FERRET BARRICA 2005 BN GRAN RESERVA
40% xarel.lo, 35% parellada, 25% macabeo.

89 Colour: bright golden. Nose: fragrant herbs, lees reduction notes, fruit preserve. Palate: powerful, flavourful, good acidity, fine bitter notes.

CELIA DE FERRET ROSADO 2003 BN GRAN RESERVA
80% pinot noir, 20% garnacha.

88 Colour: rose. Nose: lactic notes, red berry notes, floral, fresh, expressive. Palate: fresh, fruity, light-bodied, flavourful, easy to drink.

EZEQUIEL FERRET 2003 BN GRAN RESERVA
50% xarel.lo, 30% parellada, 20% macabeo.

85 Colour: bright yellow. Nose: faded flowers, sweet spices, dried herbs. Palate: slightly evolved, flavourful, rich.

FERRET BN RESERVA
40% macabeo, 40% parellada, 20% xarel.lo.

89 Colour: bright straw. Nose: medium intensity, fresh fruit, dried herbs, fine lees, floral. Palate: fresh, fruity, flavourful, good acidity.

CAVAS HILL

Bonavista, 2
08734 Moja (Olérdola) (Barcelona)
☎: +34 938 900 588 - Fax: +34 938 170 246
cavashill@cavashill.com
www.cavashill.com

CAVA 1887 BR
35% macabeo, 50% xarel.lo, 15% parellada.

85 Colour: bright straw. Nose: medium intensity, dried herbs, dry nuts, faded flowers. Palate: fruity, good acidity.

BRUTÍSIMO 2007 BN GRAN RESERVA
40% xarel.lo, 20% macabeo, 10% parellada, 30% chardonnay.

88 Colour: bright yellow. Nose: medium intensity, fresh fruit, dried herbs, fine lees, floral. Palate: fresh, fruity, flavourful, good acidity, fine bitter notes.

CAVAS HILL BRUT DE BRUT ARTESANÍA BN RESERVA
25% macabeo, 40% xarel.lo, 10% chardonnay, 25% parellada.

86 Colour: bright yellow. Nose: fresh fruit, pattiserie, floral, fine lees. Palate: powerful, flavourful, fine bitter notes.

CAVAS HILL ARTESANÍA BN
50% xarel.lo, 35% macabeo, 15% parellada.

85 Colour: bright straw. Nose: medium intensity, fresh fruit, dried herbs, fine lees. Palate: fresh, fruity, flavourful, good acidity.

CAVAS LAVERNOYA

Finca La Porxada
08729 Sant Marçal (Barcelona)
☎: +34 938 912 202 - Fax: +34 938 919 948
lavernoya@lavernoya.com
www.lavernoya.com

LÁCRIMA BACCUS HERETAT BR

88 Colour: bright yellow. Nose: white flowers, fragrant herbs, fine lees, spicy. Palate: powerful, flavourful, long, balanced, good acidity.

LÁCRIMA BACCUS PRIMERÍSIMO BR GRAN RESERVA

87 Colour: bright golden. Nose: ripe fruit, lees reduction notes, pattiserie, sweet spices. Palate: powerful, flavourful, long, fine bitter notes.

LÁCRIMA BACCUS BR

86 Colour: bright golden. Nose: lees reduction notes, ripe fruit, faded flowers, pattiserie. Palate: flavourful, ripe fruit, thin.

LÁCRIMA BACCUS SUMMUM BN GRAN RESERVA

90 Colour: bright golden. Nose: white flowers, fragrant herbs, pattiserie, dry nuts. Palate: powerful, flavourful, good acidity, fine bead.

LÁCRIMA BACCUS BN
xarel.lo, macabeo, parellada.

89 Colour: bright golden. Nose: faded flowers, dried herbs, ripe fruit, dry nuts. Palate: powerful, flavourful, long, fine bead.

LÁCRIMA BACCUS HERETAT BN

87 Colour: bright straw. Nose: fresh fruit, dried herbs, fine lees, floral. Palate: fresh, fruity, flavourful, good acidity.

CAVAS MESTRES

Plaça Ajuntament, 8
08770 Sant Sadurní D'Anoia (Barcelona)
☎: +34 938 910 043 - Fax: +34 938 911 611
cava@mestres.es
www.mestres.es

MESTRES CUPAGE ROSÉ 2008 BR RESERVA
50% trepat, 30% monastrell, 20% pinot noir.

87 Colour: rose. Nose: medium intensity, rose petals, red berry notes, elegant. Palate: fruity, good acidity, elegant, fine bitter notes.

MESTRES CUPAGE BARCELONA 2007 BR GRAN RESERVA
40% macabeo, 30% xarel.lo, 30% parellada.

91 Colour: bright golden. Nose: fine lees, dry nuts, fragrant herbs, complex. Palate: powerful, flavourful, good acidity, fine bead, fine bitter notes.

MESTRES CUPATGE PIT LANE 2007 BR GRAN RESERVA
40% xarel.lo, 35% macabeo, 25% parellada.

88 Colour: bright yellow. Nose: fine lees, dried flowers, ripe fruit. Palate: flavourful, good structure, ripe fruit, long, fine bitter notes.

MESTRES CUPAGE 50 AÑOS DE "CAVA" 2006 BR GRAN RESERVA
25% macabeo, 50% xarel.lo, 25% parellada.

91 Colour: bright yellow. Nose: dried flowers, fragrant herbs, complex, balanced. Palate: flavourful, full, ripe fruit, long.

MESTRES CUPAGE 80 ANIVERSARIO 2006 BR GRAN RESERVA
60% xarel.lo, 25% macabeo, 15% parellada.

90 Colour: bright straw, greenish rim. Nose: medium intensity, dried herbs, dried flowers, fine lees. Palate: flavourful, fruity, balanced, fine bitter notes.

MESTRES MAS VÍA 2000 BR GRAN RESERVA
75% xarel.lo, 15% macabeo, 10% parellada.

92 Colour: bright golden. Nose: fine lees, dry nuts, complex, petrol notes. Palate: powerful, flavourful, good acidity, fine bead, fine bitter notes.

MESTRES COQUET 2007 BN GRAN RESERVA
40% xarel.lo, 30% macabeo, 30% parellada.

89 Colour: bright yellow, greenish rim. Nose: elegant, balanced, dried flowers, fine lees. Palate: flavourful, fruity, good acidity.

ELENA DE MESTRES ROSADO 2007 BN GRAN RESERVA
60% trepat, 40% monastrell.

85 Colour: rose. Nose: medium intensity, dried herbs, red berry notes, balanced. Palate: fruity, flavourful.

MESTRES VISOL 2006 BN GRAN RESERVA
40% xarel.lo, 35% macabeo, 25% parellada.

90 Nose: fine lees, dry nuts, fragrant herbs, complex. Palate: powerful, flavourful, good acidity, fine bead, fine bitter notes.

MESTRE CLOS NOSTRE SENYOR 2002 BN GRAN RESERVA
60% xarel.lo, 20% macabeo, 20% parellada.

91 Colour: bright yellow. Nose: sweet spices, dark chocolate, ripe fruit, fine lees, complex. Palate: good structure, ripe fruit, fine bitter notes.

CAVES CONDE DE CARALT

Ctra. Sant Sadurní-Sant Pere de Riudebitlles, Km. 5
08775 Torrelavit (Barcelona)
☎: +34 938 917 070 - Fax: +34 938 996 006
condedecaralt@condedecaralt.com
www.condedecaralt.com

CONDE DE CARALT BLANC DE BLANCS BR
60% macabeo, 20% xarel.lo, 20% parellada.

90 Colour: bright straw. Nose: white flowers, dried herbs, expressive, fine lees, elegant. Palate: powerful, flavourful, full, long, balanced.

CONDE DE CARALT BR
50% macabeo, 30% parellada, 20% xarel.lo.

87 Colour: bright straw. Nose: dried flowers, candied fruit, fragrant herbs. Palate: light-bodied, fresh, fruity, flavourful, easy to drink.

CAVES MONASTELL

Girona, 30
08770 Sant Sadurní D'Anoia (Barcelona)
☎: +34 938 910 396 - Fax: +34 938 911 070
ferrangirones@terra.es
www.cavesmonastell.com

TERCERA DINASTÍA 2007 BR
xarel.lo, macabeo, parellada, chardonnay.

88 Colour: bright straw. Nose: medium intensity, fine lees, dry nuts, dried flowers. Palate: fresh, fruity, flavourful, good acidity.

MONTSANT ARTESA 2010 BN
macabeo, xarel.lo, parellada.

87 Colour: bright straw. Nose: medium intensity, fresh fruit, dried herbs, fine lees, floral. Palate: fresh, fruity, flavourful, good acidity.

MONASTELL 2009 BN RESERVA
xarel.lo, macabeo.

86 Colour: bright straw, greenish rim. Nose: fresh, medium intensity, faded flowers. Palate: fresh, easy to drink.

ROCA GIBERT 2009 BN RESERVA
macabeo, xarel.lo, parellada.

84

CAVES NAVERÁN

Can Parellada - Sant Martí Sadevesa
08775 Torrelavit (Barcelona)
☎: +34 938 988 400 - Fax: +34 938 989 027
sadeve@naveran.com
www.naveran.com

NAVERÁN PERLES ROSES PINOT NOIR 2010 RD
pinot noir.

91 Colour: ochre. Nose: fine lees, fragrant herbs, wild herbs, fresh fruit, expressive. Palate: correct, powerful, flavourful, complex.

NAVERAN PERLES BLANQUES 2009 BR
pinot noir, chardonnay.

92 Colour: bright yellow. Nose: expressive, complex, ripe fruit, white flowers, elegant. Palate: fruity, full, long, good acidity, fine bitter notes.

ODISEA NAVERÁN 2010 BN

91 Colour: bright straw. Nose: fresh fruit, dried herbs, fine lees, white flowers. Palate: fresh, fruity, flavourful, good acidity, fine bead, balanced.

CELLER CAN PUJOL

Duc de la Victoria, 9
08800 Vilanova i la Geltrú (Barcelona)
☎: +34 938 931 535 - Fax: +34 938 143 063
botiga@cellercanpujol.com
www.cellercanpujol.com

TORRENTS & CARBÓ CORREFOC 2007 BN
50% xarel.lo, 30% macabeo, 20% parellada.

89 Colour: bright yellow. Nose: fresh fruit, dried herbs, fine lees, white flowers. Palate: fresh, fruity, flavourful, good acidity.

TORRENTS & CARBÓ VIVACE 2005 BN RESERVA
60% xarel.lo, 20% macabeo, 20% parellada.

86 Colour: bright straw. Nose: medium intensity, dried herbs, fine lees, floral, ripe fruit. Palate: flavourful, good acidity.

CELLER CARLES ANDREU

Sant Sebastià, 19
43423 Pira (Tarragona)
☎: +34 977 887 404 - Fax: +34 977 887 427
celler@cavandreu.com
www.cavandreu.com

CAVA ROSADO TREPAT BRUT CARLES ANDREU 2010
100% trepat.

87 Colour: raspberry rose. Nose: fine lees, floral, raspberry, red berry notes. Palate: correct, good acidity, light-bodied, easy to drink.

CAVA RESERVA BARRICA BRUT NATURE CARLES ANDREU 2009
parellada, macabeo, chardonnay.

90 Colour: bright yellow. Nose: faded flowers, ripe fruit, toasty, creamy oak. Palate: flavourful, powerful, toasty, roasted-coffee afterpalate:.

CAVA BRUT CARLES ANDREU 2010 BR
parellada, macabeo.

89 Colour: bright yellow. Nose: white flowers, dried herbs, fresh, expressive. Palate: good acidity, fine bitter notes, flavourful, complex.

CAVA BRUT NATURE CARLES ANDREU 2010 BN
parellada, macabeo.

89 Colour: bright straw. Nose: medium intensity, fresh fruit, dried herbs, fine lees, floral. Palate: fresh, fruity, flavourful, good acidity.

CAVA RESERVA BRUT NATURE CARLES ANDREU 2009 BN
parellada, macabeo, chardonnay.

88 Colour: bright straw. Nose: fine lees, white flowers, fragrant herbs, expressive. Palate: balanced, fine bitter notes, powerful, flavourful.

CELLER COOPERATIU D'ARTÉS SCCL - CAVES ARTIUM

Cr. Rocafort, 44
08271 Artés (Barcelona)
☎: +34 938 305 325 - Fax: +34 938 306 289
artium@cavesartium.com
www.cavesartium.com

LLUÍS GUITART 2011 BR
40% macabeo, 40% xarel.lo, 20% parellada.

83

ARTIUM ROSAT 2010 BR RESERVA
100% trepat.

87 Colour: light cherry. Nose: balanced, red berry notes, dried herbs. Palate: flavourful, easy to drink, correct, good acidity.

ARTIUM 2010 BR RESERVA
50% macabeo, 30% xarel.lo, 20% parellada.

86 Colour: bright yellow, greenish rim. Nose: balanced, medium intensity, dried herbs, dried flowers. Palate: correct, fine bitter notes, good acidity.

ARTIUM BR GRAN RESERVA
macabeo, xarel.lo, parellada.

84

ARTIUM 2010 BN RESERVA
50% macabeo, 30% xarel.lo, 20% parellada.

87 Colour: bright yellow. Nose: dried flowers, fragrant herbs, medium intensity. Palate: correct, good acidity, fine bitter notes.

CELLER JORDI LLUCH

Barrio Les Casetes, s/n
08777 Sant Quinti de Mediona (Barcelona)
☎: +34 938 988 138 - Fax: +34 938 988 138
vinyaescude@vinyaescude.com
www.vinyaescude.com

VINYA ESCUDÉ ROSAT PINOT NOIR BN
100% pinot noir.

82

VINYA ESCUDÉ 523 EXTRA BRUT RESERVA
40% macabeo, 20% xarel.lo, 40% parellada.

89 Colour: bright yellow. Nose: medium intensity, fresh fruit, dried herbs, fine lees, floral, citrus fruit. Palate: fresh, fruity, flavourful, good acidity, powerful.

CELLER MARIOL/CASA MARIOL

Rosselló, 442
08025 (Barcelona)
☎: +34 934 367 628 - Fax: +34 934 500 281
celler@cellermariol.es
www.casamariol.com

CASA MARIOL ROSADO 2009 BR RESERVA
100% trepat.

86 Colour: light cherry. Nose: balanced, red berry notes, ripe fruit, floral. Palate: flavourful, fruity, good acidity.

CASA MARIOL ARTESANAL 36 MESOS 2009 BR RESERVA
40% macabeo, 30% xarel.lo, 30% parellada.

85 Colour: bright yellow. Nose: ripe fruit, faded flowers, medium intensity. Palate: correct, good acidity.

CASA MARIOL ARTESANAL 2010 BN
40% macabeo, 40% xarel.lo, 20% parellada.

86 Colour: bright straw, greenish rim. Nose: medium intensity, wild herbs. Palate: easy to drink, good acidity.

CASA MARIOL 2008 BN RESERVA
macabeo, xarel.lo, parellada.

87 Colour: bright yellow, greenish rim. Nose: medium intensity, balanced, ripe fruit, dried flowers, dried herbs. Palate: flavourful, good acidity, fine bitter notes.

CASA MARIOL 2005 BN GRAN RESERVA
20% macabeo, 60% xarel.lo, 20% parellada.

87 Colour: bright golden. Nose: balanced, candied fruit, dry nuts, faded flowers, lees reduction notes. Palate: fruity, fine bitter notes.

CASA MARIOL ARTESANAL 18 MESOS 2010 SS
40% macabeo, 40% xarel.lo, 20% parellada.

80

CELLER VELL

Partida Mas Solanes, s/n
08770 Sant Sadurní D'Anoia (Barcelona)
☎: +34 938 910 290 - Fax: +34 938 183 246
info@cellervell.com
www.cellervell.com

CELLER VELL EXTRA BRUT 2008 GRAN RESERVA
chardonnay, xarel.lo, macabeo, parellada.

87 Colour: bright yellow. Nose: fragrant herbs, floral, pattiserie, fine lees. Palate: powerful, flavourful, balanced.

CELLER VELL 2008 BN RESERVA
xarel.lo, macabeo, parellada.

88 Nose: medium intensity, fresh fruit, dried herbs, fine lees, floral. Palate: fresh, fruity, flavourful, good acidity, light-bodied.

ESTRUCH NATURE CLASSIC 2007 BN RESERVA
chardonnay, pinot noir, xarel.lo, parellada, macabeo.

88 Colour: bright golden. Nose: faded flowers, lees reduction notes, sweet spices. Palate: long, correct, fine bitter notes.

CELLERS CAROL VALLÈS

Can Parellada, s/n - Corral del Mestre
08739 Subirats (Barcelona)
☎: +34 938 989 078 - Fax: +34 938 988 413
info@cellerscarol.com
www.cellerscarol.com

GUILLEM CAROL MILLENIUM 2003 BR GRAN RESERVA
35% parellada, 30% xarel.lo, 20% macabeo, 15% chardonnay.

86 Colour: bright golden. Nose: dry nuts, fragrant herbs, spicy, lees reduction notes. Palate: powerful, good acidity.

PARELLADA I FAURA 2009 BN RESERVA
40% parellada, 30% macabeo, 30% xarel.lo.

87 Colour: bright straw. Nose: medium intensity, fresh fruit, dried herbs, floral. Palate: fresh, fruity, flavourful.

GUILLEM CAROL PINOT NOIR ROSAT 2009 BN RESERVA
100% pinot noir.

80

PARELLADA I FAURA MILLENIUM 2008 BN RESERVA
40% macabeo, 30% parellada, 30% xarel.lo.

87 Colour: bright straw. Nose: medium intensity, fresh fruit, fine lees, floral. Palate: fresh, fruity, good acidity.

GUILLEM CAROL 2008 BN GRAN RESERVA
40% parellada, 40% xarel.lo, 20% chardonnay.

86 Colour: bright yellow. Nose: medium intensity, dried herbs, balanced, faded flowers. Palate: flavourful, fruity, good acidity.

GUILLEM CAROL CHARDONNAY PINOT NOIR 2008 BN RESERVA
60% chardonnay, 40% pinot noir.

84

GUILLEM CAROL 2008 EXTRA BRUT GRAN RESERVA
40% parellada, 40% xarel.lo, 20% chardonnay.

82

CELLERS PLANAS ALBAREDA

Ctra. Guardiola, Km. 3
08735 Vilobí del Penedès (Barcelona)
☎: +34 938 922 143 - Fax: +34 938 922 143
planasalbareda@yahoo.es
www.planas-albareda.com

PLANAS ALBAREDA ROSAT 2010 BR

84

PLANAS ALBAREDA 2009 BN
macabeo, xarel.lo, parellada.

83

PLANAS ALBAREDA RESERVA DE L'AVI 2008 BN RESERVA
macabeo, xarel.lo, parellada, chardonnay.

86 Colour: bright yellow. Nose: powerfull, dry nuts, faded flowers. Palate: flavourful, powerful, toasty.

PLANAS ALBAREDA 2008 BN RESERVA
macabeo, xarel.lo, parellada.

85 Colour: bright yellow. Nose: fresh, fresh fruit, fine lees, dried flowers. Palate: fresh, easy to drink, good acidity.

CELLERS VIVES GAU

Mas de la Basserola
43714 El Pla de Manlleu (Barcelona)
☎: +34 977 638 619 - Fax: +34 977 639 196
mas.basserola@sct.ictnet.es
www.mas.basserola.cat

MAS DE LA BASSEROLA BN
85% parellada, 15% macabeo.

84

CHOZAS CARRASCAL

Vereda San Antonio Pol. Ind. Catastral, 16 Parcelas 136-138
46340 San Antonio de Requena (Valencia)
☎: +34 963 410 395 - Fax: +34 963 168 067
chozas@chozascarrascal.es
www.chozascarrascal.es

EL CAVA DE CHOZAS CARRASCAL 2008 BN RESERVA
chardonnay, macabeo.

93 Colour: bright yellow. Nose: dry nuts, faded flowers, dried herbs, lees reduction notes. Palate: good acidity, fine bitter notes, correct.

CODORNÍU

Avda. Jaume Codorníu, s/n
08770 Sant Sadurní D'Anoia (Barcelona)
☎: +34 938 183 232 - Fax: +34 938 910 822
s.martin@codorniu.es
www.codorniu.com

REINA Mª CRISTINA BLANC DE NOIRS 2008 BR RESERVA
87% pinot noir, 13% chardonnay.

91 Colour: bright straw. Nose: medium intensity, floral, fresh. Palate: flavourful, fruity, complex, good acidity, fine bead, balanced.

JAUME CODORNÍU BR
chardonnay, pinot noir.

92 Colour: bright yellow. Nose: complex, balanced, ripe fruit, dried flowers, dried herbs. Palate: balanced, fine bitter notes, good acidity.

CODORNÍU PINOT NOIR BR ESPUMOSO
100% pinot noir.

89 Colour: light cherry, bright. Nose: medium intensity, dried herbs, fresh, fine lees, floral. Palate: correct, balanced, fine bitter notes.

ANNA DE CODORNÍU BR
70% chardonnay, 15% parellada, 15% xarel.lo, macabeo.

88 Colour: bright yellow. Nose: fresh fruit, white flowers, medium intensity. Palate: easy to drink, fresh, good acidity.

ANNA DE CODORNÍU BLANC DE NOIRS BR
100% pinot noir.

88 Colour: coppery red, pale. Nose: dried flowers, fragrant herbs, medium intensity, fresh. Palate: easy to drink, fruity, good acidity.

ANNA DE CODORNÍU ROSÉ BR
70% pinot noir, 30% chardonnay.

87 Colour: brilliant rose. Nose: fresh fruit, fragrant herbs, dry nuts. Palate: fruity, flavourful, good acidity, balanced.

GRAN PLUS ULTRA BN RESERVA
chardonnay, parellada.

91 Colour: bright yellow. Nose: white flowers, fresh fruit, fine lees, balanced. Palate: fruity, fine bitter notes, flavourful.

COVIDES VIÑEDOS BODEGAS

Rambla Nostra Senyora, 45 - 1er
08720 Vilafranca del Penedès (Barcelona)
☎: +34 938 172 552 - Fax: +34 938 171 798
covides@covides.com
www.covides.com

DUC DE FOIX BR RESERVA ESPECIAL
chardonnay, macabeo, xarel.lo, parellada.

88 Colour: bright yellow. Nose: medium intensity, fresh fruit, dried herbs, fine lees, floral. Palate: fresh, fruity, flavourful, good acidity.

DUC DE FOIX BN
macabeo, xarel.lo, parellada.

87 Colour: bright yellow. Nose: ripe fruit, lees reduction notes, fragrant herbs. Palate: correct, good acidity, flavourful.

CUM LAUDE

Sant Sadurni D'Anoia (Barcelona)
☎: +34 941 454 050 - Fax: +34 941 454 529
bodega@bodegasriojanas.com
www.bodegasriojanas.com

CUM LAUDE S/C ESP
40% xarel.lo, 30% macabeo, 30% parellada.

86 Colour: bright straw. Nose: fresh fruit, dried herbs, fine lees, floral. Palate: fresh, fruity, flavourful, good acidity, easy to drink.

DOMINIO DE LA VEGA

Ctra. Madrid - Valencia, Km. 270,6
46390 San Antonio. (Valencia)
☎: +34 962 320 570 - Fax: +34 962 320 330
info@dominiodelavega.com
www.dominiodelavega.com

DOMINIO DE LA VEGA RESERVA ESPECIAL BR RESERVA
macabeo, chardonnay.

90 Colour: bright golden. Nose: ripe fruit, faded flowers, dry nuts, expressive. Palate: fine bitter notes, good acidity, flavourful, long. Personality.

DOMINIO DE LA VEGA BR
macabeo.

86 Colour: bright yellow. Nose: white flowers, expressive, fragrant herbs. Palate: fresh, fruity, flavourful.

DOMINIO DE LA VEGA PINOT NOIR BR
pinot noir.

86 Colour: rose. Nose: red berry notes, floral, powerfull, medium intensity. Palate: flavourful, fresh, light-bodied.

ARTEMAYOR IV CAVA BN
chardonnay, macabeo.

91 Colour: bright yellow. Nose: faded flowers, sweet spices, toasty, fragrant herbs. Palate: powerful, flavourful, rich, good acidity.

DOMINIO DE LA VEGA BN RESERVA
macabeo, chardonnay.

89 Colour: bright golden. Nose: dried herbs, dry nuts, faded flowers, spicy. Palate: rich, flavourful, balanced.

DOMINIO DE LA VEGA BN
macabeo.

87 Colour: bright yellow. Nose: medium intensity, fresh, fragrant herbs. Palate: easy to drink, good acidity.

ELVIWINES

Finca "Clos Mesorah" Ctra. T-300 Falset Marça, Km. 1
43775 Marça Priorat (Tarragona)
☎: +34 935 343 026 - Fax: +34 936 750 316
moises@elviwines.com
www.elviwines.com

ADAR CAVA 2009 BR
parellada, macabeo, xarel.lo.

87 Colour: bright straw, greenish rim. Nose: medium intensity, fragrant herbs, fresh. Palate: fruity, easy to drink.

EMENDIS

Barrio de Sant Marçal, 67
08732 Castellet i La Gornal (Barcelona)
☎: +34 938 186 119 - Fax: +34 938 918 169
avalles@emendis.es
www.emendis.es

EMENDIS ROSÉ 2010
100% pinot noir.

86 Colour: rose. Nose: rose petals, red berry notes, ripe fruit. Palate: correct, rich, flavourful.

EMENDIS 2010 BR
50% xarel.lo, 25% macabeo, 25% parellada.

88 Colour: bright yellow. Nose: white flowers, fragrant herbs, fresh fruit. Palate: correct, flavourful, complex, fresh, fruity.

EMENDIS IMUM 2009 BN RESERVA
50% xarel.lo, 25% macabeo, 25% parellada.

91 Colour: bright straw. Nose: complex, floral, fragrant herbs, fresh fruit. Palate: powerful, flavourful, fresh, fruity, balanced.

EMENDIS 2007 BN GRAN RESERVA
xarel.lo, macabeo, parellada.

89 Colour: bright golden. Nose: fine lees, dry nuts, fragrant herbs, complex. Palate: powerful, flavourful, good acidity, fine bead, fine bitter notes.

EMENDIS IMUM MAGNUM BN RESERVA

88 Colour: bright yellow. Nose: dry nuts, candied fruit, toasty, sweet spices. Palate: flavourful, powerful, fine bitter notes, good acidity.

FERRE I CATASUS

Ctra. de Sant Sadurní, Km. 8- Masía Can Gustems
08792 La Granada (Barcelona)
☎: +34 938 974 558 - Fax: +34 938 974 708
maracalvo@ferreicatasus.com
www.castelldelmirall.com

FERRÉ I CATASÚS 2008 BR RESERVA
55% xarel.lo, 35% macabeo, 10% parellada.

88 Colour: bright golden. Nose: petrol notes, lees reduction notes, dry nuts, toasty. Palate: powerful, flavourful, complex, fine bead.

CAVA ROSÉ 2008 BR
100% pinot noir.

85 Colour: light cherry. Nose: red berry notes, ripe fruit, medium intensity. Palate: balanced, easy to drink.

MAS SUAU 2011 BN CRIANZA
55% macabeo, 35% xarel.lo, 10% parellada.

87 Colour: bright golden. Nose: faded flowers, ripe fruit, dry nuts. Palate: good acidity, rich, powerful.

FERRÉ I CATASÚS 2008 BN RESERVA
55% xarel.lo, 35% macabeo, 10% parellada.

91 Colour: bright golden. Nose: fine lees, dry nuts, fragrant herbs, complex, toasty. Palate: powerful, flavourful, good acidity, fine bead, fine bitter notes.

FERRÉ I CATASÚS CLÀSSIC BN RESERVA

89 Colour: bright yellow. Nose: faded flowers, lees reduction notes, dried herbs. Palate: good acidity, fine bitter notes, flavourful.

FINCA TORREMILANOS BODEGAS PEÑALBA LÓPEZ

Finca Torremilanos, s/n
09400 Aranda de Duero (Burgos)
☎: +34 947 510 377 - Fax: +34 947 512 856
torremilanos@torremilanos.com
www.torremilanos.com

PEÑALBA-LÓPEZ BN
90% viura, 10% chardonnay.

87 Colour: bright straw. Nose: dried herbs, fine lees, floral, citrus fruit. Palate: fresh, fruity, flavourful, balanced.

PEÑALBA-LÓPEZ ROSADO BN
50% garnacha, 50% pinot noir.

87 Colour: raspberry rose. Nose: medium intensity, dried flowers, fragrant herbs. Palate: fruity, flavourful, easy to drink.

FINCA VALLDOSERA

Masia Les Garrigues, Urb. Can Trabal s/n
08734 Olèrdola (Barcelona)
☎: +34 938 143 047 - Fax: +34 938 935 590
general@fincavalldosera.com
www.fincavalldosera.com

CAVA SUBIRAT PARENT 2009 BN
100% subirat parent.

91 Colour: bright straw. Nose: dried flowers, candied fruit, citrus fruit, fine lees. Palate: flavourful, fine bitter notes, good acidity.

CAVA VALLDOSERA 2008 BN
45% xarel.lo, 10% macabeo, 10% chardonnay, 5% subirat parent.

88 Colour: bright straw. Nose: medium intensity, fresh fruit, dried herbs, floral. Palate: fresh, fruity, flavourful.

MS 4.7 BN RESERVA

88 Colour: bright yellow. Nose: balanced, dry nuts, faded flowers, medium intensity. Palate: fresh, easy to drink.

FREIXA RIGAU

Santa Llucía, 15
17750 Capmany (Girona)
☎: +34 972 549 012 - Fax: +34 972 549 106
comercial@grupoliveda.com
www.grupoliveda.com

FAMILIA OLIVEDA ROSADO 2009
50% garnacha, 50% trepat.

83

FAMILIA OLIVEDA 2010 BR
50% macabeo, 30% xarel.lo, 20% parellada.

85 Colour: bright straw. Nose: fresh fruit, dried herbs, fine lees, floral. Palate: fresh, fruity, flavourful.

GRAN RIGAU BRUT DE BRUTS 2008 BR
40% xarel.lo, 30% macabeo, 30% parellada.

86 Colour: yellow, greenish rim. Nose: dry nuts, fine lees, dried flowers. Palate: spicy, ripe fruit, balanced.

GRAN RIGAU ROSADO 2008 BR RESERVA
100% pinot noir.

83

FREIXA RIGAU NATURE MIL.LÈSSIMA RESERVA FAMILIAR 2009 BN
40% macabeo, 30% xarel.lo, 30% parellada.

86 Colour: bright straw. Nose: medium intensity, dried herbs, macerated fruit. Palate: fruity, flavourful, good acidity.

FAMILIA OLIVEDA 2009 BN RESERVA
60% macabeo, 40% xarel.lo.

85 Colour: bright yellow. Nose: floral, dried herbs, medium intensity. Palate: flavourful, unctuous, correct.

GRAN RIGAU CHARDONNAY 2008 BN
100% chardonnay.

87 Colour: yellow, greenish rim. Nose: fragrant herbs, faded flowers, spicy. Palate: flavourful, good acidity.

FREIXENET

Joan Sala, 2
08770 Sant Sadurní D'Anoia (Barcelona)
☎: +34 938 917 000 - Fax: +34 938 183 095
freixenet@freixenet.es
www.freixenet.es

FREIXENET MALVASÍA 2001 B
malvasía.

86 Colour: bright golden. Nose: dry nuts, dried fruit, sweet spices, dried herbs. Palate: rich, flavourful, long.

TREPAT 2010 BR
trepat.

90 Colour: ochre. Nose: white flowers, fragrant herbs, fine lees, fresh fruit. Palate: powerful, flavourful, complex, balanced, long.

FREIXENET MONASTRELL XAREL.LO 2009 BR
monastrell, xarel.lo.

88 Colour: bright straw. Nose: fresh fruit, dried herbs, fine lees, floral. Palate: fresh, fruity, flavourful, good acidity.

MERITUM 2007 BR GRAN RESERVA
xarel.lo, macabeo, parellada.

92 Colour: bright yellow. Nose: dried flowers, dry nuts, fragrant herbs, balanced. Palate: elegant, flavourful, complex, long.

CUVÉE D.S. 2007 BR GRAN RESERVA
macabeo, parellada, xarel.lo.

89 Colour: bright golden. Nose: petrol notes, fine lees, dry nuts. Palate: good acidity, powerful, flavourful, complex, balanced.

RESERVA REAL BR RESERVA
macabeo, xarel.lo, parellada.

94 Colour: bright straw. Nose: fragrant herbs, white flowers, dried flowers, expressive. Palate: good acidity, fine bead.

BRUT BARROCO BR GRAN RESERVA
parellada, macabeo, xarel.lo.

91 Colour: bright yellow. Nose: ripe fruit, white flowers, dried herbs, fine lees. Palate: powerful, flavourful, rich, fine bitter notes.

ELYSSIA PINOT NOIR ROSÉ BR RESERVA
pinot noir.

89 Colour: light cherry. Nose: floral, red berry notes, ripe fruit, fine lees, dried herbs. Palate: fine bitter notes, flavourful, fruity.

ELYSSIA GRAN CUVÉE BR RESERVA
chardonnay, macabeo, parellada, pinot noir.

88 Colour: bright yellow. Nose: dried flowers, dried herbs, dry nuts, pattiserie. Palate: balanced, powerful, flavourful, long.

CORDÓN NEGRO BR RESERVA
parellada, macabeo, xarel.lo.

86 Colour: bright straw. Nose: medium intensity, dried herbs, fine lees. Palate: fresh, fruity, good acidity.

FREIXENET CARTA NEVADA BR RESERVA
macabeo, xarel.lo, parellada.

85 Colour: bright straw. Nose: fine lees, citrus fruit, dried herbs. Palate: fine bitter notes, fresh, lacks expression.

FREIXENET 2007 BN GRAN RESERVA
xarel.lo, macabeo, parellada.

88 Colour: bright golden. Nose: ripe fruit, fragrant herbs, pattiserie, faded flowers. Palate: fine bitter notes, powerful, flavourful.

GASTÓN COTY

Avernó, 28-30
08770 Sant Sadurní D'Anoia (Barcelona)
☎: +34 938 183 602 - Fax: +34 938 913 461
lorigan@lorigancava.com
www.lorigancava.com

AIRE DE L'O DE L'ORIGAN 2008 BN
50% macabeo, 30% xarel.lo, 10% parellada, 10% chardonnay.

90 Colour: bright straw. Nose: powerfull, ripe fruit, sweet spices, candied fruit. Palate: flavourful, good acidity, fine bitter notes.

L'ORIGAN 2007 BN
55% macabeo, 35% xarel.lo, 10% chardonnay.

89 Colour: bright straw. Nose: powerfull, characterful, fruit preserve. Palate: fine bitter notes, good acidity, spicy.

L'ORIGAN ROSAT 2007 BN
85% pinot noir, 15% chardonnay.

88 Colour: coppery red. Nose: candied fruit, red berry notes, expressive. Palate: good acidity, fine bead, fine bitter notes.

L'ORIGAN MAGNUM 2005 BN
30% xarel.lo, 40% macabeo, 20% chardonnay, 10% parellada.

93 Colour: bright golden. Nose: fine lees, dry nuts, fragrant herbs, complex. Palate: powerful, flavourful, good acidity, fine bead, fine bitter notes.

GIRÓ DEL GORNER

Finca Giró del Gorner, s/n
08797 Puigdálber (Barcelona)
☎: +34 938 988 032
gorner@girodelgorner.com
www.girodelgorner.com

GORNER 2008 BR RESERVA
macabeo, xarel.lo, parellada.

88 Colour: bright yellow. Nose: medium intensity, dry nuts, dried flowers, fine lees. Palate: fruity, easy to drink, fresh.

GORNER 2007 BN RESERVA
macabeo, xarel.lo, parellada.

88 Colour: bright yellow. Nose: ripe fruit, white flowers, dried herbs. Palate: fresh, flavourful, good acidity, correct.

GORNER 2004 BN GRAN RESERVA
macabeo, xarel.lo, parellada.

87 Colour: bright yellow. Nose: balanced, lees reduction notes, ripe fruit, sweet spices, dry nuts. Palate: balanced, good acidity, flavourful.

GIRÓ RIBOT

Finca El Pont, s/n
08792 Santa Fe del Penedès (Barcelona)
☎: +34 938 974 050 - Fax: +34 938 974 311
giroribot@giroribot.es
www.giroribot.es

GIRÓ RIBOT AVANT BR RESERVA
45% xarel.lo, 40% chardonnay, 15% macabeo.

93 Colour: bright yellow. Nose: lees reduction notes, dry nuts, pattiserie, toasty, creamy oak, complex. Palate: powerful, flavourful, fine bitter notes, toasty. Personality.

PAUL CHENEAU BLANC DE BLANCS BR RESERVA
45% macabeo, 40% xarel.lo, 10% chardonnay, 5% parellada.

89 Colour: bright yellow. Nose: balanced, floral, fresh fruit. Palate: balanced, good acidity, fine bitter notes.

GIRÓ RIBOT AB BR RESERVA
50% macabeo, 30% xarel.lo, 10% parellada, 10% chardonnay.

86 Colour: bright yellow. Nose: dried flowers, lees reduction notes, dry nuts. Palate: fine bitter notes, light-bodied, flavourful.

GIRÓ RIBOT DIVINIS MAGNUM 2008 BN RESERVA
90% chardonnay, 10% parellada.

92 Colour: bright yellow. Nose: white flowers, fine lees, citrus fruit, ripe fruit, dried herbs. Palate: powerful, flavourful, fresh, fruity, good acidity.

GIRÓ RIBOT MARE 2007 BN GRAN RESERVA
50% xarel.lo, 30% macabeo, 20% parellada.

93 Colour: bright golden. Nose: dry nuts, fragrant herbs, complex, expressive, pattiserie. Palate: powerful, flavourful, good acidity, fine bead, fine bitter notes, balanced.

GIRÓ RIBOT AB 2007 BN GRAN RESERVA
30% macabeo, 30% xarel.lo, 10% parellada, 10% chardonnay.

88 Colour: bright golden. Nose: fine lees, dry nuts, fragrant herbs, complex. Palate: powerful, flavourful, good acidity, fine bead, fine bitter notes.

GIRÓ RIBOT MARE MAGNUM 2006 BN GRAN RESERVA
50% xarel.lo, 30% macabeo, 20% parellada.

89 Colour: bright golden. Nose: fine lees, dry nuts, fragrant herbs. Palate: powerful, flavourful, good acidity, fine bead, fine bitter notes.

GIRÓ RIBOT AB BRUT ROSADO
85% trepat, 15% pinot noir.

87 Colour: light cherry. Nose: fruit expression, jasmine, expressive. Palate: fine bitter notes, easy to drink, good acidity.

GIRÓ RIBOT AB TENDENCIAS EXTRA BRUT
40% macabeo, 30% xarel.lo, 15% parellada, 15% chardonnay.

86 Colour: bright straw. Nose: medium intensity, fresh fruit, dried herbs, fine lees, floral. Palate: fresh, fruity, flavourful, good acidity.

GRAMONA

Industria, 34-36
08770 Sant Sadurní D'Anoia (Barcelona)
☎: +34 938 910 113 - Fax: +34 938 183 284
comunicacion@gramona.com
www.gramona.com

GRAMONA ARGENT ROSÉ 2008 RD GRAN RESERVA
100% pinot noir.

90 Colour: coppery red. Nose: closed, toasty, fruit liqueur notes, fruit preserve, lees reduction notes. Palate: flavourful, fine bitter notes, powerful, fine bead.

GRAMONA ARGENT 2008 BR RESERVA
100% chardonnay.

93 Colour: bright straw. Nose: balanced, elegant, fine lees, citrus fruit, spicy. Palate: rich, complex, fine bitter notes, fresh.

GRAMONA IMPERIAL 2006 BR GRAN RESERVA
50% xarel.lo, 40% macabeo, 10% chardonnay.

91 Colour: bright yellow. Nose: balanced, expressive, fresh, floral, fine lees. Palate: fine bitter notes, balanced, good acidity.

GRAMONA CELLER BATLLE 2002 BR GRAN RESERVA
70% xarel.lo, 30% macabeo.

94 Colour: bright golden. Nose: lees reduction notes, floral, fragrant herbs, pattiserie, sweet spices. Palate: powerful, flavourful, good acidity, fine bead, long, toasty.

GRAMONA CELLER BATLLE 2001 BR GRAN RESERVA
70% xarel.lo, 30% macabeo.

96 Colour: bright golden. Nose: dry nuts, fragrant herbs, complex. Palate: powerful, flavourful, good acidity, fine bead, fine bitter notes, spicy.

GRAMONA CELLER BATLLE 2000 BR GRAN RESERVA
70% xarel.lo, 30% macabeo.

98 Colour: yellow. Nose: complex, expressive, dry nuts, spicy, faded flowers, fine lees, candied fruit. Palate: flavourful, complex, fine bitter notes, good acidity.

GRAMONA COLECCIÓN DE ARTE 2000 BR GRAN RESERVA
100% chardonnay.

95 Colour: bright golden. Nose: candied fruit, dry nuts, honeyed notes, dried herbs, sweet spices. Palate: sweetness, fresh, fine bitter notes, good acidity, fine bead.

GRAMONA ALLEGRO BR
33% chardonnay, 33% macabeo, 33% xarel.lo.

89 Colour: bright straw. Nose: fresh fruit, dried herbs, fine lees, floral. Palate: fresh, fruity, good acidity.

GRAMONA ROSÉ BR
100% pinot noir.

87 Colour: rose. Nose: floral, red berry notes, candied fruit, fresh. Palate: good acidity, fine bead, fine bitter notes, fruity, flavourful.

GRAMONA III LUSTROS 2005 BN
70% xarel.lo, 30% macabeo.

92 Colour: bright yellow. Nose: dried flowers, dry nuts, balanced, complex, faded flowers. Palate: balanced, long, good acidity.

GRAMONA III LUSTROS 2004 BN GRAN RESERVA
70% xarel.lo, 30% macabeo.

94 Colour: bright yellow. Nose: candied fruit, spicy, lees reduction notes, dry nuts, complex, dried herbs. Palate: balanced, spicy, elegant.

GRAMONA GRAN CUVÉE DE POSTRE ESP GRAN RESERVA
33% xarel.lo, 33% macabeo, 33% parellada.

88 Colour: yellow. Nose: ripe fruit, white flowers, candied fruit. Palate: balanced, rich, flavourful, correct.

GRAMONA LA SUITE SC RESERVA
33% xarel.lo, 33% macabeo, 33% parellada.

88 Colour: bright yellow. Nose: fine lees, wild herbs, dried flowers, medium intensity. Palate: fruity, flavourful.

GRAN DUCAY BODEGAS

Ctra. N-330, Km. 450
50400 Cariñena (Zaragoza)
☎: +34 976 620 400 - Fax: +34 976 620 398
bsv@sanvalero.com
www.sanvalero.com

GRAN DUCAY BN
macabeo, xarel.lo, parellada.

85 Colour: bright straw. Nose: jasmine, citrus fruit, fresh. Palate: fruity, good acidity, correct.

GRAN DUCAY ROSÉ BN
100% garnacha.

82

GRIMAU DE PUJADES

Castell de Les Pujades, s/n
08732 La Munia (Barcelona)
☎: +34 938 918 031 - Fax: +34 938 918 427
grimau@grimau.com
www.grimau.com

GRIMAU BR
macabeo, xarel.lo, parellada.

87 Colour: bright yellow. Nose: floral, dried herbs, fine lees, fresh. Palate: balanced, flavourful, easy to drink.

GRIMAU BN
macabeo, xarel.lo, parellada.

88 Colour: bright yellow. Nose: fresh fruit, dried herbs, fine lees, floral. Palate: fresh, fruity, flavourful, good acidity.

GRIMAU RESERVA FAMILIAR BN
macabeo, xarel.lo, parellada, chardonnay.

87 Colour: bright yellow. Nose: balanced, dry nuts, medium intensity. Palate: fruity, flavourful, good acidity.

TRENCADÍS BN
macabeo, xarel.lo, parellada, chardonnay.

86 Colour: bright yellow. Nose: fine lees, floral, dried herbs. Palate: fine bead, fine bitter notes, correct.

TRENCADÍS ROSAT BN
pinot noir, garnacha.

84

HACIENDAS DE ESPAÑA

Monistrol D'Anoia, s/n
08770 Sant Sadurní D'Anoia (Barcelona)
☎: +34 914 365 900
www.haciendas-espana.com

MM VINTAGE (MARQUÉS DE LA CONCORDIA FAMILY OF WINES) 2009 BR
15% macabeo, 35% xarel.lo, 25% parellada, 25% chardonnay.

86 Colour: bright yellow. Nose: white flowers, fruit expression, balanced. Palate: flavourful, good acidity, balanced.

MM ROSÉ BRUT MILLESIME (MARQUÉS DE LA CONCORDIA FAMILY OF WINES) 2008 BR
70% pinot noir, 30% monastrell.

87 Colour: light cherry. Nose: faded flowers, balanced. Palate: flavourful, easy to drink, good acidity.

MM PREMIUM CUVÉE MILLESIME (MARQUÉS DE LA CONCORDIA FAMILY OF WINES) 2008 BN
35% chardonnay, 25% macabeo, 15% xarel.lo, 25% parellada.

90 Colour: bright yellow. Nose: fine lees, white flowers, fragrant herbs, expressive. Palate: correct, fine bitter notes, fine bead, good acidity.

HERETAT MAS TINELL

Ctra. de Vilafranca a St. Martí Sarroca, Km. 0,5
08720 Vilafranca del Penedès (Barcelona)
☎: +34 938 170 586 - Fax: +34 938 170 500
info@mastinell.com
www.mastinell.com

MAS TINELL BRUT REAL MAGNUM 2006 BR RESERVA
35% macabeo, 35% parellada, 30% xarel.lo.

89 Colour: bright straw. Nose: medium intensity, fresh fruit, citrus fruit. Palate: fresh, balanced, easy to drink, fine bitter notes.

MAS TINELL BRUT REAL 2007 BR RESERVA
35% macabeo, 35% parellada, 30% xarel.lo.

87 Colour: bright straw. Nose: fresh fruit, dried herbs, fine lees, floral. Palate: fresh, fruity, flavourful, good acidity.

MAS TINELL BRUT ROSÉ 2007 BR RESERVA
100% trepat.

91 Colour: onion pink. Nose: floral, red berry notes, ripe fruit, elegant, balanced, expressive. Palate: complex, powerful, flavourful, long, fine bitter notes.

MAS TINELL CARPE DIEM RESERVA ESPECIAL 2006 BN RESERVA
40% chardonnay, 30% xarel.lo, 30% parellada.

90 Colour: bright yellow. Nose: expressive, faded flowers, ripe fruit, fragrant herbs. Palate: long, good acidity, fine bead, flavourful.

MAS TINELL NATURE REAL 2005 BN GRAN RESERVA
40% xarel.lo, 30% macabeo, 25% parellada, 5% chardonnay.

86 Colour: bright yellow. Nose: lees reduction notes, faded flowers, dry nuts, sweet spices. Palate: good acidity, long, flavourful.

MAS TINELL CRISTINA VINTAGE 2006 EXTRA BRUT GRAN RESERVA
40% xarel.lo, 30% parellada, 20% chardonnay, 10% macabeo.

89 Colour: bright straw. Nose: fresh fruit, dried herbs, floral, powerfull, spicy. Palate: fresh, fruity, flavourful, good acidity.

JANÉ VENTURA

Ctra. Calafell, 2
43700 El Vendrell (Tarragona)
☎: +34 977 660 118 - Fax: +34 977 661 239
janeventura@janeventura.com
www.janeventura.com

JANÉ VENTURA RESERVA DE LA MÚSICA 2009 BR
38% xarel.lo, 32% macabeo, 30% parellada.

89 Colour: bright straw. Nose: medium intensity, fresh fruit, dried herbs, fine lees, floral. Palate: fresh, fruity, flavourful, good acidity, easy to drink.

JANÉ VENTURA ROSÉ RESERVA DE LA MÚSICA 2009 BR RESERVA
100% garnacha.

88 Colour: rose. Nose: red berry notes, raspberry, fresh fruit, expressive. Palate: good acidity, fruity, flavourful.

JANÉ VENTURA RESERVA DE LA MÚSICA 2009 BN RESERVA
38% xarel.lo, 32% macabeo, 30% parellada.

90 Colour: bright straw. Nose: fresh fruit, dried herbs, fine lees, fresh, powerfull, dried flowers. Palate: fresh, fruity, flavourful, easy to drink, fine bitter notes.

JANÉ VENTURA VINTAGE 2008 BN GRAN RESERVA
29% macabeo, 51% xarel.lo, 20% parellada.

90 Colour: bright yellow. Nose: fine lees, white flowers, fragrant herbs, spicy. Palate: powerful, flavourful, complex, long.

JANÉ VENTURA DE L'ORGUE 2006 BN GRAN RESERVA
32% macabeo, 38% xarel.lo, 30% parellada.

92 Colour: bright yellow. Nose: expressive, powerfull, white flowers, ripe fruit, dried herbs. Palate: rich, powerful, flavourful, good acidity.

JAUME GIRÓ I GIRÓ

Montaner i Oller, 5
08770 Sant Sadurní D'Anoia (Barcelona)
☎: +34 938 910 165 - Fax: +34 938 911 271
cavagiro@cavagiro.com
www.cavagiro.com

JAUME GIRÓ I GIRÓ GRANDALLA DE LUXE 2004 GRAN RESERVA

90 Colour: bright golden. Nose: dry nuts, ripe fruit, fragrant herbs, complex. Palate: powerful, flavourful, good acidity, fine bead, fine bitter notes.

JAUME GIRÓ I GIRÓ DE CAL REI ROSAT

86 Colour: raspberry rose. Nose: fine lees, red berry notes, candied fruit, fresh. Palate: balanced, powerful, flavourful.

JAUME GIRÓ I GIRÓ GRANDALLA 2007 BR GRAN RESERVA

90 Colour: bright straw. Nose: fine lees, white flowers, fruit expression, expressive. Palate: balanced, good acidity, powerful, flavourful.

JAUME GIRÓ I GIRÓ BOMBONETTA 2005 BR GRAN RESERVA

89 Colour: yellow, greenish rim. Nose: balanced, floral, dried herbs. Palate: flavourful, ripe fruit, long, elegant.

JAUME GIRÓ I GIRÓ CAL REI 2005 BR GRAN RESERVA

88 Colour: bright yellow. Nose: fragrant herbs, ripe fruit, faded flowers. Palate: correct, fine bitter notes, powerful, flavourful.

CAN FESTIS 2010 BN
chardonnay, macabeo, xarel.lo, parellada.

85 Colour: bright straw. Nose: medium intensity, fresh fruit, dried herbs, fine lees, floral. Palate: fresh, fruity, flavourful.

CAN FESTIS 2009 BN RESERVA
xarel.lo, chardonnay, parellada, macabeo.

90 Colour: bright yellow. Nose: jasmine, white flowers, fragrant herbs, fresh. Palate: correct, fine bitter notes, flavourful.

JAUME GIRÓ I GIRÓ MONTANER 2008 BN GRAN RESERVA

87 Colour: yellow, greenish rim. Nose: fine lees, dried flowers, medium intensity. Palate: fruity, fresh, good acidity.

CAN FESTIS 2008 BN GRAN RESERVA
chardonnay, xarel.lo, macabeo, parellada.

87 Colour: bright yellow. Nose: fine lees, white flowers, fresh, balanced. Palate: correct, fine bead, flavourful.

JAUME GIRÓ I GIRÓ SELECTE 2006 BN GRAN RESERVA

91 Colour: bright yellow. Nose: complex, candied fruit, fine lees, faded flowers, expressive. Palate: correct, flavourful, fine bead, good acidity.

JAUME GIRÓ I GIRÓ 2005 BN GRAN RESERVA

89 Colour: yellow, greenish rim. Nose: balanced, ripe fruit, fine lees, faded flowers. Palate: fruity, flavourful, good acidity.

JAUME GIRÓ I GIRÓ ELABORACIÓN ARTESANA BN

87 Colour: bright straw, greenish rim. Nose: fresh, floral, citrus fruit, fine lees. Palate: correct, balanced, good acidity.

JAUME LLOPART ALEMANY

Font Rubí, 9
08736 Font-Rubí (Barcelona)
☎: +34 938 979 133 - Fax: +34 938 979 133
info@jaumellopartalemany.com
www.jaumellopartalemany.com

JAUME LLOPART ALEMANY AINA ROSADO 2010 BR RESERVA
pinot noir.

88 Colour: raspberry rose. Nose: floral, red berry notes, raspberry, expressive. Palate: good acidity, powerful.

JAUME LLOPART ALEMANY 2008 BR RESERVA
macabeo, xarel.lo, parellada.

88 Colour: bright yellow. Nose: medium intensity, dried herbs, fine lees, floral. Palate: fresh, fruity, flavourful, good acidity.

JAUME LLOPART ALEMANY VINYA D'EN FERRAN 2008 BN GRAN RESERVA
pinot noir, chardonnay.

92 Colour: bright golden. Nose: ripe fruit, balanced, elegant, dry nuts. Palate: good structure, flavourful, good acidity, fine bitter notes.

JAUME LLOPART ALEMANY 2008 BN RESERVA
macabeo, xarel.lo, parellada.

88 Colour: yellow, greenish rim. Nose: dried flowers, dry nuts, fragrant herbs, expressive. Palate: flavourful, good acidity, balanced.

JAUME LLOPART ALEMANY 2007 BN GRAN RESERVA
macabeo, xarel.lo, parellada.

90 Colour: bright yellow. Nose: dried herbs, faded flowers, ripe fruit, dry nuts. Palate: good acidity, rich, flavourful.

JAUME SERRA

Ctra. de Vilanova, Km. 2,5
08800 Vilanova i la Geltrú (Barcelona)
☎: +34 938 936 404 - Fax: +34 938 147 482
jaumeserra@jgc.es
www.garciacarrion.es

JAUME SERRA CHARDONNAY BLANC DE BLANCS 2006
100% chardonnay.

85 Colour: bright golden. Nose: toasty, honeyed notes, dry nuts. Palate: powerful, fine bitter notes, unctuous.

CRISTALINO JAUME SERRA BR
50% macabeo, 35% parellada, 15% xarel.lo.

86 Colour: bright yellow. Nose: white flowers, citrus fruit, ripe fruit. Palate: fine bitter notes, flavourful, correct.

CRISTALINO JAUME SERRA BR
trepat, pinot noir.

85 Colour: coppery red. Nose: floral, red berry notes, dry nuts, fresh. Palate: fruity, flavourful, easy to drink.

JAUME SERRA ROSADO BR
80% trepat, 20% pinot noir.

83

JAUME SERRA VINTAGE 2008 BN
30% macabeo, 30% chardonnay, 25% parellada, 15% xarel.lo.

83

JAUME SERRA BN RESERVA
45% macabeo, 25% parellada, 15% xarel.lo, 15% chardonnay.

85 Colour: bright yellow. Nose: faded flowers, honeyed notes, powerfull. Palate: light-bodied, fresh, flavourful, fine bitter notes.

JAUME SERRA BN
50% macabeo, 25% xarel.lo, 25% parellada.

82

JOAN RAVENTÓS ROSELL

Ctra. Sant Sadurní a Masquefa, Km. 6,5
08783 Masquefa (Barcelona)
☎: +34 937 725 251 - Fax: +34 937 727 191
raventosrosell@raventosrosell.com
www.raventosrosell.com

JOAN RAVENTÓS ROSELL GRAN HERETAT BR
70% chardonnay, 10% pinot noir, 10% macabeo, 10% parellada.

86 Colour: bright golden. Nose: expressive, complcx, white flowers, dry nuts, spicy, candied fruit, honeyed notes. Palate: flavourful, long.

JOAN RAVENTÓS ROSELL ROSÉ DONE'S BR
100% pinot noir.

85 Colour: raspberry rose. Nose: medium intensity, faded flowers, fine lees. Palate: balanced, easy to drink, good acidity.

JOAN RAVENTÒS ROSELL HERETAT BR RESERVA
70% chardonnay, 15% macabeo, 15% parellada.

82

JOAN SARDÀ

Ctra. Vilafranca a St. Jaume dels Domenys, Km. 8,1
08732 Castellvi de la Marca (Barcelona)
☎: +34 937 720 900 - Fax: +34 937 721 495
joansarda@joansarda.com
www.joansarda.com

JOAN SARDÀ BR RESERVA
macabeo, xarel.lo, parellada.

88 Colour: bright straw. Nose: fragrant herbs, faded flowers, fine lees, medium intensity. Palate: correct, good acidity.

JOAN SARDÀ MILLENIUM 2007 BN GRAN RESERVA
macabeo, xarel.lo, parellada.

89 Colour: bright golden. Nose: fine lees, dry nuts, fragrant herbs, complex. Palate: powerful, flavourful, good acidity, fine bead, fine bitter notes.

JOAN SARDÀ BN RESERVA
macabeo, xarel.lo, parellada.

86 Colour: bright yellow. Nose: medium intensity, fine lees, fresh fruit, dried flowers. Palate: fruity, flavourful, long.

JOAN SARDÁ ROSÉ BR RESERVA
monastrell, garnacha.

87 Colour: rose. Nose: floral, red berry notes, ripe fruit, dried herbs. Palate: powerful, flavourful, fresh, fruity, easy to drink.

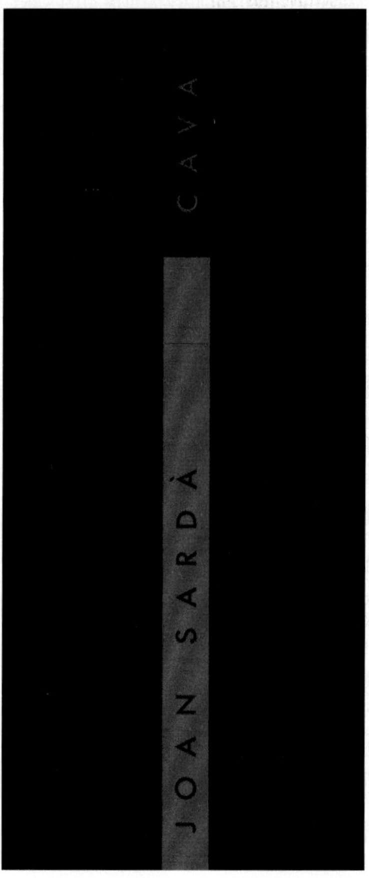

JOSEP Mª RAVENTÓS I BLANC

Plaça del Roure, s/n
08770 Sant Sadurní D'Anoia (Barcelona)
☎: +34 938 183 262 - Fax: +34 938 912 500
raventos@raventos.com
www.raventos.com

RAVENTÓS I BLANC DE NIT 2010 BR
55% macabeo, 30% xarel.lo, 10% parellada, 5% monastrell.

90 Colour: raspberry rose. Nose: medium intensity, elegant, red berry notes, fruit expression. Palate: good acidity, ripe fruit, fine bead.

RAVENTÓS I BLANC 2010 BR RESERVA
50% macabeo, 35% xarel.lo, 15% parellada.

88 Colour: bright straw, greenish rim. Nose: medium intensity, fresh fruit, dried herbs, fine lees, floral. Palate: fresh, fruity, flavourful, good acidity.

RAVENTÓS I BLANC LA FINCA 2009 BN GRAN RESERVA
40% xarel.lo, 30% macabeo, 25% parellada, 5% chardonnay.

89 Colour: bright yellow. Nose: balanced, dry nuts, fine lees, dried herbs. Palate: fresh, spicy, good acidity.

RAVENTÓS I BLANC GRAN RESERVA PERSONAL M.R.N. 2000 BN GRAN RESERVA

95 Colour: bright golden. Nose: fine lees, dry nuts, fragrant herbs, complex, candied fruit, ripe fruit, toasty. Palate: powerful, flavourful, good acidity, fine bead, fine bitter notes.

RAVENTÓS I BLANC GRAN RESERVA PERSONAL M.R.N. 1999 BN GRAN RESERVA

95 Colour: bright golden. Nose: fine lees, fragrant herbs, complex, sweet spices, dry nuts. Palate: powerful, flavourful, good acidity, fine bead, fine bitter notes.

RAVENTÓS I BLANC GRAN RESERVA PERSONAL M.R.N. 1998 BN

96 Colour: bright golden. Nose: dry nuts, fragrant herbs, complex, lees reduction notes, characterful, toasty. Palate: powerful, flavourful, good acidity, fine bead, fine bitter notes.

RAVENTÓS I BLANC LA FINCA MAGNUM BN

92 Colour: bright straw. Nose: medium intensity, fresh fruit, dried herbs, floral. Palate: fresh, fruity, flavourful, good acidity.

JUVÉ Y CAMPS

Sant Venat, 1
08770 Sant Sadurní D'Anoia (Barcelona)
☎: +34 938 911 000 - Fax: +34 938 912 100
juveycamps@juveycamps.com
www.juveycamps.com

JUVÉ & CAMPS BLANC DE NOIRS 2010
90% pinot noir, 10% xarel.lo.

88 Colour: bright yellow. Nose: dried flowers, fresh fruit, citrus fruit, fragrant herbs. Palate: fine bitter notes, correct, flavourful, fresh.

GRAN JUVÉ CAMPS 2009 BR GRAN RESERVA
40% xarel.lo, 26% macabeo, 25% chardonnay, 9% parellada.

91 Colour: bright yellow. Nose: fine lees, fragrant herbs, complex. Palate: powerful, flavourful, good acidity, fine bead, fine bitter notes.

JUVÉ & CAMPS MILESIMÉ CHARDONNAY 2009 BR RESERVA
100% chardonnay.

91 Colour: bright straw. Nose: dry nuts, fragrant herbs, complex. Palate: powerful, flavourful, good acidity, fine bead, fine bitter notes.

JUVÉ & CAMPS MILESIMÉ MAGNUM 2009 BR RESERVA
100% chardonnay.

91 Colour: bright yellow. Nose: powerfull, reduction notes, fruit preserve, citrus fruit. Palate: flavourful, good acidity, fine bitter notes.

JUVÉ & CAMPS MILLESIMÉ 2006 BR GRAN RESERVA
chardonnay.

92 Colour: bright golden. Nose: fine lees, dry nuts, fragrant herbs, complex. Palate: powerful, flavourful, good acidity, fine bead, fine bitter notes.

GRAN JUVÉ CAMPS SELECCIÓN XAREL.LO BR GRAN RESERVA
xarel.lo.

94 Colour: bright golden. Nose: fine lees, dry nuts, fragrant herbs, characterful, fresh. Palate: powerful, flavourful, good acidity, fine bead, fine bitter notes.

JUVÉ & CAMPS CINTA PÚRPURA BR RESERVA
33% macabeo, 53% xarel.lo, 14% parellada.

89 Colour: bright yellow. Nose: medium intensity, dried flowers, fragrant herbs. Palate: correct, good acidity, fine bitter notes.

JUVÉ & CAMPS ROSÉ BR
100% pinot noir.

87 Colour: light cherry. Nose: balanced, rose petals, fragrant herbs, red berry notes. Palate: fruity, easy to drink, balanced.

JUVÉ & CAMPS RESERVA DE LA FAMILIA MAGNUM 2009 BN RESERVA
30% macabeo, 50% xarel.lo, 10% parellada, 10% chardonnay.

93 Colour: bright golden. Nose: fine lees, dry nuts, fragrant herbs. Palate: powerful, flavourful, good acidity, fine bead, fine bitter notes.

JUVÉ & CAMPS RESERVA DE LA FAMILIA 2009 BN GRAN RESERVA
30% macabeo, 50% xarel.lo, 10% parellada, 10% chardonnay.

90 Colour: bright golden. Nose: fine lees, dry nuts, fragrant herbs, citrus fruit. Palate: powerful, flavourful, good acidity, fine bead, fine bitter notes.

LATIDOS DE VINO (EPILENSE DE VINOS Y VIÑEDOS)

La Quimera del oro 30 3ºD
50019 (Zaragoza)
☎: +34 669 148 771
fmora@latidosdevino.com
www.latidosdevino.com

LATIDOS DE VINO "I LOVE CAVA" BN
macabeo, chardonnay.

87 Colour: bright yellow. Nose: ripe fruit, lees reduction notes, sweet spices, dried herbs. Palate: light-bodied, fresh, flavourful.

LLOPART

Ctra. de Sant Sadurni - Ordal, Km. 4
08739 Subirats (Els Casots) (Barcelona)
☎: +34 938 993 125 - Fax: +34 938 993 038
llopart@llopart.com
www.llopart.com

LLOPART ROSÉ (375 ML) 2010 BR
60% monastrell, 20% garnacha, 20% pinot noir.

89 Colour: raspberry rose. Nose: red berry notes, white flowers, dried herbs. Palate: flavourful, balanced, good acidity, fine bitter notes.

LLOPART ROSÉ 2009 BR RESERVA
60% monastrell, 20% garnacha, 20% pinot noir.

87 Colour: raspberry rose. Nose: red berry notes, raspberry, floral, fresh. Palate: fruity, flavourful, easy to drink.

LLOPART MAGNUM IMPERIAL 2008 BR GRAN RESERVA
50% xarel.lo, 40% macabeo, 10% parellada.

90 Colour: bright straw. Nose: medium intensity, fresh fruit, dried herbs, fine lees, floral. Palate: fresh, fruity, flavourful, good acidity.

LLOPART IMPERIAL 2008 BR GRAN RESERVA
50% xarel.lo, 40% macabeo, 10% parellada.

88 Colour: bright yellow. Nose: fine lees, dry nuts, fragrant herbs, complex. Palate: powerful, flavourful, good acidity, fine bead, fine bitter notes.

LLOPART EX-VITE 2006 BR GRAN RESERVA
60% xarel.lo, 40% macabeo.

90 Colour: bright yellow. Nose: floral, dry nuts, sweet spices, fine lees, complex, expressive. Palate: good acidity, flavourful, good structure, long.

LLOPART LEOPARDI 2007 BN GRAN RESERVA
40% macabeo, 40% xarel.lo, 10% parellada, 10% chardonnay.

92 Colour: bright straw. Nose: fine lees, dry nuts, fragrant herbs. Palate: powerful, flavourful, good acidity, fine bead, fine bitter notes.

LLOPART INTEGRAL 2010 BN RESERVA
40% parellada, 40% chardonnay, 20% xarel.lo.

88 Colour: bright yellow. Nose: fine lees, dried flowers, citrus fruit, dry nuts. Palate: fine bitter notes, flavourful, balanced.

LLOPART INTEGRAL (375 ML) 2010 BN RESERVA
40% xarel.lo, 30% macabeo, 30% parellada.

88 Colour: bright straw. Nose: fresh fruit, medium intensity, balanced, dried herbs. Palate: flavourful, good acidity, balanced.

LLOPART 2009 BN RESERVA
40% xarel.lo, 30% macabeo, 20% parellada, 10% chardonnay.

87 Colour: bright straw. Nose: medium intensity, fresh fruit, dry nuts, dried flowers. Palate: flavourful, fruity, good acidity.

LLOPART MICROCOSMOS ROSÉ 2008 BN RESERVA
85% pinot noir, 15% monastrell.

89 Colour: light cherry. Nose: red berry notes, white flowers, dried herbs, balanced, elegant. Palate: flavourful, good acidity, fine bead, fine bitter notes.

LLOPART NÉCTAR TERRENAL 2010 SEMIDULCE RESERVA
70% xarel.lo, 30% parellada.

86 Colour: bright straw. Nose: white flowers, dry nuts, sweet spices. Palate: flavourful, fruity, sweetness.

LONG WINES

Avda. del Monte, 46
28120 Algete (Madrid)
☎: +34 916 221 305 - Fax: +34 916 220 029
www.longwines.com

CAN PETIT BR
55% macabeo, 45% parellada.

87 Colour: bright yellow. Nose: medium intensity, dried herbs, fine lees, floral, candied fruit. Palate: fresh, flavourful, good acidity.

DE PRÓ BR
50% xarel.lo, 30% macabeo, 20% parellada.

85 Colour: bright yellow, greenish rim. Nose: medium intensity, dried flowers, dried herbs. Palate: fresh, fruity.

DE PRÓ ROSÉ BR
100% trepat.

85 Colour: light cherry. Nose: rose petals, dried herbs. Palate: fruity, flavourful, fresh.

CAN PETIT ROSÉ BR
100% trepat.

83

LOXAREL

Can Mayol, s/n
08735 Vilobí del Penedès (Barcelona)
☎: +34 938 978 001 - Fax: +34 938 978 111
loxarel@loxarel.com
www.loxarel.com

LOXAREL VINTAGE 2009 BN RESERVA
xarel.lo, macabeo, chardonnay.

87 Colour: bright straw. Nose: fresh fruit, fine lees, floral. Palate: fresh, fruity, flavourful, good acidily.

LOXAREL VINTAGE 2008 BN RESERVA

89 Colour: bright yellow. Nose: dry nuts, dried flowers, dried herbs. Palate: correct, fine bitter notes, fruity, good acidity.

LOXAREL 2007 BN GRAN RESERVA

86 Colour: yellow. Nose: powerfull, ripe fruit, white flowers, dry nuts. Palate: flavourful, fruity, long, good acidity.

LOXAREL RESERVA FAMILIA BN GRAN RESERVA

90 Colour: bright yellow. Nose: fine lees, dry nuts, fragrant herbs, balanced. Palate: powerful, flavourful, good acidity, fine bead, fine bitter notes.

999 DE LOXAREL ROSADO BN
pinot noir, xarel.lo.

87 Colour: light cherry. Nose: dried flowers, dry nuts, fresh. Palate: fruity, flavourful, good acidity, correct, fine bitter notes.

REFUGI DE LOXAREL BN RESERVA

87 Colour: bright yellow. Nose: dry nuts, floral, medium intensity. Palate: fruity, easy to drink, good acidity.

MARCELINO DÍAZ

Mecánica, s/n
06200 Almendralejo (Badajoz)
☎: +34 924 677 548 - Fax: +34 924 660 977
bodega@madiaz.com
www.madiaz.com

PUERTA PALMA BR
macabeo.

80

PUERTA PALMA BN RESERVA
80% macabeo, 20% parellada.

80

MARQUÉS DE GELIDA - L'ALZINAR

Can Llopart de Les Alzines
08770 Sant Sadurní D'Anoia (Barcelona)
☎: +34 938 912 353 - Fax: +34 938 183 956
info@elcep.com
www.elcep.com

MARQUÉS DE GELIDA GRAN SELECCIÓ 2006 GRAN RESERVA
25% macabeo, 35% xarel.lo, 20% parellada, 20% chardonnay.

87 Colour: bright yellow. Nose: lees reduction notes, faded flowers, dried herbs, spicy. Palate: unctuous, powerful, flavourful.

L'ALZINAR 2009 BR RESERVA
35% macabeo, 35% xarel.lo, 20% parellada, 10% chardonnay.

86 Colour: bright straw. Nose: medium intensity, fresh fruit, dried herbs, floral. Palate: fresh, fruity, good acidity.

MARQUÉS DE GELIDA PINOT NOIR 2009 BR RESERVA
100% pinot noir.

86 Colour: coppery red. Nose: lactic notes, faded flowers, red berry notes. Palate: light-bodied, fresh, fruity, flavourful.

MARQUÉS DE GELIDA A. ECOLÓGICA 2008 BR RESERVA
30% macabeo, 35% xarel.lo, 25% parellada, 10% chardonnay.

88 Colour: bright yellow. Nose: balanced, fresh fruit, medium intensity, elegant, fragrant herbs. Palate: fresh, good acidity, fine bitter notes, easy to drink.

MARQUÉS DE GELIDA BRUT EXCLUSIVE 2008 BR RESERVA
30% macabeo, 35% xarel.lo, 25% parellada, 10% chardonnay.

85 Colour: bright yellow. Nose: white flowers, candied fruit, medium intensity. Palate: correct, flavourful, complex.

L'ALZINAR 2008 BN RESERVA
40% xarel.lo, 30% macabeo, parellada.

86 Colour: bright straw. Nose: medium intensity, dried herbs, floral, ripe fruit. Palate: fruity, flavourful, good acidity.

MARQUÉS DE GELIDA 2007 BN GRAN RESERVA
25% macabeo, 35% xarel.lo, 20% parellada, 20% chardonnay.

90 Colour: bright golden. Nose: fine lees, dry nuts, fragrant herbs, complex. Palate: flavourful, good acidity, fine bead.

MARQUÉS DE GELIDA CLAROR 2007 BN GRAN RESERVA
45% xarel.lo, 35% macabeo, 20% parellada.

86 Colour: bright straw. Nose: medium intensity, fresh fruit, dried herbs, floral. Palate: fresh, fruity, flavourful, good acidity.

L'ALZINAR 2006 BN GRAN RESERVA
20% macabeo, 35% xarel.lo, 25% parellada, 20% chardonnay.

86 Colour: bright yellow. Nose: candied fruit, dry nuts, balanced, faded flowers. Palate: fruity, easy to drink, correct.

MARRUGAT

Doctor Pasteur, 6
08720 Vilafranca del Penedès (Barcelona)
☎: +34 938 903 066 - Fax: +34 938 170 979
pinord@pinord.com
www.pinord.com

MARRUGAT ROSADO 2010 BR RESERVA
garnacha.

88 Colour: light cherry. Nose: medium intensity, floral, red berry notes. Palate: fresh, fruity, flavourful, good acidity.

MARRUGAT 2010 BR
xarel.lo, macabeo, parellada.

87 Colour: bright straw. Nose: medium intensity, fresh fruit, fine lees, floral. Palate: fresh, fruity, flavourful, good acidity.

DIBON 2010 BR RESERVA
macabeo, xarel.lo, parellada.

86 Colour: bright yellow. Nose: sweet spices, dried flowers, fine lees. Palate: flavourful, light-bodied, easy to drink.

MARRUGAT GRAN BRUT 2008 BR RESERVA
xarel.lo, macabeo, parellada.

86 Colour: bright yellow. Nose: fruit expression, white flowers, citrus fruit. Palate: fruity, correct, good acidity.

MARRUGAT CHARDONNAY 2007 BR RESERVA
chardonnay.

85 Colour: bright yellow. Nose: white flowers, honeyed notes, pattiserie. Palate: correct, ripe fruit, fine bitter notes.

DIBON 2010 BN
macabeo, xarel.lo, parellada.

87 Colour: bright yellow. Nose: citrus fruit, candied fruit, fine lees. Palate: powerful, flavourful, fine bitter notes.

MARRUGAT RIMA 32 2007 BN RESERVA
pinot noir, chardonnay.

90 Colour: bright yellow. Nose: dried flowers, fine lees, dry nuts, pattiserie. Palate: long, good acidity, flavourful, fine bitter notes.

MARRUGAT 2007 BN GRAN RESERVA
xarel.lo, macabeo, parellada.

86 Colour: bright yellow. Nose: ripe fruit, floral, balanced. Palate: flavourful, fruity, fine bitter notes, correct.

MARRUGAT SUSPIRUM 2006 BN
xarel.lo, macabeo, parellada, chardonnay.

85 Colour: bright straw. Nose: fresh fruit, dried herbs, fine lees, floral, citrus fruit. Palate: fresh, fruity, flavourful, correct.

MARTÍ SERDÀ

Camí Mas del Pont s/n
08792 Santa Fe del Penedès (Barcelona)
☎: +34 938 974 411 - Fax: +34 938 974 405
info@martiserda.com
www.martiserda.com

MARTÍ SERDÀ XAREL.LO 2011 B
100% xarel.lo.

88 Colour: bright straw. Nose: fresh, fresh fruit, white flowers, expressive. Palate: flavourful, fruity, good acidity, balanced.

MARTÍ SERDÀ BR
macabeo, xarel.lo, parellada.

88 Colour: bright straw. Nose: fresh fruit, dried herbs, fine lees, faded flowers. Palate: fresh, fruity, flavourful, good acidity.

MARTÍ SERDÀ CHARDONNAY BR
chardonnay.

86 Colour: bright straw, greenish rim. Nose: medium intensity, dried flowers. Palate: flavourful, rich, fruity.

MARTÍ SERDÀ 2007 BN GRAN RESERVA
40% xarel.lo, 35% chardonnay, 25% macabeo.

87 Colour: bright straw. Nose: medium intensity, dried herbs, fine lees, dried flowers. Palate: fresh, fruity, flavourful, good acidity.

MARTÍ SERDÀ CUVÉE REAL 2006 BN GRAN RESERVA
25% xarel.lo, 50% macabeo, 25% vino de reserva.

91 Colour: bright yellow. Nose: fine lees, dry nuts, fragrant herbs, complex. Palate: powerful, flavourful, good acidity, fine bead, fine bitter notes.

MARTÍ SERDÀ BN RESERVA
35% macabeo, 40% xarel.lo, 25% parellada.

87 Colour: bright straw. Nose: medium intensity, dried flowers, fine lees, balanced. Palate: easy to drink, good acidity, balanced.

MARTÍ SERDÀ BRUT ROSÉ
35% garnacha, 35% pinot noir, 30% trepat.

86 Colour: rose, bright. Nose: rose petals, dried flowers, red berry notes, medium intensity. Palate: fruity, flavourful, easy to drink, good acidity.

MAS CODINA

Barri El Gorner, s/n - Mas Codina
08797 Puigdalber (Barcelona)
☎: +34 938 988 166 - Fax: +34 938 988 166
info@mascodina.com
www.mascodina.com

MAS CODINA 2008 BR RESERVA
51% macabeo, 25% xarel.lo, 16% chardonnay, 8% pinot noir.

86 Colour: bright yellow. Nose: white flowers, fragrant herbs, ripe fruit. Palate: fresh, fruity, easy to drink.

MAS CODINA 2008 BN RESERVA
51% macabeo, 25% xarel.lo, 16% chardonnay, 8% pinot noir.

89 Colour: bright straw. Nose: powerfull, floral, dried herbs, citrus fruit, fresh fruit, fine lees. Palate: powerful, flavourful, fruity, long.

MAS CODINA 2007 BN GRAN RESERVA
40% xarel.lo, 25% chardonnay, 20% macabeo, 15% pinot noir.

89 Colour: old gold. Nose: ripe fruit, pattiserie, dried flowers, dried herbs, medium intensity. Palate: powerful, flavourful, long.

MASCARÓ

Casal, 9
08720 Vilafranca del Penedès (Barcelona)
☎: +34 938 901 628 - Fax: +34 938 901 358
mascaro@mascaro.es
www.mascaro.es

MASCARÓ ROSADO "RUBOR AURORAE" BR
100% garnacha.

88 Colour: light cherry. Nose: medium intensity, red berry notes, balanced, wild herbs. Palate: flavourful, easy to drink, fine bitter notes.

MASCARÓ NIGRUM BR RESERVA
60% parellada, 30% macabeo, 10% xarel.lo.

87 Colour: bright yellow. Nose: dried flowers, dried herbs, dry nuts. Palate: good acidity, fine bitter notes.

MASCARÓ PURE BN RESERVA
80% parellada, 20% macabeo.

88 Colour: bright straw. Nose: medium intensity, dried herbs, fine lees, floral, dry nuts. Palate: fresh, fruity, flavourful, good acidity.

CUVÉE ANTONIO MASCARÓ 2008 EXTRA BRUT GRAN RESERVA
50% parellada, 35% macabeo, 15% chardonnay.

89 Colour: bright golden. Nose: fine lees, dry nuts, fragrant herbs, complex. Palate: powerful, flavourful, good acidity, fine bead, fine bitter notes.

MASCARÓ "AMBROSIA" SS RESERVA
60% parellada, 30% macabeo, 10% xarel.lo.

85 Colour: bright yellow. Nose: ripe fruit, balanced, faded flowers. Palate: fruity, sweetness, easy to drink.

MASET DEL LLEÓ

C-244, Km. 32,5
08792 La Granada del Penedès (Barcelona)
☎: +34 902 200 250 - Fax: +34 938 921 333
info@maset.com
www.maset.com

NU BRUT DE MASET DEL LLEÓ BR
macabeo, parellada, xarel.lo.

88 Colour: bright yellow. Nose: fine lees, white flowers, fresh fruit, candied fruit. Palate: fresh, fruity, light-bodied, flavourful.

MASET DEL LLEÓ ROSÉ BR
garnacha, trepat.

84

MASET DEL LLEÓ L'AVI PAU BN RESERVA
chardonnay, macabeo, parellada, xarel.lo.

87 Colour: bright yellow. Nose: floral, ripe fruit, dried herbs, dry nuts, spicy. Palate: powerful, flavourful, correct.

MASET DEL LLEÓ BN RESERVA
macabeo, parellada, xarel.lo.

86 Colour: bright straw. Nose: floral, candied fruit, fragrant herbs, lees reduction notes. Palate: flavourful, good acidity, correct.

MASET DEL LLEÓ XAREL.LO AURUM BN RESERVA
chardonnay, xarel.lo.

85 Colour: bright yellow. Nose: lees reduction notes, faded flowers, ripe fruit, dried herbs. Palate: long, rich, flavourful.

MASET DEL LLEÓ VINTAGE BN RESERVA
macabeo, parellada, xarel.lo.

82

MATA I COLOMA

Montserrat, 73
08770 Sant Sadurní D'Anoia (Barcelona)
☎: +34 938 183 968 - Fax: +34 938 183 968
info@matacoloma.com
www.matacoloma.com

PERE MATA CUPADA Nº 6 2008 BN RESERVA
50% macabeo, 25% xarel.lo, 25% parellada.

84

PERE MATA RESERVA FAMILIA 2007 BN GRAN RESERVA
40% macabeo, 30% xarel.lo, 30% parellada.

90 Colour: bright yellow. Nose: dry nuts, fragrant herbs, sweet spices, toasty, ripe fruit. Palate: powerful, flavourful, good acidity, fine bitter notes.

PERE MATA L'ENSAMBLATGE 2007 BN GRAN RESERVA
50% xarel.lo, 30% macabeo, 20% parellada.

87 Colour: bright yellow. Nose: fragrant herbs, lees reduction notes, white flowers, ripe fruit. Palate: powerful, flavourful, fine bitter notes.

MIQUEL PONS

Baix Llobregat, 5
08792 La Granada (Barcelona)
☎: +34 938 974 541 - Fax: +34 938 974 710
miquelpons@cavamiquelpons.com
www.cavamiquelpons.com

EULÀLIA DE PONS BR RESERVA
macabeo, xarel.lo, parellada.

87 Colour: bright straw. Nose: medium intensity, fresh fruit, fine lees, floral. Palate: fresh, fruity, flavourful, good acidity.

MIQUEL PONS 2007 BN GRAN RESERVA
macabeo, xarel.lo, parellada.

90 Colour: bright yellow. Nose: petrol notes, lees reduction notes, spicy, faded flowers. Palate: round, powerful, flavourful, complex.

MIQUEL PONS MONTARGULL BN
macabeo, xarel.lo, parellada.

88 Colour: bright golden. Nose: pattiserie, sweet spices, toasty, ripe fruit, dried herbs. Palate: powerful, flavourful, toasty.

MONT MARÇAL

Finca Manlleu
08732 Castellví de la Marca (Barcelona)
☎: +34 938 918 281 - Fax: +34 938 919 045
mrivas@mont-marcal.com
www.mont-marcal.com

MONT MARÇAL GRAN CUVÉE BR
40% xarel.lo, 25% macabeo, 15% parellada, 20% chardonnay.

88 Colour: bright straw. Nose: medium intensity, dried herbs, faded flowers. Palate: fresh, fruity, flavourful, good acidity.

MONT MARÇAL EXTREMARIUM BR
35% xarel.lo, 25% macabeo, 20% parellada, 20% chardonnay.

87 Colour: bright yellow, greenish rim. Nose: medium intensity, dry nuts, dried herbs. Palate: correct, fine bitter notes, good acidity.

MONT MARÇAL RESERVA BR
40% xarel.lo, 30% macabeo, 20% parellada, 10% chardonnay.

86 Colour: bright straw. Nose: medium intensity, fresh fruit, fine lees, floral. Palate: fresh, fruity, flavourful, good acidity, easy to drink.

AUREUM DE MONT MARÇAL BN RESERVA
50% xarel.lo, 30% chardonnay, 10% pinot noir, 10% parellada.

90 Colour: bright yellow. Nose: dried flowers, pattiserie, fine lees, fragrant herbs, expressive. Palate: powerful, flavourful, good acidity, fine bitter notes.

MONT MARÇAL EXTREMARIUM ROSADO BN
100% pinot noir.

90 Colour: light cherry. Nose: balanced, red berry notes, medium intensity, dried flowers. Palate: flavourful, fine bitter notes, good acidity, long.

MONT MARÇAL BRUT ROSADO
100% trepat.

82

MONT-FERRANT

Abat Escarré, 1
17300 Blanes (Girona)
☎: +34 934 191 000 - Fax: +34 934 193 170
jcivit@montferrant.com
www.montferrant.com

AGUSTÍ VILARET 2006 GRAN RESERVA
70% chardonnay, 10% xarel.lo, 10% macabeo, 10% parellada.

90 Colour: bright yellow. Nose: white flowers, jasmine, balanced, fresh, fine lees. Palate: correct, good acidity, balanced.

BERTA BOUZY 2008 BR RESERVA
24% macabeo, 15% chardonnay, 36% xarel.lo, 25% parellada.

91 Colour: bright straw. Nose: fresh fruit, dried herbs, fine lees, floral, expressive. Palate: fresh, fruity, flavourful, good acidity, balanced.

L AMERICANO 2008 BR RESERVA
30% macabeo, 40% xarel.lo, 25% parellada, 5% chardonnay.

89 Colour: bright straw. Nose: medium intensity, fresh fruit, dried herbs, fine lees, white flowers. Palate: fresh, fruity, flavourful.

MONT FERRANT TRADICIÓ 2008 BR RESERVA
35% macabeo, 25% xarel.lo, 30% parellada, 10% chardonnay.

87 Colour: bright straw. Nose: medium intensity, fresh fruit, dried herbs, fine lees. Palate: fresh, fruity, good acidity.

MONT FERRANT BR GRAN RESERVA

89 Colour: bright yellow. Nose: fine lees, dry nuts, fragrant herbs, complex. Palate: flavourful, good acidity, fine bead, fine bitter notes.

L AMERICANO 2007 BN GRAN RESERVA
29% macabeo, 40% xarel.lo, 26% parellada, 5% chardonnay.

89 Colour: bright yellow. Nose: fine lees, dried flowers, ripe fruit, dry nuts. Palate: good acidity, fine bead, powerful, flavourful.

BLANES NATURE 2007 EXTRA BRUT GRAN RESERVA
29% macabeo, 40% xarel.lo, 26% parellada, 5% chardonnay.

87 Colour: bright yellow. Nose: fine lees, dry nuts, white flowers. Palate: powerful, flavourful, good acidity, fine bead, fine bitter notes.

MONTAU DE SADURNÍ

Masía Can Sadurní, s/n
08859 Begues (Barcelona)
☎: +34 936 392 112 - Fax: +34 936 390 161
info@montaudesadurni.com
www.montaudesadurni.com

MONTAU DE SADURNÍ RESERVA
40% xarel.lo, 30% macabeo, 30% parellada.

86 Colour: bright yellow. Nose: medium intensity, fresh, fine lees, dried flowers. Palate: light-bodied, correct, fresh, easy to drink.

MONTAU DE SADURNÍ BR GRAN RESERVA
40% xarel.lo, 30% macabeo, 30% parellada.

85 Colour: bright golden. Nose: dry nuts, fragrant herbs, lees reduction notes. Palate: powerful, flavourful, good acidity, fine bead, fine bitter notes.

MOST DORÉ

Rambla de la Generalitat, 8
08770 Sant Sadurní d'Anoia (Barcelona)
☎: +34 938 183 641 - Fax: +34 938 911 662
lodeseo@objetodedeseo.eu
www.objetodedeseo.eu

MOST - DORÉ "OBJETO DE DESEO 2009 RD RESERVA
monastrell, pinot noir, trepat.

87 Colour: coppery red. Nose: powerfull, ripe fruit, red berry notes, floral, expressive. Palate: , powerful, fruity, fresh, balanced, good acidity.

MOST - DORÉ "OBJETO DE DESEO 2009 BRUT EXTRA RESERVA
macabeo, xarel.lo, parellada.

89 Colour: bright straw. Nose: medium intensity, fresh fruit, dried herbs, fine lees, floral. Palate: fresh, fruity, flavourful, good acidity.

NADAL

Finca Nadal de la Boadella, s/n
08775 Torrelavit (Barcelona)
☎: +34 938 988 011 - Fax: +34 938 988 443
comunicacio@nadal.com
www.nadal.com

SALVATGE ROSÉ 2008 RD RESERVA
pinot noir.

88 Colour: raspberry rose. Nose: floral, fruit expression, red berry notes, ripe fruit. Palate: flavourful, correct, easy to drink, good acidity.

SALVATGE 2006 BR GRAN RESERVA
65% macabeo, 13% xarel.lo, 15% parellada.

88 Colour: bright golden. Nose: fragrant herbs, ripe fruit, sweet spices. Palate: flavourful, fresh, fruity, balanced.

R.N.G. 2004 BR GRAN RESERVA
68% xarel.lo, 32% parellada.

85 Colour: bright yellow. Nose: pattiserie, toasty, lees reduction notes, dry nuts. Palate: fine bitter notes, good acidity, flavourful.

NADAL 2007 BN GRAN RESERVA
58% parellada, 32% macabeo, 10% xarel.lo.

89 Colour: bright yellow. Nose: fine lees, dry nuts, fragrant herbs, complex. Palate: powerful, flavourful, good acidity, fine bead, fine bitter notes.

ORIOL ROSSELL

Propietat Can Cassanyes, s/n
08732 St. Marçal (Barcelona)
☎: +34 977 671 061 - Fax: +34 977 671 050
oriolrossell@oriolrossell.com
www.oriolrossell.com

ORIOL ROSSELL 2009 BN RESERVA
50% xarel.lo, 30% macabeo, 20% parellada.

87 Colour: bright straw. Nose: medium intensity, fresh fruit, dried herbs. Palate: fresh, flavourful, good acidity, fine bitter notes.

ORIOL ROSSELL 2008 BN GRAN RESERVA
70% xarel.lo, 30% macabeo.

88 Colour: bright golden. Nose: lees reduction notes, petrol notes, slightly evolved. Palate: powerful, flavourful, rich, ripe fruit.

ORIOL ROSSELL RESERVA DE LA PROPIETAT 2007 BN GRAN RESERVA
60% xarel.lo, 25% macabeo, 15% parellada.

85 Colour: bright yellow. Nose: lees reduction notes, faded flowers, dry nuts. Palate: powerful, flavourful, fine bitter notes.

ORIOL ROSSELL 2009 BRUT ROSÉ
100% trepat.

89 Colour: raspberry rose. Nose: floral, red berry notes, raspberry, dried herbs. Palate: powerful, fruity, fresh.

PAGO DE THARSYS

Ctra. Nacional III, km. 274
46340 Requena (Valencia)
☎: +34 962 303 354 - Fax: +34 962 329 000
pagodetharsys@pagodetharsys.com
www.pagodetharsys.com

PAGO DE THARSYS BRUT ROSADO 2010 BR
100% garnacha.

86 Colour: brilliant rose. Nose: fruit expression, medium intensity, fresh, red berry notes. Palate: easy to drink, correct.

PAGO DE THARSYS MILLESIME 2009 BR RESERVA
macabeo, parellada, chardonnay.

90 Colour: bright yellow. Nose: ripe fruit, white flowers, balanced. Palate: fine bitter notes, good acidity, flavourful, complex.

PAGO DE THARSYS MILLÉSIME ROSÉ RESERVA 2009 BR
100% garnacha.

90 Colour: salmon. Nose: medium intensity, red berry notes, floral, balanced. Palate: fruity, fresh, balanced, easy to drink, good acidity.

CARLOTA SURIA 2010 BN
80% macabeo, 20% parellada.

88 Colour: yellow. Nose: white flowers, ripe fruit, dry nuts. Palate: fruity, easy to drink, good acidity.

PAGO DE THARSYS 2010 BN
80% macabeo, 20% chardonnay.

87 Colour: bright straw. Nose: medium intensity, fresh fruit, dried herbs, fine lees, floral. Palate: fresh, fruity, flavourful, good acidity.

PAGO DE THARSYS 2005 BN GRAN RESERVA
macabeo, chardonnay.

86 Colour: bright golden. Nose: dry nuts, fragrant herbs, spicy. Palate: powerful, good acidity, fine bead.

PARATÓ

Can Respall de Renardes
08733 (Barcelona)
☎: +34 938 988 182 - Fax: +34 938 988 510
info@parato.es
www.parato.es

ÁTICA PINOT NOIR 2010 RD
100% pinot noir.

87 Colour: brilliant rose. Nose: red berry notes, candied fruit, floral, fragrant herbs. Palate: good acidity, fruity, flavourful.

PARATÓ 2009 BR
40% macabeo, 40% xarel.lo, 20% parellada.

89 Colour: bright straw. Nose: floral, fragrant herbs, expressive, fine lees. Palate: fruity, flavourful, complex, easy to drink.

RENARDES CUVÉE ESPECIAL 2009 BN
40% macabeo, 40% xarel.lo, 20% parellada.

87 Colour: bright yellow. Nose: white flowers, fragrant herbs, candied fruit. Palate: flavourful, correct, fine bitter notes.

PARATÓ 2008 BN RESERVA
40% parellada, 25% macabeo, 25% xarel.lo, 10% chardonnay.

86 Colour: bright straw. Nose: medium intensity, fresh fruit, dried herbs, fine lees, floral. Palate: fresh, fruity, flavourful, good acidity.

ELIAS I TERNS 2004 BN GRAN RESERVA
35% macabeo, 55% xarel.lo, 10% chardonnay, parellada.

90 Colour: bright yellow. Nose: complex, balanced, fine lees, floral. Palate: complex, good acidity, balanced.

ÁTICA 2008 EXTRA BRUT GRAN RESERVA
40% parellada, 25% macabeo, 25% xarel.lo, 10% chardonnay.

87 Colour: bright yellow. Nose: citrus fruit, dried flowers, dry nuts. Palate: long, fresh, powerful, flavourful.

PARÉS BALTÀ

Masía Can Baltá, s/n
08796 Pacs del Penedès (Barcelona)
☎: +34 938 901 399 - Fax: +34 938 901 143
paresbalta@paresbalta.com
www.paresbalta.com

ROSA CUSINE 2008 RD

90 Colour: brilliant rose. Nose: floral, fresh fruit, rcd berry notes, fragrant herbs. Palate: flavourful, fruity, tresh, good acidity, fine bitter notes.

BLANCA CUSINÉ BR

92 Colour: bright straw. Nose: medium intensity, fresh fruit, dried herbs, fine lees, floral, rose petals. Palate: fresh, fruity, flavourful, balanced.

PARÉS BALTÀ SELECTIO BR

90 Colour: bright straw. Nose: medium intensity, fresh fruit, floral, lees reduction notes. Palate: fresh, fruity, flavourful, good acidity.

PARÉS BALTÀ BN

88 Colour: bright straw. Nose: medium intensity, fresh fruit, dried herbs, fine lees, floral. Palate: fresh, fruity, flavourful, good acidity.

PARXET

Torrent, 38
08391 Tiana (Barcelona)
☎: +34 933 950 811 - Fax: +34 933 955 500
info@parxet.es
www.parxet.es

PARXET CUVÉE DESSERT 375 ML. RD
pinot noir.

85 Colour: raspberry rose. Nose: candied fruit, ripe fruit, floral, sweet spices. Palate: fresh, fruity, sweetness.

TITIANA PANSA BLANCA 2010 BR
pansa blanca.

91 Colour: bright straw. Nose: white flowers, fresh fruit, grassy, spicy. Palate: flavourful, fine bitter notes, good acidity.

PARXET 2009 BR RESERVA
macabeo, parellada, pansa blanca.

89 Colour: bright yellow. Nose: white flowers, dried herbs, fruit expression, fine lees. Palate: powerful, flavourful, fine bead, fine bitter notes.

TITIANA PINOT NOIR ROSÉ 2009 BR
pinot noir.

88 Colour: coppery red. Nose: red berry notes, ripe fruit, floral, medium intensity. Palate: light-bodied, flavourful, fresh, fruity.

PARXET BR
macabeo, parellada, pansa blanca.

89 Colour: bright straw. Nose: white flowers, fresh fruit, fragrant herbs, fresh. Palate: powerful, flavourful, fruity, easy to drink.

TITIANA VINTAGE 2009 BN
chardonnay.

89 Colour: bright golden. Nose: fragrant herbs, ripe fruit, dried flowers, expressive. Palate: good acidity, rich, flavourful.

PARXET ANIVERSARIO 2008 BN

92 Colour: bright yellow. Nose: elegant, floral, spicy, fragrant herbs, complex, characterful. Palate: powerful, flavourful, long, balanced, round.

PARXET 2008 BN
macabeo, parellada, pansa blanca.

87 Colour: bright yellow. Nose: ripe fruit, candied fruit, floral, balsamic herbs. Palate: flavourful, fruity, correct.

GRAN RESERVA MARÍA CABANE 2008 EXTRA BRUT GRAN RESERVA

90 Colour: bright golden. Nose: fine lees, dry nuts, fragrant herbs, complex, fresh fruit. Palate: powerful, flavourful, fine bead, fine bitter notes, balanced.

PARXET SS RESERVA
macabeo.

88 Colour: bright straw. Nose: candied fruit, white flowers, tropical fruit. Palate: fresh, fruity, easy to drink, sweetness.

PERE VENTURA

Ctra. de Vilafranca, Km. 0,4
08770 Sant Sadurní D'Anoia (Barcelona)
☎: +34 938 183 371 - Fax: +34 938 912 679
info@pereventura.com
www.pereventura.com

PERE VENTURA CUPATGE D'HONOR BR
60% xarel.lo, 40% chardonnay.

87 Colour: bright yellow. Nose: fresh fruit, dried herbs, fine lees, white flowers. Palate: flavourful, good acidity, fine bead, fine bitter notes.

PERE VENTURA TRESOR ROSÉ BR
100% trepat.

85 Colour: raspberry rose. Nose: dried flowers, red berry notes, ripe fruit, grassy. Palate: powerful, flavourful, fruity.

PERE VENTURA TRESOR BN RESERVA
40% macabeo, 40% xarel.lo, 20% parellada.

85 Colour: bright golden. Nose: fine lees, grassy, pattiserie, ripe fruit. Palate: correct, powerful, flavourful.

RAMÓN CANALS CANALS

Avda. Mare de Deu Montserrat, 9
08769 Castellví de Rosanes (Barcelona)
☎: +34 937 755 446 - Fax: +34 937 741 719
cava@canalscanals.com
www.canalscanals.com

MARTA DELUXE 2007 BN GRAN RESERVA
xarel.lo, macabeo, parellada.

89 Colour: bright yellow. Nose: fresh fruit, fine lees, white flowers. Palate: balanced, fine bitter notes, easy to drink, good acidity.

RAMÓN CANALS GRAN RESERVA LIMITADA 2007 BN GRAN RESERVA
xarel.lo, macabeo, parellada.

88 Colour: bright golden. Nose: fine lees, dry nuts, fragrant herbs, complex. Palate: powerful, flavourful, good acidity, fine bead, fine bitter notes.

CANALS CANALS GRAN SELECCIÓ NUMERADA BN RESERVA
xarel.lo, macabeo, parellada.

88 Colour: bright straw, greenish rim. Nose: fragrant herbs, fresh, white flowers. Palate: fresh, easy to drink, good acidity.

CANALS CANALS MAGNUM BN GRAN RESERVA
xarel.lo, macabeo, parellada.

88 Colour: bright yellow. Nose: powerfull, characterful, ripe fruit, citrus fruit, lees reduction notes. Palate: flavourful, fruity, fine bitter notes.

RECAREDO

Tamarit, 10 Apartado 15
08770 Sant Sadurní D'Anoia (Barcelona)
☎: +34 938 910 214 - Fax: +34 938 911 697
cava@recaredo.es
www.recaredo.es

RECAREDO BRUT NATURE 2008 BN GRAN RESERVA
46% xarel.lo, 40% macabeo, 14% parellada.

93 Colour: bright yellow. Nose: dried flowers, fine lees, fragrant herbs, powerfull, complex. Palate: fine bitter notes, flavourful, long, good structure.

RECAREDO INTENS ROSAT 2008 BN GRAN RESERVA
90% pinot noir, 10% monastrell.

90 Colour: light cherry. Nose: fine lees, rose petals, red berry notes, expressive. Palate: good acidity, fine bitter notes, flavourful, fruity, long.

RECAREDO SUBTIL 2007 BN GRAN RESERVA
62% xarel.lo, 30% chardonnay, 8% macabeo.

93 Colour: bright yellow. Nose: complex, balanced, dry nuts, spicy, fragrant herbs. Palate: good structure, flavourful, complex.

RECAREDO BRUT DE BRUT 2004 BN GRAN RESERVA
67% macabeo, 33% xarel.lo.

92 Colour: bright yellow. Nose: medium intensity, dry nuts, fine lees. Palate: flavourful, fine bitter notes, fine bead, good acidity.

RECAREDO RESERVA PARTICULAR 2002 BN GRAN RESERVA
72% macabeo, 28% xarel.lo.

96 Colour: bright yellow. Nose: ripe fruit, spicy, dry nuts, dried flowers, lees reduction notes. Palate: flavourful, complex, elegant, fine bitter notes.

TURO D'EN MOTA 2002 BN RESERVA
100% xarel.lo.

93 Colour: bright golden. Nose: nose:tic coffee, pattiserie, toasty, candied fruit, petrol notes. Palate: long, good acidity, powerful, flavourful. Personality.

REXACH BAQUES

Santa María, 12
08736 Guardiola de Font-Rubí (Barcelona)
☎: +34 938 979 170
info@rexachbaques.com
www.rexachbaques.com

REXACH BAQUES BRUT IMPERIAL 2008 BR RESERVA
40% xarel.lo, 30% macabeo, 30% parellada.

89 Colour: bright yellow. Nose: candied fruit, citrus fruit, fine lees, expressive. Palate: flavourful, light-bodied, fruity, fresh.

REXACH BAQUES GRAN CARTA 2008 BR
35% xarel.lo, 30% macabeo, 35% parellada.

87 Colour: bright straw. Nose: medium intensity, fresh fruit, dried herbs, fine lees, dried flowers. Palate: fresh, fruity, flavourful.

REXACH BAQUES 100 ANIVERSARI 2006 BR GRAN RESERVA
35% xarel.lo, 25% macabeo, 30% parellada, 10% pinot noir.

90 Colour: bright yellow. Nose: white flowers, dry nuts, dried herbs, spicy. Palate: correct, powerful, flavourful, complex.

REXACH BAQUES 2007 BN GRAN RESERVA
40% xarel.lo, 25% macabeo, 35% parellada.

88 Colour: bright golden. Nose: fine lees, dry nuts, fragrant herbs, complex. Palate: powerful, flavourful, fine bead, fine bitter notes.

RIMARTS

Avda. Cal Mir, 44
08770 Sant Sadurní D'Anoia (Barcelona)
☎: +34 938 912 775 - Fax: +34 938 912 775
rimarts@rimarts.net
www.rimarts.net

RIMARTS 2010 BR RESERVA
xarel.lo, macabeo, parellada.

88 Colour: bright straw, greenish rim. Nose: dried herbs, fine lees. Palate: powerful, flavourful, fruity, long.

RIMARTS 2009 BN RESERVA
xarel.lo, macabeo, parellada.

89 Colour: yellow, greenish rim. Nose: medium intensity, ripe fruit, dried flowers. Palate: good acidity, balanced.

RIMARTS CHARDONNAY 2008 BN RESERVA ESPECIAL
chardonnay.

90 Colour: bright straw. Nose: medium intensity, dried herbs, fine lees, floral, varietal. Palate: fresh, fruity, good acidity, elegant.

RIMARTS 2008 BN GRAN RESERVA
xarel.lo, macabeo, parellada, chardonnay.

89 Colour: bright golden. Nose: fine lees, dry nuts, complex, dried herbs. Palate: good acidity, fine bead, fine bitter notes.

RIMARTS UVAE 2008 BN GRAN RESERVA
xarel.lo, chardonnay.

89 Colour: bright golden. Nose: powerfull, complex, lees reduction notes, candied fruit, faded flowers. Palate: good structure, balanced, fine bitter notes, good acidity.

RIMARTS MAGNUM BN GRAN RESERVA
xarel.lo, macabeo, parellada, chardonnay.

89 Colour: bright golden. Nose: fine lees, dry nuts, fragrant herbs. Palate: powerful, flavourful, good acidity, fine bead, fine bitter notes.

ROCAMAR

Major, 80
08755 Castellbisbal (Barcelona)
☎: +34 937 720 900 - Fax: +34 937 721 495
info@rocamar.net
www.rocamar.net

CASTELL DE RIBES BR
macabeo, xarel.lo, parellada.

86 Colour: bright yellow. Nose: fine lees, white flowers, fragrant herbs, citrus fruit. Palate: fruity, fresh, light-bodied, flavourful.

ROGER GOULART

Major, s/n
08635 Sant Esteve Sesrovires (Barcelona)
☎: +34 934 191 000 - Fax: +34 934 193 170
jcivit@montferrant.com
www.rogergoulart.com

COMPTE ARNAU 2008 BR RESERVA
40% xarel.lo, 30% macabeo, 30% parellada.

90 Colour: bright straw. Nose: medium intensity, fresh fruit, dried herbs, fine lees, floral. Palate: fresh, fruity, flavourful, good acidity.

COMTE ARNAU ROSÉ 2008 BR
60% garnacha, 40% monastrell.

80

ROGER GOULART ROSÉ 2006 BR
60% garnacha, 40% monastrell.

86 Colour: brilliant rose. Nose: floral, red berry notes, ripe fruit, neat. Palate: fresh, fruity, light-bodied, flavourful.

ROGER GOULART 2006 BN RESERVA
40% xarel.lo, 30% macabeo, 25% parellada, 5% chardonnay.

88 Colour: bright straw. Nose: medium intensity, dried herbs, dry nuts, dried flowers. Palate: fruity, flavourful, good acidity.

ROGER GOULART 2006 EXTRA BRUT GRAN RESERVA

89 Colour: bright yellow. Nose: white flowers, fragrant herbs, fine lees, dry nuts. Palate: powerful, flavourful, dry wood.

ROSELL & FORMOSA

Rambla de la Generalitat, 14
08770 Sant Sadurní D'Anoia (Barcelona)
☎: +34 938 911 013 - Fax: +34 938 911 967
rformosa@roselliformosa.com
www.roselliformosa.com

ROSELL I FORMOSA 2008 BR RESERVA
40% macabeo, 35% xarel.lo, 25% parellada.

87 Colour: bright straw. Nose: medium intensity, fresh fruit, dried herbs, fine lees, floral. Palate: fresh, fruity, flavourful, good acidity.

ROSELL I FORMOSA ROSAT 2008 BR
50% garnacha, 50% monastrell.

85 Colour: rose. Nose: red berry notes, overripe fruit, faded flowers, powerfull. Palate: flavourful, fresh, fruity.

DAURAT "BRUT DE BRUTS" 2006 BR GRAN RESERVA
45% macabeo, 30% xarel.lo, 25% parellada.

90 Colour: bright golden. Nose: lees reduction notes, ripe fruit, dried herbs, pattiserie, lactic notes. Palate: powerful, flavourful, long.

ROSELL I FORMOSA 2007 BN GRAN RESERVA
45% macabeo, 30% xarel.lo, 25% parellada.

87 Colour: bright yellow. Nose: lees reduction notes, ripe fruit, dry nuts, sweet spices. Palate: long, flavourful, powerful.

ROSELL GALLART

Montserrat, 56
08770 Sant Sadurní D'Anoia (Barcelona)
☎: +34 938 912 073 - Fax: +34 938 183 539
info@rosellgallart.com
www.cavarosellgallart.com

TERESA MATA GARRIGA 2008 BN RESERVA
xarel.lo, macabeo, chardonnay, parellada.

89 Colour: bright yellow. Nose: ripe fruit, fragrant herbs, floral, expressive. Palate: good acidity, powerful, flavourful.

ROSELL GALLART 2007 BN RESERVA
xarel.lo, macabeo, parellada, chardonnay.

87 Colour: bright yellow. Nose: medium intensity, dried herbs, floral, ripe fruit, lees reduction notes. Palate: fresh, fruity, flavourful, good acidity.

ROSELL GALLART MAGNUM 2004 BN RESERVA
xarel.lo, chardonnay, macabeo, parellada.

87 Colour: bright yellow. Nose: neat, dried flowers, medium intensity, lees reduction notes. Palate: correct, good finish.

ROSELL RAVENTÓS CRISTAL 2004 BN RESERVA
xarel.lo, chardonnay, macabeo, parellada.

84

ROVELLATS

Finca Rovellats - B° La Bleda
08731 Sant Marti Sarroca (Barcelona)
☎: +34 934 880 575 - Fax: +34 934 880 819
rovellats@cavasrovellats.com
www.cavasrovellats.com

ROVELLATS COL.LECCIÓ 2007
58% parellada, 42% xarel.lo.

90 Colour: bright golden. Nose: fine lees, dry nuts, fragrant herbs, complex. Palate: powerful, flavourful, fine bead, fine bitter notes.

ROVELLATS 2010 BR
80% parellada, 10% macabeo, 10% xarel.lo.

87 Colour: bright yellow. Nose: medium intensity, fresh fruit, white flowers. Palate: correct, easy to drink, fresh.

ROVELLATS PREMIER BRUT 2010 BR
85% parellada, 15% macabeo.

85 Colour: bright yellow. Nose: white flowers, citrus fruit, fresh fruit, jasmine. Palate: fresh, flavourful, fruity, easy to drink.

ROVELLATS IMPERIAL 2009 BR
60% macabeo, 25% parellada, 15% xarel.lo.

88 Colour: yellow. Nose: fresh fruit, white flowers, fine lees, medium intensity. Palate: complex, flavourful, fruity, good acidity, fine bitter notes.

ROVELLATS ROSÉ 2009 BR
85% garnacha, 15% monastrell.

86 Colour: light cherry. Nose: ripe fruit, rose petals, balanced. Palate: correct, ripe fruit, good acidity.

ROVELLATS PREMIER 2010 BN
85% parellada, 15% macabeo.

87 Colour: bright straw. Nose: medium intensity, fresh fruit, dried herbs, fine lees. Palate: fresh, flavourful, good acidity.

ROVELLATS MAGNUM 2007 BN
60% xarel.lo, 26% macabeo, 14% parellada.

90 Colour: bright golden. Nose: fine lees, dry nuts, complex, dried herbs. Palate: flavourful, good acidity, fine bead, fine bitter notes.

ROVELLATS GRAN RESERVA 2006 BN
60% xarel.lo, 26% macabeo, 14% parellada.

88 Colour: bright yellow. Nose: fragrant herbs, medium intensity, floral, fresh fruit. Palate: flavourful, good acidity, correct.

ROVELLATS MASIA S. XV MILLESIMEE 2004 BN GRAN RESERVA
50% xarel.lo, 36% macabeo, 9% parellada, 5% chardonnay.

87 Colour: bright golden. Nose: ripe fruit, dry nuts, faded flowers. Palate: ripe fruit, long, good acidity.

SEGURA VIUDAS

Ctra. Sant Sadurní a St. Pere de Riudebitlles, Km. 5
08775 Torrelavit (Barcelona)
☎: +34 938 917 070 - Fax: +34 938 996 006
seguraviudas@seguraviudas.es
www.seguraviudas.com

SEGURA VIUDAS RESERVA HEREDAD 2008 BR GRAN RESERVA
67% macabeo, 33% parellada.

92 Colour: bright yellow. Nose: fine lees, dry nuts, fragrant herbs, complex. Palate: powerful, flavourful, good acidity, fine bead, fine bitter notes.

SEGURA VIUDAS BRUT VINTAGE 2007 BR
67% macabeo, 33% parellada.

88 Colour: bright yellow. Nose: dried flowers, ripe fruit, dried herbs. Palate: correct, good acidity, flavourful, fine bead, fine bitter notes.

LAVIT ROSADO BR
80% trepat, 10% monastrell, 10% garnacha.

87 Colour: raspberry rose. Nose: fine lees, dried herbs, floral, red berry notes. Palate: fresh, fruity, light-bodied, flavourful, easy to drink.

SEGURA VIUDAS BR RESERVA
50% macabeo, 15% xarel.lo, 35% parellada.

86 Colour: bright yellow. Nose: lees reduction notes, faded flowers, fruit liqueur notes, lactic notes. Palate: flavourful, ripe fruit, long.

LAVIT 2009 BN
60% macabeo, 40% parellada.

88 Colour: bright straw. Nose: fine lees, white flowers, fragrant herbs, fresh. Palate: good acidity, fine bead, fine bitter notes.

TORRE GALIMANY 2007 BN GRAN RESERVA
xarel.lo.

90 Colour: bright straw. Nose: floral, citrus fruit, fresh fruit, fragrant herbs, fine lees. Palate: good acidity, fine bead, fine bitter notes, fresh, fruity, flavourful.

ARIA BN
60% macabeo, 20% xarel.lo, 20% parellada.

86 Colour: bright straw. Nose: floral, ripe fruit, fragrant herbs. Palate: correct, fresh, light-bodied, easy to drink.

SOGAS MASCARÓ

Amalia Soler, 35
08720 Vilafranca del Penedès (Barcelona)
☎: +34 931 185 387
info@sogasmascaro.com
www.sogasmascaro.com

SOGAS MASCARÓ BR
40% macabeo, 40% xarel.lo, 20% parellada.

86 Colour: bright straw. Nose: medium intensity, dried herbs, floral. Palate: fresh, fruity, flavourful, good acidity.

SOGAS MASCARÓ 2008 BN RESERVA
40% xarel.lo, 30% macabeo, 30% parellada.

86 Colour: bright yellow, greenish rim. Nose: dry nuts, fragrant herbs, spicy. Palate: flavourful, correct, good acidity.

SOGAS MASCARÓ BN
40% macabeo, 40% xarel.lo, 20% parellada.

86 Colour: bright yellow. Nose: fresh fruit, wild herbs, dried flowers. Palate: correct, good acidity, balanced.

TORELLÓ

Can Martí de Baix, Ctra. de Sant Sadurni a Gélida - Apdo. Correos 8
08770 Sant Sadurní D'Anoia (Barcelona)
☎: +34 938 910 793 - Fax: +34 938 910 877
torello@torello.es
www.torello.com

TORELLÓ ROSÉ 2009 BR RESERVA
monastrell, garnacha.

86 Colour: rose, purple rim. Nose: candied fruit, powerfull. Palate: flavourful, spicy, long.

TORELLÓ 2008 BR RESERVA
macabeo, xarel.lo, parellada.

88 Colour: bright yellow, greenish rim. Nose: medium intensity, dried flowers, fresh. Palate: correct, easy to drink, good acidity.

TORELLÓ BY CUSTO BARCELONA 2007 BR GRAN RESERVA
macabeo, xarel.lo, parellada.

92 Colour: bright golden. Nose: fine lees, dry nuts, balanced. Palate: powerful, flavourful, good acidity, fine bead, fine bitter notes.

TORELLÓ ROSÉ MAGNUM 2007 BR RESERVA
monastrell, garnacha.

89 Colour: coppery red, bright. Nose: medium intensity, red berry notes, neat, balanced. Palate: flavourful, easy to drink, long.

JEROBOAM TORELLÓ 2008 BN GRAN RESERVA

94 Colour: bright straw. Nose: dried herbs, fine lees, overripe fruit, expressive, powerfull, fresh, white flowers. Palate: fruity, flavourful, good acidity, elegant, fresh, balanced.

TORELLÓ 225 2008 BN GRAN RESERVA
macabeo, xarel.lo, parellada.

92 Colour: bright yellow, greenish rim. Nose: dry nuts, dried herbs, dried flowers. Palate: good acidity, balanced, fine bitter notes.

GRAN TORELLÓ MAGNUM 2007 BN GRAN RESERVA
macabeo, xarel.lo, parellada.

91 Colour: bright straw. Nose: medium intensity, fresh fruit, dried herbs, fine lees, floral. Palate: fresh, fruity, flavourful, good acidity.

TORELLÓ 2008 BN GRAN RESERVA
macabeo, xarel.lo, parellada.

89 Colour: bright yellow. Nose: balanced, dry nuts, dried herbs. Palate: fruity, fine bitter notes, good acidity.

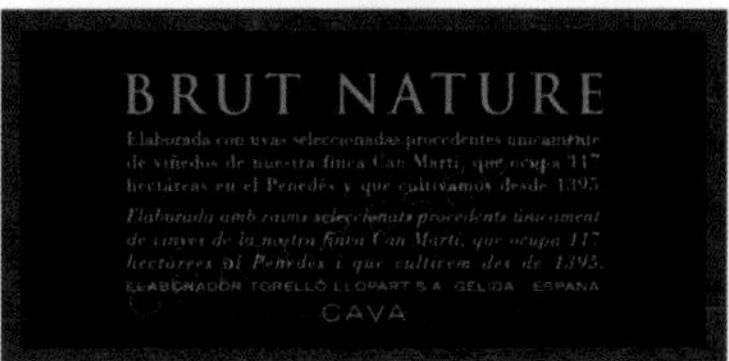

GRAN TORELLÓ 2007 BN GRAN RESERVA
macabeo, xarel.lo, parellada.

91 Colour: bright golden. Nose: fine lees, dry nuts, complex, dried herbs. Palate: powerful, flavourful, good acidity, fine bead, fine bitter notes.

TORELLÓ MAGNUM BN GRAN RESERVA
macabeo, xarel.lo, parellada.

89 Colour: bright straw. Nose: medium intensity, ripe fruit, spicy, faded flowers. Palate: balanced, good acidity, easy to drink.

TORELLÓ 37'5 CL. BN

87 Colour: bright yellow. Nose: medium intensity, fresh, fine lees, citrus fruit. Palate: fresh, easy to drink, correct.

TORRE ORIA

Ctra. Pontón - Utiel, Km. 3
46390 Derramador - Requena (Valencia)
☎: +34 962 320 289 - Fax: +34 962 320 311
info.torreoria@torreoria.es
www.torreoria.com

TORRE ORIA BR
macabeo.

84

TORRE ORIA BN
macabeo.

85 Colour: bright straw. Nose: medium intensity, dried herbs, ripe fruit, dried flowers. Palate: fresh, fruity, flavourful, good acidity.

UNIÓN VINÍCOLA DEL ESTE

Pl. Ind. El Romeral- Construcción, 74
46340 Requena (Valencia)
☎: +34 962 323 343 - Fax: +34 962 349 413
cava@uveste.es
www.uveste.es

NASOL DE RECHENNA BR
macabeo, chardonnay.

88 Colour: bright yellow. Nose: citrus fruit, fresh fruit, floral, fragrant herbs. Palate: light-bodied, fresh, flavourful, easy to drink.

LÁGRIMA REAL 2008 BN
chardonnay.

86 Colour: bright straw. Nose: medium intensity, fresh fruit, dried herbs. Palate: fresh, fruity, flavourful, good acidity.

NASOL DE RECHENNA BN
macabeo, chardonnay.

87 Colour: bright yellow. Nose: balanced, fragrant herbs, dry nuts, dried flowers. Palate: flavourful, fresh, good acidity.

VEGA MEDIEN BN
macabeo, chardonnay.

86 Colour: bright straw. Nose: medium intensity, fresh fruit, dried herbs, fine lees. Palate: fresh, fruity, flavourful, good acidity.

BESO DE RECHENNA BN RESERVA
macabeo, chardonnay.

85 Colour: bright straw. Nose: medium intensity, fresh fruit, dried herbs, fine lees, floral. Palate: fresh, fruity, flavourful.

VALL DOLINA

Plaça de la Creu, 1
08795 Olesa de Bonesvalls (Barcelona)
☎: +34 938 984 181 - Fax: +34 938 984 181
info@valldolina.com
www.valldolina.com

TUTUSAUS ECO 2008 BN GRAN RESERVA
45% xarel.lo, 38% macabeo, 8% parellada, 9% chardonnay.

87 Colour: bright yellow. Nose: balanced, powerfull, candied fruit, fine lees, faded flowers. Palate: flavourful, long.

VALL DOLINA ECO BN RESERVA
35% macabeo, 41% xarel.lo, 17% parellada, 7% chardonnay.

89 Colour: bright straw. Nose: white flowers, fresh fruit, fragrant herbs, expressive. Palate: powerful, flavourful, fruity, balanced.

VERA DE ESTENAS

Junto N-III, km. 266 - Paraje La Cabeuzela
46300 Utiel (Valencia)
☎: +34 962 171 141 - Fax: +34 962 174 352
estenas@estenas.es
www.estenas.es

ESTENAS 2010 BN
chardonnay, macabeo.

88 Colour: bright straw. Nose: medium intensity, fresh fruit, dried herbs, fine lees, floral. Palate: fresh, fruity, flavourful, good acidity.

VILARNAU

Ctra. d'Espiells, Km. 1,4 Finca "Can Petit"
08770 Sant Sadurní D'Anoia (Barcelona)
☎: +34 938 912 361 - Fax: +34 938 912 913
vilarnau@vilarnau.es
www.vilarnau.es

VILARNAU 2009 BN RESERVA
50% macabeo, 35% parellada, 15% chardonnay.

87 Colour: bright straw. Nose: medium intensity, fresh fruit, dried herbs, floral. Palate: fresh, fruity, flavourful, good acidity.

ALBERT DE VILARNAU GLOP FERMENTADO EN BARRICA 2008 BN GRAN RESERVA
60% chardonnay, 20% macabeo, 20% parellada.

93 Colour: bright golden. Nose: fine lees, dry nuts, complex, sweet spices. Palate: powerful, flavourful, good acidity, fine bead, fine bitter notes.

ALBERT DE VILARNAU GLOP 2008 BN GRAN RESERVA
50% chardonnay, 50% pinot noir.

91 Colour: bright golden. Nose: fine lees, dry nuts, fragrant herbs, complex, varietal. Palate: powerful, flavourful, good acidity, fine bead, fine bitter notes.

VILARNAU VINTAGE 2008 BN GRAN RESERVA
35% macabeo, 35% parellada, 30% chardonnay.

89 Colour: bright golden. Nose: fine lees, dry nuts, fragrant herbs, complex, floral. Palate: powerful, flavourful, good acidity, fine bead, fine bitter notes.

VILARNAU BRUT ROSÉ BRUT ROSADO
85% trepat, 15% pinot noir.

86 Colour: rose. Nose: ripe fruit, medium intensity, dried flowers. Palate: fruity, easy to drink.

VINÍCOLA DE NULLES S.C.C.L.

Estació, s/n
43887 Nulles (Tarragona)
☎: +34 977 602 622 - Fax: +34 977 602 622
botiga@vinicoladenulles.com
www.vinicoladenulles.com

ADERNATS DOLÇ 2009
50% macabeo, 25% xarel.lo, 25% parellada.

88 Colour: bright yellow. Nose: white flowers, candied fruit, fragrant herbs, sweet spices. Palate: sweetness, flavourful, fruity.

ADERNATS ROSAT 2010 BR
100% trepat.

87 Colour: coppery red. Nose: white flowers, red berry notes, ripe fruit. Palate: easy to drink, light-bodied, flavourful, fresh.

ADERNATS 2009 BR RESERVA
50% macabeo, 25% xarel.lo, 25% parellada.

88 Colour: bright yellow. Nose: floral, fresh fruit, fragrant herbs, expressive. Palate: correct, light-bodied, fresh, fine bitter notes.

ADERNATS 2008 BR GRAN RESERVA
40% macabeo, 30% xarel.lo, 30% chardonnay.

89 Colour: bright golden. Nose: fine lees, dry nuts, fragrant herbs, complex. Palate: powerful, flavourful, rich, balanced.

ADERNATS XC 2006 BR GRAN RESERVA
100% xarel.lo.

92 Colour: bright golden. Nose: petrol notes, ripe fruit, sweet spices, complex, expressive. Palate: good acidity, fine bitter notes, powerful, flavourful, long.

ADERNATS RESERVA 2009 BN
50% macabeo, 25% xarel.lo, 25% parellada.

89 Colour: bright straw. Nose: fine lees, floral, citrus fruit, dried herbs. Palate: balanced, fine bitter notes, powerful, flavourful.

ADERNATS 2008 BN GRAN RESERVA
40% macabeo, 30% xarel.lo, 30% chardonnay.

90 Colour: bright yellow. Nose: expressive, dried herbs, dried flowers, ripe fruit. Palate: balanced, powerful, flavourful, long.

ADERNATS 2006 BN GRAN RESERVA

89 Colour: bright yellow. Nose: medium intensity, balanced, dry nuts, faded flowers. Palate: fruity, good acidity, balanced.

VINÍCOLA DE SARRAL Í SELECCIÓ DE CREDIT

Avinguda de la Conca, 33
43424 Sarral (Tarragona)
☎: +34 977 890 031 - Fax: +34 977 890 136
cavaportell@covisal.es
www.cava-portell.com

PORTELL 2010 BR
70% macabeo, 30% parellada.

87 Colour: bright straw, greenish rim. Nose: medium intensity, dry nuts, dried flowers. Palate: light-bodied, fresh, easy to drink.

PORTELL ROSAT 2010 BR
100% trepat.

85 Colour: raspberry rose. Nose: red berry notes, balanced, floral. Palate: light-bodied, easy to drink, good finish, fresh.

PORTELL SUBLIM ROSADO 2009 BN
100% trepat.

90 Colour: light cherry. Nose: jasmine, sweet spices, red berry notes, fruit expression. Palate: balanced, fruity, flavourful. Personality.

PORTELL 2009 BN
80% macabeo, 20% parellada.

86 Colour: bright straw. Nose: balanced, dried flowers, dried herbs, medium intensity, fresh, dry nuts. Palate: fine bitter notes, correct, good acidity.

PORTELL PETRIGNANO BN GRAN RESERVA
80% macabeo, 20% parellada.

85 Colour: bright yellow. Nose: lees reduction notes, faded flowers, fragrant herbs. Palate: flavourful, powerful, fine bitter notes.

PORTELL ROSAT 2010 SS
100% trepat.

85 Colour: coppery red. Nose: floral, candied fruit, fresh. Palate: light-bodied, fresh, fruity, easy to drink, sweetness.

VINS I CAVES CUSCÓ BERGA

Esplugues, 7
08793 Avinyonet del Penedès (Barcelona)
☎: +34 938 970 164
cuscoberga@cuscoberga.com
www.cuscoberga.com

CUSCÓ BERGA ROSÉ 2009 BR
100% trepat.

83

CUSCÓ BERGA 2008 BR
40% xarel.lo, 30% macabeo, 30% parellada.

80

CUSCÓ BERGA 2007 BR GRAN RESERVA
50% xarel.lo, 30% macabeo, 20% parellada.

85 Colour: bright yellow. Nose: lees reduction notes, ripe fruit, dried herbs. Palate: flavourful, rich, powerful.

CUSCÓ BERGA 2009 BN RESERVA
50% xarel.lo, 30% macabeo, 20% parellada.

84

VINYA NATURA

Herrero, 32- S° 12
12005 Castellón (Castellón)
☎: +34 678 126 449
info@vinyanatura.com
www.vinyanatura.com

BABEL DE VINYA NATURA 2009 BR
100% macabeo.

83

VIVES AMBRÒS

Mayor, 39
43812 Montferri (Tarragona)
☎: +34 639 521 652 - Fax: +34 977 606 579
covives@tinet.org
www.vivesambros.com

VIVES AMBRÒS 2008 BR RESERVA
42% macabeo, 33% xarel.lo, 25% parellada.

87 Colour: bright straw. Nose: fresh fruit, dried herbs, fine lees, floral. Palate: fresh, fruity, flavourful, good acidity.

VIVES AMBRÒS 2006 BN GRAN RESERVA
39% xarel.lo, 27% macabeo, 25% chardonnay, 9% parellada.

88 Colour: bright golden. Nose: dry nuts, fragrant herbs, complex. Palate: powerful, flavourful, good acidity, fine bead, fine bitter notes.

VIVES AMBRÒS SALVATGE MAGNUM 2006 BN GRAN RESERVA
55% xarel.lo, 45% macabeo.

87 Colour: bright yellow. Nose: faded flowers, ripe fruit, powerfull. Palate: flavourful, correct.

VIVES AMBRÒS SALVATGE 2005 BN GRAN RESERVA
57% xarel.lo, 43% macabeo.

86 Colour: bright golden. Nose: medium intensity, dried herbs, fine lees, floral. Palate: fresh, flavourful, good acidity.

WINNER WINES

Avda. del Mediterráneo, 38
28007 Madrid (Madrid)
☎: +34 915 019 042 - Fax: +34 915 017 794
winnerwines@ibernoble.com
www.ibernoble.com

JUVENALS BR RESERVA
macabeo, xarel.lo, parellada.

86 Colour: bright straw. Nose: medium intensity, fresh fruit, dried herbs, fine lees, floral. Palate: fresh, fruity, flavourful, good acidity.

LOCATION:

The region stretches to the north of the Duero depression and on both sides of the Pisuerga, bordered by the Cérvalos and the Torozos hills. The vineyards are situated at an altitude of 750 m; the DO extends from part of the municipal area of Valladolid (the wine estate known as 'El Berrocal') to the municipality of Dueñas in Palencia, also including Cabezón de Pisuerga, Cigales, Corcos del Valle, Cubillas de Santa Marte, Fuensaldaña, Mucientes, Quintanilla de Trigueros, San Martín de Valvení, Santovenia de Pisuerga, Trigueros del Valle and Valoria la Buena.

CLIMATE:

The climate is continental with Atlantic influences, and is marked by great contrasts in temperature, both yearly and day/night. The summers are extremely dry; the winters are harsh and prolonged, with frequent frost and fog; rainfall is irregular.

SOIL:

The soil is sandy and limy with clay loam which is settled on clay and marl. It has an extremely variable limestone content which, depending on the different regions, ranges between 1% and 35%.

TYPES OF WINE:

ROSÉS: Cigales Nuevo. Produced with at least 60% of the *Tinta del País* variety and at least 20% of white varieties. The vintage must be displayed on the label. Cigales. Produced with at least 60% of the *Tinta del País* variety and at least 20% of white varieties. Marketed from 31st December of the following year. **REDS:** Produced with at least 85% of the Tinta del País and the *Garnacha Tinta* varieties.

GRAPE VARIETIES:

WHITE: *Verdejo*, *Albillo*, *Sauvignon Blanc* and *Viura*. **RED:** *Tinta del País* (*Tempranillo*), *Garnacha Tinta*, *Garnacha Gris*, *Merlot*, *Syrah* and *Cabernet Sauvignon*.

FIGURES:

Vineyard surface: 2,300 – **Wine-Growers:** 500 – **Wineries:** 33 – **2011 Harvest rating:** Excellent – **Production:** 5,283,761 litres – **Market percentages:** 75% domestic. 25% export

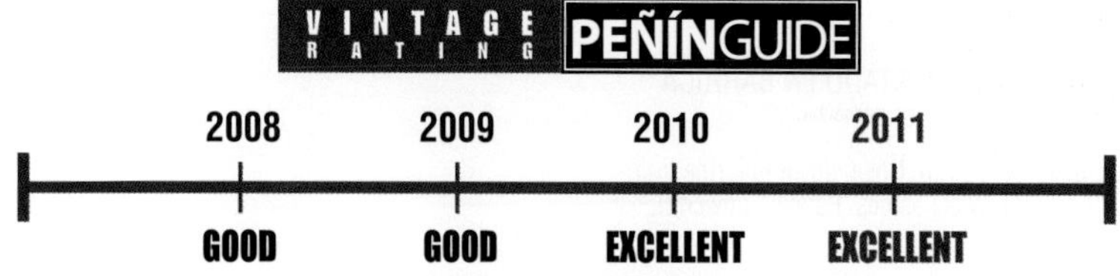

CONSEJO REGULADOR
Pza. Corro Vaca, 5 - 47270 Cigales (Valladolid) - ☎: +34 983 580 074 - Fax: +34 983 586 590
@ consejo@do-cigales.es - www.do-cigales.es

AVELINO VEGAS

Real del Pino, 36
40460 Santiuste (Segovia)
☎: +34 921 596 002 - Fax: +34 921 596 035
ana@avelinovegas.com
www.avelinovegas.com

VEGA LOS ZARZALES 2011 RD
tempranillo.

86 Colour: rose, purple rim. Nose: varietal, ripe fruit, red berry notes. Palate: flavourful, fruity, good acidity.

BODEGA CÉSAR PRÍNCIPE

Ctra. Fuensaldaña-Mucientes, s/n
47194 Fuensaldaña (Valladolid)
☎: +34 983 663 123
cesarprincipe@cesarprincipe.es
www.cesarprincipe.es

CÉSAR PRÍNCIPE 2009 TC
100% tempranillo.

93 Colour: black cherry. Nose: ripe fruit, varietal, powerfull, characterful, mineral, toasty. Palate: powerful, fine bitter notes, spicy, long.

BODEGA COOPERATIVA DE CIGALES

Las Bodegas, s/n
47270 Cigales (Valladolid)
☎: +34 983 580 135 - Fax: +34 983 580 682
bcc@bodegacooperativacigales.com
www.bodegacooperativacigales.com

TORONDOS 2011 RD
80% tempranillo, 10% garnacha, 10% albillo.

85 Colour: rose. Nose: floral, rose petals, red berry notes. Palate: flavourful, fruity.

BODEGA HIRIART

Los Cortijos, 38
47270 Cigales (Valladolid)
☎: +34 983 580 094 - Fax: +34 983 100 701
ines@bodegahiriart.es
www.bodegahiriart.es

HIRIART 2011 RD FERMENTADO EN BARRICA
70% tinta del país, 20% verdejo, 10% garnacha.

89 Colour: rose, purple rim. Nose: powerfull, ripe fruit, red berry notes, floral, sweet spices. Palate: , powerful, fruity, fresh.

HIRIART LÁGRIMA 2011 RD
70% tinta del país, 20% verdejo, 10% garnacha.

89 Colour: rose, purple rim. Nose: powerfull, ripe fruit, red berry notes, floral. Palate: , powerful, fruity, fresh.

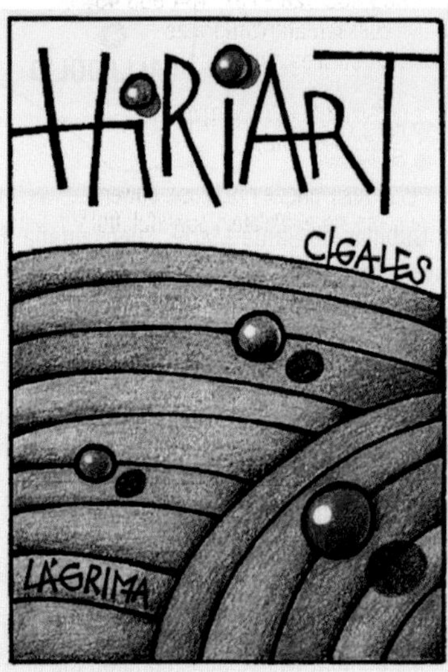

HIRIART 2010 T ROBLE
tinta del país.

88 Colour: bright cherry. Nose: sweet spices, creamy oak, fruit preserve. Palate: flavourful, fruity, toasty.

HIRIART 2009 TC
100% tinta del país.

90 Colour: bright cherry. Nose: ripe fruit, dark chocolate, nose:tic coffee. Palate: flavourful, fruity, toasty, round

BODEGA VALDELOSFRAILES

Camino de Cubillas, s/n
47290 Cubillas de Santa Marta (Valladolid)
☎: +34 983 485 028 - Fax: +34 983 485 028
valdelosfrailes@matarromera.es
www.valdelosfrailes.es

VALDELOSFRAILES 2011 RD
70% tinta del país, 30% verdejo.

88 Colour: rose, purple rim. Nose: powerfull, ripe fruit, red berry notes, floral. Palate: , powerful, fruity, fresh.

VALDELOSFRAILES TEMPRANILLO 2010 T
100% tinta del país.

89 Colour: bright cherry. Nose: ripe fruit, sweet spices, creamy oak. Palate: flavourful, fruity, toasty, round tannins.

VALDELOSFRAILES PRESTIGIO 2006 TR
100% tinta del país.

90 Colour: very deep cherry. Nose: powerfull, ripe fruit, toasty, dark chocolate, scrubland. Palate: powerful, spicy, ripe fruit.

SELECCIÓN PERSONAL CARLOS MORO VALDELOSFRAILES RESERVA ESPECIAL 2006 T
100% tinta del país.

90 Colour: deep cherry. Nose: powerfull, varietal, characterful, fruit preserve, toasty, dark chocolate. Palate: powerful, sweetness, spicy, ripe fruit.

VALDELOSFRAILES VENDIMIA SELECCIONADA 2006 TC
100% tinta del país.

88 Colour: cherry, garnet rim. Nose: spicy, creamy oak, toasty, complex, earthy notes, fruit preserve. Palate: powerful, flavourful, toasty, round tannins.

VALDELOSFRAILES PAGO DE LAS COSTANAS RESERVA ESPECIAL 2005 T
100% tinta del país.

88 Colour: cherry, garnet rim. Nose: ripe fruit, spicy, complex, roasted coffee, dark chocolate. Palate: powerful, flavourful, toasty, round tannins.

BODEGAS FERNÁNDEZ CAMARERO

Condes de Torreanaz, 45- 1ºA
28028 (Madrid)
☎: +34 677 682 426
javier.fernandez@balvinar.com
www.balvinar.com

BALVINAR PAGOS SELECCIONADOS 2007 TC
100% tempranillo.

92 Colour: cherry, garnet rim. Nose: ripe fruit, spicy, creamy oak, toasty, complex, mineral. Palate: powerful, flavourful, toasty, round tannins.

BODEGAS HIJOS DE FÉLIX SALAS

Corrales, s/n
47280 Corcos del Valle (Valladolid)
☎: +34 983 580 378 - Fax: +34 983 580 262
bodega@bodegasfelixsalas.com
www.bodegasfelixsalas.com

VIÑA PICOTA 2011 RD

84

BODEGAS LEZCANO-LACALLE

Ctra. Valoria, 2
47282 Trigueros del Valle (Valladolid)
☎: +34 629 280 515
info@lezcano-lacalle.com
www.lezcano-lacalle.com

DOCETAÑIDOS 2011 RD
tempranillo, albillo, verdejo, sauvignon blanc.

88 Colour: rose, purple rim. Nose: powerfull, red berry notes, floral, expressive. Palate: , powerful, fruity, fresh.

MAUDES 2010 TC
tempranillo, merlot, cabernet sauvignon.

87 Colour: black cherry. Nose: characterful, closed, ripe fruit, sweet spices, dark chocolate. Palate: spicy, fine bitter notes, toasty.

LEZCANO-LACALLE DÚ 2006 T
tempranillo, merlot, cabernet sauvignon.

91 Colour: deep cherry. Nose: powerfull, ripe fruit, sweet spices, toasty. Palate: flavourful, spicy, ripe fruit, fine bitter notes.

LEZCANO-LACALLE 2006 TR
tempranillo, merlot, cabernet sauvignon.

89 Colour: bright cherry. Nose: ripe fruit, spicy, cocoa bean, mineral. Palate: toasty, spicy, ripe fruit.

ÁTIMA BN
tempranillo, albillo, verdejo, sauvignon blanc.

83

BODEGAS SANTA RUFINA

Pago Fuente La Teja. Pol. Ind. 3 - Parcela 102
47290 Cubillas de Santa Marta (Valladolid)
☎: +34 983 585 202 - Fax: +34 983 585 202
info@bodegassantarufina.com
www.bodegassantarufina.com

A SOLAS 2011 B
100% verdejo.

88 Colour: bright straw. Nose: fresh, white flowers, ripe fruit. Palate: flavourful, fruity, good acidity, balanced.

VIÑA RUFINA 2009 TC
100% tempranillo.

87 Colour: bright cherry. Nose: sweet spices, creamy oak, ripe fruit. Palate: flavourful, fruity, toasty, round tannins.

BODEGAS Y VIÑEDOS ALFREDO SANTAMARÍA

Poniente, 18
47290 Cubillas de Santa Marta (Valladolid)
☎: +34 983 585 006 - Fax: +34 983 440 770
info@bodega-santamaria.com
www.bodega-santamaria.com

VALVINOSO 2011 RD
80% tempranillo, 10% albillo, 10% verdejo.

87 Colour: rose, purple rim. Nose: powerfull, ripe fruit, red berry notes, floral, expressive. Palate: , fruity, fresh.

TRASCASAS 2007 TR
tempranillo.

90 Colour: deep cherry. Nose: earthy notes, ripe fruit, toasty, sweet spices. Palate: flavourful, spicy, ripe fruit.

ALFREDO SANTAMARÍA 2007 TC
tempranillo.

88 Colour: cherry, garnet rim. Nose: spicy, creamy oak, toasty, ripe fruit. Palate: powerful, flavourful, toasty, round tannins.

BODEGAS Y VIÑEDOS ROSAN

Santa María, 6
47270 Cigales (Valladolid)
☎: +34 983 580 006 - Fax: +34 983 580 006
rodriguezsanz@telefonica.net

ROSAN 2011 RD
tinto fino, verdejo.

86 Colour: rose, purple rim. Nose: powerfull, ripe fruit, red berry notes, floral. Palate: , powerful, fruity, fresh.

ALBÉITAR 2010 T
tinto fino.

87 Colour: bright cherry. Nose: ripe fruit, fruit expression, scrubland. Palate: flavourful, ripe fruit.

BODEGAS Y VIÑEDOS SINFORIANO

San Pedro, 12
47194 Mucientes (Valladolid)
☎: +34 983 663 008 - Fax: +34 983 587 789
sinfo@sinforianobodegas.com
www.sinforianobodegas.com

SINFO 2010 T ROBLE
100% tempranillo.

85 Colour: deep cherry. Nose: powerfull, fruit liqueur notes, fruit preserve, sweet spices. Palate: powerful, good acidity, fine bitter notes.

SINFORIANO 2009 TC
100% tempranillo.

90 Colour: cherry, garnet rim. Nose: ripe fruit, spicy, creamy oak, toasty, complex. Palate: powerful, flavourful, toasty, round tannins.

SINFORIANO 2008 TR
100% tempranillo.

90 Colour: cherry, garnet rim. Nose: ripe fruit, spicy, creamy oak, toasty, characterful. Palate: powerful, flavourful, toasty, round tannins.

BODEGAS Y VIÑEDOS VALERIANO

Camino de las Bodegas, s/n
47290 Cubillas de Santa Marta (Valladolid)
☎: +34 983 585 085 - Fax: +34 983 585 186
bodegasvaleriano@yahoo.es
www.bodegasvaleriano.com

EL BERROJO 2011 RD
85% tempranillo, 10% albillo, 5% verdejo.

87 Colour: rose, purple rim. Nose: red berry notes, fruit expression, floral. Palate: flavourful, fresh, fruity.

C.H. VINOS DE CUBILLAS

Paseo Fuente la teja, 31
47290 Cubillas de Santa Marta (Valladolid)
☎: +34 983 585 203 - Fax: +34 983 585 093
info@valdecabado.com
www.bodegaschvinosdecubillas.com

VALDECABADO 2011 RD
60% tempranillo, 40 % garnacha, albillo, verdejo, viura.

87 Colour: rose, purple rim. Nose: powerfull, ripe fruit, red berry notes, floral, expressive. Palate: fleshy, powerful, fruity, fresh.

VALDECABADO 2008 T BARRICA
100% tempranillo.

88 Colour: dark-red cherry, garnet rim. Nose: ripe fruit, fruit liqueur notes, spicy, creamy oak. Palate: flavourful, fresh, spicy, long.

SELECCIÓN VIÑEDOS VIEJOS VALDECABADO 2006 T
100% tempranillo.

89 Colour: cherry, garnet rim. Nose: ripe fruit, spicy, creamy oak, fragrant herbs. Palate: powerful, flavourful, toasty, round tannins, balanced.

CONCEJO BODEGAS

Ctra. Valoria, Km. 3.6
47200 Valoria La Buena (Valladolid)
☎: +34 +34 983 502263 - Fax: +34 +34 983 502253
info@concejobodegas.com
www.concejobodegas.com

CARREDUEÑAS 2011 RD FERMENTADO EN BARRICA
100% tempranillo.

91 Colour: bright cherry. Nose: ripe fruit, sweet spices, creamy oak, expressive. Palate: flavourful, fruity, toasty, round tannins.

CARREDUEÑAS DOLCE 2011 RD
100% tempranillo.

90 Colour: rose, purple rim. Nose: powerfull, ripe fruit, red berry notes, floral, expressive. Palate: , fruity, fresh, sweetness.

CARREDUEÑAS 2011 RD
100% tempranillo.

87 Colour: rose, purple rim. Nose: powerfull, ripe fruit, red berry notes, floral. Palate: , powerful, fruity, fresh.

FINCA MUSEUM

Ctra. Cigales - Corcos, Km. 3
47270 Cigales (Valladolid)
☎: +34 983 581 029 - Fax: +34 983 581 030
info@bodegasmuseum.com
www.bodegasmuseum.com

VINEA 2009 TC
100% tinta del país.

91 Colour: cherry, garnet rim. Nose: spicy, creamy oak, toasty, complex, red berry notes. Palate: powerful, flavourful, toasty, round tannins.

MUSEUM REAL 2009 TR
tempranillo.

90 Colour: cherry, garnet rim. Nose: powerfull, characterful, ripe fruit, sweet spices, nose:tic coffee. Palate: powerful, spicy, ripe fruit.

FRUTOS VILLAR

Camino Los Barreros, s/n
47270 Cigales (Valladolid)
☎: +34 983 586 868 - Fax: +34 983 580 180
bodegasfrutosvillar@bodegasfrutosvillar.com
www.bodegasfrutosvillar.com

VIÑA CALDERONA 2011 RD
tinta del país.

87 Colour: light cherry. Nose: medium intensity, varietal, ripe fruit, red berry notes. Palate: flavourful, ripe fruit.

CONDE ANSÚREZ 2011 RD
tinta del país.

85 Colour: light cherry. Nose: ripe fruit, fruit expression, violet drops. Palate: flavourful, powerful, sweetness.

CALDERONA 2011 T
100% tinta del país.

88 Colour: cherry, purple rim. Nose: fresh fruit, red berry notes, floral, lactic notes, fresh. Palate: flavourful, fruity, good acidity.

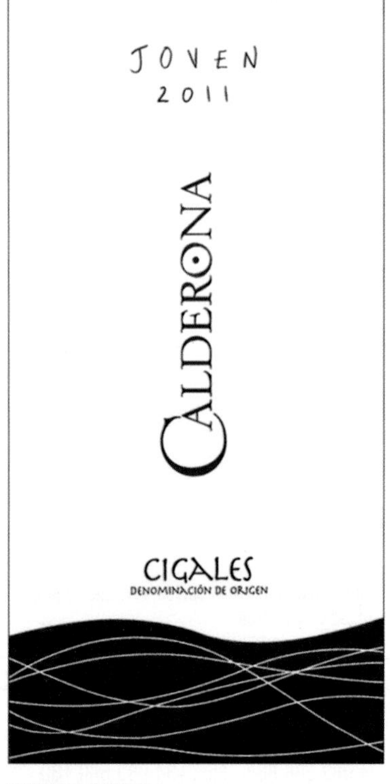

CALDERONA 2007 TC
100% tinta del país.

88 Colour: cherry, garnet rim. Nose: ripe fruit, spicy, complex, roasted coffee. Palate: powerful, flavourful, toasty, grainy tannins.

CONDE ANSÚREZ 2007 TC
100% tinta del país.

88 Colour: bright cherry. Nose: ripe fruit, sweet spices, nose:tic coffee, dark chocolate. Palate: flavourful, fruity, toasty, round tannins.

CALDERONA 2006 TR
100% tinta del país.

86 Colour: pale ruby, brick rim edge. Nose: dark chocolate, nose:tic coffee, roasted coffee, candied fruit. Palate: sweetness, spirituous, fine bitter notes.

HIJOS DE MARCOS GÓMEZ

Cuarto San Pedro, s/n
47194 Mucientes (Valladolid)
☎: +34 983 587 764 - Fax: +34 983 587 764
bodegas@salvueros.com

SALVUEROS 2011 RD

89 Colour: rose, purple rim. Nose: powerfull, ripe fruit, red berry notes, floral, expressive. Palate: fleshy, powerful, fruity, fresh.

HIJOS DE RUFINO IGLESIAS

La Canoniga, 25
47194 Mucientes (Valladolid)
☎: +34 983 587 778 - Fax: +34 983 587 778
bodega@hijosderufinoiglesias.com

CARRATRAVIESA 2011 RD
80% tempranillo, 10% garnacha, 10% albillo.

88 Colour: brilliant rose. Nose: elegant, candied fruit, dried flowers, fragrant herbs, red berry notes. Palate: light-bodied, flavourful, good acidity, long, spicy.

LA LEGUA

Ctra. Cigales, km. 1
47194 Fuensaldaña (Valladolid)
☎: +34 983 583 244 - Fax: +34 983 583 172
lalegua@lalegua.com
www.lalegua.com

LA LEGUA 2011 T
tempranillo.

83

LA LEGUA 2010 T ROBLE
tempranillo.

87 Colour: deep cherry. Nose: sweet spices, dark chocolate, ripe fruit. Palate: flavourful, powerful, ripe fruit.

LA LEGUA 2009 TC
tempranillo.

88 Colour: deep cherry. Nose: dark chocolate, cocoa bean, ripe fruit. Palate: flavourful, powerful, fine bitter notes, correct.

LA LEGUA CAPRICHO 2007 T
tempranillo.

90 Colour: deep cherry. Nose: ripe fruit, roasted coffee, dark chocolate. Palate: spicy, fine bitter notes, round tannins.

LA LEGUA 2007 TR
tempranillo.

87 Colour: cherry, garnet rim. Nose: ripe fruit, spicy, creamy oak, toasty. Palate: powerful, flavourful, toasty, round tannins.

OVIDIO GARCÍA

Malpique, s/n
47270 Cigales (Valladolid)
☎: +34 628 509 475 - Fax: +34 983 474 085
info@ovidiogarcia.com
www.ovidiogarcia.com

OVIDIO GARCÍA ESENCIA 2008 TC
100% tempranillo.

89 Colour: deep cherry. Nose: ripe fruit, sweet spices, toasty, cocoa bean. Palate: flavourful, powerful, spicy, ripe fruit.

OVIDIO GARCÍA ESENCIA 2006 TC
100% tempranillo.

90 Colour: cherry, garnet rim. Nose: powerfull, characterful, ripe fruit, toasty, dark chocolate. Palate: powerful, flavourful, concentrated.

OVIDIO GARCÍA 2006 TR
100% tempranillo.

88 Colour: deep cherry. Nose: sweet spices, roasted coffee, dark chocolate, ripe fruit. Palate: powerful, sweetness, fine bitter notes.

TRASLANZAS

Barrio de las Bodegas, s/n
47194 Mucientes (Valladolid)
☎: +34 639 641 123
traslanzas@traslanzas.com
www.traslanzas.com

TRASLANZAS 2008 T
100% tinta del país.

91 Colour: deep cherry. Nose: candied fruit, fruit expression, scrubland, spicy, cocoa bean. Palate: flavourful, good acidity, fine bitter notes.

DO CONCA DE BARBERÀ

Montblanc
TARRAGONA
Consejo Regulador
DO Boundary

LOCATION:

In the north of the province of Tarragona with a production area covering 14 municipalities, to which two new ones have recently been added: Savallà del Comtat and Vilanova de Prades.

CLIMATE:

Mediterranean and continental influences, as the vineyards occupy a river valley surrounded by mountain ranges without direct contact with the sea.

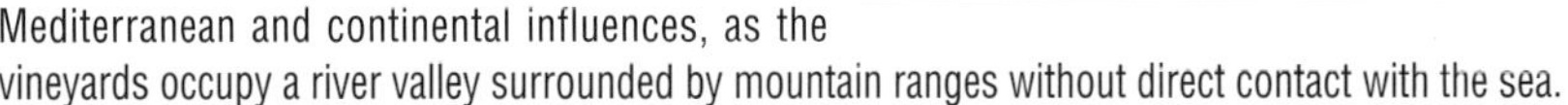

SOIL:

The soil is mainly brownish-grey and limy. The vines are cultivated on slopes protected by woodland. An important aspect is the altitude which gives the wines a fresh, light character.

GRAPE VARIETIES:

WHITE: *Macabeo, Parellada* (majority 3,300 Ha) *Chardonnay* and *Sauvignon Blanc.*
RED: *Trepat, Ull de Llebre* (*Tempranillo*), *Garnatxa, Cabernet Sauvignon, Merlot, Syrah* and *Pinot Noir.*

FIGURES:

Vineyard surface: 5,246 – **Wine-Growers:** 1,093 – **Wineries:** 20 – **2011 Harvest rating:** Very Good – **Production:** 26,569 litres – **Market percentages:** 70% domestic. 30% export

VINTAGE RATING PEÑÍNGUIDE

2008	2009	2010	2011
VERY GOOD	GOOD	GOOD	GOOD

CONSEJO REGULADOR
Torre del Portal de Sant Antoni C/ de la Volta, 2 - 43400 Montblanc - ☎: +34 977 926 905 / +34 692 596 044 - Fax: +34 977 926 906
@ cr@doconcadebarbera.com - www.doconcadebarbera.com

ABADÍA DE POBLET

Passeig de l'Abat Conill, 6
43448 Poblet (Tarragona)
☎: +34 977 870 358 - Fax: +34 977 870 191
info@abadiadepoblet.es
www.grupocodorniu.com

LES MASIES DE POBLET 2008 T
100% pinot noir.

86 Colour: bright cherry, orangey edge. Nose: medium intensity, spicy, tobacco, fruit preserve. Palate: correct, ripe fruit.

AGRÍCOLA DE BARBERÀ

Comercio, 40
43422 Barberà de la Conca (Tarragona)
☎: +34 977 887 035 - Fax: +34 977 887 035
cobarbera@doconcadebarbera.com

CABANAL TREPAT 2011 T
100% trepat.

86 Colour: cherry, purple rim. Nose: medium intensity, citrus fruit, neat, fruit expression. Palate: balanced, good acidity, easy to drink.

CABANAL TREPAT 2009 T
100% trepat.

87 Colour: very deep cherry. Nose: dried herbs, animal reductive notes, wild herbs. Palate: flavourful, correct.

BODEGA SANSTRAVÉ

De la Conca, 10
43412 Solivella (Tarragona)
☎: +34 977 892 165 - Fax: +34 977 892 073
bodega@sanstrave.com
www.sanstrave.com

SANSTRAVÉ FINCA GASSET CHARDONNAY 2011 BFB
chardonnay.

87 Colour: yellow. Nose: ripe fruit, floral, balanced, candied fruit, honeyed notes. Palate: correct, balanced, easy to drink.

SANSTRAVÉ PARTIDA DELS JUEUS 2009 TC
merlot, tempranillo, cabernet sauvignon, garnacha, trepat.

90 Colour: cherry, garnet rim. Nose: ripe fruit, spicy, creamy oak, balsamic herbs. Palate: powerful, flavourful, toasty, round tannins.

SANSTRAVÉ FINCA GASSET SYRAH 2005 TR
syrah.

84

BODEGA VEGA AIXALÁ

De la Font, 11
43439 Vilanova de Prades (Tarragona)
☎: +34 636 519 821 - Fax: +34 977 869 019
info@vegaaixala.com
www.vegaaixala.com

VEGA AIXALÁ 2010 B
garnacha blanca, pinot gris, chardonnay.

84

VEGA AIXALÁ 2009 TC
cabernet sauvignon, garnacha, syrah, cariñena, merlot.

88 Colour: very deep cherry, purple rim. Nose: expressive, balsamic herbs, cocoa bean, fruit preserve. Palate: balanced, round tannins.

BODEGAS BELLOD

Avda. Mare de Déu de Montserrat, 6
08970 Sant Joan Despí (Barcelona)
☎: +34 933 731 151 - Fax: +34 933 731 354
bodegasbellod@bodegasbellod.com
www.bodegasbellod.com

BELLOD BLANC DE BLANC 2011 B
moscatel.

84

MAS DEL NEN 2009 T
50% cabernet sauvignon, 50% syrah.

90 Colour: deep cherry, purple rim. Nose: creamy oak, dark chocolate, fragrant herbs, candied fruit. Palate: good structure, flavourful, ripe fruit.

BODEGAS TORRES

Miguel Torres i Carbó, 6
08720 Vilafranca del Penedès (Barcelona)
☎: +34 938 177 400 - Fax: +34 938 177 444
mailadmin@torres.es
www.torres.es

MILMANDA 2009 B
100% chardonnay.

90 Colour: bright yellow. Nose: powerfull, ripe fruit, sweet spices, creamy oak, fragrant herbs. Palate: rich, smoky aftertaste, flavourful, fresh, good acidity.

GRANS MURALLES 2008 TR
garnacha, cariñena, monastrell, garró, samsó.

93 Colour: deep cherry, purple rim. Nose: tobacco, ripe fruit, powerfull, scrubland, balsamic herbs, toasty. Palate: long, spirituous, spicy, ripe fruit, round tannins.

CARLANIA CELLER

Polígono 23, Parcela 93
43422 Barberà de la Conca (Tarragona)
☎: +34 977 887 375
info@carlania.com
www.carlania.com

CARLANIA 2011 B
80% macabeo, 20% trepat.

88 Colour: bright straw. Nose: balanced, expressive, medium intensity, white flowers, wild herbs. Palate: full, flavourful, long, ripe fruit.

CARLANIA 2010 RD
100% trepat.

85 Colour: coppery red, bright. Nose: wild herbs, faded flowers, expressive. Palate: flavourful, good acidity, long.

EL PETIT CARLANIA 2011 T
100% trepat.

86 Colour: bright cherry, purple rim. Nose: medium intensity, dried flowers, ripe fruit. Palate: light-bodied, easy to drink.

CARLANIA 2009 T
70% ull de llebre, 30% trepat.

87 Colour: cherry, garnet rim. Nose: medium intensity, ripe fruit, spicy. Palate: flavourful, full, fruity.

CARLANIA 2007 T
90% merlot, 10% trepat.

87 Colour: cherry, garnet rim. Nose: macerated fruit, fruit preserve, spicy, tobacco. Palate: balanced, round tannins.

CASTELL D'OR

Mare Rafols, 3- 1º 4º
08720 Vilafranca del Penedès (Barcelona)
☎: +34 938 905 446 - Fax: +34 938 905 446
castelldor@castelldor.com
www.castelldor.com

FRANCOLI 2011 B
80% macabeo, 20% parellada.

84

CASTELL DE LA COMANDA 2011 B
80% macabeo, 20% parellada.

82

FRANCOLI 2011 RD
100% trepat.

85 Colour: rose, purple rim. Nose: red berry notes, ripe fruit, rose petals. Palate: flavourful, ripe fruit.

CASTELL DE LA COMANDA 2011 RD

85 Colour: rose. Nose: red berry notes, ripe fruit, powerfull, citrus fruit. Palate: correct, easy to drink.

CASTELL DE LA COMANDA 2010 T
100% tempranillo.

86 Colour: cherry, garnet rim. Nose: fruit preserve, cocoa bean, scrubland. Palate: fruity, correct, easy to drink.

FRANCOLI 2009 T
50% trepat, 50% tempranillo.

86 Colour: cherry, garnet rim. Nose: medium intensity, wild herbs, fruit preserve, sweet spices. Palate: flavourful, ripe fruit.

FRANCOLI 2008 TC
60% tempranillo, 40% cabernet sauvignon.

85 Colour: bright cherry, garnet rim. Nose: medium intensity, ripe fruit, spicy, candied fruit. Palate: ripe fruit, round tannins.

CASTELL DE LA COMANDA 2006 T
100% tempranillo.

82

CASTELL DE LA COMANDA 2004 TR
100% cabernet sauvignon.

87 Colour: cherry, garnet rim. Nose: candied fruit, toasty, sweet spices. Palate: correct, easy to drink, spicy.

CELLER CARLES ANDREU

Sant Sebastià, 19
43423 Pira (Tarragona)
☎: +34 977 887 404 - Fax: +34 977 887 427
celler@cavandreu.com
www.cavandreu.com

PARELLADA CARLES ANDREU 2011 B
100% parellada.

87 Colour: bright yellow. Nose: medium intensity, faded flowers, ripe fruit. Palate: powerful, correct.

VINO TINTO TREPAT CARLES ANDREU 2010 T
100% trepat.

89 Colour: light cherry. Nose: woody, scrubland, fruit preserve, spicy. Palate: full, good acidity, fruity.

CELLER ESCODA SANAHUJA

Camí de Lilla a Prenafeta, s/n
43400 Montblanc (Tarragona)
☎: +34 659 478 198 - Fax: +34 977 314 897
jre@celler-escodasanahuja.com
www.celler-escodasanahuja.com

ELS BASSOTS 2009 B

89 Colour: yellow. Nose: expressive, spicy, scrubland. Palate: flavourful, rich, spicy. Personality.

LA LLOPETERA 2009 TC

89 Colour: bright cherry, garnet rim. Nose: powerfull, ripe fruit, candied fruit, dark chocolate. Palate: powerful, correct.

LES PARADETES 2007 TC

88 Colour: bright cherry, purple rim. Nose: candied fruit, powerfull, cocoa bean, sweet spices. Palate: correct, flavourful.

CELLER GUSPÍ

Avda. Arnau de Ponç, 10
43423 Pira (Tarragona)
☎: +34 636 816 724
viguspi@gmail.com
www.guspi.com

GUSPI BLANCTRESC 2011 B
60% macabeo, 30% chardonnay, 10% sauvignon blanc.

85 Colour: bright yellow. Nose: balanced, medium intensity, faded flowers, ripe fruit. Palate: powerful, flavourful, fruity.

GUSPI PINETELL 2009 T
100% merlot.

89 Colour: deep cherry, garnet rim. Nose: candied fruit, complex, spicy, creamy oak. Palate: ripe fruit, long, round tannins.

GUSPI EMBIGATS DE LA MARÍA 2009 T
100% ull de llebre.

88 Colour: cherry, garnet rim. Nose: medium intensity, spicy, ripe fruit, cocoa bean. Palate: fruity, balanced.

CELLER JORDI LLORENS

Prim, 5-7
43411 Blancafort (Tarragona)
☎: +34 629 204 672
cellerjll@gmail.com

CELLER JORDI LLORENS MACABEU PARELLADA 2011 B
50% macabeo, 50% parellada.

78

BLANKAFORTI 2011 T
20% garnacha, 80% cabernet sauvignon.

86 Colour: deep cherry, purple rim. Nose: medium intensity, candied fruit. Palate: flavourful, correct, ripe fruit.

ATIQETE CABERNET 2010 T BARRICA
100% cabernet sauvignon.

84

CELLER MAS FORASTER

Camino Ermita de Sant Josep, s/n
43400 Montblanc (Tarragona)
☎: +34 977 860 229 - Fax: +34 977 875 037
info@josepforaster.com
www.josepforaster.com

JOSEP FORASTER BLANC SELECCIÓ 2011 BFB
garnacha blanca, macabeo, chardonnay.

85 Colour: yellow. Nose: toasty, creamy oak, candied fruit. Palate: rich, toasty.

JOSEP FORASTER BLANC DEL COSTER 2011 B
90% macabeo, 10% garnacha blanca.

85 Colour: bright straw. Nose: fresh, medium intensity, floral. Palate: fruity, correct, easy to drink.

JOSEP FORASTER COLLITA 2011 T
90% ull de llebre, 10% cabernet sauvignon.

87 Colour: cherry, purple rim. Nose: medium intensity, ripe fruit, balanced. Palate: correct, fruity.

JOSEP FORASTER TREPAT 2010 T
100% trepat.

88 Colour: light cherry, garnet rim. Nose: medium intensity, balanced, ripe fruit, wild herbs. Palate: easy to drink, good acidity, correct.

JOSEP FORASTER 2009 TC
40% cabernet sauvignon, 25% ull de llebre, 25% syrah, 10% trepat.

88 Colour: cherry, garnet rim. Nose: medium intensity, wild herbs, ripe fruit, cocoa bean. Palate: flavourful, correct.

JOSEP FORASTER SELECCIÓ 2007 TR
90% cabernet sauvignon, 10% ull de llebre.

90 Colour: very deep cherry. Nose: complex, powerfull, ripe fruit, spicy, creamy oak. Palate: good structure, full, good acidity.

CELLER MOLÍ DELS CAPELLANS

Celler de Viveristes de Barberà de la Conca
43422 Barberà de la Conca (Tarragona)
☎: +34 651 034 221
info@molidelscapellans.com
www.molidelscapellans.com

MOLÍ DELS CAPELLANS PARELLADA 2011 B
parellada, moscatel.

87 Colour: bright straw. Nose: fresh, fresh fruit, white flowers, expressive. Palate: flavourful, fruity, balanced.

MOLÍ DELS CAPELLANS 2010 BFB
100% chardonnay.

87 Colour: bright yellow. Nose: candied fruit, medium intensity, creamy oak, sweet spices, floral. Palate: long, rich.

MOLÍ DELS CAPELLANS 2010 T
100% trepat.

87 Colour: light cherry, garnet rim. Nose: ripe fruit, sweet spices, creamy oak. Palate: powerful, flavourful, spicy.

MOLÍ DELS CAPELLANS SELECCIÓ 2010 T
ull de llebre, syrah, cabernet sauvignon.

86 Colour: cherry, garnet rim. Nose: dark chocolate, creamy oak, candied fruit. Palate: good structure, fruity.

MOLÍ DELS CAPELLANS PREMIUM 2007 T
100% cabernet sauvignon.

86 Colour: cherry, garnet rim. Nose: ripe fruit, spicy, old leather. Palate: powerful, flavourful, round tannins.

CELLER TINTORÉ DE VIMBODÍ I POBLET

Copèrnic, 44
08021 (Barcelona)
☎: +34 932 096 101 - Fax: +34 934 145 236
oriol@tinto-re.com

RE 2009 T
garnacha, cariñena, cabernet sauvignon.

90 Colour: cherry, garnet rim. Nose: ripe fruit, creamy oak, toasty, fragrant herbs. Palate: powerful, flavourful, toasty, round tannins.

CLOS MONTBLANC

Ctra. Montblanc-Barbera, s/n
43422 Barberà de la Conca (Tarragona)
☎: +34 977 887 030 - Fax: +34 977 887 032
club@closmontblanc.com
www.closmontblanc.com

CLOS MONTBLANC XIPELLA BLANC 2011 B
40% macabeo, 40% parellada, 20% sauvignon blanc.

88 Colour: bright straw. Nose: medium intensity, dried herbs, floral. Palate: fresh, fruity, good acidity.

CLOS MONTBLANC CHARDONNAY 2011 BFB
100% chardonnay.

87 Colour: bright yellow. Nose: powerfull, ripe fruit, sweet spices, creamy oak. Palate: rich, smoky aftertaste.

CLOS MONTBLANC SAUVIGNON BLANC PREMIUM 2011 B
100% sauvignon blanc.

86 Colour: bright straw. Nose: white flowers, ripe fruit, powerfull. Palate: flavourful, ripe fruit, fine bitter notes.

CLOS MONTBLANC ROSAT PREMIUM 2011 RD
cabernet sauvignon, merlot, pinot noir, tempranillo.

87 Colour: rose, purple rim. Nose: dried flowers, medium intensity, red berry notes. Palate: correct, good finish.

CLOS MONTBLANC CASTELL 2011 RD
cabernet sauvignon, merlot, tempranillo.

86 Colour: rose, purple rim. Nose: red berry notes, medium intensity. Palate: powerful, fruity, fresh.

CLOS MONTBLANC SYRAH PREMIUM 2009 T
100% syrah.

89 Colour: cherry, garnet rim. Nose: ripe fruit, spicy, creamy oak, complex. Palate: powerful, flavourful, toasty, round tannins.

CLOS MONTBLANC MERLOT PREMIUM 2008 TC
100% merlot.

87 Colour: cherry, garnet rim. Nose: powerfull, fruit preserve, toasty, tobacco. Palate: correct, spicy.

CLOS MONTBLANC MASÍA LES COMES 2007 TR
60% cabernet sauvignon, 40% merlot.

90 Colour: very deep cherry. Nose: dry stone, ripe fruit, candied fruit, dark chocolate, creamy oak. Palate: ripe fruit, long.

GRAN CLOS MONTBLANC UNIC TREPAT 2010
100% trepat.

88 Colour: cherry, garnet rim. Nose: ripe fruit, medium intensity, wild herbs, balanced, spicy. Palate: light-bodied, fruity, easy to drink.

GATZARA VINS

Josep M. Tossas, 47. 1º-2º
43400 Montblanc (Tarragona)
☎: +34 977 861 175 - Fax: +34 977 861 175
info@gatzaravins.com
http://viverdecelleristes.concadebarbera.cat

GATZARA BLANC 2011 B
65% macabeo, 35% chardonnay.

88 Colour: bright straw. Nose: scrubland, faded flowers, citrus fruit, ripe fruit, mineral, spicy. Palate: powerful, flavourful, long, balsamic.

GATZARA 2011 T
100% trepat.

90 Colour: cherry, purple rim. Nose: fresh fruit, red berry notes, floral, fragrant herbs, mineral. Palate: flavourful, fruity, good acidity, round tannins, balanced.

GATZARA 2009 TC
50% merlot, 30% cabernet sauvignon, 20% ull de llebre.

92 Colour: cherry, garnet rim. Nose: complex, balanced, candied fruit, dark chocolate, sweet spices. Palate: full, round tannins.

HEREDAD PALLARÉS

Ctra. Montblanc Prenafeta km 4
43415 Montblanc (Tarragona)
☎: +34 639 168 514 - Fax: +34 977 252 729
alosada@heredad-pallares.com
www.heredad-pallares.com

ARRELS DE LA CONCA 2011 B
chardonnay.

88 Colour: bright yellow. Nose: white flowers, ripe fruit, fragrant herbs. Palate: flavourful, fruity, long.

MAS DEL TOSSAL

Comerç, 2
43422 Barberà de la Conca (Tarragona)
☎: +34 618 546 050
pepburguera@yahoo.es

ESPURNA 2008 T

88 Colour: cherry, garnet rim. Nose: ripe fruit, spicy, creamy oak, cigar, complex. Palate: powerful, flavourful, toasty, round tannins.

RENDÉ MASDÉU

Avda. Catalunya, 44
43440 L'Espluga de Francolí (Tarragona)
☎: +34 977 871 361 - Fax: +34 977 871 361
rendemasdeu@terra.es
www.rendemasdeu.com

RENDÉ MASDEU 2011 RD
100% syrah.

87 Colour: rose. Nose: balanced, red berry notes, faded flowers. Palate: easy to drink, fruity, flavourful.

ARNAU 2010 T
100% syrah.

87 Colour: cherry, purple rim. Nose: powerfull, ripe fruit, faded flowers, sweet spices. Palate: ripe fruit, flavourful, good acidity.

MANUELA VENTOSA 2009 T
70% cabernet sauvignon, 30% syrah.

90 Colour: bright cherry, garnet rim. Nose: cocoa bean, tobacco, candied fruit, sweet spices. Palate: flavourful, fruity, good finish.

RENDÉ MASDEU 2009 TC
90% cabernet sauvignon, 10% syrah.

88 Colour: cherry, garnet rim. Nose: spicy, tobacco, ripe fruit. Palate: powerful, flavourful, long.

RENDÉ MASDEU 2007 TR
85% cabernet sauvignon, 15% syrah.

89 Colour: deep cherry. Nose: powerfull, fruit preserve, cocoa bean. Palate: full, good structure, round tannins, spicy.

ROSA MARÍA TORRES

Avda. Anguera, 2
43424 Sarral (Tarragona)
☎: +34 977 890 013 - Fax: +34 977 890 173
info@rosamariatorres.com
www.rosamariatorres.com

SUSEL VIOGNIER 2011 BFB
viognier.

86 Colour: bright straw. Nose: fresh, fresh fruit, white flowers. Palate: flavourful, fruity, good acidity, balanced.

VIOGNIER 2010 BFB
viognier.

87 Colour: bright yellow. Nose: ripe fruit, sweet spices, fragrant herbs. Palate: smoky aftertaste, good acidity.

SUSEL 2011 RD
cabernet sauvignon.

90 Colour: light cherry. Nose: fresh, red berry notes, fragrant herbs. Palate: flavourful, ripe fruit, balanced.

SUSEL 2011 T
cabernet sauvignon.

88 Colour: bright cherry, purple rim. Nose: medium intensity, varietal, scrubland. Palate: fruity, balanced.

RD ROURE 2010 T
cabernet sauvignon, syrah.

85 Colour: deep cherry. Nose: warm, scrubland, ripe fruit, varietal. Palate: fruity, flavourful, spicy.

VINYA PLANS 2009 TC
cabernet franc, cabernet sauvignon, syrah.

89 Colour: deep cherry, garnet rim. Nose: medium intensity, ripe fruit, spicy. Palate: good structure, full.

DOLÇ T
cabernet sauvignon.

83

VINÍCOLA DE SARRAL Í SELECCIÓ DE CREDIT

Avinguda de la Conca, 33
43424 Sarral (Tarragona)
☎: +34 977 890 031 - Fax: +34 977 890 136
cavaportell@covisal.es
www.cava-portell.com

PORTELL BLANC DE BLANCS 2011 B
80% macabeo, 20% parellada.

85 Colour: bright straw. Nose: medium intensity, fresh, fresh fruit. Palate: correct, good acidity.

PORTELL TREPAT 2011 RD
100% trepat.

86 Colour: light cherry, bright. Nose: medium intensity, fresh, red berry notes, faded flowers. Palate: light-bodied, easy to drink.

PORTELL SELECCIÓ 2º ANY 2010 T
70% tempranillo, 15% cabernet sauvignon, 15% merlot.

87 Colour: bright cherry, orangey edge. Nose: candied fruit, spicy, fragrant herbs. Palate: fruity, good acidity.

PORTELL MERLOT 2009 T
100% merlot.

89 Colour: cherry, garnet rim. Nose: expressive, balanced, ripe fruit, creamy oak, spicy. Palate: fruity, long.

PORTELL 2007 TC
40% merlot, 40% cabernet sauvignon, 20% tempranillo.

83

PORTELL 2006 TR
50% merlot, 40% cabernet sauvignon, 10% tempranillo.

86 Colour: cherry, garnet rim. Nose: spicy, tobacco, old leather, fruit preserve. Palate: fruity, balanced.

PORTELL 2011 BLANCO DE AGUJA
80% macabeo, 20% parellada.

81

PORTELL TREPAT 2011 ROSADO DE AGUJA
100% trepat.

81

VINS DE PEDRA

Sant Josep, 16
43400 Montblanc (Tarragona)
☎: +34 630 405 118
vinsdepedra@gmail.com

L'ORNI 2011 B
100% chardonnay.

87 Colour: bright straw. Nose: balanced, fresh fruit, white flowers. Palate: powerful, fruity, fine bitter notes.

LA MUSA 2010 T
70% merlot, 22% cabernet sauvignon, 8% syrah.

86 Colour: cherry, garnet rim. Nose: powerfull, fruit preserve, sweet spices, pattiserie. Palate: balanced, fine bitter notes, round tannins.

DO CONDADO DE HUELVA
Y VINO NARANJA DEL CONDADO DE HUELVA

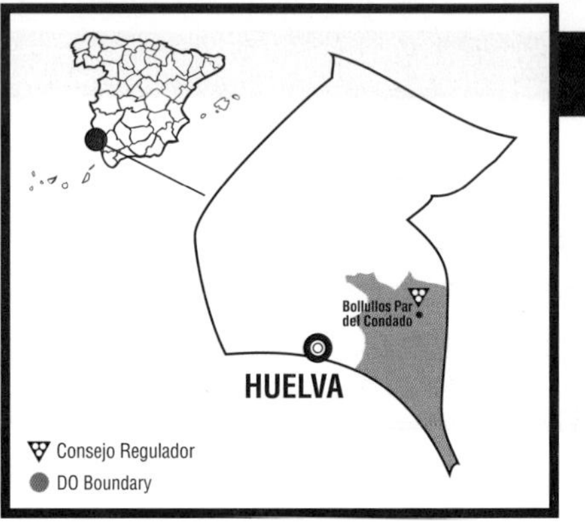

LOCATION:

In the south east of Huelva. It occupies the plain of Bajo Guadalquivir. The production area covers the municipal areas of Almonte, Beas, Bollullos Par del Condado, Bonares, Chucena, Gibraleón, Hinojos, La Palma del Condado, Lucena del Puerto, Manzanilla, Moguer, Niebla, Palos de la Frontera, Rociana del Condado, San Juan del Puerto, Villalba del Alcor, Villarrasa and Trigueros.

CLIMATE:

Mediterranean in nature, with certain Atlantic influences. The winters and springs are fairly mild, with long hot summers. The average annual temperature is 18 °C, and the average rainfall per year is around 550 mm, with a relative humidity of between 60% and 80%.

SOIL:

In general, flat and slightly rolling terrain, with fairly neutral soils of medium fertility. The soil is mainly reddish, brownish-grey with alluvium areas in the proximity of the Guadalquivir.

GRAPE VARIETIES:

WHITE: *Zalema* (majority with 86% of vineyards), *Palomino, Listán de Huelva, Garrido Fino, Moscatel de Alejandría* and *Pedro Ximénez.*
RED: *Merlot, Syrah, Tempranillo, Cabernet Sauvignon* and *Cabernet Franc.*

FIGURES:

Vineyard surface: 3,008 – **Wine-Growers:** 1,747 – **Wineries:** 30 – **2011 Harvest rating:** Good – **Production:** 9,010,774 litres – **Market percentages:** 90% domestic. 10% export

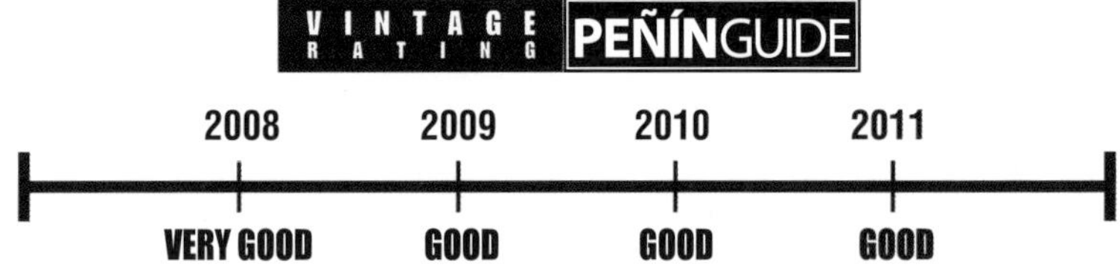

CONSEJO REGULADOR
Plaza Ildefonso Pinto, s/n. - 21710 Bollullos Par del Condado (Huelva) - ☎: +34 959 410 322 - Fax: +34 959 413 859
@ cr@condadodehuelva.es - www.condadodehuelva.es

AGROALIMENTARIA VIRGEN DEL ROCÍO

Avda. de Cabezudos, s/n
21730 Almonte (Huelva)
☎: +34 959 406 146 - Fax: +34 959 407 052
administracion@raigal.com
www.raigal.com

RAIGAL 2010 B
100% zalema.

80

MATALAGRANA 2009 T
tempranillo, merlot.

82

TEJARES CONDADO PÁLIDO FI
100% zalema.

85 Colour: bright yellow. Nose: pungent, faded flowers, balanced. Palate: balanced, fine bitter notes, long, easy to drink.

TEJARES CONDADO DULCE GE
100% zalema.

82

BODEGA MATEO L. BARBA

Ctra. Gibraleón - Trigueros, km. 2
21500 Gibraleón (Huelva)
☎: +34 658 882 699 - Fax: +34 615 031 519
mateobarba@vinicolavalverdejo.com
www.vinicolavalverdejo.com

TORREUMBRÍA 2011 B
palomino.

83

TORREUMBRÍA 2008 T
tempranillo, cabernet sauvignon, merlot.

86 Colour: cherry, garnet rim. Nose: red berry notes, ripe fruit, neat. Palate: flavourful, ripe fruit, long.

TORRECANALES NARANJA OL

86 Colour: light mahogany. Nose: balanced, jasmine, candied fruit, citrus fruit. Palate: fruity, flavourful, rich.

BODEGAS ANDRADE

Avda. Coronación, 35
21710 Bollullos del Condado (Huelva)
☎: +34 959 410 106 - Fax: +34 959 411 305
bodegas_andrade@hsoft.es
www.bodegasandrade.es

ANDRADE SELECCIÓN S/C B

83

ANDRADE SYRAH S/C T ROBLE
syrah.

86 Colour: cherry, garnet rim. Nose: ripe fruit, old leather, spicy, candied fruit. Palate: flavourful, ripe fruit, easy to drink.

DOCEAÑERO CR

87 Colour: light mahogany. Nose: candied fruit, powerfull, acetaldehyde. Palate: correct, balanced, good finish.

ANDRADE PEDRO XIMÉNEZ 1985 GE RESERVA
pedro ximénez.

88 Colour: old gold, amber rim. Nose: balanced, expressive, dried fruit, honeyed notes, sweet spices. Palate: long, unctuous, correct.

ANDRADE VINO NARANJA GE

88 Colour: light mahogany. Nose: powerfull, expressive, fruit liqueur notes, fruit liqueur notes, floral, citrus fruit. Palate: flavourful, balanced, long.

BODEGAS CONTRERAS RUIZ

Almonte, 5
21720 Rociana del Condado (Huelva)
☎: +34 959 416 426 - Fax: +34 959 416 744
contreras@bodegascontreras.com
www.bodegascontreras.com

VIÑA BARREDERO 2011 B
100% zalema.

86 Colour: bright straw. Nose: fresh, balanced, fresh fruit, white flowers. Palate: fresh, fruity, easy to drink.

BODEGAS DEL DIEZMO NUEVO

Sor Ángela de la Cruz, 56
21800 Moguer (Huelva)
☎: +34 959 370 004 - Fax: +34 959 370 004
info@bodegadiezmonuevo.com
www.bodegadiezmonuevo.com

VIÑA EL PATRIARCA 2011 B
zalema.

80

MELQUIADES SAENZ "VINO DE NARANJA" 2008 B
zalema, pedro ximénez.

86 Colour: mahogany. Nose: candied fruit, citrus fruit, jasmine, toasty, sweet spices. Palate: balanced, fruity, good finish.

BODEGAS DÍAZ

Pol. Ind. El Lirio Toneleros, 6
21710 Bollullos del Condado (Huelva)
☎: +34 959 410 340 - Fax: +34 959 408 095
diaz@bodegasdiaz.com
www.bodegasdiaz.com

VADO DEL QUEMA S/C B
100% zalema.

86 Colour: bright straw, greenish rim. Nose: dried herbs, fruit expression, fresh fruit. Palate: flavourful, ripe fruit, good finish.

DAIZ S/C T
syrah.

85 Colour: cherry, garnet rim. Nose: balanced, medium intensity, red berry notes, ripe fruit. Palate: fruity, easy to drink.

1955 CONDADO PÁLIDO CONDADO PÁLIDO
palomino.

84

ONUBIS GE
moscatel.

86 Colour: mahogany. Nose: balanced, expressive, dried fruit, candied fruit, cocoa bean, sweet spices. Palate: flavourful, ripe fruit, long.

1955 GE

86 Colour: light mahogany. Nose: powerfull, candied fruit, cocoa bean, sweet spices. Palate: flavourful, full, balanced.

NARANJA DE ORO VINO NARANJA
zalema.

86 Colour: light mahogany. Nose: balanced, candied fruit, floral, citrus fruit. Palate: fruity, flavourful, good finish.

BODEGAS DOÑANA

Labradores, 2
21710 Bollulos del Condado (Huelva)
☎: +34 959 411 513
bodegasdonana@terra.es
www.bodegasdoñana.es

VIÑA DOÑANA S/C B
zalema.

85 Colour: bright yellow. Nose: medium intensity, ripe fruit, floral. Palate: correct, flavourful, ripe fruit, fine bitter notes.

VIÑA DOÑANA 2009 B ROBLE
colombard.

86 Colour: bright yellow. Nose: powerfull, ripe fruit, sweet spices, creamy oak, toasty. Palate: rich, smoky afterpalate:, good acidity, toasty.

VIÑA DOÑANA S/C T
syrah.

80

VIÑA DOÑANA 2009 T ROBLE
syrah.

84

VIÑA DOÑANA 2007 TC
syrah.

84

BODEGAS IGLESIAS

Teniente Merchante, 2
21710 Bollullos del Condado (Huelva)
☎: +34 959 410 439 - Fax: +34 959 410 463
bodegasiglesias@bodegasiglesias.com
www.bodegasiglesias.com

% UZ CIEN X CIEN UVA ZALEMA 2011 B JOVEN
100% zalema.

85 Colour: bright straw. Nose: fresh, balanced, wild herbs, fresh fruit. Palate: ripe fruit, correct, good acidity.

UZT TARDÍA 2011 B
100% zalema.

84

RICAHEMBRA SOLERA 1980 GE
85% zalema, 15% pedro ximénez.

86 Colour: dark mahogany. Nose: powerfull, dried fruit, dark chocolate, sweet spices, toasty. Palate: sweet, flavourful, balanced.

LETRADO SOLERA 1992 GE SOLERA
100% zalema.

83

PAR VINO NARANJA VINO DE LICOR
85% zalema, 15% pedro ximénez.

87 Colour: light mahogany. Nose: candied fruit, expressive, balanced, powerfull, floral. Palate: flavourful, fruity, balsamic, correct.

BODEGAS OLIVEROS

Rábida, 12
21710 Bollullos Par del Condado (Huelva)
☎: +34 959 410 057 - Fax: +34 959 410 057
oliveros@bodegasoliveros.com
www.bodegasoliveros.com

JUAN JAIME SEMIDULCE 2011 B
100% zalema.

86 Colour: bright yellow, greenish rim. Nose: medium intensity, dried herbs, fresh fruit. Palate: easy to drink, flavourful, ripe fruit.

OLIVEROS 2007 TC
75% tempranillo, 25% syrah.

87 Colour: cherry, garnet rim. Nose: ripe fruit, spicy, creamy oak, toasty, complex. Palate: powerful, flavourful, toasty, round tannins, complex.

OLIVEROS PEDRO XIMÉNEZ PX

90 Colour: dark mahogany. Nose: complex, fruit liqueur notes, dried fruit, pattiserie, toasty. Palate: sweet, rich, unctuous, powerful.

BODEGAS SAUCI

Doctor Fleming, 1
21710 Bollullos del Condado (Huelva)
☎: +34 959 410 524 - Fax: +34 959 410 331
sauci@bodegassauci.es
www.bodegassauci.es

SAUCI 2011 B JOVEN
100% zalema.

85 Colour: bright straw. Nose: fresh fruit, floral, wild herbs, medium intensity. Palate: light-bodied, correct, fresh.

SAUCI VENDIMIA TARDÍA 2011 B JOVEN
100% zalema.

82

ESPINAPURA CONDADO PÁLIDO
100% palomino.

86 Colour: bright yellow. Nose: fresh, medium intensity, fresh fruit, dry nuts. Palate: flavourful, full, long.

RIODIEL SOLERA 1980 CONDÁDO VIEJO
100% palomino.

84

SAUCI CREAM SOLERA 1980 CR
75% palomino, 25% pedro ximénez.

85 Colour: light mahogany. Nose: medium intensity, candied fruit, pattiserie, caramel. Palate: full, balanced, fine bitter notes.

S' PX SOLERA 1989 VINO DE LICOR
100% pedro ximénez.

91 Colour: mahogany. Nose: sweet spices, fruit liqueur notes, complex, expressive, caramel. Palate: creamy, balanced, fruity, flavourful.

S' NARANJA VINO DE LICOR
80% pedro ximénez, 20% palomino.

88 Colour: mahogany. Nose: cocoa bean, sweet spices, candied fruit, citrus fruit, floral. Palate: flavourful, correct, balanced.

S' PX DULCE NATURAL VINO DE LICOR
100% pedro ximénez.

88 Colour: mahogany. Nose: candied fruit, honeyed notes, pattiserie, balanced. Palate: flavourful, concentrated, fruity.

SAUCI VINO DULCE VINO DE LICOR
palomino, pedro ximénez.

85 Colour: light mahogany. Nose: dried fruit, caramel, pattiserie. Palate: flavourful, spirituous, correct, balanced.

CONVENTO DE MORAÑINA

Avda. de la Paz, 43
21710 Bollullos Par del Condado (Huelva)
☎: +34 959 412 250
bodega@bodegasconvento.com
www.bodegasconvento.com

CONVENTO SUREÑO VIEJO 2002 CONDADO VIEJO OLOROSO
palomino, zalema.

85 Colour: iodine. Nose: medium intensity, caramel, sweet spices, candied fruit. Palate: flavourful, sweetness, fine bitter notes.

SECRETO DEL CONVENTO 1960 CR
palomino, zalema, pedro ximénez.

90 Colour: mahogany. Nose: powerfull, expressive, acetaldehyde, sweet spices, varnish. Palate: flavourful, spicy, ripe fruit, balanced.

CONVENTO PX RESERVA
100% pedro ximénez.

91 Colour: dark mahogany. Nose: complex, fruit liqueur notes, dried fruit, pattiserie, toasty. Palate: sweet, rich, unctuous, powerful.

CONVENTO NARANJA 2009 SEMIDULCE
100% zalema.

88 Colour: light mahogany. Nose: fruit liqueur notes, citrus fruit, wild herbs, sweet spices. Palate: flavourful, balanced.

MARQUÉS DE VILLALÚA

Ctra. A-472, Km. 25,2
21860 Villalba del Alcor (Huelva)
☎: +34 959 420 905 - Fax: +34 959 421 141
bodega@marquesdevillalua.com
www.marquesdevillalua.com

MARQUÉS DE VILLALÚA COLECCIÓN S/C B

87 Colour: bright straw. Nose: balanced, expressive, ripe fruit, white flowers. Palate: flavourful, fruity, long.

MARQUÉS DE VILLALÚA 2011 B
zalema, otras.

87 Colour: bright straw. Nose: fresh, balanced, medium intensity, floral, fresh fruit. Palate: fruity, flavourful, easy to drink.

SANTA AGUEDA VINO NARANJA

86 Colour: light mahogany. Nose: balanced, candied fruit, citrus fruit. Palate: fruity, easy to drink, good finish.

NUESTRA SEÑORA DEL SOCORRO

Carril de los Moriscos, 72
21720 Rociana del Condado (Huelva)
☎: +34 959 416 108 - Fax: +34 959 416 108
jl63@nuestrasenoradelsocorro.com

EL GAMO S/C B
100% zalema.

84

VIÑAGAMO S/C B

84

VIÑAGAMO S/C B

81

DON FREDE S/C RD

83

DON FREDE 2011 T
70% tempranillo, 30% syrah.

80

DON FREDE 2008 TC
70% tempranillo, 30% syrah.

87 Colour: bright cherry. Nose: ripe fruit, creamy oak, sweet spices, cocoa bean. Palate: flavourful, fruity, round tannins.

PRIMER CONSORCIO DE BODEGUEROS ESPAÑOLES

Almaraz, 44
21710 Bollullos del Condado (Huelva)
☎: +34 956 056 642
admin@emc3.es

ORANGE TREE (VINO NARANJA)

87 Colour: light mahogany. Nose: sweet spices, toasty, candied fruit, acetaldehyde. Palate: correct, ripe fruit, good finish.

VINÍCOLA DEL CONDADO

San José, 2
21710 Bollullos del Condado (Huelva)
☎: +34 959 410 261 - Fax: +34 959 410 171
comercial@vinicoladelcondado.com
www.vinicoladelcondado.com

MIORO 2011 B
100% zalema.

82

MIORO GRAN SELECCIÓN 2010 B
75% zalema, 25% moscatel.

85 Colour: bright yellow. Nose: white flowers, ripe fruit, balanced. Palate: fruity, flavourful, correct.

LANTERO 2009 RD
100% syrah.

81

LANTERO SYRAH 2010 T
100% syrah.

83

LANTERO ROBLE SYRAH 2009 T ROBLE
100% syrah.

82

VDM ORANGE
50% zalema, 50% moscatel.

88 Colour: old gold, amber rim. Nose: expressive, balanced, white flowers, fruit liqueur notes, sweet spices. Palate: flavourful.

MISTERIO DULCE GE
100% zalema.

84

MISTERIO OLOROSO SECO OL
100% zalema.

88 Colour: iodine, amber rim. Nose: powerfull, toasty, dry nuts. Palate: rich, fine bitter notes, , long, spicy.

DO COSTERS DEL SEGRE

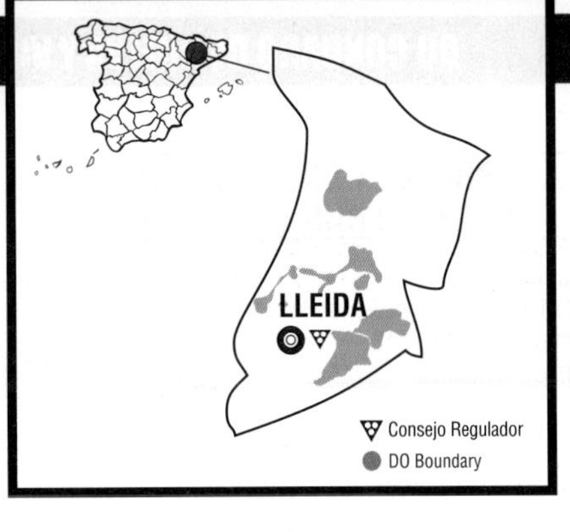

LOCATION:

In the southern regions of Lleida, and a few municipal areas of Tarragona. It covers the sub-regions of: Artesa de Segre, Garrigues, Pallars Jussà, Raimat, Segrià and Valls del Riu Corb.

CLIMATE:

Rather dry continental climate in all the sub-regions, with minimum temperatures often dropping below zero in winter, summers with maximum temperatures in excess of 35° on occasions, and fairly low rainfall figures: 385 mm/year in Lleida and 450 mm/year in the remaining regions.

SOIL:

The soil is mainly calcareous and granitic in nature. Most of the vineyards are situated on soils with a poor organic matter content, brownish-grey limestone, with a high percentage of limestone and very little clay.

GRAPE VARIETIES:

WHITE: PREFERRED: *Macabeo, Xarel·lo, Parellada, Chardonnay, Garnacha Blanca, Moscatel de Grano Menudo, Malvasía, Gewürztraminer, Albariño, Riesling* and *Sauvignon Blanc.*
RED: PREFERRED: *Garnacha Negra, Ull de Llebre* (*Tempranillo*), *Cabernet Sauvignon, Merlot, Monastrell, Trepat, Samsó, Pinot Noir* and *Syrah.*

SUB-REGIONS:

Artesa de Segre: Located on the foothills of the Sierra de Montsec, just north of the Noguera region, it has mainly limestone soils.
Urgell: Located in the central part of the province of Lleida, at an average altitude of 350 meters, its climate is a mix of mediterranean and continental features.
Garrigues: To the southeast of the province of Lleida, it is a region with a complex topography and marl soils. Its higher altitude is near 700 meters.
Pallars Jussà: Located in the Pyrinees, it is the northernmost sub-zone. Soils are predominantly limestone and its type of climate mediterranean with strong continental influence.
Raimat: Located in the province of Lleida and with predominantly limestone soils, it has a mediterranean climate with continental features, with predominantly cold winters and very hot summers.
Segrià: Is the central sub-zone of the DO, with limestone soils.
Valls del Riu Corb: Located in the southeast of the DO, its climate is primarily mediterranean-continental softened by both the beneficial effect of the sea breezes (called marinada in the region) and "el Seré", a dry sea-bound inland wind.

CONSEJO REGULADOR
Complex de la Caparrella, 97 - 25192 Lleida - ☎: +34 973 264 583 - Fax: +34 973 264 583
@ secretari@costersdelsegre.es - www.costersdelsegre.es

FIGURES:

Vineyard surface: 4,464 – **Wine-Growers:** 601 – **Wineries:** 38 – **2011 Harvest rating:** Very Good – **Production:** 10,542,100 litres – **Market percentages:** 60% domestic. 40% export

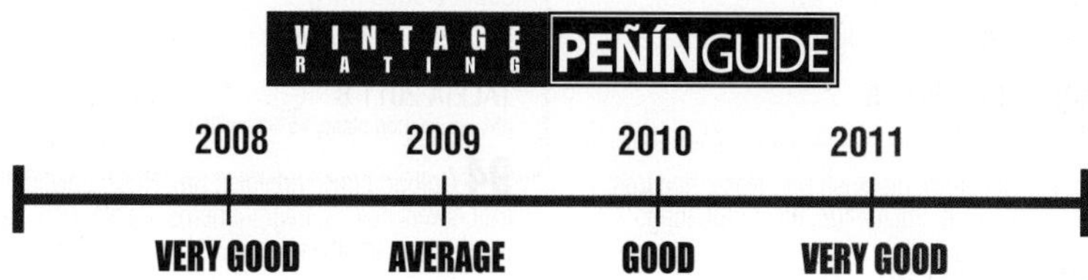

BODEGAS COSTERS DEL SIÓ

Ctra. de Agramunt, Km. 4,2
25600 Balaguer (Lleida)
☎: +34 973 424 062 - Fax: +34 973 424 112
comunicacio@costersio.com
www.costersio.com

SIÓS CHARDONNAY 2011 B
85% chardonnay, 15% otras.

88 Colour: bright yellow, greenish rim. Nose: ripe fruit, white flowers, citrus fruit. Palate: full, flavourful, long.

SIÓS GARNACHA 2011 RD
85% garnacha, 15% syrah.

87 Colour: light cherry, bright. Nose: red berry notes, ripe fruit, powerfull, wild herbs. Palate: flavourful, fruity, correct.

SIÓS SYRAH 2010 T
85% syrah, 15% garnacha.

86 Colour: very deep cherry, purple rim. Nose: roasted coffee, warm, powerfull. Palate: good structure, flavourful, long.

SIÓS SELECCIÓN 2009 T
40% syrah, 25% garnacha, 25% tempranillo, 10% cabernet sauvignon.

90 Colour: black cherry. Nose: creamy oak, toasty, complex, candied fruit, fruit preserve, dark chocolate. Palate: powerful, flavourful, toasty, round tannins.

SIÓS TEMPRANILLO 2009 T
100% tempranillo.

89 Colour: cherry, garnet rim. Nose: ripe fruit, spicy, creamy oak, toasty. Palate: powerful, flavourful, toasty, round tannins.

ALTO SIÓS 2007 T
60% syrah, 40% tempranillo.

90 Colour: deep cherry, garnet rim. Nose: candied fruit, sweet spices, cocoa bean. Palate: ripe fruit, flavourful, round tannins.

CASTELL D'ENCUS

Ctra. Tremp a Santa Engracia, Km. 5
25630 Talarn (Lleida)
☎: +34 973 252 974
celler@encus.org
www.encus.org

TALEIA 2011 B
85% sauvignon blanc, 15% semillón.

94 Colour: straw, greenish rim. Nose: powerfull, ripe fruit, sweet spices, fragrant herbs. Palate: rich, flavourful, fresh, good acidity, mineral.

EKAM 2011 B
90% riesling, 10% albariño.

88 Colour: bright straw. Nose: white flowers, ripe fruit, medium intensity. Palate: flavourful, fruity, good acidity, balanced.

THALARN 2010 T
100% syrah.

96 Colour: deep cherry. Nose: powerfull, complex, ripe fruit, fruit expression, creamy oak, sweet spices. Palate: flavourful, good acidity, fine bitter notes, long.

ACUSP 2010 T
100% pinot noir.

92 Colour: deep cherry. Nose: candied fruit, violet drops, scrubland. Palate: fruity, rich, flavourful.

QUEST 2010 T
cabernet sauvignon, cabernet franc, merlot, petit verdot.

91 Colour: very deep cherry. Nose: spicy, ripe fruit, sweet spices, creamy oak. Palate: round tannins, spicy, ripe fruit.

CASTELL DEL REMEI

Finca Castell del Remei, s/n
25300 Castell del Remei (Lleida)
☎: +34 973 580 200 - Fax: +34 973 718 312
info@castelldelremei.com
www.castelldelremei.com

CASTELL DEL REMEI ODA BLANC 2011 BFB
55% macabeo, 45% chardonnay.

90 Colour: bright yellow. Nose: roasted coffee, creamy oak, ripe fruit. Palate: powerful, flavourful, fine bitter notes.

CASTELL DEL REMEI BLANC PLANELL 2011 B

88 Colour: bright straw. Nose: powerfull, fruit expression, tropical fruit. Palate: flavourful, good acidity, easy to drink.

CASTELL DEL REMEI GOTIM BRU 2010 T
30% tempranillo, 25% garnacha, 25% cabernet sauvignon, 15% merlot, 5% syrah.

88 Colour: cherry, garnet rim. Nose: candied fruit, spicy. Palate: ripe fruit, good acidity, fine bitter notes.

CASTELL DEL REMEI ODA 2009 T

88 Colour: cherry, garnet rim. Nose: spicy, toasty, scrubland. Palate: fine bitter notes, good acidity, toasty.

CASTELL DEL REMEI 1780 2006 T

91 Colour: cherry, garnet rim. Nose: toasty, sweet spices, earthy notes. Palate: flavourful, powerful, fine bitter notes.

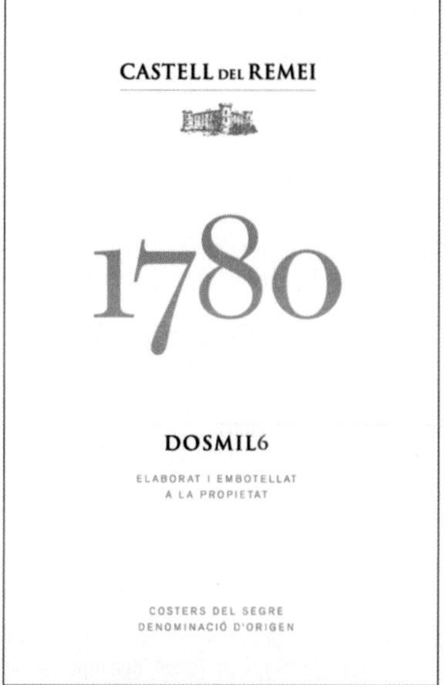

CELLER ANALEC

Ctra. a Analec, s/n
25341 Nalec (Lleida)
☎: +34 973 303 190 - Fax: +34 973 303 190
info@analec.net
www.analec.net

LA CREU VALL DEL RIU CORB 2011 B
60% macabeo, 40% chardonnay.

86 Colour: bright yellow. Nose: fresh fruit, floral, citrus fruit, fragrant herbs. Palate: correct, good finish, easy to drink.

ANALEC CINERIA B
100% macabeo.

85 Colour: bright golden. Nose: powerfull, overripe fruit, neat. Palate: fruity, flavourful.

LA CREU NEGRO 2010 T
100% tempranillo.

86 Colour: cherry, garnet rim. Nose: fruit preserve, scrubland, spicy, toasty. Palate: fruity, correct, easy to drink.

LA ROMIGUERA 2009 T
50% tempranillo, 20% syrah, 30% cabernet sauvignon.

88 Colour: cherry, garnet rim. Nose: ripe fruit, spicy, creamy oak, toasty, complex. Palate: powerful, flavourful, toasty, round tannins.

ANALEC GUALECH RESERVA ESPECIAL 2008
33% macabeo, 33% parellada, 33% chardonnay.

88 Colour: bright yellow. Nose: medium intensity, balanced, dried flowers, faded flowers. Palate: flavourful, fruity, fresh.

ANALEC 2009 BN
50% macabeo, 50% parellada.

85 Colour: bright yellow. Nose: dry nuts, medium intensity. Palate: easy to drink, good finish.

ANALEC BRUT ROSAT 2010 ESP
100% trepat.

85 Colour: light cherry. Nose: fresh, medium intensity, dried flowers. Palate: correct, easy to drink.

ANALEC SORT ABRIL 2008 ESP RESERVA
50% macabeo, 50% parellada.

85 Colour: bright yellow. Nose: medium intensity, faded flowers. Palate: correct, ripe fruit, easy to drink.

CELLER CERCAVINS

Ctra. LV-2101, km. 0,500
25340 Verdú (Lleida)
☎: +34 973 348 114 - Fax: +34 973 348 114
info@cellercercavins.com
www.cellercercavins.com

GUILLAMINA 2011 B
53% sauvignon blanc, 37% macabeo, 10% gewürztraminer.

87 Colour: bright yellow, greenish rim. Nose: powerfull, ripe fruit, dried flowers. Palate: fruity, easy to drink, good finish.

GUILLA 2009 BFB
100% macabeo.

88 Colour: bright golden. Nose: ripe fruit, powerfull, roasted coffee. Palate: flavourful, fruity, spicy, toasty, long.

VIROL 2011 RD
100% syrah.

86 Colour: light cherry. Nose: ripe fruit, powerfull, rose petals. Palate: flavourful, ripe fruit, long.

BRU DE VERDÚ 14 2008 T
56% syrah, 22% tempranillo, 22% merlot.

88 Colour: very deep cherry, garnet rim. Nose: powerfull, fruit preserve, dark chocolate, creamy oak. Palate: good structure, concentrated, spicy.

BRU DE VERDÚ 2008 T
55% tempranillo, 29% syrah, 10% cabernet sauvignon, 6% merlot.

87 Colour: cherry, garnet rim. Nose: medium intensity, ripe fruit, sweet spices. Palate: fruity, flavourful, easy to drink.

EGOM 2007 T
100% merlot.

87 Colour: cherry, garnet rim. Nose: spicy, dark chocolate, tobacco, candied fruit. Palate: rich, fruity, round tannins.

CELLER MATALLONGA

Raval, 8
25411 Fulleda (Lleida)
☎: +34 660 840 791
matallonga60@gmail.com
http://cellermatallonga.blogspot.com

ESCORÇA 2011 B
macabeo.

88 Colour: bright straw. Nose: medium intensity, wild herbs, fresh. Palate: fruity, good acidity, balanced.

CELLER TORRES DE SANUI

Camí Torres de Sanui - La Cerdera, s/n
25193 (Lleida)
☎: +34 973 050 202 - Fax: +34 973 050 202
celler@desanui.com
www.desanui.com

DE SANUI BLANC BARRICA 2008 B BARRICA
30% macabeo, 15% moscatel, 55% riesling.

87 Colour: bright yellow. Nose: medium intensity, ripe fruit, toasty, floral. Palate: correct, spicy, toasty.

DE SANUI NEGRE JOVE 2009 T
30% syrah, 35% garnacha, 35% ull de llebre.

83

DE SANUI NEGRE 2008 T BARRICA
35% syrah, 35% tempranillo, 30% garnacha.

86 Colour: cherry, garnet rim. Nose: medium intensity, dark chocolate, sweet spices, ripe fruit. Palate: fruity, spicy, easy to drink.

DE SANUI SYRAH 2006 TC
100% syrah.

87 Colour: cherry, garnet rim. Nose: balanced, warm, sweet spices. Palate: flavourful, ripe fruit, long.

DE SANUI NEGRE 2006 TC
40% syrah, 25% garnacha, 35% ull de llebre.

86 Colour: cherry, garnet rim. Nose: spicy, medium intensity, old leather. Palate: ripe fruit, balanced.

DE SANUI MERLOT 2006 TC
100% merlot.

86 Colour: cherry, garnet rim. Nose: cigar, spicy, ripe fruit. Palate: flavourful, good structure, round tannins.

CELLER VILA CORONA

Camí els Nerets, s/n
25654 Vilamitjana (Lleida)
☎: +34 973 652 638 - Fax: +34 973 652 638
vila-corona@avired.com
www.vilacorona.cat

LLABUSTES RIESLING 2011 BFB
100% riesling.

89 Colour: bright yellow. Nose: medium intensity, white flowers, varnish, sweet spices. Palate: ripe fruit, balanced, spicy.

LLABUSTES CHARDONNAY 2009 B
100% chardonnay.

86 Colour: bright yellow. Nose: candied fruit, honeyed notes, faded flowers. Palate: rich, ripe fruit, toasty.

TU RAI 2010 T
garnacha, monastrell, ull de llebre.

88 Colour: cherry, garnet rim. Nose: complex, expressive, medium intensity, ripe fruit, scrubland. Palate: balanced, spicy.

LLABUSTES ULL DE LLEBRE 2009 T
100% ull de llebre.

86 Colour: cherry, garnet rim. Nose: ripe fruit, spicy, creamy oak. Palate: powerful, flavourful, toasty, round tannins.

LLABUSTES CABERNET SAUVIGNON 2008 TC
100% cabernet sauvignon.

87 Colour: cherry, garnet rim. Nose: powerfull, macerated fruit, scrubland, spicy. Palate: flavourful, round tannins.

LLABUSTES MERLOT 2008 T
100% merlot.

87 Colour: light cherry, orangey edge. Nose: medium intensity, old leather, spicy, ripe fruit. Palate: balanced, long.

CÉRVOLES CELLER

Avda. Les Garrigues, 26
25471 La Pobla de Cèrvoles (Lleida)
☎: +34 973 175 101 - Fax: +34 973 718 312
info@cervoles.com
www.cervoles.com

CÉRVOLES NEGRE 2007 T

90 Colour: cherry, garnet rim. Nose: spicy, creamy oak, toasty, complex, mineral. Palate: powerful, flavourful, toasty, round tannins.

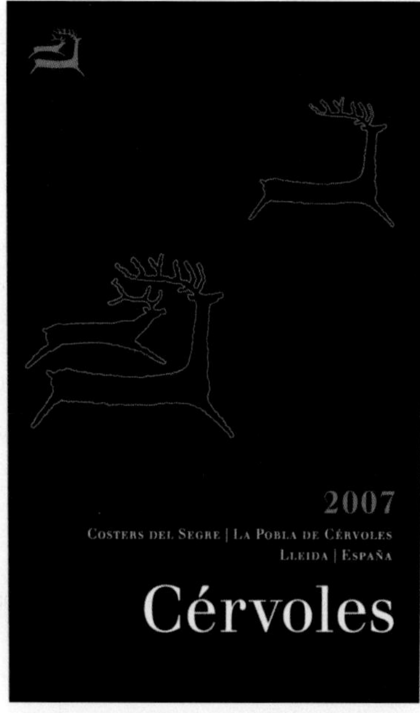

CÉRVOLES 2011 BFB
54% macabeo, 46% chardonnay.

92 Colour: bright straw. Nose: citrus fruit, ripe fruit, creamy oak, toasty. Palate: flavourful, fine bitter notes, good acidity, round.

CÉRVOLES COLOUR:S 2011 B
70% macabeo, 30% chardonnay.

90 Colour: bright straw. Nose: ripe fruit, fruit expression, white flowers. Palate: flavourful, ripe fruit, fine bitter notes.

CÉRVOLES COLOUR:S 2010 T

88 Colour: bright cherry. Nose: ripe fruit, sweet spices, creamy oak. Palate: flavourful, fruity, toasty, round tannins.

CÉRVOLES ESTRATS 2006 T
42% cabernet sauvignon, 36% tempranillo, 17% garnacha, 5% merlot.

94 Colour: very deep cherry. Nose: toasty, sweet spices, ripe fruit. Palate: flavourful, complex, sweetness.

CLOS PONS

Ctra. LV-7011, km. 4,5
25155 L'Albagés (Lleida)
☎: +34 973 070 737
clospons@grup-pons.com
www.clospons.com

CLOS PONS SISQUELLA 2010 B
garnacha blanca, albariño, moscatel de alejandría.

89 Colour: bright yellow. Nose: ripe fruit, powerfull, floral, balanced. Palate: fruity, flavourful, long.

CLOS PONS ROC NU 2009 TC
tempranillo, garnacha, cabernet sauvignon.

90 Colour: cherry, garnet rim. Nose: ripe fruit, spicy, toasty, earthy notes, balsamic herbs. Palate: powerful, flavourful, toasty, round tannins, balanced.

CLOS PONS ALGES 2009 TC
tempranillo, garnacha, syrah.

88 Colour: cherry, garnet rim. Nose: red berry notes, wild herbs, violets, creamy oak, mineral. Palate: light-bodied, fresh, fruity, flavourful.

LAGRAVERA

Ctra. de Tamarite, 9
25120 Alfarrás (Lleida)
☎: +34 973 761 374 - Fax: +34 973 760 218
info@lagravera.com
www.lagravera.com

ÓNRA MOLTA HONRA BLANC 2011 B
garnacha blanca, sauvignon blanc.

88 Colour: bright yellow. Nose: powerfull, ripe fruit, sweet spices, fragrant herbs. Palate: good acidity, ripe fruit.

ÒNRA BLANC 2011 B
garnacha blanca, chenin blanc, sauvignon blanc.

87 Colour: bright straw. Nose: fresh, scrubland, expressive, dried flowers. Palate: powerful, flavourful, long, good acidity.

LALTRE 2011 T
garnacha, merlot, monastrell.

87 Colour: cherry, garnet rim. Nose: balanced, medium intensity, red berry notes, ripe fruit. Palate: fruity, flavourful.

ÓNRA MOLTA HONRA 2010 T
garnacha, cabernet sauvignon.

91 Colour: cherry, purple rim. Nose: cocoa bean, sweet spices, candied fruit, neat. Palate: good structure, flavourful, round tannins.

ÒNRA 2010 T
garnacha, merlot, cabernet sauvignon.

90 Colour: cherry, garnet rim. Nose: medium intensity, ripe fruit, dry stone. Palate: flavourful, rich, fruity, good structure.

ÒNRA VI DE PEDRA SOLERA
garnacha blanca.

93 Colour: bright golden. Nose: candied fruit, honeyed notes, white flowers, creamy oak. Palate: good structure, rich, flavourful, good acidity.

MAS BLANCH I JOVÉ

Paratge Llinars. Pol. Ind. 9- Parc. 129
25471 La Pobla de Cérvoles (Lleida)
☎: +34 973 050 018 - Fax: +34 973 391 151
sara@masblanchijove.com
www.masblanchijove.com

SAÓ BLANC 2010 B
90% macabeo, 10% garnacha blanca.

89 Colour: bright straw. Nose: ripe fruit, fragrant herbs, balanced. Palate: flavourful, long, good acidity, fine bitter notes.

SAÓ ABRIVAT 2009 T
40% tempranillo, 35% garnacha, 15% cabernet sauvignon.

89 Colour: cherry, garnet rim. Nose: candied fruit, dark chocolate, spicy. Palate: good structure, flavourful.

SAÓ ABRIVAT 2008 T
40% tempranillo, 35% garnacha, 15% cabernet sauvignon.

90 Colour: cherry, garnet rim. Nose: medium intensity, balanced, cocoa bean, spicy, ripe fruit. Palate: fruity, good finish, easy to drink.

SAÓ EXPRESSIU 2008 T
55% garnacha, 25% cabernet sauvignon, 20% tempranillo.

89 Colour: cherry, garnet rim. Nose: medium intensity, sweet spices, candied fruit. Palate: correct, ripe fruit, easy to drink.

SAÓ EXPRESSIU 2007 T
55% garnacha, 25% cabernet sauvignon, 20% tempranillo.

92 Colour: cherry, garnet rim. Nose: complex, expressive, cocoa bean, creamy oak, ripe fruit. Palate: good structure, ripe fruit, round tannins.

OLIVERA

La Plana, s/n
25268 Vallbona de les Monges (Lleida)
☎: +34 973 330 276 - Fax: +34 973 330 276
olivera@olivera.org
www.olivera.org

BLANC DE SERÈ 2011 B
macabeo, parellada, chardonnay.

88 Colour: bright straw. Nose: medium intensity, balanced, fresh fruit, scrubland. Palate: fresh, fruity, easy to drink.

VALLISBONA 89 2010 B

92 Colour: bright yellow. Nose: powerfull, creamy oak, sweet spices, candied fruit. Palate: rich, ripe fruit, balanced.

MISSENYORA 2010 BFB

91 Colour: bright yellow. Nose: candied fruit, creamy oak, sweet spices, expressive. Palate: flavourful, full, ripe fruit, long.

AGALIU 2010 BFB
macabeo.

89 Colour: bright yellow. Nose: powerfull, ripe fruit, sweet spices, fragrant herbs. Palate: rich, smoky afterpalate:, flavourful, fresh, good acidity.

BLANC DE MARGES 2010 BFB

88 Colour: bright straw. Nose: medium intensity, balanced, dried flowers, dried herbs, sweet spices. Palate: easy to drink, good acidity.

BLANC DE ROURE 2010 B
macabeo, parellada, chardonnay.

87 Colour: bright yellow. Nose: white flowers, sweet spices, candied fruit. Palate: fruity, easy to drink.

EIXADERS 2009 BFB

92 Colour: bright yellow. Nose: balanced, complex, ripe fruit, creamy oak, sweet spices. Palate: rich, flavourful, balanced.

L'OLIVERA 2010 ESP

85 Colour: bright yellow. Nose: floral, ripe fruit, balanced. Palate: fresh, fruity, good finish.

L'OLIVERA GRAN RESERVA ESP

87 Colour: bright yellow. Nose: candied fruit, faded flowers, complex, expressive. Palate: fine bitter notes, balanced, flavourful.

RAIMAT

Ctra. Lleida, s/n
25111 (Lleida)
☎: +34 973 724 000 - Fax: +34 935 051 567
info@raimat.es
www.raimat.es

RAIMAT TERRA 2011 B
100% chardonnay.

91 Colour: bright yellow. Nose: ripe fruit, floral, balanced, expressive. Palate: flavourful, fruity, good acidity.

CASTELL DE RAIMAT CHARDONNAY 2011 B
100% chardonnay.

89 Colour: bright yellow. Nose: balanced, fruit expression, floral. Palate: flavourful, fruity, fine bitter notes.

CASTELL DE RAIMAT XAREL.LO CHARDONNAY 2011 B
50% xarel.lo, 50% chardonnay.

88 Colour: bright yellow. Nose: floral, ripe fruit, balanced. Palate: rich, flavourful, easy to drink, good acidity.

CASTELL DE RAIMAT CHARDONNAY BARRICA 2010 B
100% chardonnay.

89 Colour: bright yellow. Nose: candied fruit, jasmine, balanced, creamy oak. Palate: flavourful, rich, spicy.

RAIMAT VALLCORBA 2009 T
70% cabernet sauvignon, 30% syrah.

88 Colour: cherry, garnet rim. Nose: powerfull, warm, dark chocolate, ripe fruit. Palate: flavourful, fruity, round tannins, full.

CASTELL DE RAIMAT CABERNET SAUVIGNON 2008 TC
100% cabernet sauvignon.

87 Colour: cherry, garnet rim. Nose: medium intensity, spicy, scrubland. Palate: flavourful, correct, good acidity.

RAIMAT BRUT
chardonnay.

88 Colour: bright yellow. Nose: floral, ripe fruit, medium intensity. Palate: good acidity, balanced, correct, easy to drink.

RAIMAT GRAN BRUT BR
60% chardonnay, 40% pinot noir.

90 Colour: bright straw. Nose: fresh fruit, wild herbs, medium intensity. Palate: flavourful, correct, fine bitter notes, fresh.

TOMÁS CUSINÉ

Plaça Sant Sebastià, 13
25457 El Vilosell (Lleida)
☎: +34 973 176 029 - Fax: +34 973 175 945
info@tomascusine.com
www.tomascusine.com

AUZELLS 2011 B
31% macabeo, 27% sauvignon blanc, 16% chardonnay, 16% riesling, 5% albariño, 5% otras.

94 Colour: bright straw. Nose: expressive, floral, grassy, ripe fruit. Palate: spicy, ripe fruit, round, good acidity.

MACABEU FINCA RACONS 2010 B
100% macabeo.

92 Colour: bright straw. Nose: scrubland, ripe fruit, white flowers. Palate: flavourful, fine bitter notes, good acidity.

VILOSELL 2009 T
55% tempranillo, 18% syrah, 12% merlot, 11% cabernet sauvignon, 4% cariñena.

92 Colour: cherry, garnet rim. Nose: spicy, creamy oak, toasty, characterful. Palate: powerful, flavourful, toasty, round tannins.

FINCA COMABARRA 2009 T
50% cabernet sauvignon, 25% syrah, 25% garnacha.

92 Colour: cherry, garnet rim. Nose: ripe fruit, spicy, creamy oak, complex, sweet spices, nose:tic coffee. Palate: powerful, flavourful, toasty, round tannins.

LLEBRE 2009 T
28% tempranillo, 21% merlot, 18% cabernet sauvignon, 12% garnacha, 11% cariñena, 10% syrah.

87 Colour: deep cherry. Nose: ripe fruit, spicy, warm. Palate: fine bitter notes, toasty.

GEOL 2008 T
44% merlot, 30% cabernet sauvignon, 9% cabernet franc, 6% garnacha, 6% cariñena, 6% marselan.

92 Colour: cherry, garnet rim. Nose: earthy notes, ripe fruit, sweet spices. Palate: flavourful, powerful, fine bitter notes.

VINYA L'HEREU DE SERÓ

Molí, s/n
25739 Sero - Artesa de Segre (Lleida)
☎: +34 973 400 472 - Fax: +34 973 400 472
vinyalhereu@vinyalhereu.com
www.vinyalhereu.com

PETIT GREALÓ 2009 T
syrah, merlot, cabernet sauvignon.

88 Colour: cherry, garnet rim. Nose: powerfull, scrubland, ripe fruit, fruit preserve. Palate: correct, balanced.

PETIT GREALÓ 2008 T
syrah, merlot, cabernet sauvignon.

86 Colour: cherry, garnet rim. Nose: powerfull, scrubland, spicy. Palate: fruity, spicy, easy to drink.

FLOR DE GREALÓ 2007 T
merlot, syrah, cabernet sauvignon.

87 Colour: bright cherry, garnet rim. Nose: macerated fruit, wild herbs, old leather, tobacco. Palate: flavourful, fruity.

VINYA VILARS

Camí de Puiggrós, s/n
25140 Arbeca (Lleida)
☎: +34 973 149 144 - Fax: +34 973 160 719
vinyaelsvilars@vinyaelsvilars.com
www.vinyaelsvilars.com

LEIX 2009 T
100% syrah.

91 Colour: cherry, garnet rim. Nose: complex, expressive, elegant, ripe fruit. Palate: flavourful, spicy, round tannins.

TALLAT DE LLUNA 2009 T
100% syrah.

88 Colour: bright cherry, garnet rim. Nose: toasty, cocoa bean. Palate: ripe fruit, balanced, long.

VILARS 2009 T
50% merlot, 50% syrah.

87 Colour: cherry, garnet rim. Nose: powerfull, spicy, balanced. Palate: flavourful, ripe fruit, round tannins.

GERAR 2009 T
100% merlot.

86 Colour: cherry, garnet rim. Nose: medium intensity, ripe fruit, spicy, warm, scrubland. Palate: flavourful, ripe fruit, long.

DO EL HIERRO

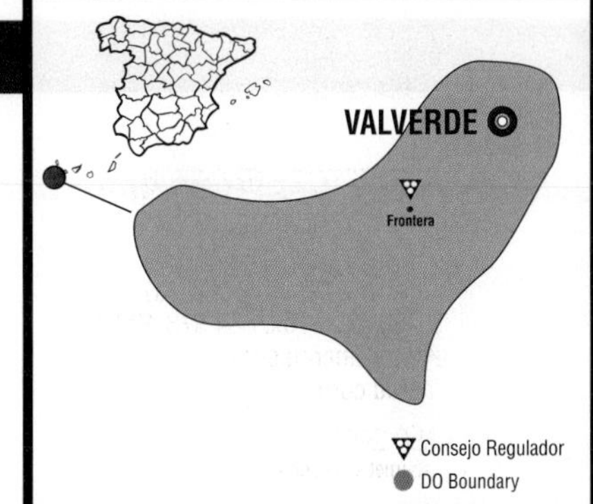

LOCATION:

On the island of El Hierro, part of the Canary Islands. The production area covers the whole island, although the main growing regions are Valle del Golfo, Sabinosa, El Pinar and Echedo.

CLIMATE:

Fairly mild in general, although higher levels of humidity are recorded in high mountainous regions. Rainfall is relatively low.

SOIL:

Volcanic in origin, with a good water retention and storage capacity. Although the vineyards were traditionally cultivated in the higher regions, at present most of them are found at low altitudes, resulting in an early ripening of the grapes.

GRAPE VARIETIES:

WHITE: *Verijadiego* (majority with 50% of all white varieties), *Listán Blanca, Bremajuelo, Uval* (*Gual*), *Pedro Ximénez, Baboso* and *Moscatel.*
RED: *Listán Negro, Negramoll, Baboso Negro* and *Verijadiego Negro.*

FIGURES:

Vineyard surface: 192 – **Wine-Growers:** 257 – **Wineries:** 7 – **2011 Harvest rating:** N/A – **Production:** 90,000 litres – **Market percentages:** 99% domestic. 1% export

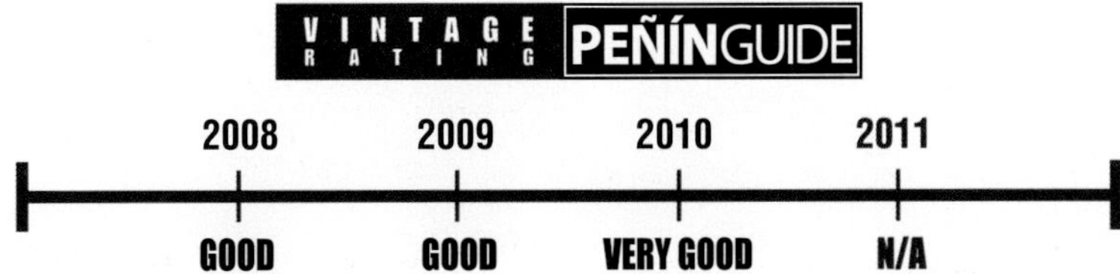

CONSEJO REGULADOR
Oficina de Agricultura. El Matorral, s/n - 38911 Frontera (Santa Cruz de Tenerife)
☎: +34 922 556 064 / +34 922 559 744 - Fax: +34 922 559 691
@ doelhierro@hotmail.com - www.elhierro.tv

SDAD. COOPERATIVA DEL CAMPO "FRONTERA" VINÍCOLA INSULAR

El Matorral, s/n
38911 Frontera - El Hierro (Tenerife)
☎: +34 922 556 016 - Fax: +34 922 556 042
coopfrontera@cooperativafrontera.com
www.cooperativafrontera.com

VIÑA FRONTERA AFRUTADO 2011 B
60% verijadiego blanco, listán blanco, 10% vidueño.

86 Colour: bright straw. Nose: dried flowers, citrus fruit, medium intensity. Palate: flavourful, balanced, good acidity, ripe fruit.

VIÑA FRONTERA 2011 B
60% verijadiego blanco, 40% listán blanco.

84

VIÑA FRONTERA 2011 T MACERACIÓN CARBÓNICA
100% listán negro.

89 Colour: cherry, purple rim. Nose: neat, fruit expression, violets, balanced. Palate: balanced, good acidity, fine bitter notes, fruity.

VIÑA FRONTERA BABOSO 2009 T
100% baboso negro.

84

VIÑA FRONTERA VERIJADIEGO 2009 T
100% verijadiego.

82

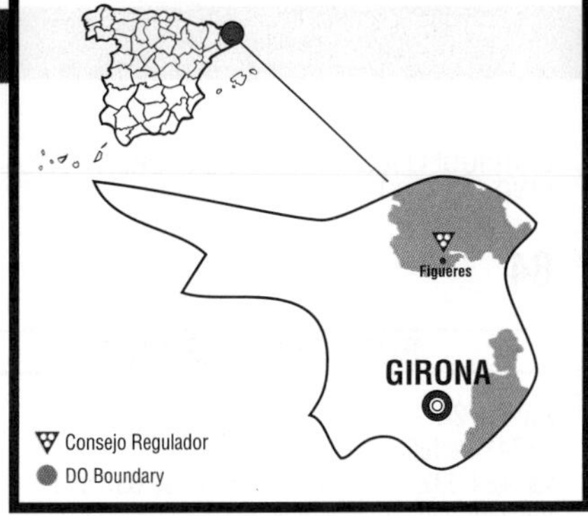

LOCATION:

In the far north west of Catalonia, in the province of Girona. The production area covers 40 municipal areas and is situated the slopes of the Rodes and Alberes mountain ranges forming an arch which leads from Cape Creus to what is known as the Garrotxa d'Empordà.

CLIMATE:

The climatology is conditioned by the 'Tramontana', a strong north wind which affects the vineyards. Furthermore, the winters are mild, with hardly any frost, and the summers hot, although somewhat tempered by the sea breezes. The average rainfall is around 600 mm.

SOIL:

The soil is in general poor, of a granitic nature in the mountainous areas, alluvial in the plains and slaty on the coastal belt.

GRAPE VARIETIES:

WHITE:
PREFERRED: *Garnacha Blanca*, *Macabeo (Viura)* and *Moscatel de Alejandría.*
AUTHORIZED: *Xarel.lo, Chardonnay, Gewürztraminer, Malvasía, Moscatel de Gra Petit, Picapoll Blanc* and *Sauvignon Blanc.*
RED:
PREFERRED: *Cariñena* and *Garnacha Tinta.*
AUTHORIZED: *Cabernet Sauvignon, Cabernet Franc, Merlot, Monastrell, Tempranillo, Syrah, Garnacha Roja (lledoner roig)* and *Garnacha Peluda.*

FIGURES:

Vineyard surface: 1,786 – **Wine-Growers:** 335 – **Wineries:** 49 – **2011 Harvest rating:** Very Good – **Production:** 6,395,900 litres – **Market percentages:** 84% domestic. 16% export

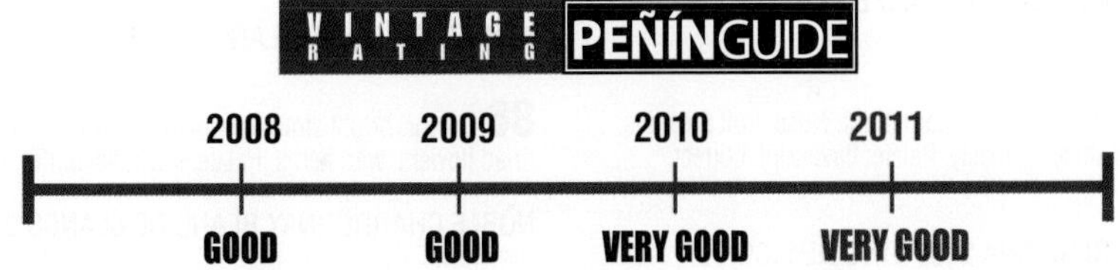

CONSEJO REGULADOR
Avda. Marignane, 2 - Apdo. de Correos 186 - 17600 Figueres (Girona) - ☎: +34 972 507 513 - Fax: +34 972 510 058
@ info@doemporda.com - www.doemporda.com

AGRÍCOLA DE GARRIGUELLA

Ctra. de Roses, s/n
17780 Garriguella (Girona)
☎: +34 972 530 002 - Fax: +34 972 531 747
lluis@cooperativagarriguella.com
www.cooperativagarriguella.com

DINARELLS 2011 B
60% macabeo, 30% garnacha blanca, 10% moscatel.

84

PUNTILS 2010 B
75% garnacha blanca, 25% moscatel.

84

DINARELLS 2011 RD
40% tempranillo, 40% mazuelo, 20% merlot.

87 Colour: light cherry, bright. Nose: balanced, red berry notes, rose petals. Palate: fruity, ripe fruit, long.

PUNTILS 2010 RD
30% mazuelo, 50% garnacha, 20% tempranillo.

83

DINARELLS NEGRE 2010 T
30% mazuelo, 30% garnacha, 20% merlot, 20% cabernet sauvignon.

85 Colour: cherry, purple rim. Nose: ripe fruit, wild herbs. Palate: correct, balanced, easy to drink, good finish.

GARRIGUELLA 2009 TC
50% cabernet sauvignon, 30% garnacha, 20% mazuelo.

86 Colour: deep cherry, garnet rim. Nose: toasty, sweet spices, cocoa bean, powerfull. Palate: ripe fruit, easy to drink.

PUNTILS 2007 T
35% merlot, 35% mazuelo, 20% garnacha, cabernet sauvignon.

85 Colour: dark-red cherry, garnet rim. Nose: toasty, dark chocolate. Palate: good structure, round tannins, toasty, ripe fruit.

GARRIGUELLA GARNATXA D'EMPORDÁ NEGRA 2007 T
100% garnacha.

85 Colour: deep cherry, garnet rim. Nose: fruit preserve, balanced, pattiserie, toasty. Palate: flavourful, correct, balanced.

DOLÇ DE GERISENA 2005 VINO DE LICOR
75% garnacha, 25% mazuelo.

90 Colour: mahogany. Nose: acetaldehyde, pattiserie, sweet spices, candied fruit. Palate: flavourful, good finish.

GARRIGUELLA GARNATXA D'EMPORDÁ ROJA S/C VINO DEL LICOR
garnacha roja.

84

BODEGAS MAS VIDA

Afuera, 24
17741 Cistella (Girona)
☎: +34 932 045 598 - Fax: +34 932 037 541
info@bodegasmasvida.com
www.bodegasmasvida.com

MAS VIDA 117 2011 B
chardonnay.

87 Colour: bright yellow. Nose: powerfull, expressive, ripe fruit, sweet spices, white flowers. Palate: flavourful, fruity, long.

MAS VIDA 17 2011 B
chardonnay.

86 Colour: bright yellow. Nose: medium intensity, ripe fruit, white flowers. Palate: flavourful, fruity, balanced.

MAS VIDA 32 2009 T ROBLE
merlot.

86 Colour: bright cherry. Nose: sweet spices, creamy oak, candied fruit. Palate: flavourful, fruity, toasty, round tannins.

MAS VIDA CABERNET SAUVIGNON 2001 T
cabernet sauvignon.

86 Colour: bright cherry, orangey edge. Nose: balanced, spicy, ripe fruit, tobacco. Palate: fruity, fine bitter notes, spicy.

BODEGAS TROBAT

Castelló, 10
17780 Garriguella (Girona)
☎: +34 972 530 092 - Fax: +34 972 552 530
bodegas.trobat@bmark.es
www.bodegastrobat.com

AMAT SAUVIGNON BLANC 2011 B
sauvignon blanc.

86 Colour: bright straw, greenish rim. Nose: balanced, dried flowers, wild herbs. Palate: fresh, flavourful, fruity.

NOBLE CHARDONNAY BLANC DE BLANCS 2011 B
chardonnay.

85 Colour: bright straw. Nose: ripe fruit, medium intensity, wild herbs. Palate: correct, fine bitter notes, ripe fruit.

AMAT MERLOT 2011 RD
merlot, garnacha.

86 Colour: light cherry, bright. Nose: medium intensity, wild herbs, floral. Palate: flavourful, fine bitter notes.

TROBAT VI NOVELL 2011 T
syrah.

88 Colour: light cherry, purple rim. Nose: violet drops, red berry notes, floral, expressive. Palate: fruity, fresh, good acidity, spicy.

AMAT NEGRE 2011 T
merlot, garnacha.

83

AMAT NEGRE 2009 TC
samsó, merlot, syrah.

88 Colour: cherry, garnet rim. Nose: ripe fruit, spicy, toasty. Palate: powerful, flavourful, toasty, round tannins.

NOBLE 2008 TR
syrah, cabernet franc, garnacha.

85 Colour: cherry, garnet rim. Nose: ripe fruit, creamy oak, toasty. Palate: powerful, flavourful, toasty, round tannins.

CASTILLO DE CAPMANY

Fort, 5
17750 Capmany (Girona)
☎: +34 972 549 043 - Fax: +34 972 549 043
info@castillodecapmany.es
www.castillodecapmany.com

CASTILLO OLIVARES 2005 T
cabernet sauvignon, merlot, garnacha.

83

MOLL DE ALBA 2003 TR
cabernet sauvignon, merlot, garnacha, syrah.

84

CASTILLO PERELADA VINOS Y CAVAS

Pl. del Carmen, 1
17491 Perelada (Girona)
☎: +34 972 538 011 - Fax: +34 972 538 277
perelada@castilloperelada.com
www.castilloperelada.com

CASTILLO PERELADA LA GARRIGA 2011 B
40% cariñena blanca, 40% chardonnay, 20% sauvignon blanc.

90 Colour: bright yellow. Nose: ripe fruit, floral, powerfull. Palate: rich, spicy, ripe fruit, long.

CASTILLO PERELADA GARNATXA BLANCA 2011 B
100% garnacha blanca.

89 Colour: bright straw. Nose: medium intensity, wild herbs, balanced, ripe fruit. Palate: balanced, correct, ripe fruit, good acidity.

CIGONYES 2011 B
90% macabeo, 10% sauvignon blanc.

89 Colour: bright straw, greenish rim. Nose: wild herbs, dried flowers, fresh. Palate: flavourful, fruity, fine bitter notes.

CASTILLO PERELADA CHARDONNAY 2011 B
100% chardonnay.

88 Colour: bright straw. Nose: ripe fruit, white flowers, medium intensity. Palate: ripe fruit, easy to drink, good finish.

CASTILLO PERELADA BLANC DE BLANCS 2011 B
50% macabeo, 15% garnacha blanca, 20% chardonnay, 15% sauvignon blanc.

87 Colour: bright straw. Nose: medium intensity, fresh, citrus fruit, dried flowers, dried herbs. Palate: balanced, ripe fruit, flavourful.

CASTILLO PERELADA SAUVIGNON BLANC 2011 B
100% sauvignon blanc.

86 Colour: bright straw. Nose: elegant, balanced, floral, fruit expression, dried herbs. Palate: correct, ripe fruit, fine bitter notes, flavourful.

CASTILLO PERELADA GARNATXA DE L'EMPORDÀ B
80% garnacha roja, 20% garnacha blanca.

92 Colour: amber. Nose: creamy oak, caramel, roasted almonds, sweet spices. Palate: rich, full, spicy.

CASTILLO PERELADA CABERNET SAUVIGNON 2011 RD
100% cabernet sauvignon.

87 Colour: rose, bright. Nose: medium intensity, wild herbs, faded flowers. Palate: flavourful, powerful, long.

CASTILLO PERELADA 2011 RD
40% garnacha, 40% samsó, 20% ull de llebre.

86 Colour: rose, purple rim. Nose: red berry notes, ripe fruit, floral, balanced. Palate: balanced, powerful, flavourful.

CASTILLO DE PERELADA EX EX 9 S/C T
50% sangiovese, 50% nero D'Avola.

94 Colour: deep cherry, purple rim. Nose: red berry notes, ripe fruit, scrubland, spicy. Palate: good structure, flavourful, long, ripe fruit. Personality.

CIGONYES 2011 T
90% garnacha, 10% syrah.

89 Colour: bright cherry, purple rim. Nose: balanced, ripe fruit, elegant. Palate: long, flavourful, good structure, fruity.

FINCA GARBET 2009 T
60% syrah, 40% cabernet sauvignon.

92 Colour: black cherry, purple rim. Nose: complex, elegant, mineral, cocoa bean, ripe fruit, warm. Palate: round, complex, good structure, round tannins.

CASTILLO PERELADA FINCA MALAVEÏNA 2008 T
50% merlot, 30% cabernet sauvignon, 10% syrah, 10% garnacha.

90 Colour: cherry, garnet rim. Nose: ripe fruit, spicy, creamy oak, toasty, complex, balsamic herbs. Palate: powerful, flavourful, toasty, round tannins.

CASTILLO PERELADA FINCA MALAVEÏNA 2009 T
40% merlot, 30% cabernet sauvignon, 20% syrah, 10% garnacha.

91 Colour: cherry, garnet rim. Nose: complex, ripe fruit, sweet spices, balsamic herbs. Palate: long, good acidity, round tannins, spicy.

CASTILLO PERELADA FINCA ESPOLLA 2009 T
60% monastrell, 40% syrah.

90 Colour: very deep cherry. Nose: expressive, balanced, balsamic herbs, dark chocolate, toasty. Palate: full, flavourful, fine bitter notes, round tannins.

CASTILLO DE PERELADA 3 FINCAS 2009 TC
35% garnacha, 35% samsó, 15% cabernet sauvignon, 15% merlot.

86 Colour: cherry, garnet rim. Nose: fruit preserve, spicy, wild herbs. Palate: ripe fruit, easy to drink.

CASTILLO PERELADA LA GARRIGA 2008 T
100% samsó.

90 Colour: bright cherry, garnet rim. Nose: mineral, spicy, complex, expressive, ripe fruit. Palate: long, fruity, rich, good acidity.

CASTILLO DE PERELADA 5 FINCAS 2007 TR
20% merlot, 25% cabernet sauvignon, 25% garnacha, 15% syrah, 15% samsó.

92 Colour: black cherry, garnet rim. Nose: complex, balanced, expressive, balsamic herbs, sweet spices. Palate: flavourful, good structure, round tannins, long.

FINCA GARBET 2006 T
90% syrah, 10% cabernet sauvignon.

91 Colour: deep cherry, garnet rim. Nose: sweet spices, cocoa bean, candied fruit, balsamic herbs, closed. Palate: complex, spicy, long, round tannins.

CASTILLO PERELADA GRAN CLAUSTRO 2006 T
40% cabernet sauvignon, 30% merlot, 15% garnacha, 15% samsó.

91 Colour: deep cherry, garnet rim. Nose: cocoa bean, sweet spices, ripe fruit, balsamic herbs, complex, expressive. Palate: fruity, good structure, elegant, fine bitter notes.

CASTILLO PERELADA CABERNET SAUVIGNON 2006 T
100% cabernet sauvignon.

87 Colour: dark-red cherry, orangey edge. Nose: candied fruit, fruit liqueur notes, spicy. Palate: ripe fruit, long.

CASTILLO PERELADA GRAN CLAUSTRO 2005 T
50% cabernet sauvignon, 20% merlot, 15% garnacha, 15% samsó.

92 Colour: deep cherry, garnet rim. Nose: complex, balanced, elegant, mineral, creamy oak, wild herbs. Palate: full, flavourful, complex, round tannins, long.

CELLER ARCHÉ PAGÈS

Sant Climent, 31
17750 Capmany (Girona)
☎: +34 626 647 251 - Fax: +34 972 549 229
bonfill@capmany.com
www.cellerarchepages.com

SÀTIRS BLANC 2011 B
100% macabeo.

84

SÀTIRS 2011 RD
49% garnacha, 46% cabernet sauvignon, 5% syrah.

82

BONFILL 2007 T
73% garnacha, 21% samsó, 6% cabernet sauvignon.

89 Colour: deep cherry, garnet rim. Nose: powerfull, balanced, dark chocolate, candied fruit, creamy oak, warm. Palate: flavourful, good structure.

SÀTIRS 2007 T
46% garnacha, 28% cabernet sauvignon, 26% samsó.

78

CARTESIUS 2006 T
63% garnacha, 21% cabernet sauvignon, 16% merlot.

87 Colour: cherry, garnet rim. Nose: fruit preserve, toasty, spicy. Palate: fruity, good finish.

CELLER CAN SAIS

Raval de Dalt, 10
17253 Vall-Llobrega (Girona)
☎: +34 647 443 873
correu@cellercansais.com
www.cellercansais.com

CAN SAIS MESTRAL 2011 B
malvasía, xarel.lo, macabeo, garnacha blanca.

84

CAN SAIS GREGAL 2011 RD
garnacha, merlot.

84

CAN SAIS MIGJORN 2011 T
merlot, ull de llebre, samsó.

85 Colour: cherry, purple rim. Nose: balanced, wild herbs, red berry notes, ripe fruit. Palate: correct, fruity, easy to drink.

CAN SAIS PRIVILEGI 2009 T
100% garnacha.

90 Colour: cherry, garnet rim. Nose: expressive, candied fruit, fruit liqueur notes, varnish, balsamic herbs. Palate: flavourful, balanced, good finish.

CAN SAIS SELECCIÓ 2009 T
ull de llebre, merlot, garnacha.

86 Colour: cherry, garnet rim. Nose: toasty, dark chocolate, fruit preserve, sweet spices. Palate: full, roasted-coffee afterpalate:.

CAN SAIS EXPRESSIÓ ZERO SULFITS 2008 T
100% garnacha.

88 Colour: cherry, garnet rim. Nose: candied fruit, creamy oak, sweet spices, cocoa bean. Palate: concentrated, fruity.

CAN SAIS SONMI ROSADO 2010 ESP
100% garnacha.

82

CELLER COOPERATIU D'ESPOLLA

Ctra. Roses, s/n
17753 Espolla (Girona)
☎: +34 972 563 049 - Fax: +34 972 563 178
ccdespolla@telefonica.es
www.cellerespolla.com

CASTELL DE PANISSARS 2011 B
45% lledoner blanc, 25% macabeo, 20% chardonnay, 10% moscatel de alejandría.

87 Colour: bright straw. Nose: balanced, medium intensity, jasmine. Palate: flavourful, easy to drink, ripe fruit.

CLOS DE LES DÒMINES 2010 BFB
40% lledoner blanco, 40% moscatel de alejandría, 20% cariñena blanca.

85 Colour: bright yellow. Nose: powerfull, ripe fruit, sweet spices, floral. Palate: rich, smoky afterpalate:, good acidity.

MUSCAT D'EMPORDÀ ESPOLLA B
100% moscatel de alejandría.

81

CASTELL DE PANISSARS 2011 RD
75% merlot, 25% lledoner.

86 Colour: rose, bright. Nose: fresh, red berry notes. Palate: fruity, flavourful, balanced, good acidity.

NEGRE JOVE 2011 T
40% lledoner, 40% lledoner roig, 20% merlot.

88 Colour: cherry, purple rim. Nose: jasmine, floral, fruit expression, expressive. Palate: flavourful, balanced, round tannins.

CASTELL DE PANISSARS 2009 TC
40% cariñena, 30% lledoner, 30% merlot.

86 Colour: deep cherry, garnet rim. Nose: creamy oak, sweet spices, toasty, ripe fruit, candied fruit. Palate: fruity, ripe fruit, long.

CLOS DE LES DÒMINES 2008 TR
45% merlot, 30% cabernet sauvignon, 25% cariñena.

87 Colour: cherry, garnet rim. Nose: ripe fruit, fruit preserve, toasty, powerfull. Palate: flavourful, ripe fruit, balanced.

GARNATXA D'EMPORDÀ ESPOLLA DULCE NATURAL GRAN RESERVA
65% lledoner blanco, 35% lledoner roig.

89 Colour: light mahogany. Nose: toasty, pattiserie, sweet spices, acetaldehyde. Palate: flavourful, full, balanced, rich.

CELLER MARIÀ PAGÈS

Pujada, 6
17750 Capmany (Girona)
☎: +34 972 549 160 - Fax: +34 972 549 160
info@cellermpages.com
www.cellermpages.com

CELLER MARÍÀ PAGÈS MOSCAT S/C B
100% moscatel.

88 Colour: bright yellow. Nose: candied fruit, pattiserie, white flowers, honeyed notes. Palate: rich, sweet, flavourful.

SERRASAGUÉ VINYA DE HORT 2011 B
garnacha blanca, chardonnay, moscatel.

85 Colour: bright straw. Nose: balanced, medium intensity, faded flowers, scrubland. Palate: fruity, easy to drink.

CELLER MARÍÀ PAGÈS GARNACHA 2010 B
50% garnacha, 50% garnacha blanca.

91 Colour: light mahogany. Nose: candied fruit, roasted almonds, sweet spices, caramel, varnish. Palate: flavourful, sweet, rich.

SERRASAGUÉ ROSA - T 2011 RD
80% garnacha, 20% merlot.

87 Colour: light cherry. Nose: white flowers, red berry notes, balanced, fresh. Palate: flavourful, fruity, fine bitter notes, correct.

SERRASAGUÉ 2011 T
60% garnacha, 30% merlot, 10% cabernet sauvignon.

88 Colour: bright cherry, purple rim. Nose: red berry notes, ripe fruit, wild herbs. Palate: balanced, correct, ripe fruit, long.

SERRASAGUÉ 2007 T
30% garnacha, 30% merlot, 30% cabernet sauvignon.

85 Colour: bright cherry, garnet rim. Nose: wild herbs, candied fruit, sweet spices, creamy oak. Palate: flavourful, correct.

SERRASAGUÉ 2006 TC
33% garnacha, 33% merlot, 33% cabernet sauvignon.

85 Colour: deep cherry, garnet rim. Nose: scrubland, balsamic herbs, powerfull, spicy. Palate: flavourful, fruity.

MARÍÀ PAGÈS GARNATXA RESERVA
garnacha, garnacha blanca.

86 Colour: light mahogany. Nose: fruit preserve, sweet spices, cocoa bean. Palate: fruity, unctuous, sweet.

CELLER MARTÍ FABRA

Barrio Vic, 26
17751 Sant Climent Sescebes (Girona)
☎: +34 972 563 011 - Fax: +34 972 563 867
info@cellermartifabra.com

VERD ALBERA 2011 B
65% garnacha blanca, 20% moscatel, 10% garnacha rosada, 5% chardonnay.

88 Colour: bright straw. Nose: fresh, fresh fruit, white flowers, fragrant herbs. Palate: flavourful, fruity, good acidity.

MASÍA CARRERAS BLANC 2010 BFB
40% cariñena blanca, 30% cariñena rosada, 10% garnacha blanca, 10% garnacha rosada, 10% picapoll.

91 Colour: bright yellow. Nose: ripe fruit, sweet spices, creamy oak, fragrant herbs. Palate: rich, smoky afterpalate:, flavourful, fresh, good acidity.

FLOR D'ALBERA 2010 BFB
100% moscatel.

88 Colour: bright straw. Nose: white flowers, citrus fruit, ripe fruit. Palate: flavourful, fruity, long, good acidity.

MASÍA PAIRAL CAN CARRERAS MOSCAT 2007 B
100% moscatel.

90 Colour: golden. Nose: powerfull, floral, honeyed notes, candied fruit, fragrant herbs. Palate: flavourful, sweet, fresh, fruity, good acidity, long.

MASÍA PAIRAL CAN CARRERAS GARNATXA DE L'EMPORDÀ B
garnacha blanca, garnacha rosada.

88 Colour: light mahogany. Nose: ripe fruit, dry nuts, powerfull, toasty, aged wood nuances, sweet spices. Palate: flavourful, fruity, spicy, toasty, long.

LLADONER 2011 RD
100% garnacha.

84

L'ORATORI 2009 T
50% garnacha, 30% cabernet sauvignon, 20% cariñena.

87 Colour: light cherry, garnet rim. Nose: spicy, balanced, ripe fruit, overripe fruit. Palate: flavourful, balsamic, good acidity.

MARTÍ FABRA SELECCIÓ VINYES VELLES 2008 T ROBLE
60% garnacha, 25% cariñena, 8% syrah, 5% cabernet sauvignon, 2% tempranillo.

88 Colour: cherry, garnet rim. Nose: spicy, tobacco, ripe fruit. Palate: balanced, fine bitter notes, flavourful.

MASÍA CARRERAS NEGRE 2007 T
80% cariñena, 20% merlot.

89 Colour: cherry, garnet rim. Nose: medium intensity, ripe fruit, sweet spices, balanced. Palate: flavourful, fine bitter notes, ripe fruit.

CELLER MAS PATIRÀS

Jardins de l'Empordà- Jardin botànic
17110 Fonteta (Girona)
☎: +34 972 642 687
info@jardinsemporda.com
www.jardinsemporda.com.com

BLAU DE TRAMUNTANA 2008 T ROBLE
syrah, garnacha, cariñena.

83

DOLÇ TRAMUNTANA MISTELA

83

CELLERS D'EN GUILLA

Camí de Perelada nº 1, Delfià
17754 Rabós d'Empordà (Girona)
☎: +34 972 545 144
info@cellersdenguilla.com
www.cellersdenguilla.com

MAGENC 2011 B
garnacha blanca, macabeo.

88 Colour: bright straw. Nose: fresh, fresh fruit, white flowers. Palate: flavourful, fruity, good acidity, balanced, fine bitter notes.

CELLERS SANTAMARÍA

Pza. Mayor, 6
17750 Capmany (Girona)
☎: +34 972 549 033 - Fax: +34 972 549 022
info@granrecosind.com
www.granrecosind.com

GRAN RECOSIND 2006 TC
garnacha, tempranillo, cabernet sauvignon, syrah, merlot.

83

GRAN RECOSIND 2005 TR
merlot.

87 Colour: deep cherry, orangey edge. Nose: balanced, candied fruit, spicy. Palate: flavourful, balanced, round tannins.

CLOS D'AGON

Afores, s/n
17251 Calonge (Girona)
☎: +34 972 661 486 - Fax: +34 972 661 462
info@closdagon.com
www.closdagon.com

AMIC DE CLOS D'AGON 2011 B
garnacha blanca.

90 Colour: bright straw. Nose: fresh, fresh fruit, white flowers, expressive. Palate: flavourful, fruity, good acidity, balanced.

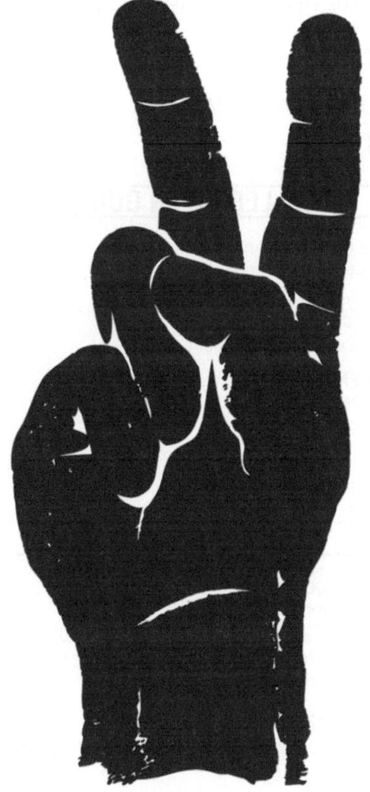

AMIC DE CLOS D'AGON 2011 T
66% garnacha, 21% cabernet sauvignon, 9% merlot, 4% syrah.

90 Colour: cherry, purple rim. Nose: medium intensity, ripe fruit, balsamic herbs, spicy. Palate: flavourful, powerful, fruity aftespalate:, long.

COLL DE ROSES

Ctra. de les Arenes, s/n
17480 Roses (Girona)
☎: +34 972 256 465 - Fax: +34 972 531 741
info@espeltviticultors.com
www.collderoses.es

COLL DE ROSES 2011 B
macabeo, chardonnay.

84

COLL DE ROSES 2010 T
garnacha, tempranillo.

89 Colour: dark-red cherry, purple rim. Nose: powerfull, balanced, ripe fruit. Palate: good structure, rich, flavourful, round tannins.

COLL DE ROSES FINCA DEL MAR 2009 T
garnacha, cabernet sauvignon.

87 Colour: deep cherry, purple rim. Nose: powerfull, ripe fruit, spicy, scrubland. Palate: flavourful, round tannins.

EMPORDÀLIA

Ctra. de Roses, s/n
17494 Pau (Girona)
☎: +34 972 530 140 - Fax: +34 972 530 528
info@empordalia.com
www.empordalia.com

SINOLS BLANC 2011 B
50% garnacha blanca, 50% macabeo.

88 Colour: bright straw. Nose: ripe fruit, spicy, white flowers. Palate: flavourful, full, ripe fruit, easy to drink.

SINOLS ROSAT 2011 RD
60% garnacha, 40% mazuelo.

84

SINOLS NEGRE 2011 T
60% garnacha, 40% mazuelo.

86 Colour: cherry, purple rim. Nose: medium intensity, red berry notes, ripe fruit. Palate: flavourful, good structure, long.

SINOLS SAMSÓ 2010 T
samsó.

86 Colour: cherry, garnet rim. Nose: dark chocolate, sweet spices, candied fruit. Palate: flavourful, full.

SINOLS 2009 TC
30% garnacha, 30% mazuelo, 25% cabernet sauvignon, 10% merlot, 5% syrah.

87 Colour: cherry, garnet rim. Nose: spicy, ripe fruit, scrubland. Palate: full, spicy.

SINOLS 2006 TR
50% cabernet sauvignon, 25% garnacha, 25% mazuelo.

85 Colour: cherry, garnet rim. Nose: sweet spices, cocoa bean, scrubland. Palate: correct, ripe fruit, spicy.

ESPELT VITICULTORS

Mas Espelt
17493 Vilajuiga (Girona)
☎: +34 972 531 727 - Fax: +34 972 531 741
info@espeltviticultors.com
www.espeltviticultors.com

ESPELT MARENY 2011 B
sauvignon blanc, moscatel.

85 Colour: bright straw. Nose: medium intensity, jasmine, white flowers, ripe fruit. Palate: correct, balanced.

ESPELT VAILET 2011 B
garnacha blanca, macabeo.

83

ESPELT QUINZE ROURES 2010 BFB
garnacha gris, garnacha blanca.

84

ESPELT CORALI 2011 RD
garnacha.

85 Colour: light cherry, bright. Nose: medium intensity, wild herbs, dried flowers. Palate: ripe fruit, balanced, correct.

ESPELT SAULÓ 2011 T
garnacha.

86 Colour: deep cherry, purple rim. Nose: ripe fruit, balanced, powerfull. Palate: ripe fruit, long, rich, round tannins.

TERRAMALA VINYES VELLES 2010 T
cariñena.

90 Colour: very deep cherry, purple rim. Nose: toasty, dark chocolate, sweet spices, ripe fruit. Palate: fruity, flavourful, round tannins.

ESPELT TERRES NEGRES 2010 T
cariñena, cabernet sauvignon.

87 Colour: black cherry, purple rim. Nose: toasty, ripe fruit, powerfull, cocoa bean. Palate: good structure, fruity, round tannins.

ESPELT VIDIVÍ 2010 T
garnacha, merlot.

85 Colour: deep cherry. Nose: scrubland, ripe fruit, powerfull. Palate: flavourful, fruity, correct, fine bitter notes.

ESPELT COMABRUNA 2009 T
cariñena, syrah.

89 Colour: bright cherry, cherry, garnet rim. Nose: ripe fruit, expressive, complex, spicy. Palate: long, ripe fruit, round tannins.

ESPELT OLD VINES 2009 T
garnacha.

87 Colour: very deep cherry, purple rim. Nose: ripe fruit, scrubland. Palate: flavourful, fruity, long.

ESPELT GARNACHA AIRAM VINO DE LICOR
garnacha, garnacha gris.

87 Colour: light mahogany. Nose: candied fruit, caramel, sweet spices, cocoa bean. Palate: sweet, balanced, spirituous, toasty.

EXPLOTACIONES AGRÍCOLAS Y FORESTALES BRUGAROL

Finca Bell-Lloc, s/n
17230 Palamós (Girona)
☎: +34 972 316 203
info@brugarol.com
www.brugarol.com

BELL-LLOC BLANC 2010 B
malvasía, xarel.lo, moscatel.

85 Colour: bright yellow. Nose: ripe fruit, candied fruit, floral. Palate: flavourful, good finish.

BELL-LLOC 2008 TC
50% garnacha, 20% cabernet franc, 20% cabernet sauvignon, 10% cariñena.

88 Colour: cherry, garnet rim. Nose: ripe fruit, spicy, dark chocolate, scrubland. Palate: full, flavourful, long.

JOAN SARDÀ

Ctra. Vilafranca a St. Jaume dels Domenys, Km. 8,1
08732 Castellvi de la Marca (Barcelona)
☎: +34 937 720 900 - Fax: +34 937 721 495
joansarda@joansarda.com
www.joansarda.com

CAP DE CREUS NACRE 2011 B
lledoner roig, lledoner blanc.

84

CAP DE CREUS CORALL 2010 T
lledoner, samsó.

85 Colour: cherry, purple rim. Nose: medium intensity, ripe fruit. Palate: fruity, flavourful, long, fruity aftespalate:.

LAVINYETA

Ctra. de Mollet de Peralada a Masarac, s/n
17752 Mollet de Peralada (Girona)
☎: +34 647 748 809 - Fax: +34 972 505 323
celler@lavinyeta.es
www.lavinyeta.es

HEUS BLANC 2011 B
44% macabeo, 20% garnacha, 20% xarel.lo, 16% moscatel.

85 Colour: bright yellow. Nose: medium intensity, scrubland, faded flowers. Palate: correct, balanced.

MICROVINS BLANC 2011 B ROBLE
100% cariñena blanca.

85 Colour: bright yellow. Nose: candied fruit, faded flowers, wild herbs, sweet spices. Palate: flavourful, easy to drink, good finish.

HEUS ROSAT 2011 RD
32% cariñena, 30% garnacha, 23% merlot, 15% syrah.

85 Colour: rose, bright. Nose: red berry notes, ripe fruit, rose petals. Palate: full, flavourful, fruity.

HEUS NEGRE 2011 T
31% syrah, 26% garnacha, 24% merlot, 19% cariñena.

90 Colour: deep cherry, purple rim. Nose: medium intensity, ripe fruit, lactic notes. Palate: fruity, flavourful, fine bitter notes.

MICROVINS NEGRE 2010 T ROBLE
100% cariñena.

90 Colour: bright cherry. Nose: ripe fruit, sweet spices, creamy oak, expressive. Palate: flavourful, fruity, toasty, round tannins.

PUNTIAPART 2010 T
85% cabernet sauvignon, 15% cariñena.

89 Colour: very deep cherry, purple rim. Nose: expressive, complex, ripe fruit, cocoa bean, creamy oak, sweet spices. Palate: long, elegant, fine bitter notes.

LLAVORS 2010 T
38% cariñena, 35% cabernet sauvignon, 20% merlot, 7% cabernet franc.

86 Colour: cherry, garnet rim. Nose: balanced, toasty, sweet spices, ripe fruit. Palate: round tannins, long, ripe fruit.

SOLS 2009 DULCE
50% garnacha roja, 50% garnacha blanca.

84

LORDINA

Ctra. de Roses, Km. 9,5
17493 Vilajuiga (Girona)
☎: +34 629 578 001
lordina@lordina.es
www.lordina.net

LORDINA MESSAGE 2011 B
90% sauvignon blanc, 10% moscatel.

86 Colour: bright straw. Nose: dried flowers, wild herbs, balanced. Palate: fruity, flavourful.

LORDINA MESSAGE 2011 RD
100% garnacha.

85 Colour: salmon, bright. Nose: wild herbs, faded flowers, balanced. Palate: ripe fruit, long.

LORDINA MESSAGE 2010 T
80% garnacha, 20% cariñena.

86 Colour: very deep cherry, purple rim. Nose: powerfull, scrubland, ripe fruit. Palate: balanced, ripe fruit, correct.

LORDINA GRANIT 2008 T
80% garnacha, 20% cariñena.

88 Colour: dark-red cherry, purple rim. Nose: medium intensity, ripe fruit, spicy, closed. Palate: flavourful, round tannins.

LORDINA "AMPHORA" 2008 T
60% syrah, 40% garnacha.

88 Colour: deep cherry, garnet rim. Nose: spicy, old leather, ripe fruit, dark chocolate. Palate: spicy, ripe fruit.

MAS LLUNES

Ctra. de Roses, s/n
17780 Garriguella (Girona)
☎: +34 972 552 684 - Fax: +34 972 530 112
masllunes@masllunes.es
www.masllunes.es

MARAGDA 2011 B
100% garnacha blanca.

85 Colour: bright yellow, greenish rim. Nose: medium intensity, scrubland. Palate: flavourful, fruity, good finish.

NIVIA 2010 BFB
63% garnacha blanca, 37% samsó blanc.

88 Colour: bright yellow. Nose: candied fruit, faded flowers, neat, complex. Palate: toasty, spicy, ripe fruit, balanced.

MARAGDA 2011 RD
55% garnacha, 45% syrah.

87 Colour: light cherry, bright. Nose: wild herbs, fresh, red berry notes. Palate: flavourful, fruity, ripe fruit, good acidity.

CERCIUM 2010 T
61% garnacha, 21% syrah, 18% samsó.

86 Colour: cherry, purple rim. Nose: balanced, medium intensity, ripe fruit. Palate: ripe fruit, easy to drink, round tannins.

RHODES 2007 T
63% samsó, 37% syrah.

90 Colour: bright cherry, garnet rim. Nose: medium intensity, ripe fruit, cocoa bean, sweet spices. Palate: balanced, fine bitter notes.

EMPÓRION 2006 T
72% cabernet sauvignon, 28% syrah.

86 Colour: black cherry, garnet rim. Nose: dark chocolate, toasty, fruit preserve, powerfull, tobacco. Palate: flavourful, good structure.

MAS OLLER

Ctra. GI-652, Km. 0,23
17123 Torrent (Girona)
☎: +34 972 300 001 - Fax: +34 972 300 001
info@masoller.es
www.masoller.es

MAS OLLER MAR 2011 B
picapoll, malvasía.

91 Colour: bright straw. Nose: fresh, fresh fruit, white flowers, expressive, fragrant herbs, mineral. Palate: flavourful, fruity, good acidity, balanced, elegant.

MAS OLLER PUR 2011 T
syrah, garnacha, cabernet sauvignon.

91 Colour: cherry, purple rim. Nose: expressive, fresh fruit, red berry notes, floral, fragrant herbs, mineral. Palate: flavourful, fruity, good acidity, round tannins.

MAS OLLER BLAU 2011 T
syrah.

90 Colour: cherry, purple rim. Nose: red berry notes, ripe fruit, scrubland, earthy notes.

MAS OLLER PLUS 2010 T
syrah, garnacha.

92 Colour: cherry, garnet rim. Nose: ripe fruit, spicy, creamy oak, toasty, balsamic herbs, earthy notes. Palate: powerful, flavourful, toasty, long, spicy.

MASIA SERRA

Dels Solés, 20
17708 Cantallops (Girona)
☎: +34 689 703 687
masiaserra@masiaserra.com
www.masiaserra.com

CTÒNIA 2011 BFB
garnacha blanca.

90 Colour: bright yellow. Nose: powerfull, ripe fruit, sweet spices. Palate: rich, smoky afterpalate:, flavourful, fresh, good acidity.

IO MASIA SERRA 2008 T
marselan, merlot, cabernet franc, garnacha.

90 Colour: cherry, garnet rim. Nose: ripe fruit, spicy, creamy oak, toasty. Palate: powerful, flavourful, toasty, round tannins.

AROA 2006 T
garnacha roja, marselan.

90 Colour: cherry, garnet rim. Nose: ripe fruit, spicy, creamy oak, toasty, characterful. Palate: powerful, flavourful, toasty, round tannins.

GNEIS 2004 T
merlot, garnacha, cabernet sauvignon.

88 Colour: cherry, garnet rim. Nose: wet leather, fruit liqueur notes, nose:tic coffee. Palate: ripe fruit, good acidity, spicy.

INO GARNATXA DE L'EMPORDÀ VINO DULCE NATURAL
garnacha roja.

94 Colour: light mahogany. Nose: candied fruit, dry nuts, acetaldehyde, sweet spices, cocoa bean, dark chocolate, toasty. Palate: powerful, flavourful, spicy, balanced, elegant.

OLIVEDA

La Roca, 3
17750 Capmany (Girona)
☎: +34 972 549 012 - Fax: +34 972 549 106
comercial@grupoliveda.com
www.grupoliveda.com

FINCA FUROT SAUVIGNON BLANC 2011 B
100% sauvignon blanc.

86 Colour: bright yellow, greenish rim. Nose: scrubland, ripe fruit, white flowers. Palate: flavourful, fruity, full.

MASIA OLIVEDA BLANC DE BLANCS 2011 B
60% macabeo, 40% chardonnay.

84

MASIA OLIVEDA ROSAT FLOR 2011 RD
20% samsó, 30% cabernet sauvignon, 50% garnacha.

86 Colour: light cherry, bright. Nose: medium intensity, fresh, red berry notes, floral. Palate: flavourful, fruity, correct, balanced.

FINCA FUROT 2008 TC
100% samsó.

87 Colour: cherry, garnet rim. Nose: red berry notes, ripe fruit, earthy notes, spicy. Palate: flavourful, good structure, easy to drink.

RIGAU ROS CABERNET SAUVIGNON 2006 TGR
90% cabernet sauvignon, 10% merlot.

86 Colour: bright cherry, garnet rim. Nose: varietal, powerfull, ripe fruit, scrubland. Palate: flavourful, fruity, round tannins.

RIGAU ROS 2006 TGR
50% cabernet sauvignon, 30% garnacha, 20% samsó.

86 Colour: cherry, garnet rim. Nose: powerfull, neat, scrubland, spicy. Palate: correct, balanced, fine bitter notes.

FINCA FUROT 2005 TR
10% cabernet sauvignon, 80% garnacha, 10% merlot.

87 Colour: cherry, garnet rim. Nose: ripe fruit, spicy, toasty, complex. Palate: powerful, flavourful, toasty, round tannins.

OLIVER CONTI

Puignau, s/n
17550 Capmany (Girona)
☎: +34 972 193 161 - Fax: +34 972 193 040
dolors@oliverconti.com
www.oliverconti.com

OLIVER CONTI TREYU 2011 B
50% gewürztraminer, 50% macabeo.

88 Colour: bright straw, greenish rim. Nose: balanced, expressive, fresh fruit, white flowers. Palate: flavourful, fruity, good finish.

ENOC BLANCO 2009 B BARRICA
60% gewürztraminer, 40% sauvignon blanc.

88 Colour: bright yellow. Nose: complex, balanced, expressive, sweet spices, white flowers, ripe fruit. Palate: balanced, fruity, rich.

ENOC TINTO 2009 TR
70% cabernet sauvignon, 20% merlot, 10% cabernet franc.

90 Colour: bright cherry. Nose: ripe fruit, sweet spices, creamy oak, expressive, scrubland. Palate: flavourful, fruity, round tannins, fruity aftespalate:.

OLIVER CONTI CARLOTA 2009 T
75% cabernet franc, 25% cabernet sauvignon.

90 Colour: bright cherry, garnet rim. Nose: ripe fruit, wild herbs, balanced, spicy. Palate: correct, balanced, fine bitter notes, good acidity.

OLIVER CONTI ARA 2009 T
20% garnacha, 22% cabernet franc, 58% cabernet sauvignon, merlot.

90 Colour: cherry, garnet rim. Nose: varietal, balanced, scrubland, ripe fruit, earthy notes. Palate: correct, ripe fruit, long.

OLIVER CONTI TURÓ NEGRE 2009 T
30% garnacha, 20% cabernet sauvignon, 40% merlot, 10% cabernet franc.

89 Colour: cherry, garnet rim. Nose: balanced, ripe fruit, dark chocolate, sweet spices. Palate: complex, good structure, round tannins.

PERE GUARDIOLA

Ctra. GI-602, Km. 2,9
17750 Capmany (Girona)
☎: +34 972 549 096 - Fax: +34 972 549 097
vins@pereguardiola.com
www.pereguardiola.com

ANHEL D'EMPORDÀ 2011 B
macabeo, garnacha blanca.

84

JONCÀRIA MOSCAT BARRICA 2010 BFB
100% moscatel de alejandría.

88 Colour: bright yellow. Nose: jasmine, white flowers, honeyed notes, sweet spices, varietal. Palate: fruity, rich, full, long.

FLORESTA 2011 RD
garnacha, cabernet sauvignon, samsó, merlot.

86 Colour: light cherry, bright. Nose: red berry notes, ripe fruit, floral, dried herbs. Palate: flavourful, ripe fruit, long.

FLORESTA 2007 TC
garnacha, merlot, syrah, cabernet sauvignon.

87 Colour: deep cherry, orangey edge. Nose: candied fruit, sweet spices, creamy oak. Palate: rich, flavourful, good finish, ripe fruit.

FLORESTA 3B8 2007 T
80% merlot, 10% garnacha, 10% mazuelo.

84

TORRE DE CAPMANY GARNATXA D'EMPORDÀ VINO DULCE NATURAL GRAN RESERVA

88 Colour: light mahogany. Nose: candied fruit, caramel, pattiserie, sweet spices. Palate: flavourful, full, rich.

FLORESTA 2011 B
macabeo, chardonnay, xarel.lo, garnacha blanca, sauvignon blanc.

86 Colour: bright straw. Nose: white flowers, fresh fruit, balanced. Palate: flavourful, easy to drink, fine bitter notes.

ROIG PARALS

Garriguella, 8
17752 Mollet de Peralada (Girona)
☎: +34 972 634 320
info@roigparals.cat
www.roigparals.cat

ROIG PARALS 2010 T
80% samsó, 20% merlot.

87 Colour: dark-red cherry, purple rim. Nose: medium intensity, ripe fruit. Palate: good structure, powerful, rich.

LA BOTERA 2009 T
80% samsó, 20% merlot.

84

CAMÍ DE CORMES 2007 T
100% samsó.

88 Colour: cherry, garnet rim. Nose: candied fruit, dark chocolate, sweet spices, warm. Palate: good structure, full, rich, round tannins.

FINCA PLA DEL MOLÍ 2007 T
50% cabernet sauvignon, 50% merlot.

87 Colour: black cherry, garnet rim. Nose: powerfull, dark chocolate, candied fruit. Palate: flavourful, spicy, balsamic, round tannins.

SETZEVINS CELLER

Relliquer, 11 Baixos
17753 Espolla (Girona)
☎: +34 639 264 313
setzevins@gmail.com
www.setzevins.cat

NÉSTOR 2010 T
garnacha, cariñena, syrah.

87 Colour: cherry, purple rim. Nose: powerfull, ripe fruit, balanced, scrubland. Palate: flavourful, ripe fruit, round tannins.

OCTUBRE 2008 T
70% garnacha, 20% cariñena, 10% syrah.

84

OCTUBRE 2007 T
cariñena, garnacha, syrah.

84

SOTA ELS ÀNGELS

Apdo. Correos 27
17100 La Bisbal (Girona)
☎: +34 872 006 976
info@sotaelsangels.com
www.sotaelsangels.com

SOTA ELS ÀNGELS 2010 BFB
picapoll, viognier.

90 Colour: bright yellow. Nose: balanced, ripe fruit, white flowers, sweet spices. Palate: fruity, correct, fine bitter notes.

SOTA ELS ÀNGELS 2007 TR
cabernet sauvignon, carménère, merlot, samsó, syrah.

89 Colour: cherry, garnet rim. Nose: ripe fruit, spicy, creamy oak, toasty, complex, earthy notes. Palate: powerful, flavourful, toasty, round tannins.

VINÍCOLA DEL NORDEST

Empolla, 9
17752 Mollet de Peralada (Girona)
☎: +34 972 563 150 - Fax: +34 972 545 134
vinicola@vinicoladelnordest.com
www.vinicoladelnordest.com

VINYA FARRIOL SEMIDULCE S/C B
63% macabeo, 16% sauvignon blanc, 11% garnacha blanca, 10% chardonnay.

82

COVEST CHARDONNAY 2010 B
100% chardonnay.

85 Colour: bright yellow. Nose: powerfull, ripe fruit, white flowers, varietal. Palate: fruity, correct, balanced.

VINYA FARRIOL S/C RD
55% garnacha, 25% ull de llebre, 20% merlot.

83

GARRIGAL 2007 TC
80% garnacha, 20% cariñena.

84

ANUBIS 2004 TR
60% garnacha, 25% merlot, 15% cabernet sauvignon.

86 Colour: bright cherry, orangey edge. Nose: spicy, toasty, complex, fruit preserve. Palate: fruity, easy to drink.

VINOS JOC - JORDI OLIVER CONTI

Mas Marti
17467 Sant Mori (Girona)
☎: +34 607 222 002
info@vinojoc.com
www.vinojoc.com

JOC BLANC EMPORDÀ 2011 B
garnacha blanca, macabeo.

88 Colour: bright straw. Nose: fresh, fresh fruit, expressive, faded flowers. Palate: flavourful, fruity, good acidity.

JOC NEGRE EMPORDÀ 2011 T
65% garnacha, 15% syrah, 10% cabernet sauvignon, 10% cabernet franc.

84

VINYES D'OLIVARDOTS

Paratge Olivadots, s/n
17750 Capmany (Girona)
☎: +34 650 395 627
vdo@olivardots.com
www.olivardots.com

VD'O 4.09 2009 T
100% cabernet sauvignon.

93 Colour: very deep cherry, purple rim. Nose: complex, balsamic herbs, cocoa bean, creamy oak, mineral. Palate: full, good structure, elegant, fine bitter notes, round tannins.

GRESA 2008 T
30% garnacha, 30% cariñena, 30% syrah, 10% cabernet sauvignon.

92 Colour: cherry, garnet rim. Nose: balanced, earthy notes, ripe fruit, candied fruit, sweet spices. Palate: good structure, complex, fine bitter notes, elegant, ripe fruit.

VD'O 2.08 2008 T
100% cariñena.

92 Colour: cherry, garnet rim. Nose: medium intensity, expressive, sweet spices, creamy oak. Palate: ripe fruit, round tannins, spicy.

VD'O 1.08 2008 T
100% cariñena.

91 Colour: cherry, garnet rim. Nose: dark chocolate, candied fruit, medium intensity, spicy, mineral. Palate: full, complex, long, creamy.

VINYES DELS ASPRES

Requesens, 7
17708 Cantallops (Girona)
☎: +34 972 463 146 - Fax: +34 972 420 662
vinyesdelsaspres@vinyesdelsaspres.cat
www.vinyesdelsaspres.cat

BLANC DELS ASPRES 2010 BC
100% garnacha blanca.

86 Colour: bright yellow. Nose: powerfull, toasty, creamy oak, sweet spices, candied fruit, floral. Palate: rich, flavourful, ripe fruit, spicy.

ORIOL NEGRE 2010 T
40% cariñena, 30% garnacha, 10% merlot, cabernet sauvignon.

86 Colour: cherry, purple rim. Nose: balanced, scrubland, ripe fruit. Palate: rich, flavourful, fruity, easy to drink.

S'ALOU 2008 TC
60% garnacha, 14% cariñena, 13% cabernet sauvignon, 13% syrah.

89 Colour: cherry, garnet rim. Nose: candied fruit, toasty, cocoa bean, complex. Palate: concentrated, fruity, flavourful, fine bitter notes, sweet tannins.

NEGRE DELS ASPRES 2007 TC
34% garnacha, 33% cariñena, 33% cabernet sauvignon.

88 Colour: cherry, garnet rim. Nose: sweet spices, ripe fruit, neat. Palate: ripe fruit, long, spicy, round tannins.

XAVIER MASET ISACH

Paratge - Pedreguers, s/n
17780 Garriguella (Alt Empordà)
☎: +34 972 505 455 - Fax: +34 972 501 948
jmaset@masetplana.com
www.masetplana.com

A21 MASETPLANA S/C B
garnacha blanca.

82

A21 MASETPLANA S/C RD
samsó.

85 Colour: light cherry. Nose: medium intensity, fresh, dried flowers. Palate: fruity, flavourful.

A21 MASETPLANA S/C T

84

A21 MASETPLANA 2009 TC
mazuelo.

86 Colour: deep cherry, garnet rim. Nose: toasty, creamy oak, sweet spices, cocoa bean. Palate: rich, flavourful, toasty.

A21 MASETPLANA 2007 TC
45% merlot, 29% garnacha, 26% samsó.

85 Colour: bright cherry, orangey edge. Nose: powerfull, candied fruit, sweet spices. Palate: fruity, flavourful, correct.

DO GETARIAKO TXAKOLINA

LOCATION:

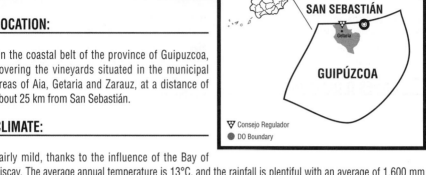

On the coastal belt of the province of Guipuzcoa, covering the vineyards situated in the municipal areas of Aia, Getaria and Zarauz, at a distance of about 25 km from San Sebastián.

CLIMATE:

Fairly mild, thanks to the influence of the Bay of Biscay. The average annual temperature is 13°C, and the rainfall is plentiful with an average of 1,600 mm per year.

SOIL:

The vineyards are situated in small valleys and gradual hillsides at altitudes of up to 200 m. They are found on humid brownish-grey limy soil, which are rich in organic matter.

GRAPE VARIETIES:

WHITE: *Hondarrabi Zuri* (majority with 90% of all vineyards), *Gros Manseng* and *Riesling.*
RED: *Hondarrabi Beltza.*

FIGURES:

Vineyard surface: 402 – **Wine-Growers:** 96 – **Wineries:** 26 – **2011 Harvest rating:** Good – **Production:** 2,284,000 litres – **Market percentages:** 95% domestic. 5% export

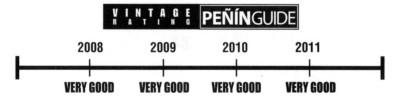

VINTAGE RATING PEÑÍNGUIDE

2008	2009	2010	2011
VERY GOOD	VERY GOOD	VERY GOOD	VERY GOOD

CONSEJO REGULADOR
Parque Aldamar, 4 bajo - 20808 Getaria (Gipuzkoa) - ☎: +34 943 140 383 - Fax: +34 943 896 030
@ info@getariakotxakolina.com - www.getariakotxakolina.com

ADUR

Paseo De Zubiaurre Nº 30 1ºIzq
20013 Donostia (Gipuzkoa)
☎: +34 617 216 677
info@adurtxakolina.com
www.adurtxakolina.com

ADUR 2011 B
100% hondarrabi zuri.

88 Colour: bright yellow. Nose: dried flowers, fresh fruit, fragrant herbs, fresh. Palate: fruity, fine bitter notes, flavourful.

AGERRE

Agerre Baserria - Bº Askizu
20808 Getaria (Gipuzkoa)
☎: +34 943 140 446 - Fax: +34 943 140 446
txakaguerre@terra.es

AGERRE 2011 B
100% hondarrabi zuri.

85 Colour: bright straw. Nose: white flowers, fresh fruit, fragrant herbs. Palate: fresh, fruity, light-bodied.

AMEZTOI

Barrio Eitzaga, 10
20808 Getaria (Gipuzkoa)
☎: +34 943 140 918 - Fax: +34 943 140 169
ameztoi@txakoliameztoi.com
www.txakoliameztoi.com

AMEZTOI 2011 B
100% hondarrabi zuri.

86 Colour: bright straw. Nose: white flowers, fruit expression, fragrant herbs. Palate: light-bodied, fresh, fruity, flavourful.

ARREGI

Talaimendi, 727- Bajo
20800 Zarautz (Gipuzkoa)
☎: +34 943 580 835
info@txakoliarregi.com
www.txakoliarregi.com

ARREGI 2011 B
100% hondarrabi zuri.

86 Colour: bright straw. Nose: floral, fruit expression, ripe fruit, grassy. Palate: fresh, fruity, easy to drink.

BASA LORE

Santa Bárbara Auzoa
Buzón 1
20800 Zarautz (Gipuzkoa)
☎: +34 943 132 231 - Fax: +34 943 834 747
basa-lore@mixmail.com

BASA LORE 2011 B
hondarrabi zuri.

82

BODEGA REZABAL

Itsas Begi Etxea, 628
20800 Zarautz (Gipuzkoa)
☎: +34 943 580 899 - Fax: +34 943 580 775
info@txakolirezabal.com
www.txakolirezabal.com

TXAKOLI REZABAL 2011 B
hondarrabi zuri.

90 Colour: bright straw. Nose: fresh, fresh fruit, white flowers, grassy. Palate: flavourful, fruity, good acidity, balanced.

BODEGAS SANTARBA

Santa Bárbara, 7- buzón Nº 8
20800 Zarautz (Gipuzkoa)
☎: +34 943 140 452

SANTARBA 2011 B
hondarrabi zuri.

87 Colour: bright straw. Nose: fresh, fresh fruit, white flowers. Palate: flavourful, fruity, balanced.

EMETERIO AIZPURUA

San Prudentzio Auzoa, 36
20808 Getaria (Gipuzkoa)
☎: +34 943 580 922
aizpuruaaialle@yahoo.es

AIZPURUA. B 2011 B
hondarrabi zuri.

87 Colour: bright straw. Nose: fresh fruit, white flowers, wild herbs. Palate: fresh, fruity, flavourful, balanced.

AIALLE 2010 B
hondarrabi zuri.

85 Colour: bright straw. Nose: fresh, fresh fruit, white flowers, expressive. Palate: flavourful, fruity, good acidity, balanced.

GAÑETA

Agerre Goikoa Baserria
20808 Getaria (Gipuzkoa)
☎: +34 943 140 174 - Fax: +34 943 140 174

GAÑETA 2011 B

88 Colour: bright straw. Nose: white flowers, fresh fruit, fragrant herbs. Palate: light-bodied, fresh, fruity, flavourful.

GOROSTI

Bio. Elorriaga s/n Itziar Deba
22750 Zumaia (Gipuzkoa)
☎: +34 670 408 439
gorostibodega@hotmail.com

FLYSCH 2011 B
hondarrabi zuri.

87 Colour: bright yellow. Nose: white flowers, candied fruit, dried herbs. Palate: correct, light-bodied, fruity.

HIRUZTA

Barrio Jaizubia, 266
20280 Hondarribia (Gipuzkoa)
☎: 349 436 466 89
info@hiruzta.com
www.hiruzta.com

HIRUZTA 2011 B
hondarrabi zuri, gros manseng.

86 Colour: bright straw. Nose: floral, fruit expression, grassy. Palate: light-bodied, fresh, fruity.

K5

Apdo. Correos 258
20800 Zarautz (Gipuzkoa)
☎: +34 943 240 005
bodega@txakolina-k5.com
www.txakolina-k5.com

K5 ARGUIÑANO 2011 B
hondarrabi zuri.

90 Colour: bright straw. Nose: fresh, fresh fruit, citrus fruit, dried flowers, dried herbs. Palate: flavourful, fruity, good acidity, balanced.

MOKOROA

Urteta Auzoa Kortaburu Baserria
20800 Zarautz (Gipuzkoa)
☎: +34 630 222 653 - Fax: +34 943 833 925
bodega@txakolimokoroa.com

MOKOROA 2011 B

86 Colour: bright straw. Nose: fresh, fresh fruit, white flowers, expressive. Palate: flavourful, fruity, good acidity.

SAGARMIÑA

Sagarmiña Baserria
20830 Mitriku (Gipuzcoa)
☎: +34 943 603 225 - Fax: +34 943 192 249
txakolisagarmina@live.com

SAGARMIÑA 2011 B
100% hondarrabi zuri.

87 Colour: bright straw. Nose: white flowers, dried herbs, fruit expression. Palate: fresh, fruity, flavourful.

TALAI BERRI

Talaimendi, 728
20800 Zarautz (Gipuzkoa)
☎: +34 943 132 750 - Fax: +34 943 132 750
info@talaiberri.com
www.talaiberri.com

TXAKOLI TALAI BERRI 2011 B
90% hondarrabi zuri, 10% hondarrabi beltza.

87 Colour: bright straw. Nose: fresh, white flowers, fresh fruit. Palate: fresh, fruity, light-bodied, easy to drink.

TXAKOLI FINCA JAKUE 2011 B
100% hondarrabi zuri.

87 Colour: bright straw. Nose: dried flowers, fruit expression, wild herbs. Palate: flavourful, fresh, fruity.

TXAKOLI ULACIA

Ctra. Meagas
20808 Getaria (Gipuzkoa)
☎: +34 943 140 893 - Fax: +34 943 140 893
nicolasulacia@euskalnet.net

ULACIA 2011 B
90% hondarrabi zuri, 10% hondarrabi beltza.

86 Colour: bright straw. Nose: dried flowers, fragrant herbs, fruit expression. Palate: fine bitter notes, fresh, fruity.

TXAKOLI ZUDUGARAI

Ctra. Zarautz - Aia B° Laurgain
20809 Aia (Gipuzkoa)
☎: +34 943 134 625 - Fax: +34 943 835 952
txakolizudugarai@euskalnet.net
www.txakolizudugarai.com

ZUDUGARAI 2011 B
90% hondarrabi zuri, 10% hondarrabi beltza.

85 Colour: bright yellow. Nose: fresh fruit, white flowers, expressive. Palate: light-bodied, fresh, fruity, easy to drink.

AMATS 2011 B
90% hondarrabi zuri, 10% hondarrabi beltza.

84

TXOMIN ETXANIZ

Txomin Etxaniz
20808 Getaria (Gipuzkoa)
☎: +34 943 140 702 - Fax: +34 943 140 462
txakoli@txominetxaniz.com
www.txominetxaniz.com

TXOMÍN ETXANÍZ BEREZIA 2011 B
90% hondarrabi zuri, 10% hondarrabi beltza.

90 Colour: bright straw. Nose: white flowers, fruit expression, complex, balanced. Palate: light-bodied, fresh, fruity, flavourful.

TXOMÍN ETXANÍZ WHITE WINE 2011 B
80% hondarrabi zuri, 20% chardonnay.

87 Colour: bright straw. Nose: dried flowers, fresh fruit, fragrant herbs. Palate: powerful, fresh, fruity.

TXOMÍN ETXANÍZ 2011 B
100% hondarrabi zuri.

89 Colour: bright straw. Nose: citrus fruit, fruit expression, floral, fragrant herbs. Palate: flavourful, fresh, fruity, balanced, elegant.

EUGENIA TXOMÍN ETXANÍZ 2010 ESP
100% hondarrabi zuri.

86 Colour: bright straw. Nose: lees reduction notes, dried flowers, fragrant herbs. Palate: fine bead, powerful, flavourful, fruity.

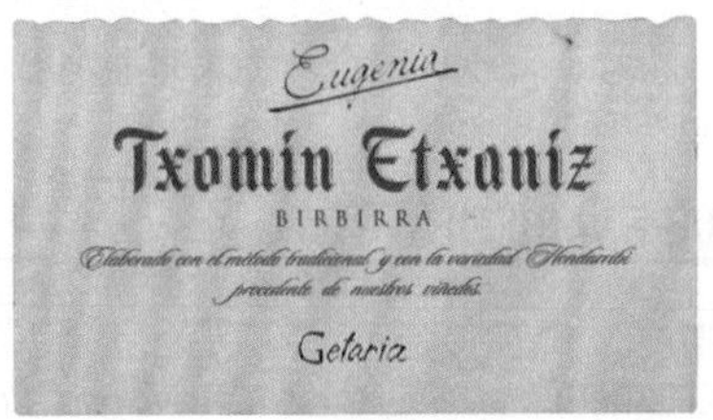

URKI

Urki Txakolina
20808 Getaria (Gipuzcoa)
☎: +34 943 140 049 - Fax: +34 943 140 049
info@urkitxakolina.com
www.urkitxakolina.com

URKI 2011 B
100% hondarrabi zuri.

86 Colour: bright straw. Nose: white flowers, fruit expression, fragrant herbs. Palate: fresh, fruity, light-bodied, easy to drink.

URKI II 2011 B
hondarrabi zuri.

83

DO GRAN CANARIA

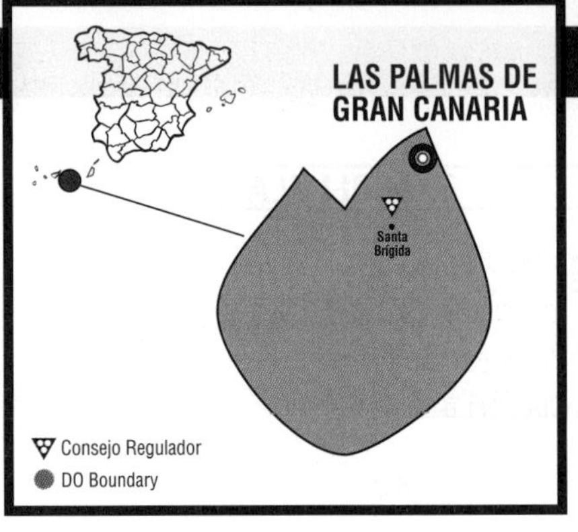

LOCATION:

The production region covers 99% of the island of Gran Canaria, as the climate and the conditions of the terrain allow for the cultivation of grapes at altitudes close to sea level up to the highest mountain tops. The DO incorporates all the municipal areas of the island, except for the Tafira Protected Landscape which falls under an independent DO, Monte de Lentiscal, also fully covered in this Guide.

CLIMATE:

As with the other islands of the archipelago, the differences in altitude give rise to several microclimates which create specific characteristics for the cultivation of the vine. Nevertheless, the climate is conditioned by the influence of the trade winds which blow from the east and whose effect is more evident in the higher-lying areas.

SOIL:

The vineyards are found both in coastal areas and on higher grounds at altitudes of up to 1500 m, resulting in a varied range of soils.

GRAPE VARIETIES:

WHITE:
PREFERRED: *Malvasía, Güal, Marmajuelo* (*Bermejuela*), *Vijariego, Albillo* and *Moscatel.*
AUTHORIZED: *Listán Blanco, Burrablanca, Torrontés, Pedro Ximénez, Brebal* and *Bastardo Blanco.*
RED:
PREFERRED: *Listán Negro, Negramoll, Tintilla, Malvasía Rosada.*
AUTHORIZED: *Moscatel Negra, Bastardo Negro, Listán Prieto, Vijariego Negro, Bastardo Negro, Listón Prieto* und *Vijariego Negro.*

FIGURES:

Vineyard surface: 238 – **Wine-Growers:** 346 – **Wineries:** 68 – **2011 Harvest rating:** Very Good – **Production:** 215,000 litres – **Market percentages:** 90% domestic. 10% export

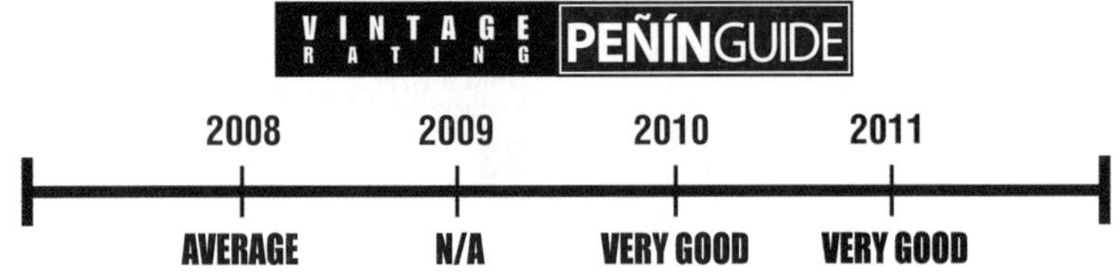

CONSEJO REGULADOR
Calvo Sotelo nº 26 - 35300 Santa Brígida (Las Palmas) - ☎: +34 928 640 462
@ crdogc@yahoo.es - www.vinosdegrancanaria.es

BENTAYGA

El Alberconcillo, s/n
35360 Tejeda (Las Palmas)
☎: +34 928 426 047 - Fax: +34 928 418 795
info@bodegasbentayga.com
www.bodegasbentayga.com

AGALA DULCELENA DULCE 2011 B
vijariego blanco, moscatel.

88 Colour: bright straw. Nose: white flowers, balanced, expressive. Palate: flavourful, fruity.

AGALA 2011 B
vijariego blanco, listán blanco, moscatel, albillo.

86 Colour: bright straw. Nose: fresh, white flowers, medium intensity, expressive. Palate: flavourful, fruity, fine bitter notes.

AGALA VIJARIEGO 2011 T
100% vijariego negro.

88 Colour: cherry, garnet rim. Nose: balanced, ripe fruit, cocoa bean, sweet spices. Palate: fruity, powerful, round tannins.

AGALA 2011 T
listán negro, negramoll, baboso negro.

87 Colour: cherry, purple rim. Nose: balanced, red berry notes, ripe fruit, fragrant herbs. Palate: balanced, fruity, flavourful.

AGALA 2009 TC
100% baboso negro.

89 Colour: cherry, garnet rim. Nose: powerfull, balanced, scrubland, spicy, complex, balsamic herbs. Palate: ripe fruit, long, round tannins, good acidity.

AGALA VENDIMIA NOCTURNA 2011 BLANCO SEMIDULCE
vijariego blanco, moscatel.

86 Colour: bright straw. Nose: floral, jasmine, neat, ripe fruit. Palate: flavourful, fruity, correct.

BODEGA LOS BERRAZALES

León y Castillo, 43
35480 Agaete (Las Palmas)
☎: +34 628 922 588 - Fax: +34 928 898 154
lugojorge3@hotmail.com
www.bodegalosberrazales.com

LOS BERRAZALES SEMISECO 2011 B
60% moscatel, 40% malvasía.

88 Colour: bright straw. Nose: medium intensity, white flowers, balanced. Palate: flavourful, fruity, sweetness, varietal.

LOS BERRAZALES SECO VENDIMIA NOCTURNA 2011 B
50% moscatel, 50% malvasía.

87 Colour: bright straw. Nose: fresh fruit, tropical fruit, balanced, floral. Palate: flavourful, fruity, good acidity.

LOS BERRAZALES DULCE VENDIMIA NOCTURNA 2010 B
moscatel.

90 Colour: bright straw. Nose: white flowers, balanced, ripe fruit, honeyed notes. Palate: fruity, flavourful, long.

LOS BERRAZALES 2010 B BARRICA
moscatel, malvasía.

89 Colour: bright yellow. Nose: floral, expressive, ripe fruit, citrus fruit, balanced. Palate: balanced, good acidity, fruity.

LOS BERRAZALES 2011 T
listán negro, tintilla.

84

LA SAVIA ECOLÓGICA

Pío XII, 221
35460 Galdar (Las Palmas)
☎: +34 617 455 863
celso@lasaviaecologica.com

CALETÓN DULCE 2010 T
listán negro, castellana.

86 Colour: cherry, garnet rim. Nose: spicy, old leather, overripe fruit. Palate: flavourful, rich, light-bodied. Personality.

CALETÓN 2009 T BARRICA
listán negro, castellana.

85 Colour: cherry, garnet rim. Nose: sweet spices, dark chocolate, candied fruit. Palate: flavourful, fruity, spicy.

VEGA DE GÁLDAR

Camino de La Longuera - La Vega de Gáldar
35460 Gáldar (Las Palmas)
☎: +34 605 043 047
lamenora1960@yahoo.es

NUBIA 2011 B
listán blanco, moscatel.

86 Colour: yellow. Nose: powerfull, earthy notes, faded flowers, wild herbs. Palate: fruity, ripe fruit.

VEGA DE GÁLDAR 2011 T
listán negro, castellana.

87 Colour: cherry, purple rim. Nose: medium intensity, red berry notes, wild herbs. Palate: flavourful, fruity, good acidity.

VIÑA AMABLE 2010 T
listán negro, castellana.

89 Colour: cherry, garnet rim. Nose: toasty, sweet spices, cocoa bean, fruit preserve. Palate: flavourful, good structure, round tannins.

EL CONVENTO DE LA VEGA 2010 T
listán negro, castellana.

85 Colour: cherry, garnet rim. Nose: ripe fruit, cocoa bean, sweet spices, balanced. Palate: flavourful, fruity.

DO JEREZ-XÉRÈS-SHERRY-MANZANILLA DE SANLÚCAR DE BARRAMEDA

LOCATION:

In the province of Cádiz. The production area covers the municipal districts of Jerez de la Frontera, El Puerto de Santa María, Chipiona, Trebujena, Rota, Puerto Real, Chiclana de la Frontera and some estates in Lebrija.

CLIMATE:

Warm with Atlantic influences. The west winds play an important role, as they provide humidity and help to temper the conditions. The average annual temperature is 17.5°C, with an average rainfall of 600 mm per year.

SOIL:

The so-called 'Albariza' soil is a key factor regarding quality. This type of soil is practically white and is rich in calcium carbonate, clay and silica. It is excellent for retaining humidity and storing winter rainfall for the dry summer months. Moreover, this soil determines the so-called 'Jerez superior'. It is found in Jerez de la Frontera, Puerto de Santa María, Sanlúcar de Barrameda and certain areas of Trebujena. The remaining soil, known as 'Zona', is muddy and sandy.arenas.

GRAPE VARIETIES:

WHITE: *Palomino* (90%), *Pedro Ximénez, Moscatel, Palomino Fino* and *Palomino de Jerez.*

FIGURES:

Vineyard surface: 7,420 – **Wine-Growers:** 1,834 – **Wineries:** 32 – **2011 Harvest rating:** N/A – **Production:** 31,400,176 litres – **Market percentages:** 29% domestic. 71% export

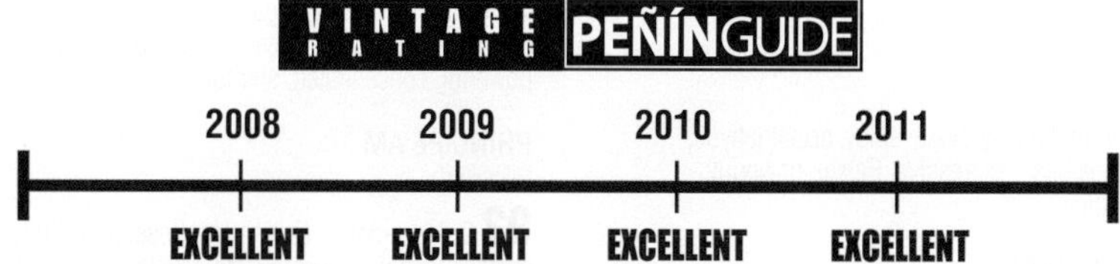

This denomination of origin, due to the wine-making process, does not make available single-year wines indicated by vintage, so the following evaluation refers to the overall quality of the wines that were palate:d this year.

CONSEJO REGULADOR
Avda. Álvaro Domecq, 2 - 11405 Jerez de la Frontera (Cádiz) - ☎: +34 956 332 050 - Fax: +34 956 338 908
@ vinjerez@sherry.org @ prensa@sherry.org - www.sherry.org

AECOVI-JEREZ

Urb. Pie de Rey, 3- Local Izquierda
11407 Jerez de la Frontera (Cádiz)
☎: +34 956 180 873 - Fax: +34 956 180 301
mpascual@aecovi-jerez.com
www.aecovi-jerez.com

ALEXANDRO MZ
100% palomino.

86 Colour: bright straw. Nose: saline, flor yeasts, dry nuts. Palate: flavourful, rich, thin.

PEDRO XIMÉNEZ ALEXANDRO PX
100% pedro ximénez.

87 Colour: mahogany. Nose: dried fruit, powerfull, caramel, sweet spices. Palate: flavourful, correct, unctuous.

ALVARO DOMECQ

Madre de Dios s/n
11401 Jerez de la Frontera (Cádiz)
☎: +34 956 339 634 - Fax: +34 956 340 402
alvarodomecqsl@alvarodomecq.com
www.alvarodomecq.com

LA JANDA FI
palomino.

88 Colour: bright straw. Nose: medium intensity, saline, pungent. Palate: fine bitter notes, correct, flavourful, dry.

1730 VORS OL
palomino.

92 Colour: light mahogany. Nose: acetaldehyde, cocoa bean, dark chocolate, spicy, toasty. Palate: powerful, flavourful, complex, long.

ALBUREJO OL
palomino.

91 Colour: mahogany. Nose: spicy, acetaldehyde, varnish, cocoa bean, expressive. Palate: powerful, flavourful, spicy.

ARANDA CREAM OL
palomino, pedro ximénez.

88 Colour: mahogany. Nose: caramel, acetaldehyde, dark chocolate, candied fruit. Palate: balanced, rich, flavourful, sweetness.

PEDRO XIMÉNEZ 1730 PX
pedro ximénez.

93 Colour: dark mahogany. Nose: dried fruit, spicy, cocoa bean, dark chocolate, aged wood nuances, complex, expressive. Palate: long, spicy, powerful, flavourful, toasty.

BODEGA DE LOS INFANTES ORLEANS BORBÓN

Baños, 1
11540 Sanlúcar de Barrameda (Cádiz)
☎: +34 956 849 002 - Fax: +34 956 849 135
info@biob.es
www.biob.es

TORREBREVA MZ

85 Colour: bright straw. Nose: flor yeasts, saline, medium intensity. Palate: light-bodied, fresh, flavourful.

CARLA PX

86 Colour: dark mahogany. Nose: dried fruit, dark chocolate, caramel. Palate: flavourful, unctuous, sweet, long.

BODEGAS BARBADILLO

Luis de Eguilaz, 11
11540 Sanlúcar de Barrameda (Cádiz)
☎: +34 956 385 500 - Fax: +34 956 385 501
barbadillo@barbadillo.com
www.barbadillo.com

RELIQUIA AM
palomino.

96 Colour: light mahogany. Nose: powerfull, complex, elegant, dry nuts, toasty, acetaldehyde. Palate: rich, fine bitter notes, , long, spicy, powerful, concentrated.

BARBADILLO AMONTILLADO VORS AM
palomino.

95 Colour: light mahogany. Nose: powerfull, warm, acetaldehyde, toasty, sweet spices. Palate: flavourful, powerful, concentrated, spirituous.

PRÍNCIPE AM
palomino.

92 Colour: iodine, amber rim. Nose: powerfull, complex, elegant, toasty, dark chocolate. Palate: rich, fine bitter notes, , long, confected.

EVA CREAM CR
palomino.

90 Colour: light mahogany. Nose: balanced, toasty, sweet spices, dark chocolate. Palate: flavourful, balanced, long, sweetness.

MANZANILLA EN RAMA SACA DE PRIMAVERA 2012 MZ
palomino.

95 Colour: bright yellow. Nose: complex, expressive, pungent, saline, dry nuts, dried herbs, spicy, iodine notes. Palate: rich, powerful, fresh, fine bitter notes, flavourful, spicy, balanced, elegant.

MANZANILLA EN RAMA SACA DE INVIERNO MZ
palomino.

96 Colour: bright golden. Nose: faded flowers, dry nuts, powerfull, flor yeasts, saline. Palate: powerful, flavourful, fine bitter notes.

SOLEAR MZ
palomino.

90 Nose: complex, pungent, saline, dry nuts. Palate: rich, powerful, fine bitter notes, complex.

MUYFINA MZ
palomino.

88 Colour: bright straw. Nose: powerfull, expressive, saline. Palate: flavourful, light-bodied, fine bitter notes.

LAURA MOSCATEL
moscatel.

88 Colour: mahogany. Nose: powerfull, dried fruit, sweet spices, caramel, fruit liqueur notes. Palate: flavourful, balanced, rich.

RELIQUIA OL
palomino.

94 Colour: iodine, amber rim. Nose: powerfull, complex, dry nuts, toasty, expressive. Palate: rich, fine bitter notes, , long, spicy.

BARBADILLO OLOROSO SECO VORS OL

90 Colour: iodine, amber rim. Nose: sweet spices, powerfull, characterful. Palate: powerful, good acidity, fine bitter notes, spicy.

CUCO OLOROSO SECO OL

90 Colour: iodine, amber rim. Nose: powerfull, complex, dry nuts, toasty. Palate: rich, fine bitter notes, , long, spicy.

BARBADILLO OLOROSO DULCE VORS OL
palomino.

89 Colour: light mahogany. Nose: powerfull, candied fruit, fruit liqueur notes, acetaldehyde, sweet spices, pattiserie.

SAN RAFAEL OL
palomino, pedro ximénez.

88 Colour: iodine, amber rim. Nose: dried fruit, honeyed notes, dark chocolate, toasty. Palate: powerful, flavourful, sweetness.

RELIQUIA PC
palomino.

94 Colour: iodine, amber rim. Nose: powerfull, complex, elegant, dry nuts, toasty, acetaldehyde. Palate: rich, fine bitter notes, , long, spicy, powerful.

BARBADILLO PALO CORTADO VORS PC
palomino.

93 Colour: light mahogany. Nose: powerfull, candied fruit, fruit liqueur notes, toasty, sweet spices. Palate: powerful, sweetness, concentrated, fine bitter notes.

OBISPO GASCÓN PC
palomino.

92 Colour: light mahogany. Nose: sweet spices, acetaldehyde, expressive, dry nuts. Palate: good structure, balanced, long, spicy.

RELIQUIA PX
pedro ximénez.

96 Colour: dark mahogany. Nose: complex, expressive, fruit liqueur notes, dried fruit, dark chocolate, cocoa bean. Palate: unctuous, fine bitter notes, complex.

LA CILLA PX
pedro ximénez.

89 Colour: dark mahogany. Nose: fruit liqueur notes, dried fruit, pattiserie, toasty, powerfull. Palate: sweet, rich, unctuous, powerful.

BODEGAS BARÓN

Molinillo 2a 2 y 3
11540 Sanlúcar de Barrameda (Cádiz)
☎: +34 956 360 796 - Fax: +34 956 363 256
baron.as@terra.es
www.bodegasbaron.net

ATALAYA AM

90 Colour: iodine, amber rim. Nose: powerfull, dry nuts, toasty, cocoa bean, dark chocolate. Palate: rich, fine bitter notes, long, spicy.

MANZANILLA PASADA BARÓN MZ
palomino.

92 Colour: bright yellow. Nose: saline, acetaldehyde, dried herbs, expressive. Palate: fine bitter notes, flavourful, complex, rich.

P.X. BARÓN PX
15% pedro ximénez.

92 Colour: dark mahogany. Nose: acetaldehyde, spicy, nose:tic coffee, dark chocolate, creamy oak. Palate: flavourful, complex, rich, long.

P.X. BARÓN VIEJO PX
pedro ximénez.

92 Colour: dark mahogany. Nose: complex, fruit liqueur notes, dried fruit, pattiserie, toasty, acetaldehyde. Palate: sweet, rich, unctuous, powerful.

BODEGAS DIEZ MÉRITO

Ctra. Morabita, Km. 2
11407 Jerez de la Frontera (Cádiz)
☎: +34 956 186 112 - Fax: +34 956 303 500
paternina@paternina.com
www.paternina.com

FINO IMPERIAL 30 AÑOS VORS AM
100% palomino.

92 Colour: iodine, amber rim. Nose: acetaldehyde, mineral, dry nuts, spicy. Palate: powerful, flavourful, complex, toasty.

BERTOLA 12 AÑOS AM
100% palomino.

90 Colour: light mahogany. Nose: balanced, sweet spices, complex, expressive. Palate: flavourful, rich, balanced, spicy.

BERTOLA CR
75% palomino, 25% pedro ximénez.

85 Colour: dark mahogany. Nose: dried fruit, acetaldehyde, medium intensity. Palate: spicy, unctuous, easy to drink.

BERTOLA FI
100% palomino.

90 Colour: bright yellow. Nose: powerfull, complex, dried flowers, pungent, saline. Palate: long, fine bitter notes, balanced.

VICTORIA REGINA VORS OL
100% palomino.

89 Colour: iodine, amber rim. Nose: powerfull, dry nuts, toasty. Palate: rich, fine bitter notes, , long, spicy.

BERTOLA 12 AÑOS OL
100% palomino.

87 Colour: light mahogany. Nose: expressive, acetaldehyde, woody. Palate: spirituous, powerful, flavourful.

VIEJA SOLERA 30 AÑOS VORS PX
100% pedro ximénez.

92 Colour: dark mahogany. Nose: expressive, varnish, spicy, aged wood nuances, acetaldehyde, nose:tic coffee. Palate: long, rich, powerful, flavourful, complex.

BERTOLA 12 AÑOS PX
100% pedro ximénez.

88 Colour: dark mahogany. Nose: complex, fruit liqueur notes, dried fruit, toasty. Palate: sweet, rich, unctuous, powerful.

BODEGAS GARVEY JEREZ

Ctra. Circunvalación, s/n
11407 Jerez de la Frontera (Cádiz)
☎: +34 956 319 650 - Fax: +34 956 319 824
marketing@grupogarvey.com
www.bodegasgarvey.com

ASALTO AMOROSO B
palomino, pedro ximénez.

90 Colour: mahogany. Nose: balanced, dried fruit, acetaldehyde, cocoa bean. Palate: flavourful, good structure, sweetness, full.

OÑANA AM
palomino.

93 Colour: bright golden. Nose: sweet spices, acetaldehyde, varnish. Palate: fine bitter notes, spirituous, round.

TIO GUILLERMO AM
palomino.

84

FLOR DEL MUSEO CR
palomino, pedro ximénez.

92 Colour: mahogany. Nose: complex, expressive, powerfull, acetaldehyde, spicy, dry nuts. Palate: good structure, flavourful, complex, fine bitter notes.

FLOR DE JEREZ CR
palomino, pedro ximénez.

86 Colour: mahogany. Nose: dried fruit, sweet spices, caramel, aged wood nuances. Palate: correct, sweet.

SAN PATRICIO FI
palomino.

90 Colour: bright straw. Nose: saline, flor yeasts, expressive. Palate: flavourful, complex, fine bitter notes.

JUNCAL MZ
palomino.

89 Colour: bright straw. Nose: saline, dried flowers, complex, dry nuts. Palate: fine bitter notes, correct, flavourful.

GARVEY 1780 VORS OL
palomino.

92 Colour: light mahogany. Nose: dry nuts, expressive, balanced, powerfull, toasty. Palate: good structure, complex, spirituous, long.

GARVEY 1780 VOS OL
palomino.

90 Colour: mahogany. Nose: powerfull, complex, spicy, balanced. Palate: fine bitter notes, spicy, long, spirituous.

PUERTA REAL OL
palomino.

90 Colour: light mahogany. Nose: cocoa bean, sweet spices, dried fruit. Palate: powerful, good structure, long, fine bitter notes, spirituous.

OCHAVICO OL
palomino.

87 Colour: light mahogany. Nose: balanced, medium intensity, caramel. Palate: spirituous, good finish.

JAUNA PC
palomino.

91 Colour: light mahogany. Nose: spicy, creamy oak, candied fruit, balanced. Palate: rich, flavourful, complex, spicy.

GRAN ORDEN PX
pedro ximénez.

95 Colour: dark mahogany. Nose: complex, fruit liqueur notes, dried fruit, acetaldehyde, spicy. Palate: sweet, rich, unctuous, powerful.

PEDRO XIMENEZ ZOILO RUIZ MATEOS PX
pedro ximénez.

95 Colour: dark mahogany. Nose: expressive, elegant, spicy, caramel, dark chocolate, toasty, creamy oak. Palate: long, spicy, complex, rich, powerful, flavourful.

GARVEY 1780 VORS PX
pedro ximénez.

92 Colour: dark mahogany. Nose: complex, fruit liqueur notes, dried fruit, pattiserie, toasty, acetaldehyde, dark chocolate, spicy, creamy oak. Palate: sweet, rich, unctuous, powerful, long, flavourful.

GARVEY 1780 VOS PX
pedro ximénez.

91 Colour: dark mahogany. Nose: complex, fruit liqueur notes, dried fruit, pattiserie, toasty, dark chocolate. Palate: sweet, rich, unctuous, powerful, balanced.

GARVEY PX
pedro ximénez.

88 Colour: dark mahogany. Nose: powerfull, balanced, dark chocolate, varietal. Palate: long, flavourful, sweetness, full.

BODEGAS GRANT

Bolos
11500 El Puerto de Santa María (Cádiz)
☎: +34 956 870 406 - Fax: +34 956 870 406
info@bodegasgrant.com
www.bodegasgrant.com

LA GARROCHA AM
palomino.

87 Colour: iodine, amber rim. Nose: powerfull, dry nuts, toasty, medium intensity. Palate: rich, , spicy, light-bodied, fine bitter notes.

LA GARROCHA CR
palomino, pedro ximénez.

88 Colour: light mahogany. Nose: medium intensity, acetaldehyde, dry nuts. Palate: flavourful, correct, fine bitter notes, sweetness.

VALEROSO FI
palomino.

87 Colour: bright yellow. Nose: complex, expressive, pungent, saline, flor yeasts. Palate: powerful, fresh, fine bitter notes.

LA GARROCHA MOSCATEL
moscatel.

85 Colour: mahogany. Nose: candied fruit, pattiserie, sweet spices, toasty. Palate: powerful, flavourful, correct.

LA GARROCHA OL
palomino.

86 Colour: iodine, amber rim. Nose: acetaldehyde, varnish, spicy, toasty. Palate: fine bitter notes, short, flavourful.

LA GARROCHA PX
pedro ximénez.

86 Colour: dark mahogany. Nose: fruit liqueur notes, dried fruit, pattiserie, toasty, fruit liqueur notes. Palate: sweet, rich, unctuous.

BODEGAS GUTIÉRREZ COLOSÍA

Avda. Bajamar, 40
11500 El Puerto de Santa María (Cádiz)
☎: +34 956 852 852 - Fax: +34 956 542 936
info@gutierrezcolosia.com
www.gutierrezcolosia.com

GUTIÉRREZ COLOSÍA MOSCATEL SOLEADO
moscatel.

88 Colour: light mahogany. Nose: varietal, jasmine, honeyed notes, dried fruit. Palate: balanced, unctuous, long, sweet, spicy.

GUTIÉRREZ COLOSÍA SOLERA FAMILIAR AM
palomino.

91 Colour: iodine, amber rim. Nose: powerfull, complex, dry nuts, toasty, dark chocolate. Palate: rich, fine bitter notes, , long, spicy.

GUTIÉRREZ COLOSÍA AM
palomino.

91 Colour: light mahogany. Nose: acetaldehyde, fruit liqueur notes, cocoa bean, spicy, creamy oak. Palate: fine bitter notes, powerful, flavourful, long.

GUTIÉRREZ COLOSÍA CR
palomino, pedro ximénez.

87 Colour: mahogany. Nose: dried fruit, medium intensity, pattiserie. Palate: sweetness, fine bitter notes.

MARI PEPA CR
palomino, pedro ximénez.

87 Colour: light mahogany. Nose: dried fruit, dry nuts, sweet spices, toasty. Palate: pruney, rich, correct.

GUTIÉRREZ COLOSÍA FI
palomino.

90 Colour: bright golden. Nose: powerfull, pungent, saline, acetaldehyde, dry nuts. Palate: flavourful, fine bitter notes, long, balanced.

GUTIÉRREZ COLOSÍA FINO EN RAMA FI
palomino.

87 Colour: bright golden. Nose: powerfull, pungent, fruit liqueur notes, slightly evolved. Palate: flavourful, fine bitter notes.

GUTIÉRREZ COLOSÍA MZ
palomino.

91 Colour: bright straw. Nose: balanced, medium intensity, saline, dry nuts. Palate: powerful, flavourful.

GUTIÉRREZ COLOSÍA SOLERA FAMILIAR OL
palomino.

92 Colour: mahogany. Nose: elegant, balanced, dry nuts, sweet spices, caramel. Palate: rich, powerful, complex.

GUTIÉRREZ COLOSÍA OL
palomino.

87 Colour: light mahogany. Nose: fruit liqueur notes, spicy, acetaldehyde. Palate: spirituous, flavourful, correct.

SANGRE Y TRABAJADERO OL
palomino.

86 Colour: light mahogany. Nose: creamy oak, roasted almonds, spicy, fruit liqueur notes. Palate: powerful, flavourful, spirituous.

GUTIÉRREZ COLOSÍA SOLERA FAMILIAR PC
palomino.

90 Colour: iodine, amber rim. Nose: nose:tic coffee, toasty, varnish, expressive. Palate: balanced, powerful, flavourful.

GUTIÉRREZ COLOSÍA SOLERA FAMILIAR PX
pedro ximénez.

90 Colour: dark mahogany. Nose: varnish, acetaldehyde, spicy, dark chocolate, aged wood nuances. Palate: sweetness, powerful, flavourful, complex.

GUTIÉRREZ COLOSÍA PX
pedro ximénez.

88 Colour: dark mahogany. Nose: complex, fruit liqueur notes, dried fruit, pattiserie, toasty. Palate: sweet, rich, unctuous, powerful.

BODEGAS HARVEYS

Pintor Muñoz Cebrián, s/n
11402 Jerez de la Frontera (Cádiz)
☎: +34 956 346 000 - Fax: +34 956 349 427
visitas@bodegasharveys.com
www.bodegasharveys.com

HARVEYS VORS AM
100% palomino.

92 Colour: iodine, amber rim. Nose: dry nuts, acetaldehyde, spicy, creamy oak. Palate: complex, flavourful, rich, spicy.

HARVEYS BRISTOL CREAM CR
80% palomino, 20% pedro ximénez.

85 Colour: mahogany. Nose: fruit preserve, dried fruit, pattiserie, toasty. Palate: flavourful, rich.

HARVEYS VORS RICH OLD OL
90% palomino, 10% pedro ximénez.

94 Colour: light mahogany. Nose: expressive, elegant, cocoa bean, dark chocolate, spicy, creamy oak. Palate: fine bitter notes, powerful, flavourful, complex.

HARVEYS VORS PC
98% palomino, 2% pedro ximénez.

93 Colour: amber. Nose: sweet spices, caramel, acetaldehyde, candied fruit. Palate: long, spicy, flavourful.

HARVEYS VORS PX
100% pedro ximénez.

90 Colour: dark mahogany. Nose: complex, fruit liqueur notes, dried fruit, pattiserie, toasty. Palate: sweet, rich, unctuous, powerful.

BODEGAS HIDALGO-LA GITANA

Banda de Playa, 42
11540 Sanlúcar de Barrameda (Cádiz)
☎: +34 956 385 304 - Fax: +34 956 363 844
bodegashidalgo@lagitana.es
www.lagitana.es

NAPOLEÓN 30 AÑOS VORS 50 CL. AM
100% palomino.

93 Colour: light mahogany. Nose: complex, expressive, dry nuts, acetaldehyde, spicy. Palate: full, flavourful, balanced, fine bitter notes.

NAPOLEÓN AM
100% palomino.

88 Colour: light mahogany. Nose: acetaldehyde, roasted almonds, slightly evolved. Palate: rich, spicy.

ALAMEDA CR
75% palomino, 25% pedro ximénez.

87 Colour: iodine, amber rim. Nose: sweet spices, fruit liqueur notes, pattiserie, toasty. Palate: correct, flavourful, concentrated.

PASTRANA MANZANILLA PASADA MZ
100% palomino.

94 Colour: bright golden. Nose: saline, pungent, dry nuts, roasted almonds, expressive. Palate: rich, powerful, flavourful, balanced.

LA GITANA MZ
100% palomino.

92 Colour: bright straw. Nose: saline, dried flowers, balanced, expressive. Palate: complex, fresh, flavourful, elegant.

FARAÓN 30 AÑOS VORS 50 CL. OL
100% palomino.

92 Colour: iodine, amber rim. Nose: dry nuts, varnish, spicy, toasty. Palate: correct, fine bitter notes, toasty, long.

FARAÓN OL
100% palomino.

86 Colour: iodine, amber rim. Nose: acetaldehyde, sweet spices, fruit liqueur notes. Palate: spirituous, powerful, flavourful.

WELLINGTON 30 AÑOS VORS PC
100% palomino.

91 Colour: mahogany. Nose: powerfull, expressive, complex, spicy, pungent, acetaldehyde. Palate: full, good structure, long, spicy.

WELLINGTON JEREZ CORTADO 20 AÑOS VOS PC
100% palomino.

90 Colour: light mahogany. Nose: medium intensity, sweet spices. Palate: light-bodied, correct, balanced, spirituous.

TRIANA 30 AÑOS VORS PX
100% pedro ximénez.

92 Colour: dark mahogany. Nose: creamy oak, dark chocolate, nose:tic coffee, toasty, expressive. Palate: long, sweet, rich, flavourful.

TRIANA PX
100% pedro ximénez.

90 Colour: dark mahogany. Nose: spicy, caramel, dark chocolate, dried fruit. Palate: rich, powerful, flavourful.

BODEGAS LA CIGARRERA

Pza. Madre de Dios, s/n
11540 Sanlúcar de Barrameda (Cádiz)
☎: +34 956 381 285 - Fax: +34 956 383 824
lacigarrera@bodegaslacigarrera.com
www.bodegaslacigarrera.com

LA CIGARRERA AM
100% palomino.

91 Colour: golden. Nose: powerfull, complex, elegant, dry nuts, toasty, acetaldehyde. Palate: rich, fine bitter notes, long, spicy.

LA CIGARRERA MZ
100% palomino.

88 Colour: bright straw. Nose: dried flowers, saline, dry nuts. Palate: long, powerful, flavourful, rich.

LA CIGARRERA MOSCATEL
100% moscatel.

92 Colour: light mahogany. Nose: dried fruit, acetaldehyde, nose:tic coffee, spicy, toasty. Palate: sweetness, powerful, flavourful, complex, balanced.

LA CIGARRERA OL
100% palomino.

88 Colour: iodine, amber rim. Nose: fruit liqueur notes, sweet spices, creamy oak. Palate: spicy, oaky, long.

LA CIGARRERA PX
100% pedro ximénez.

89 Colour: dark mahogany. Nose: toasty, dried fruit, nose:tic coffee, dark chocolate. Palate: powerful, flavourful, sweetness, spirituous.

BODEGAS OSBORNE

Fernán Caballero, 7
11500 El Puerto de Santa María (Cádiz)
☎: +34 956 869 000 - Fax: +34 925 869 026
comunicacion@osborne.es
www.osborne.es

OSBORNE RARE SHERRY AOS AM
palomino.

96 Colour: iodine, amber rim. Nose: powerfull, complex, elegant, dry nuts, toasty, acetaldehyde. Palate: rich, , spicy, long, fine biller notes.

AMONTILLADO 51-1ª V.O.R.S AM
100% palomino.

93 Colour: light mahogany. Nose: powerfull, acetaldehyde, dark chocolate, nose:tic coffee, varnish. Palate: powerful, good acidity, fine bitter notes, spicy.

SANTA MARÍA CREAM CR
pedro ximénez, palomino.

87 Colour: iodine. Nose: candied fruit, powerfull, caramel, pattiserie. Palate: flavourful, sweetness, rich.

FINO QUINTA FI
100% palomino.

93 Colour: bright straw. Nose: complex, balanced, pungent, saline. Palate: flavourful, dry, elegant, long, fine bitter notes.

COQUINERO FI
100% palomino.

92 Colour: bright yellow. Nose: dry nuts, sweet spices, white flowers. Palate: long, fine bitter notes, flavourful.

OSBORNE RARE SHERRY SOLERA BC 200 OL
pedro ximénez, palomino.

97 Colour: iodine, amber rim. Nose: powerfull, complex, dry nuts, toasty, acetaldehyde. Palate: rich, fine bitter notes, long, spicy.

SIBARITA V.O.R.S. OL
98% palomino, 2% pedro ximénez.

95 Colour: iodine, amber rim. Nose: powerfull, complex, elegant, dry nuts, toasty. Palate: rich, fine bitter notes, , long, good acidity.

OSBORNE RARE SHERRY SOLERA INDIA OL
pedro ximénez, palomino.

94 Colour: iodine, amber rim. Nose: fruit liqueur notes, fruit liqueur notes, pattiserie. Palate: spicy, spirituous, fine bitter notes.

10 RF OL
palomino, pedro ximénez.

88 Colour: light mahogany. Nose: sweet spices, toasty, dark chocolate, cocoa bean. Palate: spicy, sweetness, correct.

BAILÉN OL
100% palomino.

88 Colour: light mahogany. Nose: medium intensity, nose:tic coffee, sweet spices. Palate: flavourful, spicy, rich.

CAPUCHINO V.O.R.S PC
100% palomino.

94 Colour: iodine, amber rim. Nose: powerfull, characterful, ripe fruit, toasty. Palate: good acidity, flavourful, powerful.

OSBORNE RARE SHERRY SOLERA PAP PC
pedro ximénez, palomino.

93 Colour: light mahogany. Nose: powerfull, fruit liqueur notes, toasty, acetaldehyde. Palate: powerful, spicy, good acidity, fine bitter notes, sweetness.

VENERABLE VORS PX
100% pedro ximénez.

97 Colour: dark mahogany. Nose: acetaldehyde, varnish, nose:tic coffee, caramel, dark chocolate, toasty, aged wood nuances, expressive. Palate: powerful, flavourful, sweet, spirituous, balanced, elegant.

OSBORNE RARE SHERRY PX VORS PX
pedro ximénez.

93 Colour: dark mahogany. Nose: acetaldehyde, powerfull, expressive, varnish, nose:tic coffee, toasty, complex. Palate: long, powerful, flavourful, sweet, spicy, spirituous.

OSBORNE 1827 PX
100% pedro ximénez.

91 Colour: dark mahogany. Nose: fruit liqueur notes, dried fruit, toasty, dark chocolate, aged wood nuances. Palate: complex, powerful, flavourful.

BODEGAS PEDRO ROMERO

Trasbolsa, 84
11540 Sanlúcar de Barrameda (Cádiz)
☎: +34 956 360 736 - Fax: +34 956 361 027
pedroromero@pedroromero.es
www.pedroromero.es

DON PEDRO ROMERO VORS PRESTIGE AM
100% palomino.

94 Colour: iodine, amber rim. Nose: acetaldehyde, toasty, creamy oak, varnish, expressive, pungent. Palate: powerful, flavourful, complex, spicy.

AURORA MZ
100% palomino.

87 Colour: bright yellow. Nose: medium intensity, dried herbs, pungent. Palate: easy to drink, light-bodied.

HIJO DE PEDRO ROMERO VILLAREAL VORS PRESTIGE PC
100% palomino.

93 Colour: iodine, amber rim. Nose: spicy, creamy oak, balanced, acetaldehyde. Palate: unctuous, round, flavourful, complex, long.

TRES ÁLAMOS PX
100% pedro ximénez.

86 Colour: dark mahogany. Nose: acetaldehyde, dried fruit, nose:tic coffee, pattiserie, toasty. Palate: powerful, flavourful, spirituous, concentrated.

BODEGAS TERESA RIVERO

Puerto, 21
11540 Sanlúcar de Barrameda (Cádiz)
☎: +34 956 361 491 - Fax: +34 956 368 369
info@bodegasteresarivero.com
www.grupogarvey.com

BAJO DE GUÍA MZ
palomino.

90 Colour: bright straw. Nose: dried herbs, pungent, saline, flor yeasts. Palate: flavourful, dry, balanced, long.

LA SANLUQUEÑA MZ
palomino.

90 Colour: bright straw. Nose: medium intensity, fresh, dried herbs, pungent. Palate: flavourful, dry, long.

BODEGAS TERRY

Toneleros, s/n
11500 El Puerto de Santa María (Cádiz)
☎: +34 956 151 500 - Fax: +34 956 858 474
visitas@bodegasterry.com
www.bodegasterry.com

TERRY AMONTILLADO AM
100% palomino.

90 Colour: light mahogany. Nose: sweet spices, dry nuts, acetaldehyde. Palate: flavourful, powerful, spirituous.

TERRY FINO FI
100% palomino.

91 Colour: bright straw. Nose: pungent, fine lees, white flowers. Palate: powerful, fine bitter notes, long.

TERRY OLOROSO OL
100% palomino.

88 Colour: light mahogany. Nose: medium intensity, cocoa bean, nose:tic coffee. Palate: correct, balanced, spirituous, fine bitter notes.

TERRY PEDRO XIMÉNEZ PX
100% pedro ximénez.

90 Colour: dark mahogany. Nose: complex, fruit liqueur notes, dried fruit, pattiserie, toasty. Palate: sweet, rich, unctuous, powerful.

BODEGAS TRADICIÓN

Cordobeses, 3
11408 Jerez de la Frontera (Cádiz)
☎: +34 956 168 628 - Fax: +34 956 331 963
mllanos@bodegastradicion.com
www.bodegastradicion.com

AMONTILLADO TRADICIÓN VORS AM
palomino.

93 Colour: light mahogany. Nose: expressive, balanced, dry nuts, acetaldehyde. Palate: flavourful, dry, complex, full.

OLOROSO TRADICIÓN VORS OL
palomino.

94 Colour: light mahogany. Nose: complex, elegant, spicy, expressive, toasty. Palate: flavourful, spirituous, fine bitter notes.

PALO CORTADO TRADICIÓN VORS PC
palomino.

91 Colour: light mahogany. Nose: acetaldehyde, dark chocolate, spicy, creamy oak. Palate: fine bitter notes, complex, flavourful, spicy.

PEDRO XIMÉNEZ TRADICIÓN VOS PX
pedro ximénez.

91 Colour: dark mahogany. Nose: complex, fruit liqueur notes, pattiserie, toasty, sweet spices, dark chocolate. Palate: sweet, rich, unctuous, powerful, long, flavourful.

BODEGAS VALDIVIA

Zoilo Ruiz Mateo, s/n
11408 Jerez de la Frontera (Cádiz)
☎: +34 956 314 358 - Fax: +34 956 169 657
info@bodegasvaldivia.com
www.bodegasvaldivia.com

SACROMONTE 15 AÑOS AM
palomino.

90 Colour: iodine, amber rim. Nose: powerfull, toasty, acetaldehyde, sweet spices. Palate: rich, fine bitter notes, , long, spicy.

VALDIVIA DORIUS AM
palomino.

89 Colour: light mahogany. Nose: dry nuts, sweet spices. Palate: flavourful, good structure, full.

VALDIVIA ATRUM CR
palomino.

91 Colour: light mahogany. Nose: dried fruit, sweet spices, dark chocolate, expressive. Palate: long, flavourful, spicy, complex.

VALDIVIA FI
palomino.

91 Colour: bright straw. Nose: balanced, powerfull, complex, pungent, saline. Palate: long, flavourful, full.

LA RUBIA MZ
100% palomino.

87 Colour: bright straw. Nose: medium intensity, balanced, neat. Palate: flavourful, correct.

SACROMONTE 15 AÑOS OL
palomino.

91 Colour: iodine, amber rim. Nose: acetaldehyde, dry nuts, dark chocolate, sweet spices. Palate: complex, powerful, flavourful, spicy.

VALDIVIA PRUNE OL
palomino.

90 Colour: old gold, amber rim. Nose: spicy, toasty, dry nuts. Palate: rich, flavourful, long, balanced.

VALDIVIA ÁMBAR OL
palomino.

87 Colour: iodine, amber rim. Nose: acetaldehyde, spicy, fruit liqueur notes. Palate: fine bitter notes, spicy, toasty.

VALDIVIA SUN PALE CREAM PCR
palomino.

90 Colour: bright yellow. Nose: complex, fresh, saline. Palate: balanced, fine bitter notes, easy to drink, sweetness, good acidity.

SACROMONTE 15 AÑOS PX
pedro ximénez.

90 Colour: dark mahogany. Nose: complex, fruit liqueur notes, dried fruit, pattiserie, toasty, nose:tic coffee, cocoa bean. Palate: sweet, rich, unctuous, powerful.

VALDIVIA PX PX
pedro ximénez.

88 Colour: dark mahogany. Nose: complex, fruit liqueur notes, dried fruit, pattiserie, toasty. Palate: sweet, rich, unctuous, powerful.

CÉSAR L. FLORIDO ROMERO

Padre Lerchundi, 35-37
11550 Chipiona (Cádiz)
☎: +34 956 371 285 - Fax: +34 956 370 222
florido@bodegasflorido.com
www.bodegasflorido.com

CRUZ DEL MAR CR
75% moscatel, 25% palomino.

85 Colour: iodine, amber rim. Nose: citrus fruit, pattiserie, aged wood nuances, dark chocolate. Palate: flavourful, spirituous, pruney.

FINO CÉSAR FI
100% palomino.

91 Colour: bright yellow. Nose: complex, expressive, pungent, saline. Palate: rich, powerful, fresh, fine bitter notes, complex.

CÉSAR FLORIDO MOSCATEL ESPECIAL MOSCATEL
100% moscatel.

91 Colour: dark mahogany. Nose: powerfull, sweet spices, pattiserie, candied fruit, dark chocolate. Palate: good structure, rich, full, flavourful.

CÉSAR FLORIDO MOSCATEL PASAS MOSCATEL
100% moscatel.

88 Colour: mahogany. Nose: dried fruit, acetaldehyde, cocoa bean, sweet spices. Palate: complex, flavourful, rich.

CÉSAR FLORIDO MOSCATEL DORADO MOSCATEL
100% moscatel.

87 Colour: iodine. Nose: pattiserie, sweet spices, candied fruit, citrus fruit. Palate: rich, sweetness, correct.

CRUZ DEL MAR OL
100% palomino.

87 Colour: light mahogany. Nose: cocoa bean, expressive, toasty, honeyed notes. Palate: powerful, flavourful, spirituous.

DELGADO ZULETA

Avda. Rocío Jurado, s/n
11540 Sanlúcar de Barrameda (Cádiz)
☎: +34 956 360 133 - Fax: +34 956 360 780
direccioncomercial@delgadozuleta.com
www.delgadozuleta.com

QUO VADIS AM
100% palomino.

90 Colour: old gold, amber rim. Nose: acetaldehyde, roasted almonds, expressive. Palate: spicy, long, flavourful.

MONTEAGUDO AM
100% palomino.

90 Colour: iodine, amber rim. Nose: expressive, caramel, spicy, toasty. Palate: fine bitter notes, flavourful, long.

MONTEAGUDO PEDRO XIMÉNEZ PX
pedro ximénez.

87 Colour: dark mahogany. Nose: fruit liqueur notes, dried fruit, pattiserie, toasty. Palate: sweet, rich, unctuous, powerful.

DIOS BACO

Tecnología, A-14
11407 Jerez de la Frontera (Cádiz)
☎: +34 956 333 337 - Fax: +34 956 333 825
info@bodegasdiosbaco.com
www.bodegasdiosbaco.com

DIOS BACO AM
palomino.

89 Colour: old gold, amber rim. Nose: saline, acetaldehyde, spicy, toasty. Palate: fine bitter notes, powerful, flavourful, toasty.

BACO DE ÉLITE MEDIUM DRY AM
palomino.

89 Colour: old gold. Nose: expressive, toasty, sweet spices, dark chocolate. Palate: powerful, spicy.

DIOS BACO CR
palomino, pedro ximénez.

91 Colour: mahogany. Nose: dried fruit, caramel, pattiserie, powerfull, fruit liqueur notes. Palate: rich, flavourful, balanced.

BULERÍA FI
palomino.

88 Colour: bright straw. Nose: saline, flor yeasts, candied fruit. Palate: rich, fine bitter notes, flavourful.

RIÁ PITÁ MZ
palomino.

87 Colour: bright yellow. Nose: candied fruit, expressive, powerfull. Palate: good structure, flavourful.

ESNOBISTA MOSCATEL PASA MOSCATEL
moscatel.

87 Colour: light mahogany. Nose: dried fruit, acetaldehyde, spicy. Palate: flavourful, spicy, creamy.

DIOS BACO OL
18% palomino.

91 Colour: light mahogany. Nose: expressive, spicy, aged wood nuances. Palate: flavourful, long, fine bitter notes, rich.

BACO DE ÉLITE MEDIUM OL
palomino.

90 Colour: light mahogany. Nose: toasty, aged wood nuances, spicy. Palate: spirituous, sweetness, rich, balanced.

OXFORD 1970 PX
pedro ximénez.

90 Colour: dark mahogany. Nose: varietal, warm, fruit liqueur notes, dark chocolate, fruit liqueur notes. Palate: correct, balanced, good structure.

EL MAESTRO SIERRA

Pza. de Silos, 5
11403 Jerez de la Frontera (Cádiz)
☎: +34 956 342 433 - Fax: +34 956 342 433
info@maestrosierra.com
www.maestrosierra.com

EL MAESTRO SIERRA FI
palomino.

92 Colour: bright yellow. Nose: balanced, spicy, dried herbs, pungent. Palate: rich, full, fine bitter notes.

EL MAESTRO SIERRA OLOROSO 1/14 OL
palomino.

94 Colour: mahogany. Nose: dark chocolate, cocoa bean, spicy, toasty, expressive. Palate: long, spicy, powerful, flavourful, complex.

EMILIO LUSTAU

Arcos, 53
11402 Jerez de la Frontera (Cádiz)
☎: +34 956 341 597 - Fax: +34 956 859 204
lustau@lustau.es
www.lustau.es

LUSTAU ESCUADRILLA AM
palomino.

90 Colour: iodine, amber rim. Nose: powerfull, complex, dry nuts, toasty. Palate: rich, fine bitter notes, , long, spicy.

LUSTAU EAST INDIA CR
palomino, pedro ximénez.

90 Colour: mahogany. Nose: powerfull, dried fruit, spicy, pattiserie, dark chocolate, expressive. Palate: sweetness, powerful, flavourful.

CANDELA CR
palomino, pedro ximénez.

86 Colour: iodine, amber rim. Nose: honeyed notes, pattiserie, sweet spices, toasty. Palate: rich, powerful, spirituous.

LA INA FI
palomino.

96 Colour: bright straw. Nose: expressive, complex, pungent, saline, flor yeasts. Palate: complex, flavourful, long, fine bitter notes.

PUERTO FINO FI
palomino.

93 Colour: bright yellow. Nose: expressive, pungent, saline. Palate: rich, powerful, fresh, fine bitter notes.

LUSTAU JARANA FI
100% palomino.

91 Colour: bright straw. Nose: powerfull, complex, white flowers, pungent. Palate: long, fine bitter notes, good acidity.

LUSTAU PAPIRUSA MZ SOLERA
palomino.

94 Colour: bright yellow. Nose: saline, flor yeasts, pungent, faded flowers. Palate: complex, flavourful, rich.

MACARENA MZ
100% palomino.

90 Colour: bright straw. Nose: powerfull, characterful, pungent, flor yeasts. Palate: flavourful, good acidity, full.

LUSTAU EMILÍN MOSCATEL
100% moscatel.

91 Colour: light mahogany. Nose: acetaldehyde, dried fruit, cocoa bean, sweet spices. Palate: rich, flavourful, complex, toasty, long.

RÍO VIEJO OL
palomino.

92 Colour: iodine, amber rim. Nose: sweet spices, dark chocolate, fruit liqueur notes. Palate: long, spicy, powerful.

LUSTAU AÑADA 1997 OLOROSO DULCE OL
palomino.

92 Colour: iodine, amber rim. Nose: sweet spices, pattiserie, dried fruit, honeyed notes. Palate: powerful, flavourful, complex, sweetness.

LUSTAU EMPERATRIZ EUGENIA OL
palomino.

89 Colour: mahogany. Nose: balanced, expressive, dry nuts, sweet spices. Palate: powerful, complex, toasty, fine bitter notes.

LUSTAU DON NUÑO OL
palomino.

88 Colour: light mahogany. Nose: balanced, sweet spices, cocoa bean. Palate: good structure, balanced, spicy, correct.

LUSTAU PENÍSULA PC
palomino.

90 Colour: iodine, amber rim. Nose: powerfull, pungent, spicy, toasty. Palate: flavourful, powerful, fine bitter notes.

LUSTAU SAN EMILIO PX
pedro ximénez.

93 Colour: mahogany. Nose: powerfull, varietal, candied fruit, dark chocolate, nose:tic coffee. Palate: full, complex, good acidity, fine bitter notes.

VIÑA 25 PX
100% pedro ximénez.

88 Colour: mahogany. Nose: candied fruit, dried fruit, dark chocolate. Palate: long, toasty, unctuous, sweet.

EQUIPO NAVAZOS

Cartuja, 1 - módulo 6
11401 Jerez de la Frontera (Cádiz)
equipo@navazos.com
www.equiponavazos.com

LA BOTA DE AMONTILLADO (BOTA Nº 37) AM

95 Colour: light mahogany. Nose: powerfull, acetaldehyde, varnish, sweet spices, roasted almonds. Palate: concentrated, balanced, spicy, long.

LA BOTA DE CREAM Nº 38 CR

96 Colour: light mahogany. Nose: caramel, varnish, pattiserie, sweet spices, complex. Palate: long, rich, fine bitter notes.

LA BOTA DE FINO (BOTA Nº 35) FI

99 Colour: bright golden. Nose: complex, elegant, dry nuts, pungent, balsamic herbs, flor yeasts. Palate: long, spicy, complex, fine bitter notes.

LA BOTA DE MANZANILLA PASADA (BOTA NO) Nº39 MZ

99 Colour: bright golden. Nose: complex, expressive, dry nuts, pungent. Palate: fine bitter notes, elegant, spicy, lacks balance. Personality.

LA BOTA DE PEDRO XIMENEZ Nº36 BOTA NO PX
pedro ximénez.

96 Colour: mahogany. Nose: balanced, medium intensity, candied fruit, pattiserie, neat. Palate: unctuous, full.

LA BOTA DE MANZANILLA PASADA (BOTA NO) Nº40 MZ

99 Colour: bright golden. Nose: powerfull, expressive, candied fruit, acetaldehyde, spicy, dry nuts, honeyed notes. Palate: rich, flavourful, long, powerful.

MANZANILLA I THINK MZ

92 Colour: bright straw. Nose: fresh fruit, flor yeasts, saline, powerfull, complex, slightly evolved, dry nuts. Palate: flavourful, long, fine bitter notes, balanced.

LA BOTA DE PALO CORTADO (BOTA Nº 34) PC

94 Colour: light mahogany. Nose: medium intensity, dry nuts, roasted almonds, sweet spices, pattiserie. Palate: balanced, spicy.

LA BOTA DE DULCE Nº33 COLOUR: SOLERA

95 Colour: dark mahogany. Nose: complex, fruit liqueur notes, dried fruit, pattiserie, toasty, varnish, nose:tic coffee, dark chocolate. Palate: sweet, rich, unctuous, powerful, slightly acidic.

ESPÍRITUS DE JEREZ

Pza. Cocheras, 3
11403 Jerez de la Frontera (Cádiz)
☎: +34 649 456 990
direccion@espiritusdejerez.com

COLECCIÓN ROBERTO AMILLO AMONTILLADO AM
palomino.

95 Colour: iodine, amber rim. Nose: complex, dry nuts, toasty, acetaldehyde, pungent, expressive. Palate: rich, fine bitter notes, long, spicy.

COLECCIÓN ROBERTO AMILLO OLOROSO OL
palomino.

95 Colour: iodine, amber rim. Nose: dry nuts, toasty, pattiserie, expressive. Palate: rich, fine bitter notes, long, spicy.

COLECCIÓN ROBERTO AMILLO PALO CORTADO PC
palomino.

96 Colour: iodine, amber rim. Nose: elegant, dry nuts, toasty, expressive, warm, varnish, acetaldehyde. Palate: rich, fine bitter notes, long, spicy.

COLECCIÓN ROBERTO AMILLO PEDRO XIMÉNEZ PX
pedro ximénez.

95 Colour: dark mahogany. Nose: dried fruit, fruit liqueur notes, pattiserie, toasty, tar, varnish, characterful. Palate: rich, unctuous, powerful, spicy, long, spirituous.

FERNANDO DE CASTILLA

San Fco. Javier, 3
11404 Jerez de la Frontera (Cádiz)
☎: +34 956 182 454 - Fax: +34 956 182 222
bodegas@fernandodecastilla.com
www.fernandodecastilla.com

FERNANDO DE CASTILLA "AMONTILLADO ANTIQUE" AM
100% palomino.

94 Colour: iodine, amber rim. Nose: powerfull, complex, elegant, dry nuts, toasty. Palate: rich, fine bitter notes, fine solera notes, long, spicy.

FERNANDO DE CASTILLA "FINO ANTIQUE" FI
100% palomino.

94 Colour: bright yellow. Nose: powerfull, complex, characterful, pungent, dry nuts. Palate: powerful, complex, long, creamy.

FERNANDO DE CASTILLA FINO CLASSIC FI
100% palomino.

90 Colour: bright yellow. Nose: complex, expressive, pungent, saline. Palate: rich, powerful, fresh, fine bitter notes.

FERNANDO DE CASTILLA MANZANILLA CLASSIC MZ
100% palomino.

88 Colour: bright straw. Nose: saline, dry nuts, powerfull, floral. Palate: fine bitter notes, flavourful, unctuous.

FERNANDO DE CASTILLA "OLOROSO ANTIQUE" OL
100% palomino.

92 Colour: iodine, amber rim. Nose: powerfull, dry nuts, toasty. Palate: rich, fine bitter notes, , long, spicy.

FERNANDO DE CASTILLA "PALO CORTADO ANTIQUE" PC
100% palomino.

94 Colour: light mahogany. Nose: powerfull, dry nuts, fruit liqueur notes, creamy oak, dark chocolate, pungent. Palate: spicy, fine bitter notes, long.

FERNANDO DE CASTILLA "P.X. ANTIQUE" PX
100% pedro ximénez.

94 Colour: dark mahogany. Nose: complex, varietal, dried fruit, dark chocolate, sweet spices, spicy. Palate: balanced, spirituous, unctuous.

FERNANDO DE CASTILLA "PX PREMIUM" PX
100% pedro ximénez.

91 Colour: mahogany. Nose: balanced, dried fruit, dark chocolate, sweet spices, pattiserie. Palate: flavourful, sweetness, easy to drink.

GONZÁLEZ BYASS JEREZ

Manuel María González, 12
11403 Jerez de la Frontera (Cádiz)
☎: +34 956 357 000 - Fax: +34 956 357 043
elrincondegb@gonzalezbyass.es
www.gonzalezbyass.es

AMONTILLADO DEL DUQUE VORS AM
100% palomino.

93 Colour: mahogany. Nose: complex, powerfull, spicy, dry nuts. Palate: rich, long, fine bitter notes, spirituous.

VIÑA AB AM
100% palomino.

90 Colour: golden. Nosc: powerfull, pungent, acetaldehyde, iodine notes. Palate: flavourful, rich, long, complex.

MATUSALEM VORS CR
palomino, pedro ximénez.

92 Colour: iodine, amber rim. Nose: sweet spices, dark chocolate, dry nuts. Palate: flavourful, powerful, fine bitter notes.

SOLERA 1847 CR
palomino, pedro ximénez.

87 Colour: light mahogany. Nose: acetaldehyde, dried fruit, dark chocolate, aged wood nuances. Palate: unctuous, flavourful, sweetness.

TÍO PEPE FI
100% palomino.

93 Colour: bright yellow. Nose: pungent, saline, fresh, flor yeasts. Palate: rich, powerful, fresh, fine bitter notes.

ALFONSO OL
100% palomino.

89 Colour: light mahogany. Nose: medium intensity, dry nuts. Palate: easy to drink, spicy, fine bitter notes.

GONZALEZ BYASS AÑADA 1982 PC
100% palomino.

95 Colour: iodine. Nose: complex, elegant, expressive, acetaldehyde. Palate: good structure, rich, complex, fine bitter notes, balanced.

APÓSTOLES VORS PC
palomino, pedro ximénez.

92 Colour: light mahogany. Nose: honeyed notes, dark chocolate, sweet spices, toasty, acetaldehyde. Palate: round, powerful, flavourful, complex, sweetness.

LEONOR PC
100% palomino.

90 Nose: sweet spices, caramel, dry nuts, nose:tic coffee. Palate: flavourful, spicy, long.

NOÉ PX
100% pedro ximénez.

94 Colour: dark mahogany. Nose: complex, fruit liqueur notes, pattiserie, toasty, caramel, spicy. Palate: sweet, rich, unctuous, long, flavourful, complex.

NÉCTAR PX
100% pedro ximénez.

90 Colour: light mahogany. Nose: cocoa bean, dark chocolate, toasty, dried fruit. Palate: flavourful, rich, concentrated, complex.

HEREDEROS DE ARGÜESO

Mar, 8
11540 Sanlúcar de Barrameda (Cádiz)
☎: +34 956 385 116 - Fax: +34 956 368 169
argueso@argueso.es
www.argueso.es

ARGÜESO AMONTILLADO VIEJO AM
100% palomino.

91 Colour: light mahogany. Nose: powerfull, dry nuts, acetaldehyde. Palate: powerful, spirituous, fine bitter notes.

ARGÜESO AM
100% palomino.

88 Colour: light mahogany. Nose: candied fruit, powerfull, dry nuts, medium intensity. Palate: flavourful, balanced, correct.

SAN LEÓN RESERVA DE FAMILIA MZ
100% palomino.

95 Colour: bright yellow. Nose: complex, expressive, pungent, saline, powerfull, dry nuts. Palate: rich, powerful, fresh, fine bitter notes.

SAN LEÓN "CLÁSICA" MZ
100% palomino.

92 Colour: bright yellow. Nose: complex, expressive, pungent, saline. Palate: rich, powerful, fresh, fine bitter notes.

LAS MEDALLAS DE ARGÜESO MZ
100% palomino.

91 Colour: bright straw. Nose: saline, flor yeasts, floral, expressive. Palate: rich, powerful, flavourful.

ARGÜESO OL
100% palomino.

85 Colour: light mahogany. Nose: acetaldehyde, fruit liqueur notes, spicy. Palate: toasty, flavourful, correct.

ARGÜESO PX
100% pedro ximénez.

85 Colour: mahogany. Nose: toasty, nose:tic coffee, sweet spices, dark chocolate, fruit liqueur notes. Palate: flavourful, spirituous, full.

HIDALGO

Clavel, 29
11402 Jerez de la Frontera (Cádiz)
☎: +34 956 341 078 - Fax: +34 956 320 922
emiliohidalgo@emiliohidalgo.es
www.hidalgo.com

EL TRESILLO 1874 AMONTILLADO VIEJO AM
palomino.

93 Colour: old gold, amber rim. Nose: balanced, expressive, spicy, acetaldehyde, pungent. Palate: good structure, complex, fine bitter notes.

LA PANESA ESPECIAL FINO FI
palomino.

95 Colour: bright yellow. Nose: complex, expressive, pungent, saline, dry nuts. Palate: powerful, fresh, fine bitter notes, complex, full.

VILLAPANÉS OL
palomino.

94 Colour: iodine, amber rim. Nose: complex, elegant, dry nuts, toasty. Palate: rich, fine bitter notes, , long, spicy, complex, full.

GOBERNADOR OL
palomino.

90 Colour: light mahogany. Nose: balanced, expressive, dry nuts, acetaldehyde, spicy. Palate: long, flavourful, fine bitter notes.

MARQUÉS DE RODIL PC
palomino.

91 Colour: old gold, amber rim. Nose: medium intensity, acetaldehyde, sweet spices, pungent. Palate: fine bitter notes, balanced, flavourful.

HIDALGO PEDRO XIMÉNEZ PX
pedro ximénez.

88 Colour: mahogany. Nose: fruit liqueur notes, dried fruit, toasty, varietal, dark chocolate. Palate: sweet, rich, unctuous, powerful.

HIJOS DE RAINERA PÉREZ MARÍN

Ctra. Nacional IV, Km. 640
11406 Jerez de la Frontera (Cádiz)
☎: +34 956 321 004 - Fax: +34 956 340 829
visitas@grupoestevez.com
www.grupoestevez.com

LA GUITA MZ

89 Colour: bright yellow. Nose: complex, expressive, pungent, saline. Palate: rich, powerful, fresh, fine bitter notes.

LUIS CABALLERO

San Francisco, 24
11500 El Puerto de Santa María (Cádiz)
☎: +34 956 851 751 - Fax: +34 956 853 802
marketing@caballero.es
www.caballero.es

DON LUIS AM
palomino.

88 Colour: old gold. Nose: roasted almonds, sweet spices, creamy oak. Palate: spicy, fine bitter notes.

MANOLA CREAM CR
palomino, pedro ximénez.

88 Colour: mahogany. Nose: pattiserie, caramel, dried fruit. Palate: flavourful, sweetness, full, rich.

PAVÓN PUERTO FINO FI SOLERA
palomino.

90 Colour: bright straw. Nose: mineral, faded flowers, flor yeasts, saline. Palate: long, rich, flavourful, fresh.

LERCHUNDI MOSCATEL
100% moscatel.

89 Colour: light mahogany. Nose: dried fruit, acetaldehyde, cocoa bean, sweet spices. Palate: long, unctuous, complex, flavourful.

CABALLERO OLOROSO REAL OL
palomino.

90 Colour: light mahogany. Nose: medium intensity, sweet spices, caramel. Palate: balanced, spicy, long.

REAL TESORO

Ctra. Nacional IV, Km. 640
11406 Jerez de la Frontera (Cádiz)
☎: +34 956 321 004 - Fax: +34 956 340 829
visitas@grupoestevez.com
www.grupoestevez.es

DEL PRÍNCIPE AM

95 Colour: iodine, amber rim. Nose: powerfull, complex, elegant, dry nuts, toasty, acetaldehyde. Palate: rich, fine bitter notes, , long, spicy.

SACRISTÍA AB

Sevilla, 2 1° Izq.
11540 Sanlúcar de Barrameda (Cádiz)
☎: 607 920 337
www.sacristiaab.com

SACRISTÍA AB MZ

95 Colour: bright straw. Nose: pungent, dry nuts, toasty, pattiserie. Palate: flavourful, spirituous, fine bitter notes, long.

SÁNCHEZ ROMATE

Lealas, 26
11404 Jerez de la Frontera (Cádiz)
☎: +34 956 182 212 - Fax: +34 956 185 276
comercial@romate.com
www.romate.com

OLD & PLUS AMONTILLADO VORS AM
100% palomino.

92 Colour: light mahogany. Nose: acetaldehyde, roasted almonds, spicy, toasty. Palate: complex, flavourful, fine bitter notes, spicy.

NPU AM
100% palomino.

91 Colour: light mahogany. Nose: saline, dried herbs, spicy, roasted almonds. Palate: rich, flavourful, spicy, long.

IBERIA CR
70% palomino, 30% pedro ximénez.

89 Colour: light mahogany. Nose: nose:tic coffee, cocoa bean, dried fruit, fruit preserve, expressive. Palate: flavourful, concentrated, sweetness.

FINO PERDIDO 1/15 FI
palomino.

92 Colour: bright golden. Nose: dried flowers, saline, woody, aged wood nuances. Palate: fine bitter notes, rich, flavourful, long.

MARISMEÑO FI
100% palomino.

89 Colour: bright yellow. Nose: powerfull, pungent, balanced, dried flowers. Palate: flavourful, dry, balanced.

OLD & PLUS OLOROSO OL
100% palomino.

94 Colour: iodine. Nose: expressive, balanced, complex, spicy. Palate: good structure, rich, fine bitter notes, complex.

DON JOSÉ OL
100% palomino.

91 Colour: mahogany. Nose: cocoa bean, dark chocolate, balanced. Palate: good structure, rich, full, spicy, flavourful.

REGENTE PC
100% palomino.

90 Colour: iodine, amber rim. Nose: acetaldehyde, fruit liqueur notes, spicy, toasty. Palate: powerful.

OLD & PLUS P.X. PX
100% pedro ximénez.

93 Colour: dark mahogany. Nose: complex, fruit liqueur notes, dried fruit, pattiserie, toasty, dark chocolate, nose:tic coffee, spicy. Palate: sweet, rich, unctuous, powerful, long, flavourful.

CARDENAL CISNEROS PX
100% pedro ximénez.

91 Colour: dark mahogany. Nose: nose:tic coffee, cocoa bean, toasty, fruit liqueur notes, fruit liqueur notes. Palate: long, toasty, flavourful, concentrated, complex.

DUQUESA PX
100% pedro ximénez.

88 Colour: dark mahogany. Nose: aged wood nuances, sweet spices, pattiserie, nose:tic coffee. Palate: sweetness, rich, flavourful.

SANDEMAN JEREZ

Porrera, 3 of. 8
11403 Jerez de la Frontera (Cádiz)
☎: +34 956 151 700 - Fax: +34 956 303 534
jose.moreno@sogrape.pt
www.sandeman.eu

SANDEMAN ROYAL ESMERALDA VOS AM
100% palomino.

94 Colour: iodine, amber rim. Nose: powerfull, complex, elegant, dry nuts, toasty, varnish, pattiserie. Palate: rich, fine bitter notes, , long, spicy.

SANDEMAN ROYAL CORREGIDOR VOS OL
85% palomino, 15% pedro ximénez.

91 Colour: light mahogany. Nose: powerfull, sweet spices, dark chocolate, acetaldehyde. Palate: spicy, long, sweetness.

SANDEMAN ROYAL AMBROSANTE VOS PX
100% pedro ximénez.

92 Colour: dark mahogany. Nose: complex, fruit liqueur notes, dried fruit, toasty, nose:tic coffee, fruit preserve. Palate: sweet, rich, unctuous, powerful, flavourful.

VALDESPINO

Ctra. Nacional IV, Km.640
11406 Jerez de la Frontera (Cádiz)
☎: +34 956 321 004 - Fax: +34 956 340 829
visitas@grupoestevez.com
www.grupoestevez.es

TÍO DIEGO AM

89 Colour: old gold, amber rim. Nose: pattiserie, spicy, acetaldehyde. Palate: flavourful, good acidity, fine bitter notes.

YNOCENTE FI

95 Colour: bright yellow. Nose: complex, expressive, pungent, saline, dry nuts. Palate: rich, powerful, fresh, fine bitter notes.

DON GONZALO VOS OL

96 Colour: iodine, amber rim. Nose: powerfull, complex, elegant, dry nuts, toasty, characterful, acetaldehyde. Palate: rich, fine bitter notes, , long, spicy.

SOLERA SU MAJESTAD VORS OL

96 Colour: light mahogany. Nose: complex, elegant, expressive, spicy, dry nuts. Palate: good structure, rich, flavourful, complex, fine bitter notes.

SOLERA 1842 VOS OL

94 Colour: iodine, amber rim. Nose: acetaldehyde, toasty, dark chocolate. Palate: long, fine bitter notes, powerful.

EL CANDADO PX
pedro ximénez.

89 Colour: mahogany. Nose: powerfull, candied fruit, fruit liqueur notes, caramel, toasty. Palate: full, balanced, spirituous, sweet.

WILLIAMS & HUMBERT

Ctra. N-IV, Km. 641,75
11408 Jerez de la Frontera (Cádiz)
☎: +34 956 353 400 - Fax: +34 956 353 412
secretaria@williams-humbert.com
www.williams-humbert.com

JALIFA VORS "30 YEARS" AM

92 Colour: iodine, amber rim. Nose: powerfull, complex, elegant, dry nuts, toasty, sweet spices. Palate: rich, fine bitter notes, , long, spicy.

DRY SACK MEDIUM DRY CR
palomino, pedro ximénez.

88 Colour: iodine, amber rim. Nose: fruit liqueur notes, aged wood nuances, pattiserie. Palate: powerful, flavourful, easy to drink.

CANASTA CR
palomino, pedro ximénez.

85 Colour: iodine, amber rim. Nose: fruit liqueur notes, pattiserie, sweet spices, toasty. Palate: spicy, spirituous, flavourful.

DRY SACK FINO FI
palomino.

90 Colour: bright yellow. Nose: flor yeasts, saline, pungent, roasted almonds. Palate: powerful, flavourful, long, complex.

DRY SACK "SOLERA ESPECIAL" 15 AÑOS OL
palomino, pedro ximénez.

91 Colour: mahogany. Nose: acetaldehyde, dark chocolate, nose:tic coffee, toasty. Palate: powerful, flavourful, sweetness.

DOS CORTADOS PC
palomino.

92 Colour: iodine, amber rim. Nose: pattiserie, acetaldehyde, powerfull, sweet spices. Palate: flavourful, correct, fine bitter notes, spicy.

DON GUIDO SOLERA ESPECIAL 20 AÑOS VOS PX
pedro ximénez.

93 Colour: dark mahogany. Nose: complex, fruit liqueur notes, dried fruit, pattiserie, toasty, acetaldehyde, varnish. Palate: sweet, rich, unctuous, powerful, spicy, long.

ZOILO RUIZ-MATEOS

Pizarro 12 y 14
11403 Jerez de la Frontera (Cádiz)
☎: +34 956 310 014 - Fax: +34 956 310 014
gael.barowman@zoiloruizmateos.com
www.grupogarvey.com

AMONTILLADO ZOILO RUIZ MATEOS AM
palomino.

95 Colour: light mahogany. Nose: elegant, expressive, balanced, acetaldehyde, varnish. Palate: complex, flavourful, long, spicy.

OLOROSO ZOILO RUIZ MATEOS OL

89 Colour: light mahogany. Nose: medium intensity, balanced, sweet spices, toasty. Palate: spirituous, rich, flavourful, fine bitter notes.

DO JUMILLA

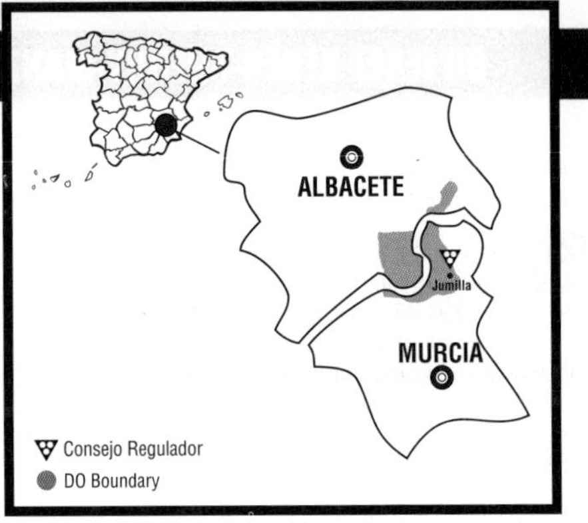

LOCATION:

Midway between the provinces of Murcia and Albacete, this DO spreads over a large region in the southeast of Spain and covers the municipal areas of Jumilla (Murcia) and Fuente Álamo, Albatana, Ontur, Hellín, Tobarra and Montealegre del Castillo (Albacete).

CLIMATE:

Continental in nature with Mediterranean influences. It is characterized by its aridity and low rainfall (270 mm) which is mainly concentrated in spring and autumn. The winters are cold and the summers dry and quite hot.

SOIL:

The soil is mainly brownish-grey, brownish-grey limestone and limy. In general, it is poor in organic matter, with great water retention capacity and medium permeability.

GRAPE VARIETIES:

RED: *Monastrell* (main 35,373 Ha), *Garnacha Tinta, Garnacha Tintorera, Cencibel* (*Tempranillo*), *Cabernet Sauvignon, Merlot, Petit Verdot* and *Syrah.*
WHITE: *Airén* (3,751 Ha), *Macabeo, Malvasía, Pedro Ximénez, Chardonnay, Sauvignon Blanc* and *Moscatel de Grano Menudo.*

FIGURES:

Vineyard surface: 25,800 – **Wine-Growers:** 2,100 – **Wineries:** 42 – **2011 Harvest rating:** Very Good – **Production:** 24,500,000 litres – **Market percentages:** 56% domestic. 44% export

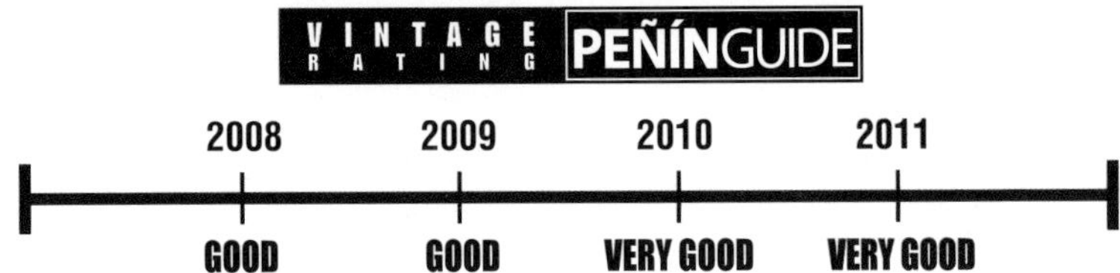

CONSEJO REGULADOR
San Roque, 15, Apdo. 66 - 30520 Jumilla (Murcia) - ☎: +34 968 781 761 - Fax: +34 968 781 900
@ info@vinosdejumilla.org - www.vinosdejumilla.org

ALTOS DEL CUADRADO

Pío Baroja, 3- Apdo. Correos 120
30510 Yecla (Murcia)
☎: +34 968 791 115 - Fax: +34 968 791 900
info@altosdelcuadrado.com
www.altosdelcuadrado.com

ALTOS DEL CUADRADO 2010 T
85% monastrell, 10% petit verdot, 5% cabernet sauvignon.

87 Colour: cherry, garnet rim. Nose: scrubland, ripe fruit, cocoa bean. Palate: flavourful, fruity.

ALTOS DEL CUADRADO VVV 2009 T
80% monastrell, 20% petit verdot.

88 Colour: bright cherry. Nose: sweet spices, creamy oak, characterful. Palate: flavourful, fruity, toasty, round tannins.

ASENSIO CARCELÉN N.C.R.

Ctra. C- 3314, Km. 8
30520 Jumilla (Murcia)
☎: +34 968 435 543 - Fax: +34 968 435 542
bodegascarcelen@terra.es

100 X 100 SYRAH 2009 T
100% syrah.

83

PURA SANGRE 2006 TR
100% monastrell.

85 Colour: light cherry, orangey edge. Nose: acetaldehyde, spicy, toasty, wet leather. Palate: good acidity, long, flavourful.

BARÓN DEL SOLAR

Paraje El Jurado
30520 Jumilla (Murcia)
☎: +34 679 874 590 - Fax: +34 968 716 197
pepita@barondelsolar.com
www.barondelsolar.com

BARÓN DEL SOLAR 2010 T
85% monastrell, 15% cabernet sauvignon.

85 Colour: cherry, garnet rim. Nose: ripe fruit, sweet spices, roasted coffee. Palate: flavourful, long, powerful.

BARÓN DEL SOLAR MANOS COLECCIÓN PRIVADA 2008 T
100% monastrell.

91 Colour: cherry, garnet rim. Nose: ripe fruit, sweet spices, cocoa bean, dark chocolate, fine reductive notes. Palate: flavourful, toasty, long, spicy.

BLEDA

Ctra. Jumilla - Ontur, Km. 2.
30520 Jumilla (Murcia)
☎: +34 968 780 012 - Fax: +34 968 782 699
vinos@bodegasbleda.com
www.bodegasbleda.com

CASTILLO DE JUMILLA 2011 B
60% sauvignon blanc, 30% macabeo, 10% airén.

89 Colour: bright straw. Nose: fresh, fresh fruit, white flowers, tropical fruit. Palate: flavourful, fruity, good acidity, balanced.

PINO DONCEL 2011 B
sauvignon blanc.

84

CASTILLO DE JUMILLA 2011 RD
100% monastrell.

88 Colour: brilliant rose. Nose: floral, red berry notes, raspberry, expressive. Palate: powerful, flavourful, fresh, fruity, easy to drink.

DIVUS 2010 T
100% monastrell.

89 Colour: bright cherry. Nose: ripe fruit, sweet spices, creamy oak, toasty, dark chocolate. Palate: flavourful, fruity, toasty.

CASTILLO DE JUMILLA MONASTRELL - TEMPRANILLO 2010 T
50% monastrell, 50% tempranillo.

88 Colour: bright cherry. Nose: ripe fruit, sweet spices, creamy oak, expressive. Palate: flavourful, fruity, toasty, round tannins.

CASTILLO DE JUMILLA MONASTRELL 2010 T
100% monastrell.

85 Colour: cherry, garnet rim. Nose: medium intensity, ripe fruit, spicy. Palate: fine bitter notes, balanced.

CASTILLO DE JUMILLA 2009 TC
90% monastrell, 10% tempranillo.

85 Colour: cherry, garnet rim. Nose: ripe fruit, spicy, creamy oak, toasty. Palate: powerful, flavourful, toasty.

CASTILLO DE JUMILLA 2007 TR
90% monastrell, 10% tempranillo.

86 Colour: bright cherry. Nose: ripe fruit, sweet spices, dark chocolate. Palate: flavourful, fruity, toasty, round tannins.

BODEGA ARTESANAL VIÑA CAMPANERO

Ctra. de Murcia, s/n- Apdo. 346
30520 Jumilla (Murcia)
☎: +34 968 780 754 - Fax: +34 968 780 754
bodegas@vinacampanero.com
www.vinacampanero.com

VEGARDAL MONASTRELL CEPAS JÓVENES 2011 T
100% monastrell.

83

VEGARDAL MONASTRELL CEPAS VIEJAS 2010 T
100% monastrell.

84

VEGARDAL CUCO DEL ARDAL EDICIÓN ESPECIAL 2010 T
100% monastrell.

83

VEGARDAL CUCO DEL ARDAL SELECCIÓN 2009 T
100% monastrell.

86 Colour: cherry, garnet rim. Nose: spicy, toasty, overripe fruit. Palate: powerful, flavourful, toasty, round tannins.

VEGARDAL CUCO DEL ARDAL 2008 TC
100% monastrell.

85 Colour: ruby red, orangey edge. Nose: ripe fruit, tobacco, old leather. Palate: powerful, flavourful, spicy.

BODEGA TORRECASTILLO

Ctra. de Bonete, s/n
02650 Montealegre del Castillo (Albacete)
☎: +34 967 582 188 - Fax: +34 967 582 339
bodega@torrecastillo.com
www.torrecastillo.com

TORRECASTILLO 2011 B
sauvignon blanc.

86 Colour: bright straw. Nose: ripe fruit, dried flowers, medium intensity. Palate: fine bitter notes, fresh, fruity.

TORRECASTILLO 2011 RD
monastrell.

86 Colour: rose, purple rim. Nose: powerfull, red berry notes, floral, lactic notes. Palate: , powerful, fruity, fresh.

TORRECASTILLO 2011 T
monastrell.

86 Colour: cherry, purple rim. Nose: ripe fruit, red berry notes, medium intensity. Palate: correct, flavourful, fruity.

TORRECASTILLO 2009 TC
monastrell.

85 Colour: cherry, garnet rim. Nose: ripe fruit, spicy, creamy oak, toasty, complex. Palate: powerful, flavourful, toasty.

BODEGAS 1890

Ctra. Venta del Olivo, Km. 2,5
30520 Jumilla (Murcia)
☎: +34 968 757 099 - Fax: +34 968 757 099
bodegas1890@jgc.es
www.vinosdefamilia.com

MAYORAL 2011 T JOVEN
70% monastrell, 20% syrah, 10% cabernet sauvignon.

89 Colour: cherry, purple rim. Nose: expressive, fresh fruit, red berry notes, floral. Palate: flavourful, fruity, good acidity, round tannins.

MAYORAL 2009 TC
70% monastrell, 30% tempranillo.

85 Colour: cherry, garnet rim. Nose: ripe fruit, spicy, toasty. Palate: powerful, flavourful, toasty.

BODEGAS CARCHELO

Casas de la Hoya, s/n
30520 Jumilla (Murcia)
☎: +34 968 435 137 - Fax: +34 968 435 200
administracion@carchelo.com
www.carchelo.com

CARCHELO 2011 T
monastrell, syrah, cabernet sauvignon.

88 Colour: deep cherry, garnet rim. Nose: ripe fruit, wild herbs, balanced. Palate: good structure, flavourful, fine bitter notes.

SIERVA 2010 T
monastrell, cabernet sauvignon, syrah.

91 Colour: deep cherry, garnet rim. Nose: balanced, ripe fruit, wild herbs, spicy. Palate: balanced, fine bitter notes, round tannins.

CARCHELO 2010 T
40% monastrell, 40% syrah, 20% cabernet sauvignon.

88 Colour: deep cherry. Nose: powerfull, warm, overripe fruit, sweet spices. Palate: powerful, concentrated.

ALTICO SYRAH 2009 T
100% syrah.

91 Colour: bright cherry. Nose: ripe fruit, sweet spices, creamy oak. Palate: flavourful, fruity, toasty, round tannins.

SIERVA 2009 TC
40% monastrell, 30% cabernet sauvignon, 30% syrah.

88 Colour: cherry, garnet rim. Nose: spicy, creamy oak, toasty, complex, overripe fruit. Palate: powerful, flavourful, toasty.

CANALIZO 2008 TC
40% monastrell, 40% syrah, 10% tempranillo.

90 Colour: cherry, garnet rim. Nose: ripe fruit, spicy, creamy oak, toasty, characterful. Palate: powerful, flavourful, toasty, round tannins.

AUTISTA 2008 TC

88 Colour: cherry, garnet rim. Nose: ripe fruit, spicy, creamy oak, toasty, complex. Palate: powerful, flavourful, toasty, round tannins.

BODEGAS EL NIDO

Ctra. de Fuentealamo - Paraje de la Aragona
30520 Jumilla (Murcia)
☎: +34 968 435 022 - Fax: +34 968 435 653
info@bodegaselnido.com
www.orowines.com

EL NIDO 2009 T
30% monastrell, 70% cabernet sauvignon.

96 Colour: black cherry. Nose: creamy oak, dark chocolate, nose:tic coffee, fruit liqueur notes, ripe fruit. Palate: fine bitter notes, powerful, concentrated, good acidity.

CLÍO 2009 T
70% monastrell, 30% cabernet sauvignon.

94 Colour: cherry, garnet rim. Nose: ripe fruit, spicy, creamy oak, toasty, characterful. Palate: powerful, flavourful, toasty, round tannins.

BODEGAS GUARDIOLA

Ctra. de Murcia, s/n Apartado 94
30520 Jumilla (Murcia)
☎: +34 968 781 711 - Fax: +34 968 781 030
info@bodegasguardiola.com
www.bodegasguardiola.com

SOLANA DEL MAYORAZGO 2008 TC
85% monastrell, 15% syrah.

83

SOLANA DEL MAYORAZGO GRAN VINO 2007 T
100% monastrell.

84

DON GUARDIOLA ALLIER 2006 T
100% monastrell.

86 Colour: deep cherry, orangey edge. Nose: ripe fruit, scrubland, tobacco, old leather. Palate: flavourful, ripe fruit, long.

BODEGAS HACIENDA DEL CARCHE

Ctra. del Carche, Km. 8,3- Apdo. Correos 257
30520 Jumilla (Murcia)
☎: +34 968 108 248 - Fax: +34 968 975 935
info@haciendadelcarche.com
www.haciendadelcarche.com

HACIENDA DEL CARCHE 2011 B
40% sauvignon blanc, 30% airén, 30% macabeo.

88 Colour: bright straw. Nose: fresh, fresh fruit, white flowers. Palate: flavourful, fruity, good acidity, balanced.

HACIENDA DEL CARCHE 2011 RD
80% monastrell, 20% syrah.

87 Colour: rose, purple rim. Nose: ripe fruit, red berry notes, floral, grassy. Palate: , powerful, fruity, fresh.

TAVS 2011 T
70% monastrell, 20% syrah, 10% garnacha.

90 Colour: cherry, purple rim. Nose: expressive, fresh fruit, ripe fruit. Palate: flavourful, fruity, good acidity, round tannins.

TAVS SELECCIÓN 2010 T
50% monastrell, 25% syrah, 25% cabernet sauvignon.

89 Colour: cherry, garnet rim. Nose: spicy, creamy oak, toasty, ripe fruit. Palate: powerful, flavourful, toasty, round tannins.

HACIENDA DEL CARCHE CEPAS VIEJAS 2009 TC
70% monastrell, 30% cabernet sauvignon.

87 Colour: cherry, garnet rim. Nose: ripe fruit, spicy, creamy oak, toasty, old leather. Palate: powerful, flavourful, toasty, round tannins.

BODEGAS HUERTAS

Avda. de Murcia, s/n
30520 Jumilla (Murcia)
☎: +34 968 783 061 - Fax: +34 968 781 180
vinos@bodegashuertas.es
www.bodegashuertas.es

RODREJO 2009 T
80% monastrell, 20% tempranillo.

85 Colour: cherry, garnet rim. Nose: ripe fruit, powerfull, scrubland, creamy oak. Palate: powerful, flavourful.

BODEGAS JUAN GIL

Ctra. Fuentealamo - Paraje de la Aragona
30520 Jumilla (Murcia)
☎: +34 968 435 022 - Fax: +34 968 716 051
info@juangil.es
www.juangil.es

JUAN GIL MOSCATEL 2011 B
100% moscatel.

90 Colour: bright straw. Nose: fresh, fresh fruit, white flowers, expressive. Palate: flavourful, fruity, good acidity, balanced.

HONORO VERA ORGANIC 2011 T
100% monastrell.

90 Colour: cherry, purple rim. Nose: red berry notes, floral, ripe fruit. Palate: flavourful, fruity, good acidity, round tannins.

JUAN GIL 4 MESES 2011 T
100% monastrell.

89 Colour: bright cherry. Nose: ripe fruit, sweet spices, creamy oak, expressive. Palate: flavourful, fruity, toasty, round tannins.

JUAN GIL 12 MESES 2010 T
100% monastrell.

93 Colour: very deep cherry. Nose: ripe fruit, powerfull, characterful, sweet spices, creamy oak, fruit expression, earthy notes. Palate: powerful, round tannins, long.

JUAN GIL 4 MESES 2010 T
100% monastrell.

90 Colour: bright cherry. Nose: ripe fruit, sweet spices, creamy oak, expressive. Palate: flavourful, fruity, toasty, round tannins.

JUAN GIL 18 MESES 2009 T
60% monastrell, 30% cabernet sauvignon, 10% syrah.

92 Colour: cherry, garnet rim. Nose: spicy, creamy oak, toasty, characterful, fruit expression. Palate: powerful, flavourful, toasty, round tannins.

BODEGAS LA ESPERANZA

Brisol, 16 bis
28230 Las Rozas (Madrid)
☎: +34 917 104 880 - Fax: +34 917 104 881
anap@swd.es
www.swd.es

NUDO MACABEO 2010 B
100% macabeo.

81

NUDO CABERNET SAUVIGNON 2010 T
100% cabernet sauvignon.

83

NUDO 2007 TC
monastrell, syrah.

87 Colour: bright cherry. Nose: ripe fruit, sweet spices, creamy oak. Palate: flavourful, fruity, toasty, round tannins.

BODEGAS LUZÓN

Ctra. Jumilla-Calasparra, Km. 3,1
30520 Jumilla (Murcia)
☎: +34 968 784 135 - Fax: +34 968 781 911
info@bodegasluzon.com
www.bodegasluzon.com

LUZÓN 2011 B
macabeo, airén.

83

LUZÓN 2011 T
70% monastrell, 30% syrah.

91 Colour: bright cherry. Nose: ripe fruit, sweet spices, expressive. Palate: flavourful, fruity, toasty, round tannins.

LUZÓN VERDE ORGANIC 2011 T
100% monastrell.

90 Colour: cherry, purple rim. Nose: fresh fruit, red berry notes, floral, expressive, varietal. Palate: flavourful, fruity, good acidity, round tannins.

CASTILLO DE LUZÓN 2009 TC
50% monastrell, 20% tempranillo, 20% cabernet sauvignon, 10% merlot.

88 Colour: cherry, garnet rim. Nose: ripe fruit, spicy, creamy oak, toasty, fine reductive notes. Palate: powerful, flavourful, toasty.

PORTÚ 2008 T
80% monastrell, 20% cabernet sauvignon.

93 Colour: cherry, garnet rim. Nose: ripe fruit, spicy, creamy oak, toasty, complex. Palate: powerful, flavourful, toasty, round tannins.

ALTOS DE LUZÓN 2008 T
50% monastrell, 25% tempranillo, 25% cabernet sauvignon.

90 Colour: cherry, garnet rim. Nose: ripe fruit, wild herbs, earthy notes, dark chocolate. Palate: flavourful, long, correct.

ALMA DE LUZÓN 2007 T
70% monastrell, 10% syrah, 20% cabernet sauvignon.

93 Colour: cherry, garnet rim. Nose: ripe fruit, spicy, creamy oak, complex, mineral, roasted coffee. Palate: powerful, flavourful, toasty, round tannins.

BODEGAS MADROÑO

Ctra., Jumilla-Ontur, km. 16
30520 Jumilla (Murcia)
☎: +34 662 380 985
gmartinez@vinocrapula.com

MADROÑO 2011 B
chardonnay.

82

MADROÑO 2010 T
monastrell, syrah.

89 Colour: cherry, purple rim. Nose: lactic notes, floral, red berry notes, expressive. Palate: good acidity, flavourful, long.

MADROÑO 2009 T
monastrell, syrah, cabernet sauvignon.

91 Colour: cherry, garnet rim. Nose: ripe fruit, spicy, creamy oak, toasty, characterful. Palate: powerful, flavourful, toasty, round tannins.

BODEGAS OLIVARES

Vereda Real, s/n
30520 Jumilla (Murcia)
☎: +34 968 780 180 - Fax: +34 968 756 474
correo@bodegasolivares.com
www.bodegasolivares.com

ALTOS DE LA HOYA 2010 T
100% monastrell.

88 Colour: bright cherry, garnet rim. Nose: ripe fruit, creamy oak, expressive, cocoa bean. Palate: flavourful, fruity, toasty, round tannins.

OLIVARES DULCE MONASTRELL 2008 T
100% monastrell.

90 Colour: cherry, garnet rim. Nose: dark chocolate, spicy, dried fruit. Palate: good acidity, powerful, flavourful, complex, long.

OLIVARES 2008 TC
100% monastrell.

88 Colour: bright cherry, garnet rim. Nose: ripe fruit, sweet spices, creamy oak, expressive. Palate: flavourful, fruity, toasty, round tannins.

BODEGAS PÍO DEL RAMO

Ctra. Almanza, s/n
02652 Ontur (Albacete)
☎: +34 967 323 230
info@piodelramo.com
www.piodelramo.com

CHARDONNAY PÍO DEL RAMO 2011 B BARRICA
chardonnay.

91 Colour: bright yellow. Nose: powerfull, ripe fruit, sweet spices, creamy oak, fragrant herbs. Palate: rich, smoky afterpalate:, flavourful, fresh, good acidity.

PÍO DEL RAMO 2010 T ROBLE
monastrell, syrah, cabernet sauvignon.

88 Colour: bright cherry. Nose: sweet spices, creamy oak, overripe fruit. Palate: flavourful, fruity, toasty, round tannins.

PÍO DEL RAMO ECOLÓGICO 2010 T
monastrell.

85 Colour: bright cherry. Nose: sweet spices, overripe fruit. Palate: flavourful, fruity, toasty, round tannins.

PÍO DEL RAMO 2008 TC
syrah, monastrell, cabernet sauvignon, petit verdot.

91 Colour: cherry, garnet rim. Nose: ripe fruit, spicy, creamy oak, toasty. Palate: powerful, flavourful, toasty, round tannins.

BODEGAS SAN DIONISIO, S. COOP.

Ctra. Higuera, s/n
02651 Fuenteálamo (Albacete)
☎: +34 967 543 032 - Fax: +34 967 543 136
sandionisio@bodegassandionisio.es
www.bodegassandinisio.es

SEÑORÍO DE FUENTEÁLAMO SYRAH 2011 RD
100% syrah.

86 Colour: raspberry rose. Nose: red berry notes, rose petals, fresh, expressive. Palate: light-bodied, fresh, fruity, easy to drink.

SEÑORÍO DE FUENTEÁLAMO SELECCIÓN 2010 T
100% monastrell.

87 Colour: cherry, garnet rim. Nose: powerfull, overripe fruit, spicy, toasty. Palate: powerful, spicy.

SEÑORÍO DE FUENTEÁLAMO MONASTRELL SYRAH 2009 TC
60% monastrell, 40% syrah.

87 Colour: cherry, garnet rim. Nose: ripe fruit, spicy, creamy oak, toasty. Palate: powerful, flavourful, toasty.

MAINETES PETIT VERDOT 2008 T ROBLE
100% petit verdot.

88 Colour: cherry, garnet rim. Nose: powerfull, ripe fruit, sweet spices. Palate: powerful, flavourful, concentrated.

BODEGAS SAN ISIDRO BSI

Ctra. Murcia, s/n
30520 Jumilla (Murcia)
☎: +34 968 780 700 - Fax: +34 968 782 351
bsi@bsi.es
www.bsi.es

SABATACHA 2009 BFB
airén.

82

SABATACHA SYRAH 2011 T
100% syrah.

87 Colour: cherry, purple rim. Nose: fresh fruit, red berry notes, floral. Palate: flavourful, fruity, good acidity.

SABATACHA MONASTRELL 2011 T
100% monastrell.

87 Colour: cherry, purple rim. Nose: red berry notes, ripe fruit, fresh, scrubland. Palate: light-bodied, fresh, fruity.

GÉMINA MONASTRELL 2010 T
100% monastrell.

87 Colour: cherry, garnet rim. Nose: ripe fruit, spicy, creamy oak. Palate: ripe fruit, powerful, flavourful.

GENUS MONASTRELL SYRAH 2010 T
80% monastrell, 20% syrah.

84

GÉMINA CUVÉE SELECCIÓN 2009 T
100% monastrell.

87 Colour: cherry, garnet rim. Nose: ripe fruit, scrubland, waxy notes, roasted coffee. Palate: correct, flavourful, powerful.

SABATACHA PETIT VERDOT 2009 T
100% petit verdot.

85 Colour: cherry, garnet rim. Nose: ripe fruit, spicy, creamy oak, toasty. Palate: powerful, flavourful, toasty.

SABATACHA 2008 TC
100% monastrell.

80

SABATACHA 2006 TR
100% monastrell.

87 Colour: pale ruby, brick rim edge. Nose: spicy, fine reductive notes, wet leather, aged wood nuances. Palate: spicy, fine tannins, elegant, ripe fruit.

GÉMINA PREMIUM 2003 TR
100% monastrell.

88 Colour: light cherry. Nose: ripe fruit, wild herbs, toasty, fine reductive notes. Palate: correct, powerful, flavourful, round tannins.

LACRIMA CHRISTI T
100% monastrell.

88 Colour: dark mahogany. Nose: spicy, nose:tic coffee, ripe fruit, dry nuts, toasty. Palate: powerful, flavourful, complex, balanced.

GÉMINA DULCE 2009 TINTO DULCE
100% monastrell.

85 Colour: cherry, garnet rim. Nose: toasty, ripe fruit, dried fruit. Palate: flavourful, sweetness, long.

BODEGAS SILVANO GARCÍA

Avda. de Murcia, 29
30520 Jumilla (Murcia)
☎: +34 968 780 767 - Fax: +34 968 716 125
bodegas@silvanogarcia.com
www.silvanogarcia.com

VIÑAHONDA 2011 B
100% macabeo.

86 Colour: bright straw. Nose: ripe fruit, tropical fruit, fragrant herbs. Palate: light-bodied, fresh, fruity.

SILVANO GARCÍA MOSCATEL 2010 B
100% moscatel.

90 Colour: golden. Nose: powerfull, floral, honeyed notes, candied fruit, fragrant herbs. Palate: flavourful, sweet, fresh, fruity, good acidity, long.

VIÑAHONDA 2011 RD
monastrell.

86 Colour: rose, purple rim. Nose: ripe fruit, red berry notes, floral, expressive. Palate: , fruity, fresh, easy to drink.

SILVANO GARCÍA DULCE MONASTRELL 2009 T
100% monastrell.

87 Colour: cherry, garnet rim. Nose: ripe fruit, dried flowers, spicy. Palate: powerful, flavourful, fruity, sweetness.

VIÑAHONDA 2008 TC
50% monastrell, 30% cabernet sauvignon, 20% tempranillo.

86 Colour: deep cherry, orangey edge. Nose: spicy, fine reductive notes, wet leather, fruit liqueur notes. Palate: spicy, fine tannins, long.

BODEGAS SIMÓN

Madrid, 15
02653 Albatana (Albacete)
☎: +34 967 323 340 - Fax: +34 967 323 340
info@bodegassimon.com
www.bodegassimon.com

GALÁN DEL SIGLO SELECCIÓN 2011 T
monastrell, petit verdot, tempranillo.

87 Colour: cherry, purple rim. Nose: floral, ripe fruit, candied fruit. Palate: flavourful, powerful, fruity, warm.

GALÁN DEL SIGLO TRADICIÓN FAMILIAR 2011 T
monastrell, tempranillo, syrah.

86 Colour: cherry, purple rim. Nose: red berry notes, raspberry, medium intensity. Palate: powerful, flavourful, easy to drink.

GALÁN DEL SIGLO MONASTRELL SYRAH 2009 T
monastrell, syrah.

82

BODEGAS VIÑA ELENA

Estrecho Marín, s/n
30520 Jumilla (Murcia)
☎: +34 968 781 340 - Fax: +34 968 435 275
info@vinaelena.com
www.vinaelena.com

LOS CUCOS DE LA ALBERQUILLA 2010 T
cabernet sauvignon.

88 Colour: bright cherry. Nose: ripe fruit, sweet spices, creamy oak. Palate: flavourful, fruity, toasty, round tannins.

FAMILIA PACHECO ORGÁNICO 2010 T
monastrell, syrah.

87 Colour: cherry, garnet rim. Nose: red berry notes, ripe fruit, slightly evolved. Palate: balanced, powerful, flavourful.

PACO PACHECO FINCA EL CALVARIO 2010 T

87 Colour: very deep cherry. Nose: powerfull, ripe fruit, toasty, scrubland. Palate: powerful, concentrated, warm.

FAMILIA PACHECO 2010 T ROBLE
monastrell, cabernet sauvignon, syrah.

85 Colour: cherry, garnet rim. Nose: fruit liqueur notes, ripe fruit, wild herbs, toasty. Palate: powerful, flavourful, toasty.

BODEGAS Y VIÑEDOS CASA DE LA ERMITA

Ctra. El Carche, Km. 11,5
30520 Jumilla (Murcia)
☎: +34 968 783 035 - Fax: +34 968 716 063
bodega@casadelaermita.com
www.casadelaermita.com

CASA DE LA ERMITA 2011 B

86 Colour: bright straw. Nose: fresh, fresh fruit, white flowers. Palate: flavourful, fruity, good acidity, balanced.

CASA DE LA ERMITA ECOLÓGICO MONASTRELL 2011 T
100% monastrell.

90 Colour: cherry, purple rim. Nose: expressive, fresh fruit, red berry notes, floral. Palate: flavourful, fruity, good acidity, round tannins.

CARACOL SERRANO 2011 T
60% monastrell, 20% syrah, 15% cabernet sauvignon, 5% petit verdot.

88 Colour: cherry, purple rim. Nose: fresh fruit, red berry notes, floral. Palate: flavourful, fruity, good acidity, round tannins.

CASA DE LA ERMITA 2011 T ROBLE
80% monastrell, 20% petit verdot.

87 Colour: bright cherry. Nose: sweet spices, creamy oak, overripe fruit. Palate: flavourful, fruity, toasty, round tannins.

ALTOS DEL CUCO 2011 T
40% monastrell, 30% syrah, 30% tempranillo.

86 Colour: cherry, purple rim. Nose: red berry notes, floral, ripe fruit. Palate: flavourful, fruity, good acidity, round tannins.

MONASTERIO DE SANTA ANA ECOLÓGICO 2011 T
60% monastrell, 40% tempranillo.

84

ALTOS DEL CUCO VERDE 2011 T
100% monastrell.

82

CASA DE LA ERMITA DULCE MONASTRELL 2010 T
100% monastrell.

86 Colour: bright cherry. Nose: sweet spices, creamy oak, overripe fruit, dried fruit. Palate: flavourful, fruity, toasty, round tannins.

CASA DE LA ERMITA 2009 TC
60% monastrell, 25% petit verdot, 15% cabernet sauvignon.

89 Colour: cherry, garnet rim. Nose: spicy, creamy oak, toasty, overripe fruit. Palate: powerful, flavourful, toasty, round tannins.

CASA DE LA ERMITA 2008 TC
100% monastrell.

88 Colour: cherry, garnet rim. Nose: spicy, creamy oak, toasty, overripe fruit. Palate: powerful, flavourful, toasty, round tannins.

CASA DE LA ERMITA PETIT VERDOT 2008 T
100% petit verdot.

87 Colour: dark-red cherry. Nose: overripe fruit, fruit liqueur notes, roasted coffee, nose:tic coffee. Palate: powerful, spirituous, fine bitter notes.

CASA DE LA ERMITA IDÍLICO 2008 TC
65% petit verdot, 35% monastrell.

87 Colour: cherry, garnet rim. Nose: spicy, creamy oak, toasty, characterful, overripe fruit. Palate: powerful, flavourful, toasty, round tannins.

CAMPOS DE RISCA

Avda. Diagonal, 590, 5 1
08021 Barcelona (Barcelona)
☎: +34 660 445 464
info@vinergia.com
www.vinergia.es

CAMPOS DE RISCA 2011 T
90% monastrell, 10% syrah.

87 Colour: cherry, garnet rim. Nose: ripe fruit, expressive, red berry notes. Palate: flavourful, fruity, toasty.

CRAPULA WINES

Avda. de la Asunción, 42 2D
30520 Jumilla (Murcia)
☎: +34 968 781 855
gmartinez@vinocrapula.com

CELEBRE 2010 T
monastrell, syrah, petit verdot.

93 Colour: bright cherry. Nose: sweet spices, creamy oak, expressive, fruit expression. Palate: flavourful, fruity, toasty, round tannins.

CÁRMINE 3 MESES 2010 T
monastrell.

90 Colour: bright cherry. Nose: ripe fruit, sweet spices, creamy oak, expressive. Palate: flavourful, fruity, toasty, round tannins.

CRÁPULA PETIT VERDOT 2010 T
petit verdot.

90 Colour: very deep cherry. Nose: powerfull, characterful, ripe fruit, violet drops. Palate: powerful, flavourful, fine bitter notes, spicy, long.

DULCE CRÁPULA 2010 T
monastrell.

87 Colour: cherry, garnet rim. Nose: ripe fruit, spicy, creamy oak, toasty, complex. Palate: powerful, flavourful, toasty, sweet.

NDQ (NACIDO DEL QUORUM) 2010 T
monastrell.

85 Colour: very deep cherry. Nose: roasted coffee, dark chocolate, fruit liqueur notes. Palate: powerful, concentrated, spirituous.

NDQ (NACIDO DEL QUORUM) 2009 T
monastrell, syrah, cabernet sauvignon.

93 Colour: cherry, garnet rim. Nose: red berry notes, expressive, dark chocolate, sweet spices, nose:tic coffee. Palate: good structure, flavourful, complex, long, toasty.

CÁRMINE 2009 T
monastrell, syrah.

93 Colour: cherry, garnet rim. Nose: spicy, creamy oak, toasty, complex, red berry notes. Palate: powerful, flavourful, toasty, round tannins, long. Personality.

CELEBRE 2009 T
monastrell, syrah.

92 Colour: cherry, garnet rim. Nose: powerfull, varietal, fruit expression, mineral. Palate: powerful, flavourful, fruity, complex.

CRÁPULA 2009 T
85% monastrell, 15% otras.

91 Colour: bright cherry. Nose: ripe fruit, sweet spices, creamy oak, expressive, nose:tic coffee. Palate: flavourful, fruity, toasty, balanced.

EGO BODEGAS

Plaza Santa Gertrudis, Nº 1, Entresuelo A
30001 (Murcia)
☎: +34 968 964 326
esther@gsdwines.com
www.egobodegas.com

TALENTO 2011 T
70% monastrell, 30% syrah.

88 Colour: cherry, purple rim. Nose: fresh fruit, red berry notes, floral, varietal. Palate: flavourful, fruity, good acidity, round tannins.

EGO MONASTRELL 2009 T
60% monastrell, 40% cabernet sauvignon.

90 Colour: cherry, garnet rim. Nose: ripe fruit, spicy, toasty, roasted coffee. Palate: powerful, flavourful, toasty, round tannins.

HACIENDA PINARES

San Juan Bautista, 18
02513 Santiago Tubarra (Albacete)
☎: +34 609 108 393
haciendapinar@gmail.com

HACIENDA PINARES 2010 T

85 Colour: very deep cherry. Nose: ripe fruit, red berry notes. Palate: powerful, flavourful, concentrated, fine bitter notes.

HACIENDA PINARES PIE FRANCO 2009 T

89 Colour: cherry, garnet rim. Nose: ripe fruit, spicy, creamy oak, toasty. Palate: powerful, flavourful, toasty, round tannins.

HACIENDA PINARES T

87 Colour: deep cherry. Nose: powerfull, candied fruit, fruit preserve. Palate: powerful, long, sweet.

ORO WINES

Ctra. de Fuentealamo - Paraje de la Aragona
30520 Jumilla (Murcia)
☎: +34 968 435 022 - Fax: +34 968 716 051
info@orowines.com
www.orowines.com

COMOLOCO 2011 T
100% monastrell.

87 Colour: cherry, purple rim. Nose: ripe fruit, spicy, earthy notes, varietal. Palate: flavourful, good acidity, spicy.

PEDRO LUIS MARTÍNEZ

Barrio Iglesias, 55
30520 Jumilla (Murcia)
☎: +34 968 780 142 - Fax: +34 968 716 256
plmsa@alceno.com
www.alceno.com

ALCEÑO 2011 B
85% macabeo, 15% airén.

85 Colour: bright straw. Nose: fresh, white flowers, ripe fruit. Palate: flavourful, fruity, good acidity, balanced.

ALCEÑO 2011 RD
55% monastrell, 30% syrah, 15% tempranillo.

88 Colour: rose, purple rim. Nose: powerfull, ripe fruit, red berry notes, floral, expressive. Palate: fleshy, powerful, fruity, fresh.

ALCEÑO PREMIUM 2011 T
85% syrah, 15% monastrell.

92 Colour: cherry, purple rim. Nose: expressive, red berry notes, floral, ripe fruit. Palate: flavourful, fruity, good acidity, round tannins.

ALCEÑO 2011 T
60% monastrell, 20% tempranillo, 20% syrah.

89 Colour: cherry, purple rim. Nose: red berry notes, fresh fruit, expressive, floral. Palate: fresh, fruity, flavourful, light-bodied.

ALCEÑO DULCE 2010 T
100% monastrell.

90 Colour: bright cherry. Nose: sweet spices, creamy oak, expressive, candied fruit. Palate: flavourful, fruity, toasty, sweet tannins.

GENIO ESPAÑOL 2010 T
60% monastrell, 25% tempranillo, 15% syrah.

83

ALCEÑO 4 MESES 2010 T ROBLE
60% monastrell, 40% syrah.

88 Colour: cherry, garnet rim. Nose: sweet spices, dark chocolate, overripe fruit. Palate: spicy, powerful, concentrated.

ALCEÑO 12 MESES 2009 T
85% monastrell, 15% syrah.

91 Colour: cherry, garnet rim. Nose: spicy, creamy oak, toasty, characterful, fruit expression. Palate: powerful, flavourful, toasty, round tannins.

ALCEÑO SELECCIÓN 2008 TC
55% monastrell, 35% syrah, 10% tempranillo.

87 Colour: bright cherry. Nose: sweet spices, creamy oak, overripe fruit. Palate: flavourful, fruity, toasty, round tannins.

PROPIEDAD VITÍCOLA CASA CASTILLO

Ctra. Jumilla - Hellín, RM-428, Km. 8
30520 Jumilla (Murcia)
☎: +34 968 781 691 - Fax: +34 968 716 238
info@casacastillo.es
www.casacastillo.es

CASA CASTILLO MONASTRELL 2011 T
100% monastrell.

92 Colour: cherry, garnet rim. Nose: fresh fruit, fruit expression, scrubland, spicy. Palate: balanced, good acidity, fine bitter notes.

VALTOSCA 2010 T
100% syrah.

92 Colour: bright cherry. Nose: ripe fruit, sweet spices, creamy oak, mineral. Palate: flavourful, fruity, toasty, round tannins.

EL MOLAR 2010 T
100% garnacha.

91 Colour: bright cherry. Nose: complex, elegant, mineral, spicy, scrubland. Palate: powerful, flavourful, spicy, balsamic.

LAS GRAVAS 2009 T
80% monastrell, 15% garnacha, 5% syrah.

95 Colour: cherry, garnet rim. Nose: spicy, creamy oak, toasty, complex, mineral, fruit expression. Palate: powerful, flavourful, toasty, round tannins.

CASA CASTILLO PIE FRANCO 2008 T
100% monastrell.

95 Colour: cherry, garnet rim. Nose: creamy oak, toasty, complex, mineral, elegant. Palate: powerful, flavourful, toasty, round tannins.

RED BOTTLE INTERNATIONAL

Rosales, 6
09400 Aranda de Duero (Burgos)
☎: +34 947 515 884 - Fax: +34 947 515 886
rbi@redbottleint.com

CASPER 2009 T BARRICA
100% monastrell.

90 Colour: cherry, garnet rim. Nose: ripe fruit, spicy, creamy oak, toasty, characterful. Palate: powerful, flavourful, toasty, round tannins.

SAN JOSÉ

Camino de Hellín, s/n
02652 Ontur (Albacete)
☎: +34 678 747 913 - Fax: +34 967 324 186
export@bodegasanjose.com
www.bodegasanjose.com

VILLA DE ONTUR 2011 B
sauvignon blanc.

85 Colour: bright straw. Nose: fresh, white flowers, expressive, ripe fruit. Palate: flavourful, fruity, good acidity, balanced.

DOMINIO DE ONTUR SYRAH 2011 T
syrah.

88 Colour: cherry, purple rim. Nose: fresh fruit, red berry notes. Palate: flavourful, fruity, good acidity, round tannins.

DOMINIO DE ONTUR MERLOT 2011 T
merlot.

86 Colour: cherry, purple rim. Nose: expressive, floral, red berry notes, wild herbs. Palate: flavourful, fruity, good acidity.

DOMINIO DE ONTUR MONASTRELL 2011 T
monastrell.

82

PATRE 2010 T
syrah, monastrell.

87 Colour: bright cherry. Nose: sweet spices, creamy oak, fruit expression. Palate: flavourful, fruity, toasty, round tannins.

VIÑAS DE LA CASA DEL RICO

Poeta Andrés Bolarin, 1- 5ºB
30011 Murcia (Murcia)
☎: +34 639 957 687
vino@gorgocil.com
www.casadelrico.com

GORGOCIL TEMPRANILLO 2009 T
100% tempranillo.

93 Colour: bright cherry. Nose: ripe fruit, sweet spices, creamy oak, fragrant herbs. Palate: flavourful, fruity, toasty, round tannins.

GORGOCIL MONASTRELL 2009 T
monastrell.

90 Colour: cherry, garnet rim. Nose: spicy, creamy oak, toasty, earthy notes, overripe fruit. Palate: powerful, flavourful, toasty, round tannins.

VIÑEDOS Y BODEGAS XENYSEL

Valle Hoya de Torres
30520 Jumilla (Murcia)
☎: +34 968 756 240 - Fax: +34 968 756 240
info@xenysel.com
www.xenysel.com

XENYSEL ORGANICALLY 2011 T
100% monastrell.

87 Colour: cherry, purple rim. Nose: expressive, fresh fruit, red berry notes, floral, medium intensity. Palate: fruity, good acidity, round tannins, easy to drink.

XENYSEL PIE FRANCO 2011 T
100% monastrell.

86 Colour: cherry, purple rim. Nose: medium intensity, ripe fruit, balanced. Palate: flavourful, fruity, correct.

CALZÁS PIE FRANCO 2008 T
100% monastrell.

89 Colour: deep cherry, garnet rim. Nose: powerfull, fruit preserve, dark chocolate, sweet spices, creamy oak, pattiserie. Palate: flavourful, good structure.

XENYSEL 12 2008 T
100% monastrell.

86 Colour: bright cherry, purple rim. Nose: medium intensity, sweet spices, candied fruit. Palate: flavourful, spicy.

DO LA GOMERA

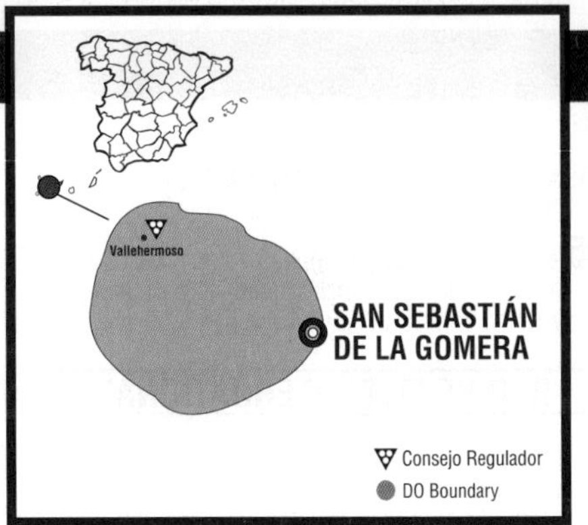

LOCATION:

The majority of the vineyards are found in the north of the island, in the vicinity of the towns of Vallehermoso (some 385 Ha) and Hermigua. The remaining vineyards are spread out over Agulo, Valle Gran Rey –near the capital city of La Gomera, San Sebastián– and Alajeró, on the slopes of the Garajonay peak.

CLIMATE:

The island benefits from a subtropical climate together with, as one approaches the higher altitudes of the Garajonay peak, a phenomenon of permanent humidity known as 'mar de nubes' (sea of clouds) caused by the trade winds. This humid air from the north collides with the mountain range, thereby creating a kind of horizontal rain resulting in a specific ecosystem made up of luxuriant valleys. The average temperature is 20°C all year round.

SOIL:

The most common soil in the higher mountain regions is deep and clayey, while, as one approaches lower altitudes towards the scrubland, the soil is more Mediterranean with a good many stones and terraces similar to those of the Priorat.

GRAPE VARIETIES:

WHITE: *Forastera* (90%), *Gomera Blanca, Listán Blanca, Marmajuelo, Malvasía* and *Pedro Ximenez.*
RED: *Listán Negra* (5%), *Negramoll* (2%); **Experimental:** *Tintilla Castellana, Cabernet Sauvignon* and *Rubí Cabernet.*

FIGURES:

Vineyard surface: 125 – **Wine-Growers:** 230 – **Wineries:** 14 – **2011 Harvest rating:** -- – **Production:** 50.000 litres – **Market percentages:** 96% domestic. 4% export

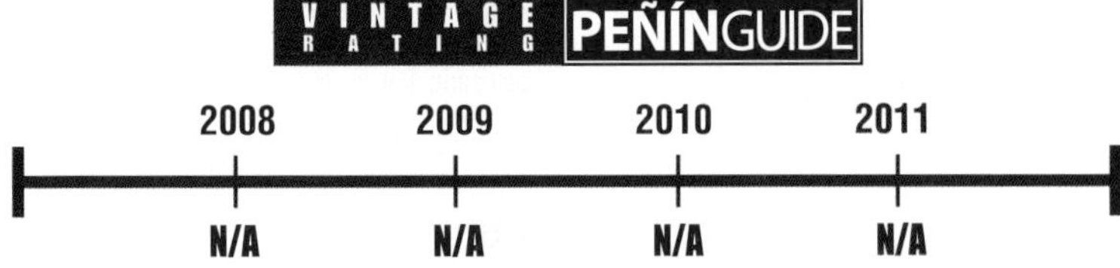

CONSEJO REGULADOR
Avda. Guillermo Ascanio,16, 1° - Vallehermoso 38840 La Gomera - ☎: +34 922 800 801 - Fax: +34 922 801 146
@ crdolagomera@mixmail.com - www.vinosdelagomera.es

LOCATION:

On the southern plateau in the provinces of Albacete, Ciudad Real, Cuenca and Toledo. It is the largest wine-growing region in Spain and in the world.

CLIMATE:

Extreme continental, with temperatures ranging between 40/45°C in summer and –10/12°C in winter. Rather low rainfall, with an average of about 375 mm per year.

SOIL:

The terrain is flat and the vineyards are situated at an altitude of about 700 m above sea level. The soil is generally sandy, limy and clayey.

GRAPE VARIETIES:

WHITE: *Airén* (majority), *Macabeo, Pardilla, Chardonnay, Sauvignon Blanc, Verdejo, Moscatel de Grano Menudo, Gewürztraminer, Parellada, Pero Ximénez, Riesling* and *Torrontés.*
RED: *Cencibel* (majority amongst red varieties), *Garnacha, Moravia, Cabernet Sauvignon, Merlot, Syrah, Cabernet Franc, Graciano, Malbec, Mencía, Monastrell, Pinot Noir, Petit Verdot* and *Bobal.*

FIGURES:

Vineyard surface: 164,449 – **Wine-Growers:** 17,222 – **Wineries:** 268 – **2011 Harvest rating:** Excellent – **Production:** 145,419,200 litres – **Market percentages:** 35% domestic. 65% export

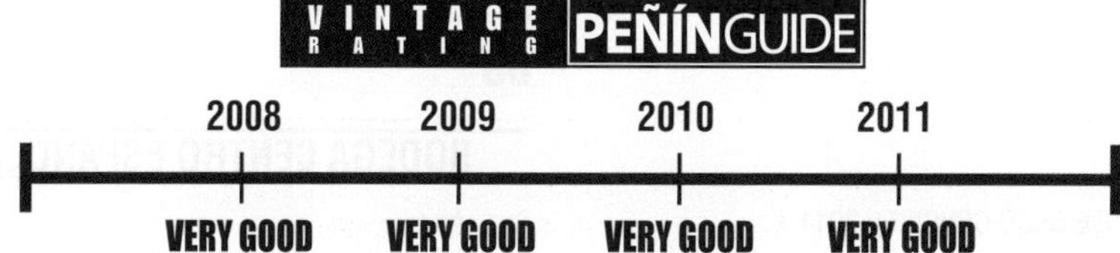

CONSEJO REGULADOR
Avda. de Criptana, 73 - 13600 Alcázar de San Juan (Ciudad Real) - ☎: +34 926 541 523 - Fax: +34 926 588 040
@ consejo@lamanchado.es @ prensa@lamanchado.es - www.lamanchawines.com

AMANCIO MENCHERO MÁRQUEZ

Legión, 27
13260 Bolaños de Calatrava (Ciudad Real)
☎: +34 926 870 076 - Fax: +34 926 871 558
amanciomenchero@hotmail.com

FINCA MORIANA 2011 B
100% airén.

80

FINCA MORIANA 2007 TC
100% cencibel.

84

BACO, BODEGAS ASOCIADAS COOPERATIVAS

Pol. Ind. Alces, Avda. de los Vinos, s/n
13600 Alcázar de San Juan (Ciudad Real)
☎: +34 926 547 404 - Fax: +34 926 547 702
info@grupobaco.com
www.grupobaco.com

DOMINIO DE BACO AIRÉN 2011 B
airén.

85 Colour: bright straw, greenish rim. Nose: medium intensity, ripe fruit, tropical fruit. Palate: fruity, easy to drink.

DOMINIO DE BACO MACABEO 2011 B
macabeo.

81

DOMINIO DE BACO 2011 RD
cencibel.

83

DOMINIO DE BACO CENCIBEL 2011 T
cencibel.

88 Colour: cherry, purple rim. Nose: expressive, fresh fruit, red berry notes, floral. Palate: flavourful, fruity, good acidity, round tannins.

DOMINIO DE BACO CABERNET 2010 T
cabernet sauvignon.

84

BERNAL GARCÍA-CHICOTE

Santo Domingo de Guzmán, 4
13620 Pedro Muñoz (Ciudad Real)
☎: +34 610 557 541
info@bodegabernal.com
www.bodegabernal.com

OVIDIO SELECTION 2008 T
tempranillo.

84

TERRUÑO CORCOLES 2007 TC
tempranillo.

87 Colour: cherry, garnet rim. Nose: ripe fruit, spicy, toasty, tobacco. Palate: flavourful, toasty, spicy.

OVIDIO 2007 T ROBLE
tempranillo.

80

TERRUÑO CORCOLES 2006 TC
tempranillo.

85 Colour: pale ruby, brick rim edge. Nose: spicy, fine reductive notes, wet leather, aged wood nuances, fruit liqueur notes. Palate: spicy, long, good acidity.

TERRUÑO CORCOLES 2006 TR
tempranillo.

85 Colour: cherry, garnet rim. Nose: ripe fruit, wet leather, cigar, creamy oak. Palate: long, spicy.

TERRUÑO CORCOLES 2005 TR
tempranillo.

83

BODEGA CENTRO ESPAÑOLAS

Ctra. Alcázar, s/n
13700 Tomelloso (Ciudad Real)
☎: +34 926 505 654 - Fax: +34 926 505 652
allozo@allozo.com
www.allozo.com

ALLOZO VERDEJO 2011 B
verdejo.

83

ALLOZO FINCA LOS FRAILES CABERNET 2011 T
100% cabernet sauvignon.

86 Colour: cherry, purple rim. Nose: red berry notes, ripe fruit, scrubland. Palate: sweetness, correct, flavourful.

ALLOZO SHYRAZ DE FINCA DE LA RAMA 2011 T
100% syrah.

84

ALLOZO 2011 T
100% tempranillo.

84

ALLOZO MERLOT DE FINCA LOMA DE LOS FRAILES 2011 T
100% merlot.

83

ALLOZO 927 2008 T
33% tempranillo, 33% merlot, 33% syrah.

89 Colour: cherry, garnet rim. Nose: ripe fruit, dark chocolate, sweet spices, balanced. Palate: long, fruity, flavourful, fruity aftespalate:.

ALLOZO 2008 TC
100% tempranillo.

86 Colour: cherry, garnet rim. Nose: spicy, medium intensity, ripe fruit. Palate: correct, fruity, flavourful.

ALLOZO 2006 TR
100% tempranillo.

87 Colour: cherry, garnet rim. Nose: medium intensity, balanced, ripe fruit, spicy. Palate: good structure, flavourful, long.

ALLOZO 2005 TGR
100% tempranillo.

86 Colour: light cherry, garnet rim. Nose: balanced, medium intensity, sweet spices. Palate: powerful, flavourful, good structure.

BODEGA LA TERCIA-VINOS ECOLÓGICOS

Pl. Santa Quiteria, 12
13600 Alcázar de San Juan (Ciudad Real)
☎: +34 926 541 512 - Fax: +34 926 550 104
administracion@bodegalatercia.com
www.bodegalatercia.com

YEMANUEVA AIRÉN ECOLÓGICO 2011 B
100% airén.

83

YEMANUEVA TEMPRANILLO ECOLÓGICO 2009 T
100% tempranillo.

81

YEMANUEVA TEMPRANILLO ECOLÓGICO 2010 T
100% tempranillo.

85 Colour: deep cherry, purple rim. Nose: powerfull, ripe fruit, expressive. Palate: flavourful, fruity, good structure.

YEMASERENA TEMPRANILLO SELECCIÓN LIMITADA 2006 T
100% tempranillo.

86 Colour: cherry, garnet rim. Nose: ripe fruit, creamy oak, sweet spices. Palate: powerful, flavourful, long.

BODEGA MATEOS HIGUERA

Ctra. CM-3127 P.k. 7,100
13240 La Solana (Ciudad Real)
☎: +34 676 920 905 - Fax: +34 926 633 826
joaquin@vegamara.es
www.vegamara.es

VEGA DEMARA 2011 B
verdejo.

80

VEGA DEMARA 2011 T
tempranillo.

82

BODEGA Y VIÑAS ALDOBA

Ctra. Alcázar, s/n
13700 Tomelloso (Ciudad Real)
☎: +34 926 505 653 - Fax: +34 926 505 652
aldoba@allozo.com

ALDOBA 2011 B
verdejo.

80

ALDOBA 2011 T
tempranillo.

84

ALDOBA 2008 TC
tempranillo.

85 Colour: cherry, garnet rim. Nose: ripe fruit, spicy, creamy oak. Palate: flavourful, toasty, thin.

ALDOBA 2007 TR
tempranillo.

88 Colour: cherry, garnet rim. Nose: ripe fruit, spicy, toasty, fine reductive notes. Palate: powerful, flavourful, toasty.

BODEGAS AYUSO

Miguel Caro, 6
02600 Villarrobledo (Albacete)
☎: +34 967 140 458 - Fax: +34 967 144 925
comercial@bodegasayuso.es
www.bodegasayuso.es

FINCA LOS AZARES SAUVIGNON BLANC 2011 B
100% sauvignon blanc.

85 Colour: bright straw, greenish rim. Nose: ripe fruit, tropical fruit. Palate: fruity, flavourful, balanced.

ESTOLA VERDEJO 2011 B
100% verdejo.

85 Colour: bright straw. Nose: tropical fruit, grassy, medium intensity. Palate: fresh, light-bodied, flavourful, easy to drink.

ESTOLA 2011 BFB
80% airén, 20% chardonnay.

84

ARMIÑO 2011 B
100% airén.

83

CASTILLO DE BENIZAR MACABEO 2011 B
100% macabeo.

82

CASTILLO DE BENIZAR CABERNET SAUVIGNON 2011 RD
100% cabernet sauvignon.

84

CASTILLO DE BENIZAR TEMPRANILLO 2011 T
100% tempranillo.

85 Colour: cherry, purple rim. Nose: floral, red berry notes, ripe fruit. Palate: powerful, flavourful, fresh, fruity.

ESTOLA 2007 TC
100% tempranillo.

85 Colour: cherry, garnet rim. Nose: medium intensity, ripe fruit, spicy. Palate: easy to drink, spicy, round tannins.

FINCA LOS AZARES 2007 T
50% cabernet sauvignon, 50% merlot.

85 Colour: pale ruby, brick rim edge. Nose: spicy, wet leather, aged wood nuances, fruit liqueur notes. Palate: spicy, long, toasty.

ESTOLA 2006 TR
75% tempranillo, 25% cabernet sauvignon.

85 Colour: pale ruby, brick rim edge. Nose: spicy, fine reductive notes, wet leather, fruit liqueur notes. Palate: spicy, fine tannins, long.

FINCA LOS AZARES PETIT VERDOT 2005 T
100% petit verdot.

87 Colour: light cherry, brick rim edge. Nose: ripe fruit, balanced, spicy, toasty. Palate: flavourful, toasty, balsamic.

ESTOLA 2001 TGR
65% tempranillo, 35% cabernet sauvignon.

85 Colour: light cherry, orangey edge. Nose: medium intensity, old leather, spicy. Palate: light-bodied, easy to drink.

BODEGAS CAMPOS REALES

Castilla La Mancha, 4
16670 El Provencio (Cuenca)
☎: +34 967 166 066 - Fax: +34 967 165 032
info@bodegascamposreales.com
www.bodegascamposreales.com

CANFORRALES SAUVIGNON BLANC 2011 B
sauvignon blanc.

85 Colour: bright straw. Nose: white flowers, fragrant herbs, ripe fruit. Palate: powerful, flavourful, fruity, fresh.

CANFORRALES ALMA VERDEJO 2011 B
verdejo.

85 Colour: bright straw. Nose: balanced, ripe fruit, floral, tropical fruit. Palate: fruity, flavourful, easy to drink.

CANFORRALES CLÁSICO TEMPRANILLO 2011 T
14% tempranillo.

87 Colour: cherry, purple rim. Nose: red berry notes, ripe fruit, violets, fruit expression. Palate: fruity, flavourful, ripe fruit, balanced.

CANFORRALES SELECCIÓN 2010 T
tempranillo.

84

CÁNFORA PIE FRANCO 2009 T
tempranillo.

92 Colour: cherry, garnet rim. Nose: ripe fruit, spicy, scrubland, creamy oak, toasty, fine reductive notes. Palate: powerful, flavourful, complex, spicy.

GLADIUM VIÑAS VIEJAS 2009 TC
tempranillo.

91 Colour: cherry, garnet rim. Nose: ripe fruit, balsamic herbs, earthy notes, mineral, dark chocolate, creamy oak, toasty. Palate: flavourful, good structure, spicy, round tannins.

GLADIUM 2009 TC
tempranillo.

88 Colour: cherry, garnet rim. Nose: ripe fruit, spicy, creamy oak, toasty. Palate: powerful, flavourful, toasty, round tannins.

CANFORRALES SYRAH 2009 T ROBLE
syrah.

86 Colour: bright cherry. Nose: ripe fruit, toasty, grassy. Palate: flavourful, fruity, toasty, round tannins.

BODEGAS CASA ANTONETE

Barrio San José, s/n
02100 Tarazona de la Mancha (Albacete)
☎: +34 967 480 074 - Fax: +34 967 480 294
launion@casaantonete.com
www.casaantonete.com

NÉGORA CHARDONNAY 2011 B
chardonnay.

85 Colour: bright yellow. Nose: dried flowers, citrus fruit, fragrant herbs. Palate: flavourful, fruity, light-bodied, easy to drink.

NÉGORA VERDEJO 2011 B
verdejo.

85 Colour: bright straw. Nose: dried flowers, fragrant herbs, ripe fruit. Palate: light-bodied, fresh, fruity, easy to drink.

NÉGORA CABERNET 2010 T
cabernet sauvignon.

86 Colour: cherry, purple rim. Nose: expressive, red berry notes, floral, balsamic herbs, sweet spices. Palate: flavourful, fruity, good acidity.

CASA ANTONETE CENCIBEL 2008 TC
100% tempranillo.

84

CASA ANTONETE CENCIBEL 2005 TR
tempranillo.

84

BODEGAS CRISTO DE LA VEGA

General Goded, 6
13630 Socuéllamos (Ciudad Real)
☎: +34 926 530 388 - Fax: +34 926 530 024
comercial@bodegascrisve.com
www.bodegascrisve.com

EL YUGO AIRÉN 2011 B
airén.

87 Colour: bright yellow. Nose: lactic notes, tropical fruit, ripe fruit. Palate: light-bodied, fresh, easy to drink.

EL YUGO 2011 RD

86 Colour: rose, purple rim. Nose: red berry notes, candied fruit, lactic notes, floral. Palate: flavourful, fruity, fresh.

EL YUGO 2011 T

88 Colour: cherry, purple rim. Nose: lactic notes, red berry notes, balanced, floral. Palate: good acidity, fruity, flavourful, easy to drink.

BODEGAS DEL SAZ

Maestro Manzanares, 57
13610 Campo de Criptana (Ciudad Real)
☎: +34 926 562 424 - Fax: +34 926 562 659
bodegasdelsaz@bodegasdelsaz.com
www.bodegasdelsaz.com

VIDAL DEL SAZ SELECCIÓN WHITE 2011 B
macabeo, sauvignon blanc, verdejo.

86 Colour: bright straw. Nose: tropical fruit, expressive, powerfull, ripe fruit. Palate: fruity, flavourful.

VIDAL DEL SAZ SELECCIÓN ROSÉ 2011 RD
merlot, syrah.

80

VIDAL DEL SAZ 2010 T ROBLE
tempranillo.

84

VIDAL DEL SAZ 2009 TC
tempranillo.

84

BODEGAS ENTREMONTES (NUESTRA SEÑORA DE LA PIEDAD)

Ctra. Circunvalación, s/n
45800 Quintanar de la Orden (Toledo)
☎: +34 925 180 930 - Fax: +34 925 180 480
comercial@bodegasentremontes.com

CLAVELITO AIRÉN 2011 B
100% airén.

84

CLAVELITO VERDEJO 2011 B
100% verdejo.

83

CLAVELITO MACABEO 2011 B
100% macabeo.

80

CLAVELITO 2011 RD
100% tempranillo.

80

ENTREMONTES GARNACHA 2011 T
100% garnacha.

84

ENTREMONTES SYRAH 2010 T
100% syrah.

84

ENTREMONTES TEMPRANILLO 2010 T

83

ENTREMONTES CABERNET SAUVIGNON 2010 T
100% cabernet sauvignon.

78

ENTREMONTES 2009 T ROBLE
100% tempranillo.

85 Colour: cherry, garnet rim. Nose: powerfull, ripe fruit, overripe fruit, sweet spices, toasty. Palate: correct, ripe fruit, long.

ENTREMONTES 2004 TC
100% tempranillo.

80

ENTREMONTES 2003 TR
100% tempranillo.

86 Colour: pale ruby, brick rim edge. Nose: scrubland, cigar, spicy, toasty. Palate: correct, flavourful, spirituous.

ENTREMONTES 2002 TGR
100% tempranillo.

85 Colour: pale ruby, brick rim edge. Nose: spicy, fine reductive notes, wet leather, aged wood nuances, fruit liqueur notes. Palate: spicy, fine tannins, elegant, long.

ENTREMONTES BN
60% macabeo, 40% verdejo.

82

ENTREMONTES S/C SS
100% airén.

81

BODEGAS HERMANOS RUBIO

Ctra. de Villamuelas, s/n
45740 Villasequilla (Toledo)
☎: +34 925 310 284 - Fax: +34 925 325 133
info@bhrubio.com
www.bhrubio.com

ZOCODOVER SELECCIÓN SAUVIGNON BLANC 2011 B
sauvignon blanc.

88 Colour: bright straw. Nose: fresh, white flowers, tropical fruit. Palate: flavourful, fruity, good acidity, balanced.

SEÑORÍO DE ZOCODOVER 2007 TC
tempranillo.

84

ZOCODOVER SELECCIÓN 2005 TR
tempranillo, cabernet sauvignon.

85 Colour: light cherry. Nose: ripe fruit, balsamic herbs, spicy. Palate: powerful, flavourful, long.

SEÑORÍO DE ZOCODOVER 2005 TR
tempranillo.

85 Colour: light cherry. Nose: ripe fruit, balsamic herbs, sweet spices. Palate: long, flavourful, easy to drink.

BODEGAS ISLA

Nuestra Señora de la Paz, 9
13210 Villarta San Juan (Ciudad Real)
☎: +34 926 640 004 - Fax: +34 926 640 004
b.isla@terra.es
www.bodegasisla.com

ISLA ORO AIRÉN 2011 B
100% airén.

77

ISLA ORO GARNACHA 2011 RD
100% garnacha.

77

ISLA ORO TEMPRANILLO SYRAH MERLOT 2011 T
33% tempranillo, 33% syrah, 33% merlot.

78

ISLA ORO TEMPRANILLO 2011 T
100% tempranillo.

75

ISLA ORO TEMPRANILLO 2009 TC
100% tempranillo.

81

BODEGAS LA REMEDIADORA

Alfredo Atieza, 149-151
02630 La Roda (Albacete)
☎: +34 967 440 600 - Fax: +34 967 441 465
export@laremediadora.com
www.laremediadora.com

TOPICO MOSCATEL 2011 B
100% moscatel.

86 Colour: golden. Nose: powerfull, floral, candied fruit, fragrant herbs. Palate: flavourful, sweet, fresh, fruity, long.

LA VILLA REAL MACABEO 2011 B
100% macabeo.

84

LA VILLA REAL VENDIMIA SELECCIONADA 2011 RD
100% tempranillo.

87 Colour: brilliant rose. Nose: faded flowers, balanced, fruit expression. Palate: flavourful, fruity, easy to drink, balanced.

LA VILLA REAL VENDIMIA SELECCIONADA 2011 T
50% tempranillo, 50% syrah.

86 Colour: cherry, purple rim. Nose: balanced, floral, red berry notes. Palate: fruity, good structure, correct, good acidity.

LA VILLA REAL 2008 TC
50% merlot, 50% cabernet sauvignon.

86 Colour: cherry, garnet rim. Nose: ripe fruit, spicy, creamy oak, toasty, complex. Palate: powerful, flavourful, toasty.

LA VILLA REAL SUMILLER 2008 TR
merlot, cabernet sauvignon.

83

BODEGAS LAHOZ

Ctra. N-310, km. 108,5
13630 Socuéllamos (Ciudad Real)
☎: +34 926 699 083 - Fax: +34 926 514 929
info@bodegaslahoz.com
www.bodegaslahoz.com

VEGA CÓRCOLES SAUVIGNON BLANC 2011 B
sauvignon blanc.

88 Colour: bright straw, greenish rim. Nose: fragrant herbs, balanced, expressive, ripe fruit. Palate: fruity, flavourful, full.

VEGA CÓRCOLES AIRÉN 2011 B
airén.

81

VEGA CÓRCOLES 2011 RD
tempranillo.

86 Colour: rose, bright. Nose: red berry notes, ripe fruit, powerfull. Palate: flavourful, full, balanced, ripe fruit.

VEGA CÓRCOLES TEMPRANILLO 2011 T
tempranillo.

86 Colour: cherry, purple rim. Nose: medium intensity, fruit expression, floral. Palate: good structure, fruity.

VEGA CÓRCOLES TEMPRANILLO 2007 T ROBLE
tempranillo.

86 Colour: cherry, garnet rim. Nose: medium intensity, spicy, ripe fruit, fruit preserve. Palate: fruity, flavourful, spicy.

BODEGAS MARTÍNEZ SÁEZ

06200 Villarrobledo (Albacete)
☎: +34 967 443 088 - Fax: +34 967 440 204
bodegas@lapina.es
www.bodegasmartinezsaez.es

VIÑA ORCE MACABEO 2011 B
macabeo.

84

VIÑA ORCE 2011 RD
merlot.

85 Colour: brilliant rose. Nose: floral, candied fruit, fragrant herbs, lactic notes. Palate: powerful, flavourful, fresh.

VIÑA ORCE 2011 T ROBLE
tempranillo.

83

VIÑA ORCE 2008 TC
60% tempranillo, 40% cabernet sauvignon.

85 Colour: cherry, garnet rim. Nose: ripe fruit, spicy, toasty, scrubland. Palate: powerful, flavourful, toasty.

BODEGAS NARANJO

Felipe II, 5
13150 Carrión de Calatrava (Ciudad Real)
☎: +34 926 814 155 - Fax: +34 926 815 335
info@bodegasnaranjo.com
www.bodegasnaranjo.com

VIÑA CUERVA AIRÉN 2011 B
airén.

85 Colour: bright straw. Nose: ripe fruit, white flowers, dried herbs. Palate: light-bodied, fresh, flavourful, easy to drink.

VIÑA CUERVA 2011 RD
tempranillo.

82

VIÑA CUERVA 2007 TR
tempranillo.

86 Colour: cherry, garnet rim. Nose: ripe fruit, woody, toasty, balsamic herbs. Palate: powerful, flavourful, correct

BODEGAS ROMERO DE ÁVILA SALCEDO

Avda. Constitución, 4
13200 La Solana (Ciudad Real)
☎: +34 926 631 426
comercial@bodegasromerodeavila.com
www.bodegasromerodeavila.com

GRAN MAJESTAD SAUVIGNON BLANC 2011 B
sauvignon blanc.

84

PORTENTO SAUVIGNON BLANC 2011 B
sauvignon blanc.

84

PORTENTO SYRAH 2011 T
syrah.

88 Colour: cherry, purple rim. Nose: fresh fruit, red berry notes, floral, lactic notes. Palate: flavourful, fruity, good acidity, round tannins.

PORTENTO TEMPRANILLO 2011 T
tempranillo.

87 Colour: cherry, purple rim. Nose: expressive, fresh fruit, red berry notes, floral. Palate: flavourful, fruity, good acidity, round tannins.

GRAN MAJESTAD SYRAH 2011 T
syrah.

86 Colour: cherry, purple rim. Nose: expressive, fresh fruit, red berry notes, floral. Palate: flavourful, fruity, good acidity.

GRAN MAJESTAD TEMPRANILLO 2011 T
tempranillo.

85 Colour: cherry, purple rim. Nose: lactic notes, red berry notes, ripe fruit, grassy. Palate: fine bitter notes, flavourful.

PORTENTO 2008 TC
tempranillo, cabernet sauvignon.

77

BODEGAS SAN ISIDRO DE PEDRO MUÑOZ

Ctra. El Toboso, 1
13620 Pedro Muñoz (Ciudad Real)
☎: +34 926 586 057 - Fax: +34 926 568 380
administracion@viacotos.com
www.viacotos.com

LA HIJUELA 2011 B
airén.

82

LA HIJUELA TEMPRANILLO 2010 T
100% tempranillo.

80

GRAN AMIGO SANCHO 2008 T
100% tempranillo.

87 Colour: cherry, garnet rim. Nose: powerfull, balanced, sweet spices. Palate: fruity, good structure, ripe fruit, long.

BODEGAS VERDÚGUEZ

Los Hinojosos, 1
45810 Villanueva de Alcardete (Toledo)
☎: +34 925 167 493 - Fax: +34 925 166 148
verduguez@bodegasverduguez.com
www.bodegasverduguez.com

PALACIOS REALES VERDEJO 2011 B
100% verdejo.

83

VEREDA MAYOR TEMPRANILLO 2011 T
100% tempranillo.

87 Colour: cherry, purple rim. Nose: fresh fruit, red berry notes, floral. Palate: flavourful, fruity, good acidity.

IMPERIAL TOLEDO OLD VINE SELECTION 2009 T
100% tempranillo.

88 Colour: very deep cherry. Nose: ripe fruit, dark chocolate, sweet spices, fruit preserve. Palate: good structure, ripe fruit, long.

PALACIOS REALES OAKED SELECTION 2009 T ROBLE
60% tempranillo, 20% syrah, 20% merlot.

85 Colour: bright cherry. Nose: ripe fruit, sweet spices, creamy oak. Palate: flavourful, fruity, toasty.

IMPERIAL TOLEDO 2006 TR
100% tempranillo.

86 Colour: deep cherry, garnet rim. Nose: sweet spices, ripe fruit, toasty. Palate: flavourful, fruity.

BODEGAS VERUM

Juan Antonio López Ramírez, 4
13700 Tomelloso (Ciudad Real)
☎: +34 926 511 404 - Fax: +34 926 515 047
administracion@bodegasverum.com
www.bodegasverum.com

VERUM GRAN CUEVA 2007 ESP
100% chardonnay.

86 Colour: bright golden. Nose: fine lees, dry nuts, fragrant herbs. Palate: flavourful, good acidity, fine bead, fine bitter notes.

BODEGAS VOLVER

Pza. de Grecia, 1 Local 1B
45005 Toledo (Toledo)
☎: +34 925 167 493 - Fax: +34 925 167 059
export@bodegasvolver.com
www.bodegasvolver.com

PASO A PASO VERDEJO 2011 B
100% verdejo.

87 Colour: bright straw. Nose: ripe fruit, tropical fruit, floral. Palate: flavourful, fruity, full.

PASO A PASO TEMPRANILLO 2011 T
100% tempranillo.

89 Colour: very deep cherry. Nose: expressive, varietal, ripe fruit, cocoa bean. Palate: flavourful, powerful, concentrated, sweetness.

VOLVER 2010 T
100% tempranillo.

90 Colour: bright cherry. Nose: ripe fruit, sweet spices, creamy oak, varietal, characterful, earthy notes. Palate: flavourful, fruity, toasty, round tannins.

VOLVER 2009 T
100% tempranillo.

90 Colour: cherry, garnet rim. Nose: balanced, ripe fruit, sweet spices, expressive. Palate: ripe fruit, long, round tannins, toasty.

BODEGAS Y VIÑEDOS BRO VALERO

Ctra. Las Mesas, Km. 11
02600 Villarrobledo (Albacete)
☎: +34 649 985 103 - Fax: +34 914 454 675
bodegas@brovalero.es
www.brovalero.es

BRO VALERO SYRAH ECO 2009 T
100% syrah.

84

BODEGAS Y VIÑEDOS DE CINCO CASAS

Virgen de las Nieves, 2
13720 Cinco Casas (Ciudad Real)
☎: +34 926 529 010 - Fax: +34 926 526 070
bodega@bodegascasadelavina.com
www.bodegascasadelavina.com

VIÑA SANTA ELENA 2011 B
macabeo.

80

VIÑA SANTA ELENA TEMPRANILLO 2011 T
tempranillo.

84

VIÑA SANTA ELENA 2007 TR
tempranillo.

85 Colour: cherry, garnet rim. Nose: fruit preserve, sweet spices, creamy oak. Palate: spicy, flavourful, correct.

BODEGAS Y VIÑEDOS LADERO

Ctra. Alcázar, s/n
13700 Tomelloso (Ciudad Real)
☎: +34 926 505 653 - Fax: +34 926 505 652
ladero@allozo.com

LADERO VERDEJO 2011 B
100% verdejo.

82

LADERO 2011 T
tempranillo.

86 Colour: cherry, purple rim. Nose: medium intensity, red berry notes. Palate: light-bodied, round tannins, correct.

LADERO 2008 TC
100% tempranillo.

86 Colour: cherry, garnet rim. Nose: ripe fruit, wild herbs, spicy. Palate: long, flavourful, spicy.

LADERO 2006 TR
100% tempranillo.

85 Colour: cherry, garnet rim. Nose: medium intensity, warm, ripe fruit, spicy. Palate: flavourful, fruity.

LADERO 2005 TGR
100% tempranillo.

87 Colour: cherry, garnet rim. Nose: ripe fruit, spicy, toasty. Palate: powerful, flavourful, toasty, round tannins.

BODEGAS YUNTERO

Pol. Ind. Ctra. Alcázar, s/n
13200 Manzanares (Ciudad Real)
☎: +34 926 610 309 - Fax: +34 926 610 516
yuntero@yuntero.com
www.yuntero.com

YUNTERO 2011 B
85% macabeo, 15% sauvignon blanc.

86 Colour: bright straw. Nose: floral, citrus fruit, tropical fruit, ripe fruit. Palate: fruity, flavourful, easy to drink.

YUNTERO 2011 B
50% verdejo, 50% sauvignon blanc.

83

YUNTERO 2011 RD

85 Colour: rose, purple rim. Nose: lactic notes, red berry notes, medium intensity. Palate: fruity, fresh, easy to drink.

YUNTERO 2011 T
85% tempranillo, 15% syrah.

85 Colour: cherry, purple rim. Nose: red berry notes, ripe fruit, balsamic herbs. Palate: light-bodied, fresh, fruity, flavourful.

YUNTERO 2011 T ROBLE
85% tempranillo, 15% merlot.

84

YUNTERO 2008 TC
85% tempranillo, 15% syrah.

86 Colour: cherry, garnet rim. Nose: ripe fruit, spicy, toasty, fine reductive notes. Palate: powerful, flavourful, toasty.

YUNTERO 2007 TR
100% tempranillo.

85 Colour: cherry, garnet rim. Nose: red berry notes, ripe fruit, sweet spices. Palate: long, spicy, harsh oak tannins.

BOGARVE 1915

Reyes Católicos, 10
45710 Madridejos (Toledo)
☎: +34 925 460 820 - Fax: +34 925 467 006
bogarve@bogarve1915.com
www.bogarve1915.com

LACRUZ VEGA 2011 B
sauvignon blanc, verdejo, syrah, chardonnay.

86 Colour: bright straw. Nose: fresh, fresh fruit, white flowers, expressive. Palate: flavourful, fruity, good acidity, balanced.

CAMPOS DE VIENTO

Avda. Diagonal, 590 - 5º 1ª
08021 (Barcelona)
☎: +34 660 445 464
info@vinergia.com
www.vinergia.com

CAMPOS DE VIENTO 2011 T
100% tempranillo.

86 Colour: cherry, purple rim. Nose: raspberry, red berry notes, floral, lactic notes. Palate: light-bodied, fresh, fruity, easy to drink.

CASA GUALDA

Tapias, 8
16708 Pozoamargo (Cuenca)
☎: +34 969 387 173 - Fax: +34 969 387 202
info@casagualda.com
www.casagualda.com

CASA GUALDA TEMPRANILLO 2011 T
tempranillo.

83

CASA GUALDA SELECCIÓN C&J 2008 T
tempranillo.

86 Colour: cherry, garnet rim. Nose: powerfull, ripe fruit, spicy. Palate: flavourful, fruity, full.

CASA GUALDA 2008 TC
tempranillo, cabernet sauvignon.

85 Colour: deep cherry, garnet rim. Nose: powerfull, toasty, grassy, ripe fruit. Palate: fruity, correct.

CASA GUALDA SELECCIÓN 50 ANIVERSARIO 2008 T
tempranillo, syrah, petit verdot.

85 Colour: cherry, garnet rim. Nose: ripe fruit, medium intensity, dried herbs. Palate: fruity, flavourful, balanced.

COOPERATIVA SAN ANTONIO ABAD

Afueras, 17
45860 Villacañas (Toledo)
☎: +34 925 160 414 - Fax: +34 925 162 015
export@sanantonioabad.es
www.sanantonioabad.es

VILLA ABAD 2011 T ROBLE
tempranillo.

88 Colour: cherry, purple rim. Nose: red berry notes, ripe fruit, spicy, floral. Palate: correct, flavourful, fruity, spicy, harsh oak tannins.

ALBARDIALES 2011 T
tempranillo.

88 Colour: cherry, purple rim. Nose: expressive, red berry notes, lactic notes, raspberry. Palate: good acidity, powerful, flavourful, balanced.

VILLA ABAD TEMPRANILLO 2011 T
tempranillo.

86 Colour: cherry, purple rim. Nose: fresh fruit, red berry notes, floral. Palate: flavourful, fruity, easy to drink.

EL PROGRESO SOCIEDAD COOP. CLM

Avda. de la Virgen, 89
13670 Villarubia de los Ojos (Ciudad Real)
☎: +34 926 896 088 - Fax: +34 926 896 135
administracion@bodegaselprogreso.com
www.bodegaselprogreso.com

OJOS DEL GUADIANA VERDEJO 2011 B
100% verdejo.

84

OJOS DEL GUADIANA AIRÉN 2011 B
100% airén.

81

OJOS DEL GUADIANA SYRAH 2011 T ROBLE
100% syrah.

87 Colour: cherry, garnet rim. Nose: spicy, red berry notes, ripe fruit, cocoa bean. Palate: flavourful, spicy, good finish.

OJOS DEL GUADIANA TEMPRANILLO 2011 T
100% tempranillo.

87 Colour: cherry, purple rim. Nose: red berry notes, fresh fruit, violets. Palate: round tannins, correct, fine bitter notes.

OJOS DEL GUADIANA SELECCIÓN 2010 T
33% cabernet sauvignon, 33% merlot, 33% syrah.

85 Colour: bright cherry. Nose: ripe fruit, sweet spices, creamy oak, scrubland. Palate: flavourful, fruity, toasty.

OJOS DEL GUADIANA 2008 TR
100% tempranillo.

88 Colour: cherry, garnet rim. Nose: red berry notes, ripe fruit, sweet spices, toasty. Palate: correct, powerful, flavourful.

OJOS DEL GUADIANA 2008 TC
100% tempranillo.

84

OJOS DEL GUADIANA 2004 TGR
100% tempranillo.

85 Colour: dark-red cherry, orangey edge. Nose: ripe fruit, cigar, old leather, toasty, fruit preserve. Palate: long, powerful, flavourful.

FÉLIX SOLÍS

Autovía del Sur, Km. 199
13300 Valdepeñas (Ciudad Real)
☎: +34 926 322 400 - Fax: +34 926 322 417
fsa@felixsolisavantis.com
www.felixsolisavantis.com

VIÑA SAN JUAN 2011 B
35% chardonnay, 33% verdejo, 32% viura.

85 Colour: bright straw. Nose: fresh, white flowers, expressive, tropical fruit. Palate: flavourful, fruity, fine bitter notes.

CALIZA 2011 B
35% chardonnay, 33% verdejo, 32% viura.

84

CALIZA 2011 RD
100% tempranillo.

86 Colour: rose, purple rim. Nose: powerfull, ripe fruit, red berry notes, floral. Palate: , powerful, fruity, fresh, good acidity.

VIÑA SAN JUAN 2011 RD
100% tempranillo.

85 Colour: rose. Nose: ripe fruit, floral, fragrant herbs. Palate: light-bodied, fresh, fruity.

CALIZA 2011 T
50% tempranillo, 25% syrah, 25% merlot.

87 Colour: cherry, purple rim. Nose: warm, red berry notes, ripe fruit, earthy notes. Palate: light-bodied, fruity, flavourful, balanced.

FINCA ANTIGUA

Ctra. Quintanar - Los Hinojosos, Km. 11,5
16417 Los Hinojosos (Cuenca)
☎: +34 969 129 700 - Fax: +34 969 129 496
info@fincaantigua.com
www.familiamartinezbujanda.com

FINCA ANTIGUA MOSCATEL 2011 B
100% moscatel.

90 Colour: bright golden. Nose: jasmine, ripe fruit, citrus fruit, fragrant herbs. Palate: long, powerful, flavourful, sweetness.

FINCA ANTIGUA VIURA 2011 B
100% viura.

86 Colour: bright straw. Nose: medium intensity, dried flowers, fresh, tropical fruit. Palate: fresh, correct, fine bitter notes.

FINCA ANTIGUA SYRAH 2010 T
100% syrah.

91 Colour: cherry, purple rim. Nose: balanced, powerfull, sweet spices, ripe fruit. Palate: good structure, flavourful, good acidity.

FINCA ANTIGUA MERLOT 2010 T ROBLE
100% merlot.

86 Colour: bright cherry. Nose: ripe fruit, sweet spices, creamy oak, expressive, toasty. Palate: flavourful, fruity, toasty, round tannins.

FINCA ANTIGUA PETIT VERDOT 2009 T
100% petit verdot.

89 Colour: deep cherry. Nose: ripe fruit, powerfull, spicy, toasty, neat. Palate: fruity, flavourful, round tannins.

FINCA ANTIGUA 2009 TC
50% tempranillo, 20% merlot, 20% cabernet sauvignon, 10% syrah.

88 Colour: cherry, garnet rim. Nose: sweet spices, ripe fruit, cocoa bean, balanced. Palate: ripe fruit, easy to drink.

FINCA ANTIGUA GARNACHA 2009 T
100% garnacha.

88 Colour: bright cherry. Nose: ripe fruit, sweet spices, creamy oak, cocoa bean. Palate: flavourful, fruity, toasty, round tannins.

FINCA ANTIGUA TEMPRANILLO 2009 T
100% tempranillo.

87 Colour: bright cherry. Nose: ripe fruit, sweet spices, creamy oak, expressive. Palate: flavourful, fruity, toasty, round tannins.

FINCA ANTIGUA CABERNET SAUVIGNON 2009 T
100% cabernet sauvignon.

86 Colour: bright cherry, garnet rim. Nose: balsamic herbs, ripe fruit, sweet spices. Palate: correct, good structure, full.

CLAVIS VIÑEDO PICO GARBANZO 2006 TR

91 Colour: deep cherry, garnet rim. Nose: sweet spices, creamy oak, cocoa bean, ripe fruit. Palate: round, balanced, long, ripe fruit, spicy.

FINCA ANTIGUA CICLOS 2005 T
merlot, syrah, cabernet sauvignon.

88 Colour: cherry, garnet rim. Nose: ripe fruit, spicy, creamy oak, complex. Palate: powerful, flavourful, toasty, round tannins.

FINCA LA BLANCA

Princesa, 84
45840 Puebla de Almoradiel (Toledo)
☎: +34 925 178 437 - Fax: +34 925 178 432
montedonlucio@terra.es
www.capel-vinos.es

MONTE DON LUCIO SAUVIGNON BLANC 2011 B
100% sauvignon blanc.

82

MONTE DON LUCIO CABERNET SAUVIGNON 2011 T
100% cabernet sauvignon.

85 Colour: cherry, garnet rim. Nose: grassy, ripe fruit, green pepper. Palate: balanced, flavourful, spicy.

MONTE DON LUCIO TEMPRANILLO 2011 T
tempranillo.

84

FONTANA

Extramuros, s/n
16411 Fuente de Pedro Naharro (Cuenca)
☎: +34 969 125 433 - Fax: +34 969 125 387
gemag@bodegasfontana.com
www.bodegasfontana.com

FONTAL 2011 B
60% verdejo, 40% sauvignon blanc.

87 Colour: bright straw, greenish rim. Nose: fresh fruit, fragrant herbs, citrus fruit. Palate: correct, balanced, fresh.

FONTAL TEMPRANILLO 2010 T ROBLE
100% tempranillo.

88 Colour: cherry, purple rim. Nose: medium intensity, balanced, red berry notes, ripe fruit. Palate: spicy, long, fruity, round tannins.

FONTAL 2008 TC
85% tempranillo, 15% cabernet sauvignon.

88 Colour: cherry, garnet rim. Nose: ripe fruit, spicy, toasty, medium intensity. Palate: powerful, flavourful, toasty, round tannins.

GRAN CASTILLO ROYAL

Nicanor Piñole, 6
33420 Lugones (Asturias)
☎: +34 984 041 246
info@bullanddragon.es
www.grancastilloroyal.bullanddragon.es

GRAN CASTILLO ROYAL 2008 TR
100% tempranillo.

86 Colour: cherry, garnet rim. Nose: ripe fruit, balsamic herbs, creamy oak, toasty. Palate: round tannins, powerful, flavourful.

GRAN CASTILLO ROYAL 2008 TC
100% tempranillo.

84

J. GARCÍA CARRIÓN LA MANCHA

Guarnicionero, s/n
13250 Daimiel (Ciudad Real)
☎: +34 926 260 104 - Fax: +34 926 260 091
jalcaide@jgc.es
www.garciacarrion.es

OPERA PRIMA CHARDONNAY B
chardonnay.

82

OPERA PRIMA MERLOT 2011 T
merlot.

85 Colour: cherry, purple rim. Nose: red berry notes, floral, wild herbs. Palate: flavourful, fruity, good acidity.

OPERA PRIMA SHIRAZ 2011 T
syrah.

84

OPERA PRIMA TEMPRANILLO 2011 T
tempranillo.

84

OPERA PRIMA CABERNET 2011 T
cabernet sauvignon.

81

DON LUCIANO 2009 TC
tempranillo.

85 Colour: cherry, garnet rim. Nose: fruit liqueur notes, wild herbs, roasted coffee. Palate: powerful, flavourful.

DON LUCIANO 2007 TR
tempranillo.

87 Colour: pale ruby, brick rim edge. Nose: spicy, wet leather, toasty, nose:tic coffee, sweet spices. Palate: long, powerful, flavourful, easy to drink.

LA VID Y LA ESPIGA

San Antón, 30
16415 Villamayor de Santiago (Cuenca)
☎: +34 969 139 069 - Fax: +34 969 139 069
export@vidyespiga.es
www.vidyespiga.es

VEGABRISA SAUVIGNON/VERDEJO 2011 B
sauvignon blanc, verdejo.

83

VEGABRISA AIREN 2011 B
airén.

81

VEGABRISA 2011 RD
tempranillo.

84

VEGABRISA 2011 T
tempranillo.

84

NUESTRA SEÑORA DE MANJAVACAS SOC. COOP.

Camino del Campo de Criptana, s/n
16630 Mota del Cuervo (Cuenca)
☎: +34 967 180 025 - Fax: +34 967 181 120
enologia@zagarron.com
www.zagarron.com

ZAGARRON SAUVIGNON BLANC 2011 B
sauvignon blanc.

86 Colour: bright straw. Nose: floral, fragrant herbs, medium intensity. Palate: fresh, flavourful, correct, easy to drink.

ZAGARRON VERDEJO 2011 B
100% verdejo.

86 Colour: bright straw. Nose: floral, citrus fruit, ripe fruit, tropical fruit. Palate: flavourful, fresh, correct, fine bitter notes.

ZAGARRON TEMPRANILLO 2011 T
100% tempranillo.

87 Colour: cherry, purple rim. Nose: medium intensity, red berry notes, floral, violets. Palate: easy to drink, correct, fresh.

PAGO DE LA JARABA

Ctra. Nacional 310, Km. 142,7
02600 Villarrobledo (Albacete)
☎: +34 967 138 250 - Fax: +34 967 138 252
info@lajaraba.com
www.lajaraba.com

VIÑA JARABA 2008 TC
70% tempranillo, 30% otras.

87 Colour: cherry, garnet rim. Nose: sweet spices, dark chocolate, toasty, ripe fruit. Palate: correct, flavourful, long.

PAGO DE LA JARABA 2008 TC
70% tempranillo, 30% otras.

87 Colour: cherry, garnet rim. Nose: ripe fruit, spicy, creamy oak, toasty. Palate: powerful, flavourful, toasty.

S.C.V. DE C-LM VIRGEN DE LAS VIÑAS

Ctra. Argamasilla de Alba, s/n
13700 Tomelloso (Ciudad Real)
☎: +34 926 510 865 - Fax: +34 926 512 130
atencion.cliente@vinostomillar.com
www.vinostomillar.com

TOMILLAR CHARDONNAY 2011 B
chardonnay.

87 Colour: bright yellow. Nose: white flowers, earthy notes, ripe fruit. Palate: long, flavourful, varietal, balanced.

TOMILLAR SAUVIGNON BLANC 2011 B
100% sauvignon blanc.

84

LORENZETE 2011 B
airén.

83

TOMILLAR 2011 B

81

TOMILLAR 2011 RD

84

TOMILLAR TEMPRANILLO 2011 T
tempranillo.

87 Colour: cherry, purple rim. Nose: expressive, fresh fruit, red berry notes, floral. Palate: flavourful, fruity, good acidity.

TOMILLAR 2008 TR
cabernet sauvignon, cencibel.

86 Colour: cherry, garnet rim. Nose: ripe fruit, spicy, creamy oak, toasty. Palate: powerful, flavourful, toasty, round tannins.

SAN ISIDRO LABRADOR SOC. COOP. CLM

Ramón y Cajal, 42
16640 Belmonte (Cuenca)
☎: +34 967 170 289 - Fax: +34 967 170 289
isbelmonte@ucaman.es
www.castibell.es

VISIBEL 2010 B
airén.

84

CASTIBELL 2010 T
tempranillo.

81

SAN ISIDRO S.C.C.L.M. - BODEGAS LATÚE

Camino Esperilla, s/n
45810 Villanueva de Alcardete (Toledo)
☎: +34 925 166 350 - Fax: +34 925 166 673
gerencia@latue.com
www.latue.com

PINGOROTE SAUVIGNON BLANC 2011 B
100% sauvignon blanc.

87 Colour: bright straw. Nose: fresh, fresh fruit, white flowers, expressive. Palate: flavourful, fruity, good acidity, balanced.

LATÚE AIRÉN 2011 B
100% airén.

83

LATÚE TEMPRANILLO 2011 T
100% tempranillo.

86 Colour: cherry, purple rim. Nose: fresh fruit, red berry notes, floral. Palate: flavourful, fruity, good acidity, round tannins.

LATÚE CABERNET SAUVIGNON & SYRAH 2010 T
50% cabernet sauvignon, 50% syrah.

87 Colour: cherry, purple rim. Nose: expressive, fresh fruit, red berry notes, floral. Palate: flavourful, fruity, good acidity, round tannins.

PINGOROTE 2008 TR
100% tempranillo.

86 Colour: cherry, garnet rim. Nose: ripe fruit, spicy, creamy oak, toasty, complex. Palate: powerful, flavourful, toasty, round tannins.

LATÚE BRUT NATURE 2009 ESP
100% airén.

86 Colour: bright straw. Nose: white flowers, fine lees, fragrant herbs, balanced. Palate: light-bodied, fresh, flavourful, good acidity.

SANTA CATALINA

Cooperativa, 2
13240 La Solana (Ciudad Real)
☎: +34 926 632 194 - Fax: +34 926 631 085
compras@santacatalina.es
www.santacatalina.es

CAMPECHANO 2011 B
100% airén.

85 Colour: bright straw. Nose: floral, fragrant herbs, medium intensity. Palate: flavourful, fresh, light-bodied.

LOS GALANES AIRÉN 2011 B
100% airén.

84

LOS GALANES VERDEJO 2011 B
100% verdejo.

82

CAMPECHANO 2011 T
100% tempranillo.

86 Colour: cherry, purple rim. Nose: red berry notes, floral, ripe fruit. Palate: flavourful, fruity, good acidity, easy to drink.

LOS GALANES 2008 TR
100% tempranillo.

86 Colour: cherry, garnet rim. Nose: spicy, ripe fruit, warm. Palate: fruity, flavourful.

LOS GALANES 2008 TC
100% tempranillo.

84

LOS GALANES 2011 T
100% tempranillo.

86 Colour: cherry, garnet rim. Nose: ripe fruit, herbaceous, red berry notes. Palate: easy to drink, light-bodied, fresh, fruity, flavourful.

SOCIEDAD COOPERATIVA ANGEL DEL ALCAZAR

Ctra. de Lillo, s/n
45860 Villacañas (Toledo)
☎: +34 925 160 548 - Fax: +34 925 160 548
angeldelalcazar@terra.es

HACEDOR AIRÉN 2011 B
100% airén.

81

HACEDOR CENCIBEL 2011 T
100% cencibel.

81

VIHUCAS

Mayor, 3
45860 Villacañas (Toledo)
☎: +34 925 160 309 - Fax: +34 925 160 176
info@vihucas.com
www.vihucas.com

VIHUCAS CENCIBEL [TEMPRANILLO] 2010 T

86 Colour: cherry, purple rim. Nose: medium intensity, fruit expression, balanced. Palate: correct, easy to drink.

VIHUCAS COLECCIÓN FAMILIAR 2009 T
100% merlot.

89 Colour: cherry, garnet rim. Nose: balanced, expressive, spicy, dark chocolate. Palate: good structure, fruity, flavourful, full.

VIHUCAS FINCA DETRÉS 2009 T
merlot, tempranillo, graciano.

84

VIHUCAS MERLOT 18 MESES 2008 TR
merlot.

88 Colour: deep cherry, garnet rim. Nose: balanced, powerfull, creamy oak, sweet spices, ripe fruit. Palate: fruity, flavourful, round tannins.

VIHUCAS QUINCE 2007 T ROBLE

87 Colour: cherry, garnet rim. Nose: warm, ripe fruit, dark chocolate, sweet spices. Palate: fruity, flavourful, ripe fruit, long.

VIHUCAS DOBLE 08/09 T
merlot.

88 Colour: bright cherry. Nose: ripe fruit, sweet spices, creamy oak, expressive. Palate: flavourful, fruity, toasty, round tannins.

VINÍCOLA DE CASTILLA

Pol. Ind. Calle I, s/n
13200 Manzanares (Ciudad Real)
☎: +34 926 647 800 - Fax: +34 926 610 466
nacional@vinicoladecastilla.com
www.vinicoladecastilla.com

SEÑORÍO DE GUADIANEJA SAUVIGNON BLANC 2011 B
100% sauvignon blanc.

82

SEÑORÍO DE GUADIANEJA CHARDONNAY 2011 B
chardonnay.

82

SEÑORÍO DE GUADIANEJA MACABEO 2011 B
macabeo.

82

SEÑORÍO DE GUADIANEJA VERDEJO 2011 B
100% verdejo.

75

SEÑORÍO DE GUADIANEJA SYRAH 2011 T
100% syrah.

86 Colour: cherry, purple rim. Nose: ripe fruit, warm, faded flowers. Palate: warm, correct, flavourful.

SEÑORÍO DE GUADIANEJA TEMPRANILLO 2011 T
100% tempranillo.

85 Colour: cherry, purple rim. Nose: red berry notes, ripe fruit, wild herbs. Palate: spicy, warm, easy to drink.

SEÑORÍO DE GUADIANEJA CABERNET SAUVIGNON 2011 T
cabernet sauvignon.

85 Colour: cherry, purple rim. Nose: red berry notes, ripe fruit, scrubland. Palate: flavourful, fruity, good acidity.

SEÑORÍO DE GUADIANEJA MERLOT 2011 T
100% merlot.

85 Colour: cherry, purple rim. Nose: scrubland, ripe fruit, floral. Palate: fine bitter notes, balsamic, flavourful.

SEÑORÍO DE GUADIANEJA 2007 TC
tempranillo.

85 Colour: cherry, garnet rim. Nose: ripe fruit, spicy, toasty, fine reductive notes. Palate: powerful, flavourful, toasty.

SEÑORÍO DE GUADIANEJA CABERNET 2004 TGR
cabernet sauvignon.

86 Colour: light cherry, orangey edge. Nose: old leather, spicy, fruit liqueur notes. Palate: spicy, reductive nuances.

GUADIANEJA RESERVA ESPECIAL 2003 TR
tempranillo.

85 Colour: deep cherry. Nose: medium intensity, spicy, ripe fruit. Palate: long, spicy, correct, fine bitter notes.

VINÍCOLA DE TOMELLOSO

Ctra. Toledo - Albacete, Km. 130,8
13700 Tomelloso (Ciudad Real)
☎: +34 926 513 004 - Fax: +34 926 538 001
vinicola@vinicolatomelloso.com
www.vinicolatomelloso.com

AÑIL 2011 B
100% macabeo.

87 Colour: bright straw. Nose: floral, citrus fruit, fresh. Palate: correct, flavourful, fruity, easy to drink, good acidity.

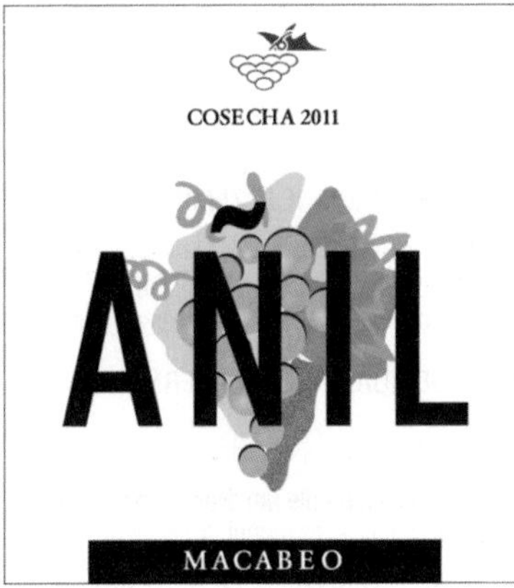

GAZATE SAUVIGNON BLANC 2011 B
100% sauvignon blanc.

86 Colour: bright straw. Nose: dried flowers, dried herbs, fruit expression. Palate: easy to drink, fine bitter notes, fresh, flavourful.

GAZATE VERDEJO 2011 B
100% verdejo.

83

TORRE DE GAZATE AIRÉN 2011 B
100% airén.

82

FINCA CERRADA 2011 RD
100% tempranillo.

84

TORRE DE GAZATE 2011 RD
100% cabernet sauvignon.

83

TORRE DE GAZATE 2006 TC
60% tempranillo, 40% cabernet sauvignon.

84

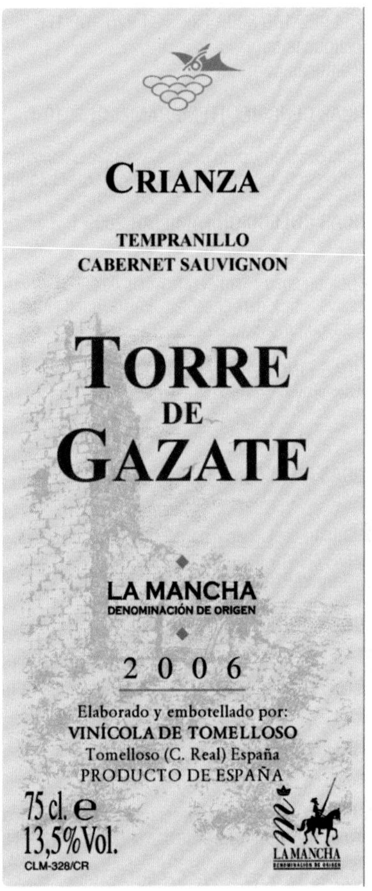

GAZATE MERLOT 2011 T
100% merlot.

86 Colour: cherry, purple rim. Nose: red berry notes, ripe fruit, fragrant herbs. Palate: light-bodied, fresh, fruity, easy to drink.

TORRE DE GAZATE CENCIBEL 2011 T
100% tempranillo.

85 Colour: cherry, purple rim. Nose: fresh fruit, red berry notes, floral. Palate: flavourful, fruity, good acidity, grainy tannins.

GAZATE SYRAH 2011 T
100% syrah.

85 Colour: cherry, purple rim. Nose: red berry notes, fruit liqueur notes, scrubland. Palate: powerful, fruity, fresh.

TORRE DE GAZATE 2010 T ROBLE
100% tempranillo.

86 Colour: bright cherry. Nose: ripe fruit, sweet spices, creamy oak, expressive. Palate: flavourful, fruity, toasty, round tannins.

FINCA CERRADA 2006 TC
tempranillo, cabernet sauvignon, syrah.

85 Colour: cherry, garnet rim. Nose: ripe fruit, spicy, toasty. Palate: powerful, flavourful, toasty, round tannins.

TORRE DE GAZATE 2002 TR
60% cabernet sauvignon, 40% tempranillo.

85 Colour: dark-red cherry, orangey edge. Nose: medium intensity, balanced, old leather, spicy, balsamic herbs. Palate: flavourful, full.

TORRE DE GAZATE 2000 TGR
100% cabernet sauvignon.

83

MANTOLÁN ESP
100% macabeo.

83

VINOS ALMAGUER

Sol, 11
45880 Corral de Almaguer (Toledo)
☎: +34 925 191 143
gonzalez@estudio880.com
www.vinos880.com

880 VIURA 2011 B
viura.

84

880 TEMPRANILLO 2011 T
tempranillo.

87 Colour: cherry, purple rim. Nose: floral, red berry notes, ripe fruit, lactic notes. Palate: flavourful, fruity, good acidity, round tannins.

VINOS COLOMAN

Goya, 17
13620 Pedro Muñoz (Ciudad Real)
☎: +34 926 586 410 - Fax: +34 926 586 656
coloman@satcoloman.com
www.satcoloman.com

BESANA REAL MACABEO 2011 B
100% macabeo.

77

BESANA REAL 2011 RD
100% tempranillo.

84

BESANA REAL TEMPRANILLO 2011 T
100% tempranillo.

86 Colour: cherry, purple rim. Nose: expressive, fresh fruit, red berry notes, floral. Palate: flavourful, fruity, fine bitter notes.

BESANA REAL 2009 TC
100% tempranillo.

87 Colour: cherry, purple rim. Nose: red berry notes, ripe fruit, creamy oak. Palate: long, powerful, flavourful.

BESANA REAL SYRAH 2008 T ROBLE
100% syrah.

85 Colour: cherry, garnet rim. Nose: ripe fruit, creamy oak, spicy. Palate: ripe fruit, long, correct.

BESANA REAL CABERNET SAUVIGNON 2007 T ROBLE
100% cabernet sauvignon.

82

VIÑEDOS MEJORANTES

Ctra. de Villafranca, Km. 2
45860 Villacañas (Toledo)
☎: +34 925 201 036 - Fax: +34 925 200 023
portillejo@portillejo.com
www.portillejo.es

PORTILLEJO MERLOT 2009 T ROBLE
100% merlot.

84

PORTILLEJO CABERNET SAUVIGNON 2009 T ROBLE
100% cabernet sauvignon.

81

PORTILLEJO 6675 2006 TC
100% cabernet sauvignon.

86 Colour: cherry, garnet rim. Nose: ripe fruit, spicy, toasty, balsamic herbs. Palate: powerful, flavourful, toasty, round tannins.

PORTILLEJO CABERNET SAUVIGNON 2005 TC
100% cabernet sauvignon.

85 Colour: cherry, garnet rim. Nose: ripe fruit, spicy, woody, balsamic herbs. Palate: powerful, flavourful, toasty.

PORTILLEJO CABERNET SAUVIGNON 2003 TR
100% cabernet sauvignon.

83

VIÑEDOS Y BODEGAS MUÑOZ

Ctra. Villarrubia, 11
45350 Noblejas (Toledo)
☎: +34 925 140 070 - Fax: +34 925 141 334
info@bodegasmunoz.com
www.bodegasmunoz.com

ARTERO MACABEO 2011 B
100% macabeo.

83

BLAS MUÑOZ CHARDONNAY 2010 BFB
100% chardonnay.

91 Colour: bright golden. Nose: sweet spices, ripe fruit, fragrant herbs, citrus fruit, creamy oak. Palate: powerful, flavourful, spicy, toasty, balanced.

ARTERO 2011 RD
100% tempranillo.

83

ARTERO TEMPRANILLO 2011 T
100% tempranillo.

85 Colour: cherry, purple rim. Nose: lactic notes, red berry notes, macerated fruit, floral. Palate: flavourful, fresh, correct.

ARTERO 2009 TC
50% merlot, 50% tempranillo.

88 Colour: bright cherry. Nose: ripe fruit, sweet spices, creamy oak, toasty. Palate: flavourful, fruity, toasty, round tannins.

ARTERO MERLOT 2007 TR
100% merlot.

88 Colour: cherry, garnet rim. Nose: ripe fruit, spicy, creamy oak, toasty, complex. Palate: powerful, flavourful, toasty, round tannins.

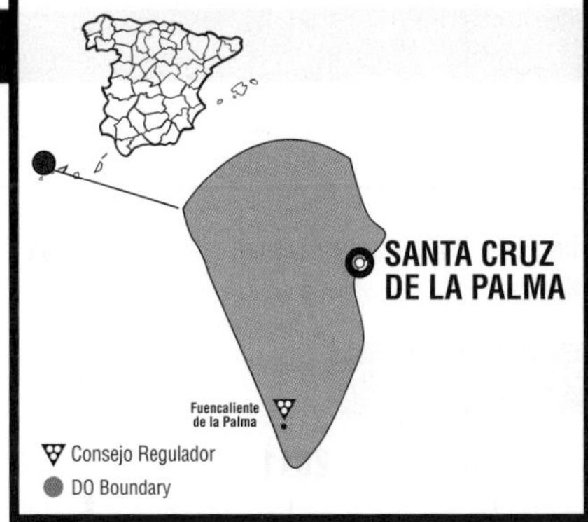

LOCATION:

The production area covers the whole island of San Miguel de La Palma, and is divided into three distinct sub-regions: Hoyo de Mazo, Fuencaliente and Northern La Palma.

CLIMATE:

Variable according to the altitude and the direction that the vineyards face. The relief is a fundamental aspect in La Palma, seeing as it gives rise to different climates and microclimates; one must not forget that it has the highest altitudes in relation to surface area of all the Canary Islands. Nevertheless, as it is situated in the Atlantic, it benefits from the effects of the trade winds (humid and from the northwest), which temper the temperatures and tone down the climatic contrasts.

SOIL:

The vineyards are situated at altitudes of between 200 m and 1,400 m above sea level in a coastal belt ranging in width which surrounds the whole island. Due to the ragged topography, the vineyards occupy the steep hillsides in the form of small terraces. The soil is mainly of volcanic origin.

GRAPE VARIETIES:

WHITE: *Malvasía, Güal and Verdello* (main); *Albillo, Bastardo Blanco, Bermejuela, Bujariego, Burra Blanca, Forastera Blanca, Listán Blanco, Moscatel, Pedro Ximénez, Sabro* and *Torrontés.*
RED: *Negramol* (main), *Listán Negro* (Almuñeco), *Bastardo Negro, Malvasía Rosada, Moscatel Negro, Tintilla, Castellana, Listán Prieto* and *Vijariego Negro.*

SUB-REGIONS:

Hoyo de Mazo: It comprises the municipal districts of Villa de Mazo, Breña Baja, Breña Alta and Santa Cruz de La Palma, at altitudes of between 200 m and 700 m. The vines grow over the terrain on hillsides covered with volcanic stone ('Empedrados') or with volcanic gravel ('Picón Granado'). White and mainly red varieties are grown.
Fuencaliente: It comprises the municipal districts of Fuencaliente, El Paso, Los Llanos de Aridane and Tazacorte. The vines grow over terrains of volcanic ash at altitudes of between 200 m and 1900 m. The white varieties and the sweet Malvasia stand out.
Northern La Palma: Situated at an altitude of between 100 m and 200 m, It comprises the municipal areas of Puntallana, San Andrés and Sauces, Barlovento, Garafía, Puntagorda and Tijarafe. The region is richer in vegetation and the vines grow on trellises and using the goblet system. The traditional 'Tea' wines are produced here.

CONSEJO REGULADOR
Acosta Gómez, 7 - 38740 Fuencaliente (La Palma) - ☎: +34 922 444 432 - Fax: +34 922 444 404
@ cr.vinoslapalma@terra.es - www.malvasiadelapalma.com

FIGURES:

Vineyard surface: 713 – **Wine-Growers:** 1,200 – **Wineries:** 18 – **2011 Harvest rating:** N/A – **Production:** 668,327 litres – **Market percentages:** 99% domestic. 1% export

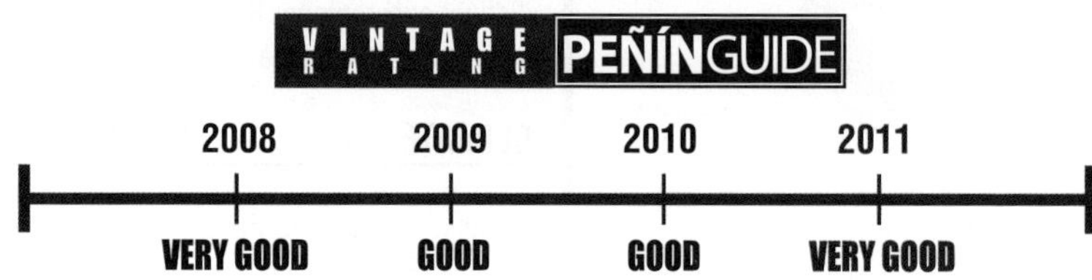

BODEGA PERDOMO S.A.T.

Joaquina, 12 (Las Tricias)
38738 Garafia (La Palma)
☎: +34 922 400 089 - Fax: +34 922 400 689

PIEDRA JURADA 2011 B

87 Colour: bright straw. Nose: fresh fruit, citrus fruit, wild herbs, medium intensity. Palate: flavourful, good acidity, fine bitter notes, balanced.

BODEGAS CARBALLO

Ctra. a Las Indias de la Palma, 74
38740 Fuencaliente de La Palma
(Santa Cruz de Tenerife)
☎: +34 922 444 140 - Fax: +34 922 211 744
info@bodegascarballo.com
www.bodegascarballo.com

MALVASÍA DULCE CARBALLO 2009 B
malvasía.

93 Colour: old gold, amber rim. Nose: spicy, candied fruit, tobacco, white flowers. Palate: flavourful, unctuous, balanced, long.

MALVASÍA DULCE CARBALLO 1997 B
malvasía.

97 Colour: light mahogany. Nose: complex, expressive, candied fruit, floral, acetaldehyde, caramel, pattiserie, aromatic coffee. Palate: concentrated, balanced, unctuous.

BODEGAS NOROESTE DE LA PALMA

Bellido Alto, s/n
38780 Tijarafe (Santa Cruz de Tenerife)
☎: +34 922 491 075 - Fax: +34 922 491 075
administracion@vinosveganorte.com
www.vinosveganorte.com

VEGA NORTE ALBILLO 2011 B

90 Colour: bright straw. Nose: fresh, fresh fruit, white flowers, expressive. Palate: flavourful, fruity, good acidity, balanced, fine bitter notes.

VEGA NORTE 2011 B
listán blanco, albillo.

89 Colour: bright straw. Nose: medium intensity, floral, citrus fruit, fresh fruit, wild herbs. Palate: fruity, flavourful, fine bitter notes.

VEGA NORTE 2011 RD

88 Colour: rose, bright. Nose: expressive, fruit expression, rose petals. Palate: balanced, powerful, flavourful, good acidity.

VEGA NORTE 2011 T

87 Colour: cherry, purple rim. Nose: medium intensity, red berry notes, ripe fruit, neat, warm. Palate: good structure, flavourful, long.

VEGA NORTE "VINO DE TEA" T
negramoll.

88 Colour: light cherry, purple rim. Nose: balanced, fruit expression, floral, balsamic herbs, fragrant herbs. Palate: fruity, easy to drink, good finish.

BODEGAS TAMANCA

Ctra. Gral. Tamanca, 75
38750 El Paso (Santa Cruz de Tenerife)
☎: +34 922 494 155 - Fax: +34 922 494 296
bioaad@telefonica.net

TAMANCA 2011 B

88 Colour: bright straw. Nose: balanced, scrubland, fresh fruit, wild herbs. Palate: flavourful, fruity, balanced, good acidity.

TAMANCA SABRO 2011 B

87 Colour: old gold. Nose: candied fruit, jasmine, expressive, pattiserie. Palate: flavourful, rich, fruity, balsamic.

TAMANCA MALVASÍA 2008 B

90 Colour: old gold, amber rim. Nose: medium intensity, balanced, floral, candied fruit, varietal. Palate: flavourful, fruity.

TAMANCA PEDREGAL 2011 T BARRICA

86 Colour: light cherry, garnet rim. Nose: scrubland, balsamic herbs, ripe fruit, spicy. Palate: flavourful, fruity, good acidity.

BODEGAS TENEGUÍA

Los Canarios, s/n
38740 Fuencaliente de La Palma
(Santa Cruz de Tenerife)
☎: +34 922 444 078 - Fax: +34 922 444 394
enologia@vinosteneguia.com
www.vinosteneguia.com

TENEGUÍA SABRO DULCE 2011 B

91 Colour: old gold, amber rim. Nose: candied fruit, dry nuts, faded flowers, toasty. Palate: flavourful, rich, full, good acidity.

TENEGUÍA MALVASÍA AROMÁTICA 2011 B
malvasía.

89 Colour: bright golden. Nose: medium intensity, balanced, candied fruit, overripe fruit, white flowers. Palate: flavourful, fruity, unctuous.

TENEGUÍA LISTÁN BLANCO 2011 B
listán blanco.

86 Colour: bright straw. Nose: medium intensity, fresh fruit, citrus fruit. Palate: balanced, fruity, good acidity.

TENEGUÍA LA GOTA 2011 B

86 Colour: bright straw. Nose: balanced, fresh, medium intensity. Palate: fruity, fresh, fine bitter notes, easy to drink.

TENEGUÍA 2011 B

85 Colour: bright straw. Nose: floral, fresh, balanced. Palate: flavourful, fruity, good acidity, correct, easy to drink.

TENEGUÍA MALVASÍA 2010 BFB

86 Colour: bright yellow. Nose: candied fruit, sweet spices, honeyed notes, floral. Palate: fruity, flavourful.

TENEGUÍA MALVASÍA BOTRYTIS PARCIAL 2008 B
malvasía.

92 Colour: old gold, amber rim. Nose: balanced, sweet spices, candied fruit, honeyed notes, cocoa bean. Palate: flavourful, balanced, long.

TENEGUÍA MALVASÍA DULCE 2006 B RESERVA
malvasía.

93 Colour: light mahogany. Nose: neat, expressive, candied fruit, acetaldehyde, sweet spices, pattiserie, cocoa bean. Palate: balanced, flavourful, unctuous, long.

TENEGUÍA MALVASÍA DULCE 1996 B RESERVA

95 Colour: light mahogany. Nose: candied fruit, pattiserie, caramel, sweet spices, acetaldehyde, dark chocolate. Palate: flavourful, full, good structure, balanced.

TENEGUÍA NEGRAMOLL 2011 T
negramoll.

83

EUFROSINA PÉREZ RODRÍGUEZ

Briesta, 3- El Castillo
38787 El Castillo (La Palma)
☎: +34 922 400 447
adali_12@msn.com

EL NÍSPERO 2011 B

91 Colour: bright straw. Nose: fresh fruit, neat, varietal, citrus fruit, white flowers. Palate: powerful, flavourful, fruity, balanced, fine bitter notes.

JUAN JESÚS PÉREZ Y ADRIÁN

Bajada al Puerto de Santo Domingo
38787 Garafia (Santa Cruz de Tenerife)
☎: +34 618 309 374
tagalguen@hotmail.com

TAGALGUÉN 2011 B
albillo, listán blanco.

88 Colour: bright straw. Nose: white flowers, fresh fruit, candied fruit, fresh. Palate: light-bodied, fresh, fruity, flavourful.

TAGALGUÉN 2011 T
listán negro, tintilla.

88 Colour: cherry, garnet rim. Nose: scrubland, ripe fruit, earthy notes. Palate: fine bitter notes, powerful, flavourful, spicy.

JUAN MATÍAS TORRES

Ciudad Real, 10- Los Canarios
38740 Fuentecaliente de la Palma
(Santa Cruz de Tenerife)
☎: +34 922 444 219
bodega@matiasitorres.com
www.matiastorres.com

MATÍAS TORRES ALBILLO 2011 B
albillo.

90 Colour: bright straw. Nose: expressive, fragrant herbs, fresh fruit, balanced, floral. Palate: balanced, fine bitter notes, easy to drink, good acidity.

MATIAS I TORRES MALVASÍA AROMÁTICA 2010 B
malvasía.

93 Colour: old gold, amber rim. Nose: dried fruit, expressive, balanced, varietal, honeyed notes. Palate: flavourful, balanced, long.

VID SUR DULCE 2008 B
malvasía.

93 Colour: old gold, amber rim. Nose: expressive, candied fruit, honeyed notes, complex, varietal. Palate: balanced, good acidity, complex.

VID SUR DULCE 2006 B
malvasía.

93 Colour: old gold, amber rim. Nose: balanced, expressive, toasty, honeyed notes. Palate: good structure, flavourful, full.

MATÍAS I TORRES NEGRAMOLL 2011 T
negramoll.

80

ONÉSIMA PÉREZ RODRÍGUEZ

Las Tricias
38738 Garafia (La Palma)
☎: +34 922 463 481 - Fax: +34 922 463 481
vinosvitega@terra.es

VITEGA ALBILLO 2011 B

89 Colour: bright straw. Nose: fresh, varietal, wild herbs, balanced, medium intensity. Palate: good acidity, correct, balanced, fine bitter notes.

VITEGA 2011 B

85 Colour: bright straw. Nose: white flowers, fresh fruit, medium intensity. Palate: fruity, balanced, good acidity.

DO LANZAROTE

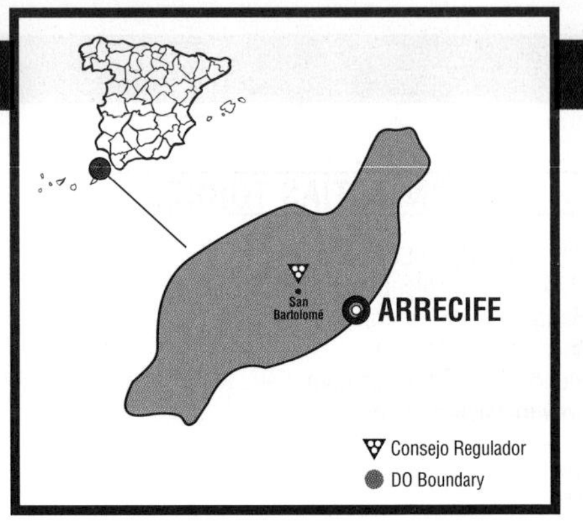

LOCATION:

On the island of Lanzarote. The production area covers the municipal areas of Tinajo, Yaiza, San Bartolomé, Haría and Teguise.

CLIMATE:

Dry subtropical in nature, with low rainfall (about 200 mm per year) which is spread out irregularly throughout the year. On occasions, the Levante wind (easterly), characterised by its low humidity and which carries sand particles from the African continent, causes a considerable increase in the temperatures.

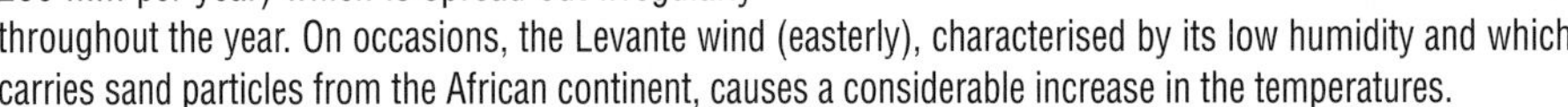

SOIL:

Volcanic in nature (locally known as 'Picón'). In fact, the cultivation of vines is made possible thanks to the ability of the volcanic sand to perfectly retain the water from dew and the scant rainfall. The island is relatively flat (the maximum altitude is 670 m) and the most characteristic form of cultivation is in 'hollows' surrounded by semicircular walls which protect the plants from the wind. This singular trainig system brings about an extremaly low density.

GRAPE VARIETIES:

WHITE: *Malvasía* (majority 75%), *Pedro Ximénez, Diego, Listán Blanco, Moscatel, Burrablanca, Breval.*
RED: *Listán Negra* (15%) and *Negramoll.*

FIGURES:

Vineyard surface: 1,976 – **Wine-Growers:** 1,723 – **Wineries:** 17 – **2011 Harvest rating:** Very Good – **Production:** 503,382 – **Market percentages:** 99% domestic. 1% export

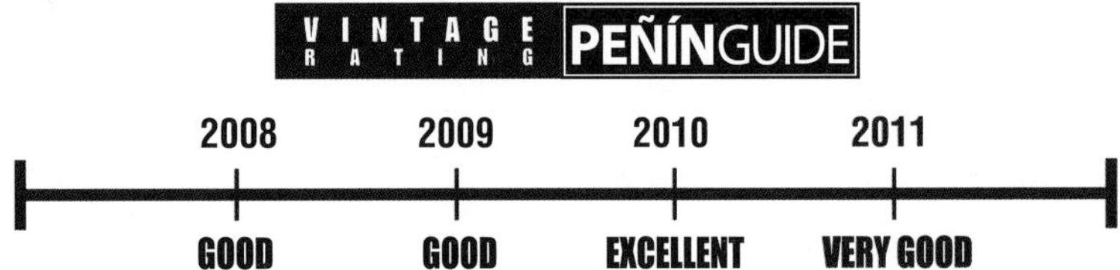

CONSEJO REGULADOR
Arrecife, 9 - 35550 San Bartolomé (Las Palmas) - ☎: +34 928 521 048 - Fax: +34 928 521 049
@ info@dolanzarote.com - www.dolanzarote.com

BODEGA LA GERIA

Ctra. de la Geria, Km. 19
35570 Yaiza (Las Palmas de Gran Canaria)
☎: +34 928 171 378 - Fax: +34 928 511 370
bodega@lageria.com
www.lageria.com

MANTO 2011 B
malvasía.

88 Colour: bright straw. Nose: balanced, expressive, varietal, fresh fruit, white flowers. Palate: flavourful, fruity, long, good acidity.

LA GERIA 2011 RD
listán negro.

81

LA GERIA S/C T
listán negro.

84

LA GERIA MALVASÍA S/C DULCE
malvasía.

84

BODEGA MARTINON

Camino del Mentidero, 2
35572 Masdache Tías (Las Palmas)
☎: +34 928 834 160 - Fax: +34 928 834 160
info@bodegasmartinon.com
www.bodegasmartinon.com

MARTINÓN MALVASÍA SECO S/C B

86 Colour: bright yellow. Nose: balanced, medium intensity, white flowers. Palate: flavourful, fruity, good acidity.

MARTINÓN S/C T

84

BODEGA STRATVS

Ctra. La Geria, Km. 18
35570 Yaiza (Las Palmas)
☎: +34 928 809 977 - Fax: +34 928 524 651
bodega@stratvs.com
www.stratvs.com

STRATVS 2007 TC
60% tinta conejera, 40% listán negro.

87 Colour: cherry, garnet rim. Nose: balanced, powerfull, ripe fruit, old leather. Palate: good structure.

STRATVS MALVASÍA NATURALMENTE DULCE S/C B
100% malvasía.

94 Colour: old gold. Nose: elegant, expressive, faded flowers, candied fruit, sweet spices, honeyed notes. Palate: rich, flavourful, long.

STRATVS MOSCATEL LICOR S/C B
moscatel de alejandría.

92 Colour: light mahogany. Nose: candied fruit, expressive, powerfull, sweet spices, pattiserie, caramel. Palate: balanced, unctuous, complex.

STRATVS MALVASÍA SELECCIÓN 2011 B
100% malvasía.

88 Colour: bright yellow. Nose: faded flowers, balanced, slightly evolved. Palate: fruity, balanced, good acidity, flavourful.

STRATVS MOSCATEL SEMIDULCE 2010 B
85% moscatel, 15% diego.

91 Colour: bright yellow. Nose: white flowers, expressive, varietal, neat. Palate: good acidity.

STRATVS MOSCATEL DULCE 2010 B
moscatel de alejandría.

90 Colour: bright yellow. Nose: medium intensity, citrus fruit, floral, varietal. Palate: balanced, good acidity, long.

STRATVS DIEGO SEMIDULCE 2009 B
85% diego, 15% moscatel de alejandría.

89 Colour: bright yellow. Nose: ripe fruit, white flowers, balanced, expressive. Palate: fruity, flavourful, balanced.

STRATVS 2011 RD
100% tinta conejera.

87 Colour: light cherry. Nose: fresh fruit, red berry notes, floral, balanced. Palate: fruity, flavourful, good acidity, correct.

STRATVS 2010 T
40% tinta conejera, 60% listán negro.

90 Colour: cherry, garnet rim. Nose: balanced, expressive, ripe fruit, scrubland. Palate: balanced, fine bitter notes, balsamic.

STRATVS MALVASÍA SECO 2010
100% malvasía.

91 Colour: bright yellow. Nose: white flowers, ripe fruit, balanced, varietal, expressive. Palate: flavourful, rich, fruity, balanced, fine bitter notes, good acidity.

BODEGA VULCANO DE LANZAROTE

Victor Fernández Gopar, 5
35572 Tías (Las Palmas)
☎: +34 928 834 456 - Fax: +34 928 524 384
info@bodegavulcano.es
www.bodegavulcano.es

VULCANO DOLCE 2011 B
moscatel de alejandría.

90 Colour: bright yellow. Nose: candied fruit, honeyed notes, varietal, pattiserie. Palate: flavourful, balanced, unctuous.

VULCANO DE LANZAROTE 2011 B
malvasía.

87 Colour: bright straw. Nose: fresh, dried flowers, medium intensity. Palate: fresh, correct, easy to drink.

VULCANO DE LANZAROTE 2011 B
malvasía.

87 Colour: bright straw. Nose: medium intensity, floral, fresh. Palate: flavourful, fruity, good acidity, balanced.

VULCANO DE LANZAROTE 2011 RD
listán negro, negramoll.

84

VULCANO DE LANZAROTE 2011 T
listán negro, negramoll.

85 Colour: cherry, garnet rim. Nose: red berry notes, ripe fruit, sweet spices. Palate: fine bitter notes, flavourful.

BODEGAS GUIGUAN

Avda. Los Volcanes, 116
35560 Tinajo (Las Palmas)
☎: +34 928 840 715 - Fax: +34 928 840 715
bodegaguiguan@hotmail.com
www.bodegasguiguan.com

GUIGUAN MOSCATEL DULCE 2011 B

88 Colour: bright yellow. Nose: balanced, varietal, white flowers, honeyed notes. Palate: fruity, flavourful, rich, long.

GUIGUAN MALVASÍA SECO 2011 B

86 Colour: bright straw. Nose: medium intensity, dried flowers. Palate: fruity, easy to drink, good acidity.

BODEGAS LOS BERMEJOS

Camino a Los Bermejos, 7
35550 San Bartolomé de Lanzarote (Las Palmas)
☎: +34 928 522 463 - Fax: +34 928 522 641
bodegas@losbermejos.com
www.losbermejos.com

BERMEJO MALVASIA NATURALMENTE DULCE S/C B
malvasía.

93 Colour: bright yellow. Nose: complex, expressive, balanced, toasty, candied fruit, acetaldehyde. Palate: balanced, good structure, flavourful.

BERMEJO MOSCATEL NATURALMENTE DULCE S/C B
100% moscatel.

87 Colour: bright yellow. Nose: white flowers, candied fruit, powerfull. Palate: flavourful, rich, sweet, long.

BERMEJO DIEGO 2011 B
100% diego.

87 Colour: bright straw. Nose: balanced, neat, floral, fresh fruit. Palate: good acidity, balanced.

BERMEJO DIEGO ECOLÓGICO 2011 B
100% diego.

87 Colour: bright straw. Nose: medium intensity, fresh, fresh fruit, citrus fruit. Palate: correct, easy to drink, light-bodied.

BERMEJO MALVASÍA 2011 BFB
100% malvasía.

87 Colour: yellow. Nose: white flowers, sweet spices, balanced. Palate: fruity, flavourful, good acidity, correct.

BERMEJO MALVASÍA SEMIDULCE 2011 B
malvasía.

87 Colour: bright straw. Nose: medium intensity, white flowers, fresh. Palate: fruity, correct, good acidity.

BERMEJO MALVASÍA SECO 2011 B
100% malvasía.

86 Colour: bright straw. Nose: medium intensity, fresh, citrus fruit. Palate: flavourful, good acidity, correct.

LISTÁN ROSADO BERMEJO 2011 RD
100% listán negro.

86 Colour: light cherry, bright. Nose: medium intensity, red berry notes, balanced, fresh. Palate: fruity, correct, easy to drink.

BERMEJO LISTÁN NEGRO 2011 T MACERACIÓN CARBÓNICA
100% listán negro.

86 Colour: cherry, purple rim. Nose: red berry notes, expressive, violets. Palate: fruity, easy to drink, good finish.

BERMEJO 2010 T BARRICA
100% listán negro.

87 Colour: cherry, garnet rim. Nose: ripe fruit, spicy, powerfull. Palate: correct, fruity, flavourful.

BERMEJO MALVASIA 2010 BN
100% malvasía.

86 Colour: bright yellow. Nose: powerfull, fine lees, faded flowers, dry nuts. Palate: long, easy to drink, good acidity.

BERMEJO ROSADO BN
100% listán negro.

84

BODEGAS RUBICÓN

Ctra. Teguise - Yaiza, 2
35570 La Geria - Yaiza (Las Palmas)
☎: +34 928 173 708
bodegasrubicon@gmail.com
www.vinosrubicon.com

RUBICÓN SECO 2011 B
malvasía.

88 Colour: bright straw. Nose: medium intensity, fresh fruit, white flowers. Palate: correct, flavourful, good finish.

RUBICÓN MOSCATEL 2011 B
moscatel.

88 Colour: bright yellow. Nose: medium intensity, varietal, fresh, white flowers. Palate: balanced, ripe fruit, long.

AMALIA 2011 B
malvasía.

87 Colour: bright straw. Nose: fresh fruit, white flowers, varietal. Palate: balanced, flavourful, fruity, good acidity.

RUBICÓN SEMIDULCE 2011 B
malvasía, moscatel.

87 Colour: bright straw. Nose: candied fruit, floral, citrus fruit, toasty. Palate: fruity, flavourful, good acidity, fine bitter notes.

SWEET GOLD 2009 B

91 Colour: bright yellow. Nose: balanced, expressive, white flowers, sweet spices, honeyed notes. Palate: rich, flavourful, full.

EL GRIFO

Lugar de El Grifo, s/n
35550 San Bartolomé (Las Palmas de Gran Canaria)
☎: +34 928 524 036 - Fax: +34 928 832 634
malvasia@elgrifo.com
www.elgrifo.com

EL GRIFO CANARI DULCE DE LICOR S/C B
100% malvasía.

95 Colour: old gold, amber rim. Nose: pattiserie, complex, expressive, candied fruit, acetaldehyde, floral, sweet spices. Palate: flavourful, elegant, rich, full.

EL GRIFO MALVASÍA SECO COLECCIÓN 2011 B
100% malvasía.

88 Colour: bright yellow. Nose: balanced, fresh, white flowers. Palate: balanced, fine bitter notes, good acidity.

EL GRIFO MALVASÍA 2011 BFB
100% malvasía.

88 Colour: bright yellow. Nose: balanced, ripe fruit, sweet spices, creamy oak, white flowers. Palate: fruity, flavourful, good acidity.

EL GRIFO 2011 T
100% listán negro.

89 Colour: cherry, purple rim. Nose: red berry notes, balanced, expressive, violets. Palate: fruity, flavourful, long, balanced, good acidity.

ARIANA 2010 T
60% listán negro, 40% syrah.

93 Colour: deep cherry, purple rim. Nose: red berry notes, ripe fruit, wild herbs, sweet spices. Palate: flavourful, fruity, correct.

EL GRIFO MALVASÍA COLECCIÓN 2011 SEMIDULCE
100% malvasía.

88 Colour: bright straw. Nose: medium intensity, balanced, varietal, floral, fresh. Palate: flavourful, fruity, good acidity, balanced.

DO MÁLAGA Y SIERRAS DE MÁLAGA

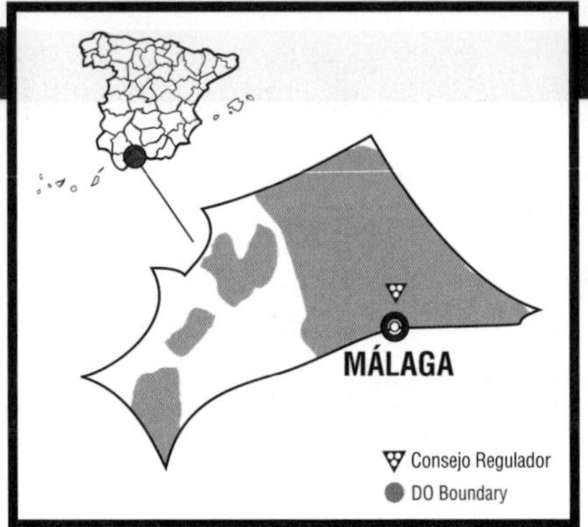

LOCATION:

In the province of Málaga. It covers 54 municipal areas along the coast (in the vicinity of Málaga and Estepona) and inland (along the banks of the river Genil), together with the new sub-region of Serranía de Ronda, a region to which the two new municipal districts of Cuevas del Becerro and Cortes de la Frontera have been added.

CLIMATE:

Varies depending on the production area. In the northern region, the summers are short with high temperatures, and the average rainfall is in the range of 500 mm; in the region of Axarquía, protected from the northerly winds by the mountain ranges and facing south, the climate is somewhat milder due to the influence of the Mediterranean; whilst in the west, the climate can be defined as dry subhumid.

SOIL:

It varies from red Mediterranean soil with limestone components in the northern region to decomposing slate on steep slopes of the Axarquía.

GRAPE VARIETIES:

WHITE: DO Málaga: *Pedro Ximénez* and *Moscatel*; DO Sierras de Málaga: *Chardonnay, Moscatel, Pedro Ximénez, Macabeo*, *Sauvignon Blanc* and *Colombard*.
RED (only DO Sierras de Málaga): *Romé, Cabernet Sauvignon*, *Merlot, Syrah, Tempranillo, Petit Verdot*.

FIGURES:

Vineyard surface: 1,305 – **Wine-Growers:** 470 – **Wineries:** 37 – **2011 Harvest rating:** N/A – **Production:** 2,750,000 litres – **Market percentages:** 60% domestic. 40% export

TYPOLOGY OF CLASSIC WINES:

A) LIQUEUR WINES: from 15 to 22% vol.
B) NATURAL SWEET WINES: from 15 to 22 % vol. obtained from the *Moscatel* or *Pedro Ximénez* varieties, from musts with a minimum sugar content of 244 grams/litre.

CONSEJO REGULADOR
Plaza de los Viñeros,1 - 29008 Málaga - ☎: +34 952 227 990 - Fax: +34 952 227 990
@ info@vinomalaga.com - www.vinomalaga.com

C) NATURALLY SWEET WINES (with the same varieties, over 13% vol. and from musts with 300 grams of sugar/litre) and still wines (from 10 to 15% vol.).
Depending on their ageing:

- **Málaga Joven:** Unaged still wines.
- **Málaga Pálido:** Unaged non-still wines.
- **Málaga:** Wines aged for between 6 and 24 months.
- **Málaga Noble:** Wines aged for between 2 and 3 years.
- **Málaga Añejo:** Wines aged for between 3 and 5 years.
- **Málaga Trasañejo:** Wines aged for over 5 years.

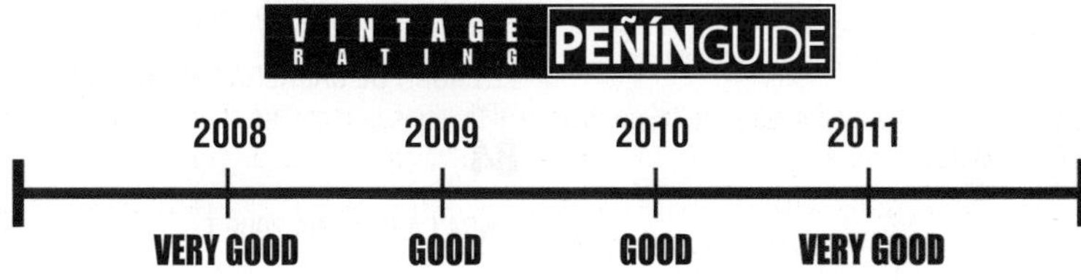

BODEGA ANTIGUA CASA DE GUARDIA

Ctra. Olias - Comares- El Romerillo
29197 (Málaga)
☎: +34 952 030 714 - Fax: +34 952 252 150
info@casadeguardia.com
www.casadeguardia.com

VERDIALES CR
100% pedro ximénez.

87 Colour: light mahogany. Nose: candied fruit, honeyed notes, pattiserie. Palate: balanced, spirituous, unctuous, long.

ISABEL II TRASAÑEJO
100% moscatel de alejandría.

93 Colour: mahogany. Nose: nose:tic coffee, creamy oak, sweet spices, roasted almonds, candied fruit. Palate: flavourful, full, long.

PAJARETE 1908 VINO DE LICOR
100% pedro ximénez.

87 Colour: light mahogany. Nose: fruit liqueur notes, sweet spices, dark chocolate, roasted almonds. Palate: correct, sweet, rich, good finish.

VERDIALES SECO VINO DE LICOR
100% pedro ximénez.

87 Colour: light mahogany. Nose: spicy, toasty, dry nuts, candied fruit, medium intensity, caramel. Palate: flavourful, complex.

PEDRO XIMENEZ 1908 VINO DE LICOR
100% pedro ximénez.

86 Colour: mahogany. Nose: sweet spices, nose:tic coffee, caramel. Palate: fruity, sweet, easy to drink, balanced.

VERDIALES CONARTE VINO DE LICOR DULCE
70% pedro ximénez, 30% moscatel de alejandría.

90 Colour: mahogany. Nose: sweet spices, creamy oak, pattiserie, dark chocolate. Palate: flavourful, sweet, rich, spicy.

BODEGA ANTONIO MUÑOZ CABRERA

San Bartolomé, 5
29738 Moclinejo (Málaga)
☎: +34 952 400 594 - Fax: +34 952 400 743
bodega@dimobe.es
www.dimobe.es

EL LAGAR DEL ZAR 2011 T
tempranillo, syrah, romé.

87 Colour: light cherry. Nose: medium intensity, floral, overripe fruit. Palate: rich, sweet.

EL LAGAR DE CABRERA SYRAH 2010 T
syrah.

84

FINCA LA INDIANA 2009 T
petit verdot.

87 Colour: cherry, garnet rim. Nose: ripe fruit, spicy, creamy oak, toasty. Palate: powerful, flavourful, toasty, round tannins.

LAGAR DE CABRERA 2009 TC
syrah.

86 Colour: cherry, garnet rim. Nose: powerfull, spicy, fruit preserve. Palate: long, good acidity.

LAGAR DE CABRERA 2011 MOSCATEL
moscatel de alejandría.

86 Colour: bright straw. Nose: expressive, varietal, jasmine, white flowers. Palate: fruity, easy to drink, good finish.

SEÑORÍO DE BROCHES 2010 MOSCATEL
moscatel de alejandría.

86 Colour: bright yellow. Nose: medium intensity, white flowers, fresh fruit, citrus fruit. Palate: rich, flavourful, sweet, balanced.

ZUMBRAL 2009 MOSCATEL
moscatel de alejandría.

85 Colour: old gold. Nose: caramel, sweet spices, honeyed notes. Palate: flavourful, rich, easy to drink.

RUJAQ ANDALUSI TRASAÑEJO
moscatel de alejandría.

88 Colour: mahogany. Nose: balanced, candied fruit, honeyed notes, sweet spices, pattiserie. Palate: unctuous, balanced, complex.

BODEGA CUESTA LA VIÑA

Antigua Ctra. Ronda-Sevilla, km. 21,6. A-2300
Montecorto
29400 Ronda (Málaga)
☎: +34 629 589 336 - Fax: +34 952 870 719
vinosjorgebonet@gmail.com

JORGE BONET 2010 T
syrah.

87 Colour: cherry, garnet rim. Nose: medium intensity, ripe fruit, sweet spices, cocoa bean. Palate: flavourful, good structure, spicy.

JORGE BONET TSMC 2007 T

86 Colour: cherry, garnet rim. Nose: medium intensity, fruit preserve, spicy, cocoa bean. Palate: fruity, easy to drink.

BODEGA DOÑA FELISA

Apartado 432
29400 Ronda (Málaga)
☎: +34 951 166 033 - Fax: +34 951 166 033
jlosantos@chinchillawine.com
www.chinchillawine.com

CHINCHILLA SEIS + SEIS 2009 T ROBLE
tempranillo, syrah.

84

CHINCHILLA 2007 T
cabernet sauvignon, merlot.

88 Colour: bright cherry. Nose: ripe fruit, sweet spices, creamy oak. Palate: flavourful, fruity, toasty, round tannins.

BODEGA GONZALO BELTRÁN

Finca La Nogalera, Hoya de los Molinos
29670 San Pedro de Alcántara (Málaga)
☎: +34 629 455 558
info@bodegagonzalobeltran.com
www.bodegagonzalobeltran.com

PEREZOSO 2010 T
100% syrah.

87 Colour: cherry, garnet rim. Nose: ripe fruit, powerfull, warm. Palate: flavourful, fruity, correct, good finish.

BODEGA JOAQUÍN FERNÁNDEZ

Finca Los Frutales Paraje de los Frontones
29400 Ronda (Málaga)
☎: +34 665 899 200 - Fax: +34 951 166 043
info@bodegajf.es
www.bodegajf.com

ROSADO FINCA LOS FRUTALES 2011 RD
50% merlot, 50% syrah.

87 Colour: light cherry. Nose: balanced, expressive, ripe fruit, sweet spices. Palate: rich, flavourful, long, spicy, ripe fruit.

FINCA LOS FRUTALES GARNACHA 2010 T
90% garnacha, 10% cabernet sauvignon.

89 Colour: cherry, garnet rim. Nose: ripe fruit, cocoa bean, creamy oak, scrubland. Palate: balanced, ripe fruit, spicy.

HACIENDA VIZCONDESA 2009 T
40% merlot, 40% cabernet sauvignon, 20% syrah.

85 Colour: cherry, garnet rim. Nose: ripe fruit, medium intensity, scrubland. Palate: fruity, easy to drink.

FINCA LOS FRUTALES IGUALADO 2008 T
50% cabernet sauvignon, 20% merlot, 20% syrah, 10% garnacha.

87 Colour: cherry, garnet rim. Nose: medium intensity, ripe fruit, spicy, scrubland. Palate: light-bodied, easy to drink, good finish.

FINCA LOS FRUTALES MERLOT SYRAH 2007 TC
50% merlot, 50% syrah.

86 Colour: cherry, garnet rim. Nose: toasty, woody, medium intensity. Palate: correct, fruity, easy to drink.

BODEGA KIENINGER

Los Frontones, 67
29400 Ronda (Málaga)
☎: +34 952 879 554
martin@bodegakieninger.com
www.bodegakieninger.com

VINANA CUVÉE COUPAGE 2010 T
cabernet sauvignon, cabernet franc, pinot noir, merlot.

91 Colour: cherry, garnet rim. Nose: ripe fruit, spicy, creamy oak, toasty, complex. Palate: powerful, flavourful, toasty, round tannins.

BODEGA LOS BUJEOS

Ctra. Ronda El Burgo, Km 1
29400 Ronda (Málaga)
☎: +34 610 269 422 - Fax: +34 952 161 160
bodegapasoslargos@gmail.com
www.bodegapasoslargos.com

A PASOS 2008 T

90 Colour: bright cherry. Nose: ripe fruit, sweet spices, creamy oak, expressive. Palate: flavourful, fruity, toasty, round tannins.

PASOS LARGOS 2005 T ROBLE
cabernet sauvignon, petit verdot, merlot, syrah.

91 Colour: cherry, garnet rim. Nose: dark chocolate, nose:tic coffee, ripe fruit. Palate: flavourful, good structure, round tannins, spicy.

BODEGA LOS VILLALONES

Médico Luis Peralta, 2
29400 Ronda (Málaga)
☎: +34 628 698 870
isidoro@sierrahidalga.com

MORILLAS 2007 T
tempranillo, cabernet sauvignon, syrah, merlot, petit verdot.

86 Colour: cherry, garnet rim. Nose: ripe fruit, spicy, toasty, balsamic herbs. Palate: fruity, balanced, good acidity.

BODEGA VETAS

Camino Nador " El Baco", s/n
29350 Arriate (Málaga)
☎: +34 647 177 620
info@bodegavetas.com
www.bodegavetas.com

VETAS PETIT VERDOT 2006 T
100% petit verdot.

93 Colour: deep cherry, garnet rim. Nose: elegant, balanced, creamy oak, sweet spices, dried herbs. Palate: good structure, round tannins, long.

VETAS SELECCIÓN 2006 T
cabernet franc, cabernet sauvignon, petit verdot.

93 Colour: black cherry, garnet rim. Nose: balanced, expressive, ripe fruit, cocoa bean, creamy oak. Palate: flavourful, good structure, fruity, long, round tannins.

VETAS SELECCIÓN 2005 T
cabernet franc, cabernet sauvignon, petit verdot.

93 Colour: cherry, garnet rim. Nose: medium intensity, ripe fruit, scrubland, sweet spices, earthy notes. Palate: balanced, powerful.

VETAS PETIT VERDOT 2004 T
100% petit verdot.

92 Colour: cherry, garnet rim. Nose: expressive, medium intensity, ripe fruit, spicy, mineral. Palate: flavourful, balanced, spicy.

BODEGAS BENTOMIZ

29752 Sayalonga (Málaga)
☎: +34 658 845 285
info.bodegasbentomiz@gmail.com
www.bodegasbentomiz.com

ARIYANAS SECO SOBRE LÍAS 2011 B
moscatel de alejandría.

89 Colour: bright straw. Nose: medium intensity, balanced, white flowers, citrus fruit. Palate: flavourful, fruity, long, balanced.

ARIYANAS TERRUÑO PIZARROSO 2008 B
moscatel de alejandría.

94 Colour: old gold. Nose: candied fruit, honeyed notes, white flowers, sweet spices, citrus fruit. Palate: flavourful, balanced, complex.

ARIYANAS TINTO DE ENSAMBLAJE 2010 T
romé, petit verdot, tempranillo.

88 Colour: deep cherry, garnet rim. Nose: powerfull, fruit expression. Palate: flavourful, balanced, easy to drink.

ARIYANAS NATURALMENTE DULCE 2008 BLANCO DULCE
100% moscatel de alejandría.

92 Colour: bright yellow. Nose: candied fruit, faded flowers, dried herbs. Palate: balanced, rich, long.

BODEGAS EXCELENCIA

Almendra, 40-42
29400 Ronda (Málaga)
☎: +34 952 870 960 - Fax: +34 952 877 002
jlbravo@bodegasexcelencia.com
www.bodegasexcelencia.com

TAGUS 2011 T
cabernet franc.

84

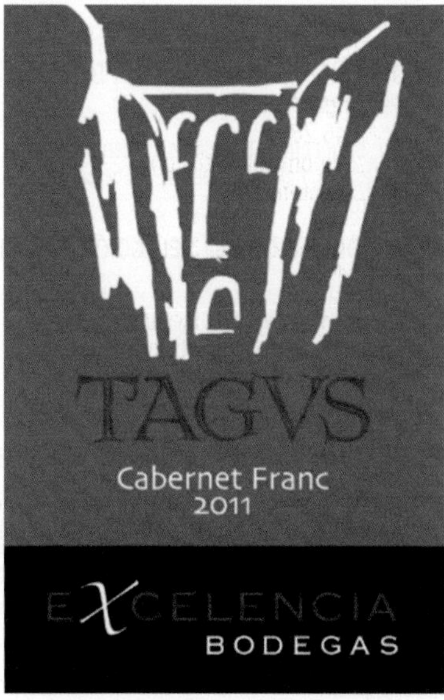

LOS FRONTONES 2008 T
syrah, cabernet franc, cabernet sauvignon, tempranillo.

87 Colour: cherry, garnet rim. Nose: powerfull, fruit preserve, dark chocolate. Palate: fruity, flavourful.

LOS FRONTONES 2009 T
tempranillo, syrah, cabernet franc, cabernet sauvignon.

88 Colour: cherry, garnet rim. Nose: toasty, spicy, ripe fruit. Palate: good structure, flavourful, fruity, balanced.

BODEGAS GARCÍA HIDALGO

Partido Rural Los Morales- LLano de la Cruz
29400 Ronda (Málaga)
☎: +34 670 940 693
info@bodegasgarciahidalgo.es
www.bodegasgarciahidalgo.es

ALCOBACÍN 2010 T ROBLE
cabernet sauvignon, syrah, merlot.

85 Colour: cherry, garnet rim. Nose: toasty, dark chocolate, ripe fruit. Palate: flavourful, fruity, round tannins.

BODEGAS GOMARA

Diseminado Maqueda Alto, 59
29590 Maqueda - Campanillas (Málaga)
☎: +34 952 434 195 - Fax: +34 952 626 312
bodegas@gomara.com
www.gomara.com

MOSCATEL MÁLAGA B
moscatel de alejandría.

86 Colour: old gold. Nose: candied fruit, medium intensity, sweet spices, pattiserie. Palate: unctuous, correct, good finish.

SECO AÑEJO GOMARA
100% pedro ximénez.

86 Colour: light mahogany. Nose: candied fruit, dry nuts, caramel. Palate: flavourful, correct, fine bitter notes.

PAJARETE GOMARA
100% pedro ximénez.

85 Colour: light mahogany. Nose: candied fruit, balanced, fruit liqueur notes, sweet spices. Palate: flavourful, good finish, easy to drink.

MÁLAGA DULCE MÁLAGA
90% pedro ximénez, 10% moscatel de alejandría.

85 Colour: dark mahogany. Nose: dried fruit, fruit liqueur notes, spicy. Palate: rich, flavourful, easy to drink.

LACRIMAE CHRISTI NOBLE SOLERA
90% pedro ximénez, 10% moscatel de alejandría.

87 Colour: dark mahogany. Nose: dried fruit, sweet spices, honeyed notes. Palate: correct, easy to drink.

SECO GOMARA NOBLE
100% pedro ximénez.

86 Colour: bright yellow. Nose: medium intensity, candied fruit, faded flowers, pungent. Palate: flavourful, powerful, long.

GOMARA PEDRO XIMÉNEZ PX
100% pedro ximénez.

85 Colour: dark mahogany. Nose: dried fruit, fruit liqueur notes, caramel, sweet spices. Palate: balanced, good structure, rich.

GRAN GOMARA TRASAÑEJO SOLERA
70% pedro ximénez, 30% moscatel de alejandría.

92 Colour: mahogany. Nose: acetaldehyde, varnish, dark chocolate, sweet spices, fruit liqueur notes. Palate: full, flavourful, complex, long, balanced.

MÁLAGA TRASAÑEJO GOMARA TRASAÑEJO
100% pedro ximénez.

90 Colour: dark mahogany. Nose: balanced, cocoa bean, pattiserie, candied fruit. Palate: flavourful, long, spirituous, complex.

BODEGAS JORGE ORDÓÑEZ & CO

Bartolome Esteban Murillo, 11
29700 Velez-Málaga (Málaga)
☎: +34 952 504 706 - Fax: +34 951 284 796
office@jorge-ordonez.es
www.jorge-ordonez.es

JORGE ORDÓÑEZ & CO BOTANI 2011 B
100% moscatel de alejandría.

92 Colour: bright straw. Nose: fresh, fresh fruit, white flowers, expressive. Palate: flavourful, fruity, balanced, good acidity, round.

JORGE ORDÓÑEZ & CO Nº 1 SELECCIÓN ESPECIAL 2010 B
moscatel de alejandría.

93 Colour: bright straw. Nose: white flowers, fragrant herbs, candied fruit, citrus fruit, elegant. Palate: fresh, fruity, rich, flavourful, round.

JORGE ORDÓÑEZ & CO. Nº3 VIÑAS VIEJAS 2008 B
moscatel de alejandría.

96 Colour: golden. Nose: powerfull, floral, honeyed notes, candied fruit, fragrant herbs. Palate: flavourful, sweet, fresh, fruity, good acidity, long, balanced.

JORGE ORDÓÑEZ & CO Nº 2 VICTORIA 2010 BLANCO DULCE
moscatel de alejandría.

94 Colour: bright yellow. Nose: pattiserie, candied fruit, honeyed notes, floral, mineral, expressive. Palate: fruity, complex, flavourful, good acidity, unctuous, long, sweet, elegant.

BODEGAS LUNARES DE RONDA

Almendra, 3
29400 Ronda (Málaga)
☎: +34 952 877 180
vinos@bodegaslunares.com
www.bodegaslunares.com

ALTOCIELO 2009 T
syrah, cabernet sauvignon.

89 Colour: cherry, garnet rim. Nose: balanced, cocoa bean, dark chocolate, wild herbs. Palate: good structure, flavourful, round tannins, good acidity.

BODEGAS MÁLAGA VIRGEN

Autovía A-92, Málaga-Sevilla, Km. 132
29520 Fuente de Piedra (Málaga)
☎: +34 952 319 454 - Fax: +34 952 359 819
didier.bricout@bodegasmalagavirgen.com
www.bodegasmalagavirgen.com

TRES LEONES S/C B
moscatel de alejandría.

85 Colour: bright yellow. Nose: powerfull, varietal, jasmine, complex. Palate: rich, flavourful, fruity.

BARÓN DE RIVERO 2011 B
chardonnay, pedro ximénez.

84

SECO TRASAÑEJO B

93 Colour: old gold. Nose: toasty, fruit liqueur notes, candied fruit, honeyed notes, sweet spices, acetaldehyde. Palate: full, flavourful, spicy, elegant, fine bitter notes.

PERNALES SYRAH S/C T
syrah.

88 Colour: cherry, garnet rim. Nose: powerfull, ripe fruit, dark chocolate, spicy. Palate: flavourful, fruity, good acidity, balanced.

EL VIVILLO 2010 T
syrah.

83

SOL DE MÁLAGA

88 Colour: dark mahogany. Nose: candied fruit, cocoa bean, sweet spices, creamy oak. Palate: correct, balanced, spicy, good finish.

CHORRERA CREAM AÑEJO

91 Colour: mahogany. Nose: cocoa bean, roasted almonds, pattiserie, candied fruit, complex. Palate: flavourful, rich, good structure, long.

TRAJINERO AÑEJO

89 Colour: old gold. Nose: dark chocolate, sweet spices, pattiserie, varnish, candied fruit. Palate: balanced, round, toasty.

MOSCATEL IBERIA S/C MALAGA

86 Colour: light mahogany. Nose: medium intensity, candied fruit, sweet spices. Palate: fruity, flavourful, sweet, easy to drink.

MOSCATEL 30 AÑOS MOSCATEL

93 Colour: mahogany. Nose: complex, expressive, candied fruit, fruit liqueur notes, honeyed notes, varnish, pattiserie, tobacco. Palate: unctuous, long, spicy, toasty.

MOSCATEL RESERVA DE FAMILIA MOSCATEL

89 Colour: light mahogany. Nose: powerfull, dried fruit, honeyed notes, pattiserie, sweet spices. Palate: unctuous, correct, spicy.

CARTOJAL PÁLIDO

86 Colour: bright straw. Nose: white flowers, medium intensity, citrus fruit. Palate: correct, easy to drink, good finish.

PEDRO XIMÉNEZ RESERVA DE FAMILIA PX

91 Colour: light mahogany. Nose: candied fruit, medium intensity, cocoa bean, varietal. Palate: long, flavourful, sweet, correct.

MÁLAGA VIRGEN PX

87 Colour: mahogany. Nose: medium intensity, sweet spices, candied fruit. Palate: fruity, sweet, good finish.

DON JUAN TRASAÑEJO

93 Colour: dark mahogany. Nose: complex, expressive, nose:tic coffee, caramel, creamy oak, pattiserie. Palate: flavourful, creamy, long.

BODEGAS QUITAPENAS

Ctra. de Guadalmar, 12
29004 Málaga (Málaga)
☎: +34 952 247 595 - Fax: +34 952 105 138
ventas@quitapenas.es
www.quitapenas.es

MÁLAGA PX NOBLE

87 Colour: light mahogany. Nose: pattiserie, caramel, candied fruit, fruit liqueur notes, honeyed notes. Palate: unctuous, flavourful.

MÁLAGA PAJARETE NOBLE

86 Colour: old gold. Nose: balanced, varnish, acetaldehyde, sweet spices. Palate: flavourful, balanced, good finish.

QUITAPENAS MOSCATEL DORADO PÁLIDO

85 Colour: bright golden. Nose: candied fruit, fruit liqueur notes, white flowers, citrus fruit. Palate: rich, flavourful, sweet.

SOL SALERO SOLERA

87 Colour: old gold. Nose: balanced, roasted almonds, sweet spices, creamy oak. Palate: flavourful, correct, good finish.

MÁLAGA ORO VIEJO 5 AÑOS TRASAÑEJO

86 Colour: mahogany. Nose: candied fruit, fruit liqueur notes, dark chocolate, pattiserie, varnish. Palate: full, good structure.

BODEGAS SÁNCHEZ ROSADO

Parcela 47- Polígono 14
29570 Cartama (Málaga)
☎: +34 600 504 302 - Fax: +34 952 213 644
info@bodegassanchezrosado.com
www.bodegassanchezrosado.com

CARTIMA CSXXI 2011 T ROBLE
tempranillo, garnacha, syrah.

85 Colour: cherry, garnet rim. Nose: balanced, ripe fruit, scrubland, sweet spices. Palate: fruity, spicy, easy to drink.

BODEGAS VILORIA

Médico Luis Peralta, 2- Ofic.5
29400 Ronda (Málaga)
☎: +34 637 531 800
bodegasviloria@hotmail.es
www.bodegasviloria.com

LAGAREJO 2011 RD
petit verdot, syrah.

79

LAGAREJO 2011 T
tempranillo.

83 Colour: cherry, garnet rim. Nose: medium intensity, red berry notes, ripe fruit, fragrant herbs. Palate: light-bodied, fruity, easy to drink.

LAGAREJO 2010 T
cabernet sauvignon.

83

LAGAREJO SELECCIÓN 2007 T
petit verdot, cabernet sauvignon, tempranillo, merlot, syrah.

86 Colour: cherry, garnet rim. Nose: powerfull, sweet spices, candied fruit, balsamic herbs, dark chocolate. Palate: fruity, flavourful.

LAGAREJO 2006 T
petit verdot, cabernet sauvignon, tempranillo, merlot, syrah.

86 Colour: bright cherry. Nose: ripe fruit, sweet spices, creamy oak. Palate: flavourful, fruity, toasty, round tannins.

LAGAREJO 2005 T
petit verdot, cabernet sauvignon, tempranillo, merlot, syrah.

86 Colour: cherry, garnet rim. Nose: ripe fruit, toasty, spicy, scrubland, tobacco. Palate: powerful, good structure, ripe fruit.

BODEGAS Y VIÑEDOS CONRAD

Ctra. El Burgo, Km. 4,5
29400 Ronda (Málaga)
☎: +34 672 290 742 - Fax: +34 951 166 035
conrad@vinosconrad.com
www.vinosconrad.com

SAN LORENZO 2010 T
pinot noir, tempranillo.

87 Colour: cherry, garnet rim. Nose: ripe fruit, sweet spices, dried herbs. Palate: flavourful, good acidity, correct.

CRISTINA 2008 T
malbec, cabernet franc.

89 Colour: cherry, garnet rim. Nose: balanced, ripe fruit, sweet spices. Palate: fruity, good structure, balanced.

SOLEÓN 2008 T
cabernet sauvignon, merlot, cabernet franc.

88 Colour: cherry, garnet rim. Nose: spicy, ripe fruit, dark chocolate, medium intensity. Palate: good structure, round tannins.

COMPAÑÍA DE VINOS TELMO RODRÍGUEZ

El Monte
01308 Lanciego (Álava)
☎: +34 945 628 315 - Fax: +34 945 628 314
contact@telmorodriguez.com
www.telmorodriguez.com

MR 2010 B
100% moscatel.

93 Colour: bright yellow. Nose: candied fruit, fruit expression, citrus fruit, white flowers. Palate: flavourful, sweet, fruity, fresh.

MOUNTAIN 2010 B
moscatel.

93 Colour: bright straw. Nose: fresh, fresh fruit, white flowers, varietal. Palate: flavourful, fruity, good acidity, balanced.

MOLINO REAL 2008 B
100% moscatel.

96 Colour: golden. Nose: powerfull, floral, honeyed notes, candied fruit, fragrant herbs. Palate: flavourful, sweet, fresh, fruity, good acidity, long.

CORTIJO LA FUENTE

Avda. La Fuente, 10
29532 Mollina (Málaga)
☎: +34 663 045 906
cortijolafuente@terra.es

CORTIJO LA FUENTE GRAN SOLERA 2002 B
moscatel de alejandría.

85 Colour: mahogany. Nose: balanced, dried fruit, cocoa bean, caramel. Palate: unctuous, balanced, long, fruity.

CORTIJO LA FUENTE 2010 BLANCO AFRUTADO
moscatel.

87 Colour: bright yellow. Nose: expressive, fresh fruit, white flowers. Palate: fruity, balanced, easy to drink.

CORTIJO LA FUENTE 2008 PX
pedro ximénez.

84

CORTIJO LOS AGUILARES

Ctra. Ronda a Campillo, km. 5
29400 Ronda (Málaga)
☎: +34 952 874 457 - Fax: +34 951 166 000
info@cortijolosaguilares.com
www.cortijolosaguilares.com

CORTIJO LOS AGUILARES 2011 RD
33% tempranillo, 33% merlot, 34% petit verdot.

87 Colour: rose, purple rim. Nose: balanced, red berry notes, ripe fruit. Palate: flavourful, ripe fruit, long.

CORTIJO LOS AGUILARES PINOT NOIR 2011 T
pinot noir.

93 Colour: bright cherry, purple rim. Nose: floral, red berry notes, expressive. Palate: flavourful, fruity, good acidity, fine bitter notes. Personality.

CORTIJO LOS AGUILARES 2011 T
54% tempranillo, 28% merlot, 18% syrah.

88 Colour: cherry, purple rim. Nose: balanced, ripe fruit, neat. Palate: flavourful, fruity, balanced.

CORTIJO LOS AGUILARES TADEO 2009 T
100% petit verdot.

94 Colour: cherry, garnet rim. Nose: fruit preserve, sweet spices, cocoa bean, creamy oak. Palate: balanced, long, round tannins.

CORTIJO LOS AGUILARES TADEO 2008 T
petit verdot.

94 Colour: deep cherry, garnet rim. Nose: complex, elegant, expressive, sweet spices. Palate: full, good structure, ripe fruit, long, round tannins.

CORTIJO LOS AGUILARES PAGO EL ESPINO 2008 T
25% tempranillo, 25% merlot, 29% petit verdot, 21% cabernet sauvignon.

91 Colour: cherry, garnet rim. Nose: sweet spices, creamy oak, ripe fruit, cocoa bean. Palate: good structure, ripe fruit, long, good acidity.

DESCALZOS VIEJOS

Finca Descalzos Viejos- Partido de los Molinos, s/n
29400 Ronda (Málaga)
☎: +34 952 874 696 - Fax: +34 952 874 696
info@descalzosviejos.com
www.descalzosviejos.com

DV CHARDONNAY 2010 B
chardonnay.

87 Colour: bright straw. Nose: ripe fruit, spicy, dry nuts. Palate: flavourful, good finish, ripe fruit, rich.

DV DESCALZOS VIEJOS 2009 T
garnacha, syrah, merlot.

84

DV CONARTE 2007 TC
petit verdot, cabernet sauvignon, syrah, merlot.

92 Colour: deep cherry, garnet rim. Nose: medium intensity, creamy oak, sweet spices, ripe fruit. Palate: complex, good structure, flavourful, long, round tannins.

DV DESCALZOS VIEJOS (+) 2007 TC
cabernet sauvignon, graciano, merlot.

88 Colour: cherry, garnet rim. Nose: ripe fruit, spicy, creamy oak, toasty. Palate: powerful, flavourful, round tannins.

FINCA LA MELONERA

Paraje Los Frontones, Camino Ronda-Setenil s/n
29400 Ronda (Malaga)
☎: +34 932 097 514 - Fax: +34 932 011 068
info@lamelonera.com
www.lamelonera.com

PAYOYA NEGRA 2009 T
garnacha, tintilla de rota.

92 Colour: cherry, garnet rim. Nose: balanced, cocoa bean, ripe fruit, earthy notes. Palate: good structure, fruity, long, good acidity, round tannins.

LA DONAIRA

Pza. Portugal, 23
29400 Ronda (Málaga)
☎: +34 678 733 286
info@mapa7g.com
www.ladonaira.com

LA DONAIRA PETIT VERDOT 2010 T
petit verdot.

89 Colour: cherry, garnet rim. Nose: toasty, sweet spices, aged wood nuances. Palate: correct, ripe fruit, round tannins, balanced.

LA DONAIRA PETIT VERDOT CABERNET FRANC 2009 T
petit verdot, cabernet franc.

91 Colour: deep cherry, garnet rim. Nose: sweet spices, creamy oak, cocoa bean, fruit preserve. Palate: full, ripe fruit, toasty, long.

LA DONAIRA CABERNET FRANC 2009 T
cabernet franc.

89 Colour: cherry, garnet rim. Nose: complex, wild herbs, ripe fruit, spicy, cocoa bean, warm. Palate: balanced, round tannins, long.

LA DONAIRA SYRAH CABERNET FRANC 2009 T
syrah, cabernet franc.

89 Colour: cherry, garnet rim. Nose: balanced, ripe fruit, creamy oak, cocoa bean. Palate: powerful, round tannins, balanced.

LA DONAIRA SYRAH 2009 T
syrah.

88 Colour: cherry, garnet rim. Nose: creamy oak, toasty, sweet spices, candied fruit, faded flowers. Palate: good structure, powerful, long.

TIERRAS DE MOLLINA

Avda. de las Américas, s/n- Cortijo Colarte
29532 Mollina (Málaga)
☎: +34 952 841 451 - Fax: +34 952 842 555
ajimena@hojiblanca.es
www.tierrasdemollina.net

CARPE DIEM DULCE NATURAL 2011 B
100% moscatel.

88 Colour: bright straw. Nose: candied fruit, honeyed notes, floral. Palate: flavourful, ripe fruit, sweet.

MONTESPEJO 2011 B
60% lairén, 30% moscatel, 10% doradilla.

87 Colour: bright straw. Nose: fresh fruit, white flowers. Palate: flavourful, fruity, good acidity, balanced, correct.

MONTESPEJO 2011 T
100% syrah.

86 Colour: cherry, purple rim. Nose: fruit expression, floral. Palate: flavourful, fruity, balanced.

MONTESPEJO 2010 T ROBLE
85% syrah, 15% merlot.

85 Colour: cherry, garnet rim. Nose: powerfull, ripe fruit, candied fruit, sweet spices. Palate: long, ripe fruit.

CARPE DIEM MÁLAGA TRASAÑEJO MÁLAGA
90% pedro ximénez, 10% moscatel.

88 Colour: mahogany. Nose: candied fruit, roasted almonds, pattiserie. Palate: rich, correct, balanced, spicy, toasty.

CARPE DIEM MÁLAGA AÑEJO
90% pedro ximénez, 10% moscatel.

87 Colour: mahogany. Nose: candied fruit, honeyed notes, dark chocolate, sweet spices, acetaldehyde. Palate: balanced, rich, flavourful.

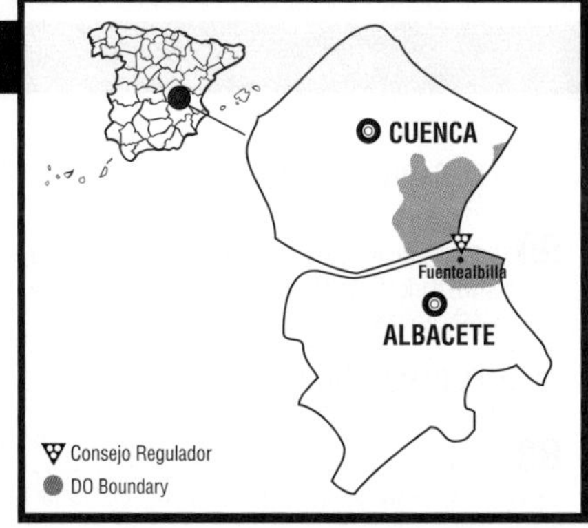

LOCATION:

The production area covers the territory situated in the southeast of the province of Cuenca and the northeast of Albacete, between the rivers Júcar and Cabriel. It comprises 70 municipal districts, 26 of which are in Albacete and the rest in Cuenca.

CLIMATE:

The climate is continental in nature, with cold winters and hot summers, although the cool and humid winds from the Mediterranean during the summer help to lower the temperatures at night, so creating favourable day-night temperature contrasts for a slow ripening of the grapes.

SOIL:

The vineyards are situated at an altitude ranging between 600 and 700 m above sea level. The terrain is mainly flat, except for the ravines outlined by the rivers. Regarding the composition of the terrain, below a clayey surface of gravel or sand, the soil is limy, which is an important quality factor for the region.

GRAPE VARIETIES:

WHITE: *Albillo, Chardonnay, Macabeo, Sauvignon Blanc, Verdejo, Pardillo, Viognier* and *Moscatel de Grano Menudo.*
RED: *Bobal, Cabernet Sauvignon, Cencibel (Tempranillo), Garnacha, Merlot, Monastrell, Moravia Dulce, Syrah, Garnacha Tintorera, Malbec, Moravia agria, Mazuelo, Graciano, Rojal, Frasco (Tinto Velasco), Petit Verdot, Cabernet Franc* and *Pinot Noir.*

FIGURES:

Vineyard surface: 4,674 – **Wine-Growers:** 797 – **Wineries:** 33 – **2011 Harvest rating:** Excellent – **Production:** 26,605,575 litres – **Market percentages:** 20% domestic. 80% export

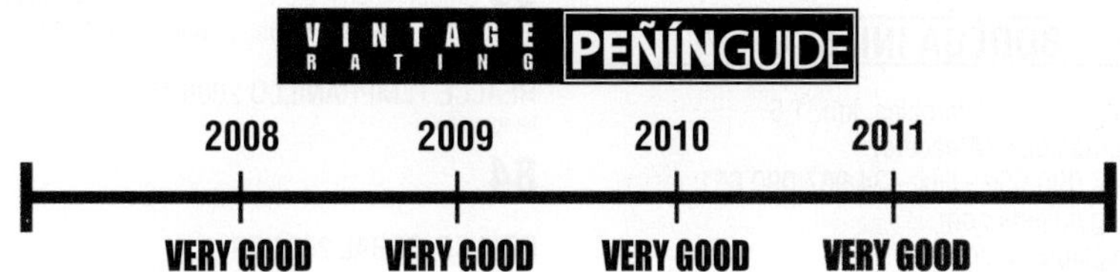

CONSEJO REGULADOR
Matadero, 5 - 02260 Fuentealbilla (Albacete) - ☎: +34 967 477 535 - Fax: +34 967 477 505
@ domanchuela@lamanchuela.es. - www.do-manchuela.com

ALTOLANDÓN

Ctra. N-330, km. 242
16330 Landete (Cuenca)
☎: +34 962 300 662 - Fax: +34 962 300 662
altolandon@altolandon.com
www.altolandon.com

ALTOLANDÓN 2010 BFB
petit manseng, chardonnay.

92 Colour: bright golden. Nose: white flowers, fruit expression, citrus fruit, sweet spices, creamy oak. Palate: elegant, fruity, flavourful, balanced.

RAYUELO 2009 T
80% bobal, 20% malbec, monastrell.

92 Colour: cherry, purple rim. Nose: floral, red berry notes, citrus fruit, scrubland, spicy, creamy oak. Palate: flavourful, fruity, long, toasty.

BODEGA CIEN Y PICO

San Francisco, 19
02240 Mahora (Albacete)
☎: +34 967 494 336 - Fax: +34 967 494 336
luisjimenaz@gmail.com
www.cienypico.com

CIEN Y PICO DOBLE PASTA 2009 T
100% garnacha tintorera.

88 Colour: bright cherry. Nose: ripe fruit, sweet spices, creamy oak. Palate: flavourful, fruity, toasty, round tannins.

CIEN Y PICO KNIGHTS-ERRANT 2008 T
100% garnacha tintorera.

90 Colour: cherry, garnet rim. Nose: ripe fruit, spicy, creamy oak, toasty, complex. Palate: powerful, flavourful, toasty, round tannins.

BODEGA INIESTA

Ctra. Fuentealbilla - Villamalea, km. 1,5
02260 Fuentealbilla (Albacete)
☎: +34 967 090 650 - Fax: +34 967 090 651
info@bodegainiesta.com
www.bodegainiesta.com

FINCA EL CARRIL 2010 B
macabeo.

87 Colour: bright straw. Nose: dried flowers, fragrant herbs, ripe fruit. Palate: rich, flavourful, long.

FINCA EL CARRIL 2010 T ROBLE
tempranillo, petit verdot.

90 Colour: bright cherry. Nose: ripe fruit, sweet spices, expressive, dark chocolate, mineral. Palate: flavourful, fruity, toasty, round tannins.

FINCA EL CARRIL 2010 TC
petit verdot, syrah, tempranillo.

88 Colour: cherry, garnet rim. Nose: ripe fruit, spicy, creamy oak, toasty, complex. Palate: powerful, flavourful, toasty, round tannins.

BODEGA SC. "UNION CAMPESINA INIESTENSE"

San Idefonso, 1
16235 Iniesta (Cuenca)
☎: +34 967 490 120 - Fax: +34 967 490 777
comercial@cooperativauci.com
www.cooperativauci.com

REALCE VIURA 2011 B
viura.

80

REALCE BOBAL 2011 RD
bobal.

84

REALCE TEMPRANILLO 2011 T
tempranillo.

88 Colour: cherry, purple rim. Nose: lactic notes, floral, red berry notes, expressive. Palate: flavourful, fruity, easy to drink, balanced.

REALCE BOBAL 2007 TR
bobal.

85 Colour: cherry, garnet rim. Nose: spicy, creamy oak, aged wood nuances. Palate: powerful, flavourful, spicy.

REALCE TEMPRANILLO 2006 TC
tempranillo.

84

REALCE BOBAL 2004 TR
bobal.

83

BODEGA SEÑORÍO DEL JÚCAR

Pol. Ind. Parc 64-70
02200 Casas Ibáñez (Albacete)
☎: +34 967 460 632 - Fax: +34 967 460 564
info@bsjucar.es
www.senoriodeljucar.com

SEÑORÍO DEL JÚCAR 2005 TR
tempranillo, merlot, syrah.

80

SEÑORÍO DEL JÚCAR 2005 TC
tempranillo, merlot, syrah.

80

BODEGAS RECIAL

Libertad, 1
02153 Pozo Lorente (Albacete)
☎: +34 630 418 264 - Fax: +34 967 572 063
gerencia@bodegasrecial.com
www.bodegasrecial.com

PÚRPURA POZO LORENTE 2011 B
sauvignon blanc.

84

PÚRPURA POZO LORENTE 2008 TC
garnacha tintorera.

83

BODEGAS SAAC

Valencia, 41
02270 Villamalea (Albacete)
☎: +34 967 483 023 - Fax: +34 967 483 536
saac@bodegas-saac.com
www.bodegas-saac.com

ALTOS DEL CABRIEL SELECCIÓN 2011 B
macabeo.

82

ALTOS DEL CABRIEL 2011 RD
bobal.

88 Colour: rose, purple rim. Nose: powerfull, ripe fruit, red berry notes, floral, expressive, lactic notes. Palate: , powerful, fruity, fresh, easy to drink.

VIÑAMALEA 2006 TC
syrah, tempranillo.

81

BODEGAS SAN GREGORIO MAGNO SOC. COOP. DE CLM

Ctra. de Ledaña, s/n
02246 Navas de Jorquera (Albacete)
☎: +34 967 482 134 - Fax: +34 967 482 134
sangregorio@amialbacete.com

MONTE MIRÓN 2006 TC
cencibel.

86 Colour: cherry, garnet rim. Nose: ripe fruit, spicy, waxy notes, fine reductive notes. Palate: correct, powerful, flavourful, reductive nuances.

BODEGAS VILLAVID, DULCE NOMBRE DE JESÚS SOC. COOP. DE C-LM

Niño Jesús, 25
16280 Villarta (Cuenca)
☎: +34 962 189 006 - Fax: +34 962 189 125
info@villavid.com
www.villavid.com

VILLAVID 2011 B
verdejo, macabeo.

84

VILLAVID 2011 RD
bobal.

85 Colour: rose, purple rim. Nose: powerfull, red berry notes, floral, lactic notes. Palate: , powerful, fruity, fresh.

BODEGAS Y VIÑEDOS PONCE

La Virgen, 34
16235 Iniesta (Cuenca)
☎: +34 677 434 523 - Fax: +34 967 220 876
bodegasponce@gmail.com

RETO 2011 B
albilla.

88 Colour: bright straw. Nose: medium intensity, dried flowers, fresh. Palate: correct, easy to drink, balanced.

CLOS LOJEN 2011 T
100% bobal.

92 Colour: cherry, purple rim. Nose: red berry notes, raspberry, floral, balsamic herbs, expressive. Palate: light-bodied, fresh, fruity, flavourful, easy to drink.

PINO 2010 T
bobal.

94 Colour: cherry, garnet rim. Nose: mineral, ripe fruit, sweet spices, expressive. Palate: flavourful, fruity, round tannins.

P.F. 2010 T
100% bobal.

93 Colour: cherry, garnet rim. Nose: powerfull, ripe fruit, scrubland, spicy. Palate: good structure, fruity, fine bitter notes, harsh oak tannins.

LA CASILLA (ESTRECHA) 2010 T
100% bobal.

92 Colour: cherry, garnet rim. Nose: balanced, red berry notes, ripe fruit, violets, scrubland. Palate: fruity, good structure.

COOP VIRGEN DE LAS NIEVES, S.C. DE CLM

Paseo Virgen de las Nieves, 1
02247 Cenizate (Albacete)
☎: +34 967 482 006 - Fax: +34 967 482 805
comercial@virgendelasnives.com
www.virgendelasnieves.com

ARTESONES DE CENIZATE SEMIDULCE 2011 B
macabeo.

85 Colour: golden. Nose: powerfull, floral, candied fruit. Palate: flavourful, sweet, fresh, fruity, long.

ARTESONES DE CENIZATE 2011 B
macabeo.

83

ARTESONES DE CENIZATE 2011 RD
bobal.

87 Colour: rose, purple rim. Nose: lactic notes, floral, red berry notes, ripe fruit. Palate: powerful, flavourful, easy to drink.

ARTESONES DE CENIZATE TEMPRANILLO 2011 T
tempranillo.

85 Colour: cherry, purple rim. Nose: red berry notes, floral, balsamic herbs. Palate: flavourful, fruity, good acidity.

ARTESONES DE CENIZATE 2011 T
100% syrah.

84

ARTESONES DE CENIZATE TEMPRANILLO 2008 TC
tempranillo.

81

ARTESONES DE CENIZATE BOBAL 2007 TC
bobal.

84

COOP. DEL CAMPO SAN ISIDRO DE ALBOREA

Extramuros, s/n
02215 Alborea (Albacete)
☎: +34 967 477 096 - Fax: +34 967 477 076
coopalborea@telefonica.net

ALTERÓN 2007 TC
100% cencibel.

83

ALTERÓN 2005 TR
100% bobal.

85 Colour: cherry, garnet rim. Nose: ripe fruit, spicy, creamy oak, toasty. Palate: powerful, flavourful, toasty, round tannins.

ALTERÓN 2005 TGR
100% bobal.

84

COOP. SAN ISIDRO

Ctra. Valencia, s/n
02240 Mahora (Albacete)
☎: +34 967 494 058 - Fax: +34 967 494 058
info@vinosmahora.com
www.vinosmahora.com

MAHORA 2007 T BARRICA
tempranillo.

78

COOPERATIVA NUESTRA SEÑORA DE LA ESTRELLA

Elías Fernández, 10
16290 El Herrumbar (Cuenca)
☎: +34 962 313 029 - Fax: +34 962 313 232
laestrella@ucaman.es

ANTARES 2011 B
80% macabeo, 10% verdejo, 10% sauvignon blanc.

84

ANTARES 2011 RD
100% bobal.

83

ANTARES 2011 T

89 Colour: cherry, purple rim. Nose: red berry notes, spicy, expressive, balsamic herbs. Palate: good acidity, easy to drink, powerful, flavourful.

ANTARES 2009 T ROBLE
100% syrah.

85 Colour: bright cherry. Nose: ripe fruit, sweet spices, creamy oak. Palate: flavourful, fruity, toasty.

FINCA SANDOVAL

Ctra. CM-3222, Km. 26,800
16237 Ledaña (Cuenca)
☎: +34 616 444 805
fincasandoval@gmail.com
www.grandespagos.com/sandoval.html

SIGNO GARNACHA 2010 T
garnacha.

93 Colour: cherry, garnet rim. Nose: red berry notes, ripe fruit, mineral, sweet spices, creamy oak. Palate: powerful, flavourful, complex, long, toasty.

SALIA 2009 T

93 Colour: cherry, garnet rim. Nose: red berry notes, ripe fruit, nose:tic coffee, spicy, expressive. Palate: powerful, flavourful, complex, long, toasty.

SIGNO BOBAL 2009 T
bobal.

93 Colour: cherry, garnet rim. Nose: red berry notes, earthy notes, spicy, balanced, expressive. Palate: powerful, flavourful, complex, long, toasty.

FINCA SANDOVAL CUVEE TNS MAGNUM 2008 T
67% touriga nacional, 33% syrah.

95 Colour: cherry, garnet rim. Nose: earthy notes, red berry notes, ripe fruit, sweet spices, creamy oak, balanced, expressive. Palate: elegant, flavourful, complex, long, fine tannins.

FINCA SANDOVAL 2008 T
77% syrah, 16% monastrell, 7% bobal.

94 Colour: cherry, garnet rim. Nose: ripe fruit, spicy, creamy oak, toasty, complex, mineral. Palate: powerful, flavourful, toasty, round tannins.

NUESTRA SEÑORA DE LA CABEZA SOC. COOP.

Avda. del Vino, 10
02200 Casas Ibáñez (Albacete)
☎: +34 967 460 105 - Fax: +34 967 460 266
info@coop-cabeza.com
www.coop-cabeza.com

VIARIL 2011 BFB
100% macabeo.

87 Colour: bright yellow. Nose: ripe fruit, sweet spices, creamy oak, fragrant herbs. Palate: rich, smoky afterpalate:, flavourful, fresh.

VIARIL CABERNET SAUVIGNON 2010 T
100% cabernet sauvignon.

82

VIARIL 2007 TC

83

PAGOS DE FAMILIA VEGA TOLOSA

Correos, 6
02200 Casas Ibáñez (Albacete)
☎: +34 617 379 328 - Fax: +34 967 461 331
info@vegatolosa.com
www.vegatolosa.com

VEGA TOLOSA CHARDONNAY 2011 B BARRICA
100% chardonnay.

88 Colour: bright yellow. Nose: powerfull, ripe fruit, sweet spices, creamy oak, fragrant herbs. Palate: rich, flavourful, fresh, good acidity.

VEGA TOLOSA SELECCIÓN 2011 B
50% macabeo, 35% sauvignon blanc, 15% chardonnay.

85 Colour: bright straw. Nose: fresh, fresh fruit, white flowers, expressive. Palate: flavourful, fruity, good acidity.

VEGA TOLOSA LÁGRIMA DE SYRAH 2011 RD
100% syrah.

84

VEGA TOLOSA BOBAL VIÑAS VIEJAS 2011 T
bobal.

88 Colour: cherry, purple rim. Nose: expressive, fresh fruit, red berry notes, sweet spices, dark chocolate. Palate: flavourful, fruity, good acidity, warm.

VEGA TOLOSA NATURE 2011 T
50% syrah, 50% tempranillo.

85 Colour: cherry, purple rim. Nose: ripe fruit, balsamic herbs, floral, warm. Palate: flavourful, fruity, good acidity.

VEGA TOLOSA BOBAL VIÑAS VIEJAS 2010 T
100% bobal.

86 Colour: bright cherry. Nose: ripe fruit, creamy oak, expressive. Palate: flavourful, fruity, toasty, harsh oak tannins.

VEGA TOLOSA BOBAL VIÑAS VIEJAS 2009 T
100% bobal.

85 Colour: cherry, garnet rim. Nose: red berry notes, ripe fruit, sweet spices, creamy oak. Palate: flavourful, spicy.

VEGA TOLOSA BOBAL VIÑAS VIEJAS 2007 T
100% bobal.

88 Colour: dark-red cherry, orangey edge. Nose: ripe fruit, sweet spices, toasty. Palate: flavourful, long, toasty.

SEÑORÍO DE MONTERRUIZ

La Plaza
16234 Casas de Santa Cruz (Cuenca)
☎: +34 967 493 828
reservas@monterruiz.com
www.señoriodemonterruiz.es

SEÑORIO DE MONTERRUIZ 2011 T
bobal.

87 Colour: cherry, garnet rim. Nose: red berry notes, ripe fruit, scrubland. Palate: light-bodied, fresh, flavourful, easy to drink.

SEÑORIO DE MONTERRUIZ 2011 T MACERACIÓN CARBÓNICA

85 Colour: cherry, purple rim. Nose: fruit expression, floral, lactic notes, red berry notes. Palate: powerful, flavourful, good finish.

VINOS DE ALBOREA (BODEGA PARDO TOLOSA)

Villatolla, 26
02215 Alborea (Albacete)
☎: +34 963 517 067 - Fax: +34 963 517 091
mj.veses@bodegapardotolosa.com
www.bodegapardotolosa.com

MIZARAN TEMPRANILLO 2009 T
100% tempranillo.

83

SENDA DE LAS ROCHAS 2008 T
100% tempranillo.

85 Colour: cherry, garnet rim. Nose: ripe fruit, spicy, creamy oak, toasty. Palate: powerful, flavourful, toasty.

VITIVINOS ANUNCIACIÓN SC DE CLM

Camino de Cabezuelas, s/n
02270 Villamalea (Albacete)
☎: +34 967 483 114 - Fax: +34 967 483 964
info@vitivinos.com
www.vitivinos.com

AZUA MACABEO 2011 B
100% macabeo.

85 Colour: bright straw. Nose: fresh, fresh fruit, white flowers, fragrant herbs. Palate: flavourful, fruity, good acidity.

AZUA BOBAL 2011 RD
100% bobal.

86 Colour: rose, purple rim. Nose: powerfull, ripe fruit, red berry notes, floral, fragrant herbs. Palate: , fruity, fresh, light-bodied, easy to drink.

AZUA SYRAH 2010 T ROBLE
100% syrah.

88 Colour: cherry, purple rim. Nose: red berry notes, raspberry, violets. Palate: light-bodied, fresh, fruity, balanced.

AZUA BOBAL 2010 T ROBLE
100% bobal.

88 Colour: cherry, garnet rim. Nose: ripe fruit, floral, earthy notes, spicy. Palate: powerful, flavourful, complex, harsh oak tannins.

AZUA CABERNET 2010 T ROBLE
100% cabernet sauvignon.

87 Colour: cherry, garnet rim. Nose: red berry notes, ripe fruit, balsamic herbs, spicy. Palate: powerful, flavourful, correct, balsamic.

AZUA CRIANZA SELECCIÓN BOBAL VIEJO 2008 TC
100% bobal.

87 Colour: cherry, garnet rim. Nose: ripe fruit, spicy, creamy oak, toasty, fine reductive notes. Palate: powerful, flavourful, toasty, round tannins.

AZUA RESERVA SELECCIÓN BOBAL VIEJO 2008 TR
100% bobal.

87 Colour: cherry, garnet rim. Nose: ripe fruit, spicy, creamy oak, toasty, complex. Palate: powerful, flavourful, toasty, harsh oak tannins.

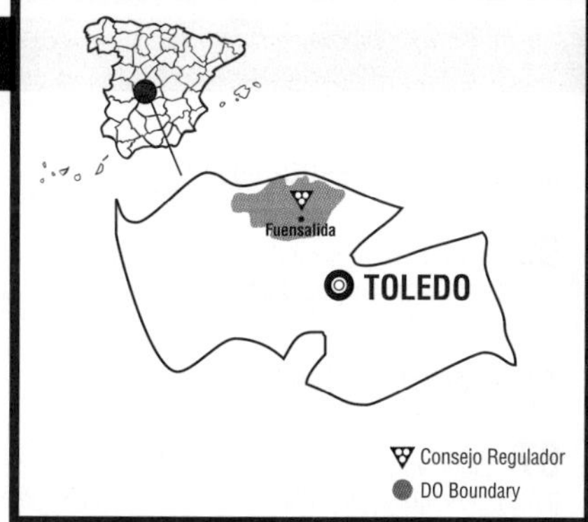

LOCATION:

In the north of the province of Toledo. It borders with the provinces of Ávila and Madrid to the north, with the Tajo to the south, and with the Sierra de San Vicente to the west. It is made up of 51 municipal areas of the province of Toledo.

CLIMATE:

Continental, dry and extreme, with long, cold winters and hot summers. Late frosts in spring are quite common. The average rainfall is between 300 mm and 500 mm, and is irregularly distributed throughout the year.

SOIL:

The vineyards are at an altitude of between 400 m and 600 m, although some municipal districts of the Sierra de San Vicente reach an altitude of 800 m. The soil is mainly sandy-clayey, with a medium to loose texture.

GRAPE VARIETIES:

WHITE: *Albillo, Macabeo, Sauvignon Blanc, Chardonnay* and *Moscatel de Grano Menudo.*
RED: *Garnacha* (majority 85% of total), *Cencibel* (*Tempranillo*), *Cabernet Sauvignon, Merlot, Syrah, Petit Verdot, Cabernet Franc* and *Graciano.*

FIGURES:

Vineyard surface: 5,000 – **Wine-Growers:** 1,200 – **Wineries:** 26 – **2011 Harvest rating:** Good – **Production:** 4,320,903 litres – **Market percentages:** 75% domestic. 25% export

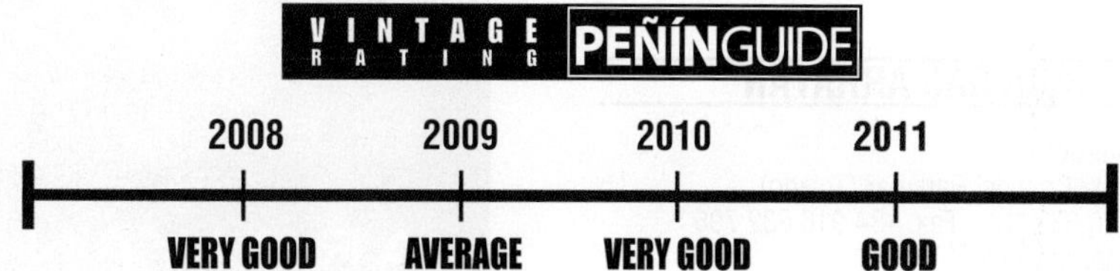

CONSEJO REGULADOR
Avda. Cristo del Amparo, 16 - 45510 Fuensalida (Toledo) - ☎: +34 925 785 185 - Fax: +34 925 784 154
@ administracion@domentrida.es - www.domentrida.es

AGROVILLARTA

Ctra. Toledo-Ávila, Km. 48
45910 Escalona (Toledo)
☎: +34 913 441 990
comunicacion@haciendavillarta.com

BESANAS 2007 TC

85 Colour: deep cherry. Nose: spicy, toasty, nose:tic coffee. Palate: flavourful, fine bitter notes, round tannins.

BESANAS 2006 TR

85 Colour: cherry, garnet rim. Nose: toasty, dark chocolate, fruit liqueur notes. Palate: fine bitter notes, good acidity.

ALONSO CUESTA

Pza. de la Constitución, 4
45920 La Torre de Esteban Hambrán (Toledo)
☎: +34 925 795 742 - Fax: +34 925 795 742
comercial@alonsocuesta.com
www.alonsocuesta.com

HACIENDA VALPRIMERO 2010 T
garnacha, syrah, cabernet sauvignon.

85 Colour: deep cherry. Nose: powerfull, fruit preserve, red berry notes, toasty. Palate: powerful, good acidity, round tannins.

ALONSO CUESTA 2009 T
garnacha, tempranillo, cabernet sauvignon.

93 Color cherry, garnet rim. Nose: ripe fruit, spicy, creamy oak, toasty, complex. Palate: powerful, flavourful, toasty, round tannins.

BODEGAS ARRAYÁN

Finca La Verdosa
45513 Santa Cruz del Retamar (Toledo)
☎: +34 916 633 131 - Fax: +34 916 632 796
comercial@arrayan.es
www.arrayan.es

ARRAYÁN 2011 RD
syrah, merlot, cabernet sauvignon, petit verdot.

88 Color rose, purple rim. Nose: powerfull, ripe fruit, red berry notes, floral, expressive. Palate: fleshy, powerful, fruity, fresh.

ARRAYÁN PETIT VERDOT 2009 T
100% petit verdot.

90 Colour: cherry, garnet rim. Nose: ripe fruit, fruit expression, scrubland. Palate: toasty, fine bitter notes, good acidity.

ARRAYÁN SYRAH 2009 T
100% syrah.

87 Colour: very deep cherry. Nose: fruit liqueur notes, grassy, powerfull, spicy. Palate: powerful, fine bitter notes, balsamic.

ARRAYÁN SELECCIÓN 2009 T
syrah, merlot, cabernet sauvignon, petit verdot.

86 Colour: very deep cherry. Nose: candied fruit, stalky, grassy, toasty. Palate: flavourful, powerful, good acidity.

ESTELA DE ARRAYÁN 2008 T
syrah, merlot, cabernet sauvignon, petit verdot.

93 Colour: very deep cherry. Nose: powerfull, characterful, ripe fruit, toasty, sweet spices. Palate: spicy, ripe fruit, fine bitter notes, good acidity.

ARRAYÁN PREMIUM 2008 T
syrah, merlot, cabernet sauvignon, petit verdot.

91 Colour: deep cherry. Nose: spicy, fruit liqueur notes, ripe fruit, toasty, dark chocolate. Palate: flavourful, good acidity, fine bitter notes.

BODEGAS CANOPY

Avda. Barber, 71
45004 (Toledo)
☎: +34 619 244 878 - Fax: +34 925 283 681
achacon@bodegascanopy.com

LOCO 2011 B
garnacha blanca.

93 Colour: bright straw. Nose: white flowers, ripe fruit, fine lees. Palate: flavourful, powerful, good acidity, long, round.

CONGO 2009 T
100% garnacha.

93 Colour: bright cherry. Nose: red berry notes, overripe fruit, balsamic herbs, scrubland. Palate: flavourful, light-bodied, good acidity.

MALPASO 2008 T
syrah.

94 Colour: very deep cherry. Nose: sweet spices, mineral, balsamic herbs, scrubland, floral. Palate: flavourful, fine bitter notes, good acidity, round tannins.

LA VIÑA ESCONDIDA 2008 T
garnacha.

94 Colour: cherry, garnet rim. Nose: balsamic herbs, scrubland, ripe fruit, warm, characterful. Palate: flavourful, powerful, fine bitter notes, good acidity.

TRES PATAS 2008 T
90% garnacha, 10% syrah.

93 Colour: cherry, garnet rim. Nose: expressive, red berry notes, sweet spices, scrubland, mineral. Palate: flavourful, powerful, fine bitter notes, good acidity.

BODEGAS JIMÉNEZ LANDI

Avda. Solana, 39-41
45930 Méntrida (Toledo)
☎: +34 918 178 213 - Fax: +34 918 178 213
jose@jimenezlandi.com
www.jimenezlandi.com

ATAULFOS 2010 T
garnacha.

96 Colour: light cherry. Nose: dried flowers, candied fruit, fruit liqueur notes, cocoa bean, dark chocolate, sweet spices, mineral. Palate: flavourful, long, round, balanced, ripe fruit, sweetness.

THE END 2010 T
garnacha.

95 Colour: ruby red, orangey edge. Nose: scrubland, red berry notes, ripe fruit, earthy notes, mineral, creamy oak. Palate: elegant, round, good acidity, flavourful, fresh, fruity, complex.

PIÉLAGO 2010 T
garnacha.

94 Colour: cherry, garnet rim. Nose: dry stone, wild herbs, balsamic herbs, spicy, creamy oak, expressive. Palate: complex, flavourful, spicy, mineral, elegant, balanced.

SOTORRONDERO 2010 T
garnacha, syrah.

93 Colour: cherry, garnet rim. Nose: ripe fruit, fruit preserve, balsamic herbs, mineral. Palate: long, spicy, flavourful, fine bitter notes, balanced.

BODEGAS TORRESTEBAN

Ctra. Méntrida, s/n
45920 La Torre de Esteban Hambrán (Toledo)
☎: +34 925 795 114 - Fax: +34 925 795 163
coopcristo@gmail.com

SEÑORÍO DE ESTEBAN HAMBRÁN 2011 T
garnacha, tempranillo.

82

TORRESTEBAN 2011 T

75

REMURI TEMPRANILLO SYRAH 2010 T
tempranillo, syrah.

83

REMURI 2010 T ROBLE
syrah.

81

TORRESTEBAN 2009 TC
70% tempranillo, 30% garnacha.

83

BODEGAS Y VIÑEDOS TAVERA

Ctra. Valmojado - Toledo, Km. 22
45182 Arcicóllar (Toledo)
☎: +34 666 294 012
info@bodegastavera.com
www.bodegastavera.com

TAVERA ROSADO ANTIGUOS VIÑEDOS 2011 RD
100% garnacha.

85 Colour: brilliant rose. Nose: red berry notes, ripe fruit, candied fruit, floral. Palate: flavourful, fine bitter notes, good acidity.

TAVERA 2011 T MACERACIÓN CARBÓNICA
tempranillo, syrah, garnacha.

83

TAVERA TEMPRANILLO SYRAH 2010 T
tempranillo, syrah.

85 Colour: very deep cherry. Nose: powerfull, warm, fruit liqueur notes. Palate: sweetness, fine bitter notes, ripe fruit.

TAVERA EDICCIÓN SYRAH 2009 T FERMENTADO EN BARRICA
100% syrah.

88 Colour: cherry, garnet rim. Nose: powerfull, characterful, ripe fruit, new oak, roasted coffee. Palate: powerful, sweetness, fine bitter notes.

COOPERATIVA CONDES DE FUENSALIDA

Avda. San Crispín, 129
45510 Fuensalida (Toledo)
☎: +34 925 784 823 - Fax: +34 925 784 823
condesdefuensalida@hotmail.com
www.condesdefuensalida.iespana.es

CONDES DE FUENSALIDA 2010 RD
garnacha.

83

CONDES DE FUENSALIDA 2010 T

82

CONDES DE FUENSALIDA 2007 TC

84

COOPERATIVA NUESTRA SEÑORA DE LA NATIVIDAD

Puente San Roque, 1
45930 Méntrida (Toledo)
☎: +34 918 177 004 - Fax: +34 918 177 004
coopnatividad@gmail.com

VEGA BERCIANA 2011 RD

83

VEGA BERCIANA 2011 T

83

VEGA BERCIANA 2008 TR
100% tempranillo.

87 Colour: cherry, garnet rim. Nose: ripe fruit, powerfull, characterful, toasty. Palate: ripe fruit, flavourful.

VALLE PEDROMORO 2006 T BARRICA
garnacha.

80

LAS CAÑADAS DE CARTEMA

Mahonia, 2
28043 (Madrid)
☎: +34 913 433 026 - Fax: +34 913 433 090
info@cartema.es
www.cartema.com

CARTEMA 2008 TC
cabernet sauvignon, syrah, tempranillo.

86 Colour: deep cherry. Nose: ripe fruit, toasty, spicy, dark chocolate. Palate: flavourful, fine bitter notes.

SANTO DOMINGO DE GUZMÁN SOC. COOP.

Alameda del Fresno, 14
45940 Valmojado (Toledo)
☎: +34 918 170 904 - Fax: +34 918 170 904
valdejuana2011@hotmail.com
www.santodomingodeguzman.es

VALDEJUANA 2011 T
syrah.

88 Colour: cherry, purple rim. Nose: powerfull, raspberry, ripe fruit. Palate: powerful, flavourful, ripe fruit.

UNVINOBENAYAS

José Antonio, 16
45542 El Casar de Escalona (Toledo)
☎: +34 655 907 640
info@unvinobenayas.com
www.unvinobenayas.es

ENCASTAO 2008 TC
garnacha, tempranillo.

81

CODICIOSO 2007 TC
syrah.

83

VIÑEDOS DE CAMARENA, SDAD. COOPERATIVA DE CLM

Ctra. Toledo - Valmojado, km. 24,6
45180 Camarena (Toledo)
☎: +34 918 174 347 - Fax: +34 918 174 632
vdecamarena@hotmail.com
www.vdecamarena.com

BASTIÓN DE CAMARENA 2011 B
verdejo.

83

BASTIÓN DE CAMARENA 2011 RD
garnacha, cencibel.

85 Colour: light cherry. Nose: fresh fruit, red berry notes, fragrant herbs. Palate: flavourful, fruity.

BASTIÓN DE CAMARENA 2011 T
cencibel, syrah.

86 Colour: cherry, purple rim. Nose: floral, ripe fruit, violet drops. Palate: flavourful, good acidity, ripe fruit.

BASTIÓN DE CAMARENA 2009 T ROBLE
merlot.

84

VIÑEDOS Y BODEGAS GONZÁLEZ

Real, 86
45180 Camarena (Toledo)
☎: +34 918 174 063 - Fax: +34 918 174 136
bodegasgonzalez@yahoo.es
www.vinobispo.com

VIÑA BISPO 2011 B
sauvignon blanc, moscatel grano menudo, verdejo.

81

VIÑA BISPO 2011 RD
garnacha, cabernet sauvignon.

81

VIÑA BISPO 2011 T
syrah.

85 Colour: cherry, purple rim. Nose: powerfull, varietal, ripe fruit. Palate: flavourful, fruity, good acidity.

DO MONDÉJAR

LOCATION:

In the southwest of the province of Guadalajara. It is made up of the municipal districts of Albalate de Zorita, Albares, Almoguera, Almonacid de Zorita, Driebes, Escariche, Escopete, Fuenteovilla, Illana, Loranca de Tajuña, Mazuecos, Mondéjar, Pastrana, Pioz, Pozo de Almoguera, Sacedón, Sayatón, Valdeconcha, Yebra and Zorita de los Canes.

CLIMATE:

Temperate Mediterranean. The average annual temperature is around 18°C and the average rainfall is 500 mm per year.

SOIL:

The south of the Denomination is characterized by red soil on lime-clayey sediments, and the north (the municipal districts of Anguix, Mondéjar, Sacedón, etc.) has brown limestone soil on lean sandstone and conglomerates.

GRAPE VARIETIES:

WHITE (40%): *Malvar* (majority 80% of white varieties), *Macabeo* and *Torrontés*.
RED (60%): *Cencibel* (*Tempranillo* – represents 95% of red varieties), *Cabernet Sauvignon* (5%) and *Syrah*.

FIGURES:

Vineyard surface: 3,000 – **Wine-Growers:** 300 – **Wineries:** 2 – **2011 Harvest rating:** N/A – **Production:** 421,130 litres – **Market percentages:** 100% domestic

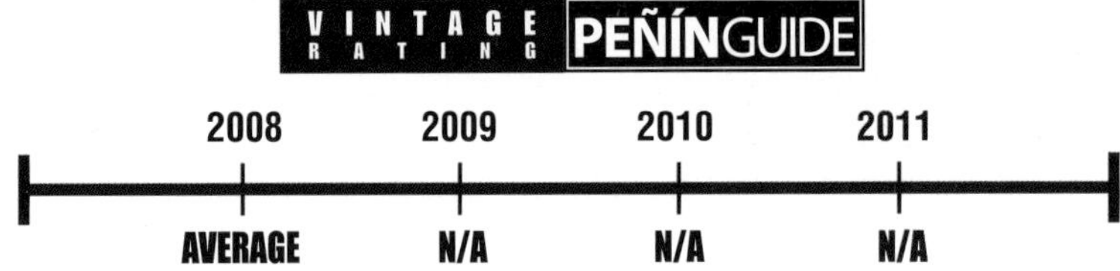

CONSEJO REGULADOR
Pza. Mayor, 10 - 19110 Mondéjar (Guadalajara) - ☎: 949 385 284 - Fax: 949 385 284
@ crdom@crdomondejar.com - www.crdomondejar.com

DO MONTERREI

LOCATION:

In the east of the province of Orense, on the border with Portugal. The vineyards occupy the valley of Monterrei, and it is made up of the municipal districts of Verín, Monterrei, Oimbra and Castrelo do Vall.

CLIMATE:

Midway between the Atlantic and Continental influences. Drier than in the rest of Galicia, with maximum temperatures of 35°C in summer and minimum of –5°C in winter.

SOIL:

The vineyards cover the slopes of the mountains and valleys irrigated by the Támega river and its tributaries. The soil is quite clayey, deep, rather heavy and, in some places, somewhat sandy.

GRAPE VARIETIES:

WHITE: *Dona Blanca, Verdello* (*Godello*) and *Treixadura* (*Verdello Louro*), *Albariño, Caiño Blanco, Loureira* and *Blanca de Monterrei.*
RED: *Aranxa (Tempranillo), Caiño Tinto, Mencía, Bastardo* (or *María Ardoña*) and *Sousón.*

FIGURES:

Vineyard surface: 400 – **Wine-Growers:** 320 – **Wineries:** 24 – **2011 Harvest rating:** Very Good – **Production:** 1,456,075 – **Market percentages:** 87% domestic. 13% export

SUB-REGIONS:

Val de Monterrei. Comprising the vineyards situated in the valley region (therefore, more level terrains) and covering the parishes and municipal districts belonging to the following city councils: Castrelo do Val (Castrelo do Val, Pepín and Nocedo); Monterrei (Albarellos, Infesta, Monterrei and Vilaza); Oimbra (Oimbra, Rabal, O Rosal and San Cibrao); Verín (Abedes, Cabreiroa, Feces da Baixo, Feces de Cima, Mandín, Mourazos, Pazos, Queizás, A Rasela, Tamagos, Tamaguelos, Tintores, Verín, Vilela and Vilamaior do Val).
Ladeira de Monterrei. These vineyards occupy the hills. The parishes and municipal districts that make up this sub-region are: Castrelo do Val (Gondulfes and Servoi), Oimbra (As Chas and A Granxa), Monterrey (Flariz, Medeiros, Mixós, Estevesiños and Vences) and Verín (Queirugas).

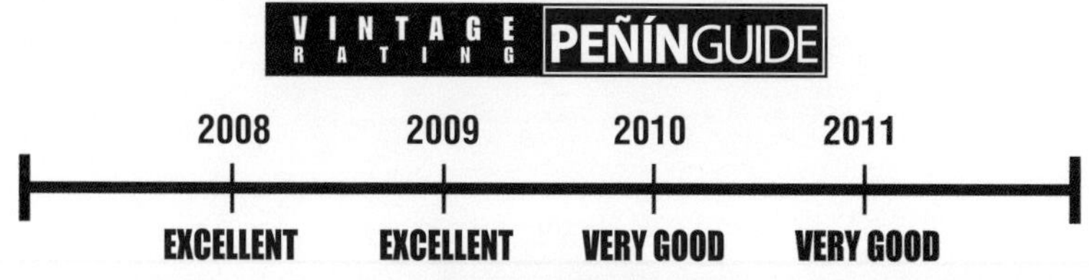

CONSEJO REGULADOR
Mercado Comarcal, 1 - 32600 Verín (Ourense) - ☎: +34 988 590 007 - Fax: +34 988 410 634
@ info@domonterrei.com - www.domonterrei.com

ADEGA ABELEDOS

Avda. Portugal, 110 2ºA
32600 Verín (Ourense)
☎: +34 988 414 075 - Fax: +34 988 414 075
cristinabooparadela@hotmail.com

ABELEDO 2011 T
mencía.

88 Colour: cherry, purple rim. Nose: red berry notes, floral, ripe fruit. Palate: flavourful, fruity, good acidity, round tannins.

ADEGAS CHICHENO

Quintá de Arriba, s/n
32600 Queizas Verin (Ourense)
☎: +34 988 411 949
bodegaschicheno@gmail.com
www.bodegaschicheno.com

GALVÁN 2011 B
treixadura, godello.

85 Colour: bright straw. Nose: powerfull, floral, grassy. Palate: ripe fruit, easy to drink.

GALVÁN 2011 T
mencía, tempranillo.

88 Colour: cherry, purple rim. Nose: expressive, fresh fruit, red berry notes, floral, balsamic herbs. Palate: flavourful, fruity, good acidity.

ADEGAS O CABILDO

Cabildo, 10
32613 Oimbra (Ourense)
☎: +34 670 601 625
casaldocabildo@casaldocabildo.com
www.casaldocabildo.com

CASAL DO CABILDO 2001 B
godello, treixadura, dona blanca.

85 Colour: bright straw. Nose: fresh, ripe fruit, dried flowers, scrubland. Palate: flavourful, fruity, good acidity.

CASAL DO CABILDO 2009 T
mencía.

80

ALMA ATLÁNTICA

Ctra. N- 525
36618 Albarellos de Monterrei (Ourense)
☎: +34 986 526 040 - Fax: +34 986 526 901
comercial@martincodax.com
www.almaatlantica.com

MARA MARTIN GODELLO 2011 B
100% godello.

90 Colour: bright straw. Nose: fresh, fresh fruit, white flowers, fragrant herbs, expressive. Palate: flavourful, fruity, good acidity, balanced.

BODEGA GARGALO

Rua Do Castelo, 59
32619 Pazos Verín (Ourense)
☎: +34 988 590 203 - Fax: +34 988 590 295
gargalo@verino.es
www.gargalo.es

GARGALO GODELLO 2011 B
godello.

91 Colour: bright straw. Nose: fresh, white flowers, ripe fruit, mineral. Palate: flavourful, fruity, good acidity, balanced.

TERRA DO GARGALO SOBRE LÍAS 2011 B
godello, treixadura.

91 Colour: bright straw. Nose: fresh, white flowers, expressive, lactic notes, ripe fruit. Palate: flavourful, fruity, good acidity, balanced.

GARGALO ALBARIÑO & TREIXADURA 2011 B
albariño, treixadura.

90 Colour: bright straw. Nose: fresh, expressive, ripe fruit, citrus fruit, grassy. Palate: flavourful, fruity, good acidity, balanced.

TERRA DO GARGALO CARBALLO 2009 TC
mencía.

89 Colour: bright cherry. Nose: ripe fruit, sweet spices, creamy oak, aged wood nuances, new oak. Palate: flavourful, fruity, toasty, round tannins.

BODEGA TABÚ

Plaza A Carreira, 6 O Rosal
32613 Oimbra (Ourense)
☎: +34 665 644 500
bodegatabu@gmail.com

STIBADÍA 2011 B
godello, treixadura.

87 Colour: bright straw. Nose: fresh, fresh fruit, floral. Palate: flavourful, fruity, good acidity, balanced.

STIBADÍA 2011 T
mencía, tempranillo.

87 Colour: cherry, purple rim. Nose: fresh fruit, red berry notes, floral, fragrant herbs. Palate: flavourful, fruity, round tannins, correct.

STIBADÍA 2010 T BARRICA
mencía, tempranillo.

88 Colour: bright cherry. Nose: ripe fruit, sweet spices, creamy oak, expressive. Palate: flavourful, fruity, toasty, long.

BODEGAS ABANICO

Pol. Ind Ca l'Avellanet - Susany, 6
08553 Seva (Barcelona)
☎: +34 938 125 676 - Fax: +34 938 123 213
info@exportiberia.com
www.bodegasabanico.com

VIÑA TOEN 2011 B
50% godello, 50% treixadura.

90 Colour: bright straw. Nose: white flowers, fresh fruit, dried herbs, expressive. Palate: balanced, fine bitter notes, flavourful, fruity, long.

BODEGAS LADAIRO

Ctra. Ladairo, 42
32613 O'Rosal (Oimbra) (Ourense)
☎: +34 988 422 757 - Fax: +34 988 422 757
info@bodegasladairo.com
www.ladairo.com

LADAIRO 2011 B
80% godello, 20% treixadura.

89 Colour: bright straw. Nose: white flowers, fresh fruit, dried herbs, medium intensity. Palate: light-bodied, fresh, fruity, flavourful.

LADAIRO 2010 BFB
50% godello, 50% treixadura.

88 Colour: bright yellow. Nose: powerfull, ripe fruit, sweet spices, fragrant herbs, white flowers. Palate: rich, flavourful, fresh, good acidity.

LADAIRO 2011 T
80% mencía, 20% merenzao.

89 Colour: cherry, purple rim. Nose: red berry notes, floral, ripe fruit. Palate: flavourful, fruity, good acidity, round tannins.

LADAIRO 2010 T BARRICA
70% mencía, 30% sousón.

89 Colour: bright cherry. Nose: sweet spices, expressive, toasty, ripe fruit, fruit liqueur notes. Palate: flavourful, fruity, toasty.

BODEGAS Y VIÑEDOS QUINTA DA MURADELLA

Avda. Luis Espada, 99- Entresuelo, dcha.
32600 Verín (Ourense)
☎: +34 988 411 724 - Fax: +34 988 590 427
muradella@verin.net

MURADELLA 2011 B
treixadura, dona blanca.

91 Colour: bright yellow. Nose: spicy, creamy oak, dried herbs, floral, ripe fruit, mineral. Palate: balsamic, long, powerful, flavourful, spicy.

ALANDA 2011 B BARRICA
dona blanca, treixadura, godello.

89 Colour: bright yellow. Nose: ripe fruit, sweet spices, creamy oak, fragrant herbs. Palate: rich, flavourful, fresh, good acidity.

GORVIA FERMENTADO EN BARRICA 2010 BFB
100% dona blanca.

92 Colour: bright golden. Nose: balanced, floral, wild herbs, spicy, creamy oak, expressive. Palate: round, fine bitter notes, powerful, flavourful, balanced.

GORVIA 2010 T
100% mencía.

92 Colour: bright cherry. Nose: mineral, earthy notes, balsamic herbs, scrubland, fruit expression. Palate: flavourful, fruity, fresh, good acidity.

MURADELLA 2010 T
mencía, bastardo, sousón.

91 Colour: deep cherry. Nose: mineral, fruit expression, spicy, floral. Palate: flavourful, fruity, fine bitter notes, good acidity.

ALANDA 2009 T BARRICA
mencía, bastardo, sousón.

89 Colour: deep cherry. Nose: balsamic herbs, scrubland, red berry notes. Palate: ripe fruit, fine bitter notes, good acidity.

CREGO E MONAGUILLO

Rua Nova, 24
32618 Salgueira (Ourense)
☎: +34 988 418 164 - Fax: +34 988 418 164
tito@cregoemonaguillo.com
www.cregoemonaguillo.com

CREGO E MONAGUILLO 2011 B
godello, treixadura.

89 Colour: bright yellow. Nose: white flowers, ripe fruit, fragrant herbs. Palate: powerful, flavourful, rich, fruity.

MAROVA 2010 B
treixadura, godello.

90 Colour: bright straw. Nose: ripe fruit, citrus fruit, sweet spices. Palate: flavourful, fruity, fine bitter notes, good acidity.

CREGO E MONAGUILLO 2011 T
mencía, arauxa.

90 Colour: cherry, purple rim. Nose: red berry notes, floral, ripe fruit. Palate: flavourful, good acidity, ripe fruit.

MANUEL GUERRA JUSTO

Ctra. Albarellos, 61
32618 Villaza (Monterrei) (Ourense)
☎: +34 687 409 618
viaarxentea@viaarxentea.com

VÍA ARXÉNTEA 2011 B
treixadura, godello.

91 Colour: bright yellow. Nose: white flowers, fragrant herbs, citrus fruit, fresh fruit, balanced. Palate: powerful, flavourful, fruity, complex.

PAZO BLANCO (TAPIAS-MARIÑÁN)

Ctra. N-525, Km. 170,4
32619 Pazos (Ourense)
☎: +34 988 411 693 - Fax: +34 988 411 693
pazoblanco@yahoo.es
www.tapiasmarinhan.com

QUINTAS DAS TAPIAS 2011 B
treixadura, godello, albariño.

90 Colour: bright straw. Nose: floral, fresh fruit, citrus fruit, grassy. Palate: flavourful, fruity, fresh, full.

PAZO DE MARIÑAN 2011 B
godello, treixadura, albariño.

89 Colour: bright straw. Nose: fresh, fresh fruit, white flowers, grassy. Palate: flavourful, fruity, good acidity, balanced.

PAZO DE MARIÑAN 2011 T
mencía, tempranillo.

86 Colour: cherry, purple rim. Nose: ripe fruit, red berry notes, scrubland. Palate: flavourful, fruity.

QUINTAS DAS TAPIAS 2010 T
mencía, tempranillo.

86 Colour: cherry, garnet rim. Nose: ripe fruit, warm, characterful, scrubland. Palate: flavourful, powerful, fine bitter notes, good acidity.

TAPIAS 10 2009 T
mencía.

84

PAZO DAS TAPIAS

As Tapias - Pazos
32600 Verin (Ourense)
☎: +34 988 261 256 - Fax: +34 988 261 264
info@pazodomar.com
www.pazodastapias.com

FINCA OS COBATOS 2011 B
godello.

89 Colour: bright straw. Nose: fresh, fresh fruit, white flowers, elegant. Palate: flavourful, fruity, good acidity, light-bodied.

ALMA DE BLANCO GODELLO 2011 B
godello.

87 Colour: bright straw. Nose: fresh, fresh fruit, faded flowers. Palate: flavourful, fruity, balanced.

FINCA OS COBATOS 2011 T
mencía.

88 Colour: cherry, purple rim. Nose: floral, fresh fruit, red berry notes, balsamic herbs. Palate: fresh, fruity, light-bodied, easy to drink.

ALMA DE TINTO 2011 T
mencía.

87 Colour: cherry, purple rim. Nose: red berry notes, ripe fruit, balsamic herbs, medium intensity. Palate: powerful, flavourful, correct.

PAZOS DEL REY

Carrero Blanco, 33- Albarellos
32618 Monterrei (Ourense)
☎: +34 988 425 959 - Fax: +34 988 425 949
info@pazosdelrey.com
www.pazosdelrey.com

PAZO DE MONTERREY 2011 B
godello.

90 Colour: bright straw. Nose: expressive, ripe fruit, citrus fruit, grassy, balsamic herbs. Palate: flavourful, fruity, fresh.

SILA GODELLO 2011 B
100% godello.

88 Colour: bright straw. Nose: ripe fruit, dried herbs, white flowers. Palate: flavourful, fruity, good acidity.

SILA MENCÍA 2010 T BARRICA
100% mencía.

88 Colour: deep cherry. Nose: spicy, toasty, scrubland, candied fruit, red berry notes. Palate: powerful, fine bitter notes, good acidity.

QUINTA DO BUBLE

Ladeira A Machada s/n Casas dos Montes
32689 Oimbra (Ourense)
☎: +34 988 422 960
info@quintadobuble.com
www.quintadobuble.com

QUINTA DO BUBLE 2011 B
godello.

87 Colour: bright yellow. Nose: powerfull, candied fruit, fruit preserve. Palate: flavourful, fine bitter notes, good acidity.

TERRAS DO CIGARRÓN

Ctra. N- 525
32618 Albarellos de Monterrei (Ourense)
☎: +34 988 418 703
bodega@terrasdocigarron.com
www.terrasdocigarron.com

TERRAS DO CIGARRÓN 2011 B
100% godello.

87 Colour: bright straw. Nose: fresh, fresh fruit, dried flowers, medium intensity. Palate: flavourful, fruity, correct.

DO MONTILLA-MORILES

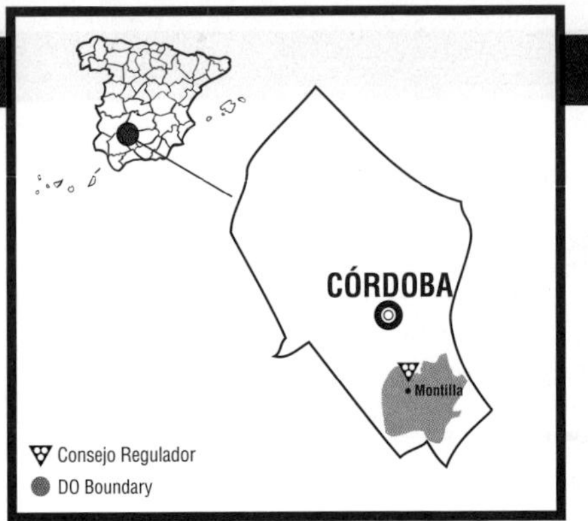

LOCATION:

To the south of Córdoba. It covers all the vineyards of the municipal districts of Montilla, Moriles, Montalbán, Puente Genil, Montruque, Nueva Carteya and Doña Mencía, and part of the municipal districts of Montemayor, Fernán-Núñez, La Rambla, Santaella, Aguilar de la Frontera, Lucena, Cabra, Baena, Castro del Río and Espejo.

CLIMATE:

Semi-continental Mediterranean, with long, hot, dry summers and short winters. The average annual temperature is 16.8°C and the average rainfall is between 500 mm and 1,000 mm per year.

SOIL:

The vineyards are situated at an altitude of between 125 m and 640 m. The soils are franc, franc-sandy and, in the higher regions, calcareous ('Albarizas'), which are precisely those of best quality, and which predominate in what is known as the Upper Sub-Region, which includes the municipal districts of Montilla, Moriles, Castro del Río, Cabra and Aguilar de la Frontera.

GRAPE VARIETIES:

WHITE: *Pedro Ximénez* (main variety), *Airén, Baladí, Moscatel, Torrontés* and *Verdejo.*
RED: *Tempranillo, Syrah* and *Cabernet Sauvignon.*

SUB-REGIONS:

We have to differentiate between the vineyards in the flatlands and those in higher areas –such as Sierra de Montilla and Moriles Alto–, prominently limestone soils of higher quality and hardly 2000 hectares planted.

FIGURES:

Vineyard surface: 5,483 – **Wine-Growers:** 2,592 – **Wineries:** 84 – **2011 Harvest rating:** N/A – **Production:** 32,654,427 litres – **Market percentages:** 88% domestic. 12% export

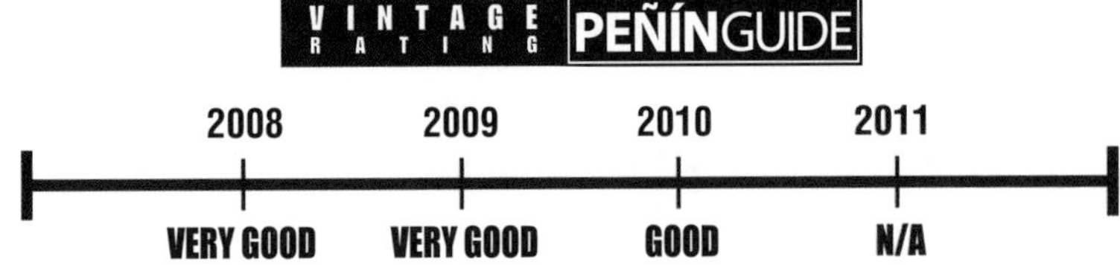

CONSEJO REGULADOR
Rita Pérez, s/n - 14550 Montilla (Córdoba) - ☎: +34 957 699 957 - Fax: +34 957 652 866
@ consejo.montillamoriles @juntadeandalucia.es - www.montilla-moriles.org

ALVEAR

María Auxiliadora, 1
14550 Montilla (Córdoba)
☎: +34 957 650 100 - Fax: +34 957 650 135
alvearsa@alvear.es
www.alvear.es

ALVEAR SOLERA FUNDACIÓN AM
100% pedro ximénez.

94 Colour: light mahogany. Nose: complex, powerfull, neat, caramel, acetaldehyde, sweet spices. Palate: good structure, rich, full, fine bitter notes.

CARLOS VII AM
100% pedro ximénez.

90 Colour: old gold. Nose: balanced, sweet spices, candied fruit. Palate: balanced, fine bitter notes, flavourful.

ALVEAR SOLERA CREAM CR
100% pedro ximénez.

90 Colour: light mahogany. Nose: spicy, dry nuts, acetaldehyde, candied fruit, cocoa bean. Palate: complex, flavourful, long, elegant, balanced.

ALVEAR FINO EN RAMA 2006 FI
100% pedro ximénez.

90 Colour: bright yellow. Nose: complex, expressive, saline, pungent, faded flowers. Palate: fresh, easy to drink, long, fine bitter notes.

C.B. FI
100% pedro ximénez.

90 Colour: bright straw. Nose: pungent, saline, floral, dry nuts, complex, expressive. Palate: flavourful, long, fine bitter notes, elegant.

ASUNCIÓN OL
100% pedro ximénez.

91 Colour: light mahogany. Nose: elegant, candied fruit, sweet spices, caramel. Palate: complex, rich, full, fine bitter notes.

ALVEAR PX 1927 S/C PX SOLERA
100% pedro ximénez.

90 Colour: dark mahogany. Nose: fruit liqueur notes, pattiserie, toasty, acetaldehyde, varnish, dry nuts, dried fruit. Palate: sweet, rich, unctuous, flavourful, long, toasty.

ALVEAR PX COSECHA 2008 PX
100% pedro ximénez.

90 Colour: light mahogany. Nose: fruit liqueur notes, fruit liqueur notes, expressive, powerfull, caramel, pattiserie. Palate: balanced, unctuous.

ALVEAR PX 1830 PX RESERVA
100% pedro ximénez.

98 Colour: dark mahogany. Nose: complex, dried fruit, pattiserie, toasty, acetaldehyde, tobacco. Palate: sweet, rich, unctuous, powerful.

ALVEAR DULCE VIEJO PX RESERVA
100% pedro ximénez.

94 Colour: dark mahogany. Nose: dried fruit, complex, varietal, expressive, nose:tic coffee, tobacco. Palate: concentrated, rich, good structure.

BODEGAS CRUZ CONDE

Ronda Canillo, 4
14550 Montilla (Córdoba)
☎: +34 957 651 250 - Fax: +34 957 653 619
info@bodegascruzconde.es
www.bodegascruzconde.es

CRUZ CONDE FI
100% pedro ximénez.

85 Colour: bright yellow. Nose: medium intensity, wild herbs, saline. Palate: flavourful, rich.

MERCEDES OL
100% pedro ximénez.

83

CRUZ CONDE SOLERA FUNDACIÓN 1902 PX
pedro ximénez.

92 Colour: mahogany. Nose: complex, tobacco, dark chocolate, pattiserie, dried fruit. Palate: flavourful, balanced, unctuous, spicy.

BODEGAS DELGADO

Cosano, 2
14500 Puente Genil (Córdoba)
☎: +34 957 600 085 - Fax: +34 957 604 571
fino@bodegasdelgado.com
www.bodegasdelgado.com

DELGADO 1874 AMONTILLADO NATURAL MUY VIEJO AM
100% pedro ximénez.

90 Colour: old gold, amber rim. Nose: acetaldehyde, sweet spices, cocoa bean, caramel. Palate: long, spicy, rich, flavourful.

SEGUNDA BOTA FI
100% pedro ximénez.

87 Colour: bright straw, greenish rim. Nose: dry nuts, medium intensity, balanced, saline. Palate: flavourful, correct, fine bitter notes.

F.E.O. FINO EXTRA OLOROSO OL
pedro ximénez.

85 Colour: bright yellow. Nose: powerfull, nose:tic coffee, spicy, toasty, dry nuts. Palate: correct, flavourful.

DELGADO 1874 PX
pedro ximénez.

94 Colour: dark mahogany. Nose: complex, powerfull, dark chocolate, pattiserie, expressive, varnish. Palate: fruity, flavourful, spicy, creamy.

CALIFA PX
100% pedro ximénez.

88 Colour: light mahogany. Nose: dried fruit, honeyed notes, toasty, sweet spices, powerfull. Palate: good structure, full, long.

BODEGAS JESÚS NAZARENO

Avda. Cañete de las Torres, 33
14850 Baena (Córdoba)
☎: +34 957 670 225 - Fax: +34 957 690 873
bjn@bjn1963.com
www.bjn1963.com

DON BUENO S/C B
baldi, torrontés.

80 Colour: bright straw. Nose: slightly evolved, medium intensity, faded flowers. Palate: flavourful, fruity.

PEDRO XIMÉNEZ PX

88 Colour: dark mahogany. Nose: fruit liqueur notes, dried fruit, pattiserie, toasty. Palate: sweet, rich, unctuous, powerful.

BODEGAS LA AURORA

Avda. de Europa, 7
14550 Montilla (Córdoba)
☎: +34 957 650 362 - Fax: +34 957 654 642
administracion@bodegaslaaurora.com
www.bodegaslaaurora.com

FINO AMANECER FI

86 Colour: bright yellow. Nose: balanced, neat, dried herbs. Palate: correct, easy to drink.

AMANECER SOLERA DRY OLOROSO OL

87 Colour: light mahogany. Nose: balanced, complex, toasty, spicy, acetaldehyde. Palate: correct, balanced, good finish.

SOLERA 1981 PX

91 Colour: mahogany. Nose: toasty, sweet spices, fruit liqueur notes, fruit liqueur notes, dark chocolate. Palate: flavourful, unctuous.

AMANECER PX

87 Colour: light mahogany. Nose: balanced, powerfull, dried fruit, fruit liqueur notes, caramel. Palate: sweet.

BODEGAS MÁLAGA VIRGEN

Autovía A-92, Málaga-Sevilla, Km. 132
29520 Fuente de Piedra (Málaga)
☎: +34 952 319 454 - Fax: +34 952 359 819
didier.bricout@bodegasmalagavirgen.com
www.bodegasmalagavirgen.com

LAGAR DE BENAVIDES FI

84

BODEGAS MORENO

Fuente de la Salud, 2
14006 (Córdoba)
☎: +34 957 767 605 - Fax: +34 957 279 907
moreno@morenosa.com
www.morenosa.com

CABRIOLA AMONTILLADO VIEJO AM
100% pedro ximénez.

89 Colour: light mahogany. Nose: sweet spices, nose:tic coffee, acetaldehyde, complex. Palate: rich, flavourful, concentrated, long.

SIETE SABIOS AM
100% pedro ximénez.

88 Colour: old gold. Nose: medium intensity, sweet spices, candied fruit, acetaldehyde. Palate: flavourful, rich, long.

MUSA AM
100% pedro ximénez.

86 Colour: old gold. Nose: balanced, complex, acetaldehyde, spicy. Palate: full, flavourful, spicy.

BENAVIDES FI
100% pedro ximénez.

85 Colour: bright yellow. Nose: balanced, faded flowers, saline. Palate: easy to drink, good finish.

MUSA FI
100% pedro ximénez.

82

MUSA OL
100% pedro ximénez.

90 Colour: light mahogany. Nose: medium intensity, sweet spices, cocoa bean, candied fruit. Palate: flavourful, spicy, fine bitter notes.

PLATINO SOLERA OLOROSA OL
100% pedro ximénez.

90 Colour: iodine, amber rim. Nose: powerfull, complex, elegant, dry nuts, toasty. Palate: rich, fine bitter notes, fine solera notes, long, spicy.

OLOROSO VIEJO FUNDACIÓN 1819 OL
100% pedro ximénez.

88 Colour: iodine, amber rim. Nose: powerfull, elegant, dry nuts, toasty, caramel. Palate: rich, fine bitter notes, , long, spicy.

ALBOROQUE PC
100% pedro ximénez.

89 Colour: light mahogany. Nose: balanced, powerfull, acetaldehyde, sweet spices, candied fruit. Palate: rich, full.

VIRGILIO PX
100% pedro ximénez.

90 Colour: dark mahogany. Nose: dried fruit, honeyed notes, caramel, nose:tic coffee, dark chocolate. Palate: rich, flavourful.

MUSA PX
100% pedro ximénez.

87 Colour: dark mahogany. Nose: complex, fruit liqueur notes, dried fruit, pattiserie, toasty. Palate: sweet, rich, unctuous, powerful.

UNA VIDA PX
100% pedro ximénez.

86 Colour: dark mahogany. Nose: sweet spices, caramel, dark chocolate, dried fruit, powerfull. Palate: rich, flavourful, long.

BODEGAS MORILES 47

Ctra. de la Estación, 11 Apdo. 534
14900 Lucena (Córdoba)
☎: +34 957 500 046 - Fax: +34 957 502 935
ventas@moriles47.com
www.moriles47.com

LAGAR DE CAMPOARAS 2011 B
vidueño.

79

PACORRITO AM
pedro ximénez.

88 Colour: light mahogany. Nose: sweet spices, acetaldehyde, candied fruit. Palate: flavourful, rich, full, complex, spicy, long.

PATRICIA CREAM CR
pedro ximénez.

86 Colour: light mahogany. Nose: old leather, tobacco, candied fruit, sweet spices. Palate: flavourful, easy to drink.

MORILES 47 FI
pedro ximénez.

86 Colour: bright yellow. Nose: expressive, neat, faded flowers, saline. Palate: fine bitter notes, correct, balanced.

PX ARACELI VIEJO PX
pedro ximénez.

87 Colour: dark mahogany. Nose: pattiserie, dark chocolate, dried fruit, spicy. Palate: flavourful, unctuous, balanced, good structure.

BODEGAS ROBLES

Ctra. Córdoba-Málaga, Km. 44,7
14550 Montilla (Córdoba)
☎: +34 957 650 063 - Fax: +34 957 653 140
info@bodegasrobles.com
www.bodegasrobles.com

SELECCIÓN ROBLES 1927 PX PX

90 Colour: dark mahogany. Nose: complex, dried fruit, toasty, fruit liqueur notes, dark chocolate, nose:tic coffee. Palate: sweet, rich, unctuous, powerful.

CÍA. VINÍCOLA DEL SUR - TOMÁS GARCÍA

Avda. Luis de Góngora y Argote, s/n
14550 Montilla (Córdoba)
☎: +34 957 650 204 - Fax: +34 957 652 335
info@vinicoladelsur.com
www.vinicoladelsur.com

MONTE CRISTO AM
100% pedro ximénez.

89 Colour: light mahogany. Nose: pattiserie, sweet spices, caramel, acetaldehyde. Palate: flavourful, balanced, long.

MONTE CRISTO FI
100% pedro ximénez.

89 Colour: bright yellow. Nose: powerfull, balanced, expressive, saline, pungent, faded flowers. Palate: fine bitter notes, balanced, long.

VERBENERA FI
pedro ximénez.

89 Colour: bright straw. Nose: elegant, dried flowers, saline. Palate: correct, fine bitter notes, easy to drink.

MONTE CRISTO OL
100% pedro ximénez.

92 Colour: iodine, amber rim. Nose: powerfull, toasty, sweet spices. Palate: rich, fine bitter notes, , balanced, long.

TOMÁS GARCÍA PX
100% pedro ximénez.

89 Colour: dark mahogany. Nose: powerfull, fruit liqueur notes, fruit liqueur notes, dried fruit, toasty. Palate: full, flavourful.

MONTE CRISTO PX
100% pedro ximénez.

87 Colour: mahogany. Nose: dried fruit, balanced, powerfull, varietal, pattiserie. Palate: long, creamy, correct, spirituous, sweet.

EQUIPO NAVAZOS

Cartuja, 1 - módulo 6
11401 Jerez de la Frontera (Cádiz)
equipo@navazos.com
www.equiponavazos.com

OVNI 2011 B
100% pedro ximénez.

89 Colour: bright yellow. Nose: dried flowers, dry nuts, dried herbs, saline. Palate: powerful, flavourful, complex, balanced.

CASA DEL INCA 2010 PX
pedro ximénez.

95 Colour: mahogany. Nose: candied fruit, dried fruit, balanced, sweet spices, pattiserie. Palate: rich, concentrated, long, balanced.

GRACIA HERMANOS

Avda. Marqués de la Vega de Armijo, 103
14550 Montilla (Córdoba)
☎: +34 957 650 162 - Fax: +34 957 652 335
info@bodegasgracia.com
www.bodegasgracia.com

VIÑAVERDE 2011 B
pedro ximénez, verdejo, moscatel, macabeo, torrontés.

84

TAUROMAQUIA AMONTILLADO VIEJO AM
100% pedro ximénez.

89 Colour: light mahogany. Nose: complex, expressive, sweet spices, acetaldehyde, candied fruit, dry nuts, toasty. Palate: balanced, fine bitter notes, long.

SOLERA FINA TAUROMAQUIA FI
100% pedro ximénez.

89 Colour: bright yellow. Nose: medium intensity, balanced, faded flowers. Palate: flavourful, full, easy to drink, fine bitter notes.

SOLERA FINA MARÍA DEL VALLE FI
100% pedro ximénez.

87 Colour: bright yellow. Nose: floral, saline, pungent, complex, elegant. Palate: flavourful, long, balanced, fine bitter notes.

FINO CORREDERA FI
100% pedro ximénez.

87 Colour: bright yellow. Nose: medium intensity, dried flowers. Palate: flavourful, full, good structure, long.

TAUROMAQUIA OL
100% pedro ximénez.

88 Colour: iodine, amber rim. Nose: powerfull, elegant, dry nuts, toasty, sweet spices, spicy. Palate: rich, fine bitter notes, , long, spicy.

TAUROMAQUIA PX
100% pedro ximénez.

90 Colour: dark mahogany. Nose: complex, fruit liqueur notes, dried fruit, pattiserie, toasty. Palate: sweet, rich, unctuous, powerful.

GRACIA DULCE VIEJO PX
100% pedro ximénez.

89 Colour: dark mahogany. Nose: dried fruit, expressive, powerfull, sweet spices, pattiserie. Palate: rich, good structure, balanced.

NAVISA

Ctra. Montalbán, s/n
14550 Montilla (Córdoba)
☎: +34 957 650 450 - Fax: +34 957 651 747
abaena@navisa.es
www.navisa.es

VEGA MARÍA 2010 B
chardonnay, moscatel, macabeo.

82

COBOS FI
100% pedro ximénez.

85 Colour: bright straw. Nose: balanced, medium intensity, pungent, saline. Palate: light-bodied, easy to drink.

TRES PASAS PX
100% pedro ximénez.

87 Colour: light mahogany. Nose: spicy, nose:tic coffee, fruit liqueur notes, dried fruit, balanced. Palate: fruity, unctuous.

PÉREZ BARQUERO

Avda. Andalucía, 27
14550 Montilla (Córdoba)
☎: +34 957 650 500 - Fax: +34 957 650 208
info@perezbarquero.com
www.perezbarquero.com

VIÑA AMALIA 2011 B
pedro ximénez, moscatel, verdejo, torrontés.

84

GRAN BARQUERO AM
100% pedro ximénez.

91 Colour: old gold. Nose: neat, sweet spices, caramel, candied fruit. Palate: flavourful, balanced, spicy.

GRAN BARQUERO FI
100% pedro ximénez.

89 Colour: bright yellow. Nose: balanced, saline, dried flowers, dry nuts. Palate: flavourful, dry, long.

FINO LOS AMIGOS FI
100% pedro ximénez.

86 Colour: bright straw. Nose: balanced, medium intensity, saline, faded flowers. Palate: flavourful, rich, long, fine bitter notes.

GRAN BARQUERO OL
100% pedro ximénez.

90 Colour: old gold. Nose: candied fruit, sweet spices, caramel, medium intensity. Palate: ripe fruit, balanced, fine bitter notes.

PÉREZ BARQUERO PEDRO XIMÉNEZ DE COSECHA 2010 PX
100% pedro ximénez.

89 Colour: light mahogany. Nose: candied fruit, dried fruit, honeyed notes, varietal, pattiserie. Palate: balanced, unctuous, long.

LA CAÑADA PX
100% pedro ximénez.

96 Colour: dark mahogany. Nose: complex, fruit liqueur notes, dried fruit, pattiserie, toasty. Palate: sweet, rich, unctuous, powerful.

GRAN BARQUERO PX
100% pedro ximénez.

90 Colour: mahogany. Nose: pattiserie, toasty, dark chocolate, powerfull, dried fruit. Palate: flavourful, sweet, correct, balanced.

TORO ALBALÁ

Avda. Antonio Sánchez Romero, 1
14920 Aguilar de la Frontera (Córdoba)
☎: +34 957 660 046 - Fax: +34 957 661 494
info@toroalbala.com
www.toroalbala.com

ELÉCTRICO FINO DEL LAGAR FI
100% pedro ximénez.

87 Colour: bright yellow. Nose: expressive, pungent, saline, dry nuts. Palate: long, fine bitter notes, balanced.

DON P.X. 2008 PX
100% pedro ximénez.

90 Colour: mahogany. Nose: cocoa bean, sweet spices, fruit liqueur notes, honeyed notes. Palate: spirituous, flavourful, toasty, spicy, balanced.

DON P.X. 1985 PX GRAN RESERVA
100% pedro ximénez.

94 Colour: dark mahogany. Nose: complex, expressive, floral, balsamic herbs, balanced, dried fruit, fruit liqueur notes. Palate: full, flavourful, elegant, unctuous.

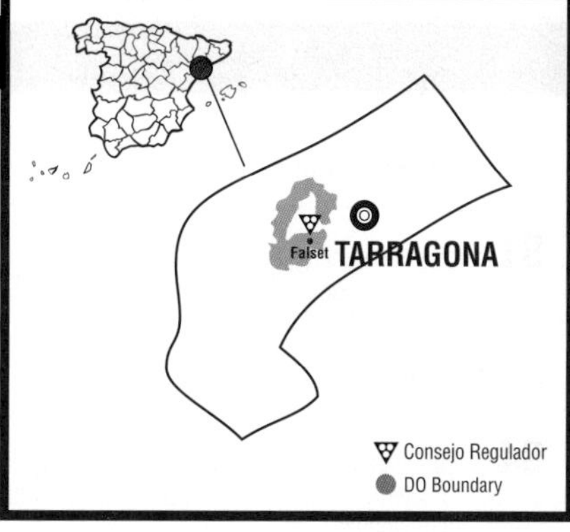

LOCATION:

In the region of Priorat (Tarragona). It is made up of Baix Priorat, part of Alt Priorat and various municipal districts of Ribera d'Ebre that were already integrated into the Falset sub-region. In total, 16 municipal districts: La Bisbal de Falset, Cabaces, Capçanes, Cornudella de Montsant, La Figuera, Els Guiamets, Marçá, Margalef, El Masroig, Pradell, La Torre de Fontaubella, Ulldemolins, Falset, El Molar, Darmós and La Serra d'Almos. The vineyards are located at widely variable altitudes, ranging between 200 m to 700 m above sea level.

CLIMATE:

Although the vineyards are located in a Mediterranean region, the mountains that surround the region isolate it from the sea to a certain extent, resulting in a somewhat more Continental climate. Due to this, it benefits from the contrasts in day/night temperatures, which is an important factor in the ripening of the grapes. However, it also receives the sea winds, laden with humidity, which help to compensate for the lack of rainfall in the summer. The average rainfall is between 500 and 600 mm per year.

SOIL:

There are mainly three types of soil: compact calcareous soils with pebbles on the borders of the DO; granite sands in Falset; and siliceous slate (the same stony slaty soil as Priorat) in certain areas of Falset and Cornudella.

GRAPE VARIETIES:

WHITE: *Chardonnay, Garnacha Blanca, Macabeo, Moscatel, Pansal, Parellada.*
RED: *Cabernet Sauvignon, Cariñena, Garnacha Tinta, Garnacha Peluda, Merlot, Monastrell, Picapoll, Syrah, Tempranillo* and *Mazuela.*

FIGURES:

Vineyard surface: 1,857 – **Wine-Growers:** 700 – **Wineries:** 59 – **2011 Harvest rating:** Very Good – **Production:** 5,900,000 litres – **Market percentages:** 38% domestic. 62% export

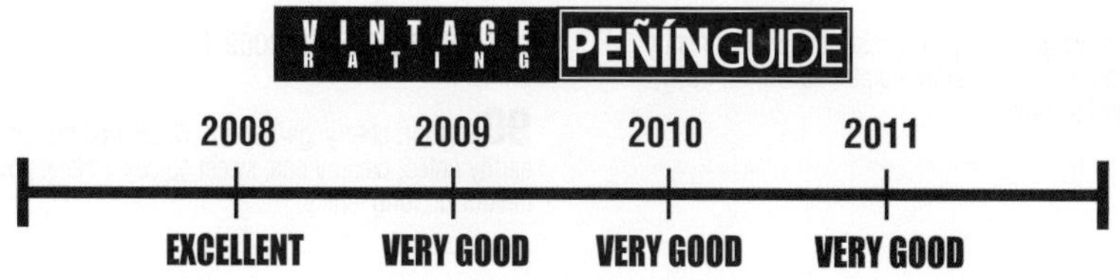

CONSEJO REGULADOR
Plaça de la Quartera, 6 - 43730 Falset (Tarragona) - ☎: +34 977 831 742 - Fax: +34 977 830 676
@ info@domontsant.com - www.domontsant.com

ACÚSTIC CELLER

Progrés s/n
43775 Marça (Tarragona)
☎: +34 672 432 691 - Fax: +34 977 660 867
acustic@acusticceller.com
www.acusticceller.com

ACÚSTIC 2011 BFB
60% garnacha, 10% garnacha roja, 25% macabeo, 5% pansal.

90 Colour: bright yellow. Nose: balanced, expressive, wild herbs, spicy. Palate: flavourful, good acidity, balanced, fine bitter notes, full.

ACÚSTIC 2010 B
60% garnacha, 10% garnacha roja, 25% macabeo, pansal.

91 Colour: bright yellow. Nose: floral, toasty, sweet spices, fresh fruit. Palate: balanced, good acidity, rich, flavourful, long.

+RITME 2010 B
70% garnacha blanca, 30% macabeo.

89 Colour: yellow, greenish rim. Nose: ripe fruit, balanced, dried herbs. Palate: flavourful, fruity, fine bitter notes.

ACÚSTIC ROSAT 2011 RD
40% garnacha, 40% cariñena, 20% garnacha roja.

88 Colour: rose, purple rim. Nose: powerfull, red berry notes, ripe fruit, floral. Palate: flavourful, fruity, fresh.

AUDITORI 2010 T
100% garnacha.

93 Colour: deep cherry, purple rim. Nose: balanced, complex, scrubland, expressive. Palate: good structure, flavourful, round tannins.

BRAÓ 2010 T
55% cariñena, 45% garnacha.

92 Colour: deep cherry, garnet rim. Nose: sweet spices, creamy oak, elegant, balanced, ripe fruit. Palate: good structure, long, round tannins.

RITME NEGRE 2010 T
70% cariñena, 30% garnacha.

92 Colour: bright cherry. Nose: sweet spices, creamy oak, mineral, fruit expression. Palate: flavourful, fruity, toasty, round tannins.

ACÚSTIC 2010 T ROBLE
35% garnacha, 65% cariñena.

91 Colour: black cherry, purple rim. Nose: ripe fruit, balsamic herbs, elegant, spicy. Palate: balanced, good acidity, ripe fruit, long.

AUDITORI 2009 T
100% garnacha.

94 Colour: cherry, garnet rim. Nose: spicy, creamy oak, toasty, characterful, mineral. Palate: powerful, flavourful, toasty, round tannins.

BRAÓ 2009 T
55% cariñena, 45% garnacha.

93 Colour: cherry, garnet rim. Nose: ripe fruit, spicy, creamy oak, toasty, complex, dark chocolate, mineral, scrubland. Palate: powerful, flavourful, toasty, round tannins.

ACÚSTIC 2009 T ROBLE
35% garnacha, 65% cariñena.

91 Colour: bright cherry. Nose: sweet spices, creamy oak, overripe fruit. Palate: flavourful, fruity, toasty, round tannins.

AGRÍCOLA D'ULLDEMOLINS SANT JAUME

Avda. Verge de Montserrat, s/n
43363 Ulldemolins (Tarragona)
☎: +34 977 561 613 - Fax: +34 977 561 613
coopulldemolins@omo.com
www.coopulldemolins.com

LES PEDRENYERES 2011 B
macabeo, garnacha.

88 Colour: bright straw. Nose: fresh, fresh fruit, white flowers, mineral. Palate: flavourful, fruity, good acidity, balanced.

ULLDEMOLINS 2011 T
100% garnacha.

85 Colour: deep cherry, purple rim. Nose: ripe fruit, scrubland. Palate: flavourful, ripe fruit, long.

LES PEDRENYERES 2009 T
garnacha.

90 Colour: cherry, garnet rim. Nose: ripe fruit, mineral, earthy notes, creamy oak, sweet spices. Palate: powerful, flavourful, long, spicy.

ALFREDO ARRIBAS

Sort dels Capellans, 5
43730 Falset (Tarragona)
☎: +34 932 531 760 - Fax: +34 934 173 591
info@portaldelpriorat.com
www.portaldelpriorat.com

TROSSOS SANTS 2011 B
90% garnacha blanca, 10% garnacha gris.

93 Colour: bright straw. Nose: floral, fragrant herbs, mineral, spicy, creamy oak. Palate: rich, flavourful, fruity, long, spicy, balanced.

TROSSOS TROS BLANC 2010 B
garnacha blanca.

92 Colour: bright yellow. Nose: ripe fruit, sweet spices, creamy oak, fragrant herbs, white flowers, mineral, expressive. Palate: rich, flavourful, fresh, good acidity, long, balanced.

TROSSOS TROS BLANC MAGNUM 2009 B
garnacha blanca.

96 Colour: bright yellow. Nose: dried flowers, ripe fruit, mineral, wild herbs, sweet spices, creamy oak, balanced. Palate: long, spicy, flavourful, fresh, mineral, elegant.

TROSSOS TROS NEGRE 2009 T
garnacha.

95 Colour: light cherry, garnet rim. Nose: balanced, cocoa bean, sweet spices, expressive. Palate: flavourful, fruity, round tannins.

TROSSOS TROS NEGRE MAGNUM 2008 T
garnacha.

95 Colour: light cherry, orangey edge. Nose: complex, elegant, balanced, wild herbs, sweet spices. Palate: good structure, flavourful, elegant, fine bitter notes.

BODEGAS ORDÓÑEZ

Bartolomé Esteban Murillo, 11
29700 Vélez- Málaga (Málaga)
☎: +34 952 504 706 - Fax: +34 951 284 796
office@jorge-ordonez.es
www.grupojorgeordonez.com

ZERRÁN GARNATXA BLANCA 2011 B
garnacha blanca.

87 Colour: bright straw. Nose: candied fruit, citrus fruit, balsamic herbs. Palate: fine bitter notes, good acidity.

ZERRÁN 2010 T
50% garnacha, 40% mazuelo, 10% syrah.

88 Colour: bright cherry. Nose: ripe fruit, creamy oak, mineral. Palate: flavourful, fruity, toasty, round tannins.

BUIL & GINÉ

Ctra. de Gratallops - Vilella Baixa, Km. 11,5
43737 Gratallops (Tarragona)
☎: +34 977 839 810 - Fax: +34 977 839 811
info@builgine.com
www.builgine.com

17-XI 2009 T ROBLE
garnacha, cariñena, tempranillo.

88 Colour: cherry, garnet rim. Nose: fruit expression, floral, balanced. Palate: flavourful, fruity, easy to drink.

BABOIX 2008 T
garnacha, cariñena, tempranillo, cabernet sauvignon.

90 Colour: very deep cherry. Nose: sweet spices, ripe fruit, mineral. Palate: flavourful, spicy, good acidity.

CASTELL D'OR

Mare Rafols, 3- 1º 4º
08720 Vilafranca del Penedès (Barcelona)
☎: +34 938 905 446 - Fax: +34 938 905 446
castelldor@castelldor.com
www.castelldor.com

TEMPLER 2007 TC
50% garnacha, 50% tempranillo.

85 Colour: cherry, garnet rim. Nose: toasty, spicy, nose:tic coffee, fruit liqueur notes. Palate: fine bitter notes, sweetness.

TEMPLER 2006 TR
40% cabernet sauvignon, 30% garnacha, 30% tempranillo.

85 Colour: cherry, garnet rim. Nose: ripe fruit, spicy, roasted coffee, nose:tic coffee. Palate: powerful, flavourful, toasty.

CELLER ANGUERA DOMENECH

Sant Pere, 2
43743 Darmós (Tarragona)
☎: +34 977 405 857 - Fax: +34 977 404 106
angueradomenech@wanadoo.es
www.vianguera.com

RECLOT 2011 T
garnacha, tempranillo, monastrell.

85 Colour: cherry, garnet rim. Nose: ripe fruit, fruit preserve, balsamic herbs. Palate: fruity, flavourful, correct.

VINYA GASÓ 2008 TC
garnacha, tempranillo, samsó.

89 Colour: bright cherry. Nose: ripe fruit, sweet spices, creamy oak, expressive. Palate: flavourful, fruity, toasty, round tannins.

CELLER CAIRATS

Vista Alegre, 9 2n Organyá
25794 Cornudella de Montsant (Tarragona)
☎: +34 606 995 952

SAURÍ 2010 T

88 Colour: cherry, garnet rim. Nose: ripe fruit, fruit liqueur notes, scrubland, earthy notes. Palate: good acidity, flavourful, balsamic, spicy, long.

CELLER CEDÓ ANGUERA

Ctra. La Serra d'Almos-Darmós, Km. 0,2
43746 La Serra d'Almos (Tarragona)
☎: +34 699 694 728 - Fax: +34 977 417 369
celler@cedoanguera.com
www.cedoanguera.com

ANEXE 2011 T
samsó, garnacha, syrah.

86 Colour: cherry, purple rim. Nose: medium intensity, ripe fruit, scrubland. Palate: fruity, good acidity.

CLÒNIC 2009 T
samsó, cabernet sauvignon, syrah.

88 Colour: cherry, garnet rim. Nose: spicy, creamy oak, toasty, fruit preserve. Palate: powerful, flavourful, toasty.

CELLER COOPERATIU CORNUDELLA

Comte de Rius, 2
43360 Cornudella de Montsant (Tarragona)
☎: +34 977 821 329 - Fax: +34 977 821 329
info@cornudella.net
www.cornudella.net

LES TROIES 2011 B
macabeo, garnacha rosa.

89 Colour: bright straw. Nose: fresh, fresh fruit, white flowers, expressive. Palate: flavourful, fruity, good acidity, balanced.

LES TROIES 2011 RD
60% garnacha, 40% cariñena.

89 Colour: rose, purple rim. Nose: powerfull, ripe fruit, red berry notes, floral. Palate: , powerful, fruity, fresh, easy to drink, balanced.

LES TROIES 2011 T
50% garnacha, 50% cariñena.

91 Colour: dark-red cherry, garnet rim. Nose: fresh, ripe fruit, balsamic herbs, mineral, earthy notes. Palate: powerful, flavourful, complex, spicy.

CASTELL DE SIURANA SELECCIÓ DE COSTERS 2009 T
70% garnacha, 30% cariñena.

90 Colour: cherry, garnet rim. Nose: ripe fruit, spicy, creamy oak, earthy notes. Palate: powerful, flavourful, toasty.

CODOLAR 2009 T
50% garnacha, 50% cariñena.

87 Colour: cherry, garnet rim. Nose: ripe fruit, balsamic herbs, spicy, creamy oak. Palate: correct, powerful, flavourful.

CASTELL DE SIURANA GARNATXA DEL MONTSANT 2010
100% garnacha roja.

90 Colour: light mahogany. Nose: fruit liqueur notes, fruit liqueur notes, caramel, pattiserie, toasty, varnish. Palate: powerful, flavourful, long, spicy.

CASTELLA DE SIURANA MISTELA 2010 VINO DE LICOR
100% garnacha.

88 Colour: ruby red. Nose: candied fruit, floral, sweet spices, powerfull, acetaldehyde. Palate: spicy, long, powerful, flavourful.

CELLER DE CAPÇANES

Celler de Capçanes
43776 Capçanes (Tarragona)
☎: +34 977 178 319 - Fax: +34 977 178 319
cellercapcanes@cellercapcanes.com
www.cellercapcanes.com

MAS DONÍS 2011 RD
80% garnacha, 10% syrah, 10% merlot.

88 Colour: rose, bright. Nose: balanced, red berry notes, fragrant herbs. Palate: ripe fruit, good acidity.

MAS PICOSA 2011 T
garnacha, merlot, tempranillo.

90 Colour: cherry, purple rim. Nose: powerfull, ripe fruit, fruit expression. Palate: powerful, flavourful, ripe fruit.

MAS DONÍS 2011 T
80% garnacha, 10% syrah, 5% tempranillo, 5% merlot.

86 Colour: cherry, purple rim. Nose: warm, ripe fruit, spicy. Palate: good acidity, fine bitter notes, warm.

COSTERS DEL GRAVET 2010 TC
60% cabernet sauvignon, 30% garnacha, 10% cariñena.

92 Colour: deep cherry, purple rim. Nose: expressive, red berry notes, ripe fruit, balsamic herbs, sweet spices. Palate: good structure, good acidity, fine bitter notes, round tannins.

FLOR DE PRIMAVERA PERAJ HA'ABIB KOSHER 2010 T
33% cabernet sauvignon, 33% cariñena, 33% garnacha.

91 Colour: cherry, garnet rim. Nose: complex, expressive, balanced, ripe fruit, creamy oak. Palate: good structure, flavourful, full.

MAS TORTÓ 2010 TC
70% garnacha, 10% syrah, 10% merlot, 10% cabernet sauvignon.

91 Colour: cherry, purple rim. Nose: complex, balanced, ripe fruit, spicy, scrubland. Palate: good structure, flavourful, complex.

LASENDAL GARNATXA 2010 T BARRICA
85% garnacha, 15% syrah.

90 Colour: deep cherry, purple rim. Nose: spicy, balsamic herbs, ripe fruit. Palate: correct, ripe fruit, good finish.

MAS COLLET 2010 T BARRICA
30% garnacha, 30% cariñena, 20% tempranillo, 20% cabernet sauvignon.

88 Colour: bright cherry. Nose: ripe fruit, sweet spices, expressive. Palate: flavourful, fruity, toasty, round tannins.

CABRIDA VIÑAS VIEJAS 2009 T
100% garnacha.

91 Colour: cherry, garnet rim. Nose: wild herbs, ripe fruit, sweet spices. Palate: flavourful, good structure, good acidity.

VALL DEL CALÀS 2009 T
50% merlot, 30% garnacha, 20% tempranillo.

90 Colour: cherry, garnet rim. Nose: ripe fruit, spicy, creamy oak, complex. Palate: powerful, flavourful, toasty, round tannins.

PANSAL DEL CALÀS VINO DE POSTRE 2008 T
70% garnacha, 30% cariñena.

90 Colour: cherry, garnet rim. Nose: ripe fruit, fruit liqueur notes, dark chocolate, cocoa bean, sweet spices, toasty. Palate: powerful, flavourful, long, balanced.

CELLER DOSTERRAS

Ctra. Falset a Marça, Km. 2
43775 Marça (Tarragona)
☎: +34 678 730 596
jgrau@dosterras.com
www.dosterras.com

DOSTERRAS 2010 T
garnacha.

92 Colour: bright cherry. Nose: sweet spices, creamy oak, expressive, red berry notes, ripe fruit. Palate: flavourful, fruity, toasty, round tannins.

VESPRES 2010 T
80% garnacha, 20% samsó.

89 Colour: cherry, garnet rim. Nose: ripe fruit, spicy, roasted coffee, scrubland. Palate: correct, powerful, flavourful.

CELLER EL MASROIG

Passeig de L'Arbre, 3
43736 El Masroig (Tarragona)
☎: +34 977 825 026
celler@cellermasroig.com
www.cellermasroig.com

SOLA FRED 2011 B
75% macabeo, 25% garnacha blanca.

86 Colour: bright yellow. Nose: dried flowers, dried herbs, citrus fruit, ripe fruit. Palate: powerful, flavourful, long.

ETNIC 2010 BFB
100% garnacha blanca.

90 Colour: bright yellow. Nose: powerfull, ripe fruit, sweet spices, creamy oak, fragrant herbs. Palate: rich, smoky afterpalate:, flavourful, fresh, good acidity.

LES SORTS 2010 BFB
100% garnacha blanca.

88 Colour: bright yellow. Nose: ripe fruit, citrus fruit, dried herbs, spicy, creamy oak, toasty. Palate: powerful, flavourful, rich, long.

LES SORTS ROSAT 2011 RD
90% garnacha, 10% mazuelo.

89 Colour: rose, bright. Nose: fresh, balanced, wild herbs, red berry notes, ripe fruit. Palate: flavourful, fruity, long.

SOLA FRED 2011 RD
90% garnacha, 10% syrah.

87 Colour: light cherry, bright. Nose: fresh, citrus fruit. Palate: correct, flavourful, good acidity, fine bitter notes.

LES SORTS 2011 T MACERACIÓN CARBÓNICA
50% mazuelo, 30% garnacha, 20% syrah.

89 Colour: cherry, purple rim. Nose: expressive, fresh fruit, red berry notes, floral. Palate: flavourful, fruity, good acidity, round tannins.

FINCA CUCÓ 2011 T
50% garnacha, 40% mazuelo, 10% syrah.

87 Colour: deep cherry. Nose: powerfull, warm, fruit preserve. Palate: flavourful, powerful, fine bitter notes.

SOLÀ FRED 2011 T
90% mazuelo, 10% garnacha.

86 Colour: cherry, purple rim. Nose: ripe fruit, mineral, balsamic herbs. Palate: correct, powerful, flavourful.

FINCA CUCÓ SELECCIÓ 2010 T
65% mazuelo, 30% garnacha, 5% syrah.

89 Colour: cherry, garnet rim. Nose: ripe fruit, fruit preserve, dark chocolate. Palate: balanced, fine bitter notes, ripe fruit.

CASTELL DE LES PINYERES 2009 T
40% garnacha, 40% mazuelo, 20% cabernet sauvignon, merlot, tempranillo.

91 Colour: cherry, garnet rim. Nose: ripe fruit, spicy, toasty, complex, mineral, earthy notes. Palate: powerful, flavourful, toasty, balanced.

LES SORTS VINYES VELLES 2007 TC
60% samsó, 30% garnacha, 10% cabernet sauvignon.

90 Colour: deep cherry, garnet rim. Nose: cocoa bean, sweet spices, ripe fruit. Palate: good structure, balanced, fine bitter notes, good acidity.

CELLER ELS GUIAMETS

Avinguda Ctra., 23
43777 Els Guiamets (Tarragona)
☎: +34 977 413 018
eguasch@cellerelsguiamets.com
www.cellerelsguiamets.com

LOMETS 2011 B
garnacha blanca.

83

MAS DELS METS 2011 T
garnacha, cariñena, tempranillo.

86 Colour: cherry, garnet rim. Nose: ripe fruit, balsamic herbs, medium intensity. Palate: powerful, flavourful, long.

GRAN METS 2008 TC
cabernet sauvignon, merlot, ull de llebre.

92 Colour: cherry, garnet rim. Nose: ripe fruit, spicy, creamy oak, toasty, complex, balsamic herbs. Palate: powerful, flavourful, toasty, round tannins, balanced.

GRAN METS 2007 TC
cabernet sauvignon, merlot, tempranillo.

89 Colour: cherry, garnet rim. Nose: spicy, creamy oak, toasty, mineral. Palate: powerful, flavourful, toasty, round tannins.

ISIS 2006 T
syrah, garnacha, cariñena.

88 Colour: cherry, garnet rim. Nose: fruit liqueur notes, ripe fruit, fine reductive notes, spicy, toasty, earthy notes. Palate: long, powerful, flavourful.

CELLER LAURONA

Ctra. Bellmunt s/n
43730 Falset (Tarragona)
☎: +34 977 830 221 - Fax: +34 977 831 797
laurona@cellerlaurona.com
www.cellerlaurona.com

LAURONA 2007 T
garnacha, cariñena, merlot, syrah, cabernet sauvignon.

91 Colour: cherry, garnet rim. Nose: ripe fruit, spicy, creamy oak, toasty, complex. Palate: powerful, flavourful, toasty, round tannins.

6 VINYES DE LAURONA 2006 T
garnacha, cariñena.

92 Colour: cherry, garnet rim. Nose: creamy oak, toasty, complex, earthy notes, mineral. Palate: powerful, flavourful, toasty, round tannins.

CELLER LOS TROVADORES

Avda. de las Encinas, 25
28707 San Sebastián de los Reyes (Madrid)
☎: +34 679 459 074
cgomez@lostrovadores.com
www.lostrovadores.com

GALLICANT 2005 T
garnacha, carignan, syrah.

88 Colour: cherry, garnet rim. Nose: ripe fruit, spicy, smoky, mineral, damp earth. Palate: powerful, flavourful, toasty, round tannins.

CELLER MAS DE LES VINYES

Mas de les Vinyes, s/n
43373 Cabacés (Tarragona)
☎: +34 652 568 848 - Fax: +34 977 718 543
josep@masdelesvinyes.com
www.masdelesvinyes.com

MAS DE LES VINYES NEGRE 2010 T
100% garnacha.

87 Colour: cherry, garnet rim. Nose: balanced, dried herbs, ripe fruit. Palate: flavourful, good structure, good acidity.

CELLER SUI GENERIS

Mas de l'Aleix
43886 Renau (Tarragona)
☎: +34 977 260 192 - Fax: +34 932 254 904
info@suigenerismontsant.com
www.suigenerismontsant.com

SUI GENERIS 2009 TC
90% cariñena, 10% garnacha.

87 Colour: cherry, garnet rim. Nose: medium intensity, balanced, ripe fruit, scrubland, spicy. Palate: ripe fruit, flavourful.

SUI GENERIS VIN DE GARAGE 2009 T
garnacha, tempranillo, cariñena, cabernet sauvignon, merlot.

84

SUI GENERIS 2008 TC
36% garnacha, 24% cariñena, 16% tempranillo, 16% cabernet sauvignon, 8% merlot.

87 Colour: cherry, garnet rim. Nose: spicy, toasty, fruit preserve, dark chocolate. Palate: powerful, flavourful, toasty, round tannins.

CELLER VENDRELL RIVED

Bassa, 10
43775 Marçà (Tarragona)
☎: +34 637 537 383 - Fax: +34 977 263 053
celler@vendrellrived.com
www.vendrellrived.com

SERE 2011 T
80% garnacha, 20% cariñena.

86 Colour: cherry, purple rim. Nose: ripe fruit, medium intensity, warm. Palate: fine bitter notes, flavourful.

L'ALLEU 2010 T
60% garnacha, 40% cariñena.

89 Colour: bright cherry. Nose: ripe fruit, sweet spices, creamy oak, expressive, earthy notes, mineral. Palate: flavourful, fruity, toasty.

CELLER VERMUNVER

Dalt, 29
43775 Marçà (Tarragona)
☎: +34 977 178 288 - Fax: +34 977 178 288
info@genesi.cat
www.genesi.cat

GÈNESI VARIETAL 2009 T
100% samsó.

95 Colour: cherry, garnet rim. Nose: ripe fruit, spicy, creamy oak, toasty, complex, mineral, elegant. Palate: powerful, flavourful, toasty, round tannins, balanced, elegant.

GÈNESI SELECCIÓ 2007 T
garnacha, cariñena.

90 Colour: cherry, garnet rim. Nose: ripe fruit, scrubland, earthy notes, spicy, fine reductive notes. Palate: powerful, flavourful, complex, long, toasty.

CELLERS BARONÍA DEL MONTSANT

Comte de Rius, 1
43360 Cornudella de Montsant (Tarragona)
☎: +34 977 821 483 - Fax: +34 977 821 483
englora@baronia-m.com
www.baronia-m.com

FLOR D'ENGLORA ROURE 2010 T
60% garnacha, 35% cariñena, 2% mencía, 2% syrah, 1% ull de llebre.

88 Colour: bright cherry. Nose: ripe fruit, sweet spices, creamy oak. Palate: flavourful, fruity, toasty.

ENGLORA 2009 TC
49% garnacha, 24% cariñena, 7% syrah, 19% cabernet sauvignon, 1% ull de llebre.

92 Colour: cherry, garnet rim. Nose: ripe fruit, spicy, creamy oak, toasty, complex. Palate: powerful, flavourful, toasty, round tannins.

CLOS D'ENGLORA AV 14 2008 T
38% garnacha, 18% cariñena, 14% merlot, 11% cabernet sauvignon, 11% syrah, 8% otras.

91 Colour: deep cherry. Nose: candied fruit, spicy, toasty. Palate: flavourful, spicy, ripe fruit.

CELLERS CAN BLAU

Ctra. Bellmunt, s/n
43730 Falset (Tarragona)
☎: +34 629 261 379 - Fax: +34 968 716 051
info@orowines.com
www.orowines.com

BLAU 2010 T
50% cariñena, 25% syrah, 25% garnacha.

91 Colour: deep cherry. Nose: sweet spices, red berry notes, ripe fruit, toasty, creamy oak. Palate: flavourful, balsamic, spicy, ripe fruit.

CAN BLAU 2010 T
50% mazuelo, 30% garnacha, 20% syrah.

89 Colour: cherry, garnet rim. Nose: roasted coffee, dark chocolate, ripe fruit. Palate: spicy, ripe fruit, mineral, harsh oak tannins.

MAS DE CAN BLAU 2009 T
50% mazuelo, 30% garnacha, 20% syrah.

94 Colour: cherry, garnet rim. Nose: creamy oak, dark chocolate, ripe fruit, earthy notes. Palate: powerful, flavourful, concentrated, fine bitter notes, good acidity.

CELLERS SANT RAFEL

Ctra. La Torre, Km. 1,7
43774 Pradell de la Teixeta (Tarragona)
☎: +34 689 792 305 - Fax: +34 977 323 078
info@solpost.com
www.solpost.com

SOLPOST BLANC 2011 B
100% garnacha blanca.

84

SOLPOST 2011 RD
50% garnacha, 50% syrah.

86 Colour: rose, purple rim. Nose: powerfull, ripe fruit, dried herbs. Palate: , powerful, fruity, fresh.

SOLPOST FRESC 2009 TC
80% garnacha, 35% cariñena, 15% cabernet sauvignon.

90 Colour: cherry, garnet rim. Nose: ripe fruit, spicy, toasty, mineral. Palate: powerful, flavourful, toasty, round tannins.

JOANA 2009 T
80% garnacha, 10% merlot, 10% cabernet sauvignon.

90 Colour: bright cherry. Nose: ripe fruit, sweet spices, expressive, dark chocolate. Palate: flavourful, fruity, toasty, round tannins.

SOLPOST 2007 TC
50% garnacha, 35% cariñena, 15% cabernet sauvignon.

92 Colour: cherry, garnet rim. Nose: ripe fruit, balsamic herbs, mineral, earthy notes, creamy oak, sweet spices. Palate: round, powerful, flavourful, complex, toasty.

CELLERS UNIÓ

Joan Oliver, 16-24
43206 Reus (Tarragona)
☎: +34 977 330 055 - Fax: +34 977 330 070
info@cellersunio.com
www.cellersunio.com

DAIRO 2010 TC
40% garnacha, 40% mazuelo, 20% syrah.

89 Colour: cherry, garnet rim. Nose: ripe fruit, spicy, creamy oak, toasty. Palate: powerful, flavourful, toasty.

PERLAT 2010 T
40% garnacha, 40% mazuelo, 20% syrah.

88 Colour: cherry, garnet rim. Nose: ripe fruit, balsamic herbs, spicy, creamy oak, mineral. Palate: flavourful, long.

PERLAT SYRAH 2009 T
100% syrah.

87 Colour: deep cherry. Nose: fruit preserve, nose:tic coffee, dark chocolate, fruit liqueur notes. Palate: powerful, spirituous, sweetness.

PERLAT GARNATXA 2009 T
100% garnacha.

87 Colour: deep cherry. Nose: spicy, ripe fruit, fruit expression. Palate: spicy, ripe fruit, round tannins.

CINGLES BLAUS

Finca Mas de les Moreres (Afueras de Cornudella)
43360 Cornudella de Montsant (Tarragona)
☎: +34 977 326 080 - Fax: +34 977 323 928
cinglesblaus@cinglesblaus.com
www.cinglesblaus.com

CINGLES BLAUS OCTUBRE 2010 B
50% garnacha blanca, 50% macabeo.

84

SINGLES BLAUS OCTUBRE 2010 RD
100% garnacha.

84

CINGLES BLAUS OCTUBRE 2010 T
60% garnacha, 20% cariñena, 20% syrah.

92 Colour: very deep cherry. Nose: scrubland, ripe fruit, red berry notes, violet drops. Palate: flavourful, powerful, fine bitter notes, good acidity.

CINGLES BLAUS MAS DE LES MORERES 2009 T
garnacha, syrah, cariñena, cabernet sauvignon.

89 Colour: bright cherry. Nose: ripe fruit, sweet spices, creamy oak, mineral. Palate: flavourful, fruity, toasty, round tannins.

COCA I FITÓ

Avda. 11 de Setembre s/n
43736 El Masroig (Tarragona)
☎: +34 619 776 948 - Fax: +34 935 457 092
info@cocaifito.cat
www.cocaifito.com

COCA I FITÓ ROSA 2011 RD
100% syrah.

89 Colour: rose, purple rim. Nose: powerfull, ripe fruit, red berry notes, floral, expressive. Palate: fleshy, powerful, fruity, fresh.

JASPI NEGRE 2010 T
45% garnacha, 25% cariñena, 15% cabernet sauvignon, 15% syrah.

90 Colour: bright cherry. Nose: ripe fruit, sweet spices, creamy oak, mineral. Palate: flavourful, fruity, spicy.

JASPI MARAGDA 2010 T
55% garnacha, 25% cariñena, 20% syrah.

90 Colour: cherry, garnet rim. Nose: red berry notes, ripe fruit, balsamic herbs, sweet spices, creamy oak, mineral. Palate: powerful, flavourful, long, spicy.

COCA I FITÓ NEGRE 2009 T
50% syrah, 30% garnacha, 20% cariñena.

93 Colour: cherry, garnet rim. Nose: ripe fruit, spicy, creamy oak, toasty, complex, earthy notes, mineral. Palate: powerful, flavourful, toasty, round tannins.

COOPERATIVA FALSET - MARÇA

Miquel Barceló, 31
43730 Falset (Tarragona)
☎: +34 977 830 105 - Fax: +34 977 830 363
info@etim.es
www.etim.cat

ÈTIM 2011 B
garnacha blanca.

89 Colour: bright yellow. Nose: spicy, wild herbs, ripe fruit. Palate: balanced, good acidity, fine bitter notes.

ÈTIM VEREMA TARDANA BLANC 2009 B
garnacha blanca.

90 Colour: bright yellow. Nose: candied fruit, white flowers, balanced. Palate: flavourful, rich, sweet, balanced, good acidity.

CASTELL DE FALSET 2009 BFB
100% garnacha blanca.

90 Colour: bright yellow. Nose: powerfull, sweet spices, toasty. Palate: rich, flavourful, toasty, good acidity.

IMUS SELECCIÓ DE VINYES 2011 T
garnacha, cariñena.

85 Colour: cherry, garnet rim. Nose: ripe fruit, balsamic herbs, warm, medium intensity. Palate: correct, flavourful.

ÈTIM VEREMA TARDANA NEGRE 2009 T
garnacha.

91 Colour: cherry, garnet rim. Nose: sweet spices, cocoa bean, candied fruit. Palate: fruity, long, good acidity.

ÈTIM NEGRE 2009 T
garnacha, samsó, syrah.

88 Colour: cherry, garnet rim. Nose: balanced, ripe fruit, wild herbs, warm. Palate: correct, good acidity.

ÈTIM GRENACHE 2008 T
85% garnacha, 15% cabernet sauvignon.

89 Colour: cherry, garnet rim. Nose: balanced, ripe fruit, balsamic herbs, spicy. Palate: flavourful, ripe fruit, good acidity.

ÈTIM SELECTION SYRAH 2006 T
syrah.

90 Colour: black cherry, garnet rim. Nose: toasty, sweet spices, ripe fruit. Palate: flavourful, powerful, fine bitter notes, round tannins.

CASTELL DE FALSET 2006 T
garnacha, samsó, cabernet sauvignon.

89 Colour: black cherry. Nose: ripe fruit, spicy, creamy oak, toasty, complex. Palate: powerful, flavourful, toasty, round tannins.

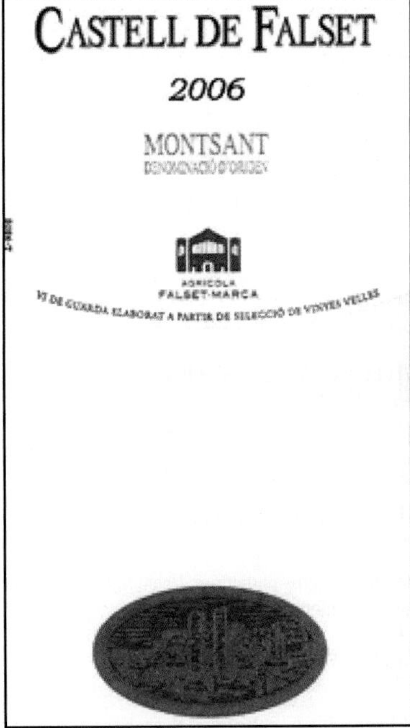

ÈTIM L'ESPARVER 2006 T
garnacha, cariñena, syrah, cabernet sauvignon.

88 Colour: cherry, garnet rim. Nose: dark chocolate, creamy oak, fruit preserve. Palate: flavourful, balanced.

ÈTIM RANCI
garnacha, cariñena.

92 Colour: bright golden. Nose: complex, balanced, varnish, roasted almonds, acetaldehyde. Palate: long, balanced.

DIT CELLER

Avda. Setembre, s/n Baixos
43736 El Masroig (Tarragona)
☎: +34 619 777 419
tonicoca@gmail.com
www.ditceller.com

SELENITA 2011 RD
garnacha, syrah.

87 Colour: brilliant rose. Nose: candied fruit, dried flowers, fragrant herbs, red berry notes. Palate: light-bodied, flavourful, good acidity.

CABIROL 2011 T
tempranillo, garnacha.

88 Colour: cherry, purple rim. Nose: fresh fruit, red berry notes, floral. Palate: flavourful, fruity, good acidity, round tannins.

CABIROL 10 2010 T ROBLE
garnacha, tempranillo.

90 Colour: cherry, garnet rim. Nose: red berry notes, ripe fruit, balsamic herbs, sweet spices, creamy oak. Palate: powerful, flavourful, long, toasty.

SELENITA 2010 T
garnacha, syrah, cabernet sauvignon.

85 Colour: cherry, garnet rim. Nose: ripe fruit, fruit preserve, sweet spices, creamy oak. Palate: powerful, flavourful, toasty.

SELENITA TERRER 2009 T
garnacha, cariñena.

91 Colour: cherry, garnet rim. Nose: ripe fruit, sweet spices, creamy oak, earthy notes. Palate: powerful, flavourful, complex, toasty.

EDICIONES I-LIMITADAS

Claravall n.2
08022 (Barcelona)
☎: +34 629 341 231
info@edicionesi.limitadas.com
www.edicionesi.limitadas.com

NÚVOL 2011 B
garnacha blanca, macabeo.

91 Colour: bright straw. Nose: dried flowers, fragrant herbs, tropical fruit, fruit expression, creamy oak. Palate: powerful, flavourful, long, spicy.

FAUNUS 2010 T
ull de llebre, syrah, merlot, cariñena.

91 Colour: cherry, garnet rim. Nose: balanced, ripe fruit, expressive, spicy. Palate: good structure, balanced, elegant.

SIURALTA 2008 T
cariñena.

91 Colour: deep cherry, garnet rim. Nose: balanced, elegant, ripe fruit, spicy, creamy oak. Palate: balanced, fine bitter notes, round tannins.

ELVIWINES

Finca "Clos Mesorah" Ctra. T-300 Falset Marça, Km. 1
43775 Marça Priorat (Tarragona)
☎: +34 935 343 026 - Fax: +34 936 750 316
moises@elviwines.com
www.elviwines.com

CLOS MESORAH 2009 TR
40% cariñena, 30% garnacha, 30% syrah.

88 Colour: cherry, garnet rim. Nose: ripe fruit, spicy, toasty, balsamic herbs, earthy notes. Palate: powerful, flavourful, toasty.

ESPECTACLE VINS

Camí Manyetes, s/n
43737 Gratallops (Tarragona)
☎: +34 977 839 171 - Fax: +34 977 839 426
jordi@espectaclevins.com
www.espectaclevins.com

ESPECTACLE 2009 T
garnacha.

96 Colour: bright cherry. Nose: red berry notes, fruit expression, floral, scrubland, balsamic herbs, sweet spices. Palate: good acidity, fine bitter notes, elegant, fine tannins.

LA COVA DELS VINS

Hermenegild Pallejà, 6
43730 Falset (Tarragona)
☎: +34 636 395 386
info@lacovadelsvins.com
www.lacovadelsvins.cat

OMBRA BLANCA 2010 B
garnacha blanca.

88 Colour: bright straw. Nose: candied fruit, honeyed notes. Palate: powerful, flavourful, fine bitter notes.

OMBRA 2010 T BARRICA
garnacha, cariñena, syrah.

87 Colour: cherry, garnet rim. Nose: ripe fruit, balsamic herbs, spicy, new oak. Palate: correct, powerful, flavourful.

TERRÒS 2009 T
garnacha, cariñena, syrah.

90 Colour: cherry, garnet rim. Nose: ripe fruit, spicy, earthy notes, balsamic herbs, creamy oak. Palate: powerful, flavourful, complex.

MAS D'EN CANONGE

Pol. Ind. 7, Parc. 27
43775 Marça (Tarragona)
☎: +34 977 054 071 - Fax: +34 977 054 971
celler@masdencanonge.com
www.masdencanonge.com

SOLEIES D'EN CANONGE 2011 B
garnacha blanca.

85 Colour: bright straw. Nose: dried flowers, fragrant herbs, ripe fruit. Palate: flavourful, fruity, good acidity.

SONS D'EN CANONGE 2011 T
garnacha, cariñena, syrah.

87 Colour: very deep cherry. Nose: ripe fruit, red berry notes, scrubland. Palate: flavourful, powerful, fine bitter notes.

RESSONS CLOT DE LA VELLA 2009 TC
garnacha.

90 Colour: cherry, garnet rim. Nose: ripe fruit, balanced, sweet spices, cocoa bean. Palate: ripe fruit, long, good acidity.

SONS D'EN CANONGE 2009 TC
garnacha, cariñena, tempranillo.

88 Colour: cherry, garnet rim. Nose: balanced, sweet spices, ripe fruit, dark chocolate. Palate: good structure, flavourful, fruity.

RESSONS D'EN CANONGE 2009 T
garnacha, syrah.

86 Colour: deep cherry, garnet rim. Nose: warm, sweet spices, fruit preserve, animal reductive notes. Palate: good structure.

MAS PERINET

Finca Mas Perinet, s/n
43660 Cornudella de Montsant (Tarragona)
☎: +34 977 827 113 - Fax: +34 977 827 180
info@masperinet.com
www.masperinet.com

GOTIA 2006 T

93 Colour: bright cherry. Nose: sweet spices, creamy oak, fruit liqueur notes. Palate: flavourful, fruity, toasty, round tannins.

GOTIA 2005 T

93 Colour: cherry, garnet rim. Nose: ripe fruit, spicy, creamy oak, toasty, complex, earthy notes. Palate: powerful, flavourful, toasty, round tannins.

NOGUERALS

Tou, 5
43360 Cornudella de Montsant (Tarragona)
☎: +34 650 033 546 - Fax: +34 934 419 879
noguerals@hotmail.com
www.noguerals.com

CORBATERA 2009 T
70% garnacha, 30% cabernet sauvignon.

91 Colour: cherry, garnet rim. Nose: ripe fruit, spicy, creamy oak. Palate: powerful, flavourful, toasty, round tannins.

ORTO VINS

Major, 10
43736 El Masroig (Tarragona)
☎: +34 629 171 246
info@ortovins.com

BLANC D'ORTO BRISAT 2011 B
garnacha blanca.

91 Colour: bright golden. Nose: ripe fruit, fragrant herbs, dried flowers, mineral, sweet spices, creamy oak. Palate: rich, flavourful, complex, spicy, long, toasty.

BLANC D'ORTO FLOR 2011 B
garnacha blanca.

88 Colour: bright yellow. Nose: powerfull, ripe fruit, creamy oak, fragrant herbs. Palate: rich, flavourful, fresh, good acidity.

PALELL 2010 TC
100% garnacha peluda.

93 Colour: bright cherry. Nose: ripe fruit, sweet spices, creamy oak, earthy notes. Palate: flavourful, fruity, toasty, round tannins.

LA CARRERADA 2010 T
100% samsó.

93 Colour: cherry, garnet rim. Nose: ripe fruit, spicy, creamy oak, toasty, complex, mineral, earthy notes. Palate: powerful, flavourful, toasty, round tannins.

LES TALLADES DE CAL NICOLAU 2010 TC
picapoll negro.

92 Colour: very deep cherry. Nose: spicy, fruit liqueur notes, scrubland, earthy notes. Palate: flavourful, spicy, ripe fruit, fine bitter notes. Personality.

LES PUJOLES 2010 TC
100% ull de llebre.

90 Colour: very deep cherry. Nose: scrubland, ripe fruit, sweet spices. Palate: flavourful, powerful, fine bitter notes.

ORTO 2010 T
55% samsó, 29% garnacha, 10% ull de llebre, 5% cabernet sauvignon.

88 Colour: deep cherry. Nose: powerfull, ripe fruit, spicy, scrubland, warm. Palate: fine bitter notes, spicy, ripe fruit, sweet tannins.

LES COMES D'ORTO 2010 T
50% garnacha, 45% samsó, 5% ull de llebre.

88 Colour: deep cherry. Nose: fruit expression, ripe fruit, toasty, spicy. Palate: sweetness, spicy, warm.

DOLÇ D'ORTO 2011 DULCE NATURAL
80% garnacha blanca, 20% macabeo, tripó de gat, mamella de monja, trobat.

92 Colour: bright golden. Nose: faded flowers, honeyed notes, candied fruit, citrus fruit. Palate: flavourful, sweet, long.

PORTAL DEL MONTSANT

Carrer de Dalt, s/n
43775 Marça (Tarragona)
☎: +34 933 950 811 - Fax: +34 933 955 500
info@parxet.es
www.parxet.es

BRUBERRY 2011 B
100% garnacha blanca.

90 Colour: bright straw. Nose: fresh, fresh fruit, white flowers, expressive, complex. Palate: flavourful, fruity, good acidity, balanced.

SANTBRU BLANC 2010 B
garnacha.

92 Colour: bright straw. Nose: fresh, fresh fruit, white flowers, scrubland, spicy, mineral. Palate: flavourful, fruity, good acidity, balanced.

BRUNUS ROSÉ 2011 RD
garnacha.

90 Colour: rose, purple rim. Nose: powerfull, ripe fruit, red berry notes, floral, mineral, balanced. Palate: , powerful, fruity, fresh, fine bitter notes.

SANTES NEGRE 2011 T
tempranillo.

89 Colour: cherry, purple rim. Nose: red berry notes, scrubland, mineral, dried flowers. Palate: light-bodied, fresh, fruity, balsamic, balanced.

BRUBERRY 2010 T
cariñena, garnacha, merlot.

89 Colour: bright cherry, cherry, garnet rim. Nose: medium intensity, ripe fruit, scrubland. Palate: balanced, fine bitter notes.

BRUNUS 2009 T
cariñena, garnacha, syrah, cabernet sauvignon.

90 Colour: bright cherry. Nose: ripe fruit, sweet spices, creamy oak, mineral, expressive. Palate: flavourful, fruity, toasty, round tannins.

SANTBRU 2008 T
cariñena, garnacha, syrah.

93 Colour: bright cherry, garnet rim. Nose: expressive, balanced, ripe fruit, spicy, scrubland. Palate: good structure, fine bitter notes, round tannins.

RONADELLES

Finca La Plana, s/n
43360 Cornudella del Montsant (Tarragona)
☎: +34 977 821 104 - Fax: +34 977 274 913
info@ronadelles.com
www.ronadelles.com

PETIT BLANC 2009 B
garnacha blanca, macabeo.

90 Colour: bright yellow. Nose: fine lees, ripe fruit, dried herbs, earthy notes, dried flowers. Palate: powerful, flavourful, complex, fine bitter notes.

PETIT DOLÇ 2009 B
garnacha roja.

89 Colour: golden. Nose: powerfull, floral, honeyed notes, candied fruit, fragrant herbs, caramel. Palate: flavourful, sweet, fresh, fruity, good acidity, long.

PETIT ROSAT 2011 RD
garnacha, syrah.

86 Colour: light cherry. Nose: red berry notes, fruit expression. Palate: flavourful, ripe fruit.

CAP DE RUC GARNACHA 2011 T
garnacha.

87 Colour: cherry, purple rim. Nose: balanced, ripe fruit, dried herbs. Palate: flavourful, fruity, good structure.

PETIT NEGRE 2009 T
garnacha, cariñena.

90 Colour: deep cherry, garnet rim. Nose: balanced, wild herbs, ripe fruit, spicy. Palate: good structure, good acidity.

CAP DE RUC GARNACHA 2009 TC
garnacha, samsó.

88 Colour: cherry, garnet rim. Nose: medium intensity, ripe fruit, spicy. Palate: balanced, correct, toasty.

GIRAL VINYES VELLES 2005 TR
garnacha, cariñena.

89 Colour: pale ruby, brick rim edge. Nose: spicy, fine reductive notes, wet leather, aged wood nuances, fruit liqueur notes. Palate: spicy, fine tannins, long.

VENUS LA UNIVERSAL

Ctra. Porrera, s/n
43730 Falset (Tarragona)
☎: +34 699 435 154 - Fax: +34 639 121 244
info@venuslauniversal.com
www.venuslauniversal.com

DIDO 2011 B
macabeo, garnacha blanca.

92 Colour: bright straw. Nose: ripe fruit, faded flowers, dried herbs, earthy notes, mineral, toasty, creamy oak. Palate: powerful, flavourful, rich, spicy, good acidity.

DIDO 2010 T

91 Colour: cherry, purple rim. Nose: ripe fruit, dried flowers. Palate: good structure, ripe fruit, good acidity, balanced, fine bitter notes.

VENUS 2008 T

92 Colour: bright cherry, garnet rim. Nose: expressive, balanced, spicy, complex, cocoa bean, mineral. Palate: good structure, full, balanced, fine bitter notes, round tannins.

VINATERRERS DEL COLL DE MORA

Pol. Ind. Sort dels Capellans Nau, 14
43730 Falset (Tarragona)
☎: +34 692 114 451
info@vinaterrers.com
www.vinaterrers.com

LLUNARA 2009 T
garnacha, syrah, cabernet sauvignon, cariñena.

89 Colour: cherry, garnet rim. Nose: powerfull, fruit preserve, spicy. Palate: flavourful, powerful.

VINS DE MAS SERSAL

Pl. Sort dels Capellans, Nau Bahaus
43730 Falset (Tarragona)
☎: +34 666 415 735
vins@massersal.com
www.massersal.com

ESTONES 2010 T
70% garnacha, 30% samsó.

87 Colour: black cherry, purple rim. Nose: fruit preserve, dark chocolate, creamy oak. Palate: flavourful, balsamic, long.

VINYES D'EN GABRIEL

Ctra. Darmós - La Serra, s/n
43746 Darmós (Tarragona)
☎: +34 609 989 345
info@vinyesdengabriel.com
www.vinyesdengabriel.com

L'HERAVI 2011 RD

81

DOLCET DE MIREIA 2011 T

90 Colour: black cherry, purple rim. Nose: candied fruit, pattiserie, fruit liqueur notes, sweet spices, cocoa bean. Palate: flavourful, fruity.

L'HERAVI 2011 T
60% garnacha, 20% cariñena, 20% syrah.

86 Colour: black cherry, purple rim. Nose: ripe fruit, fruit preserve, powerfull, warm. Palate: sweetness, good acidity.

MANS DE SAMSÓ 2010 T
samsó.

90 Colour: black cherry, purple rim. Nose: sweet spices, fruit liqueur notes, fruit preserve, red berry notes. Palate: warm, sweetness, concentrated.

L'HERAVI 2010 TC
garnacha, samsó.

88 Colour: cherry, garnet rim. Nose: spicy, creamy oak, toasty, earthy notes, fruit preserve. Palate: powerful, flavourful, toasty, round tannins.

L'HERAVI SELECCIÓ 2010 T
cariñena, syrah.

87 Colour: deep cherry. Nose: powerfull, characterful, fruit preserve. Palate: sweetness, fine bitter notes.

VINYES DOMÈNECH

Camí del Collet, km. 3,8
43776 Capçanes (Tarragona)
☎: +34 670 297 395 - Fax: +34 932 127 759
jidomenech@vinyesdomenech.com
www.vinyesdomenech.com

BANCAL RITA 2011 B
80% garnacha blanca, 20% macabeo.

90 Colour: bright straw. Nose: white flowers, ripe fruit, balanced, expressive. Palate: rich, flavourful, ripe fruit, spicy.

TEIXAR 2010 T
100% garnacha peluda.

95 Colour: bright cherry. Nose: sweet spices, creamy oak, expressive, varietal, mineral, ripe fruit, fragrant herbs. Palate: flavourful, fruity, toasty, round tannins.

BANCAL DEL BOSC 2010 T
60% garnacha, 20% syrah, 20% cabernet sauvignon.

90 Colour: cherry, garnet rim. Nose: medium intensity, balanced, scrubland, fruit expression. Palate: long, ripe fruit, round tannins.

TEIXAR 2009 T
100% garnacha peluda.

94 Colour: cherry, garnet rim. Nose: mineral, earthy notes, ripe fruit, spicy. Palate: fine bitter notes, good acidity, long, spicy, ripe fruit.

FURVUS 2009 T
85% garnacha, 15% merlot.

92 Colour: cherry, garnet rim. Nose: ripe fruit, spicy, creamy oak, toasty, characterful. Palate: powerful, flavourful, toasty, round tannins.

VIÑAS DEL MONTSANT

Partida Coll de Mora , s/n
43775 Marça (Tarragona)
☎: +34 977 831 309 - Fax: +34 977 831 356
mariajose.bajon@morlanda.com
www.fraguerau.com

GARBÓ 2011 RD
13,5% garnacha, syrah.

87 Colour: rose, bright. Nose: red berry notes, rose petals, balanced. Palate: flavourful, fruity.

GARBÓ 2011 T
garnacha, merlot, syrah, cabernet sauvignon.

86 Colour: cherry, purple rim. Nose: medium intensity, ripe fruit, balsamic herbs. Palate: flavourful, fruity, good acidity.

FRA GUERAU 2007 TC
garnacha, merlot, syrah, cabernet sauvignon.

87 Colour: cherry, garnet rim. Nose: scrubland, overripe fruit, spicy. Palate: fruity, correct, fine bitter notes.

DO NAVARRA

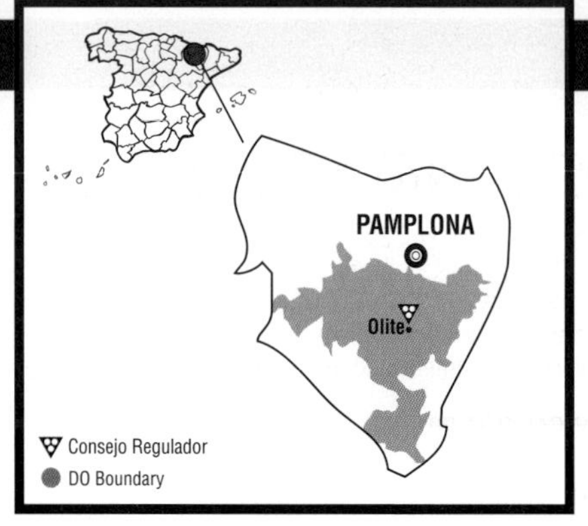

LOCATION:

In the province of Navarra. It draws together areas of different climates and soils, which produce wines with diverse characteristics.

CLIMATE:

Typical of dry, sub-humid regions in the northern fringe, with average rainfall of between 593 mm and 683 mm per year. The climate in the central region is transitional and changes to drier conditions in southern regions, where the average annual rainfall is a mere 448 mm.

SOIL:

The diversity of the different regions is also reflected in the soil. Reddish or yellowish and stony in the Baja Montaña, brownish-grey limestone and limestone in Valdizarbe and Tierra Estella, limestone and alluvium marl in the Ribera Alta, and brown and grey semi-desert soil, brownish-grey limestone and alluvium in the Ribera Baja.

GRAPE VARIETIES:

WHITE: *Chardonnay* (2%), *Garnacha Blanca, Malvasía, Moscatel de Grano Menudo, Viura* (6% of total) and *Sauvignon Blanc.*
RED: *Cabernet Sauvignon* (9%), *Garnacha Tinta* (majority 42% of total), *Graciano, Mazuelo, Merlot, Tempranillo* (29%), *Syrah* and *Pinot Noir.*

SUB-REGIONS:

Baja Montaña. Situated northeast of Navarra, it comprises 22 municipal districts with around 2,500 Ha under cultivation.
Tierra Estella. In western central Navarra, it stretches along the Camino de Santiago. It has 1,800 Ha of vineyards in 38 municipal districts.
Valdizarbe. In central Navarra. It is the key centre of the Camino de Santiago. It comprises 25 municipal districts and has 1,100 Ha of vineyards.
Ribera Alta. In the area around Olite, it takes in part of central Navarra and the start of the southern region. There are 26 municipal districts and 3,300 Ha of vineyards.
Ribera Baja. In the south of the province, it is the most important in terms of size (4,600 Ha). It comprises 14 municipal districts.

CONSEJO REGULADOR
Rúa Romana, s/n - 31690 Olite (Navarra) - ☎: +34 948 741 812 - Fax: +34 948 741 776
@ consejoregulador@vinonavarra.com / info@navarrawine.com - www.vinonavarra.com

FIGURES:

Vineyard surface: 11,700 – **Wine-Growers:** 2,716 – **Wineries:** 113 – **2011 Harvest rating:** Very Good – **Production:** 47,796,986 litres – **Market percentages:** 68% domestic. 32% export

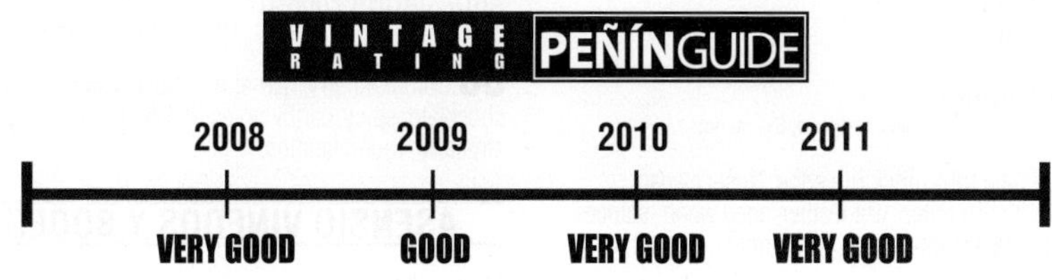

ARDOA

Las Mercedes, 31- 4º Depto. 4
48930 Las Arenas-Getxo (Bizkaia)
☎: +34 944 315 872 - Fax: +34 944 315 873
info@ardoa.com
www.ardoa.com

AGA 2011 T ROBLE
85% tempranillo, 10% cabernet sauvignon, 5% merlot.

86 Colour: pale ruby, brick rim edge. Nose: elegant, spicy, fine reductive notes, wet leather, aged wood nuances, fruit liqueur notes. Palate: spicy, fine tannins, elegant, long.

AZCÚNAGA 2009 TC
85% tempranillo, 10% cabernet sauvignon, 5% merlot.

85 Colour: cherry, garnet rim. Nose: creamy oak, dark chocolate, fruit preserve. Palate: flavourful, fruity, good finish.

AZCÚNAGA SELECCIÓN PRIVADA 2007 TR
100% cabernet sauvignon.

85 Colour: cherry, garnet rim. Nose: ripe fruit, spicy, creamy oak, toasty. Palate: powerful, flavourful, toasty.

AROA BODEGAS

Apalaz, 13
31292 Gorozin-Zurukoain (Navarra)
☎: +34 948 921 867
info@aroawines.com
www.aroawines.com

AROA LAIA 2011 B
100% garnacha blanca.

86 Colour: bright straw. Nose: fresh fruit, white flowers, expressive, citrus fruit. Palate: flavourful, fruity, correct.

AROA LARROSA 2011 RD
50% garnacha, 50% tempranillo.

89 Colour: rose, purple rim. Nose: powerfull, ripe fruit, red berry notes, floral, expressive. Palate: fleshy, powerful, fruity, fresh.

AROA MUTIKO 2011 T
100% tempranillo.

87 Colour: cherry, purple rim. Nose: balanced, red berry notes, ripe fruit. Palate: correct, easy to drink, good finish.

AROA GORENA 18M 2008 TR
70% cabernet sauvignon, 30% merlot.

90 Colour: cherry, garnet rim. Nose: spicy, balsamic herbs, varietal, ripe fruit. Palate: balanced, ripe fruit, long, toasty.

AROA JAUNA 2008 TC
39% merlot, 20% tempranillo, 41% cabernet sauvignon.

88 Colour: cherry, garnet rim. Nose: candied fruit, dark chocolate, spicy, earthy notes. Palate: flavourful, good structure, round tannins.

ASENSIO VIÑEDOS Y BODEGAS

Mayor, 84
31293 Sesma (Navarra)
☎: +34 948 698 078 - Fax: +34 948 698 097
info@bodegasasensio.com

JAVIER ASENSIO 2011 B
chardonnay, sauvignon blanc.

87 Colour: bright straw. Nose: fresh, fresh fruit, white flowers, expressive. Palate: fruity, good acidity, fine bitter notes.

JAVIER ASENSIO 2009 TC

88 Colour: cherry, garnet rim. Nose: ripe fruit, balsamic herbs, spicy. Palate: powerful, flavourful, correct.

JAVIER ASENSIO 2006 TR
merlot, tempranillo.

87 Colour: cherry, garnet rim. Nose: fruit preserve, spicy, tobacco, scrubland. Palate: flavourful, easy to drink, correct.

JAVIER ASENSIO MERLOT 2005 TR
merlot.

86 Colour: cherry, garnet rim. Nose: balanced, scrubland, tobacco, spicy. Palate: flavourful, spicy, round tannins.

AZUL Y GARANZA BODEGAS

San Juan, 19
31310 Carcastillo (Navarra)
☎: +34 636 406 939 - Fax: +34 948 725 677
info@azulygaranza.com
www.azulygaranza.com

VIURA DE AZUL Y GARANZA 2011 B
viura.

90 Colour: bright straw. Nose: fresh, fresh fruit, expressive, fragrant herbs. Palate: flavourful, fruity, good acidity, balanced.

ROSA DE AZUL Y GARANZA 2011 RD
60% tempranillo, 40% garnacha.

88 Colour: rose, purple rim. Nose: ripe fruit, red berry notes, floral, balsamic herbs. Palate: , powerful, fruity, fresh.

ABRIL DE AZUL Y GARANZA 2011 T
80% tempranillo, 20% cabernet sauvignon.

89 Colour: cherry, purple rim. Nose: medium intensity, ripe fruit, scrubland. Palate: flavourful, fruity, easy to drink.

SEIS DE AZUL Y GARANZA 2009 T
90% merlot, 10% cabernet sauvignon.

87 Colour: cherry, garnet rim. Nose: earthy notes, fine reductive notes, scrubland, spicy. Palate: powerful, flavourful, balanced.

DESIERTO DE AZUL Y GARANZA 2008 T
cabernet sauvignon.

91 Colour: bright cherry. Nose: ripe fruit, fragrant herbs, sweet spices, varietal, expressive. Palate: flavourful, good acidity, spicy, long.

BODEGA COSECHEROS REUNIDOS S. COOP.

Pza. San Antón, 1
31390 Olite (Navarra)
☎: +34 948 740 067 - Fax: +34 948 740 067
info@bodegacosecheros.com
www.bodegacosecheros.com

VIÑA JUGUERA GARNACHA 2011 T
100% garnacha.

87 Colour: cherry, purple rim. Nose: floral, red berry notes, lactic notes, expressive. Palate: fresh, fruity, light-bodied, flavourful, easy to drink.

VIÑA JUGUERA TEMPRANILLO 2011 T
100% tempranillo.

82

VIÑA JUGUERA 2008 T
tempranillo, cabernet sauvignon.

84

BODEGA DE SADA

Arrabal, 2
31491 Sada (Navarra)
☎: +34 948 877 013 - Fax: +34 948 877 433
bodega@bodegadesada.com
www.bodegadesada.com

PALACIO DE SADA 2011 RD
garnacha.

87 Colour: rose. Nose: balanced, elegant, red berry notes, scrubland. Palate: flavourful, balanced, fruity.

PALACIO DE SADA GARNACHA 2011 T
garnacha.

86 Colour: cherry, purple rim. Nose: fruit expression, red berry notes, balanced. Palate: fruity, easy to drink, correct.

PALACIO DE SADA 2009 TC
90% garnacha, 10% tempranillo, cabernet sauvignon.

89 Colour: deep cherry, garnet rim. Nose: powerfull, toasty, creamy oak, sweet spices. Palate: ripe fruit, flavourful.

BODEGA DE SARRÍA

Finca Señorío de Sarría, s/n
31100 Puente La Reina (Navarra)
☎: +34 948 202 200 - Fax: +34 948 202 202
info@taninia.com
www.bodegadesarria.com

SEÑORÍO DE SARRÍA CHARDONNAY 2011 B
chardonnay.

86 Colour: bright straw. Nose: white flowers, ripe fruit, fragrant herbs. Palate: powerful, flavourful, fine bitter notes.

SEÑORÍO DE SARRÍA VIÑEDO Nº 3 2009 BFB
chardonnay.

91 Colour: bright yellow. Nose: ripe fruit, jasmine, fragrant herbs, sweet spices, toasty, creamy oak. Palate: rich, flavourful, fruity, spicy.

SEÑORÍO DE SARRÍA 2011 RD
garnacha.

86 Colour: rose. Nose: expressive, fresh, red berry notes, scrubland, medium intensity. Palate: flavourful, balanced, easy to drink.

SEÑORÍO DE SARRÍA VIÑEDO Nº 5 2011 RD
garnacha.

85 Colour: rose, purple rim. Nose: powerfull, red berry notes, floral, balsamic herbs. Palate: , powerful, fruity, easy to drink.

SEÑORÍO DE SARRÍA 2009 TC
tempranillo, cabernet sauvignon.

87 Colour: cherry, garnet rim. Nose: scrubland, ripe fruit, spicy. Palate: flavourful, balanced, easy to drink.

SEÑORÍO DE SARRÍA VIÑEDO Nº 8 2009 TC
mazuelo.

87 Colour: bright cherry, purple rim. Nose: medium intensity, red berry notes, ripe fruit, wild herbs. Palate: balanced, ripe fruit.

SEÑORÍO DE SARRÍA VIÑEDO Nº 7 2008 TC
graciano.

87 Colour: cherry, garnet rim. Nose: old leather, tobacco, scrubland. Palate: ripe fruit, long, spicy.

SEÑORÍO DE SARRÍA 2005 TR
merlot, cabernet sauvignon.

88 Colour: cherry, garnet rim. Nose: ripe fruit, spicy, toasty. Palate: powerful, flavourful, toasty, round tannins.

SEÑORÍO DE SARRÍA VIÑEDO SOTÉS 2005 T
merlot, graciano, mazuelo, tempranillo, garnacha, cabernet sauvignon.

87 Colour: cherry, garnet rim. Nose: nose:tic coffee, sweet spices, ripe fruit, fine reductive notes. Palate: fruity, correct, balanced.

SEÑORÍO DE SARRÍA RESERVA ESPECIAL 2004 TR
cabernet sauvignon.

90 Colour: cherry, garnet rim. Nose: balanced, varietal, ripe fruit, balsamic herbs, spicy. Palate: good structure, round tannins.

SEÑORÍO DE SARRÍA 2001 TGR
merlot, cabernet sauvignon.

90 Colour: pale ruby, brick rim edge. Nose: elegant, spicy, fine reductive notes, aged wood nuances, fruit liqueur notes. Palate: spicy, fine tannins, elegant, long.

SEÑORÍO DE SARRÍA MOSCATEL 2010 BLANCO DULCE
moscatel grano menudo.

87 Colour: bright yellow. Nose: medium intensity, white flowers, honeyed notes. Palate: rich, confected, flavourful.

BODEGA INURRIETA

Ctra. Falces-Miranda de Arga, km. 30
31370 Falces (Navarra)
☎: +34 948 737 309 - Fax: +34 948 737 310
info@bodegainurrieta.com
www.bodegainurrieta.com

INURRIETA ORCHÍDEA 2011 B
sauvignon blanc.

90 Colour: bright straw. Nose: floral, citrus fruit, fruit expression, fragrant herbs, balanced, expressive. Palate: light-bodied, fresh, fruity, flavourful, good acidity, balanced.

INURRIETA ORCHÍDEA CUVÉE 2009 B
sauvignon blanc.

92 Colour: bright yellow. Nose: powerfull, ripe fruit, sweet spices, creamy oak, fragrant herbs. Palate: rich, smoky afterpalate:, flavourful, fresh, good acidity.

INURRIETA MEDIODÍA 2011 RD
garnacha.

89 Colour: rose, purple rim. Nose: red berry notes, ripe fruit, scrubland. Palate: flavourful, fruity, balanced, fine bitter notes.

INURRIETA "SUR" 2010 T ROBLE
garnacha, graciano.

90 Colour: very deep cherry. Nose: creamy oak, sweet spices, cocoa bean. Palate: good structure, ripe fruit, round tannins.

INURRIETA NORTE 2010 T ROBLE
cabernet sauvignon, merlot.

88 Colour: cherry, garnet rim. Nose: ripe fruit, spicy, creamy oak, medium intensity. Palate: powerful, flavourful, long.

INURRIETA PV 2009 T

92 Colour: deep cherry, garnet rim. Nose: complex, balanced, ripe fruit, sweet spices. Palate: good structure, flavourful.

LADERAS DE INURRIETA 2009 T
graciano.

91 Colour: cherry, garnet rim. Nose: ripe fruit, earthy notes, nose:tic coffee, sweet spices. Palate: balanced, round, powerful, flavourful.

INURRIETA CUATROCIENTOS 2009 TC
cabernet sauvignon, merlot.

90 Colour: cherry, garnet rim. Nose: ripe fruit, powerfull, sweet spices, toasty. Palate: powerful, flavourful, balanced, toasty.

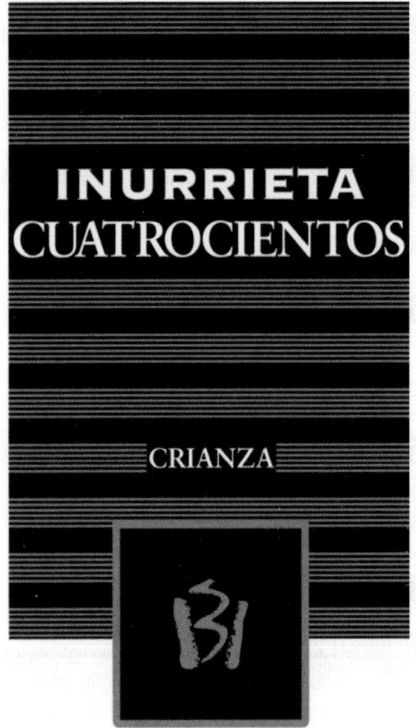

ALTOS DE INURRIETA 2008 TR
graciano, garnacha, syrah.

91 Colour: cherry, garnet rim. Nose: ripe fruit, spicy, creamy oak, toasty, complex. Palate: powerful, flavourful, toasty, round tannins.

BODEGA MARQUÉS DE MONTECIERZO

San José, 62
31590 Castejón (Navarra)
☎: +34 948 814 414 - Fax: +34 948 814 420
info@marquesdemontecierzo.com
www.marquesdemontecierzo.com

EMERGENTE MOSCATEL 2011 B
100% moscatel grano menudo.

88 Colour: bright straw. Nose: candied fruit, honeyed notes, floral. Palate: flavourful, rich, long.

EMERGENTE 2011 B
chardonnay.

84

EMERGENTE 2010 BFB
100% chardonnay.

85 Colour: yellow, coppery red. Nose: candied fruit, sweet spices, pattiserie. Palate: lacks balance.

EMERGENTE ROSADO DE LÁGRIMA 2011 RD
garnacha, cabernet sauvignon, merlot.

84

EMERGENTE GARNACHA 2011 T
100% garnacha.

85 Colour: light cherry, purple rim. Nose: wild herbs, ripe fruit, medium intensity. Palate: fruity, easy to drink.

EMERGENTE 2011 T
tempranillo, cabernet sauvignon, merlot, garnacha.

85 Colour: bright cherry, purple rim. Nose: balanced, scrubland, warm. Palate: flavourful, easy to drink, good finish.

EMERGENTE GARNACHA SELECCIÓN 2010 T ROBLE
100% garnacha.

87 Colour: cherry, garnet rim. Nose: jasmine, cocoa bean, sweet spices, toasty. Palate: powerful, flavourful, fruity aftespalate:, balanced.

EMERGENTE 2008 TC
tempranillo, cabernet sauvignon, merlot.

84

EMERGENTE 2007 TC
tempranillo, cabernet sauvignon, merlot, garnacha.

85 Colour: cherry, garnet rim. Nose: ripe fruit, spicy, balanced, scrubland. Palate: good structure, fruity.

MARQUES DE MONTECIERZO MERLOT SELECCIÓN 2005 TC
100% merlot.

90 Colour: deep cherry, garnet rim. Nose: powerfull, ripe fruit, sweet spices, tobacco, fragrant herbs. Palate: flavourful, ripe fruit, long.

EMERGENTE RESERVA NUMERADA 2005 TR
tempranillo, merlot, cabernet sauvignon.

87 Colour: deep cherry, orangey edge. Nose: spicy, fine reductive notes, aged wood nuances, fruit liqueur notes. Palate: spicy, fine tannins, balanced.

BODEGA MÁXIMO ABETE

Ctra. Estella-Sangüesa, Km. 43,5
31495 San Martín de Unx (Navarra)
☎: +34 948 738 120 - Fax: +34 948 738 120
info@bodegasmaximoabete.com
www.bodegasmaximoabete.com

GUERINDA CHARDONNAY 2011 B
chardonnay.

86 Colour: bright straw. Nose: balanced, expressive, fresh, citrus fruit, white flowers, tropical fruit. Palate: flavourful, ripe fruit.

GUERINDA 2011 RD
100% garnacha.

83

GUERINDA 2009 TC
garnacha, graciano, cabernet sauvignon, merlot.

86 Colour: cherry, garnet rim. Nose: ripe fruit, balsamic herbs, spicy, creamy oak. Palate: light-bodied, flavourful, spicy.

GUERINDA 2009 T ROBLE
garnacha, tempranillo, merlot, cabernet sauvignon.

86 Colour: cherry, garnet rim. Nose: spicy, ripe fruit, tobacco. Palate: balanced, long.

GUERINDA GRACIANO 2007 T ROBLE
100% graciano.

84

BODEGA NUESTRA SEÑORA DEL ROMERO

Ctra. de Tarazona, 33
31520 Cascante (Navarra)
☎: +34 948 851 411 - Fax: +34 948 844 504
info@bodegasdelromero.com
www.bodegasdelromero.com

MALÓN DE ECHAIDE 2011 B
70% chardonnay, 30% viura.

86 Colour: bright straw. Nose: ripe fruit, white flowers. Palate: correct, balanced, ripe fruit.

MALÓN DE ECHAIDE 2011 RD
100% garnacha.

86 Colour: rose, purple rim. Nose: ripe fruit, red berry notes, floral, expressive. Palate: , powerful, fruity, fresh.

CORAZÓN DE MALON 2011 RD
100% garnacha.

84

MALÓN DE ECHAIDE TEMPRANILLO 2011 T
100% tempranillo.

87 Colour: cherry, garnet rim. Nose: ripe fruit, fragrant herbs, balanced. Palate: flavourful, fruity, easy to drink.

MALÓN DE ECHAIDE GARNACHA 2009 T ROBLE
100% garnacha.

85 Colour: bright cherry. Nose: ripe fruit, sweet spices, creamy oak. Palate: flavourful, fruity, toasty.

SEÑOR DE CASCANTE 2008 TC
85% tempranillo, 15% cabernet sauvignon.

86 Colour: cherry, garnet rim. Nose: balanced, fruit preserve, spicy. Palate: flavourful, correct.

MALÓN DE ECHAIDE 2008 TC
80% tempranillo, 15% cabernet sauvignon, 5% merlot.

85 Colour: cherry, garnet rim. Nose: powerfull, candied fruit, spicy. Palate: ripe fruit, spicy, good finish.

SEÑOR DE CASCANTE 2005 TGR
85% tempranillo, 15% cabernet sauvignon.

83

VIÑA PAROT 2003 TR
85% cabernet sauvignon, 15% tempranillo.

86 Colour: deep cherry, orangey edge. Nose: balanced, fruit preserve, old leather, waxy notes. Palate: correct, spicy.

BODEGA OTAZU

Señorío de Otazu, s/n
31174 Etxauri (Navarra)
☎: +34 948 329 200 - Fax: +34 948 329 353
otazu@otazu.com
www.otazu.com

OTAZU CHARDONNAY 2010 B
chardonnay.

90 Colour: bright straw. Nose: white flowers, expressive, ripe fruit, fragrant herbs. Palate: flavourful, fruity, good acidity.

PALACIO DE OTAZU CHARDONNAY 2009 BFB

91 Colour: bright yellow. Nose: powerfull, ripe fruit, sweet spices, fragrant herbs, new oak. Palate: rich, smoky afterpalate:, flavourful, fresh, good acidity.

OTAZU 2011 RD
merlot.

87 Colour: rose. Nose: characterful, ripe fruit, red berry notes. Palate: flavourful, powerful, sweetness.

OTAZU PREMIUM CUVEE 2007 T
cabernet sauvignon, tempranillo, merlot.

92 Colour: cherry, garnet rim. Nose: spicy, creamy oak, toasty, dark chocolate, ripe fruit. Palate: powerful.

BODEGA SAN MARTÍN S. COOP.

Ctra. de Sanguesa, s/n
31495 San Martín de Unx (Navarra)
☎: +34 948 738 294 - Fax: +34 948 738 297
admon@bodegasanmartin.com
www.bodegasanmartin.com

ILAGARES 2011 B
viura, chardonnay.

85 Colour: bright straw. Nose: ripe fruit, faded flowers, dried herbs. Palate: powerful, flavourful, correct.

ILAGARES 2011 RD
garnacha.

86 Colour: rose, purple rim. Nose: powerfull, ripe fruit, floral. Palate: , powerful, fruity, fresh, balanced.

SEÑORÍO DE UNX GARNACHA 2011 T
garnacha.

88 Colour: cherry, purple rim. Nose: expressive, fresh fruit, red berry notes, floral. Palate: flavourful, fruity, good acidity.

ILAGARES 2011 T
tempranillo, garnacha, merlot, cabernet sauvignon.

83

ALMA DE UNX 2008 T
garnacha.

88 Colour: cherry, garnet rim. Nose: ripe fruit, sweet spices, waxy notes, fine reductive notes, scrubland. Palate: ripe fruit, flavourful. Personality.

SEÑORÍO DE UNX 2008 TC
tempranillo, garnacha.

82

SEÑORÍO DE UNX 2006 TR
90% tempranillo, 10% garnacha.

88 Colour: cherry, garnet rim. Nose: powerfull, candied fruit, sweet spices, dark chocolate. Palate: flavourful, fruity, good finish.

BODEGA TÁNDEM

Ctra. Pamplona - Logroño Km. 35,9
31292 Lácar (Navarra)
☎: +34 948 536 031 - Fax: +34 948 536 068
bodega@tandem.es
www.tandem.es

INMÁCULA 2011 B
viura.

87 Colour: bright straw. Nose: balanced, expressive, citrus fruit, fragrant herbs. Palate: fruity, flavourful, good acidity, fine bitter notes.

ARS NOVA 2006 T
tempranillo, merlot, cabernet sauvignon.

88 Colour: cherry, garnet rim. Nose: spicy, ripe fruit, fragrant herbs. Palate: flavourful, fruity.

ARS MÁCULA 2005 T
cabernet sauvignon, merlot.

90 Colour: pale ruby, brick rim edge. Nose: spicy, fine reductive notes, aged wood nuances, cocoa bean, dark chocolate. Palate: spicy, fine tannins, long.

BODEGA Y VIÑAS VALDELARES

Ctra. Eje del Ebro, km. 60
31579 Carcar (Navarra)
☎: +34 656 849 602
valdelares@terra.es
www.valdelares.com

VALDELARES 2011 RD
garnacha.

89 Colour: rose, purple rim. Nose: rose petals, red berry notes, ripe fruit, balsamic herbs. Palate: powerful, flavourful, fruity aftespalate:. Personality.

VALDELARES 2011 T

88 Colour: cherry, purple rim. Nose: expressive, fresh fruit, red berry notes, floral. Palate: flavourful, fruity, good acidity, round tannins.

VALDELARES 2009 TC
tempranillo, cabernet sauvignon, merlot.

90 Colour: cherry, garnet rim. Nose: red berry notes, ripe fruit, cocoa bean, sweet spices, toasty. Palate: balanced, powerful, flavourful.

VALDELARES ALTA EXPRESIÓN 2009 TC
cabernet sauvignon.

89 Colour: bright cherry. Nose: ripe fruit, sweet spices, creamy oak, expressive. Palate: flavourful, fruity, toasty, round tannins.

BODEGAS 1877

Brisol, 16 bis
28230 Las Rozas (Madrid)
☎: +34 917 104 880 - Fax: +34 917 104 881
anap@swd.es
www.swd.es

MARQUÉS DE LUZ TEMPRANILLO CABERNET SAUVIGNON 2010 T
60% tempranillo, 40% cabernet sauvignon.

82

BODEGAS AZPEA

Camino Itúrbero, s/n
31440 Lumbier (Navarra)
☎: +34 948 880 433 - Fax: +34 948 880 433
info@bodegasazpea.com
www.bodegasazpea.com

AZPEA VINO DULCE DE MOSCATEL 2011 B
100% moscatel.

87 Colour: bright yellow. Nose: candied fruit, white flowers, expressive, grapey. Palate: flavourful, rich, fruity.

AZPEA VIURA 2011 B
viura, moscatel.

82

AZPEA JOVEN 2011 T
tempranillo, cabernet sauvignon, garnacha.

85 Colour: cherry, purple rim. Nose: warm, ripe fruit, scrubland, spicy. Palate: good structure, flavourful.

AZPEA SELECCIÓN 2007 T
cabernet sauvignon, garnacha, merlot.

85 Colour: cherry, garnet rim. Nose: warm, scrubland, spicy, fine reductive notes, ripe fruit. Palate: powerful, flavourful, toasty.

AZPEA GARNACHA 2006 T
100% garnacha.

87 Colour: light cherry, orangey edge. Nose: ripe fruit, balsamic herbs, spicy, fine reductive notes. Palate: powerful, flavourful, long.

BODEGAS CAMILO CASTILLA

Santa Bárbara, 40
31591 Corella (Navarra)
☎: +34 948 780 006 - Fax: +34 948 780 515
info@bodegascamilocastilla.com
www.bodegascamilocastilla.com

MONTECRISTO 2011 B
100% moscatel grano menudo.

84

PINK 2011 RD
100% garnacha.

86 Colour: rose, purple rim. Nose: red berry notes, ripe fruit, dried flowers, balsamic herbs. Palate: correct, light-bodied, flavourful, easy to drink.

MONTECRISTO 2011 RD
100% garnacha.

85 Colour: rose, bright. Nose: medium intensity, red berry notes, fragrant herbs. Palate: correct, easy to drink.

MONTECRISTO 2009 TC
70% tempranillo, 30% cabernet sauvignon.

86 Colour: cherry, garnet rim. Nose: red berry notes, sweet spices, creamy oak, expressive. Palate: powerful, flavourful, spicy.

MONTECRISTO MOSCATEL 2011 BLANCO DULCE
100% moscatel grano menudo.

88 Colour: bright straw. Nose: balanced, candied fruit, jasmine, citrus fruit. Palate: rich.

CAPRICHO DE GOYA VINO DE LICOR
100% moscatel grano menudo.

91 Colour: dark mahogany. Nose: dark chocolate, caramel, sweet spices, creamy oak, dry nuts, acetaldehyde. Palate: rich, powerful, flavourful, spirituous.

BODEGAS CAMPOS DE ENANZO S.C.

Mayor, 189
31521 Murchante (Navarra)
☎: +34 948 838 030 - Fax: +34 948 838 677
info@enanzo.com
www.enanzo.com

ENANZO CHARDONNAY 2011 B BARRICA
chardonnay.

86 Colour: yellow. Nose: toasty, sweet spices, candied fruit, white flowers. Palate: flavourful, spicy.

REMONTE VIURA 2011 B
viura.

84

ENANZO 2011 RD
garnacha.

86 Colour: rose, purple rim. Nose: red berry notes, medium intensity. Palate: fruity, correct, good acidity.

REMONTE JUNTOS 2010 T
graciano.

84

ENANZO 2007 TC
tempranillo, cabernet sauvignon.

83

BODEGAS CASTILLO DE MONJARDÍN

Viña Rellanada, s/n
31242 Villamayor de Monjardín (Navarra)
☎: +34 948 537 412 - Fax: +34 948 537 436
sonia@monjardin.es
www.monjardin.es

CASTILLO DE MONJARDÍN CHARDONNAY 2011 B
chardonnay.

86 Colour: bright straw. Nose: medium intensity, ripe fruit, faded flowers. Palate: fruity, flavourful, easy to drink.

CASTILLO DE MONJARDÍN CHARDONNAY 2009 BFB
chardonnay.

93 Colour: bright yellow. Nose: powerfull, ripe fruit, creamy oak, fragrant herbs, citrus fruit, toasty. Palate: rich, flavourful, fresh, good acidity.

CASTILLO DE MONJARDÍN CHARDONNAY 2008 B RESERVA
100% chardonnay.

89 Colour: bright golden. Nose: honeyed notes, balsamic herbs, aged wood nuances, creamy oak, floral. Palate: rich, powerful, flavourful, spicy, long.

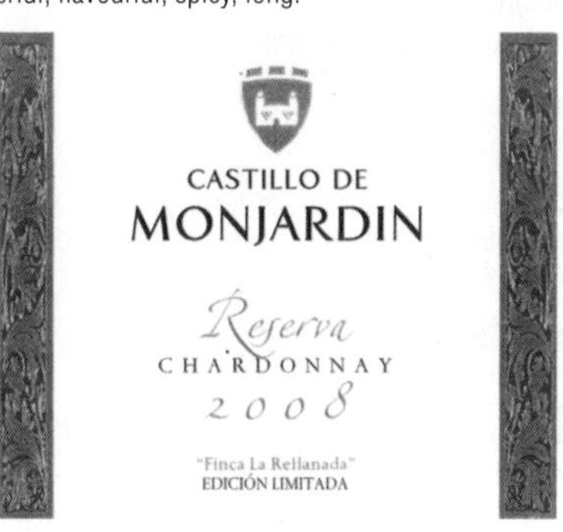

ESENCIA MONJARDÍN 2007 B
chardonnay.

93 Colour: bright golden. Nose: elegant, expressive, candied fruit, dried flowers, sweet spices. Palate: balanced, spicy.

CASTILLO DE MONJARDÍN 2009 TC
cabernet sauvignon, merlot, tempranillo.

88 Colour: cherry, garnet rim. Nose: ripe fruit, spicy, toasty. Palate: powerful, flavourful, balanced.

CASTILLO DE MONJARDÍN DEYO 2008 TC
merlot.

88 Colour: cherry, garnet rim. Nose: ripe fruit, spicy, medium intensity, warm. Palate: powerful, flavourful, toasty, round tannins.

CASTILLO DE MONJARDÍN CABERNET SAUVIGNON 1998 TGR
cabernet sauvignon, merlot, tempranillo.

88 Colour: pale ruby, brick rim edge. Nose: spicy, fine reductive notes, wet leather, aged wood nuances, fruit liqueur notes. Palate: spicy, fine tannins, long.

BODEGAS CAUDALIA

San Francisco, 7
Najera (La Rioja)
☎: +34 670 833 340 - Fax: +34 941 145 394
info@bodegascaudalia.com
www.bodegascaudalia.com

PAAL 01 2011 T
100% syrah.

92 Colour: cherry, purple rim. Nose: powerfull, varietal, ripe fruit, fruit expression, scrubland. Palate: flavourful, powerful, spicy, ripe fruit.

PAAL 01 2010 T
100% syrah.

89 Colour: bright cherry. Nose: ripe fruit, sweet spices, creamy oak, expressive. Palate: flavourful, fruity, toasty, round tannins.

BODEGAS CORELLANAS

Santa Bárbara, 29
31591 Corella (Navarra)
☎: +34 948 780 029 - Fax: +34 948 781 542
info@bodegascorellanas.com
www.bodegascorellanas.com

MOSCATEL SARASATE EXPRESIÓN 2011 B
moscatel grano menudo.

87 Colour: bright yellow. Nose: candied fruit, faded flowers, citrus fruit. Palate: rich, flavourful.

VIÑA RUBICÁN 2011 B
40% viura, 60% moscatel grano menudo.

82

VIÑA RUBICÁN ÚNICO 2007 T
15% tempranillo, 85% garnacha.

90 Colour: cherry, garnet rim. Nose: ripe fruit, spicy, creamy oak, toasty, complex. Palate: powerful, flavourful, toasty, fine tannins.

VIÑA RUBICÁN 2005 TR
cabernet sauvignon, tempranillo, merlot.

86 Colour: cherry, garnet rim. Nose: balanced, ripe fruit, spicy, tobacco. Palate: correct, good finish, easy to drink.

BODEGAS DE LA CASA DE LÚCULO

Ctra. Larraga, s/n
31150 Mendigorría (Navarra)
☎: +34 948 343 148 - Fax: +34 948 343 148
bodega@luculo.es
www.luculo.es

CÁTULO 2010 T
90% garnacha, 10% syrah.

87 Colour: cherry, garnet rim. Nose: ripe fruit, mineral, wild herbs. Palate: powerful, flavourful, fruity.

JARDÍN DE LÚCULO 2008 T
garnacha.

91 Colour: light cherry, garnet rim. Nose: fruit liqueur notes, earthy notes, spicy, fine reductive notes. Palate: elegant, balanced, round, powerful, flavourful.

BODEGAS FERNÁNDEZ DE ARCAYA

La Serna, 31
31210 Los Arcos (Navarra)
☎: +34 948 640 811 - Fax: +34 948 441 060
info@fernandezdearcaya.com
www.fernandezdearcaya.com

VIÑA PERGUITA 2011 T ROBLE
85% tempranillo, 10% cabernet sauvignon, 5% merlot.

85 Colour: cherry, garnet rim. Nose: ripe fruit, balsamic herbs, spicy, creamy oak. Palate: good acidity, flavourful, toasty.

VIÑA PERGUITA 2009 TC
80% tempranillo, 15% cabernet sauvignon, 5% merlot.

88 Colour: cherry, garnet rim. Nose: ripe fruit, spicy, creamy oak. Palate: powerful, flavourful, toasty, round tannins, balanced.

FERNÁNDEZ DE ARCAYA 2008 TR
100% cabernet sauvignon.

90 Colour: cherry, garnet rim. Nose: spicy, creamy oak, fragrant herbs. Palate: toasty, flavourful, ripe fruit.

BODEGAS GRAN FEUDO

Calle de la Ribera 32
31592 Cintruénigo (Navarra)
☎: +34 948 811 000
info@bodegaschivite.com

GRAN FEUDO EDICIÓN DULCE DE MOSCATEL 2011 B
moscatel.

92 Colour: golden. Nose: powerfull, floral, candied fruit, fragrant herbs. Palate: flavourful, sweet, fruity, good acidity.

GRAN FEUDO EDICIÓN CHARDONNAY SOBRE LÍAS 2011 B
100% chardonnay.

91 Colour: bright straw. Nose: fresh, fresh fruit, white flowers, floral, mineral. Palate: flavourful, fruity, good acidity, balanced.

GRAN FEUDO CHARDONNAY 2011 B
chardonnay.

89 Colour: bright straw. Nose: fresh, fresh fruit, white flowers. Palate: flavourful, fruity, good acidity, balanced.

GRAN FEUDO SUAVE 2011 B
chardonnay, moscatel.

88 Colour: bright straw. Nose: citrus fruit, ripe fruit, expressive. Palate: flavourful, fruity, fresh.

GRAN FEUDO 2011 RD
garnacha.

88 Colour: brilliant rose. Nose: medium intensity, red berry notes, floral. Palate: light-bodied, fruity, good acidity.

GRAN FEUDO 2009 TC
tempranillo, garnacha, cabernet sauvignon.

88 Colour: very deep cherry. Nose: spicy, dark chocolate, ripe fruit, toasty. Palate: ripe fruit, long, spicy.

GRAN FEUDO EDICIÓN SELECCIÓN ESPECIAL 2008 TC
tempranillo, merlot, cabernet sauvignon.

91 Colour: cherry, garnet rim. Nose: ripe fruit, toasty, complex, sweet spices, mineral. Palate: powerful, flavourful, toasty, round tannins.

GRAN FEUDO 2008 TR
tempranillo, garnacha, cabernet sauvignon.

90 Colour: cherry, garnet rim. Nose: ripe fruit, spicy, toasty, complex, elegant. Palate: powerful, flavourful, toasty, round tannins.

GRAN FEUDO EDICIÓN VIÑAS VIEJAS 2007 TR
tempranillo, garnacha, merlot.

89 Colour: cherry, garnet rim. Nose: creamy oak, toasty, spicy. Palate: powerful, flavourful, toasty, round tannins.

BODEGAS IRACHE

Monasterio de Irache, 1
31240 Ayegui (Navarra)
☎: +34 948 551 932 - Fax: +34 948 554 954
irache@irache.com
www.irache.com

CASTILLO IRACHE 2011 B
chardonnay.

85 Colour: bright straw. Nose: fresh, white flowers. Palate: flavourful, fruity, balanced.

CASTILLO IRACHE 2011 RD
garnacha.

85 Colour: rose, purple rim. Nose: lactic notes, floral, red berry notes, ripe fruit. Palate: powerful, flavourful, fruity, easy to drink.

CASTILLO IRACHE TEMPRANILLO 2011 T
tempranillo.

83

FUENTE CERRADA 2010 T
tempranillo, cabernet sauvignon, merlot.

85 Colour: cherry, garnet rim. Nose: ripe fruit, spicy, toasty. Palate: correct, fruity, good finish.

GRAN IRACHE 2008 TC
tempranillo, merlot, cabernet sauvignon.

85 Colour: cherry, garnet rim. Nose: ripe fruit, spicy, creamy oak. Palate: powerful, flavourful, toasty, spicy.

CASTILLO IRACHE 2007 TC
cabernet sauvignon, merlot.

85 Colour: cherry, garnet rim. Nose: ripe fruit, spicy, nose:tic coffee. Palate: powerful, flavourful, ripe fruit.

IRACHE 2004 TR
tempranillo, cabernet sauvignon, merlot.

84

BODEGAS ITURBIDE

Término la Torre, s/n
31350 Peralta (Navarra)
☎: +34 948 750 537 - Fax: +34 647 742 368
bodegasiturbide@bodegasiturbide.com
www.bodegasiturbide.com

NOVEM 2011 RD
100% garnacha.

82

NOVEM 2010 T
80% garnacha, 20% tempranillo.

83

NOVEM 2009 T
100% cabernet sauvignon.

83

BODEGAS LASIERPE

Ribera, s/n
31592 Cintruénigo (Navarra)
☎: +34 948 811 033 - Fax: +34 948 815 160
comercial@dominiolasierpe.com
www.dominiolasierpe.com

FINCA LASIERPE BLANCO DE VIURA 2011 B
100% viura.

83

FINCA LASIERPE GARNACHA 2011 RD
100% garnacha.

85 Colour: rose, purple rim. Nose: floral, candied fruit, fresh, expressive. Palate: easy to drink, light-bodied, fruity, flavourful.

FINCA LASIERPE TEMPRANILLO GARNACHA 2011 T
60% tempranillo, 40% garnacha.

81

FLOR DE LASIERPE GRACIANO 2009 T
100% graciano.

88 Colour: bright cherry. Nose: ripe fruit, sweet spices, creamy oak, expressive. Palate: flavourful, fruity, toasty, round tannins.

DOMINIO LASIERPE 2009 TC
85% tempranillo, 15% cabernet sauvignon.

85 Colour: cherry, garnet rim. Nose: ripe fruit, aged wood nuances, sweet spices. Palate: easy to drink, flavourful, correct.

FLOR DE LASIERPE GARNACHA VIÑAS VIEJAS 2008 T
100% garnacha.

87 Colour: cherry, garnet rim. Nose: fruit preserve, sweet spices, dark chocolate. Palate: powerful, powerful tannins.

BODEGAS LEZAUN

Egiarte, 1
31292 Lakar (Navarra)
☎: +34 948 541 339 - Fax: +34 948 536 055
info@lezaun.com
www.lezaun.com

LEZAUN TXURIA 2011 B
garnacha.

84

LEZAUN TEMPRANILLO 2011 T MACERACIÓN CARBÓNICA
100% tempranillo.

89 Colour: cherry, purple rim. Nose: red berry notes, lactic notes, floral, expressive. Palate: good acidity, powerful, flavourful, fruity, balanced.

LEZAUN 0,0 SULFITOS 2011 T
100% tempranillo.

84

LEZAUN GAZAGA 2009 T ROBLE
50% tempranillo, 15% merlot, 35% cabernet sauvignon.

89 Colour: cherry, garnet rim. Nose: powerfull, creamy oak, sweet spices, dark chocolate, candied fruit. Palate: balanced, long, round tannins.

LEZAUN 2009 TC
50% tempranillo, 15% merlot, 35% cabernet sauvignon.

88 Colour: bright cherry. Nose: ripe fruit, sweet spices, creamy oak, expressive. Palate: flavourful, fruity, toasty, round tannins.

LEZAUN 2007 TR
33% tempranillo, 33% garnacha, 33% graciano.

88 Colour: deep cherry, garnet rim. Nose: ripe fruit, dark chocolate. Palate: ripe fruit, balanced, long, round tannins.

BODEGAS LOGOS

Avda. de los Fueros, 18
31522 Monteagudo (Navarra)
☎: +34 948 843 102 - Fax: +34 948 843 161
inma@bodegasescudero.com
www.familiaescudero.com

PEDRO DE IVAR 2008 TC
70% tempranillo, 20% garnacha, 10% mazuelo.

88 Colour: cherry, garnet rim. Nose: ripe fruit, red berry notes, sweet spices, creamy oak. Palate: flavourful, fruity, easy to drink.

LOGOS II 2006 TC
40% garnacha, 30% tempranillo, 30% cabernet sauvignon.

87 Colour: cherry, garnet rim. Nose: spicy, fruit preserve, fine reductive notes. Palate: powerful, flavourful, toasty, round tannins.

LOGOS I 2004 T
40% garnacha, 30% tempranillo, 30% cabernet sauvignon.

91 Colour: bright cherry, garnet rim. Nose: macerated fruit, candied fruit, cocoa bean, sweet spices. Palate: good structure, full, ripe fruit, long.

BODEGAS MACAYA

Ctra. Berbinzana, 74
31251 Larraga (Navarra)
☎: +34 948 711 549 - Fax: +34 948 711 788
info@bodegasmacaya.com
www.bodegasmacaya.com

CONDADO DE ALMARA FINCA LINTE 2010 T
100% tempranillo.

88 Colour: light cherry, garnet rim. Nose: mineral, ripe fruit, balsamic herbs, spicy. Palate: powerful, flavourful, balanced.

CONDADO DE ALMARA SELECCIÓN 2009 T
100% tempranillo.

87 Colour: cherry, garnet rim. Nose: balanced, ripe fruit, cocoa bean. Palate: flavourful, fruity, good acidity.

CONDADO DE ALMARA 2008 TC
50% tempranillo, 50% cabernet sauvignon.

88 Colour: bright cherry, purple rim. Nose: new oak, cocoa bean, sweet spices. Palate: balanced, ripe fruit, round tannins.

CONDADO DE ALMARA 2007 TR
70% tempranillo, 30% cabernet sauvignon.

89 Colour: cherry, garnet rim. Nose: ripe fruit, earthy notes, creamy oak, toasty. Palate: long, balanced, flavourful.

ALMARA CABERNET SAUVIGNON 2005 TR
100% cabernet sauvignon.

88 Colour: pale ruby, brick rim edge. Nose: spicy, fine reductive notes, wet leather, aged wood nuances, fruit liqueur notes. Palate: spicy, fine tannins, long.

BODEGAS MUSEO ONTAÑÓN

Avda. de Aragón, 3
26006 Logroño (La Rioja)
☎: +34 941 234 200 - Fax: +34 941 270 482
enoturismo@ontanon.es
www.ontanon.es

MEDIEL 2011 RD
garnacha, tempranillo.

85 Colour: rose. Nose: medium intensity, red berry notes, scrubland. Palate: fresh, fruity, easy to drink.

BODEGAS NAPARRALDE

Crtra. de Madrid s/n
31591 Corella (Navarra)
☎: +34 948 782 255 - Fax: +34 948 401 182
administracion@naparralde.com
www.upain.es

UPAIN 2011 RD
100% garnacha.

84

UPAIN SYRAH SELECCIÓN PRIVADA 2010 T
100% syrah.

86 Colour: cherry, purple rim. Nose: red berry notes, ripe fruit, sweet spices, creamy oak. Palate: flavourful, toasty.

UPAIN GARNACHA SELECCIÓN PRIVADA 2009 T
100% garnacha.

87 Nose: ripe fruit, sweet spices, creamy oak. Palate: flavourful, fruity, toasty.

UPAINBERRI 2009 T ROBLE
tempranillo, garnacha, cabernet sauvignon.

86 Colour: bright cherry. Nose: ripe fruit, sweet spices, creamy oak. Palate: flavourful, fruity, toasty, round tannins.

UPAIN TRES VARIEDADES SELECCIÓN PRIVADA 2008 T
33% tempranillo, 33% garnacha, 33% cabernet sauvignon.

87 Colour: cherry, garnet rim. Nose: ripe fruit, spicy, toasty. Palate: powerful, flavourful, toasty, round tannins.

UPAIN TEMPRANILLO MERLOT 2005 T
70% tempranillo, 30% merlot.

84

BODEGAS OCHOA

Alcalde Maillata, 2
31390 Olite (Navarra)
☎: +34 948 740 006 - Fax: +34 948 740 048
info@bodegasochoa.com
www.bodegasochoa.com

MOSCATO DE OCHOA 2011 B
moscatel grano menudo.

87 Colour: bright straw. Nose: medium intensity, fresh, floral. Palate: fresh, fruity, flavourful.

OCHOA CALENDAS 2011 B
viura, chardonnay.

83

OCHOA ROSADO DE LÁGRIMA 2011 RD
50% garnacha, 50% cabernet sauvignon.

87 Colour: light cherry, bright. Nose: fresh fruit, citrus fruit, wild herbs. Palate: fruity, flavourful, good acidity.

OCHOA TEMPRANILLO 2009 TC
tempranillo.

86 Colour: cherry, garnet rim. Nose: ripe fruit, spicy, toasty. Palate: flavourful, correct, spicy.

OCHOA CALENDAS 2010 T ROBLE
tempranillo, syrah.

84

OCHOA 2006 TR
55% tempranillo, 15% merlot, 30% cabernet sauvignon.

89 Colour: cherry, garnet rim. Nose: sweet spices, creamy oak, cocoa bean, ripe fruit. Palate: good structure, flavourful, good acidity.

OCHOA MOSCATEL 2011 BLANCO DULCE
moscatel grano menudo.

90 Colour: bright yellow. Nose: candied fruit, citrus fruit, white flowers, balanced, expressive. Palate: rich, flavourful, elegant.

BODEGAS ORVALAIZ

Ctra. Pamplona-Logroño, s/n
31151 Óbanos (Navarra)
☎: +34 948 344 437 - Fax: +34 948 344 401
bodega@orvalaiz.es
www.orvalaiz.es

ORVALAIZ CHARDONNAY 2011 B
100% chardonnay.

86 Colour: bright straw. Nose: fresh, fresh fruit, white flowers, balsamic herbs. Palate: flavourful, fruity, good acidity.

VIÑA ORVALAIZ 2011 B
50% viura, 45% chardonnay, 5% malvasía.

82

ORVALAIZ ROSADO DE LÁGRIMA 2011 RD
100% cabernet sauvignon.

83

VIÑA ORVALAIZ ROSADO 2011 RD
90% garnacha, 10% tempranillo.

83

VIÑA ORVALAIZ 2011 T
75% tempranillo, 25% cabernet sauvignon.

84

ORVALAIZ CABERNET SAUVIGNON 2010 T ROBLE
100% cabernet sauvignon.

86 Colour: cherry, garnet rim. Nose: ripe fruit, scrubland, spicy, creamy oak. Palate: powerful, flavourful, toasty.

ORVALAIZ TEMPRANILLO 2010 T ROBLE
100% tempranillo.

85 Colour: cherry, garnet rim. Nose: toasty, spicy, ripe fruit. Palate: easy to drink, good finish, fruity.

ORVALAIZ GARNACHA 2010 T ROBLE
100% garnacha.

80

ORVALAIZ MERLOT 2009 T ROBLE
100% merlot.

87 Colour: bright cherry. Nose: ripe fruit, sweet spices, creamy oak, balsamic herbs. Palate: flavourful, fruity, toasty.

SEPTENTRIÓN 2008 TC
85% tempranillo, 15% cabernet sauvignon.

87 Colour: bright cherry. Nose: expressive, sweet spices, cocoa bean, ripe fruit. Palate: flavourful, correct.

ORVALAIZ 2008 TC
40% tempranillo, 30% cabernet sauvignon, 30% merlot.

85 Colour: cherry, garnet rim. Nose: ripe fruit, spicy, toasty. Palate: powerful, flavourful, toasty.

ORVALAIZ 2006 TR
50% tempranillo, 30% cabernet sauvignon, merlot.

86 Colour: cherry, garnet rim. Nose: ripe fruit, spicy, old leather. Palate: flavourful, toasty, round tannins.

BODEGAS PAGOS DE ARÁIZ

Camino de Araiz, s/n
31390 Olite (Navarra)
☎: +34 948 399 182
info@bodegaspagosdearaiz.com
www.bodegaspagosdearaiz.com

PAGOS DE ARÁIZ 2011 RD
90% garnacha, 10% graciano.

86 Colour: rose, purple rim. Nose: red berry notes, floral, expressive, lactic notes. Palate: , flavourful, fresh, fruity.

BODEGAS PALACIO DE LA VEGA

Condesa de la Vega de Pozo, s/n
31263 Dicastillo (Navarra)
☎: +34 948 527 009 - Fax: +34 948 527 333
infopalaciodelavega@ambrosiovelasco.es
www.palaciodelavega.com

PALACIO DE LA VEGA CHARDONNAY 2011 B
chardonnay.

88 Colour: bright straw. Nose: white flowers, fragrant herbs, fruit expression. Palate: flavourful, rich, fruity, balanced.

PALACIO DE LA VEGA GARNACHA 2011 RD
garnacha.

87 Colour: rose, bright. Nose: red berry notes, fragrant herbs, balanced. Palate: fruity, balanced, good acidity.

PALACIO DE LA VEGA CABERNET SAUVIGNON TEMPRANILLO 2009 TC
cabernet sauvignon, tempranillo.

87 Colour: cherry, garnet rim. Nose: ripe fruit, spicy, creamy oak, toasty. Palate: powerful, flavourful, toasty, balanced.

CONDE DE LA VEGA DEL POZO 2005 TR
tempranillo, cabernet sauvignon, merlot.

82

BODEGAS PIEDEMONTE

Rua Romana, s/n
31390 Olite (Navarra)
☎: +34 948 712 406 - Fax: +34 948 740 090
bodega@piedemonte.com
www.piedemonte.com

PIEDEMONTE MOSCATEL 2011 B
moscatel grano menudo.

90 Colour: golden. Nose: powerfull, floral, honeyed notes, candied fruit. Palate: flavourful, sweet, fresh, fruity, long.

PIEDEMONTE CHARDONNAY 2011 B
chardonnay.

88 Colour: bright yellow. Nose: medium intensity, floral, fruit expression. Palate: correct, ripe fruit, good finish, balanced.

PIEDEMONTE GAMMA 2011 B
viura, chardonnay, moscatel.

83

PIEDEMONTE 2011 RD
garnacha.

86 Colour: rose, bright. Nose: balanced, fresh, red berry notes, floral. Palate: fruity, easy to drink, good acidity.

PIEDEMONTE TEMPRANILLO 2011 T
tempranillo.

84

PIEDEMONTE MERLOT 2011 T
merlot.

81

PIEDEMONTE GAMMA 2010 T
merlot, tempranillo, cabernet sauvignon.

85 Colour: cherry, garnet rim. Nose: ripe fruit, balsamic herbs, spicy. Palate: correct, powerful, flavourful.

PIEDEMONTE 2008 TC
tempranillo, merlot, cabernet sauvignon.

85 Colour: cherry, garnet rim. Nose: spicy, creamy oak, toasty. Palate: powerful, flavourful, ripe fruit.

PIEDEMONTE CABERNET SAUVIGNON 2007 TC
cabernet sauvignon.

87 Colour: cherry, garnet rim. Nose: ripe fruit, spicy, creamy oak, toasty. Palate: powerful, flavourful, toasty.

PIEDEMONTE MERLOT 2007 TC
merlot.

86 Colour: cherry, garnet rim. Nose: ripe fruit, spicy, toasty, balsamic herbs. Palate: powerful, flavourful, toasty, round tannins.

PIEDEMONTE 2006 TR
merlot, tempranillo, cabernet sauvignon.

87 Colour: cherry, garnet rim. Nose: ripe fruit, spicy, creamy oak. Palate: powerful, flavourful, toasty, spicy.

BODEGAS PRÍNCIPE DE VIANA

Mayor, 191
31521 Murchante (Navarra)
☎: +34 948 838 640 - Fax: +34 948 818 574
info@principedeviana.com
www.principedeviana.com

PRÍNCIPE DE VIANA CHARDONNAY 2011 B
100% chardonnay.

88 Colour: bright yellow. Nose: jasmine, sweet spices, ripe fruit. Palate: ripe fruit, flavourful.

PRÍNCIPE DE VIANA EDICIÓN LIMITADA 2008 TC
50% merlot, 25% tempranillo, 25% cabernet sauvignon.

90 Colour: cherry, garnet rim. Nose: ripe fruit, spicy, creamy oak. Palate: powerful, flavourful, toasty, round tannins.

PRÍNCIPE DE VIANA 2007 TR
65% tempranillo, 20% merlot, 15% cabernet sauvignon.

88 Colour: cherry, garnet rim. Nose: ripe fruit, spicy, cocoa bean, creamy oak. Palate: powerful, spicy, long.

BODEGAS URABAIN

Ctra. Estella, 21
31262 Allo (Navarra)
☎: +34 948 523 011 - Fax: +34 948 523 409
vinos@bodegasurabain.com
www.bodegasurabain.com

URABAIN CHARDONNAY 2011 B
chardonnay.

87 Colour: bright straw. Nose: balanced, dried flowers, ripe fruit, citrus fruit. Palate: fruity, long, balanced.

URABAIN ROSADO DE LÁGRIMA 2011 RD
merlot.

87 Colour: rose, bright. Nose: powerfull, fruit expression, balanced, rose petals. Palate: powerful, flavourful, ripe fruit, long.

URABAIN CABERNET SAUVIGNON TEMPRANILLO 2011 T
tempranillo, cabernet sauvignon.

85 Colour: cherry, purple rim. Nose: red berry notes, fruit liqueur notes, scrubland. Palate: flavourful, light-bodied, fresh, fruity.

UN PASO MÁS 2009 T
tempranillo, cabernet sauvignon, merlot.

91 Colour: deep cherry, garnet rim. Nose: creamy oak, cocoa bean, sweet spices. Palate: good structure, full, ripe fruit.

PRADO DE CHICA 2009 T
merlot.

87 Colour: bright cherry. Nose: ripe fruit, creamy oak, expressive, balsamic herbs. Palate: flavourful, long, varietal.

URABAIN FINCA SANTA BÁRBARA 2009 T
merlot, cabernet sauvignon, tempranillo.

87 Colour: cherry, garnet rim. Nose: balanced, dark chocolate, ripe fruit. Palate: flavourful, correct, balanced.

BODEGAS VALCARLOS

Ctra. Circunvalación, s/n
31210 Los Arcos (Navarra)
☎: +34 948 640 806
info@bodegasvalcarlos.com
www.bodegasvalcarlos.com

FORTIUS CHARDONNAY 2011 B
100% chardonnay.

86 Colour: bright yellow. Nose: balanced, dried flowers, dried herbs. Palate: flavourful, correct.

FORTIUS 2011 B
viura, chardonnay.

84

MARQUÉS DE VALCARLOS 2011 B
viura, chardonnay.

84

MARQUÉS DE VALCARLOS CHARDONNAY 2011 B
100% chardonnay.

82

MARQUÉS DE VALCARLOS 2011 RD
tempranillo, merlot.

84

FORTIUS 2011 RD
tempranillo, merlot.

84

FORTIUS TEMPRANILLO 2009 T
tempranillo.

87 Colour: cherry, garnet rim. Nose: ripe fruit, wild herbs, spicy, creamy oak. Palate: light-bodied, flavourful, long.

MARQUÉS DE VALCARLOS TEMPRANILLO 2009 T
100% tempranillo.

87 Colour: cherry, garnet rim. Nose: ripe fruit, spicy, balanced, toasty, sweet spices. Palate: fruity, balanced.

MARQUÉS DE VALCARLOS 2008 TC
tempranillo, cabernet sauvignon.

85 Colour: cherry, garnet rim. Nose: medium intensity, ripe fruit, dried herbs. Palate: fruity, spicy.

FORTIUS 2008 TC
tempranillo, cabernet sauvignon.

84

FORTIUS MERLOT 2007 TC
100% merlot.

88 Colour: cherry, garnet rim. Nose: medium intensity, balanced, ripe fruit. Palate: correct, balanced, round tannins.

FORTIUS 2005 TR
tempranillo, cabernet sauvignon.

87 Colour: cherry, garnet rim. Nose: balanced, medium intensity, ripe fruit, spicy, tobacco. Palate: flavourful, long.

MARQUÉS DE VALCARLOS 2005 TR
tempranillo, cabernet sauvignon.

84

ÉLITE DE FORTIUS 2004 TR
merlot, cabernet sauvignon.

90 Colour: pale ruby, brick rim edge. Nose: ripe fruit, fragrant herbs, earthy notes, spicy, fine reductive notes. Palate: elegant, good structure, flavourful.

FORTIUS 2001 TGR
tempranillo, cabernet sauvignon.

89 Colour: pale ruby, brick rim edge. Nose: scrubland, spicy, aged wood nuances, fruit liqueur notes, fine reductive notes. Palate: fine tannins, balanced, powerful, flavourful.

MARQUÉS DE VALCARLOS 2001 TGR
tempranillo, cabernet sauvignon.

88 Colour: cherry, garnet rim. Nose: balanced, ripe fruit, sweet spices. Palate: flavourful, reductive nuances, spicy.

BODEGAS VEGA DEL CASTILLO

Rua Romana, 3
31390 Olite (Navarra)
☎: +34 948 740 012
info@vegadelcastillo.com
www.vegadelcastillo.com

VEGA DEL CASTILLO GARNACHA CEPAS VIEJAS 2011 T
100% garnacha.

88 Colour: cherry, purple rim. Nose: fruit expression, balanced, violets. Palate: flavourful, fruity, correct, balanced.

AUZOLÁN LLAVERO ECOLÓGICO 2008 TC
cabernet sauvignon.

86 Colour: cherry, garnet rim. Nose: candied fruit, cocoa bean, sweet spices. Palate: flavourful, correct.

VEGA DEL CASTILLO 2007 TR
25% merlot, 50% tempranillo, 25% cabernet sauvignon.

90 Colour: cherry, garnet rim. Nose: ripe fruit, balsamic herbs, sweet spices, toasty. Palate: spicy, long, powerful, flavourful.

DUBHE 2007 T ROBLE
50% merlot, 25% cabernet sauvignon, 25% tempranillo.

90 Colour: cherry, garnet rim. Nose: complex, sweet spices, cocoa bean, creamy oak. Palate: full, toasty, round tannins.

MERAK VEGA DEL CASTILLO 2007 T
50% merlot, 25% tempranillo, 25% cabernet sauvignon.

89 Colour: cherry, garnet rim. Nose: ripe fruit, spicy, creamy oak, toasty, complex. Palate: powerful, flavourful, toasty, round tannins.

BODEGAS VIÑA MAGAÑA

San Miguel, 9
31523 Barillas (Navarra)
☎: +34 948 850 034 - Fax: +34 948 851 536
bodegas@vinamagana.com
www.vinamagana.com

BARÓN DE MAGAÑA 2009 TC

91 Colour: cherry, garnet rim. Nose: ripe fruit, creamy oak, toasty, balsamic herbs, wild herbs. Palate: powerful, flavourful, toasty, balanced.

MAGAÑA MERLOT 2009 TR
merlot.

91 Colour: cherry, garnet rim. Nose: creamy oak, mineral, fragrant herbs, ripe fruit, spicy, balanced. Palate: long, spicy, flavourful, fresh, fruity, round tannins.

MAGAÑA CALCHETAS 2008 T

92 Colour: cherry, garnet rim. Nose: ripe fruit, earthy notes, spicy, balsamic herbs, expressive, creamy oak. Palate: powerful, flavourful, complex, long, spicy.

MAGAÑA DIGNUS 2007 TC

90 Colour: cherry, garnet rim. Nose: ripe fruit, spicy, creamy oak, toasty, complex, fine reductive notes. Palate: powerful, flavourful, toasty, round tannins.

VIÑA MAGAÑA 2004 TR

88 Colour: bright cherry, orangey edge. Nose: spicy, fine reductive notes, creamy oak, acetaldehyde, balsamic herbs. Palate: spicy, fine tannins, long.

BODEGAS Y VIÑEDOS ARTAZU

Mayor, 3
31109 Artazu (Navarra)
☎: +34 945 600 119 - Fax: +34 945 600 850
artazu@artadi.com

SANTA CRUZ DE ARTAZU 2010 T
garnacha.

95 Colour: cherry, purple rim. Nose: floral, fragrant herbs, balsamic herbs, toasty, spicy, mineral. Palate: round, good acidity, powerful, round tannins.

CRIANZAS Y VIÑEDOS R. REVERTE

Lejalde, 43
31593 Fitero (Navarra)
☎: +34 948 366 031 - Fax: +34 948 183 487
comercial@rafaelreverte.es
www.rafaelreverte.es

REVERTE 2011 B
garnacha blanca.

86 Colour: bright straw. Nose: fresh, fresh fruit, white flowers, expressive. Palate: flavourful, fruity, good acidity, balanced.

REVERTE 2011 T MACERACIÓN CARBÓNICA
tempranillo.

87 Colour: cherry, purple rim. Nose: expressive, red berry notes, floral. Palate: flavourful, fruity, balanced.

TIFERO 2011 T
garnacha.

83

ODIPUS CABERNET SAUVIGNON 2010 T
cabernet sauvignon.

88 Colour: bright cherry. Nose: ripe fruit, sweet spices, scrubland. Palate: flavourful, fruity, toasty, round tannins.

ODIPUS MAZUELO 2010 T
mazuelo.

86 Colour: cherry, garnet rim. Nose: powerfull, ripe fruit, dried herbs. Palate: flavourful, fruity, spicy.

ODIPUS GARNACHA 2009 T
garnacha.

88 Colour: cherry, garnet rim. Nose: ripe fruit, sweet spices, creamy oak, expressive. Palate: flavourful, fruity, toasty, round tannins.

CISTUM 2009 T
garnacha.

87 Colour: bright cherry. Nose: ripe fruit, sweet spices, creamy oak, dark chocolate. Palate: flavourful, fruity, toasty, harsh oak tannins.

SEPTO 2008 TC
garnacha, tempranillo, mazuelo, otras.

87 Colour: cherry, garnet rim. Nose: ripe fruit, toasty, sweet spices. Palate: powerful, flavourful, harsh oak tannins.

SEPTO 2008 TR
garnacha.

85 Colour: cherry, garnet rim. Nose: powerfull, dark chocolate, fruit preserve. Palate: correct, flavourful, full.

DISTRIBUCIONES B. IÑAKI NÚÑEZ

Ctra. de Ablitas a Ribafora, Km. 5
31523 Ablitas (Navarra)
☎: +34 948 386 210 - Fax: +34 629 354 190
bodegasin@pagodecirsus.com
www.pagodecirsus.com

PAGO DE CIRSUS CHARDONNAY 2011 B
100% chardonnay.

89 Colour: bright straw. Nose: powerfull, faded flowers, wild herbs. Palate: flavourful, powerful, ripe fruit, balanced, long.

PAGO DE CIRSUS DE IÑAKI NÚÑEZ SELECCIÓN DE FAMILIA 2007 T
tempranillo, syrah.

92 Colour: cherry, purple rim. Nose: powerfull, cocoa bean, creamy oak, ripe fruit. Palate: full, flavourful, long, good acidity.

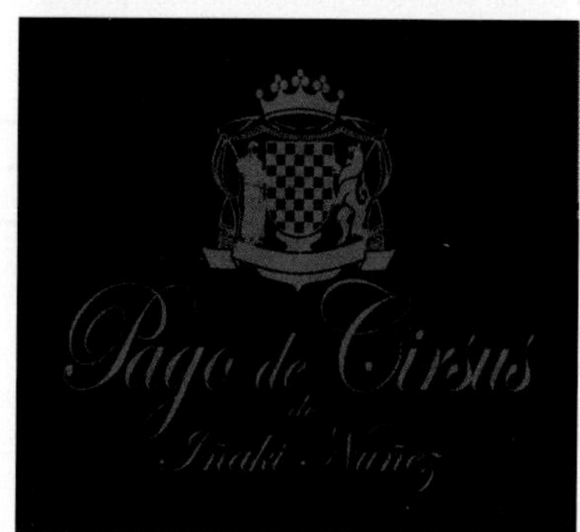

PAGO DE CIRSUS CHARDONNAY 2010 BFB
100% chardonnay.

91 Colour: bright yellow. Nose: balanced, expressive, ripe fruit, white flowers. Palate: flavourful, spicy, ripe fruit, long.

PAGO DE CIRSUS MOSCATEL VENDIMIA TARDÍA 2007 BFB
100% moscatel grano menudo.

91 Colour: golden. Nose: honeyed notes, candied fruit, elegant, faded flowers, sweet spices. Palate: flavourful, sweet, fruity, long, rich.

PAGO DE CIRSUS DE IÑAKI NUÑEZ VENDIMIA SELECCIONADA 2009 TC
tempranillo, merlot, syrah.

90 Colour: cherry, garnet rim. Nose: closed, ripe fruit, spicy, nose:tic coffee. Palate: balanced, good structure, round tannins.

PAGO DE CIRSUS OPUS 11 2008 T
syrah, tempranillo.

92 Colour: dark-red cherry, garnet rim. Nose: powerfull, fruit preserve, sweet spices. Palate: good structure, rich, complex, round tannins.

PAGO DE CIRSUS DE IÑAKI NÚÑEZ CUVÉE ESPECIAL 2008 TR
tempranillo, merlot, syrah.

88 Colour: bright cherry, garnet rim. Nose: powerfull, dried herbs, spicy. Palate: flavourful, fine bitter notes, round tannins.

DOMAINES LUPIER

Monseñor Justo Goizueta, 4
31495 San Martín de Unx (Navarra)
☎: +34 639 622 111
info@domaineslupier.com
www.domaineslupier.com

DOMAINES LUPIER EL TERROIR 2009 T
100% garnacha.

94 Colour: cherry, garnet rim. Nose: balanced, ripe fruit, floral, fragrant herbs, spicy, cocoa bean, creamy oak. Palate: fresh, fruity, flavourful, long, toasty.

DOMAINES LUPIER LA DAMA VIÑAS VIEJAS 2009 T
100% garnacha.

93 Colour: cherry, garnet rim. Nose: ripe fruit, balsamic herbs, varietal, mineral, sweet spices, creamy oak. Palate: long, balanced, fresh, fruity, flavourful, round tannins.

DSG VINEYARDS

Ctra. Assa
01309 Elvillar (Alava)
☎: +34 619 600 425
www.dsgvineyards.es

LIBIDO 2011 RD
100% garnacha.

88 Colour: rose, purple rim. Nose: powerfull, ripe fruit, red berry notes, floral, expressive. Palate: fleshy, powerful, fruity, fresh.

LIBIDO 2010 T
100% garnacha.

87 Colour: cherry, garnet rim. Nose: ripe fruit, scrubland, wild herbs, spicy, creamy oak. Palate: flavourful, fresh, fruity.

PASOLASMONJAS 2008 T
100% garnacha.

89 Colour: cherry, garnet rim. Nose: earthy notes, scrubland, spicy, toasty, creamy oak, ripe fruit. Palate: powerful, flavourful, long, balsamic.

FINCA ALBRET

Ctra. Cadreita-Villafranca, s/n
31515 Cadreita (Navarra)
☎: +34 948 406 806 - Fax: +34 948 406 699
info@fincaalbret.com
www.fincaalbret.com

JUAN DE ALBRET 2009 T
50% tempranillo, 30% cabernet sauvignon, 20% merlot.

90 Colour: cherry, garnet rim. Nose: ripe fruit, sweet spices, creamy oak. Palate: flavourful, complex, rich, balanced.

ALBRET LA VIÑA DE MI MADRE 2007 TR
95% cabernet sauvignon, 5% merlot.

89 Colour: cherry, garnet rim. Nose: ripe fruit, candied fruit, balsamic herbs, sweet spices. Palate: balanced, flavourful, toasty.

GARCÍA BURGOS

Finca La Cantera de Santa Ana, s/n
31521 Murchante (Navarra)
☎: +34 948 847 734 - Fax: +34 948 847 734
info@bodegasgarciaburgos.com
www.bodegasgarciaburgos.com

GARCÍA BURGOS SH 2009 T
100% syrah.

91 Colour: bright cherry. Nose: ripe fruit, sweet spices, creamy oak, expressive. Palate: flavourful, fruity, toasty, round tannins.

GARCÍA BURGOS VENDIMIA SELECCIONADA 2009 T
40% cabernet sauvignon, 40% merlot, 20% syrah.

90 Colour: cherry, garnet rim. Nose: ripe fruit, fragrant herbs, expressive, creamy oak. Palate: round, powerful, flavourful.

FINCA LA CANTERA DE SANTA ANA 2007 T
100% cabernet sauvignon.

92 Colour: bright cherry, garnet rim. Nose: complex, elegant, balanced, sweet spices, creamy oak. Palate: full, good acidity, round tannins.

LOLA GARCÍA AS RESERVA 2007 TR
100% merlot.

91 Colour: cherry, garnet rim. Nose: spicy, creamy oak, toasty, ripe fruit, earthy notes. Palate: powerful, flavourful, toasty, round tannins, elegant.

HACIENDA UVANIS

Avda. Estella, 61
31300 Tafalla (Navarra)
☎: +34 948 700 088 - Fax: +34 948 755 433
haciendauvanis@grupoan.com
www.grupoan.com

HACIENDA UVANIS SELECCIÓN 2008 T
tempranillo, merlot, syrah.

88 Colour: cherry, garnet rim. Nose: ripe fruit, spicy, creamy oak, earthy notes, balsamic herbs. Palate: powerful, flavourful, toasty, round tannins.

J. CHIVITE PAGOS & ESTATES

31292 Aberin (Navarra)
☎: +34 948 555 285
info@bodegaschivite.com
www.bodegaschivite.com

CHIVITE FINCA DE VILLATUERTA 2010 B
chardonnay.

93 Colour: bright straw. Nose: fresh fruit, ripe fruit, mineral, sweet spices, white flowers. Palate: flavourful, good acidity, fine bitter notes, spicy, long.

CHIVITE COLECCIÓN 125 2009 BFB
chardonnay.

95 Colour: bright yellow. Nose: powerfull, ripe fruit, sweet spices, fragrant herbs, mineral. Palate: rich, smoky afterpalate:, flavourful, fresh, good acidity.

CHIVITE COLECCIÓN 125 VENDIMIA TARDÍA B
moscatel.

95 Colour: golden. Nose: powerfull, honeyed notes, candied fruit, fragrant herbs, balanced, expressive. Palate: flavourful, sweet, fresh, fruity, good acidity, long, balanced.

CHIVITE COLECCIÓN 125 2007 RD

92 Colour: onion pink. Nose: scrubland, red berry notes, ripe fruit, sweet spices, toasty. Palate: flavourful, ripe fruit, creamy, fine bitter notes.

CHIVITE FINCA DE VILLATUERTA SYRAH 2010 T
100% syrah.

93 Colour: cherry, garnet rim. Nose: ripe fruit, spicy, toasty, red berry notes, fruit expression, creamy oak, cocoa bean. Palate: powerful, flavourful, toasty, round tannins.

CHIVITE BIOLÓGICO MERLOT 2008 T
merlot.

90 Colour: cherry, garnet rim. Nose: ripe fruit, spicy, creamy oak, toasty, balsamic herbs. Palate: powerful, flavourful, toasty, round tannins.

CHIVITE FINCA DE VILLATUERTA SELECCIÓN ESPECIAL 2008 T
67% tempranillo, 33% merlot.

88 Colour: cherry, garnet rim. Nose: ripe fruit, sweet spices, toasty, scrubland. Palate: flavourful, fine bitter notes, good acidity.

CHIVITE COLECCIÓN 125 2006 TR
tempranillo, merlot, cabernet sauvignon.

92 Colour: cherry, garnet rim. Nose: toasty, nose:tic coffee, scrubland, ripe fruit. Palate: flavourful, fine bitter notes, good acidity, spicy, long.

LA CALANDRIA. PURA GARNACHA

Camino de Aspra, s/n
31521 Murchante (Navarra)
☎: +34 630 904 327
luis@lacalandria.org
www.lacalandria.org

SONROJO 2011 RD
100% garnacha.

89 Colour: rose, purple rim. Nose: powerfull, ripe fruit, red berry notes, floral, expressive. Palate: fleshy, powerful, fruity, fresh.

CIENTRUENOS 2011 T BARRICA
100% garnacha.

91 Colour: light cherry, purple rim. Nose: elegant, red berry notes, scrubland, mineral. Palate: flavourful, balanced, complex, spicy.

VOLANDERA 2011 T MACERACIÓN CARBÓNICA
100% garnacha.

89 Colour: cherry, purple rim. Nose: expressive, fresh fruit, red berry notes, floral. Palate: flavourful, fruity, good acidity, balanced.

LADERAS DE MONTEJURRA

Paraje de Argonga, s/n
31263 Dicastillo (Navarra)
☎: +34 638 218 727
info@laderasdemontejurra.com
www.laderasdemontejurra.com

VIÑA DE SAN MARTÍN 2010 T

93 Colour: bright cherry. Nose: ripe fruit, sweet spices, creamy oak, expressive, balsamic herbs, mineral. Palate: flavourful, fruity, toasty, good acidity, balanced.

VIÑA DE LEORÍN 2010 T

92 Colour: black cherry, garnet rim. Nose: earthy notes, fruit liqueur notes, spicy, balsamic herbs, balanced. Palate: powerful, flavourful, spicy, long, fine bitter notes.

EMILIO VALERIO LADERAS DE MONTEJURRA 2010 T

91 Colour: dark-red cherry, garnet rim. Nose: ripe fruit, dried flowers, fragrant herbs, earthy notes. Palate: fresh, fruity, flavourful, spicy, long, balsamic.

USUARAN 2010 T

91 Colour: cherry, garnet rim. Nose: spicy, creamy oak, red berry notes, ripe fruit, earthy notes, balsamic herbs. Palate: powerful, flavourful, toasty, spicy.

AMBURZA 2009 T

88 Colour: cherry, garnet rim. Nose: ripe fruit, spicy, creamy oak, scrubland, fine reductive notes. Palate: powerful, flavourful, toasty, round tannins.

LUIS GURPEGUI MUGA

Ctra. Pamplona, s/n
31330 Villafranca (Navarra)
☎: +34 948 670 050 - Fax: +34 948 670 259
bodegas@gurpegui.es
www.gurpegui.es

MONTE ORY 2011 RD
garnacha.

86 Colour: rose, purple rim. Nose: powerfull, red berry notes, floral, expressive. Palate: , powerful, fresh, flavourful.

MONTE ORY TEMPRANILLO - CABERNET SAUVIGNON 2011 T
tempranillo, cabernet sauvignon.

85 Colour: deep cherry, purple rim. Nose: medium intensity, ripe fruit, scrubland. Palate: correct, flavourful.

MONTE ORY 2008 TC
tempranillo, garnacha, cabernet sauvignon.

85 Colour: cherry, garnet rim. Nose: sweet spices, cocoa bean, candied fruit. Palate: powerful, fruity.

Mª LUISA JANICES

Ctra. Tafalla, s/n
31495 San Martín de Unx (Navarra)
☎: +34 948 738 262 - Fax: +34 948 738 080
info@bodegasberamendi.com
www.bodegasberamendi.com

BERAMENDI 3F 2011 B
60% chardonnay, 40% moscatel.

85 Colour: bright straw. Nose: ripe fruit, floral, medium intensity. Palate: correct, good finish.

BERAMENDI 3F 2011 RD
100% garnacha.

86 Colour: rose, bright. Nose: floral, red berry notes, ripe fruit, balanced, expressive. Palate: good acidity, balanced, flavourful.

BERAMENDI 2011 RD
100% garnacha.

84

BERAMENDI 2011 T
80% tempranillo, 20% garnacha.

86 Colour: cherry, purple rim. Nose: ripe fruit, powerfull, warm, wild herbs. Palate: flavourful, balsamic, correct.

BERAMENDI TEMPRANILLO 2009 TC
100% tempranillo.

87 Colour: cherry, garnet rim. Nose: sweet spices, cocoa bean, ripe fruit, wild herbs. Palate: powerful, flavourful, fruity, long.

BERAMENDI 2005 TR
80% merlot, 20% graciano.

84

MARCO REAL

Ctra. Pamplona-Zaragoza, Km. 38
31390 Olite (Navarra)
☎: +34 948 712 193 - Fax: +34 948 712 343
info@familiabelasco.com
www.familiabelasco.com

HOMENAJE 2011 B
viura, chardonnay.

86 Colour: yellow. Nose: white flowers, fresh fruit, citrus fruit. Palate: balanced, good finish, easy to drink.

HOMENAJE 2011 RD
garnacha.

88 Colour: rose, purple rim. Nose: powerfull, ripe fruit, red berry notes, floral, lactic notes. Palate: , powerful, fruity, fresh, easy to drink.

HOMENAJE 2011 T
tempranillo, cabernet sauvignon.

86 Colour: cherry, purple rim. Nose: warm, red berry notes, fruit liqueur notes, balsamic herbs. Palate: powerful, flavourful, easy to drink.

MARCO REAL COLECCIÓN PRIVADA 2009 TC
tempranillo, cabernet sauvignon, merlot, graciano.

91 Colour: bright cherry, garnet rim. Nose: expressive, balanced, elegant, cocoa bean, ripe fruit, dry stone. Palate: flavourful, good structure, good acidity.

HOMENAJE 2008 TC
tempranillo, merlot.

88 Colour: bright cherry. Nose: ripe fruit, sweet spices, creamy oak, expressive. Palate: flavourful, fruity, toasty, round tannins.

MARCO REAL RESERVA DE FAMILIA 2007 TR
tempranillo, cabernet sauvignon, merlot, graciano.

91 Colour: cherry, garnet rim. Nose: complex, balanced, sweet spices. Palate: good structure, flavourful, round tannins.

NEKEAS

Las Huertas, s/n
31154 Añorbe (Navarra)
☎: +34 948 350 296 - Fax: +34 948 350 300
nekeas@nekeas.com
www.nekeas.com

NEKEAS CHARDONNAY 2011 B
100% chardonnay.

90 Colour: bright straw. Nose: fresh, fresh fruit, white flowers, expressive. Palate: flavourful, fruity, good acidity, balanced, elegant.

NEKEAS 2011 RD
100% garnacha.

88 Colour: rose, bright. Nose: scrubland, red berry notes, expressive. Palate: fruity, flavourful, good acidity.

NEKEAS CEPA X CEPA (CXC) 2010 T
100% garnacha.

90 Colour: bright cherry, garnet rim. Nose: balanced, medium intensity, scrubland, spicy. Palate: good structure, fruity, round tannins.

EL CHAPARRAL DE VEGA SINDOA OLD VINE GARNACHA 2010 T
100% garnacha.

85 Colour: cherry, garnet rim. Nose: ripe fruit, aged wood nuances, new oak, toasty. Palate: balanced, flavourful, easy to drink.

NEKEAS 2009 TC
40% tempranillo, 60% cabernet sauvignon.

89 Colour: cherry, garnet rim. Nose: ripe fruit, toasty, complex, cocoa bean. Palate: powerful, flavourful, toasty, balanced.

NUEVOS VINOS CB

C/ Alfafara, 12
03803 Alcoy (Alicante)
☎: +34 965 549 172 - Fax: +34 965 549 173
josecanto@nuevosvinos.es
www.nuevosvinos.es

TERRAPLEN BLANCO VIURA 2011 B
100% viura.

85 Colour: bright straw. Nose: white flowers, ripe fruit, dried herbs. Palate: flavourful, fruity, fine bitter notes.

TERRAPLEN ROSADO GARNACHA 2011 RD
100% garnacha.

86 Colour: light cherry, bright. Nose: red berry notes, wild herbs. Palate: correct, fine bitter notes, easy to drink, good finish.

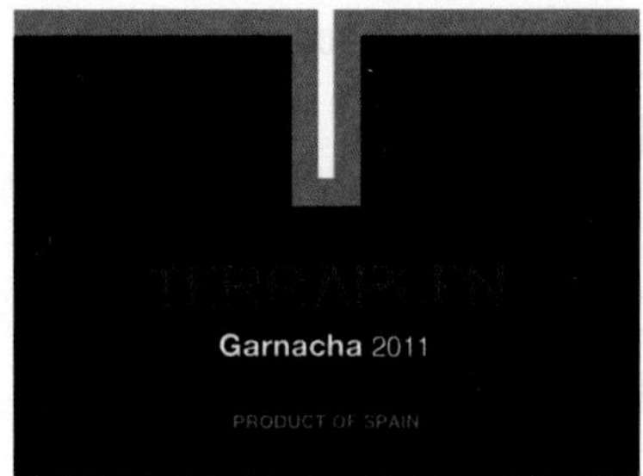

TERRAPLEN TINTO GARNACHA 2011 T
100% garnacha.

83

PAGO DE LARRÁINZAR

Camino de la Corona, s/n
31240 Ayegui (Navarra)
☎: +34 948 550 421 - Fax: +34 948 556 210
info@pagodelarrainzar.com
www.pagodelarrainzar.com

RASO DE LARRAINZAR 2008 T
43% tempranillo, merlot, 23% cabernet sauvignon, 3% garnacha.

91 Colour: cherry, garnet rim. Nose: ripe fruit, spicy, creamy oak, toasty. Palate: powerful, flavourful, toasty, round tannins.

PAGO DE LARRAINZAR 2007 T
40% merlot, 40% cabernet sauvignon, 15% tempranillo, 5% garnacha.

93 Colour: bright cherry. Nose: complex, spicy, creamy oak, cocoa bean, ripe fruit. Palate: flavourful, fruity, round tannins.

PAGO DE SAN GABRIEL

Paraje La Sarda. N-232, Km. 83,4
31590 Castejón (Navarra)
☎: +34 659 620 209
socoymanu@hotmail.com
www.pagosangabriel.com

ZUBIOLA 2009 T
90% cabernet sauvignon, 5% merlot, 5% cabernet franc.

90 Colour: cherry, garnet rim. Nose: elegant, balanced, sweet spices, ripe fruit, scrubland. Palate: good structure, flavourful.

PRADOMAYOR DE ZUBIOLA 2009 T
80% cabernet sauvignon, 20% merlot.

88 Colour: bright cherry. Nose: ripe fruit, sweet spices, creamy oak, expressive. Palate: flavourful, fruity, toasty, round tannins.

ZUBIOLA EDICIÓN LIMITADA 2007 T
95% cabernet sauvignon, 5% merlot.

92 Colour: cherry, garnet rim. Nose: ripe fruit, mineral, sweet spices, creamy oak, elegant. Palate: powerful, flavourful, long, balanced.

SEÑORÍO DE ANDIÓN

Ctra. Pamplona-Zaragoza, Km. 38
31390 Olite (Navarra)
☎: +34 948 712 193 - Fax: +34 948 712 343
info@familiabelasco.com
www.familiabelasco.com

SEÑORÍO DE ANDIÓN MOSCATEL VENDIMIA TARDÍA 2007 B
100% moscatel grano menudo.

93 Colour: golden. Nose: powerfull, floral, honeyed notes, candied fruit, fragrant herbs, citrus fruit, spicy. Palate: flavourful, sweet, fresh, fruity, good acidity, long.

SEÑORÍO DE ANDIÓN 2005 T
tempranillo, merlot, cabernet sauvignon, graciano.

92 Colour: cherry, garnet rim. Nose: neat, toasty, sweet spices, ripe fruit. Palate: flavourful, ripe fruit, spicy, round tannins.

THE TAPAS WINE COLLECTION

Casas de la Hoya, s/n
30520 Jumilla (Murcia)
☎: +34 968 437 137 - Fax: +34 968 437 200
export@thetapaswinecollection.com
www.thetapaswinecollection.com

THE TAPAS WINE COLLECTION 2011 B
verdejo.

83

THE TAPAS WINE COLLECTION 2011 RD

84

UNZU PROPIEDAD

Avda. de la Poveda, 16
01306 Lapuebla (Álava)
☎: +34 948 812 297
info@unzupropiedad.com
www.unzupropiedad.com

FINCAS DE UNZU 2011 RD
75% merlot, 25% garnacha.

89 Colour: rose, purple rim. Nose: ripe fruit, red berry notes, expressive, fragrant herbs. Palate: , fruity, fresh, flavourful.

VINÍCOLA CORELLANA

Ctra. del Villar, s/n
31591 Corella (Navarra)
☎: +34 948 780 617 - Fax: +34 948 401 894
info@vinicolacorellana.com
www.vinicolacorellana.com

VIÑA ZORZAL GARNACHA VIÑAS VIEJAS 2010 T
100% garnacha.

86 Colour: cherry, garnet rim. Nose: ripe fruit, sweet spices, creamy oak. Palate: powerful, flavourful, correct.

VIÑA ZORZAL GRACIANO 2010 T
100% graciano.

85 Colour: cherry, garnet rim. Nose: medium intensity, dried herbs, ripe fruit, spicy. Palate: balanced, spicy, long.

VINÍCOLA NAVARRA

Avda. Pamplona, 25
31398 Tiebas (Navarra)
☎: +34 948 360 131 - Fax: +34 948 360 544
vinicolanavarra@domecqbodegas.com
www.vinicolanavarra.com

LAS CAMPANAS CHARDONNAY 2011 B
chardonnay, viura.

85 Colour: bright straw. Nose: fresh, fresh fruit, white flowers. Palate: flavourful, fruity, good acidity.

CASTILLO DE JAVIER 2011 RD
garnacha.

87 Colour: rose, purple rim. Nose: red berry notes, floral, expressive, wild herbs. Palate: flavourful, fruity, easy to drink.

LAS CAMPANAS 2011 RD
garnacha.

85 Colour: rose, purple rim. Nose: floral, red berry notes, balsamic herbs. Palate: fresh, fruity, light-bodied, flavourful, easy to drink.

LAS CAMPANAS TEMPRANILLO 2011 T
tempranillo.

89 Colour: cherry, purple rim. Nose: red berry notes, raspberry, balsamic herbs, expressive. Palate: powerful, flavourful, fresh, fruity, easy to drink.

VIÑA ALIAGA

Camino del Villar. N-161, Km. 3
31591 Corella (Navarra)
☎: +34 948 401 321 - Fax: +34 948 781 414
sales@vinaaliaga.com
www.vinaaliaga.com

ALIAGA DOSCARLOS 2011 B
sauvignon blanc.

87 Colour: bright straw. Nose: white flowers, citrus fruit, ripe fruit. Palate: flavourful, full, balanced.

ALIAGA MOSCATEL VENDIMIA TARDÍA 2010 B
100% moscatel grano menudo.

88 Colour: bright yellow. Nose: ripe fruit, citrus fruit, honeyed notes, white flowers. Palate: long, powerful, flavourful, balanced.

ALIAGA LÁGRIMA DE GARNACHA 2011 RD
100% garnacha.

87 Colour: rose, purple rim. Nose: powerfull, ripe fruit, red berry notes, floral, expressive. Palate: fleshy, powerful, fruity, fresh.

ALIAGA TEMPRANILLO 2010 T
100% tempranillo.

81

ALIAGA CUVÉE 2008 T
85% tempranillo, 15% cabernet sauvignon.

84

ALIAGA COLECCIÓN PRIVADA 2007 TC
80% tempranillo, 20% cabernet sauvignon.

87 Colour: cherry, garnet rim. Nose: ripe fruit, sweet spices, aged wood nuances, creamy oak. Palate: long, balsamic, flavourful.

ALIAGA GARNACHA VIEJA 2007 T
100% garnacha.

84

ALIAGA RESERVA DE LA FAMILIA 2005 TR
75% tempranillo, 25% cabernet sauvignon.

87 Colour: cherry, garnet rim. Nose: ripe fruit, spicy, creamy oak, toasty, fine reductive notes. Palate: powerful, flavourful, toasty.

VIÑA ALIAGA ANTONIO CORPUS 2002 T
100% garnacha.

85 Colour: cherry, garnet rim. Nose: creamy oak, fruit preserve, dark chocolate, spicy. Palate: powerful, toasty, round tannins.

VIÑA ALIAGA VENDIMIA SELECCIONADA 2001 TR
tempranillo, merlot, cabernet sauvignon.

87 Colour: pale ruby, brick rim edge. Nose: spicy, fine reductive notes, wet leather, aged wood nuances, fruit liqueur notes. Palate: spicy, fine tannins, elegant, long.

VIÑA VALDORBA

Ctra. de la Estación, s/n
31395 Garinoain (Navarra)
☎: +34 948 720 505 - Fax: +34 948 720 505
bodegasvaldorba@bodegasvaldorba.com
www.bodegasvaldorba.com

EOLO CHARDONNAY 2011 B
100% chardonnay.

87 Colour: bright straw. Nose: white flowers, fragrant herbs, expressive, varietal. Palate: flavourful, fruity, easy to drink.

EOLO MOSCATEL 2009 B
100% moscatel de alejandría.

88 Colour: bright yellow. Nose: dried flowers, ripe fruit, citrus fruit, honeyed notes, fragrant herbs. Palate: powerful, flavourful, rich, complex.

EOLO ROSADO SANGRADO 2011 RD
100% garnacha.

85 Colour: rose, bright. Nose: fragrant herbs, red berry notes. Palate: correct, easy to drink.

EOLO GARNACHA 2011 T
100% garnacha.

83

EOLO ROBLE 2010 T
50% garnacha, 50% cabernet sauvignon.

85 Colour: bright cherry. Nose: ripe fruit, sweet spices, creamy oak. Palate: flavourful, fruity, toasty, round tannins.

EOLO SYRAH 2009 T
100% syrah.

89 Colour: bright cherry, garnet rim. Nose: red berry notes, ripe fruit, sweet spices. Palate: balanced, good acidity.

EOLO 2009 TC
cabernet sauvignon, merlot, graciano, garnacha.

85 Colour: cherry, garnet rim. Nose: fruit expression, spicy. Palate: fruity, flavourful, balanced.

GRAN EOLO 2006 TR
merlot, graciano, cabernet sauvignon.

87 Colour: cherry, garnet rim. Nose: ripe fruit, spicy, creamy oak. Palate: flavourful, correct, long.

GRAN EOLO CAURO 2002 TR
50% cabernet sauvignon, 50% graciano.

88 Colour: pale ruby, brick rim edge. Nose: fruit preserve, fruit liqueur notes, spicy, creamy oak. Palate: long, balsamic, flavourful.

VIÑEDOS DE CALIDAD

Ctra. Tudela, s/n
31591 Corella (Navarra)
☎: +34 948 782 014 - Fax: +34 948 782 164
inf@vinosalex.com
www.vinosalex.com

ALEX VIURA 2011 B
viura.

84

ALEX GARNACHA 2011 RD
garnacha.

86 Colour: rose, purple rim. Nose: medium intensity, red berry notes, rose petals. Palate: flavourful, easy to drink.

ALEX TEMPRANILLO 2011 T
tempranillo.

87 Colour: cherry, purple rim. Nose: expressive, fresh fruit, red berry notes, floral. Palate: flavourful, fruity, good acidity.

ONTINAR 14 BARRICAS 2009 T
50% tempranillo, 50% merlot.

90 Colour: cherry, garnet rim. Nose: creamy oak, toasty, new oak. Palate: flavourful, good structure, ripe fruit, good acidity, long.

ALEX 2009 TC
70% tempranillo, 20% merlot, 10% graciano.

86 Colour: cherry, garnet rim. Nose: ripe fruit, spicy, creamy oak, toasty. Palate: flavourful, round tannins.

ALEX 2005 TR
tempranillo.

87 Colour: cherry, garnet rim. Nose: powerfull, ripe fruit, spicy. Palate: flavourful, fruity, balanced.

ALEX 2011 MOSCATEL
moscatel grano menudo.

88 Colour: bright yellow. Nose: white flowers, ripe fruit, honeyed notes, medium intensity. Palate: powerful, flavourful, rich.

VIÑEDOS Y BODEGAS ALCONDE

Ctra. de Calahorra, s/n
31260 Lerín (Navarra)
☎: +34 948 530 058 - Fax: +34 948 530 589
info@bodegasalconde.com
www.bodegasalconde.com

VIÑA SARDASOL 2011 RD
garnacha.

84

VIÑA SARDASOL TEMPRANILLO MERLOT 2010 T ROBLE
tempranillo, merlot.

86 Colour: cherry, garnet rim. Nose: spicy, ripe fruit, medium intensity. Palate: fruity, flavourful.

BODEGAS ALCONDE SELECCIÓN 2008 TC
tempranillo, garnacha, cabernet sauvignon.

87 Colour: cherry, garnet rim. Nose: fruit preserve, toasty, sweet spices, scrubland. Palate: balanced, correct, flavourful.

VIÑA SARDASOL 2008 TC
tempranillo.

84

BODEGAS ALCONDE PREMIUM 2005 TR
tempranillo, garnacha, merlot.

89 Colour: cherry, garnet rim. Nose: complex, balanced, candied fruit, dark chocolate. Palate: flavourful, ripe fruit, long.

DO PENEDÈS

LOCATION:

In the province of Barcelona, between the pre-coastal Catalonian mountain range and the plains that lead to the Mediterranean coast. There are three different areas: Penedès Superior, Penedès Central or Medio and Bajo Penedès.

CLIMATE:

Mediterranean, in general warm and mild; warmer in the Bajo Penedès region due to the influence of the Mediterranean Sea, with slightly lower temperatures in Medio Penedès and Penedès Superior, where the climate is typically pre-coastal (greater contrasts between maximum and minimum temperatures, more frequent frosts and annual rainfall which at some places can reach 990 litres per square metre).

SOIL:

There is deep soil, not too sandy or too clayey, permeable, which retains the rainwater well. The soil is poor in organic matter and not very fertile.

GRAPE VARIETIES:

WHITE: *Macabeo* (6,622 Ha), *Xarel·lo* (7,833 Ha), *Parellada* (6,045 Ha), *Chardonnay* (1,038 Ha), *Riesling, Gewürztraminer, Chenin Blanc, Moscatel de Alejandría* and *Garnacha Blanca.*
RED: *Garnacha, Merlot* (1,554 Ha), *Cariñena, Ull de Llebre* (*Tempranillo* – 1,507 Ha), *Pinot Noir, Monastrell, Cabernet Sauvignon* (11,487 Ha), *Syrah* and *Sumoll.*

SUB-REGIONS:

Penedès Superior. The vineyards reach an altitude of 800 m; the traditional, characteristic variety is the Parellada, which is better suited to the cooler regions.
Penedès Central or Medio. Cava makes up a large part of the production in this region; the most abundant traditional varieties are *Macabeo* and *Xarel-lo.*
Bajo Penedès. This is the closest region to the sea, with a lower altitude and wines with a markedly Mediterranean character.

FIGURES:

Vineyard surface: 23,000 – **Wine-Growers:** 3,700 – **Wineries:** 161 – **2011 Harvest rating:** N/A – **Production:** 14,062,770 litres – **Market percentages:** 71% domestic. 29% export

CONSEJO REGULADOR
Pol. Industrial Domenys II. Plaça Àgora. Apdo. 226 - 08720 Vilafranca del Penedès (Barcelona)
☎: +34 938 904 811 - Fax: +34 938 904 754
@ dopenedes@dopenedes.es - www.dopenedes.es

1 + 1 = 3

Masía Navinés
08736 Guardiola de Font-Rubí (Barcelona)
☎: +34 938 974 069 - Fax: +34 938 974 724
umesu@umesufan3.com
www.umesufan3.com

1+1=3 XAREL.LO 2011 B
xarel.lo.

88 Colour: bright straw. Nose: fresh, white flowers, expressive, citrus fruit. Palate: flavourful, fruity, good acidity, balanced.

DAHLIA 1 + 1 = 3 2010 B
75% viognier, 25% xarel.lo.

88 Colour: bright straw, greenish rim. Nose: white flowers, balanced, expressive. Palate: correct, fine bitter notes, full.

DÉFORA 1 + 1 = 3 2009 T
75% garnacha, 25% cariñena.

90 Colour: cherry, garnet rim. Nose: ripe fruit, spicy, creamy oak, toasty, complex. Palate: powerful, flavourful, toasty, round tannins.

AGUSTÍ TORELLÓ MATA

La Serra, s/n PO Box 35
08770 Sant Sadurní D'Anoia (Barcelona)
☎: +34 938 911 173 - Fax: +34 938 912 616
comunicacio@agustitorellomata.com
www.agustitorellomata.com

APTIÀ D'AGUSTÍ TORELLÓ MATA "COL.LECCIÓ TERRERS" 2011 B
100% macabeo.

93 Colour: bright straw. Nose: fresh, fresh fruit, white flowers, expressive, creamy oak. Palate: flavourful, fruity, good acidity, balanced.

XAREL.LO D'AGUSTÍ TORELLÓ MATA "COL.LECCIÓ TERRERS" 2011 B
100% xarel.lo.

91 Colour: bright straw. Nose: ripe fruit, powerfull, expressive. Palate: good acidity, powerful, light-bodied, ripe fruit.

XII SUBIRAT PARENT D'AGUSTÍ TORELLÓ MATA "COL.LECCIÓ TERRERS" 2011 B
100% subirat parent.

90 Colour: bright straw. Nose: mineral, ripe fruit, fruit expression, citrus fruit, earthy notes. Palate: flavourful, fruity, good acidity.

ALBET I NOYA

Can Vendrell de la Codina, s/n
08739 Sant Pau D'Ordal (Barcelona)
☎: +34 938 994 812 - Fax: +34 938 994 930
albetinoya@albetinoya.cat
www.albetinoya.cat

ALBET I NOYA COL.LECCIÓ CHARDONNAY 2011 B
chardonnay.

92 Colour: bright yellow. Nose: ripe fruit, sweet spices, creamy oak, fragrant herbs. Palate: rich, smoky afterpalate:, flavourful, good acidity.

ALBET I NOYA EL BLANC XXV "ECOLÓGICO" 2011 B

91 Colour: bright yellow. Nose: ripe fruit, dried flowers, mineral, dry stone, wild herbs. Palate: powerful, flavourful, rich, long, balanced.

ALBET I NOYA LIGNUM 2011 B
chardonnay, sauvignon blanc, xarel.lo.

90 Colour: bright yellow. Nose: white flowers, sweet spices, creamy oak, balsamic herbs, mineral. Palate: long, balanced, elegant, flavourful.

ALBET I NOYA XAREL-LO CLÀSSIC 2011 B
xarel.lo.

90 Colour: bright straw. Nose: fresh, fresh fruit, white flowers, expressive. Palate: flavourful, fruity, good acidity, balanced.

ALBET I NOYA 3 MACABEUS 2011 B
macabeo.

90 Colour: bright straw. Nose: white flowers, fresh fruit, mineral, balsamic herbs. Palate: fresh, fruity, flavourful, balanced.

ALBET I NOYA EL FANIO 2011 B
xarel.lo.

89 Colour: bright yellow. Nose: ripe fruit, white flowers, fragrant herbs, expressive. Palate: warm, correct, fruity, flavourful.

ALBET I NOYA PETIT ALBET 2011 B
xarel.lo, chardonnay.

88 Colour: bright yellow. Nose: citrus fruit, ripe fruit, floral, fragrant herbs. Palate: light-bodied, fresh, fruity, flavourful.

ALBET I NOYA DOLÇ LES TIMBES 2010 B
viognier.

86 Colour: golden. Nose: powerfull, floral, honeyed notes, candied fruit, fragrant herbs. Palate: flavourful, sweet, fresh, fruity, good acidity, long.

ALBET I NOYA PINOT NOIR MERLOT CLÀSSIC 2011 RD
pinot noir, merlot.

88 Colour: light cherry, bright. Nose: balanced, red berry notes, powerfull, rose petals. Palate: ripe fruit, long, flavourful.

ALBET I NOYA TEMPRANILLO CLÀSSIC 2011 T
tempranillo.

90 Colour: cherry, purple rim. Nose: expressive, fresh fruit, red berry notes, floral. Palate: flavourful, fruity, good acidity, round tannins.

ALBET I NOYA LIGNUM 2010 T
cabernet sauvignon, garnacha, merlot, ull de llebre, syrah.

90 Colour: bright cherry. Nose: ripe fruit, sweet spices, creamy oak, expressive. Palate: flavourful, fruity, toasty, round tannins.

BELAT 2008 T
belat.

93 Colour: cherry, garnet rim. Nose: ripe fruit, spicy, complex, mineral. Palate: powerful, flavourful, toasty, round tannins.

ALBET I NOYA COL.LECCIÓ SYRAH 2008 T
syrah.

92 Colour: cherry, garnet rim. Nose: ripe fruit, spicy, creamy oak, toasty, earthy notes. Palate: powerful, flavourful, toasty, round tannins.

ALBET I NOYA RESERVA MARTÍ 2007 T

93 Colour: cherry, garnet rim. Nose: ripe fruit, spicy, creamy oak, toasty, characterful. Palate: powerful, flavourful, toasty, round tannins.

FINCA LA MILANA 2006 T
caladoc, ull de llebre, cabernet sauvignon, merlot.

91 Colour: cherry, garnet rim. Nose: creamy oak, toasty, characterful, ripe fruit. Palate: powerful, flavourful, toasty, round tannins.

ALBET I NOYA DOLÇ ADRIÀ 2007 TINTO DULCE

87 Colour: cherry, garnet rim. Nose: ripe fruit, fragrant herbs, spicy, aged wood nuances, varnish. Palate: powerful, flavourful, spirituous, toasty.

ALEMANY I CORRIO

Melió, 78
08720 Vilafranca del Penedès (Barcelona)
☎: +34 938 922 746 - Fax: +34 938 172 587
sotlefriec@sotlefriec.com

PRINCIPIA MATHEMATICA 2011 B
xarel.lo.

87 Colour: bright yellow. Nose: faded flowers, candied fruit, spicy. Palate: fine bitter notes, good acidity, correct.

PAS CURTEI 2010 T

92 Colour: very deep cherry. Nose: ripe fruit, overripe fruit, sweet spices. Palate: flavourful, powerful, good acidity, fine bitter notes.

SOT LEFRIEC 2007 T
cabernet sauvignon, cariñena, merlot.

96 Colour: cherry, garnet rim. Nose: spicy, creamy oak, toasty, complex, earthy notes, ripe fruit. Palate: powerful, flavourful, toasty, round tannins.

ALSINA SARDÁ

Barrio Les Tarumbas, s/n
08733 Pla del Penedès (Barcelona)
☎: +34 938 988 132 - Fax: +34 938 988 671
alsina@alsinasarda.com
www.alsinasarda.com

ALSINA & SARDÁ FINCA LA BOLTANA 2011 B
100% xarel.lo.

90 Colour: bright straw. Nose: expressive, ripe fruit, white flowers. Palate: flavourful, fruity, fresh, good acidity, fine bitter notes.

ALSINA & SARDÁ BLANC DE BLANCS 2011 B
70% macabeo, 30% parellada.

86 Colour: bright straw. Nose: expressive, ripe fruit, candied fruit. Palate: flavourful, sweetness, fine bitter notes.

ALSINA & SARDÁ MUSCAT LLÀGRIMA 2011 B
100% moscatel.

86 Colour: bright straw. Nose: ripe fruit, white flowers. Palate: flavourful, good acidity, sweetness.

ALSINA & SARDÁ MERLOT LLÀGRIMA 2011 RD
100% merlot.

87 Colour: rose, purple rim. Nose: powerfull, ripe fruit, red berry notes, floral. Palate: , powerful, fruity, fresh.

ARNAU 2011 T
100% merlot.

86 Colour: bright cherry, purple rim. Nose: red berry notes, ripe fruit, scrubland. Palate: correct, easy to drink.

ALSINA & SARDÁ FINCA CAL JANES 2009 T
100% merlot.

86 Colour: cherry, garnet rim. Nose: powerfull, fruit preserve, wild herbs, dark chocolate. Palate: flavourful, ripe fruit, long.

ALSINA & SARDÁ RESERVA DE FAMILIA 2007 T
100% merlot.

88 Colour: cherry, garnet rim. Nose: ripe fruit, spicy, toasty, wild herbs. Palate: powerful, flavourful, toasty, round tannins.

ALSINA & SARDÁ FINCA OLERDOLA 2007 TR
100% cabernet sauvignon.

88 Colour: cherry, garnet rim. Nose: expressive, varietal, medium intensity, scrubland. Palate: good structure, flavourful, good acidity, round tannins.

AVINYÓ CAVAS

Masia Can Fontanals
08793 Avinyonet del Penedès (Barcelona)
☎: +34 938 970 055 - Fax: +34 938 970 691
avinyo@avinyo.com
www.avinyo.com

AVINYÓ CABERNET SAUVIGNON 2007 TC
100% cabernet sauvignon.

87 Colour: cherry, garnet rim. Nose: ripe fruit, balsamic herbs, spicy, fine reductive notes. Palate: flavourful, spicy, long.

AVINYÓ MERLOT 2007 T
100% merlot.

85 Colour: light cherry, orangey edge. Nose: ripe fruit, balsamic herbs, spicy. Palate: flavourful, long, correct.

BLANCHER-CAPDEVILA PUJOL

Plaça Pont Romà, Edificio Blancher
08770 Sant Sadurní D'Anoia (Barcelona)
☎: +34 938 183 286 - Fax: +34 938 911 961
blancher@blancher.es
www.blancher.es

GUIXERES 2011 B
xarel.lo, macabeo.

84

BODEGAS CA N'ESTELLA

Masia Ca N'Estella, s/n
08635 Sant Esteve Sesrovires (Barcelona)
☎: +34 934 161 387 - Fax: +34 934 161 620
j.rodriguez@fincacanestella.com
www.fincacanestella.com

PETIT CLOT DELS OMS 2011 B
20% macabeo, 40% xarel.lo, 30% chardonnay, 10% moscatel.

86 Colour: bright straw. Nose: fresh fruit, expressive, dried flowers. Palate: flavourful, fruity, good acidity.

CLOT DELS OMS 2011 B
80% chardonnay, 10% malvasía.

85 Colour: bright yellow. Nose: ripe fruit, dried flowers, fragrant herbs. Palate: powerful, flavourful, ripe fruit.

GRAN CLOT DELS OMS 2010 BFB
chardonnay.

87 Colour: bright yellow. Nose: powerfull, ripe fruit, sweet spices, fragrant herbs, roasted coffee. Palate: rich, flavourful, fresh.

GRAN CLOT DELS OMS XAREL.LO 2008 BFB
xarel.lo.

90 Colour: bright yellow. Nose: ripe fruit, faded flowers, fragrant herbs, sweet spices, creamy oak. Palate: fruity, flavourful, spicy, long.

PETIT CLOT DELS OMS 2011 RD
cabernet sauvignon.

87 Colour: rose, purple rim. Nose: powerfull, ripe fruit, red berry notes, floral. Palate: , powerful, fruity, fresh, easy to drink.

CLOT DELS OMS 2011 RD
100% merlot.

87 Colour: rose, purple rim. Nose: floral, grassy, red berry notes, ripe fruit. Palate: powerful, flavourful, fruity.

CLOT DELS OMS VI DOLÇ DE FRED ROSAT 2010 RD
merlot.

85 Colour: rose, purple rim. Nose: powerfull, ripe fruit, red berry notes, floral. Palate: , powerful, fruity, fresh, sweet.

PETIT CLOT DELS OMS 2010 T
80% cabernet sauvignon, 20% merlot.

88 Colour: cherry, garnet rim. Nose: roasted coffee, powerfull, warm. Palate: powerful, fine bitter notes, good acidity.

CLOT DELS OMS 2008 TC
merlot, cabernet sauvignon.

88 Colour: cherry, garnet rim. Nose: ripe fruit, spicy, creamy oak, toasty. Palate: powerful, flavourful, toasty, round tannins.

GRAN CLOT DELS OMS 2006 TR
40% merlot, 60% cabernet sauvignon.

90 Colour: cherry, garnet rim. Nose: ripe fruit, spicy, creamy oak, toasty, complex. Palate: powerful, flavourful, toasty, round tannins.

BODEGAS CAPITÀ VIDAL

Ctra. Villafranca-Igualada, Km. 21
08733 Pla del Penedès (Barcelona)
☎: +34 938 988 630 - Fax: +34 938 988 625
capitavidal@capitavidal.com
www.capitavidal.com

CLOS VIDAL BLANC DE BLANCS 2011 B
58% xarel.lo, 18% parellada, 14% macabeo, 10% moscatel.

86 Colour: bright straw. Nose: fresh, fresh fruit, white flowers, tropical fruit. Palate: flavourful, fruity, good acidity.

CLOS VIDAL ROSÉ CUVÉE 2011 RD
45% syrah, 30% merlot, 25% garnacha.

86 Colour: coppery red. Nose: red berry notes, ripe fruit, fragrant herbs. Palate: light-bodied, fresh, fruity.

CLOS VIDAL MERLOT 2010 TC
85% merlot, 15% tempranillo.

85 Colour: cherry, garnet rim. Nose: ripe fruit, fragrant herbs, spicy, toasty. Palate: long, balsamic, flavourful.

CLOS VIDAL CABERNET SAUVIGNON 2008 T ROBLE
90% cabernet sauvignon, 10% tempranillo.

86 Colour: cherry, garnet rim. Nose: ripe fruit, spicy, creamy oak, toasty. Palate: powerful, flavourful, spicy.

BODEGAS MUR BARCELONA

Rambla de la Generalitat, 1-9
08770 Sant Sadurni D'Anoia (Barcelona)
☎: +34 938 183 641 - Fax: +34 938 914 366
info@mur-barcelona.com
www.mur-barcelona.com

ROBERT MUR BLANCO SECO 2011 B
xarel.lo, parellada, macabeo.

84

ROBERT J. MUR ROSADO SECO 2011 RD
garnacha, monastrell, tempranillo.

84

ROBERT J. MUR 2011 T
ull de llebre, merlot, cabernet sauvignon.

87 Colour: cherry, purple rim. Nose: fresh fruit, red berry notes, floral. Palate: flavourful, fruity, round tannins.

BODEGAS PINORD

Doctor Pasteur, 6
08720 Vilafranca del Penedès (Barcelona)
☎: +34 938 903 066 - Fax: +34 938 170 979
pinord@pinord.es
www.pinord.es

PINORD DIORAMA CHARDONNAY 2011 B
chardonnay.

89 Colour: bright straw. Nose: fresh, white flowers. Palate: flavourful, fruity, good acidity, balanced.

PINORD +NATURA 2011 B
xarel.lo.

88 Colour: bright straw. Nose: fresh, white flowers, ripe fruit. Palate: flavourful, fruity, good acidity, balanced.

PINORD CLOS DE TORRIBAS 2011 B
xarel.lo, macabeo, gewürztraminer.

87 Colour: bright straw. Nose: fresh, white flowers, ripe fruit. Palate: flavourful, fruity, good acidity, balanced.

PINORD DIORAMA SYRAH 2009 T
syrah.

87 Colour: deep cherry. Nose: balanced, ripe fruit, fruit preserve, sweet spices. Palate: correct, balanced, fine bitter notes.

PINORD DIORAMA MERLOT 2009 T
merlot.

86 Colour: cherry, garnet rim. Nose: balanced, medium intensity, toasty, spicy. Palate: correct, spicy, ripe fruit.

+ NATURA 2009 T
cabernet sauvignon, merlot.

85 Colour: cherry, garnet rim. Nose: medium intensity, fruit preserve, warm, scrubland. Palate: flavourful, fruity.

PINORD CLOS DE TORRIBAS 2008 TC
tempranillo.

87 Colour: cherry, garnet rim. Nose: ripe fruit, spicy. Palate: powerful, flavourful, toasty, round tannins.

PINORD CLOS DE TORRIBAS 2005 TR
85% tempranillo, 10% cabernet sauvignon, 5% merlot.

86 Colour: dark-red cherry, orangey edge. Nose: tobacco, fine reductive notes, ripe fruit, warm. Palate: correct, easy to drink, ripe fruit.

PINORD CHATELDON 2004 TR
cabernet sauvignon, merlot.

79

PINORD PI DEL NORD CABERNET SAUVIGNON 2003 T
cabernet sauvignon.

87 Colour: cherry, garnet rim. Nose: balanced, varietal, spicy, fine reductive notes. Palate: balanced, spicy, easy to drink.

PINORD LA NANSA 2011 BLANCO DE AGUJA
macabeo, chardonnay.

85 Colour: bright straw. Nose: expressive, fresh fruit, citrus fruit. Palate: flavourful, fruity, fresh.

BODEGAS TORRE DEL VEGUER

Urb. Torre de Veguer, s/n
08810 Sant Pere de Ribes (Barcelona)
☎: +34 938 963 190 - Fax: +34 938 962 967
torredelveguer@torredelveguer.com
www.torredelveguer.com

TORRE DEL VEGUER DULCE VENDIMIA TARDÍA 2011 B
90% moscatel de frontignan, 10% chardonnay.

92 Colour: golden. Nose: powerfull, floral, candied fruit, fragrant herbs, complex, citrus fruit. Palate: flavourful, sweet, fresh, fruity, good acidity, long.

TORRE DEL VEGUER MUSCAT 2011 B
100% moscatel de frontignan.

88 Colour: bright straw. Nose: white flowers, ripe fruit. Palate: flavourful, fruity, fresh.

TORRE DEL VEGUER XAREL.LO 2011 B
100% xarel.lo.

88 Colour: bright straw. Nose: burnt matches, powerfull, ripe fruit, citrus fruit, characterful. Palate: fine bitter notes, sweetness, powerful.

TORRE DEL VEGUER ROSAT DE LLÁGRIMA 2011 RD
100% syrah.

84

TORRE DEL VEGUER ECLECTIC 2009 T
cabernet sauvignon, syrah, merlot.

87 Colour: bright cherry. Nose: ripe fruit, sweet spices, creamy oak. Palate: flavourful, fruity, toasty, round tannins.

TORRE DEL VEGUER MARTA 2010 ESP
100% moscatel de frontignan.

87 Colour: bright yellow. Nose: white flowers, fresh fruit, candied fruit, fragrant herbs. Palate: fresh, fruity, flavourful, good acidity.

BODEGAS TORRES

Miguel Torres i Carbó, 6
08720 Vilafranca del Penedès (Barcelona)
☎: +34 938 177 400 - Fax: +34 938 177 444
mailadmin@torres.es
www.torres.es

WALTRAUD 2011 B
100% riesling.

89 Colour: bright straw. Nose: medium intensity, fresh fruit, white flowers. Palate: flavourful, sweetness.

ATRIUM MERLOT 2010 T
100% merlot.

90 Colour: cherry, garnet rim. Nose: red berry notes, ripe fruit, fragrant herbs, expressive. Palate: powerful, flavourful, spicy, long.

ATRIUM CABERNET SAUVIGNON 2009 T
85% cabernet sauvignon, 15% tempranillo.

88 Colour: cherry, garnet rim. Nose: ripe fruit, complex, balsamic herbs, sweet spices. Palate: powerful, flavourful, toasty.

ATRIUM CHARDONNAY 2011 B
85% chardonnay, 15% parellada.

92 Colour: bright straw. Nose: fresh, fresh fruit, white flowers, expressive. Palate: flavourful, fruity, good acidity, balanced.

MAS LA PLANA CABERNET SAUVIGNON 2008 TR
100% cabernet sauvignon.

93 Colour: deep cherry, garnet rim. Nose: complex, elegant, spicy, scrubland. Palate: balanced, fine bitter notes, round tannins.

FRANSOLA 2011 B
95% sauvignon blanc, 5% parellada.

91 Colour: bright straw. Nose: floral, citrus fruit, candied fruit, balsamic herbs, wild herbs. Palate: light-bodied, fresh, fruity, flavourful, easy to drink.

GRAN CORONAS 2008 TC
85% cabernet sauvignon, 15% tempranillo.

88 Colour: cherry, garnet rim. Nose: ripe fruit, spicy, creamy oak, balsamic herbs. Palate: powerful, flavourful, toasty.

RESERVA REAL 2003 TGR
cabernet sauvignon, merlot, cabernet franc.

90 Colour: pale ruby, brick rim edge. Nose: elegant, spicy, fine reductive notes, wet leather, aged wood nuances, fruit liqueur notes. Palate: spicy, fine tannins, elegant, long.

BODEGUES AMETLLER CIVILL

Caspe, 139 Entr 1ª
08013 (Barcelona)
☎: +34 933 208 439 - Fax: +34 933 208 437
ametller@ametller.com
www.ametller.com

AMETLLER BLANC FLORAL 2011 B
50% moscatel, 50% sauvignon blanc.

87 Colour: bright straw. Nose: ripe fruit, white flowers. Palate: flavourful, fruity, fresh.

AMETLLER BLANC DE BLANCS 2011 B
85% xarel.lo, 15% chardonnay.

87 Colour: bright straw. Nose: fresh fruit, fruit expression. Palate: flavourful, fruity, fresh.

BODEGUES SUMARROCA

Barrio El Rebato, s/n
08739 Subirats (Barcelona)
☎: +34 938 911 092 - Fax: +34 938 911 778
info@sumarroca.com
www.sumarroca.com

SUMARROCA GEWÜRZTRAMINER 2011 B
gewürztraminer.

89 Colour: bright straw. Nose: fresh, fresh fruit, expressive, rose petals, floral. Palate: flavourful, fruity, good acidity, balanced.

SUMARROCA TEMPS DE FLORS 2011 B
moscatel, gewürztraminer, xarel.lo.

88 Colour: bright straw. Nose: fresh fruit, citrus fruit, varietal. Palate: flavourful, fruity, sweetness.

SUMARROCA MUSCAT 2011 B
moscatel.

87 Colour: bright straw. Nose: fresh fruit, citrus fruit, floral, varietal. Palate: fine bitter notes, good acidity.

SUMARROCA BLANC DE BLANCS 2011 B
macabeo, xarel.lo, parellada, moscatel.

87 Colour: bright straw. Nose: white flowers, fresh fruit, citrus fruit. Palate: flavourful, fruity, fresh.

SUMARROCA 2011 RD
tempranillo, merlot, syrah.

88 Colour: rose, purple rim. Nose: lactic notes, floral, candied fruit, balsamic herbs. Palate: easy to drink, powerful, flavourful.

SUMARROCA TEMPS DE FRUITS Nº 2 2011 T

90 Colour: cherry, purple rim. Nose: red berry notes, ripe fruit, balsamic herbs, mineral, floral. Palate: light-bodied, fresh, fruity, flavourful, balanced.

SUMARROCA TEMPS DE FRUITS Nº 1 2011 T

89 Colour: rose. Nose: red berry notes, raspberry, fragrant herbs, floral, fresh. Palate: light-bodied, fresh, fruity, flavourful.

SUMARROCA 2011 T
merlot, tempranillo, cabernet sauvignon.

88 Colour: deep cherry. Nose: powerfull, ripe fruit, warm, spicy. Palate: flavourful, powerful, ripe fruit.

SUMARROCA TEMPS DE FRUITS Nº 3 2011 T

88 Colour: cherry, purple rim. Nose: violets, jasmine, floral, wild herbs, raspberry, spicy. Palate: powerful, flavourful, fresh, balsamic.

TERRAL 2009 T
syrah, cabernet franc, merlot, cabernet sauvignon.

92 Colour: very deep cherry. Nose: sweet spices, ripe fruit, fruit expression, toasty, mineral. Palate: fruity, flavourful, fine bitter notes, good acidity.

SUMARROCA SANTA CREU DE CREIXÀ 2009 T
syrah, garnacha, cabernet sauvignon, cabernet franc.

90 Colour: cherry, garnet rim. Nose: sweet spices, cocoa bean, red berry notes, ripe fruit. Palate: flavourful, powerful, fine bitter notes.

BÒRIA 2008 T
syrah, cabernet sauvignon, merlot.

91 Colour: bright cherry. Nose: ripe fruit, sweet spices, creamy oak, characterful, mineral. Palate: flavourful, fruity, toasty, round tannins.

CAL RASPALLET VITICULTORS

Barri Sabanell, 11
08736 Font Rubí (Barcelona)
☎: +34 607 262 779
calraspallet@vinifera.cat

NUN VINYA DELS TAUS 2010 B
xarel.lo.

94 Colour: bright yellow. Nose: characterful, expressive, varietal, ripe fruit, citrus fruit. Palate: good acidity, fine bitter notes, round.

IMPROVISACIÓ 2010 B
xarel.lo.

91 Colour: bright straw. Nose: candied fruit, citrus fruit, spicy. Palate: flavourful, ripe fruit, fine bitter notes, good acidity.

CAN BONASTRE WINE RESORT

Finca Can Bonastre de Sta Magdalena
Ctra. B 224 Km 13.2

08783 Masquefa (Barcelona)
☎: +34 937 726 167 - Fax: +34 937 727 929
bodega@canbonastre.com
www.canbonastre.com

MAUREL 2008 B

89 Colour: bright yellow. Nose: powerfull, ripe fruit, fragrant herbs, sweet spices, roasted coffee. Palate: rich, smoky afterpalate:, flavourful, fresh, good acidity.

CAN BONASTRE 2006 TC

87 Colour: bright cherry, orangey edge. Nose: ripe fruit, sweet spices, creamy oak, toasty, fine reductive notes. Palate: round, balsamic, spicy, flavourful.

CAN CREDO

Tamarit, 10 Apartado 15
08770 Sant Sadurní D'Anoia (Barcelona)
☎: +34 938 910 214 - Fax: +34 938 911 697
cava@recaredo.es
www.recaredo.es

CAN CREDO 2010 B
100% xarel.lo.

90 Colour: bright yellow. Nose: candied fruit, citrus fruit, spicy. Palate: flavourful, spicy, ripe fruit.

ALOERS 2010 B
65% xarel.lo, 24% macabeo, 11% parellada.

88 Colour: bright straw. Nose: candied fruit, citrus fruit, faded flowers. Palate: powerful, fine bitter notes, spicy.

CAN DESCREGUT

Masia Can Descregut, s/n
08735 Vilobi del Penedès (Barcelona)
☎: +34 938 978 273 - Fax: +34 938 170 786
info@descregut.com
www.montdarac.com

DESCREGUT X 100 2011 B
xarel.lo.

87 Colour: bright straw. Nose: dried flowers, dried herbs, fresh fruit, citrus fruit. Palate: correct, fresh, flavourful.

DESCREGUT 30(3) 2011 B
xarel.lo, macabeo, chardonnay.

85 Colour: bright straw. Nose: white flowers, fragrant herbs, ripe fruit. Palate: flavourful, fruity, good acidity.

DESCREGUT 100 MERLOT 2011 RD
100% merlot.

84

CAN FEIXES (HUGUET)

Finca Can Feixes, s/n
08718 Cabrera D'Anoia (Barcelona)
☎: +34 937 718 227 - Fax: +34 937 718 031
canfeixes@canfeixes.com
www.canfeixes.com

CAN FEIXES SELECCIÓ 2011 B
parellada, macabeo, chardonnay, malvasía.

86 Colour: bright yellow. Nose: ripe fruit, fruit preserve, dried herbs, faded flowers. Palate: correct, fine bitter notes, flavourful.

CAN FEIXES CHARDONNAY 2007 BFB
chardonnay.

91 Colour: bright golden. Nose: ripe fruit, dry nuts, powerfull, toasty, honeyed notes. Palate: flavourful, fruity, spicy, toasty, long, balanced.

CAN FEIXES SELECCIÓ 2010 T JOVEN
tempranillo, merlot.

88 Colour: cherry, garnet rim. Nose: red berry notes, ripe fruit, fragrant herbs. Palate: light-bodied, fresh, flavourful, balsamic.

CAN FEIXES TRADICIÓ 2007 TC
merlot, cabernet sauvignon, tempranillo, petit verdot.

87 Colour: cherry, garnet rim. Nose: ripe fruit, spicy, creamy oak, toasty, complex. Palate: powerful, flavourful, toasty, round tannins.

CAN FEIXES RESERVA ESPECIAL 2005 TR
cabernet sauvignon, merlot.

89 Colour: dark-red cherry, orangey edge. Nose: ripe fruit, spicy, balsamic herbs, medium intensity. Palate: powerful, flavourful, round tannins.

CAN RÀFOLS DELS CAUS

Can Rafols del Caus s/n
08792 Avinyonet del Penedès (Barcelona)
☎: +34 938 970 013 - Fax: +34 938 970 370
canrafolsdelscaus@canrafolsdelscaus.com
www.canrafolsdelscaus.com

PETIT CAUS 2011 B
xarel.lo, macabeo, chardonnay, chenin blanc.

86 Colour: bright straw. Nose: medium intensity, white flowers, ripe fruit. Palate: fruity, correct, good finish.

VINYA LA CALMA 2009 BFB
chenin blanc.

93 Colour: bright yellow. Nose: elegant, complex, petrol notes, ripe fruit, sweet spices, creamy oak. Palate: fruity, flavourful, complex. Personality.

EL ROCALLÍS 2009 BFB
Incrozio manzoni.

90 Colour: bright yellow. Nose: candied fruit, toasty, spicy, honeyed notes. Palate: rich, flavourful, good structure, spicy, long.

XAREL.LO PAIRAL 2008 BFB
xarel.lo, macabeo.

89 Colour: bright yellow. Nose: powerfull, ripe fruit, sweet spices, creamy oak, fragrant herbs. Palate: rich, smoky afterpalate:, flavourful, fresh, good acidity.

PETIT CAUS 2011 RD
merlot, ull de llebre, cabernet franc, syrah.

87 Colour: coppery red. Nose: candied fruit, dried flowers, fragrant herbs. Palate: correct, light-bodied, fresh, fruity.

CAN RAFOLS SUMOLL 2009 T
sumoll.

88 Colour: bright cherry. Nose: overripe fruit, scrubland, balsamic herbs. Palate: flavourful, spicy, ripe fruit.

CANALS & MUNNÉ

Ctra. de Sant Sadurni a Vilafranca, km. 0,5
08770 Sant Sadurní D'Anoia (Barcelona)
☎: +34 938 910 318 - Fax: +34 938 911 945
info@canalsimunne.com
www.canalsimunne.com

BLANC PRÍNCEPS MUSCAT 2011 B
100% moscatel.

87 Colour: yellow, greenish rim. Nose: white flowers, candied fruit, dried herbs. Palate: fresh, fruity, flavourful.

BLANC PRÍNCEPS ECOLOGIC 2011 B
xarel.lo, chardonnay, sauvignon blanc.

86 Colour: bright straw. Nose: fresh, fresh fruit, white flowers, expressive. Palate: flavourful, fruity, good acidity, correct.

GRAN BLANC PRÍNCEPS 2010 BFB
xarel.lo, chardonnay.

88 Colour: bright yellow. Nose: sweet spices, dried herbs, faded flowers, toasty. Palate: good acidity, fresh, rich, flavourful.

NOIR PRÍNCEPS 2004 TC
cabernet sauvignon, tempranillo, merlot.

85 Colour: dark-red cherry, orangey edge. Nose: medium intensity, ripe fruit, dark chocolate, tobacco. Palate: flavourful, aged character.

GRAN PRÍNCEPS 2002 TGR
cabernet sauvignon, tempranillo, merlot.

85 Colour: dark-red cherry, orangey edge. Nose: toasty, woody. Palate: fruity, spicy, easy to drink.

CANALS NADAL

Ponent, 2
08733 El Pla del Penedès (Barcelona)
☎: +34 938 988 081 - Fax: +34 938 989 050
cava@canalsnadal.com
www.canalsnadal.com

CANALS NADAL GRAN XAREL.LO 2010 BFB
100% xarel.lo.

86 Colour: yellow, greenish rim. Nose: dried flowers, fragrant herbs, ripe fruit. Palate: rich, flavourful, fruity.

ANTONI CANALS NADAL CABERNET SAUVIGNON MERLOT 2009 TC
50% cabernet sauvignon, 50% merlot.

85 Colour: pale ruby, brick rim edge. Nose: ripe fruit, scrubland, old leather, cigar. Palate: flavourful, long, spicy.

CASA RAVELLA

Ravella, 1
08739 Ordal (Barcelona)
☎: +34 938 179 173 - Fax: +34 938 179 245
bodega@condedeolzinellas.com
www.casaravella.com

HEREDEROS DEL CONDE DE OLZINELLAS 2011 B
80% xarel.lo, 20% chardonnay.

86 Colour: bright straw. Nose: ripe fruit, white flowers, grassy. Palate: flavourful, fine bitter notes, good acidity.

CASA RAVELLA 2010 BFB
70% xarel.lo, 30% chardonnay.

88 Colour: bright straw. Nose: toasty, ripe fruit, powerfull. Palate: flavourful, powerful, sweetness.

CASA RAVELLA 2009 BFB
70% xarel.lo, 30% chardonnay.

88 Colour: bright yellow. Nose: ripe fruit, citrus fruit, dried herbs. Palate: flavourful, spicy, ripe fruit.

CASA RAVELLA TINTO SELECCIÓN 2008 T
cabernet sauvignon.

89 Colour: very deep cherry. Nose: balanced, spicy, candied fruit, powerfull. Palate: flavourful, full, long, round tannins.

CASA RAVELLA TINTO SELECCIÓN 2007 T
cabernet sauvignon.

88 Colour: deep cherry, garnet rim. Nose: balanced, ripe fruit, characterful, wild herbs. Palate: flavourful, fine bitter notes.

CASTELL D'AGE

Ctra.de Martorell a Capellades, 6-8
08782 La Beguda Baixa (Barcelona)
☎: +34 937 725 181 - Fax: +34 937 727 061
info@castelldage.com
www.castelldage.com

L'ESSÈNCIA DEL XAREL.LO 2011 B
100% xarel.lo.

88 Colour: bright straw. Nose: fresh, fresh fruit, white flowers, expressive, fragrant herbs. Palate: flavourful, fruity, good acidity, balanced.

CASTELL D'AGE BLANC DE BLANCS 2011 B
100% macabeo.

84

CASTELL D'AGE ROSAT MERLOT 2011 RD
100% merlot.

85 Colour: rose, purple rim. Nose: powerfull, ripe fruit, red berry notes, floral. Palate: , powerful, fruity, fresh.

CASTELL D'AGE CABERNET SAUVIGNON 2006 T
100% cabernet sauvignon.

89 Colour: cherry, garnet rim. Nose: powerfull, balanced, ripe fruit, fruit preserve, spicy. Palate: flavourful, good structure, good acidity.

CASTELL D'AGE MERLOT 2006 T
100% merlot.

87 Colour: cherry, garnet rim. Nose: medium intensity, closed, spicy. Palate: flavourful, fruity, good acidity.

CASTELL D'AGE TEMPRANILLO 2006 T
100% tempranillo.

86 Colour: cherry, garnet rim. Nose: medium intensity, fruit preserve, spicy. Palate: fruity, correct.

FRUIT DE CASTELL D'AGE 2004 T
cabernet sauvignon, merlot, syrah.

89 Colour: deep cherry, orangey edge. Nose: ripe fruit, medium intensity, spicy. Palate: balanced, good acidity, round tannins.

CASTELL D'OR

Mare Rafols, 3- 1º 4º
08720 Vilafranca del Penedès (Barcelona)
☎: +34 938 905 446 - Fax: +34 938 905 446
castelldor@castelldor.com
www.castelldor.com

COSSETÀNIA XAREL.LO 2011 B
100% xarel.lo.

86 Colour: bright straw. Nose: fresh fruit, citrus fruit. Palate: flavourful, fruity, fresh.

COSSETÀNIA CHARDONNAY 2011 B
100% chardonnay.

86 Colour: bright straw. Nose: powerfull, varietal, ripe fruit, citrus fruit. Palate: flavourful, fruity, fresh.

COSSETÀNIA 2011 RD
100% merlot.

84

COSSETÀNIA 2010 T
60% cabernet sauvignon, 40% merlot.

87 Colour: cherry, garnet rim. Nose: ripe fruit, scrubland, earthy notes, green pepper. Palate: round tannins, powerful, flavourful.

COSSETÀNIA 2008 TC
80% tempranillo, 20% merlot.

86 Colour: cherry, garnet rim. Nose: ripe fruit, spicy, scrubland. Palate: powerful, flavourful, toasty, balsamic.

COSSETÀNIA 2006 TR
100% cabernet sauvignon.

86 Colour: dark-red cherry, garnet rim. Nose: ripe fruit, spicy, creamy oak, medium intensity. Palate: powerful, flavourful, toasty.

CASTELLROIG - FINCA SABATÉ I COCA

Ctra. Sant Sadurní d'Anoia a Vilafranca del Penedès, Km. 1
08739 Subirats (Barcelona)
☎: +34 938 911 927 - Fax: +34 938 914 055
info@castellroig.com
www.castellroig.com

TERROJA DE SABATÉ I COCA 2011 B
xarel.lo.

91 Colour: bright straw. Nose: fresh, white flowers, fresh fruit. Palate: flavourful, fruity, good acidity, balanced.

CASTELLROIG XAREL.LO 2011 B
xarel.lo.

88 Colour: bright straw. Nose: mineral, powerfull, ripe fruit, citrus fruit. Palate: flavourful, fruity, fresh.

CASTELLROIG SELECCIÓ 2010 B
xarel.lo, chardonnay.

90 Colour: bright straw. Nose: powerfull, ripe fruit, spicy. Palate: flavourful, powerful, complex, long.

CASTELLROIG ULL DE LLEBRE 2009 T
tempranillo.

87 Colour: cherry, garnet rim. Nose: ripe fruit, spicy, complex, scrubland. Palate: powerful, flavourful, long.

CAVA JOSEP M. FERRET GUASCH

Barri L'Alzinar, 68
08739 Font-Rubí (Barcelona)
☎: +34 938 979 037 - Fax: +34 938 979 414
ferretguasch@ferretguasch.com
www.ferretguasch.com

NA DIA SAUVIGNON BLANC 2011 B

89 Colour: bright straw. Nose: fresh, fresh fruit, expressive, dried herbs, faded flowers. Palate: flavourful, fruity, good acidity, balanced.

GEBRE CABERNET SAUVIGNON 2011 RD
100% cabernet sauvignon.

84

CAVAS FERRET

Avda. de Catalunya, 36
08736 Guardiola de Font-Rubí (Barcelona)
☎: +34 938 979 148 - Fax: +34 938 979 285
ferret@cavasferret.com
www.cavasferret.com

ABAC 2011 B
100% xarel.lo.

90 Colour: yellow, greenish rim. Nose: saline, ripe fruit, floral, fragrant herbs. Palate: light-bodied, fresh, fruity, flavourful.

IGNEA DE FERRET 2011 B
40% parellada, 30% macabeo, 20% xarel.lo.

85 Colour: bright straw. Nose: fresh, fresh fruit, dried flowers. Palate: flavourful, fruity, good acidity, balanced.

FERRET BLANC SELECCIÓ DE BARRIQUES 2007 B
50% xarel.lo, 50% chardonnay.

83

IGNEA DE FERRET 2011 RD
40% ull de llebre, 30% cabernet sauvignon, 30% merlot.

79

IGNEA DE FERRET 2010 T
40% cabernet sauvignon, 40% merlot, 20% ull de llebre.

87 Colour: deep cherry. Nose: powerfull, characterful, overripe fruit, roasted coffee. Palate: fine bitter notes, good acidity, ripe fruit.

FERRET NEGRE SELECCIÓ DE BARRIQUES 2006 T
40% cabernet franc, 24% merlot, 36% tempranillo.

85 Colour: cherry, garnet rim. Nose: ripe fruit, spicy, creamy oak, toasty, warm. Palate: powerful, flavourful, toasty, round tannins.

CAVAS HILL

Bonavista, 2
08734 Moja (Olérdola) (Barcelona)
☎: +34 938 900 588 - Fax: +34 938 170 246
cavashill@cavashill.com
www.cavashill.com

ORO PENEDÈS 2011 B
40% moscatel, 60% xarel.lo.

86 Colour: yellow. Nose: white flowers, medium intensity, dried herbs. Palate: fresh, fruity, light-bodied.

CHARDONNAY HILL 2011 B
chardonnay.

85 Colour: bright yellow. Nose: powerfull, ripe fruit, sweet spices, creamy oak, fragrant herbs. Palate: rich, smoky afterpalate:, flavourful, good acidity.

BLANC BRUC 2011 BFB
35% chardonnay, 65% xarel.lo.

84

GRAN CIVET 2009 TC
70% cabernet sauvignon, 30% tempranillo.

85 Colour: cherry, garnet rim. Nose: ripe fruit, spicy, creamy oak, toasty. Palate: powerful, flavourful, toasty.

GRAN TOC 2008 TR
70% merlot, 30% tempranillo.

84

CAVES GRAMONA

Industria, 36
08770 Sant Sadurní D'Anoia (Barcelona)
☎: +34 938 910 113 - Fax: +34 938 183 284
comunicacion@gramona.com
www.gramona.com

GRAMONA SAUVIGNON BLANC 2011 BFB
100% sauvignon blanc.

94 Colour: bright yellow. Nose: elegant, white flowers, citrus fruit, fruit expression, sweet spices, mineral. Palate: balanced, fresh, fruity, flavourful, complex. Personality.

GRAMONA MAS ESCORPÍ CHARDONNAY 2011 B
100% chardonnay.

92 Colour: bright yellow. Nose: ripe fruit, floral, citrus fruit, wild herbs, complex, mineral. Palate: flavourful, rich, fruity, long, elegant.

GRAMONA XAREL.LO FONT JUI 2010 B
100% xarel.lo.

93 Colour: bright yellow. Nose: ripe fruit, sweet spices, creamy oak, fragrant herbs, complex, expressive. Palate: rich, smoky afterpalate:, flavourful, fresh, good acidity.

VI DE GLASS GEWÜRZTRAMINER 0,375 2010 B
100% gewürztraminer.

90 Colour: bright yellow. Nose: powerfull, candied fruit, honeyed notes, white flowers. Palate: flavourful, sweet, good acidity.

VI DE GLASS RIESLING 2010 B
100% riesling.

90 Colour: bright straw. Nose: powerfull, candied fruit, fruit preserve, citrus fruit. Palate: flavourful, sweet, fruity.

VI DE GLASS GEWÜRZTRAMINER 0,75 2007 BC
100% gewürztraminer.

94 Colour: bright yellow. Nose: powerfull, floral, honeyed notes, candied fruit, fragrant herbs. Palate: flavourful, sweet, fresh, fruity, good acidity, long.

CAVES NAVERÁN

Can Parellada - Sant Martí Sadevesa
08775 Torrelavit (Barcelona)
☎: +34 938 988 400 - Fax: +34 938 989 027
sadeve@naveran.com
www.naveran.com

CLOS ANTONIA 2011 B
viognier.

93 Colour: bright yellow. Nose: ripe fruit, sweet spices, creamy oak, fragrant herbs, elegant. Palate: rich, flavourful, fresh, good acidity. Personality.

MANUELA DE NAVERÁN 2011 B
chardonnay.

89 Colour: bright straw. Nose: fresh, white flowers, expressive, ripe fruit. Palate: flavourful, fruity, good acidity, balanced.

NAVERÁN CLOS DELS ANGELS 2010 T
syrah, merlot, cabernet sauvignon.

93 Colour: light cherry, garnet rim. Nose: red berry notes, ripe fruit, fragrant herbs, expressive. Palate: light-bodied, fresh, balsamic, elegant.

NAVERÁN DON PABLO 2005 TR
cabernet sauvignon.

90 Colour: cherry, garnet rim. Nose: ripe fruit, spicy, creamy oak, balsamic herbs. Palate: powerful, flavourful, toasty, round tannins.

CLOS DEL PI 2001 T

89 Colour: pale ruby, brick rim edge. Nose: elegant, spicy, fine reductive notes, wet leather, aged wood nuances, fruit liqueur notes. Palate: spicy, fine tannins, elegant, long.

CELLER CAL SERRADOR

Montserrat, 87
08770 Sant Sadurní D'Anoia (Barcelona)
☎: +34 938 912 073 - Fax: +34 938 183 539
vinuet@terra.es
www.vinuet.com

VINUET CHARDONNAY 2011 B
100% chardonnay.

86 Colour: bright yellow. Nose: citrus fruit, ripe fruit, floral, dried herbs. Palate: powerful, flavourful, fresh, fruity.

VINUET XAREL.LO 2011 B
100% xarel.lo.

84

VINUET ROSAT 2011 RD
90% merlot, 10% syrah.

85 Colour: rose, purple rim. Nose: ripe fruit, red berry notes, floral. Palate: , powerful, fruity, fresh.

VINUET MERLOT 2011 T JOVEN
merlot.

87 Colour: cherry, purple rim. Nose: red berry notes, floral, wild herbs. Palate: flavourful, fruity, good acidity.

CELLER JORDI LLUCH

Barrio Les Casetes, s/n
08777 Sant Quinti de Mediona (Barcelona)
☎: +34 938 988 138 - Fax: +34 938 988 138
vinyaescude@vinyaescude.com
www.vinyaescude.com

VINYA ESCUDÉ MAIOLES 2008 BFB

88 Colour: bright yellow. Nose: sweet spices, fine lees, candied fruit, honeyed notes, expressive. Palate: fruity, flavourful.

VINYA ESCUDÉ NOGUERA 2005 TC
cabernet sauvignon, merlot.

88 Colour: pale ruby, brick rim edge. Nose: elegant, spicy, fine reductive notes, ripe fruit. Palate: fine tannins, long, spicy.

CELLERS AVGVSTVS FORVM

Ctra. Sant Vicenç, s/n
43700 El Vendrell (Tarragona)
☎: +34 977 666 910 - Fax: +34 977 666 590
albert@avgvstvs.es
www.avgvstvs.es

AVGVSTVS CHARDONNAY 2011 BFB
100% chardonnay.

92 Colour: bright yellow. Nose: powerfull, ripe fruit, sweet spices, creamy oak, fragrant herbs. Palate: rich, smoky afterpalate:, flavourful, fresh, good acidity.

AVGVSTVS XAREL.LO 2011 BFB
100% xarel.lo.

90 Colour: bright yellow. Nose: ripe fruit, sweet spices, creamy oak, fragrant herbs, mineral. Palate: rich, smoky afterpalate:, flavourful, fresh.

AVGVSTVS CHARDONNAY MAGNUM 2010 B
100% chardonnay.

94 Colour: bright straw. Nose: fragrant herbs, warm, complex, expressive, ripe fruit, citrus fruit. Palate: ripe fruit, fine bitter notes, good acidity, spicy.

AVGVSTVS CABERNET SAUVIGNON ROSÉ 2011 RD
100% cabernet sauvignon.

82

AVGVSTVS MERLOT SYRAH 2011 T
merlot, syrah.

88 Colour: cherry, purple rim. Nose: expressive, fresh fruit, red berry notes, floral. Palate: flavourful, fruity, good acidity, round tannins.

AVGVSTVS CABERNET SAUVIGNON-MERLOT 2010 T ROBLE
cabernet sauvignon, merlot.

90 Colour: very deep cherry. Nose: balanced, expressive, mineral, ripe fruit. Palate: good structure, complex, ripe fruit, spicy, round tannins.

AVGVSTVS CABERNET FRANC 2010 T ROBLE
100% cabernet franc.

89 Colour: cherry, garnet rim. Nose: balanced, medium intensity, spicy, closed. Palate: full, flavourful, good structure, ripe fruit.

AVGVSTVS TRAJANVS 2009 TR
cabernet sauvignon, merlot, cabernet franc, garnacha.

90 Colour: deep cherry, garnet rim. Nose: closed, ripe fruit, spicy, scrubland. Palate: full, good structure, round tannins.

AVGVSTVS CABERNET SAUVIGNON-MERLOT 2009 T
cabernet sauvignon, merlot.

89 Colour: very deep cherry, garnet rim. Nose: medium intensity, varietal, scrubland. Palate: ripe fruit, fine bitter notes, balanced.

AVGVSTVS TRAJANVS 2007 TR
cabernet sauvignon, merlot, cabernet franc.

89 Colour: deep cherry, orangey edge. Nose: fruit preserve, dark chocolate, creamy oak. Palate: flavourful, full, long, round tannins.

COLET

Cami del Salinar, s/n
08739 Pacs del Penedès (Barcelona)
☎: +34 938 170 809 - Fax: +34 938 170 809
info@colet.cat
www.colet.cat

COLET ASSEMBLAGE BLANC DE NOIR ESP
chardonnay, pinot noir.

92 Colour: coppery red. Nose: powerfull, candied fruit, spicy, toasty, dry nuts. Palate: flavourful, fine bitter notes, good acidity, fine bead.

COLET TRADICIONAL ESP
55% xarel.lo, 40% macabeo, 5% parellada.

92 Colour: bright straw. Nose: powerfull, expressive, characterful, fine lees. Palate: flavourful, powerful, sweetness, fine bitter notes, balanced.

COLET GRAND CUVEÉ ESP
chardonnay, macabeo, xarel.lo.

92 Colour: bright straw. Nose: ripe fruit, fine lees, pattiserie, spicy. Palate: flavourful, fine bitter notes, ripe fruit.

VATUA ! ESP
moscatel, parellada, gewürztraminer.

90 Colour: bright straw. Nose: medium intensity, fresh fruit, dried herbs, fine lees, floral. Palate: fresh, fruity, flavourful, good acidity.

A POSTERIORI ROSAT ESP
100% merlot.

89 Colour: coppery red. Nose: medium intensity, fresh fruit, dried herbs, fine lees, floral. Palate: fresh, fruity, flavourful, good acidity.

A PRIORI ESP
macabeo, chardonnay, riesling, gewürztraminer, moscatel.

89 Colour: bright straw. Nose: medium intensity, ripe fruit, fine lees. Palate: flavourful, ripe fruit, fine bitter notes.

COLET NAVAZOS EXTRA BRUT 2009 EXTRA BRUT

92 Colour: bright straw. Nose: spicy, medium intensity, balanced, balsamic herbs, dry nuts. Palate: flavourful, long, fine bitter notes.

COLET NAVAZOS EXTRA BRUT 2008 EXTRA BRUT RESERVA
chardonnay.

94 Colour: bright yellow. Nose: complex, expressive, candied fruit, pattiserie, saline. Palate: flavourful, long, spicy, fine bitter notes.

EMENDIS

Barrio de Sant Marçal, 67
08732 Castellet i La Gornal (Barcelona)
☎: +34 938 186 119 - Fax: +34 938 918 169
avalles@emendis.es
www.emendis.es

EMENDIS TRÍO VARIETAL 2011 B
macabeo, chardonnay, moscatel.

87 Colour: bright straw. Nose: fresh, fresh fruit, white flowers, expressive. Palate: flavourful, fruity, good acidity.

EMENDIS NOX 2011 RD
50% syrah, 50% pinot noir.

84

EMENDIS DUET VARIETAL 2010 T

91 Colour: cherry, garnet rim. Nose: ripe fruit, spicy, creamy oak, toasty, complex. Palate: powerful, flavourful, toasty, round tannins.

EMENDIS MATER 2006 TC
100% merlot.

91 Colour: cherry, garnet rim. Nose: spicy, creamy oak, toasty, characterful. Palate: powerful, flavourful, toasty, round tannins.

FINCA VALLDOSERA

Masia Les Garrigues, Urb. Can Trabal s/n
08734 Olèrdola (Barcelona)
☎: +34 938 143 047 - Fax: +34 938 935 590
general@fincavalldosera.com
www.fincavalldosera.com

FINCA VALLDOSERA SUBIRAT PARENT 2011 B
100% subirat parent.

90 Colour: bright straw. Nose: expressive, candied fruit, powerfull. Palate: flavourful, sweetness, fine bitter notes. Personality.

FINCA VALLDOSERA XAREL.LO 2011 B
xarel.lo.

88 Colour: bright straw. Nose: faded flowers, candied fruit, dried herbs. Palate: light-bodied, fresh, fruity, flavourful.

FINCA VALLDOSERA SYRAH MERLOT 2011 RD
60% syrah, 40% merlot.

87 Colour: light cherry, bright. Nose: red berry notes, ripe fruit, floral. Palate: flavourful, fruity, ripe fruit.

FINCA VALLDOSERA 2011 T
syrah, merlot, cabernet sauvignon.

90 Colour: cherry, purple rim. Nose: fruit expression, expressive, balanced. Palate: correct, fruity, easy to drink.

FINCA VALLDOSERA 2008 T
merlot, cabernet sauvignon, tempranillo.

91 Colour: cherry, garnet rim. Nose: dark chocolate, ripe fruit, powerfull, red berry notes. Palate: good structure, full, round tannins.

FINCA VILADELLOPS

Celler Gran Viladellops
08734 Olérdola (Barcelona)
☎: +34 938 188 371 - Fax: +34 938 188 371
md@viladellops.com
www.viladellops.com

FINCA VILADELLOPS XAREL.LO 2010 BFB
100% xarel.lo.

89 Colour: bright yellow. Nose: ripe fruit, citrus fruit, fragrant herbs, sweet spices. Palate: powerful, flavourful, fruity.

FINCA VILADELLOPS 2008 T
60% garnacha, 40% syrah.

86 Colour: cherry, garnet rim. Nose: ripe fruit, spicy, creamy oak, toasty. Palate: powerful, flavourful, toasty.

VILADELLOPS GARNATXA 2011 T
garnacha.

92 Colour: cherry, garnet rim. Nose: ripe fruit, balsamic herbs, scrubland, fresh, expressive. Palate: powerful, flavourful, complex, balsamic, balanced.

TURÓ DE LES ABELLES 2008 T
50% garnacha, 50% syrah.

91 Colour: cherry, garnet rim. Nose: ripe fruit, spicy, creamy oak, toasty, earthy notes. Palate: powerful, flavourful, toasty.

GIRÓ DEL GORNER

Finca Giró del Gorner, s/n
08797 Puigdàlber (Barcelona)
☎: +34 938 988 032
gorner@girodelgorner.com
www.girodelgorner.com

BLANC GORNER 2011 B
macabeo, xarel.lo, parellada, chardonnay.

85 Colour: bright straw. Nose: white flowers, ripe fruit, dried herbs. Palate: flavourful, fruity, good acidity.

XAREL.LO GORNER 2010 B
100% xarel.lo.

90 Colour: bright yellow. Nose: dried flowers, wild herbs, ripe fruit, spicy. Palate: powerful, rich, flavourful, toasty.

GORNER 2006 TR
cabernet sauvignon, merlot.

88 Colour: deep cherry, garnet rim. Nose: sweet spices, balsamic herbs, toasty. Palate: ripe fruit, good acidity, fine bitter notes.

GIRÓ RIBOT

Finca El Pont, s/n
08792 Santa Fe del Penedès (Barcelona)
☎: +34 938 974 050 - Fax: +34 938 974 311
giroribot@giroribot.es
www.giroribot.es

GIRÓ RIBOT MUSCAT DE FRONTIGNAC 2011 B
100% moscatel de frontignan.

90 Colour: bright straw. Nose: fresh, fresh fruit, white flowers, expressive, candied fruit. Palate: flavourful, fruity, good acidity, balanced.

GIRÓ RIBOT GIRO 2 2011 B
100% giró.

89 Colour: bright yellow. Nose: fresh fruit, citrus fruit, white flowers, fragrant herbs. Palate: fruity, light-bodied, flavourful, good acidity, balanced.

GIRÓ RIBOT BLANC DE BLANCS 2011 B
50% xarel.lo, 30% macabeo, 15% parellada, 5% chardonnay.

85 Colour: bright yellow. Nose: ripe fruit, fragrant herbs, medium intensity. Palate: light-bodied, fresh, fruity.

HERETAT MAS TINELL

Ctra. de Vilafranca a St. Martí Sarroca, Km. 0,5
08720 Vilafranca del Penedès (Barcelona)
☎: +34 938 170 586 - Fax: +34 938 170 500
info@mastinell.com
www.mastinell.com

MAS TINELL GISELE 2011 BFB
100% xarel.lo.

88 Colour: bright yellow. Nose: powerfull, ripe fruit, sweet spices, fragrant herbs. Palate: rich, flavourful, fresh.

MAS TINELL CHARDONNAY 2011 B
100% chardonnay.

87 Colour: yellow, greenish rim. Nose: citrus fruit, dried herbs, floral. Palate: fresh, fruity, easy to drink.

MAS TINELL ALBA BLANC DE LLUNA 2011 B
20% macabeo, 25% parellada, 25% xarel.lo, 30% moscatel.

87 Colour: bright straw. Nose: fresh fruit, white flowers, fragrant herbs. Palate: flavourful, fruity, good acidity.

MAS TINELL GISELE 2009 BFB
100% xarel.lo.

91 Colour: bright yellow, yellow, greenish rim. Nose: dried flowers, dry nuts, scrubland, spicy. Palate: powerful, flavourful, round, long, complex.

MAS TINELL CLOS SANT PAU 2008 B
100% moscatel.

87 Colour: golden. Nose: powerfull, candied fruit, fragrant herbs, white flowers. Palate: flavourful, sweet, fresh, fruity, good acidity, long.

MAS TINELL ARTE 2006 TR
34% cabernet sauvignon, 33% garnacha, 33% merlot.

86 Colour: pale ruby, brick rim edge. Nose: spicy, fine reductive notes, wet leather, aged wood nuances, fruit liqueur notes. Palate: spicy, long, flavourful.

HERETAT MONT-RUBÍ

L'Avellà, 1
08736 Font- Rubí (Barcelona)
☎: +34 938 979 066 - Fax: +34 938 979 066
hmr@montrubi.com
www.montrubi.com

WHITE HMR 2011 B
100% xarel.lo.

89 Colour: bright straw. Nose: white flowers, fresh fruit, fragrant herbs. Palate: light-bodied, fresh, fruity, flavourful, easy to drink.

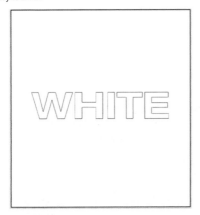

BLACK HMR 2011 T
60% garnacha, 40% otras.

91 Colour: cherry, purple rim. Nose: floral, raspberry, red berry notes, lactic notes, expressive. Palate: good acidity, powerful, flavourful, balanced.

GAINTUS 2007 T
sumoll.

91 Colour: cherry, garnet rim. Nose: spicy, creamy oak, toasty, expressive, characterful, ripe fruit. Palate: powerful, flavourful, toasty, round tannins.

ADVENT XAREL.LO 2009 B
xarel.lo.

90 Colour: bright golden. Nose: ripe fruit, dry nuts, citrus fruit, fragrant herbs, dried flowers. Palate: powerful, flavourful, concentrated, balanced, round.

ADVENT SAMSÓ DULCE NATURAL 2010 RD
samsó.

92 Colour: light mahogany. Nose: ripe fruit, fruit liqueur notes, varnish, cocoa bean, toasty, sweet spices. Palate: round, rich, flavourful.

ADVENT SUMOLL DULCE NATURAL 2009 RD
sumoll.

94 Colour: coppery red. Nose: candied fruit, raspberry, floral, sweet spices, creamy oak, dark chocolate. Palate: powerful, flavourful, spicy, toasty, roasted-coffee afterpalate:.

DURONA 2007 T
sumoll, garnacha, cariñena.

90 Colour: cherry, garnet rim. Nose: ripe fruit, spicy, creamy oak, toasty, earthy notes. Palate: powerful, flavourful, toasty, round tannins.

J. MIQUEL JANÉ

Masia Cal Costas, s/n
08736 Font- Rubí (Barcelona)
☎: +34 934 140 948 - Fax: +34 932 015 901
info@jmiqueljane.com
www.jmiqueljane.com

J. MIQUEL JANÉ SAUVIGNON BLANC 2011 B
100% sauvignon blanc.

89 Colour: bright yellow. Nose: dried flowers, fragrant herbs, citrus fruit, expressive. Palate: rich, flavourful, fruity, long.

BLANC BALTANA 2011 B
50% macabeo, 35% parellada, 15% sauvignon blanc.

85 Colour: bright yellow. Nose: ripe fruit, fragrant herbs, dried flowers. Palate: flavourful, fresh, fruity.

J. MIQUEL JANÉ CABERNET SAUVIGNON 2011 RD
85% cabernet sauvignon, 15% garnacha.

83

BALTANA NEGRE 2010 T
50% cabernet sauvignon, 30% garnacha, 20% syrah.

85 Colour: cherry, garnet rim. Nose: spicy, ripe fruit, medium intensity. Palate: flavourful, fruity, round tannins.

BALTANA SELECCIO 2008 T
60% cabernet sauvignon, 40% merlot.

89 Colour: cherry, garnet rim. Nose: medium intensity, scrubland, spicy, sweet spices. Palate: flavourful, fine bitter notes.

JANÉ VENTURA

Ctra. Calafell, 2
43700 El Vendrell (Tarragona)
☎: +34 977 660 118 - Fax: +34 977 661 239
janeventura@janeventura.com
www.janeventura.com

JANÉ VENTURA MALVASÍA DE SITGES 2011 B BARRICA
malvasía.

92 Colour: bright straw. Nose: elegant, complex, white flowers, ripe fruit, sweet spices. Palate: balanced, good acidity, fine bitter notes. Personality.

JANÉ VENTURA "FINCA ELS CAMPS" SERRA DEL MOMTMELL 2011 B
macabeo.

91 Colour: bright straw. Nose: fresh, white flowers, expressive, ripe fruit. Palate: flavourful, fruity, good acidity, balanced.

JANÉ VENTURA BLANC SELECCIÓ 15 VINYES 2011 B
xarel.lo, malvasía, moscatel, sauvignon blanc.

89 Colour: bright straw. Nose: fresh, fresh fruit, white flowers, mineral. Palate: flavourful, fruity, good acidity, balanced.

JANÉ VENTURA "FINCA ELS CAMPS" MACABEU 2010 BFB

90 Colour: bright straw. Nose: wild herbs, elegant, ripe fruit, complex. Palate: fruity, good acidity, fine bitter notes.

JANÉ VENTURA ROSAT SELECCIÓ 2011 RD
sumoll, merlot, syrah, ull de llebre.

87 Colour: rose, bright. Nose: red berry notes, ripe fruit, rose petals. Palate: balanced, fine bitter notes, fruity, flavourful.

JANÉ VENTURA "MAS VILELLA" COSTERS DEL ROTLLAN 2009 T
cabernet sauvignon.

92 Colour: cherry, garnet rim. Nose: scrubland, ripe fruit, earthy notes, expressive, spicy, creamy oak. Palate: round, powerful, flavourful, long, balanced.

JANÉ VENTURA "FINCA ELS CAMPS" ULL DE LLEBRE 2007 T
ull de llebre.

91 Colour: cherry, garnet rim. Nose: ripe fruit, spicy, creamy oak, toasty, complex. Palate: powerful, flavourful, toasty, round tannins.

JAUME GIRÓ I GIRÓ

Montaner i Oller, 5
08770 Sant Sadurní D'Anoia (Barcelona)
☎: +34 938 910 165 - Fax: +34 938 911 271
cavagiro@cavagiro.com
www.cavagiro.com

JAUME GIRÓ I GIRÓ XAREL.LO MACERADO 2011 B
88% xarel.lo, 10% chardonnay, 1% moscatel, 1% sauvignon blanc.

86 Colour: bright straw. Nose: fresh, fresh fruit, white flowers, expressive. Palate: flavourful, fruity, good acidity, balanced.

JAUME GIRÓ I GIRÓ CABERNET MERLOT 2009 T
45% cabernet sauvignon, 45% merlot, 10% syrah.

87 Colour: cherry, garnet rim. Nose: ripe fruit, spicy, toasty, scrubland. Palate: powerful, flavourful, round tannins.

JAUME SERRA

Ctra. de Vilanova, Km. 2,5
08800 Vilanova i la Geltru (Barcelona)
☎: +34 938 936 404 - Fax: +34 938 147 482
jaumeserra@jgc.es
www.garciacarrion.es

JAUME SERRA MACABEO 2011 B
macabeo.

85 Colour: bright straw. Nose: medium intensity, candied fruit. Palate: flavourful, fine bitter notes, good acidity.

JAUME SERRA 2011 B

82

JAUME SERRA CHARDONNAY 2010 BFB
100% chardonnay.

87 Colour: bright yellow. Nose: toasty, spicy, ripe fruit. Palate: powerful, flavourful.

JAUME SERRA MERLOT 2011 RD
100% merlot.

86 Colour: light cherry. Nose: ripe fruit, balanced, powerfull. Palate: flavourful, fruity, correct, fine bitter notes.

JAUME SERRA TEMPRANILLO 2010 T
100% tempranillo.

86 Colour: cherry, garnet rim. Nose: medium intensity, ripe fruit, spicy. Palate: correct, easy to drink.

JAUME SERRA 2007 TC
65% cabernet sauvignon, 20% merlot, 15% tempranillo.

82

JEAN LEON

Pago Jean León, s/n
08775 Torrelavit (Barcelona)
☎: +34 938 995 512 - Fax: +34 938 995 517
jeanleon@jeanleon.com
www.jeanleon.com

JEAN LEÓN PETIT CHARDONNAY 2011 B
100% chardonnay.

90 Colour: bright yellow. Nose: expressive, ripe fruit, jasmine, powerfull, varietal. Palate: flavourful, rich, long, good acidity, balanced.

JEAN LEÓN VIÑA GIGI CHARDONNAY 2009 BC
100% chardonnay.

90 Colour: bright yellow. Nose: elegant, balanced, candied fruit, creamy oak. Palate: flavourful, toasty, ripe fruit.

JEAN LEÓN 3055 PETIT MERLOT 2011 T ROBLE
100% merlot.

87 Colour: bright cherry. Nose: ripe fruit, creamy oak, expressive, balsamic herbs. Palate: flavourful, fruity, toasty, round tannins.

JEAN LEÓN VINYA PALAU MERLOT 2007 TC
100% merlot.

91 Colour: cherry, garnet rim. Nose: ripe fruit, spicy, creamy oak, toasty, wild herbs. Palate: powerful, flavourful, toasty, round tannins, elegant.

JEAN LEÓN CABERNET SAUVIGNON 2005 TR
85% cabernet sauvignon, 15% cabernet franc.

92 Colour: dark-red cherry, orangey edge. Nose: ripe fruit, balsamic herbs, earthy notes, fine reductive notes. Palate: long, flavourful, spicy, balanced.

JEAN LEÓN VINYA LA SCALA CABERNET SAUVIGNON 2001 TGR
100% cabernet sauvignon.

92 Colour: pale ruby, brick rim edge. Nose: elegant, spicy, fine reductive notes, wet leather, aged wood nuances, fruit liqueur notes. Palate: spicy, fine tannins, elegant, long.

JOAN SARDÀ

Ctra. Vilafranca a St. Jaume dels Domenys, Km. 8,1
08732 Castellvi de la Marca (Barcelona)
☎: +34 937 720 900 - Fax: +34 937 721 495
joansarda@joansarda.com
www.joansarda.com

BLANC MARINER 2011 B
xarel.lo, chardonnay.

87 Colour: bright straw. Nose: fresh, white flowers, citrus fruit. Palate: flavourful, fruity, good acidity, balanced.

VINYA SARDÀ 2011 B
xarel.lo, chardonnay.

87 Colour: bright straw. Nose: fresh, white flowers, ripe fruit. Palate: flavourful, fruity, good acidity, balanced.

JOAN SARDÀ CHARDONNAY 2011 B
chardonnay.

87 Colour: bright straw. Nose: powerfull, ripe fruit, citrus fruit, mineral. Palate: flavourful, fruity, fresh.

VINYA SARDÀ 2011 RD
merlot.

86 Colour: rose, purple rim. Nose: powerfull, ripe fruit, red berry notes, floral, expressive. Palate: fleshy, powerful, fruity, fresh.

JOAN SARDÀ CABERNET SAUVIGNON 2011 RD
cabernet sauvignon.

84

VINYA SARDÀ 2010 T
merlot, tempranillo.

84

JOAN SARDÀ 2009 TC
merlot, cabernet sauvignon.

88 Colour: cherry, garnet rim. Nose: ripe fruit, spicy, fragrant herbs. Palate: powerful, flavourful, toasty, round tannins.

JOAN SARDÀ CABERNET SAUVIGNON 2009 TC
cabernet sauvignon.

87 Colour: cherry, garnet rim. Nose: medium intensity, cocoa bean, ripe fruit. Palate: correct, good acidity.

JOAN SARDÀ 2008 TR
cabernet sauvignon, tempranillo, merlot.

88 Colour: cherry, garnet rim. Nose: balanced, ripe fruit, balsamic herbs, expressive. Palate: fruity, good structure, round tannins.

JORDI ALEMANY BONASTRE

Ctra. Gélida a St. Llorenç d'Hortons, km. 5,25
08790 Gelida (Barcelona)
☎: +34 935 039 318
jalemany@matadabello.com
www.matadabello.com

MATA D'ABELLO "TOIETES" 2010 B
xarel.lo.

88 Colour: bright yellow. Nose: dried flowers, ripe fruit, fragrant herbs, expressive. Palate: powerful, flavourful, rich, complex, long.

MATA D'ABELLO TOTTÓ 2010 BFB
xarel.lo.

87 Colour: bright yellow. Nose: powerfull, ripe fruit, sweet spices, creamy oak, fragrant herbs. Palate: rich, smoky afterpalate:, flavourful.

MATA D'ABELLO BALLÓ 2009 TC

83

JOSEP GUILERA RIAMBAU

Can Guilera, s/n
08739 Sant Pau D'Ordal (Subirats) (Barcelona)
☎: +34 938 993 094 - Fax: +34 938 993 094
canguilera@comnose:.net
www.comnose:.net

COMA ROMÀ 2011 B
xarel.lo.

84

COMA ROMÀ XAREL.LO MACERACIÓ 2010 B
xarel.lo.

84

COMA ROMÀ 2011 RD
merlot, ull de llebre.

83

COMA ROMÀ 2009 T
merlot.

86 Colour: cherry, garnet rim. Nose: ripe fruit, spicy, creamy oak, toasty. Palate: powerful, flavourful, toasty.

JOSEP Mª RAVENTÓS I BLANC

Plaça del Roure, s/n
08770 Sant Sadurní D'Anoia (Barcelona)
☎: +34 938 183 262 - Fax: +34 938 912 500
raventos@raventos.com
www.raventos.com

SILENCIS 2011 B
100% xarel.lo.

90 Colour: bright straw. Nose: white flowers, varietal, ripe fruit, balanced. Palate: flavourful, fruity, good acidity, balanced.

PERFUM DE VI BLANC 2011 B
60% macabeo, 40% moscatel.

89 Colour: bright straw. Nose: fresh, fresh fruit, white flowers, expressive. Palate: flavourful, fruity, good acidity, balanced.

LA ROSA DE RAVENTÓS I BLANC 2011 RD
100% pinot noir.

86 Colour: raspberry rose. Nose: dried herbs, floral, fruit expression. Palate: flavourful, fruity, fresh.

ISABEL NEGRA 2009 T
45% cabernet sauvignon, 43% syrah, 12% monastrell.

89 Colour: cherry, garnet rim. Nose: ripe fruit, spicy, creamy oak, toasty, earthy notes. Palate: powerful, flavourful, toasty, round tannins.

JUVÉ Y CAMPS

Sant Venat, 1
08770 Sant Sadurní D'Anoia (Barcelona)
☎: +34 938 911 000 - Fax: +34 938 912 100
juveycamps@juveycamps.com
www.juveycamps.com

MIRANDA D'ESPIELLS 2011 B
100% chardonnay.

90 Colour: bright straw. Nose: fresh, fresh fruit, white flowers, expressive. Palate: flavourful, fruity, good acidity, balanced.

ERMITA D'ESPIELLS 2011 B
56% xarel.lo, 32% macabeo, 12% parellada.

88 Colour: bright straw. Nose: ripe fruit, fruit expression, dried herbs, floral. Palate: flavourful, fruity, fresh.

FLOR D'ESPIELLS 2010 BFB
100% chardonnay.

88 Colour: bright yellow. Nose: spicy, creamy oak, toasty, ripe fruit. Palate: flavourful, powerful, fine bitter notes, good acidity.

IOHANNES 2008 T
55% merlot, 45% cabernet sauvignon.

91 Colour: cherry, garnet rim. Nose: scrubland, ripe fruit, spicy, balanced. Palate: long, balsamic, flavourful, round tannins.

CASA VELLA D'ESPIELLS MAGNUM 2008 T
80% cabernet sauvignon, 20% merlot.

89 Colour: cherry, garnet rim. Nose: ripe fruit, spicy, toasty. Palate: powerful, flavourful, toasty, round tannins.

VIÑA ESCARLATA 2008 T
100% merlot.

89 Colour: cherry, garnet rim. Nose: ripe fruit, spicy, toasty, dark chocolate. Palate: powerful, flavourful, toasty, round tannins.

CASA VELLA D'ESPIELLS 2008 T
80% cabernet sauvignon, 20% merlot.

89 Colour: cherry, garnet rim. Nose: ripe fruit, sweet spices, creamy oak, balsamic herbs. Palate: long, complex, powerful, flavourful.

LLOPART

Ctra. de Sant Sadurni - Ordal, Km. 4
08739 Subirats (Els Casots) (Barcelona)
☎: +34 938 993 125 - Fax: +34 938 993 038
llopart@llopart.com
www.llopart.com

LLOPART CLOS DELS FÒSSILS CHARDONNAY 2011 B
85% chardonnay, 15% xarel.lo.

87 Colour: bright straw. Nose: varietal, white flowers, medium intensity, sweet spices. Palate: balanced, fine bitter notes.

LLOPART VITIS 2011 B
60% xarel.lo, 30% subirat parent, 10% moscatel.

86 Colour: bright straw. Nose: fresh, white flowers, expressive. Palate: flavourful, fruity, good acidity, balanced, fine bitter notes.

LLOPART CASTELL DE SUBIRATS 2008 T ROBLE
40% merlot, 30% tempranillo, 30% cabernet sauvignon.

87 Colour: cherry, garnet rim. Nose: ripe fruit, new oak, aged wood nuances. Palate: spicy, flavourful, balsamic, long.

LOXAREL

Can Mayol, s/n
08735 Vilobí del Penedès (Barcelona)
☎: +34 938 978 001 - Fax: +34 938 978 111
loxarel@loxarel.com
www.loxarel.com

GAIA DE LOXAREL 2011 B
sauvignon blanc.

88 Colour: bright straw. Nose: powerfull, ripe fruit, fresh fruit. Palate: flavourful, fruity, fresh.

AMALTEA DE LOXAREL 2011 B
garnacha blanca.

88 Colour: bright straw. Nose: fresh, white flowers, citrus fruit. Palate: flavourful, fruity, good acidity, balanced.

CORA DE LOXAREL 2011 B
xarel.lo, moscatel.

87 Colour: bright straw. Nose: fresh fruit, fruit expression, powerfull. Palate: flavourful, powerful, easy to drink.

A PÉL 2011 RD
pinot noir, chardonnay.

89 Colour: onion pink. Nose: candied fruit, dried flowers, fragrant herbs, red berry notes. Palate: light-bodied, good acidity, spicy.

GAL GRAN ARNAU DE LOXAREL 2011 RD
merlot.

86 Colour: rose, purple rim. Nose: powerfull, ripe fruit, red berry notes. Palate: , powerful, fruity, fresh.

PETIT ARNAU DE LOXAREL 2011 RD
cabernet sauvignon, merlot.

83

EOS DE LOXAREL SYRAH 2011 T
syrah.

89 Colour: cherry, purple rim. Nose: fresh fruit, red berry notes, balsamic herbs. Palate: flavourful, fruity, good acidity, warm.

OPS DE LOXAREL 2010 T

89 Colour: cherry, garnet rim. Nose: spicy, creamy oak, toasty, characterful, ripe fruit. Palate: powerful, flavourful, round tannins.

AMALTEA DE LOXAREL 2009 T
cabernet sauvignon, merlot.

88 Colour: cherry, garnet rim. Nose: spicy, creamy oak, toasty, ripe fruit. Palate: powerful, flavourful, toasty, round tannins.

790 LOXAREL 2008 T
cabernet sauvignon.

88 Colour: deep cherry. Nose: ripe fruit, sweet spices, toasty, nose:tic coffee. Palate: flavourful, fine bitter notes, round tannins.

LOXAREL CABERNET 2007 TR
cabernet sauvignon.

88 Colour: cherry, garnet rim. Nose: ripe fruit, spicy, toasty. Palate: powerful, flavourful, toasty, round tannins.

MAS CARGOLS DE LOXAREL 2007 T
pinot noir.

87 Colour: cherry, garnet rim. Nose: ripe fruit, spicy, creamy oak, mineral. Palate: powerful, flavourful, toasty, round tannins.

MARTÍ SERDÀ

Camí Mas del Pont s/n
08792 Santa Fe del Penedès (Barcelona)
☎: +34 938 974 411 - Fax: +34 938 974 405
info@martiserda.com
www.martiserda.com

VINYET BLANC 2011 B JOVEN
50% macabeo, 35% parellada, 15% moscatel.

87 Colour: bright straw. Nose: fresh, white flowers, citrus fruit. Palate: flavourful, fruity, good acidity, balanced.

MASÍA D'OR MEDIUM 2011 B
50% macabeo, 35% xarel.lo, 15% moscatel.

85 Colour: golden. Nose: powerfull, floral, candied fruit, fragrant herbs. Palate: flavourful, sweet, fruity.

MASÍA D'OR BLANC 2011 B
35% macabeo, 35% xarel.lo, 30% parellada.

85 Colour: bright straw. Nose: fresh, fresh fruit, white flowers. Palate: flavourful, fruity, good acidity, balanced.

MARE NOSTRUM VINO DE AGUJA 2011 B
40% macabeo, 30% xarel.lo, 25% parellada.

84

VINYET 2011 RD JOVEN
50% garnacha, 50% merlot.

86 Colour: rose, purple rim. Nose: powerfull, ripe fruit, red berry notes, floral, expressive. Palate: fleshy, powerful, fruity, fresh.

MASÍA D'OR ROSAT 2011 RD
50% garnacha, 50% tempranillo.

84

MARE NOSTRUM VINO DE AGUJA 2011 RD
60% garnacha, 40% tempranillo.

80

MASÍA D'OR 2011 T
50% garnacha, 50% tempranillo.

82

VINYET NEGRE 2008 TC
75% garnacha, 25% cabernet sauvignon.

85 Colour: cherry, garnet rim. Nose: ripe fruit, spicy, creamy oak. Palate: powerful, flavourful, toasty.

MARTÍ SERDÁ MERLOT 2007 TC
100% merlot.

86 Colour: pale ruby, brick rim edge. Nose: spicy, fine reductive notes, aged wood nuances, fruit liqueur notes. Palate: spicy, fine tannins, long.

MAS BERTRAN

Ctra. BP - 2121, km. 7,7
08731 St. Martí Sarroca (Barcelona)
☎: +34 938 990 859 - Fax: +34 938 990 859
info@masbertran.com
www.masbertran.com

NUTT 2010 B
xarel.lo.

87 Colour: bright straw. Nose: candied fruit, citrus fruit, dried herbs. Palate: flavourful, fruity, fresh.

NUTT SUMOLL 2011 RD
100% sumoll.

90 Colour: salmon, bright. Nose: floral, fruit expression, expressive, balanced. Palate: fruity, flavourful, long, good acidity.

ARGILA ROSÉ 2009 BN RESERVA
100% sumoll.

88 Colour: coppery red. Nose: fragrant herbs, fine lees, fruit preserve, candied fruit. Palate: fine bitter notes, flavourful.

BALMA 2008 BN RESERVA
macabeo, xarel.lo, parellada.

88 Colour: bright straw. Nose: faded flowers, candied fruit, fruit preserve. Palate: fine bitter notes, good acidity.

ARGILA 2007 BN GRAN RESERVA
xarel.lo.

92 Colour: bright golden. Nose: fine lees, dry nuts, fragrant herbs, complex. Palate: powerful, flavourful, good acidity, fine bead, fine bitter notes.

MAS CAN COLOMÉ

Masies Sant Marçal s/n
08720 Castellet i La Gornal (Barcelona)
☎: +34 938 918 203 - Fax: +34 938 918 203
info@mascancolome.com
www.mascancolome.com

TURONET 2011 B
chardonnay, xarel.lo, sauvignon blanc.

89 Colour: bright yellow. Nose: dried herbs, faded flowers, citrus fruit, ripe fruit. Palate: correct, powerful, fruity, flavourful.

BLANC MEDITERRANI 2011 B
xarel.lo, macabeo, parellada, moscatel.

86 Colour: bright straw. Nose: fresh, fresh fruit, white flowers, fragrant herbs. Palate: flavourful, fruity, good acidity.

ROSADENC 2011 RD
garnacha, syrah, pinot noir.

87 Colour: light cherry. Nose: red berry notes, ripe fruit, rose petals. Palate: balanced, long, ripe fruit.

TURÓ 2010 T
garnacha, syrah, samsó.

87 Colour: bright cherry. Nose: powerfull, warm, fruit liqueur notes, toasty. Palate: fine bitter notes, spicy.

MAS CAN COLOMÉ VITICULTORS 2010 BN
macabeo, xarel.lo, parellada, chardonnay.

87 Colour: bright straw. Nose: candied fruit, dried flowers, dried herbs, medium intensity. Palate: fresh, light-bodied, flavourful, easy to drink.

SERENOR 2010 ESP
xarel.lo, chardonnay, parellada, macabeo.

90 Colour: bright straw. Nose: fresh fruit, dried herbs, fine lees, floral, citrus fruit. Palate: fresh, fruity, flavourful, good acidity, complex.

MAS CANDÍ

Ctra. de Les Gunyoles, s/n
08793 Avinyonet (Barcelona)
☎: +34 680 765 275
info@mascandi.com
www.mascandi.com

MAS CANDI DESIG 2011 B
xarel.lo.

89 Colour: bright straw. Nose: neat, ripe fruit, scrubland, expressive. Palate: fruity, good structure, complex, rich.

MAS CANDI PECAT NOBLE 2010 B
malvasía.

92 Colour: bright yellow. Nose: citrus fruit, fruit liqueur notes, varnish, creamy oak, fragrant herbs. Palate: powerful, flavourful, fruity, sweet, balanced.

MAS CANDÍ QUATRE XAREL.LO QX 2010 BFB
100% xarel.lo.

90 Colour: bright yellow. Nose: toasty, spicy, candied fruit, wild herbs. Palate: balanced, fruity, full.

MAS CANDÍ SOL+SOL 2009 T
cabernet sauvignon, sumoll, otras.

89 Colour: cherry, garnet rim. Nose: ripe fruit, spicy, creamy oak, toasty, complex. Palate: powerful, flavourful, toasty.

MAS CANDÍ LES FORQUES 2008 T
cabernet sauvignon, sumoll, otras.

89 Colour: cherry, garnet rim. Nose: scrubland, ripe fruit, spicy, fine reductive notes. Palate: balsamic, correct, powerful, flavourful.

MAS CODINA

Barri El Gorner, s/n - Mas Codina
08797 Puigdalber (Barcelona)
☎: +34 938 988 166 - Fax: +34 938 988 166
info@mascodina.com
www.mascodina.com

MAS CODINA 2011 B

88 Colour: bright straw. Nose: powerfull, ripe fruit, citrus fruit. Palate: flavourful, fine bitter notes, good acidity.

MAS CODINA 2011 RD
merlot, cabernet sauvignon.

83

MAS CODINA VINYA MIQUEL 2009 T
syrah.

87 Colour: deep cherry. Nose: toasty, spicy, overripe fruit. Palate: round tannins, spicy, ripe fruit.

MAS CODINA VINYA FERRER 2008 TC
cabernet sauvignon.

87 Colour: cherry, garnet rim. Nose: spicy, dark chocolate, toasty. Palate: flavourful, spicy, ripe fruit.

MAS COMTAL

Mas Comtal, 1
08793 Avinyonet del Penedès (Barcelona)
☎: +34 938 970 052 - Fax: +34 938 970 591
mascomtal@mascomtal.com
www.mascomtal.com

POMELL DE BLANCS 2011 B
50% xarel.lo, 50% chardonnay.

87 Colour: bright straw. Nose: fresh, fresh fruit, white flowers, warm. Palate: flavourful, fruity, good acidity.

PÉTREA 2008 BFB
85% chardonnay, 15% xarel.lo.

91 Colour: bright yellow. Nose: powerfull, ripe fruit, sweet spices, creamy oak, fragrant herbs. Palate: rich, flavourful, fresh, good acidity, long.

MAS COMTAL ROSAT DE LLÀGRIMA 2011 RD
100% merlot.

88 Colour: rose, bright. Nose: powerfull, ripe fruit, floral, balanced. Palate: flavourful, full, ripe fruit.

MAS COMTAL S/C T ROBLE
merlot, cabernet sauvignon, cabernet franc.

85 Colour: cherry, garnet rim. Nose: spicy, scrubland, warm. Palate: flavourful, fruity, good finish.

ANTISTIANA 2008 T
85% merlot, 15% cabernet sauvignon.

90 Colour: cherry, garnet rim. Nose: ripe fruit, spicy, creamy oak, toasty, dark chocolate. Palate: powerful, flavourful, toasty, round tannins.

MAS COMTAL PREMIUM 2009 BR
50% xarel.lo, 50% chardonnay.

87 Colour: bright straw. Nose: medium intensity, fresh fruit, dried herbs, fine lees. Palate: fresh, fruity, flavourful, easy to drink.

MAS COMTAL CUVÈE PRESTIGE 2006 BN
50% xarel.lo, 50% chardonnay.

88 Colour: bright yellow. Nose: candied fruit, dry nuts, floral, dried herbs. Palate: light-bodied, flavourful, complex, long, toasty.

MAS RODÓ

Finca Mas Rodo, km. 2 Ctra. Sant Pere Sacarrera a Sant Joan de Mediona
08773 Sant Joan de Mediona (Barcelona)
☎: +34 932 385 780 - Fax: +34 932 174 356
info@masrodo.com
www.masrodo.com

MAS RODÓ RIESLING 2011 BFB
85% riesling, 15% montonega.

90 Colour: bright yellow. Nose: ripe fruit, sweet spices, creamy oak, fragrant herbs. Palate: rich, flavourful, fresh, good acidity, toasty.

MAS RODÓ MONTONEGA 2010 B
100% montonega.

87 Colour: bright yellow. Nose: ripe fruit, scrubland, earthy notes. Palate: light-bodied, fresh, flavourful.

MAS RODÓ MACABEO 2010 B
100% macabeo.

85 Colour: bright yellow. Nose: powerfull, ripe fruit, sweet spices, creamy oak, fragrant herbs. Palate: rich, flavourful, fresh, good acidity.

MAS RODÓ CABERNET SAUVIGNON 2009 T
100% cabernet sauvignon.

88 Colour: bright cherry. Nose: ripe fruit, sweet spices, creamy oak, expressive. Palate: flavourful, fruity, toasty.

MAS RODÓ MERLOT 2009 TC
100% merlot.

80 Colour: cherry, garnet rim. Nose: fruit preserve, grassy, herbaceous, spicy. Palate: flavourful, spirituous.

MASET DEL LLEÓ

C-244, Km. 32,5
08792 La Granada del Penedès (Barcelona)
☎: +34 902 200 250 - Fax: +34 938 921 333
info@maset.com
www.maset.com

MASET DEL LLEÓ XAREL.LO BLANC DE BLANCS 2011 B
xarel.lo.

87 Colour: bright straw. Nose: white flowers, ripe fruit, fruit expression. Palate: flavourful, fruity, fresh.

MASET DEL LLEÓ CHARDONNAY FLOR DE MAR 2011 B
chardonnay.

87 Colour: bright straw. Nose: white flowers, fresh fruit, expressive. Palate: flavourful, fruity, fresh.

MASET DEL LLEÓ MERLOT 2011 RD
merlot.

85 Colour: light cherry. Nose: floral, ripe fruit, fragrant herbs, fresh. Palate: powerful, flavourful, fresh, fruity.

MASET DEL LLEÓ TEMPRANILLO SELECCIÓN 2010 T
tempranillo.

86 Colour: deep cherry. Nose: fruit preserve, sweet spices, powerfull, toasty. Palate: fine bitter notes, sweetness, powerful.

MASET DEL LLEÓ MERLOT FOC 2008 TR
merlot.

88 Colour: cherry, garnet rim. Nose: toasty, spicy, fruit liqueur notes. Palate: ripe fruit, fine bitter notes, good acidity.

MASET DEL LLEÓ CABERNET SAUVIGNON 2008 TR
cabernet sauvignon.

87 Colour: cherry, garnet rim. Nose: toasty, creamy oak, ripe fruit. Palate: good acidity, fine bitter notes, ripe fruit.

MATA D'ABELLÓ

Can Mata D'Abelló
08790 Gélida (Barcelona)
☎: +34 935 039 318 - Fax: +34 935 039 3189
jalemany@matadabello.com
www.matadabello.com

FINCA AVELLÓ MERLOT 2010 T
merlot.

86 Colour: cherry, garnet rim. Nose: powerfull, fruit preserve, cocoa bean. Palate: flavourful, fruity, good structure.

MIQUEL PONS

Baix Llobregat, 5
08792 La Granada (Barcelona)
☎: +34 938 974 541 - Fax: +34 938 974 710
miquelpons@cavamiquelpons.com
www.cavamiquelpons.com

MONTARGULL 2011 BFB
100% xarel.lo.

90 Colour: bright yellow. Nose: powerfull, ripe fruit, sweet spices, creamy oak, floral. Palate: rich, smoky afterpalate:, flavourful, fresh, good acidity.

NURIA DE MONTARGULL 2011 BFB
moscatel, chardonnay.

85 Colour: bright straw, greenish rim. Nose: floral, ripe fruit, neat, medium intensity. Palate: correct, easy to drink.

MIQUEL PONS 2007 T
cabernet sauvignon.

84

MONT MARÇAL

Finca Manlleu
08732 Castellví de la Marca (Barcelona)
☎: +34 938 918 281 - Fax: +34 938 919 045
mrivas@mont-marcal.com
www.mont-marcal.com

MONT MARÇAL 2011 B
50% xarel.lo, 30% sauvignon blanc, 20% chardonnay.

85 Colour: bright straw. Nose: fresh, white flowers, ripe fruit, citrus fruit. Palate: flavourful, fruity, good acidity.

MONT MARÇAL 2011 RD
50% merlot, 35% cabernet sauvignon, 15% syrah.

85 Colour: light cherry, bright. Nose: powerfull, ripe fruit, expressive. Palate: fruity, good finish.

MONT MARÇAL 2011 T
40% merlot, 20% tempranillo, 15% syrah.

87 Colour: cherry, purple rim. Nose: balanced, ripe fruit, powerfull. Palate: flavourful, ripe fruit, correct.

NADAL

Finca Nadal de la Boadella, s/n
08775 Torrelavit (Barcelona)
☎: +34 938 988 011 - Fax: +34 938 988 443
comunicacio@nadal.com
www.nadal.com

NADAL XAREL.LO 2011 B
100% xarel.lo.

85 Colour: bright straw. Nose: characterful, candied fruit, white flowers, faded flowers. Palate: flavourful, fruity, good acidity, balanced.

ORIOL ROSSELL

Propietat Can Cassanyes, s/n
08732 St. Marçal (Barcelona)
☎: +34 977 671 061 - Fax: +34 977 671 050
oriolrossell@oriolrossell.com
www.oriolrossell.com

VIROLET XAREL.LO 2011 B
100% xarel.lo.

90 Colour: bright yellow. Nose: balanced, expressive, ripe fruit, wild herbs, faded flowers. Palate: balanced, rich, fine bitter notes, long.

ROCAPLANA 2010 T
syrah.

87 Colour: deep cherry, purple rim. Nose: balanced, ripe fruit, cocoa bean. Palate: concentrated, flavourful, ripe fruit, long.

PARATÓ

Can Respall de Renardes
08733 (Barcelona)
☎: +34 938 988 182 - Fax: +34 938 988 510
info@parato.es
www.parato.es

FINCA RENARDES BLANC MACABEU + COUPAGE 2011 B
46% macabeo, 43% chardonnay, 11% xarel.lo.

90 Colour: bright straw. Nose: fresh, fresh fruit, white flowers, expressive. Palate: flavourful, fruity, good acidity, balanced.

PARATÓ XAREL.LO 2011 B
100% xarel.lo.

88 Colour: bright straw. Nose: fresh, white flowers, grassy, ripe fruit. Palate: flavourful, fruity, good acidity, balanced.

PARATÓ ÁTICA TRES X TRES 2010 B
62% xarel.lo, 33% chardonnay, 5% macabeo.

87 Colour: bright straw. Nose: powerfull, candied fruit, citrus fruit. Palate: flavourful, fine bitter notes, warm.

PARATÓ PINOT NOIR 2011 RD
100% pinot noir.

87 Colour: rose, purple rim. Nose: powerfull, ripe fruit, red berry notes, floral. Palate: , powerful, fruity, fresh.

FINCA RENARDES 2011 T
tempranillo, cabernet sauvignon, cariñena.

88 Colour: cherry, purple rim. Nose: ripe fruit, balanced. Palate: fruity, flavourful, good finish, spicy.

PARATÓ SAMSÓ 2008 TR
cariñena.

89 Colour: cherry, garnet rim. Nose: ripe fruit, spicy, creamy oak, toasty, complex. Palate: powerful, flavourful, toasty, round tannins.

PARATÓ ÁTICA PINOT NOIR 2007 TR
100% pinot noir.

88 Colour: pale ruby, brick rim edge. Nose: ripe fruit, earthy notes, fine reductive notes, spicy. Palate: powerful, flavourful, long, spicy.

PARATÓ NEGRE CLÀSSIC 2004 TR
70% cabernet sauvignon, 30% tempranillo.

88 Colour: cherry, garnet rim. Nose: ripe fruit, spicy, old leather, cigar. Palate: powerful, flavourful, toasty.

PARDAS

Finca Can Comas, s/n
08775 Torrelavit (Barcelona)
☎: +34 938 995 005
pardas@cancomas.com
www.pardas.net

PARDAS RUPESTRIS 2011 B
68% xarel.lo, 17% malvasía, 15% xarel.lo.

88 Colour: bright straw. Nose: expressive, fruit expression, citrus fruit. Palate: balanced, flavourful, fine bitter notes.

PARDAS ASPRIU 2010 B
100% xarel.lo.

92 Colour: bright straw. Nose: faded flowers, ripe fruit, creamy oak, sweet spices. Palate: flavourful, sweetness, fine bitter notes, good acidity.

PARDAS XAREL.LO 2009 B
100% xarel.lo.

88 Colour: bright yellow. Nose: faded flowers, candied fruit, fruit preserve. Palate: fine bitter notes, powerful, ripe fruit.

PARDAS ASPRIU 2009 T
100% cabernet franc.

94 Colour: deep cherry. Nose: toasty, spicy, earthy notes, ripe fruit, fruit expression, scrubland. Palate: flavourful, spicy, ripe fruit, fine bitter notes.

PARDAS NEGRE FRANC 2009 T
66% cabernet franc, 23% cabernet sauvignon, 11% sumoll.

91 Colour: deep cherry. Nose: ripe fruit, sweet spices, mineral. Palate: flavourful, powerful, fine bitter notes, round tannins.

COLLITA ROJA 2009 T
90% sumoll, 10% marselan.

89 Colour: bright cherry. Nose: ripe fruit, sweet spices, creamy oak. Palate: flavourful, fruity, toasty, round tannins.

PARÉS BALTÀ

Masía Can Baltá, s/n
08796 Pacs del Penedès (Barcelona)
☎: +34 938 901 399 - Fax: +34 938 901 143
paresbalta@paresbalta.com
www.paresbalta.com

INDÍGENA 2011 B
100% garnacha blanca.

94 Colour: bright straw. Nose: ripe fruit, citrus fruit, dried herbs. Palate: flavourful, good acidity, fine bitter notes, easy to drink, long.

CALCARI XAREL.LO 2011 B
100% xarel.lo.

89 Colour: bright straw. Nose: white flowers, expressive. Palate: flavourful, fruity, good acidity, balanced.

GINESTA 2011 B
100% gewürztraminer.

88 Colour: bright yellow. Nose: balanced, expressive, neat, citrus fruit, ripe fruit. Palate: correct, fine bitter notes, easy to drink.

BLANC DE PACS 2011 B
45% parellada, 21% xarel.lo, 34% macabeo.

87 Colour: bright straw. Nose: fresh, fresh fruit, white flowers, expressive. Palate: flavourful, fruity, good acidity, balanced.

ELECTIO XAREL.LO 2009 B
100% xarel.lo.

90 Colour: bright yellow. Nose: faded flowers, fruit preserve, citrus fruit. Palate: flavourful, fine bitter notes, good acidity, long.

RADIX 2011 RD
100% syrah.

88 Colour: rose, purple rim. Nose: powerfull, red berry notes, floral, candied fruit. Palate: , powerful, fruity, fresh.

ROS DE PACS 2011 RD
45% syrah, 41% merlot, 14% cabernet sauvignon.

82

INDÍGENA 2010 T
100% garnacha.

91 Colour: deep cherry. Nose: ripe fruit, spicy, toasty, mineral. Palate: round tannins, spicy, ripe fruit.

MAS ELENA 2009 T
merlot, cabernet sauvignon, cabernet franc.

91 Colour: cherry, garnet rim. Nose: spicy, creamy oak, toasty, characterful. Palate: powerful, flavourful, toasty, round tannins.

HISENDA MIRET GARNATXA 2009 T
100% garnacha.

90 Colour: deep cherry. Nose: fruit preserve, toasty, spicy, nose:tic coffee. Palate: flavourful, powerful, spicy, long.

PARÉS BALTÀ MAS PETIT 2009 T
76% cabernet sauvignon, 24% garnacha.

88 Colour: cherry, garnet rim. Nose: spicy, creamy oak, fruit expression. Palate: powerful, flavourful, toasty, round tannins.

MAS IRENE 2007 T
72% merlot, 28% cabernet franc.

92 Colour: cherry, garnet rim. Nose: ripe fruit, spicy, creamy oak, toasty, characterful. Palate: powerful, flavourful, toasty, round tannins.

MARTA DE BALTÀ 2007 T
100% syrah.

91 Colour: cherry, garnet rim. Nose: spicy, toasty, complex, nose:tic coffee, fruit expression. Palate: powerful, flavourful, toasty, round tannins.

PUIG ROMEU

Barri Piscina, 5
08779 La Llacuna (Barcelona)
☎: +34 938 976 206 - Fax: +34 938 977 087
info@puig-romeu.com
www.puig-romeu.com

VINYA JORDINA 2011 B
50% viognier, 30% sauvignon blanc, 20% garnacha blanca.

91 Colour: bright yellow. Nose: ripe fruit, floral, fragrant herbs, sweet spices, spicy. Palate: good acidity, correct, elegant, powerful, flavourful.

3 NEGRES 2007 T
50% merlot, 30% syrah, 20% ull de llebre.

89 Colour: cherry, garnet rim. Nose: ripe fruit, spicy, creamy oak, toasty, complex. Palate: powerful, flavourful, toasty, round tannins.

HAUTE LA MASUCA 2008 BN
25% pinot noir, 25% viognier, 15% chenin blanc, 10% albariño, 10% parellada, 15% otras.

89 Colour: bright straw. Nose: powerfull, candied fruit, lees reduction notes. Palate: fine bitter notes, good acidity, spicy.

BIEL.LO ESP RESERVA
50% pinot noir, 50% parellada.

88 Colour: bright straw. Nose: medium intensity, fresh fruit, dried herbs, fine lees, floral. Palate: fresh, fruity, flavourful, good acidity.

RENÉ BARBIER

Ctra. Sant Sadurní a St. Pere Riudebitlles, km. 5
08775 Torrelavit (Barcelona)
☎: +34 938 917 070 - Fax: +34 938 996 006
renebarbier@renebarbier.es
www.renebarbier.com

RENÉ BARBIER CHARDONNAY SELECCIÓN 2009 BFB
chardonnay.

87 Colour: bright yellow. Nose: toasty, spicy, dry nuts, candied fruit, creamy oak. Palate: fine bitter notes, rich, varietal.

RENÉ BARBIER SELECCIÓN CABERNET SAUVIGNON SELECCIÓN 2007 TC
cabernet sauvignon.

87 Colour: deep cherry. Nose: ripe fruit, spicy, scrubland, toasty. Palate: ripe fruit, spicy.

ROCAMAR

Major, 80
08755 Castellbisbal (Barcelona)
☎: +34 937 720 900 - Fax: +34 937 721 495
info@rocamar.net
www.rocamar.net

ROCAMAR TEMPRANILLO 2009 T
tempranillo.

85 Colour: cherry, garnet rim. Nose: balanced, sweet spices, ripe fruit. Palate: correct, fruity, easy to drink.

ROVELLATS

Finca Rovellats - Bº La Bleda
08731 Sant Marti Sarroca (Barcelona)
☎: +34 934 880 575 - Fax: +34 934 880 819
rovellats@cavasrovellats.com
www.cavasrovellats.com

ROVELLATS BLANC PRIMAVERA 2011 B
50% xarel.lo, 30% parellada, 20% macabeo.

85 Colour: bright yellow. Nose: faded flowers, ripe fruit, dried herbs. Palate: powerful, flavourful, fruity.

ROVELLATS MERLOT 2011 RD
100% merlot.

81

ROVELLATS BRUT DE TARDOR 2008 T
39% garnacha, 35% cabernet sauvignon, 26% merlot.

86 Colour: cherry, garnet rim. Nose: spicy, creamy oak, balsamic herbs, fruit preserve. Palate: powerful, flavourful, toasty.

SEGURA VIUDAS

Ctra. Sant Sadurní a St. Pere de Riudebitlles, Km. 5
08775 Torrelavit (Barcelona)
☎: +34 938 917 070 - Fax: +34 938 996 006
seguraviudas@seguraviudas.es
www.seguraviudas.com

CREU DE LAVIT 2010 BFB
xarel.lo.

87 Colour: bright yellow, greenish rim. Nose: floral, citrus fruit, balanced, spicy. Palate: flavourful, fruity, fine bitter notes, good acidity.

CLOS JUVÈNCIA 2011 RD
garnacha, merlot, syrah, tempranillo.

87 Colour: light cherry. Nose: powerfull, candied fruit, scrubland. Palate: flavourful, powerful, good acidity.

MAS D'ARANYÓ
2005 TR
tempranillo, cabernet sauvignon, cariñena.

87 Colour: cherry, garnet rim. Nose: spicy, creamy oak, toasty, warm. Palate: powerful, flavourful, toasty, round tannins.

SURIOL

Can Suriol del Castell
08736 Font-Rubí (Barcelona)
☎: +34 938 978 426 - Fax: +34 938 978 426
cansuriol@suriol.com
www.suriol.com

CASTELL DE GRABUAC 2010 B
xarel.lo.

88 Colour: bright yellow. Nose: citrus fruit, ripe fruit, dried herbs, floral. Palate: flavourful, balanced, round.

SURIOL DONZELLA 2010 B
xarel.lo.

86 Colour: bright straw. Nose: white flowers, expressive, ripe fruit. Palate: flavourful, fruity, good acidity, warm.

SURIOL SELECCIÓ ROSAT 2011 RD
garnacha.

82

SURIOL SELECCIO 2011 T
merlot, garnacha, ull de llebre.

84

SURIOL DOLC 2010 T
merlot.

88 Colour: dark mahogany. Nose: ripe fruit, dry nuts, varnish, aged wood nuances, toasty. Palate: correct, fine bitter notes, sweet, spicy, long.

CASTELL DE GRABUAC 2006 TC
pinot noir.

88 Colour: cherry, garnet rim. Nose: ripe fruit, spicy, toasty, complex, damp earth. Palate: flavourful, toasty, long, round tannins.

TERRAPRIMA

Can Ràfols dels Caus, s/n
08792 Avinyonet del Penedès (Barcelona)
☎: +34 938 970 013 - Fax: +34 938 970 370
info@terraprima.es
www.terraprima.es

TERRAPRIMA 2011 B
xarel.lo, riesling.

88 Colour: bright yellow. Nose: fresh, balanced, floral, citrus fruit. Palate: fruity, flavourful, fine bitter notes, good acidity.

TERRAPRIMA 2009 T
cabernet franc, garnacha, syrah.

88 Colour: cherry, garnet rim. Nose: ripe fruit, spicy, creamy oak, characterful. Palate: powerful, flavourful, toasty, round tannins.

TORELLÓ

Can Martí de Baix, Ctra. de Sant Sadurni a Gélida - Apdo. Correos 8
08770 Sant Sadurní D'Anoia (Barcelona)
☎: +34 938 910 793 - Fax: +34 938 910 877
torello@torello.es
www.torello.com

CRISALYS 2011 B
xarel.lo.

88 Colour: bright straw. Nose: powerfull, characterful, toasty, spicy, ripe fruit. Palate: flavourful, powerful, fine bitter notes.

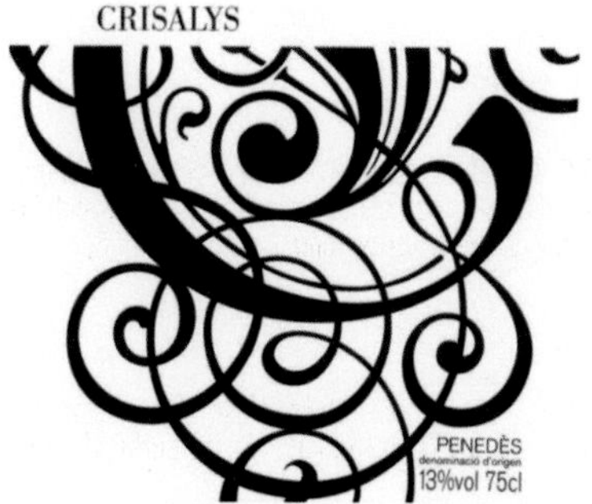

VITTIOS VENDIMIA TARDÍA 2011 B
xarel.lo.

88 Colour: golden. Nose: powerfull, honeyed notes, candied fruit, fragrant herbs, white flowers. Palate: flavourful, sweet, fresh, fruity, good acidity, long.

PETJADES 2011 RD
merlot.

90 Colour: rose, purple rim. Nose: powerfull, ripe fruit, red berry notes, floral, expressive, mineral. Palate: , powerful, fruity, fresh.

RAIMONDA 2006 TR
cabernet sauvignon, merlot.

89 Colour: cherry, garnet rim. Nose: powerfull, characterful, ripe fruit, overripe fruit, dark chocolate. Palate: powerful, sweetness, fine bitter notes, round tannins.

VALL DOLINA

Plaça de la Creu, 1
08795 Olesa de Bonesvalls (Barcelona)
☎: +34 938 984 181 - Fax: +34 938 984 181
info@valldolina.com
www.valldolina.com

VALL DOLINA XAREL.LO "ECOLÓGICO" 2011 B
xarel.lo.

90 Colour: yellow, greenish rim. Nose: floral, ripe fruit, dried herbs, expressive, mineral. Palate: powerful, flavourful, balanced, good acidity.

VALL DOLINA ROSAT ECO 2011 RD
merlot.

86 Colour: rose. Nose: powerfull, ripe fruit, red berry notes, floral. Palate: flavourful, fine bitter notes, ripe fruit, easy to drink.

VALL DOLINA MERLOT CABERNET SAUVIGNON 2010 T
merlot, cabernet sauvignon.

83

BONES VALLS CABERNET SAUVIGNON 2009 T
cabernet sauvignon.

89 Colour: cherry, garnet rim. Nose: ripe fruit, spicy, creamy oak, toasty, complex. Palate: powerful, flavourful, toasty, round tannins, balanced.

VALLFORMOSA

La Sala, 45
08735 Vilobi del Penedès (Barcelona)
☎: +34 938 978 286 - Fax: +34 938 978 355
vallformosa@vallformosa.es
www.vallformosa.com

DOMÈNECH VIDAL - MASIA FREYÈ PARELLADA MUSCAT 2011 B
parellada, moscatel.

89 Colour: bright straw. Nose: expressive, ripe fruit, fruit expression. Palate: flavourful, fruity, fresh.

DOMÈNECH VIDAL - LA SALA XAREL.LO MACABEO CHARDONNAY 2011 B
xarel.lo, macabeo, chardonnay.

89 Colour: bright straw. Nose: fresh, fresh fruit, white flowers, expressive. Palate: flavourful, fruity, good acidity, balanced.

DOMÈNECH VIDAL - MASIA FREYÈ XAREL.LO CHARDONNAY 2011 B
xarel.lo, chardonnay.

88 Colour: bright straw. Nose: fresh fruit, white flowers, ripe fruit. Palate: flavourful, fruity, good acidity, balanced.

MARINA DE VALLFORMOSA 2011 B

86 Colour: pale. Nose: expressive, fresh fruit, citrus fruit. Palate: fine bead, good acidity, ripe fruit.

DOMÈNECH VIDAL - LA SALA MERLOT SUMOLL TEMPRANILLO 2011 RD
merlot, sumoll, tempranillo.

89 Colour: rose, purple rim. Nose: powerfull, ripe fruit, red berry notes, floral, expressive. Palate: fleshy, powerful, fruity, fresh.

DOMÈNECH VIDAL - MASIA FREYÈ MERLOT SUMOLL 2011 RD
merlot, sumoll.

88 Colour: rose, purple rim. Nose: powerfull, ripe fruit, red berry notes, floral. Palate: , powerful, fruity, fresh.

MARINA DE VALLFORMOSA 2011 RD

85 Colour: rose. Nose: floral, red berry notes, candied fruit. Palate: flavourful, sweetness, good acidity.

DOMÈNECH VIDAL - LA SALA TEMPRANILLO CABERNET SAUVIGNON GARNACHA 2010 T
tempranillo, cabernet sauvignon, garnacha.

88 Colour: cherry, purple rim. Nose: red berry notes, ripe fruit, expressive. Palate: correct, fine bitter notes, flavourful.

VINS I CAVES CUSCÓ BERGA

Esplugues, 7
08793 Avinyonet del Penedès (Barcelona)
☎: +34 938 970 164
cuscoberga@cuscoberga.com
www.cuscoberga.com

CUSCÓ BERGA MUSCAT 2011 B
100% moscatel.

83

CUSCÓ BERGA CHARDONNAY 2010 B
100% chardonnay.

82

CUSCÓ BERGA MERLOT SELECCIÓ 2011 RD
100% merlot.

83

CUSCÓ BERGA CABERNET 2007 TC
80% cabernet sauvignon, 20% merlot.

86 Colour: cherry, garnet rim. Nose: powerfull, warm, ripe fruit, toasty. Palate: spirituous, sweetness, fine bitter notes.

LOCATION:

Covering one of the eastern extremes of the Central Catalonian Depression; it covers the natural region of Bages, of which the city of Manresa is the urban centre. To the south the region is bordered by the Montserrat mountain range, the dividing line which separates it from Penedés. It comprises the municipal areas of Fonollosa, Monistrol de Caldres, Sant Joan de Vilatorrada, Artés, Avinyó, Balsareny, Calders, Callús, Cardona, Castellgalí, Castellfollit del Boix, Castellnou de Bages, Manresa, Mura, Navarcles, Navàs, El Pont de Vilomara, Rajadell, Sallent, Sant Fruitós de Bages, Sant Mateu de Bages, Sant Salvador de Guardiola, Santpedor, Santa María d'Oló, Súria and Talamanca.

CLIMATE:

Mid-mountain Mediterranean, with little rainfall (500 mm to 600 mm average annual rainfall) and greater temperature contrasts than in the Penedès.

SOIL:

The vineyards are situated at an altitude of about 400 m. The soil is franc-clayey, franc-sandy and franc-clayey-sandy.

GRAPE VARIETIES:

WHITE: *Chardonnay, Gewürztraminer, Macabeo, Picapoll, Parellada, Sauvignon Blanc.*
RED: *Sumoll, Ull de Llebre* (*Tempranillo*), *Merlot, Cabernet Franc, Cabernet Sauvignon, Syrah* and *Garnacha.*

FIGURES:

Vineyard surface: 450 – **Wine-Growers:** 94 – **Wineries:** 11 – **2011 Harvest rating:** Excellent – **Production:** 874,976 litres – **Market percentages:** 70% domestic. 30% export

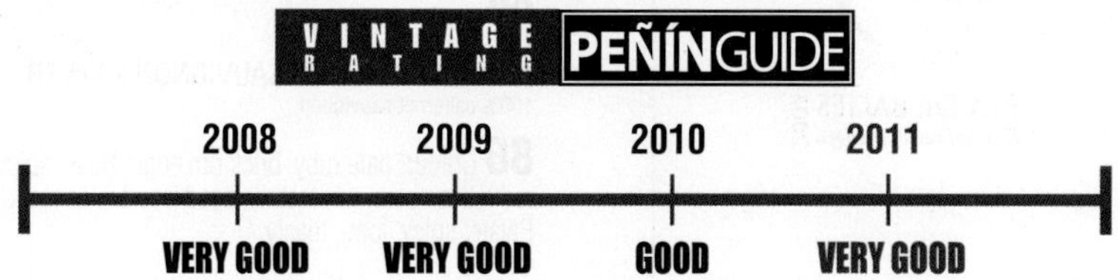

CONSEJO REGULADOR
Casa de La Culla - La Culla, s/n - 08240 Manresa (Barcelona) - ☎: +34 938 748 236 - Fax: +34 938 748 094
@ info@dopladebages.com - www.dopladebages.com

ABADAL

Santa María d'Horta d'Avinyó
08279 Santa María D'Horta D'Avinyó (Barcelona)
☎: +34 938 743 511 - Fax: +34 938 737 204
info@abadal.net
www.abadal.net

ABADAL PICAPOLL 2011 B
100% picapoll.

91 Colour: bright straw. Nose: fresh, fresh fruit, white flowers, expressive, fragrant herbs, citrus fruit, mineral. Palate: flavourful, fruity, good acidity, balanced.

NUAT 2009 B
80% picapoll, 20% macabeo.

89 Colour: bright yellow. Nose: powerfull, ripe fruit, creamy oak, fragrant herbs. Palate: rich, flavourful, fresh, good acidity, toasty.

ABADAL CABERNET SAUVIGNON 2011 RD
90% cabernet sauvignon, 10% sumoll.

86 Colour: rose, purple rim. Nose: powerfull, red berry notes, floral, candied fruit, fragrant herbs. Palate: , easy to drink, light-bodied, fruity.

ABADAL 3.9 2008 TR
85% cabernet sauvignon, 15% syrah.

93 Colour: cherry, garnet rim. Nose: ripe fruit, spicy, fine reductive notes, earthy notes, scrubland. Palate: powerful, flavourful, complex, balanced.

ABADAL 5 MERLOT 2008 TR
100% merlot.

89 Colour: dark-red cherry, garnet rim. Nose: mineral, ripe fruit, old leather, spicy. Palate: powerful, flavourful, balsamic, long.

ABADAL SELECCIÓ 2007 TR
40% cabernet sauvignon, 40% cabernet franc, 15% syrah, 5% sumoll, 5% mandó.

93 Colour: cherry, garnet rim. Nose: ripe fruit, spicy, toasty, nose:tic coffee, earthy notes, scrubland. Palate: powerful, flavourful, toasty.

CELLER COOPERATIU D'ARTÉS SCCL - CAVES ARTIUM

Cr. Rocafort, 44
08271 Artés (Barcelona)
☎: +34 938 305 325 - Fax: +34 938 306 289
artium@cavesartium.com
www.cavesartium.com

ARTIUM MERLOT CAPRICI 2010 T
100% merlot.

85 Colour: cherry, garnet rim. Nose: mineral, fruit preserve, damp earth, scrubland. Palate: spirituous, powerful, flavourful, spicy.

ARTIUM CABERNET SAUVIGNON 2009 T ROBLE
90% cabernet sauvignon, 10% merlot.

85 Colour: cherry, garnet rim. Nose: ripe fruit, fruit preserve, dried herbs, spicy. Palate: ripe fruit, long, flavourful.

ARTIUM ROQUES ALBES 2008 TC
50% cabernet sauvignon, 50% merlot.

83

ARTIUM MERLOT 2006 TC
100% merlot.

84

ARTIUM CABERNET SAUVIGNON 2005 TR
100% cabernet sauvignon.

86 Colour: pale ruby, brick rim edge. Nose: spicy, fine reductive notes, wet leather, aged wood nuances, ripe fruit. Palate: spicy, long, toasty.

EL MOLI

Camí de Rajadell, Km. 3
08241 Manresa (Barcelona)
☎: +34 931 021 965 - Fax: +34 931 021 965
collbaix@cellerelmoli.com
www.cellerelmoli.com

COLLBAIX SINGULAR 2011 B
90% macabeo, 10% picapoll.

90 Colour: bright straw. Nose: floral, citrus fruit, spicy, expressive, ripe fruit. Palate: flavourful, rich, complex, long, good acidity, balanced.

COLLBAIX MACABEO PICAPOLL 2011 B
65% picapoll, 35% macabeo.

87 Colour: bright straw. Nose: medium intensity, fresh, fragrant herbs. Palate: flavourful, fruity, fine bitter notes.

U D'URPINA 2009 T
100% cabernet sauvignon.

89 Colour: cherry, garnet rim. Nose: ripe fruit, spicy, toasty, earthy notes, smoky. Palate: powerful, flavourful, toasty, round tannins, long.

COLLBAIX SINGULAR 2008 T
100% cabernet sauvignon.

91 Colour: cherry, garnet rim. Nose: ripe fruit, spicy, creamy oak, complex, wild herbs. Palate: powerful, flavourful, toasty, round tannins.

COLLBAIX CUPATGE 2008 T
30% cabernet sauvignon, 30% merlot, 30% tempranillo, 10% cabernet franc.

88 Colour: cherry, garnet rim. Nose: ripe fruit, toasty, earthy notes, sweet spices, balsamic herbs. Palate: powerful, flavourful, toasty, round tannins.

COLLBAIX LA LLOBETA 2007 T
60% cabernet sauvignon, 40% merlot.

87 Colour: cherry, garnet rim. Nose: ripe fruit, balsamic herbs, earthy notes, creamy oak. Palate: long, round, powerful, flavourful.

HERETAT OLLER DEL MAS

Ctra. de Igualada (C-37), km. 91
08241 Manresa (Barcelona)
☎: +34 938 768 315 - Fax: +34 932 056 949
info@ollerdelmas.com
www.ollerdelmas.com

BERNAT OLLER BLANC DE PICAPOLLS 2011 B
50% picapoll, 50% picapoll negro.

89 Colour: bright straw. Nose: white flowers, fragrant herbs, mineral, citrus fruit, ripe fruit. Palate: fresh, fruity, light-bodied, easy to drink.

PETIT BERNAT 2011 T
40% syrah, 30% cabernet franc, 20% merlot, 10% picapoll negro.

87 Colour: bright cherry. Nose: ripe fruit, sweet spices, creamy oak, expressive. Palate: flavourful, fruity, toasty, round tannins.

ARNAU OLLER SELECCIÓ DE LA FAMILIA 2007 T
100% merlot.

90 Colour: cherry, garnet rim. Nose: ripe fruit, earthy notes, fragrant herbs, spicy. Palate: complex, powerful, flavourful, balanced.

BERNAT OLLER 2007 T
90% merlot, picapoll negro.

89 Colour: cherry, garnet rim. Nose: ripe fruit, wild herbs, creamy oak, medium intensity. Palate: flavourful, spicy, good finish.

JAUME GRAU - VINS GRAU

Ctra. C-37 de Igualada a Manresa, Km. 75,5
08255 Maians (Barcelona)
☎: +34 938 356 002 - Fax: +34 938 356 812
info@vinsgrau.com
www.vinsgrau.com

JAUME GRAU I GRAU PICAPOLL 2011 B
picapoll.

89 Colour: bright straw. Nose: dried flowers, ripe fruit, dried herbs, varietal. Palate: powerful, flavourful, correct.

JAUME GRAU I GRAU AVRVM 2011 B
sauvignon blanc, chardonnay.

86 Colour: bright straw. Nose: white flowers, candied fruit, fragrant herbs. Palate: light-bodied, fresh, fruity, easy to drink.

JAUME GRAU AVRVM SELECCIÓN 2007 BC
chardonnay, sauvignon blanc.

83

JAUME GRAU I GRAU MERLOT 2011 RD
merlot.

86 Colour: rose. Nose: floral, red berry notes, ripe fruit, lactic notes, fragrant herbs. Palate: fresh, fruity, light-bodied, easy to drink.

JAUME GRAU SELECCIÓN ESPECIAL 2011 T
tempranillo, merlot, cabernet franc, syrah.

88 Colour: cherry, purple rim. Nose: red berry notes, floral, ripe fruit, mineral, balsamic herbs. Palate: flavourful, fruity, good acidity, round tannins.

JAUME GRAU I GRAU SENSVS 2007 TC
cabernet franc, syrah.

88 Colour: pale ruby, brick rim edge. Nose: mineral, ripe fruit, scrubland, spicy, faded flowers. Palate: flavourful, spicy, round tannins.

JAUME GRAU I GRAU “GRATVS” 2006 TC
merlot, tempranillo.

87 Colour: pale ruby, brick rim edge. Nose: spicy, fine reductive notes, wet leather, aged wood nuances, balsamic herbs. Palate: spicy, long, flavourful.

JAUME GRAU I GRAU SENSVS 2004 TR
cabernet sauvignon.

88 Colour: pale ruby, brick rim edge. Nose: fine reductive notes, fruit liqueur notes, spicy, ripe fruit, toasty. Palate: spicy, elegant, long, toasty.

LOCATION:

The production region covers the eastern part of Majorca and consists of 18 municipal districts: Algaida, Ariany, Artá, Campos, Capdepera, Felanitx, Lluchamajor, Manacor, Mª de la Salud, Montuiri, Muro, Petra, Porreres, Sant Joan, Sant Llorens des Cardasar, Santa Margarita, Sineu and Vilafranca de Bonany.

CLIMATE:

Mediterranean, with an average temperature of 16°C and with slightly cool winters and dry, hot summers. The constant sea breeze during the summer has a notable effect on these terrains close to the coast. The wet season is in autumn and the average annual rainfall is between 450 mm and 500 mm.

SOIL:

The soil is made up of limestone rocks, which give limy-clayey soils. The reddish Colour: of the terrain is due to the presence of iron oxide. The clays and calcium and magnesium carbonates, in turn, provide the whitish Colour: which can also be seen in the vineyards.

GRAPE VARIETIES:

WHITE: *Prensal Blanc, Macabeo, Parellada, Moscatel* and *Chardonnay.*
RED: *Callet* (majority), *Manto Negro, Fogoneu, Tempranillo, Monastrell, Cabernet Sauvignon, Merlot* and *Syrah.*

FIGURES:

Vineyard surface: 356 – **Wine-Growers:** 105 – **Wineries:** 14 – **2011 Harvest rating:** N/A – **Production:** 1,121,000 litres – **Market percentages:** 91% domestic. 9% export

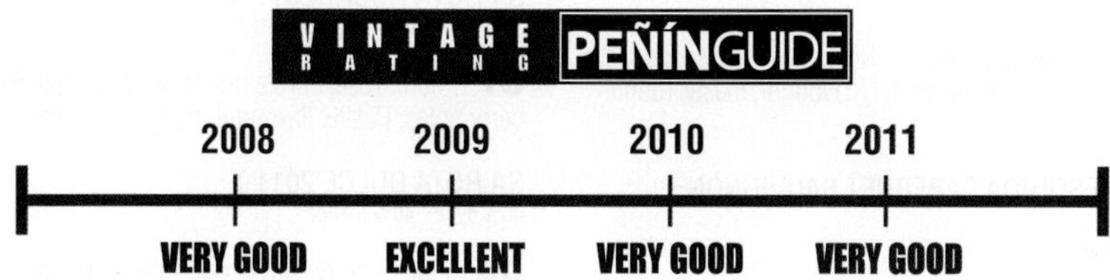

CONSEJO REGULADOR
Molí de N'Amengual. Dusai, 3 - 07260 Porreres (Illes Balears) - ☎: +34 971 168 569 - Fax: +34 971 168 569
@ info@plaillevantmallorca.es - www.plaillevantmallorca.es

BODEGA JAUME MESQUIDA

Vileta, 7
07260 Porreres (Illes Ballears)
☎: +34 971 647 106 - Fax: +34 971 168 205
info@jaumemesquida.com
www.jaumemesquida.com

MOLÍ DE VENT 2011 B
prensal, chardonnay, parellada.

89 Colour: bright straw. Nose: fresh, wild herbs, fresh fruit, citrus fruit. Palate: flavourful, fruity, good acidity, balanced, fine bitter notes.

MOLÍ DE VENT 2011 RD
callet, manto negro.

85 Colour: rose, purple rim. Nose: scrubland, medium intensity, ripe fruit. Palate: correct, ripe fruit.

MOLÍ DE VENT NEGRE 2009 T
callet, manto negro.

90 Colour: bright cherry. Nose: ripe fruit, sweet spices, creamy oak, scrubland. Palate: flavourful, fruity, round tannins, good acidity.

VIÑA DEL ALBARICOQUE 2009 T

90 Colour: deep cherry, garnet rim. Nose: complex, balanced, ripe fruit, sweet spices, creamy oak. Palate: flavourful, spicy.

JAUME MESQUIDA NEGRE 2008 T
callet, manto negro, cabernet sauvignon, syrah.

89 Colour: bright cherry, garnet rim. Nose: powerfull, balanced, expressive, ripe fruit. Palate: balanced, good acidity, round tannins.

JAUME MESQUIDA CABERNET SAUVIGNON 2007 TC
cabernet sauvignon.

90 Colour: cherry, garnet rim. Nose: ripe fruit, spicy, toasty, complex. Palate: powerful, flavourful, toasty, round tannins.

JAUME MESQUIDA CABERNET SAUVIGNON 2006 TC
100% cabernet sauvignon.

93 Colour: cherry, garnet rim. Nose: complex, spicy, earthy notes, ripe fruit, fragrant herbs, dark chocolate, elegant. Palate: balanced, good acidity.

BODEGA MESQUIDA MORA

Vileta, 7
07260 Porreres (Mallorca)
☎: +34 687 971 457
info@mesquidamora.com
www.mesquidamora.com

ACROLLAM BLANC 2011 B

89 Colour: bright yellow. Nose: balanced, wild herbs, fresh fruit. Palate: ripe fruit, balanced, good acidity.

ACROLLAM ROSAT 2011 RD

83

TRISPOL 2010 T

90 Colour: bright cherry, purple rim. Nose: powerfull, ripe fruit, spicy. Palate: powerful, flavourful, full, good acidity.

BODEGAS BORDOY

Camí de Muntanya s/n
07609 Lluchmajor (Illes Ballears)
☎: +34 971 774 081 - Fax: +34 971 771 246
sarota@bodegasbordoy.es

SA ROTA BLANC 2011 B
80% chardonnay, 20% prensal.

87 Colour: bright yellow, greenish rim. Nose: powerfull, fresh fruit, scrubland, dried flowers. Palate: ripe fruit, easy to drink.

SA ROTA BLANC CHARDONNAY 2010 BFB
100% chardonnay.

87 Colour: bright yellow. Nose: creamy oak, sweet spices, ripe fruit, varietal. Palate: flavourful, balanced, rich.

SA ROTA ROSAT 2011 RD
85% cabernet sauvignon, 15% merlot.

87 Colour: rose, purple rim. Nose: powerfull, fresh, red berry notes. Palate: flavourful, fruity, balanced.

SA ROTA DULCE 2011 T
60% syrah, 40% merlot.

85 Colour: cherry, purple rim. Nose: medium intensity, candied fruit, scrubland. Palate: flavourful, fruity.

SA ROTA 2010 T
90% cabernet sauvignon, 10% callet.

87 Colour: bright cherry, purple rim. Nose: spicy, scrubland, ripe fruit, fruit preserve. Palate: good structure, flavourful.

SA ROTA MERLOT 2008 T
100% merlot.

88 Colour: bright cherry, garnet rim. Nose: spicy, candied fruit, powerfull. Palate: rich, full, round tannins.

SA ROTA 2007 TR
60% merlot, 20% cabernet sauvignon, 20% syrah.

88 Colour: cherry, garnet rim. Nose: ripe fruit, spicy, creamy oak, toasty, complex. Taste powerful, flavourful, toasty, round tannins.

SA ROTA SYRAH 2007 T
100% syrah.

87 Colour: bright cherry, purple rim. Nose: cocoa bean, sweet spices, candied fruit. Palate: flavourful, easy to drink, round tannins.

SA ROTA 2007 TC
75% cabernet sauvignon, 15% merlot, 10% syrah.

86 Colour: cherry, garnet rim. Nose: ripe fruit, scrubland. Palate: powerful, flavourful, spicy.

BODEGAS PERE SEDA

Cid Campeador, 22
07500 Manacor (Illes Ballears)
☎: +34 971 605 087 - Fax: +34 971 604 856
pereseda@pereseda.com
www.pereseda.com

CHARDONNAY PERE SEDA 2011 B
100% chardonnay.

87 Colour: bright yellow. Nose: balanced, ripe fruit, white flowers. Palate: flavourful, easy to drink, good acidity.

PERE SEDA BLANC 2011 B
macabeo, prensal, chardonnay, parellada.

86 Colour: bright yellow. Nose: floral, ripe fruit, balanced. Palate: fruity, easy to drink, correct.

L'ARXIDUC PERE SEDA 2011 B
parellada, moscatel, chardonnay.

85 Colour: bright straw. Nose: balanced, medium intensity, fresh fruit, tropical fruit. Palate: flavourful, ripe fruit.

L'ARXIDUC PERE SEDA 2011 RD
70% merlot, 30% tempranillo.

86 Colour: rose. Nose: red berry notes, ripe fruit, powerfull. Palate: flavourful, fruity, balanced, powerful.

PERE SEDA ROSAT 2011 RD
callet, tempranillo, merlot.

86 Colour: coppery red, bright. Nose: balanced, ripe fruit, scrubland. Palate: flavourful, fruity, easy to drink.

PERE SEDA NEGRE 2010 T
merlot, tempranillo, callet, cabernet sauvignon.

87 Colour: bright cherry, purple rim. Nose: medium intensity, red berry notes, violets. Palate: fruity, correct, easy to drink.

GVIVM MERLOT-CALLET 2009 T
70% merlot, 30% callet.

90 Colour: bright cherry, garnet rim. Nose: ripe fruit, candied fruit, sweet spices. Palate: long, balanced, full.

L'ARXIDUC PERE SEDA NEGRE 2009 T
merlot, tempranillo, cabernet sauvignon, callet.

87 Colour: bright cherry, garnet rim. Nose: powerfull, creamy oak, sweet spices, cocoa bean, ripe fruit. Palate: flavourful, round tannins.

PERE SEDA 2008 TC
cabernet sauvignon, merlot, syrah, callet.

90 Colour: bright cherry. Nose: sweet spices, cocoa bean, balanced, red berry notes, ripe fruit. Palate: good structure, flavourful, long.

MOSSÈN ALCOVER 2008 T
73% cabernet sauvignon, 27% callet.

89 Colour: cherry, garnet rim. Nose: balanced, scrubland, spicy, ripe fruit. Palate: balanced, fruity aftestaste, long.

PERE SEDA 2007 TR
merlot, syrah, cabernet sauvignon, callet.

87 Colour: bright cherry. Nose: sweet spices, cocoa bean, candied fruit. Palate: fruity, flavourful, good acidity.

PERE SEDA BN
95% parellada, 5% chardonnay.

84

VINS MIQUEL GELABERT

Carrer d'en Sales, 50
07500 Manacor (Illes Balears)
☎: +34 971 821 444 - Fax: +34 971 596 441
vinsmg@vinsmiquelgelabert.com
www.vinsmiquelgelabert.com

GOLÓS BLANC 2010 B
60% riesling, 40% moscatel.

87 Colour: bright yellow. Nose: ripe fruit, white flowers, varietal. Palate: fruity, good acidity, correct.

SA VALL SELECCIÓ PRIVADA 2009 BFB
40% prensal, 40% chardonnay, 20% moscatel.

87 Colour: bright yellow. Nose: candied fruit, jasmine, honeyed notes, balanced, toasty. Palate: fruity, good finish, easy to drink.

CHARDONNAY ROURE BFB
100% chardonnay.

90 Colour: bright yellow. Nose: powerfull, ripe fruit, sweet spices, creamy oak. Palate: rich, smoky aftertaste, flavourful, fresh, good acidity.

GOLÓS 2009 T
callet, manto negro, fogoneu.

92 Colour: bright cherry, garnet rim. Nose: balsamic herbs, wild herbs, ripe fruit, mineral, spicy. Palate: complex, good structure, flavourful, good acidity.

AUTÓCTON 2009 T
60% callet, 30% manto negro, 10% fogoneu.

91 Colour: bright cherry, garnet rim. Nose: elegant, balanced, wild herbs, ripe fruit, mineral. Palate: long, round tannins, good acidity.

GRAN VINYA SON CAULES 2006 T
95% callet, 5% manto negro, fogoneu.

90 Colour: bright cherry, orangey edge. Nose: powerfull, toasty, scrubland. Palate: ripe fruit, spicy, long, good acidity.

VINYA DES MORÉ 2006 T
100% pinot noir.

90 Colour: cherry, garnet rim. Nose: ripe fruit, spicy, creamy oak, dark chocolate. Palate: powerful, flavourful, toasty, round tannins.

TORRENT NEGRE 2006 T
40% cabernet sauvignon, 30% merlot, 30% syrah.

89 Colour: cherry, garnet rim. Nose: balanced, complex, balsamic herbs, sweet spices, cocoa bean. Palate: ripe fruit, round tannins.

TORRENT NEGRE SELECCIÓ PRIVADA SYRAH 2005 T
100% syrah.

91 Colour: bright cherry. Nose: ripe fruit, creamy oak, sweet spices. Palate: flavourful, ripe fruit, long, round tannins.

PETIT TORRENT 2005 T
70% cabernet sauvignon, 15% merlot, 15% callet.

90 Colour: cherry, garnet rim. Nose: balsamic herbs, ripe fruit, balanced, sweet spices. Palate: flavourful, long.

TORRENT NEGRE CABERNET SELECCIÓ PRIVADA 2005 T
100% cabernet sauvignon.

88 Colour: cherry, garnet rim. Nose: powerfull, wild herbs, warm, spicy. Palate: flavourful, round tannins, good acidity.

VINS TONI GELABERT

Camí dels Horts de Llodrá Km. 1,3
07500 Manacor (Illes Balears)
☎: +34 610 789 531
info@vinstonigelabert.com
www.vinstonigelabert.com

TONI GELABERT CHARDONNAY 2011 BFB
100% chardonnay.

90 Colour: bright yellow. Nose: creamy oak, roasted coffee. Palate: good structure, rich, flavourful, ripe fruit, spicy.

FANGOS BLANC 2011 B
prensal, moscatel.

88 Colour: bright straw. Nose: faded flowers, balanced, expressive, fragrant herbs. Palate: flavourful, fruity, good acidity.

NEGRE DE SA COLONIA 2010 T
100% callet.

90 Colour: bright cherry. Nose: expressive, scrubland, ripe fruit. Palate: spicy, fruity, easy to drink, elegant.

EQUILIBRI 2009 T
callet, cabernet sauvignon, syrah.

89 Colour: bright cherry. Nose: ripe fruit, sweet spices, expressive, scrubland. Palate: flavourful, fruity, toasty, round tannins.

TONI GELABERT COLONIA U 2008 TC
cabernet sauvignon, otras.

90 Colour: cherry, purple rim. Nose: balanced, scrubland, ripe fruit. Palate: full, flavourful, good structure.

FANGOS NEGRE 2008 T
callet, merlot, cabernet sauvignon, syrah.

90 Colour: cherry, garnet rim. Nose: powerfull, warm, ripe fruit, sweet spices. Palate: flavourful, round tannins.

TONI GELABERT NEGRE SELECCIO 2007 T
cabernet sauvignon, manto negro.

91 Colour: bright cherry, garnet rim. Nose: complex, balsamic herbs, spicy, ripe fruit. Palate: full, flavourful, round tannins, long.

TONI GELABERT MERLOT 2007 T
100% merlot.

88 Colour: bright cherry. Nose: powerfull, spicy, warm, ripe fruit. Palate: flavourful, fruity, balanced.

SES HEREVES 2005 T
cabernet sauvignon, merlot, syrah.

90 Colour: bright cherry, orangey edge. Nose: spicy, creamy oak, warm, scrubland, fruit liqueur notes. Palate: powerful, flavourful, toasty, round tannins.

VINYES I BODEGUES MIQUEL OLIVER

Font, 26
07520 Petra-Mallorca (Illes Ballears)
☎: +34 971 561 117 - Fax: +34 971 561 117
bodega@miqueloliver.com
www.miqueloliver.com

AIA 2009 T
100% merlot.

91 Colour: bright cherry, garnet rim. Nose: ripe fruit, powerfull, expressive, scrubland. Palate: fruity, full, spicy, long.

ORIGINAL MUSCAT MIQUEL OLIVER 2011 B
100% moscatel.

89 Colour: bright yellow. Nose: white flowers, varietal, balanced, citrus fruit. Palate: fresh, fruity, good acidity, fine bitter notes.

ALEGRÍA 2011 RD
100% merlot.

86 Colour: light cherry. Nose: expressive, balanced, wild herbs, ripe fruit. Palate: correct, easy to drink.

XPERIMENT 2009 T
100% callet.

90 Colour: bright cherry, purple rim. Nose: ripe fruit, complex, balanced, cocoa bean. Palate: fruity, good acidity.

SES FERRITGES 2008 TC
callet, cabernet sauvignon, merlot, syrah.

92 Colour: bright cherry. Nose: cocoa bean, creamy oak, ripe fruit, balsamic herbs. Palate: balanced, good acidity, spicy, ripe fruit.

SYRAH NEGRE MIQUEL OLIVER 2007 T
100% syrah.

89 Colour: cherry, garnet rim. Nose: ripe fruit, spicy, creamy oak, toasty. Palate: powerful, flavourful, toasty, round tannins.

DO Ca. PRIORAT

TARRAGONA
Torroja
Consejo Regulador
DO Boundary

LOCATION:

In the province of Tarragona. It is made up of the municipal districts of La Morera de Montsant, Scala Dei, La Vilella, Gratallops, Bellmunt, Porrera, Poboleda, Torroja, Lloá, Falset and Mola.

CLIMATE:

Although with Mediterranean influences, it is temperate and dry. One of the most important characteristics is the practical absence of rain during the summer, which ensures very healthy grapes. The average rainfall is between 500 and 600 mm per year.

SOIL:

This is probably the most distinctive characteristic of the region and precisely what has catapulted it to the top positions in terms of quality, not only in Spain, but around the world. The soil, thin and volcanic, is composed of small pieces of slate (llicorella), which give the wines a markedly mineral character. The vineyards are located on terraces and very steep slopes.

GRAPE VARIETIES:

WHITE: *Chenin Blanc, Macabeo, Garnacha Blanca, Pedro Ximénez.*
RED: *Cariñena, Garnacha, Garnacha Peluda, Cabernet Sauvignon, Merlot, Syrah.*

FIGURES:

Vineyard surface: 1,887 – **Wine-Growers:** 637 – **Wineries:** 96 – **2011 Harvest rating:** N/A – **Production:** 3,292,593 litres – **Market percentages:** 51% domestic. 49% export

CONSEJO REGULADOR
Major, 2 - 43737 Torroja del Priorat (Tarragona) - ☎: +34 977 83 94 95 - Fax. +34 977 83 94 72
@ info@doqpriorat.org - www.doqpriorat.org

AGNÈS DE CERVERA

Ctra. El Molar - El Lloar, Km. 10
43736 El Molar (Tarragona)
☎: +34 977 054 851 - Fax: +34 977 054 851
comunicacion@agnesdecervera.com
www.agnesdecervera.com

LA PETITE AGNÈS 2011 T
85% garnacha, 15% mazuelo.

87 Colour: very deep cherry, purple rim. Nose: powerfull, ripe fruit, fruit preserve, scrubland. Palate: good structure, flavourful.

LYTOS 2010 T
45% mazuelo, 30% garnacha, 15% syrah, 5% cabernet sauvignon.

91 Colour: cherry, garnet rim. Nose: red berry notes, ripe fruit, mineral, creamy oak. Palate: spicy, powerful, flavourful, balanced.

KALOS 2010 T
85% mazuelo, 15% syrah.

90 Colour: bright cherry. Nose: sweet spices, creamy oak, mineral. Palate: flavourful, fruity, toasty, round tannins.

ARGELES 2010 T
50% garnacha, 40% mazuelo, 10% cabernet sauvignon.

89 Colour: deep cherry, purple rim. Nose: balanced, wild herbs, mineral. Palate: good structure, ripe fruit, long.

ALVARO PALACIOS

Afores, s/n
43737 Gratallops (Tarragona)
☎: +34 977 839 195 - Fax: +34 977 839 197
info@alvaropalacios.com

CAMINS DEL PRIORAT 2011 T
40% garnacha, 30% samsó, 5% syrah, 20% cabernet sauvignon, 5% merlot.

90 Colour: bright cherry. Nose: ripe fruit, raspberry, scrubland. Palate: flavourful, fruity, toasty, round tannins.

L'ERMITA 2010 TC
garnacha.

97 Colour: very deep cherry. Nose: scrubland, characterful, expressive, ripe fruit, toasty, sweet spices. Palate: flavourful, fine bitter notes, spicy, fine tannins.

FINCA DOFÍ 2010 TC
80% garnacha, 15% syrah, 5% cabernet sauvignon.

95 Colour: deep cherry. Nose: expressive, complex, elegant, scrubland, sweet spices. Palate: flavourful, ripe fruit, spicy, good acidity, fine bitter notes.

GRATALLOPS VI DE LA VILA 2010 T
65% garnacha, 15% samsó, 10% syrah, 10% cabernet sauvignon.

94 Colour: very deep cherry. Nose: sweet spices, ripe fruit, fruit expression, mineral. Palate: flavourful, spicy, ripe fruit, long, round tannins.

LES TERRASSES VINYES VELLES 2010 T
40% garnacha, 45% samsó, 10% cabernet sauvignon, 5% syrah.

93 Colour: cherry, garnet rim. Nose: toasty, sweet spices, fruit expression, earthy notes. Palate: flavourful, spicy, fine bitter notes, good acidity.

AUTOR

Balandra, 6
43737 Torroja de Priorat (Tarragona)
☎: +34 977 839 285
adminbodega@rotllantorra.com
www.rotllantorra.com

AUTOR 2008 TR
garnacha, mazuelo, cabernet sauvignon.

91 Colour: deep cherry, garnet rim. Nose: balanced, expressive, cocoa bean, creamy oak. Palate: balanced, good acidity, fine bitter notes.

BLAI FERRÉ JUST

Piró, 28
43737 Gratallops (Tarragona)
☎: +34 647 217 751 - Fax: +34 977 839 507
blaiferrejust@yahoo.es

BILLO 2010 T
35% syrah, 35% garnacha, 20% cariñena, 10% cabernet sauvignon.

88 Colour: deep cherry, garnet rim. Nose: ripe fruit, balanced, dried herbs. Palate: flavourful, fruity, long.

DESNIVELL 2009 TC
80% garnacha, 20% cariñena.

90 Colour: cherry, garnet rim. Nose: powerfull, warm, ripe fruit. Palate: flavourful, concentrated, sweetness.

BODEGAS BORDALÁS GARCÍA (BG)

Ctra. T-710, Km. 9,5
43737 Gratallops (Tarragona)
☎: +34 977 839 434 - Fax: +34 977 839 434
bodegasbg@yahoo.es
www.bodegasbg.es

EL SI DEL MOLÍ 2011 B
garnacha blanca, macabeo.

85 Colour: bright straw. Nose: ripe fruit, dried flowers, fragrant herbs. Palate: light-bodied, fresh, fruity, fine bitter notes.

PAMATURA VI DE FAMILIA 2010 T
garnacha, cariñena, merlot.

85 Colour: black cherry, purple rim. Nose: slightly evolved, powerfull, sweet spices. Palate: flavourful, fruity.

GUETA LUPIA 2009 T
garnacha, cariñena, merlot, cabernet sauvignon.

88 Colour: cherry, garnet rim. Nose: spicy, creamy oak, overripe fruit, fine reductive notes. Palate: powerful, flavourful, toasty.

FRA FORT 2009 T
garnacha, cariñena.

87 Colour: deep cherry, garnet rim. Nose: powerfull, tobacco, spicy, overripe fruit. Palate: powerful, fine bitter notes.

GUETA LUPIA 2008 T
garnacha, cariñena, merlot, cabernet sauvignon.

88 Colour: cherry, garnet rim. Nose: powerfull, characterful, warm, toasty. Palate: powerful, fine bitter notes, good acidity.

BODEGAS MAS ALTA

Ctra. T-702, Km. 16,8
43375 La Vilella Alta (Tarragona)
☎: +34 977 054 151 - Fax: +34 977 817 194
info@bodegasmasalta.com
www.bodegasmasalta.com

ARTIGAS 2011 BFB
garnacha blanca, macabeo, pedro ximénez.

93 Colour: bright yellow. Nose: powerfull, ripe fruit, sweet spices, fragrant herbs. Palate: rich, flavourful, fresh, good acidity.

ELS PICS 2010 T

91 Colour: very deep cherry. Nose: characterful, ripe fruit, spicy, creamy oak. Palate: flavourful, powerful, fine bitter notes.

ARTIGAS 2009 T
garnacha, mazuelo, cabernet sauvignon.

94 Colour: cherry, garnet rim. Nose: ripe fruit, spicy, creamy oak, toasty, mineral. Palate: powerful, flavourful, toasty, round tannins.

LA BASSETA 2009 T

92 Colour: very deep cherry. Nose: ripe fruit, sweet spices, toasty, mineral. Palate: flavourful, powerful, fine bitter notes, good acidity, round tannins.

CIRERETS 2009 T

91 Colour: cherry, garnet rim. Nose: spicy, creamy oak, toasty, complex, mineral. Palate: powerful, flavourful, toasty, round tannins.

LA CREU ALTA 2005 T
50% cariñena, 35% garnacha, 15% cabernet sauvignon.

94 Colour: cherry, garnet rim. Nose: spicy, complex, fruit expression, new oak, earthy notes. Palate: powerful, flavourful, toasty, round tannins.

BUIL & GINÉ

Ctra. de Gratallops - Vilella Baixa, Km. 11,5
43737 Gratallops (Tarragona)
☎: +34 977 839 810 - Fax: +34 977 839 811
info@builgine.com
www.builgine.com

PLERET BLANC DOLÇ 2010 B
macabeo, garnacha blanca, pedro ximénez.

90 Colour: bright yellow. Nose: powerfull, fruit preserve, sweet spices. Palate: flavourful, sweetness, fine bitter notes.

JOAN GINÉ 2010 B BARRICA
garnacha blanca, pedro ximénez, macabeo.

84

GINÉ ROSAT 2010 RD
garnacha, merlot.

87 Colour: rose. Nose: red berry notes, fruit expression. Palate: flavourful, fruity.

GINÉ GINÉ 2009 T
garnacha, cariñena.

88 Colour: cherry, purple rim. Nose: fresh fruit, red berry notes, floral, spicy. Palate: flavourful, fruity, good acidity.

JOAN GINÉ 2007 T
garnacha, cariñena, cabernet sauvignon.

88 Colour: cherry, garnet rim. Nose: mineral, toasty, spicy, dark chocolate, ripe fruit. Palate: spicy, fine bitter notes, round tannins.

PLERET 2005 T
garnacha, cariñena, cabernet sauvignon, merlot, syrah.

88 Colour: dark-red cherry, garnet rim. Nose: balanced, powerfull, ripe fruit, wild herbs. Palate: fruity, easy to drink.

BURGOS PORTA

Mas Sinén, s/n
43376 Poboleda (Tarragona)
☎: +34 696 094 509
burgosporta@massinen.com
www.massinen.com

PETIT MAS SINÉN 2009 T
garnacha, cariñena, cabernet sauvignon, syrah, merlot.

89 Colour: black cherry, purple rim. Nose: medium intensity, spicy, ripe fruit. Palate: good acidity, balanced, fine bitter notes.

MAS SINÉN 2008 T
garnacha, cariñena, cabernet sauvignon, syrah.

90 Colour: cherry, garnet rim. Nose: toasty, spicy, overripe fruit. Palate: spicy, ripe fruit, fine bitter notes.

CASA GRAN DEL SIURANA

Mayor, 3
43738 Bellmunt del Priorat (Tarragona)
☎: +34 932 233 022 - Fax: +34 932 231 370
perelada@castilloperelada.com
www.castilloperelada.com

GR-174 2011 T
42% garnacha, 38% cariñena, 20% cabernet sauvignon.

90 Colour: bright cherry. Nose: sweet spices, expressive, fruit preserve. Palate: flavourful, fruity, toasty, round tannins.

GRAN CRUOR 2008 T
70% syrah, 20% cariñena, 10% garnacha.

93 Colour: cherry, garnet rim. Nose: ripe fruit, spicy, creamy oak, complex, mineral, dark chocolate. Palate: powerful, flavourful, toasty, round tannins.

CRUOR 2008 T
30% garnacha, 20% syrah, 10% merlot, 20% cabernet sauvignon, 20% cariñena.

91 Colour: bright cherry. Nose: sweet spices, creamy oak, expressive, overripe fruit. Palate: flavourful, fruity, toasty, round tannins.

CASTELL D'OR

Mare Rafols, 3- 1º 4º
08720 Vilafranca del Penedès (Barcelona)
☎: +34 938 905 446 - Fax: +34 938 905 446
castelldor@castelldor.com
www.castelldor.com

ABADÍA MEDITERRÀNIA 2010 TC
60% garnacha, 40% cariñena.

90 Colour: cherry, purple rim. Nose: balanced, spicy, wild herbs. Palate: good structure, flavourful, long.

GRAN ABADÍA MEDITERRÀNIA 2009 TR
50% garnacha, 35% cariñena, 15% cabernet sauvignon.

90 Colour: cherry, garnet rim. Nose: ripe fruit, spicy, creamy oak, toasty. Palate: powerful, flavourful, toasty, round tannins.

CELLER AIXALÀ I ALCAIT

Balandra, 43
43737 Torroja del Priorat (Tarragona)
☎: +34 977 839 516
pardelasses@gmail.com
www.pardelasses.com

DESTRANKIS 2010 T
80% garnacha, 20% cariñena.

88 Colour: cherry, garnet rim. Nose: ripe fruit, spicy, creamy oak, toasty. Palate: powerful, flavourful, toasty, round tannins.

PARDELASSES 2009 T
50% garnacha, 50% cariñena.

88 Colour: cherry, garnet rim. Nose: ripe fruit, spicy, creamy oak, fine reductive notes. Palate: powerful, flavourful, toasty.

LES CLIVELLES DE TORROJA 2009 TC
100% cariñena.

88 Colour: very deep cherry. Nose: ripe fruit, warm, toasty. Palate: powerful, flavourful, sweetness.

CELLER BARTOLOMÉ

Major, 23
43738 Bellmunt del Priorat (Tarragona)
☎: +34 616 478 581 - Fax: +34 977 320 448
cellerbartolome@hotmail.com
www.cellerbartolome.com

CLOS BARTOLOME 2008 T
45% garnacha, 45% cariñena, 10% cabernet sauvignon.

90 Colour: deep cherry, garnet rim. Nose: powerfull, expressive, cigar, dark chocolate, varnish. Palate: balanced, fine bitter notes, round tannins.

PRIMITIU DE BELLMUNT 2007 T
50% garnacha, 50% cariñena.

91 Colour: cherry, garnet rim. Nose: cocoa bean, sweet spices, ripe fruit. Palate: good structure, flavourful, fruity, round tannins.

PRIMITIU DE BELLMUNT 2005 T
50% garnacha, 50% cariñena.

89 Colour: deep cherry, garnet rim. Nose: ripe fruit, fruit preserve, spicy, varnish, cocoa bean. Palate: powerful, flavourful.

CELLER CASTELLET

Font de Dalt, 11
43739 Porrera (Tarragona)
☎: +34 977 828 044
info@cellercastellet.com
www.cellercastellet.com

EMPIT 2009 TC
50% garnacha, 30% cabernet sauvignon, 20% cariñena.

89 Colour: deep cherry. Nose: spicy, toasty, ripe fruit, mineral. Palate: flavourful, ripe fruit, spicy.

FERRAL 2009 T
65% garnacha, 15% cabernet sauvignon, 12% syrah, 8% merlot.

89 Colour: cherry, garnet rim. Nose: ripe fruit, sweet spices, balsamic herbs, mineral. Palate: flavourful, good structure, round tannins.

EMPIT SELECCIÓ 2009 TC
95% cariñena, 5% garnacha.

89 Colour: cherry, garnet rim. Nose: spicy, creamy oak, toasty, balsamic herbs, fruit liqueur notes. Palate: powerful, flavourful, toasty.

CELLER CECILIO

Piró, 28
43737 Gratallops (Tarragona)
☎: +34 977 839 181 - Fax: +34 977 839 507
celler@cellercecilio.com
www.cellercecilio.com

CELLER CECILIO BLANC 2011 B
100% garnacha blanca.

84

CELLER CECILIO NEGRE 2010 T
garnacha, cariñena, cabernet sauvignon.

88 Colour: deep cherry. Nose: ripe fruit, sweet spices, toasty. Palate: ripe fruit, good acidity, spicy.

L'ESPILL 2008 TC
garnacha, cariñena, cabernet sauvignon.

88 Colour: cherry, garnet rim. Nose: spicy, ripe fruit, balanced. Palate: fruity, good structure, round tannins.

L'ESPILL 2007 TC
garnacha, cariñena, cabernet sauvignon.

87 Colour: cherry, garnet rim. Nose: fruit preserve, sweet spices, powerfull. Palate: fruity, fine bitter notes, round tannins.

CELLER DE L'ABADÍA

De la Font, 38
43737 Gratallops (Tarragona)
☎: +34 627 032 134
jeroni@cellerabadia.com
www.cellerabadia.com

SANT JERONI DOLC 2010 T
80% cabernet sauvignon, 20% cariñena.

88 Colour: cherry, garnet rim. Nose: fruit preserve, aged wood nuances, nose:tic coffee, creamy oak. Palate: rich, flavourful, spirituous.

SANT JERONI "GARNATXA DE L'HORT 2010 T
70% garnacha, 30% syrah.

88 Colour: cherry, garnet rim. Nose: complex, ripe fruit, balsamic herbs, spicy, mineral. Palate: good structure, flavourful.

SANT JERONI CARINYENA I CABERNET 2009 T
80% cariñena, 20% cabernet sauvignon.

89 Colour: deep cherry, garnet rim. Nose: balsamic herbs, ripe fruit, mineral. Palate: ripe fruit, long, round tannins.

ALICE 2007 T
30% garnacha, 40% cariñena, 10% syrah, 10% cabernet sauvignon.

90 Colour: bright cherry. Nose: sweet spices, creamy oak, overripe fruit. Palate: flavourful, fruity, toasty, round tannins.

CLOS CLARA 2007 TC
40% garnacha, 40% cariñena, 10% syrah, 10% cabernet sauvignon.

90 Colour: cherry, garnet rim. Nose: mineral, earthy notes, ripe fruit, fruit expression, toasty. Palate: mineral, long, spicy, ripe fruit.

CELLER DE L'ENCASTELL

Castell, 13
43739 Porrera (Tarragona)
☎: +34 630 941 959
roquers@roquers.com
www.roquers.com

MARGE 2010 T

88 Colour: bright cherry. Nose: ripe fruit, sweet spices, creamy oak. Palate: flavourful, fruity, toasty, round tannins.

ROQUERS DE PORRERA 2009 TC

93 Colour: cherry, garnet rim. Nose: spicy, creamy oak, toasty, red berry notes, raspberry. Palate: powerful, flavourful, toasty, round tannins.

CELLER DEL PONT

Del Riu, 1- Baixos
43374 La Vilella Baixa (Tarragona)
☎: +34 977 828 231 - Fax: +34 977 828 231
cellerdelpont@gmail.com
www.cellerdelpont.com

LO GIVOT 2008 T
33% garnacha, 32% mazuelo, 25% cabernet sauvignon, syrah.

93 Colour: cherry, garnet rim. Nose: ripe fruit, spicy, toasty, complex, mineral. Palate: powerful, flavourful, toasty, round tannins, elegant.

CELLER DELS PINS VERS

Afores, s/n
43736 El Molar (Tarragona)
☎: +34 977 825 458 - Fax: +34 977 825 458
info@lafuina.com
www.lafuina.com

ELS PINS VERS 2008 T
garnacha, samsó, cabernet sauvignon, syrah.

90 Colour: cherry, garnet rim. Nose: spicy, creamy oak, toasty, complex, fruit preserve. Palate: powerful, flavourful, toasty, round tannins.

CELLER DEVINSSI

Masets, 1
43737 Gratallops (Tarragona)
☎: +34 977 839 523
devinssi@il-lia.com
www.devinssi.com

CUPATGE 2009 T
garnacha, cariñena, cabernet sauvignon, merlot, syrah.

90 Colour: cherry, garnet rim. Nose: overripe fruit, creamy oak, sweet spices. Palate: flavourful, powerful, ripe fruit.

ROCAPOLL 2008 T
cariñena.

90 Colour: dark-red cherry, garnet rim. Nose: balanced, ripe fruit, expressive, spicy, scrubland. Palate: powerful, flavourful, long.

MAS DE LES VALLS 2008 T
garnacha, cariñena, cabernet sauvignon.

88 Colour: cherry, garnet rim. Nose: ripe fruit, spicy, cocoa bean. Palate: flavourful, long, round tannins.

IL.LIA 2007 T
garnacha, cariñena, cabernet sauvignon.

87 Colour: cherry, garnet rim. Nose: fruit preserve, balsamic herbs, creamy oak. Palate: flavourful, spicy, long.

CELLER HIDALGO ALBERT

Finca Les Salanques, Pol. Ind. 14, Parc. 102
43376 Poboleda (Tarragona)
☎: +34 977 842 064 - Fax: +34 977 842 064
hialmi@yahoo.es

1270 A VUIT 2010 B
80% garnacha blanca, 20% viognier.

90 Colour: bright yellow. Nose: expressive, candied fruit, floral, powerfull. Palate: flavourful, fruity, rich, balanced.

1270 A VUIT 2008 T
garnacha, cariñena, merlot, syrah, cabernet sauvignon.

89 Colour: cherry, garnet rim. Nose: ripe fruit, spicy, scrubland. Palate: powerful, flavourful, round tannins, good acidity.

1270 A VUIT 2007 T
garnacha, cariñena, merlot, syrah, cabernet sauvignon.

92 Colour: cherry, garnet rim. Nose: ripe fruit, scrubland, earthy notes, spicy. Palate: powerful, flavourful, long, balsamic, spicy.

CELLER JORDI DOMENECH

Finca Les Comes
43376 Poboleda (Tarragona)
☎: +34 646 169 210
jordidomenech@live.com
www.cellerjordidomenech.com

CLOS PENAT 2009 TC
garnacha, syrah.

87 Colour: cherry, garnet rim. Nose: ripe fruit, sweet spices, dark chocolate, powerfull, characterful. Palate: flavourful, concentrated, fine bitter notes, good acidity.

PETIT CLOS PENAT 2008 T
garnacha, syrah.

91 Colour: cherry, garnet rim. Nose: spicy, creamy oak, toasty, overripe fruit. Palate: powerful, flavourful, toasty, round tannins.

CELLER MAS BASTE

Font, 38
43737 Gratallops (Tarragona)
☎: +34 629 300 291
info@cellermasbaste.com
www.cellermasbaste.com

PEITES 2011 T
80% garnacha, 20% syrah.

90 Colour: very deep cherry, purple rim. Nose: balanced, powerfull, balsamic herbs, ripe fruit. Palate: fruity, balanced.

PEITES 2010 TC
80% cariñena, 20% cabernet sauvignon.

87 Colour: cherry, garnet rim. Nose: fruit liqueur notes, balsamic herbs, earthy notes, creamy oak. Palate: powerful, flavourful, ripe fruit.

CLOS PEITES 2009 T
80% cariñena, 20% cabernet sauvignon.

90 Colour: cherry, garnet rim. Nose: ripe fruit, balanced, expressive, balsamic herbs. Palate: fruity, flavourful, round tannins.

CELLER MAS DE LES PERERES

Mas de Les Pereres, s/n
43376 Poboleda (Tarragona)
☎: +34 977 827 257 - Fax: +34 977 827 257
dirk@nunci.com
www.nunci.com

NUNCI ABOCAT 2010 B
macabeo, garnacha, moscatel de alejandría, moscatel grano menudo.

88 Colour: bright yellow. Nose: powerfull, candied fruit, citrus fruit. Palate: flavourful, long, ripe fruit.

NUNCI BLANC 2009 BFB
garnacha blanca, macabeo.

90 Colour: bright yellow. Nose: powerfull, ripe fruit, sweet spices, creamy oak, fragrant herbs. Palate: rich, flavourful, fresh, good acidity.

NUNCI ABOCAT 2009 B
macabeo, garnacha, moscatel de alejandría, moscatel grano menudo.

90 Colour: bright yellow. Nose: white flowers, fruit expression, tropical fruit, fragrant herbs. Palate: fresh, fruity, light-bodied, flavourful.

NUNCI BLANC 2008 BFB
garnacha, macabeo.

91 Colour: bright yellow. Nose: powerfull, ripe fruit, creamy oak, dried herbs. Palate: rich, smoky aftertaste, flavourful, fresh.

NUNCITO 2009 T BARRICA
garnacha, syrah, mazuelo.

92 Colour: cherry, garnet rim. Nose: ripe fruit, spicy, creamy oak, scrubland, expressive. Palate: powerful, flavourful, toasty, round tannins.

NUNCITO 2008 T BARRICA
garnacha, syrah, mazuelo.

91 Colour: cherry, garnet rim. Nose: powerfull, scrubland, ripe fruit. Palate: good structure, flavourful, full.

NUNCI COSTERO 2006 T
55% mazuelo, 40% garnacha, 5% merlot.

91 Colour: cherry, garnet rim. Nose: ripe fruit, spicy, creamy oak, toasty, earthy notes, expressive. Palate: powerful, flavourful, toasty, round tannins, balanced.

NUNCI NEGRE 2006 T
garnacha, syrah, mazuelo, cabernet franc, cabernet sauvignon.

91 Colour: cherry, garnet rim. Nose: ripe fruit, spicy, creamy oak, complex. Palate: powerful, flavourful, toasty, round tannins.

NUNCI COSTERO 2005 T
40% garnacha, 45% mazuelo, 5% cabernet franc, 5% merlot, 5% cabernet sauvignon.

89 Colour: bright cherry, garnet rim. Nose: ripe fruit, tobacco, spicy. Palate: good structure, ripe fruit, fine bitter notes.

NUNSWEET 2007 TINTO DULCE
garnacha, merlot, syrah.

88 Colour: deep cherry. Nose: complex, ripe fruit, candied fruit. Palate: powerful, sweet, fine bitter notes.

CELLER MAS DOIX

Carme, 115
43376 Poboleda (Tarragona)
☎: +34 639 356 172 - Fax: +34 933 216 790
info@masdoix.com
www.masdoix.com

DOIX 2010 TC
55% cariñena, 45% garnacha.

94 Colour: cherry, garnet rim. Nose: sweet spices, ripe fruit, red berry notes, toasty. Palate: flavourful, good acidity, fine bitter notes, round tannins.

SALANQUES 2010 T

92 Colour: cherry, garnet rim. Nose: earthy notes, fruit expression, ripe fruit, creamy oak, spicy. Palate: ripe fruit, good acidity, fine bitter notes.

LES CRESTES 2010 T

91 Colour: bright cherry. Nose: sweet spices, creamy oak, ripe fruit. Palate: flavourful, fruity, toasty, round tannins.

CELLER PRIOR PONS

Rey, 4
43375 La Vilella Alta (Tarragona)
☎: +34 606 547 865
info@priorpons.com
www.priorpons.com

PRIOR PONS 2009 T
40% garnacha, 45% mazuelo, 15% cabernet sauvignon.

91 Colour: cherry, garnet rim. Nose: ripe fruit, spicy, complex, mineral, earthy notes. Palate: powerful, flavourful, toasty, round tannins.

PLANETS DE PRIOR PONS 2009 T
40% garnacha, 40% mazuelo, 10% cabernet sauvignon, 5% syrah, 5% merlot.

90 Colour: cherry, garnet rim. Nose: ripe fruit, spicy, creamy oak, toasty, balsamic herbs. Palate: powerful, flavourful, toasty, balanced.

CELLER SABATÉ

Nou, 6
43374 La Vilella Baixa (Tarragona)
☎: +34 977 839 209 - Fax: +34 977 839 209
cellersabate@cellersabate.com
www.cellersabate.com

MAS PLANTADETA 2011 BFB
100% garnacha blanca.

88 Colour: bright yellow. Nose: powerfull, ripe fruit, sweet spices, fragrant herbs. Palate: flavourful, fresh, good acidity.

MAS PLANTADETA 2009 T ROBLE
100% garnacha.

90 Colour: bright cherry. Nose: ripe fruit, sweet spices, creamy oak, expressive. Taste flavourful, fruity, toasty, round tannins.

MAS PLANTADETA 2006 TC
50% garnacha, 25% cariñena, 25% cabernet sauvignon.

87 Colour: cherry, garnet rim. Nose: spicy, balanced, fruit preserve. Palate: good structure, full, spicy, good acidity.

CELLER VALL-LLACH

Del Pont, 9
43739 Porrera (Tarragona)
☎: +34 977 828 244 - Fax: +34 977 828 325
celler@vallllach.com
www.vallllach.com

EMBRUIX DE VALL-LLACH 2009 T

93 Colour: cherry, garnet rim. Nose: spicy, creamy oak, toasty, fruit expression. Palate: powerful, flavourful, toasty, round tannins.

IDUS DE VALL-LLACH 2009 T

88 Colour: bright cherry. Nose: sweet spices, creamy oak. Palate: flavourful, fruity, toasty, round tannins.

VALL-LLACH 2009 T

88 Colour: cherry, garnet rim. Nose: spicy, complex, fruit liqueur notes. Palate: powerful, flavourful, toasty, round tannins.

CELLERS DE SCALA DEI

Rambla de la Cartoixa, s/n
43379 Scala Dei (Tarragona)
☎: +34 977 827 027 - Fax: +34 977 827 044
codinfo@codorniu.es
www.grupocodorniu.com

SCALA DEI PRIOR 2009 TC
45% garnacha, 20% samsó, 20% cabernet sauvignon, 15% syrah.

88 Colour: cherry, garnet rim. Nose: overripe fruit, toasty, earthy notes. Palate: fine bitter notes, good acidity, pruney.

SCALA DEI CARTOIXA 2007 TR
60% garnacha, 25% cariñena, 10% syrah, 5% cabernet sauvignon.

91 Colour: cherry, garnet rim. Nose: ripe fruit, spicy, creamy oak, toasty. Palate: flavourful, toasty, round tannins.

CELLERS RIPOLL SANS - CAL BATLLET

Consolació, 16
43737 Gratallops (Tarragona)
☎: +34 687 638 951
mripoll@closabatllet.com
www.closabatllet.com

GRATALLOPS ESCANYA VELLA 2010 B
100% escanya-vella.

91 Colour: bright yellow. Nose: candied fruit, faded flowers, expressive, dried herbs. Palate: flavourful, fine bitter notes. Personality.

TORROJA RONÇAVALL 2009 T
cariñena.

93 Colour: deep cherry. Nose: powerfull, varietal, ripe fruit, sweet spices, creamy oak. Palate: flavourful, powerful, good structure, long, mineral.

GRATALLOPS 5 PARTIDES 2009 T
100% cariñena.

92 Colour: cherry, garnet rim. Nose: ripe fruit, sweet spices, mineral, spicy, balsamic herbs, expressive. Palate: long, powerful, flavourful, complex, balanced.

ARTAI 2009 T
47% garnacha, 28% cariñena, 23% cabernet sauvignon, 2% syrah.

90 Colour: cherry, garnet rim. Nose: ripe fruit, scrubland, sweet spices, cocoa bean. Palate: ripe fruit, spicy, fine bitter notes, round tannins.

CELLERS UNIÓ

Joan Oliver, 16-24
43206 Reus (Tarragona)
☎: +34 977 330 055 - Fax: +34 977 330 070
info@cellersunio.com
www.cellersunio.com

ROUREDA LLICORELLA BLANC PEDRO XIMÉNEZ 2010 B
100% pedro ximénez.

88 Colour: bright yellow. Nose: balanced, expressive, mineral. Palate: rich, flavourful, fine bitter notes.

TENDRAL SELECCIÓN 2008 T
40% cariñena, 60% garnacha.

89 Colour: deep cherry. Nose: toasty, spicy, ripe fruit, earthy notes. Palate: spicy, ripe fruit, long.

ROUREDA LLICORELLA CLASSIC 2007 T
40% garnacha, 40% cariñena, 15% cabernet sauvignon, 5% merlot.

89 Colour: cherry, garnet rim. Nose: powerfull, fruit liqueur notes, toasty, dark chocolate. Palate: fine bitter notes, ripe fruit, spicy.

ROUREDA LLICORELLA VITIS 60 2006 T
40% garnacha, 40% cariñena, 10% cabernet sauvignon, 10% syrah.

90 Colour: cherry, garnet rim. Nose: ripe fruit, spicy, creamy oak, toasty, complex. Taste powerful, flavourful, toasty, round tannins.

CLOS DE L'OBAC

Camí Manyetes, s/n
43737 Gratallops (Tarragona)
☎: +34 977 839 276 - Fax: +34 977 839 371
info@obac.es
www.obac.es

KYRIE 2008 BC
garnacha blanca, macabeo, xarel.lo, moscatel.

93 Colour: bright yellow. Nose: ripe fruit, sweet spices, creamy oak, fragrant herbs, dry stone. Palate: rich, flavourful, fresh, good acidity, balanced.

MISERERE 2008 TC
garnacha, cabernet sauvignon, tempranillo, cariñena, merlot.

92 Colour: cherry, garnet rim. Nose: ripe fruit, spicy, toasty, mineral, fragrant herbs. Palate: flavourful, toasty, complex, spicy.

CLOS DE L'OBAC 2008 TC
garnacha, cabernet sauvignon, cariñena, merlot, syrah.

91 Colour: cherry, garnet rim. Nose: ripe fruit, spicy, scrubland. Palate: toasty, long, spicy, balanced.

CLOS DEL PORTAL

Pista del Lloar a Bellmunt
43376El Molar Solanes del Molar (Tarragona)
☎: +34 932 531 760 - Fax: +34 934 173 591
info@portaldelpriorat.com
www.portaldelpriorat.com

GOTES DEL PRIORAT 2011 T
garnacha, cariñena.

89 Colour: cherry, garnet rim. Nose: red berry notes, fragrant herbs, mineral, spicy, fresh. Palate: fresh, fruity, flavourful, good acidity.

TROS DE CLOS 2010 T
cariñena.

94 Colour: bright cherry. Nose: ripe fruit, sweet spices, creamy oak, dark chocolate, cocoa bean, dry stone. Palate: flavourful, fruity, toasty, round tannins, balanced, elegant.

NEGRE DE NEGRES 2010 T
garnacha, cariñena, cabernet sauvignon.

93 Colour: bright cherry. Nose: ripe fruit, sweet spices, creamy oak, mineral, balsamic herbs. Palate: flavourful, fruity, toasty, round tannins, good acidity, long.

SOMNI 2010 T

92 Colour: bright cherry. Nose: ripe fruit, sweet spices, creamy oak, cocoa bean, dark chocolate, toasty, mineral. Palate: flavourful, fruity, toasty, round tannins.

GOTES DEL PRIORAT MAGNUM 2010 T
cariñena, garnacha.

91 Colour: cherry, purple rim. Nose: expressive, fresh fruit, red berry notes, floral, mineral, cocoa bean, spicy. Palate: flavourful, fruity, balanced, spicy.

TROS DE CLOS MAGNUM 2009 T
cariñena.

93 Colour: cherry, garnet rim. Nose: ripe fruit, spicy, creamy oak, toasty, balsamic herbs, complex. Palate: powerful, flavourful, toasty, round tannins, good acidity, balanced, elegant.

SOMNI MAGNUM 2009 T
cariñena, syrah.

93 Colour: cherry, garnet rim. Nose: red berry notes, ripe fruit, fragrant herbs, mineral, nose:tic coffee, toasty. Palate: powerful, complex, fresh, fruity, flavourful.

NEGRE DE NEGRES MAGNUM 2009 T
garnacha, cariñena, cabernet sauvignon.

93 Colour: cherry, garnet rim. Nose: dry stone, earthy notes, red berry notes, ripe fruit, cocoa bean, dark chocolate, spicy, balanced. Palate: good acidity, elegant, flavourful, fresh, fruity.

CLOS FIGUERAS

Carrer La Font, 38
43737 Gratallops (Tarragona)
☎: +34 977 830 217 - Fax: +34 977 830 422
info@closfigueras.com
www.desfigueras.com

SERRAS DEL PRIORAT 2010 T
65% garnacha, 15% mazuelo, 10% syrah, 10% cabernet sauvignon.

91 Colour: bright cherry, garnet rim. Nose: powerfull, ripe fruit, spicy. Palate: good structure, round tannins, long.

CLOS FIGUERES 2009 T

91 Colour: cherry, garnet rim. Nose: spicy, creamy oak, toasty, complex, earthy notes, overripe fruit. Palate: powerful, flavourful, toasty, round tannins.

FONT DE LA FIGUERA 2009 T

89 Colour: bright cherry. Nose: sweet spices, creamy oak, expressive, mineral, toasty, overripe fruit. Palate: flavourful, fruity, toasty, round tannins.

CLOS MOGADOR

Camí Manyetes, s/n
43737 Gratallops (Tarragona)
☎: +34 977 839 171 - Fax: +34 977 839 426
closmogador@closmogador.com
www.closmogador.com

NELIN 2010 B
garnacha, macabeo, viognier, escanyavelles.

90 Colour: bright yellow. Nose: balanced, expressive, spicy, ripe fruit. Palate: rich, flavourful, fruity, fine bitter notes.

MANYETES 2009 T
cariñena, garnacha.

94 Colour: cherry, garnet rim. Nose: powerfull, ripe fruit, toasty, creamy oak, mineral. Palate: powerful, flavourful, fine bitter notes, good acidity, mineral, spicy.

CLOS MOGADOR 2009 T
garnacha, cariñena, cabernet sauvignon, syrah.

93 Colour: cherry, garnet rim. Nose: earthy notes, overripe fruit, dark chocolate. Palate: powerful, flavourful, fine bitter notes, good acidity, round tannins.

COMBIER-FISCHER-GERIN

Baixa Font, 18
43737 Torroja del Priorat (Tarragona)
☎: +34 600 753 840 - Fax: +34 977 828 380
yalellamaremos@yahoo.es
www.trioinfernal.es

TRÍO INFERNAL Nº 0/3 2010 B
garnacha blanca, macabeo.

84

RIU DEL TRÍO INFERNAL 2009 T
garnacha, cariñena, syrah.

89 Colour: cherry, garnet rim. Nose: ripe fruit, spicy, toasty, earthy notes, fine reductive notes. Palate: powerful, flavourful, toasty, round tannins.

TRÍO INFERNAL Nº 2/3 2007 T
100% cariñena.

91 Colour: very deep cherry, garnet rim. Nose: powerfull, dark chocolate, ripe fruit, fruit preserve, sweet spices. Palate: good structure, round tannins.

COSTERS DEL PRIORAT

Finca Sant Martí
43738 Bellmunt del Priorat (Tarragona)
☎: +34 618 203 473
info@costersdelpriorat.com
www.costersdelpriorat.com

CLOS CYPRES 2010 T
90% cariñena, 10% garnacha.

91 Colour: deep cherry. Nose: spicy, toasty, mineral, ripe fruit. Palate: flavourful, ripe fruit, fine bitter notes.

PISSARRES 2010 T
55% cariñena, 30% garnacha, 15% cabernet sauvignon, syrah.

90 Colour: cherry, garnet rim. Nose: ripe fruit, spicy, toasty, mineral. Palate: powerful, flavourful, round tannins.

ELIOS 2010 T
55% garnacha, cariñena.

89 Colour: cherry, garnet rim. Nose: powerfull, ripe fruit, wild herbs. Palate: good structure, flavourful, long.

DE MULLER

Camí Pedra Estela, 34
43205 Reus (Tarragona)
☎: +34 977 757 473 - Fax: +34 977 771 129
lab@demuller.es
www.demuller.es

LEGITIM 2009 TC
50% garnacha, 35% merlot, 10% syrah, 5% cariñena.

87 Colour: deep cherry, orangey edge. Nose: fruit preserve, balsamic herbs, wild herbs. Palate: powerful, spicy.

LES PUSSES DE MULLER 2007 TC
50% merlot, 50% syrah.

89 Colour: cherry, garnet rim. Nose: ripe fruit, spicy, creamy oak, toasty, earthy notes. Palate: powerful, flavourful, toasty.

LO CABALÓ 2006 TR
70% garnacha, 10% merlot, 10% syrah, 10% cariñena.

87 Colour: deep cherry, brick rim edge. Nose: roasted coffee, fruit liqueur notes, fruit liqueur notes. Palate: fine bitter notes, warm, round tannins.

DOM JOAN FORT 1865 SOLERA
moscatel de alejandría, garnacha, garnacha blanca.

94 Colour: bright golden. Nose: dry nuts, saline, acetaldehyde, aged wood nuances, creamy oak. Palate: balanced, powerful, flavourful, spicy, long.

DOMINI DE LA CARTOIXA

Camino de la Solana, s/n
43736 El Molar (Tarragona)
☎: +34 606 443 736 - Fax: +34 977 771 737
info@closgalena.com
www.closgalena.com

FORMIGA DE VELLUT 2010 T

90 Colour: cherry, garnet rim. Nose: balanced, ripe fruit, powerfull, mineral. Palate: balanced, fine bitter notes, good structure.

CROSSOS 2010 T
60% garnacha, 20% cabernet sauvignon, 20% cariñena.

90 Colour: bright cherry. Nose: ripe fruit, sweet spices, creamy oak, scrubland, mineral. Palate: flavourful, fruity, toasty, round tannins.

CLOS GALENA 2009 TC
garnacha, cariñena, syrah, cabernet sauvignon.

93 Colour: cherry, garnet rim. Nose: ripe fruit, spicy, creamy oak, toasty, complex, earthy notes, mineral. Palate: powerful, flavourful, toasty, round tannins.

GALENA 2009 T

91 Colour: cherry, garnet rim. Nose: ripe fruit, creamy oak, toasty, complex. Palate: powerful, flavourful, toasty, round tannins, balanced.

ELVIWINES

Finca "Clos Mesorah" Ctra. T-300 Falset Marça, Km. 1
43775 Marça Priorat (Tarragona)
☎: +34 935 343 026 - Fax: +34 936 750 316
moises@elviwines.com
www.elviwines.com

EL26 2008 TR
40% cabernet sauvignon, 25% syrah, 20% garnacha, 15% cariñena.

91 Colour: cherry, garnet rim. Nose: ripe fruit, spicy, creamy oak, toasty, complex. Taste powerful, flavourful, toasty, round tannins.

FERRER BOBET

Ctra. Falset a Porrera, Km. 6,5
43730 Falset (Tarragona)
☎: +34 609 945 532 - Fax: +34 935 044 265
eguerre@ferrerbobet.com
www.ferrerbobet.com

FERRER BOBET VINYES VELLES 2010 T
70% cariñena, 30% garnacha.

95 Colour: cherry, garnet rim. Nose: ripe fruit, spicy, creamy oak, toasty. Palate: powerful, flavourful, toasty, round tannins.

FERRER BOBET SELECCIÓ ESPECIAL 2010 T
100% cariñena.

94 Colour: bright cherry. Nose: ripe fruit, sweet spices, creamy oak, expressive, earthy notes. Palate: flavourful, fruity, toasty, round tannins.

FERRER BOBET SELECCIÓ ESPECIAL 2009 T
100% cariñena.

96 Colour: cherry, garnet rim. Nose: ripe fruit, spicy, creamy oak, complex, mineral, new oak. Palate: powerful, flavourful, toasty, round tannins.

FERRER BOBET VINYES VELLES 2009 T
70% cariñena, 30% garnacha.

95 Colour: cherry, garnet rim. Nose: ripe fruit, spicy, creamy oak, toasty, mineral. Palate: powerful, flavourful, toasty, round tannins, fruity, good acidity, long.

GENIUM CELLER

Nou, 92- Bajos
43376 Poboleda (Tarragona)
☎: +34 977 827 146 - Fax: +34 977 827 146
genium@geniumceller.com
www.geniumceller.com

GENIUM XIMENIS 2010 BFB
90% pedro ximénez, 10% garnacha blanca.

88 Colour: bright straw. Nose: fresh fruit, ripe fruit, citrus fruit, white flowers. Palate: flavourful, fine bitter notes.

GENIUM FRESC 2010 T ROBLE
80% garnacha, 20% cariñena.

86 Colour: cherry, purple rim. Nose: balanced, powerfull, overripe fruit. Palate: fruity, flavourful, fine bitter notes.

POBOLEDA VI DE VILA 2008 TR
70% garnacha, 30% cariñena.

88 Colour: cherry, garnet rim. Nose: ripe fruit, spicy, toasty, fine reductive notes, earthy notes. Palate: powerful, flavourful, toasty, round tannins.

GENIUM COSTERS 2008 TR
60% garnacha, 20% cariñena, 10% merlot, 10% syrah.

86 Colour: deep cherry. Nose: overripe fruit, fruit liqueur notes, toasty, nose:tic coffee. Palate: sweetness, concentrated, fine bitter notes.

GENIUM ECOLÒGIC 2007 T
50% garnacha, 30% merlot, 10% cariñena, 10% syrah.

88 Colour: bright cherry, garnet rim. Nose: expressive, mineral, ripe fruit, spicy, fruit preserve. Palate: long, round tannins, balanced.

GENIUM CELLER 2006 TC
60% garnacha, 20% cariñena, 15% merlot, 5% syrah.

89 Colour: cherry, garnet rim. Nose: ripe fruit, spicy, creamy oak, fine reductive notes, mineral. Palate: powerful, flavourful, toasty, round tannins.

GRAN CLOS

Montsant, 2
43738 Bellmunt (Tarragona)
☎: +34 977 830 675
cellersfuentes@granclos.com
www.granclos.com

GRAN CLOS 2008 B
50% garnacha blanca, 50% macabeo.

87 Colour: bright yellow. Nose: fruit preserve, citrus fruit. Palate: flavourful, good acidity, fine bitter notes.

SOLLUNA 2009 T
65% garnacha, 15% syrah, 10% cabernet sauvignon, 5% cariñena, 5% merlot.

86 Colour: black cherry, garnet rim. Nose: overripe fruit, powerfull, sweet spices. Palate: balanced, fine bitter notes.

LES MINES SOLLUNA 2009 T
65% garnacha, 15% syrah, 10% cabernet sauvignon, 5% merlot, 5% cariñena.

85 Colour: cherry, garnet rim. Nose: ripe fruit, creamy oak, fruit liqueur notes, slightly evolved. Palate: powerful, flavourful, toasty.

SOLLUNA 2008 T
75% garnacha, 15% cariñena, 10% merlot.

87 Colour: cherry, purple rim. Nose: balanced, ripe fruit, sweet spices. Palate: correct, good acidity, ripe fruit.

FINCA EL PUIG 2006 T
50% garnacha, 20% syrah, 15% cabernet sauvignon, 15% cariñena.

88 Colour: pale ruby, brick rim edge. Nose: elegant, spicy, fine reductive notes, wet leather, aged wood nuances, fruit liqueur notes. Palate: spicy, long, balanced.

GRAN CLOS 2005 T
55% garnacha, 25% cariñena, 20% cabernet sauvignon.

92 Colour: pale ruby, brick rim edge. Nose: elegant, spicy, fine reductive notes, aged wood nuances, fruit liqueur notes, earthy notes. Palate: spicy, fine tannins, elegant, long.

CARTUS 2005 T
garnacha, 25% cariñena.

91 Colour: very deep cherry. Nose: powerfull, fruit liqueur notes, overripe fruit, toasty, spicy. Palate: powerful, fine bitter notes, good acidity.

GRATAVINUM

Mas D'en Serres, s/n
43737 Gratallops (Tarragona)
☎: +34 938 901 399 - Fax: +34 938 901 143
gratavinum@gratavinum.com
www.gratavinum.com

GRATAVINUM GV5 2009 T
cariñena, garnacha, cabernet sauvignon.

92 Colour: cherry, garnet rim. Nose: ripe fruit, spicy, creamy oak, toasty, complex, mineral. Palate: powerful, flavourful, toasty, round tannins.

GRATAVINUM 2 PI R 2009 T
garnacha, cariñena, cabernet sauvignon, syrah.

88 Colour: black cherry, purple rim. Nose: creamy oak, fruit preserve. Palate: good structure, flavourful.

GRATAVINUM COSTER 2007 T
100% cariñena.

92 Colour: black cherry, garnet rim. Nose: balanced, ripe fruit, tobacco, spicy. Palate: good structure, powerful, round tannins, balanced.

HUELLAS

De la Mora de Sant Pere, 26- 2º
08880 Cubelles (Barcelona)
☎: +34 609 428 507
franckmassard@epicure-wines.com

AMIC 2011 T
garnacha, merlot, cabernet sauvignon.

91 Colour: cherry, garnet rim. Nose: spicy, creamy oak, toasty, characterful, fruit expression. Palate: powerful, flavourful, toasty, round tannins.

JOAN AMETLLER

Ctra. La Morera de Monsant - Cornudella, km. 3,2
43361 La Morera de Monsant (Tarragona)
☎: +34 933 208 439 - Fax: +34 933 208 437
ametller@ametller.com
www.ametller.com

CLOS CORRIOL 2011 B
garnacha blanca.

88 Colour: bright straw. Nose: candied fruit, citrus fruit, dried flowers. Palate: long, easy to drink.

CLOS MUSTARDÓ 2010 B
garnacha blanca.

91 Colour: bright straw. Nose: fresh, fresh fruit, white flowers, characterful. Palate: flavourful, fruity, good acidity, balanced.

CLOS CORRIOL 2011 RD
80% cabernet sauvignon, 20% garnacha.

87 Colour: rose, purple rim. Nose: powerfull, ripe fruit, red berry notes, floral, expressive. Taste fleshy, powerful, fruity, fresh.

CLOS CORRIOL 2009 T
garnacha, cabernet sauvignon, merlot.

90 Colour: bright cherry, garnet rim. Nose: powerfull, fruit expression, balsamic herbs, spicy. Palate: fruity, flavourful.

JOAN SIMÓ

11 de Setembre, 7
43739 Porrera (Tarragona)
☎: +34 627 563 713 - Fax: +34 977 830 993
leseres@cellerjoansimo.com
www.cellerjoansimo.com

LES ERES 2008 T
60% cariñena, 30% garnacha, 10% cabernet sauvignon.

92 Colour: cherry, garnet rim. Nose: ripe fruit, spicy, creamy oak, toasty. Palate: powerful, flavourful, toasty, round tannins.

SENTIUS 2008 T
55% garnacha, 25% syrah, 20% cabernet sauvignon.

88 Colour: deep cherry. Nose: powerfull, warm, overripe fruit, toasty. Palate: flavourful, powerful, good structure.

LES ERES ESPECIAL DELS CARNERS 2007 T
75% garnacha, 25% cariñena.

91 Colour: cherry, garnet rim. Nose: ripe fruit, balsamic herbs, mineral, sweet spices, creamy oak. Palate: powerful, flavourful, complex, long, spicy.

LA CONRERIA D'SCALA DEI

Carrer Mitja Galta, s/n - Finca Les Brugueres
43379 Scala Dei (Tarragona)
☎: +34 977 827 055 - Fax: +34 977 827 055
laconreria@vinslaconreria.com
www.vinslaconreria.com

LES BRUGUERES 2011 B
garnacha blanca.

90 Colour: bright straw. Nose: fresh, white flowers, ripe fruit. Palate: flavourful, fruity, good acidity, balanced.

LA CONRERIA 2010 T
garnacha, syrah, merlot, cabernet sauvignon.

88 Colour: cherry, garnet rim. Nose: ripe fruit, spicy, toasty, warm. Palate: powerful, flavourful, toasty, round tannins.

IUGITER 2008 T
garnacha, merlot, cabernet sauvignon, cariñena.

89 Colour: cherry, garnet rim. Nose: ripe fruit, spicy, creamy oak, toasty, complex, mineral. Palate: powerful, flavourful, spicy.

IUGITER SELECCIÓ VINYES VELLES 2007 TC
garnacha, cariñena, cabernet sauvignon.

90 Colour: cherry, garnet rim. Nose: ripe fruit, spicy, creamy oak, toasty, characterful. Palate: powerful, flavourful, toasty, round tannins.

LA PERLA DEL PRIORAT

Mas dels Frares, s/n
43736 El Molar (Tarragona)
☎: +34 977 825 202
frares@laperladelpriorat.com
www.laperladelpriorat.com

NOSTER INICIAL 2008 T
garnacha, carignan, cabernet sauvignon.

88 Colour: cherry, garnet rim. Nose: ripe fruit, spicy, creamy oak, complex, dry stone, toasty. Palate: powerful, flavourful, toasty.

NOSTER 2007 TC
garnacha, carignan.

89 Colour: light cherry, garnet rim. Nose: mineral, ripe fruit, spicy, creamy oak. Palate: good acidity, powerful, flavourful.

CLOS LES FITES 2006 T
garnacha, carignan, cabernet sauvignon.

91 Colour: light cherry, garnet rim. Nose: dry stone, ripe fruit, fragrant herbs, spicy, creamy oak. Palate: elegant, round, flavourful, spicy.

LLICORELLA VINS

Carrer de l'Era, 11
43737 Torroja del Priorat (Tarragona)
☎: +34 977 839 049 - Fax: +34 977 839 049
comercial@llicorellavins.com
www.llicorellavins.com

AÒNIA 2009 T
garnacha, cariñena, cabernet sauvignon.

92 Colour: cherry, garnet rim. Nose: ripe fruit, spicy, creamy oak, toasty, complex. Taste powerful, flavourful, toasty, round tannins.

MAS SAURA 2008 TC
garnacha, cabernet sauvignon, syrah, cariñena.

91 Colour: cherry, garnet rim. Nose: spicy, toasty, scrubland, ripe fruit, mineral. Palate: powerful, flavourful, toasty, round tannins, balanced.

GRAN NASARD 2008 TC
garnacha, cariñena.

90 Colour: very deep cherry. Nose: dark chocolate, sweet spices, ripe fruit, fruit preserve. Palate: full, flavourful, ripe fruit, balanced, fine bitter notes, round tannins.

MARCO ABELLA

Ctra. de Porrera a Cornudella del Montsant, Km. 0,7
43739 Porrera (Tarragona)
☎: +34 933 712 407 - Fax: +34 933 712 407
admin@marcoabella.com
www.marcoabella.com

MAS MALLOLA 2008 T
38% cariñena, 45% garnacha, 10% cabernet sauvignon, 5% syrah, 2% merlot.

88 Colour: deep cherry. Nose: sweet spices, spicy, toasty, dark chocolate. Palate: powerful, fine bitter notes, warm.

MAS MALLOLA 2007 T
38% cariñena, 45% garnacha, 10% cabernet sauvignon, 5% syrah, 2% merlot.

88 Colour: deep cherry. Nose: fruit liqueur notes, warm, toasty, spicy. Palate: flavourful, powerful, fine bitter notes.

CLOS ABELLA 2006 T
40% cariñena, 40% garnacha, 15% cabernet sauvignon, 5% syrah.

90 Colour: cherry, garnet rim. Nose: spicy, creamy oak, dried herbs, tobacco. Palate: flavourful, fruity, good structure.

CLOS ABELLA 2005 T
40% cariñena, 40% garnacha, 10% cabernet sauvignon, 10% syrah.

92 Colour: cherry, garnet rim. Nose: ripe fruit, spicy, creamy oak, toasty, characterful. Palate: powerful, flavourful, toasty, round tannins.

MAS IGNEUS

Ctra. Falset a Vilella Baixa T-710, Km. 11,1
43737 Gratallops (Tarragona)
☎: +34 977 262 259 - Fax: +34 977 054 027
celler@masigneus.com
www.masigneus.com

BARRANC DELS CLOSOS BLANC 2010 B
30% garnacha blanca, 50% macabeo, 15% pedro ximénez, 5% moscatel.

88 Colour: bright straw, greenish rim. Nose: ripe fruit, white flowers, candied fruit. Palate: flavourful, rich.

FA 104 BLANC 2010 B

88 Colour: bright yellow. Nose: candied fruit, citrus fruit, white flowers. Palate: flavourful, spicy, ripe fruit.

FA 206 NEGRE 2010 T

88 Colour: bright cherry, purple rim. Nose: balanced, ripe fruit, complex. Palate: good structure, flavourful, balanced.

FA 112 2008 T
garnacha, cariñena, cabernet sauvignon, syrah.

88 Colour: cherry, garnet rim. Nose: ripe fruit, spicy, toasty, balsamic herbs, earthy notes. Palate: powerful, flavourful, toasty, round tannins, correct.

COSTERS DE L'ERMITA 2006 T
80% garnacha, 20% cariñena.

88 Colour: cherry, garnet rim. Nose: ripe fruit, spicy, creamy oak, fine reductive notes. Palate: powerful, flavourful, toasty, round tannins.

MAS MARTINET

Ctra. Falset - Gratallops, Km. 6
43730 Falset (Tarragona)
☎: +34 629 238 236 - Fax: +34 977 262 348
masmartinet@masmartinet.com
www.masmartinet.com

ELS ESCURÇONS 2009 T

94 Colour: deep cherry, garnet rim. Nose: complex, earthy notes, scrubland, ripe fruit. Palate: good structure, balanced, fine bitter notes, elegant.

CAMI PESSEROLES 2009 T

93 Colour: deep cherry, garnet rim. Nose: complex, balanced, expressive, ripe fruit, creamy oak, varnish, dry stone. Palate: good structure, ripe fruit, long.

CLOS MARTINET 2009 T

92 Colour: cherry, garnet rim. Nose: ripe fruit, spicy, acetaldehyde, fragrant herbs, dried flowers, mineral. Palate: flavourful, toasty, long, mineral, elegant, fine tannins. Personality.

MARTINET BRU 2009 T

90 Colour: cherry, garnet rim. Nose: warm, ripe fruit, scrubland, spicy, creamy oak, fine reductive notes. Palate: flavourful, complex, long, spicy, balsamic, round tannins.

MAS MARTINET ASSESSORAMENTS

Vidal i Barraquer, 8
43739 Porrera (Tarragona)
☎: +34 609 715 004 - Fax: +34 977 262 348
info@masmartinet-ass.com
www.masmartinet-ass.com

MARTINET DEGUSTACIÓ 2 2005 T

92 Colour: bright cherry. Nose: ripe fruit, sweet spices, creamy oak, nose:tic coffee, balsamic herbs, mineral. Palate: flavourful, fruity, toasty, spicy, long, ripe fruit, elegant, fine tannins.

MARTINET DEGUSTACIÓ 1 2004 T

92 Colour: cherry, garnet rim. Nose: creamy oak, toasty, scrubland, fruit liqueur notes, mineral, acetaldehyde. Palate: powerful, flavourful, toasty, balanced, round.

MAS PERINET

Finca Mas Perinet, s/n - T-702, Km. 1,6
43361 La Morera de Montsant (Tarragona)
☎: +34 977 827 113 - Fax: +34 977 827 180
info@masperinet.com
www.masperinet.com

PERINET + PLUS 2006 T

94 Colour: cherry, garnet rim. Nose: spicy, creamy oak, toasty, mineral, earthy notes. Palate: powerful, flavourful, toasty, round tannins.

PERINET 2006 T

92 Colour: cherry, garnet rim. Nose: ripe fruit, creamy oak, toasty, characterful. Palate: powerful, flavourful, toasty, round tannins.

PERINET 2005 T

92 Colour: cherry, garnet rim. Nose: spicy, creamy oak, toasty, overripe fruit, earthy notes. Palate: powerful, flavourful, toasty, round tannins.

MASET DEL LLEÓ

C-244, Km. 32,5
08792 La Granada del Penedès (Barcelona)
☎: +34 902 200 250 - Fax: +34 938 921 333
info@maset.com
www.maset.com

MAS VILÓ 2008 T

90 Colour: black cherry, garnet rim. Nose: medium intensity, cocoa bean, dried herbs. Palate: good structure, flavourful, round tannins.

CLOS VILÓ 2007 T

89 Colour: very deep cherry. Nose: balanced, scrubland, spicy, creamy oak, smoky. Palate: good structure, flavourful.

CLOS GRAN VILÓ 2006 T

89 Colour: black cherry. Nose: medium intensity, fruit preserve, sweet spices. Palate: balanced, fine bitter notes, good acidity.

MASÍA DUCH

Ctra. de las Vilellas, Km. 13
Finca el Tancat
43379 Scala Dei (Tarragona)
☎: +34 977 773 513 - Fax: +34 977 341 215
mduch@masiaduch.com

BRESSOL 2011 T

88 Colour: cherry, purple rim. Nose: red berry notes, floral, ripe fruit. Palate: flavourful, fruity, good acidity, round tannins.

MAYOL VITICULTORS

De la Bassa, 24
43737 Torroja del Priorat (Tarragona)
☎: +34 977 839 395 - Fax: +34 977 839 317
celler@mayol.eu
www.mayol.eu

ROSER 2011 BFB
75% macabeo, 25% garnacha blanca.

88 Colour: bright straw. Nose: ripe fruit, citrus fruit, white flowers. Palate: ripe fruit, good acidity, fine bitter notes.

GLOP 2010 T
60% garnacha, 20% cariñena, 20% syrah.

89 Colour: cherry, garnet rim. Nose: ripe fruit, spicy, toasty, mineral. Palate: powerful, flavourful, toasty, round tannins.

BROGIT 2009 TC
50% garnacha, 15% cariñena, 15% syrah, 15% cabernet sauvignon, 5% merlot.

89 Colour: cherry, garnet rim. Nose: overripe fruit, sweet spices, creamy oak. Palate: balanced, fine bitter notes, ripe fruit, long.

TORROJA DES DE DINS 2009 TC
60% garnacha, 20% cariñena, 15% syrah, 5% cabernet sauvignon.

86 Colour: cherry, garnet rim. Nose: spicy, fruit preserve, creamy oak. Palate: powerful, flavourful, toasty.

MELIS

Balandra, 54
43737 Torroja del Priorat (Tarragona)
☎: +34 937 313 021 - Fax: +34 937 312 371
javier@melispriorat.com
www.melispriorat.com

MELIS 2009 T

92 Colour: cherry, garnet rim. Nose: ripe fruit, scrubland, earthy notes, mineral, spicy, creamy oak. Palate: balanced, round, flavourful, long, elegant.

ELIX 2009 T

92 Colour: cherry, garnet rim. Nose: ripe fruit, balsamic herbs, floral, sweet spices, creamy oak, expressive. Palate: powerful, flavourful, spicy, long, balanced.

OBRADOR 2009 T

90 Colour: cherry, garnet rim. Nose: ripe fruit, spicy, creamy oak, fragrant herbs, mineral. Palate: powerful, flavourful, toasty, round tannins.

MERITXELL PALLEJÀ

Major, 32
43737 Gratallops (Tarragona)
☎: +34 670 960 735
info@nita.cat
www.nita.cat

NITA 2011 T

88 Colour: bright cherry. Nose: candied fruit, balsamic herbs, scrubland, toasty, dark chocolate. Palate: fine bitter notes, powerful tannins, spicy.

MERUM PRIORATI

Ctra. a Falset (T-740), km. 9,3
43739 Porrera (Tarragona)
☎: +34 977 828 307 - Fax: +34 977 828 324
info@merumpriorati.com
www.merumpriorati.com

OSMIN 2007 T
garnacha, cariñena, cabernet sauvignon, syrah, merlot.

90 Colour: deep cherry. Nose: creamy oak, earthy notes, overripe fruit, fruit liqueur notes. Palate: flavourful, powerful, fine bitter notes.

ARDILES 2007 T
garnacha, cariñena, cabernet sauvignon, syrah.

88 Colour: cherry, garnet rim. Nose: spicy, creamy oak, toasty, characterful, overripe fruit, mineral. Palate: powerful, flavourful, toasty, round tannins.

NOGUERALS

Tou, 5
43360 Cornudella de Montsant (Tarragona)
☎: +34 650 033 546 - Fax: +34 934 419 879
noguerals@hotmail.com
www.noguerals.com

ABELLARS 2009 T
50% garnacha, 25% samsó, 15% cabernet sauvignon, 10% syrah.

90 Colour: cherry, garnet rim. Nose: balanced, old leather, earthy notes. Palate: flavourful, fine bitter notes, long, round tannins.

R.TI 2 2009 T
garnacha, cabernet sauvignon, syrah.

91 Colour: cherry, garnet rim. Nose: ripe fruit, creamy oak, toasty, earthy notes, mineral. Palate: powerful, flavourful, toasty, balanced.

ROCA DE LES DOTZE

Turó, 5
08328 Alella (Barcelona)
☎: +34 662 302 214
info@rocadelesdotze.cat
www.rocadelesdotze.cat

NORAY 2007 T
garnacha, samsó, cabernet sauvignon, syrah.

90 Colour: cherry, garnet rim. Nose: ripe fruit, balsamic herbs, spicy, creamy oak, mineral. Palate: correct, powerful, flavourful, long.

ROCA BRUIXA 2007 T
garnacha, syrah.

89 Colour: cherry, garnet rim. Nose: spicy, creamy oak, toasty, overripe fruit. Palate: powerful, flavourful, toasty, round tannins.

RODRÍGUEZ SANZO

Manuel Azaña, 9
47014 (Valladolid)
☎: +34 983 150 150 - Fax: +34 983 150 151
comunicacion@valsanzo.com
www.rodriguezsanzo.com

NASSOS 2009 T
100% garnacha.

93 Colour: cherry, garnet rim. Nose: spicy, creamy oak, toasty, earthy notes, mineral, ripe fruit. Palate: powerful, flavourful, toasty, round tannins.

ROTLLAN TORRA

Balandra, 6
43737 Torroja del Priorat (Tarragona)
☎: +34 977 839 285 - Fax: +34 933 050 112
comercial@rotllantorra.com
www.rotllantorra.com

ROTLLAN TORRA 2009 T

88 Colour: deep cherry. Nose: spicy, dark chocolate, toasty, ripe fruit. Palate: flavourful, powerful, ripe fruit, spicy.

MISTIK 2008 T

90 Colour: cherry, garnet rim. Nose: ripe fruit, spicy, creamy oak, toasty, complex. Palate: powerful, flavourful, toasty, balanced.

ROTLLAN TORRA 2008 TR

88 Colour: black cherry. Nose: toasty, dark chocolate, aged wood nuances, overripe fruit. Palate: flavourful, powerful, fine bitter notes.

BALANDRA 2007 TR

84

SANGENÍS I VAQUÉ

Pl. Catalunya, 3
43739 Porrera (Tarragona)
☎: +34 977 828 252
celler@sangenisivaque.com
www.sangenisivaque.com

LO COSTER BLANC 2010 B
garnacha blanca, macabeo.

90 Colour: bright yellow. Nose: ripe fruit, fragrant herbs, floral, expressive. Palate: powerful, flavourful, complex, long.

DARA 2008 TR
45% garnacha, 45% cariñena, 10% merlot.

89 Colour: cherry, garnet rim. Nose: spicy, creamy oak, toasty, complex. Palate: powerful, flavourful, toasty, round tannins.

SAÓ DEL COSTER

De Les Valls, 28
43737 Gratallops (Priorat)
☎: +34 977 839 298
info@saodelcoster.com
www.saodelcoster.com

"S" 2009 T
garnacha, merlot, cabernet sauvignon, syrah.

90 Colour: bright cherry, purple rim. Nose: fresh fruit, expressive, earthy notes. Palate: good structure, flavourful, balsamic, spicy.

TERRAM 2008 T
garnacha, cariñena, syrah, cabernet sauvignon.

91 Colour: bright cherry. Nose: sweet spices, creamy oak, overripe fruit. Palate: flavourful, fruity, toasty, round tannins.

PLANASSOS 2006 T
cariñena.

90 Colour: pale ruby, brick rim edge. Nose: elegant, spicy, fine reductive notes, fruit liqueur notes, mineral. Palate: spicy, fine tannins, elegant, long.

SOLA CLASSIC

Clos, 1
43738 Bellmunt del Priorat (Tarragona)
☎: +34 977 831 134
info@solaclassic.com
www.solaclassic.com

SOLÀ2 CLASSIC 2011 B
macabeo.

85 Colour: bright straw. Nose: ripe fruit, faded flowers, dried herbs, mineral. Palate: flavourful, fruity, correct.

SOLÀ2 CLASSIC 2010 T
50% garnacha, 50% mazuelo.

87 Colour: very deep cherry, purple rim. Nose: powerfull, sweet spices, creamy oak, overripe fruit. Palate: good structure, flavourful.

SOLÀ CLASSIC 2010 T
50% mazuelo, 50% garnacha.

84

VINYES JOSEP 2008 T
50% garnacha, 50% mazuelo.

88 Colour: cherry, garnet rim. Nose: fruit preserve, dark chocolate, sweet spices, creamy oak. Palate: powerful, flavourful, spicy.

TERRA PERSONAS

Apartado 96
43730 Falset (Tarragona)
☎: +34 662 214 291
ruud@terrapersonas.com
www.terrapersonas.festis.cat

TERRA BLANCA 2011 B
60% macabeo, 40% garnacha blanca.

87 Colour: bright yellow. Nose: ripe fruit, white flowers, citrus fruit. Palate: flavourful, easy to drink, good finish.

TERRA VERMELLA 2011 T
45% cariñena, 40% garnacha, 15% syrah.

88 Colour: deep cherry, garnet rim. Nose: red berry notes, ripe fruit, medium intensity, scrubland. Palate: ripe fruit, good finish.

TERRA NEGRA 2010 T
80% cariñena, 10% garnacha, 10% syrah.

87 Colour: cherry, garnet rim. Nose: powerfull, toasty, spicy, fruit preserve. Palate: ripe fruit, long.

TERRES DE VIDALBA

Partida Foreses
43376 Poboleda (Tarragona)
☎: +34 616 413 722
info@terresdevidalba.com

TOCS 2008 T
62% garnacha, 35% syrah, 3% cabernet sauvignon.

88 Colour: cherry, garnet rim. Nose: ripe fruit, spicy, creamy oak, toasty, characterful. Palate: powerful, flavourful, toasty, round tannins.

TOCS 2007 T
30% garnacha, 35% syrah, 35% cabernet sauvignon, 5% merlot.

90 Colour: very deep cherry. Nose: powerfull, ripe fruit, sweet spices, nose:tic coffee, dark chocolate, earthy notes, mineral. Palate: powerful, flavourful, fine bitter notes.

TERROIR AL LIMIT

Baixa Tont, 10
43737 Torroja del Priorat (Tarragona)
☎: +34 699 732 707
vi@terroir-al-limit.com
www.terroir-al-limit.com

PEDRA DE GUIX 2009 B
garnacha blanca, macabeo, pedro ximénez.

90 Colour: bright straw. Nose: mineral, ripe fruit, citrus fruit, dried herbs, faded flowers. Palate: spicy, ripe fruit, long.

TORROJA VI DE LA VILA 2009 T
50% garnacha, 50% cariñena.

96 Colour: cherry, garnet rim. Nose: ripe fruit, spicy, creamy oak, toasty, complex, mineral, scrubland. Palate: powerful, flavourful, toasty, round tannins.

ARBOSSAR 2009 T
cariñena.

95 Colour: cherry, garnet rim. Nose: powerfull, characterful, candied fruit. Palate: flavourful, powerful, good acidity, fine bitter notes, elegant, mineral, balsamic.

LES TOSSES 2009 T
cariñena.

94 Colour: cherry, garnet rim. Nose: expressive, elegant, red berry notes, scrubland. Palate: ripe fruit, long, fine bitter notes, elegant.

LES MANYES 2009 T
garnacha.

93 Colour: cherry, garnet rim. Nose: balsamic herbs, ripe fruit, elegant. Palate: ripe fruit, long, good structure, round tannins.

DITS DEL TERRA 2009 T
cariñena.

92 Colour: very deep cherry. Nose: ripe fruit, characterful, powerfull, creamy oak. Palate: flavourful, good acidity, ripe fruit.

TORRES PRIORAT

Finca La Soleta, s/n
43737 El Lloar (Tarragona)
☎: +34 938 177 400 - Fax: +34 938 177 444
admin@torres.es
www.torres.es

SALMOS 2010 TC
garnacha, syrah, cariñena.

89 Colour: cherry, purple rim. Nose: balanced, medium intensity, ripe fruit, toasty. Palate: flavourful, round tannins.

PERPETUAL 2009 TC
cariñena, garnacha.

92 Colour: deep cherry. Nose: ripe fruit, creamy oak, toasty, spicy. Palate: flavourful, powerful, good acidity, round.

TROSSOS DEL PRIORAT

Ctra. Gratallops a La Vilella Baixa, Km. 10,65
43737 Gratallops (Tarragona)
☎: +34 670 590 788 - Fax: +34 933 704 154
celler@trossosdelpriorat.com
www.trossosdelpriorat.com

ABRACADABRA 2010 B
70% garnacha blanca, 30% macabeo.

90 Colour: bright straw. Nose: mineral, ripe fruit, citrus fruit, floral. Palate: flavourful, fruity, fresh.

LO MÓN 2009 T
garnacha, cariñena, cabernet sauvignon, syrah.

92 Colour: cherry, garnet rim. Nose: spicy, creamy oak, toasty, complex, earthy notes, ripe fruit. Palate: powerful, flavourful, toasty, long.

UN PAM DE NAS 2009 T
garnacha, cariñena, cabernet sauvignon, syrah.

92 Colour: cherry, garnet rim. Nose: complex, mineral, ripe fruit, spicy. Palate: good structure, balanced, fine bitter notes.

VINÍCOLA DEL PRIORAT

Piró, s/n
43737 Gratallops (Tarragona)
☎: +34 977 839 167 - Fax: +34 977 839 201
info@vinicoladelpriorat.com
www.jordimirodiego.blogsopt.com

ÒNIX CLÁSSIC 2011 B
garnacha blanca, viura, pedro ximénez.

90 Colour: bright straw, greenish rim. Nose: ripe fruit, balanced, floral. Palate: flavourful, ripe fruit, fine bitter notes.

ÒNIX CLÁSSIC 2011 T
garnacha, mazuelo.

91 Colour: cherry, purple rim. Nose: expressive, fresh fruit, red berry notes. Palate: flavourful, fruity, good acidity, round tannins.

CLOS GEBRAT 2011 T
garnacha, mazuelo, merlot, cabernet sauvignon, syrah.

89 Colour: deep cherry, purple rim. Nose: ripe fruit, mineral, balanced. Palate: balanced, good structure, fruity, flavourful.

NADIU 2011 T
garnacha, mazuelo, cabernet sauvignon, merlot, syrah.

88 Colour: cherry, purple rim. Nose: ripe fruit, balsamic herbs, mineral, medium intensity. Palate: powerful, flavourful, long.

ÒNIX FUSIÓ 2010 T
garnacha, syrah, mazuelo.

92 Colour: cherry, garnet rim. Nose: spicy, toasty, red berry notes, ripe fruit, mineral. Palate: powerful, flavourful, toasty, round tannins.

L'OBAGA 2010 T
garnacha, syrah.

88 Colour: cherry, garnet rim. Nose: ripe fruit, balsamic herbs, earthy notes. Palate: powerful, flavourful, correct, long.

CLOS GEBRAT 2010 T BARRICA
garnacha, mazuelo, merlot, cabernet sauvignon, syrah.

87 Colour: cherry, garnet rim. Nose: fruit liqueur notes, sweet spices, creamy oak, mineral. Palate: powerful, flavourful, complex, balanced.

ÒNIX EVOLUCIÓ 2009 T
garnacha, mazuelo, cabernet sauvignon.

90 Colour: cherry, garnet rim. Nose: ripe fruit, spicy, creamy oak, toasty. Palate: powerful, flavourful, toasty, round tannins.

NADIU 2009 TC
garnacha, mazuelo, cabernet sauvignon, merlot, syrah.

90 Colour: cherry, garnet rim. Nose: ripe fruit, spicy, creamy oak, toasty, complex. Taste powerful, flavourful, toasty, round tannins.

CLOS GEBRAT 2009 TC
garnacha, mazuelo, cabernet sauvignon.

88 Colour: cherry, garnet rim. Nose: ripe fruit, spicy, creamy oak, complex, earthy notes. Palate: powerful, flavourful, toasty.

VINNICO EXPORT

Muela, 16
03730 Jávea (Alicante)
☎: +34 965 791 967 - Fax: +34 966 461 471
info@vinnico.com
www.vinnico.com

TOSALET 2011 T
50% garnacha, 30% carignan, 20% cabernet sauvignon.

87 Colour: cherry, purple rim. Nose: red berry notes, ripe fruit, mineral, scrubland. Palate: long, ripe fruit, flavourful.

VINYES ALTAIR

Les Eres, s/n
43375 La Villeta Alta (Tarragona)
☎: +34 646 748 500
info@masperla.com
www.masperla.com

MASPERLA 2007 T
garnacha, cariñena, syrah, merlot, cabernet sauvignon.

91 Colour: cherry, garnet rim. Nose: powerfull, characterful, complex, ripe fruit. Palate: flavourful, powerful, concentrated, fine bitter notes.

MASPERLA 2006 T
garnacha, cariñena, syrah, merlot, cabernet sauvignon.

91 Colour: deep cherry. Nose: sweet spices, cocoa bean, toasty, spicy, earthy notes. Palate: flavourful, powerful, fine bitter notes, good acidity.

MAGINACIO 2006 T
garnacha, cariñena, syrah, merlot, cabernet sauvignon.

87 Colour: dark-red cherry, orangey edge. Nose: ripe fruit, sweet spices, fine reductive notes, balsamic herbs. Palate: long, spicy, flavourful.

VINYES DE MANYETES

Camí Manyetes, s/n
43737 Gratallops (Tarragona)
☎: +34 977 839 171 - Fax: +34 977 839 426
euroseleccio@euroseleccio.com
www.vinyesdemanyetes.com

SOLERTIA 2009 T
garnacha, cariñena, cabernet sauvignon, syrah.

88 Colour: bright cherry. Nose: ripe fruit, sweet spices, creamy oak, expressive. Palate: flavourful, fruity, toasty.

VITICULTORS DEL PRIORAT

Partida Palells - Mas Subirat
43738 Bellmunt del Priorat (Tarragona)
☎: +34 977 262 268 - Fax: +34 977 262 268
morlanda@morlanda.com
www.morlanda.com

MORLANDA 2011 B
garnacha blanca, macabeo.

88 Colour: bright straw. Nose: fresh, fresh fruit, white flowers, earthy notes. Palate: flavourful, fruity, good acidity, balanced.

COSTERS DEL PRIOR 2009 T

89 Colour: cherry, garnet rim. Nose: ripe fruit, spicy, creamy oak, scrubland. Palate: powerful, flavourful, toasty, round tannins.

MORLANDA 2007 TR
garnacha, cariñena.

89 Colour: cherry, garnet rim. Nose: ripe fruit, balsamic herbs, mineral, creamy oak, cocoa bean. Palate: powerful, flavourful, long, toasty.

VITICULTORS MAS D'EN GIL

Finca Mas d'en Gil
43738 Bellmunt del Priorat (Tarragona)
☎: +34 977 830 192 - Fax: +34 977 830 152
mail@masdengil.com
www.masdengil.com

COMA BLANCA 2011 BC
50% macabeo, 50% garnacha blanca.

91 Colour: bright straw. Nose: balanced, spicy, scrubland, toasty. Palate: rich, fruity, flavourful, ripe fruit, good acidity.

CLOS FONTÀ 2009 T
60% cariñena, 30% garnacha peluda, 10% garnacha.

91 Colour: cherry, garnet rim. Nose: ripe fruit, creamy oak, complex, mineral. Palate: powerful, flavourful, toasty, round tannins.

COMA VELLA 2009 T
50% garnacha peluda, 20% garnacha, 20% cariñena, 10% syrah.

89 Colour: very deep cherry. Nose: ripe fruit, overripe fruit, toasty, sweet spices. Palate: flavourful, powerful, fine bitter notes.

NUS 2010 DULCE NATURAL
80% garnacha, 15% syrah, 5% viognier.

92 Colour: ruby red. Nose: ripe fruit, dark chocolate, sweet spices, creamy oak, toasty, expressive. Palate: powerful, flavourful, spicy, sweet, toasty.

DO RÍAS BAIXAS

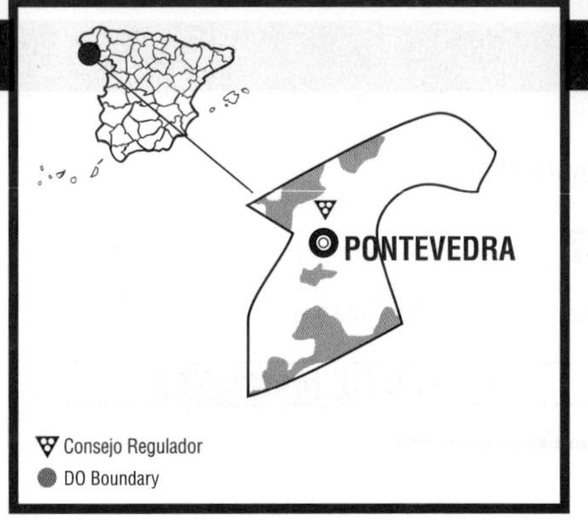

LOCATION:

In the southwest of the province of Pontevedra, covering five distinct sub-regions: Val do Salnés, O Rosal, Condado do Tea, Soutomaior and Ribeira do Ulla.

CLIMATE:

Atlantic, with moderate, mild temperatures due to the influence of the sea, high relative humidity and abundant rainfall (the annual average is around 1600 mm). There is less rainfall further downstream of the Miño (Condado de Tea), and as a consequence the grapes ripen earlier.

SOIL:

Sandy, shallow and slightly acidic, which makes fine soil for producing quality wines. The predominant type of rock is granite, and only in the Concellos of Sanxenxo, Rosal and Tomillo is it possible to find a narrow band of metamorphous rock. Quaternary deposits are very common in all the sub-regions.

GRAPE VARIETIES:

WHITE: *Albariño* (majority), *Loureira Blanca* or *Marqués*, *Treixadura* and Caíño *Blanco* (preferred); *Torrontés* and *Godello* (authorized).
RED: *Caíño Tinto, Espadeiro, Loureira Tinta* and *Sousón* (preferred); *Tempranillo, Mouratón, Garnacha Tintorera, Mencía* and *Brancellao* (authorized).

SUB-REGIONS:

Val do Salnés. This is the historic sub-region of the *Albariño* (in fact, here, almost all the white wines are produced as single-variety wines from this variety) and is centred around the municipal district of Cambados. It has the flattest relief of the four sub-regions.
Condado do Tea. The furthest inland, it is situated in the south of the province on the northern bank of the Miño. It is characterized by its mountainous terrain. The wines must contain a minimum of 70% of *Albariño* and *Treixadura.*
O Rosal. In the extreme southwest of the province, on the right bank of the Miño river mouth. The warmest sub-region, where river terraces abound. The wines must contain a minimum of 70% of *Albariño* and *Loureira.*
Soutomaior. Situated on the banks of the Verdugo River, about 10 km from Pontevedra, it consists only of the municipal district of Soutomaior. It produces only single-varietals of *Albariño.*
Ribeira do Ulla. A new sub-region along the Ulla River, which forms the landscape of elevated valleys further inland. It comprises the municipal districts of Vedra and part of Padrón, Deo, Boquixon, Touro, Estrada, Silleda and Vila de Cruce. Red wines predominate.

CONSEJO REGULADOR
Centro de Apoyo de Cabanas - 36143 Salcedo (Pontevedra) - ☎: +34 986 854 850 / +34 864 530 - Fax: +34 986 864 546
@ consejo@doriasbaixas.com - www.doriasbaixas.com

FIGURES:

Vineyard surface: 3,966 – **Wine-Growers:** 6,617 – **Wineries:** 181 – **2011 Harvest rating:** Very Good – **Production:** 28,699,843 litres – **Market percentages:** 77% domestic. 23% export

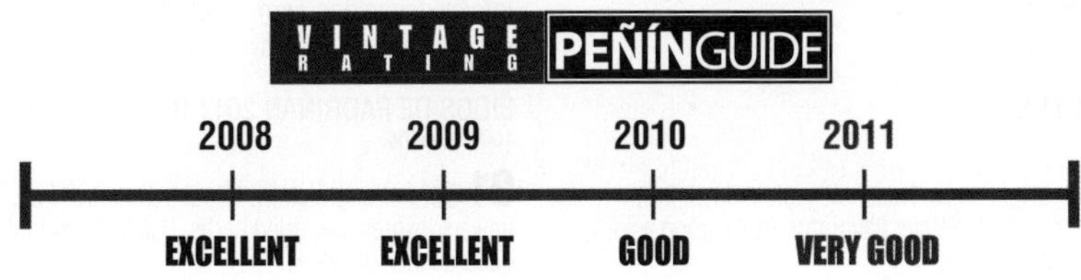

A. PAZOS DE LUSCO

Grixó - Alxén s/n
36458 Salvaterra do Miño (Pontevedra)
☎: +34 987 514 550 - Fax: +34 987 514 570
info@lusco.es
www.lusco.es

LUSCO 2011 B
100% albariño.

92 Colour: bright straw. Nose: elegant, varietal, fruit expression, ripe fruit. Palate: flavourful, fruity, good acidity, fine bitter notes.

ZIOS DE LUSCO 2011 B
100% albariño.

91 Colour: bright straw. Nose: white flowers, fresh fruit, fragrant herbs, mineral. Palate: correct, fresh, fruity, flavourful, balanced.

PAZO DE PIÑEIRO 2010 B
100% albariño.

95 Colour: bright straw. Nose: white flowers, scrubland, mineral, ripe fruit. Palate: flavourful, fine bitter notes, good acidity, spicy, ripe fruit.

ADEGA CONDES DE ALBAREI

Lugar a Bouza, 1 Castrelo
36639 Cambados (Pontevedra)
☎: +34 986 543 535 - Fax: +34 986 524 251
inf@condesdealbarei.com
www.condesdealbarei.com

CONDES DE ALBAREI 2011 B
100% albariño.

90 Colour: bright straw. Nose: ripe fruit, citrus fruit, white flowers. Palate: flavourful, fruity, fine bitter notes, good acidity.

CARBALLO GALEGO 2010 BFB
100% albariño.

92 Colour: bright yellow. Nose: powerfull, ripe fruit, sweet spices, fragrant herbs, dried flowers. Palate: rich, smoky aftertaste, flavourful, fresh, good acidity.

ENXEBRE 2010 B
100% albariño.

90 Colour: bright straw. Nose: white flowers, grassy, fresh fruit, citrus fruit. Palate: light-bodied, fresh, flavourful.

ADEGA DOS EIDOS

Padriñán, 65
36960 Sanxenxo (Pontevedra)
☎: +34 986 690 009 - Fax: +34 986 720 307
info@adegaeidos.com
www.adegaeidos.com

EIDOS DE PADRIÑÁN 2011 B
100% albariño.

91 Colour: bright straw. Nose: fresh, fresh fruit, white flowers, expressive, dried herbs. Palate: flavourful, fruity, good acidity, balanced.

VEIGAS DE PADRIÑÁN 2010 B
100% albariño.

91 Colour: bright straw. Nose: characterful, varietal, ripe fruit, grassy. Palate: flavourful, fine bitter notes, good acidity.

CONTRAAPAREDE 2008 B
100% albariño.

93 Colour: bright yellow. Nose: dry nuts, fragrant herbs, ripe fruit, complex, petrol notes. Palate: powerful, flavourful, long, balanced.

ADEGA VALDÉS

Santa Cruz de Rivadulla, s/n
15885 Vedra (A Coruña)
☎: +34 981 512 439 - Fax: +34 981 509 226
ventas@gundian.com
www.adegavaldes.com

ALBARIÑO GUNDIAN 2011 B
100% albariño.

90 Colour: bright straw. Nose: fresh, fresh fruit, white flowers, expressive, fine lees. Palate: flavourful, fruity, good acidity, balanced.

PAZO VILADOMAR 2011 B
treixadura, albariño.

90 Colour: bright straw. Nose: fresh, fresh fruit, white flowers, expressive. Taste flavourful, fruity, good acidity, balanced.

XIRADELLA 2011 B
100% albariño.

90 Colour: bright straw. Nose: fresh, fresh fruit, white flowers, expressive. Taste flavourful, fruity, good acidity, balanced.

ADEGAS AROUSA

Tirabao, 15 - Baión
36614 Vilanova de Arousa (Pontevedra)
☎: +34 986 506 113 - Fax: +34 986 715 454
grupoarousaboucina@gmail.com
www.adegasarousa.com

PAZO DA BOUCIÑA 2011 B
albariño.

91 Colour: bright straw. Nose: fresh, fresh fruit, white flowers, expressive, fragrant herbs. Palate: flavourful, fruity, good acidity, balanced.

ADEGAS CASTROBREY

Camanzo, s/n
36587 Vila de Cruces (Pontevedra)
☎: +34 986 583 643 - Fax: +34 986 583 722
bodegas@castrobrey.com
www.castrobrey.com

SIN PALABRAS CASTRO VALDÉS 2011 B
100% albariño.

92 Colour: bright straw. Nose: fresh, fresh fruit, white flowers, balsamic herbs, grassy. Palate: flavourful, fruity, good acidity, balanced.

SEÑORÍO DE CRUCES 2011 B
100% albariño.

89 Colour: bright straw. Nose: grassy, fresh fruit, citrus fruit. Palate: ripe fruit, easy to drink.

SEÑORÍO DA REGAS 2011 B
albariño, treixadura, godello, torrontés.

88 Colour: bright straw. Nose: grassy, ripe fruit, fresh fruit. Palate: flavourful, light-bodied, fruity.

ADEGAS GALEGAS

Meder, s/n
36457 Salvaterra de Miño (Pontevedra)
☎: +34 986 657 143 - Fax: +34 986 526 901
comercial@adegasgalegas.es
www.adegasgalegas.es

DON PEDRO SOUTOMAIOR 2011 B
100% albariño.

91 Colour: bright straw. Nose: fresh, white flowers, ripe fruit, citrus fruit, dry stone. Palate: flavourful, fruity, good acidity, balanced.

DIONISOS 2011 B
100% albariño.

89 Colour: bright straw. Nose: fresh, fresh fruit, white flowers, expressive. Taste flavourful, fruity, good acidity, balanced.

BAGO AMARELO 2011 B
100% albariño.

89 Colour: bright straw. Nose: white flowers, fresh fruit, fragrant herbs. Palate: light-bodied, fresh, fruity, flavourful.

ADEGAS GRAN VINUM

Fermín Bouza Brei, 9 - 5ºB
36600 Vilagarcía de Arousa (Pontevedra)
☎: +34 986 555 742 - Fax: +34 986 555 742
info@adegasgranvinum.com
www.adegasgranvinum.com

ESENCIA DIVIÑA 2011 B
albariño.

91 Colour: bright straw. Nose: fresh, fresh fruit, white flowers, expressive, fragrant herbs. Palate: flavourful, fruity, good acidity, balanced.

GRAN VINUM 2010 B
albariño.

88 Colour: bright yellow. Nose: grassy, fine lees, floral, expressive. Palate: powerful, flavourful, long.

ADEGAS MORGADÍO

Albeos s/n
36429 Creciente (Pontevedra)
☎: +34 988 261 212 - Fax: +34 988 261 213
info@morgadio.com
www.morgadio.com

MORGADÍO 2011 B
albariño.

89 Colour: bright straw. Nose: fresh, fresh fruit, white flowers, grassy. Palate: flavourful, fruity, good acidity, balanced.

ADEGAS TOLLODOURO

Ctra. Tui-A Guarda, Km. 45
36760 O Rosal (Pontevedra)
☎: +34 986 609 810 - Fax: +34 986 609 811
bodega@tollodouro.com
www.tollodouro.com

PONTELLÓN ALBARIÑO 2011 B
albariño.

90 Colour: bright straw. Nose: fresh, white flowers, ripe fruit. Palate: flavourful, fruity, good acidity, balanced.

TOLLODOURO ROSAL 2011 B
albariño, treixadura, loureiro, caiño.

87 Colour: bright straw. Nose: dried flowers, grassy, fresh, medium intensity. Palate: flavourful, correct, fine bitter notes.

ADEGAS VALMIÑOR

A Portela, s/n - San Juan de Tabagón
36760 O'Rosal (Pontevedra)
☎: +34 986 609 060 - Fax: +34 986 609 313
valminor@valminorebano.com
www.adegasvalminor.com

TORROXAL 2011 B
albariño.

88 Colour: bright straw. Nose: fresh, fresh fruit, white flowers, expressive. Taste flavourful, fruity, good acidity, balanced.

SERRA DA ESTRELA 2011 B
albariño.

86 Colour: bright straw. Nose: floral, fragrant herbs, medium intensity. Palate: flavourful, fresh, fruity.

DÁVILA L100 2010 B
loureiro.

92 Colour: bright straw. Nose: ripe fruit, citrus fruit, grassy. Palate: flavourful, fine bitter notes, ripe fruit.

DÁVILA 2010 B
albariño, loureiro, treixadura.

90 Colour: bright yellow. Nose: fine lees, ripe fruit, fragrant herbs, expressive. Palate: long, rich, flavourful, balanced.

DÁVILA M.100 2009 B
albariño, loureiro, treixadura.

90 Colour: bright straw. Nose: mineral, ripe fruit, grassy. Palate: easy to drink, ripe fruit, good acidity.

VALMIÑOR 2011 B
albariño.

90 Colour: bright straw. Nose: ripe fruit, citrus fruit, white flowers. Palate: flavourful, fine bitter notes, good acidity.

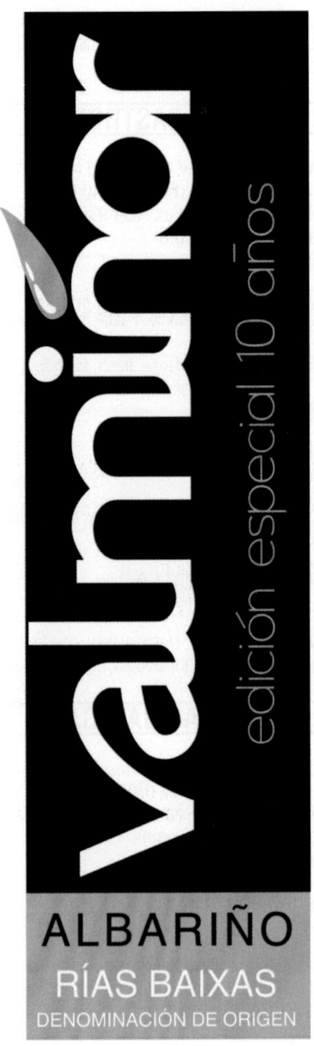

valmiñor
edición especial 10 años
ALBARIÑO
RÍAS BAIXAS
DENOMINACIÓN DE ORIGEN

ADEGAS VALTEA

Lg. Portela, 14
36429 Crecente (Pontevedra)
☎: +34 986 666 344 - Fax: +34 986 644 914
vilarvin@vilarvin.com
www.vilarvin.com

VALTEA 2011 B
100% albariño.

90 Colour: bright yellow. Nose: fruit expression, fine lees, fragrant herbs, expressive. Palate: correct, fine bitter notes, powerful, flavourful.

VALTEA 2010 B
100% albariño.

90 Colour: bright yellow. Nose: faded flowers, fragrant herbs, ripe fruit. Palate: powerful, flavourful, rich, long.

FINCA GARABATO 2010 B
100% albariño.

87 Colour: bright golden. Nose: dried flowers, ripe fruit, fragrant herbs, slightly evolved. Palate: powerful, flavourful, rich.

FINCA GARABATO 2009 B
100% albariño.

89 Colour: bright yellow. Nose: fine lees, ripe fruit, dried herbs, sweet spices. Palate: powerful, flavourful, rich, long.

ALBARIÑO BAIÓN

Lg. Abelleira 4,5,6 - Baión
36614 Vilanova de Arousa (Pontevedra)
☎: +34 986 543 535 - Fax: +34 986 524 251
info@pazobaion.com
www.pazobaion.com

PAZO BAIÓN 2011 B
100% albariño.

91 Colour: bright straw. Nose: fresh, white flowers, expressive, varietal, ripe fruit, mineral. Palate: flavourful, fruity, good acidity, balanced.

ALTOS DE CRISTIMIL

Cristimil 5 Padrenda
36638 Meaño (Pontevedra)
☎: +34 986 747 267 - Fax: +34 986 747 267
altosdecristimil@gmail.com

ALTOS DE CRISTIMIL 2011 B
100% albariño.

88 Colour: bright straw. Nose: dried flowers, grassy, citrus fruit. Palate: fresh, fruity, flavourful.

ATTIS BODEGAS Y VIÑEDOS

Morouzos - Dena
36967 Meaño (Pontevedra)
☎: +34 986 744 164
info@attisbyv.com
www.attisbyv.com

ATTIS 2011 B
100% albariño.

89 Colour: bright straw. Nose: fresh fruit, white flowers, ripe fruit. Palate: flavourful, fruity, good acidity, balanced.

XIÓN 2011 B
100% albariño.

88 Colour: bright straw. Nose: dried flowers, fragrant herbs, medium intensity. Palate: powerful, flavourful, long.

NANA 2009 B
100% albariño.

87 Colour: bright yellow. Nose: dried flowers, fragrant herbs, spicy. Palate: powerful, flavourful, rich, slightly evolved.

BENJAMÍN MIGUEZ NOVAL

Porto de Abaixo, 10 - Porto
36458 Salvaterra de Miño (Pontevedra)
☎: +34 986 122 705
enoturismo@mariabargiela.com
www.mariabargiela.com

MARÍA BARGIELA 2010 B
90% albariño, 8% treixadura, 2% loureiro.

88 Colour: bright straw. Nose: fresh, fresh fruit, white flowers, fragrant herbs. Palate: flavourful, fruity, balanced.

BODEGA CASTRO BAROÑA

Cabeiro - San Martín
36637 Meis (Pontevedra)
☎: +34 981 134 847 - Fax: +34 981 174 030
castrobarona@castrobarona.com
www.castrobarona.com

LAGAR DO CASTELO 2011 B
100% albariño.

90 Colour: bright straw. Nose: fresh, white flowers, ripe fruit, citrus fruit. Palate: flavourful, fruity, balanced.

CASTRO BAROÑA 2011 B
100% albariño.

90 Colour: bright straw. Nose: fresh, white flowers, ripe fruit. Palate: flavourful, fruity, good acidity, balanced.

MONTELOURO 2011 B
100% albariño.

88 Colour: bright straw. Nose: fresh, fresh fruit, white flowers, varietal. Palate: flavourful, fruity, good acidity.

CASTRO BAROÑA SELECCIÓN ÚNICA 2010 B
100% albariño.

91 Colour: bright yellow. Nose: floral, dried herbs, mineral, balanced. Palate: powerful, flavourful, complex, fine bitter notes, balanced.

BODEGA FORJAS DEL SALNÉS

As Covas, 5
36968 Meaño (Pontevedra)
☎: +34 699 446 113 - Fax: +34 986 744 428
rodri@movistar.net

LEIRANA 2011 B
albariño.

91 Colour: bright straw. Nose: saline, white flowers, fruit expression, fragrant herbs. Palate: elegant, flavourful, fresh, fruity, balanced.

LEIRANA FINCA GENOVEVA 2010 B
albariño.

94 Colour: bright yellow. Nose: powerfull, ripe fruit, sweet spices, creamy oak, fragrant herbs, dried flowers, mineral. Palate: rich, flavourful, fresh, good acidity, complex, round, balanced.

GOLIARDO ATELLEIRA 2010 B BARRICA
100% albariño.

93 Colour: bright yellow. Nose: powerfull, ripe fruit, sweet spices, creamy oak, fragrant herbs, varnish, cocoa bean, dry stone. Palate: rich, flavourful, fresh, good acidity, long, elegant.

GOLIARDO CAIÑO 2010 T
caiño.

92 Colour: cherry, garnet rim. Nose: ripe fruit, creamy oak, cocoa bean, dark chocolate, scrubland, toasty. Palate: powerful, flavourful, round tannins, balsamic.

GOLIARDO ESPADEIRO 2010 T
espadeiro.

91 Colour: cherry, garnet rim. Nose: ripe fruit, fruit liqueur notes, balsamic herbs, spicy, creamy oak, mineral, floral. Palate: flavourful, long, fine bitter notes, round, good acidity.

GOLIARDO LOUREIRO 2010 T
loureiro.

90 Colour: cherry, garnet rim. Nose: balsamic herbs, mineral, dried flowers, spicy, creamy oak. Palate: fresh, flavourful, long, spicy, balanced.

BASTIÓN DE LA LUNA 2010 T
espadeiro, loureiro, caiño.

90 Colour: bright cherry. Nose: ripe fruit, sweet spices, creamy oak, wild herbs, roasted coffee. Palate: flavourful, fruity, toasty, round tannins, balsamic.

BODEGA GRANBAZÁN

Tremoedo, 46
36628 Vilanova de Arousa (Pontevedra)
☎: +34 986 555 562 - Fax: +34 986 555 799
agrodebazan@agrodebazansa.es
www.agrodebazansa.es

GRANBAZÁN ETIQUETA ÁMBAR 2011 B
100% albariño.

91 Colour: bright straw. Nose: wild herbs, ripe fruit, dried flowers, fresh. Palate: powerful, flavourful, rich, fine bitter notes, balanced.

GRANBAZÁN ETIQUETA VERDE 2011 B
100% albariño.

90 Colour: bright straw. Nose: fresh, white flowers, fragrant herbs, ripe fruit. Palate: flavourful, fruity, good acidity.

CONTRAPUNTO 2011 B
100% albariño.

87 Colour: bright straw. Nose: fresh, fresh fruit, white flowers, citrus fruit. Palate: flavourful, fruity, good acidity, easy to drink.

GRANBAZÁN LIMOUSIN 2010 B
100% albariño.

93 Colour: bright golden. Nose: powerfull, toasty, honeyed notes, ripe fruit, sweet spices. Palate: flavourful, fruity, spicy, toasty, long.

GRANBAZÁN DON ALVARO DE BAZÁN 2010 B
100% albariño.

92 Colour: bright yellow. Nose: powerfull, ripe fruit, sweet spices, creamy oak, fragrant herbs. Palate: rich, flavourful, fresh, balanced.

BODEGAS ABANICO

Pol. Ind Ca l'Avellanet - Susany, 6
08553 Seva (Barcelona)
☎: +34 938 125 676 - Fax: +34 938 123 213
info@exportiberia.com
www.bodegasabanico.com

DILUVIO 2011 B
100% albariño.

89 Colour: bright straw. Nose: fresh, fresh fruit, white flowers, dried herbs, citrus fruit. Palate: flavourful, fruity, good acidity, balanced.

BODEGAS AGUIUNCHO

Las Pedreiras, 1º Villalonga
36990 Sanxenxo (Pontevedra)
☎: +34 986 720 980 - Fax: +34 986 727 063
info@aguiuncho.com
www.aguiuncho.com

MAR DE ONS 2011 B
100% albariño.

86 Colour: bright straw. Nose: fruit expression, dried herbs, floral. Palate: light-bodied, fruity, easy to drink.

AGUIUNCHO 2010 B BARRICA
albariño.

89 Colour: bright straw. Nose: white flowers, ripe fruit, citrus fruit, grassy. Palate: flavourful, good acidity, easy to drink.

AGUIUNCHO SELECCIÓN 2010 B
100% albariño.

89 Colour: bright yellow. Nose: creamy oak, sweet spices, ripe fruit. Palate: flavourful, powerful, spicy, ripe fruit.

BODEGAS ALBAMAR

O Adro, 11 - Castrelo
36639 Cambados (Pontevedra)
☎: +34 660 292 750 - Fax: +34 986 520 048
info@bodegasalbamar.com

ALBAMAR 2011 B
albariño.

90 Colour: bright straw. Nose: fresh fruit, white flowers, fragrant herbs. Palate: flavourful, fruity, good acidity, fine bitter notes.

ALMA DE MAR SOBRE LÍAS 2011 B
albariño.

89 Colour: bright straw. Nose: fresh, white flowers, ripe fruit. Palate: flavourful, fruity, good acidity, balanced.

PEPE LUIS SOBRE LÍAS 2010 B
albariño.

92 Colour: bright yellow. Nose: powerfull, ripe fruit, sweet spices, creamy oak, fragrant herbs. Taste rich, smoky aftertaste, flavourful, fresh, good acidity.

ALBAMAR 2010 B
albariño.

89 Colour: bright straw. Nose: candied fruit, citrus fruit, fragrant herbs. Palate: flavourful, ripe fruit, long.

BODEGAS ALTOS DE TORONA

Vilachán s/n
36740 Tomiño (Pontevedra)
☎: +34 986 288 212 - Fax: +34 986 401 185
info@reginaviarum.es
www.altosdetorona.com

ALTOS DE TORONA 2011 B
85% albariño, 10% caiño blanco, 5% loureiro.

90 Colour: bright straw. Nose: white flowers, dried herbs, fresh fruit, expressive. Palate: powerful, flavourful, fresh, balanced.

TORRES DE ERMELO 2011 B
100% albariño.

88 Colour: bright straw. Nose: expressive, ripe fruit, white flowers, grassy. Palate: flavourful, fruity, fine bitter notes.

ALBANTA 2011 B
100% albariño.

88 Colour: bright straw. Nose: fresh, fresh fruit, white flowers. Palate: flavourful, fruity, good acidity, balanced.

BODEGAS AQUITANIA

Bauza, 17 Castrelo
36639 Cambados (Pontevedra)
☎: +34 986 520 895 - Fax: +34 986 520 895
info@bodegasaquitania.com
www.bodegasaquitania.com

AQUITANIA 2011 B
albariño.

89 Colour: bright straw. Nose: fresh, white flowers, ripe fruit, fruit expression. Palate: flavourful, fruity, good acidity.

BERNON 2011 B
albariño.

89 Colour: bright straw. Nose: white flowers, candied fruit, fragrant herbs. Palate: correct, fresh, fruity.

RAIOLAS D'OUTONO 2011 B
albariño.

86 Colour: bright straw. Nose: white flowers, fresh fruit, fresh. Palate: flavourful, fresh, fruity.

AQUITANIA 2011 T
mencía.

82

BODEGAS AS LAXAS

As Laxas, 16
36430 Arbo (Pontevedra)
☎: +34 986 665 444 - Fax: +34 986 665 554
info@bodegasaslaxas.com
www.bodegasaslaxas.com

BÁGOA DO MIÑO 2011 B
100% albariño.

91 Colour: bright straw. Nose: fresh, fresh fruit, white flowers. Palate: flavourful, fruity, good acidity, balanced.

LAXAS 2011 B
100% albariño.

91 Colour: bright straw. Nose: fruit expression, floral, fragrant herbs, mineral, balanced. Palate: powerful, flavourful, good structure, correct.

VAL DO SOSEGO 2011 B
100% albariño.

90 Colour: bright straw. Nose: fresh, fresh fruit, white flowers, varietal, complex. Palate: flavourful, fruity, good acidity.

ALVINTE 2011 B
100% albariño.

89 Colour: bright straw. Nose: powerfull, fresh fruit, ripe fruit, grassy. Palate: flavourful, fruity, good acidity.

CONDADO LAXAS 2011 B
60% albariño, 30% treixadura, 10% loureiro.

88 Colour: bright straw. Nose: white flowers, fragrant herbs, expressive, tropical fruit. Palate: correct, flavourful.

VALDOCEA 2011 B
100% albariño.

88 Colour: pale. Nose: floral, ripe fruit, citrus fruit. Palate: flavourful, fruity, light-bodied.

BODEGAS CASTRO MARTÍN

Puxafeita, 3
36636 Ribadumia (Pontevedra)
☎: +34 986 710 202 - Fax: +34 986 710 607
info@castromartin.com
www.castromartin.com

CASAL CAEIRO ALBARIÑO 2011 B
100% albariño.

89 Colour: bright straw. Nose: fine lees, white flowers, fragrant herbs, mineral. Palate: fine bitter notes, flavourful, fresh, fruity, balanced.

BODEGA CASTRO MARTÍN ALBARIÑO 2011 B
100% albariño.

88 Colour: bright straw. Nose: fresh, white flowers, ripe fruit. Palate: flavourful, fruity, good acidity, balanced.

BODEGAS COTO REDONDO

Bouza do Rato, s/n - Rubiós
36449 As Neves (Pontevedra)
☎: +34 986 667 212 - Fax: +34 986 648 279
info@bodegas-cotoredondo.com
www.bodegas-cotoredondo.com

SEÑORÍO DE RUBIÓS CONDADO BLANCO DO TEA 2011 B
treixadura, albariño, loureiro, godello, torrontés.

91 Colour: bright yellow. Nose: powerfull, ripe fruit, citrus fruit, white flowers. Palate: flavourful, fruity, fresh.

SEÑORÍO DE RUBIÓS ALBARIÑO 2011 B
100% albariño.

88 Colour: bright straw. Nose: fresh, white flowers, ripe fruit. Palate: flavourful, fruity, good acidity, balanced.

SEÑORÍO DE RUBIÓS CONDADO DO TEA BARRICA 2007 B
treixadura, albariño, loureiro, godello, torrontés.

91 Colour: bright yellow. Nose: powerfull, ripe fruit, sweet spices, creamy oak, fragrant herbs. Taste rich, smoky aftertaste, flavourful, fresh, good acidity.

SEÑORÍO DE RUBIÓS SOUSÓN 2011 T
100% sausón.

90 Colour: cherry, purple rim. Nose: balsamic herbs, scrubland, red berry notes, fruit expression. Palate: fine bitter notes, balsamic.

SEÑORÍO DE RUBIÓS CONDADO TINTO 2011 T
sousón, espadeiro, caiño, mencía, pedral, loureiro tinto.

89 Colour: cherry, purple rim. Nose: balsamic herbs, red berry notes, ripe fruit. Palate: flavourful, fruity, fresh.

SEÑORÍO DE RUBIÓS MENCÍA 2011 T
100% mencía.

88 Colour: cherry, purple rim. Nose: fresh fruit, red berry notes, floral. Palate: flavourful, fruity, good acidity, round tannins.

MANUEL D'AMARO PEDRAL 2011 T
100% pedral.

88 Colour: deep cherry. Nose: red berry notes, floral, balsamic herbs. Palate: flavourful, fruity, fresh.

BODEGAS DEL PALACIO DE FEFIÑANES

Pza. de Fefiñanes, s/n
36630 Cambados (Pontevedra)
☎: +34 986 542 204 - Fax: +34 986 524 512
fefinanes@fefinanes.com
www.fefinanes.com

1583 ALBARIÑO DE FEFIÑANES 2011 BFB
100% albariño.

92 Colour: bright yellow. Nose: faded flowers, candied fruit, citrus fruit. Palate: flavourful, fruity, ripe fruit.

ALBARIÑO DE FEFIÑANES III AÑO 2009 B
100% albariño.

95 Colour: bright yellow. Nose: spicy, candied fruit, characterful, powerfull. Palate: long, ripe fruit, spicy, fine bitter notes.

ALBARIÑO DE FEFIÑANES 2011 B
100% albariño.

92 Colour: bright straw. Nose: ripe fruit, citrus fruit, white flowers, varietal. Palate: flavourful, fruity, fine bitter notes, good acidity.

BODEGAS EIDOSELA

Eidos de Abaixo, s/n - Sela
36494 Arbo (Pontevedra)
☎: +34 986 665 550 - Fax: +34 986 665 299
info@bodegaseidosela.com
www.bodegaseidosela.com

EIDOSELA 2011 B
100% albariño.

91 Colour: bright straw. Nose: fresh, white flowers, ripe fruit. Palate: flavourful, fruity, good acidity, balanced.

ETRA CONDADO 2011 B
70% albariño, 20% treixadura, 10% loureiro.

90 Colour: bright straw. Nose: fresh, fresh fruit, white flowers, fragrant herbs. Palate: flavourful, fruity, good acidity, balanced.

ARBASTRUM 2011 B
70% albariño, 20% treixadura, 10% loureiro.

88 Colour: bright straw. Nose: grassy, powerfull, varietal, ripe fruit, citrus fruit. Palate: flavourful, powerful, fruity.

BODEGAS FILLABOA

Lugar de Fillaboa, s/n
36450 Salvaterra do Miño (Pontevedra)
☎: +34 986 658 132
info@bodegasfillaboa.masaveu.com
www.bodegasfillaboa.com

FILLABOA 2011 B
albariño.

91 Colour: bright straw. Nose: ripe fruit, white flowers, citrus fruit, mineral. Palate: flavourful, fruity, fresh, ripe fruit.

FILLABOA SELECCIÓN FINCA MONTEALTO 2010 B
albariño.

92 Colour: bright yellow. Nose: grassy, fragrant herbs, ripe fruit, fruit expression, citrus fruit. Palate: flavourful, powerful, ripe fruit, fine bitter notes.

BODEGAS GERARDO MÉNDEZ

Galiñanes, 10 - Lores
36968 Meaño (Pontevedra)
☎: +34 986 747 046 - Fax: +34 986 748 915
info@bodegasgerardomendez.com
www.bodegasgerardomendez.com

ALBARIÑO DO FERREIRO 2011 B
albariño.

92 Colour: bright straw. Nose: grassy, fragrant herbs, dried flowers, mineral. Palate: powerful, flavourful, complex, long.

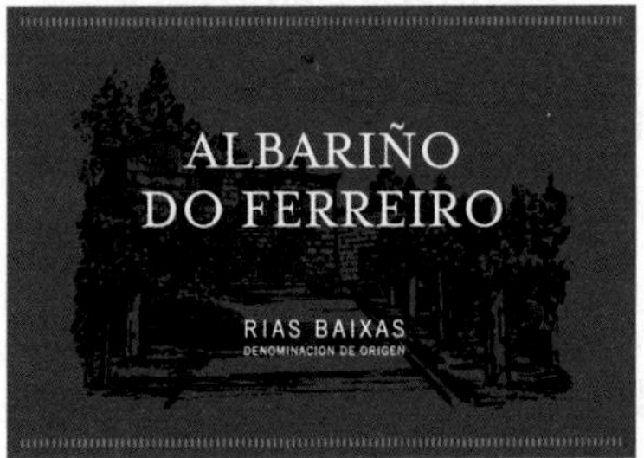

BODEGAS LA CANA

Bartolome Esteban Murillo, 11 - Pol Ind La Pañoleta
29700 Vélez (Málaga)
☎: +34 952 504 706 - Fax: +34 951 284 796
office@jorge-ordonez.es
www.lacana.es

LA CANA 2011 B
100% albariño.

92 Colour: bright straw. Nose: fresh, fresh fruit, white flowers, expressive. Taste flavourful, fruity, good acidity, balanced.

BODEGAS LA VAL

Lugar Muguiña, s/n - Arantei
36458 Salvaterra de Miño (Pontevedra)
☎: +34 986 610 728 - Fax: +34 986 611 635
laval@bodegaslaval.com
www.bodegaslaval.com

LA VAL ALBARIÑO 2011 B
100% albariño.

91 Colour: bright straw. Nose: dried flowers, fragrant herbs, mineral, expressive. Palate: rich, flavourful, correct, balanced.

ORBALLO 2011 B
100% albariño.

90 Colour: bright straw. Nose: fresh, white flowers, ripe fruit. Palate: flavourful, fruity, good acidity, balanced.

FINCA ARANTEI 2011 B
100% albariño.

88 Colour: bright straw. Nose: fresh, white flowers, characterful, ripe fruit. Palate: flavourful, fruity, good acidity, balanced.

TABOEXA 2011 B
100% albariño.

88 Colour: bright straw. Nose: fresh, white flowers, ripe fruit, citrus fruit. Palate: flavourful, fruity, good acidity, balanced.

LA VAL ALBARIÑO 2010 BFB
100% albariño.

90 Colour: bright yellow. Nose: creamy oak, sweet spices, candied fruit, citrus fruit. Palate: flavourful, powerful, fine bitter notes, balanced.

LA VAL CRIANZA SOBRE LÍAS 2005 BC
100% albariño.

92 Colour: bright yellow. Nose: powerfull, expressive, complex, candied fruit, citrus fruit, dried flowers. Palate: rich, powerful, flavourful, fine bitter notes, good acidity.

BODEGAS MAR DE FRADES

Lg. Arosa, 16 - Finca Valiñas
36637 Meis (Pontevedra)
☎: +34 986 680 911 - Fax: +34 986 680 926
info@mardefrades.es
www.mardefrades.es

FINCA VALIÑAS "CRIANZA SOBRE LÍAS" 2010 B
albariño.

93 Colour: bright yellow. Nose: citrus fruit, candied fruit, dried herbs, mineral, fragrant herbs. Palate: good acidity, flavourful, fresh, fruity, balanced, elegant.

MAR DE FRADES 2011 B
albariño.

89 Colour: bright straw. Nose: fresh, fresh fruit, white flowers, fragrant herbs. Palate: flavourful, fruity, good acidity, balanced.

BODEGAS MARQUÉS DE VIZHOJA

Finca La Moreira s/n
36438 Arbo (Pontevedra)
☎: +34 986 665 825 - Fax: +34 986 665 960
marquesdevizhoja@marquesdevizhoja.com
www.marquesdevizhoja.com

TORRE LA MOREIRA 2011 B
100% albariño.

90 Colour: bright straw. Nose: grassy, fruit expression, citrus fruit, fresh fruit. Palate: flavourful, good acidity.

SEÑOR DA FOLLA VERDE 2011 B
70% albariño, 15% treixadura, 15% loureiro.

89 Colour: bright straw. Nose: fruit expression, grassy, dried flowers. Palate: fine bitter notes, powerful, flavourful.

BODEGAS MARTÍN CÓDAX

Burgans, 91
36633 Vilariño-Cambados (Pontevedra)
☎: +34 986 526 040 - Fax: +34 986 526 901
comercial@martincodax.com
www.martincodax.com

ANXO MARTÍN 2011 B
85% albariño, 10% caiño blanco, 5% loureiro.

93 Colour: bright straw. Nose: fresh, fresh fruit, white flowers, expressive, grassy, balsamic herbs, mineral. Palate: flavourful, fruity, good acidity, balanced.

ALBA MARTÍN 2011 B
100% albariño.

91 Colour: bright straw. Nose: fresh, white flowers, varietal, ripe fruit, mineral. Palate: flavourful, fruity, good acidity, balanced.

BURGÁNS 2011 B
100% albariño.

90 Colour: bright straw. Nose: fresh, white flowers, expressive, fruit expression. Palate: flavourful, fruity, good acidity.

MARTÍN CÓDAX 2011 B
100% albariño.

89 Colour: bright straw. Nose: fresh, fresh fruit, white flowers, varietal. Palate: flavourful, fruity, good acidity, balanced.

MARTÍN CÓDAX GALLAECIA 2009 B
100% albariño.

90 Colour: bright yellow. Nose: powerfull, ripe fruit, sweet spices, creamy oak. Palate: rich, smoky aftertaste, flavourful, fresh, good acidity.

ORGANISTRUM 2009 B
100% albariño.

89 Colour: bright straw. Nose: white flowers, ripe fruit, citrus fruit, grassy. Palate: long, ripe fruit, good acidity.

MARTIN CODAX LÍAS 2008 B
100% albariño.

90 Colour: bright yellow. Nose: powerfull, ripe fruit, sweet spices, fragrant herbs. Palate: rich, smoky aftertaste, flavourful, fresh, good acidity.

BODEGAS NANCLARES

Castriño, 13 - Castrelo
36639 Cambados (Pontevedra)
☎: +34 986 520 763
bodega@bodegasnanclares.es
www.bodegasnanclares.com

TEMPUS VIVENDI 2011 B
100% albariño.

88 Colour: bright straw. Nose: fresh, white flowers, ripe fruit. Palate: flavourful, fruity, good acidity, balanced.

DANDELION 2011 B
100% albariño.

88 Colour: bright straw. Nose: fresh, fresh fruit, grassy, dried flowers. Palate: flavourful, fruity, balanced.

ALBERTO NANCLARES ALBARIÑO 2010 B
100% albariño.

89 Colour: bright yellow. Nose: ripe fruit, white flowers, dried herbs, fresh, citrus fruit. Palate: powerful, flavourful, long, balanced.

SOVERRIBAS DE NANCLARES BFB
100% albariño.

87 Colour: bright yellow. Nose: powerfull, ripe fruit, sweet spices, fragrant herbs. Palate: rich, smoky aftertaste, flavourful, fresh.

BODEGAS SANTIAGO ROMA

Catariño, 5 - Besomaño
36636 Ribadumia (Pontevedra)
☎: +34 679 469 218
bodega@santiagoroma.com
www.santiagoroma.com

ALBARIÑO SANTIAGO ROMA SELECCIÓN 2011 B
100% albariño.

91 Colour: bright yellow. Nose: ripe fruit, dried flowers, fragrant herbs, sweet spices. Palate: rich, fruity, flavourful, long.

COLLEITA DE MARTIS ALBARIÑO 2011 B
100% albariño.

90 Colour: bright straw. Nose: white flowers, citrus fruit, dried herbs. Palate: flavourful, fruity, fine bitter notes, easy to drink.

ALBARIÑO SANTIAGO ROMA 2011 B
100% albariño.

89 Colour: bright straw. Nose: citrus fruit, fragrant herbs, floral, balanced. Palate: fresh, fruity, light-bodied, flavourful, long.

BODEGAS SEÑORÍO DE VALEI

La Granja, s/n
36494 Sela - Arbo (Pontevedra)
☎: +34 698 146 950 - Fax: +34 986 665 390
info@bodegasenoriodevalei.com
www.bodegasenoriodevalei.com

PAZO DE VALEI 2011 B
100% albariño.

91 Colour: bright straw. Nose: fresh, fresh fruit, white flowers, citrus fruit. Palate: flavourful, fruity, good acidity, balanced.

SEÑORÍO DE VALEI 2011 B
100% albariño.

90 Colour: bright straw. Nose: fresh, fresh fruit, white flowers. Palate: flavourful, fruity, good acidity, balanced.

ESTELA 2011 B
100% albariño.

88 Colour: bright straw. Nose: white flowers, fruit expression, fine lees, fragrant herbs. Palate: flavourful, rich, balanced.

ORO VALEI 2011 B
100% albariño.

88 Colour: bright straw. Nose: fresh, fresh fruit, white flowers. Palate: flavourful, fruity, good acidity, balanced.

BODEGAS TERRAS GAUDA

Ctra. Tui - A Guarda, Km. 55
36760 O Rosal (Pontevedra)
☎: +34 986 621 001 - Fax: +34 986 621 084
terrasgauda@terrasgauda.com
www.terrasgauda.com

ABADÍA DE SAN CAMPIO 2011 B
albariño.

90 Colour: bright straw. Nose: fresh, fresh fruit, white flowers, expressive, grassy. Palate: flavourful, fruity, good acidity, balanced.

TERRAS GAUDA ETIQUETA NEGRA 2010 BFB
70% albariño, 20% loureiro, 10% caiño blanco.

92 Colour: bright yellow. Nose: sweet spices, cocoa bean, ripe fruit, fruit expression, citrus fruit. Palate: long, ripe fruit, spicy.

TERRAS GAUDA 2011 B
70% albariño, 18% loureiro, 12% caiño blanco.

91 Colour: bright yellow. Nose: fresh, neat, varietal, complex, dry stone. Palate: fruity, full, fine bitter notes.

LA MAR 2010 B
85% caiño blanco, 10% albariño, 5% loureiro.

89 Colour: bright yellow. Nose: powerfull, candied fruit, citrus fruit. Palate: spicy, ripe fruit, fine bitter notes.

BODEGAS VICENTE GANDÍA

Ctra. Cheste a Godelleta, s/n
46370 Chiva (Valencia)
☎: +34 962 524 242 - Fax: +34 962 524 243
vuboldi@vicentegandia.com
www.vicentegandia.es

CON UN PAR (WITH A PAIR) 2010 B
100% albariño.

89 Colour: bright yellow. Nose: floral, dried herbs, earthy notes, citrus fruit, ripe fruit. Palate: fine bitter notes, flavourful, long.

BODEGAS VINUM TERRAE

Lugar de Axis - Simes, s/n
36968 Meaño (Pontevedra)
☎: +34 986 747 566 - Fax: +34 986 747 621
pepa.formoso@vinumterrae.com
www.vinumterrae.com

YOU & ME WHITE EXPERIENCE 2011 B
100% albariño.

91 Colour: bright straw. Nose: ripe fruit, citrus fruit, white flowers, fragrant herbs, expressive. Palate: rich, fresh, fruity, flavourful.

AGNUSDEI ALBARIÑO 2011 B
100% albariño.

90 Colour: bright straw. Nose: ripe fruit, floral, fragrant herbs. Palate: fruity, rich, flavourful, easy to drink.

BODEGAS Y VIÑEDOS DON OLEGARIO

Refoxos, s/n - Corvillón
36634 Cambados (Pontevedra)
☎: +34 986 520 886 - Fax: +34 986 520 886
info@donolegario.com
www.donolegario.com

DON OLEGARIO ALBARIÑO 2011 B
albariño.

92 Colour: bright straw. Nose: grassy, balsamic herbs, citrus fruit, ripe fruit. Palate: good acidity, fine bitter notes, round.

BOUZA DO REI

Lugar de Puxafeita, s/n
36636 Ribadumia (Pontevedra)
☎: +34 986 710 257 - Fax: +34 986 718 393
bouzadorei@bouzadorei.com
www.bouzadorei.com

ALBARIÑO BOUZA DO REI 2011 B
100% albariño.

90 Colour: bright straw. Nose: fresh, fresh fruit, white flowers, expressive. Taste flavourful, fruity, good acidity, balanced.

CASTEL DE BOUZA 2011 B
100% albariño.

90 Colour: bright straw. Nose: white flowers, fresh fruit, fragrant herbs, fresh, complex. Palate: flavourful, fruity, long.

CAMPOS DE CELTAS

Avda. Diagonal, 590, 5º 1ª
08021 (Barcelona)
☎: +34 660 445 464
info@vinergia.com
www.vinergia.com

CAMPOS DE CELTAS 2011 B
100% albariño.

90 Colour: bright straw. Nose: fresh, fresh fruit, white flowers, expressive. Taste flavourful, fruity, good acidity, balanced.

CODORNÍU

Avda. Jaume Codorníu, s/n
08770 Sant Sadurní D'Anoia (Barcelona)
☎: +34 938 183 232 - Fax: +34 938 910 822
s.martin@codorniu.es
www.codorniu.com

LEIRAS 2011 B
100% albariño.

88 Colour: pale. Nose: characterful, varietal, ripe fruit, citrus fruit. Palate: flavourful, fruity, good acidity.

COMERCIAL GRUPO FREIXENET

Joan Sala, 2
08770 Sant Sadurní D'Anoia (Barcelona)
☎: +34 938 917 000 - Fax: +34 938 183 095
freixenet@freixenet.es
www.freixenet.es

VIONTA 2011 B
100% albariño.

90 Colour: bright straw. Nose: fresh, fresh fruit, citrus fruit, fragrant herbs. Palate: flavourful, fruity, good acidity, fine bitter notes.

CRUCEIRO VELLO

Raul Alfonsin, 3 - Lugar Cruceiro Vello
36636 Ribadumia (Pontevedra)
☎: +34 941 454 050 - Fax: +34 941 454 529
bodega@bodegasriojanas.com
www.bodegasriojanas.com

CRUCEIRO VELLO 2011 B
100% albariño.

91 Colour: bright yellow. Nose: candied fruit, ripe fruit, faded flowers. Palate: flavourful, good acidity, ripe fruit.

DAVIDE

Serantes, 36 Bayón
36614 Vilanova de Arousa (Pontevedra)
☎: +34 620 248 165 - Fax: +34 986 506 330
info@davide.es
www.davide.es

DAVIDE DUO 2011 B
50% albariño, 50% godello.

91 Colour: bright straw. Nose: fresh, fresh fruit, white flowers, expressive, fragrant herbs. Palate: flavourful, fruity, good acidity, balanced.

DAVIDE TRADICIÓN 2011 B
100% albariño.

90 Colour: bright straw. Nose: fresh, fresh fruit, white flowers. Palate: flavourful, fruity, good acidity, balanced.

DOMECQ WINES

Vía Rápida do Salnés, Km. 5
36637 (Pontevedra)
☎: +34 986 710 827 - Fax: +34 986 710 827
info@domecqbodegas.com
www.domecqbodegas.com

VILLAREI 2011 B
100% albariño.

90 Colour: bright straw. Nose: fresh, fresh fruit, white flowers, expressive. Taste flavourful, fruity, good acidity, balanced.

GRUPO VINÍCOLA MARQUÉS DE VARGAS - PAZO DE SAN MAURO

Pombal, 3 - Lugar de Porto
36458 Salvaterra de Miño (Pontevedra)
☎: +34 986 658 285 - Fax: +34 986 664 208
info@pazosanmauro.com
www.marquesdevargas.com

PAZO SAN MAURO 2011 B
albariño.

88 Colour: bright straw. Nose: fresh, white flowers, ripe fruit, varietal. Palate: flavourful, fruity, good acidity, balanced.

SANAMARO 2009 B
95% albariño, 5% loureiro.

91 Colour: bright yellow. Nose: dried herbs, white flowers, mineral. Palate: balanced, powerful, flavourful.

JOSÉ CARLOS QUINTAS PÉREZ

Fonte, 20 Quintela
36492 Crecente (Pontevedra)
☎: +34 669 485 271 - Fax: +34 986 267 145
plus-mer@plus-mer.es
www.oreidecampoverde.es

DAINSUA 2011 B
albariño, loureiro, treixadura.

88 Colour: bright straw. Nose: fresh, fresh fruit, white flowers, grassy. Palate: flavourful, fruity, good acidity, balanced.

O REI DE CAMPOVERDE 2011 B
100% albariño.

88 Colour: bright straw. Nose: fresh, fresh fruit, white flowers, varietal. Palate: flavourful, fruity, good acidity, fine bitter notes.

LAGAR DE BESADA

Pazo, 11
36968 Xil-Meaño (Pontevedra)
☎: +34 986 747 473 - Fax: +34 986 747 826
info@lagardebesada.com
www.lagardebesada.com

BALADIÑA 2011 B
100% albariño.

90 Colour: bright straw. Nose: medium intensity, fresh fruit, citrus fruit. Palate: flavourful, full.

EX-LIBRIS 2011 B
100% albariño.

89 Colour: bright straw. Nose: fresh, white flowers, ripe fruit. Palate: flavourful, fruity, good acidity, balanced.

LAGAR DE BESADA 2011 B
100% albariño.

88 Colour: bright yellow. Nose: dried herbs, dried flowers, ripe fruit. Palate: powerful, flavourful, long, good acidity.

AÑADA DE BALADIÑA 2004 B
100% albariño.

91 Colour: bright yellow. Nose: powerfull, characterful, candied fruit. Palate: ripe fruit, spicy, fine bitter notes, good acidity.

LAGAR DE COSTA

Sartaxes, 8 - Castrelo
36639 Cambados (Pontevedra)
☎: +34 986 543 526 - Fax: +34 986 982 342
contacto@lagardecosta.com
www.lagardecosta.com

LAGAR DE COSTA 2011 B
100% albariño.

89 Colour: bright straw. Nose: fresh, fresh fruit, white flowers, expressive. Taste flavourful, fruity, good acidity, balanced.

MAIO5 DE LAGAR COSTA 2010 B
100% albariño.

91 Colour: bright straw. Nose: white flowers, fresh fruit, fragrant herbs, mineral, balanced. Palate: powerful, flavourful, long, balanced.

LAGAR DE COSTA 2010 B BARRICA
100% albariño.

89 Colour: bright yellow. Nose: powerfull, ripe fruit, sweet spices, fragrant herbs, lees reduction notes. Palate: rich, flavourful, fresh, good acidity.

LAGAR DE FORNELOS

Barrio de Cruces - Fornelos
36770 O Rosal (Pontevedra)
☎: +34 986 625 875 - Fax: +34 986 625 011
lagar@riojalta.com
www.riojalta.com

LAGAR DE CERVERA 2011 B
100% albariño.

91 Colour: bright straw. Nose: white flowers, ripe fruit, fragrant herbs, expressive, varietal. Palate: powerful, flavourful, long.

LAGAR DO REI

Carballoso s/n - Xil
36968 Meaño (Pontevedra)
☎: +34 986 743 189
correo@lagarderei.com
www.ecogalicia.com/lagarderei

LAGAR DE REI 2011 B
albariño.

86 Colour: bright straw. Nose: dried herbs, dried flowers, medium intensity. Palate: flavourful, fine bitter notes, correct.

LUAR DE MINARELLOS

Plaza de Matute 12, - 3º
28012 (Madrid)
☎: +34 609 119 248
info@miravinos.es
www.miravinos.es

MINARELLOS 2011 B
albariño.

91 Colour: bright yellow. Nose: powerfull, mineral, candied fruit, citrus fruit. Palate: flavourful, ripe fruit, fine bitter notes.

M. CONSTANTINA SOTELO ARES

Castelo Castriño,
36639 Cambados (Pontevedra)
☎: +34 639 835 073
adegasotelo@yahoo.es

ROSALÍA 2011 B
albariño.

90 Colour: bright straw. Nose: fresh, fresh fruit, white flowers. Palate: flavourful, fruity, good acidity, balanced.

MAIOR DE MENDOZA

Rúa de Xiabre, 58
36613 Villagarcía de Arosa (Pontevedra)
☎: +34 986 508 896 - Fax: +34 986 507 924
maiordemendoza@hotmail.es
www.maiordemendoza.com

FULGET 2011 B
100% albariño.

90 Colour: bright straw. Nose: ripe fruit, white flowers, mineral. Palate: flavourful, fruity, fresh.

MAIOR DE MENDOZA "SOBRE LÍAS" 2011 B
100% albariño.

89 Colour: bright straw. Nose: fine lees, dried flowers, grassy. Palate: flavourful, fresh, fruity, balanced.

MAIOR DE MENDOZA MACERACIÓN CARBÓNICA 2011 B MACERACIÓN CARBÓNICA
100% albariño.

85 Colour: bright straw. Nose: dried flowers, medium intensity, fragrant herbs. Palate: flavourful, fresh, fine bitter notes.

MAIOR DE MENDOZA 3 CRIANZAS 2010 B
100% albariño.

88 Colour: bright yellow. Nose: fine lees, fruit expression, fragrant herbs. Palate: correct, fruity, flavourful.

MAR DE ENVERO

Lugar Quintáns, 17
36638 Ribadumia (Pontevedra)
☎: +34 981 577 083 - Fax: +34 981 569 552
bodega@mardeenvero.es
www.mardeenvero.es

TROUPE 2011 B

90 Colour: bright straw. Nose: fresh, fresh fruit, white flowers. Palate: flavourful, fruity, good acidity, balanced.

MAR DE ENVERO 2009 B
albariño.

91 Colour: bright yellow. Nose: dried flowers, fragrant herbs, ripe fruit, balanced. Palate: powerful, flavourful,

PACO & LOLA

Valdamor, 18 - XII
36968 Meaño (Pontevedra)
☎: +34 986 747 779 - Fax: +34 986 748 940
internacional@pacolola.com
www.pacolola.com

IWINE 2009 B
albariño.

88 Colour: bright yellow. Nose: ripe fruit, dried herbs, faded flowers. Palate: long, powerful, flavourful, fine bitter notes.

PACO & LOLA 2011 B
albariño.

92 Colour: bright straw. Nose: mineral, fragrant herbs, dried flowers, varietal. Palate: good acidity, flavourful, fruity.

FOLLAS NOVAS 2011 B
albariño.

90 Colour: bright straw. Nose: fresh, fresh fruit, white flowers. Palate: flavourful, fruity, good acidity, balanced.

LOLO 2011 B
albariño.

88 Colour: bright straw. Nose: fresh, fresh fruit, white flowers, expressive. Taste flavourful, fruity, good acidity, balanced.

PAZO DE BARRANTES

Finca Pazo de Barrantes
36636 Barrantes (Pontevedra)
☎: +34 986 718 211 - Fax: +34 986 710 424
bodega@pazodebarrantes.com
www.pazodebarrantes.com

PAZO DE BARRANTES ALBARIÑO 2011 B
100% albariño.

93 Colour: bright straw. Nose: fresh, white flowers, ripe fruit, varietal, expressive. Palate: flavourful, fruity, good acidity, balanced.

LA COMTESSE 2009 B
100% albariño.

94 Colour: bright yellow. Nose: powerfull, ripe fruit, sweet spices, creamy oak, fragrant herbs, mineral. Palate: rich, flavourful, fresh, good acidity.

PAZO DE SEÑORANS

Vilanoviña,s/n
36616 Meis (Pontevedra)
☎: +34 986 715 373 - Fax: +34 986 715 569
info@pazodesenorans.com
www.pazodesenorans.com

PAZO SEÑORANS 2011 B
100% albariño.

92 Colour: bright straw. Nose: fresh, fresh fruit, white flowers, expressive, mineral. Palate: flavourful, fruity, good acidity, balanced.

PAZO SEÑORANS SELECCIÓN DE AÑADA 2005 B
100% albariño.

96 Colour: bright yellow. Nose: mineral, ripe fruit, fruit expression, white flowers, complex, varietal. Palate: good acidity, flavourful, ripe fruit, long.

PRIMA VINIA

Soutelo, 3
36750 Goián (Pontevedra)
☎: +34 902 100 723 - Fax: +34 986 620 071

LEIRA VELLA 2011 B
albariño.

90 Colour: bright straw. Nose: fresh, fresh fruit, white flowers, expressive. Taste flavourful, fruity, good acidity, balanced.

GAUDILA 2009 B
albariño.

92 Colour: bright yellow. Nose: ripe fruit, floral, fine lees, fragrant herbs, complex. Palate: powerful, flavourful, long, balanced.

QUINTA COUSELO

Barrio de Couselo, 13
36770 O'Rosal (Pontevedra)
☎: +34 986 625 051 - Fax: +34 986 626 267
quintacouselo@quintacouselo.com
www.quintacouselo.com

QUINTA DE COUSELO 2011 B
albariño, loureiro.

90 Colour: bright straw. Nose: fresh, fresh fruit, white flowers, varietal. Palate: flavourful, fruity, good acidity, balanced.

TVRONIA 2011 B
albariño.

90 Colour: bright straw. Nose: fresh, white flowers, ripe fruit, varietal. Palate: flavourful, fruity, good acidity, balanced.

QUINTA DE LA ERRE

As Eiras, s/n
36778 O'Rosal (Pontevedra)
☎: +34 986 620 292 - Fax: +34 986 620 121
labodega@quintadelaerre.com
www.aforado.com

ALBARIÑO QUINTA DE LA ERRE 2011 B
albariño.

88 Colour: bright straw. Nose: candied fruit, citrus fruit, white flowers. Palate: easy to drink, ripe fruit.

RECTORAL DO UMIA

Plg. de Rua do Pan, 9
36636 Ribadumia (Pontevedra)
☎: +34 986 716 360 - Fax: +34 986 718 252
jmanuel@rectoraldoumia.com
www.rectoraldoumia.com

MIUDIÑO 2011 B

88 Colour: bright straw. Nose: grassy, white flowers. Palate: flavourful, fine bitter notes.

PÓRTICO DA RIA 2011 B

88 Colour: bright straw. Nose: floral, grassy, medium intensity, fruit expression. Palate: powerful, flavourful, fine bitter notes.

RECTORAL DO UMIA 2011 B
albariño.

87 Colour: bright straw. Nose: floral, citrus fruit, ripe fruit, medium intensity. Palate: flavourful, fruity, ripe fruit.

RED BOTTLE INTERNATIONAL

Rosales, 6
09400 Aranda de Duero (Burgos)
☎: +34 947 515 884 - Fax: +34 947 515 886
rbi@redbottleint.com

ELAS 2011 B
100% albariño.

90 Colour: bright straw. Nose: citrus fruit, floral, fragrant herbs, expressive. Palate: balanced, fresh, fruity, flavourful.

RICARDO ABAL PADIN

Avda. La Pastora, 24
36630 Cambados (Pontevedra)
☎: +34 670 452 929 - Fax: +34 986 542 882
lagardacachada@gmail.com

LAGAR DA CACHADA 2011 B
albariño.

83

SANTIAGO RUIZ

Rua do Vinicultor Santiago Ruiz
36760 San Miguel de Tabagón - O Rosal (Pontevedra)
☎: +34 986 614 083 - Fax: +34 986 614 142
info@bodegasantiagoruiz.com
www.bodegasantiagoruiz.com

SANTIAGO RUIZ 2011 B
albariño, loureiro, treixadura, caiño, godello.

91 Colour: bright straw. Nose: fresh, fresh fruit, white flowers, fragrant herbs. Palate: flavourful, fruity, good acidity, balanced.

SEÑORÍO DE SOBRAL

Lg. Porto - Finca Sobral
36458 Salvaterra do Miño (Pontevedra)
☎: +34 986 415 144 - Fax: +34 986 421 744
info@ssobral.net
www.ssobral.net

CANTARCIÑO 2011 B
100% albariño.

88 Colour: bright straw. Nose: fresh, fresh fruit, white flowers. Palate: flavourful, fruity, good acidity, balanced.

SEÑORÍO DE SOBRAL 2011 B
100% albariño.

87 Colour: bright straw. Nose: fresh, fresh fruit, white flowers, dried herbs. Palate: flavourful, fruity, good acidity.

TERRA DE ASOREI

Rúa San Francisco, 2 - 1º C-D
36630 Cambados (Pontevedra)
☎: +34 986 198 882 - Fax: +34 986 520 813
info@terradeasorei.com
www.terradeasorei.com

NAI 2011 B
albariño.

90 Colour: bright straw. Nose: fresh, fresh fruit, white flowers. Palate: flavourful, fruity, good acidity.

TERRA DE ASOREI 2011 B
albariño.

88 Colour: bright straw. Nose: fresh, fresh fruit, white flowers. Palate: flavourful, fruity, good acidity, balanced.

TOMADA DE CASTRO

Travesía do Freixo, 3
36636 Ribadumia (Pontevedra)
☎: +34 986 710 550 - Fax: +34 986 718 552
info@tomadadecastro.com
www.tomadadecastro.com

SILFIDE 2011 B
100% albariño.

88 Colour: bright straw. Nose: ripe fruit, citrus fruit, grassy. Palate: flavourful, good acidity.

TOMADA DE CASTRO 2011 B
100% albariño.

87 Colour: bright straw. Nose: fresh, fresh fruit, white flowers, characterful, mineral. Palate: flavourful, fruity, good acidity, balanced.

VALDAMOR

Valdamor, 8
36968 Xil - Meaño (Pontevedra)
☎: +34 986 747 111 - Fax: +34 986 747 743
clientes@valdamor.es
www.valdamor.es

VALDAMOR 2011 B
albariño.

89 Colour: bright straw. Nose: characterful, varietal, ripe fruit, citrus fruit. Palate: flavourful, good acidity, balanced.

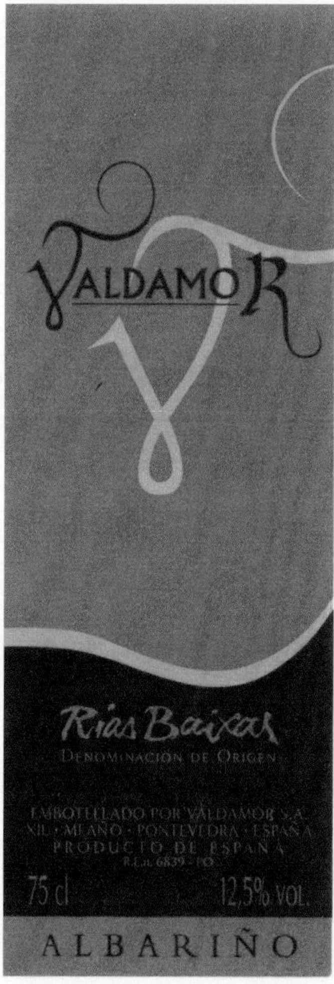

NAMORÍO 2011 B
albariño.

89 Colour: bright straw, greenish rim. Nose: floral, fragrant herbs, fresh fruit. Palate: fresh, fruity, flavourful, fine bitter notes.

VALDAMOR BARRICA 2009 B
albariño.

89 Colour: bright yellow. Nose: powerfull, ripe fruit, sweet spices, fragrant herbs, toasty. Palate: rich, flavourful, fresh, good acidity.

VEIGA NAÚM

Villarreis, 21 - Dena
36967 Meaño (Pontevedra)
☎: +34 941 454 050 - Fax: +34 941 454 529
bodega@bodegasriojanas.com
www.bodegasriojanas.com

VEIGA NAÚM 2011 B
100% albariño.

87 Colour: bright straw. Nose: white flowers, grassy, citrus fruit. Palate: flavourful, fruity, easy to drink.

VIÑA ALMIRANTE

Peroxa, 5
36658 Portas (Pontevedra)
☎: +34 620 294 293 - Fax: +34 986 541 471
info@vinaalmirante.com
www.vinaalmirante.com

PIONERO MUNDI 2011 B
100% albariño.

90 Colour: bright straw. Nose: balsamic herbs, grassy, ripe fruit, citrus fruit. Palate: flavourful, fruity, fresh.

VANIDADE 2011 B
100% albariño.

90 Colour: bright straw. Nose: grassy, ripe fruit, citrus fruit, fruit expression. Palate: flavourful, fruity, ripe fruit.

PIONERO MACCERATO 2011 B
100% albariño.

89 Colour: bright straw. Nose: citrus fruit, ripe fruit, floral, fragrant herbs. Palate: fine bitter notes, flavourful, fresh.

VIÑA CARTIN

Baceiro, 1 - Lantaño
36657 Portas (Pontevedra)
☎: +34 615 646 442
bodegas@montino.es
www.terrasdelantano.com

TERRAS DE LANTAÑO 2011 B
100% albariño.

90 Colour: bright straw. Nose: ripe fruit, citrus fruit, white flowers. Palate: flavourful, good acidity, fine bitter notes.

VIÑA CARTIN 2011 B
100% albariño.

89 Colour: bright straw. Nose: fresh, fresh fruit, white flowers, grassy. Palate: flavourful, fruity, good acidity, balanced.

VIÑA NORA

Bruñeiras, 7
36440 As Neves (Pontevedra)
☎: +34 986 667 210 - Fax: +34 986 664 610
info@vinanora.com
www.vinanora.com

NORA 2011 B
albariño.

90 Colour: bright straw. Nose: fresh, fresh fruit, white flowers, mineral. Palate: flavourful, fruity, good acidity, balanced.

VAL DE NORA 2011 B
albariño.

90 Colour: bright straw. Nose: fresh, fresh fruit, white flowers, lactic notes. Palate: flavourful, fruity, good acidity, balanced.

NORA DA NEVE 2009 BFB
albariño.

95 Colour: bright yellow. Nose: complex, characterful, candied fruit, fruit expression, mineral. Palate: fine bitter notes, good acidity, balanced, round.

VIÑEDOS SINGULARES

Cuzco, 26 - 28, Nave 8
08030 (Barcelona)
☎: +34 609 168 191 - Fax: +34 934 807 076
info@vinedossingulares.com
www.vinedossingulares.com

LUNA CRECIENTE 2011 B
albariño.

90 Colour: bright straw. Nose: fresh, fresh fruit, white flowers, citrus fruit, fragrant herbs. Palate: flavourful, fruity, good acidity, balanced.

ZÁRATE

Bouza, 23
36668 Padrenda - Meaño (Pontevedra)
☎: +34 986 718 503 - Fax: +34 986 718 549
info@zarate.es
www.albarino-zarate.com

ZÁRATE 2011 B
albariño.

89 Colour: bright straw. Nose: candied fruit, dried herbs. Palate: spicy, ripe fruit, fine bitter notes.

ZÁRATE EL BALADO 2010 B
albariño.

90 Colour: bright straw. Nose: candied fruit, fruit expression, floral. Palate: flavourful, powerful, fine bitter notes.

ZÁRATE CAIÑO TINTO 2010 T
caiño.

90 Colour: deep cherry. Nose: stalky, ripe fruit, spicy, balsamic herbs. Palate: flavourful, fine bitter notes.

ZÁRATE LOUREIRO TINTO 2010 T
loureiro.

89 Colour: deep cherry. Nose: stalky, sweet spices, scrubland. Palate: flavourful, powerful, fine bitter notes.

DO RIBEIRA SACRA

LOCATION:

The region extends along the banks of the rivers Miño and Sil in the south of the province of Lugo and the northern region of the province of Orense; it is made up of 17 municipal districts in this region.

CLIMATE:

Quite variable depending on the specific area. Less rain and slightly cooler climate and greater Continental influence in the Sil valley, and greater Atlantic character in the Miño valley. Altitude, on the other hand, also has an effect, with the vineyards closer to the rivers and with a more favourable orientation (south-southeast) being slightly warmer.

SOIL:

In general, the soil is highly acidic, although the composition varies greatly from one area to another. The vineyards are located on steep terraces and are no higher than 400 m to 500 m above sea level.

GRAPE VARIETIES:

WHITE: *Albariño, Loureira, Treixadura, Godello, Dona Blanca* and *Torrontés*.
RED: Main: *Mencía, Brancellao Merenzao*, *Garnacha Tintorera, Tempranillo, Sausón, Caiño Tinto* and *Mouratón*.

SUB-REGIONS:

Amandi, Chantada, Quiroga-Bibei, Ribeiras do Miño (in the province of Lugo) and **Ribeiras do Sil**.

FIGURES:

Vineyard surface: 1,265 – **Wine-Growers:** 2,896 – **Wineries:** 93 – **2011 Harvest rating:** Very Good – **Production:** 4,735,019 litres – **Market percentages:** 90% domestic. 10% export

CONSEJO REGULADOR
Rúa do Comercio, 6-8 - 27400 Monforte de Lemos (Lugo) - ☎: +34 982 410 968 - Fax: +34 982 411 265
@ info@ribeirasacra.org - www.ribeirasacra.org

ADEGAS MOURE

Buenos Aires, 12 - Bajo
27540 Escairón (Lugo)
☎: +34 982 452 031 - Fax: +34 982 452 700
abadiadacova@adegasmoure.com
www.adegasmoure.com

ABADÍA DA COVA ALBARIÑO 2011 B
85% albariño, 15% godello.

91 Colour: bright straw. Nose: white flowers, expressive, ripe fruit. Palate: flavourful, fruity, good acidity, balanced.

ABADÍA DA COVA DE AUTOR 2011 T
mencía.

94 Colour: cherry, purple rim. Nose: elegant, mineral, balsamic herbs, spicy. Palate: balanced, fine bitter notes, good finish, round tannins.

ABADÍA DA COVA 2011 T BARRICA
mencía.

91 Colour: bright cherry. Nose: ripe fruit, sweet spices, expressive, toasty, mineral. Palate: flavourful, fruity, toasty, round tannins.

ABADÍA DA COVA MENCÍA 2011 T
100% mencía.

90 Colour: cherry, garnet rim. Nose: red berry notes, balsamic herbs, mineral, medium intensity. Palate: light-bodied, fresh, fruity, easy to drink.

CEPA VELLA 2011 T
mencía.

89 Colour: cherry, purple rim. Nose: mineral, raspberry, floral, fresh, balsamic herbs. Palate: flavourful, fruity, easy to drink.

A FUGA 2011 T
mencía.

87 Colour: cherry, purple rim. Nose: red berry notes, balsamic herbs, floral, expressive. Palate: flavourful, fruity, easy to drink.

ABADÍA DA COVA 2010 T BARRICA
mencía.

92 Colour: cherry, garnet rim. Nose: ripe fruit, spicy, creamy oak, toasty, red berry notes, characterful. Palate: powerful, flavourful, toasty, round tannins, mineral.

ALGUEIRA

Doade, s/n
27460 Sober (Lugo)
☎: +34 629 208 917 - Fax: +34 982 410 299
info@adegaalgueira.com
www.adegaalgueira.com

ALGUEIRA MERENZAO 2010 T ROBLE
merenzao.

95 Colour: bright cherry. Nose: ripe fruit, varietal, dry stone, floral, balsamic herbs, expressive. Palate: fruity, toasty, round tannins, round. Personality.

ALGUEIRA FINCAS 2010 T ROBLE
caiño, sousón.

94 Colour: bright cherry. Nose: ripe fruit, sweet spices, creamy oak, fragrant herbs. Palate: flavourful, fruity, toasty, round tannins, balanced, elegant.

BODEGA CASTRO BAROÑA

Cabeiro - San Martín
36637 Meis (Pontevedra)
☎: +34 981 134 847 - Fax: +34 981 174 030
castrobarona@castrobarona.com
www.castrobarona.com

PAZO DE BEXÁN 2011 T
100% mencía.

88 Colour: cherry, purple rim. Nose: expressive, fresh fruit, red berry notes, balsamic herbs. Palate: flavourful, fruity, good acidity.

BODEGA VICTORINO ÁLVAREZ

Luis Carballo, 74
32765 A Teixeira (Ourense)
☎: +34 639 787 665
adegasollio@yahoo.es

SOLLIO GODELLO 2011 B
100% godello.

88 Colour: bright straw. Nose: white flowers, ripe fruit, fragrant herbs. Palate: flavourful, fruity, good acidity, balanced.

SOLLÍO 2011 T
95% mencía, 5% brancellao.

88 Colour: cherry, garnet rim. Nose: red berry notes, ripe fruit, scrubland. Palate: powerful, flavourful, rich.

BODEGAS ALBAMAR

O Adro, 11 - Castrelo
36639 Cambados (Pontevedra)
☎: +34 660 292 750 - Fax: +34 986 520 048
info@bodegasalbamar.com

FUSCO 2011 T
mencía.

90 Colour: cherry, purple rim. Nose: medium intensity, fruit expression, fragrant herbs, mineral. Palate: flavourful, fruity, long, good acidity.

BODEGAS RECTORAL DE AMANDI

Amandi
27423 Sober (Lugo)
☎: +34 988 384 200 - Fax: +34 988 384 068
vinos@bodegasgallegas.com
www.bodegasgallegas.com

RECTORAL DE AMANDI 2011 T
mencía.

88 Colour: cherry, purple rim. Nose: neat, dried herbs, medium intensity, earthy notes. Palate: flavourful, fruity, good acidity.

CASA MOREIRAS

San Martín de Siós, s/n
27430 Pantón (Lugo)
☎: +34 982 456 129 - Fax: +34 982 456 129
bodega@casamoreiras.com
www.casamoreiras.com

CASA MOREIRAS GODELLO 2011 B
godello, albariño.

89 Colour: bright straw. Nose: fresh, white flowers, varietal, ripe fruit. Palate: flavourful, fruity, good acidity, balanced.

CASA MOREIRAS 2011 T
mencía, tempranillo.

88 Colour: cherry, purple rim. Nose: red berry notes, expressive, balanced, powerfull, violets. Palate: fruity, full, correct.

DOMINIO DO BIBEI

Langullo, s/n
32781 Manzaneda (Ourense)
☎: +34 988 294 453 - Fax: +34 988 519 494
info@dominiodobibei.com
www.dominiodobibei.com

LAPOLA 2010 B

93 Colour: bright straw. Nose: mineral, ripe fruit, fruit expression, sweet spices. Palate: flavourful, ripe fruit, long.

LAPENA 2009 B

93 Colour: bright yellow. Nose: candied fruit, citrus fruit, medium intensity, sweet spices. Palate: good acidity, balanced, round.

LACIMA 2009 T

94 Colour: cherry, garnet rim. Nose: creamy oak, sweet spices, ripe fruit, fruit expression, dried herbs. Palate: good acidity, fine bitter notes, spicy, powerful tannins.

LALAMA 2009 T

92 Colour: bright cherry. Nose: ripe fruit, red berry notes, fruit expression, balsamic herbs. Palate: flavourful, spicy, ripe fruit.

DOMINIO DO BIBEI B 2008 T
brancellao.

96 Colour: deep cherry. Nose: spicy, balsamic herbs, scrubland, fresh, complex, expressive. Palate: flavourful, fresh, fruity, light-bodied, long.

DOMINIO DE BIBEI MT 2008 T

93 Colour: deep cherry. Nose: scrubland, powerfull, ripe fruit, raspberry, sweet spices. Palate: flavourful, powerful, complex, round tannins.

ERNESTO RODRÍGUEZ PÉREZ

Barrio Figueiroá, 13
27460 Sober (Lugo)
☎: +34 600 687 107
ernestoribadent@yahoo.es

VIÑA PEÓN 2010 T
mencía.

83

FINCA MILLARA BODEGAS Y VIÑEDOS

Millara Ribeiras do Miño
27430 Pantón (Lugo)
☎: +34 981 648 161 - Fax: +34 981 648 259
yordisl@teleline.es

FINCA MILLARA 2009 T BARRICA
mencía.

88 Colour: cherry, garnet rim. Nose: wild herbs, ripe fruit, spicy. Palate: flavourful, ripe fruit, long.

NAZ

Naz de Abaixo, 55 (Rosende)
27466 Sober (Lugo)
☎: +34 982 460 110
comercial@naz.es
www.naz.es

NAZ 2011 T
90% mencía, 3% garnacha, 7% tempranillo.

89 Colour: bright cherry, garnet rim. Nose: balanced, mineral, ripe fruit, balsamic herbs. Palate: balanced, fine bitter notes, good finish.

PEDRO MANUEL RODRÍGUEZ PÉREZ

Sanmil, 43 - Santa Cruz de Brosmos
27425 Sober (Lugo)
☎: +34 982 152 508 - Fax: +34 982 402 000
adegasguimaro@gmail.com

GUIMARO B1P 2011 B
100% godello.

89 Colour: bright yellow. Nose: ripe fruit, fragrant herbs, dried herbs, earthy notes. Palate: powerful, flavourful, balsamic.

GUIMARO MENCÍA 2011 T
100% mencía.

91 Colour: cherry, garnet rim. Nose: ripe fruit, spicy, toasty, complex, balsamic herbs, scrubland. Palate: powerful, flavourful, round tannins.

FINCA CAPELIÑOS 2010 T
100% mencía.

93 Colour: bright cherry. Nose: ripe fruit, creamy oak, spicy, balsamic herbs, mineral. Palate: flavourful, fruity, toasty, fresh, balanced.

FINCA MEIXEMAN 2010 T
100% mencía.

93 Colour: cherry, garnet rim. Nose: ripe fruit, spicy, dried flowers. Palate: powerful, flavourful, toasty, balsamic, round tannins.

PONTE DA BOGA

15178 Castro Caldelas (Ourense)
☎: +34 988 203 306 - Fax: +34 988 203 299
ruben@pontedaboga.es
www.pontedaboga.es

PONTE DA BOGA BLANCO DE BLANCOS 2011 B
albariño, godello, dona blanca.

91 Colour: bright straw. Nose: fresh, fresh fruit, white flowers, expressive, balsamic herbs, mineral. Palate: flavourful, fruity, good acidity, balanced.

PONTE DA BOGA MENCÍA 2011 T
mencía.

87 Colour: cherry, purple rim. Nose: ripe fruit, balsamic herbs, warm. Palate: good structure, fruity, good finish, balanced.

PONTE DA BOGA EXPRESIÓN HISTÓRICA 2010 T
mencía, merenzao, sausón, brancellao.

91 Colour: cherry, garnet rim. Nose: spicy, complex, red berry notes, ripe fruit. Palate: powerful, flavourful, toasty, round tannins.

PONTE DA BOGA CAPRICHO DE MERENZAO 2009 T
merenzao, brancellao, sousón.

93 Colour: cherry, garnet rim. Nose: ripe fruit, spicy, scrubland, expressive, creamy oak. Palate: round, flavourful, long, spicy, elegant.

PONTE DA BOGA BANCALES OLVIDADOS MENCÍA 2009 T
mencía.

91 Colour: cherry, garnet rim. Nose: red berry notes, ripe fruit, scrubland, spicy. Palate: flavourful, long, balanced, balsamic.

ALAIS 2009 T
mencía.

89 Colour: cherry, garnet rim. Nose: medium intensity, closed, ripe fruit. Palate: good structure, powerful, spicy.

RAMÓN MARCOS FERNÁNDEZ

Vilachá de Doade, 140
27400 Sober (Lugo)
☎: +34 982 152 285
info@adegacruceiro.es
www.adegacruceiro.es

CRUCEIRO 2011 T
mencía.

88 Colour: cherry, garnet rim. Nose: red berry notes, fresh fruit, scrubland. Palate: correct, fresh, fruity, balsamic.

CRUCEIRO REXIO 2009 T
mencía.

84

REGINA VIARUM

Doade, s/n
27424 Sober (Lugo)
☎: +34 986 288 212 - Fax: +34 986 401 185
info@reginaviarum.es
www.reginaviarum.es

REGINA VIARUM GODELLO 2011 B
85% godello, 10% loureiro, 5% treixadura.

85 Colour: bright straw. Nose: fresh, fresh fruit, white flowers, expressive. Palate: flavourful, fruity, good acidity, balanced.

REGINA VIARUM 2011 T
100% mencía.

88 Colour: cherry, purple rim. Nose: fresh fruit, red berry notes, balsamic herbs. Palate: flavourful, fruity, good acidity.

VÍA IMPERIAL 2001 T
100% mencía.

84

S.A.T. VIRXEN DOS REMEDIOS

Diomondi, 56
27548 O Saviñao (Lugo)
☎: +34 982 171 720 - Fax: +34 982 171 720
info@virxendosremedios.es
www.virxendosremedios.es

VIÑA VELLA 2011 B
60% godello, 20% albariño, 20% treixadura.

86 Colour: bright straw. Nose: fresh fruit, citrus fruit, grassy. Palate: flavourful, fruity, fresh.

VIÑA VELLA MENCÍA 2011 T
100% mencía.

86 Colour: cherry, purple rim. Nose: red berry notes, ripe fruit, balanced, scrubland. Palate: flavourful, fruity, good finish.

VÍA ROMANA

A Ermida - Belesar, s/n
27500 Chantada (Lugo)
☎: +34 982 454 005 - Fax: +34 982 454 094
vinose:na@vinose:na.es
www.vinose:na.es

VÍA ROMANA 2011 B
godello.

86 Colour: bright straw. Nose: varietal, expressive, ripe fruit, citrus fruit. Palate: good acidity, fine bitter notes, light-bodied.

VÍA ROMANA MENCÍA S/C T
100% mencía.

87 Colour: cherry, garnet rim. Nose: ripe fruit, fruit preserve, powerfull, scrubland. Palate: correct, fruity, round tannins.

VÍA ROMANA MENCÍA 2009 T BARRICA
mencía.

89 Colour: cherry, garnet rim. Nose: red berry notes, ripe fruit, scrubland, floral, spicy. Palate: light-bodied, flavourful, spicy, balanced.

VÍA ROMANA SELECCIÓN DE AÑADA MAGNUM 2008 T
mencía.

86 Colour: cherry, garnet rim. Nose: ripe fruit, fragrant herbs, balsamic herbs, floral, spicy. Palate: long, balsamic, correct.

LOCATION:

In the west of the province of Ourense. The region comprises 13 municipal districts marked by the Miño and its tributaries.

CLIMATE:

Atlantic, with low temperatures in winter, a certain risk of spring frosts, and high temperatures in the summer months. The average annual rainfall varies between 800 mm and 1,000 mm.

SOIL:

Predominantly granite, deep and rich in organic matter, although in some areas clayey soils predominate. The vineyards are on the slopes of the mountains (where higher quality wines are produced) and on the plains.

GRAPE VARIETIES :

WHITE: Preferred: *Treixadura, Torrontés, Palomino, Godello, Macabeo, Loureira* and *Albariño.* Authorized: *Albilla, Macabeo, Jerez.* Experimental: *Lado.*
RED: Preferred: *Caíño, Alicante, Sousón, Ferrón, Mencía, Tempranillo, Brancellao.*
Authorized: *Tempranillo, Garnacha.*

FIGURES:

Vineyard surface: 2,805 – **Wine-Growers:** 6,053 – **Wineries:** 116 – **2011 Harvest rating:** N/A – **Production:** 13,473,204 litres – **Market percentages:** 95% domestic. 5% export

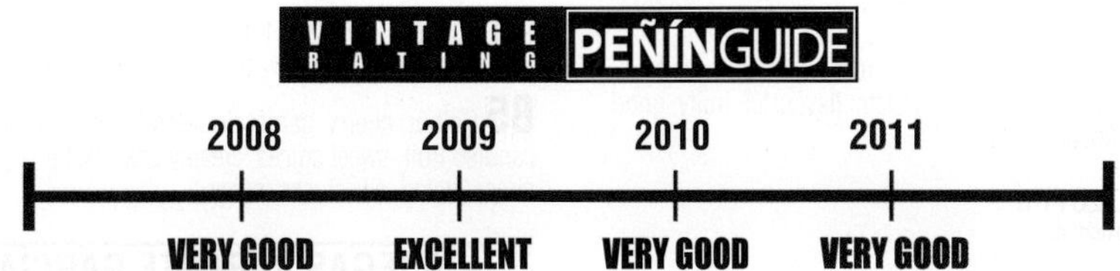

CONSEJO REGULADOR
Salgado Moscoso, 9 - 32400 Ribadavia (Ourense) - ☎: +34 988 477 200 - Fax: +34 988 477 201
@ info@ribeiro.es - www.ribeiro.es

A PORTELA

Piñeiros, s/n
32431 Beade (Ourense)
☎: +34 988 480 050 - Fax: +34 988 480 050
beade@beadeprimacia.com
www.beadeprimacia.com

BEADE PRIMACÍA 2011 B
95% treixadura, 3% albariño, 2% loureiro.

88 Colour: bright straw. Nose: fresh, white flowers, fresh fruit. Palate: flavourful, fruity, good acidity, balanced.

SEÑORÍO DE BEADE 2011 B
treixadura, godello, torrontés, otras.

87 Colour: bright straw. Nose: fresh, fresh fruit, white flowers, dried herbs, citrus fruit. Palate: flavourful, fruity, good acidity.

SEÑORÍO DE BEADE 2011 T
50% mencía, 40% caiño, 10% otras.

89 Colour: cherry, purple rim. Nose: expressive, fresh fruit, red berry notes, floral, raspberry. Palate: flavourful, fruity, good acidity, round tannins.

ADEGA MANUEL FORMIGO

Cabo de Vila, 49
32431 Beade (Ourense)
☎: +34 627 569 885
info@fincateira.com
www.fincateira.com

FINCA TEIRA 2011 B
treixadura, godello, torrontés.

90 Colour: bright straw. Nose: fresh, fresh fruit, white flowers, characterful, grassy. Palate: flavourful, fruity, good acidity, balanced.

FORMIGO 2011 B
treixadura, palomino.

86 Colour: bright straw. Nose: medium intensity, ripe fruit, white flowers. Palate: flavourful, fruity, ripe fruit.

TEIRA X 2010 B
treixadura, loureiro, albariño, albillo.

87 Colour: bright yellow. Nose: ripe fruit, citrus fruit, dried herbs, floral. Palate: powerful, flavourful, long, correct.

TOSTADO DE TEIRA 2006 B
treixadura.

94 Colour: golden. Nose: powerfull, honeyed notes, fragrant herbs, dark chocolate, cocoa bean. Palate: flavourful, sweet, fresh, fruity, good acidity, long.

FINCA TEIRA 2011 T
caiño, sousón, brancellao.

82

ADEGAS ÁUREA LUX

Rúa do Ribeiro, 29
32400 Ribadavia (Ourense)
☎: +34 655 393 673
info@aurealux.com
www.aurealux.com

PARADIGMA LEIVE 2011 B
50% treixadura, 35% albariño, 15% loureiro.

89 Colour: bright yellow. Nose: burnt matches, rose petals, faded flowers, ripe fruit. Palate: fine bitter notes, good acidity, correct.

LEIVE TREIXADURA 2011 B
100% treixadura.

83

LEIVE RELIQUIA 2010 BFB
50% treixadura, 35% albariño, 15% loureiro.

87 Colour: bright straw. Nose: powerfull, candied fruit, honeyed notes, roasted coffee, dark chocolate. Palate: powerful, sweetness, long.

PRETO DE LEIVE 2011 T
25% caiño, 25% sausón, 25% brancellao, 25% mencía.

85 Colour: cherry, garnet rim. Nose: fruit preserve, candied fruit, sweet spices, creamy oak. Palate: concentrated, sweetness, spicy.

ADEGAS PARENTE GARCÍA

Lugar As Chabolas, 22
32454 Cenlle (Ourense)
☎: +34 660 411 350 - Fax: +34 986 330 443
info@parentegarcia.com
www.parentegarcia.com

QUINTA DO AVELINO 2011 B
100% treixadura.

88 Colour: bright straw. Nose: fresh, white flowers, dried herbs. Palate: flavourful, fruity, good acidity, easy to drink.

ADEGAS PAZO DO MAR

Ctra. Ourense-Castrelo, Km. 12,5
32940 Toén (Ourense)
☎: +34 988 261 256 - Fax: +34 988 261 264
info@pazodomar.com
www.pazodomar.com

EXPRESIÓN DE PAZO DO MAR 2011 B
treixadura.

89 Colour: bright straw. Nose: fresh, fresh fruit, white flowers, neat, varietal. Palate: flavourful, fruity, good acidity, balanced.

PAZO DO MAR 2011 B
torrontés, treixadura, godello.

88 Colour: bright straw. Nose: fresh, fresh fruit, white flowers, dried herbs. Palate: flavourful, fruity, good acidity, balanced.

PAZO DO MAR 2011 T
mencía, garnacha.

83

ADEGAS VALDAVIA

Cuñas, s/n
32454 Cenlle (Ourense)
☎: +34 669 892 681 - Fax: +34 986 367 016
comercial@adegasvaldavia.com
www.adegasvaldavia.com

CUÑAS DAVIA 2011 B JOVEN
treixadura, albariño, godello, lado.

91 Colour: bright straw. Nose: fresh, white flowers, fresh fruit, ripe fruit, citrus fruit. Palate: flavourful, fruity, good acidity, balanced.

CUÑAS DAVIA 2010 BFB
treixadura, albariño.

92 Colour: bright straw. Nose: powerfull, ripe fruit, citrus fruit, white flowers, mineral. Palate: flavourful, ripe fruit, long, fine bitter notes, good acidity.

CUÑAS DAVIA 2010 T
mencía, brancellao, caiño, sousón.

87 Colour: cherry, purple rim. Nose: red berry notes, floral, ripe fruit, sweet spices. Palate: flavourful, fruity, good acidity, round tannins.

AILALA-AILALELO

Lugar o Cotiño, s/n
32415 Ribadavia (Ourense)
☎: +34 695 220 256 - Fax: +34 988 488 741
info@ailalawine.com
www.ailalawine.com

AILALÁ 2011 B
100% treixadura.

88 Colour: bright straw. Nose: fresh, fresh fruit, mineral, floral, jasmine. Palate: flavourful, fruity, good acidity, balanced.

ALECRÍN

Pza. da Cruz, 7
32454 Cenlle (Ourense)
☎: +34 670 522 346 - Fax: +34 988 471 566
info@bolasalecrin.com
www.bolasalecrin.com

ALECRIN 2011 B
treixadura, albariño.

84

BENITO ELADIO RODRÍGUEZ FERNÁNDEZ

Arco da Vella a Adega de Eladio
32431 Beade (Ourense)
☎: +34 607 487 060 - Fax: +34 986 376 800
bodega@bodegaeladio.com
www.bodegaeladio.com

TORQUES DO CASTRO 2011 B
60% treixadura, 20% torrontés, 15% godello, 5% loureiro.

88 Colour: bright straw, greenish rim. Nose: dried flowers, dried herbs, ripe fruit. Palate: powerful, flavourful, balsamic.

TARABELO 2010 TC
60% sousón, 10% caiño, 15% brancellao, 15% garnacha.

82

BERNARDO ESTÉVEZ

Outeiro Cruz, 56
32417 Arnoia (Ourense)
☎: +34 649 541 711
bernardoestevezvillar@yahoo.es

ISSUE 2009 B
lado, treixadura, silveiriña, verdejo, albilla, otras.

89 Colour: bright yellow. Nose: ripe fruit, citrus fruit, floral, fragrant herbs, sweet spices, toasty. Palate: rich, flavourful, balanced, toasty.

BODEGA ALANÍS

Lg. Santa Cruz de Arrabaldo, s/n
32990 (Ourense)
☎: +34 988 384 200 - Fax: +34 988 384 068
vinos@bodegasgallegas.com
www.bodegasgallegas.com

GRAN ALANÍS 2011 B
treixadura, godello.

90 Colour: bright straw. Nose: fresh, fresh fruit, white flowers, expressive, complex, varietal, grassy. Palate: flavourful, fruity, good acidity, balanced.

BODEGA COOP. SAN ROQUE DE BEADE

Ctra. Ribadavia - Carballiño, Km. 4
32431 Beade (Ourense)
☎: +34 988 471 522 - Fax: +34 988 471 502
adegas@terradocastelo.com
www.terradocastelo.com

TERRA DO CASTELO "SENSACIÓN" 2011 B
50% treixadura, 45% palomino, 5% godello.

90 Colour: bright straw. Nose: white flowers, fresh fruit, fragrant herbs. Palate: correct, balanced, fresh, fruity.

TERRA DO CASTELO TREIXADURA 2011 B
100% treixadura.

88 Colour: bright straw. Nose: fresh, fresh fruit, white flowers, expressive. Palate: flavourful, fruity, easy to drink.

TERRA DO CASTELO GODELLO 2011 B
100% godello.

88 Colour: bright straw. Nose: fresh, fresh fruit, candied fruit. Palate: flavourful, fruity, good acidity, balanced.

BODEGAS CAMPANTE

Finca Reboreda, s/n
32941 Puga (Ourense)
☎: +34 988 261 212 - Fax: +34 988 261 213
info@campante.com
www.campante.com

GRAN REBOREDA 2011 B
treixadura, godello, loureiro.

90 Colour: bright straw. Nose: fresh, fresh fruit, white flowers, scrubland. Palate: flavourful, fruity, good acidity, balanced.

BODEGAS DOCAMPO

Lg. Sampaio
32414 Ribadavia (Ourense)
☎: +34 988 470 258 - Fax: +34 988 470 421
admin@bodegasdocampo.com
www.bodegasdocampo.com

VIÑA DO CAMPO 2011 B
treixadura, torrontés.

86 Colour: bright straw. Nose: powerfull, lactic notes, grassy. Palate: fine bitter notes, good acidity, long.

SEÑORÍO DA VILA 2010 B
treixadura.

91 Colour: bright yellow. Nose: ripe fruit, citrus fruit, fragrant herbs. Palate: flavourful, fruity, rich, balanced.

BODEGAS EL PARAGUAS

Lugar de Esmelle, 111
15594 Ferrol (A Coruña)
☎: +34 636 161 479
info@bodegaselparaguas.com
www.bodegaselparaguas.com

EL PARAGUAS ATLÁNTICO 2011 B
85% treixadura, 10% godello, 5% albariño.

90 Colour: bright straw. Nose: fresh, fresh fruit, fragrant herbs, dried flowers. Palate: flavourful, fruity, good acidity, balanced.

BODEGAS NAIROA

A Ponte, 2
32417 Arnoia (Ourense)
☎: +34 988 492 867
info@bodegasnairoa.com
www.bodegasnairoa.com

ALBERTE 2011 B
80% treixadura, 20% albariño.

90 Colour: bright straw. Nose: ripe fruit, citrus fruit, grassy. Palate: ripe fruit, flavourful, powerful.

VAL DE NAIROA 2011 B
80% treixadura, 10% albariño, 5% lado, 5% loureiro.

89 Colour: bright straw. Nose: fresh, fresh fruit, white flowers, expressive, lactic notes. Palate: flavourful, fruity, good acidity, balanced.

NAIROA 2011 B
treixadura, torrontés, palomino.

88 Colour: bright straw. Nose: powerfull, ripe fruit, citrus fruit, balsamic herbs. Palate: flavourful, ripe fruit.

VAL DO COUSO 2011 B
treixadura, torrontés, palomino.

88 Colour: bright straw. Nose: dried flowers, dried herbs, ripe fruit, citrus fruit. Palate: correct, light-bodied, fresh, fruity.

TERRALONGA 2011 T
mencía, garnacha.

86 Colour: cherry, purple rim. Nose: red berry notes, floral, ripe fruit, balsamic herbs. Palate: flavourful, fruity, correct.

BODEGAS O'VENTOSELA

Ctra. Ribadavia - Carballiño, km. 8,8 San Clodio
32420 Leiro (Ourense)
☎: +34 981 635 829 - Fax: +34 981 635 870
bodegasydestilerias@oventosela.com
www.oventosela.com

GRAN LEIRIÑA 2011 B
treixadura, albariño, godello, torrontés.

86 Colour: bright straw. Nose: fresh, floral, grassy. Palate: flavourful, fruity, good acidity, easy to drink.

GRAN LEIRIÑA 2010 BFB
treixadura, albariño, godello.

87 Colour: bright yellow. Nose: ripe fruit, sweet spices, creamy oak, fragrant herbs. Palate: rich, flavourful, fresh, good acidity.

GRAN LEIRIÑA VENDIMIA TARDÍA 2010 B
treixadura.

86 Colour: bright yellow. Nose: ripe fruit, faded flowers, balsamic herbs, saline. Palate: correct, rich, flavourful, fine bitter notes.

BODEGAS PEÑA

Rua da Igrexa, 4 - Vide
23430 Castrelo de Miño (Ourense)
☎: +34 988 489 094
info@lanceroribeiro.com
www.lancero.com

SEÑORÍO DO LANCERO 2011 B
70% treixadura, 15% godello, 10% torrontés, 5% lado, albariño, otras.

88 Colour: bright straw. Nose: ripe fruit, citrus fruit, mineral, grassy, sweet spices. Palate: flavourful, fine bitter notes, good acidity.

VIÑA ENXIDO 2011 B
75% jerez, 25% otras.

80 Colour: bright yellow. Nose: grassy, slightly evolved, short. Palate: lacks expression.

SEÑORÍO DO LANCERO 2010 B
70% treixadura, 15% godello, 10% torrontés, 5% lado, albariño, otras.

84

CASAL DE ARMÁN

Lugar O Cotiño, s/n. San Andrés de Camporredondo
32400 Ribadavia (Ourense)
☎: +34 699 060 464 - Fax: +34 988 491 809
bodega@casaldearman.net
www.casaldearman.net

CASAL DE ARMÁN 2011 B
90% treixadura, 5% albariño, 5% godello.

92 Colour: bright straw. Nose: fresh, fresh fruit, white flowers, scrubland, varietal, mineral. Palate: flavourful, fruity, good acidity, balanced.

7 CUPOS 2011 B
treixadura.

89 Colour: bright straw. Nose: candied fruit, ripe fruit, citrus fruit. Palate: flavourful, sweetness, fine bitter notes.

ARMAN FINCA OS LOUREIROS 2010 B
100% treixadura.

90 Colour: bright straw. Nose: mineral, dry stone, floral, citrus fruit, ripe fruit. Palate: flavourful, round, sweetness.

ARMÁN FINCA MISENHORA 2010 B
treixadura, godello, albariño.

88 Colour: bright straw. Nose: faded flowers, candied fruit, citrus fruit. Palate: spicy, flavourful, sweetness.

CASAL DE ARMÁN 2011 T
brancellao, sousón, caiño.

91 Colour: cherry, purple rim. Nose: fruit expression, red berry notes, scrubland. Palate: flavourful, fruity, fresh, good acidity.

COTO DE GOMARIZ

Barrio de Gomariz
32429 Leiro (Ourense)
☎: +34 671 641 982 - Fax: +34 988 488 174
gomariz@cotodegomariz.com
www.cotodegomariz.com

GOMARIZ X 2011 B
95% albariño, 5% treixadura.

91 Colour: bright straw. Nose: powerfull, varietal, characterful, ripe fruit. Palate: flavourful, powerful, good acidity, carbonic notes.

COTO DE GOMARIZ 2011 B
treixadura, godello, loureiro, torrontés.

91 Colour: bright straw. Nose: fresh, white flowers, varietal, complex, citrus fruit, dried herbs. Palate: flavourful, fruity, good acidity, balanced.

THE FLOWER AND THE BEE (TREIXADURA) 2011 B
treixadura.

89 Colour: bright straw. Aroma fresh, fresh fruit, white flowers, expressive. Palate: flavourful, fruity, good acidity, balanced.

THE FLOWER AND THE BEE (SOUSÓN) 2011 T
sousón.

88 Colour: bright cherry. Nose: sweet spices, creamy oak, expressive, balsamic herbs, red berry notes. Palate: flavourful, fruity, toasty, round tannins.

CUNQUEIRO

Prado de Miño, 4
32430 Castrelo de Miño (Ourense)
☎: +34 988 489 023 - Fax: +34 988 489 082
info@bodegascunqueiro.es
www.bodegascunqueiro.es

CUQUEIRA 2011 B
treixadura, torrontés, godello.

86 Colour: bright straw. Nose: ripe fruit, floral, dried herbs. Palate: light-bodied, fresh, easy to drink.

CUNQUEIRO III MILENIUM 2011 B
treixadura, loureiro, godello, albariño.

89 Colour: bright straw. Nose: dried flowers, citrus fruit, fruit expression. Palate: fresh, fruity, light-bodied, flavourful, balanced.

EDUARDO PEÑA

Carrero Blanco, s/n - Barral
Castelo de Miño (Ourense)
☎: +34 629 872 130
bodega@bodegaeduardopenha.es
www.bodegaeduardopenha.es

EDUARDO PEÑA 2011 B

90 Colour: bright straw. Nose: ripe fruit, fruit expression, balsamic herbs, scrubland, mineral. Palate: flavourful, spicy, ripe fruit.

ELOI LORENZO

A Ponte, 37
32417 Arnoia (Ourense)
☎: +34 677 457 614
gerente@eloilorenzo.es
eloilorenzo.es

ELOI LORENZO 2011 B
treixadura, lado, loureiro, torrontés.

85 Colour: bright straw. Nose: white flowers, ripe fruit, citrus fruit, floral. Palate: good acidity, fine bitter notes.

EMILIO DOCAMPO DIÉGUEZ

San Andrés, 57
32415 Ribadavia (Ourense)
☎: +34 639 332 790 - Fax: +34 988 275 318
edocampodieguez@hotmail.com

CASAL DE PAULA 2011 B
treixadura, torrontés, albariño, godello.

90 Colour: bright straw, greenish rim. Nose: white flowers, fresh fruit, fragrant herbs, mineral, citrus fruit. Palate: powerful, flavourful, rich, fruity.

EMILIO ROJO

Lugar de Remoiño, s/n
32233 Arnoia (Ourense)
☎: +34 988 488 050
vinoemiliorojo@hotmail.com

EMILIO ROJO 2011 B

91 Colour: bright straw, greenish rim. Nose: citrus fruit, white flowers, fragrant herbs, sweet spices, creamy oak, mineral. Palate: fresh, fruity, flavourful, spicy, long.

FERNÁNDEZ RODRÍGUEZ S.C.

Darral
32430 Castrelo de Miño (Ourense)
☎: +34 988 493 053
sefero@terra.es

POUSADOIRO 2011 B

87 Colour: bright straw. Nose: ripe fruit, citrus fruit, scrubland. Palate: flavourful, good acidity, balanced.

FINCA VIÑOA

A Viñoa,s/n, Banga
O Carballiño (Ourense)
☎: +34 695 220 256 - Fax: +34 988 488 741
info@fincavinoa.com
www.fincavinoa.com

FINCA VIÑOA 2011 B
treixadura, godello, loureiro, albariño.

91 Colour: bright straw. Nose: fresh, fresh fruit, floral, varietal, grassy. Palate: flavourful, fruity, good acidity, balanced.

FRANCISCO FERNÁNDEZ SOUSA

Prado, 14
32430 Castrelo do Miño (Ourense)
☎: +34 988 489 077
info@terraminei.com
www.terraminei.com

LAGAR DE BRAIS 2011 B
palomino, torrontés.

88 Colour: bright straw. Nose: powerfull, ripe fruit, white flowers. Palate: flavourful, ripe fruit.

TERRA MINEI 2010 B
100% treixadura.

89 Colour: bright yellow. Nose: balsamic herbs, candied fruit, citrus fruit. Palate: good acidity, fruity, spicy, ripe fruit.

JOSÉ ESTÉVEZ FERNÁNDEZ

Ponte, 21
32417 Arnoia (Ourense)
☎: +34 696 402 970
joseestevezarnoia@gmail.com

MAURO ESTEVEZ 2011 B
albariño, lado, treixadura, loureiro.

88 Colour: bright straw. Nose: white flowers, fresh fruit, dried herbs, medium intensity. Palate: correct, powerful, flavourful.

JOSÉ GONZÁLEZ ALVAREZ

Pazo Lalón Barro de Gomariz
32427 Leiro (Ourense)
☎: +34 653 131 487
eduardogonzalezbravo@gmail.com
www.eduardobravo.es

EDUARDO BRAVO 2011 B
treixadura, albariño, torrontés.

89 Colour: bright straw. Nose: fresh, white flowers, ripe fruit. Palate: flavourful, fruity, good acidity, balanced.

PAZO LALÓN 2011 B
treixadura.

83

LAGAR DO MERENS

Chaos
32430 Arnoia (Ourense)
☎: +34 607 533 314
info@lagardomerens.com
www.lagardomerens.com

LAGAR DO MERENS 2010 BFB
treixadura, lado, torrontés.

92 Colour: bright yellow. Nose: powerfull, ripe fruit, sweet spices, creamy oak, fragrant herbs. Palate: rich, flavourful, fresh, good acidity.

LAGAR DO MERENS 2010 B
treixadura, lado, torrontés.

91 Colour: bright straw. Nose: candied fruit, fruit expression, dried herbs, balsamic herbs. Palate: flavourful, powerful, good acidity, fine bitter notes.

30 COPELOS 2010 T
sousón, brancellao, caiño, ferrón.

90 Colour: cherry, purple rim. Nose: expressive, fresh fruit, red berry notes, floral, balsamic herbs. Palate: flavourful, fruity, good acidity, round tannins.

LUIS A. RODRÍGUEZ VÁZQUEZ

Laxa, 7
32417 Arnoia (Ourense)
☎: +34 988 492 977 - Fax: +34 988 492 977

VIÑA DE MARTÍN "OS PASÁS" 2010 B
treixadura, lado, albariño, torrontés.

91 Colour: bright straw. Nose: fresh, dried flowers, dried herbs, citrus fruit. Palate: flavourful, fruity, balanced, good acidity.

VIÑA DE MARTÍN ESCOLMA 2008 BFB
treixadura, albariño, lado, torrontés.

92 Colour: bright yellow. Nose: creamy oak, candied fruit, fruit liqueur notes, toasty. Palate: powerful, sweetness, fine bitter notes, good acidity.

A TORNA DOS PASAS 2009 T
brancellao, ferrol, caiño longo, caiño redondo.

89 Colour: cherry, garnet rim. Nose: ripe fruit, spicy, creamy oak, toasty, wild herbs, mineral. Palate: flavourful, toasty, light-bodied, easy to drink.

VIÑA DE MARTÍN ESCOLMA 2008 T
brancellao, ferrol, otras.

87 Colour: deep cherry. Nose: closed, candied fruit, spicy. Palate: fine bitter notes, good acidity, spicy.

PAZO CASANOVA

Camiño Souto do Río, 1 Santa Cruz de Arrabaldo
32990 (Ourense)
☎: +34 988 384 196 - Fax: +34 988 384 196
casanova@pazocasanova.com
www.pazocasanova.com

CASANOVA 2011 B
80% treixadura, 20% godello, albariño, loureiro.

89 Colour: bright straw. Nose: fresh, white flowers, ripe fruit, floral. Palate: flavourful, fruity, good acidity, balanced.

PAZO DE VIEITE

Ctra. Ribadavia a Carbadiño, Km. 6
32419 Vieite Leiro (Ourense)
☎: +34 988 488 229 - Fax: +34 988 488 229
info@pazodevieite.es
www.pazodevieite.es

VIÑA FARNADAS 2011 B
85% treixadura, 15% godello, albariño.

88 Colour: bright straw. Nose: floral, ripe fruit, fruit expression, grassy. Palate: flavourful, easy to drink, ripe fruit.

VIÑA FARNADAS 2010 B
treixadura, godello, albariño, loureiro.

87 Colour: bright yellow. Nose: ripe fruit, dried flowers, fragrant herbs. Palate: flavourful, fresh, ripe fruit.

PAZO TIZÓN

Pol. Ind. Aimayor - Estaño, 4
28330 San Martín de la Vega (Madrid)
☎: +34 639 788 788
admon@pazotizon.com
www.pazotizon.com

EXTRAMUNDI 2011 B
treixadura, albariño.

88 Colour: bright straw, greenish rim. Nose: floral, dried herbs, citrus fruit, fruit expression. Palate: fresh, light-bodied, flavourful.

PAZO TIZON 2009 T
tempranillo, garnacha.

86 Colour: cherry, garnet rim. Nose: ripe fruit, spicy, toasty, balsamic herbs. Palate: powerful, flavourful, toasty.

PRODUCCIONES A MODIÑO

Cubilledo-Gomariz
32420 Leiro (Ourense)
☎: +34 686 961 681
sanclodiovino@gmail.com
www.vinosanclodio.com

SANCLODIO 2011 B
treixadura, godello, loureiro, albariño, torrontés.

92 Colour: bright straw. Nose: white flowers, dry stone, mineral, fruit expression, fragrant herbs. Palate: flavourful, fresh, fruity, rich, balanced.

SAMEIRÁS

San Andrés, 98
32415 Ribadavia (Ourense)
☎: +34 988 491 812 - Fax: +34 988 470 591
sameiras@terra.es

1040 SAMEIRÁS 2011 B

90 Colour: bright straw. Nose: fresh, fresh fruit, white flowers, expressive, creamy oak, spicy. Palate: flavourful, fruity, good acidity, balanced.

SAMEIRÁS 2011 B
albariño, godello, lado, loureiro.

88 Colour: bright straw. Nose: white flowers, fresh fruit, citrus fruit, grassy. Palate: flavourful, fruity, fresh.

SAMEIRÁS 2011 T

89 Colour: cherry, purple rim. Nose: red berry notes, fruit liqueur notes, fragrant herbs, floral, expressive. Palate: powerful, flavourful, fresh, fruity.

VALDEPUGA

Ctra. Ourense a Cortegada, km 14
32940 Alongos -Toén (Ourense)
☎: +34 988 235 817 - Fax: +34 988 235 817
valdepuga@grupopuga.com
www.bodegasvaldepuga.com

VALDEPUGA SELECCIÓN 2011 B
treixadura, loureiro, albariño, godello.

87 Colour: bright straw. Nose: dried flowers, fragrant herbs, tropical fruit. Palate: flavourful, fruity, balanced.

VILERMA

Villerma
32429 Leiro (Ourense)
☎: +34 988 228 951 - Fax: +34 988 248 580
arsenio@vilerma.com

VILERMA 2011 B
treixadura, albariño, godello, loureiro, torrontés, lado.

89 Colour: bright straw. Nose: white flowers, ripe fruit, fragrant herbs, balanced. Palate: flavourful, fruity, balanced.

VIÑA MEIN

Mein, s/n
32420 Leiro (Ourense)
☎: +34 617 326 248 - Fax: +34 988 488 732
info.bodega@vinamein.com
www.vinamein.com

VIÑA MEIN 2011 B

94 Colour: bright straw. Nose: fresh, fresh fruit, white flowers, fragrant herbs, mineral. Palate: flavourful, fruity, good acidity, balanced, elegant.

VIÑA MEIN 2011 BFB

91 Colour: bright yellow. Nose: ripe fruit, sweet spices, creamy oak, balsamic herbs, balanced. Palate: rich, flavourful, fresh, good acidity, spicy, long.

VIÑOS DE ENCOSTAS

Florentino Cuevillas Nº6, 1ºC
32500 O Carballiño (Ourense)
☎: +34 647 468 464
xlsebio@gmail.com
http://vinosdeencostas.blogspot.com.es/

SALVAXE 2010 B
treixadura, albariño, lado, loureiro.

92 Colour: bright yellow. Nose: floral, ripe fruit, dried herbs, dry stone, fine lees. Palate: rich, flavourful, fresh, long, balanced, elegant.

HUSH 2009 T
100% sousón.

92 Colour: cherry, garnet rim. Nose: earthy notes, mineral, fragrant herbs, ripe fruit, spicy, toasty. Palate: powerful, flavourful, long, spicy, balanced, elegant.

VITIVINÍCOLA DEL RIBEIRO - VIÑA COSTEIRA

Valdepereira, s/n
32415 Ribadavia (Ourense)
☎: +34 988 477 210 - Fax: +34 988 470 330
info@pazoribeiro.com
www.vinoribeiro.com

COLECCIÓN COSTEIRA TREIXADURA DO RIBEIRO 2011 B
treixadura.

90 Colour: bright straw. Nose: white flowers, fruit expression, fragrant herbs, expressive. Palate: flavourful, fruity, fresh, balanced.

COLECCIÓN COSTEIRA TREIXADURA BARRICA 2011 BFB
treixadura.

90 Colour: bright yellow. Nose: powerfull, ripe fruit, creamy oak, toasty. Palate: rich, smoky afterpalate:, flavourful, good acidity.

COLECCIÓN COSTEIRA ALBARIÑO DO RIBEIRO 2011 B
albariño.

88 Colour: bright straw. Nose: fresh, white flowers, ripe fruit. Palate: flavourful, fruity, good acidity, balanced.

VIÑA COSTEIRA 2011 B
treixadura, torrontés, otras.

88 Colour: bright straw. Nose: complex, characterful, ripe fruit, citrus fruit. Palate: flavourful, fruity, fresh.

PAZO 2011 B
palomino, torrontés.

85 Colour: bright straw. Nose: fresh, ripe fruit, dried flowers, dried herbs. Palate: flavourful, fruity, good acidity.

ALÉN DA ISTORIA 2011 T
caiño, brancellao, sousón, mencía.

85 Colour: cherry, purple rim. Nose: fresh fruit, red berry notes, floral. Palate: flavourful, fruity, good acidity.

DO RIBERA DEL DUERO

LOCATE:

Between the provinces of Burgos, Valladolid, Segovia and Soria. This region comprises 19 municipal districts in the east of Valladolid, 5 in the north west of Segovia, 59 in the south of Burgos (most of the vineyards are concentrated in this province with 10,000 Ha) and 6 in the west of Soria.en la parte occidental de Soria.

CLIMATE:

Continental in nature, with slight Atlantic influences. The winters are rather cold and the summers hot, although mention must be made of the significant difference in day-night temperatures contributing to the slow ripening of the grapes, enabling excellent acidity indexes to be achieved. The greatest risk factor in the region is the spring frosts, which are on many occasions responsible for sharp drops in production. The average annual rainfall is between 450 mm and 500 mm.

SOIL:

In general, the soils are loose, not very fertile and with a rather high limestone content. Most of the sediment is composed of layers of sandy limestone or clay. The vineyards are located on the interfluvial hills and in the valleys at an altitude of between 700 and 850 m.

GRAPE VARIETIES:

WHITE: *Albillo.*
RED: *Tinta del País* (*Tempranillo* – majority with 81% of all vineyards), *Garnacha Tinta, Cabernet Sauvignon, Malbec* and *Merlot*.

FIGURES:

Vineyard surface: 21,381 – **Wine-Growers:** 8,356 – **Wineries:** 264 – **2011 Harvest rating:** Excellent – **Production:** 67,653,245 litres – **Market percentages:** 68% domestic. 32% export

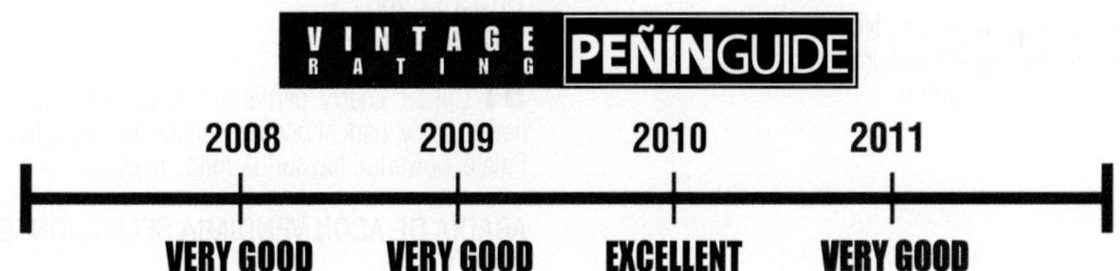

CONSEJO REGULADOR
Hospital, 6 - 09300 Roa (Burgos) - ☎: +34 947 541 221 - Fax: +34 947 541 116
@ info@riberadelduero.es - www.riberadelduero.es

3 ASES

Carretera, 7
09315 Fuentemolinos (Burgos)
☎: +34 670 601 118
info@3asesvino.com
www.3asesvino.com

3 ASES 2010 T ROBLE
tempranillo.

88 Colour: bright cherry. Nose: sweet spices, creamy oak, expressive, fruit expression, grassy. Palate: flavourful, fruity, toasty, round tannins.

3 ASES 2009 TC
tempranillo.

90 Colour: cherry, garnet rim. Nose: spicy, creamy oak, toasty, characterful, mineral. Palate: powerful, flavourful, toasty, round tannins.

4U WINES

Aranda,11
09471 Fuentelcesped (Burgos)
☎: +34 665 305 666
4uwines@gmail.com

4 U + 2009 T
tempranillo.

91 Colour: cherry, garnet rim. Aroma ripe fruit, spicy, creamy oak, toasty, complex. Palate: powerful, flavourful, toasty, round tannins.

4U 2008 T
tempranillo.

91 Colour: cherry, garnet rim. Nose: ripe fruit, spicy, creamy oak, toasty, varietal. Palate: powerful, flavourful, toasty, round tannins.

4U VENDIMIA SELECCIONADA 2007 T
tempranillo.

91 Colour: cherry, garnet rim. Nose: ripe fruit, spicy, creamy oak, toasty, characterful. Palate: powerful, flavourful, toasty, round tannins.

AALTO BODEGAS Y VIÑEDOS

Paraje Vallejo de Carril, s/n
47360 Quintanilla de Arriba (Valladolid)
☎: +34 620 351 182 - Fax: +34 983 036 949
aalto@aalto.es
www.aalto.es

AALTO PS 2009 T
tempranillo.

94 Colour: bright cherry. Nose: ripe fruit, sweet spices, creamy oak, cocoa bean, dark chocolate, mineral, expressive. Palate: flavourful, fruity, toasty, balanced, elegant.

AALTO 2009 T
tempranillo.

93 Colour: cherry, garnet rim. Nose: ripe fruit, creamy oak, toasty, sweet spices, expressive. Palate: powerful, flavourful, toasty, round tannins, balanced.

ABADÍA DE ACÓN

Ctra. Hontangas, Km. 09400
09391 Castrillo de la Vega (Burgos)
☎: +34 947 509 292 - Fax: +34 947 508 586
info@abadiadeacon.com
www.abadiadeacon.com

ACÓN 2009 TC
100% tempranillo.

90 Colour: bright cherry. Nose: ripe fruit, sweet spices, creamy oak, varietal. Palate: flavourful, fruity, toasty, round tannins.

ACÓN 2007 TR
90% tempranillo, 10% cabernet sauvignon.

91 Colour: bright cherry. Nose: sweet spices, creamy oak, earthy notes. Palate: flavourful, fruity, toasty, round tannins.

TARGÚM 2007 T
100% tempranillo.

91 Colour: cherry, garnet rim. Nose: ripe fruit, balsamic herbs, spicy, dark chocolate, toasty, fine reductive notes. Palate: powerful, flavourful, long, spicy.

ABADÍA DE ACÓN VENDIMIA SELECCIONADA 2005 T
100% tempranillo.

90 Colour: dark-red cherry, orangey edge. Nose: ripe fruit, powerfull, wet leather, tobacco, spicy, toasty. Palate: flavourful, powerful, spicy, long.

ALEJANDRO FERNÁNDEZ TINTO PESQUERA

Real, 2
47315 Pesquera de Duero (Valladolid)
☎: +34 983 870 037 - Fax: +34 983 870 088
pesquera@pesqueraafernandez.com
www.grupopesquera.com

TINTO PESQUERA 2009 TC
tempranillo.

89 Colour: cherry, garnet rim. Nose: ripe fruit, fruit liqueur notes, spicy, aged wood nuances, toasty, balsamic herbs. Palate: powerful, flavourful, long, spicy.

ALTOS DEL TERRAL

Barrionuevo, 11
09400 Aranda de Duero (Burgos)
☎: +34 616 953 451
bodega@altosdelterral.com
www.altosdelterral.com

ALTOS DEL TERRAL T1 2009 T
100% tinto fino.

93 Colour: cherry, garnet rim. Aroma ripe fruit, spicy, creamy oak, toasty, complex. Palate: powerful, flavourful, toasty, round tannins.

CUVÉE JULIA ALTOS DEL TERRAL 2009 T
100% tinto fino.

93 Colour: black cherry, garnet rim. Nose: red berry notes, ripe fruit, balsamic herbs, mineral, sweet spices, creamy oak. Palate: balanced, powerful, flavourful,

ASTRALES

Ctra. Olmedillo, Km. 7
09313 Anguix (Burgos)
☎: +34 947 554 222 - Fax: +34 947 554 222
administracio@astrales.es
www.astrales.es

ASTRALES CHRISTINA 2009 T
tempranillo.

92 Colour: cherry, garnet rim. Nose: creamy oak, complex, sweet spices, red berry notes, ripe fruit. Palate: powerful, flavourful, toasty, round tannins, balanced.

ASTRALES 2009 T
tempranillo.

91 Colour: cherry, garnet rim. Nose: ripe fruit, spicy, creamy oak, complex, mineral. Palate: powerful, flavourful, toasty, balanced.

BADEN NUMEN

Carreterilla, s/n
47359 San Bernardo Valbuena de Duero (Valladolid)
☎: +34 615 995 552 - Fax: +34 983 683 041
bodega@badennumen.es
www.badennumen.es

BADEN NUMEN "B" 2011 T

89 Colour: deep cherry, purple rim. Nose: creamy oak, sweet spices, ripe fruit. Palate: balanced, ripe fruit.

BADEN NUMEN ORO "AU" 2009 T

92 Colour: cherry, garnet rim. Nose: ripe fruit, mineral, sweet spices, creamy oak, toasty. Palate: powerful, flavourful, spicy, toasty.

BADEN NUMEN "N" 2009 TC

91 Colour: cherry, garnet rim. Nose: ripe fruit, balsamic herbs, sweet spices, creamy oak. Palate: powerful, flavourful, good structure, long, toasty.

BODEGA CONVENTO SAN FRANCISCO

Calvario, 22
47300 Peñafiel (Valladolid)
☎: +34 983 878 052 - Fax: +34 983 873 052
bodega@bodegaconvento.com
www.bodegaconvento.com

CONVENTO SAN FRANCISCO 2008 T
100% tinta del país.

88 Colour: cherry, garnet rim. Nose: spicy, creamy oak, toasty, characterful. Palate: powerful, flavourful, toasty, round tannins.

CONVENTO SAN FRANCISCO SELECCIÓN ESPECIAL 2005 T BARRICA
90% tinta del país, 10% cabernet sauvignon.

91 Colour: dark-red cherry, cherry, garnet rim. Nose: ripe fruit, spicy, fine reductive notes, dark chocolate, earthy notes, expressive. Palate: powerful, flavourful, spicy.

BODEGA DE BLAS SERRANO

Ctra. Santa Cruz, s/n
09471 Fuentelcésped (Burgos)
☎: +34 606 338 632
dbs@bodegasdeblasserrano.com
www.bodegasdeblasserrano.com

PHYLOS 2009 T
100% tinta del país.

91 Colour: cherry, garnet rim. Nose: red berry notes, ripe fruit, sweet spices, cocoa bean, creamy oak, expressive. Palate: powerful, flavourful, long, toasty, balanced.

DE BLAS SERRANO BODEGAS 2008 T
100% tinta del país.

90 Colour: bright cherry. Nose: ripe fruit, sweet spices, creamy oak, aromatic coffee. Palate: flavourful, fruity, toasty, balanced.

MATHIS 2007 T
100% tinta del país.

91 Colour: cherry, garnet rim. Nose: ripe fruit, spicy, creamy oak, toasty, complex. Palate: powerful, flavourful, toasty, round tannins, elegant.

BODEGA HNOS. PÁRAMO ARROYO

Ctra. de Roa Pedrosa, Km. 4
09314 Pedrosa de Duero (Burgos)
☎: +34 947 530 041 - Fax: +34 947 530 036
bodega@paramoarroyo.com
www.paramoarroyo.com

EREMUS 2011 T
100% tempranillo.

87 Colour: cherry, purple rim. Nose: expressive, fresh fruit, red berry notes, floral. Palate: flavourful, fruity, good acidity.

EREMUS 2008 TC
100% tempranillo.

87 Colour: cherry, garnet rim. Nose: ripe fruit, spicy, creamy oak, iodine notes. Palate: powerful, flavourful, toasty.

BODEGA MARQUÉS DE VELILLA

Ctra. de Sotillo de la Ribera, s/n
09311 La Horra (Burgos)
☎: +34 947 542 166 - Fax: +34 947 542 165
bodega@marquesdevelilla.com
www.marquesdevelilla.com

MARQUÉS DE VELILLA 2011 T
100% tinta del país.

87 Colour: cherry, purple rim. Nose: fresh fruit, red berry notes, floral. Palate: flavourful, fruity, good acidity, round tannins.

MARQUÉS DE VELILLA FINCA LA MARÍA 2009 T
100% tinta del país.

90 Colour: bright cherry. Nose: sweet spices, creamy oak, red berry notes, ripe fruit. Palate: flavourful, fruity, toasty, balanced.

MARQUÉS DE VELILLA 2008 TC
100% tinta del país.

88 Colour: cherry, garnet rim. Nose: ripe fruit, warm, spicy. Palate: flavourful, ripe fruit, correct.

DONCEL DE MATAPERRAS 2005 TC
100% tinta del país.

93 Colour: cherry, garnet rim. Nose: spicy, creamy oak, toasty, fruit preserve, fine reductive notes. Palate: powerful, flavourful, toasty, round tannins, balanced.

BODEGA MATARROMERA

Ctra. Renedo-Pesquera, Km. 30
47359 Valbuena de Duero (Valladolid)
☎: +34 902 430 170 - Fax: +34 902 430 189
matarromera@matarromera.es
www.grupomatarromera.com

MELIOR 2011 T ROBLE
100% tempranillo.

87 Colour: bright cherry. Nose: ripe fruit, sweet spices, creamy oak. Palate: flavourful, fruity, toasty, round tannins.

MATARROMERA PRESTIGIO 2009 T
100% tempranillo.

91 Colour: cherry, garnet rim. Nose: red berry notes, ripe fruit, balsamic herbs, sweet spices, toasty. Palate: long, powerful, flavourful.

MATARROMERA 2009 TC
100% tempranillo.

90 Colour: cherry, garnet rim. Nose: spicy, creamy oak, toasty, ripe fruit. Palate: powerful, flavourful, toasty, round tannins.

MATARROMERA 2005 TGR
100% tempranillo.

91 Colour: cherry, garnet rim. Nose: elegant, creamy oak, sweet spices, old leather. Palate: spicy, fine tannins, elegant, long.

BODEGA NEXUS

Santiago, 17 - 4º
47001 (Valladolid)
☎: +34 983 360 284 - Fax: +34 983 345 546
info@bodegasfrontaura.es
www.bodegasfrontaura.es

NEXUS 2010 T
100% tempranillo.

91 Colour: cherry, garnet rim. Nose: ripe fruit, spicy, creamy oak, toasty, varietal. Palate: powerful, flavourful, toasty, round tannins.

NEXUS + 2006 T
100% tempranillo.

93 Colour: very deep cherry. Nose: sweet spices, mineral, balanced, expressive. Palate: good structure, flavourful, good acidity, round tannins.

NEXUS 2006 TC
100% tempranillo.

92 Colour: cherry, garnet rim. Nose: spicy, creamy oak, toasty. Palate: toasty, round tannins, flavourful.

BODEGA RENACIMIENTO

Santa María, 36
47359 Olivares de Duero (Valladolid)
☎: +34 902 430 170 - Fax: +34 902 430 189
emina@emina.es
www.bodegarento.es

RENTO 2005 TC
100% tempranillo.

90 Colour: cherry, garnet rim. Nose: dark chocolate, toasty, fruit preserve. Palate: balanced, good structure, round tannins.

BODEGA S. ARROYO

Avda. del Cid, 99
09441 Sotillo de la Ribera (Burgos)
☎: +34 947 532 444 - Fax: +34 947 532 444
info@tintoarroyo.com
www.tintoarroyo.com

VIÑARROYO 2011 RD
tempranillo.

88 Colour: rose, purple rim. Nose: expressive, fruit expression, balanced. Palate: flavourful, fruity, good acidity.

TINTO ARROYO 2011 T
100% tempranillo.

87 Colour: cherry, purple rim. Nose: red berry notes, floral, ripe fruit. Palate: flavourful, fruity, good acidity, round tannins.

TINTO ARROYO 2010 T ROBLE
100% tempranillo.

86 Colour: bright cherry. Nose: ripe fruit, sweet spices. Palate: flavourful, fruity, round tannins.

TINTO ARROYO 2007 TR
100% tempranillo.

88 Colour: cherry, garnet rim. Nose: spicy, creamy oak, toasty, scrubland. Palate: powerful, flavourful, toasty, round tannins.

TINTO ARROYO 2005 TGR
100% tempranillo.

88 Colour: bright cherry, garnet rim. Nose: medium intensity, ripe fruit, spicy, cocoa bean. Palate: flavourful, fruity.

TINTO ARROYO 2009 TC
100% tempranillo.

90 Colour: cherry, garnet rim. Nose: ripe fruit, spicy, creamy oak, toasty, elegant. Palate: powerful, flavourful, toasty, good acidity, round.

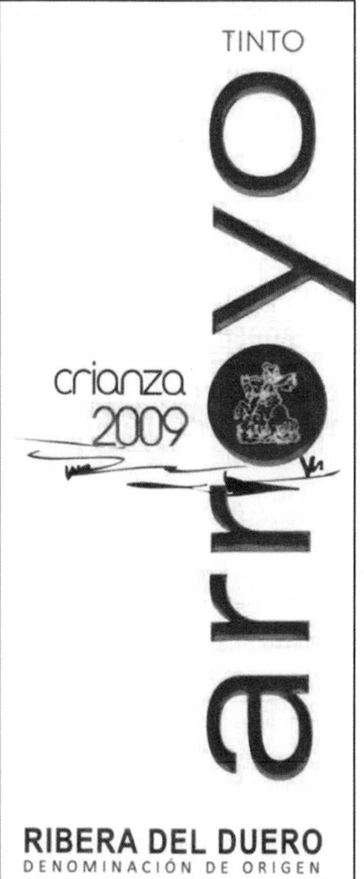

BODEGA SAN MAMÉS

Ctra. Valladolid, s/n
09315 Fuentecén (Burgos)
☎: +34 947 532 693 - Fax: +34 947 532 653
info@bodegasanmames.com
www.bodegasanmames.com

DOBLE R (5 MESES) 2010 T
tempranillo.

88 Colour: cherry, garnet rim. Nose: spicy, creamy oak, toasty, expressive. Palate: powerful, flavourful, toasty, round tannins.

DOBLE R 2010 T
tempranillo.

87 Colour: cherry, garnet rim. Nose: medium intensity, ripe fruit, scrubland. Palate: flavourful, fruity, correct.

DOBLE R 2009 T
tempranillo.

90 Colour: cherry, garnet rim. Nose: red berry notes, ripe fruit, mineral, sweet spices, creamy oak. Palate: powerful, flavourful, spicy.

BODEGA SAN ROQUE DE LA ENCINA, SDAD. COOP.

San Roque, 73
09391 Castrillo de la Vega (Burgos)
☎: +34 947 536 001 - Fax: +34 947 536 001
info@bodegasanroquedelaencina.com
www.bodegasanroquedelaencina.com

MONTE DEL CONDE 2009 TC

89 Colour: cherry, garnet rim. Nose: ripe fruit, spicy, creamy oak, aromatic coffee. Palate: powerful, flavourful, toasty.

MONTE PINADILLO 2009 TC

88 Colour: deep cherry, purple rim. Nose: balanced, ripe fruit, dark chocolate, toasty. Palate: flavourful, good structure, good acidity.

CERRO PIÑEL 2009 TC

87 Colour: cherry, garnet rim. Nose: ripe fruit, spicy, toasty, aged wood nuances. Palate: powerful, flavourful, toasty.

BODEGA VALLEBUENO

Ctra. Valbuena, 20
47315 Pesquera de Duero (Valladolid)
☎: +34 983 868 116 - Fax: +34 983 868 432
info@taninia.com
www.vallebueno.com

VALLEBUENO 2010 T ROBLE
100% tinto fino.

87 Colour: cherry, garnet rim. Nose: balsamic herbs, red berry notes, ripe fruit, sweet spices. Palate: powerful, flavourful, fruity.

VALLEBUENO 2008 TC
100% tinto fino.

87 Colour: cherry, garnet rim. Nose: ripe fruit, spicy, toasty, balsamic herbs. Palate: powerful, flavourful, toasty, correct.

BODEGA VIÑA VILANO S. COOP.

Ctra. de Anguix, 10
09314 Pedrosa de Duero (Burgos)
☎: +34 947 530 029 - Fax: +34 947 530 037
info@vinavilano.com
www.vinavilano.com

VIÑA VILANO 2011 RD
tempranillo.

85 Colour: rose, purple rim. Nose: floral, lactic notes, ripe fruit, balsamic herbs. Palate: fruity, fresh, light-bodied.

VIÑA VILANO 2011 T
tempranillo.

85 Colour: cherry, purple rim. Nose: red berry notes, ripe fruit, balsamic herbs. Palate: light-bodied, fruity, easy to drink.

BODEGA Y VIÑEDO FUENTECÉN

La Iglesia, 48
09315 Fuentecén (Burgos)
☎: +34 947 532 718 - Fax: +34 947 532 768
info@bodegahemar.com
www.bodegahemar.com

HEMAR 12 MESES 2007 T
tempranillo.

85 Colour: cherry, garnet rim. Nose: ripe fruit, spicy, toasty, fine reductive notes. Palate: powerful, toasty, correct.

LLANUM 2006 T
tempranillo.

90 Colour: dark-red cherry, orangey edge. Nose: ripe fruit, earthy notes, fine reductive notes, aged wood nuances, sweet spices. Palate: long, powerful, flavourful, complex.

BODEGAS ABADÍA LA ARROYADA

La Tejera, s/n
09442 Terradillos de Esgueva (Burgos)
☎: +34 947 545 309 - Fax: +34 947 545 309
bodegas@abadialaarroyada.es
www.abadialaarroyada.es

ABADÍA LA ARROYADA 2011 T
tempranillo.

88 Colour: cherry, purple rim. Nose: red berry notes, ripe fruit. Palate: flavourful, fruity, good acidity, round tannins.

ABADÍA LA ARROYADA 2009 T ROBLE
tempranillo.

87 Colour: cherry, garnet rim. Nose: fragrant herbs, floral, candied fruit, sweet spices. Palate: correct, powerful, flavourful, toasty.

ABADÍA LA ARROYADA 2007 TC
tempranillo.

90 Colour: cherry, garnet rim. Nose: ripe fruit, spicy, creamy oak, toasty, complex, balsamic herbs, violets. Palate: powerful, flavourful, toasty, round tannins. Personality.

BODEGAS ABANICO

Pol. Ind Ca l'Avellanet - Susany, 6
08553 Seva (Barcelona)
☎: +34 938 125 676 - Fax: +34 938 123 213
info@exportiberia.com
www.bodegasabanico.com

CATHAR 2011 T
100% tempranillo.

89 Colour: cherry, purple rim. Nose: powerfull, red berry notes, ripe fruit, mineral, balsamic herbs. Palate: flavourful, fresh, fruity, long, correct.

CATHAR 2009 T ROBLE
100% tempranillo.

88 Colour: bright cherry. Nose: ripe fruit, sweet spices, creamy oak, medium intensity. Palate: flavourful, fruity, toasty, balanced.

CATHAR 2007 TC
100% tempranillo.

87 Colour: cherry, garnet rim. Nose: ripe fruit, spicy, toasty, fine reductive notes, old leather. Palate: powerful, flavourful, toasty, round tannins, long.

CATHAR 2006 TR
100% tempranillo.

90 Colour: ruby red, orangey edge. Nose: ripe fruit, fruit liqueur notes, balsamic herbs, spicy, creamy oak, fine reductive notes. Palate: balanced, powerful, flavourful, long, spicy.

BODEGAS ALTA PAVINA

Camino de Santibáñez, s/n
47328 La Parrilla (Valladolid)
☎: +34 983 681 521
bodegas@altapavina.com
www.altapavina.com

VALDRINAL 6 2011 T ROBLE

88 Colour: bright cherry. Nose: ripe fruit, sweet spices, creamy oak, expressive. Palate: flavourful, fruity, toasty, round.

VALDRINAL 2010 TC

88 Colour: cherry, garnet rim. Nose: ripe fruit, creamy oak, dry stone, sweet spices. Palate: powerful, flavourful, toasty, long.

VALDRINAL SQR 2008 T
100% tempranillo.

89 Colour: cherry, garnet rim. Nose: ripe fruit, spicy, creamy oak, fine reductive notes. Palate: powerful, flavourful, toasty, round tannins.

VALDRINAL 2007 TR

89 Colour: cherry, garnet rim. Nose: ripe fruit, toasty, complex, fine reductive notes, sweet spices. Palate: powerful, flavourful, toasty, round tannins.

BODEGAS ARCO DE CURIEL

Calvario, s/n
47316 Curiel del Duero (Valladolid)
☎: +34 983 880 481 - Fax: +34 983 881 766
info@arcocuriel.com
www.arcocuriel.com

ARCO DE CURIEL 2011 T ROBLE
100% tempranillo.

87 Colour: bright cherry. Nose: ripe fruit, sweet spices, creamy oak. Palate: flavourful, fruity, toasty, round tannins.

ARCO DE CURIEL 2009 TC
100% tempranillo.

89 Colour: cherry, garnet rim. Nose: ripe fruit, sweet spices, creamy oak, cocoa bean. Palate: powerful, flavourful, balanced, toasty.

NEPTIS EXPRESION 2009 T
100% tempranillo.

88 Colour: cherry, garnet rim. Nose: ripe fruit, sweet spices, creamy oak, toasty. Palate: powerful, long, toasty.

BODEGAS ARROCAL

Eras de Santa María, s/n
09443 Gumiel de Mercado (Burgos)
☎: +34 606 292 102 - Fax: +34 947 561 290
arrocal@arrocal.com
www.arrocal.com

ROSA DE ARROCAL 2011 RD
50% tempranillo, 50% albillo.

88 Colour: light cherry. Nose: red berry notes, fragrant herbs, expressive, balanced, rose petals. Palate: flavourful, ripe fruit, long.

ARROCAL 2010 T
tempranillo.

87 Colour: cherry, garnet rim. Nose: red berry notes, ripe fruit, dark chocolate, toasty. Palate: harsh oak tannins, flavourful, powerful.

ARROCAL PASSIÓN 2009 T
tempranillo.

90 Colour: cherry, garnet rim. Nose: red berry notes, ripe fruit, sweet spices, creamy oak. Palate: powerful, flavourful, long, toasty, balanced.

ARROCAL ANGEL 2008 T
tempranillo.

90 Colour: cherry, garnet rim. Nose: ripe fruit, creamy oak, toasty, mineral. Palate: flavourful, toasty, round tannins, long, balanced.

ARROCAL SELECCIÓN 2007 T
tempranillo.

89 Colour: dark-red cherry, garnet rim. Nose: ripe fruit, balsamic herbs, spicy, creamy oak. Palate: correct, flavourful, long.

ARROCAL MÁXIMO 2006 T
tempranillo.

92 Colour: cherry, garnet rim. Nose: ripe fruit, balsamic herbs, creamy oak, toasty, expressive. Palate: balanced, elegant, flavourful, spicy.

BODEGAS ARZUAGA NAVARRO

Ctra. N-122, Km. 325
47350 Quintanilla de Onésimo (Valladolid)
☎: +34 983 681 146 - Fax: +34 983 681 147
bodeg@arzuaganavarro.com
www.arzuaganavarro.com

VIÑEDOS Y BODEGAS LA PLANTA 2011 T
100% tempranillo.

87 Colour: deep cherry. Nose: roasted coffee, tar. Palate: flavourful, toasty, ripe fruit, long.

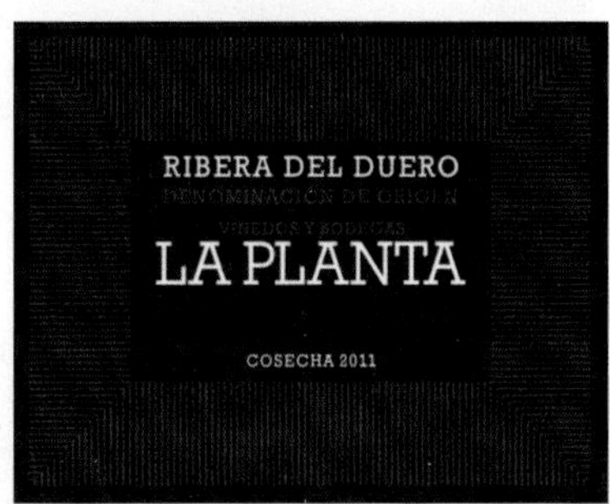

ARZUAGA 2010 TC
90% tinto fino, 7% cabernet sauvignon, 3% merlot.

91 Colour: very deep cherry. Nose: sweet spices, aromatic coffee, ripe fruit, red berry notes. Palate: round, good acidity, spicy, ripe fruit.

ARZUAGA ECOLÓGICO 2010 TC
100% tinto fino.

90 Colour: cherry, garnet rim. Nose: ripe fruit, spicy, creamy oak, characterful, roasted coffee. Palate: powerful, flavourful, toasty, round tannins.

GRAN ARZUAGA 2009 T
75% tinto fino, 25% cabernet sauvignon, albillo.

94 Colour: cherry, garnet rim. Nose: spicy, creamy oak, toasty, characterful, ripe fruit. Palate: powerful, flavourful, toasty, round tannins.

ARZUAGA RESERVA ESPECIAL 2009 TR
95% tinto fino, 5% albillo.

93 Colour: cherry, garnet rim. Nose: ripe fruit, fruit expression, spicy, balanced. Palate: flavourful, powerful, fruity.

ARZUAGA 2009 TR
95% tinto fino, 5% cabernet sauvignon, merlot.

92 Colour: cherry, garnet rim. Nose: ripe fruit, spicy, creamy oak, toasty, characterful, mineral. Palate: powerful, flavourful, toasty, round tannins.

ARZUAGA 2009 TC
90% tinto fino, 7% cabernet sauvignon, 3% merlot.

90 Colour: bright cherry. Nose: ripe fruit, sweet spices, creamy oak, roasted coffee. Palate: flavourful, fruity, toasty, round tannins.

AMAYA ARZUAGA AUTOR 2009 T
95% tinto fino, 5% albillo.

90 Colour: very deep cherry. Nose: powerfull, overripe fruit, toasty, dark chocolate. Palate: flavourful, fine bitter notes, good acidity, spicy, toasty.

ARZUAGA RESERVA ESPECIAL 2008 TR
95% tinto fino, 5% albillo.

92 Colour: cherry, garnet rim. Nose: mineral, ripe fruit, red berry notes, fruit expression, creamy oak. Palate: ripe fruit, spicy, fine bitter notes.

AMAYA ARZUAGA AUTOR 2008 T
95% tinto fino, 5% albillo.

92 Colour: bright cherry. Nose: ripe fruit, sweet spices, creamy oak, expressive, roasted coffee. Palate: flavourful, fruity, toasty, balanced.

ARZUAGA 2008 TR
95% tinto fino, 5% cabernet sauvignon, merlot.

88 Colour: cherry, garnet rim. Nose: ripe fruit, spicy, creamy oak, toasty, complex, scrubland. Palate: powerful, flavourful, toasty, round tannins.

AMAYA ARZUAGA AUTOR 2007 T
95% tinto fino, 5% albillo.

92 Colour: cherry, garnet rim. Nose: ripe fruit, spicy, aromatic coffee, sweet spices, toasty. Palate: long, powerful, flavourful, balanced.

ARZUAGA 2004 TGR
90% tinto fino, 10% cabernet sauvignon, merlot.

90 Colour: cherry, garnet rim. Nose: creamy oak, sweet spices, ripe fruit. Palate: flavourful, powerful, spicy, ripe fruit.

BODEGAS ASENJO & MANSO

09311 La Horra (Burgos)
☎: +34 636 972 421 - Fax: +34 947 505 269
info@asenjo-manso.com
www.asenjo-manso.com

SILVANUS 2008 TC
100% tempranillo.

89 Colour: cherry, garnet rim. Nose: ripe fruit, spicy, toasty, earthy notes. Palate: powerful, flavourful, toasty, round tannins.

CERES 2008 TC
100% tempranillo.

87 Colour: cherry, garnet rim. Nose: spicy, creamy oak, toasty, overripe fruit. Palate: powerful, flavourful, toasty.

SILVANUS EDICIÓN LIMITADA 2008 T
100% tempranillo.

85 Colour: pale ruby, brick rim edge. Nose: powerfull, ripe fruit, roasted coffee. Palate: flavourful, fine bitter notes, good acidity.

CERES ECOLÓGICO 2007 T ROBLE
100% tempranillo.

88 Colour: cherry, garnet rim. Nose: toasty, spicy, ripe fruit, creamy oak. Palate: flavourful, fine bitter notes, good acidity.

A&M AUTOR 2006 T
100% tempranillo.

92 Colour: cherry, garnet rim. Nose: ripe fruit, spicy, creamy oak, toasty, characterful, varietal. Palate: powerful, flavourful, toasty, round tannins.

BODEGAS BALBÁS

La Majada, s/n
09311 La Horra (Burgos)
☎: +34 947 542 111 - Fax: +34 947 542 112
bodegas@balbas.es
www.balbas.es

RITUS 2009 T
75% tempranillo, 25% merlot.

90 Colour: cherry, garnet rim. Nose: medium intensity, creamy oak, dark chocolate. Palate: balanced, ripe fruit, long.

ARDAL 2009 TC
80% tempranillo, 20% cabernet sauvignon.

89 Colour: cherry, garnet rim. Nose: ripe fruit, cocoa bean, sweet spices, creamy oak. Palate: powerful, flavourful, balanced, toasty.

BALBÁS 2009 TC
90% tempranillo, 10% cabernet sauvignon.

86 Colour: bright cherry. Nose: sweet spices, creamy oak, ripe fruit. Palate: flavourful, fruity, toasty, round tannins.

ARDAL 2006 TR
80% tempranillo, 20% cabernet sauvignon.

91 Colour: bright cherry. Nose: sweet spices, creamy oak, red berry notes, ripe fruit. Palate: flavourful, fruity, toasty, round tannins.

ALITUS 2004 T
75% tempranillo, 20% cabernet sauvignon, 5% merlot.

91 Colour: cherry, garnet rim. Nose: spicy, creamy oak, toasty, ripe fruit. Palate: powerful, flavourful, toasty, round tannins.

BODEGAS BALUARTE

Calle de la Ribera 32
31592 Cintruénigo (Navarra)
☎: +34 948 811 000
info@bodegaschivite.com

BALUARTE 2009 T ROBLE
tinta del país.

87 Colour: deep cherry. Nose: ripe fruit, neat, varietal, toasty. Palate: flavourful, powerful, good acidity, fine bitter notes.

BALUARTE 2008 TC
tinta del país.

91 Colour: cherry, garnet rim. Nose: ripe fruit, spicy, creamy oak, toasty, mineral, floral. Palate: powerful, flavourful, toasty, round tannins.

BODEGAS BRIEGO

Del Rosario, 32
47311 Fompedraza (Valladolid)
☎: +34 983 892 156 - Fax: +34 983 892 156
info@bodegasbriego.com
www.bodegasbriego.com

BRIEGO VENDIMIA SELECCIONADA 2009 T ROBLE
100% tempranillo.

92 Colour: very deep cherry. Nose: creamy oak, dark chocolate, ripe fruit, balanced. Palate: good structure, flavourful, good acidity, long.

SUPERNOVA ROBLE 2009 T ROBLE
100% tempranillo.

92 Colour: cherry, garnet rim. Nose: spicy, creamy oak, toasty, characterful, ripe fruit. Palate: powerful, flavourful, toasty, round tannins.

SUPERNOVA 2008 TC
100% tempranillo.

88 Colour: bright cherry, garnet rim. Nose: sweet spices, cocoa bean, ripe fruit, powerfull. Palate: flavourful, round tannins.

BRIEGO 2005 TR
100% tempranillo.

88 Colour: deep cherry, garnet rim. Nose: powerfull, fruit preserve, spicy, creamy oak. Palate: good structure, flavourful.

BODEGAS CASTILLO DE GUMIEL

Avda. de Extremadura, 55
09400 Aranda de Duero (Burgos)
☎: +34 947 510 839 - Fax: +34 947 510 839
castillodegumiel@hotmail.com
www.silenciovaldiruela.com

SILENCIO DE VALDIRUELA 2011 RD
25% albillo, 75% tempranillo.

86 Colour: light cherry. Nose: red berry notes, ripe fruit, lactic notes. Palate: fruity, correct, good finish.

SILENCIO DE VALDIRUELA 2011 T
100% tinta del país.

87 Colour: deep cherry, purple rim. Nose: medium intensity, red berry notes, ripe fruit. Palate: flavourful, balanced.

SILENCIO DE VALDIRUELA 2010 T ROBLE
tempranillo.

88 Colour: cherry, purple rim. Nose: expressive, ripe fruit, sweet spices. Palate: flavourful, good acidity, spicy.

SILENCIO DE VALDIRUELA 2009 TC
tempranillo.

86 Colour: cherry, garnet rim. Nose: ripe fruit, balsamic herbs, aged wood nuances, spicy. Palate: powerful, flavourful, spicy, long.

SILENCIO DE VALDIRUELA 2007 TR
tempranillo.

90 Colour: ruby red, orangey edge. Nose: ripe fruit, creamy oak, sweet spices, fine reductive notes. Palate: correct, balanced, powerful, flavourful.

BODEGAS CASTILLO DE LA DUQUESA

Calle Mar, 116
12181 Benlloch (Castellón)
☎: +34 693 299 449 - Fax: +34 964 339 958
info@banus.eu
www.banus.eu

QUINTADO TEMPRANILLO 2009 TC
87% tempranillo, 8% cabernet sauvignon, 4% merlot.

88 Colour: bright cherry. Nose: ripe fruit, sweet spices, creamy oak, toasty. Palate: flavourful, fruity, toasty, round tannins.

QUINTADO TEMPRANILLO 2008 TR
94% tempranillo, 6% merlot.

90 Colour: cherry, garnet rim. Nose: ripe fruit, spicy, creamy oak, toasty, fine reductive notes. Palate: powerful, flavourful, toasty, round tannins, balanced.

BODEGAS CEPA 21

Ctra. N-122, Km. 297
47318 Castrillo de Duero (Valladolid)
☎: +34 983 484 083 - Fax: +34 983 480 017
bodega@cepa21.com
www.cepa21.com

HITO 2011 RD
100% tinto fino.

86 Colour: rose, purple rim. Nose: powerfull, ripe fruit, red berry notes. Palate: flavourful, fruity.

MALABRIGO 2010 T
100% tinto fino.

93 Colour: very deep cherry. Nose: powerfull, dark chocolate, roasted coffee, ripe fruit. Palate: powerful, fine bitter notes, good acidity, round tannins.

CEPA 21 2009 T
100% tinto fino.

92 Colour: cherry, garnet rim. Nose: spicy, creamy oak, toasty, ripe fruit. Palate: powerful, flavourful, toasty, round tannins.

BODEGAS CRUZ DE ALBA

Síndico, 4 y 5
47350 Quintanilla de Onésimo (Valladolid)
☎: +34 941 310 295 - Fax: +34 941 310 832
info@cruzdealba.es
www.cruzdealba.es

LUCERO DE ALBA 2011 T ROBLE
100% tempranillo.

89 Colour: bright cherry. Nose: ripe fruit, sweet spices, creamy oak, balsamic herbs. Palate: flavourful, fruity, toasty, balanced.

CRUZ DE ALBA 2009 TC
100% tempranillo.

91 Colour: cherry, garnet rim. Nose: ripe fruit, creamy oak, toasty, sweet spices. Palate: powerful, flavourful, toasty, round tannins, balanced.

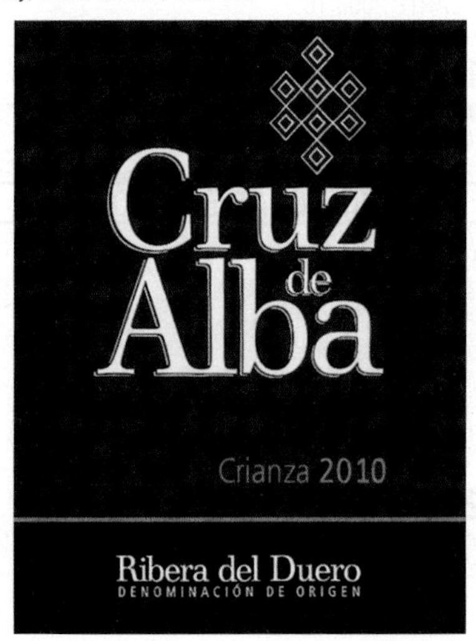

BODEGAS CUEVAS JIMÉNEZ - FERRATUS

Ctra. Madrid-Irún, A-I km. 165
09370 Gumiel de Izán (Burgos)
☎: +34 947 679 999 - Fax: +34 947 613 873
bodega@ferratus.es
www.ferratus.es

FERRATUS A0 2010 T ROBLE

89 Colour: cherry, garnet rim. Nose: varietal, medium intensity, ripe fruit, sweet spices, lactic notes. Palate: flavourful, good structure, spicy.

FERRATUS 2008 T
100% tempranillo.

94 Colour: bright cherry, garnet rim. Nose: balanced, ripe fruit, sweet spices. Palate: flavourful, good acidity, round tannins.

FERRATUS 2007 T
100% tempranillo.

93 Colour: cherry, garnet rim. Nose: spicy, creamy oak, toasty, ripe fruit, mineral. Palate: powerful, flavourful, toasty, round tannins.

FERRATUS SENSACIONES 2007 T
100% tempranillo.

93 Colour: deep cherry, garnet rim. Nose: cocoa bean, creamy oak, complex. Palate: ripe fruit, long, good structure.

FERRATUS SENSACIONES 2006 T
100% tempranillo.

93 Colour: cherry, garnet rim. Nose: spicy, creamy oak, toasty, characterful, ripe fruit, earthy notes. Palate: powerful, flavourful, toasty, round tannins.

BODEGAS DE LOS RÍOS PRIETO

Ctra. Pesquera - Renedo, 1
47315 Pesquera de Duero (Valladolid)
☎: +34 983 880 383 - Fax: +34 983 878 032
info@bodegasdelosriosprieto.com
www.bodegasdelosriosprieto.com

PRIOS MAXIMUS 2011 T ROBLE
100% tempranillo.

88 Colour: bright cherry. Aroma ripe fruit, sweet spices, creamy oak, expressive. Palate: flavourful, fruity, toasty, round tannins.

PRIOS MAXIMUS 2010 TC
100% tempranillo.

88 Colour: cherry, garnet rim. Nose: creamy oak, cocoa bean, balanced, ripe fruit. Palate: flavourful, toasty, round tannins.

LARA PRIOS MAXIMUS VINO DE AUTOR 2006 T
100% tempranillo.

90 Colour: cherry, garnet rim. Nose: ripe fruit, spicy, creamy oak, toasty, fragrant herbs, characterful. Palate: powerful, flavourful, toasty, round tannins.

PRIOS MAXIMUS 2006 TR
100% tempranillo.

87 Colour: pale ruby, brick rim edge. Nose: fruit liqueur notes, fragrant herbs, fine reductive notes, spicy. Palate: powerful, flavourful, toasty.

BODEGAS DOMINIO DE CAIR

Ctra. Aranda a la Aguilera. km. 9
09370 La Aguilera (Burgos)
☎: +34 947 545 276
bodegas@dominiodecair.com
www.dominiodecair.com

LU&BE 2009 T
90% tempranillo, 10% merlot.

89 Colour: cherry, garnet rim. Nose: ripe fruit, fragrant herbs, spicy, toasty. Palate: good acidity, powerful, flavourful.

CAIR 2008 T
100% tempranillo.

88 Colour: cherry, garnet rim. Nose: ripe fruit, balsamic herbs, sweet spices, creamy oak. Palate: correct, flavourful, toasty.

BODEGAS EMILIO MORO

Ctra. Peñafiel - Valoria, s/n
47315 Pesquera de Duero (Valladolid)
☎: +34 983 878 400 - Fax: +34 983 870 195
bodega@emiliomoro.com
www.emiliomoro.com

FINCA RESALSO 2011 T
100% tinto fino.

90 Colour: bright cherry. Nose: ripe fruit, sweet spices, creamy oak, varietal. Palate: flavourful, fruity, toasty, round tannins.

EMILIO MORO 2009 TC
100% tinto fino.

93 Colour: cherry, garnet rim. Nose: ripe fruit, spicy, creamy oak, toasty, characterful. Palate: powerful, flavourful, toasty, round tannins.

MALLEOLUS 2009 T
100% tinto fino.

93 Colour: cherry, garnet rim. Nose: creamy oak, toasty, characterful, ripe fruit, spicy. Palate: powerful, flavourful, toasty, round tannins.

MALLEOLUS DE SANCHOMARTÍN 2008 T
100% tinto fino.

94 Colour: cherry, garnet rim. Aroma ripe fruit, spicy, creamy oak, toasty, complex. Palate: powerful, flavourful, toasty, round tannins.

MALLEOLUS DE VALDERRAMIRO 2008 T
100% tinto fino.

93 Colour: cherry, garnet rim. Nose: ripe fruit, mineral, dark chocolate, cocoa bean, sweet spices, creamy oak. Palate: balanced, powerful, flavourful, toasty.

BODEGAS EPIFANIO RIVERA

Onésimo Redondo, 1
47315 Pesquera de Duero (Valladolid)
☎: +34 983 870 109 - Fax: +34 983 870 109
comercial@epifaniorivera.com
www.epifaniorivera.com

ERIAL TF 2009 T
tinto fino.

89 Colour: bright cherry. Nose: ripe fruit, sweet spices, creamy oak, toasty. Palate: flavourful, fruity, toasty.

ERIAL 2009 T
tinto fino.

88 Colour: cherry, purple rim. Nose: medium intensity, toasty, sweet spices. Palate: flavourful, fruity.

BODEGAS FÉLIX CALLEJO

Avda. del Cid, km. 16
09441 Sotillo de la Ribera (Burgos)
☎: +34 947 532 312 - Fax: +34 947 532 304
callejo@bodegasfelixcallejo.com
www.bodegasfelixcallejo.com

VIÑA PILAR 2011 RD
100% tempranillo.

86 Colour: rose, purple rim. Nose: powerfull, ripe fruit, red berry notes, floral. Palate: , powerful, fruity, fresh.

FLORES DE CALLEJO 2010 T
tempranillo.

87 Colour: bright cherry, purple rim. Nose: ripe fruit, sweet spices, creamy oak. Palate: flavourful, fruity, spicy.

FÉLIX CALLEJO SELECCIÓN 2009 TC
tempranillo.

92 Colour: deep cherry, garnet rim. Nose: balanced, complex, spicy, ripe fruit. Palate: good structure, long, balanced.

MAJUELOS DE CALLEJO 2009 T
tempranillo.

90 Colour: deep cherry, purple rim. Nose: medium intensity, red berry notes, ripe fruit, sweet spices. Palate: flavourful, good structure.

CALLEJO 2009 TC
100% tempranillo.

89 Colour: cherry, purple rim. Nose: medium intensity, ripe fruit, sweet spices. Palate: flavourful, ripe fruit, correct.

GRAN CALLEJO 2006 TGR
tempranillo.

91 Colour: cherry, garnet rim. Nose: ripe fruit, creamy oak, expressive. Palate: powerful, flavourful, toasty, round tannins.

BODEGAS FUENTENARRO

Constitución, 32
09311 La Horra (Burgos)
☎: +34 947 542 092 - Fax: +34 947 542 083
bodegas@fuentenarro.com
www.fuentenarro.com

FUENTENARRO VENDIMIA SELECCIONADA 2010 T
100% tempranillo.

91 Colour: cherry, garnet rim. Nose: spicy, creamy oak, toasty, characterful, ripe fruit. Palate: powerful, flavourful, toasty, round tannins.

FUENTENARRO CUATRO MESES BARRICA 2010 T BARRICA
100% tempranillo.

86 Colour: cherry, garnet rim. Nose: powerfull, dark chocolate, ripe fruit. Palate: correct, balanced.

FUENTENARRO 2009 TC
100% tempranillo.

90 Colour: cherry, garnet rim. Aroma ripe fruit, spicy, creamy oak, toasty, complex. Palate: powerful, flavourful, toasty, round tannins.

FUENTENARRO 2006 TR
100% tempranillo.

91 Colour: cherry, garnet rim. Nose: ripe fruit, spicy, fine reductive notes, cocoa bean. Palate: powerful, flavourful, toasty, round tannins.

BODEGAS FUENTESPINA

Camino Cascajo, s/n
09470 Fuentespina (Burgos)
☎: +34 921 596 002 - Fax: +34 921 596 035
ana@avelinovegas.com
www.avelinovegas.com

FUENTESPINA 2011 T ROBLE
100% tempranillo.

87 Colour: deep cherry, purple rim. Nose: expressive, ripe fruit, sweet spices. Palate: good structure, good finish.

FUENTESPINA GRANATE 2011 T
tempranillo.

87 Colour: bright cherry. Nose: ripe fruit, sweet spices, creamy oak. Palate: flavourful, fruity, toasty, spicy.

CORONA DE CASTILLA PRESTIGIO 2009 TC
tempranillo.

91 Colour: cherry, garnet rim. Nose: spicy, creamy oak, toasty, characterful, ripe fruit. Palate: powerful, flavourful, toasty, round tannins.

FUENTESPINA SELECCIÓN 2009 T
tempranillo.

90 Colour: cherry, garnet rim. Nose: ripe fruit, spicy, toasty, complex, mineral, cocoa bean, dark chocolate. Palate: powerful, flavourful, toasty, harsh oak tannins.

FUENTESPINA 2009 TC
tempranillo.

88 Colour: cherry, garnet rim. Nose: spicy, creamy oak, toasty, complex, characterful, ripe fruit. Palate: powerful, flavourful, toasty, round tannins.

FUENTESPINA 2006 TR
tempranillo.

88 Colour: cherry, garnet rim. Nose: balanced, spicy, creamy oak, ripe fruit. Palate: balanced, ripe fruit.

F DE FUENTESPINA 2004 TR
tempranillo.

90 Colour: cherry, garnet rim. Nose: ripe fruit, creamy oak, dark chocolate. Palate: powerful, flavourful, toasty, round tannins.

BODEGAS GARCÍA DE ARANDA

Ctra. de Soria, s/n
09400 Aranda de Duero (Burgos)
☎: +34 947 501 817 - Fax: +34 947 506 355
bodega@bodegasgarcia.com
www.bodegasgarcia.com

SEÑORÍO DE LOS BALDÍOS DON ANASTASIO GARCÍA 2011 RD
tempranillo.

87 Colour: rose, purple rim. Aroma powerfull, ripe fruit, red berry notes, floral, expressive. Palate: fleshy, powerful, fruity, fresh.

SEÑORÍO DE LOS BALDÍOS 2011 T
tempranillo.

86 Colour: cherry, purple rim. Nose: fresh, red berry notes, raspberry, floral. Palate: fresh, light-bodied, fruity, flavourful.

SEÑORÍO DE LOS BALDÍOS 2011 T ROBLE
tempranillo.

82

PEDRO GARCÍA 2009 T
tempranillo.

92 Colour: bright cherry. Aroma ripe fruit, sweet spices, creamy oak, expressive. Palate: flavourful, fruity, toasty, round tannins.

SEÑORÍO DE LOS BALDÍOS 2009 TC
tempranillo.

88 Colour: cherry, garnet rim. Nose: ripe fruit, aged wood nuances, spicy, roasted coffee. Palate: powerful, flavourful, spicy.

SEÑORÍO DE LOS BALDÍOS 2007 TR
tempranillo.

88 Colour: bright cherry, garnet rim. Nose: old leather, ripe fruit, spicy. Palate: flavourful, spicy, ripe fruit.

BODEGAS HACIENDA MONASTERIO

Ctra. Pesquera - Valbuena, km. 38
47315 Pesquera de Duero (Valladolid)
☎: +34 983 484 002 - Fax: +34 983 484 079
bmonasterio@haciendamonasterio.com
www.haciendamonasterio.com

HACIENDA MONASTERIO 2009 T
80% tempranillo, 10% cabernet sauvignon, 10% merlot.

92 Colour: cherry, garnet rim. Nose: ripe fruit, spicy, creamy oak, toasty, characterful, elegant. Palate: powerful, flavourful, toasty, round tannins.

HACIENDA MONASTERIO RESERVA ESPECIAL 2009 TR
80% tempranillo, 20% cabernet sauvignon.

93 Colour: cherry, garnet rim. Nose: ripe fruit, spicy, creamy oak, toasty, complex, expressive. Palate: powerful, flavourful, toasty, round tannins.

HACIENDA MONASTERIO 2007 TR
80% tempranillo, 20% cabernet sauvignon.

92 Colour: cherry, garnet rim. Nose: ripe fruit, spicy, creamy oak, toasty, complex, wet leather. Palate: powerful, flavourful, toasty, round tannins.

BODEGAS HERMANOS PÉREZ PASCUAS

Ctra. Roa, s/n
09314 Pedrosa de Duero (Burgos)
☎: +34 947 530 100 - Fax: +34 947 530 002
vinapedrosa@perezpascuas.com
www.perezpascuas.com

VIÑA PEDROSA 2010 TC
100% tinta del país.

90 Colour: cherry, garnet rim. Nose: sweet spices, creamy oak, cocoa bean, ripe fruit. Palate: long, powerful, flavourful, fruity, balsamic, spicy.

CEPA GAVILÁN 2010 T
100% tinta del país.

89 Colour: bright cherry. Nose: ripe fruit, creamy oak, spicy, balanced. Palate: flavourful, fruity, toasty, long, spicy.

VIÑA PEDROSA LA NAVILLA 2009 T
100% tinta del país.

95 Colour: cherry, garnet rim. Nose: creamy oak, toasty, red berry notes, ripe fruit, sweet spices, mineral. Palate: powerful, flavourful, toasty, round tannins, balanced.

VIÑA PEDROSA 2009 TR
90% tinta del país, 10% cabernet sauvignon.

94 Colour: cherry, garnet rim. Nose: ripe fruit, spicy, creamy oak, toasty, characterful, varietal. Palate: flavourful, toasty, round tannins, good acidity, elegant.

PÉREZ PASCUAS GRAN SELECCIÓN 2006 TGR

93 Colour: pale ruby, brick rim edge. Nose: ripe fruit, balsamic herbs, dark chocolate, sweet spices, creamy oak, expressive, elegant. Palate: spicy, long, flavourful, balanced, elegant, good acidity.

VIÑA PEDROSA 2006 TGR
90% tinta del país, 10% cabernet sauvignon.

92 Colour: pale ruby, brick rim edge. Nose: elegant, spicy, fine reductive notes, wet leather, aged wood nuances, ripe fruit. Palate: spicy, fine tannins, elegant, long, balanced.

BODEGAS HERMANOS SASTRE

San Pedro, s/n
09311 La Horra (Burgos)
☎: +34 947 542 108 - Fax: +34 947 542 108
sastre@vinasastre.com
www.vinasastre.com

REGINA VIDES 2009 T
100% tinta del país.

97 Colour: bright cherry, garnet rim. Nose: complex, creamy oak, spicy, cocoa bean, ripe fruit. Palate: good structure, full, round tannins.

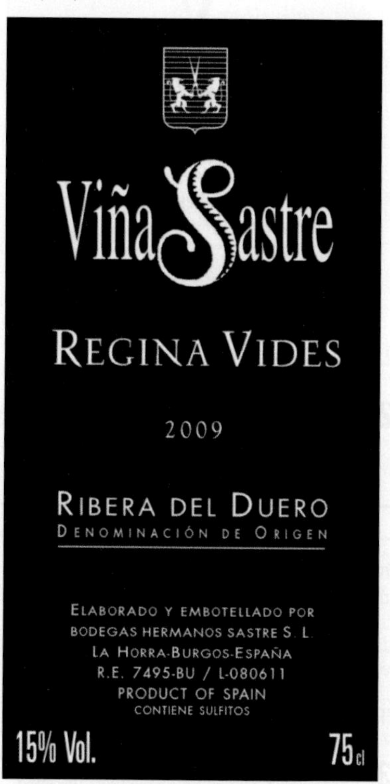

VIÑA SASTRE PESUS 2009 T
80% tinta del país, 10% merlot, 10% cabernet sauvignon.

96 Colour: cherry, garnet rim. Nose: spicy, creamy oak, characterful, fruit expression, toasty, cocoa bean. Palate: powerful, flavourful, toasty, round tannins.

VIÑA SASTRE PAGO DE SANTA CRUZ 2009 T
100% tinta del país.

95 Colour: cherry, garnet rim. Nose: ripe fruit, spicy, creamy oak, toasty, mineral. Palate: powerful, flavourful, toasty, round tannins.

VIÑA SASTRE 2009 TC
tinta del país.

93 Colour: cherry, garnet rim. Nose: spicy, creamy oak, toasty, characterful, ripe fruit, mineral. Palate: powerful, flavourful, toasty, round tannins.

BODEGAS HESVERA

Ctra. Peñafiel - Pesquera, Km. 5,5
47315 Pesquera de Duero (Valladolid)
☎: +34 626 060 516 - Fax: +34 983 870 201
bodegashesvera@gmail.com
www.hesvera.es

HESVERA SEIS MESES 2010 T
tempranillo.

86 Colour: deep cherry. Nose: ripe fruit, toasty, medium intensity. Palate: fine bitter notes, ripe fruit.

HESVERA 2009 TC
tempranillo.

88 Colour: cherry, garnet rim. Nose: ripe fruit, spicy, creamy oak, toasty. Palate: powerful, flavourful, toasty, round tannins.

BODEGAS IMPERIALES

Ctra. Madrid - Irun, Km. 171
09370 Gumiel de Izán (Burgos)
☎: +34 947 544 070 - Fax: +34 947 525 759
direccion@bodegasimperiales.com
www.bodegasimperiales.com

ABADÍA DE SAN QUIRCE 2010 T
100% tinta del país.

90 Colour: deep cherry. Nose: powerfull, ripe fruit, toasty, spicy. Palate: flavourful, spicy, ripe fruit, fine bitter notes.

ABADÍA DE SAN QUIRCE 2009 TC
100% tinta del país.

92 Colour: cherry, garnet rim. Nose: red berry notes, ripe fruit, balsamic herbs, sweet spices, toasty, mineral. Palate: powerful, flavourful, complex, toasty.

FINCA HELENA AUTOR 2006 T
100% tinta del país.

92 Colour: cherry, garnet rim. Nose: spicy, ripe fruit, aromatic coffee, creamy oak. Palate: flavourful, good structure, fruity.

ABADÍA DE SAN QUIRCE 2005 TR
100% tinta del país.

90 Colour: cherry, garnet rim. Nose: complex, balanced, powerfull, warm, ripe fruit, old leather. Palate: flavourful, fruity.

ABADÍA DE SAN QUIRCE 2001 TGR
100% tinta del país.

91 Colour: pale ruby, brick rim edge. Nose: elegant, spicy, wet leather, aged wood nuances, fruit liqueur notes. Palate: spicy, elegant, balanced, fine bitter notes.

BODEGAS ISMAEL ARROYO - VALSOTILLO

Los Lagares, 71
09441 Sotillo de la Ribera (Burgos)
☎: +34 947 532 309 - Fax: +34 947 532 487
bodega@valsotillo.com
www.valsotillo.com

MESONEROS DE CASTILLA 2011 RD
90% tinta del país, 10% albillo.

87 Colour: rose, purple rim. Nose: red berry notes, raspberry, fresh, medium intensity. Palate: flavourful, fresh, fruity.

MESONEROS DE CASTILLA 2011 T
100% tinta del país.

87 Colour: cherry, purple rim. Nose: expressive, ripe fruit. Palate: flavourful, fruity, good acidity, round tannins.

VALSOTILLO 2009 TC
100% tinta del país.

91 Colour: cherry, garnet rim. Nose: spicy, creamy oak, toasty, ripe fruit. Palate: powerful, flavourful, toasty, round tannins.

VALSOTILLO 2005 TR
100% tinta del país.

87 Colour: deep cherry. Nose: powerfull, dark chocolate, toasty, ripe fruit. Palate: flavourful, fruity, full.

VALSOTILLO 2004 TGR
100% tinta del país.

91 Colour: cherry, garnet rim. Nose: spicy, creamy oak, toasty, complex, animal reductive notes, fine reductive notes. Palate: powerful, flavourful, toasty, round tannins.

VALSOTILLO VS 2004 TR
100% tinta del país.

90 Colour: cherry, garnet rim. Nose: spicy, creamy oak, toasty, complex, characterful, ripe fruit. Palate: powerful, flavourful, toasty, round tannins.

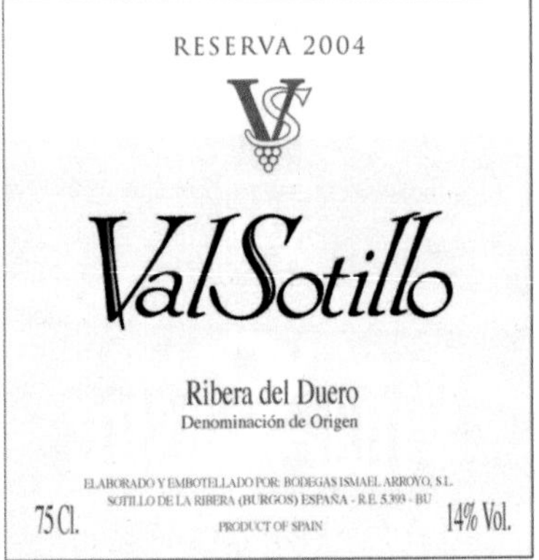

VALSOTILLO VS 2001 TR
100% tinta del país.

92 Colour: cherry, garnet rim. Nose: spicy, creamy oak, toasty, wet leather, ripe fruit, fine reductive notes. Palate: powerful, flavourful, round tannins, spicy.

BODEGAS LA HORRA

Camino de Anguix s/n
09311 La Horra (Burgos)
☎: +34 947 613 963 - Fax: +34 947 613 963
rodarioja@roda.es
www.bodegaslahorra.es

CORIMBO I 2010 T
tinta del país.

93 Colour: cherry, garnet rim. Nose: ripe fruit, spicy, creamy oak, toasty, characterful. Palate: powerful, flavourful, toasty, round tannins.

CORIMBO 2010 T
tempranillo.

91 Colour: cherry, garnet rim. Nose: ripe fruit, fruit expression, toasty, new oak. Palate: flavourful, ripe fruit, spicy, long.

CORIMBO I 2009 T
tempranillo.

92 Colour: cherry, garnet rim. Nose: creamy oak, toasty, ripe fruit, mineral. Palate: powerful, flavourful, toasty, round tannins.

BODEGAS LAMBUENA

Ctra. Fuentecén, s/n
09300 Roa (Burgos)
☎: +34 947 540 034 - Fax: +34 947 540 614
lambuena@bodegaslambuena.com
www.bodegaslambuena.com

LAMBUENA 2010 T ROBLE

84

LAMBUENA 2009 TC

87 Colour: cherry, garnet rim. Nose: ripe fruit, spicy, creamy oak, toasty. Palate: powerful, flavourful, spicy.

LAMBUENA 2005 TR
tinto fino.

87 Colour: pale ruby, brick rim edge. Nose: spicy, fine reductive notes, aged wood nuances, fruit liqueur notes, fruit preserve. Palate: spicy, ripe fruit, long.

BODEGAS LIBA Y DELEITE

Paseo De Zorrilla, 77 – 3º Dcha.
47007 (Valladolid)
☎: +34 983 355 543 - Fax: +34 983 340 824
acontia@acontia.es
www.acontia.es

ACONTIA '06 ROBLE ESPAÑOL 2010 T
100% tempranillo.

89 Colour: cherry, garnet rim. Nose: ripe fruit, spicy, toasty, cocoa bean, dark chocolate. Palate: powerful, flavourful, toasty.

ACONTIA '12 ROBLE ESPAÑOL 2008 T
100% tempranillo.

89 Colour: cherry, garnet rim. Aroma ripe fruit, spicy, creamy oak, toasty, complex. Palate: powerful, flavourful, toasty, round tannins.

BODEGAS LÓPEZ CRISTÓBAL

Barrio Estación, s/n
09300 Roa de Duero (Burgos)
☎: +34 947 561 139 - Fax: +34 947 540 606
info@lopezcristobal.com
www.lopezcristobal.com

LÓPEZ CRISTOBAL 2011 T ROBLE
95% tinta del país, 5% merlot.

91 Colour: bright cherry. Nose: ripe fruit, sweet spices, creamy oak, expressive, red berry notes. Palate: flavourful, fruity, toasty, round tannins.

LÓPEZ CRISTOBAL 2009 TC
95% tempranillo, 5% merlot.

92 Colour: cherry, garnet rim. Nose: red berry notes, ripe fruit, sweet spices, creamy oak. Palate: powerful, flavourful, long, spicy.

BAGÚS VENDIMIA SELECCIONADA 2009 T
100% tempranillo.

91 Colour: bright cherry, garnet rim. Nose: toasty, new oak, powerfull, ripe fruit. Palate: good structure, full, flavourful, round tannins.

BODEGAS MARQUÉS DE VALPARAISO

Paraje los Llanillos, s/n
09370 Quintana del Pidío (Burgos)
☎: +34 947 545 286 - Fax: +34 947 545 163
paternina@paternina.com
www.paternina.com

MARQUÉS DE VALPARAÍSO 2011 T ROBLE
tinta del país.

87 Colour: cherry, purple rim. Nose: ripe fruit, creamy oak, mineral, spicy. Palate: powerful, flavourful, ripe fruit.

FINCA EL ENCINAL 2011 T ROBLE
tinto fino.

85 Colour: cherry, purple rim. Nose: ripe fruit, sweet spices, creamy oak. Palate: long, spicy, flavourful.

BODEGAS MUÑOZ Y MAZÓN

Avda. Valle Esgueva, 12
09310 Villatuelda (Burgos)
☎: +34 941 454 050 - Fax: +34 941 454 529
bodega@bodegasriojanas.com
www.bodegasriojanas.com

AZUEL ROBLE 2011 T
100% tempranillo.

87 Colour: bright cherry. Nose: ripe fruit, sweet spices, creamy oak. Palate: flavourful, fruity, toasty.

AZUEL 2009 TC
100% tempranillo.

88 Colour: cherry, garnet rim. Nose: ripe fruit, spicy, toasty. Palate: powerful, flavourful, toasty.

BODEGAS MUSEO ONTAÑÓN

Avda. de Aragón, 3
26006 Logroño (La Rioja)
☎: +34 941 234 200 - Fax: +34 941 270 482
enoturismo@ontanon.es
www.ontanon.es

TEÓN DEL CONDADO 2010 T ROBLE

88 Colour: deep cherry, purple rim. Nose: powerfull, dark chocolate, sweet spices, ripe fruit. Palate: good structure, flavourful, round tannins.

TEÓN DEL CONDADO 2008 TC

88 Colour: cherry, garnet rim. Nose: spicy, creamy oak, toasty, ripe fruit. Palate: powerful, flavourful, toasty, round tannins.

BODEGAS PAGOS DE MOGAR

Ctra. Pesquera, km. 0,2
47359 Valbuena de Duero (Valladolid)
☎: +34 983 683 011 - Fax: +34 983 683 011
comercial@bodegaspagosdemogar.com
www.bodegaspagosdemogar.com

MOGAR 2010 T ROBLE
100% tinta del país.

88 Colour: bright cherry. Nose: ripe fruit, creamy oak, expressive, balsamic herbs, sweet spices. Palate: flavourful, fruity, toasty, round tannins.

BODEGAS PASCUAL

Ctra. de Aranda, Km. 5
09471 Fuentelcesped (Burgos)
☎: +34 947 557 351 - Fax: +34 947 557 312
export@bodegaspascual.com
www.bodegaspascual.com

HEREDAD DE PEÑALOSA 2011 T ROBLE
100% tempranillo.

85 Colour: cherry, purple rim. Nose: ripe fruit, sweet spices, toasty. Palate: correct, fruity aftespalate:.

BURÓ SELECCIÓN 2009 T
100% tempranillo.

92 Colour: cherry, garnet rim. Nose: ripe fruit, balsamic herbs, earthy notes, spicy, toasty. Palate: powerful, flavourful, spicy, long, toasty.

BURÓ DE PEÑALOSA 2009 TC
100% tempranillo.

89 Colour: cherry, garnet rim. Nose: ripe fruit, spicy, creamy oak, toasty. Palate: powerful, flavourful, toasty, round tannins.

BURÓ DE PEÑALOSA 2007 TR
100% tempranillo.

88 Colour: cherry, garnet rim. Nose: balanced, ripe fruit, spicy. Palate: flavourful, round tannins.

BODEGAS PEÑAFIEL

Ctra. N-122, Km. 311
47300 Peñafiel (Valladolid)
☎: +34 983 881 622 - Fax: +34 983 881 944
bodegaspenafiel@bodegaspenafiel.com
www.bodegaspenafiel.com

MIROS 2009 T ROBLE
82% tempranillo, 12% merlot, 6% cabernet sauvignon.

88 Colour: cherry, garnet rim. Nose: ripe fruit, spicy, balanced, scrubland. Palate: flavourful, fruity, good acidity.

MIROS DE RIBERA 2007 TC
90% tempranillo, 7% merlot, 3% cabernet sauvignon.

88 Colour: cherry, garnet rim. Nose: ripe fruit, spicy, toasty, aromatic coffee, dark chocolate. Palate: powerful, flavourful, toasty, round tannins.

MIROS DE RIBERA 2006 TR
100% tempranillo.

89 Colour: cherry, garnet rim. Nose: ripe fruit, spicy, creamy oak, mineral. Palate: correct, powerful, flavourful, spicy.

MIRO RANCI VINO DE LICOR

84

BODEGAS PEÑALBA HERRAIZ

Sol de las Moreras, 3
09400 Aranda de Duero (Burgos)
☎: +34 947 508 249 - Fax: +34 947 511 145
miguelpma@ono.com

APTUS 2010 T ROBLE
tempranillo.

88 Colour: bright cherry. Nose: ripe fruit, sweet spices, toasty. Palate: flavourful, fruity, toasty, round tannins.

CARRAVID 2009 T
95% tempranillo, 5% garnacha.

87 Colour: cherry, garnet rim. Nose: fruit preserve, sweet spices, fragrant herbs. Palate: flavourful, round tannins.

BODEGAS PINGÓN

Ctra. N-122, Km. 311
47300 Peñafiel (Valladolid)
☎: +34 983 880 623 - Fax: +34 983 880 623
carramimbre@bodegaspingon.com
www.bodegaspingon.com

CARRAMIMBRE 2011 T ROBLE
95% tinto fino, 5% cabernet sauvignon.

89 Colour: bright cherry. Nose: sweet spices, creamy oak, ripe fruit. Palate: flavourful, fruity, toasty, round tannins.

ALTAMIMBRE 2009 T
100% tinto fino.

92 Colour: cherry, garnet rim. Nose: ripe fruit, mineral, sweet spices, creamy oak. Palate: powerful, flavourful, complex, long, toasty.

CARRAMIMBRE 2006 TR
95% tinto fino, 5% cabernet sauvignon.

88 Colour: cherry, garnet rim. Aroma ripe fruit, spicy, creamy oak, toasty, complex. Palate: powerful, flavourful, toasty, round tannins.

CARRAMIMBRE 2009 TC
95% tinto fino, 5% cabernet sauvignon.

91 Colour: cherry, garnet rim. Nose: ripe fruit, creamy oak, toasty, balsamic herbs. Palate: powerful, flavourful, toasty, round tannins.

BODEGAS PORTIA

Antigua Ctra. N-I, km. 170
09370 Gumiel de Izán (Burgos)
☎: +34 947 102 700 - Fax: +34 947 107 004
info@bodegasportia.com
www.bodegasportia.com

PORTIA 2009 TC
tempranillo.

89 Colour: cherry, garnet rim. Nose: medium intensity, expressive, balanced, ripe fruit, scrubland. Palate: fruity, balanced.

PORTIA PRIMA 2010 T
tempranillo.

92 Colour: cherry, garnet rim. Nose: balanced, expressive, sweet spices, ripe fruit, cocoa bean. Palate: flavourful, good structure, round tannins.

TRIENNIA 2010 T
tempranillo.

91 Colour: cherry, garnet rim. Nose: mineral, spicy, ripe fruit, toasty. Palate: flavourful, ripe fruit, good acidity, round tannins.

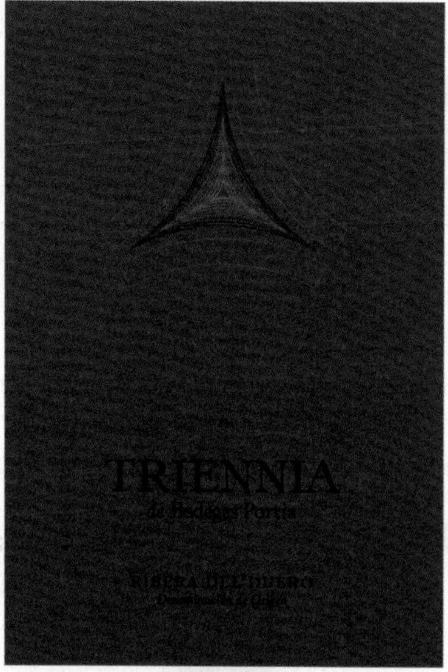

EBEIA DE PORTIA 2011 T ROBLE
tempranillo.

88 Colour: cherry, purple rim. Nose: balanced, ripe fruit, creamy oak, sweet spices. Palate: balanced, flavourful.

BODEGAS RESALTE DE PEÑAFIEL

Ctra. N-122, Km. 312
47300 Peñafiel (Valladolid)
☎: +34 983 878 160 - Fax: +34 983 880 601
info@resalte.com
www.resalte.com

RESALTE VENDIMIA SELECCIONADA 2011 T
100% tempranillo.

88 Colour: cherry, purple rim. Nose: ripe fruit, lactic notes, fragrant herbs. Palate: powerful, flavourful, fruity, long.

PEÑA ROBLE 2011 T
100% tempranillo.

86 Colour: cherry, purple rim. Nose: fresh fruit, red berry notes, floral, lactic notes. Palate: flavourful, fruity, balanced.

RESALTE 2007 TC
100% tempranillo.

89 Colour: cherry, garnet rim. Nose: ripe fruit, red berry notes, sweet spices, creamy oak, toasty. Palate: powerful, flavourful, correct, long.

PEÑA ROBLE 2006 TC
100% tempranillo.

87 Colour: dark-red cherry, orangey edge. Nose: spicy, fine reductive notes, waxy notes, ripe fruit. Palate: correct, long, flavourful.

RESALTE 2005 TR
100% tempranillo.

90 Colour: ruby red, orangey edge. Nose: ripe fruit, scrubland, earthy notes, cocoa bean, dark chocolate, creamy oak. Palate: powerful, flavourful, long, spicy.

PEÑA ROBLE 2004 TR
100% tempranillo.

90 Colour: dark-red cherry, orangey edge. Nose: elegant, spicy, fine reductive notes, aged wood nuances. Palate: spicy, fine tannins, elegant, long.

GRAN RESALTE 2001 T
100% tempranillo.

87 Colour: pale ruby, brick rim edge. Nose: fruit liqueur notes, scrubland, tobacco, waxy notes, old leather, aged wood nuances. Palate: spicy, long, flavourful, spirituous.

BODEGAS REYES

Ctra. Valladolid - Soria, Km. 54
47300 Peñafiel (Valladolid)
☎: +34 983 873 015 - Fax: +34 983 873 017
info@teofiloreyes.com
www.bodegasreyes.com

TAMIZ 2010 T ROBLE
100% tempranillo.

87 Colour: cherry, purple rim. Nose: ripe fruit, spicy, creamy oak. Palate: spicy, fruity aftespalate:, correct.

TEÓFILO REYES 2009 TC
100% tempranillo.

89 Colour: cherry, garnet rim. Nose: ripe fruit, spicy, creamy oak, toasty, fine reductive notes. Palate: powerful, flavourful, toasty.

BODEGAS RODERO

Ctra. Boada, s/n
09314 Pedrosa de Duero (Burgos)
☎: +34 947 530 046 - Fax: +34 947 530 097
rodero@bodegasrodero.com
www.bodegasrodero.com

CARMELO RODERO 2011 T
100% tempranillo.

89 Colour: cherry, purple rim. Nose: fresh fruit, red berry notes, floral. Palate: flavourful, fruity, good acidity, round tannins.

CARMELO RODERO 9 MESES 2011 T
100% tempranillo.

88 Colour: cherry, purple rim. Nose: powerfull, ripe fruit, fruit preserve, toasty. Palate: flavourful, powerful, fine bitter notes.

CARMELO RODERO 2009 TR
90% tempranillo, 10% cabernet sauvignon.

93 Colour: cherry, garnet rim. Nose: ripe fruit, spicy, creamy oak, toasty, characterful, varietal. Palate: powerful, flavourful, toasty, round tannins.

CARMELO RODERO 2009 TC
90% tempranillo, 10% cabernet sauvignon.

91 Colour: cherry, garnet rim. Nose: creamy oak, sweet spices, tobacco. Palate: flavourful, full, round tannins, complex.

CARMELO RODERO TSM 2006 T
75% tempranillo, 10% cabernet sauvignon, 15% merlot.

93 Colour: cherry, garnet rim. Nose: ripe fruit, spicy, creamy oak, toasty, dark chocolate. Palate: powerful, flavourful, toasty, round tannins.

PAGO DE VALTARREÑA 2005 T
100% tempranillo.

94 Colour: cherry, garnet rim. Nose: ripe fruit, spicy, creamy oak, toasty, complex, fine reductive notes. Palate: powerful, flavourful, toasty, round tannins, balanced, elegant.

BODEGAS SANTA EULALIA

Malpica, s/n
09311 La Horra (Burgos)
☎: +34 983 586 868 - Fax: +34 947 580 180
bodegasfrutosvillar@bodegasfrutosvillar.com
www.bodegasfrutosvillar.com

CONDE DE SIRUELA 2008 TC
100% tinta del país.

90 Colour: cherry, garnet rim. Nose: balanced, creamy oak, overripe fruit. Palate: flavourful, round tannins.

CONDE DE SIRUELA 2011 T
100% tinta del país.

89 Colour: cherry, purple rim. Nose: fresh fruit, red berry notes, floral. Palate: flavourful, fruity, good acidity, round tannins.

CONDE DE SIRUELA 2010 T ROBLE
100% tinta del país.

85 Colour: cherry, purple rim. Nose: toasty, medium intensity, ripe fruit. Palate: correct, easy to drink, spicy.

BODEGAS SEÑORÍO DE NAVA

Ctra. Valladolid - Soria, s/n
09318 Nava de Roa (Burgos)
☎: +34 987 209 712 - Fax: +34 947 550 003
snava@senoriodenava.es
www.senoriodenava.es

SEÑORÍO DE NAVA 2011 RD
95% tinta del país, 5% albillo.

88 Colour: rose, purple rim. Nose: powerfull, ripe fruit, red berry notes, floral, lactic notes. Palate: , powerful, fruity, fresh.

SEÑORÍO DE NAVA 2011 T
100% tinta del país.

85 Colour: cherry, purple rim. Nose: fresh fruit, red berry notes, floral. Palate: flavourful, fruity, correct.

DON ÁLVARO 2011 T
100% tinta del país.

83

SEÑORÍO DE NAVA 2009 T ROBLE
85% tinta del país, 15% cabernet sauvignon.

87 Colour: bright cherry. Nose: ripe fruit, sweet spices, creamy oak, spicy. Palate: flavourful, fruity, toasty.

VEGA CUBILLAS 2009 T ROBLE
85% tinta del país, 15% cabernet sauvignon.

85 Colour: bright cherry. Nose: ripe fruit, creamy oak, medium intensity. Palate: flavourful, fruity, toasty.

SEÑORÍO DE NAVA 2008 TC
100% tinta del país.

90 Colour: cherry, garnet rim. Nose: ripe fruit, earthy notes, scrubland, fine reductive notes, aged wood nuances, toasty. Palate: powerful, flavourful, balanced, long, spicy.

VEGA CUBILLAS 2008 TC
100% tinta del país.

86 Colour: cherry, garnet rim. Nose: ripe fruit, spicy, toasty, fine reductive notes. Palate: powerful, flavourful, toasty.

DON ÁLVARO 2008 TC
100% tinta del país.

86 Colour: bright cherry. Nose: ripe fruit, sweet spices, creamy oak, fine reductive notes. Palate: flavourful, fruity, toasty.

SEÑORÍO DE NAVA 2006 TR
100% tinta del país.

88 Colour: cherry, garnet rim. Nose: spicy, creamy oak, fine reductive notes. Palate: powerful, flavourful, toasty.

SEÑORÍO DE NAVA FINCA SAN COBATE 2005 TR
100% tinta del país.

90 Colour: ruby red, orangey edge. Nose: ripe fruit, spicy, aged wood nuances, varnish, creamy oak, tobacco, old leather. Palate: powerful, flavourful, spicy, round.

BODEGAS TAMARAL

Ctra. N-122, Km. 310,6
47300 Peñafiel (Valladolid)
☎: +34 983 878 017 - Fax: +34 983 878 089
exterior@tamaral.com
www.tamaral.com

TAMARAL 2011 RD
tempranillo.

87 Colour: rose, purple rim. Nose: red berry notes, lactic notes, floral. Palate: powerful, fruity, fresh, easy to drink.

TAMARAL 2010 T ROBLE

88 Colour: cherry, garnet rim. Nose: sweet spices, expressive, ripe fruit, cocoa bean. Palate: balanced, good acidity, ripe fruit, long.

TAMARAL 2009 TC

88 Colour: cherry, garnet rim. Nose: ripe fruit, spicy, creamy oak, toasty. Palate: powerful, flavourful, toasty, round tannins.

TAMARAL 2008 TR

92 Colour: deep cherry. Nose: powerfull, characterful, ripe fruit. Palate: flavourful, powerful, concentrated, ripe fruit, long.

TAMARAL FINCA LA MIRA 2005 T

90 Colour: deep cherry, garnet rim. Nose: overripe fruit, fragrant herbs, sweet spices. Palate: flavourful, long.

BODEGAS TARSUS

Ctra. de Roa - Anguix, Km. 3
09313 Anguix (Burgos)
☎: +34 947 554 218 - Fax: +34 947 541 804
tarsus@pernod-ricard.com
www.domecqbodegas.com

TARSUS 2010 T ROBLE
100% tinta del país.

90 Colour: cherry, garnet rim. Nose: ripe fruit, dark chocolate, spicy, creamy oak. Palate: powerful, flavourful, toasty, long.

QUINTA DE TARSUS 2009 TC
100% tempranillo.

90 Colour: cherry, garnet rim. Nose: balanced, expressive, ripe fruit, neat. Palate: flavourful, full, good acidity.

QUINTA DE TARSUS 2008 TC
tempranillo.

87 Colour: cherry, garnet rim. Nose: ripe fruit, spicy, creamy oak, toasty, old leather. Palate: powerful, flavourful, toasty, round tannins.

TARSUS 2006 TR
98% tempranillo, 2% cabernet sauvignon.

91 Colour: cherry, garnet rim. Nose: spicy, creamy oak, toasty, complex, dark chocolate. Palate: powerful, flavourful, toasty, round tannins.

BODEGAS THESAURUS

Ctra. Cuellar - Villafuerte, s/n
47359 Olivares de Duero (Valladolid)
☎: +34 983 250 319 - Fax: +34 983 250 329
exportacion@ciadevinos.com
www.bodegasthesaurus.com.com

DORIVM 2010 T ROBLE
100% tempranillo.

89 Colour: cherry, garnet rim. Nose: ripe fruit, spicy, creamy oak, mineral. Palate: powerful, flavourful, correct, toasty.

CASTILLO DE PEÑAFIEL 2010 T ROBLE
tempranillo.

86 Colour: cherry, garnet rim. Nose: ripe fruit, sweet spices, creamy oak. Palate: flavourful, fruity, toasty.

DORIVM 2009 TC
tempranillo.

89 Colour: cherry, garnet rim. Nose: ripe fruit, creamy oak, sweet spices, roasted coffee. Palate: powerful, flavourful, toasty, round tannins.

CASA CASTILLA 2008 TC
tempranillo.

88 Colour: cherry, garnet rim. Nose: ripe fruit, spicy, creamy oak, toasty. Palate: powerful, flavourful, long, spicy.

CASTILLO DE PEÑAFIEL 2008 TC

86 Colour: cherry, garnet rim. Nose: ripe fruit, creamy oak, roasted coffee. Palate: powerful, flavourful, toasty.

CASTILLO DE PEÑAFIEL 2004 TR
100% tempranillo.

88 Colour: cherry, garnet rim. Nose: ripe fruit, spicy, creamy oak, toasty, balsamic herbs, fine reductive notes. Palate: powerful, flavourful, toasty.

BODEGAS TIONIO

Ctra. de Valoria, Km. 7
47315 Pesquera de Duero (Valladolid)
☎: +34 933 950 811 - Fax: +34 983 870 185
info@parxet.es
www.parxet.es

AUSTUM 2011 T
100% tinto fino.

89 Colour: bright cherry. Nose: ripe fruit, sweet spices, expressive. Palate: flavourful, fruity, round tannins.

TIONIO 2009 T
100% tinto fino.

91 Colour: cherry, garnet rim. Nose: ripe fruit, creamy oak, toasty. Palate: powerful, flavourful, toasty, round tannins.

BODEGAS TORREDEROS

Ctra. Valladolid, Km. 289,300
09318 Fuentelisendo (Burgos)
☎: +34 947 532 627 - Fax: +34 947 532 731
administracion@torrederos.com
www.torrederos.com

TORREDEROS 2009 TC
100% tempranillo.

90 Colour: cherry, garnet rim. Nose: spicy, creamy oak, toasty, characterful, ripe fruit. Palate: powerful, flavourful, toasty, round tannins.

TORREDEROS SELECCIÓN 2009 T
100% tempranillo.

90 Colour: cherry, garnet rim. Nose: ripe fruit, spicy, creamy oak, toasty, complex, aromatic coffee. Palate: powerful, flavourful, toasty, good acidity.

BODEGAS TORREMORÓN

Ctra. Boada, s/n
09314 Quintanamanvirgo (Burgos)
☎: +34 947 554 075 - Fax: +34 947 554 036
torremoron@wanadoo.es
www.torremoron.com

SENDERILLO 2011 T
100% tempranillo.

86 Colour: cherry, purple rim. Nose: red berry notes, floral, ripe fruit. Palate: flavourful, fruity, good acidity, round tannins.

TORREMORÓN TEMPRANILLO 2011 T
100% tempranillo.

85 Colour: cherry, purple rim. Nose: ripe fruit, dried flowers, balsamic herbs. Palate: powerful, flavourful, fruity.

TORREMORÓN 2009 TC
100% tempranillo.

91 Colour: cherry, garnet rim. Nose: spicy, creamy oak, toasty, characterful, ripe fruit. Palate: powerful, flavourful, toasty, round tannins, fine bitter notes.

SENDERILLO 2009 TC
100% tempranillo.

88 Colour: cherry, garnet rim. Nose: ripe fruit, aromatic coffee, sweet spices, creamy oak. Palate: correct, flavourful, toasty.

TORREMORÓN 2008 TR
100% tempranillo.

86 Colour: cherry, garnet rim. Nose: ripe fruit, spicy, toasty, wet leather. Palate: powerful, flavourful, toasty.

BODEGAS TRASLASCUESTAS

Ctra. Mambrilla-Pedrosa
09317 Valcavado de Roa (Burgos)
☎: +34 945 622 480
export@pierola.com

TRASLASCUESTAS 2009 TC
tinta del país.

89 Colour: very deep cherry. Nose: powerfull, varietal, sweet spices, cocoa bean, red berry notes, overripe fruit. Palate: flavourful, powerful, fine bitter notes, fruity, round tannins.

BODEGAS TRUS

Ctra. Pesquera - Encinas, Km. 3
47316 Piñel de Abajo (Valladolid)
☎: +34 913 872 033 - Fax: +34 902 302 340
trus@bodegastrus.com
www.bodegastrus.com

KREL 2010 T ROBLE
100% tinto fino.

91 Colour: cherry, garnet rim. Nose: ripe fruit, red berry notes, toasty, spicy. Palate: flavourful, powerful, spicy, ripe fruit.

KREL 2009 T ROBLE
100% tinto fino.

90 Colour: bright cherry, purple rim. Nose: creamy oak, sweet spices, ripe fruit, cocoa bean. Palate: good structure, flavourful, fruity.

TRUS 2005 TR
100% tinto fino.

92 Colour: very deep cherry. Nose: dark chocolate, creamy oak, ripe fruit, candied fruit. Palate: good structure, flavourful, full.

BODEGAS VALDAYA

Ctra. de Burgos, s/n
09441 Sotillo de la Ribera (Burgos)
☎: +34 947 532 450 - Fax: +34 947 532 476
info@valdaya.com
www.valdaya.com

VALDAYA 2010 T ROBLE
100% tinto fino.

88 Colour: bright cherry. Aroma ripe fruit, sweet spices, creamy oak, expressive. Palate: flavourful, fruity, toasty, round tannins.

VALDAYA VENDIMIA SELECCIONADA 2009 TC
100% tinto fino.

90 Colour: cherry, garnet rim. Nose: ripe fruit, spicy, creamy oak, toasty, expressive. Palate: powerful, flavourful, toasty, round tannins.

VALDAYA 2009 TC
100% tinto fino.

87 Colour: cherry, garnet rim. Nose: ripe fruit, spicy, creamy oak, toasty, complex. Palate: powerful, flavourful, toasty, round tannins.

BODEGAS VALDEVIÑAS

Ctra. Nacional 122, Km. 245
42320 Langa de Duero (Soria)
☎: +34 975 186 000 - Fax: +34 975 186 012
info@valdevinas.es
www.valdevinas.es

MIRAT 2005 TC
100% tempranillo.

88 Colour: dark-red cherry, orangey edge. Nose: wet leather, cigar, spicy, varnish, fruit liqueur notes. Palate: flavourful, ripe fruit, long.

TINAR DE MIRAT 2005 TC
100% tempranillo.

87 Colour: cherry, garnet rim. Nose: medium intensity, fruit preserve, spicy. Palate: spicy, good finish.

MIRAT 2004 TR
100% tempranillo.

90 Colour: cherry, garnet rim. Nose: earthy notes, powerfull, ripe fruit, sweet spices. Palate: flavourful, fruity, good acidity.

MIRAT 2004 TC
100% tempranillo.

89 Colour: cherry, garnet rim. Nose: spicy, creamy oak, toasty, ripe fruit. Palate: powerful, flavourful, toasty, round tannins.

TINAR DE MIRAT 2004 TC
100% tempranillo.

87 Colour: bright cherry. Nose: sweet spices, creamy oak, expressive, wet leather. Palate: flavourful, fruity, toasty, round tannins.

BODEGAS VALDUBÓN

Antigua N-I, Km. 151
09460 Milagros (Burgos)
☎: +34 947 546 251 - Fax: +34 947 546 250
valdubon@valdubon.es
www.valdubon.es

VALDUBÓN 2009 TC
100% tempranillo.

88 Colour: bright cherry. Nose: ripe fruit, sweet spices, creamy oak, expressive. Palate: flavourful, fruity, toasty.

HONORIS DE VALDUBÓN 2006 T
85% tempranillo, 9% merlot, 6% cabernet sauvignon.

92 Colour: ruby red, garnet rim. Nose: ripe fruit, balsamic herbs, spicy, creamy oak, expressive. Palate: powerful, flavourful, spicy, long, balanced.

VALDUBÓN DIEZ T
100% tempranillo.

91 Colour: cherry, garnet rim. Nose: ripe fruit, spicy, creamy oak, toasty, complex, mineral, balsamic herbs. Palate: powerful, flavourful, toasty, balanced.

BODEGAS VALLE DE MONZÓN

Paraje El Salegar, s/n
09370 Quintana del Pidío (Burgos)
☎: +34 947 545 694 - Fax: +34 947 545 694
bodega@vallemonzon.com
www.vallemonzon.com

HOYO DE LA VEGA 2009 TC

89 Colour: cherry, garnet rim. Nose: ripe fruit, toasty, sweet spices. Palate: powerful, flavourful, toasty, round tannins.

HOYO DE LA VEGA 2009 TR

89 Colour: cherry, garnet rim. Nose: ripe fruit, spicy, toasty, smoky. Palate: powerful, flavourful, toasty, balanced, long.

BODEGAS VALPINCIA

Ctra. de Melida, 3,5
47300 Peñafiel (Valladolid)
☎: +34 983 878 007 - Fax: +34 983 880 620
comunicacion@bodegasvalpincia.com
www.bodegasvalpincia.com

PAGOS DE VALCERRACÍN 2011 T
100% tempranillo.

87 Colour: cherry, purple rim. Nose: red berry notes, raspberry, lactic notes. Palate: fresh, fruity, powerful, flavourful.

VALPINCIA 2011 T
100% tempranillo.

85 Colour: cherry, purple rim. Nose: ripe fruit, dried flowers, medium intensity. Palate: correct, fruity, fresh.

PAGOS DE VALCERRACÍN 2010 T ROBLE
100% tempranillo.

86 Colour: bright cherry. Nose: ripe fruit, sweet spices, creamy oak. Palate: flavourful, fruity, toasty, round tannins.

VALPINCIA 2010 T ROBLE
100% tinta del país.

85 Colour: bright cherry. Nose: ripe fruit, creamy oak, medium intensity. Palate: flavourful, fruity, toasty.

GLORIA MAYOR 2009 T
100% tempranillo.

88 Colour: deep cherry. Nose: powerfull, ripe fruit, sweet spices, cocoa bean. Palate: flavourful, fine bitter notes, good acidity.

PAGOS DE VALCERRACÍN 2009 TC
100% tempranillo.

88 Colour: bright cherry, garnet rim. Nose: expressive, ripe fruit, sweet spices. Palate: good structure, fruity, easy to drink.

VALPINCIA 2009 TC
100% tinta del país.

85 Colour: cherry, garnet rim. Nose: ripe fruit, balsamic herbs, spicy, toasty. Palate: powerful, flavourful, toasty.

VALPINCIA 2006 TR
100% tempranillo.

85 Colour: bright cherry, garnet rim. Nose: toasty, varnish, overripe fruit. Palate: flavourful, correct.

BODEGAS VALSARDO

Pago de Fuentecilla, s/n Aptdo. 56
47300 Peñafiel (Valladolid)
☎: +34 983 878 080 - Fax: +34 983 880 618
valsardo@valsardo.com
www.valsardo.com

VALDEYUSO 2002 T
100% tempranillo.

82

VALDEYUSO 2001 T
100% tempranillo.

87 Colour: cherry, garnet rim. Nose: medium intensity, spicy, tobacco, creamy oak. Palate: ripe fruit, spicy, good finish.

BODEGAS VEGA SICILIA

Ctra. N-122, Km. 323
47359 Valbuena de Duero (Valladolid)
☎: +34 983 680 147 - Fax: +34 983 680 263
vegasicilia@vega-sicilia.com
www.vega-sicilia.com

VEGA SICILIA RESERVA ESPECIAL 94/99/00 T

97 Colour: cherry, garnet rim. Nose: complex, fruit preserve, spicy, dark chocolate, elegant. Palate: spicy, classic aged character, good acidity, balanced, fine bitter notes, round.

VALBUENA 5º 2008 T
93% tinto fino, 7% merlot, malbec.

94 Colour: cherry, garnet rim. Nose: creamy oak, sweet spices, cocoa bean, mineral, ripe fruit. Palate: rich, flavourful, full, complex.

VEGA SICILIA ÚNICO 2003 T
92% tinto fino, 8% cabernet sauvignon.

96 Colour: deep cherry, garnet rim. Nose: sweet spices, balanced, ripe fruit, toasty, fine reductive notes. Palate: rich, good acidity, elegant, fine bitter notes, long.

BODEGAS VEGARANDA

Avda. Arangón, s/n
09400 Aranda de Duero (Burgos)
☎: +34 626 996 974
comercial@bodegasvegaranda.com
www.bodegasvegaranda.com

VEGARANDA 2011 T ROBLE
tempranillo.

89 Colour: bright cherry. Aroma ripe fruit, sweet spices, creamy oak, expressive. Palate: flavourful, fruity, toasty, round tannins.

VEGARANDA 2011 T
tempranillo.

88 Colour: cherry, purple rim. Nose: expressive, fresh fruit, red berry notes, floral. Palate: flavourful, fruity, good acidity.

VEGARANDA 2009 TC
tempranillo.

87 Colour: cherry, garnet rim. Nose: ripe fruit, spicy, creamy oak. Palate: powerful, flavourful, round tannins.

VEGARANDA 2007 TR
tempranillo.

88 Colour: cherry, garnet rim. Nose: fruit liqueur notes, scrubland, old leather, tobacco, spicy, toasty. Palate: correct, powerful, flavourful.

BODEGAS VICENTE GANDÍA

Ctra. Cheste a Godelleta, s/n
46370 Chiva (Valencia)
☎: +34 962 524 242 - Fax: +34 962 524 243
vuboldi@vicentegandia.com
www.vicentegandia.es

DOLMO TEMPRANILLO 2011 T
100% tempranillo.

87 Colour: bright cherry. Aroma ripe fruit, sweet spices, creamy oak, expressive. Palate: flavourful, fruity, toasty, round tannins.

DOLMO TEMPRANILLO 2009 TC
100% tempranillo.

88 Colour: cherry, garnet rim. Nose: red berry notes, ripe fruit, sweet spices, creamy oak. Palate: powerful, flavourful, toasty, harsh oak tannins.

BODEGAS VITULIA

Sendín, 49
09400 Aranda de Duero (Burgos)
☎: +34 947 515 051 - Fax: +34 947 515 051
bvitulia@bodegasvitulia.com
www.bodegasvitulia.com

VITULIA 2011 RD
90% tinto fino, 10% otras.

86 Colour: rose, purple rim. Nose: powerfull, ripe fruit, red berry notes, floral. Palate: , powerful, fruity, fresh.

VITULIA 2009 TC
90% tinto fino, 10% otras.

90 Colour: cherry, garnet rim. Nose: red berry notes, ripe fruit, sweet spices, creamy oak. Palate: powerful, flavourful, harsh oak tannins.

VITULIA 2009 T ROBLE
tinto fino.

88 Colour: cherry, purple rim. Nose: balanced, ripe fruit, violets, sweet spices. Palate: flavourful, fruity, good acidity.

VITULIA 2006 TR
tinto fino.

88 Colour: cherry, garnet rim. Nose: spicy, creamy oak, toasty, ripe fruit. Palate: powerful, flavourful, toasty, round tannins.

BODEGAS VIYUELA

Ctra. de Quintanamanvirgo, s/n
09314 Boada de Roa (Burgos)
☎: +34 947 530 072 - Fax: +34 947 530 075
viyuela@bodegasviyuela.com
www.bodegasviyuela.com

VIYUELA 2011 T
100% tempranillo.

89 Colour: cherry, garnet rim. Nose: ripe fruit, violet drops, sweet spices. Palate: flavourful, good acidity, ripe fruit.

VIYUELA 3 + 3 2010 T
100% tempranillo.

87 Colour: cherry, purple rim. Nose: medium intensity, red berry notes, ripe fruit, sweet spices, cocoa bean. Palate: flavourful, balanced, good acidity.

VIYUELA 2007 TC
100% tempranillo.

88 Colour: cherry, garnet rim. Nose: balanced, ripe fruit, fine reductive notes, spicy, toasty. Palate: correct, powerful, flavourful, toasty.

VIYUELA 10 2007 T
100% tempranillo.

88 Colour: cherry, garnet rim. Nose: medium intensity, balanced, ripe fruit. Palate: fruity, good acidity.

VIYUELA SELECCIÓN 2005 T
100% tempranillo.

89 Colour: dark-red cherry, orangey edge. Nose: ripe fruit, fruit liqueur notes, balsamic herbs, waxy notes, tobacco, wet leather, spicy. Palate: long, powerful, flavourful, spicy.

VIYUELA 2004 TR
100% tempranillo.

88 Colour: cherry, garnet rim. Aroma ripe fruit, spicy, creamy oak, toasty, complex. Palate: powerful, flavourful, toasty, round tannins.

BODEGAS VIZCARRA

Finca Chirri, s/n
09317 Mambrilla de Castrejón (Burgos)
☎: +34 947 540 340 - Fax: +34 947 540 340
bodegas@vizcarra.es
www.vizcarra.es

VIZCARRA SENDA DEL ORO 2011 T
100% tinto fino.

90 Colour: cherry, purple rim. Nose: expressive, fresh fruit, red berry notes, floral. Palate: flavourful, fruity, good acidity, balanced.

INÉS VIZCARRA 2010 T
90% tinto fino, 10% merlot.

96 Colour: cherry, garnet rim. Nose: red berry notes, ripe fruit, mineral, sweet spices, aromatic coffee, balsamic herbs. Palate: powerful, flavourful, long, toasty, balanced.

CELIA VIZCARRA 2010 T
90% tinto fino, 10% garnacha.

95 Colour: cherry, garnet rim. Nose: ripe fruit, creamy oak, toasty, earthy notes, mineral, sweet spices. Palate: powerful, flavourful, toasty, round tannins, long, balanced.

VIZCARRA TORRALVO 2010 T
100% tinto fino.

94 Colour: bright cherry. Nose: ripe fruit, creamy oak, dark chocolate, caramel, mineral. Palate: flavourful, fruity, toasty, round, long, spicy.

VIZCARRA 2010 T
100% tinto fino.

92 Colour: bright cherry. Nose: ripe fruit, sweet spices, creamy oak, dark chocolate. Palate: flavourful, fruity, toasty, round tannins.

BODEGAS Y VIÑEDOS ACEÑA

Pol. Ind. Las Carretas, calle C, s/n
42330 San Esteban de Gormaz (Soria)
☎: +34 667 784 220
bodega@terraesteban.com
www.terraesteban.com

TERRAESTEBAN 2011 T JOVEN
100% tempranillo.

84

TERRAESTEBAN 2009 TC
100% tempranillo.

91 Colour: cherry, garnet rim. Nose: expressive, elegant, mineral, earthy notes. Palate: flavourful, good acidity, spicy.

TERRAESTEBAN 2009 T ROBLE
100% tempranillo.

88 Colour: bright cherry. Nose: sweet spices, creamy oak, expressive. Palate: flavourful, toasty, round tannins.

BODEGAS Y VIÑEDOS ALIÓN

Ctra. N-122, Km. 312,4 Padilla de Duero
47300 Peñafiel (Valladolid)
☎: +34 983 881 236 - Fax: +34 983 881 246
imartin@bodegasalion.com
www.bodegasalion.com

ALIÓN 2009 T
100% tinto fino.

95 Colour: deep cherry, garnet rim. Nose: expressive, balanced, complex, ripe fruit, sweet spices. Palate: long, ripe fruit, round tannins, fine bitter notes.

BODEGAS Y VIÑEDOS DEL JARO

Ctra. Pesquera - Valbuena, s/n. Finca El Quiñón
47315 Pesquera de Duero (Valladolid)
☎: +34 900 505 855 - Fax: +34 956 852 339
vinos@gvitivinicola.com
www.grupohebe.com

SEMBRO 2010 T

88 Colour: cherry, purple rim. Nose: expressive, fresh fruit, red berry notes, floral, sweet spices. Palate: flavourful, fruity, good acidity, round tannins.

SED DE CANÁ 2009 T

93 Colour: cherry, garnet rim. Nose: ripe fruit, spicy, dark chocolate, cocoa bean, earthy notes. Palate: powerful, flavourful, toasty, long, spicy, good acidity, balanced.

CHAFANDÍN 2009 T

92 Colour: bright cherry. Nose: ripe fruit, sweet spices, creamy oak, toasty. Palate: flavourful, fruity, toasty, round tannins, balanced.

JAROS 2009 T

89 Colour: cherry, garnet rim. Nose: ripe fruit, spicy, creamy oak, toasty. Palate: powerful, flavourful, toasty, round tannins.

BODEGAS Y VIÑEDOS ESCUDERO

Camino El Ramo, s/n
09311 Olmedillo de Roa (Burgos)
☎: +34 629 857 575 - Fax: +34 947 551 070
info@costaval.com
www.costaval.com

COSTAVAL 2010 T
100% tempranillo.

85 Colour: cherry, garnet rim. Nose: red berry notes, ripe fruit, balsamic herbs. Palate: correct, fruity, flavourful.

COSTAVAL 2009 TC
100% tempranillo.

88 Colour: deep cherry, purple rim. Nose: ripe fruit, sweet spices, dark chocolate. Palate: good structure, flavourful.

COSTAVAL 2005 TR
100% tempranillo.

90 Colour: bright cherry, orangey edge. Nose: ripe fruit, fruit liqueur notes, spicy, fine reductive notes. Palate: long, spicy, powerful, flavourful.

BODEGAS Y VIÑEDOS GALLEGO ZAPATERO

Segunda Travesía de la Olma, 4
09312 Anguix (Burgos)
☎: +34 648 180 777
info@bodegasgallegozapatero.com
www.bodegasgallegozapatero.com

YOTUEL 2010 T ROBLE
100% tinta del país.

88 Colour: cherry, purple rim. Nose: expressive, ripe fruit, dark chocolate. Palate: good structure, flavourful, round tannins.

YOTUEL SELECCIÓN 2009 T
100% tinta del país.

90 Colour: cherry, garnet rim. Nose: spicy, creamy oak, toasty, characterful, ripe fruit. Palate: powerful, flavourful, toasty, round tannins.

YOTUEL FINCA SAN MIGUEL 2008 T
100% tinta del país.

90 Colour: cherry, garnet rim. Nose: scrubland, spicy, ripe fruit, expressive. Palate: powerful, flavourful, long, toasty.

YOTUEL FINCA VALDEPALACIOS 2007 T
100% tinta del país.

92 Colour: cherry, garnet rim. Nose: spicy, creamy oak, toasty, complex, fragrant herbs, candied fruit. Palate: powerful, flavourful, toasty, round tannins.

BODEGAS Y VIÑEDOS LLEIROSO

Ctra. Monasterio, s/n
47359 Valbuena del Duero (Valladolid)
☎: +34 983 683 300 - Fax: +34 983 683 301
enologia@bodegaslleiroso.com
www.bodegaslleiroso.com

LVZMILLAR 2009 TC
tempranillo.

90 Colour: black cherry, garnet rim. Nose: red berry notes, ripe fruit, dark chocolate, aromatic coffee, creamy oak. Palate: long, powerful, flavourful, toasty.

LLEIROSO DE AUTOR 2006 TC
tempranillo.

89 Colour: cherry, garnet rim. Nose: spicy, creamy oak, toasty, overripe fruit, dark chocolate. Palate: powerful, flavourful, toasty, round tannins.

BODEGAS Y VIÑEDOS MARTÍN BERDUGO

Ctra. de la Colonia, s/n
09400 Aranda de Duero (Burgos)
☎: +34 947 506 331 - Fax: +34 947 506 602
bodega@martinberdugo.com
www.martinberdugo.com

MARTÍN BERDUGO 2011 RD
tempranillo.

87 Colour: rose, purple rim. Nose: powerfull, ripe fruit, red berry notes. Palate: ripe fruit, good acidity.

MARTÍN BERDUGO 2011 T
tempranillo.

88 Colour: cherry, purple rim. Nose: red berry notes, floral, ripe fruit. Palate: flavourful, fruity, good acidity, round tannins.

MARTÍN BERDUGO 2010 T BARRICA
tempranillo.

87 Colour: cherry, purple rim. Nose: medium intensity, ripe fruit, sweet spices. Palate: flavourful, fruity, good structure.

MB MARTÍN BERDUGO 2006 T
tempranillo.

92 Colour: cherry, garnet rim. Nose: medium intensity, dark chocolate, sweet spices. Palate: ripe fruit, long, round tannins.

BODEGAS Y VIÑEDOS MONTE AIXA

Ctra. Palencia - Aranda, km. 58,7
09311 La Horra (Burgos)
☎: +34 610 227 123 - Fax: +34 947 542 067
info@monteaixa.com
www.monteaixa.com

MONTE AIXA 2011 T
tempranillo.

85 Colour: cherry, purple rim. Nose: balanced, red berry notes, dried herbs. Palate: fruity, flavourful, balanced.

MONTE AIXA 2009 TC
tempranillo.

88 Colour: cherry, garnet rim. Nose: ripe fruit, creamy oak, toasty, complex. Palate: powerful, flavourful, toasty.

MONTE AIXA 2005 TR
tempranillo.

87 Colour: dark-red cherry, orangey edge. Nose: spicy, fine reductive notes, wet leather, aged wood nuances, fruit liqueur notes. Palate: spicy, long, correct.

BODEGAS Y VIÑEDOS MONTEABELLÓN

Calvario, s/n
09318 Nava de Roa (Burgos)
☎: +34 947 550 000 - Fax: +34 947 550 219
info@monteabellon.com
www.monteabellon.com

MONTEABELLÓN 5 MESES EN BARRICA 2011 T
100% tempranillo.

88 Colour: bright cherry. Nose: sweet spices, creamy oak, ripe fruit. Palate: flavourful, fruity, toasty, round tannins.

MONTEABELLÓN 14 MESES EN BARRICA 2009 T
tempranillo.

91 Colour: cherry, garnet rim. Nose: creamy oak, toasty, characterful, ripe fruit, sweet spices. Palate: powerful, flavourful, toasty, round tannins.

MONTEABELLÓN 24 MESES EN BARRICA 2007 T
tempranillo.

92 Colour: cherry, garnet rim. Nose: spicy, creamy oak, toasty, complex, scrubland, balsamic herbs. Palate: powerful, flavourful, toasty, round tannins.

MONTEABELLÓN FINCA LA BLANQUERA 2006 T
tempranillo.

90 Colour: black cherry. Nose: warm, overripe fruit, fruit preserve, aromatic coffee, dark chocolate. Palate: powerful, sweetness.

BODEGAS Y VIÑEDOS MONTECASTRO

Ctra. VA-130, s/n
47318 Castrillo de Duero (Valladolid)
☎: +34 983 484 013 - Fax: +34 983 443 939
info@bodegasmontecastro.es
www.bodegasmontecastro.com

ALCONTE 2009 TC
tempranillo.

88 Colour: cherry, garnet rim. Nose: ripe fruit, spicy, creamy oak, toasty. Palate: powerful, flavourful, toasty.

MONTECASTRO Y LLANAHERMOSA 2008 T
tempranillo, merlot, cabernet sauvignon, garnacha.

88 Colour: cherry, garnet rim. Nose: balanced, expressive, spicy, dark chocolate. Palate: good structure, flavourful, round tannins.

ALCONTE 2008 TC
tempranillo.

86 Colour: cherry, garnet rim. Nose: ripe fruit, spicy, roasted coffee. Palate: powerful, flavourful, toasty.

BODEGAS Y VIÑEDOS NEO

Ctra. N-122, Km. 274,5
09391 Castrillo de la Vega (Burgos)
☎: +34 947 514 393 - Fax: +34 947 515 445
info@bodegasconde.com
www.bodegasneo.com

NEO 2009 T
100% tempranillo.

90 Colour: cherry, garnet rim. Nose: ripe fruit, creamy oak, toasty, sweet spices, dark chocolate. Palate: powerful, flavourful, toasty, round tannins, long.

Neo
Botella 1291 de 22,000
Ribera del Duero
Denominación de Origen
SPANISH RED WINE
Elaborado y embotellado por
Bodegas y Viñedos Neo S.L.
Castrillo de la Vega - España
R.E. Nº 8322 - BU
75cl
14% vol

DISCO 2011 T
100% tempranillo.

89 Colour: bright cherry. Nose: ripe fruit, sweet spices, creamy oak, cocoa bean, mineral. Palate: flavourful, fruity, toasty, round tannins.

EL ARTE DE VIVIR 2011 T
100% tempranillo.

88 Colour: cherry, purple rim. Nose: expressive, floral, red berry notes, ripe fruit. Palate: flavourful, fruity, good acidity, round tannins.

SENTIDO 2010 T
100% tempranillo.

90 Colour: bright cherry. Nose: ripe fruit, sweet spices, mineral, balsamic herbs, creamy oak. Palate: flavourful, fruity, toasty, balanced.

NEO PUNTA ESENCIA 2009 T
100% tempranillo.

92 Colour: cherry, garnet rim. Nose: red berry notes, ripe fruit, spicy, creamy oak, mineral, elegant. Palate: round, flavourful, long, fine tannins, balanced.

BODEGAS Y VIÑEDOS ORTEGA FOURNIER

Finca El Pinar, s/n
09316 Berlangas de Roa (Burgos)
☎: +34 947 533 006 - Fax: +34 947 533 010
jmortega@ofournier.com
www.ofournier.com

URBAN RIBERA 2009 T ROBLE
100% tinta del país.

89 Colour: bright cherry. Nose: sweet spices, creamy oak, ripe fruit. Palate: flavourful, fruity, toasty, round tannins.

SPIGA 2007 T
100% tinta del país.

90 Colour: cherry, garnet rim. Nose: spicy, creamy oak, toasty, sweet spices, fragrant herbs. Palate: powerful, flavourful, toasty, round tannins.

ALFA SPIGA 2006 T
100% tinta del país.

93 Colour: cherry, garnet rim. Nose: spicy, creamy oak, toasty, characterful, mineral, ripe fruit. Palate: powerful, flavourful, toasty, round tannins.

BODEGAS Y VIÑEDOS QUMRÁN

Pago de las Bodegas, s/n
47300 Padilla de Duero (Valladolid)
☎: +34 983 882 103 - Fax: +34 983 881 514
info@bodegasqumran.es
www.bodegasqumran.es

PROVENTUS 2009 T
100% tempranillo.

90 Colour: cherry, garnet rim. Nose: ripe fruit, spicy, varietal. Palate: powerful, flavourful, toasty, round tannins.

QUMRÁN 2008 TC
100% tempranillo.

90 Colour: bright cherry. Nose: ripe fruit, sweet spices, creamy oak. Palate: flavourful, fruity, toasty, round tannins.

BODEGAS Y VIÑEDOS RAUDA

Ctra. de Pedrosa, s/n
09300 Roa (Burgos)
☎: +34 947 540 224 - Fax: +34 947 541 811
informacion@vinosderauda.com
www.vinosderauda.com

TINTO ROA 2011 T
100% tempranillo.

86 Colour: cherry, purple rim. Nose: ripe fruit, balanced. Palate: flavourful, fruity, balanced.

TINTO ROA 2010 T ROBLE
100% tempranillo.

84

TINTO ROA 2009 TC
100% tempranillo.

89 Colour: cherry, garnet rim. Nose: medium intensity, ripe fruit, spicy. Palate: fruity, flavourful, good acidity.

TINTO ROA 2006 TR
100% tempranillo.

89 Colour: cherry, garnet rim. Nose: ripe fruit, scrubland, spicy, creamy oak. Palate: powerful, flavourful, round tannins.

MUSAI DE TINTO ROA 2006 TR
100% tempranillo.

89 Colour: cherry, garnet rim. Nose: spicy, creamy oak, toasty, complex, overripe fruit. Palate: powerful, flavourful, toasty, round tannins.

BODEGAS Y VIÑEDOS RECOLETAS

Ctra. Quintanilla, s/n
47359 Olivares de Duero (Valladolid)
☎: +34 983 687 017 - Fax: +34 983 687 017
bodegas@gruporecoletas.com
www.bodegasrecoletas.com

RECOLETAS 2010 T ROBLE
tempranillo.

86 Colour: bright cherry. Nose: ripe fruit, sweet spices, creamy oak. Palate: flavourful, fruity, toasty, round tannins.

RECOLETAS 2006 TC
tempranillo.

89 Colour: cherry, garnet rim. Nose: ripe fruit, spicy, toasty, complex. Palate: powerful, flavourful, toasty.

RECOLETAS VENDIMIA SELECCIONADA 2005 T
tempranillo.

92 Colour: cherry, garnet rim. Nose: ripe fruit, dark chocolate, aromatic coffee, creamy oak, toasty, fine reductive notes. Palate: powerful, flavourful, long, round.

RECOLETAS 2005 TR
tempranillo.

88 Colour: dark-red cherry, orangey edge. Nose: fruit preserve, scrubland, wet leather, cigar, spicy. Palate: long, flavourful, spicy, toasty.

BODEGAS Y VIÑEDOS ROBEAL

Ctra. Anguix, s/n
09300 Roa (Burgos)
☎: +34 947 484 606 - Fax: +34 947 482 817
info@bodegasrobeal.com
www.bodegasrobeal.com

BUEN MIÑÓN 2011 T
tempranillo.

87 Colour: cherry, purple rim. Nose: expressive, fresh fruit, red berry notes. Palate: flavourful, fruity, good acidity, easy to drink.

VALNOGAL 2010 T ROBLE
tempranillo.

86 Colour: cherry, purple rim. Nose: medium intensity, ripe fruit, spicy. Palate: flavourful, correct.

VALNOGAL 16 MESES 2009 T BARRICA
tempranillo.

91 Colour: cherry, garnet rim. Nose: balanced, ripe fruit, sweet spices. Palate: good structure, fruity, flavourful, round tannins.

LA CAPILLA 2009 TC
tempranillo.

88 Colour: deep cherry, garnet rim. Nose: ripe fruit, spicy, dried herbs. Palate: balanced, good acidity.

BODEGAS Y VIÑEDOS TÁBULA

Ctra. de Valbuena, km. 2
47359 Olivares de Duero (Valladolid)
☎: +34 608 219 019 - Fax: +34 983 107 300
armando@bodegastabula.es
www.bodegastabula.es

DAMANA 5 2010 T
100% tempranillo.

89 Colour: bright cherry. Aroma ripe fruit, sweet spices, creamy oak, expressive. Palate: flavourful, fruity, toasty, round tannins.

TÁBULA 2009 T
100% tempranillo.

93 Colour: cherry, garnet rim. Nose: spicy, creamy oak, toasty, characterful, varietal, red berry notes. Palate: powerful, flavourful, toasty, round tannins.

Tábula

RIBERA DEL DUERO
denominación de origen

CLAVE DE TÁBULA 2009 T
100% tempranillo.

93 Colour: cherry, garnet rim. Nose: ripe fruit, spicy, creamy oak, complex. Palate: powerful, flavourful, toasty, round tannins.

DAMANA 2009 TC
100% tempranillo.

91 Colour: bright cherry. Nose: ripe fruit, sweet spices, creamy oak. Palate: flavourful, fruity, toasty, round tannins.

GRAN TÁBULA 2008 T
100% tempranillo.

92 Colour: cherry, purple rim. Nose: characterful, ripe fruit, creamy oak, sweet spices, varietal. Palate: flavourful, fine bitter notes, round tannins.

BODEGAS Y VIÑEDOS VALDERIZ

Ctra. Pedrosa, km 1
09300 Roa (Burgos)
☎: +34 947 540 460 - Fax: +34 947 541 032
bodega@valderiz.com
www.valderiz.com

VALDEHERMOSO 2011 T
tinto fino.

88 Colour: cherry, purple rim. Nose: red berry notes, ripe fruit, violets. Palate: flavourful, fruity, balanced.

Bodegas y Viñedos Valderiz
VALDEHERMOSO
JOVEN 2011
Ribera del Duero
Denominación de origen

VALDERIZ JUEGALOBOS 2010 T
tinto fino.

93 Colour: dark-red cherry, garnet rim. Nose: red berry notes, ripe fruit, red clay notes, mineral, expressive, medium intensity, sweet spices, creamy oak. Palate: complex, flavourful, round, round tannins.

VALDERIZ 2010 T
tinto fino.

91 Colour: cherry, garnet rim. Nose: closed, expressive, mineral, ripe fruit, cocoa bean, scrubland, roasted coffee. Palate: good structure, round tannins, long.

VALDEHERMOSO 2010 TC
tinto fino.

90 Colour: cherry, garnet rim. Nose: neat, balanced, ripe fruit, spicy. Palate: good structure, complex, full, flavourful, good acidity, balanced.

VALDEHERMOSO 2010 T ROBLE
tinto fino.

88 Colour: cherry, purple rim. Nose: balanced, fruit preserve, sweet spices. Palate: flavourful, fruity, spicy.

BODEGAS Y VIÑEDOS VEGA DE YUSO

Basilón, 9 - Cañada Real, s/n
47350 Quintanilla de Onésimo (Valladolid)
☎: +34 983 680 054 - Fax: +34 983 680 294
bodega@vegadeyuso.com
www.vegadeyuso.com

POZO DE NIEVE 2011 T
100% tempranillo.

88 Colour: cherry, purple rim. Nose: fresh fruit, red berry notes, spicy, creamy oak. Palate: fresh, fruity, balanced.

VEGANTIGUA 10 MESES 2010 T BARRICA
100% tempranillo.

85 Colour: cherry, garnet rim. Nose: ripe fruit, spicy, creamy oak. Palate: powerful, flavourful, toasty.

TRES MATAS VENDIMIA SELECCIONADA 2009 T
100% tempranillo.

91 Colour: cherry, garnet rim. Nose: ripe fruit, spicy, creamy oak, toasty, complex. Palate: powerful, flavourful, toasty, round tannins, elegant.

TRES MATAS 2009 TC
100% tempranillo.

91 Colour: cherry, garnet rim. Nose: spicy, creamy oak, toasty, characterful, ripe fruit. Palate: powerful, flavourful, toasty, round tannins.

TRES MATAS 2007 TR
100% tempranillo.

88 Colour: deep cherry, garnet rim. Nose: balanced, expressive, creamy oak, cocoa bean, overripe fruit. Palate: fruity, balanced, good finish.

BODEGAS Y VIÑEDOS VEGA REAL

Ctra. N-122, Km. 298,6
47318 Castrillo de Duero (Valladolid)
☎: +34 983 881 580 - Fax: +34 983 873 188
bodegas@vegareal.net
www.vegareal.net

VEGA REAL 2011 T ROBLE

85 Colour: cherry, purple rim. Nose: medium intensity, red berry notes, ripe fruit, balanced, spicy. Palate: balanced, fruity, easy to drink.

VEGA REAL 2008 TC

86 Colour: dark-red cherry, garnet rim. Nose: scrubland, fine reductive notes, earthy notes, spicy. Palate: flavourful, long, spicy.

BODEGAS Y VIÑEDOS VIÑA MAYOR

Ctra. Valladolid - Soria, Km. 325,6
47350 Quintanilla de Onésimo (Valladolid)
☎: +34 983 680 461 - Fax: +34 983 027 217
rrpp@vina-mayor.com
www.vina-mayor.es

VIÑA MAYOR 2011 T ROBLE
100% tempranillo.

88 Colour: cherry, garnet rim. Nose: powerfull, ripe fruit, red berry notes, sweet spices. Palate: flavourful, good acidity.

SECRETO VENDIMIA SELECCIONADA 2010 T ROBLE
100% tempranillo.

89 Colour: bright cherry. Nose: sweet spices, creamy oak, red berry notes. Palate: flavourful, fruity, toasty, round tannins.

VIÑA MAYOR 2009 TC
100% tempranillo.

89 Colour: cherry, garnet rim. Nose: balanced, ripe fruit, sweet spices. Palate: fruity, flavourful, fruity aftespalate:.

VIÑA MAYOR 2007 TR
100% tempranillo.

89 Colour: cherry, garnet rim. Nose: spicy, fine reductive notes, wet leather, aged wood nuances, fruit liqueur notes. Palate: spicy, long, flavourful, toasty.

CEPAS Y BODEGAS

Paseo de Zorrilla, 77 - 3º D
47001 Valladolid (Valladolid)
☎: +34 983 355 543 - Fax: +34 983 340 824
info@cepasybodegas.com
www.cepasybodegas.com

VILLACAMPA DEL MARQUÉS 2010 T ROBLE
100% tempranillo.

88 Colour: bright cherry. Nose: ripe fruit, sweet spices, creamy oak. Palate: flavourful, fruity, toasty, round tannins.

VILLACAMPA DEL MARQUÉS 2008 TC
100% tempranillo.

88 Colour: cherry, garnet rim. Nose: ripe fruit, aromatic coffee, creamy oak, roasted coffee. Palate: flavourful, long, toasty.

VILLACAMPA DEL MARQUÉS 2006 TR
100% tempranillo.

89 Colour: cherry, garnet rim. Nose: ripe fruit, spicy, creamy oak, fine reductive notes. Palate: powerful, flavourful, toasty.

CINEMA WINES

Felipe Gómez, 1
47140 Laguna de Duero (Valladolid)
☎: +34 983 544 696 - Fax: +34 983 545 539
info@cinemawines.es
www.cinemawines.es

CINEMA 2009 TC
100% tempranillo.

91 Colour: cherry, garnet rim. Nose: spicy, creamy oak, toasty, ripe fruit. Palate: powerful, flavourful, toasty, round tannins.

CINEMA 2010 T ROBLE
100% tempranillo.

86 Colour: cherry, purple rim. Nose: medium intensity, ripe fruit, sweet spices. Palate: flavourful, long, spicy.

COMENGE BODEGAS Y VIÑEDOS

Camino del Castillo, s/n
47316 Curiel de Duero (Valladolid)
☎: +34 983 880 363 - Fax: +34 983 880 717
admin@comenge.com
www.comenge.com

BIBERIUS 2011 T
tempranillo.

89 Colour: bright cherry. Nose: ripe fruit, sweet spices. Palate: flavourful, fruity, toasty, round tannins.

DON MIGUEL COMENGE 2009 T
tempranillo.

96 Colour: cherry, garnet rim. Nose: ripe fruit, spicy, creamy oak, toasty, complex, earthy notes, mineral. Palate: powerful, flavourful, toasty, round tannins.

COMENGE 2009 T
tempranillo.

89 Colour: cherry, garnet rim. Nose: ripe fruit, spicy, creamy oak, toasty, characterful. Palate: powerful, flavourful, toasty, round tannins.

COMENGE 2008 T
tempranillo.

88 Colour: cherry, garnet rim. Nose: powerfull, overripe fruit, toasty, cocoa bean. Palate: flavourful, powerful, concentrated.

COMENGE 2007 T
tempranillo.

88 Colour: bright cherry. Nose: sweet spices, creamy oak, ripe fruit, aromatic coffee. Palate: flavourful, fruity, toasty, round tannins.

COMPAÑÍA DE VINOS TELMO RODRÍGUEZ

El Monte
01308 Lanciego (Álava)
☎: +34 945 628 315 - Fax: +34 945 628 314
contact@telmorodriguez.com
www.telmorodriguez.com

M2 DE MATALLANA 2009 T
100% tinta del país.

92 Colour: cherry, garnet rim. Nose: sweet spices, ripe fruit, earthy notes, mineral, toasty. Palate: flavourful, powerful, round tannins.

MATALLANA 2007 T
100% tinto fino.

92 Colour: cherry, garnet rim. Nose: ripe fruit, spicy, creamy oak, toasty. Palate: powerful, flavourful, toasty, round tannins.

COMPAÑÍA VINÍCOLA SOLTERRA

Ctra. Pedrosa, Km. 1,5
09300 Roa (Burgos)
☎: +34 915 196 651 - Fax: +34 914 135 907
m.antonia@cvsolterra.com
www.cvsolterra.com

ALTO DE LOS ZORROS 2010 T ROBLE
100% tempranillo.

85 Colour: bright cherry. Nose: ripe fruit, creamy oak, spicy. Palate: flavourful, fruity, toasty, correct.

ALTO DE LOS ZORROS AUTOR 2009 T
100% tempranillo.

89 Colour: cherry, garnet rim. Nose: ripe fruit, spicy, toasty, cocoa bean, expressive, mineral. Palate: powerful, flavourful, toasty, round tannins.

ALTO DE LOS ZORROS 2009 TC
100% tempranillo.

87 Colour: cherry, garnet rim. Nose: ripe fruit, spicy, toasty, wild herbs. Palate: powerful, flavourful, toasty.

CONVENTO DE LAS CLARAS

Calvario s/n
47316 Curiel de Duero (Valladolid)
☎: +34 983 880 481
info@bodegasconventodelasclaras.com
www.bodegasconventodelasclaras.com

CONVENTO LAS CLARAS TEMPRANILLO 2011 T
100% tempranillo.

88 Colour: bright cherry. Nose: ripe fruit, sweet spices, creamy oak. Palate: flavourful, fruity, toasty, round tannins.

CONVENTO DE OREJA

Avda. Palencia, 1
47010 (Valladolid)
☎: +34 685 990 596 - Fax: +34 913 710 098
convento@conventooreja.es
www.conventooreja.net

CONVENTO OREJA 2010 T ROBLE
100% tinta del país.

87 Colour: bright cherry. Nose: ripe fruit, sweet spices, creamy oak. Palate: flavourful, fruity, toasty, round tannins.

CONVENTO OREJA 2009 TC
100% tinta del país.

90 Colour: cherry, garnet rim. Nose: medium intensity, balanced, ripe fruit, sweet spices. Palate: flavourful, fruity, good acidity.

CONVENTO OREJA MEMORIA 2007 TR
100% tinta del país.

92 Colour: cherry, garnet rim. Nose: ripe fruit, spicy, creamy oak, toasty, complex, mineral. Palate: powerful, flavourful, toasty, round tannins, balanced.

CVNE - COMPAÑÍA VINÍCOLA DEL NORTE DE ESPAÑA

Barrio de la Estación, s/n
26200 Haro (La Rioja)
☎: +34 941 304 800 - Fax: +34 941 304 815
marketing@cvne.com
www.cvne.com

BLACK 2010 T ROBLE
100% tempranillo.

88 Colour: bright cherry. Nose: sweet spices, creamy oak, ripe fruit. Palate: flavourful, fruity, toasty, round tannins.

BLACK 2009 TC
100% tempranillo.

89 Colour: cherry, garnet rim. Nose: ripe fruit, spicy, creamy oak, toasty. Palate: powerful, flavourful, spicy.

DEHESA DE LOS CANÓNIGOS

Ctra. Renedo - Pesquera, Km. 39
47315 Pesquera de Duero (Valladolid)
☎: +34 983 484 001 - Fax: +34 983 484 040
bodega@dehesacanonigos.com
www.bodegadehesadeloscanonigos.com

DEHESA DE LOS CANÓNIGOS 2008 T
88% tinto fino, 12% cabernet sauvignon.

88 Colour: cherry, garnet rim. Nose: ripe fruit, creamy oak, toasty, fine reductive notes. Palate: powerful, flavourful, toasty.

BODEGA
DEHESA DE LOS CANONIGOS
Dehesa de los Canonigos
18 meses en barrica

DEHESA DE LOS CANÓNIGOS MAGNUM SELECCIÓN ESPECIAL 2006 T
88% tinto fino, 12% cabernet sauvignon.

89 Colour: pale ruby, brick rim edge. Nose: ripe fruit, fruit liqueur notes, balsamic herbs, sweet spices, creamy oak, fine reductive notes. Palate: long, spicy, powerful, flavourful.

DEHESA DE LOS CANÓNIGOS 2005 TR
85% tempranillo, 12% cabernet sauvignon, 3% albillo.

90 Colour: dark-red cherry, orangey edge. Nose: ripe fruit, spicy, creamy oak. Palate: elegant, flavourful, spicy, long.

DEHESA VALDELAGUNA

Ctra. Valoria, Km. 16
Pesquera de Duero (Valladolid)
☎: +34 619 460 308 - Fax: +34 921 142 325
montelaguna@montelaguna.es
www.montelaguna.es

MONTELAGUNA 6 MESES 2010 T
tempranillo.

88 Colour: bright cherry. Nose: ripe fruit, sweet spices, creamy oak, toasty. Palate: flavourful, fruity, toasty, easy to drink.

MONTELAGUNA SELECCIÓN 2009 T
tempranillo.

92 Colour: bright cherry, garnet rim. Nose: ripe fruit, sweet spices, creamy oak, expressive. Palate: flavourful, fruity, toasty, round tannins, balanced.

MONTELAGUNA 2009 TC
tempranillo.

90 Colour: cherry, garnet rim. Nose: ripe fruit, aromatic coffee, sweet spices, creamy oak. Palate: powerful, flavourful, spicy, toasty.

RA 08 2008 TR
tempranillo.

91 Colour: cherry, garnet rim. Nose: ripe fruit, spicy, creamy oak, toasty, expressive. Palate: powerful, flavourful, toasty, round tannins, elegant.

DÍAZ BAYO HERMANOS

Camino de los Anarinos, s/n
09471 Fuentelcésped (Burgos)
☎: +34 947 561 020 - Fax: +34 947 561 204
info@bodegadiazbayo.com
www.bodegadiazbayo.com

DARDANELOS 2011 RD
tempranillo.

88 Colour: rose, bright. Nose: balanced, fruit expression, violets. Palate: fresh, fruity, flavourful.

DARDANELOS 2011 T BARRICA
tempranillo.

88 Colour: cherry, purple rim. Nose: ripe fruit, sweet spices, creamy oak, expressive. Palate: flavourful, fruity, toasty, round tannins.

NUESTRO 12 MESES 2010 T BARRICA
tempranillo.

91 Colour: bright cherry. Aroma ripe fruit, sweet spices, creamy oak, expressive. Palate: flavourful, fruity, toasty, round tannins.

DIAZ BAYO MAJUELO DE LA HOMBRÍA 2009 T BARRICA
100% tempranillo.

93 Colour: cherry, garnet rim. Nose: ripe fruit, spicy, creamy oak, toasty, complex, mineral. Palate: powerful, flavourful, toasty, round tannins. Personality.

NUESTRO CRIANZA 2008 TC
tempranillo.

91 Colour: black cherry, garnet rim. Nose: mineral, ripe fruit, citrus fruit, fragrant herbs, spicy, creamy oak. Palate: powerful, flavourful, balanced, long.

NUESTRO 20 MESES 2006 T BARRICA
tempranillo.

92 Colour: cherry, garnet rim. Nose: spicy, creamy oak, toasty, complex, overripe fruit. Palate: powerful, flavourful, toasty, round tannins.

FDB 2006 T BARRICA
tempranillo.

91 Colour: cherry, garnet rim. Nose: powerfull, fruit preserve, toasty, dark chocolate, aromatic coffee. Palate: flavourful, ripe fruit, fine bitter notes, good acidity.

DISTRIBUCIONES B. IÑAKI NÚÑEZ

Ctra. de Ablitas a Ribafora, Km. 5
31523 Ablitas (Navarra)
☎: +34 948 386 210 - Fax: +34 629 354 190
bodegasin@pagodecirsus.com
www.pagodecirsus.com

SENDA DE LOS OLIVOS FINCA LA CARRASCA 2009 T
100% tinto fino.

89 Colour: cherry, garnet rim. Nose: ripe fruit, spicy, creamy oak, toasty. Palate: powerful, flavourful, toasty, round tannins.

SENDA DE LOS OLIVOS VENDIMIA SELECCIONADA 2009 T
100% tinto fino.

88 Colour: cherry, garnet rim. Nose: spicy, creamy oak, toasty, complex, overripe fruit, warm. Palate: powerful, flavourful, toasty, round tannins.

SENDA DE LOS OLIVOS EDICIÓN ESPECIAL 2006 T
100% tinto fino.

88 Colour: black cherry, garnet rim. Nose: fruit preserve, scrubland, spicy, creamy oak. Palate: powerful, flavourful, concentrated.

DOMINIO DE ATAUTA

Ctra. a Morcuera, s/n
42345 Atauta (Soria)
☎: +34 975 351 349
dominiodeatauta.ribera@arrakis.es
www.dominiodeatauta.com

VIRIDIANA 2011 T
tempranillo.

88 Colour: very deep cherry. Nose: expressive, red berry notes, floral. Palate: flavourful, fine bitter notes, grainy tannins.

DOMINIO DE ATAUTA LLANOS DEL ALMENDRO 2009 T
100% tinto fino.

96 Colour: cherry, garnet rim. Nose: expressive, ripe fruit, mineral, sweet spices. Palate: flavourful, fine bitter notes, good acidity, elegant.

DOMINIO DE ATAUTA 2009 TC
100% tinto fino.

93 Colour: cherry, garnet rim. Nose: ripe fruit, spicy, creamy oak, toasty, characterful. Palate: powerful, flavourful, toasty, round tannins.

DOMINIO DE ATAUTA VALDEGATILES 2009 T
100% tinto fino.

94 Colour: cherry, garnet rim. Nose: spicy, creamy oak, toasty, complex, expressive, overripe fruit. Palate: powerful, flavourful, toasty, round tannins.

PARADA DE ATAUTA 2009 T
100% tinto fino.

94 Colour: cherry, garnet rim. Nose: spicy, creamy oak, toasty, characterful, fruit expression. Palate: powerful, flavourful, toasty, round tannins.

DOMINIO DE ATAUTA LA MALA 2009 TC
100% tinto fino.

93 Colour: cherry, garnet rim. Nose: spicy, creamy oak, toasty, characterful, fruit expression. Palate: powerful, flavourful, toasty, round tannins.

TORRE DE GOLBAN 2009 TC
100% tinto fino.

90 Colour: cherry, garnet rim. Nose: ripe fruit, spicy, creamy oak, toasty, dark chocolate. Palate: powerful, flavourful, toasty, round tannins.

TORRE DE GOLBAN 2008 TC
100% tinto fino.

88 Colour: cherry, garnet rim. Nose: balanced, ripe fruit, cocoa bean. Palate: flavourful, fruity, good finish.

DOMINIO DE PINGUS

Hospital, s/n - Apdo. 93, Peñafiel
47350 Quintanilla de Onésimo (Valladolid)
☎: +34 639 833 854
www.dominiopingus.com

PINGUS 2010 T
100% tinto fino.

97 Colour: cherry, garnet rim. Nose: ripe fruit, spicy, toasty, complex, sweet spices, earthy notes, mineral, fruit expression. Palate: powerful, flavourful, toasty, round tannins, round, fine bitter notes.

FLOR DE PINGUS 2010 T
100% tinto fino.

95 Colour: cherry, garnet rim. Nose: spicy, creamy oak, toasty, complex, scrubland, fruit expression, red berry notes. Palate: powerful, flavourful, toasty, powerful tannins, good acidity.

PSI 2010 T
100% tinto fino.

92 Colour: bright cherry. Nose: sweet spices, creamy oak, varietal, red berry notes. Palate: flavourful, fruity, toasty, round tannins.

DOMINIO ROMANO

Los Lagares, s/n
47319 Rábano (Valladolid)
☎: +34 983 871 661 - Fax: +34 938 901 143
dominioromano@dominioromano.com
www.dominioromano.com

DOMINIO ROMANO 2009 T
tinto fino.

90 Colour: bright cherry. Nose: sweet spices, creamy oak, expressive, fruit preserve. Palate: flavourful, fruity, toasty, round tannins.

CAMINO ROMANO 2009 T
tinto fino.

90 Colour: cherry, garnet rim. Nose: expressive, ripe fruit, fruit expression, toasty, spicy. Palate: flavourful, spicy, ripe fruit.

DURÓN

Ctra. Roa - La Horra, km. 3,800
09300 Roa (Burgos)
☎: +34 902 227 700 - Fax: +34 902 227 701
bodega@cofradiasamaniego.com
www.bodegasduron.com

DURÓN 2008 TC
90% tinta del país, 10% cabernet sauvignon.

87 Colour: cherry, garnet rim. Nose: powerfull, warm, ripe fruit, sweet spices. Palate: flavourful, correct, ripe fruit.

DURÓN 2008 TR
75% tinta del país, 15% cabernet sauvignon, 10% merlot.

86 Colour: cherry, garnet rim. Nose: ripe fruit, spicy, creamy oak, fine reductive notes. Palate: powerful, flavourful, toasty.

ÉBANO VIÑEDOS Y BODEGAS

Ctra. N-122 Km., 299,6 Pol. Ind. 1 Parcela 32
47318 Castrillo de Duero (Valladolid)
☎: +34 983 106 440 - Fax: +34 986 609 313
ebano@valminorebano.com
www.ebanovinedosybodegas.com

ÉBANO 2008 T
100% tempranillo.

90 Colour: cherry, garnet rim. Nose: medium intensity, balanced, ripe fruit. Palate: flavourful, correct.

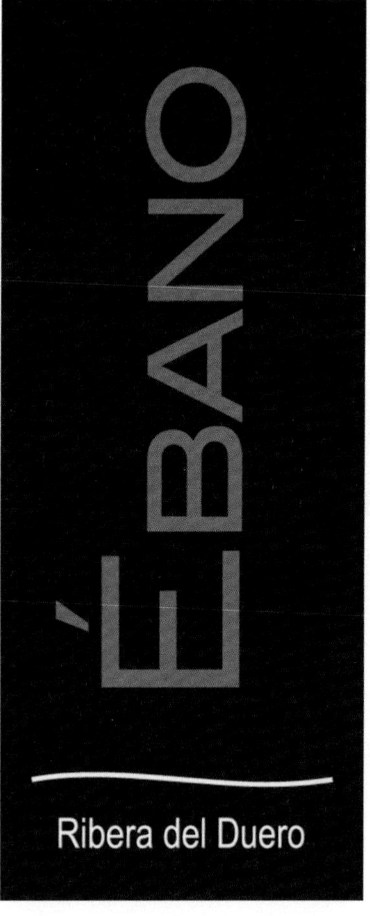

ÉBANO 6 2010 T
100% tempranillo.

87 Colour: cherry, purple rim. Nose: red berry notes, ripe fruit, spicy, creamy oak. Palate: correct, powerful, flavourful, toasty.

EL LAGAR DE ISILLA

Camino Real, 1
09471 La Vid (Burgos)
☎: +34 947 530 434 - Fax: +34 947 504 316
bodegas@lagarisilla.es
www.lagarisilla.es

EL LAGAR DE ISILLA 2011 T
100% tempranillo.

87 Colour: cherry, purple rim. Nose: red berry notes, floral, ripe fruit. Palate: flavourful, fruity, good acidity, round tannins.

EL LAGAR DE ISILLA 2010 T ROBLE
95% tinta del país, 5% cabernet sauvignon.

88 Colour: bright cherry. Nose: ripe fruit, sweet spices, creamy oak, expressive. Palate: flavourful, fruity, toasty, balanced.

EL LAGAR DE ISILLA 9 MESES GESTACIÓN 2010 T ROBLE
100% tinta del país.

87 Colour: deep cherry, garnet rim. Nose: balanced, ripe fruit, dark chocolate, sweet spices, medium intensity.

EL LAGAR DE ISILLA VENDIMIA SELECCIONADA 2009 T
100% tinta del país.

91 Colour: cherry, garnet rim. Nose: spicy, creamy oak, toasty, ripe fruit. Palate: powerful, flavourful, toasty, round tannins.

EL LAGAR DE ISILLA 2009 TC
100% tinta del país.

88 Colour: bright cherry. Nose: sweet spices, creamy oak, ripe fruit. Palate: flavourful, fruity, toasty, round tannins.

EMINA RIBERA

Ctra. San Bernardo, s/n
47359 Valbuena de Duero (Valladolid)
☎: +34 983 683 315 - Fax: +34 902 430 189
emina@emina.es
www.emina.es

EMINA PASIÓN 2011 T
100% tempranillo.

86 Colour: cherry, purple rim. Nose: ripe fruit, sweet spices. Palate: good structure, spicy, good finish.

EMINA 12 MESES 2010 T
100% tempranillo.

88 Colour: bright cherry. Nose: ripe fruit, sweet spices, creamy oak, expressive. Palate: flavourful, fruity, toasty.

EMINA PRESTIGIO 2006 TR
100% tempranillo.

89 Colour: cherry, garnet rim. Nose: spicy, creamy oak, toasty, complex, overripe fruit. Palate: powerful, toasty, round tannins.

EMINA ATIO 2005 T
100% tempranillo.

89 Colour: dark-red cherry, orangey edge. Nose: fruit preserve, scrubland, fine reductive notes, spicy, toasty. Palate: long, powerful, flavourful, toasty.

FINCA CAMPOS GÓTICOS

Parcela 622
09312 Anguix (Burgos)
☎: +34 979 165 121 - Fax: +34 979 712 343
clientedirecto@camposgoticos.es
www.camposgoticos.es

CAMPOS GÓTICOS 2009 TC
100% tempranillo.

88 Colour: cherry, garnet rim. Nose: creamy oak, complex, ripe fruit. Palate: powerful, flavourful, toasty, round tannins.

CAMPOS GÓTICOS 2009 T ROBLE
100% tempranillo.

88 Colour: bright cherry. Nose: sweet spices, creamy oak, red berry notes, ripe fruit, fragrant herbs. Palate: flavourful, fruity, toasty.

FINCA TORREMILANOS BODEGAS PEÑALBA LÓPEZ

Finca Torremilanos, s/n
09400 Aranda de Duero (Burgos)
☎: +34 947 510 377 - Fax: +34 947 512 856
torremilanos@torremilanos.com
www.torremilanos.com

MONTE CASTRILLO 7 MESES 2010 T ROBLE
100% tempranillo.

88 Colour: bright cherry. Nose: ripe fruit, sweet spices, creamy oak, expressive. Palate: flavourful, fruity, toasty.

LOS CANTOS DE TORREMILANOS 2009 T
100% tempranillo.

92 Colour: cherry, garnet rim. Nose: ripe fruit, spicy, creamy oak, mineral. Palate: powerful, flavourful, toasty, round tannins, good acidity, balanced.

CYCLO 2009 T
85% tempranillo, 10% garnacha, 5% blanca del pais.

92 Colour: cherry, garnet rim. Nose: ripe fruit, spicy, creamy oak, complex, sweet spices, earthy notes. Palate: powerful, flavourful, toasty, round tannins, balanced.

TORREMILANOS 2009 TC
100% tempranillo.

88 Colour: cherry, garnet rim. Nose: ripe fruit, spicy, toasty, balsamic herbs. Palate: powerful, flavourful, toasty, round tannins.

CYCLO 2008 T
tempranillo, garnacha, blanca del pais.

91 Colour: cherry, garnet rim. Nose: spicy, creamy oak, cocoa bean, dark chocolate, balsamic herbs, mineral, ripe fruit. Palate: powerful, flavourful, long, spicy.

TORRE - ALBENIZ 2008 TR
100% tempranillo.

88 Colour: cherry, garnet rim. Aroma ripe fruit, spicy, creamy oak, toasty, complex. Palate: powerful, flavourful, toasty, round tannins.

TORREMILANOS COLECCIÓN 2006 T
100% tempranillo.

90 Colour: cherry, garnet rim. Nose: ripe fruit, spicy, creamy oak, toasty, balsamic herbs. Palate: powerful, flavourful, round tannins, spicy, balanced.

FINCA VILLACRECES

Ctra. N-122 Km. 322
47350 Quintanilla de Onésimo (Valladolid)
☎: +34 983 680 437 - Fax: +34 983 683 314
villacreces@villacreces.com
www.villacreces.com

PRUNO 2010 T
90% tinto fino, 10% cabernet sauvignon.

92 Colour: cherry, garnet rim. Nose: creamy oak, red berry notes, fruit expression, cocoa bean. Palate: flavourful, good acidity, fine bitter notes, round.

FINCA VILLACRECES 2007 T
86% tinto fino, 10% cabernet sauvignon, 4% merlot.

91 Colour: cherry, garnet rim. Nose: spicy, toasty, complex, overripe fruit, dark chocolate. Palate: powerful, flavourful, toasty, round tannins.

GRUPO VINÍCOLA MARQUÉS DE VARGAS - CONDE SAN CRISTÓBAL

Ctra. Valladolid a Soria, Km. 303
47300 Peñafiel (Valladolid)
☎: +34 983 878 055 - Fax: +34 983 878 196
bodega@condesancristobal.com
www.marquesdevargas.com

CONDE DE SAN CRISTÓBAL 2009 T
80% tinto fino, 10% merlot, 10% cabernet sauvignon.

90 Colour: cherry, garnet rim. Nose: powerfull, balanced, ripe fruit, scrubland. Palate: fruity, good structure, round tannins.

CONDE DE SAN CRISTÓBAL RAÍCES 2007 T RESERVA ESPECIAL
90% tinto fino, 10% merlot.

91 Colour: cherry, garnet rim. Nose: ripe fruit, toasty, wet leather, earthy notes. Palate: spicy, balanced, toasty, long.

GRUPO YLLERA

Autovía A-6, Km. 173, 5
47490 Rueda (Valladolid)
☎: +34 983 868 097 - Fax: +34 983 868 177
grupoyllera@grupoyllera.com
www.grupoyllera.com

BRACAMONTE 2006 TC
tempranillo.

90 Colour: pale ruby, brick rim edge. Nose: scrubland, spicy, ripe fruit, creamy oak. Palate: powerful, flavourful, spicy, long.

VIÑA DEL VAL 2011 T
tempranillo.

88 Colour: cherry, purple rim. Aroma expressive, fresh fruit, red berry notes, floral. Palate: flavourful, fruity, good acidity, round tannins.

BRACAMONTE 2010 T ROBLE
tempranillo.

89 Colour: bright cherry. Nose: ripe fruit, sweet spices, creamy oak, expressive. Palate: flavourful, fruity, toasty, round tannins.

HACIENDA SOLANO

La Solana, 6
09370 La Aguilera (Burgos)
☎: +34 947 545 582 - Fax: +34 947 545 582
administracion@haciendasolano.com
www.haciendasolano.com

HACIENDA ERNESTINA SOLANO 6 MESES 2010 T ROBLE
100% tempranillo.

85 Colour: cherry, purple rim. Nose: medium intensity, ripe fruit, sweet spices. Palate: correct, easy to drink, good finish.

HACIENDA ERNESTINA SOLANO 12 MESES SELECCIÓN VIÑAS VIEJAS 2009 TC
100% tempranillo.

92 Colour: cherry, garnet rim. Nose: ripe fruit, spicy, creamy oak, toasty, lactic notes. Palate: powerful, flavourful, toasty, round tannins.

HACIENDA ERNESTINA SOLANO FINCA CASCORRALES 2007 T
100% tempranillo.

89 Colour: deep cherry, garnet rim. Nose: medium intensity, ripe fruit. Palate: ripe fruit, long, spicy.

HACIENDA URBIÓN

Ctra. Nalda
26120 Albelda de Iregua (Rioja)
☎: +34 941 444 223 - Fax: +34 941 444 427
info@vinicolareal.com

VEGA VIEJA 2011 T ROBLE
100% tempranillo.

85 Colour: bright cherry. Nose: ripe fruit, sweet spices, creamy oak. Palate: flavourful, fruity, spicy.

VEGA VIEJA COSECHA 2011 T
100% tempranillo.

84

VEGA VIEJA 2010 TC
90% tempranillo, 10% garnacha.

88 Colour: cherry, garnet rim. Nose: ripe fruit, aromatic coffee, sweet spices, roasted coffee. Palate: powerful, flavourful, toasty.

HACIENDAS DE ESPAÑA

Hacienda Abascal, N-122, Km. 321,5
47360 Quintanilla de Onésimo (Valladolid)
☎: +34 914 365 924
comunicacion@arcoinvest-group.com
www.haciendas-espana.com

HACIENDA ABASCAL PREMIUM (MARQUÉS DE LA CONCORDIA FAMILY OF WINES) 2008 T
100% tempranillo.

91 Colour: cherry, garnet rim. Nose: ripe fruit, spicy, toasty, cocoa bean, expressive. Palate: powerful, flavourful, toasty, round tannins.

HACIENDA ABASCAL (MARQUÉS DE LA CONCORDIA FAMILY OF WINES) 2008 TC
100% tempranillo.

89 Colour: cherry, garnet rim. Nose: ripe fruit, creamy oak, toasty, sweet spices. Palate: powerful, flavourful, toasty, round tannins.

HORNILLOS BALLESTEROS

Camino Tenerías, 9
09300 Roa de Duero (Burgos)
☎: +34 947 541 071 - Fax: +34 947 541 071
hornillosballesteros@telefonica.net
www.hornillosballesteros.es

MIBAL 2010 T
100% tempranillo.

86 Colour: cherry, purple rim. Nose: expressive, red berry notes, floral. Palate: flavourful, fruity, good acidity, round tannins.

PERFIL 2009 T
100% tempranillo.

91 Colour: cherry, garnet rim. Nose: cocoa bean, sweet spices, ripe fruit. Palate: good structure, complex, flavourful, ripe fruit.

MIBAL SELECCIÓN 2008 T
100% tempranillo.

88 Colour: deep cherry. Nose: medium intensity, ripe fruit, spicy. Palate: flavourful, fine bitter notes, good acidity.

MIBAL 2008 TC
100% tempranillo.

87 Colour: cherry, garnet rim. Nose: spicy, creamy oak, toasty. Palate: powerful, flavourful, toasty, round tannins.

LA COLECCIÓN DE VINOS

Domingo Martínez, 6- Bajo
47007 (Valladolid)
☎: +34 983 271 595 - Fax: +34 983 271 608
info@lacolecciondevinos.com
www.lacolecciondevinos.com

VALLIS 2011 T ROBLE
100% tinta del país.

89 Colour: cherry, purple rim. Nose: expressive, fresh fruit, red berry notes, toasty, spicy. Palate: flavourful, fruity, good acidity, round tannins.

1492 SANTAFÉ 2009 TC
100% tempranillo.

87 Colour: cherry, garnet rim. Nose: ripe fruit, spicy, creamy oak, toasty. Palate: powerful, flavourful, spicy.

LA VIÑA DEL LOCO

Plaza de Matute 12, - 3°
28012 (Madrid)
☎: +34 609 119 248
info@miravinos.es
www.miravinos.es

TOGA 2010 T
tinto fino.

94 Colour: cherry, garnet rim. Nose: spicy, complex, new oak, earthy notes, fruit expression, ripe fruit. Palate: powerful, flavourful, toasty, round tannins.

VENTA EL LOCO 2009 T
tinto fino.

91 Colour: bright cherry. Nose: ripe fruit, sweet spices, creamy oak, characterful, varietal. Palate: flavourful, fruity, toasty, round tannins.

LEGARIS

Ctra. Peñafiel - Encinas de Esgueva, km. 4,3
47316 Curiel de Duero (Valladolid)
☎: +34 983 878 088 - Fax: +34 983 881 034
info@legaris.com
www.grupocodorniu.com

LEGARIS 2011 T ROBLE
100% tinto fino.

89 Colour: bright cherry. Nose: sweet spices, creamy oak, red berry notes, expressive. Palate: flavourful, fruity, toasty.

LEGARIS 2009 TC
100% tinto fino.

90 Colour: cherry, garnet rim. Nose: ripe fruit, spicy, creamy oak, toasty, complex. Palate: powerful, flavourful, toasty, long, balanced.

LEGARIS 2006 TR
100% tinto fino.

91 Colour: cherry, garnet rim. Nose: ripe fruit, spicy, creamy oak, toasty, complex, elegant. Palate: powerful, flavourful, toasty, round tannins, balanced.

LOESS

El Monte, 7- Bajo
47195 Arroyo de la Encomienda (Valladolid)
☎: +34 983 664 898 - Fax: +34 983 406 579
loess@loess.es
www.loess.es

LOESS COLLECTION 2009 T
100% tempranillo.

92 Colour: deep cherry, garnet rim. Nose: ripe fruit, creamy oak, sweet spices, balanced. Palate: fine bitter notes, round tannins.

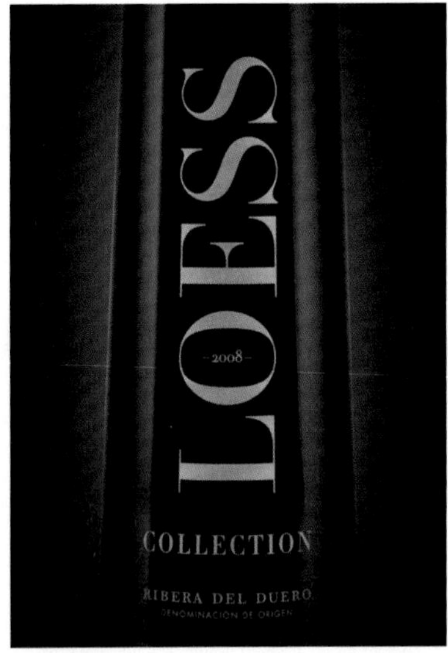

LOESS 2009 T
100% tempranillo.

90 Colour: cherry, garnet rim. Nose: ripe fruit, spicy, creamy oak, complex. Palate: flavourful, round tannins, balanced, good acidity.

LYNUS VIÑEDOS Y BODEGAS

Camino de las Pozas, s/n
47350 Quintanilla de Onésimo (Valladolid)
☎: +34 661 879 016 - Fax: +34 983 680 224
info@lynus.es
www.lynus.es

PAGOS DEL INFANTE 2009 TC
100% tempranillo.

88 Colour: cherry, garnet rim. Nose: ripe fruit, spicy, toasty. Palate: correct, powerful, flavourful.

LYNUS 2008 TC
100% tempranillo.

88 Colour: cherry, garnet rim. Nose: fruit liqueur notes, earthy notes, fine reductive notes, spicy. Palate: flavourful, long, correct.

LYNUS ÁUREA 2007 TR
100% tempranillo.

91 Colour: bright cherry, garnet rim. Nose: warm, ripe fruit, dark chocolate. Palate: fruity, round tannins.

Mª AMPARO REPISO VALLEJO

Avda. de la Estación, 47
47360 Quintanilla de Arriba (Valladolid)
☎: +34 983 476 126 - Fax: +34 983 476 126
amparorepiso@vinosarmentero.com
www.vinosarmentero.com

SARMENTERO 2010 T ROBLE
tempranillo.

86 Colour: bright cherry. Nose: ripe fruit, sweet spices, balsamic herbs. Palate: flavourful, fruity, toasty, correct.

SARMENTERO VENDIMIA SELECCIONADA 2009 T
tempranillo.

88 Colour: cherry, garnet rim. Nose: ripe fruit, creamy oak, toasty, sweet spices. Palate: powerful, flavourful, toasty.

MARQUÉS DE IRÚN

Juan de Mena, 10
28014 (Madrid)
☎: +34 956 851 711 - Fax: +34 956 859 204
mirun@marquesdeirun.es
www.marquesdeirun.com

MARQUÉS DE IRÚN 2010 T ROBLE
100% tempranillo.

85 Colour: cherry, garnet rim. Nose: medium intensity, sweet spices, fruit preserve, toasty. Palate: flavourful, balanced.

MARQUÉS DE IRÚN 2009 T ROBLE
tempranillo.

87 Colour: cherry, garnet rim. Nose: ripe fruit, spicy, creamy oak. Palate: powerful, flavourful, toasty, round tannins.

MARQUÉS DE IRÚN 2008 TC
100% tempranillo.

88 Colour: cherry, garnet rim. Nose: powerfull, fruit liqueur notes, ripe fruit, toasty. Palate: balanced, easy to drink, fruity.

MONTEBACO

Finca Montealto
47359 Valbuena de Duero (Valladolid)
☎: +34 983 485 128 - Fax: +34 983 485 033
montebaco@bodegasmontebaco.com
www.bodegasmontebaco.com

MONTEBACO 2010 TC
tempranillo.

91 Colour: cherry, garnet rim. Nose: ripe fruit, spicy, creamy oak, toasty, complex, varietal. Palate: powerful, flavourful, toasty, round tannins.

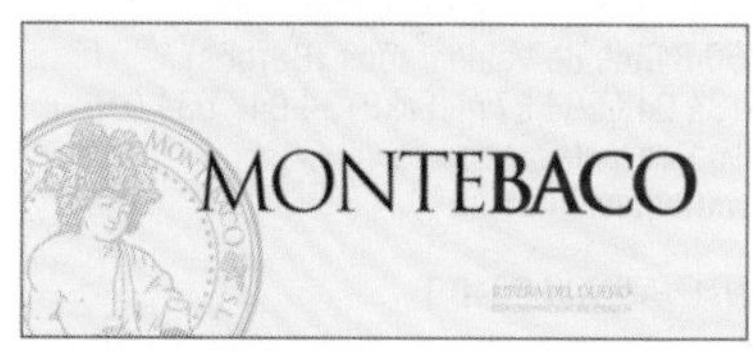

MONTEBACO 2009 TC
tempranillo.

92 Colour: cherry, garnet rim. Aroma ripe fruit, spicy, creamy oak, toasty, complex. Palate: powerful, flavourful, toasty, round tannins.

MONTEBACO VENDIMIA SELECCIONADA 2008 T
tempranillo.

91 Colour: cherry, garnet rim. Nose: powerfull, varietal, ripe fruit, creamy oak. Palate: flavourful, fine bitter notes, good acidity.

SEMELE 2010 TC
90% tempranillo, 10% merlot.

91 Colour: cherry, garnet rim. Nose: ripe fruit, spicy, creamy oak, toasty. Palate: powerful, flavourful, toasty, round tannins.

MONTEGAREDO

Ctra. Boada a Pedrosa, s/n
09314 Boada de Roa (Burgos)
☎: +34 947 530 003 - Fax: +34 947 530 140
info@montegaredo.com
www.montegaredo.com

MONTEGAREDO 2011 T ROBLE
tinto fino.

86 Colour: bright cherry. Nose: ripe fruit, sweet spices, creamy oak, roasted coffee. Palate: flavourful, fruity, toasty, round tannins.

PIRÁMIDE 2010 T
tinto fino.

91 Colour: bright cherry. Nose: ripe fruit, sweet spices, creamy oak, expressive. Palate: flavourful, fruity, toasty, balanced, long.

MONTEGAREDO 2010 TC
tinto fino.

87 Colour: cherry, garnet rim. Nose: ripe fruit, spicy, creamy oak, toasty. Palate: powerful, flavourful, toasty.

MONTEVANNOS

Santiago, s/n
09450 Baños de Valdearados (Burgos)
☎: +34 947 534 277 - Fax: +34 947 534 016
bodega@montevannos.es
www.montevannos.es

MONTEVANNOS 2010 T

85 Colour: cherry, garnet rim. Nose: ripe fruit, fruit preserve, balsamic herbs, spicy. Palate: powerful, flavourful, fruity.

MONTEVANNOS 2009 T BARRICA
85% tempranillo, 15% merlot.

84

OPIMIUS SELECCIÓN ESPECIAL 2006 T

89 Colour: cherry, garnet rim. Nose: ripe fruit, spicy, wet leather, cigar. Palate: powerful, flavourful, toasty, round tannins.

MONTEVANNOS 2006 TR

88 Colour: pale ruby, brick rim edge. Nose: spicy, fine reductive notes, aged wood nuances, fruit liqueur notes. Palate: spicy, fine tannins, long.

MONTEVANNOS 2006 TC

85 Colour: pale ruby, brick rim edge. Nose: spicy, fine reductive notes, wet leather, aged wood nuances, fruit liqueur notes. Palate: spicy, long, fine bitter notes.

OLID INTERNACIONAL

Juan García Hortelano, 21-7ºC
47014 (Valladolid)
☎: +34 983 132 690
olidinternacional@gmail.com
www.olidinternacional.com

983 2006 TC
100% tinta del país.

89 Colour: cherry, garnet rim. Nose: ripe fruit, candied fruit, sweet spices, creamy oak. Palate: powerful, flavourful, fresh, fruity.

PAGO DE CARRAOVEJAS

Camino de Carraovejas, s/n
47300 Peñafiel (Valladolid)
☎: +34 983 878 020 - Fax: +34 983 878 022
administracion@pagodecarraovejas.com
www.pagodecarraovejas.com

PAGO DE CARRAOVEJAS 2009 TC
96% tinto fino, 4% cabernet sauvignon.

93 Colour: cherry, garnet rim. Nose: ripe fruit, fruit expression, red berry notes, lactic notes, creamy oak. Palate: flavourful, powerful, complex, creamy, round tannins.

PAGO DE CARRAOVEJAS 2010 TC
95% tinto fino, 5% cabernet sauvignon.

92 Colour: cherry, garnet rim. Nose: ripe fruit, creamy oak, sweet spices. Palate: good structure, flavourful, full, toasty.

PAGO DE CARRAOVEJAS EL ANEJÓN DE LA CUESTA DE LAS LIEBRES 2009 T
93% tinto fino, 6% cabernet sauvignon, 1% merlot.

96 Colour: cherry, garnet rim. Nose: spicy, creamy oak, toasty, characterful, ripe fruit, mineral. Palate: powerful, flavourful, toasty, round tannins.

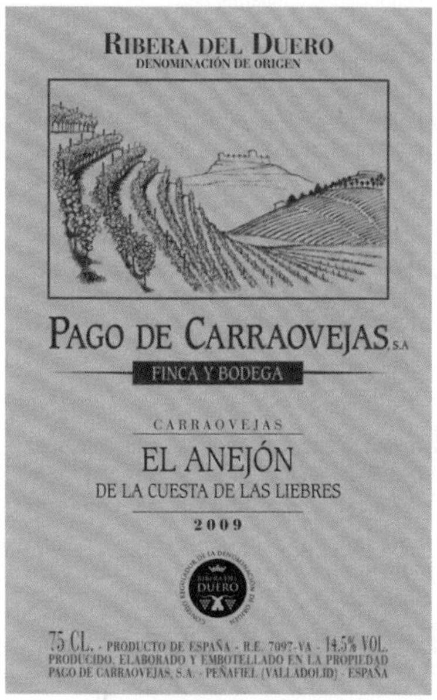

PAGO DE INA

Ctra. Pesquera km.26
47359 Olivares de Duero (Valladolid)
☎: +34 933 576 658 - Fax: +34 933 576 658
pagodeina@pagodeina.com
www.pagodeina.com

PAGO DE INA 2009 T
100% tempranillo.

88 Colour: deep cherry, purple rim. Nose: ripe fruit, sweet spices, creamy oak, premature reduction notes. Palate: flavourful, fruity, long.

ZOÑAN EDICIÓN LIMITADA 2009 T
100% tempranillo.

88 Colour: bright cherry. Nose: sweet spices, creamy oak, expressive, powerfull. Palate: flavourful, fruity, toasty, round tannins.

PAGO DE LOS CAPELLANES

Camino de la Ampudia, s/n
09314 Pedrosa de Duero (Burgos)
☎: +34 947 530 068 - Fax: +34 947 530 111
bodega@pagodeloscapellanes.com
www.pagodeloscapellanes.com

PAGO DE LOS CAPELLANES 2011 T ROBLE
100% tempranillo.

90 Colour: deep cherry, purple rim. Nose: toasty, creamy oak, sweet spices. Palate: balanced, ripe fruit, good acidity.

PAGO DE LOS CAPELLANES 2009 TC
100% tempranillo.

93 Colour: cherry, garnet rim. Nose: ripe fruit, spicy, creamy oak, toasty, complex, mineral, earthy notes. Palate: powerful, flavourful, toasty, round tannins.

PAGO DE LOS CAPELLANES 2008 TR
100% tempranillo.

91 Colour: cherry, garnet rim. Nose: fruit preserve, balanced, sweet spices. Palate: balanced, spicy, ripe fruit, long.

PAGO DE LOS CAPELLANES PARCELA EL PICÓN 2006 T
100% tempranillo.

93 Colour: cherry, garnet rim. Nose: creamy oak, characterful, overripe fruit. Palate: powerful, flavourful, toasty, round tannins.

PAGO DE LOS CAPELLANES PARCELA EL NOGAL 2006 T
100% tempranillo.

92 Colour: cherry, garnet rim. Nose: spicy, creamy oak, toasty, characterful, overripe fruit. Palate: powerful, flavourful, toasty, round tannins.

PAGOS DE MATANEGRA

Ctra. Santa María, 27
09311 Olmedillo de Roa (Burgos)
☎: +34 947 551 310 - Fax: +34 947 551 309
info@pagosdematanegra.es
www.pagosdematanegra.es

MATANEGRA VENDIMIA SELECCIONADA MM 2009 T
100% tempranillo.

93 Colour: cherry, garnet rim. Nose: red berry notes, ripe fruit, elegant, cocoa bean, dark chocolate, toasty. Palate: balanced, powerful, flavourful, long, toasty.

MATANEGRA VENDIMIA SELECCIONADA 2009 T
tempranillo.

91 Colour: cherry, garnet rim. Nose: ripe fruit, creamy oak, roasted coffee. Palate: flavourful, toasty, long, balanced.

MATANEGRA 2009 TC
100% tempranillo.

90 Colour: bright cherry. Nose: ripe fruit, sweet spices, roasted coffee, dark chocolate. Palate: flavourful, fruity, toasty.

PAGOS DEL REY

Ctra. Palencia-Aranda, Km. 53
09311 Olmedillo de Roa (Burgos)
☎: +34 947 551 111 - Fax: +34 947 551 311
pdr@pagosdelrey.com
www.pagosdelrey.com

LA ÚNICA AUTOR S/C T
100% tempranillo.

92 Colour: bright cherry, garnet rim. Nose: elegant, expressive, cocoa bean, sweet spices. Palate: good structure, good acidity, ripe fruit, long.

CONDADO DE ORIZA 2011 T ROBLE
100% tempranillo.

88 Colour: bright cherry. Nose: ripe fruit, sweet spices, creamy oak, aged wood nuances. Palate: flavourful, fruity, toasty, harsh oak tannins.

ALTOS DE TAMARÓN FUEGO Y HIELO 2011 T JOVEN
100% tempranillo.

88 Colour: cherry, purple rim. Nose: expressive, fresh fruit, red berry notes, floral, lactic notes. Palate: flavourful, fruity, good acidity, easy to drink.

CONDADO DE ORIZA 2011 T
100% tempranillo.

86 Colour: cherry, purple rim. Nose: fresh fruit, red berry notes, floral, balsamic herbs. Palate: flavourful, fruity, easy to drink.

ALTOS DE TAMARÓN 2011 T ROBLE
100% tempranillo.

85 Colour: cherry, garnet rim. Nose: ripe fruit, toasty, sweet spices. Palate: powerful, flavourful, toasty.

CONDADO DE ORIZA 2010 TC
100% tempranillo.

90 Colour: bright cherry. Nose: ripe fruit, sweet spices, creamy oak, dark chocolate. Palate: flavourful, fruity, toasty.

ALTOS DE TAMARÓN 2010 TC
100% tempranillo.

86 Colour: cherry, garnet rim. Nose: ripe fruit, spicy, creamy oak, medium intensity. Palate: powerful, flavourful, toasty.

CONDADO DE ORIZA 409 2008 T
100% tempranillo.

91 Colour: cherry, garnet rim. Nose: sweet spices, creamy oak, ripe fruit, candied fruit. Palate: powerful, flavourful, fruity, balanced.

ALTOS DE TAMARÓN 2008 TR
100% tempranillo.

88 Colour: cherry, garnet rim. Aroma ripe fruit, spicy, creamy oak, toasty, complex. Palate: powerful, flavourful, toasty, round tannins.

CONDADO DE ORIZA 2008 TR
100% tempranillo.

88 Colour: cherry, garnet rim. Nose: ripe fruit, balsamic herbs, sweet spices, creamy oak. Palate: powerful, flavourful, spicy, toasty.

CONDADO DE ORIZA 2006 TGR
100% tempranillo.

90 Colour: ruby red, garnet rim. Nose: ripe fruit, sweet spices, creamy oak, powerfull, fine reductive notes. Palate: long, spicy, flavourful, fruity.

ALTOS DE TAMARÓN 2006 TGR
100% tempranillo.

88 Colour: pale ruby, brick rim edge. Nose: spicy, fine reductive notes, wet leather, aged wood nuances, fruit liqueur notes. Palate: spicy, fine tannins, long, correct.

PÁRAMO DE GUZMÁN

Ctra. Circunvalación R-30, s/n
09300 Roa (Burgos)
☎: +34 947 541 191 - Fax: +34 947 541 192
paramodeguzman@paramodeguzman.com
www.paramodeguzman.es

RAÍZ 2011 RD
tempranillo.

90 Colour: rose, purple rim. Aroma powerfull, ripe fruit, red berry notes, floral, expressive. Palate: fleshy, powerful, fruity, fresh.

RAÍZ 2011 T ROBLE
100% tempranillo.

90 Colour: bright cherry. Aroma ripe fruit, sweet spices, creamy oak, expressive. Palate: flavourful, fruity, toasty, round tannins.

RAÍZ VINO DE AUTOR 2009 T
tempranillo.

94 Colour: cherry, garnet rim. Nose: ripe fruit, spicy, creamy oak, toasty, complex, mineral, earthy notes. Palate: powerful, flavourful, toasty, round tannins.

RAÍZ 2009 TC
tempranillo.

92 Colour: cherry, garnet rim. Nose: ripe fruit, spicy, creamy oak, toasty, characterful, expressive. Palate: powerful, flavourful, toasty, round tannins.

RAÍZ 2008 TR
tempranillo.

90 Colour: deep cherry, orangey edge. Nose: creamy oak, aromatic coffee, fine reductive notes, fruit liqueur notes. Palate: spicy, ripe fruit, round tannins.

RAÍZ DE GUZMÁN 2007 T
100% tempranillo.

94 Colour: dark-red cherry, garnet rim. Nose: ripe fruit, earthy notes, mineral, aromatic coffee, creamy oak. Palate: powerful, flavourful, spicy, long, balanced, round tannins.

PARÍS TRIMIÑO BODEGA Y VIÑEDOS

Barrio San Roque, s/n
09300 Roa de Duero (Burgos)
☎: +34 947 540 033 - Fax: +34 947 540 033
bodegaparis@bodegaparis.com
www.bodegaparis.com

PARÍS PLUS 2009 TC
100% tempranillo.

86 Colour: cherry, garnet rim. Nose: ripe fruit, fruit preserve, spicy, toasty. Palate: correct, powerful, flavourful.

PEPE LÓPEZ VINOS Y VIÑEDOS

Avda. Soria, 53 - Bajos Buzón 136
47300 Peñafiel (Valladolid)
☎: +34 983 106 207 - Fax: +34 916 048 322
info@arrotos.es
www.arrotos.es

ARROTOS 2010 T
95% tempranillo, 5% cabernet sauvignon.

88 Colour: bright cherry. Nose: sweet spices, creamy oak, ripe fruit. Palate: flavourful, fruity, toasty, round tannins.

PICO CUADRO

Del Río, 22
47350 Quintanilla de Onésimo (Valladolid)
☎: +34 620 547 057
picocuadro@picocuadro.com
www.picocuadro.com

PICO CUADRO ORIGINAL 2009 T
tinto fino.

93 Colour: cherry, garnet rim. Nose: red berry notes, ripe fruit, wild herbs, sweet spices, creamy oak. Palate: balanced, long, powerful, flavourful.

PICO CUADRO VENDIMIA SELECCIONADA 2009 T
tinto fino.

92 Colour: cherry, garnet rim. Nose: red berry notes, ripe fruit, balsamic herbs, spicy, aromatic coffee, mineral. Palate: powerful, flavourful, long, toasty, balanced.

PICO CUADRO WILD 2009 T
tinto fino.

92 Colour: bright cherry. Nose: ripe fruit, sweet spices, creamy oak, expressive, dark chocolate, roasted coffee, new oak. Palate: flavourful, fruity, toasty, balanced.

PICO CUADRO 2009 T
tinto fino.

89 Colour: cherry, garnet rim. Nose: ripe fruit, spicy, toasty, cocoa bean, dark chocolate. Palate: powerful, flavourful, toasty.

PINNA FIDELIS

Camino Llanillos, s/n
47300 Peñafiel (Valladolid)
☎: +34 983 878 034 - Fax: +34 983 878 035
info@pinnafidelis.com
www.pinnafidelis.com

PINNA FIDELIS 2011 T ROBLE
100% tinta del país.

89 Colour: cherry, purple rim. Nose: toasty, ripe fruit, sweet spices, creamy oak. Palate: flavourful, good structure.

PINNA FIDELIS ROBLE ESPAÑOL 2007 T
100% tinta del país.

90 Colour: cherry, garnet rim. Nose: ripe fruit, earthy notes, spicy, medium intensity. Palate: powerful, flavourful, long, toasty.

PINNA FIDELIS 2007 TC
100% tinta del país.

86 Colour: cherry, garnet rim. Nose: ripe fruit, creamy oak, toasty, fine reductive notes. Palate: powerful, flavourful, toasty, correct.

PINNA FIDELIS VENDIMIA SELECCIONADA 2006 T
100% tinta del país.

90 Colour: cherry, garnet rim. Nose: ripe fruit, spicy, creamy oak, toasty. Palate: powerful, flavourful, toasty, fine tannins.

PINNA FIDELIS 2005 TR
100% tinta del país.

88 Colour: cherry, garnet rim. Nose: ripe fruit, spicy, creamy oak, fine reductive notes. Palate: powerful, flavourful, toasty, round tannins.

PINNA FIDELIS 2004 TGR
100% tinta del país.

90 Colour: pale ruby, brick rim edge. Nose: spicy, wet leather, fruit liqueur notes, scrubland. Palate: spicy, fine tannins, long.

PROTOS BODEGAS RIBERA DUERO DE PEÑAFIEL

Bodegas Protos, 24-28
47300 Peñafiel (Valladolid)
☎: +34 983 878 011 - Fax: +34 983 878 012
bodega@bodegasprotos.com
www.bodegasprotos.com

PROTOS 2010 T ROBLE
100% tinta del país.

91 Colour: bright cherry. Nose: sweet spices, creamy oak, ripe fruit. Palate: flavourful, fruity, toasty, round tannins.

PROTOS 2010 TC
100% tinta del país.

91 Colour: cherry, garnet rim. Nose: ripe fruit, spicy, toasty, characterful, new oak. Palate: powerful, flavourful, toasty, round tannins.

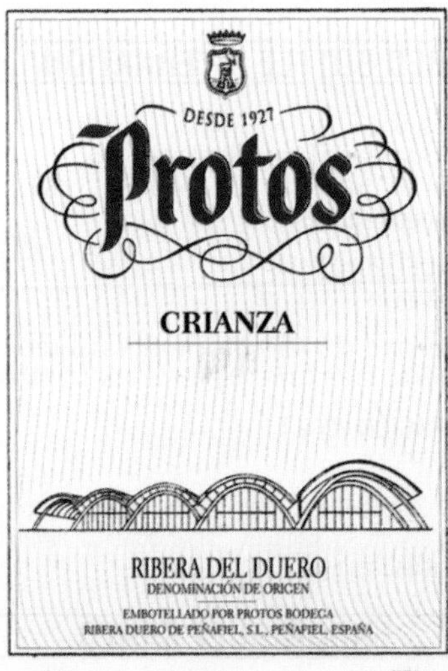

PROTOS SELECCIÓN FINCA EL GRAJO VIEJO 2009 T
100% tinta del país.

95 Colour: very deep cherry. Nose: mineral, varietal, powerfull, characterful, ripe fruit, sweet spices, dark chocolate, creamy oak. Palate: flavourful, powerful, concentrated, good acidity, fine bitter notes.

PROTOS 2006 TR
100% tinto fino.

92 Colour: very deep cherry. Nose: powerfull, elegant, ripe fruit, toasty, sweet spices. Palate: flavourful, good acidity, fine bitter notes.

PROTOS 2005 TGR
100% tinto fino.

91 Colour: deep cherry, garnet rim. Nose: powerfull, characterful, complex, ripe fruit, creamy oak, toasty. Palate: flavourful, powerful, good acidity, fine bitter notes.

QUINTA MILÚ

Camino El Val, s/n
La Aguilera (Burgos)
☎: +34 661 328 504
info@quintamilu.com
www.quintamilu.com

MILÚ 2011 T
tempranillo.

88 Colour: very deep cherry, purple rim. Nose: balanced, ripe fruit, medium intensity. Palate: correct, ripe fruit.

QUINTA MILÚ LA COMETA 2010 TC
tempranillo.

89 Colour: deep cherry, purple rim. Nose: balsamic herbs, earthy notes, spicy, ripe fruit. Palate: balanced, flavourful, powerful.

QUINTA MILÚ EL MALO 2009 TC
tinta del país.

90 Colour: cherry, garnet rim. Nose: spicy, creamy oak, toasty, complex, fragrant herbs, red berry notes. Palate: powerful, flavourful, toasty, round tannins.

REAL SITIO DE VENTOSILLA

Ctra. CL-619 (Magaz Aranda) Km. 66,1
09443 Gumiel del Mercado (Burgos)
☎: +34 947 546 900 - Fax: +34 947 546 999
bodega@pradorey.com
www.pradorey.com

PRADOREY 2011 RD FERMENTADO EN BARRICA
50% merlot, 50% tinto fino.

89 Colour: rose. Nose: balanced, red berry notes, ripe fruit, toasty, creamy oak. Palate: fruity, flavourful, full.

PRADOREY ÉLITE 2010 T
100% tinto fino.

95 Colour: cherry, garnet rim. Nose: ripe fruit, spicy, creamy oak, toasty, complex, varietal, expressive, mineral. Palate: powerful, flavourful, toasty, round tannins.

ADARO DE PRADOREY 2010 TC
100% tempranillo.

93 Colour: cherry, garnet rim. Nose: ripe fruit, creamy oak, toasty, complex, expressive, mineral. Palate: powerful, flavourful, toasty, round tannins.

PRADOREY 2010 T ROBLE
95% tinto fino, 3% cabernet sauvignon, 2% merlot.

86 Colour: bright cherry. Nose: ripe fruit, sweet spices, medium intensity. Palate: fruity, round tannins, easy to drink.

PRADOREY 2009 TC
95% tinto fino, 3% cabernet sauvignon, 2% merlot.

90 Colour: cherry, garnet rim. Nose: medium intensity, balanced, spicy, ripe fruit. Palate: good structure, good acidity, round tannins.

PRADOREY 2006 TR
95% tinto fino, 3% cabernet sauvignon, 2% merlot.

89 Colour: cherry, garnet rim. Nose: ripe fruit, spicy, creamy oak, fine reductive notes. Palate: powerful, flavourful, toasty, round tannins.

PRADOREY ÉLITE 2009 T
100% tinto fino.

94 Colour: cherry, garnet rim. Nose: spicy, creamy oak, toasty, complex, fruit expression, characterful. Palate: powerful, flavourful, toasty, round tannins.

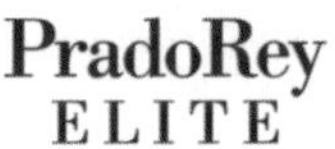

PRADOREY 2004 TGR
95% tinto fino, 3% cabernet sauvignon, 2% merlot.

92 Colour: cherry, garnet rim. Nose: balanced, expressive, ripe fruit, dark chocolate, sweet spices. Palate: good structure, flavourful, round tannins.

RED BOTTLE INTERNATIONAL

Rosales, 6
09400 Aranda de Duero (Burgos)
☎: +34 947 515 884 - Fax: +34 947 515 886
rbi@redbottleint.com

RIVENDEL 2010 T
100% tempranillo.

88 Colour: bright cherry. Nose: sweet spices, creamy oak, varietal. Palate: flavourful, fruity, toasty, round tannins.

ADMIRACIÓN 2009 T
100% tempranillo.

90 Colour: cherry, garnet rim. Aroma ripe fruit, spicy, creamy oak, toasty, complex. Palate: powerful, flavourful, toasty, round tannins.

RODRÍGUEZ SANZO

Manuel Azaña, 9
47014 (Valladolid)
☎: +34 983 150 150 - Fax: +34 983 150 151
comunicacion@valsanzo.com
www.rodriguezsanzo.com

VALL SANZO 2009 TC
tempranillo.

91 Colour: very deep cherry. Nose: characterful, ripe fruit, dark chocolate, sweet spices, creamy oak. Palate: ripe fruit, spicy, round tannins.

VALL SANZO 2009 T ROBLE
100% tempranillo.

88 Colour: cherry, garnet rim. Nose: ripe fruit, overripe fruit, dark chocolate, toasty. Palate: powerful, flavourful, toasty, ripe fruit.

RUDELES

Trasterrera, 10
42345 Peñalba de San Esteban (Soria)
☎: +34 618 644 633 - Fax: +34 975 350 582
jmartin@rudeles.com
www.rudeles.com

RUDELES "23" 2009 T
95% tempranillo, 5% garnacha.

92 Colour: cherry, garnet rim. Nose: ripe fruit, balsamic herbs, aromatic coffee, sweet spices, toasty, mineral. Palate: powerful, flavourful, toasty, balanced.

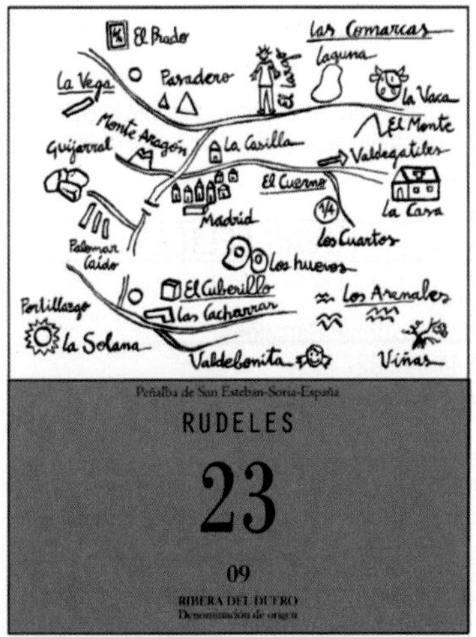

RUDELES CERRO EL CUBERILLO 2009 T
100% tempranillo.

90 Colour: cherry, garnet rim. Nose: spicy, creamy oak, balanced, dark chocolate. Palate: flavourful, full, fine bitter notes.

RUDELES SELECCIÓN 2006 T
97% tempranillo, 3% garnacha.

90 Colour: cherry, garnet rim. Nose: ripe fruit, spicy, creamy oak, toasty, complex, sweet spices, varnish. Palate: powerful, flavourful, toasty, round tannins.

SÁNCHEZ ROMATE

Lealas, 26
11404 Jerez de la Frontera (Cádiz)
☎: +34 956 182 212 - Fax: +34 956 185 276
comercial@romate.com
www.romate.com

MOMO 2008 T
85% tempranillo, 12% cabernet sauvignon, 3% merlot.

87 Colour: light cherry, garnet rim. Nose: ripe fruit, fruit liqueur notes, fine reductive notes, spicy, toasty. Palate: flavourful, long, toasty.

SELECCIÓN CÉSAR MUÑOZ

Acera de Recoletos, 14
47004 (Valladolid)
☎: +34 666 548 751
info@cesarmunoz.es
www.cesarmunoz.es

MAGALLANES 2009 TC
tempranillo.

90 Colour: cherry, garnet rim. Nose: ripe fruit, warm, powerfull, closed. Palate: flavourful, powerful, good structure, round tannins.

SELECCIÓN TORRES

Del Rosario, 56
47311 Fompedraza (Valladolid)
☎: +34 938 177 400 - Fax: +34 938 177 444
mailadmin@torres.es
www.torres.es

CELESTE 2011 T ROBLE
100% tinto fino.

88 Colour: bright cherry. Nose: sweet spices, creamy oak, ripe fruit. Palate: flavourful, fruity, toasty, round tannins.

CELESTE 2009 TC
100% tinto fino.

90 Colour: cherry, garnet rim. Nose: ripe fruit, dark chocolate, sweet spices, creamy oak. Palate: powerful, flavourful, long, toasty.

TERROIR 34

Castellote 26
Aranda de Duero (Burgos)
☎: +34 606 941 434
info@terroir34.com
www.terroir34.com

TERROIR 34 "DREAMS FROM LIMESTONE" 2009 T
100% tinto fino.

88 Colour: deep cherry. Nose: medium intensity, ripe fruit, red berry notes, sweet spices. Palate: flavourful, fruity, fresh, good acidity.

TOMÁS POSTIGO

Estación, 12
47300 Peñafiel (Valladolid)
☎: +34 983 873 019 - Fax: +34 983 880 258
administracion@tomaspostigo.es

TOMÁS POSTIGO 2009 TC
85% tinto fino, 10% cabernet sauvignon, 5% merlot.

93 Colour: cherry, garnet rim. Nose: red berry notes, sweet spices, toasty, balanced, expressive. Palate: powerful, flavourful, spicy, complex, elegant.

TORRES DE ANGUIX

Camino La Tejera, s/n
09312 Anguix (Burgos)
☎: +34 947 554 008 - Fax: +34 947 554 129
enologia@torresdeanguix.com
www.torresdeanguix.com

R D'ANGUIX 2011 RD
tinta del país.

88 Colour: light cherry, bright. Nose: balanced, red berry notes. Palate: fruity, flavourful.

T D'ANGUIX 2010 T ROBLE
tinta del país.

85 Colour: deep cherry, garnet rim. Nose: medium intensity, ripe fruit, spicy. Palate: flavourful, balanced.

GALLERY 101 BARRICA 2010 T ROBLE
tinta del país.

85 Colour: bright cherry. Nose: ripe fruit, fruit liqueur notes, spicy, toasty. Palate: flavourful, fruity, spicy.

GALLERY 101 2009 TC
tinta del país.

89 Colour: bright cherry. Nose: ripe fruit, spicy, creamy oak. Palate: powerful, flavourful, toasty, round tannins.

T D'ANGUIX 2007 TC
tinta del país.

87 Colour: cherry, garnet rim. Nose: sweet spices, old leather, toasty. Palate: ripe fruit, good finish.

T D'ANGUIX 2006 T
tinta del país.

88 Colour: cherry, garnet rim. Nose: ripe fruit, spicy, toasty. Palate: flavourful, fine bitter notes, spicy, ripe fruit.

T D'ANGUIX 2004 TR
tinta del país.

90 Colour: cherry, garnet rim. Nose: creamy oak, toasty. Palate: powerful, flavourful, toasty, round tannins.

T D'ANGUIX 2001 TGR
tinta del país.

87 Colour: bright cherry. Nose: medium intensity, old leather, ripe fruit. Palate: spicy, ripe fruit, fine bitter notes, good acidity.

UVAS FELICES

Agullers, 7
08003 Barcelona (Barcelona)
☎: +34 902 327 777
www.vilaviniteca.es

VENTA LAS VACAS 2010 T
tempranillo.

91 Colour: bright cherry. Aroma ripe fruit, sweet spices, creamy oak, expressive. Palate: flavourful, fruity, toasty, round tannins.

VALTRAVIESO

Finca La Revilla, s/n
47316 Piñel de Arriba (Valladolid)
☎: +34 983 484 030 - Fax: +34 983 484 037
valtravieso@valtravieso.com
www.valtravieso.com

VALTRAVIESO 2011 T
90% tinto fino, 5% cabernet sauvignon, 5% merlot.

86 Colour: cherry, purple rim. Nose: balanced, overripe fruit. Palate: good structure, flavourful.

VALTRAVIESO VT VENDIMIA SELECCIONADA 2009 T
75% tinto fino, 15% cabernet sauvignon, 10% merlot.

90 Colour: cherry, garnet rim. Nose: ripe fruit, spicy, creamy oak, toasty, characterful. Palate: powerful, flavourful, toasty, round tannins.

VALTRAVIESO VT TINTA FINA 2009 T
100% tinto fino.

88 Colour: cherry, garnet rim. Nose: ripe fruit, spicy, creamy oak, toasty, characterful. Palate: powerful, flavourful, toasty, round tannins.

VALTRAVIESO 2008 TC
90% tinto fino, 5% cabernet sauvignon, 5% merlot.

87 Colour: cherry, garnet rim. Nose: powerfull, ripe fruit, sweet spices. Palate: flavourful, fine bitter notes, ripe fruit.

GRAN VALTRAVIESO 2006 TR
100% tinto fino.

93 Colour: cherry, garnet rim. Nose: ripe fruit, spicy, creamy oak, toasty, characterful, dark chocolate. Palate: powerful, flavourful, toasty, round tannins.

VEGA CLARA

Ctra. N-122 Km 328 (Entrada por c/Estación)
47350 Quintanilla De Onesimo (Valladolid)
☎: +34 677 570 779 - Fax: +34 983 361 005
vegaclara@vegaclara.com
www.vegaclara.com

MARIO VC 2009 T
tempranillo, cabernet sauvignon.

90 Colour: cherry, garnet rim. Nose: spicy, creamy oak, toasty, ripe fruit. Palate: powerful, flavourful, toasty, round tannins.

VELVETY WINES

Ctra. Peñafiel (Valoria), s/n
47315 Pesquera de Duero (Valladolid)
www.velvetywines.com

VELVETY 2011 T
100% tempranillo.

87 Colour: bright cherry. Nose: ripe fruit, sweet spices, creamy oak, roasted coffee. Palate: flavourful, fruity, long.

VINNICO EXPORT

Muela, 16
03730 Jávea (Alicante)
☎: +34 965 791 967 - Fax: +34 966 461 471
info@vinnico.com
www.vinnico.com

AVENTINO 200 BARRELS 2009 T
100% tinta del país.

91 Colour: cherry, garnet rim. Nose: spicy, creamy oak, toasty, ripe fruit. Palate: powerful, flavourful, toasty, round tannins.

VINOS HERCAL

Santo Domingo, 2
09300 Roa (Burgos)
☎: +34 947 541 281
ventas@somanilla.es
www.somanilla.es

BOCCA 2011 RD
albilla, tempranillo.

83

BOCCA 2009 T ROBLE
tempranillo.

90 Colour: cherry, garnet rim. Nose: spicy, creamy oak, toasty, ripe fruit. Palate: powerful, flavourful, toasty, round tannins.

SOMANILLA 2008 TC
tinto fino.

90 Colour: bright cherry. Nose: ripe fruit, sweet spices, creamy oak. Palate: flavourful, fruity, toasty, round tannins.

VINOS SANTOS ARRANZ (LÁGRIMA NEGRA)

Ctra. de Valbuena, s/n
47315 Pesquera de Duero (Valladolid)
☎: +34 983 870 008 - Fax: +34 983 870 008
lagrimanegra82@hotmail.com
www.lagrima-negra.com

LÁGRIMA NEGRA 2010 T ROBLE
95% tempranillo, 5% cabernet sauvignon.

87 Colour: cherry, garnet rim. Nose: dried herbs, macerated fruit, spicy. Palate: flavourful, ripe fruit, good finish.

LÁGRIMA NEGRA 2009 TC
95% tempranillo, 5% cabernet sauvignon.

87 Colour: cherry, garnet rim. Nose: powerfull, creamy oak, dark chocolate, ripe fruit. Palate: flavourful, balanced, good acidity.

LÁGRIMA NEGRA 2004 TR
95% tempranillo, 5% cabernet sauvignon.

88 Colour: cherry, garnet rim. Nose: ripe fruit, creamy oak. Palate: powerful, flavourful, toasty, round tannins.

VIÑA ARNAIZ

Ctra. N-122, km. 281
09463 Haza (Burgos)
☎: +34 947 536 227 - Fax: +34 947 536 216
www.vinosdefamilia.com

MAYOR DE CASTILLA 2011 RD
100% tempranillo.

86 Colour: rose, purple rim. Nose: floral, ripe fruit, red berry notes. Palate: ripe fruit, easy to drink.

CASTILLO DE AZA 2011 T
100% tempranillo.

88 Colour: cherry, purple rim. Nose: expressive, fresh fruit, red berry notes, floral, lactic notes. Palate: flavourful, fruity, good acidity.

MAYOR DE CASTILLA 2011 T
100% tempranillo.

85 Colour: bright cherry, purple rim. Nose: balanced, red berry notes. Palate: correct, flavourful, good finish.

CASTILLO DE AZA 2010 T ROBLE
100% tempranillo.

87 Colour: cherry, garnet rim. Nose: ripe fruit, sweet spices, creamy oak. Palate: powerful, flavourful, correct, toasty.

MAYOR DE CASTILLA 2010 T ROBLE
100% tempranillo.

83

VIÑA ARNÁIZ 2009 T ROBLE
95% tempranillo, 3% cabernet sauvignon, 2% merlot.

87 Colour: bright cherry. Nose: ripe fruit, sweet spices, creamy oak. Palate: flavourful, fruity, toasty.

VIÑA ARNÁIZ 2008 TC
100% tempranillo.

87 Colour: cherry, garnet rim. Nose: cocoa bean, toasty, ripe fruit. Palate: round tannins, fine bitter notes.

MAYOR DE CASTILLA 2008 TC
100% tempranillo.

86 Colour: cherry, garnet rim. Nose: balanced, ripe fruit, sweet spices. Palate: correct, good finish.

CASTILLO DE AZA 2008 TC
100% tempranillo.

84

VIÑA ARNÁIZ 2007 TR
85% tempranillo, 10% cabernet sauvignon, 5% merlot.

90 Colour: bright cherry. Nose: ripe fruit, sweet spices, creamy oak, expressive, red berry notes. Palate: flavourful, fruity, toasty, round tannins.

CASTILLO DE AZA 2007 TR
100% tempranillo.

88 Colour: cherry, garnet rim. Nose: ripe fruit, powerfull, neat, creamy oak. Palate: flavourful, balanced.

MAYOR DE CASTILLA 2007 TR
100% tempranillo.

86 Colour: cherry, garnet rim. Nose: ripe fruit, sweet spices. Palate: fruity, easy to drink.

VIÑA MAMBRILLA

Ctra. Pedrosa s/n
09317 Mambrilla de Castrejón (Burgos)
☎: +34 947 540 234 - Fax: +34 947 540 234
bodega@mambrilla.com
www.mambrilla.com

ALIDIS 2011 T
100% tempranillo.

87 Colour: cherry, purple rim. Nose: fresh fruit, red berry notes, balsamic herbs. Palate: flavourful, fruity, correct, easy to drink.

ALIDIS 6 MESES BARRICA 2010 T
100% tempranillo.

89 Colour: bright cherry. Aroma ripe fruit, sweet spices, creamy oak, expressive. Palate: flavourful, fruity, toasty, round tannins.

ALIDIS EXPRESIÓN 2009 T
100% tempranillo.

93 Colour: cherry, garnet rim. Nose: red berry notes, mineral, expressive, sweet spices, creamy oak. Palate: powerful, flavourful, balanced, long, elegant.

ALIDIS CRIANZA 2009 TC
100% tempranillo.

88 Colour: cherry, garnet rim. Nose: ripe fruit, spicy, creamy oak, toasty. Palate: powerful, flavourful, toasty, spicy.

ALIDIS RESERVA 2008 TR
100% tempranillo.

90 Colour: cherry, garnet rim. Aroma ripe fruit, spicy, creamy oak, toasty, complex. Palate: powerful, flavourful, toasty, round tannins.

ALIDIS GRAN RESERVA 2006 TGR
100% tempranillo.

92 Colour: pale ruby, brick rim edge. Nose: spicy, fine reductive notes, dark chocolate, ripe fruit. Palate: spicy, elegant, long, balanced.

VIÑA SOLORCA

Ctra. Circunvalación, s/n
09300 Roa (Burgos)
☎: +34 947 541 823 - Fax: +34 947 540 035
info@bodegassolorca.com
www.bodegassolorca.com

ZARÚS 2010 T BARRICA
100% tempranillo.

85 Colour: deep cherry. Nose: candied fruit, toasty, spicy. Palate: powerful, fine bitter notes, good acidity.

VIÑA SOLORCA 2008 TC
100% tempranillo.

87 Colour: cherry, garnet rim. Nose: ripe fruit, dark chocolate, sweet spices. Palate: flavourful, good structure.

GRAN SOLORCA 2006 TR
100% tempranillo.

91 Colour: cherry, garnet rim. Aroma ripe fruit, spicy, creamy oak, toasty, complex. Palate: powerful, flavourful, toasty, round tannins.

VIÑA VALDEMAZÓN

Pza. Sur, 3
47359 Olivares de Duero (Valladolid)
☎: +34 983 680 220
info@valdemazon.com
www.valdemazon.com

VIÑA VALDEMAZÓN VENDIMIA SELECCIONADA 2009 T
100% tempranillo.

90 Colour: cherry, garnet rim. Aroma ripe fruit, spicy, creamy oak, toasty, complex. Palate: powerful, flavourful, toasty, round tannins.

VIÑEDOS ALONSO DEL YERRO

Finca Santa Marta - Ctra. Roa-Anguix, Km. 1,8
09300 Roa (Burgos)
☎: +34 913 160 121 - Fax: +34 913 160 121
mariadelyerro@vay.es
www.alonsodelyerro.com

"MARÍA" ALONSO DEL YERRO 2009 T
100% tempranillo.

95 Colour: cherry, garnet rim. Nose: spicy, creamy oak, toasty, complex, mineral, ripe fruit. Palate: powerful, flavourful, toasty, round tannins.

ALONSO DEL YERRO 2009 T
100% tempranillo.

94 Colour: cherry, garnet rim. Nose: ripe fruit, spicy, creamy oak, toasty, characterful, expressive. Palate: powerful, flavourful, toasty, round tannins.

VIÑEDOS SINGULARES

Cuzco, 26 - 28, Nave 8
08030 (Barcelona)
☎: +34 609 168 191 - Fax: +34 934 807 076
info@vinedossingulares.com
www.vinedossingulares.com

ENTRELOBOS 2010 T
tinto fino.

89 Colour: cherry, purple rim. Nose: red berry notes, ripe fruit, spicy, toasty. Palate: powerful, flavourful, long, spicy.

VIÑEDOS Y BODEGAS ÁSTER

Ctra. Aranda-Palencia-, Término El Caño
09312 Anguix (Burgos)
☎: +34 947 522 700 - Fax: +34 947 522 701
aster@riojalta.com
www.riojalta.com

ÁSTER FINCA EL OTERO 2010 T FERMENTADO EN BARRICA
100% tinta del país.

94 Colour: very deep cherry. Nose: mineral, characterful, elegant, floral, fruit expression, creamy oak, sweet spices. Palate: flavourful, complex, good acidity, round.

ÁSTER 2008 TC
100% tinta del país.

89 Colour: cherry, garnet rim. Nose: spicy, creamy oak, toasty, ripe fruit. Palate: flavourful, toasty, round tannins.

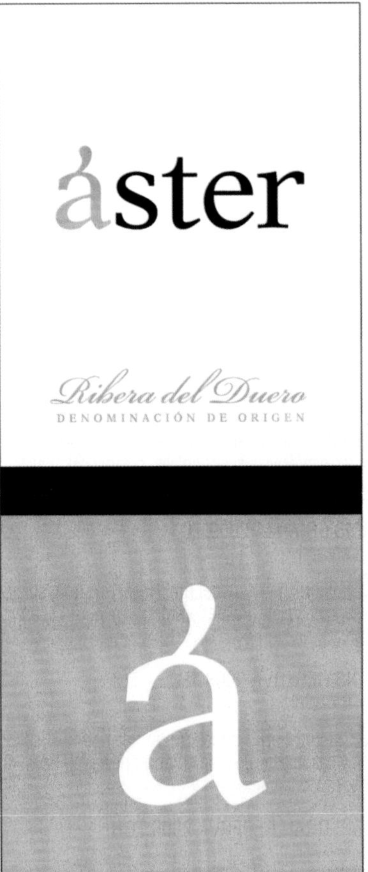

VIÑEDOS Y BODEGAS GARCÍA FIGUERO

Ctra. La Horra - Roa, Km. 2,2
09311 La Horra (Burgos)
☎: +34 947 542 127 - Fax: +34 947 542 033
bodega@tintofiguero.com
www.tintofiguero.com

FIGUERO TINUS 2009 T
100% tempranillo.

93 Colour: cherry, garnet rim. Nose: ripe fruit, fruit preserve, cocoa bean, dark chocolate, sweet spices, creamy oak. Palate: flavourful, fruity, long, good acidity, fine tannins, elegant.

TINTO FIGUERO 12 MESES BARRICA 2009 TC
100% tempranillo.

89 Colour: cherry, garnet rim. Nose: ripe fruit, spicy, toasty, balsamic herbs, mineral. Palate: powerful, flavourful, toasty, fine bitter notes, balanced.

TINTO FIGUERO 15 MESES BARRICA 2008 TR
100% tempranillo.

90 Colour: cherry, garnet rim. Nose: ripe fruit, spicy, aged wood nuances, fine reductive notes, earthy notes. Palate: powerful, flavourful, toasty, round tannins, balanced.

VIÑEDOS Y BODEGAS GORMAZ

Ctra. de Soria, s/n
42330 San Esteban de Gormaz (Soria)
☎: +34 975 350 404 - Fax: +34 975 351 313
info@hispanobodegas.com
www.hispanobodegas.com

CATANIA 2011 T
tempranillo.

88 Colour: cherry, purple rim. Nose: red berry notes, floral, fresh, balsamic herbs. Palate: flavourful, fruity, good acidity, round tannins.

12 LINAJES 2010 T ROBLE
tempranillo.

87 Colour: bright cherry. Aroma ripe fruit, sweet spices, creamy oak, expressive. Palate: flavourful, fruity, toasty, round tannins.

VIÑA GORMAZ 2009 TC
tempranillo.

89 Colour: cherry, garnet rim. Nose: balanced, medium intensity, ripe fruit. Palate: flavourful, fruity.

VIÑA GORMAZ 2011 T
tempranillo.

88 Colour: cherry, purple rim. Nose: medium intensity, varietal, red berry notes, ripe fruit. Palate: flavourful, fruity, good finish.

ANIER VENDIMIA SELECCIONADA 2010 T
tempranillo.

93 Colour: cherry, garnet rim. Nose: spicy, creamy oak, toasty, complex, fruit expression, red berry notes, mineral, varietal. Palate: powerful, flavourful, toasty, round tannins.

12 LINAJES 2009 TC
tempranillo.

88 Colour: cherry, garnet rim. Nose: ripe fruit, spicy, toasty. Palate: powerful, flavourful, toasty, correct.

CATANIA 2009 TC
tempranillo.

88 Colour: cherry, garnet rim. Nose: ripe fruit, spicy, toasty. Palate: powerful, flavourful, toasty, balsamic.

12 LINAJES 2007 TR
tempranillo.

90 Colour: bright cherry. Nose: ripe fruit, spicy, creamy oak, toasty, expressive. Palate: powerful, flavourful, toasty, round tannins.

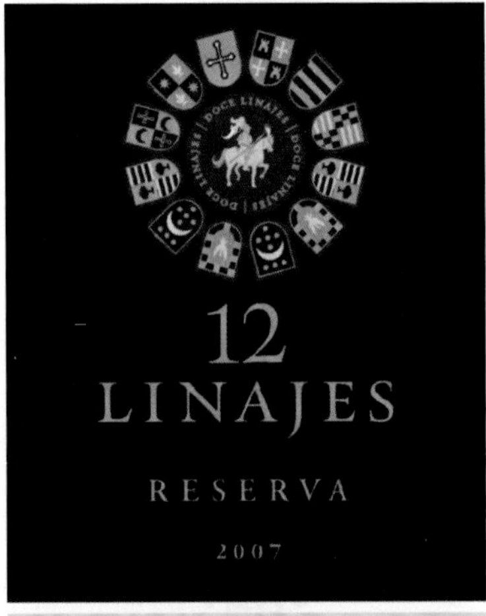

VIÑEDOS Y BODEGAS RIBÓN

Basilón, 15
47350 Quintanilla de Onésimo (Valladolid)
☎: +34 983 680 015 - Fax: +34 983 680 015
info@bodegasribon.com
www.bodegasribon.com

TINTO RIBÓN 2009 TC
100% tempranillo.

90 Colour: cherry, garnet rim. Nose: spicy, creamy oak, toasty, varietal. Palate: powerful, flavourful, toasty, round tannins.

WINNER WINES

Avda. del Mediterráneo, 38
28007 Madrid (Madrid)
☎: +34 915 019 042 - Fax: +34 915 017 794
winnerwines@ibernoble.com
www.ibernoble.com

IBERNOBLE 2011 T

85 Colour: cherry, purple rim. Nose: ripe fruit, red berry notes, sweet spices. Palate: flavourful, powerful, ripe fruit.

IBERNOBLE 2010 T ROBLE

86 Colour: deep cherry. Nose: ripe fruit, sweet spices, toasty. Palate: ripe fruit, spicy.

IBERNOBLE 2008 TC

88 Colour: cherry, garnet rim. Nose: ripe fruit, toasty, varietal, sweet spices. Palate: powerful, flavourful, toasty, round tannins.

IBERNOBLE 2006 TR
tinta del país.

88 Colour: cherry, garnet rim. Nose: toasty, sweet spices, aromatic coffee. Palate: flavourful, powerful, concentrated.

DO RIBERA DEL GUADIANA

LOCATION:

Covering the 6 wine-growing regions of Extremadura, with a total surface of more than 87,000 Ha as described below.

GRAPE VARIETIES:

WHITE: *Alarije, Borba, Cayetana Blanca, Pardina, Macabeo, Chardonnay, Chelva or Montua, Malvar, Parellada, Pedro Ximénez, Verdejo, Eva, Cigüente, Perruno, Moscatel de Alejandría, Moscatel de Grano Menudo, Sauvignon Blanc* and *Bobal Blanca.*
RED: *Garnacha Tinta, Tempranillo, Bobal, Cabernet Sauvignon, Garnacha Tintorera, Graciano, Mazuela, Merlot, Monastrell, Syrah, Pinot Noir* and *Jaén Tinto.*

SUB-REGIONS:

Cañamero. To the south east of the province of Cáceres, in the heart of the Sierra de Guadalupe. It comprises the municipal districts of Alia, Berzocana, Cañamero, Guadalupe and Valdecaballeros. The vineyards are located on the mountainside, at altitudes of between 600 m to 800 m. The terrain is rugged and the soil is slaty and loose. The climate is mild without great temperature contrasts, and the average annual rainfall is 750 mm to 800 mm. The main grape variety is the white *Alarije.*

Montánchez. Comprising 27 municipal districts. It is characterised by its complex terrain, with numerous hills and small valleys. The vineyards are located on brown acidic soil. The climate is Continental in nature and the average annual rainfall is between 500 mm and 600 mm. The white grape variety *Borba* occupies two thirds of the vineyards in the region.
Ribera Alta. This covers the Vegas del Guadiana and the plains of La Serena and Campo de Castuera and comprises 38 municipal districts. The soil is very sandy. The most common varieties are *Alarije*, *Borba* (white), *Tempranillo* and *Garnacha* (red).
Ribera Baja. Comprising 11 municipal districts. The vineyards are located on clayey-limy soil. The climate is Continental, with a moderate Atlantic influence and slight contrasts in temperature. The most common varieties are: *Cayetana Blanca* and *Pardina* among the whites, and *Tempranillo* among the reds.
Matanegra. Rather similar to Tierra de Barros, but with a milder climate. It comprises 8 municipal districts, and the most common grape varieties are *Beba*, *Montua* (whites), *Tempranillo*, *Garnacha* and *Cabernet Sauvignon* (reds).
Tierra de Barros. Situated in the centre of the province of Badajoz and the largest (4475 Ha and 37 municipal districts). It has flat plains with fertile soils which are rich in nutrients and have great water retention capacity (Rainfall is low: 350 mm to 450 mm per year). The most common varieties are the white *Cayetana Blanca* and *Pardina*, and the red *Tempranillo*, *Garnacha* and *Cabernet Sauvignon.*

CONSEJO REGULADOR
Ctra. Sevilla-Gijón - ☎: +34 924 671 302 - Fax: +34 924 664 703
@ informacion@riberadelguadiana.org - www.riberadelguadiana.eu

FIGURES:

Vineyard surface: 30,392 – **Wine-Growers:** 2,826 – **Wineries:** 22 – **2011 Harvest rating:** N/A – **Production:** 8,615,116 litres – **Market percentages:** --% domestic. --% export

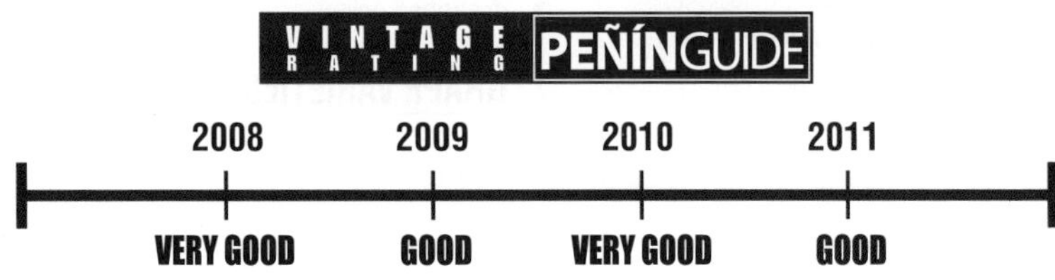

BODEGA SAN MARCOS

Ctra. Aceuchal, s/n
06200 Almendralejo (Badajoz)
☎: +34 924 670 410 - Fax: +34 924 665 505
ventas@bodegasanmarcos.com
www.campobarro.com

CAMPOBARRO MACABEO 2011 B
100% macabeo.

83

CAMPOBARRO 2011 RD
100% tempranillo.

84

CAMPOBARRO TEMPRANILLO 2011 T
100% tempranillo.

85 Colour: deep cherry, purple rim. Nose: powerfull, ripe fruit, balanced. Palate: correct, ripe fruit, flavourful.

CAMPOBARRO SELECCIÓN 2010 T
50% tempranillo, 50% mazuelo.

85 Colour: very deep cherry, purple rim. Nose: ripe fruit, sweet spices, candied fruit, balanced. Palate: flavourful, good structure, full.

HEREDAD DE BARROS 2007 TC
100% tempranillo.

85 Colour: deep cherry, garnet rim. Nose: ripe fruit, medium intensity, warm, spicy. Palate: easy to drink, spicy.

CAMPOBARRO 2007 TC
100% tempranillo.

84

HEREDAD DE BARROS 2005 TR
100% tempranillo.

85 Colour: cherry, garnet rim. Nose: candied fruit, sweet spices, cocoa bean, creamy oak. Palate: fruity, flavourful.

CAMPOBARRO 2004 TR
100% tempranillo.

85 Colour: deep cherry, orangey edge. Nose: candied fruit, sweet spices, cocoa bean. Palate: ripe fruit, flavourful.

BODEGAS CAÑALVA

Coto, 54
10136 Cañamero (Cáceres)
☎: +34 927 369 405 - Fax: +34 927 369 405
info@bodegascanalva.com
www.bodegascañalva.com

FUENTE CORTIJO 2005 TC
100% tempranillo.

87 Colour: cherry, garnet rim. Nose: balanced, sweet spices, cocoa bean, ripe fruit. Palate: fruity, correct, easy to drink.

BODEGAS CASTELAR

Avda. de Extremadura, 1
06228 Hornachos (Badajoz)
☎: +34 924 533 073 - Fax: +34 924 533 493
bodega@bodegascastelar.com
www.bodegascastelar.com

PAGO DE LAS MONJAS 2011 T
tempranillo.

87 Colour: very deep cherry. Nose: expressive, powerfull, ripe fruit, candied fruit. Palate: good structure, fruity, long.

CASTELAR 2008 TC
tempranillo, otras.

85 Colour: cherry, garnet rim. Nose: spicy, creamy oak, candied fruit, cocoa bean. Palate: powerful, flavourful,

BODEGAS MARTÍNEZ PAIVA SAT

Ctra. Gijón - Sevilla N-630, Km. 646
Apdo. Correos 87
06200 Almendralejo (Badajoz)
☎: +34 924 671 130 - Fax: +34 924 663 056
info@payva.es
www.payva.es

PAYVA MOSCATEL 2011 B
moscatel.

87 Colour: bright yellow. Nose: ripe fruit, white flowers, varietal, medium intensity. Palate: flavourful, fruity, balanced, sweetness.

PAYVA MACABEO 2011 B
100% macabeo.

85 Colour: bright yellow. Nose: ripe fruit, balanced, tropical fruit. Palate: flavourful, fruity, easy to drink.

DOÑA FRANCISQUITA 2011 T
100% tempranillo.

85 Colour: cherry, purple rim. Nose: powerfull, balanced, ripe fruit, violets. Palate: flavourful, fruity, easy to drink.

PAYVA 2011 T
100% tempranillo.

85 Colour: deep cherry, purple rim. Nose: powerfull, warm, ripe fruit. Palate: good structure, flavourful, good finish, easy to drink.

PAYVA 2008 TC
80% tempranillo, 10% graciano, 10% cabernet sauvignon.

84

56 BARRICAS 2008 TC
100% tempranillo.

83

PAYVA 2007 TR
90% tempranillo, 10% graciano.

86 Colour: cherry, garnet rim. Nose: dark chocolate, fruit preserve, old leather. Palate: spicy, flavourful, ripe fruit.

BODEGAS MEDINA

Ctra. N-432, Km. 76
06310 Puebla de Sancho Pérez (Badajoz)
☎: +34 924 575 060 - Fax: +34 924 575 076
info@bodegasmedina.net
www.bodegasmedina.net

JALOCO 2010 T ROBLE
100% cabernet sauvignon.

83

BODEGAS ORAN

Hiedra, 21
06200 Almendralejo (Badajoz)
☎: +34 662 952 800
info@bodegasoran.com
www.bodegasoran.com

FLOR DEL SEÑORÍO DE ORÁN 2010 T
tempranillo.

88 Colour: cherry, purple rim. Nose: red berry notes, floral, ripe fruit, medium intensity, balanced. Palate: flavourful, fruity, good acidity, round tannins.

VIÑA ROJA TEMPRANILLO 2010 T
tempranillo.

85 Colour: cherry, garnet rim. Nose: powerfull, ripe fruit, neat. Palate: fruity, flavourful, easy to drink.

SEÑORÍO DE ORÁN 2008 TC
tempranillo.

84

VIÑA ROJA COUPAGE 2005 TC
tempranillo, cabernet sauvignon.

88 Colour: bright cherry, orangey edge. Nose: complex, expressive, sweet spices, cocoa bean, creamy oak. Palate: good structure, ripe fruit.

SEÑORÍO DE ORÁN 2004 TGR
cabernet sauvignon.

88 Colour: very deep cherry, orangey edge. Nose: spicy, fine reductive notes, aged wood nuances, fruit liqueur notes. Palate: spicy, elegant, long.

VIÑA ROJA SELECCIÓN 2004 TR
tempranillo.

85 Colour: cherry, garnet rim. Nose: ripe fruit, spicy, toasty, warm. Palate: powerful, flavourful, toasty, round tannins.

BODEGAS PARADELLS

Finca El Charro, junto a pista canal de Lobón
06187 Guadajira (Badajoz)
☎: +34 924 105 006 - Fax: +34 924 220 016
bodega@bodegasparadells.com
www.bodegasparadells.com

ZAOS 2009 TC
90% tempranillo, 10% cabernet sauvignon.

81

BODEGAS ROMALE

Pol. Ind. Parc. 6, Manz. D
06200 Almendralejo (Badajoz)
☎: +34 924 667 255 - Fax: +34 924 665 877
romale@romale.com
www.romale.com

PRIVILEGIO DE ROMALE 2006 TR
100% tempranillo.

85 Colour: cherry, garnet rim. Nose: ripe fruit, spicy. Palate: correct, flavourful, balanced.

BODEGAS RUIZ TORRES

Ctra. EX 116, km.33,8
10136 Cañamero (Cáceres)
☎: +34 927 369 027 - Fax: +34 927 369 302
info@ruiztorres.com
www.ruiztorres.com

ATTELEA 2010 B
macabeo.

80

ATTELEA 2010 T ROBLE
tempranillo.

83

ATTELEA 2007 TC
tempranillo, cabernet sauvignon.

84

BODEGAS TORIBIO VIÑA PUEBLA

Luis Chamizo, 12-21
06310 Puebla de Sancho Pérez (Badajoz)
☎: +34 924 551 449 - Fax: +34 924 551 449
info@bodegastoribio.com
www.bodegastoribio.com

VIÑA PUEBLA MACABEO 2011 B
macabeo.

85 Colour: bright straw. Nose: fresh, white flowers, expressive, ripe fruit. Palate: flavourful, fruity, good acidity.

VIÑA PUEBLA 2010 BFB
macabeo.

90 Colour: bright yellow. Nose: powerfull, ripe fruit, sweet spices, creamy oak, fragrant herbs. Palate: rich, flavourful, good acidity.

VIÑA PUEBLA TEMPRANILLO 2011 T
tempranillo.

86 Colour: cherry, purple rim. Nose: fresh fruit, red berry notes, floral. Palate: flavourful, fruity, good acidity, round tannins.

VIÑA PUEBLA SELECCIÓN 2010 T
tempranillo, cabernet sauvignon, garnacha, syrah.

86 Colour: cherry, garnet rim. Nose: fruit preserve, scrubland, sweet spices. Palate: flavourful, long, toasty.

MADRE DEL AGUA 2009 TC
70% garnacha tintorera, 10% tempranillo, 10% cabernet sauvignon, 10% garnacha.

93 Colour: deep cherry, garnet rim. Nose: balanced, complex, expressive, ripe fruit, cocoa bean, scrubland. Palate: fruity, powerful.

VIÑA PUEBLA ESENZIA 2008 TC

90 Colour: cherry, garnet rim. Aroma ripe fruit, spicy, creamy oak, toasty, complex. Palate: powerful, flavourful, toasty, round tannins.

VIÑA PUEBLA 2008 TC
tempranillo.

87 Colour: cherry, garnet rim. Nose: ripe fruit, spicy, creamy oak, toasty. Palate: powerful, flavourful, toasty.

BODEGAS VITICULTORES DE BARROS

Ctra. de Badajoz, s/n
06200 Almendralejo (Badajoz)
☎: +34 924 664 852 - Fax: +34 924 664 852
bodegas@vbarros.com
www.viticultoresdebarros.com

EMPERADOR DE BARROS CAYETANA 2011 B
100% cayetana blanca.

86 Colour: bright yellow. Nose: ripe fruit, jasmine, citrus fruit. Palate: flavourful, full, fruity, balanced.

EMPERADOR DE BARROS TEMPRANILLO 2011 T
100% tempranillo.

86 Colour: bright cherry, purple rim. Nose: warm, balanced, candied fruit, ripe fruit. Palate: flavourful, ripe fruit, long.

VIZANA 2009 TC
100% tempranillo.

86 Colour: cherry, garnet rim. Nose: ripe fruit, sweet spices. Palate: powerful, flavourful, toasty, round tannins.

CRASH WINES

Juan de la Cierva
06830 La Zarza (Badajoz)
☎: +34 916 295 841
info@pagolosbalancines.com
www.pagolosbalancines.com

CRASH WHITE 2011 B
eva beba, verdejo, macabeo.

85 Colour: bright straw. Nose: fresh, white flowers, candied fruit. Palate: flavourful, fruity, good acidity, balanced.

CRASH PINK 2011 RD
cabernet sauvignon, garnacha.

86 Colour: brilliant rose. Nose: medium intensity, red berry notes, dried herbs. Palate: fruity, fresh.

CRASH RED 2010 T
tempranillo, syrah, garnacha tintorera, garnacha.

88 Colour: bright cherry. Nose: sweet spices, medium intensity, ripe fruit. Palate: flavourful, fruity, round tannins.

HIJOS DE FRANCISCO ESCASO

Ctra. Villafranca, 15
06360 Fuente del Maestre (Badajoz)
☎: +34 924 530 012 - Fax: +34 924 531 703
franciscoescaso@infonegocio.com

VALLARCAL 2010 B
100% cayetana blanca.

84

VALLARCAL 2010 T ROBLE
100% tempranillo.

86 Colour: deep cherry, garnet rim. Nose: candied fruit, ripe fruit, powerfull. Palate: flavourful, correct, fine bitter notes, sweet tannins.

VALLARCAL 2009 TC
100% tempranillo.

83

VALLARCAL 2007 TR
100% tempranillo.

82

LUIS GURPEGUI MUGA

Avda. Celso Muerza, 8
31560 San Adrián (Navarra)
☎: +34 948 670 050 - Fax: +34 948 670 259
bodegas@gurpegui.es
www.gurpegui.es

GURPEGUI 2011 T
tempranillo, cabernet sauvignon.

87 Colour: deep cherry, cherry, purple rim. Nose: scrubland, ripe fruit, powerfull. Palate: good structure, fruity, flavourful.

CINCO VIÑAS 2011 T
tempranillo, garnacha.

86 Colour: cherry, purple rim. Nose: expressive, red berry notes, floral. Palate: flavourful, fruity, good acidity, round tannins.

MARCELINO DÍAZ

Mecánica, s/n
06200 Almendralejo (Badajoz)
☎: +34 924 677 548 - Fax: +34 924 660 977
bodega@madiaz.com
www.madiaz.com

PUERTA PALMA 2011 B
pardina.

82

PUERTA PALMA 2011 T
tempranillo, cabernet sauvignon, graciano.

84

PAGO LOS BALANCINES

Paraje la Agraria, s/n
06475 Oliva de Mérida (Badajoz)
☎: +34 924 367 399 - Fax: +34 924 367 399
alunado@pagolosbalancines.com
www.pagolosbalancines.com

ALUNADO 2009 BFB
chardonnay.

92 Colour: bright yellow. Nose: ripe fruit, sweet spices, fragrant herbs, cocoa bean. Palate: rich, smoky afterpalate:, flavourful, fresh, good acidity.

LOS BALANCINES FINCA DE MATANEGRA 2009 TC
tempranillo, cabernet sauvignon, garnacha tintorera.

96 Colour: cherry, garnet rim. Nose: spicy, dark chocolate, elegant, expressive, balanced, earthy notes, ripe fruit. Palate: flavourful, ripe fruit, spicy, long, fine tannins.

SALITRE 2009 T
100% garnacha tintorera.

94 Colour: cherry, garnet rim. Nose: ripe fruit, spicy, creamy oak, toasty, complex, characterful, expressive, varietal. Palate: powerful, flavourful, toasty, round tannins.

VASO DE LUZ 2009 TR
cabernet sauvignon.

94 Colour: deep cherry, garnet rim. Nose: red berry notes, ripe fruit, sweet spices, cocoa bean, elegant. Palate: good structure, complex, round tannins, good acidity.

HUNO 2008 T
tempranillo, cabernet sauvignon, merlot, garnacha tintorera.

92 Colour: cherry, garnet rim. Nose: balanced, complex, spicy, dark chocolate, ripe fruit. Palate: long, good structure.

PALACIO QUEMADO

Ctra. Almendralejo - Palomas, km 6,900 - Apdo. 231
06200 Almendralejo (Badajoz)
☎: +34 924 120 082 - Fax: +34 924 120 028
palacioquemado@alvear.es
www.palacioquemado.com

ALANGE TEMPRANILLO 2011 T
tempranillo.

88 Colour: deep cherry, purple rim. Nose: balanced, red berry notes, ripe fruit, scrubland. Palate: flavourful, good structure, ripe fruit.

"PQ" PRIMICIA 2010 T
tempranillo, garnacha, syrah.

89 Colour: deep cherry, purple rim. Nose: ripe fruit, sweet spices, neat. Palate: flavourful, ripe fruit, spicy, fruity aftespalate:.

P.Q. ENSAMBLAJE 2010 T
tempranillo, garnacha.

85 Colour: bright cherry. Nose: ripe fruit, sweet spices. Palate: flavourful, fruity, toasty, round tannins.

PALACIO QUEMADO 2009 TC
tempranillo.

85 Colour: cherry, garnet rim. Nose: ripe fruit, creamy oak, cocoa bean. Palate: powerful, round tannins, correct, easy to drink.

P.Q. 2008 T
syrah, tempranillo.

87 Colour: cherry, garnet rim. Aroma ripe fruit, spicy, creamy oak, toasty, complex. Palate: powerful, flavourful, toasty, round tannins.

PALACIO QUEMADO 2005 TR
tempranillo.

88 Colour: cherry, garnet rim. Nose: ripe fruit, spicy, creamy oak, toasty, complex, dark chocolate. Palate: powerful, flavourful, toasty, round tannins.

SANTA MARTA VIRGEN

Cooperativa, s/n
06150 Santa Marta de los Barros (Badajoz)
☎: +34 924 690 218 - Fax: +34 924 690 043
info@bodegasantamarta.com
www.bodegasantamarta.com

BLASÓN DEL TURRA 2011 B
pardina.

85 Colour: bright straw. Nose: fresh, fresh fruit, white flowers. Palate: flavourful, fruity, good acidity, balanced.

BLASÓN DEL TURRA 2011 T
tempranillo.

84

COMPASS 2010 T
tempranillo.

83

VALDEAURUM 2008 T
tempranillo.

85 Colour: cherry, garnet rim. Nose: ripe fruit, spicy, fragrant herbs. Palate: powerful, flavourful, spicy.

SOCIEDAD COOPERATIVA VIÑAOLIVA

Pol. Ind., Parcela 4-17
06200 Almendralejo (Badajoz)
☎: +34 924 677 321
acoex@bme.es
www.vinaoliva.com

ZALEO MOSCATEL 2011 B
100% moscatel.

83

ZALEO PARDINA 2011 B
100% pardina.

82

ZALEO 2011 RD
100% tempranillo.

84

ZALEO TEMPRANILLO 2011 T
100% tempranillo.

86 Colour: deep cherry, purple rim. Nose: ripe fruit, fruit expression, scrubland, expressive. Palate: good structure, fruity, easy to drink.

ZALEO PREMIUM 2009 T
100% tempranillo.

87 Colour: cherry, garnet rim. Nose: balanced, sweet spices, cocoa bean, ripe fruit. Palate: fruity, flavourful, long.

ZALEO SELECCIÓN 2009 T
100% tempranillo.

85 Colour: cherry, garnet rim. Nose: candied fruit, warm, creamy oak, sweet spices. Palate: fruity, flavourful.

ZALEO SEMIDULCE 2011

84

VIÑEDOS Y BODEGA CARABAL

Ctra. Alía - Castilblanco, Km. 10
10137 Alía (Cáceres)
☎: +34 917 346 152 - Fax: +34 913 720 440
info@carabal.es
www.carabal.es

RASGO 2009 T ROBLE
70% syrah, 30% tempranillo.

87 Colour: bright cherry. Nose: ripe fruit, sweet spices, creamy oak. Palate: flavourful, fruity, toasty, round tannins.

CARABAL 2008 TC
46% cabernet sauvignon, 38% syrah, 10% graciano, 6% tempranillo.

89 Colour: very deep cherry. Nose: ripe fruit, fruit preserve, spicy, powerfull. Palate: good structure,

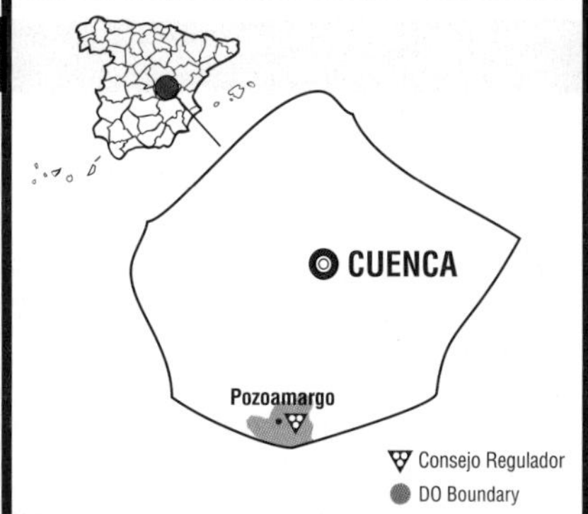

DO RIBERA DEL JÚCAR

LOCATION:

The 7 wine producing municipal districts that make up the DO are located on the banks of the Júcar, in the south of the province of Cuenca. They are: Casas de Benítez, Casas de Guijarro, Casas de Haro, Casas de Fernando Alonso, Pozoamargo, Sisante and El Picazo. The region is at an altitude of between 650 and 750 m above sea level.

CLIMATE:

Continental in nature, dry, and with very cold winters and very hot summers. The main factor contributing to the quality of the wine is the day-night temperature contrasts during the ripening season of the grapes, which causes the process to be carried out slowly.

SOIL:

The most common type of soil consists of pebbles on the surface and a clayey subsoil, which provides good water retention capacity in the deeper levels.

GRAPE VARIETIES:

RED: *Cencibel* or *Tempranillo, Cabernet Sauvignon, Merlot, Syrah*, *Bobal, Cabernet Franc* and *Petit Verdot.*
WHITE: *Moscatel de Grano Menudo* and *Sauvignon Blanc.*

FIGURES:

Vineyard surface: 9,141 – **Wine-Growers:** 970 – **Wineries:** 11 – **2011 Harvest rating:** Very Good – **Production:** 631,507 litres – **Market percentages:** 35% domestic. 65% export

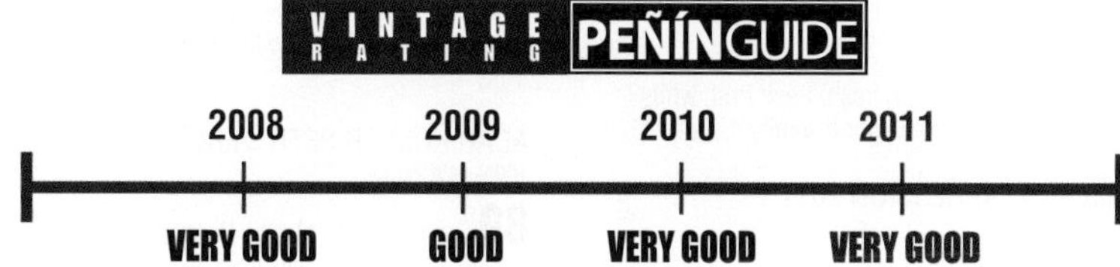

CONSEJO REGULADOR
Pza. del Ayuntamiento, s/n - 16708 Pozoamargo (Cuenca) - ☎: +34 969 387 182 - Fax: +34 969 387 208
@ do@vinosriberadeljucar.com - www.vinosriberadeljucar.com

BODEGA SAN GINÉS

Virgen del Carmen, 6
16707 Casas de Benítez (Cuenca)
☎: +34 969 382 037 - Fax: +34 969 382 998
juancarlos@bodegasangines.es
www.cincoalmudes.es

5 ALMUDES TEMPRANILLO 2011 T
tempranillo.

86 Colour: deep cherry. Nose: powerfull, varietal, warm. Palate: flavourful, powerful, good acidity.

LAS ERAS TRADICIÓN 2009 T
bobal.

89 Colour: very deep cherry. Nose: powerfull, characterful, ripe fruit. Palate: flavourful, powerful, fine bitter notes, toasty.

5 ALMUDES 2009 TC
tempranillo.

85 Colour: deep cherry. Nose: powerfull, ripe fruit, spicy, dark chocolate. Palate: flavourful, fine bitter notes, good acidity.

ALMUDES 5 DÉCADAS 2008 TR
tempranillo.

87 Colour: deep cherry. Nose: candied fruit, spicy, dark chocolate. Palate: fine bitter notes, good acidity, round tannins.

BODEGAS ILLANA

Finca Buenavista, s/n
16708 Pozoamargo (Cuenca)
☎: +34 969 147 039 - Fax: +34 969 147 057
info@bodegasillana.com
www.bodegasillana.com

CASA DE ILLANA ALMA 2011 B
sauvignon blanc, moscatel.

87 Colour: bright straw. Nose: fresh, fresh fruit, white flowers. Palate: flavourful, fruity, good acidity, balanced.

CASA DE ILLANA EXPRESSION 2011 T
tempranillo, bobal.

84

CASA DE ILLANA SELECCIÓN 2008 T
petit verdot, syrah.

89 Colour: cherry, garnet rim. Nose: ripe fruit, spicy, creamy oak, toasty, complex. Palate: powerful, flavourful, toasty, round tannins.

CASA DE ILLANA TRADICIÓN 2007 T ROBLE
tempranillo, bobal.

85 Colour: deep cherry. Nose: spicy, nose:tic coffee, toasty, fruit liqueur notes. Palate: spicy, ripe fruit, fine bitter notes.

CASA DE ILLANA TRESDECINCO 2006 TC
merlot, cabernet sauvignon, syrah.

87 Colour: cherry, garnet rim. Nose: spicy, creamy oak, toasty. Palate: powerful, flavourful, toasty, round tannins.

CASA GUALDA

Tapias, 8
16708 Pozoamargo (Cuenca)
☎: +34 969 387 173 - Fax: +34 969 387 202
info@casagualda.com
www.casagualda.com

CASA GUALDA SYRAH 2011 T
syrah.

84

ELVIWINES

Finca “Clos Mesorah” Ctra. T-300 Falset Marça, Km. 1
43775 Marça Priorat (Tarragona)
☎: +34 935 343 026 - Fax: +34 936 750 316
moises@elviwines.com
www.elviwines.com

NESS 2011 B
56% sauvignon blanc, 44% moscatel.

87 Colour: bright straw. Nose: fresh fruit, white flowers. Palate: flavourful, fine bitter notes, good acidity.

NESS KOSHER 2011 RD
100% syrah.

90 Colour: rose, purple rim. Nose: powerfull, ripe fruit, red berry notes, floral, expressive. Palate: fleshy, powerful, fruity, fresh.

ADAR KOSHER PETIT VERDOT 2008 T
100% petit verdot.

89 Colour: bright cherry. Nose: ripe fruit, sweet spices, creamy oak, grassy, balsamic herbs. Palate: flavourful, fruity, toasty, round tannins.

ADAR KOSHER 2008 T
37% cabernet sauvignon, 35% petit verdot, 28% syrah.

88 Colour: very deep cherry. Nose: powerfull, ripe fruit, dark chocolate, earthy notes, mineral. Palate: flavourful, powerful, fine bitter notes.

NUESTRO PADRE JESÚS DE NAZARENO SDAD. COOP.

Deportes, 4
16700 Sisante (Cuenca)
☎: +34 969 387 094 - Fax: +34 969 387 094
sisante_nazareno@yahoo.es
www.cooperativasisante.com

CASA DON JUAN 2011 T
tempranillo, syrah, merlot.

88 Colour: very deep cherry. Nose: expressive, ripe fruit, fruit expression. Palate: flavourful, fruity, good acidity.

TEATINOS

Ctra. Minaya - San Clemente, Km. 10
16610 Casas de Fernando Alonso (Cuenca)
☎: +34 969 383 043 - Fax: +34 969 383 153
info@vinoteatinos.com
www.vinoteatino.com

TEATINOS BOBAL 2011 RD
bobal.

86 Colour: light cherry. Nose: red berry notes, fruit expression, medium intensity. Palate: sweet, fruity.

TEATINOS TEMPRANILLO 2011 T
100% tempranillo.

89 Colour: cherry, purple rim. Nose: powerfull, varietal, red berry notes, fruit expression. Palate: flavourful, good acidity, round tannins.

TEATINOS SYRAH 2011 T
100% syrah.

88 Colour: cherry, purple rim. Nose: red berry notes, floral, ripe fruit. Palate: flavourful, fruity, good acidity, round tannins.

TEATINOS SELECCIÓN 40 BARRICAS TEMPRANILLO 2007 TR
100% tempranillo.

88 Colour: cherry, garnet rim. Nose: ripe fruit, spicy, creamy oak, toasty, characterful. Palate: powerful, flavourful, toasty, round tannins.

TEATINOS SIGNVM 2007 TC
100% tempranillo.

85 Colour: very deep cherry. Nose: toasty, sweet spices, fruit preserve. Palate: fine bitter notes, powerful.

TEATINOS CLAROS DE CUBA 2006 TR
100% tempranillo.

88 Colour: bright cherry. Nose: sweet spices, creamy oak, overripe fruit. Palate: flavourful, fruity, toasty, round tannins.

TEATINOS DULCE MOSCATEL 2010 BLANCO DULCE
100% moscatel grano menudo.

80

VIÑEDOS Y BODEGAS LA MAGDALENA

Ctra. La Roda, s/n
16611 Casas de Haro (Cuenca)
☎: +34 969 380 722 - Fax: +34 969 380 722
vinos@vegamoragona.com
www.vegamoragona.com

VEGA MORAGONA DULCE 2011 B
100% moscatel grano menudo.

88 Colour: golden. Nose: powerfull, floral, honeyed notes, candied fruit. Palate: flavourful, sweet, fresh, fruity, good acidity, long.

VEGA MORAGONA 2011 B
moscatel grano menudo.

88 Colour: bright straw. Nose: fresh, fresh fruit, white flowers, expressive. Palate: flavourful, fruity, good acidity, balanced.

VEGA MORAGONA TEMPRANILLO 2011 T JOVEN
100% tempranillo.

88 Colour: cherry, purple rim. Nose: varietal, ripe fruit, floral. Palate: flavourful, good acidity, round.

VEGA MORAGONA CABERNET SAUVIGNON 2010 T ROBLE
100% cabernet sauvignon.

86 Colour: deep cherry. Nose: spicy, toasty, ripe fruit. Palate: flavourful, spicy, ripe fruit.

VEGA MORAGONA SYRAH 2010 T ROBLE
100% syrah.

85 Colour: deep cherry. Nose: powerfull, ripe fruit, roasted coffee. Palate: powerful, concentrated, roasted-coffee afterpalate:.

VEGA MORAGONA ALTA SELECCIÓN 2005 TR
65% tempranillo, 35% cabernet sauvignon.

88 Colour: cherry, garnet rim. Nose: toasty, sweet spices, dark chocolate, nose:tic coffee. Palate: sweetness, fine bitter notes, round tannins.

DO CA. RIOJA

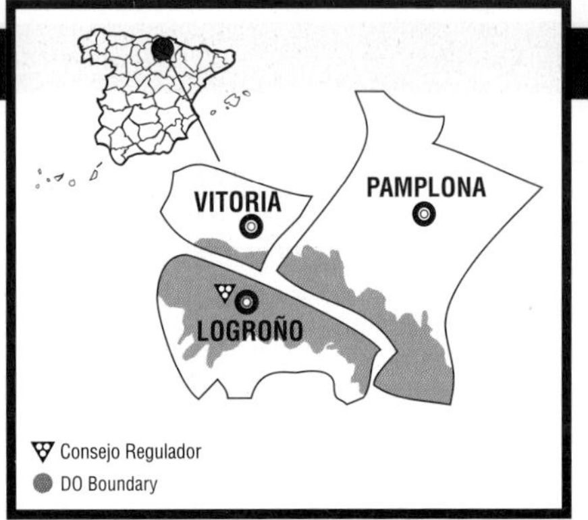

LOCATION:

Occupying the Ebro valley. To the north it borders with the Sierra de Cantabria and to the south with the Sierra de la Demanda, and is made up of different municipal districts of La Rioja, the Basque Country and Navarra. The most western region is Haro and the easternmost, Alfaro, with a distance of 100 km between the two. The region is 40 km wide.es de 40 kilómetros.

CLIMATE:

Quite variable depending on the different sub-regions. In general, there is a combination of Atlantic and Mediterranean influences, the latter becoming more dominant as the terrain descends from west to east, becoming drier and hotter. The average annual rainfall is slightly over 400 mm.

SOIL:

Various types: the clayey calcareous soil arranged in terraces and small plots which are located especially in Rioja Alavesa, la Sonsierra and some regions of Rioja Alta; the clayey ferrous soil, scattered throughout the region, with vineyards located on reddish, strong soil with hard, deep rock; and the alluvial soil in the area close to the rivers; these are the most level vineyards with larger plots; here the soil is deeper and has pebbles.

GRAPE VARIETIES:

WHITE: *Viura* (7,045 Ha), *Malvasía* and *Garnacha Blanca, Chardonnay, Sauvignon Blanc, Verdejo, Maturana Blanca, Tempranillo Blanco* and *Torrontés.*
RED: *Tempranillo* (majority with 38,476 Ha), *Garnacha, Graciano, Mazuelo, Maturana Tinta, Maturano* and *Monastrell.*

SUB-REGIONS:

Rioja Alta. This has Atlantic influences; it is the most extensive with some 20,500 Ha and produces wines well suited for ageing.
Rioja Alavesa. A mixture of Atlantic and Mediterranean influences, with an area under cultivation of some 11,500 Ha; both young wines and wines suited for ageing are produced.
Rioja Baja. With approximately 18,000 Ha, the climate is purely Mediterranean; white wines and rosés with a higher alcohol content and extract are produced.

CONSEJO REGULADOR
Estambrera, 52 - 26006 Logroño (La Rioja) - ☎: +34 941 500 400 - Fax: +34 941 500 672
@ info@riojawine.com - www.riojawine.com

FIGURES:

Vineyard surface: 63,824 – **Wine-Growers:** 17,296 – **Wineries:** 820 – **2011 Harvest rating:** Excellent – **Production:** 267 Million litres – **Market percentages:** 66% domestic. 34% export

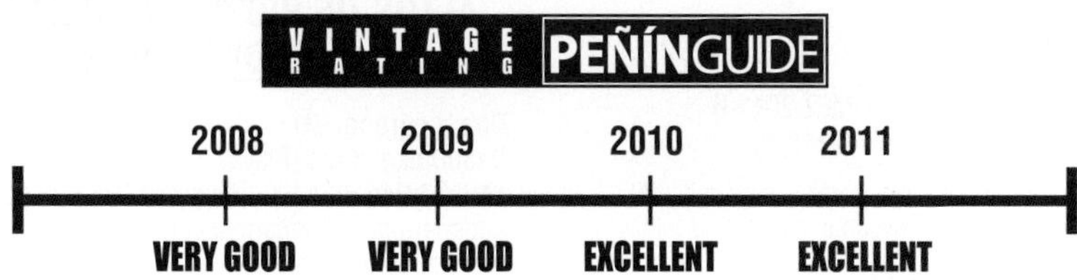

AGRÍCOLA LABASTIDA

El Olmo, 8
01330 Labastida (Álava)
☎: +34 945 331 230 - Fax: +34 945 331 257
info@tierrayvino.com
www.tierrayvino.com

TIERRA DE FERNÁNDEZ GÓMEZ 2011 B
70% viura, 20% garnacha blanca, 10% malvasía.

88 Colour: bright straw. Nose: fresh, fragrant herbs, medium intensity. Palate: flavourful, fresh, good acidity.

TIERRA DE FIDEL 2010 B
20% garnacha blanca, 20% viura, 20% malvasía, 40% otras.

89 Colour: bright straw. Nose: fresh, fresh fruit, white flowers, expressive. Palate: flavourful, fruity, good acidity, balanced.

EL PRIMAVERA 2011 T
100% tempranillo.

90 Colour: cherry, purple rim. Nose: expressive, fresh fruit, red berry notes, floral, spicy. Palate: flavourful, fruity, good acidity, round tannins.

LA HOJA TEMPRANILLO 2011 T
100% tempranillo.

88 Colour: cherry, purple rim. Nose: balanced, red berry notes, ripe fruit, powerfull. Palate: flavourful, fruity, good acidity.

FERNÁNDEZ GÓMEZ 2011 T
80% tempranillo, 10% viura, 10% garnacha.

87 Colour: cherry, purple rim. Nose: medium intensity, scrubland, ripe fruit. Palate: fruity, good finish.

EL BELISARIO 2009 T
100% tempranillo.

93 Colour: cherry, garnet rim. Nose: ripe fruit, spicy, creamy oak, toasty, complex, earthy notes, mineral. Palate: powerful, flavourful, toasty, balanced.

TIERRA 2009 TC
100% tempranillo.

90 Colour: cherry, garnet rim. Nose: balanced, ripe fruit, sweet spices. Palate: flavourful, fruity, round tannins.

LA HOJA 2009 TC
90% tempranillo, 5% garnacha, 5% viura.

89 Colour: light cherry. Nose: cocoa bean, spicy, cedar wood, fruit expression, fresh fruit, complex. Palate: fruity, powerful, flavourful, spicy, roasted-coffee afterpalate:.

TIERRA FIDEL 2009 T
50% graciano, 50% garnacha.

88 Colour: cherry, garnet rim. Nose: toasty, ripe fruit. Palate: spicy, ripe fruit, good acidity.

ALTOS DE RIOJA VITICULTORES Y BODEGUEROS

Ctra. Logroño, s/n
01300 Laguardia (Alava)
☎: +34 945 600 693 - Fax: +34 945 600 692
altosderioja@altosderioja.com
www.altosderioja.com

ALTOS R 2008 TC
100% tempranillo.

89 Colour: cherry, garnet rim. Nose: spicy, creamy oak, toasty. Palate: powerful, flavourful, toasty, round tannins.

ALTOS R 2011 B
60% viura, 40% malvasía.

90 Colour: bright straw. Nose: fresh fruit, fragrant herbs, citrus fruit. Palate: fruity, flavourful, good acidity.

ALTOS R PIGEAGE 2009 T
90% tempranillo, 10% graciano.

93 Colour: deep cherry, garnet rim. Nose: balanced, ripe fruit, sweet spices, creamy oak. Palate: good structure, flavourful, ripe fruit, good acidity.

ALTOS R 2006 TR
100% tempranillo.

90 Colour: cherry, garnet rim. Nose: balanced, ripe fruit, spicy. Palate: fruity, balanced, fine bitter notes, fine tannins.

ALTOS R TEMPRANILLO 2009 T
100% tempranillo.

88 Colour: deep cherry, garnet rim. Nose: medium intensity, ripe fruit, cocoa bean. Palate: flavourful, good acidity, fine bitter notes.

ALTÚN

Las Piscinas, 30
01307 Baños de Ebro (Álava)
☎: +34 945 609 317 - Fax: +34 945 609 309
altun@bodegasaltun.com
www.bodegasaltun.com

ALTÚN 2009 TC
100% tempranillo.

90 Colour: cherry, garnet rim. Nose: red berry notes, ripe fruit, sweet spices, creamy oak. Palate: flavourful, spicy, long, correct.

RIOJA
DENOMINACION DE ORIGEN CALIFICADA
ALTÚN
CRIANZA
2009
BODEGAS ALTÚN, S.L.

ANA DE ALTÚN 2011 B
75% viura, 25% malvasía.

88 Colour: bright straw. Nose: grassy, white flowers. Palate: flavourful, fruity, fresh.

ALBIKER 2011 T MACERACIÓN CARBÓNICA
95% tempranillo, 5% viura.

90 Colour: deep cherry. Nose: powerfull, expressive, varietal, candied fruit, fruit liqueur notes. Palate: spirituous, sweetness, flavourful, powerful, fruity, complex.

EVEREST 2010 T
100% tempranillo.

94 Colour: cherry, garnet rim. Nose: red berry notes, ripe fruit, expressive, mineral, balsamic herbs, spicy, toasty. Palate: powerful, flavourful, complex, balanced, long, toasty.

SECRETO DE ALTÚN 2010 T
100% tempranillo.

92 Colour: cherry, garnet rim. Nose: mineral, ripe fruit, red berry notes. Palate: powerful, flavourful, fine bitter notes, round tannins.

ALTÚN 2007 TR
100% tempranillo.

90 Colour: bright cherry. Nose: ripe fruit, new oak, toasty. Palate: flavourful, fruity, toasty, round tannins.

ALVAREZ ALFARO

Ctra. Comarcal 384, Km. 0,8
26559 Aldeanueva de Ebro (La Rioja)
☎: +34 941 144 210 - Fax: +34 941 144 210
info@bodegasalvarezalfaro.com
www.bodegasalvarezalfaro.com

ALVAREZ ALFARO SELECCIÓN FAMILIAR 2009 T
100% tempranillo.

90 Colour: cherry, garnet rim. Nose: ripe fruit, spicy, creamy oak, toasty, complex. Palate: powerful, flavourful, toasty, round tannins.

ALVAREZ ALFARO 2009 TC
80% tempranillo, 10% garnacha, 8% mazuelo, 2% graciano.

88 Colour: cherry, garnet rim. Nose: ripe fruit, sweet spices. Palate: powerful, flavourful, toasty, round tannins.

AMADOR GARCÍA CHAVARRI

Avda. Río Ebro, 68 - 70
01307 Baños de Ebro (Álava)
☎: +34 945 290 385 - Fax: +34 975 290 373
bodegasamadorgarcia@gmail.com
www.bodegasamadorgarcia.com

PEÑAGUDO 2011 T

86 Colour: cherry, garnet rim. Nose: earthy notes, powerfull, ripe fruit. Palate: flavourful, powerful, fruity, spirituous, sweetness.

PEÑAGUDO 2008 TC

86 Colour: cherry, garnet rim. Nose: ripe fruit, balsamic herbs, fine reductive notes, spicy. Palate: powerful, flavourful, long, toasty.

AMADOR GARCÍA 2008 TC

90 Colour: cherry, garnet rim. Nose: ripe fruit, spicy, creamy oak, toasty. Palate: powerful, flavourful, round tannins, balanced, long.

ARIBAU CUVÉE

Doctor Azcarraga, 27-29
26350 Cenicero (La Rioja)
☎: +34 933 134 347 - Fax: +34 933 050 112
comercial@rotllantorra.com
www.aribaurioja.com

ARIBAU CUVÉE 2008 TC
85% tempranillo, 10% mazuelo, 5% graciano.

88 Colour: cherry, garnet rim. Nose: ripe fruit, creamy oak, toasty, balsamic herbs. Palate: powerful, flavourful, toasty, balanced.

ARIBAU CUVÉE 2007 TR
85% tempranillo, 10% mazuelo, 5% graciano.

86 Colour: ruby red, orangey edge. Nose: ripe fruit, scrubland, spicy. Palate: fresh, flavourful, toasty.

ARRIAGA Y MIMÉNDEZ COMPAÑÍA DE VINOS

Capitán Cortés, 6. Piso 4º Puerta 3
26003 Logroño (La Rioja)
☎: +34 687 421 306 - Fax: +34 941 287 072
administracion@arriagaymimendez.com
www.arriagaymimendez.com

LA INVIERNA CORTE UNO 2007 T
100% tempranillo.

91 Colour: cherry, garnet rim. Nose: spicy, ripe fruit, tobacco. Palate: good structure, good acidity, fine bitter notes, full.

LA INVIERNA CORTE DOS 2007 T
100% tempranillo.

88 Colour: cherry, garnet rim. Nose: balanced, ripe fruit, spicy, tobacco. Palate: good structure, ripe fruit, good acidity.

ARTUKE BODEGAS Y VIÑEDOS

La Serna, 24
01307 Baños de Ebro (Álava)
☎: +34 945 623 323 - Fax: +34 945 623 323
artuke@artuke.com
www.artuke.com

ARTUKE 2011 T MACERACIÓN CARBÓNICA
95% tempranillo, 5% viura.

91 Colour: cherry, purple rim. Nose: lactic notes, raspberry, red berry notes, balanced, expressive. Palate: fresh, fruity, light-bodied, good acidity, flavourful, balanced.

ARTUKE SELECCIÓN 2011 T
90% tempranillo, 10% graciano.

89 Colour: cherry, purple rim. Nose: ripe fruit, red berry notes, fragrant herbs. Palate: flavourful, fruity, fresh.

ARTUKE K4 2010 T
75% tempranillo, 25% graciano.

96 Colour: cherry, garnet rim. Nose: spicy, creamy oak, toasty, mineral, characterful, ripe fruit, red berry notes. Palate: powerful, flavourful, toasty, round tannins.

ARTUKE FINCA DE LOS LOCOS 2010 T
80% tempranillo, 20% graciano.

95 Colour: bright cherry. Nose: expressive, cocoa bean, toasty, ripe fruit, dark chocolate. Palate: flavourful, fruity, toasty, round tannins.

ARTUKE PIES NEGROS 2010 TC
90% tempranillo, 10% graciano.

93 Colour: cherry, garnet rim. Nose: ripe fruit, spicy, creamy oak, toasty, complex, mineral. Palate: powerful, flavourful, toasty, round tannins.

BAIGORRI

Ctra. Vitoria-Logroño, Km. 53
01307 Samaniego (Álava)
☎: +34 945 609 420 - Fax: +34 945 609 407
mail@bodegasbaigorri.com
www.bodegasbaigorri.com

BAIGORRI 2010 BFB
90% viura, 10% malvasía.

91 Colour: bright yellow. Nose: powerfull, ripe fruit, sweet spices, dried herbs. Palate: rich, smoky afterpalate:, flavourful, fresh, good acidity.

BAIGORRI 2011 RD
50% tempranillo, 50% garnacha.

87 Colour: rose, purple rim. Nose: powerfull, ripe fruit, red berry notes, floral, expressive. Palate: fleshy, powerful, fruity, fresh.

BAIGORRI 2011 T MACERACIÓN CARBÓNICA
100% tempranillo.

86 Colour: deep cherry. Nose: ripe fruit, scrubland. Palate: flavourful, fine bitter notes.

BAIGORRI GARNACHA 2009 T
100% garnacha.

93 Colour: very deep cherry, garnet rim. Nose: powerfull, balanced, creamy oak, ripe fruit. Palate: good structure, flavourful.

BAIGORRI 2006 TR
100% tempranillo.

91 Colour: deep cherry. Nose: powerfull, macerated fruit, expressive, spicy, roasted coffee. Palate: powerful, flavourful, good structure, creamy, spicy.

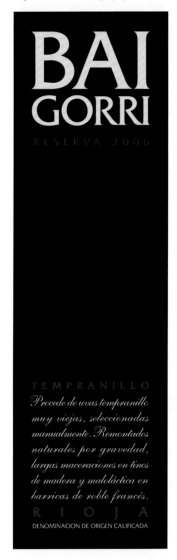

BAIGORRI 2008 TC
90% tempranillo, 10% otras.

91 Colour: deep cherry. Nose: ripe fruit, spicy, creamy oak, toasty, complex, dark chocolate. Palate: powerful, flavourful, toasty, round tannins.

BAIGORRI BELUS 2008 T
70% tempranillo, 20% mazuelo, 10% garnacha.

90 Colour: cherry, garnet rim. Nose: ripe fruit, spicy, toasty, complex. Palate: powerful, flavourful, toasty, round.

BAIGORRI DE GARAGE 2007 T
100% tempranillo.

93 Colour: cherry, garnet rim. Nose: complex, balanced, expressive, nose:tic coffee, ripe fruit, mineral. Palate: good structure, flavourful, good acidity, balanced.

BARÓN DE LEY

Ctra. Mendavia - Lodosa, Km. 5,5
31587 Mendavia (Navarra)
☎: +34 948 694 303 - Fax: +34 948 694 304
info@barondeley.com
www.barondeley.com

BARÓN DE LEY 2011 B
85% viura, 15% malvasía.

90 Colour: bright straw. Nose: white flowers, fruit expression, fresh, neat, varietal. Palate: powerful, flavourful, fruity, complex.

BARÓN DE LEY 2011 RD
100% tempranillo.

88 Colour: rose, purple rim. Nose: powerfull, ripe fruit, red berry notes, floral, expressive. Palate: fleshy, powerful, fruity, fresh.

BARÓN DE LEY VARIETALES TEMPRANILLO 2010 T
100% tempranillo.

91 Colour: cherry, garnet rim. Nose: ripe fruit, spicy, creamy oak, toasty, complex. Palate: powerful, flavourful, toasty, round tannins.

BARÓN DE LEY VARIETALES MATURANA 2009 T
100% maturana.

88 Colour: cherry, garnet rim. Nose: ripe fruit, sweet spices, nose:tic coffee. Palate: powerful, concentrated, warm.

BARÓN DE LEY VARIETALES GRACIANO 2009 T
100% graciano.

87 Colour: cherry, garnet rim. Nose: ripe fruit, complex, fragrant herbs. Palate: flavourful, round tannins, balsamic.

BARÓN DE LEY FINCA MONASTERIO 2008 T
90% tempranillo, 10% otras.

91 Colour: cherry, garnet rim. Nose: spicy, tobacco, ripe fruit, balanced. Palate: balanced, good acidity, fruity.

BARÓN DE LEY 2007 TR
tempranillo.

87 Colour: cherry, garnet rim. Nose: spicy, toasty, ripe fruit, balanced. Palate: correct, toasty, spicy.

BARÓN DE LEY 2004 TGR
tempranillo.

89 Colour: dark-red cherry, orangey edge. Nose: spicy, nose:tic coffee, animal reductive notes, old leather. Palate: round, flavourful, rich, spicy, roasted-coffee afterpalate:.

BODEGA CONTADOR

Ctra. Baños de Ebro, Km. 1
26338 San Vicente de la Sonsierra (La Rioja)
☎: 941 334 228 - Fax: 941 334 537
info@bodegacontador.com
www.bodegacontador.com

CONTADOR 2010 T
99% tempranillo, 1% garnacha.

97 Colour: cherry, purple rim. Nose: new oak, toasty, sweet spices, dark chocolate, earthy notes, mineral, fruit expression, ripe fruit. Palate: long, ripe fruit, spicy, balsamic, round tannins, round.

LA VIÑA DE ANDRÉS ROMEO 2010 T
100% tempranillo.

96 Colour: cherry, purple rim. Nose: ripe fruit, fruit expression, fresh, complex, new oak, toasty, scrubland. Palate: fine bitter notes, round, long, ripe fruit, harsh oak tannins.

LA CUEVA DEL CONTADOR 2010 T
100% tempranillo.

95 Colour: cherry, purple rim. Nose: powerfull, characterful, complex, ripe fruit, creamy oak, cocoa bean. Palate: flavourful, fine bitter notes, good acidity, round tannins.

PREDICADOR 2010 T

93 Colour: cherry, purple rim. Nose: red berry notes, fruit expression, creamy oak, sweet spices. Palate: round tannins, ripe fruit, spicy.

BODEGA DEL MONGE-GARBATI

Ctra. Rivas de Tereso, s/n
26338 San Vicente de la Sonsierra (La Rioja)
☎: +34 659 167 653 - Fax: +34 941 311 870
bodegamg@yahoo.es
www.vinaane.com

VIÑA ANE CENTENARIA 2011 B
80% viura, 20% malvasía.

83

EL LABERINTO DE VIÑA ANE 2009 T
100% tempranillo.

90 Colour: deep cherry, garnet rim. Nose: red berry notes, ripe fruit, sweet spices, violets. Palate: powerful, flavourful, good structure.

VIÑA ANE AUTOR 2009 T
100% tempranillo.

87 Colour: dark-red cherry, orangey edge. Nose: spicy, aged wood nuances, ripe fruit. Palate: harsh oak tannins, flavourful, powerful, fruity, spicy.

VIÑA ANE VENDIMIA SELECCIONADA 2007 T
100% tempranillo.

88 Colour: bright cherry, garnet rim. Nose: ripe fruit, sweet spices, toasty. Palate: fruity, easy to drink, good finish.

BODEGA I. PETRALANDA

Avda. La Estación, 44
26360 Fuenmayor (La Rioja)
☎: +34 941 450 462 - Fax: +34 941 450 620
nonno@vinoart.es
www.vinoart.es

NONNO 2007 T
tempranillo, mazuelo.

91 Colour: cherry, garnet rim. Nose: complex, medium intensity, balanced, tobacco, ripe fruit, spicy. Palate: flavourful, good structure, good acidity.

BODEGA MONTEALTO

Las Piscinas, s/n
01307 Baños del Ebro (Alava)
☎: +34 918 427 013 - Fax: +34 918 427 013
contacta@meddissl.com
www.meddissl.com

ROBATIE 2011 T
95% tempranillo, 5% viura.

90 Colour: cherry, purple rim. Nose: expressive, fresh fruit, red berry notes, floral. Palate: flavourful, fruity, good acidity, round tannins.

ROBATIE VENDIMIA SELECCIONADA 2009 T
100% tempranillo.

92 Colour: cherry, garnet rim. Nose: ripe fruit, spicy, creamy oak, toasty, characterful. Palate: powerful, flavourful, toasty, round tannins.

ROBATIE 2008 TC
100% tempranillo.

88 Colour: cherry, garnet rim. Nose: spicy, creamy oak, toasty, characterful. Palate: powerful, flavourful, toasty, round tannins.

ROBATIE 2005 TR
100% tempranillo.

88 Colour: cherry, garnet rim. Nose: spicy, creamy oak, toasty, characterful, fruit expression. Palate: powerful, flavourful, toasty, round tannins.

BODEGA SAN MARTÍN DE ABALOS

Camino del Prado s/n
26211 Fonzaleche (La Rioja)
☎: +34 941 300 423 - Fax: +34 941 300 423
comercial@bodegasanmartindeabalos.com
www.sanmartindeabalos.com

PORTALON DE SAN MARTÍN 2008 T
15% viura, 5% garnacha, 80% tempranillo.

90 Colour: cherry, garnet rim. Nose: ripe fruit, cocoa bean, sweet spices. Palate: good structure, flavourful, spicy.

VIÑA VEREDA DEL RÍO 2008 TC
80% tempranillo, 15% garnacha, 5% viura.

85 Colour: cherry, garnet rim. Nose: ripe fruit, spicy, nose:tic coffee, dark chocolate. Palate: powerful, flavourful, toasty.

VR GOLD 2007 TR
80% tempranillo, 5% garnacha, 15% viura.

87 Colour: bright cherry, orangey edge. Nose: ripe fruit, medium intensity, sweet spices, fine reductive notes. Palate: correct, flavourful, spicy.

PRADO DE FONZALECHE 2006 TR
85% tempranillo, 10% garnacha, 5% viura.

86 Colour: cherry, garnet rim. Nose: spicy, cigar, wet leather. Palate: flavourful, toasty, round tannins, long.

BODEGA SAN PRUDENCIO

Ctra. Viana, Km. 1
01322 Moreda (Álava)
☎: +34 945 622 451 - Fax: +34 945 601 034
info@bodegasanprudencio.es
www.bodegasanprudencio.com

CUETO 2011 B
90% viura, 10% malvasía.

86 Colour: bright yellow. Nose: dried flowers, fragrant herbs. Palate: balanced, good acidity, fine bitter notes.

ENVITE 2011 B
90% viura, 10% malvasía.

84

CONCLAVE ESENCIA 2010 B
90% viura, 10% malvasía.

89 Colour: bright yellow. Nose: spicy, new oak, fresh fruit. Palate: fruity, powerful, flavourful, sweetness.

CUETO 2011 RD
75% tempranillo, 25% garnacha.

88 Colour: rose, purple rim. Nose: powerfull, ripe fruit, red berry notes, floral, expressive. Palate: fleshy, powerful, fruity, fresh.

ENVITE 2011 RD
75% tempranillo, 25% garnacha.

87 Colour: rose, purple rim. Nose: powerfull, ripe fruit, red berry notes, floral, expressive. Palate: fleshy, powerful, fruity, fresh.

ENVITE 2011 T
70% tempranillo, 25% garnacha, 5% graciano.

85 Colour: deep cherry. Nose: powerfull, ripe fruit, spicy, floral. Palate: flavourful, fine bitter notes, good acidity.

CUETO 2011 T
65% tempranillo, 25% garnacha, 10% mazuelo, 5% graciano.

83

ENVITE 2009 TC
60% tempranillo, 25% garnacha, 15% mazuelo.

85 Colour: cherry, garnet rim. Nose: spicy, creamy oak, toasty, ripe fruit. Palate: powerful, flavourful, toasty, round tannins.

CUETO 2008 TC
60% tempranillo, 25% garnacha, 10% mazuelo, 5% graciano.

89 Colour: deep cherry. Nose: sweet spices, dark chocolate. Palate: spicy, ripe fruit, fine bitter notes.

DEPADRE 2008 T
50% tempranillo, 50% garnacha.

89 Colour: cherry, garnet rim. Nose: cocoa bean, dark chocolate, creamy oak, sweet spices. Palate: rich, flavourful, round tannins.

CONCLAVE 2005 TR
60% tempranillo, 35% garnacha, 5% mazuelo.

88 Colour: deep cherry. Nose: powerfull, toasty, spicy, nose:tic coffee. Palate: fine bitter notes, spicy, ripe fruit.

CUETO 2005 TR
65% tempranillo, 20% garnacha, 15% mazuelo.

87 Colour: deep cherry. Nose: toasty, nose:tic coffee, fruit liqueur notes. Palate: fine bitter notes, ripe fruit, spicy.

MALIZIA (VINO DE HIELO) 2009
60% tempranillo, 40% garnacha.

89 Colour: coppery red. Nose: overripe fruit, candied fruit, floral, honeyed notes. Palate: rich, flavourful, sweet.

ENVITE SEDUCCIÓN 2011 SEMIDULCE
90% viura, 10% malvasía.

89 Colour: bright straw. Nose: jasmine, citrus fruit, fragrant herbs, fresh fruit. Palate: full, flavourful, sweet, spirituous.

BODEGA VIÑA EGUILUZ

Camino de San Bartolomé, 10
26339 Abalos (La Rioja)
☎: +34 941 334 064 - Fax: +34 941 583 022
info@bodegaseguiluz.es
www.bodegaseguiluz.es

EGUILUZ 2011 T
100% tempranillo.

86 Colour: cherry, garnet rim. Nose: ripe fruit, wild herbs, maceration notes. Palate: flavourful, light-bodied, powerful.

EGUILUZ 2007 TC
100% tempranillo.

87 Colour: cherry, garnet rim. Nose: spicy, creamy oak, toasty. Palate: powerful, flavourful, toasty, round tannins.

EGUILUZ 2006 TR
100% tempranillo.

90 Colour: cherry, garnet rim. Nose: ripe fruit, spicy, old leather. Palate: flavourful, toasty, round tannins, balanced.

BODEGA Y VIÑEDOS SOLABAL

Camino San Bartolomé, 6
26339 Abalos (La Rioja)
☎: +34 941 334 492 - Fax: +34 941 308 164
solabal@solabal.com
www.solabal.es

MUÑARRATE 2011 B
viura, malvasía.

90 Colour: bright straw. Nose: fragrant herbs, fresh fruit, floral. Palate: fruity, fresh, complex, flavourful, powerful.

MUÑARRATE 2011 RD
garnacha.

87 Colour: rose, purple rim. Nose: powerfull, ripe fruit, red berry notes, expressive. Palate: , powerful, fruity, fresh.

MUÑARRATE 2011 T
tempranillo.

88 Colour: cherry, garnet rim. Nose: ripe fruit, macerated fruit, powerfull, varietal. Palate: sweetness, fruity, flavourful, ripe fruit, spirituous.

SOLABAL 2009 TC
tempranillo.

89 Colour: cherry, garnet rim. Nose: creamy oak, toasty, ripe fruit. Palate: good structure, round tannins.

VALA DE SOLABAL 2008 T
tempranillo.

90 Colour: cherry, garnet rim. Nose: ripe fruit, spicy, creamy oak, toasty, characterful. Palate: powerful, flavourful, toasty, round tannins.

ESCULLE DE SOLABAL 2008 T
tempranillo.

87 Colour: cherry, garnet rim. Nose: ripe fruit, spicy, creamy oak, toasty, dark chocolate. Palate: powerful, flavourful, toasty, round tannins.

SOLABAL 2007 TR
tempranillo.

90 Colour: cherry, garnet rim. Nose: spicy, creamy oak, toasty, characterful. Palate: powerful, flavourful, toasty, round tannins.

BODEGAS 1808

Ctra. El Villar Polígono 7 Biribil, 33
01300 Laguardia (Alava)
☎: +34 945 293 450 - Fax: +34 945 293 450
1808@rioja1808.com
www.rioja1808.com

1808 VIURA 2010 B
100% viura.

87 Colour: bright yellow. Nose: candied fruit, honeyed notes, powerfull, faded flowers. Palate: ripe fruit, correct.

1808 2008 TC
100% tempranillo.

87 Colour: cherry, garnet rim. Nose: ripe fruit, spicy, creamy oak, toasty. Palate: powerful, flavourful, toasty, round tannins.

BODEGAS ABANICO

Pol. Ind Ca l'Avellanet - Susany, 6
08553 Seva (Barcelona)
☎: +34 938 125 676 - Fax: +34 938 123 213
info@exportiberia.com
www.bodegasabanico.com

HAZAÑA 2010 T
100% tempranillo.

85 Colour: cherry, purple rim. Nose: red berry notes, floral, balsamic herbs, spicy. Palate: flavourful, fruity, balanced.

HAZAÑA 2007 TC
100% tempranillo.

84

BODEGAS ABEL MENDOZA MONGE

Ctra. Peñacerrada, 7
26338 San Vicente de la Sonsierra (La Rioja)
☎: +34 941 308 010 - Fax: +34 941 308 010
jarrarte.abelmendoza@gmail.com

ABEL MENDOZA MALVASÍA 2011 BFB
malvasía.

90 Colour: bright yellow. Nose: medium intensity, balanced, fresh fruit, citrus fruit, fragrant herbs. Palate: fruity, rich, good acidity, spicy.

ABEL MENDOZA VIURA 2011 BFB
100% viura.

87 Colour: bright yellow. Nose: ripe fruit, candied fruit, sweet spices. Palate: rich, flavourful, sweetness, toasty.

JARRARTE 2011 T MACERACIÓN CARBÓNICA
tempranillo.

88 Colour: cherry, purple rim. Nose: fresh fruit, red berry notes, floral, fragrant herbs. Palate: flavourful, fruity, good acidity.

ABEL MENDOZA SELECCIÓN PERSONAL 2009 T
tempranillo.

93 Colour: dark-red cherry, garnet rim. Nose: cocoa bean, fruit expression, complex, varietal, elegant. Palate: full, rich, flavourful, powerful, spicy, creamy, smoky afterpalate:.

ABEL MENDOZA TEMPRANILLO GRANO A GRANO 2009 T
tempranillo.

93 Colour: very deep cherry. Nose: medium intensity, closed, fruit expression, dark chocolate, creamy oak. Palate: powerful, flavourful, complex, balsamic, smoky afterpalate:.

JARRARTE 2008 T
tempranillo.

88 Colour: cherry, garnet rim. Nose: ripe fruit, spicy, creamy oak, toasty, complex. Palate: powerful, flavourful, toasty, round tannins.

BODEGAS AGE

Barrio de la Estación, s/n
26360 Fuenmayor (La Rioja)
☎: +34 941 293 500 - Fax: +34 941 293 501
bodegasage@pernod-ricard.com
www.bodegasage.com

SIGLO SACO 2008 TC
tempranillo, garnacha, mazuelo.

88 Colour: deep cherry. Nose: toasty, spicy, ripe fruit. Palate: spicy, ripe fruit.

SIGLO 2006 TR
tempranillo, mazuelo, graciano.

86 Colour: dark-red cherry. Nose: slightly evolved, warm, short, reduction notes. Palate: round, powerful, good structure, roasted-coffee afterpalate:, ripe fruit, classic aged character.

SIGLO 2004 TGR
tempranillo, mazuelo, graciano.

87 Colour: pale ruby, brick rim edge. Nose: old leather, waxy notes, fruit liqueur notes. Palate: spicy, ripe fruit, fine bitter notes.

BODEGAS ALABANZA

Pol. Ind. El Sequero , Avda. de Cameros, 27
26150 Agoncillo (La Rioja)
☎: +34 941 437 051 - Fax: +34 941 437 077
bodegasalabanza@bodegasalabanza.com
www.bodegasalabanza.com

ALABANZA 2011 T
100% tempranillo.

84

ALABANZA 2006 TC
85% tempranillo, 15% garnacha.

87 Colour: cherry, garnet rim. Nose: spicy, ripe fruit, toasty, sweet spices. Palate: powerful, flavourful, fine bitter notes.

ALABANZA 2006 TR
100% tempranillo.

86 Colour: bright cherry, garnet rim. Nose: medium intensity, ripe fruit, spicy. Palate: fruity, good acidity.

ALABANZA SELECCIÓN 2005 TC
75% tempranillo, 15% mazuelo, 10% graciano.

88 Colour: deep cherry, orangey edge. Nose: tobacco, fruit preserve, spicy. Palate: flavourful, ripe fruit, round tannins.

BODEGAS ALADRO

Barco, 23
01340 Elciego (Álava)
☎: +34 679 822 754
aladro@aladro.es
www.aladro.es

ALADRO 2011 T
100% tempranillo.

88 Colour: cherry, purple rim. Nose: expressive, fresh fruit, red berry notes, floral. Palate: flavourful, fruity, good acidity, round tannins.

BODEGAS ALONSO GONZÁLEZ

Hospital, 9
26339 Abalos (La Rioja)
☎: +34 669 897 630 - Fax: +34 941 334 554
bodegasalonsogonzalez@hotmail.com
www.bodegasalonsogonzalez.es

ALMA DE CANTAURI 2001 T
90% tempranillo, 10% graciano, mazuelo.

89 Colour: dark-red cherry, bright ochre rim. Nose: old leather, cigar, waxy notes, sweet spices, creamy oak. Palate: round, flavourful, spicy, soft tannins.

BODEGAS ALTANZA

Ctra. Nacional 232, Km. 419
26360 Fuenmayor (Rioja)
☎: +34 941 450 860 - Fax: +34 941 450 804
altanza@bodegasaltanza.com
www.bodegasaltanza.com

LEALTANZA 2011 B
viura, sauvignon blanc.

90 Colour: bright straw. Nose: ripe fruit, citrus fruit, scrubland. Palate: flavourful, fruity, fresh.

LEALTANZA 2011 RD
100% tempranillo.

87 Colour: rose, purple rim. Nose: ripe fruit, red berry notes, floral. Palate: , powerful, fruity, fresh.

EDULIS 2009 TC
tempranillo.

86 Colour: cherry, garnet rim. Nose: spicy, creamy oak, toasty, fine reductive notes. Palate: powerful, flavourful, toasty, correct.

LEALTANZA AUTOR 2008 T
tempranillo.

90 Colour: cherry, garnet rim. Nose: ripe fruit, spicy, creamy oak, toasty, balanced. Palate: powerful, flavourful, toasty, round tannins.

HACIENDA VALVARÉS 2008 TC
tempranillo.

87 Colour: cherry, garnet rim. Nose: ripe fruit, spicy, creamy oak. Palate: powerful, flavourful, toasty.

LEALTANZA 2007 TR
tempranillo.

90 Colour: cherry, garnet rim. Nose: ripe fruit, spicy, creamy oak, toasty, complex. Palate: powerful, flavourful, toasty, round tannins.

CLUB LEALTANZA 2005 TR
tempranillo.

89 Colour: ruby red, orangey edge. Nose: spicy, fruit liqueur notes, balsamic herbs, creamy oak, tobacco, waxy notes. Palate: long, flavourful, balanced.

ALTANZA RESERVA ESPECIAL 2004 TR
tempranillo.

90 Colour: deep cherry, garnet rim. Nose: spicy, fruit preserve, tobacco, toasty. Palate: balanced, good acidity, fine bitter notes.

LEALTANZA 2004 TGR
tempranillo.

90 Colour: pale ruby, brick rim edge. Nose: spicy, fine reductive notes, wet leather, aged wood nuances, fruit liqueur notes, fragrant herbs. Palate: spicy, fine tannins, elegant, long.

BODEGAS ALTOS DEL MARQUÉS

Ctra. Navarrete, 1
26372 Hornos de Moncalvillo (La Rioja)
☎: +34 941 286 728 - Fax: +34 941 286 729
info@altosdelmarques.com
www.altosdelmarques.com

ALTOS DEL MARQUÉS 2010 T
85% tempranillo, 10% garnacha, 5% mazuelo.

86 Colour: cherry, garnet rim. Nose: ripe fruit, spicy, toasty. Palate: powerful, flavourful, toasty, spicy.

ALTOS DEL MARQUÉS 2008 TC
100% tempranillo.

88 Colour: bright cherry. Nose: sweet spices, creamy oak, expressive, red berry notes. Palate: flavourful, fruity, toasty, round tannins.

BODEGAS AMAREN

Ctra. Baños de Ebro, s/n,
01307 Villabuena (Álava)
☎: +34 945 175 240 - Fax: +34 945 174 566
bodegas@bodegasamaren.com
www.bodegasamaren.com

AMAREN TEMPRANILLO 2006 TR
100% tempranillo.

91 Colour: cherry, garnet rim. Nose: spicy, creamy oak, toasty, fruit liqueur notes, wet leather. Palate: powerful, flavourful, toasty, round tannins.

AMAREN 2010 BFB
85% viura, 15% malvasía.

91 Colour: bright yellow. Nose: complex, fresh, powerfull, fragrant herbs, candied fruit. Palate: good acidity, elegant, fresh, fruity, full.

ÁNGELES DE AMAREN 2008 T
85% tempranillo, 15% graciano.

92 Colour: cherry, garnet rim. Nose: ripe fruit, spicy, creamy oak, complex. Palate: powerful, flavourful, toasty, round tannins.

BODEGAS AMBROSIO CASTRO

Ignacio Aldecoa, 18
01340 Elciego (Álava)
☎: +34 618 326 982
riojanova@gmail.com

STIMULUS DE JUANITO OIARZABAL 2010 T JOVEN
100% tempranillo.

86 Colour: cherry, garnet rim. Nose: powerfull, ripe fruit, toasty, spicy. Palate: flavourful, powerful.

BODEGAS AMÉZOLA DE LA MORA

Paraje Viña Vieja, s/n
26359 Torremontalbo (La Rioja)
☎: +34 941 454 532 - Fax: +34 941 454 537
info@bodegasamezola.es
www.bodegasamezola.es

IÑIGO AMÉZOLA 2009 BFB
100% viura.

88 Colour: bright yellow. Nose: powerfull, ripe fruit, sweet spices, creamy oak. Palate: rich, smoky afterpalate:, flavourful, fresh, good acidity.

IÑIGO AMÉZOLA 2010 T
100% tempranillo.

88 Colour: bright cherry. Nose: ripe fruit, sweet spices, creamy oak, expressive. Palate: flavourful, fruity, toasty, round tannins.

VIÑA AMÉZOLA 2008 TC
85% tempranillo, 10% mazuelo, 5% graciano.

89 Colour: light cherry. Nose: cocoa bean, toasty, fruit expression. Palate: soft tannins, light-bodied, flavourful, fruity.

SEÑORÍO AMÉZOLA 2006 TR
85% tempranillo, 10% mazuelo, 5% graciano.

88 Colour: pale ruby, brick rim edge. Nose: sweet spices, creamy oak, toasty, fine reductive notes. Palate: long, spicy, balanced.

SOLAR AMÉZOLA 2001 TGR
85% tempranillo, 10% mazuelo, 5% graciano.

88 Colour: pale ruby, brick rim edge. Nose: cocoa bean, sweet spices, candied fruit. Palate: round, flavourful, spicy.

BODEGAS ANTONIO ALCARAZ

Ctra. Vitoria-Logroño, Km. 57
01300 Laguardia (Álava)
☎: +34 658 959 745 - Fax: +34 965 888 359
rioja@antonio-alcaraz.es
www.antonio-alcaraz.es

GLORIA ANTONIO ALCARAZ 2009 TC
100% tempranillo.

90 Colour: deep cherry. Nose: expressive, ripe fruit, creamy oak, sweet spices. Palate: balanced, ripe fruit, round tannins.

ANTONIO ALCARAZ 2007 TR
90% tempranillo, 10% graciano, mazuelo.

91 Colour: cherry, garnet rim. Nose: ripe fruit, spicy, toasty, complex. Palate: powerful, flavourful, toasty, round tannins.

ANTONIO ALCARAZ 2009 TC
90% tempranillo, 10% mazuelo.

91 Colour: bright cherry, garnet rim. Nose: spicy, ripe fruit. Palate: fruity, flavourful, round tannins.

BODEGAS ARACO

Ctra. Lapuebla, s/n
01300 Laguardia (Álava)
☎: +34 945 600 209 - Fax: +34 945 600 067
araco@bodegasaraco.com
www.bodegasaraco.com

ARACO 2011 B
viura.

88 Colour: bright straw. Nose: fresh, fresh fruit, white flowers. Palate: flavourful, fruity, good acidity, balanced.

ARACO 2011 RD

85 Colour: salmon. Nose: red berry notes, ripe fruit, wild herbs, citrus fruit. Palate: fruity, fresh.

ARACO + 2010 T
tempranillo.

87 Colour: cherry, garnet rim. Nose: medium intensity, ripe fruit, dark chocolate. Palate: fruity, good structure, round tannins.

ARACO 2011 T
tempranillo.

87 Colour: cherry, garnet rim. Nose: neat, fresh, varietal, violets. Palate: powerful, flavourful, fruity, fresh, balsamic.

ARACO 2009 TC
tempranillo.

86 Colour: cherry, garnet rim. Nose: ripe fruit, spicy, creamy oak, toasty, complex. Palate: powerful, flavourful, toasty, round tannins.

ARACO 2005 TR
tempranillo.

87 Colour: dark-red cherry, orangey edge. Nose: scrubland, spicy, fruit liqueur notes. Palate: flavourful, long, spicy, balanced.

BODEGAS BASAGOITI

Mas Parxet, s/n
08391 Tiana (Barcelona)
☎: +34 933 950 811 - Fax: +34 933 955 500
info@parxet.es
www.parxet.es

NABARI 2011 T
70% tempranillo, 30% garnacha.

90 Colour: cherry, purple rim. Nose: ripe fruit, balsamic herbs. Palate: flavourful, fine bitter notes, good acidity.

BASAGOITI 2009 TC
75% tempranillo, 25% garnacha.

90 Colour: cherry, garnet rim. Nose: ripe fruit, scrubland, spicy. Palate: powerful, flavourful, long, spicy.

BODEGAS BENJAMÍN DE ROTHSCHILD & VEGA SICILIA

Ctra. Logroño - Vitoria, km. 61
01309 Leza (Alava)
☎: +34 983 680 147 - Fax: 983 680 263
irodriguez@vega-sicilia.com
www.vegasicilia.com

MACÁN CLÁSICO 2009 T
100% tempranillo.

95 Colour: cherry, purple rim. Nose: expressive, balanced, elegant, red berry notes, ripe fruit. Palate: flavourful, good acidity, fine tannins, long.

MACÁN 2009 T
100% tempranillo.

93 Colour: cherry, garnet rim. Nose: cocoa bean, spicy, ripe fruit, complex, closed. Palate: flavourful, full, balanced, good acidity, fine tannins.

BODEGAS BERBERANA

Ctra. El Ciego s/n
26350 Cenicero (La Rioja)
☎: +34 914 365 924
gromero@arcoinvest-group.com
www.berberana.com

BERBERANA VIÑA ALARDE 2008 TC
100% tempranillo.

87 Colour: ruby red, orangey edge. Nose: ripe fruit, balsamic herbs, sweet spices, fine reductive notes. Palate: fresh, flavourful, spicy.

BERBERANA VIÑA ALARDE 2007 TR
80% tempranillo, 20% garnacha.

88 Colour: cherry, garnet rim. Nose: ripe fruit, toasty, dark chocolate, fine reductive notes. Palate: powerful, flavourful, toasty, round tannins.

BODEGAS BERCEO

Cuevas, 32-34-36
26200 Haro (La Rioja)
☎: +34 941 310 744 - Fax: +34 948 670 259
bodegas@gurpegui.es
www.gurpegui.es

VIÑA BERCEO 2011 BFB
viura, malvasía, garnacha blanca.

85 Colour: bright straw. Nose: medium intensity, ripe fruit, citrus fruit, spicy. Palate: flavourful, fruity, fresh.

VIÑA BERCEO 2011 RD
garnacha, tempranillo, viura.

88 Colour: rose, purple rim. Nose: varietal, powerfull, complex, red berry notes, fruit expression. Palate: fresh, fruity, light-bodied, flavourful, powerful, sweetness.

LOS DOMINIOS DE BERCEO 2010 TC
tempranillo.

92 Colour: cherry, garnet rim. Nose: ripe fruit, spicy, creamy oak, toasty. Palate: powerful, flavourful, toasty, round tannins.

VIÑA BERCEO 2008 TC
tempranillo, garnacha, graciano.

91 Colour: deep cherry. Nose: ripe fruit, sweet spices, scrubland. Palate: spicy, fine bitter notes.

BERCEO "NUEVA GENERACIÓN" 2008 TC
tempranillo, graciano, mazuelo.

91 Colour: cherry, garnet rim. Nose: ripe fruit, spicy, creamy oak, toasty, complex. Palate: powerful, flavourful, toasty, round tannins, balanced.

LOS DOMINIOS DE BERCEO "RESERVA 36" 2006 TR
tempranillo.

90 Colour: deep cherry. Nose: sweet spices, creamy oak, toasty, ripe fruit. Palate: spirituous, good structure, flavourful, powerful, spicy.

GONZALO DE BERCEO 2006 TR
tempranillo, graciano, mazuelo, garnacha.

88 Colour: deep cherry, orangey edge. Nose: scrubland, spicy, fruit preserve, old leather, tobacco. Palate: flavourful, long, balsamic.

GONZALO DE BERCEO 2004 TGR
tempranillo, graciano, mazuelo.

88 Colour: dark-red cherry. Nose: sweet spices, slightly evolved, fruit preserve. Palate: creamy, ripe fruit, flavourful, soft tannins.

BODEGAS BERONIA

Ctra. Ollauri - Nájera, Km. 1,8
26220 Ollauri (La Rioja)
☎: +34 941 338 000 - Fax: +34 941 338 266
beronia@beronia.es
www.beronia.es

BERONIA 2011 RD
100% tempranillo.

84

BERONIA TEMPRANILLO ELABORACIÓN ESPECIAL 2009 T
100% tempranillo.

91 Colour: cherry, garnet rim. Nose: spicy, creamy oak, red berry notes, roasted coffee. Palate: powerful, flavourful, toasty, round tannins.

BERONIA ECOLÓGICO 2009 T
100% tempranillo.

88 Colour: cherry, garnet rim. Nose: ripe fruit, balsamic herbs, spicy. Palate: correct, good acidity, good finish.

BERONIA 2007 TR
90% tempranillo, 5% graciano, 5% mazuelo.

90 Colour: dark-red cherry, orangey edge. Nose: cocoa bean, spicy, elegant. Palate: creamy, ripe fruit, powerful, flavourful.

BERONIA GRACIANO 2009 T
100% graciano.

88 Colour: cherry, garnet rim. Nose: ripe fruit, fruit expression, expressive, powerfull. Palate: creamy, spicy, fruity, spirituous, complex.

III A.C., BERONIA 2008 T
92% tempranillo, 4% graciano, 4% mazuelo.

92 Colour: dark-red cherry. Nose: ripe fruit, fruit expression, powerfull, characterful, expressive, toasty, creamy oak. Palate: powerful, flavourful, complex, creamy, toasty.

BERONIA 2008 TC
83% tempranillo, 15% garnacha, 2% mazuelo.

87 Colour: cherry, garnet rim. Nose: ripe fruit, spicy, toasty, tobacco, waxy notes. Palate: powerful, flavourful, toasty, round tannins.

BERONIA MAZUELO 2006 TR
100% mazuelo.

87 Colour: cherry, garnet rim. Nose: sweet spices, earthy notes, fruit preserve. Palate: fine bitter notes, good acidity, ripe fruit.

BERONIA SELECCIÓN 198 BARRICAS 2005 TR
90% tempranillo, 7% mazuelo, graciano.

92 Colour: dark-red cherry. Nose: ripe fruit, powerfull, damp earth, truffle notes. Palate: elegant, round, full, rich, soft tannins.

BERONIA 2005 TGR
90% tempranillo, 8% mazuelo, 2% graciano.

91 Colour: deep cherry, garnet rim. Nose: caramel, spicy, elegant, ripe fruit. Palate: spicy, classic aged character, powerful, good structure.

BODEGAS BILBAÍNAS

Estación, 3
26200 Haro (La Rioja)
☎: +34 941 310 147 - Fax: +34 935 051 567
m.oyono@bodegasbilbainas.com
www.bodegasbilbainas.com

LA VICALANDA 2007 TR
100% tempranillo.

93 Colour: cherry, garnet rim. Nose: elegant, complex, spicy, ripe fruit. Palate: good structure, flavourful, balanced, good acidity, full.

BODEGAS BILBAINAS GARNACHA 2010 T
100% garnacha.

92 Colour: cherry, purple rim. Nose: floral, ripe fruit, fresh, balanced, balsamic herbs. Palate: flavourful, fruity, fresh, easy to drink.

VIÑA ZACO 2010 T
100% tempranillo.

90 Colour: bright cherry, garnet rim. Nose: balanced, complex, ripe fruit, cocoa bean. Palate: balanced, ripe fruit, long.

VIÑA ZACO 2009 T
100% tempranillo.

90 Colour: cherry, garnet rim. Nose: balanced, ripe fruit, sweet spices, complex. Palate: good structure, flavourful.

VIÑA POMAL 2009 TC
100% tempranillo.

88 Colour: cherry, garnet rim. Nose: spicy, fine reductive notes, wet leather, fruit liqueur notes. Palate: spicy, long, flavourful.

VIÑA POMAL "ALTO DE LA CASETA" 2008 T
100% tempranillo.

91 Colour: cherry, garnet rim. Nose: ripe fruit, wild herbs, spicy, creamy oak, fine reductive notes. Palate: balanced, flavourful.

BODEGAS BILBAINAS GRACIANO 2007 T
100% graciano.

92 Colour: cherry, garnet rim. Nose: ripe fruit, spicy, creamy oak. Palate: powerful, flavourful, toasty, round tannins.

LA VICALANDA 2005 TGR
100% tempranillo.

94 Colour: cherry, garnet rim. Nose: spicy, toasty, complex, nose:tic coffee, dark chocolate, ripe fruit. Palate: powerful, flavourful, toasty, round tannins.

VIÑA POMAL 2007 TR
100% tempranillo.

91 Colour: cherry, garnet rim. Nose: spicy, creamy oak, toasty, characterful, candied fruit. Palate: powerful, flavourful, toasty, round tannins.

BODEGAS BRETÓN CRIADORES

Ctra. de Fuenmayor, Km. 1,5
26370 Navarrete (La Rioja)
☎: +34 941 440 840 - Fax: +34 941 440 812
info@bodegasbreton.com
www.bodegasbreton.com

IUVENE 2011 T
85% tempranillo, 15% garnacha.

88 Colour: cherry, purple rim. Nose: fruit expression, wild herbs, expressive. Palate: balanced, flavourful, long.

LORIÑÓN 2009 TC
100% tempranillo.

88 Colour: cherry, garnet rim. Nose: spicy, creamy oak, toasty, ripe fruit. Palate: powerful, flavourful, toasty, round tannins.

L 5 LORIÑÓN 2008 TC
85% tempranillo, 15% graciano.

90 Colour: cherry, garnet rim. Nose: ripe fruit, spicy, creamy oak, toasty, characterful. Palate: powerful, flavourful, toasty, round tannins.

LORIÑÓN 2006 TR
90% tempranillo, 10% graciano.

88 Colour: bright cherry, garnet rim. Nose: balanced, ripe fruit, spicy. Palate: fruity, flavourful, round tannins.

ALBA DE BRETÓN 2005 TR
85% tempranillo, 15% graciano.

91 Colour: deep cherry. Nose: undergrowth, damp earth, candied fruit, creamy oak, toasty. Palate: round, powerful, flavourful, spicy, toasty.

DOMINIO DE CONTE 2005 TR
90% tempranillo, 10% graciano.

91 Colour: dark-red cherry. Nose: earthy notes, damp earth, fine reductive notes, dark chocolate, sweet spices, cedar wood. Palate: flavourful, rich, complex, spicy, reductive nuances.

BODEGAS CAMPILLO

Ctra. de Logroño, s/n
01300 Laguardia (Álava)
☎: +34 945 600 826 - Fax: +34 945 600 837
info@bodegascampillo.es
www.bodegascampillo.es

CAMPILLO 2011 BFB
85% viura, 10% malvasía, 5% chardonnay.

91 Colour: bright yellow. Nose: ripe fruit, sweet spices, creamy oak, fragrant herbs. Palate: rich, flavourful, fresh, good acidity.

CAMPILLO 2011 RD
100% tempranillo.

86 Colour: rose. Nose: fresh fruit, red berry notes, powerfull. Palate: fresh, fruity, powerful, flavourful.

CAMPILLO 2008 TC
100% tempranillo.

89 Colour: cherry, garnet rim. Nose: ripe fruit, waxy notes, old leather, powerfull, spicy. Palate: long, flavourful, spicy, correct.

CAMPILLO RESERVA SELECTA 2005 TR
100% tempranillo.

93 Colour: cherry, garnet rim. Nose: ripe fruit, spicy, creamy oak, toasty, red berry notes, mineral. Palate: powerful, flavourful, toasty, round tannins.

CAMPILLO FINCA CUESTA CLARA 2005 TR
100% tempranillo.

93 Colour: cherry, garnet rim. Nose: ripe fruit, spicy, creamy oak, toasty, dark chocolate. Palate: powerful, flavourful, toasty, round tannins.

CAMPILLO RESERVA ESPECIAL 2005 TR
85% tempranillo, 10% graciano, 5% cabernet sauvignon.

91 Colour: cherry, garnet rim. Nose: ripe fruit, scrubland, sweet spices, creamy oak. Palate: correct, ripe fruit, round tannins.

CAMPILLO 2001 TGR
95% tempranillo, 5% graciano.

90 Colour: dark-red cherry. Nose: fruit preserve, old leather, damp earth. Palate: powerful, flavourful, toasty, roasted-coffee afterpalate:, ripe fruit.

BODEGAS CAMPO VIEJO

Camino de la Puebla, 50
26006 Logroño (La Rioja)
☎: +34 941 279 900 - Fax: +34 941 279 901
campoviejo@domecqbodegas.com
www.domecqbodegas.com

FÉLIX AZPILICUETA COLECCIÓN PRIVADA 2011 BFB
viura.

90 Colour: bright yellow. Nose: powerfull, ripe fruit, sweet spices, creamy oak, fragrant herbs. Palate: rich, smoky afterpalate:, flavourful, fresh, good acidity.

ALCORTA & CARMEN RUSCADELLA 2011 B
viura.

88 Colour: bright straw. Nose: fresh, fresh fruit, white flowers. Palate: flavourful, fruity, good acidity, balanced.

CV DE CAMPO VIEJO 2011 B
viura.

84

ALCORTA & FRIENDS 2011 B

82

ALCORTA & CARMEN RUSCADELLA 2011 RD
tempranillo.

88 Colour: onion pink. Nose: red berry notes, raspberry. Palate: good acidity, powerful, flavourful.

ALCORTA GARNACHA 2011 T
garnacha.

86 Colour: deep cherry. Nose: ripe fruit, fruit expression, scrubland. Palate: flavourful, fine bitter notes, good acidity.

ALCORTA & FRIENDS 2011 T

86 Colour: cherry, purple rim. Nose: fresh fruit, red berry notes, floral, fruit expression. Palate: flavourful, fruity, good acidity, round tannins.

AZPILICUETA 2009 TC
tempranillo, graciano, mazuelo.

91 Colour: cherry, garnet rim. Nose: spicy, creamy oak, toasty, complex, ripe fruit. Palate: powerful, flavourful, toasty, round tannins.

FÉLIX AZPILICUETA COLECCIÓN PRIVADA 2008 T
tempranillo, graciano, mazuelo.

93 Colour: cherry, garnet rim. Nose: ripe fruit, spicy, creamy oak, toasty, complex, characterful. Palate: powerful, flavourful, toasty, round tannins.

CV DE CAMPO VIEJO 2011 RD
tempranillo.

87 Colour: rose, purple rim. Nose: powerfull, ripe fruit, red berry notes, floral, expressive. Palate: fleshy, powerful, fruity, fresh.

ALCORTA & CARMEN RUSCADELLA 2008 T
tempranillo.

90 Colour: cherry, garnet rim. Nose: ripe fruit, spicy, creamy oak, toasty. Palate: powerful, flavourful, toasty, round tannins.

CV DE CAMPO VIEJO 2008 TC
tempranillo, garnacha, mazuelo.

89 Colour: dark-red cherry. Nose: spicy, cedar wood, toasty, ripe fruit, fruit expression. Palate: powerful, flavourful, balanced, balsamic.

ALCORTA 2008 TC
tempranillo.

88 Colour: dark-red cherry. Nose: spicy, creamy oak, ripe fruit, fruit expression. Palate: powerful, flavourful.

AZPILICUETA 2007 TR
tempranillo, graciano, mazuelo.

91 Colour: cherry, garnet rim. Nose: balanced, expressive, elegant, ripe fruit, spicy. Palate: fruity, round tannins, good acidity.

CAMPO VIEJO 2008 TC
tempranillo, garnacha, mazuelo.

87 Colour: dark-red cherry. Nose: spicy, toasty, short, closed, ripe fruit. Palate: flavourful, good structure, spicy, lacks expression.

DOMINIO CAMPO VIEJO 2007 T
tempranillo, graciano, mazuelo.

89 Colour: dark-red cherry. Nose: characterful, expressive, creamy oak, toasty, dark chocolate, cedar wood. Palate: spicy, ripe fruit.

CAMPO VIEJO 2007 TR
tempranillo, graciano, mazuelo.

87 Colour: cherry, garnet rim. Nose: ripe fruit, creamy oak, nose:tic coffee, fruit expression. Palate: ripe fruit, round, spicy, creamy.

ALCORTA 2006 TR
tempranillo.

88 Colour: cherry, garnet rim. Nose: fruit liqueur notes, sweet spices, creamy oak, toasty, fine reductive notes. Palate: correct, flavourful, long, spicy.

CAMPO VIEJO 2004 TGR
tempranillo, graciano, mazuelo.

90 Colour: pale ruby, brick rim edge. Nose: ripe fruit, tobacco, old leather. Palate: spicy, powerful, flavourful, round.

BODEGAS CASA PRIMICIA

Camino de la Hoya, 1
01300 Laguardia (Álava)
☎: +34 945 600 296 - Fax: +34 945 621 252
info@bodegascasaprimicia.com
www.bodegasprimicia.com

VIÑA DIEZMO 2009 TC
100% tempranillo.

88 Colour: cherry, garnet rim. Nose: ripe fruit, sweet spices, mineral. Palate: flavourful, powerful.

PRIMICIA 2007 TR
100% tempranillo.

89 Colour: dark-red cherry. Nose: nose:tic coffee, spicy, creamy oak, fruit expression, elegant, expressive. Palate: elegant, round, powerful, flavourful, fruity, spicy, ripe fruit.

CASA PRIMICIA GRACIANO 2007 T
100% graciano.

88 Colour: deep cherry. Nose: toasty, dark chocolate, spicy, ripe fruit. Palate: fruity, aged character, oaky.

CASA PRIMICIA TEMPRANILLO 2007 T
100% tempranillo.

88 Colour: cherry, garnet rim. Nose: spicy, creamy oak, toasty. Palate: powerful, flavourful, toasty, round tannins.

CASA PRIMICIA MAZUELO 2007 TC
100% mazuelo.

87 Colour: dark-red cherry, orangey edge. Nose: spicy, aged wood nuances, ripe fruit. Palate: ripe fruit, spicy, toasty.

JULIÁN MADRID 2007 TR
80% tempranillo, 20% otras.

87 Colour: deep cherry. Nose: spicy, roasted coffee, ripe fruit. Palate: ripe fruit, creamy, oaky.

CASA PRIMICIA GARNACHA 2007 TC
100% garnacha.

80

COFRADÍA 2005 TR
100% tempranillo.

93 Colour: dark-red cherry, orangey edge. Nose: earthy notes, scrubland, spicy, smoky, cigar, sweet spices. Palate: balanced, flavourful, long, spicy, round tannins.

BODEGAS CASTILLO DE SAJAZARRA

Del Río, s/n
26212 Sajazarra (La Rioja)
☎: +34 941 320 066 - Fax: +34 941 320 251
bodega@castillodesajazarra.com
www.castillodesajazarra.com

SOLAR DE LÍBANO 2009 TC
97% tempranillo, 3% graciano.

87 Colour: cherry, garnet rim. Nose: spicy, creamy oak, toasty. Palate: powerful, flavourful, toasty, round tannins.

SOLAR DE LÍBANO 2008 TC
97% tempranillo, 3% graciano, garnacha.

90 Colour: cherry, garnet rim. Nose: ripe fruit, spicy, creamy oak, toasty, earthy notes. Palate: powerful, flavourful, toasty, round tannins.

SOLAR DE LÍBANO 2008 TR
97% tempranillo, 3% graciano, garnacha.

91 Colour: cherry, garnet rim. Nose: ripe fruit, spicy, creamy oak, toasty. Palate: powerful, flavourful, toasty, round tannins.

CASTILLO DE SAJAZARRA 2006 TR
100% tempranillo.

90 Colour: cherry, garnet rim. Nose: spicy, creamy oak, toasty. Palate: powerful, flavourful, toasty, round tannins.

DIGMA AUTOR 2006 TR
100% tempranillo.

94 Colour: deep cherry, garnet rim. Nose: balanced, complex, elegant, ripe fruit, creamy oak. Palate: flavourful, balanced, mineral.

BODEGAS CERROLAZA

Ctra. de Burgos, km. 5 Salida 10 La Grajera
26007 Logroño (La Rioja)
☎: +34 941 286 728 - Fax: +34 941 286 729
info@bodegascerrolaza.com
www.bodegascerrolaza.com

ATICUS VENDIMIA SELECCIONADA 2008 T
100% tempranillo.

88 Colour: cherry, garnet rim. Nose: ripe fruit, expressive, spicy, old leather. Palate: flavourful, fruity, round tannins.

ATICUS 2007 TC
100% tempranillo.

85 Colour: cherry, garnet rim. Nose: ripe fruit, spicy, creamy oak, slightly evolved. Palate: powerful, flavourful, toasty.

ATICUS 2006 TR
100% tempranillo.

85 Colour: dark-red cherry, bright ochre rim. Nose: rancio notes, aged wood nuances, spicy. Palate: round, flavourful, spicy, lacks expression.

BODEGAS CONSEJO DE LA ALTA

Avda. de Fuenmayor, s/n
26350 Cenicero (La Rioja)
☎: +34 941 455 005 - Fax: +34 941 455 010
comercial@consejodelaalta.com
www.consejodelaalta.com

CONSEJO DE LA ALTA 2009 TC
100% tempranillo.

89 Colour: cherry, garnet rim. Nose: ripe fruit, spicy, creamy oak, toasty, balsamic herbs. Palate: powerful, flavourful, toasty, round tannins, balanced.

ALTA RÍO 2008 TC
100% tempranillo.

86 Colour: cherry, garnet rim. Nose: ripe fruit, spicy, toasty. Palate: powerful, flavourful, toasty, fine bitter notes.

CONSEJO DE LA ALTA 2006 TR
tempranillo.

90 Colour: dark-red cherry, orangey edge. Nose: ripe fruit, spicy, creamy oak, fine reductive notes. Palate: good acidity, round, flavourful, spicy.

BODEGAS CORRAL

Ctra. de Logroño, Km. 10
26370 Navarrete (La Rioja)
☎: +34 941 440 193 - Fax: +34 941 440 195
info@donjacobo.es
www.donjacobo.es

DON JACOBO 2011 B
100% viura.

86 Colour: bright straw. Nose: medium intensity, fresh fruit, dried herbs. Palate: fresh, correct, good acidity, easy to drink.

DON JACOBO 2011 RD
50% tempranillo, 40% garnacha, 10% mazuelo.

86 Colour: rose. Nose: fresh fruit, neat, varietal. Palate: powerful, light-bodied, fruity, fresh.

DON JACOBO ECOLÓGICO 2010 T
50% tempranillo, 50% mazuelo.

88 Colour: cherry, garnet rim. Nose: balanced, red berry notes, ripe fruit, violets. Palate: correct, balanced.

ALTOS DE CORRAL 2008 T FERMENTADO EN BARRICA
100% tempranillo.

91 Colour: deep cherry. Nose: ripe fruit, sweet spices, dark chocolate. Palate: flavourful, spicy, ripe fruit.

DON JACOBO 2007 TC
85% tempranillo, 10% garnacha, 5% mazuelo, graciano.

88 Colour: light cherry. Nose: sweet spices, creamy oak, ripe fruit. Palate: fruity, flavourful, powerful.

ALTOS DE CORRAL SINGLE ESTATE 2004 T
100% tempranillo.

89 Colour: cherry, garnet rim. Nose: wet leather, cigar, waxy notes, spicy, scrubland. Palate: long, spicy, flavourful, balanced.

DON JACOBO 2004 TR
85% tempranillo, 10% garnacha, mazuelo.

86 Colour: pale ruby, brick rim edge. Nose: spicy, creamy oak, wet leather, cigar. Palate: long, flavourful, balanced.

DON JACOBO 1996 TGR
85% tempranillo, 15% garnacha.

89 Colour: pale ruby, brick rim edge. Nose: elegant, spicy, fine reductive notes, wet leather, aged wood nuances, fruit liqueur notes. Palate: spicy, fine tannins, elegant, long.

BODEGAS COVILA

Camino del Soto, 26
01306 La Puebla de Labarca (Álava)
☎: +34 945 627 232 - Fax: +34 945 627 295
comercial@covila.es
www.covila.es

COVILA 2005 TGR
100% tempranillo.

89 Colour: very deep cherry, garnet rim. Nose: balanced, complex, ripe fruit, spicy, fine reductive notes. Palate: balanced, fine bitter notes.

PAGOS DE LABARCA AEX 2009 T
100% tempranillo.

91 Colour: cherry, garnet rim. Nose: spicy, creamy oak, toasty, characterful, ripe fruit, mineral. Palate: powerful, flavourful, toasty, round tannins.

BODEGAS CUNA DE REYES

Ctra. de Uruñuela, s/n
26300 Najera (La Rioja)
☎: +34 941 360 280 - Fax: +34 941 410 423
bodegas@cunadereyes.es
www.cunadereyes.es

CUNA DE REYES EDICIÓN LIMITADA 2008 T
100% tempranillo.

89 Colour: dark-red cherry, garnet rim. Nose: ripe fruit, sweet spices, creamy oak, closed. Palate: flavourful, spicy, long.

BODEGAS DARIEN

Ctra. Logroño-Zaragoza, Km. 7
26006 Logroño (La Rioja)
☎: +34 941 258 130 - Fax: +34 941 265 285
info@darien.es
www.darien.es

DARIEN 2007 TR
87% tempranillo, 13% graciano.

90 Colour: cherry, garnet rim. Nose: spicy, creamy oak, toasty, characterful. Palate: powerful, flavourful, toasty, round tannins.

DELIUS 2004 TR
80% tempranillo, 20% graciano.

90 Colour: cherry, garnet rim. Nose: spicy, creamy oak, toasty, characterful. Palate: powerful, flavourful, toasty, round tannins.

DARIEN SELECCIÓN 2003 T
68% tempranillo, 32% mazuelo.

88 Colour: cherry, garnet rim. Nose: ripe fruit, spicy, creamy oak, toasty, characterful. Palate: powerful, flavourful, toasty, round tannins.

BODEGAS DE CRIANZA MARQUÉS DE GRIÑÓN

Ctra. de El Ciego, s/n
26350 Cenicero (La Rioja)
☎: +34 914 365 924
gromero@arcoinvest-group.com

MARQUÉS DE GRIÑÓN ALEA 2008 T
100% tempranillo.

87 Colour: bright cherry. Nose: ripe fruit, sweet spices, creamy oak, cocoa bean. Palate: flavourful, fruity, toasty, correct.

MARQUÉS DE GRIÑÓN COLECCIÓN PRIVADA 2008 TC
100% tempranillo.

88 Colour: cherry, garnet rim. Nose: ripe fruit, spicy, fine reductive notes. Palate: flavourful, toasty, round tannins, balanced.

BODEGAS DE FAMILIA BURGO VIEJO

Concordia, 8
26540 Alfaro (La Rioja)
☎: +34 941 183 405 - Fax: +34 941 181 603
bodegas@burgoviejo.com
www.burgoviejo.com

BURGO VIEJO 2011 T
85% tempranillo, 10% garnacha, 5% mazuelo.

82

BURGO VIEJO 2006 TR
85% tempranillo, 10% graciano, 5% mazuelo.

87 Colour: light cherry, orangey edge. Nose: spicy, scrubland, old leather. Palate: correct, flavourful, long.

BURGO VIEJO 2002 TGR
100% tempranillo.

84

BURGO VIEJO 2009 TC
90% tempranillo, 10% graciano.

84

BODEGAS DE LOS HEREDEROS DEL MARQUÉS DE RISCAL

Bodegas de los Herederos del Marqués de Riscal
01340 Elciego (Álava)
☎: +34 945 606 000 - Fax: +34 945 606 023
marquesderiscal@marquesderiscal.com
www.marquesderiscal.com

FINCA TORREA 2007 TR
tempranillo, graciano.

94 Colour: dark-red cherry, orangey edge. Nose: nose:tic coffee, creamy oak, toasty, fruit expression, damp earth. Palate: round, powerful, spirituous, balsamic, spicy, ripe fruit.

MARQUÉS DE RISCAL 2007 TR
90% tempranillo, 10% graciano, mazuelo.

89 Colour: cherry, garnet rim. Nose: ripe fruit, spicy, creamy oak, toasty, complex. Palate: powerful, flavourful, toasty, round tannins, balanced.

MARQUÉS DE RISCAL 150 ANIVERSARIO 2004 TGR
tempranillo, graciano, otras.

92 Colour: deep cherry. Nose: ripe fruit, nose:tic coffee, spicy, wet leather. Palate: flavourful, fine bitter notes, good acidity, fine tannins.

MARQUÉS DE ARIENZO 2008 TC
tempranillo, graciano, mazuelo.

88 Colour: cherry, garnet rim. Nose: spicy, toasty, sweet spices, cocoa bean. Palate: powerful, flavourful, toasty, round tannins.

BARÓN DE CHIREL 2006 TR
80% tempranillo, 20% otras.

92 Colour: bright cherry, orangey edge. Nose: balanced, expressive, ripe fruit, spicy, tobacco. Palate: good structure, flavourful, spicy, long.

BODEGAS DEL MEDIEVO

Circunvalación San Roque, s/n
26559 Aldeanueva de Ebro (La Rioja)
☎: +34 941 163 141 - Fax: +34 941 144 204
info@bodegasdelmedievo.com
www.bodegasdelmedievo.com

MEDIEVO 2009 TC
80% tempranillo, 20% graciano.

88 Colour: cherry, garnet rim. Nose: ripe fruit, spicy, fine reductive notes. Palate: powerful, flavourful, toasty.

COFRADE 2011 B
100% viura.

88 Colour: straw. Nose: varietal, elegant, fresh fruit. Palate: light-bodied, powerful, fresh, flavourful.

TUERCE BOTAS 2009 TC
100% graciano.

90 Colour: deep cherry. Nose: fruit expression, ripe fruit, fruit liqueur notes, cocoa bean. Palate: fruity, powerful, flavourful, ripe fruit, balsamic.

MEDIEVO 2007 TR
80% tempranillo, 20% graciano.

88 Colour: cherry, garnet rim. Nose: spicy, creamy oak, toasty. Palate: powerful, flavourful, toasty, round tannins.

MEDIEVO 2006 TGR
80% tempranillo, 10% garnacha, 5% graciano, 5% mazuelo.

87 Colour: bright cherry. Nose: powerfull, ripe fruit, spicy. Palate: powerful, fine bitter notes, good acidity.

BODEGAS DINASTÍA VIVANCO

Ctra. Nacional 232, s/n
26330 Briones (La Rioja)
☎: +34 941 322 013 - Fax: +34 941 322 316
infobodega@dinastiavivanco.es
www.dinastiavivanco.es

VIVANCO VIURA MALVASÍA TEMPRANILLO 2011 B
60% viura, 20% malvasía, 20% tempranillo blanco.

88 Colour: bright yellow, greenish rim. Nose: fresh, wild herbs, ripe fruit. Palate: flavourful, fruity, good acidity.

VIVANCO TEMPRANILLO GARNACHA 2011 RD
80% tempranillo, 20% garnacha.

90 Colour: rose, purple rim. Nose: powerfull, ripe fruit, red berry notes, floral, expressive. Palate: fleshy, powerful, fruity, fresh.

COLECCIÓN VIVANCO PARCELAS DE MAZUELO 2010 T
100% mazuelo.

89 Colour: deep cherry, purple rim. Nose: medium intensity, ripe fruit, sweet spices. Palate: flavourful, fruity, long.

COLECCIÓN VIVANCO 4 VARIETALES 2009 TC
70% tempranillo, 15% graciano, 10% garnacha, 5% mazuelo.

91 Colour: very deep cherry, garnet rim. Nose: cocoa bean, creamy oak, balanced, ripe fruit. Palate: long, ripe fruit, spicy, balanced, good acidity.

COLECCIÓN VIVANCO DULCE DE INVIERNO 2009 T
50% tempranillo, 20% graciano, 20% garnacha, 10% mazuelo.

94 Colour: coppery red. Nose: balanced, expressive, complex, dried fruit, floral. Palate: rich, flavourful, long, balanced, elegant.

COLECCIÓN VIVANCO PARCELAS DE MATURANA 2009 T
100% maturana.

92 Colour: black cherry. Nose: scrubland, grassy, powerfull, expressive. Palate: correct, good acidity, round tannins, fine bitter notes.

DINASTÍA VIVANCO 2009 TC
100% tempranillo.

89 Colour: cherry, garnet rim. Nose: balanced, ripe fruit, spicy, roasted coffee. Palate: flavourful, ripe fruit, good acidity.

DINASTÍA VIVANCO 2007 TR
90% tempranillo, 10% graciano.

87 Colour: dark-red cherry. Nose: spicy, aged wood nuances, dark chocolate, ripe fruit. Palate: good structure, powerful, spicy, classic aged character.

COLECCIÓN VIVANCO PARCELAS DE GARNACHA 2008 T
100% garnacha.

93 Colour: cherry, garnet rim. Nose: red berry notes, ripe fruit, earthy notes, sweet spices, toasty. Palate: powerful, flavourful, long, balanced.

COLECCIÓN VIVANCO PARCELAS DE GRACIANO 2007 T
100% graciano.

90 Colour: cherry, garnet rim. Nose: earthy notes, ripe fruit, spicy, creamy oak. Palate: powerful, flavourful, spicy, long, balanced.

BODEGAS DON SANCHO DE LONDOÑO

Ctra. Ollauri - Nájera s/n
26323 Hormilla (La Rioja)
☎: +34 941 058 976 - Fax: +34 941 058 976
info@dslbodegas.es
www.dslbodegas.es

LONDOÑO VENDIMIA SELECCIONADA 2010 BFB
viura, malvasía, garnacha blanca.

92 Colour: bright yellow. Nose: ripe fruit, sweet spices, creamy oak, fragrant herbs. Palate: rich, flavourful, fresh, good acidity, elegant.

LONDOÑO 2011 T
tempranillo, garnacha.

88 Colour: cherry, purple rim. Nose: expressive, fresh fruit, red berry notes, floral. Palate: flavourful, fruity, good acidity, round tannins.

LONDOÑO GRACIANO 2010 T
100% graciano.

89 Colour: cherry, garnet rim. Nose: fragrant herbs, balsamic herbs, ripe fruit, varietal. Palate: good structure, fresh, fruity, flavourful.

LONDOÑO 2009 TC
100% tempranillo.

90 Colour: cherry, garnet rim. Nose: ripe fruit, spicy, creamy oak, toasty, complex. Palate: powerful, flavourful, toasty, balanced.

LONDOÑO SELECCIÓN 2008 T
tempranillo, graciano.

89 Colour: cherry, garnet rim. Nose: spicy, toasty, fine reductive notes, ripe fruit. Palate: powerful, spicy, long.

BODEGAS ESTRAUNZA

Avda. La Poveda, 25
01306 Lapuebla de Labarca (Álava)
☎: +34 945 627 245 - Fax: +34 945 627 293
bodegasestraunza@euskatel.net
www.bodegasestraunza.com

SOLAR DE ESTRAUNZA 2011 B
100% viura.

87 Colour: bright straw. Nose: fresh, medium intensity, fresh fruit, fragrant herbs. Palate: fruity, fresh, flavourful.

SOLAR DE ESTRAUNZA 2011 T
100% tempranillo.

87 Colour: cherry, garnet rim. Nose: ripe fruit, red berry notes, varietal, fresh. Palate: sweetness, fruity, powerful, flavourful.

SOLAR DE ESTRAUNZA 2009 TC
100% tempranillo.

87 Colour: cherry, garnet rim. Nose: roasted coffee, fruit preserve. Palate: flavourful, round tannins.

SOLAR DE ESTRAUNZA 2005 TGR
100% tempranillo.

88 Colour: cherry, garnet rim. Nose: ripe fruit, spicy, creamy oak, toasty. Palate: powerful, flavourful, toasty, round tannins.

SOLAR DE ESTRAUNZA SELECCIÓN 2005 T
100% tempranillo.

88 Colour: cherry, garnet rim. Nose: medium intensity, tobacco, old leather. Palate: flavourful, spicy, easy to drink.

SOLAR DE ESTRAUNZA 2005 TR
100% tempranillo.

86 Colour: bright cherry, garnet rim. Nose: medium intensity, ripe fruit, spicy, tobacco. Palate: light-bodied, fine tannins.

BODEGAS EXOPTO

Ctra. de Elvillar, 26
01300 Laguardia (Álava)
☎: +34 650 213 993
info@exopto.net
www.exopto.net

HORIZONTE DE EXOPTO 2010 B
80% viura, 10% malvasía, 10% garnacha blanca.

90 Colour: bright yellow. Nose: balanced, complex, elegant, ripe fruit, floral. Palate: rich, spicy, fine bitter notes.

BOZETO DE EXOPTO 2011 T
50% garnacha, 40% tempranillo, 10% graciano.

88 Colour: cherry, purple rim. Nose: fresh fruit, red berry notes, floral. Palate: flavourful, fruity, good acidity, round tannins.

EXOPTO CUVÉE LUCA 2009 T
60% graciano, 30% tempranillo, 10% garnacha.

92 Colour: cherry, garnet rim. Nose: ripe fruit, spicy, creamy oak, toasty. Palate: powerful, flavourful, toasty, round tannins.

HORIZONTE DE EXOPTO 2009 T
80% tempranillo, 10% garnacha, 10% graciano.

91 Colour: cherry, garnet rim. Nose: spicy, ripe fruit. Palate: flavourful, good acidity, round tannins, light-bodied.

BODEGAS FAUSTINO

Ctra. de Logroño, s/n
01320 Oyón (Álava)
☎: +34 945 622 500 - Fax: +34 945 622 511
info@bodegasfaustino.es
www.bodegasfaustino.es

FAUSTINO V 2011 B
75% viura, 25% chardonnay.

88 Colour: bright straw. Nose: fresh, fresh fruit, white flowers, expressive. Palate: flavourful, fruity, balanced.

FAUSTINO DE AUTOR RESERVA ESPECIAL 2006 TR
86% tempranillo, 14% graciano.

91 Colour: deep cherry, orangey edge. Nose: spicy, creamy oak, balsamic herbs, fine reductive notes. Palate: flavourful, long, correct, round.

FAUSTINO I 75 ANIVERSARIO 2004 TGR
92% tempranillo, 8% graciano.

92 Colour: pale ruby, brick rim edge. Nose: spicy, wet leather, aged wood nuances, fruit liqueur notes, balanced. Palate: spicy, fine tannins, elegant, long.

FAUSTINO V 2006 TR
92% tempranillo, 8% mazuelo.

88 Colour: dark-red cherry. Nose: fruit preserve, powerfull, aged wood nuances, spicy. Palate: soft tannins, powerful, good structure, spicy.

FAUSTINO EDICIÓN ESPECIAL 2001 T
100% tempranillo.

93 Colour: pale ruby, brick rim edge. Nose: elegant, spicy, fine reductive notes, wet leather, aged wood nuances, fruit liqueur notes. Palate: spicy, fine tannins, elegant, long.

FAUSTINO I 2000 TGR
85% tempranillo, 10% graciano, 5% mazuelo.

88 Colour: pale ruby, brick rim edge. Nose: spicy, wet leather, aged wood nuances, fruit liqueur notes. Palate: spicy, fine tannins, elegant, long.

FAUSTINO V 2011 RD
100% tempranillo.

86 Colour: rose, purple rim. Nose: floral, lactic notes, red berry notes, ripe fruit. Palate: light-bodied, fresh, fruity, easy to drink.

FAUSTINO 2009 TC
100% tempranillo.

87 Colour: cherry, garnet rim. Nose: ripe fruit, medium intensity, sweet spices, creamy oak. Palate: warm, round, fruity, spicy.

BODEGAS FERNÁNDEZ EGUILUZ

Los Morales, 7 bajo
26339 Abalos (La Rioja)
☎: +34 941 334 166 - Fax: +34 941 308 055
p.larosa@hotmail.es
www.penalarosa.com

PEÑA LA ROSA 2011 B
viura, malvasía.

86 Colour: bright straw. Nose: fresh, fresh fruit, fragrant herbs. Palate: flavourful, fruity, good acidity, balanced.

PEÑA LA ROSA 2011 T MACERACIÓN CARBÓNICA
tempranillo.

87 Colour: cherry, purple rim. Nose: red berry notes, fresh fruit, balsamic herbs, floral. Palate: light-bodied, fresh, fruity, flavourful.

PEÑA LA ROSA VENDIMIA SELECCIONADA 2006 T
tempranillo.

88 Colour: bright cherry, orangey edge. Nose: fruit preserve, spicy. Palate: flavourful, fruity, good acidity, balanced.

BODEGAS FIN DE SIGLO

Camino Arenzana de Arriba
26311 Arenzana de Abajo (La Rioja)
☎: +34 941 410 042 - Fax: +34 941 410 043
bfs@bodegasfindesiglo.com
www.bodegasfindesiglo.com

RIBAGUDA GARNACHA 2010 TC
100% garnacha.

87 Colour: cherry, garnet rim. Nose: spicy, ripe fruit, scrubland. Palate: flavourful, concentrated, sweetness.

RIBAGUDA CEPAS VIEJAS 2007 TC
70% tempranillo, 25% garnacha, 5% mazuelo.

88 Colour: cherry, garnet rim. Nose: medium intensity, ripe fruit, spicy. Palate: fruity, flavourful, good acidity.

RIBAGUDA CEPAS VIEJAS 2005 TR
70% tempranillo, 25% garnacha, 5% mazuelo.

87 Colour: cherry, garnet rim. Nose: toasty, spicy, ripe fruit. Palate: spicy, ripe fruit.

RIBAGUDA 2008 TC
100% tempranillo.

88 Colour: cherry, garnet rim. Nose: ripe fruit, spicy, creamy oak, toasty. Palate: powerful, flavourful, toasty.

BODEGAS FINCA MANZANOS

Ctra. NA-134,km. 49
31560 Azagra (Navarra)
☎: +34 948 692 500 - Fax: +34 948 692 700
info@fincamanzanos.com
www.fincamanzanos.com

FINCA MANZANOS 2011 B
100% viura.

89 Colour: bright straw. Nose: neat, fresh, varietal, floral, fresh fruit. Palate: powerful, flavourful, fruity, fresh, smoky afterpalate:.

FINCA MANZANOS 2010 B BARRICA
100% viura.

89 Colour: bright yellow. Nose: ripe fruit, sweet spices, creamy oak, fragrant herbs. Palate: rich, flavourful, fresh, good acidity.

FINCA MANZANOS 2011 T JOVEN
80% tempranillo, 20% garnacha.

87 Colour: cherry, purple rim. Nose: medium intensity, red berry notes, wild herbs. Palate: fruity, flavourful, correct, fine bitter notes.

FINCA MANZANOS 2008 TC
90% tempranillo, 5% garnacha, 5% mazuelo.

86 Colour: cherry, garnet rim. Nose: ripe fruit, old leather, spicy, balsamic herbs. Palate: flavourful, fruity.

BODEGAS FLORENTINO MARTÍNEZ

Ermita, 33
26311 Cordovín (La Rioja)
☎: +34 941 418 614 - Fax: +34 941 418 614
bodegas@florentinomartinez.com
www.florentinomartinez.com

FLORENTIUS 2011 B
viura, malvasía.

90 Colour: bright straw. Nose: fruit expression, complex, varietal, fragrant herbs. Palate: light-bodied, full, flavourful, powerful, fresh, fruity.

FLORENTINO MARTÍNEZ 2011 B
viura.

84

FLORENTINO MARTÍNEZ 2011 T
tempranillo.

86 Colour: cherry, purple rim. Nose: medium intensity, ripe fruit, dried herbs. Palate: flavourful, long.

FLORENTINO MARTÍNEZ 2008 TC
tempranillo.

89 Colour: cherry, garnet rim. Nose: ripe fruit, spicy, medium intensity. Palate: flavourful, toasty, round tannins.

TANKA 2005 T
tempranillo.

91 Colour: cherry, garnet rim. Nose: ripe fruit, spicy, creamy oak, toasty, characterful. Palate: powerful, flavourful, toasty, round tannins.

FLORENTINO MARTÍNEZ 2011 CLARETE
viura, garnacha.

75

BODEGAS FOS

Término de Vialba, s/n
01340 Elciego (Álava)
☎: +34 945 606 681 - Fax: +34 945 606 608
fos@bodegasfos.com
www.bodegasfos.com

FOS 2011 B

89 Colour: bright yellow. Nose: powerfull, ripe fruit, sweet spices, fragrant herbs. Palate: rich, flavourful, fresh, good acidity.

FOS 2009 TC
90% tempranillo, 10% graciano.

89 Colour: cherry, garnet rim. Nose: ripe fruit, spicy, creamy oak, toasty, complex. Palate: powerful, flavourful, toasty, round tannins.

FOS BARANDA 2008 T
100% tempranillo.

91 Colour: deep cherry, garnet rim. Nose: balanced, expressive, ripe fruit, dark chocolate, creamy oak. Palate: good structure, complex, flavourful.

FOS 2007 TR
80% tempranillo, 20% graciano.

89 Colour: cherry, garnet rim. Nose: ripe fruit, spicy, creamy oak, complex. Palate: powerful, flavourful, round tannins, fruity aftespalate:.

BODEGAS FRANCISCO GARCÍA RAMÍREZ E HIJOS

Ctra. Ventas, s/n
26143 Murillo del Río Leza (La Rioja)
☎: +34 941 432 372 - Fax: +34 941 432 156
info@bodegasgarciaramirez.com

HEREDAD GARBLO 2008 T
85% tempranillo, 5% graciano, 5% mazuelo, 5% garnacha.

90 Colour: cherry, garnet rim. Nose: spicy, creamy oak, toasty, ripe fruit. Palate: powerful, flavourful, toasty, round tannins.

HEREDAD GARBLO 2005 TR
80% tempranillo, 10% garnacha, 5% mazuelo, 5% graciano.

87 Colour: deep cherry, orangey edge. Nose: medium intensity, ripe fruit, spicy, tobacco, dark chocolate. Palate: fruity, spicy.

BODEGAS FRANCO ESPAÑOLAS

Cabo Noval, 2
26009 Logroño (La Rioja)
☎: +34 941 251 300 - Fax: +34 941 262 948
francoespanolas@francoespanolas.com
www.francoespanolas.com

RIOJA BORDÓN 2008 TC
tempranillo, garnacha.

85 Colour: cherry, garnet rim. Nose: spicy, ripe fruit, scrubland, fine reductive notes. Palate: flavourful, long, spicy.

BARBARO 2007 T
garnacha, tempranillo, mazuelo.

91 Colour: cherry, garnet rim. Nose: ripe fruit, spicy, creamy oak, toasty, fine reductive notes. Palate: powerful, flavourful, toasty, fine tannins.

RIOJA BORDÓN 2007 TR
tempranillo, garnacha, mazuelo.

89 Colour: cherry, garnet rim. Nose: ripe fruit, spicy, creamy oak, toasty, fine reductive notes. Palate: powerful, flavourful, toasty, round tannins.

BARON D'ANGLADE 2005 TR
tempranillo, mazuelo, graciano.

92 Colour: dark-red cherry, garnet rim. Nose: fine reductive notes, animal reductive notes, tobacco, ripe fruit, cocoa bean, spicy. Palate: round, rich, powerful, toasty, soft tannins.

RIOJA BORDÓN 2004 TGR
mazuelo, tempranillo, graciano.

88 Colour: cherry, garnet rim. Nose: spicy, creamy oak, complex, wet leather. Palate: powerful, flavourful, toasty, round tannins.

BODEGAS GARCÍA DE OLANO

Ctra. Vitoria, s/n
01309 Paganos - La Guardia (Álava)
☎: +34 945 621 146 - Fax: +34 945 621 146
garciadeolano@telefonica.net
www.bodegasgarciadeolano.com

HEREDAD GARCÍA DE OLANO 2011 B
100% viura.

82

HEREDAD GARCÍA DE OLANO 2011 T
95% tempranillo, 5% viura.

87 Colour: cherry, purple rim. Nose: red berry notes, fragrant herbs, floral, medium intensity. Palate: powerful, flavourful, fruity.

HEREDAD GARCÍA DE OLANO 2010 T BARRICA
100% tempranillo.

86 Colour: bright cherry. Nose: ripe fruit, sweet spices. Palate: flavourful, fruity, toasty, round tannins.

3 DE OLANO 2009 T
100% tempranillo.

90 Colour: cherry, garnet rim. Nose: ripe fruit, creamy oak, toasty, cocoa bean. Palate: powerful, flavourful, toasty, balanced.

HEREDAD GARCÍA DE OLANO 2007 TC
100% tempranillo.

86 Colour: cherry, garnet rim. Nose: ripe fruit, spicy. Palate: powerful, flavourful, toasty, fruity, round tannins.

MAULEÓN 2005 TR
100% tempranillo.

83

BODEGAS GÓMEZ CRUZADO

Avda. Vizcaya, 6
26200 Haro (La Rioja)
☎: +34 941 312 502 - Fax: +34 941 303 567
bodega@gomezcruzado.com
www.gomezcruzado.com

HONORABLE GÓMEZ CRUZADO 2010 T
90% tempranillo, 10% garnacha.

91 Colour: bright cherry. Nose: ripe fruit, sweet spices, creamy oak. Palate: flavourful, fruity, toasty, round tannins.

GÓMEZ CRUZADO "GC" 2009 TC
80% tempranillo, 20% garnacha.

92 Colour: bright cherry. Nose: ripe fruit, sweet spices, creamy oak, expressive. Palate: flavourful, fruity, toasty, round tannins.

GÓMEZ CRUZADO 2007 TR
100% tempranillo.

88 Colour: dark-red cherry, orangey edge. Nose: ripe fruit, balsamic herbs, earthy notes, spicy, wet leather. Palate: balanced, powerful, flavourful, long.

BODEGAS GREGORIO MARTÍNEZ

Polígono 1 Parcela, 12
26190 Nalda (La Rioja)
☎: +34 941 220 266 - Fax: +34 941 203 849
bodegas@gregoriomartinez.com
www.gregoriomartinez.com

GREGORIO MARTÍNEZ 2010 BFB
100% viura.

84

GREGORIO MARTÍNEZ 2007 TC
100% tempranillo.

85 Colour: dark-red cherry. Nose: sweet spices, aged wood nuances, dried fruit. Palate: spirituous, powerful, good structure, spicy, pruney.

GREGORIO MARTÍNEZ 2005 TR
100% tempranillo.

87 Colour: cherry, garnet rim. Nose: ripe fruit, spicy, toasty, wet leather, balsamic herbs. Palate: powerful, flavourful, toasty.

GREGORIO MARTÍNEZ VENDIMIA SELECCIONADA 2005 TC
100% tempranillo.

87 Colour: dark-red cherry, orangey edge. Nose: scrubland, spicy, old leather, cigar. Palate: correct, flavourful, long.

BODEGAS HEREDAD BAÑOS BEZARES

Solana, s/n
26290 Briñas (La Rioja)
☎: +34 941 312 423 - Fax: +34 941 303 020
bodega@banosbezares.com
www.banosbezares.com

GRAN BOHEDAL 2011 BFB
100% viura.

89 Colour: bright straw. Nose: fresh fruit, fruit expression, smoky. Palate: creamy, smoky afterpalate:, flavourful.

BOHEDAL 2011 B
100% viura.

88 Colour: bright straw. Nose: fragrant herbs, fresh fruit, damp earth. Palate: powerful, flavourful, fruity, fresh.

BOHEDAL 2011 T MACERACIÓN CARBÓNICA
100% tempranillo.

87 Colour: cherry, garnet rim. Nose: fragrant herbs, ripe fruit. Palate: correct, balanced, fruity, good acidity.

BOHEDAL 2011 T JOVEN
100% tempranillo.

85 Colour: cherry, purple rim. Nose: ripe fruit, wild herbs, warm. Palate: fruity, flavourful, correct.

GRAN BOHEDAL 2009 TC
100% tempranillo.

87 Colour: cherry, garnet rim. Nose: ripe fruit, spicy, creamy oak, toasty. Palate: powerful, flavourful, toasty.

HEBABE 2008 T
100% graciano.

89 Colour: cherry, garnet rim. Nose: ripe fruit, scrubland, mineral, varietal, spicy. Palate: correct, flavourful, balsamic, long.

GRAN BOHEDAL 2007 TR
100% tempranillo.

87 Colour: cherry, garnet rim. Nose: ripe fruit, spicy, creamy oak, toasty, complex. Palate: powerful, flavourful, toasty, round tannins.

GRAN BOHEDAL 2004 TGR
100% tempranillo.

88 Colour: pale ruby, brick rim edge. Nose: spicy, fine reductive notes, wet leather, aged wood nuances, fruit liqueur notes. Palate: spicy, fine tannins, elegant, long.

BODEGAS HERMANOS PECIÑA

Ctra. de Vitoria, Km. 47
26338 San Vicente de la Sonsierra (La Rioja)
☎: +34 941 334 366 - Fax: +34 941 334 180
info@bodegashermanospecina.com
www.bodegashermanospecina.com

CHOBEO DE PECIÑA 2010 BFB
100% viura.

88 Colour: bright yellow. Nose: powerfull, ripe fruit, sweet spices, fragrant herbs. Palate: rich, flavourful, fresh, good acidity.

SEÑORÍO DE P. PECIÑA 2011 T
95% tempranillo, 3% garnacha, 2% graciano.

82

CHOBEO DE PECIÑA 2008 T
100% tempranillo.

90 Colour: cherry, garnet rim. Nose: ripe fruit, spicy, creamy oak, toasty, complex. Palate: powerful, flavourful, toasty, round tannins.

GRAN CHOBEO DE PECIÑA 2008 T
100% tempranillo.

90 Colour: deep cherry. Nose: characterful, fruit preserve, spicy. Palate: fine bitter notes, spicy, ripe fruit.

SEÑORÍO DE P. PECIÑA 2007 TC
95% tempranillo, 3% garnacha, 2% graciano.

88 Colour: cherry, garnet rim. Nose: spicy, creamy oak, toasty, ripe fruit. Palate: powerful, flavourful, toasty, round tannins.

SEÑORÍO DE P. PECIÑA 2001 TGR
95% tempranillo, 3% garnacha, 2% graciano.

90 Colour: pale ruby, brick rim edge. Nose: elegant, spicy, fine reductive notes, wet leather, aged wood nuances, fruit liqueur notes. Palate: spicy, fine tannins, elegant, long.

PECIÑA VENDIMIA SELECCIONADA 2001 TR
95% tempranillo, 3% garnacha, 2% graciano.

88 Colour: pale ruby, brick rim edge. Nose: elegant, fine reductive notes, wet leather. Palate: spicy, long.

SEÑORÍO DE P. PECIÑA 2001 TR

86 Colour: deep cherry, brick rim edge. Nose: fruit liqueur notes, old leather, spicy. Palate: correct, fine bitter notes, easy to drink.

BODEGAS IZADI

Herrería Travesía II, 5
01307 Villabuena de Álava (Álava)
☎: +34 945 609 086 - Fax: +34 945 609 261
club@grupoartevino.com
www.grupoartevino.com

IZADI 2011 BFB
80% viura, 20% malvasía.

88 Colour: straw. Nose: fresh fruit, grassy, smoky. Palate: good acidity, fruity, fresh, flavourful.

IZADI 2008 TC
100% tempranillo.

90 Colour: very deep cherry. Nose: ripe fruit, fruit expression, creamy oak, cocoa bean. Palate: flavourful, fruity, fresh, spicy, round tannins.

IZADI EL REGALO 2006 TR
90% tempranillo, 10% graciano, mazuelo, garnacha.

91 Colour: cherry, garnet rim. Nose: creamy oak, dark chocolate, candied fruit, ripe fruit. Palate: spicy, ripe fruit, fine bitter notes.

BODEGAS LA CATEDRAL - BODEGAS OLARRA

Avda. de Mendavia, 30
26009 Logroño (La Rioja)
☎: +34 941 235 299 - Fax: +34 941 253 703

GRAN EPULUM 2011 T
100% tempranillo.

89 Colour: cherry, purple rim. Nose: expressive, fresh fruit, red berry notes, floral. Palate: flavourful, fruity, good acidity.

GRAN EPULUM 2009 TC
80% tempranillo, 10% garnacha, mazuelo, graciano.

85 Colour: cherry, garnet rim. Nose: ripe fruit, balsamic herbs, premature reduction notes, spicy. Palate: powerful, flavourful, correct.

GRAN EPULUM 2006 TR
90% tempranillo, 5% garnacha, mazuelo, graciano.

87 Colour: bright cherry, brick rim edge. Nose: balanced, spicy, toasty. Palate: light-bodied, correct, good finish.

BODEGAS LA EMPERATRIZ

Ctra. Santo Domingo - Haro, Km. 31,5
26241 Baños de Rioja (La Rioja)
☎: +34 941 300 105 - Fax: +34 941 300 231
correo@bodegaslaemperatriz.com
www.bodegaslaemperatriz.com

FINCA LA EMPERATRIZ VIURA 2011 B
viura.

90 Colour: bright straw. Nose: fresh, fresh fruit, white flowers. Palate: flavourful, fruity, good acidity, balanced.

FINCA LA EMPERATRIZ VIURA CEPAS VIEJAS 2010 B
viura.

92 Colour: bright yellow. Nose: varietal, powerfull, complex, smoky, scrubland. Palate: elegant, spirituous, sweetness, fresh, fruity.

FINCA LA EMPERATRIZ TEMPRANILLO 2011 T
tempranillo.

88 Colour: cherry, purple rim. Nose: expressive, fresh fruit, red berry notes, floral. Palate: flavourful, fruity, good acidity, round tannins.

FINCA LA EMPERATRIZ PARCELA Nº 1 2010 T
tempranillo.

94 Colour: deep cherry. Nose: fruit expression, violet drops, fresh fruit, powerfull, varietal, complex. Palate: creamy, balsamic, complex, fruity.

Finca La Emperatriz
PARCELA nº 1
20
10

FINCA LA EMPERATRIZ GARNACHA CEPAS VIEJAS 2010 T
garnacha.

93 Colour: cherry, garnet rim. Nose: balanced, expressive, varietal, balsamic herbs, ripe fruit. Palate: good structure, full, round tannins.

FINCA LA EMPERATRIZ TERRUÑO 2009 T
tempranillo.

94 Colour: cherry, garnet rim. Nose: red berry notes, ripe fruit, sweet spices, creamy oak, toasty. Palate: powerful, flavourful, balanced, toasty.

RIOJA
Denominación de Origen Calificada
Rioja Alta
2009
Finca La Emperatriz
terruño

FINCA LA EMPERATRIZ 2008 TC
95% tempranillo, 3% garnacha, 2% viura.

88 Colour: cherry, garnet rim. Nose: ripe fruit, spicy, toasty. Palate: flavourful, long, fine bitter notes.

FINCA LA EMPERATRIZ 2009 TC
95% tempranillo, 3% garnacha, 2% viura.

94 Colour: dark-red cherry. Nose: complex, elegant, expressive, fruit expression, sweet spices, cocoa bean. Palate: powerful, flavourful, round, rich, full, toasty, fruity aftespalate:.

FINCA LA EMPERATRIZ 2007 TR
90% tempranillo, 10% graciano, mazuelo, garnacha.

91 Colour: deep cherry. Nose: creamy oak, spicy, cocoa bean, fruit expression. Palate: full, powerful, flavourful, complex.

BODEGAS LACUS

Cervantes, 18
26559 Aldeanueva de Ebro (La Rioja)
☎: +34 649 331 799 - Fax: +34 941 144 128
inedito@bodegaslacus.com
www.bodegaslacus.com

INÉDITO 2010 BFB
garnacha blanca.

89 Colour: bright yellow. Nose: candied fruit, sweet spices, citrus fruit. Palate: rich, toasty, fruity, good acidity.

INÉDITO 3/3 2010 T
50% tempranillo, 30% garnacha, 20% graciano.

91 Colour: bright cherry. Nose: ripe fruit, sweet spices, creamy oak, fragrant herbs. Palate: flavourful, fruity, toasty, round tannins.

INÉDITO H12 2008 T
75% graciano, 25% garnacha.

91 Colour: cherry, garnet rim. Nose: creamy oak, toasty, fruit expression. Palate: powerful, flavourful, toasty, round tannins.

INÉDITO S 2008 T
50% graciano, 40% tempranillo, 10% garnacha.

90 Colour: cherry, garnet rim. Nose: spicy, creamy oak, toasty, characterful, ripe fruit. Palate: powerful, flavourful, toasty, round tannins.

BODEGAS LAGAR DE ZABALA

Pza. Mayor, 2
26338 San Vicente de la Sonsierra (La Rioja)
☎: +34 941 334 435 - Fax: +34 941 334 435
bodegaslagardezabala@hotmail.com
www.bodegaslagardezabala.com

LAGAR DE ZABALA 2011 B
viura.

84

LAGAR DE ZABALA 2011 T
95% tempranillo, 5% garnacha.

86 Colour: cherry, purple rim. Nose: fresh fruit, red berry notes, floral, medium intensity. Palate: fresh, fruity, flavourful.

LAGAR DE ZABALA 2008 TC
95% tempranillo, 5% garnacha.

85 Colour: cherry, garnet rim. Nose: spicy, toasty, nose:tic coffee. Palate: flavourful, spicy, ripe fruit.

BODEGAS LAGUNILLA

Ctra. de Elciego, s/n
26350 Cenicero (La Rioja)
☎: +34 914 365 924 - Fax: +34 941 453 114
gromero@arcoinvest-group.com
www.berberana.com

LAGUNILLA OPTIMUS (MARQUÉS DE LA CONCORDIA FAMILY OF WINES) 2008 T
100% tempranillo.

91 Colour: garnet rim. Nose: ripe fruit, balsamic herbs, nose:tic coffee, creamy oak, toasty. Palate: spicy, powerful, flavourful, balanced, round tannins.

LAGUNILLA CASA DEL COMENDADOR (MARQUÉS DE LA CONCORDIA FAMILY OF WINES) 2008 TC
80% tempranillo, 20% garnacha.

89 Colour: cherry, garnet rim. Nose: ripe fruit, spicy, toasty, complex, cocoa bean, dark chocolate. Palate: powerful, flavourful, toasty, balanced.

LAGUNILLA CASA DEL COMENDADOR (MARQUÉS DE LA CONCORDIA FAMILY OF WINES) 2007 TR
80% tempranillo, 20% garnacha.

89 Colour: pale ruby, brick rim edge. Nose: ripe fruit, fruit liqueur notes, spicy, creamy oak, toasty, fine reductive notes. Palate: flavourful, long, spicy, balanced.

BODEGAS LANDALUCE

Ctra. Los Molinos, s/n
01300 Laguardia (Álava)
☎: +34 620 824 314
asier@bodegaslandaluce.es
www.bodegaslandaluce.es

ELLE DE LANDALUCE 2011 B
60% viura, 40% malvasía.

90 Colour: bright straw. Nose: floral, fragrant herbs, balanced, expressive, powerfull. Palate: rich, powerful, flavourful, sweetness, fresh, fruity.

LANDALUCE 2011 T MACERACIÓN CARBÓNICA
95% tempranillo, 5% viura.

87 Colour: cherry, purple rim. Nose: red berry notes, fresh fruit, fragrant herbs, floral. Palate: powerful, flavourful, fresh, fruity.

FINCAS DE LANDALUCE 2008 TC
100% tempranillo.

91 Colour: cherry, garnet rim. Nose: spicy, creamy oak, toasty, complex, balsamic herbs. Palate: powerful, flavourful, toasty, round tannins.

ELLE DE LANDALUCE 2008 TC
100% tempranillo.

89 Colour: dark-red cherry. Nose: sweet spices, aged wood nuances, ripe fruit. Palate: round tannins, flavourful, good structure, spicy.

CAPRICHO DE LANDALUCE 2006 T
100% tempranillo.

88 Colour: cherry, garnet rim. Nose: ripe fruit, spicy, creamy oak, toasty, wet leather. Palate: powerful, flavourful, toasty, round tannins.

BODEGAS LAR DE PAULA

Coscojal, s/n
01309 Elvillar (Álava)
☎: +34 945 604 068 - Fax: +34 945 604 105
info@lardepaula.com
www.lardepaula.com

LAR DE PAULA 2011 BFB
60% malvasía, 40% viura.

88 Colour: bright straw. Nose: fresh fruit, grassy, varietal, fresh, neat, expressive. Palate: powerful, flavourful, light-bodied, fruity, fresh.

LAR DE PAULA MADURADO 2010 T
100% tempranillo.

87 Colour: bright cherry. Nose: ripe fruit, sweet spices, creamy oak. Palate: flavourful, fruity, toasty, round tannins.

4 BESOS TEMPRANILLO 2008 T
100% tempranillo.

90 Colour: cherry, garnet rim. Nose: ripe fruit, spicy, creamy oak, toasty, red berry notes. Palate: powerful, flavourful, toasty, round tannins.

LAR DE PAULA 2008 TC
100% tempranillo.

89 Colour: deep cherry. Nose: medium intensity, ripe fruit, spicy. Palate: flavourful, spicy, ripe fruit.

MERUS.4 2007 T
100% tempranillo.

91 Colour: dark-red cherry, orangey edge. Nose: ripe fruit, spicy, creamy oak, fine reductive notes, balsamic herbs. Palate: long, powerful, flavourful.

LAR DE PAULA 2005 TR
100% tempranillo.

89 Colour: dark-red cherry, orangey edge. Nose: fine reductive notes, complex, cocoa bean, dark chocolate. Palate: flavourful, round, spicy, creamy.

LAR DE PAULA CEPAS VIEJAS 2005 TC
100% tempranillo.

88 Colour: cherry, garnet rim. Nose: spicy, creamy oak, toasty, characterful. Palate: powerful, flavourful, toasty, round tannins.

BODEGAS LARRAZ

Paraje Ribarrey. Pol. 12- Parcela 50
26350 Cenicero (La Rioja)
☎: +34 639 728 581
info@bodegaslarraz.com
www.bodegaslarraz.com

CAUDUM BODEGAS LARRAZ 2008 T
tempranillo.

87 Colour: cherry, garnet rim. Nose: balanced, fruit preserve, dark chocolate. Palate: long, balanced, round tannins.

CAUDUM BODEGAS LARRAZ SELECCIÓN ESPECIAL 2007 T
tempranillo.

87 Nose: balanced, powerfull, fruit preserve, spicy. Palate: fruity, flavourful, balanced, round tannins.

CAUDUM BODEGAS LARRAZ SELECCIÓN ESPECIAL 2009 T
tempranillo.

91 Colour: cherry, garnet rim. Nose: spicy, creamy oak, toasty, expressive, ripe fruit. Palate: powerful, flavourful, toasty, round tannins.

BODEGAS LEZA GARCÍA

San Ignacio, 26
26313 Uruñuela (La Rioja)
☎: +34 941 371 142 - Fax: +34 941 371 035
bodegasleza@bodegasleza.com
www.bodegasleza.com

VALDEPALACIOS 2011 T
85% tempranillo, 10% garnacha, 5% mazuelo.

87 Colour: cherry, purple rim. Nose: expressive, fresh fruit, red berry notes, floral. Palate: flavourful, fruity, easy to drink.

BARÓN DE VILLACAMPA 2011 T
85% tempranillo, 10% garnacha, 5% mazuelo.

86 Colour: cherry, garnet rim. Nose: candied fruit, powerfull, varietal, fruit expression. Palate: sweetness, spirituous, fruity, powerful.

VALDEPALACIOS VENDIMIA SELECCIONADA 2010 T
95% tempranillo, 5% garnacha.

86 Colour: bright cherry. Nose: fresh fruit, cocoa bean, smoky, damp earth. Palate: round, spirituous, powerful, flavourful.

LEZA GARCÍA TINTO FAMILIA 2009 T
100% tempranillo.

88 Colour: cherry, garnet rim. Nose: ripe fruit, balsamic herbs, spicy, creamy oak. Palate: long, powerful, flavourful.

BARÓN DE VILLACAMPA 2008 TC
90% tempranillo, 10% garnacha.

88 Colour: cherry, garnet rim. Nose: ripe fruit, scrubland, mineral, spicy. Palate: flavourful, balanced, spicy.

VALDEPALACIOS 2008 TC
90% tempranillo, 10% garnacha.

87 Colour: cherry, garnet rim. Nose: medium intensity, ripe fruit, spicy. Palate: balanced, good acidity.

LG DE LEZA GARCÍA 2009 T
100% tempranillo.

91 Colour: cherry, garnet rim. Nose: ripe fruit, sweet spices, dark chocolate, balsamic herbs. Palate: good structure, flavourful, round tannins.

LEZA GARCÍA 2006 TR
90% tempranillo, 10% garnacha.

88 Colour: cherry, garnet rim. Nose: spicy, creamy oak, toasty, ripe fruit, wet leather. Palate: powerful, flavourful, toasty, round tannins.

BARÓN DE VILLACAMPA 2004 TR
90% tempranillo, 10% garnacha.

89 Colour: dark-red cherry, orangey edge. Nose: old leather, cigar, medium intensity, elegant, spicy, cedar wood. Palate: fine tannins, full, flavourful, spicy.

BODEGAS LOA

Camino de la Hoya, s/n
01300 Laguardia (Alava)
☎: +34 954 975 375
casalbor@casalbor.es

SPES 2008 TC
tempranillo.

88 Colour: deep cherry. Nose: medium intensity, warm, sweet spices, roasted coffee. Palate: spicy, ripe fruit, fine bitter notes.

LOA 2007 T
tempranillo.

93 Colour: cherry, garnet rim. Nose: spicy, creamy oak, toasty, ripe fruit, mineral. Palate: powerful, flavourful, toasty, round tannins.

BODEGAS LOLI CASADO

Avda. La Poveda, 46
01306 Lapuebla de Labarca (Álava)
☎: +34 945 607 096 - Fax: +34 945 607 412
loli@bodegaslolicasado.com
www.bodegaslolicasado.com

POLUS VIURA VENDIMIA TARDÍA 2011 B
100% viura.

91 Colour: bright yellow. Nose: ripe fruit, wild herbs, candied fruit. Palate: sweet, fruity, powerful, flavourful, complex.

POLUS VIURA 2011 B
100% viura.

86 Colour: bright straw. Nose: fresh, fresh fruit, white flowers, expressive. Palate: flavourful, fruity, good acidity, balanced.

POLUS 2010 BFB
100% viura.

86 Colour: straw. Nose: dried herbs, ripe fruit, slightly evolved, aged wood nuances. Palate: flavourful, fruity, fresh, creamy.

POLUS VIURA 2008 BC
100% viura.

89 Colour: bright yellow. Nose: floral, fragrant herbs, smoky. Palate: fresh, fruity, light-bodied, creamy, smoky afterpalate:.

JAUN DE ALZATE 2011 T JOVEN
90% tempranillo, 5% mazuelo, 5% graciano.

86 Colour: cherry, purple rim. Nose: balanced, red berry notes, ripe fruit. Palate: fruity, good finish.

POLUS TEMPRANILLO 2010 T
100% tempranillo.

89 Colour: cherry, garnet rim. Nose: creamy oak, sweet spices, ripe fruit, balanced. Palate: good structure, flavourful, fruity.

JAUN DE ALZATE 2009 TC
90% tempranillo, 5% mazuelo, 5% graciano.

89 Colour: bright cherry. Nose: balanced, fruit expression, sweet spices, wild herbs. Palate: correct, fruity, easy to drink.

POLUS 2009 TC
100% tempranillo.

85 Colour: deep cherry. Nose: slightly evolved, woody, spicy. Palate: spirituous, fruity, powerful, flavourful.

POLUS GRACIANO 2008 T
85% graciano, 15% tempranillo.

84

JAUN DE ALZATE 2005 TR
90% tempranillo, 5% graciano, 5% mazuelo.

89 Colour: cherry, garnet rim. Nose: ripe fruit, spicy, creamy oak, toasty, complex. Palate: powerful, flavourful, toasty, round tannins.

JAUN DE ALZATE 2004 TGR
90% tempranillo, 5% graciano, mazuelo.

87 Colour: deep cherry. Nose: powerfull, fruit preserve, spicy. Palate: fine bitter notes, good acidity, spicy.

BODEGAS LUIS ALEGRE

Ctra. Navaridas, s/n
01300 Laguardia (Álava)
☎: +34 945 600 089 - Fax: +34 945 600 729
luisalegre@bodegasluisalegre.com
www.luisalegre.com

FINCA LA REÑANA 2010 BFB
90% viura, 10% malvasía.

90 Colour: bright yellow. Nose: powerfull, ripe fruit, sweet spices, creamy oak. Palate: rich, flavourful, fresh, good acidity.

KODEN DE LUIS ALEGRE 2010 T
100% tempranillo.

91 Colour: cherry, garnet rim. Nose: spicy, creamy oak, toasty, ripe fruit. Palate: powerful, flavourful, toasty, round tannins.

PONTAC DE PORTILES 2009 T
90% tempranillo, 10% garnacha.

92 Colour: bright cherry, garnet rim. Nose: ripe fruit, sweet spices, creamy oak, expressive, earthy notes. Palate: flavourful, fruity, toasty, round tannins, balanced.

LUIS ALEGRE 2009 TC
85% tempranillo, 15% graciano, mazuelo, garnacha.

87 Colour: cherry, garnet rim. Nose: ripe fruit, spicy, toasty. Palate: powerful, flavourful, toasty.

GRAN VINO PONTAC 2008 T
95% tempranillo, 5% graciano.

92 Colour: cherry, garnet rim. Nose: ripe fruit, spicy, creamy oak, cocoa bean, dark chocolate. Palate: powerful, flavourful, toasty, balanced.

LUIS ALEGRE PARCELA Nº 5 2008 TR
100% tempranillo.

90 Colour: black cherry, garnet rim. Nose: creamy oak, dark chocolate, sweet spices, ripe fruit. Palate: flavourful, long, round tannins.

LUIS ALEGRE SELECCIÓN ESPECIAL 2008 TR
95% tempranillo, 5% graciano, mazuelo.

90 Colour: dark-red cherry, garnet rim. Nose: ripe fruit, spicy, creamy oak, toasty, complex. Palate: powerful, flavourful, toasty, round tannins.

BODEGAS LUIS CAÑAS

Ctra. Samaniego, 10
01307 Villabuena (Álava)
☎: +34 945 623 373 - Fax: +34 945 609 289
bodegas@luiscanas.com
www.luiscanas.com

LUIS CAÑAS 2009 TC
95% tempranillo, 5% garnacha.

88 Colour: cherry, garnet rim. Nose: ripe fruit, spicy, creamy oak, complex, fragrant herbs. Palate: powerful, flavourful, toasty, round tannins.

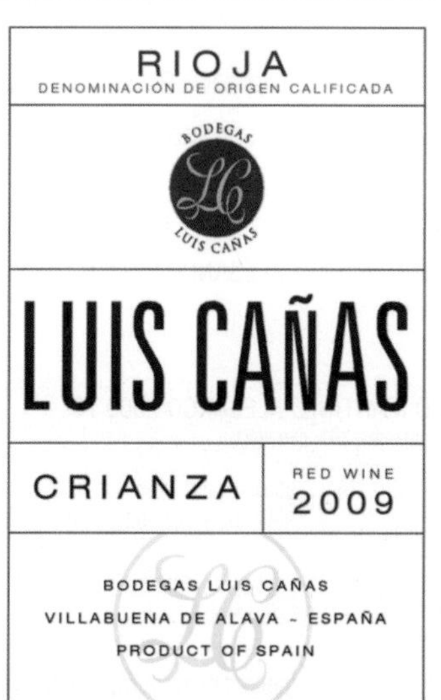

HIRU 3 RACIMOS 2006 T
100% tempranillo.

94 Colour: cherry, garnet rim. Nose: spicy, creamy oak, toasty, complex, earthy notes. Palate: powerful, flavourful, toasty, round tannins.

LUIS CAÑAS SELECCIÓN DE FAMILIA 2005 TR
85% tempranillo, 15% otras.

91 Colour: cherry, garnet rim. Nose: spicy, creamy oak, toasty, characterful, fruit liqueur notes. Palate: powerful, flavourful, toasty, round tannins.

LUIS CAÑAS 2005 TR
95% tempranillo, 5% graciano.

90 Colour: bright cherry, garnet rim. Nose: complex, balanced, elegant, spicy. Palate: balanced, ripe fruit, spicy.

LUIS CAÑAS 2004 TGR
95% tempranillo, 5% graciano.

93 Colour: bright cherry, garnet rim. Nose: spicy, expressive, fine reductive notes, fruit preserve. Palate: balanced, spicy, full.

LUIS CAÑAS 2011 BFB
85% viura, 15% malvasía.

88 Colour: bright yellow. Nose: balanced, medium intensity, expressive, ripe fruit, fragrant herbs. Palate: balanced, fine bitter notes.

BODEGAS MARQUÉS CAMPO NUBLE

Avda. del Ebro, s/n
26540 Alfaro (La Rioja)
☎: +34 941 183 502 - Fax: +34 941 183 157
marquesdecamponuble@marquesdecamponuble.com
www.marquesdecamponuble.com

MARQUÉS CAMPO NUBLE 2007 TC
90% tempranillo, 10% garnacha.

88 Colour: dark-red cherry. Nose: cedar wood, creamy oak, ripe fruit. Palate: fruity, flavourful, round, balanced.

CONDE DE ROMANONES 2007 TR
100% tempranillo.

88 Colour: cherry, garnet rim. Nose: balanced, ripe fruit, dark chocolate, sweet spices. Palate: flavourful, good structure.

MARQUÉS CAMPO NUBLE 2006 TR
100% tempranillo.

89 Colour: bright cherry, brick rim edge. Nose: balanced, ripe fruit, tobacco, spicy. Palate: flavourful, good structure, good acidity, balanced.

BODEGAS MARQUÉS DE VITORIA

Camino de Santa Lucía, s/n
01320 Oyón (Álava)
☎: +34 945 622 134 - Fax: +34 945 601 496
info@bodegasmarquesdevitoria.es
www.marquesdevitoria.com

MARQUÉS DE VITORIA 2005 TR
100% tempranillo.

91 Colour: dark-red cherry. Nose: nose:tic coffee, spicy, ripe fruit, fruit expression. Palate: full, powerful, flavourful, round, spicy, toasty.

MARQUÉS DE VITORIA 2011 B
100% viura.

87 Colour: straw. Nose: powerfull, varietal, fresh fruit. Palate: fresh, fruity, dry, flavourful.

ECCO DE MARQUÉS DE VITORIA 2011 T
100% tempranillo.

87 Colour: cherry, garnet rim. Nose: fresh, neat, varietal, ripe fruit. Palate: spirituous, sweetness, flavourful, powerful.

MARQUÉS DE VITORIA 2009 TC
100% tempranillo.

90 Colour: cherry, garnet rim. Nose: ripe fruit, balanced, dry stone, spicy, toasty. Palate: fruity, flavourful, creamy, balsamic.

MARQUÉS DE VITORIA 2004 TGR
100% tempranillo.

90 Colour: cherry, garnet rim. Nose: medium intensity, balanced, spicy, neat. Palate: fruity, spicy, good acidity, fine bitter notes.

MARQUÉS DE VITORIA 2011 RD
100% tempranillo.

84

BODEGAS MARTÍNEZ ALESANCO

José García, 20
26310 Badarán (La Rioja)
☎: +34 941 367 075 - Fax: +34 941 367 075
info@bodegasmartinezalesanco.com
www.bodegasmartinezalesanco.com

PEDRO MARTÍNEZ ALESANCO 2011 BFB
100% viura.

80

PEDRO MARTÍNEZ ALESANCO 2011 T
100% tempranillo.

84

PEDRO MARTÍNEZ ALESANCO 2009 TC
80% tempranillo, 20% garnacha.

89 Colour: cherry, garnet rim. Nose: ripe fruit, spicy, creamy oak, toasty. Palate: powerful, flavourful, toasty, round tannins.

NADA QUE VER 2008 TC
100% maturana.

90 Colour: cherry, garnet rim. Nose: ripe fruit, scrubland, sweet spices. Palate: powerful, flavourful, balanced, long.

PEDRO MARTÍNEZ ALESANCO 2007 TR
90% tempranillo, 10% garnacha.

90 Colour: deep cherry, garnet rim. Nose: balanced, fine reductive notes, ripe fruit, spicy. Palate: good structure, flavourful, long.

PEDRO MARTÍNEZ ALESANCO 2005 TGR
50% tempranillo, 50% garnacha.

87 Colour: cherry, garnet rim. Nose: ripe fruit, spicy, toasty, complex, wet leather. Palate: powerful, flavourful, toasty, round tannins.

BODEGAS MARTÍNEZ CORTA

Ctra. Cenicero, s/n
20313 Uruñuela (La Rioja)
☎: +34 670 937 520 - Fax: +34 941 374 368
enologia@bodegasmartinezcorta.com
www.bodegasmartinezcorta.com

MARTÍNEZ CORTA CEPAS ANTIGUAS 2011 T
100% tempranillo.

88 Colour: cherry, purple rim. Nose: expressive, red berry notes, floral, raspberry. Palate: flavourful, fruity, balanced.

MARTÍNEZ CORTA 2011 T
100% tempranillo.

86 Colour: bright cherry. Nose: ripe fruit, creamy oak, aged wood nuances. Palate: flavourful, fruity, toasty, round tannins.

SOROS 2009 TC
100% tempranillo.

89 Colour: bright cherry. Nose: ripe fruit, sweet spices, creamy oak, expressive. Palate: flavourful, fruity, toasty, round tannins.

MARTÍNEZ CORTA 2009 TC
100% tempranillo.

89 Colour: deep cherry. Nose: ripe fruit, toasty, sweet spices, red berry notes. Palate: flavourful, ripe fruit, fine bitter notes.

MARTÍNEZ CORTA CEPAS ANTIGUAS 2009 TC
100% tempranillo.

89 Colour: cherry, garnet rim. Nose: ripe fruit, spicy, toasty. Palate: powerful, flavourful, toasty, round tannins.

SOROS 2007 T
100% tempranillo.

90 Colour: cherry, garnet rim. Nose: ripe fruit, spicy, cocoa bean, creamy oak. Palate: powerful, flavourful, long, spicy.

MARTÍNEZ CORTA SELECCIÓN ESPECIAL 2007 T
100% tempranillo.

87 Colour: dark-red cherry, orangey edge. Nose: ripe fruit, balsamic herbs, fine reductive notes, spicy. Palate: correct, powerful, flavourful, toasty.

MC CEPAS ANTIGUAS SELECCIÓN PRIVADA 2010
100% tempranillo.

88 Colour: cherry, garnet rim. Nose: fruit preserve, roasted coffee. Palate: good structure, full, ripe fruit, round tannins.

BODEGAS MARTÍNEZ PALACIOS

Real, 23
26220 Ollauri (Rioja)
☎: +34 941 338 023 - Fax: +34 941 338 023
bodega@bodegasmartinezpalacios.com
www.bodegasmartinezpalacios.com

ORMAEGUI 2011 BFB
garnacha blanca, viura, malvasía.

77

MARTÍNEZ PALACIOS 2011 T
tempranillo.

86 Colour: cherry, purple rim. Nose: fresh fruit, red berry notes, floral, balsamic herbs. Palate: flavourful, fruity, good acidity.

MARTÍNEZ PALACIOS 2008 TC
tempranillo.

87 Colour: cherry, garnet rim. Nose: ripe fruit, creamy oak, toasty, complex. Palate: powerful, flavourful, toasty, round tannins.

MARTÍNEZ PALACIOS 2006 TR
tempranillo.

86 Colour: bright cherry, brick rim edge. Nose: medium intensity, tobacco, ripe fruit. Palate: flavourful, fruity, good acidity.

MARTÍNEZ PALACIOS PAGO CANDELA 2005 T
90% tempranillo, 10% graciano.

88 Colour: cherry, garnet rim. Nose: spicy, creamy oak, toasty, characterful, ripe fruit. Palate: powerful, flavourful, toasty, round tannins.

BODEGAS MEDRANO IRAZU

San Pedro, 14
01309 Elvillar (Álava)
☎: +34 945 604 066 - Fax: +34 945 604 126
amador@bodegasmedranoirazu.com
www.bodegasmedranoirazu.com

MEDRANO IRAZU SELECCIÓN 2011 T
tempranillo.

88 Colour: deep cherry, purple rim. Nose: red berry notes, expressive, balanced, floral. Palate: long, balanced, good acidity, fruity aftespalate:.

LUIS MEDRANO 2009 T
tempranillo.

92 Colour: bright cherry, garnet rim. Nose: closed, ripe fruit, spicy. Palate: flavourful, good structure, ripe fruit, good acidity.

MAS DE MEDRANO 2009 T
tempranillo.

90 Colour: cherry, garnet rim. Nose: ripe fruit, spicy, toasty, complex, mineral. Palate: powerful, flavourful, toasty, round tannins.

MEDRANO IRAZU 2009 TC
100% tempranillo.

89 Colour: bright cherry, garnet rim. Nose: balanced, ripe fruit, spicy. Palate: fruity, good finish.

MEDRANO IRAZU RESERVA DE FAMILIA 2006 TR
tempranillo.

90 Colour: cherry, garnet rim. Nose: ripe fruit, spicy, creamy oak, toasty, complex. Palate: powerful, flavourful, toasty, round tannins, balanced.

MEDRANO IRAZU 2006 TR
tempranillo.

89 Colour: cherry, garnet rim. Nose: ripe fruit, spicy, toasty, wet leather, tobacco, scrubland. Palate: powerful, flavourful, toasty, round tannins.

BODEGAS MENTOR

San Antón, 4-Entpta. dcha.
26002 Logroño (La Rioja)
☎: +34 941 270 795 - Fax: +34 941 244 577
info@puertagotica.es
www.puertagotica.es

MENTOR 2007 TC

90 Colour: cherry, garnet rim. Nose: ripe fruit, spicy, creamy oak. Palate: powerful, flavourful, toasty, round tannins.

MENTOR 2005 TR
100% tempranillo.

92 Colour: dark-red cherry, orangey edge. Nose: ripe fruit, wild herbs, spicy, fine reductive notes. Palate: powerful, flavourful, spicy, round tannins.

BODEGAS MITARTE

Avda. San Ginés, 15
01330 Labastida (Álava)
☎: +34 945 331 069 - Fax: +34 945 331 069
bodegas@mitarte.com
www.mitarte.com

MITARTE 2011 B
100% viura.

88 Colour: bright straw. Nose: fresh, white flowers, ripe fruit. Palate: flavourful, fruity, good acidity, balanced.

MITARTE 2011 BFB
100% viura.

85 Colour: bright yellow. Nose: powerfull, ripe fruit, sweet spices. Palate: rich, flavourful, fresh, good acidity, correct.

S Y C (SANTIAGO Y CARMEN) DE MITARTE 2008 BFB
100% viura.

88 Colour: bright yellow. Nose: powerfull, sweet spices, creamy oak, fragrant herbs, candied fruit. Palate: rich, smoky afterpalate:, flavourful, fresh, good acidity.

MITARTE 2011 RD
50% garnacha, 50% tempranillo.

87 Colour: rose, purple rim. Nose: powerfull, ripe fruit, red berry notes, floral, expressive. Palate: fleshy, powerful, fruity, fresh.

MITARTE 2011 T MACERACIÓN CARBÓNICA
80% tempranillo, 12% garnacha, 8% viura.

88 Colour: cherry, purple rim. Nose: macerated fruit, ripe fruit, powerfull, varietal. Palate: powerful, flavourful, fruity, sweetness, spirituous.

MITARTE 3 HOJA 2011 T
100% tempranillo.

87 Colour: dark-red cherry, purple rim. Nose: macerated fruit, ripe fruit, powerfull, varietal. Palate: good acidity, powerful, flavourful, fruity, sweetness.

MITARTE VENDIMIA SELECCIONADA 2009 TC
100% tempranillo.

88 Colour: cherry, garnet rim. Nose: spicy, creamy oak, toasty, characterful. Palate: powerful, flavourful, toasty, round tannins.

MITARTE MAZUELO 2008 T
100% mazuelo.

88 Colour: cherry, garnet rim. Nose: spicy, creamy oak, toasty, fruit expression. Palate: powerful, flavourful, toasty, round tannins.

S Y C (SANTIAGO Y CARMEN) DE MITARTE 2008 T
100% tempranillo.

88 Colour: very deep cherry. Nose: closed, dark chocolate, ripe fruit. Palate: balanced, flavourful, good structure, round tannins.

DE FAULA 2006 TR
100% tempranillo.

90 Colour: cherry, garnet rim. Nose: ripe fruit, creamy oak, toasty, complex. Palate: powerful, flavourful, toasty, round tannins.

MITARTE 2006 TR
100% tempranillo.

89 Colour: deep cherry, garnet rim. Nose: medium intensity, ripe fruit, sweet spices, cocoa bean. Palate: good structure, ripe fruit, long.

BODEGAS MUGA

Barrio de la Estación, s/n
26200 Haro (La Rioja)
☎: +34 941 311 825 - Fax: +34 941 312 867
info@bodegasmuga.com
www.bodegasmuga.com

MUGA 2011 BFB
90% viura, 10% malvasía.

91 Colour: bright yellow. Nose: balanced, expressive, ripe fruit, sweet spices. Palate: flavourful, rich, fruity, spicy, good acidity.

MUGA 2011 RD
60% garnacha, 30% viura, 10% tempranillo.

88 Colour: onion pink. Nose: elegant, candied fruit, dried flowers, fragrant herbs, red berry notes. Palate: light-bodied, flavourful, good acidity, long, spicy.

MUGA 2008 TC
70% tempranillo, 20% garnacha, 10% mazuelo, graciano.

92 Colour: cherry, garnet rim. Nose: spicy, balanced, medium intensity, ripe fruit. Palate: balanced, fine bitter notes, good acidity.

ARO 2006 T
70% tempranillo, 30% graciano.

93 Colour: bright cherry. Nose: mineral, powerfull, varietal, characterful, ripe fruit, toasty. Palate: powerful, flavourful, spicy, ripe fruit.

TORRE MUGA 2006 T
75% tempranillo, 15% mazuelo, 10% graciano.

93 Colour: deep cherry. Nose: cocoa bean, spicy, toasty, fruit expression, elegant, expressive, complex. Palate: long, spicy, round, elegant.

MUGA SELECCIÓN ESPECIAL 2006 TR
70% tempranillo, 20% garnacha, 10% mazuelo, graciano.

91 Colour: deep cherry. Nose: roasted coffee, spicy, dark chocolate, ripe fruit, complex. Palate: sweetness, spirituous, powerful, flavourful, spicy.

PRADO ENEA 2005 TGR
80% tempranillo, 20% garnacha, mazuelo, graciano.

94 Colour: cherry, garnet rim. Nose: complex, elegant, fine reductive notes, waxy notes, spicy. Palate: balanced, fine bitter notes, spicy, long.

BODEGAS MURÚA

Ctra. Laguardia
01340 Elciego (Álava)
☎: +34 945 606 260
info@bodegasmurua.com
www.bodegasmurua.com

MURÚA 2008 BFB
50% viura, 30% malvasía, 20% garnacha blanca.

88 Colour: bright yellow. Nose: fine reductive notes, wet leather, wild herbs, cedar wood. Palate: fresh, powerful, flavourful, spicy, aged character.

MURÚA 2004 TR
90% tempranillo, 8% graciano, 2% mazuelo.

90 Colour: bright cherry, orangey edge. Nose: balanced, neat, medium intensity, fine reductive notes. Palate: balanced, fine bitter notes, good acidity.

BODEGAS MUSEO ONTAÑÓN

Avda. de Aragón, 3
26006 Logroño (La Rioja)
☎: +34 941 234 200 - Fax: +34 941 270 482
enoturismo@ontanon.es
www.ontanon.es

VETIVER 2010 B
100% viura.

90 Colour: bright yellow. Nose: ripe fruit, fragrant herbs, white flowers, fine lees. Palate: powerful, rich, flavourful.

VETIVER 2011 RD
100% tempranillo.

88 Colour: rose, purple rim. Nose: powerfull, ripe fruit, red berry notes, floral, expressive. Palate: , powerful, fruity, fresh, balanced, easy to drink.

ONTAÑÓN 2005 TR
tempranillo, graciano.

90 Colour: cherry, garnet rim. Nose: ripe fruit, spicy, creamy oak, toasty, complex. Palate: powerful, flavourful, toasty, round tannins.

ARTESO 2008 TC
75% tempranillo, 15% graciano, 10% garnacha.

92 Colour: cherry, garnet rim. Nose: red berry notes, ripe fruit, balsamic herbs, spicy, creamy oak. Palate: balanced, round, powerful, flavourful, round tannins.

COLECCIÓN MITOLÓGICA ONTAÑÓN 2004 TGR
95% tempranillo, 5% graciano.

91 Colour: dark-red cherry, orangey edge. Nose: spicy, creamy oak, fruit liqueur notes, balsamic herbs, fine reductive notes. Palate: correct, balanced, flavourful, long.

ONTAÑÓN 2004 TGR
tempranillo, graciano.

90 Colour: deep cherry, orangey edge. Nose: fruit preserve, creamy oak, sweet spices. Palate: flavourful, ripe fruit.

ONTAÑÓN 2009 TC
90% tempranillo, 10% garnacha.

89 Colour: deep cherry. Nose: ripe fruit, creamy oak, dark chocolate, spicy. Palate: powerful, flavourful, fruity, full, spicy, creamy.

BODEGAS NAVA-RIOJA S.A.T.

Ctra. Eje del Ebro, s/n
31261 Andosilla (Navarra)
☎: +34 948 690 454 - Fax: +34 948 674 491
info@bodegasnavarioja.com
www.bodegasnavarioja.com

OTIS TARDA 2009 TC
tempranillo.

88 Colour: cherry, garnet rim. Nose: ripe fruit, spicy, creamy oak. Palate: powerful, flavourful, toasty, round tannins.

OTIS TARDA 2011 T BARRICA
tempranillo.

87 Colour: bright cherry. Nose: sweet spices, creamy oak, red berry notes. Palate: flavourful, fruity, toasty.

PARDOÑO 2011 T
tempranillo, garnacha.

86 Colour: cherry, purple rim. Nose: red berry notes, ripe fruit, balsamic herbs, mineral. Palate: light-bodied, fresh, fruity.

BODEGAS NAVAJAS

Camino Balgarauz, 2
26370 Navarrete (La Rioja)
☎: +34 941 440 140 - Fax: +34 941 440 657
info@bodegasnavajas.com
www.bodegasnavajas.com

NAVAJAS 2008 TC
95% tempranillo, 5% mazuelo.

88 Colour: dark-red cherry. Nose: sweet spices, nose:tic coffee, powerfull. Palate: balsamic, spicy, toasty, roasted-coffee afterpalate:.

NAVAJAS GRACIANO 2008 TC
100% graciano.

88 Colour: deep cherry. Nose: expressive, sweet spices, cedar wood, ripe fruit. Palate: complex, powerful, flavourful, balsamic, oaky.

NAVAJAS 2004 TGR
85% tempranillo, 10% graciano, 5% mazuelo.

91 Colour: dark-red cherry, orangey edge. Nose: fine reductive notes, tobacco, expressive, elegant, cocoa bean. Palate: round, full, rich, flavourful, toasty, soft tannins.

BODEGAS NESTARES EGUIZÁBAL

Alberto Villanueva 82-84
26144 Galilea (La Rioja)
☎: +34 941 480 351 - Fax: +34 941 480 351
info@nestareseguizabal.com
www.nestareseguizabal.com

SEGARES 2011 T
100% tempranillo.

85 Colour: cherry, garnet rim. Nose: ripe fruit, fresh, dry stone. Palate: ripe fruit, easy to drink, powerful, flavourful, spirituous.

SEGARES LAS LLECAS 2009 T
100% tempranillo.

86 Colour: cherry, garnet rim. Nose: fine reductive notes, ripe fruit, cocoa bean. Palate: sweetness, fruity, powerful, flavourful, lacks expression.

SEGARES 2008 TC
100% tempranillo.

88 Colour: cherry, garnet rim. Nose: ripe fruit, spicy, creamy oak, toasty. Palate: powerful, flavourful, toasty, round tannins.

ARZOBISPO DIEGO DE TEJADA 2007 T
100% tempranillo.

89 Colour: cherry, garnet rim. Nose: ripe fruit, spicy, toasty, complex. Palate: powerful, flavourful, toasty, fine tannins.

SEGARES 2007 TR
100% tempranillo.

88 Colour: cherry, garnet rim. Nose: spicy, toasty. Palate: powerful, flavourful, toasty, round tannins.

BODEGAS OBALO

Ctra. 232 A, Km. 26
26339 Abalos (Rioja)
☎: +34 941 744 056
www.bodegaobalo.com

OBALO 2009 TC
100% tempranillo.

93 Colour: cherry, garnet rim. Nose: spicy, creamy oak, toasty, characterful, roasted coffee. Palate: powerful, flavourful, toasty, round tannins.

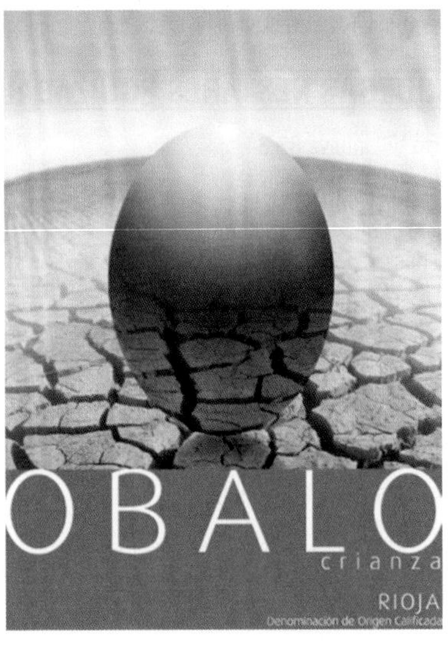

OBALO 2011 T
100% tempranillo.

91 Colour: cherry, purple rim. Nose: expressive, red berry notes, floral, balsamic herbs, mineral, spicy. Palate: flavourful, fruity, good acidity, round tannins.

ALTINO 2009 TC
100% tempranillo.

92 Colour: cherry, garnet rim. Nose: spicy, creamy oak, toasty, characterful. Palate: powerful, flavourful, toasty, round tannins.

PINTURAS 2009 TC
tempranillo.

88 Colour: bright cherry. Nose: varietal, ripe fruit, spicy, toasty. Palate: flavourful, ripe fruit, good acidity.

OBALO 2007 TR
100% tempranillo.

90 Colour: cherry, garnet rim. Nose: ripe fruit, spicy, toasty, complex. Palate: flavourful, toasty, round tannins, good structure.

BODEGAS OLARRA

Avda. de Mendavia, 30
26009 Logroño (La Rioja)
☎: +34 941 235 299 - Fax: +34 941 253 703
bodegasolarra@bodegasolarra.es
www.bodegasolarra.es

CERRO AÑÓN 2009 TC
80% tempranillo, 10% garnacha, mazuelo, graciano.

89 Colour: dark-red cherry. Nose: spicy, cedar wood, roasted coffee, ripe fruit. Palate: sweet tannins, powerful, flavourful.

SUMMA 2006 TR
85% tempranillo, 10% graciano, 5% mazuelo.

91 Colour: dark-red cherry. Nose: creamy oak, toasty, sweet spices, nose:tic coffee, ripe fruit, elegant. Palate: balanced, round, powerful, flavourful.

CERRO AÑÓN 2005 TR
80% tempranillo, mazuelo, graciano, garnacha.

91 Colour: deep cherry. Nose: ripe fruit, undergrowth, spicy, creamy oak, toasty. Palate: round, powerful, flavourful, good structure, spicy, balsamic, ripe fruit, round tannins.

BODEGAS ONDALÁN

Ctra. de Logroño, 22
01320 Oyón - Oion (Álava)
☎: +34 945 622 537 - Fax: +34 945 622 538
ondalan@ondalan.es
www.ondalan.es

ONDALÁN 2011 B
100% viura.

87 Colour: bright straw. Nose: medium intensity, fresh fruit, tropical fruit. Palate: fruity, correct, good acidity.

ONDALÁN 2011 T
90% tempranillo, 10% garnacha.

87 Colour: cherry, garnet rim. Nose: red berry notes, raspberry, powerfull, fresh. Palate: flavourful, light-bodied, fruity, fresh.

ONDALÁN TEMPRANILLO SELECCIÓN 2009 T
100% tempranillo.

90 Colour: cherry, garnet rim. Nose: ripe fruit, spicy, creamy oak, toasty, complex. Palate: powerful, flavourful, toasty, round tannins.

ONDALÁN 2009 TC
80% tempranillo, 20% graciano.

87 Colour: cherry, garnet rim. Nose: ripe fruit, spicy, creamy oak. Palate: powerful, flavourful, toasty, correct.

100 ABADES GRACIANO SELECCIÓN 2009 T
100% graciano.

86 Colour: dark-red cherry. Nose: complex, expressive, nose:tic coffee, aged wood nuances, dark chocolate. Palate: powerful, flavourful, grainy tannins.

ONDALÁN 2007 TR
70% tempranillo, 30% garnacha.

88 Colour: deep cherry. Nose: powerfull, sweet spices, creamy oak, ripe fruit. Palate: powerful, flavourful, spirituous, spicy, balsamic, good finish.

BODEGAS ONDARRE

Ctra. de Aras, s/n
31230 Viana (Navarra)
☎: +34 948 645 300 - Fax: +34 948 646 002
bodegasondarre@bodegasondarre.es
www.bodegasondarre.es

MAYOR DE ONDARRE 2006 TR
88% tempranillo, 12% mazuelo.

90 Colour: cherry, garnet rim. Nose: ripe fruit, spicy, creamy oak, toasty. Palate: powerful, flavourful, toasty, round tannins.

ONDARRE 2006 TR
85% tempranillo, 10% garnacha, 5% mazuelo.

90 Colour: dark-red cherry. Nose: spicy, creamy oak, toasty, ripe fruit. Palate: soft tannins, elegant, round, flavourful, spicy, creamy.

BODEGAS ORBEN

Ctra. Laguardia, Km. 60
01300 Laguardia (Álava)
☎: +34 945 609 086 - Fax: +34 945 609 261
club@grupoartevino.com
www.grupoartevino.com

MALPUESTO 2010 T
100% tempranillo.

96 Colour: deep cherry. Nose: fruit preserve, creamy oak, sweet spices, new oak. Palate: flavourful, powerful, fine bitter notes, good acidity, ripe fruit, round tannins.

ORBEN 2007 T
97% tempranillo, 3% graciano.

92 Colour: dark-red cherry. Nose: complex, elegant, toasty, creamy oak. Palate: spicy, creamy, toasty, ripe fruit.

BODEGAS ORTUBIA

Camino de Uriso, s/n
26292 Villalba de Rioja (La Rioja)
☎: +34 660 975 323 - Fax: +34 941 310 842
ortubia@bodegasortubia.com
www.bodegasortubia.com

PARLAZA 2009 TC
100% tempranillo.

87 Colour: cherry, garnet rim. Nose: ripe fruit, spicy, creamy oak, medium intensity. Palate: powerful, flavourful, toasty, round tannins.

ORTUBIA 2007 TR
100% tempranillo.

87 Colour: cherry, garnet rim. Nose: ripe fruit, spicy, fine reductive notes. Palate: powerful, flavourful, toasty.

BODEGAS OSTATU

Ctra. Vitoria, 1
01307 Samaniego (Álava)
☎: +34 945 609 133 - Fax: +34 945 623 338
ostatu@ostatu.com
www.ostatu.com

OSTATU 2011 B
viura, malvasía.

90 Colour: bright straw, greenish rim. Nose: balanced, expressive, fresh fruit, citrus fruit. Palate: fruity, flavourful, good acidity.

OSTATU 2011 T MACERACIÓN CARBÓNICA
tempranillo, graciano, mazuelo, viura.

88 Colour: cherry, purple rim. Nose: balanced, fruit expression. Palate: flavourful, fruity, balanced.

OSTATU SELECCIÓN 2008 T
tempranillo.

91 Colour: cherry, garnet rim. Nose: ripe fruit, spicy, toasty, complex, earthy notes, new oak. Palate: powerful, flavourful, toasty, round tannins.

OSTATU LADERAS DEL PORTILLO 2008 T
tempranillo, viura.

90 Colour: cherry, garnet rim. Nose: ripe fruit, nose:tic coffee, sweet spices, creamy oak, expressive. Palate: powerful, flavourful, toasty, balanced.

OSTATU 2009 TC
tempranillo, graciano, mazuelo, garnacha.

91 Colour: cherry, purple rim. Nose: ripe fruit, balanced, sweet spices, fragrant herbs. Palate: good structure, flavourful, good acidity.

OSTATU 2007 TR
tempranillo.

93 Colour: cherry, garnet rim. Nose: ripe fruit, spicy, toasty, complex, earthy notes, new oak, nose:tic coffee. Palate: powerful, flavourful, toasty, round tannins.

GLORIA DE OSTATU 2006 T
100% tempranillo.

94 Colour: very deep cherry, garnet rim. Nose: undergrowth, damp earth, fruit expression, cocoa bean, roasted coffee. Palate: complex, powerful, flavourful, round, reductive nuances.

BODEGAS PACO GARCÍA

Crta. Ventas s/n
26143 Murillo de Rio Leza (La Rioja)
☎: +34 941 432 372 - Fax: +34 941 432 156
info@bodegaspacogarcia.com
www.bodegaspacogarcia.com

PACO GARCÍA SEIS 2010 T
100% tempranillo.

92 Colour: dark-red cherry. Nose: ripe fruit, expressive, powerfull, varietal, nose:tic coffee. Palate: powerful, flavourful, fruity, sweetness, creamy.

PACO GARCÍA 2008 TC
90% tempranillo, 10% garnacha.

91 Colour: cherry, garnet rim. Nose: spicy, creamy oak, toasty, ripe fruit. Palate: powerful, flavourful, toasty, round tannins.

BEAUTIFUL THINGS DE PACO GARCÍA 2008 T
90% tempranillo, 10% graciano.

90 Colour: dark-red cherry. Nose: characterful, expressive, ripe fruit, sweet spices. Palate: powerful, flavourful, rich, fruity, complex.

BODEGAS PALACIO

San Lázaro, 1
01300 Laguardia (Álava)
☎: +34 945 600 057 - Fax: +34 945 600 297
rrpp@bodegaspalacio.es
www.bodegaspalacio.es

COSME PALACIO 2010 B
100% viura.

87 Colour: bright straw. Nose: fresh, fresh fruit, white flowers. Palate: flavourful, fruity, good acidity, balanced.

COSME PALACIO 1984 2009 B
92% viura, 8% malvasía.

89 Colour: bright yellow. Nose: medium intensity, candied fruit, sweet spices. Palate: flavourful, ripe fruit, spicy, fine bitter notes.

MILFLORES 2011 T
100% tempranillo.

89 Colour: cherry, purple rim. Nose: balanced, powerfull, ripe fruit. Palate: flavourful, fruity, long.

GLORIOSO 2009 TC
100% tempranillo.

88 Colour: dark-red cherry. Nose: ripe fruit, spicy, nose:tic coffee, creamy oak. Palate: creamy, spicy, toasty, spirituous, slightly dry, soft tannins.

COSME PALACIO VENDIMIA SELECCIONADA 2009 TC
100% tempranillo.

87 Colour: cherry, garnet rim. Nose: fruit expression, aged wood nuances, spicy. Palate: powerful, flavourful, sweetness, spirituous, grainy tannins.

GLORIOSO 2007 TR
100% tempranillo.

91 Colour: dark-red cherry, orangey edge. Nose: nose:tic coffee, cocoa bean, ripe fruit, fruit expression. Palate: round, elegant, balanced, powerful, flavourful, rich, creamy.

COSME PALACIO 2007 TR
100% tempranillo.

90 Colour: cherry, garnet rim. Nose: ripe fruit, earthy notes, balsamic herbs, fine reductive notes, sweet spices. Palate: powerful, flavourful, spicy, long.

GLORIOSO 2005 TGR
100% tempranillo.

90 Colour: pale ruby, brick rim edge. Nose: spicy, fine reductive notes, wet leather, aged wood nuances, fruit liqueur notes. Palate: spicy, fine tannins, elegant, long.

BODEGAS PALACIOS REMONDO

Avda. Zaragoza, 8
26540 Alfaro (La Rioja)
☎: +34 941 180 207 - Fax: +34 941 181 628
info@palaciosremondo.com

PLÁCET VALTOMELLOSO 2009 B

93 Colour: bright yellow. Nose: elegant, ripe fruit, wild herbs, dried flowers. Palate: flavourful, rich, fruity, good acidity.

LA VENDIMIA 2011 T

87 Colour: cherry, purple rim. Nose: red berry notes, floral, ripe fruit. Palate: flavourful, fruity, good acidity, round tannins.

PROPIEDAD VIÑAS TRADICIONALES 2010 T

93 Colour: cherry, garnet rim. Nose: spicy, creamy oak, toasty, complex, fruit preserve, violet drops. Palate: powerful, flavourful, toasty, round tannins.

LA MONTESA 2010 TC

92 Colour: cherry, garnet rim. Nose: spicy, creamy oak, toasty, characterful. Palate: powerful, flavourful, toasty, round tannins.

BODEGAS PATERNINA

Avda. Santo Domingo, 11
26200 Haro (La Rioja)
☎: +34 941 310 550 - Fax: +34 941 312 778
paternina@paternina.com
www.paternina.com

BANDA DORADA 2011 B
viura.

85 Colour: bright straw. Nose: fresh, fresh fruit, white flowers. Palate: flavourful, fruity, good acidity, balanced.

BANDA ROSA 2011 RD
garnacha, viura.

88 Colour: rose, purple rim. Nose: fresh, varietal, fruit expression, violet drops, red berry notes. Palate: powerful, flavourful, balsamic, fruity, good acidity.

MONTE HARO "TEMPRANILLO" 2011 T
100% tempranillo.

85 Colour: dark-red cherry. Nose: aged wood nuances, sweet spices, ripe fruit. Palate: ripe fruit, dry wood, spicy.

FEDERICO PATERNINA SELECCIÓN ESPECIAL 2009 T
tempranillo.

90 Colour: light cherry. Nose: roasted coffee, spicy, characterful. Palate: fruity, powerful, harsh oak tannins, creamy, spicy.

PATERNINA BANDA AZUL 2008 TC
tempranillo, garnacha.

87 Colour: cherry, garnet rim. Nose: woody, spicy, ripe fruit. Palate: correct, easy to drink, good finish.

PATERNINA BANDA ORO 2008 TC
tempranillo, mazuelo.

86 Colour: light cherry, orangey edge. Nose: ripe fruit, tobacco, old leather, spicy. Palate: powerful, flavourful, ripe fruit.

CONDES DE LOS ANDES 2007 TR
tempranillo, mazuelo, garnacha.

90 Colour: cherry, garnet rim. Nose: ripe fruit, creamy oak, toasty, wet leather. Palate: powerful, flavourful, toasty, round tannins.

VIÑA VIAL 2007 TR
tempranillo, garnacha, mazuelo.

87 Colour: deep cherry. Nose: spicy, ripe fruit, wet leather. Palate: flavourful, fine bitter notes.

CONDES DE LOS ANDES 2004 TGR
tempranillo, mazuelo, graciano.

87 Colour: pale ruby, brick rim edge. Nose: closed, short, caramel, sweet spices. Palate: round, lacks expression, spicy.

BODEGAS PATROCINIO

Ctra. Cenicero
26313 Uruñuela (La Rioja)
☎: +34 941 371 319 - Fax: +34 941 371 435
info@bodegaspatrocinio.com

ZINIO 2011 B
100% viura.

90 Colour: bright straw. Nose: balanced, medium intensity, floral, fragrant herbs. Palate: balanced, fine bitter notes, fruity.

SEÑORÍO DE UÑUELA 2011 B
100% viura.

89 Colour: bright straw. Nose: fresh, medium intensity, fresh fruit, wild herbs. Palate: fruity, good acidity, fresh.

LÁGRIMAS DE MARÍA 2011 B
100% viura.

86 Colour: bright straw. Nose: fresh, white flowers, ripe fruit. Palate: flavourful, fruity, good acidity, balanced.

LÁGRIMAS DE MARÍA 2011 RD
100% tempranillo.

88 Colour: brilliant rose. Nose: powerfull, fresh, characterful, fruit expression. Palate: powerful, flavourful, fruity, fresh.

ZINIO 2011 RD
100% tempranillo.

88 Colour: rose. Nose: fresh, red berry notes, medium intensity, dried flowers. Palate: flavourful, fruity, balanced.

SEÑORÍO DE UÑUELA 2011 RD
100% tempranillo.

86 Colour: rose, purple rim. Nose: powerfull, ripe fruit, red berry notes, floral. Palate: , powerful, fruity, fresh.

SANCHO GARCÉS 2011 T
100% tempranillo.

89 Colour: dark-red cherry. Nose: powerfull, elegant, characterful, fruit expression. Palate: flavourful, powerful, fruity, fresh, complex.

SEÑORÍO DE UÑUELA 2011 T
100% tempranillo.

88 Colour: cherry, purple rim. Nose: expressive, varietal, fresh, powerfull. Palate: fruity, fresh, powerful, flavourful.

LÁGRIMAS DE MARÍA 2011 T
100% tempranillo.

86 Colour: dark-red cherry. Nose: fresh fruit, fruit expression, varietal, expressive. Palate: sweetness, powerful, flavourful.

LÁGRIMAS DE MARÍA 2009 TC
85% tempranillo, 15% graciano.

90 Colour: cherry, garnet rim. Nose: ripe fruit, scrubland, nose:tic coffee, spicy. Palate: correct, powerful, flavourful.

ZINIO GARNACHA 2011 T
100% garnacha.

83

SANCHO GARCÉS 2009 TC
100% tempranillo.

85 Colour: cherry, garnet rim. Nose: ripe fruit, spicy, premature reduction notes. Palate: powerful, flavourful, toasty.

ZINIO VENDIMIA SELECCIONADA 2009 TC
100% tempranillo.

90 Colour: cherry, garnet rim. Nose: ripe fruit, toasty, spicy. Palate: spicy, ripe fruit, round tannins.

ZINIO TEMPRANILLO GRACIANO 2009 T
85% tempranillo, 15% graciano.

88 Colour: cherry, garnet rim. Nose: ripe fruit, wild herbs, creamy oak. Palate: powerful, flavourful, spicy, long.

SANCHO GARCÉS 2007 TR
100% tempranillo.

88 Colour: deep cherry. Nose: ripe fruit, spicy, cocoa bean, scrubland. Palate: flavourful, good acidity, fine bitter notes.

SEÑORÍO DE UÑUELA 2009 TC
100% tempranillo.

87 Colour: cherry, garnet rim. Nose: ripe fruit, spicy, toasty, medium intensity. Palate: toasty, long, spicy.

ZINIO VENDIMIA SELECCIONADA 2005 TR
100% tempranillo.

88 Colour: cherry, garnet rim. Nose: powerfull, fruit preserve, spicy, wet leather. Palate: fine bitter notes, good acidity, spicy.

ZINIO ORGÁNICO 2009 T
70% tempranillo, 30% garnacha.

86 Colour: cherry, garnet rim. Nose: spicy, creamy oak, toasty. Palate: powerful, flavourful, toasty, round tannins.

SEÑORÍO DE UÑUELA 2007 TR
100% tempranillo.

87 Colour: deep cherry. Nose: ripe fruit, sweet spices, roasted coffee. Palate: powerful, flavourful, creamy, ripe fruit.

BODEGAS PERICA

Avda. de la Rioja, 59
26340 San Asensio (La Rioja)
☎: +34 941 457 152 - Fax: +34 941 457 240
info@bodegasperica.com
www.bodegasperica.com

OLAGOSA 2011 BFB
95% viura, 5% malvasía.

87 Colour: bright yellow. Nose: powerfull, ripe fruit, sweet spices, creamy oak. Palate: rich, smoky afterpalate:, flavourful, fresh, good acidity.

6 CEPAS 6 2011 T
100% tempranillo.

90 Colour: cherry, purple rim. Nose: earthy notes, red berry notes, ripe fruit, balsamic herbs, spicy. Palate: powerful, flavourful, long, balanced.

MI VILLA 2011 T
85% tempranillo, 15% garnacha.

88 Colour: dark-red cherry, garnet rim. Nose: fresh, neat, varietal, fresh fruit. Palate: fruity, light-bodied, flavourful.

OLAGOSA 2009 TC
90% tempranillo, 5% garnacha, 5% mazuelo.

89 Colour: cherry, garnet rim. Nose: ripe fruit, spicy, toasty, balsamic herbs. Palate: powerful, flavourful, toasty, long.

OLAGOSA 2007 TR
90% tempranillo, 5% garnacha, 5% mazuelo.

87 Colour: deep cherry. Nose: aged wood nuances, spicy, creamy oak, ripe fruit. Palate: good structure, powerful, flavourful, spicy, creamy.

PERICA ORO RESERVA ESPECIAL 2006 TR
95% tempranillo, 5% graciano.

90 Colour: deep cherry. Nose: powerfull, spicy, toasty, creamy oak. Palate: fine bitter notes, good acidity, toasty.

OLAGOSA 2004 TGR
90% tempranillo, 5% garnacha, 5% mazuelo.

90 Colour: deep cherry. Nose: nose:tic coffee, characterful. Palate: flavourful, spirituous, long.

BODEGAS PUELLES

Camino de los Molinos, s/n
26339 Ábalos (La Rioja)
☎: +34 941 334 415 - Fax: +34 941 334 132
informacion@bodegaspuelles.com
www.bodegaspuelles.com

PUELLES 2010 B
95% viura, 5% otras.

87 Colour: bright straw. Nose: fragrant herbs, fresh fruit, expressive. Palate: fresh, fruity, light-bodied.

PUELLES 2009 TC
95% tempranillo, 5% otras.

87 Colour: cherry, garnet rim. Nose: medium intensity, ripe fruit, creamy oak. Palate: flavourful, ripe fruit, good acidity.

PUELLES 2006 TR
95% tempranillo.

89 Colour: cherry, garnet rim. Nose: spicy, creamy oak, toasty, ripe fruit, wet leather. Palate: powerful, flavourful, toasty, round tannins.

MOLINO DE PUELLES ECOLÓGICO 2006 T
100% tempranillo.

88 Colour: cherry, garnet rim. Nose: fruit liqueur notes, spicy, creamy oak, wet leather, tobacco. Palate: long, correct, flavourful.

PUELLES 2004 TGR
95% tempranillo, 5% otras.

88 Colour: pale ruby, brick rim edge. Nose: spicy, wet leather, aged wood nuances, fruit liqueur notes. Palate: spicy, fine tannins, elegant, long.

PUELLES ZENUS 2004 T
95% tempranillo.

86 Colour: pale ruby, brick rim edge. Nose: wet leather, waxy notes, cigar, spicy, scrubland. Palate: flavourful, long, spicy, balsamic.

BODEGAS RAMÍREZ DE LA PISCINA

Ctra. Vitoria-Laguardia, s/n
26338 San Vicente de la Sonsierra (La Rioja)
☎: +34 941 334 505 - Fax: +34 941 334 506
rampiscina@knet.es
www.ramirezdelapiscina.es

RAMÍREZ DE LA PISCINA 2011 B
viura.

84

RAMÍREZ DE LA PISCINA 2011 RD
50% viura, 50% garnacha.

87 Colour: onion pink. Nose: elegant, candied fruit, dried flowers, fragrant herbs, red berry notes. Palate: light-bodied, flavourful, good acidity, long, spicy.

RAMÍREZ DE LA PISCINA SELECCIÓN 2008 TC
100% tempranillo.

87 Colour: cherry, garnet rim. Nose: ripe fruit, balsamic herbs, spicy, toasty. Palate: powerful, flavourful, correct, toasty.

RAMÍREZ DE LA PISCINA 2011 T
tempranillo.

87 Colour: deep cherry. Nose: ripe fruit, red berry notes, balsamic herbs. Palate: flavourful, spicy, ripe fruit.

ENTARI 2011 T
tempranillo.

87 Colour: cherry, purple rim. Nose: expressive, fresh fruit, red berry notes, balsamic herbs. Palate: flavourful, fruity, good acidity.

RAMÍREZ DE LA PISCINA SELECCIÓN 2009 T
tempranillo.

89 Colour: cherry, garnet rim. Nose: balanced, tobacco, spicy, ripe fruit. Palate: ripe fruit, long, round tannins.

RAMÍREZ DE LA PISCINA 2008 T
100% tempranillo.

87 Colour: cherry, garnet rim. Nose: medium intensity, ripe fruit, sweet spices. Palate: flavourful, good acidity.

RAMÍREZ DE LA PISCINA 2006 TR
tempranillo.

86 Colour: deep cherry. Nose: spicy, toasty, dark chocolate, ripe fruit. Palate: flavourful, fine bitter notes, toasty.

BODEGAS RAMÓN BILBAO

Avda. Santo Domingo, 34
26200 Haro (La Rioja)
☎: +34 941 310 295 - Fax: +34 941 310 832
info@bodegasramonbilbao.es
www.bodegasramonbilbao.es

RAMÓN BILBAO TEMPRANILLO EDICIÓN LIMITADA 2010 TC
100% tempranillo.

92 Colour: cherry, garnet rim. Nose: spicy, creamy oak, toasty, ripe fruit, characterful, earthy notes. Palate: powerful, flavourful, toasty, round tannins.

RAMÓN BILBAO VIÑEDOS DE ALTURA 2010 TC
50% tempranillo, 50% garnacha.

90 Colour: bright cherry. Nose: sweet spices, creamy oak, red berry notes. Palate: flavourful, fruity, toasty, round tannins.

RAMÓN BILBAO 2010 TC
100% tempranillo.

90 Colour: cherry, garnet rim. Nose: spicy, creamy oak, toasty, characterful, ripe fruit. Palate: powerful, flavourful, toasty, round tannins.

RAMÓN BILBAO 2008 TR
90% tempranillo, 5% mazuelo, 5% graciano.

90 Colour: bright cherry. Nose: ripe fruit, sweet spices, creamy oak, spicy. Palate: flavourful, fruity, toasty, round tannins.

RAMÓN BILBAO 2004 TGR
90% tempranillo, 5% mazuelo, 5% graciano.

90 Colour: cherry, garnet rim. Nose: spicy, creamy oak, toasty, complex, wet leather. Palate: powerful, flavourful, toasty, round tannins.

MIRTO DE RAMÓN BILBAO 2008 T
100% tempranillo.

93 Colour: cherry, garnet rim. Nose: spicy, creamy oak, toasty, complex, earthy notes, mineral, ripe fruit. Palate: powerful, flavourful, toasty, round tannins.

BODEGAS REAL DIVISA

Divisa Real, s/n
26339 Abalos (La Rioja)
☎: +34 941 258 133 - Fax: +34 941 258 155
realdivisa@fer.es
www.realdivisa.com

MARQUÉS DE LEGARDA 2008 TC
91% tempranillo, 7% graciano, 2% mazuelo.

83

MARQUÉS DE LEGARDA 2007 TR
100% tempranillo.

88 Colour: dark-red cherry, orangey edge. Nose: spicy, balsamic herbs, wet leather, cigar. Palate: balanced, powerful, flavourful.

DRACO REAL DIVISA 2004 TR
100% tempranillo.

88 Colour: deep cherry. Nose: spicy, wet leather, fruit liqueur notes. Palate: spicy, ripe fruit.

MARQUÉS DE LEGARDA 2001 TGR
91% tempranillo, 7% graciano, 2% mazuelo.

90 Colour: pale ruby, brick rim edge. Nose: elegant, spicy, fine reductive notes, wet leather, aged wood nuances, fruit liqueur notes. Palate: spicy, fine tannins, elegant, long.

BODEGAS REGALÍA DE OLLAURI

Ctra. de Nájera, Km. 1
26220 Ollauri (La Rioja)
☎: +34 941 338 373 - Fax: +34 941 338 374
info@bodegasregalia.es
www.bodegasregalia.es

MARQUÉS DE TERÁN SELECCIÓN ESPECIAL 2009 T
tempranillo.

91 Colour: bright cherry. Nose: ripe fruit, sweet spices, creamy oak, expressive. Palate: flavourful, fruity, toasty, round tannins.

VERSUM 2008 T
tempranillo.

89 Colour: cherry, garnet rim. Nose: ripe fruit, earthy notes, scrubland, spicy. Palate: flavourful, long, toasty, correct.

OLLAMENDI 2007 T
tempranillo.

91 Colour: cherry, garnet rim. Nose: ripe fruit, spicy, creamy oak, toasty, mineral. Palate: powerful, flavourful, toasty, round tannins.

MARQUÉS DE TERÁN 2007 TC
tempranillo.

86 Colour: pale ruby, brick rim edge. Nose: ripe fruit, spicy, creamy oak, cigar, wet leather. Palate: correct, flavourful, toasty.

MARQUÉS DE TERÁN 2006 TR
tempranillo.

86 Colour: cherry, garnet rim. Nose: balanced, ripe fruit, spicy, old leather. Palate: ripe fruit, good finish.

AZENTO 2006 TR
tempranillo.

85 Colour: dark-red cherry, garnet rim. Nose: spicy, wet leather, cigar, waxy notes. Palate: correct, long, flavourful.

BODEGAS REMÍREZ DE GANUZA

Constitución, 1
01307 Samaniego (Álava)
☎: +34 945 609 022 - Fax: +34 945 623 335
cristina@remirezdeganuza.com
www.remirezdeganuza.com

REMÍREZ DE GANUZA 2006 TR
90% tempranillo, 5% graciano, 5% viura, malvasía.

95 Colour: dark-red cherry. Nose: undergrowth, damp earth, toasty, complex, balanced. Palate: mineral, creamy, spicy, powerful, flavourful.

Remírez de Ganuza
RIOJA
Denominación de Origen Calificada
•Reserva 2006•
Estate Bottled by
Bodegas Fernando Remírez de Ganuza, S.L.
Samaniego - España
Product of Spain
OLD VINES - UNFILTERED

TRASNOCHO 2007 T
tempranillo, 10% graciano.

94 Colour: dark-red cherry. Nose: ripe fruit, fruit expression, expressive, powerfull, undergrowth, damp earth. Palate: powerful, flavourful, good structure.

ERRE PUNTO 2010 BFB
70% viura, 30% malvasía.

89 Colour: bright straw, greenish rim. Nose: fresh, ripe fruit, sweet spices. Palate: balanced, fresh, good acidity.

ERRE PUNTO 2011 T MACERACIÓN CARBÓNICA
90% tempranillo, 5% graciano, 5% viura, malvasía.

91 Colour: cherry, purple rim. Nose: floral, red berry notes, lactic notes, fresh, expressive. Palate: powerful, flavourful, fresh, fruity, good acidity, balanced.

VIÑA COQUETA 2007 TR
90% tempranillo, 5% graciano, 5% viura, malvasía.

93 Colour: cherry, garnet rim. Nose: ripe fruit, spicy, creamy oak, fine reductive notes, sweet spices. Palate: powerful, flavourful, long, toasty.

FINCAS DE GANUZA 2005 TR
90% tempranillo, 10% graciano.

92 Colour: cherry, garnet rim. Nose: spicy, creamy oak, fine reductive notes, balsamic herbs, sweet spices. Palate: powerful, flavourful, toasty, round tannins.

BODEGAS RIOJANAS

Estación, 1 - 21
26350 Cenicero (La Rioja)
☎: +34 941 454 050 - Fax: +34 941 454 529
bodega@bodegasriojanas.com
www.bodegasriojanas.com

PUERTA VIEJA 2011 B
100% viura.

87 Colour: straw. Nose: fruit expression, grassy, fresh fruit. Palate: light-bodied, powerful, fresh, fruity.

VIÑA ALBINA SEMIDULCE 2001 B RESERVA
90% viura, 10% malvasía.

92 Colour: bright golden. Nose: candied fruit, creamy oak, toasty, sweet spices. Palate: flavourful, long, ripe fruit.

CANCHALES 2011 T
100% tempranillo.

88 Colour: dark-red cherry. Nose: expressive, varietal, powerfull, violet drops, fruit expression. Palate: spirituous, sweetness, powerful, flavourful.

ARTACHO 4M 2010 T
100% tempranillo.

87 Colour: cherry, garnet rim. Nose: ripe fruit, spicy, toasty. Palate: powerful, flavourful, toasty, round tannins.

MONTE REAL 2009 TC
100% tempranillo.

87 Colour: cherry, garnet rim. Nose: spicy, creamy oak, toasty, wet leather. Palate: powerful, flavourful, toasty, round tannins.

PUERTA VIEJA 2009 TC
80% tempranillo, 15% mazuelo, 5% graciano.

87 Colour: cherry, garnet rim. Nose: ripe fruit, spicy, toasty, fine reductive notes. Palate: powerful, flavourful, toasty.

GRAN ALBINA VENDIMIA 2007 T
34% tempranillo, 33% mazuelo, 33% graciano.

90 Colour: light cherry. Nose: fine reductive notes, expressive, creamy oak, toasty, ripe fruit. Palate: creamy, ripe fruit, flavourful, powerful, fruity.

GRAN ALBINA 2006 TR
34% tempranillo, 33% mazuelo, 33% graciano.

90 Colour: cherry, garnet rim. Nose: spicy, creamy oak, toasty. Palate: powerful, flavourful, toasty, round tannins.

VIÑA ALBINA SELECCIÓN 2006 TR
80% tempranillo, 15% mazuelo, 5% graciano.

90 Colour: cherry, garnet rim. Nose: creamy oak, toasty, spicy. Palate: powerful, flavourful, toasty, round tannins.

MONTE REAL RESERVA DE FAMILIA 2006 TR
100% tempranillo.

90 Colour: dark-red cherry, orangey edge. Nose: spicy, aged wood nuances, fruit preserve, dry nuts. Palate: round, powerful, flavourful, spirituous, spicy, smoky afterpalate:, ripe fruit.

MONTE REAL 2006 TR
100% tempranillo.

89 Colour: dark-red cherry. Nose: spicy, cedar wood, powerfull, ripe fruit. Palate: good structure, powerful, flavourful, classic aged character, round tannins.

VIÑA ALBINA 2006 TR
80% tempranillo, 15% mazuelo, 5% graciano.

89 Colour: cherry, garnet rim. Nose: spicy, creamy oak, toasty. Palate: powerful, flavourful, toasty, round tannins.

VIÑA ALBINA 2004 TGR
80% tempranillo, 15% mazuelo, 5% graciano.

88 Colour: cherry, garnet rim. Nose: ripe fruit, spicy, creamy oak, toasty, cigar, wet leather. Palate: powerful, flavourful, toasty, round tannins.

VIÑA ALBINA 2011 SEMIDULCE
95% viura, 5% malvasía.

85 Colour: bright straw. Nose: balanced, citrus fruit, faded flowers, ripe fruit. Palate: fruity, easy to drink.

MONTE REAL 2004 TGR
100% tempranillo.

87 Colour: dark-red cherry, orangey edge. Nose: spicy, sweet spices, wet leather, reduction notes. Palate: smoky afterpalate:, classic aged character, spicy.

BODEGAS RIOLANC

Curillos, 36
01308 Lanciego (Álava)
☎: +34 945 608 140 - Fax: +34 945 608 140
riolanc@riolanc.com
www.riolanc.com

RIOLANC VENDIMIA SELECCIONADA 2011 T
85% tempranillo, 15% mazuelo.

88 Colour: cherry, purple rim. Nose: red berry notes, floral. Palate: flavourful, fruity, good acidity, round tannins.

RIOLANC 2009 TC
100% tempranillo.

84

BODEGAS RODA

Avda. de Vizcaya, 5
26200 Haro (La Rioja)
☎: +34 941 303 001 - Fax: +34 941 312 703
rodarioja@roda.es
www.roda.es

CIRSION 2010 T
tempranillo.

95 Colour: cherry, purple rim. Nose: sweet spices, creamy oak, ripe fruit, red berry notes, mineral. Palate: flavourful, powerful, concentrated, spicy.

SELA 2010 T
tempranillo.

89 Colour: bright cherry. Nose: ripe fruit, sweet spices, creamy oak. Palate: flavourful, fruity, toasty, round tannins, fine bitter notes.

CIRSION 2009 T
tempranillo.

96 Colour: cherry, garnet rim. Nose: ripe fruit, spicy, creamy oak, toasty, complex, earthy notes. Palate: powerful, flavourful, toasty, round tannins.

RODA 2008 TR
90% tempranillo, 6% graciano, 4% garnacha.

91 Colour: cherry, garnet rim. Nose: elegant, dark chocolate, sweet spices, ripe fruit. Palate: good structure, flavourful, round tannins.

RODA I 2007 TR
100% tempranillo.

94 Colour: deep cherry. Nose: undergrowth, elegant, complex, fruit expression, toasty, nose:tic coffee. Palate: round, elegant, flavourful, powerful, full, roasted-coffee afterpalate:.

RODA 2007 TR
89% tempranillo, 8% garnacha, 3% graciano.

93 Colour: dark-red cherry. Nose: complex, elegant, expressive, fruit expression. Palate: flavourful, powerful, spirituous, complex, roasted-coffee afterpalate:, spicy.

BODEGAS RUCONIA

Ctra. de San Asensio, s/n junto N-120
26300 Nájera (La Rioja)
☎: +34 941 362 059 - Fax: +34 941 362 467
info@bodegasruconia.com
www.bodegasruconia.com

RUCONIA 2011 T
100% tempranillo.

84

TUBAL 2007 TC
100% tempranillo.

89 Colour: cherry, garnet rim. Nose: ripe fruit, spicy, creamy oak, toasty, complex. Palate: powerful, flavourful, toasty, round tannins.

RUCONIA 2007 TC
100% tempranillo.

88 Colour: cherry, garnet rim. Nose: balanced, sweet spices, creamy oak, ripe fruit. Palate: flavourful, balanced, good acidity.

BODEGAS RUIZ DE VIÑASPRE

Camino De La Hoya , s/n
01300 Laguardia (Álava)
☎: +34 945 600 626
info@bodegaruizdevinaspre.com
www.bodegaruizdevinaspre.com

RV DE RUIZ DE VIÑASPRE 2010 BFB
viura.

89 Colour: yellow, greenish rim. Nose: balanced, expressive, ripe fruit, sweet spices. Palate: rich, flavourful, balanced.

RUIZ DE VIÑASPRE 2008 T
100% tempranillo.

87 Colour: deep cherry. Nose: ripe fruit, spicy, scrubland. Palate: flavourful, spicy, ripe fruit.

RV DE RUIZ DE VIÑASPRE 2007 T FERMENTADO EN BARRICA
100% tempranillo.

86 Colour: cherry, garnet rim. Nose: overripe fruit, scrubland, spicy, fine reductive notes. Palate: correct, powerful, flavourful, toasty.

BODEGAS SANTALBA

Avda. de la Rioja, s/n
26221 Gimileo (La Rioja)
☎: +34 941 304 231 - Fax: +34 941 304 326
santalba@santalba.com
www.santalba.com

SANTALBA ECOLÓGICO 2010 T
100% tempranillo.

91 Colour: cherry, garnet rim. Nose: balanced, ripe fruit, sweet spices, varietal. Palate: good structure, flavourful, fresh.

ABANDO VENDIMIA SELECCIONADA 2008 T
100% tempranillo.

89 Colour: cherry, garnet rim. Nose: ripe fruit, spicy, creamy oak, toasty, fine reductive notes. Palate: powerful, flavourful, toasty.

VIÑA HERMOSA 2008 TC
100% tempranillo.

88 Colour: cherry, garnet rim. Nose: spicy, creamy oak, toasty, characterful. Palate: powerful, flavourful, toasty, round tannins.

ERMITA DE SAN FELICES 2007 TR
100% tempranillo.

90 Colour: bright cherry. Nose: ripe fruit, sweet spices, creamy oak, dry stone. Palate: flavourful, fruity, round tannins.

IREP TEMPRANILLO 2007 T
100% tempranillo.

88 Colour: cherry, garnet rim. Nose: ripe fruit, spicy, creamy oak, toasty. Palate: powerful, flavourful, toasty, round tannins.

SANTALBA SINGLE VINEYARD 2005 T
100% tempranillo.

92 Colour: deep cherry, orangey edge. Nose: spicy, cocoa bean, mineral, scrubland. Palate: flavourful, long, round tannins.

BODEGAS SEÑORÍA DE YERGA

Barrio Bodegas, s/n
26142 Villamediana (La Rioja)
☎: +34 941 435 003 - Fax: +34 941 435 003
info@senoriodeyerga.com

CASTILLO DE YERGA 2008 TC
90% tempranillo, 10% garnacha.

86 Colour: cherry, garnet rim. Nose: ripe fruit, spicy, toasty, tobacco. Palate: powerful, flavourful, toasty, round tannins.

CASTILLO YERGA 2006 TR
90% tempranillo, 10% mazuelo.

85 Colour: dark-red cherry. Nose: spicy, toasty, ripe fruit, short. Palate: correct, round, powerful, flavourful, lacks expression.

CASTILLO YERGA 2004 TGR
85% tempranillo, 10% graciano, 5% mazuelo.

88 Colour: pale ruby, brick rim edge. Nose: fruit liqueur notes, wet leather, waxy notes. Palate: fine bitter notes, spirituous.

BODEGAS SOLAR DE SAMANIEGO

Ctra. De Elciego s/n
01300 Laguardia (Álava)
☎: +34 902 227 700 - Fax: +34 902 227 701
bodega@cofradiasamaniego.com
www.solardesamaniego.com

SOLAR DE SAMANIEGO 2008 TC
tempranillo.

86 Colour: cherry, garnet rim. Nose: balanced, sweet spices. Palate: flavourful, full, correct.

VALCAVADA 2006 TR
80% tempranillo, 20% graciano.

90 Colour: cherry, garnet rim. Nose: spicy, dried herbs, tobacco. Palate: flavourful, good acidity, fine bitter notes.

LA OLVIDADA 2009

93 Colour: cherry, garnet rim. Nose: ripe fruit, cream oak, sweet spices, mineral, complex. Palate: powerful, flavourful, toasty, round tannins, balanced.

SOLAR DE SAMANIEGO 2005 TR
95% tempranillo, 5% graciano.

86 Colour: cherry, garnet rim. Nose: spicy, tobacco, dark chocolate, ripe fruit, fruit preserve. Palate: flavourful, correct.

BODEGAS SOLAR VIEJO

Camino de la Hoya, s/n
01300 Laguardia (Álava)
☎: +34 945 600 113 - Fax: +34 945 600 600
solarviejo@solarviejo.com
www.solarviejo.com

SOLAR VIEJO 2011 T
tempranillo.

89 Colour: cherry, garnet rim. Nose: expressive, fresh, varietal, ripe fruit. Palate: fruity, fresh, sweetness, flavourful, powerful.

SOLAR VIEJO VENDIMIA SELECCIONADA 2009 T
tempranillo.

88 Colour: cherry, garnet rim. Nose: balanced, ripe fruit, sweet spices. Palate: flavourful, fruity, good acidity.

ORUBE 2009 T
100% tempranillo.

88 Colour: deep cherry. Nose: ripe fruit, cedar wood, sweet spices, undergrowth. Palate: round, warm, powerful, flavourful, fruity.

SOLAR VIEJO 2009 TC
tempranillo.

86 Colour: cherry, garnet rim. Nose: ripe fruit, balsamic herbs, roasted coffee. Palate: powerful, flavourful, toasty.

SOLAR VIEJO 2007 TR
85% tempranillo, 15% graciano.

89 Colour: cherry, garnet rim. Nose: medium intensity, balanced, expressive, spicy, ripe fruit. Palate: flavourful, good acidity, long.

BODEGAS SONSIERRA, S. COOP.

El Remedio, s/n
26338 San Vicente de la Sonsierra (La Rioja)
☎: +34 941 334 031 - Fax: +34 941 334 245
sonsierra@sonsierra.com
www.sonsierra.com

SONSIERRA 2011 B
100% viura.

87 Colour: bright straw. Nose: fresh, white flowers, dried herbs. Palate: flavourful, fruity, good acidity, correct.

SONSIERRA 2011 RD
100% tempranillo.

87 Colour: brilliant rose. Nose: fresh fruit, red berry notes, neat, varietal. Palate: powerful, flavourful, sweetness, complex.

SONSIERRA TEMPRANILLO 2011 T
100% tempranillo.

88 Colour: cherry, purple rim. Nose: balanced, red berry notes, expressive. Palate: fruity, flavourful, good finish.

PERFUME DE SONSIERRA DAVID DELFÍN 2009 T
100% tempranillo.

92 Colour: bright cherry. Nose: ripe fruit, creamy oak, toasty, complex, sweet spices. Palate: powerful, flavourful, round tannins.

SONSIERRA VENDIMIA SELECCIONADA 2009 TC
100% tempranillo.

90 Colour: cherry, garnet rim. Nose: spicy, creamy oak, toasty, characterful. Palate: powerful, flavourful, toasty, round tannins.

SONSIERRA 2009 TC
100% tempranillo.

88 Colour: cherry, garnet rim. Nose: ripe fruit, spicy, creamy oak, toasty. Palate: powerful, flavourful, toasty, round tannins.

PAGOS DE LA SONSIERRA 2008 TR
100% tempranillo.

90 Colour: black cherry, garnet rim. Nose: ripe fruit, nose:tic coffee, sweet spices, toasty. Palate: spicy, long, toasty, flavourful.

SONSIERRA 2008 TR
100% tempranillo.

88 Colour: cherry, garnet rim. Nose: ripe fruit, spicy, creamy oak, toasty, complex. Palate: powerful, flavourful, toasty, round tannins.

BODEGAS TARÓN

Ctra. de Miranda, s/n
26211 Tirgo (La Rioja)
☎: +34 941 301 650 - Fax: +34 941 301 817
info@bodegastaron.com
www.bodegastaron.com

TARÓN 2011 B
100% viura.

88 Colour: bright straw. Nose: fresh, fresh fruit, white flowers. Palate: flavourful, fruity, good acidity, balanced.

TARÓN 2011 RD
50% garnacha, 50% viura.

88 Colour: light cherry. Nose: elegant, candied fruit, dried flowers, fragrant herbs, red berry notes. Palate: light-bodied, flavourful, good acidity, long, spicy.

TARÓN 2008 TC
95% tempranillo, 5% mazuelo.

86 Colour: cherry, garnet rim. Nose: ripe fruit, spicy, toasty. Palate: powerful, flavourful, toasty, round tannins.

TARÓN TEMPRANILLO 2011 T
100% tempranillo.

87 Colour: cherry, purple rim. Nose: red berry notes, ripe fruit, balsamic herbs, floral. Palate: fresh, fruity, light-bodied, easy to drink.

TARÓN VIÑAS VIEJAS 2010 TR
100% tempranillo.

92 Colour: cherry, garnet rim. Nose: ripe fruit, spicy, creamy oak, toasty, complex, mineral. Palate: powerful, flavourful, toasty, round tannins.

TARÓN 4MB 2009 T
100% tempranillo.

91 Colour: cherry, garnet rim. Nose: ripe fruit, sweet spices, violets, balanced. Palate: good structure, flavourful.

TARÓN 2005 TR
85% tempranillo, 10% mazuelo, 5% graciano.

90 Colour: cherry, garnet rim. Nose: ripe fruit, spicy, creamy oak, toasty, complex. Palate: powerful, flavourful, toasty, round tannins.

BODEGAS TOBÍA

Paraje Senda Rutia, s/n
26214 Cuzcurrita de Río Tirón (La Rioja)
☎: +34 941 301 789 - Fax: +34 941 328 045
tobia@bodegastobia.com
www.bodegastobia.com

VIÑA TOBÍA 2011 B
95% viura, 5% malvasía.

89 Colour: bright straw. Nose: ripe fruit, citrus fruit, faded flowers. Palate: fine bitter notes, good acidity, fruity.

DAIMON 2011 B
60% viura, 30% malvasía, 10% tempranillo blanco.

88 Colour: golden. Nose: powerfull, floral, candied fruit, tropical fruit, wild herbs, sweet spices. Palate: flavourful, fresh, fruity, balanced.

ALMA DE TOBÍA 2011 RD FERMENTADO EN BARRICA
55% tempranillo, 35% graciano, 10% otras.

88 Colour: rose, purple rim. Nose: ripe fruit, red berry notes, floral, expressive, creamy oak, sweet spices. Palate: , powerful, fruity, fresh.

VIÑA TOBÍA 2011 RD
100% garnacha.

88 Colour: rose, purple rim. Nose: fresh, red berry notes, ripe fruit, wild herbs. Palate: flavourful, fruity, fresh.

VIÑA TOBÍA 2011 T
100% tempranillo.

89 Colour: cherry, purple rim. Nose: expressive, fresh fruit, red berry notes, floral. Palate: flavourful, fruity, good acidity, round tannins.

DAIMON 2010 T
56% tempranillo, 22% graciano, 16% garnacha, 6% merlot.

90 Colour: cherry, garnet rim. Nose: balanced, complex, ripe fruit, creamy oak, cocoa bean. Palate: flavourful, full, round tannins.

TOBÍA SELECCIÓN 2008 TC
80% tempranillo, 10% graciano, 10% garnacha.

90 Colour: bright cherry. Nose: ripe fruit, spicy, creamy oak, cocoa bean. Palate: powerful, flavourful, toasty, round tannins.

OSCAR TOBÍA 2007 T
95% tempranillo, 5% graciano.

89 Colour: cherry, garnet rim. Nose: cigar, spicy, balanced. Palate: good structure, long, good acidity.

BODEGAS URBINA

Campillo, 33
26214 Cuzcurrita de Río Tirón (La Rioja)
☎: +34 941 224 272 - Fax: +34 941 224 272
urbina@fer.es
www.urbinavinos.com

URBINA VIURA 2011 B
100% viura.

84

URBINA 2011 RD
100% tempranillo.

85 Colour: light cherry. Nose: fruit expression, candied fruit. Palate: flavourful, fruity.

URBINA GARNACHA 2011 T
100% garnacha.

86 Colour: cherry, garnet rim. Nose: ripe fruit, wild herbs, balanced. Palate: flavourful, powerful, fine bitter notes.

URBINA TEMPRANILLO 2011 T
100% tempranillo.

83

URBINA 2007 TC
95% tempranillo, 2,5% mazuelo, 2,5% graciano.

82

URBINA RESERVA ESPECIAL RAISINS 2005 TR
95% tempranillo, 2,5% mazuelo, 2,5% graciano.

87 Colour: pale ruby, brick rim edge. Nose: overripe fruit, medium intensity, spicy. Palate: flavourful, fruity.

URBINA RESERVA ESPECIAL 2004 TR
95% tempranillo, 2,5% graciano, 2,5% mazuelo.

86 Colour: deep cherry. Nose: expressive, dark chocolate, creamy oak. Palate: spicy, fine bitter notes, correct.

URBINA RESERVA ESPECIAL 2001 TR
95% tempranillo, 2,5% mazuelo, 2,5% graciano.

88 Colour: pale ruby, brick rim edge. Nose: warm, fruit liqueur notes, spicy. Palate: light-bodied, good acidity, elegant.

URBINA 1995 TGR
95% tempranillo, 2,5% mazuelo, 2,5% graciano.

86 Colour: dark-red cherry, orangey edge. Nose: fruit liqueur notes, cigar, fine reductive notes. Palate: spicy, aged character.

BODEGAS VALDELACIERVA

Ctra. Burgos, Km. 13
26370 Navarrete (La Rioja)
☎: +34 941 440 620 - Fax: +34 941 440 787
info@hispanobodegas.com
www.hispanobodegas.com

CAMPO ALTO 2011 T
tempranillo.

85 Colour: cherry, purple rim. Nose: expressive, red berry notes, floral, fragrant herbs. Palate: flavourful, fruity, easy to drink.

IMPAR VENDIMIA SELECCIONADA 2010 T
tempranillo.

90 Colour: cherry, garnet rim. Nose: fruit expression, complex, elegant, varietal, cocoa bean. Palate: complex, fruity, powerful, flavourful, balsamic.

VALDELACIERVA 2009 TC
tempranillo.

86 Colour: cherry, garnet rim. Nose: ripe fruit, spicy, toasty. Palate: powerful, flavourful, long.

IMPAR EDICIÓN LIMITADA 2007 TR
tempranillo.

88 Colour: dark-red cherry. Nose: cocoa bean, nose:tic coffee, creamy oak, aged wood nuances, ripe fruit. Palate: powerful, flavourful, spirituous, good structure.

BODEGAS VALDELANA

Puente Barricuelo, 67-69
01340 Elciego (Álava)
☎: +34 945 606 055 - Fax: +34 945 606 587
info@bodegasvaldelana.com
www.bodegasvaldelana.com

VALDELANA 2011 B
100% malvasía.

88 Colour: bright straw. Nose: fresh, ripe fruit, white flowers, dried herbs. Palate: fresh, fruity, easy to drink, good acidity.

LADRÓN DE GUEVARA 2011 B
100% viura.

85 Colour: bright straw. Nose: fresh, fresh fruit, white flowers, dried herbs. Palate: flavourful, fruity, easy to drink.

DUQUESA DE LA VICTORIA 2011 T
95% tempranillo, 5% viura.

91 Colour: cherry, purple rim. Nose: red berry notes, balanced, expressive. Palate: fruity, flavourful, long.

VALDELANA 2011 T
95% tempranillo, 5% viura.

88 Colour: cherry, purple rim. Nose: balanced, expressive, red berry notes. Palate: good structure, flavourful, good acidity.

AGNUS DE VALDELANA DE AUTOR 2011 T
95% tempranillo, 5% graciano.

88 Colour: cherry, purple rim. Nose: ripe fruit, red berry notes, toasty, creamy oak. Palate: powerful, fine bitter notes, good acidity.

LADRÓN DE GUEVARA DE AUTOR 2011 T
95% tempranillo, 5% graciano.

88 Colour: cherry, purple rim. Nose: toasty, spicy, ripe fruit. Palate: flavourful, fine bitter notes, ripe fruit.

LADRÓN DE GUEVARA 2011 T
95% tempranillo, 5% viura.

87 Colour: cherry, purple rim. Nose: ripe fruit, red berry notes. Palate: ripe fruit.

LADRÓN DE GUEVARA DE AUTOR 2009 TC
95% tempranillo, 5% graciano.

92 Colour: cherry, garnet rim. Nose: spicy, creamy oak, toasty. Palate: powerful, flavourful, toasty, round tannins.

AGNUS D VALDELANA 2009 TC
95% tempranillo, 5% graciano.

89 Colour: bright cherry. Nose: ripe fruit, sweet spices, creamy oak, roasted coffee. Palate: flavourful, fruity, toasty, balanced.

DUQUESA DE LA VICTORIA 2009 TC
95% tempranillo, 5% mazuelo.

89 Colour: cherry, garnet rim. Nose: ripe fruit, sweet spices, dark chocolate, creamy oak, toasty. Palate: powerful, flavourful, toasty, spicy.

VALDELANA 2009 TC
95% tempranillo, 5% mazuelo.

88 Colour: deep cherry, garnet rim. Nose: sweet spices, balanced, ripe fruit, roasted coffee. Palate: toasty, harsh oak tannins.

LADRÓN DE GUEVARA 2009 TC
95% tempranillo, 5% mazuelo.

87 Colour: cherry, garnet rim. Nose: toasty, creamy oak. Palate: flavourful, spicy, harsh oak tannins.

DUQUESA DE LA VICTORIA 2006 TR
95% tempranillo, 5% graciano.

91 Colour: deep cherry, garnet rim. Nose: cocoa bean, sweet spices, ripe fruit. Palate: balanced, fine bitter notes, round tannins.

VALDELANA 2006 TR
95% tempranillo, 5% graciano.

90 Colour: deep cherry, garnet rim. Nose: creamy oak, toasty, ripe fruit. Palate: balanced, fine bitter notes, round tannins.

BARON LADRÓN DE GUEVARA 2006 TR
95% tempranillo, 5% graciano.

88 Colour: deep cherry, orangey edge. Nose: woody, spicy, ripe fruit. Palate: powerful, flavourful, oaky, ripe fruit.

BODEGAS VALDEMAR

Camino Viejo, s/n
01320 Oyón (Álava)
☎: +34 945 622 188 - Fax: +34 945 622 111
info@valdemar.es
www.valdemar.es

INSPIRACIÓN VALDEMAR TEMPRANILLO BLANCO 2011 BFB
100% tempranillo blanco.

88 Colour: bright yellow. Nose: candied fruit, spicy, medium intensity. Palate: fruity, flavourful, good finish.

CONDE DE VALDEMAR VIURA 2011 B
100% viura.

85 Colour: bright straw. Nose: fresh, fresh fruit, white flowers. Palate: flavourful, fruity, good acidity, balanced.

CONDE DE VALDEMAR FINCA ALTO CANTABRIA 2011 BFB
100% viura.

85 Colour: bright yellow. Nose: ripe fruit, candied fruit, floral. Palate: fresh, fruity, flavourful.

CONDE DE VALDEMAR 2011 RD
85% garnacha, 15% tempranillo.

85 Colour: rose, purple rim. Nose: fruit expression, red berry notes, floral. Palate: flavourful, fruity, fresh, good acidity.

VALDEMAR TEMPRANILLO 2011 T
100% tempranillo.

90 Colour: cherry, purple rim. Nose: expressive, fresh fruit, red berry notes, floral. Palate: flavourful, fruity, good acidity, round tannins.

CONDE DE VALDEMAR GARNACHA 2010 T
100% garnacha.

89 Colour: cherry, garnet rim. Nose: red berry notes, fruit liqueur notes, fragrant herbs, floral, nose:tic coffee, toasty, creamy oak. Palate: powerful, flavourful, long, spicy.

INSPIRACIÓN VALDEMAR 2010 T
80% tempranillo, 10% graciano, 5% maturana, 5% garnacha.

87 Colour: deep cherry. Nose: ripe fruit, sweet spices, creamy oak, expressive, aged wood nuances. Palate: flavourful, fruity, toasty, round tannins, good structure, powerful, spirituous.

CONDE DE VALDEMAR 2009 TC
90% tempranillo, 10% mazuelo.

88 Colour: cherry, garnet rim. Nose: spicy, creamy oak, toasty, fruit expression. Palate: powerful, flavourful, toasty, round tannins.

INSPIRACIÓN VALDEMAR EDICIÓN LIMITADA 2008 T
70% tempranillo, 20% experimental, 10% graciano.

92 Colour: cherry, garnet rim. Nose: ripe fruit, spicy, creamy oak, toasty, mineral, characterful. Palate: powerful, flavourful, toasty, round tannins.

INSPIRACIÓN VALDEMAR MATURANA 2008 T
92% maturana, 8% tempranillo.

92 Colour: cherry, garnet rim. Nose: ripe fruit, spicy, creamy oak, toasty, characterful. Palate: powerful, flavourful, toasty, round tannins.

INSPIRACIÓN VALDEMAR 2008 T
90% tempranillo, 10% graciano.

88 Colour: cherry, garnet rim. Nose: spicy, creamy oak, toasty, fruit preserve. Palate: powerful, flavourful, toasty, round tannins.

CONDE DE VALDEMAR 2007 TR
90% tempranillo, 5% mazuelo, 5% graciano.

88 Colour: cherry, garnet rim. Nose: ripe fruit, spicy, toasty, fine reductive notes. Palate: powerful, flavourful, toasty, balanced.

INSPIRACIÓN VALDEMAR GRACIANO 2005 T
100% graciano.

90 Colour: cherry, garnet rim. Nose: scrubland, spicy, wet leather, cigar, earthy notes. Palate: flavourful, long, balanced, spicy.

CONDE DE VALDEMAR 2005 TGR
85% tempranillo, 5% mazuelo, 10% graciano.

88 Colour: deep cherry. Nose: toasty, spicy, fruit liqueur notes, ripe fruit. Palate: fine bitter notes, good acidity, spicy.

BODEGAS VALLEMAYOR

Ctra. Logroño-Vitoria, 38
26360 Fuenmayor (La Rioja)
☎: +34 941 450 142 - Fax: +34 941 450 376
vallemayor@fer.es
www.vallemayor.com

VALLE MAYOR WHITE RIOJA 2011 B
100% viura.

84

VALLEMAYOR 2011 RD
50% garnacha, 50% tempranillo.

80

SEÑORÍO DE LA LUZ 2011 T
100% tempranillo.

85 Colour: cherry, purple rim. Nose: fragrant herbs, red berry notes. Palate: flavourful, fruity, fresh.

COLECCIÓN VALLE MAYOR VIÑA ENCINEDA VENDIMIA SELECCIONADA 2010 T
100% tempranillo.

86 Colour: light cherry. Nose: red clay notes, earthy notes, ripe fruit, spicy. Palate: sweetness, spirituous, powerful, flavourful, spicy.

VALLEMAYOR 2008 TC
90% tempranillo, 5% mazuelo, 5% graciano.

85 Colour: deep cherry. Nose: spicy, nose:tic coffee, ripe fruit. Palate: flavourful, ripe fruit, fine bitter notes.

VALLEMAYOR 2007 TR
85% tempranillo, 10% mazuelo, 5% graciano.

86 Colour: cherry, garnet rim. Nose: toasty, spicy, ripe fruit. Palate: spicy, ripe fruit.

COLECCIÓN VALLE MAYOR VIÑA CERRADILLA VENDIMIA SELECCIONADA 2006 TC
90% tempranillo, 10% mazuelo.

86 Colour: cherry, garnet rim. Nose: old leather, tobacco, spicy. Palate: fruity, correct, spicy.

VALLEMAYOR 2005 TGR
80% tempranillo, 10% mazuelo, 10% graciano.

88 Colour: bright cherry, orangey edge. Nose: spicy, fine reductive notes, fruit preserve. Palate: balanced, fine bitter notes, good acidity.

BODEGAS VICENTE GANDÍA

Ctra. Cheste a Godelleta, s/n
46370 Chiva (Valencia)
☎: +34 962 524 242 - Fax: +34 962 524 243
vuboldi@vicentegandia.com
www.vicentegandia.es

ALTOS DE RAIZA TEMPRANILLO 2011 T
100% tempranillo.

85 Colour: cherry, garnet rim. Nose: ripe fruit, spicy, creamy oak, balsamic herbs. Palate: flavourful, fresh, easy to drink.

RAIZA TEMPRANILLO 2008 TC
100% tempranillo.

87 Colour: cherry, garnet rim. Nose: ripe fruit, spicy, creamy oak, toasty. Palate: powerful, flavourful, toasty, round tannins.

RAIZA TEMPRANILLO 2006 TR
100% tempranillo.

87 Colour: light cherry, garnet rim. Nose: spicy, fine reductive notes, wet leather, aged wood nuances, ripe fruit. Palate: spicy, fine tannins, long.

RAIZA TEMPRANILLO 2005 TGR
100% tempranillo.

88 Colour: pale ruby, brick rim edge. Nose: spicy, wet leather, aged wood nuances, fruit liqueur notes. Palate: spicy, powerful, flavourful, long, balanced.

BODEGAS VINÍCOLA REAL

Ctra. Nalda, km. 9
26120 Albelda de Iregua (La Rioja)
☎: +34 941 444 233 - Fax: +34 941 444 427
info@vinicolareal.com
www.vinicolareal.com

VIÑA LOS VALLES 2011 T
100% tempranillo.

87 Colour: cherry, garnet rim. Nose: red berry notes, ripe fruit, balsamic herbs, fresh, expressive. Palate: powerful, flavourful, fresh, fruity.

VIÑA LOS VALLES 50 & 50 2009 T
50% garnacha, 50% graciano.

89 Colour: light cherry, garnet rim. Nose: ripe fruit, earthy notes, spicy. Palate: powerful, flavourful, fruity, round tannins.

VIÑA LOS VALLES 70 & 30 2009 TC
70% tempranillo, 30% graciano.

88 Colour: cherry, garnet rim. Nose: ripe fruit, spicy, creamy oak, toasty, smoky. Palate: powerful, flavourful, toasty, round tannins, long.

VIÑA LOS VALLES 80 & 20 2009 TC
80% tempranillo, 20% mazuelo.

88 Colour: cherry, garnet rim. Nose: ripe fruit, spicy, balsamic herbs. Palate: powerful, flavourful, balsamic, spicy.

CUEVA DEL MONGE 2009 T
100% tempranillo.

86 Colour: bright cherry. Nose: ripe fruit, sweet spices, creamy oak. Palate: flavourful, fruity, toasty, balanced.

200 MONGES 2006 TR
85% tempranillo, 10% graciano, 5% mazuelo.

89 Colour: cherry, garnet rim. Nose: ripe fruit, spicy, toasty, complex, fine reductive notes. Palate: powerful, flavourful, toasty, spicy, long.

200 MONGES SELECCIÓN ESPECIAL 2005 TR
100% tempranillo.

92 Colour: dark-red cherry, orangey edge. Nose: ripe fruit, earthy notes, balsamic herbs, spicy, fine reductive notes. Palate: flavourful, long, spicy, round tannins.

200 MONGES 2001 TGR
85% tempranillo, 10% graciano, 5% mazuelo.

91 Colour: pale ruby, brick rim edge. Nose: elegant, spicy, fine reductive notes, wet leather, aged wood nuances. Palate: spicy, fine tannins, elegant, long.

BODEGAS VIÑA BERNEDA

Ctra. Somalo, 59
26313 Uruñuela (La Rioja)
☎: +34 941 371 304 - Fax: +34 941 371 304
berneda@vinaberneda.com
www.vinaberneda.com

VIÑA BERNEDA 2011 BFB
100% viura.

88 Colour: bright yellow. Nose: powerfull, ripe fruit, sweet spices, creamy oak, toasty. Palate: rich, flavourful, sweetness.

VIÑA BERNEDA 2011 T MACERACIÓN CARBÓNICA
100% tempranillo.

87 Colour: cherry, purple rim. Nose: medium intensity, red berry notes, violets. Palate: fruity, good acidity.

BERNEDA VENDIMIA SELECCIONADA 2007 TC
100% tempranillo.

88 Colour: cherry, garnet rim. Nose: ripe fruit, spicy, creamy oak. Palate: powerful, flavourful, toasty, round tannins.

VIÑA BERNEDA 2006 TR
100% tempranillo.

89 Colour: cherry, garnet rim. Nose: ripe fruit, spicy, toasty, complex. Palate: powerful, flavourful, toasty, round tannins.

BODEGAS VIÑA HERMINIA

Camino de los Agudos, 1
26559 Aldeanueva de Ebro (La Rioja)
☎: +34 941 142 305 - Fax: +34 941 142 303
marketing@caballero.es
www.viñaherminia.es

VIÑA HERMINIA EXCELSUS 2010 T
50% garnacha, 50% tempranillo.

91 Colour: cherry, garnet rim. Nose: ripe fruit, spicy, creamy oak, toasty. Palate: powerful, flavourful, toasty, round tannins.

VIÑA HERMINIA GRACIANO 2009 T
100% graciano.

88 Colour: cherry, garnet rim. Nose: ripe fruit, spicy, creamy oak, toasty. Palate: powerful, flavourful, toasty, round tannins.

VIÑA HERMINIA 2009 TC
85% tempranillo, 15% garnacha.

87 Colour: cherry, garnet rim. Nose: powerfull, ripe fruit, toasty. Palate: flavourful, fine bitter notes, good acidity.

VIÑA HERMINIA GARNACHA 2009 T
100% garnacha.

87 Colour: dark-red cherry. Nose: sweet spices, aged wood nuances, spicy, ripe fruit. Palate: powerful, flavourful, smoky afterpalate:, ripe fruit.

VIÑA HERMINIA 2007 TR
85% tempranillo, 10% garnacha, 5% graciano.

88 Colour: dark-red cherry. Nose: creamy oak, ripe fruit, damp earth, fruit expression. Palate: powerful, full, flavourful.

BODEGAS VIRGEN DEL VALLE

Ctra. a Villabuena, 3
01307 Samaniego (Álava)
☎: +34 945 609 033 - Fax: +34 945 609 106
cincel@cincel.net
www.cincel.net

CINCEL 2007 TC
95% tempranillo, 5% mazuelo, graciano.

84

CINCEL 2004 TR
95% tempranillo, 5% graciano, mazuelo.

84

CINCEL 2002 TR
90% tempranillo, 10% graciano, mazuelo.

84

CINCEL 2000 TGR
95% tempranillo, 5% graciano, mazuelo.

85 Colour: pale ruby, brick rim edge. Nose: fruit liqueur notes, spicy, wet leather. Palate: spicy, fine bitter notes.

CINCEL 1995 TGR
95% tempranillo, 5% mazuelo, graciano.

89 Colour: pale ruby, brick rim edge. Nose: spicy, aged wood nuances, fruit liqueur notes, tobacco. Palate: spicy, fine tannins, elegant, long.

BODEGAS Y VIÑAS SENDA GALIANA

Barrio Bodegas, s/n
26142 Villamediana (La Rioja)
☎: +34 941 435 375 - Fax: +34 941 436 072
info@sendagaliana.com

SENDA GALIANA 2008 TC

82

SENDA GALIANA 2006 TR

80

SENDA GALIANA 2004 TGR
80% tempranillo, 10% graciano, 10% mazuelo.

92 Colour: pale ruby, brick rim edge. Nose: elegant, spicy, fine reductive notes, wet leather, aged wood nuances, fruit liqueur notes. Palate: spicy, fine tannins, elegant, long.

BODEGAS Y VIÑEDOS ALUÉN

Robledal, 18
26320 Baños de Río Tobia (La Rioja)
☎: +34 607 166 152 - Fax: +34 941 374 851
info@bodegasaluen.com
www.bodegasaluen.com

ALUÉN + 2008 T
100% tempranillo.

90 Colour: cherry, garnet rim. Nose: ripe fruit, creamy oak, fine reductive notes, scrubland. Palate: powerful, flavourful, toasty, balanced.

BODEGAS Y VIÑEDOS ALVAR

Camino de Ventosa, s/n
26371 Ventosa (La Rioja)
☎: +34 941 441 905 - Fax: +34 941 441 917
alvar@bodegasalvar.com
www.bodegasalvar.com

PRIMUM VITAE TEMPRANILLO 2011 T
100% tempranillo.

86 Colour: cherry, purple rim. Nose: medium intensity, red berry notes. Palate: fruity, flavourful, correct.

MILETO 2008 T
85% tempranillo, 15% garnacha.

86 Colour: cherry, garnet rim. Nose: fruit preserve, balsamic herbs, sweet spices. Palate: powerful, flavourful, spicy.

PRIMUM VITAE TEMPRANILLO 2008 TC
100% tempranillo.

84

LIVIUS GRACIANO 2007 T
100% graciano.

91 Colour: bright cherry, garnet rim. Nose: sweet spices, creamy oak, ripe fruit, balsamic herbs. Palate: balanced, ripe fruit, long.

LIVIUS TEMPRANILLO 2007 T
100% tempranillo.

88 Colour: cherry, garnet rim. Nose: ripe fruit, spicy, creamy oak, toasty, wet leather, waxy notes, tobacco. Palate: powerful, flavourful, toasty.

BODEGAS Y VIÑEDOS ARRANZ-ARGOTE

Mayor Alta, 43
26370 Navarrete (La Rioja)
☎: +34 699 046 043
bodega@vinoarar.com
www.vinoarar.com

ARAR 2010 T
tempranillo, graciano.

84

ARAR 2008 T
tempranillo, graciano, garnacha.

88 Colour: bright cherry. Nose: ripe fruit, sweet spices, creamy oak, expressive. Palate: flavourful, fruity, toasty, round tannins.

ARAR 2004 T
tempranillo, graciano, garnacha, mazuelo, maturana.

90 Colour: cherry, garnet rim. Nose: ripe fruit, spicy, creamy oak, toasty, dark chocolate. Palate: powerful, flavourful, toasty, round tannins.

ARAR 2003 T
tempranillo, graciano, garnacha, mazuelo, maturana.

88 Colour: pale ruby, brick rim edge. Nose: elegant, spicy, fine reductive notes, wet leather, aged wood nuances, fruit liqueur notes. Palate: spicy, fine tannins, elegant, long.

BODEGAS Y VIÑEDOS ARTADI

Ctra. de Logroño, s/n
01300 Laguardia (Álava)
☎: +34 945 600 119 - Fax: +34 945 600 850
info@artadi.com
www.artadi.com

ARTADI EL CARRETIL 2010 T
100% tempranillo.

98 Colour: cherry, purple rim. Nose: fruit expression, red berry notes, dry stone, creamy oak, sweet spices. Palate: flavourful, powerful, complex, spicy.

VIÑA EL PISÓN 2010 T
100% tempranillo.

96 Colour: cherry, purple rim. Nose: varietal, characterful, complex, ripe fruit, red berry notes, creamy oak. Palate: flavourful, fruity, good acidity, fine bitter notes.

ARTADI LA POZA DE BALLESTEROS 2010 T
tempranillo.

96 Colour: cherry, garnet rim. Nose: creamy oak, ripe fruit, fruit expression, red berry notes. Palate: flavourful, powerful, good acidity, fine bitter notes, round.

ARTADI PAGOS VIEJOS 2010 T
100% tempranillo.

95 Colour: cherry, garnet rim. Nose: ripe fruit, powerfull, characterful, creamy oak. Palate: flavourful, powerful, fine bitter notes, good acidity, round tannins.

ARTADI VALDEGINÉS 2010 T
tempranillo.

95 Colour: bright cherry. Nose: sweet spices, creamy oak, mineral, fruit expression, elegant. Palate: flavourful, fruity, toasty, fine tannins.

ARTADI VIÑAS DE GAIN 2010 T
100% tempranillo.

92 Colour: bright cherry. Nose: sweet spices, creamy oak, red berry notes, ripe fruit. Palate: flavourful, fruity, toasty, round tannins.

BODEGAS Y VIÑEDOS ILURCE

Ctra. Alfaro - Grávalos (LR-289), km. 23
26540 Alfaro (La Rioja)
☎: +34 941 180 829 - Fax: +34 941 183 897
info@ilurce.com
www.ilurce.com

ILURCE GRACIANO 2006 TC
100% graciano.

84

ILURCE VENDIMIA SELECCIONADA 2005 TC
60% garnacha, 40% tempranillo.

88 Colour: deep cherry. Nose: spicy, ripe fruit, wet leather. Palate: fine bitter notes, spicy, ripe fruit.

ILURCE 2011 RD
100% garnacha.

89 Colour: rose, purple rim. Nose: powerfull, ripe fruit, red berry notes, floral, expressive. Palate: fleshy, powerful, fruity, fresh

ILURCE 2004 TC
70% tempranillo, 15% garnacha, 15% graciano.

85 Colour: cherry, garnet rim. Nose: ripe fruit, spicy, creamy oak, toasty, complex. Palate: powerful, flavourful, toasty, round tannins.

ILURCE VENDIMIA SELECCIONADA 2001 TR
60% tempranillo, 40% garnacha.

87 Colour: deep cherry, bright ochre rim. Nose: fruit liqueur notes, dark chocolate, tobacco. Palate: flavourful, spicy, fine bitter notes.

BODEGAS Y VIÑEDOS LABASTIDA

Avda. Diputación, 22
01330 Labastida (Álava)
☎: +34 945 331 161 - Fax: +34 945 331 118
info@bodegaslabastida.com
www.bodegaslabastida.com

SOLAGÜEN 2008 TC
100% tempranillo.

89 Colour: cherry, garnet rim. Nose: balanced, complex, ripe fruit, spicy. Palate: fruity, good acidity, easy to drink.

SOLAGÜEN 2004 TGR
100% tempranillo.

89 Colour: cherry, garnet rim. Nose: spicy, creamy oak, toasty, wet leather. Palate: powerful, flavourful, toasty, round tannins.

BODEGAS Y VIÑEDOS MARQUÉS DE CARRIÓN

Ctra. Logroño, s/n
01330 Labastida (Álava)
☎: +34 945 331 643 - Fax: +34 945 331 694
eromero@jgc.es
www.garciacarrion.es

ANTAÑO 2011 B
viura.

87 Colour: bright straw. Nose: fresh, white flowers, ripe fruit. Palate: flavourful, fruity, good acidity, balanced.

ANTAÑO 2009 TC
tempranillo, garnacha, mazuelo, graciano.

84

MARQUÉS DE CARRIÓN 2009 TC
tempranillo, mazuelo, graciano.

84

ANTAÑO GRACIANO EDICIÓN LIMITADA 2008 T
graciano.

89 Colour: bright cherry, garnet rim. Nose: ripe fruit, balsamic herbs, earthy notes, spicy. Palate: flavourful, long, toasty, balanced.

ANTAÑO 2008 TR
tempranillo, garnacha, mazuelo, graciano.

82

MARQUÉS DE CARRIÓN 2008 TR
tempranillo, mazuelo, graciano.

81

BODEGAS Y VIÑEDOS PUENTE DEL EA

Camino Aguachal s/n
26212 Sajazarra (La Rioja)
☎: +34 941 320 405 - Fax: +34 941 320 406
puentedelea@gmail.com
www.puentedelea.com

PUENTE DEL EA 2011 BFB
90% viura, 10% chardonnay.

90 Colour: bright yellow. Nose: powerfull, ripe fruit, sweet spices, creamy oak, fragrant herbs. Palate: rich, smoky afterpalate:, flavourful, fresh, good acidity.

ERIDANO VIURA SOBRE LÍAS 2011 B
100% viura.

88 Colour: bright straw. Nose: fresh, fresh fruit, white flowers. Palate: flavourful, fruity, good acidity, balanced.

PUENTE DEL EA 2011 RD
85% tempranillo, 15% garnacha.

88 Colour: rose, purple rim. Nose: powerfull, ripe fruit, red berry notes, floral, expressive. Palate: fleshy, powerful, fruity, fresh.

PUENTE DEL EA GRACIANO 2010 T
100% graciano.

92 Colour: cherry, garnet rim. Nose: complex, elegant, powerfull, varietal, ripe fruit, fruit expression. Palate: elegant, round, powerful, flavourful, spicy.

PUENTE DEL EA GARNACHA 2010 T
100% garnacha.

91 Colour: cherry, garnet rim. Nose: ripe fruit, spicy, creamy oak, toasty, sweet spices. Palate: powerful, flavourful, toasty, round tannins.

ERIDANO SELECCIÓN 2009 T
90% tempranillo, 10% garnacha.

90 Colour: cherry, garnet rim. Nose: smoky, nose:tic coffee, elegant, fresh, complex, dry stone. Palate: round tannins, fruity, flavourful, powerful, balsamic.

PUENTE DEL EA AUTOR 2009 T
100% tempranillo.

90 Colour: cherry, garnet rim. Nose: ripe fruit, spicy, creamy oak, toasty, complex. Palate: powerful, flavourful, toasty, round tannins.

ERIDANO CRIANZA PLATA 2008 TC
100% tempranillo.

90 Colour: deep cherry. Nose: complex, expressive, ripe fruit, fruit expression, spicy, creamy oak. Palate: powerful, flavourful, complex.

PUENTE DEL EA MONOVARIETAL 2008 T
100% tempranillo.

88 Colour: cherry, garnet rim. Nose: ripe fruit, spicy, dried herbs. Palate: fruity, round tannins.

ERIDANO EDICIÓN ESPECIAL 2005 TR
90% tempranillo, 10% garnacha.

88 Colour: cherry, garnet rim. Nose: spicy, creamy oak, toasty, characterful. Palate: powerful, flavourful, toasty, round tannins.

ERIDANO 2005 TR
90% tempranillo, 10% garnacha.

88 Colour: deep cherry, garnet rim. Nose: balanced, tobacco, neat, spicy. Palate: flavourful, fine tannins.

BODEGAS Y VIÑEDOS PUJANZA

Ctra. del Villar, s/n
01300 Laguardia (Álava)
☎: +34 945 600 548 - Fax: +34 945 600 522
gerencia@bodegaspujanza.com
www.bodegaspujanza.com

PUJANZA AÑADAS FRÍAS 2010 B
100% viura.

92 Colour: bright straw. Nose: fresh fruit, citrus fruit, white flowers, mineral. Palate: flavourful, fruity, fresh, good acidity.

PUJANZA HADO 2010 T
tempranillo.

92 Colour: bright cherry. Nose: ripe fruit, sweet spices, creamy oak, expressive, mineral. Palate: flavourful, fruity, toasty, round tannins.

PUJANZA NORTE 2009 T
tempranillo.

96 Colour: cherry, garnet rim. Nose: ripe fruit, spicy, creamy oak, toasty, powerfull. Palate: powerful, flavourful, toasty, round tannins.

PUJANZA CISMA 2009 T
tempranillo.

94 Colour: very deep cherry. Nose: red berry notes, fruit expression, scrubland, sweet spices, elegant. Palate: fine bitter notes, good acidity, ripe fruit.

PUJANZA 2009 T
100% tempranillo.

93 Colour: cherry, garnet rim. Nose: mineral, ripe fruit, sweet spices. Palate: flavourful, fine bitter notes, good acidity, round tannins.

BODEGAS Y VIÑEDOS VARAL

San Vicente, 40
01307 Baños de Ebro (Álava)
☎: +34 945 623 321 - Fax: +34 945 623 321
bodegasvaral@bodegasvaral.com
www.bodegasvaral.com

ESENCIAS DE VARAL 2011 B
100% viura.

87 Colour: bright yellow. Nose: aged wood nuances, smoky, fresh fruit. Palate: round, rich, fruity, spirituous, sweetness.

JOVEN DE VARAL 2011 T MACERACIÓN CARBÓNICA
95% tempranillo, 5% viura.

87 Colour: cherry, purple rim. Nose: medium intensity, ripe fruit, neat. Palate: full, flavourful, fruity.

VARAL VENDIMIA SELECCIONADA 2008 T
100% tempranillo.

92 Colour: cherry, garnet rim. Nose: ripe fruit, sweet spices, nose:tic coffee, earthy notes. Palate: powerful, flavourful, long, toasty, balanced.

CRIANZA DE VARAL 2008 T
100% tempranillo.

90 Colour: deep cherry, garnet rim. Nose: sweet spices, red berry notes, ripe fruit. Palate: fruity, good acidity, flavourful.

ESENCIAS DE VARAL 2007 T
100% tempranillo.

91 Colour: cherry, garnet rim. Nose: ripe fruit, spicy, creamy oak, toasty, complex. Palate: powerful, flavourful, toasty, round tannins, balanced.

RESERVA DE VARAL 2006 TR
100% tempranillo.

88 Colour: bright cherry, garnet rim. Nose: medium intensity, ripe fruit, spicy. Palate: balanced, ripe fruit.

BODEGAS Y VIÑEDOS ZUAZO GASTÓN

Las Norias, 2
01320 Oyón (Álava)
☎: +34 945 601 526 - Fax: +34 945 622 917
zuazogaston@zuazogaston.com
www.zuazogaston.com

ZUAZO GASTÓN 2011 B
viura.

87 Colour: straw. Nose: fresh fruit, fresh, neat. Palate: correct, balanced, powerful, flavourful.

FINCA COSTANILLAS 2010 T
tempranillo, graciano.

89 Colour: bright cherry, garnet rim. Nose: cocoa bean, creamy oak, ripe fruit. Palate: flavourful, ripe fruit, long.

ZUAZO GASTÓN 2009 TC
100% tempranillo.

88 Colour: cherry, garnet rim. Nose: ripe fruit, spicy, creamy oak, toasty. Palate: powerful, flavourful, toasty, round tannins, easy to drink.

ZUAZO GASTÓN 2007 TR
100% tempranillo.

90 Colour: light cherry, orangey edge. Nose: nose:tic coffee, creamy oak, fruit expression, fresh fruit. Palate: powerful, flavourful, sweetness, spicy, creamy.

BODEGAS YSIOS

Camino de la Hoya, s/n
01300 Laguardia (Álava)
☎: +34 945 600 640 - Fax: +34 945 600 520
ysios@pernod-ricard.com
www.ysios.com

YSIOS EDICIÓN LIMITADA 2007 TR
100% tempranillo.

94 Colour: bright cherry, garnet rim. Nose: ripe fruit, mineral, spicy, cocoa bean, creamy oak. Palate: powerful, flavourful, long, balanced, elegant.

YSIOS 2007 TR
100% tempranillo.

92 Colour: cherry, garnet rim. Nose: ripe fruit, spicy, creamy oak, toasty, complex. Palate: powerful, flavourful, toasty, round tannins.

BODEGAS ZUGOBER

Tejerías, 13-15
01306 Lapuebla de Labarca (Álava)
☎: +34 945 627 228 - Fax: +34 945 627 281
contacto@belezos.com
www.zugober.com

BELEZOS ACUARELA 2011 T
tempranillo.

85 Colour: bright cherry. Nose: candied fruit, short. Palate: sweetness, fruity, flavourful.

BELEZOS ECOLÓGICO 2010 T ROBLE
85% tempranillo, 15% graciano.

90 Colour: cherry, garnet rim. Nose: balanced, powerfull, complex, cocoa bean. Palate: good structure, ripe fruit, spicy.

BELEZOS VENDIMIA SELECCIONADA 2008 T
90% tempranillo, 5% graciano.

90 Colour: cherry, garnet rim. Nose: spicy, creamy oak, toasty, ripe fruit. Palate: powerful, flavourful, toasty, round tannins.

BELEZOS 2008 TC
95% tempranillo, 5% graciano, mazuelo.

88 Colour: cherry, garnet rim. Nose: ripe fruit, spicy, creamy oak, toasty. Palate: powerful, flavourful, toasty, round tannins.

BELEZOS 2007 TR
95% tempranillo, 5% graciano, mazuelo.

87 Colour: cherry, garnet rim. Nose: powerfull, fruit preserve, spicy, wild herbs. Palate: flavourful, good acidity.

CARLOS SAN PEDRO PÉREZ DE VIÑASPRE

Páganos, 44- Bajo
01300 Laguardia (Álava)
☎: +34 945 600 146 - Fax: +34 945 600 146
info@bodegascarlossampedro.com
www.bodegascarlossampedro.com

BRILLADOR 2011 T MACERACIÓN CARBÓNICA
95% tempranillo, 5% viura.

84

VIÑASPERI 2008 TC
tempranillo.

84

CARLOS SAN PEDRO 2009 T
tempranillo.

90 Colour: cherry, garnet rim. Nose: ripe fruit, spicy, toasty, complex, fine reductive notes. Palate: powerful, flavourful, toasty, harsh oak tannins.

CARLOS SERRES

Avda. Santo Domingo, 40
26200 Haro (La Rioja)
☎: +34 941 310 294 - Fax: +34 941 310 418
info@carlosserres.com
www.carlosserres.com

SERRES VIURA 2011 B
100% viura.

88 Colour: yellow. Nose: medium intensity, fresh fruit, dried herbs, dried flowers. Palate: fruity, fine bitter notes, good acidity.

CARLOS SERRES 2009 TC
85% tempranillo, 15% garnacha.

88 Colour: cherry, garnet rim. Nose: ripe fruit, old leather, spicy. Palate: flavourful, spicy, long.

ONOMÁSTICA 2007 B RESERVA
100% viura.

88 Colour: bright golden. Nose: powerfull, candied fruit, white flowers, faded flowers, creamy oak, sweet spices. Palate: rich, roasted-coffee afterpalate:, full.

SERRES TEMPRANILLO GARNACHA 2011 RD
80% tempranillo, 20% garnacha.

88 Colour: rose, purple rim. Nose: powerfull, ripe fruit, red berry notes, floral. Palate: , powerful, fruity, fresh.

SERRES TEMPRANILLO 2011 T
100% tempranillo.

89 Colour: cherry, purple rim. Nose: balanced, varietal, red berry notes. Palate: flavourful, balanced, good acidity.

CARLOS SERRES 2007 TR
90% tempranillo, 10% graciano.

89 Colour: cherry, garnet rim. Nose: spicy, creamy oak, toasty, wet leather. Palate: powerful, flavourful, toasty, round tannins.

ONOMÁSTICA 2007 TR
80% tempranillo, 10% graciano, 10% mazuelo.

87 Colour: cherry, garnet rim. Nose: spicy, creamy oak, toasty, characterful, ripe fruit. Palate: powerful, flavourful, toasty, round tannins.

CARLOS SERRES 2005 TGR
85% tempranillo, 10% graciano, 5% mazuelo.

89 Colour: cherry, garnet rim. Nose: ripe fruit, spicy, creamy oak, toasty, nose:tic coffee. Palate: powerful, flavourful, toasty, round tannins.

CASTILLO CLAVIJO

Ctra. de Clavijo, s/n
26141 Alberite (La Rioja)
☎: +34 941 436 702 - Fax: +34 941 436 430
info@castilloclavijo.com
www.criadoresderioja.com

CASTILLO CLAVIJO 2010 BFB
100% viura.

87 Colour: bright yellow. Nose: scrubland, fresh, neat, powerfull, fresh fruit, smoky. Palate: fresh, fruity, smoky afterpalate:.

CASTILLO CLAVIJO 2008 TC
90% tempranillo, 10% garnacha.

86 Colour: cherry, garnet rim. Nose: toasty, spicy, ripe fruit. Palate: flavourful, easy to drink, ripe fruit.

CASTILLO CLAVIJO 2007 TR
90% tempranillo, 10% mazuelo.

87 Colour: cherry, garnet rim. Nose: ripe fruit, creamy oak, toasty, fine reductive notes. Palate: powerful, flavourful, toasty, round tannins, long.

CASTILLO CLAVIJO 2004 TGR
80% tempranillo, 10% graciano, 10% mazuelo.

88 Colour: pale ruby, brick rim edge. Nose: spicy, fine reductive notes, wet leather, aged wood nuances, fruit liqueur notes. Palate: spicy, fine tannins, elegant, long.

CASTILLO DE CUZCURRITA

San Sebastián, 1
26214 Cuzcurrita del Río Tirón (La Rioja)
☎: +34 941 328 022 - Fax: +34 941 301 620
info@castillodecuzcurrita.com
www.castillodecuzcurrita.com

SEÑORÍO DE CUZCURRITA 2007 T
100% tempranillo.

92 Colour: dark-red cherry. Nose: closed, spicy, aged wood nuances, fruit expression. Palate: creamy, mineral, flavourful, powerful.

COMPAÑÍA DE VINOS TELMO RODRÍGUEZ

El Monte
01308 Lanciego (Álava)
☎: +34 945 628 315 - Fax: +34 945 628 314
contact@telmorodriguez.com
www.telmorodriguez.com

LZ 2011 T
tempranillo, garnacha, graciano.

93 Colour: cherry, garnet rim. Nose: red berry notes, balsamic herbs, scrubland, spicy. Palate: flavourful, good acidity, fine bitter notes, fine tannins.

ALTOS DE LANZAGA 2008 T
tempranillo, garnacha, graciano.

93 Colour: cherry, garnet rim. Nose: toasty, nose:tic coffee, fruit liqueur notes, earthy notes. Palate: flavourful, fine bitter notes, good acidity, round tannins.

LANZAGA 2008 T
tempranillo, graciano, garnacha.

90 Colour: cherry, garnet rim. Nose: spicy, nose:tic coffee, toasty, ripe fruit. Palate: fine bitter notes, good acidity, round.

CREACIONES EXEO

Costanilla del Hospital s/n
01330 Labastida (Álava)
☎: +34 649 940 040
carlos@bodegasexeo.com
www.bodegasexeo.com

CIFRAS 2010 B
100% garnacha blanca.

91 Colour: bright straw, greenish rim. Nose: fresh fruit, citrus fruit, balanced, fine lees, wild herbs. Palate: rich, fruity, spicy, long.

LETRAS MINÚSCULAS 2010 T
70% tempranillo, 30% garnacha.

93 Colour: cherry, garnet rim. Nose: spicy, creamy oak, toasty, fruit expression, red berry notes. Palate: powerful, flavourful, toasty, round tannins.

CIFRAS 2010 T
100% garnacha.

92 Colour: cherry, purple rim. Nose: red berry notes, raspberry, ripe fruit, powerfull, expressive, floral. Palate: powerful, flavourful, fruity, complex, long.

LETRAS 2008 T
100% tempranillo.

94 Colour: cherry, garnet rim. Nose: red berry notes, ripe fruit, spicy, dark chocolate, cocoa bean, toasty, expressive, mineral. Palate: powerful, flavourful, toasty, balanced.

CVNE - COMPAÑÍA VINÍCOLA DEL NORTE DE ESPAÑA

Barrio de la Estación, s/n
26200 Haro (La Rioja)
☎: +34 941 304 800 - Fax: +34 941 304 815
marketing@cvne.com
www.cvne.com

CUNE CVC B
85% viura, 15% garnacha blanca, malvasía.

89 Colour: straw. Nose: fragrant herbs, fresh fruit, varietal. Palate: powerful, flavourful, unctuous, fresh, fruity.

CUNE WHITE 2011 B
100% viura.

90 Colour: bright straw. Nose: fruit expression, fragrant herbs, smoky. Palate: sweetness, fruity, rich, flavourful.

IMPERIAL 2007 TR
85% tempranillo, 10% graciano, 5% mazuelo.

93 Colour: dark-red cherry. Nose: damp earth, complex, expressive, cocoa bean, creamy oak, toasty. Palate: spicy, creamy, roasted-coffee afterpalate:, ripe fruit.

MONOPOLE 2011 B
100% viura.

89 Colour: bright straw. Nose: fresh, white flowers, expressive, citrus fruit, fragrant herbs. Palate: flavourful, fruity, good acidity, balanced.

CORONA SEMIDULCE 2010 B
85% viura, 15% garnacha blanca, malvasía.

92 Colour: pale. Nose: floral, fresh fruit, fragrant herbs. Palate: sweet, good acidity, powerful, flavourful, fruity, fresh.

CUNE 2011 RD
100% tempranillo.

86 Colour: rose, purple rim. Nose: powerfull, ripe fruit, red berry notes, floral, expressive. Palate: fleshy, powerful, fruity, fresh.

CUNE 2008 TR
85% tempranillo, 15% mazuelo, graciano, garnacha.

90 Colour: light cherry, orangey edge. Nose: ripe fruit, spicy, cedar wood, creamy oak. Palate: round, rich, flavourful, powerful.

IMPERIAL 2001 TGR
85% tempranillo, 10% graciano, 5% mazuelo.

93 Colour: dark-red cherry. Nose: dark chocolate, old leather, waxy notes, tobacco. Palate: round, powerful, flavourful, spicy, reductive nuances.

CUNE 2006 TGR
85% tempranillo, 10% graciano, 5% mazuelo.

90 Colour: pale ruby, brick rim edge. Nose: spicy, wet leather, aged wood nuances, elegant. Palate: spicy, fine tannins, elegant, long.

REAL DE ASÚA 2005 T
100% tempranillo.

93 Colour: very deep cherry. Nose: fine reductive notes, damp earth, undergrowth. Palate: round, complex, powerful, full, flavourful, sweet tannins.

DIEZ-CABALLERO

Barrihuelo, 73
01340 Elciego (Álava)
☎: +34 944 807 295 - Fax: +34 944 630 938
diez-caballero@diez-caballero.es
www.diez-caballero.es

DÍEZ-CABALLERO 2011 T
100% tempranillo.

81

DÍEZ-CABALLERO 2009 TC
tempranillo.

88 Colour: cherry, garnet rim. Nose: spicy, creamy oak, toasty, characterful. Palate: powerful, flavourful, toasty, round tannins.

DÍEZ-CABALLERO VENDIMIA SELECCIONADA 2005 TR
100% tempranillo.

90 Colour: cherry, garnet rim. Nose: spicy, creamy oak, toasty, characterful, fruit liqueur notes. Palate: powerful, flavourful, toasty, round tannins.

DÍEZ-CABALLERO 2005 TR
tempranillo.

88 Colour: cherry, garnet rim. Nose: medium intensity, spicy, ripe fruit. Palate: correct, fine bitter notes, fine tannins.

DÍEZ-CABALLERO VICTORIA 2010 T
100% tempranillo.

92 Colour: cherry, garnet rim. Nose: spicy, creamy oak, toasty. Palate: powerful, flavourful, toasty, round tannins.

DIOS ARES

Ctra. de Navaridas s/n
01300 Laguardia (Alava)
☎: +34 945 600 678 - Fax: +34 945 600 619
export@bodegasdiosares.com

ARES 2011 B
viura.

88 Colour: bright straw. Nose: varietal, fruit expression, white flowers. Palate: flavourful, fruity, fresh.

ARES 2009 TC
tempranillo.

92 Colour: bright cherry. Nose: ripe fruit, sweet spices, creamy oak, expressive. Palate: flavourful, fruity, toasty, round tannins.

ARES 2008 TR
tempranillo.

90 Colour: very deep cherry. Nose: sweet spices, dark chocolate, nose:tic coffee. Palate: flavourful, powerful, fine bitter notes.

DOMINIO DE BERZAL

Término Río Salado, s/n
01307 Baños de Ebro (Álava)
☎: +34 945 623 368 - Fax: +34 945 623 368
info@dominioberzal.com
www.dominioberzal.com

DOMINIO DE BERZAL 2011 B
viura, malvasía.

88 Colour: bright straw. Nose: medium intensity, fresh, fragrant herbs, dried flowers. Palate: balanced, fine bitter notes, good acidity.

DOMINIO DE BERZAL 2011 T MACERACIÓN CARBÓNICA
tempranillo, viura.

88 Colour: deep cherry. Nose: ripe fruit, red berry notes, floral. Palate: flavourful, good acidity.

DOMINIO DE BERZAL SELECCIÓN PRIVADA 2009 T
tempranillo.

90 Colour: cherry, garnet rim. Nose: spicy, creamy oak, toasty, ripe fruit. Palate: powerful, flavourful, toasty, round tannins.

DOMINIO DE BERZAL 2009 TC
tempranillo, graciano.

89 Colour: cherry, garnet rim. Nose: ripe fruit, spicy, toasty. Palate: powerful, flavourful, toasty.

DOMINIO DE BERZAL 7 VARIETALES 2009 T MACERACIÓN CARBÓNICA
maturana, garnacha, graciano, cabernet sauvignon, merlot, syrah, prieto picudo.

88 Colour: cherry, garnet rim. Nose: ripe fruit, scrubland, spicy, creamy oak. Palate: powerful, flavourful, long, toasty.

DSG VINEYARDS

Ctra. Assa
01309 Elvillar (Alava)
☎: +34 619 600 425
www.dsgvineyards.es

TERCAS 2009 BFB
viura, garnacha blanca, malvasía.

90 Colour: bright yellow. Nose: powerfull, ripe fruit, sweet spices, creamy oak, fragrant herbs, roasted coffee. Palate: rich, flavourful, fresh, good acidity.

VUELTA DE TERCAS 2009 T
tempranillo, graciano, garnacha.

91 Colour: cherry, garnet rim. Nose: red berry notes, ripe fruit, expressive, mineral, creamy oak, sweet spices, cocoa bean, dark chocolate. Palate: flavourful, fruity, good acidity, balanced, round tannins.

PHINCA ABEJERA 2008 T
tempranillo, graciano, viura.

94 Colour: light cherry, garnet rim. Nose: red berry notes, ripe fruit, balsamic herbs, sweet spices, creamy oak, expressive, mineral. Palate: flavourful, fresh, fruity, spicy, long, balanced.

PHINCAS 2008 T
tempranillo, garnacha, viura, graciano.

90 Colour: cherry, garnet rim. Nose: ripe fruit, spicy, creamy oak, toasty. Palate: powerful, flavourful, toasty, long.

DUNVIRO S.C.

Ctra. Logroño, Km. 362,80
26500 Calahorra (La Rioja)
☎: +34 941 130 626 - Fax: +34 941 130 626
info@bodegasdunviro.com
www.bodegasdunviro.com

DUNVIRO 2011 BFB
viura.

84

DUNVIRO VENDIMIA SELECCIONADA 2011 T
tempranillo.

87 Colour: bright cherry. Nose: ripe fruit, sweet spices, creamy oak, expressive. Palate: flavourful, fruity, toasty, round tannins.

DUNVIRO TEMPRANILLO 2011 T
tempranillo.

84

DUNVIRO 2005 TR
tempranillo, graciano, mazuelo.

86 Colour: bright cherry, orangey edge. Nose: fruit preserve, spicy, old leather. Palate: balanced, fine bitter notes.

DUNVIRO VIÑAS VIEJAS 2009 TC
tempranillo, graciano.

87 Colour: light cherry. Nose: varietal, medium intensity, expressive, fresh fruit. Palate: soft tannins, fruity, powerful, flavourful, spicy.

EL COTO DE RIOJA

Camino Viejo de Logroño, 26
01320 Oyón (Álava)
☎: +34 945 622 216 - Fax: +34 945 622 315
cotorioja@elcoto.com
www.elcoto.com

EL COTO 2011 B
viura.

87 Colour: bright straw. Nose: white flowers, fresh fruit, candied fruit. Palate: flavourful, fruity, ripe fruit.

EL COTO 2011 RD
50% garnacha, 50% tempranillo.

88 Colour: light cherry. Nose: scrubland, ripe fruit. Palate: good acidity, fruity, fresh.

COTO MAYOR 2008 TC
90% tempranillo, 10% graciano.

90 Colour: cherry, garnet rim. Nose: ripe fruit, spicy, balanced. Palate: flavourful, fruity, easy to drink, spicy.

COTO REAL 2005 TR
80% tempranillo, 10% garnacha, 10% graciano.

91 Colour: cherry, garnet rim. Nose: spicy, creamy oak, toasty, complex, fruit liqueur notes, balsamic herbs. Palate: powerful, flavourful, toasty, round tannins.

COTO DE IMAZ 2005 TR
100% tempranillo.

91 Colour: cherry, garnet rim. Nose: ripe fruit, spicy, creamy oak, toasty, wet leather. Palate: powerful, flavourful, toasty, round tannins.

EL COTO 2009 TC
100% tempranillo.

89 Colour: cherry, garnet rim. Nose: nose:tic coffee, expressive, medium intensity, fresh fruit. Palate: fruity, flavourful, creamy, roasted-coffee afterpalate:.

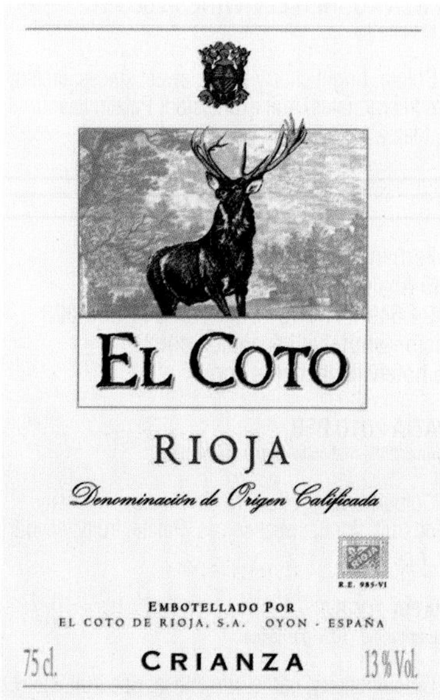

COTO DE IMAZ SELECCIÓN ANIVERSARIO 2005 TR
100% tempranillo.

90 Colour: dark-red cherry, orangey edge. Nose: spicy, creamy oak, toasty, balsamic herbs. Palate: good structure, flavourful, long.

COTO DE IMAZ 2001 TGR
100% tempranillo.

90 Colour: dark-red cherry, brick rim edge. Nose: elegant, complex, fine reductive notes, spicy. Palate: soft tannins, round, full, good structure, flavourful, creamy, toasty.

ELVIWINES

Finca "Clos Mesorah"
Ctra. T-300 Falset Marça, Km. 1
43775 Marça Priorat (Tarragona)
☎: +34 935 343 026 - Fax: +34 936 750 316
moises@elviwines.com
www.elviwines.com

MATI KOSHER ELVIWINES 2010 T
100% tempranillo.

90 Colour: cherry, garnet rim. Nose: floral, scrubland, grassy, lactic notes, complex, elegant, cocoa bean, spicy. Palate: creamy, fruity, full, light-bodied, flavourful, complex.

HERENZA KOSHER ELVIWINES 2009 TC
100% tempranillo.

92 Colour: bright cherry. Nose: sweet spices, creamy oak, red berry notes, fruit expression. Palate: flavourful, fruity, toasty, round tannins.

EMPATÍA

Pza. Fermín Gurbindo, 2
26339 Abalos (La Rioja)
☎: +34 649 841 746 - Fax: +34 941 308 023
direccion@hotelvilladeabalos.com
www.hotelvilladeabalos.com

EMPATÍA 2010 BFB
75% viura, 25% malvasía, garnacha blanca.

87 Colour: bright yellow. Nose: medium intensity, candied fruit, floral, sweet spices. Palate: fruity, flavourful, spicy, ripe fruit.

EMPATÍA 2008 T
90% tempranillo, 10% garnacha.

88 Colour: cherry, garnet rim. Nose: ripe fruit, spicy, creamy oak, toasty. Palate: powerful, flavourful, toasty, round tannins.

EMPATÍA VENDIMIA SELECCIONADA 2007 T
90% tempranillo, 10% garnacha.

86 Colour: deep cherry. Nose: powerfull, ripe fruit, creamy oak. Palate: powerful, flavourful, oaky, spicy.

FINCA ALLENDE

Pza. Ibarra, 1
26330 Briones (La Rioja)
☎: +34 941 322 301 - Fax: +34 941 322 302
info@finca-allende.com
www.finca-allende.com

MÁRTIRES 2011 B
100% viura.

94 Colour: bright yellow. Nose: powerfull, ripe fruit, sweet spices, creamy oak. Palate: rich, smoky afterpalate:, flavourful, fresh, good acidity.

MÁRTIRES 2010 B
100% viura.

97 Colour: bright yellow. Nose: complex, neat, expressive, ripe fruit, citrus fruit, white flowers, sweet spices. Palate: rich, flavourful, good structure, ripe fruit, good acidity.

ALLENDE 2010 B
90% viura, 10% malvasía.

93 Colour: straw. Nose: faded flowers, wild herbs, powerfull, expressive, complex, fresh. Palate: flavourful, powerful, rich, fruity, complex, smoky afterpalate:, sweetness, spirituous.

ALLENDE 2009 B
90% viura, 10% malvasía.

92 Colour: bright yellow. Nose: fresh fruit, fragrant herbs, dry stone, smoky. Palate: good acidity, fresh, fruity, sweetness, smoky afterpalate:.

ALLENDE 2010 T
100% tempranillo.

92 Colour: cherry, garnet rim. Nose: ripe fruit, spicy, creamy oak, toasty, varietal. Palate: powerful, flavourful, toasty, round tannins.

AVRVS 2009 T
85% tempranillo, 15% graciano.

96 Colour: deep cherry. Nose: damp earth, mineral, expressive, complex, closed, creamy oak, toasty. Palate: round, elegant, warm, spirituous, ripe fruit, round tannins.

CALVARIO 2009 T
90% tempranillo, 8% garnacha, 2% graciano.

94 Colour: cherry, garnet rim. Nose: ripe fruit, mineral, spicy, creamy oak, balsamic herbs, expressive. Palate: flavourful, long, round, spicy, balanced.

ALLENDE 2009 T
100% tempranillo.

91 Colour: dark-red cherry. Nose: damp earth, complex, elegant, spicy, cocoa bean. Palate: creamy, powerful, flavourful, fruity, elegant.

ALLENDE 2008 T
100% tempranillo.

92 Colour: dark-red cherry. Nose: cocoa bean, creamy oak, toasty, ripe fruit. Palate: round, elegant, full, flavourful, fine tannins.

CALVARIO 2008 T
90% tempranillo, 8% garnacha, 2% graciano.

92 Colour: cherry, garnet rim. Nose: spicy, creamy oak, toasty, ripe fruit, earthy notes. Palate: powerful, flavourful, toasty, round tannins.

AVRVS 2008
85% tempranillo, 15% graciano.

94 Colour: dark-red cherry. Nose: fruit preserve, fruit liqueur notes, powerfull, complex, spicy, sweet spices, creamy oak. Palate: spirituous, powerful, flavourful, round tannins.

FINCA DE LA RICA

Las Cocinillas, s/n
01330 Labastida (Rioja)
☎: +34 941 509 406
info@fincadelarica.com
www.fincadelarica.com

EL GUÍA DE FINCA DE LA RICA 2011 T
tempranillo, viura.

88 Colour: cherry, purple rim. Nose: powerfull, ripe fruit, sweet spices. Palate: flavourful, fruity, fine bitter notes, good acidity.

EL GUÍA DE FINCA DE LA RICA 2010 T
tempranillo, viura.

89 Colour: bright cherry. Nose: ripe fruit, sweet spices, creamy oak, expressive, undergrowth, truffle notes. Palate: flavourful, fruity, toasty, round tannins, powerful.

EL NÓMADA 2010 T
tempranillo, graciano.

88 Colour: bright cherry. Nose: sweet spices, creamy oak, expressive, fruit preserve. Palate: flavourful, fruity, toasty, round tannins.

EL BUSCADOR DE FINCA DE LA RICA 2010 T ROBLE
tempranillo, garnacha.

87 Colour: bright cherry. Nose: ripe fruit, sweet spices, creamy oak, expressive, nose:tic coffee. Palate: flavourful, fruity, toasty, round tannins, powerful.

EL NÓMADA 2009 T
tempranillo, graciano.

90 Colour: cherry, garnet rim. Nose: ripe fruit, spicy, creamy oak, toasty, characterful, varietal, expressive. Palate: powerful, flavourful, toasty, round tannins.

EL BUSCADOR DE FINCA DE LA RICA 2009 T
tempranillo, garnacha.

89 Colour: cherry, garnet rim. Nose: powerfull, balanced, ripe fruit, sweet spices. Palate: good structure, fruity.

FINCA DE LOS ARANDINOS

Ctra. LP 137, km. 4,6
26375 Entrena (La Rioja)
☎: +34 941 446 065 - Fax: +34 941 446 256
bodega@fincadelosarandinos.com
www.fincadelosarandinos.com

VIERO SOBRE LÍAS 2010 BFB
100% viura.

91 Colour: bright straw. Nose: expressive, complex, fresh fruit, fragrant herbs. Palate: fresh, fruity, light-bodied, powerful, flavourful, spirituous.

FINCA DE LOS ARANDINOS 2009 TC
75% tempranillo, 20% garnacha, 5% mazuelo.

91 Colour: bright cherry. Nose: ripe fruit, sweet spices, creamy oak. Palate: flavourful, fruity, toasty, round tannins.

FINCA EGOMEI

Ctra. Corella, s/n
26240 Alfaro (La Rioja)
☎: +34 948 780 006 - Fax: +34 948 780 515
info@egomei.es
www.bodegasab.com

EGOMEI 2009 T
85% tempranillo, 15% graciano.

89 Colour: deep cherry, garnet rim. Nose: scrubland, ripe fruit, creamy oak, roasted coffee. Palate: ripe fruit, long.

EGOMEI ALMA 2007 T
75% tempranillo, 25% graciano.

93 Colour: very deep cherry, garnet rim. Nose: elegant, wild herbs, ripe fruit, mineral. Palate: flavourful, good structure, round tannins.

FINCA NUEVA

Las Eras, 16
26330 Briones (La Rioja)
☎: +34 941 322 301 - Fax: +34 941 322 302
info@fincanueva.com
www.fincanueva.com

FINCA NUEVA VIURA 2011 B
100% viura.

88 Colour: bright straw. Nose: fresh, fruit expression, fragrant herbs. Palate: good acidity, fruity, fresh, powerful.

FINCA NUEVA 2008 TC
100% tempranillo.

88 Colour: cherry, garnet rim. Nose: candied fruit, cocoa bean, sweet spices. Palate: balanced, fruity, flavourful.

FINCA NUEVA 2010 BFB
100% viura.

91 Colour: bright yellow. Nose: expressive, elegant, fruit expression, fragrant herbs. Palate: creamy, rich, fresh, fruity, powerful, full.

FINCA NUEVA 2011 RD
60% garnacha, 40% tempranillo.

88 Colour: rose, purple rim. Nose: powerfull, ripe fruit, red berry notes, floral. Palate: , fruity, fresh.

FINCA NUEVA TEMPRANILLO 2011 T
100% tempranillo.

90 Colour: dark-red cherry. Nose: sweet spices, creamy oak, ripe fruit. Palate: fruity, powerful, flavourful, fresh.

FINCA NUEVA 2007 TR
100% tempranillo.

90 Colour: cherry, garnet rim. Nose: spicy, ripe fruit, balsamic herbs, old leather. Palate: flavourful, spicy, good acidity.

FINCA NUEVA 2007 TC
100% tempranillo.

90 Colour: cherry, garnet rim. Nose: ripe fruit, spicy, creamy oak, toasty, complex. Palate: powerful, flavourful, toasty, round tannins.

FINCA NUEVA 2005 TR
100% tempranillo.

90 Colour: cherry, garnet rim. Nose: ripe fruit, spicy, toasty, complex. Palate: powerful, flavourful, toasty, round tannins.

FINCA VALPIEDRA

Término El Montecillo, s/n
26360 Fuenmayor (La Rioja)
☎: +34 941 450 876 - Fax: +34 941 450 875
info@bujanda.com
www.familiamartinezbujanda.com

FINCA VALPIEDRA 2007 TR
92% tempranillo, 6% graciano, 2% maturana.

91 Colour: pale ruby, brick rim edge. Nose: ripe fruit, spicy, toasty, complex, wet leather, cigar, dry stone. Palate: powerful, flavourful, toasty, round tannins.

CANTOS DE VALPIEDRA 2009 T
100% tempranillo.

92 Colour: cherry, garnet rim. Nose: mineral, fruit expression, elegant, sweet spices, creamy oak. Palate: balanced, fruity, easy to drink.

GÓMEZ DE SEGURA

Barrio El Campillar
01300 Laguardia (Álava)
☎: +34 615 929 828 - Fax: +34 945 600 227
info@gomezdesegura.com
www.gomezdesegura.com

GÓMEZ DE SEGURA 2011 B
viura.

84

GÓMEZ DE SEGURA 2011 RD
tempranillo.

85 Colour: rose, purple rim. Nose: powerfull, ripe fruit, red berry notes, floral. Palate: , powerful, fruity, fresh.

GÓMEZ DE SEGURA 2011 T MACERACIÓN CARBÓNICA
tempranillo.

78

GÓMEZ DE SEGURA VENDIMIA SELECCIONADA 2010 T
100% tempranillo.

90 Colour: cherry, garnet rim. Nose: red berry notes, ripe fruit, toasty, sweet spices. Palate: flavourful, fruity, good acidity.

GÓMEZ DE SEGURA 2010 TC
tempranillo.

88 Colour: cherry, garnet rim. Nose: ripe fruit, spicy, creamy oak, fine reductive notes, balsamic herbs. Palate: powerful, flavourful, toasty, balanced.

GÓMEZ DE SEGURA 2007 TR
tempranillo.

89 Colour: cherry, garnet rim. Nose: medium intensity, sweet spices, ripe fruit. Palate: flavourful, fruity, good acidity.

GONZÁLEZ TESO

El Olmo, 34-36
01330 Labastida (Álava)
☎: +34 656 745 954 - Fax: +34 945 331 321
j.gontes@hotmail.com
www.bodegasgonzalezteso.com

GONTÉS 2011 T
85% tempranillo, 10% garnacha, 3% graciano, 2% mazuelo.

86 Colour: cherry, purple rim. Nose: red berry notes, ripe fruit, medium intensity, lactic notes. Palate: correct, good finish.

GONTÉS MEDIA CRIANZA 2010 T FERMENTADO EN BARRICA
100% tempranillo.

88 Colour: bright cherry. Nose: ripe fruit, sweet spices, creamy oak, expressive. Palate: fruity, round tannins, good acidity.

OLMO 34 2008 T
50% tempranillo, 30% garnacha, 20% graciano.

88 Colour: cherry, garnet rim. Nose: ripe fruit, spicy, medium intensity. Palate: powerful, flavourful, round tannins.

GONTÉS 2007 TC
85% tempranillo, 15% garnacha.

88 Colour: light cherry. Nose: spicy, sweet spices, creamy oak, fresh fruit. Palate: elegant, round, rich, powerful, flavourful.

GONTÉS EXPRESIÓN 2007 T
100% tempranillo.

87 Colour: dark-red cherry. Nose: fruit preserve, powerfull, spicy, creamy oak. Palate: spirituous, good structure, powerful, flavourful, ripe fruit.

GONTÉS EXPRESIÓN 2005 T
100% tempranillo.

88 Colour: cherry, garnet rim. Nose: ripe fruit, spicy, creamy oak, toasty, wet leather. Palate: powerful, flavourful, toasty, round tannins.

GRANJA NUESTRA SEÑORA DE REMELLURI

Ctra. Rivas de Tereso, s/n
01330 Labastida (Álava)
☎: +34 945 331 801 - Fax: +34 945 331 802
info@remelluri.com
www.remelluri.com

LINDES DE REMELLURI 2009 T
tempranillo, garnacha, graciano.

94 Colour: cherry, garnet rim. Nose: fruit expression, ripe fruit, varietal, expressive, cocoa bean. Palate: powerful, flavourful, complex, balsamic, creamy.

REMELLURI 2007 TR
tempranillo, garnacha, graciano.

93 Colour: cherry, garnet rim. Nose: ripe fruit, spicy, creamy oak, toasty. Palate: powerful, flavourful, toasty, round tannins.

LA GRANJA REMELLURI 2005 TGR
tempranillo, garnacha, graciano.

93 Colour: cherry, garnet rim. Nose: spicy, creamy oak, toasty, overripe fruit, wet leather. Palate: powerful, flavourful, toasty, round tannins.

GRUPO VINÍCOLA MARQUÉS DE VARGAS

Ctra. Zaragoza, Km. 6
26006 Logroño (La Rioja)
☎: +34 941 261 401 - Fax: +34 941 238 696
bodega@marquesdevargas.com
www.marquesdevargas.com

MARQUÉS DE VARGAS 2007 TR
75% tempranillo, 10% mazuelo, 5% garnacha, 10% otras.

91 Colour: deep cherry. Nose: spicy, aged wood nuances, fruit expression, damp earth, undergrowth. Palate: powerful tannins, flavourful, fruity, powerful, complex, toasty.

MARQUÉS DE VARGAS HACIENDA PRADOLAGAR 2005 TR
40% tempranillo, 10% mazuelo, 10% garnacha, 40% otras.

94 Colour: deep cherry. Nose: cocoa bean, spicy, fruit expression, complex, fine reductive notes, damp earth. Palate: flavourful, powerful, round, toasty, roasted-coffee afterpalate:, fine tannins.

MARQUÉS DE VARGAS RESERVA PRIVADA 2005 TR
60% tempranillo, 10% mazuelo, 10% garnacha, 20% otras.

93 Colour: cherry, garnet rim. Nose: spicy, creamy oak, toasty, ripe fruit. Palate: powerful, flavourful, toasty, round tannins.

GRUPO YLLERA

Autovía A-6, Km. 173, 5
47490 Rueda (Valladolid)
☎: +34 983 868 097 - Fax: +34 983 868 177
grupoyllera@grupoyllera.com
www.grupoyllera.com

COELUS JOVEN 2011 T
tempranillo.

87 Colour: cherry, purple rim. Nose: balsamic herbs, red berry notes, fruit liqueur notes, floral. Palate: powerful, flavourful, fresh, fruity.

COELUS 2009 TC
tempranillo.

83

COELUS 2004 TR
tempranillo.

84

HACIENDA GRIMÓN

Gallera, 6
26131 Ventas Blancas (La Rioja)
☎: +34 941 482 184 - Fax: +34 941 482 184
info@haciendagrimon.com
www.haciendagrimon.com

HACIENDA GRIMÓN 2009 TC
85% tempranillo, 10% garnacha, 5% graciano.

89 Colour: cherry, garnet rim. Nose: fresh fruit, balanced, spicy. Palate: correct, good acidity, ripe fruit.

LABARONA 2007 TR
85% tempranillo, 15% graciano.

90 Colour: cherry, garnet rim. Nose: spicy, creamy oak, toasty, dark chocolate. Palate: powerful, flavourful, toasty, round tannins.

FINCA LA ORACIÓN 2010 T
100% tempranillo.

92 Colour: cherry, garnet rim. Nose: ripe fruit, spicy, creamy oak, complex, earthy notes. Palate: powerful, flavourful, toasty, round tannins, long, balanced.

FINCA
LA ORACION
2010

ESTE VINO HA SIDO ELABORADO CON LAS MEJORES UVAS DE LA VARIEDAD TEMPRANILLO: BAYAS PEQUEÑAS Y UVAS SUELTAS.

SU MADURACIÓN EN BODEGA Y SU POSTERIOR AFINAMIENTO EN BOTELLA, CONFIEREN A ESTE VINO UNAS CARACTERÍSTICAS SINGULARES.

ES POSIBLE QUE CON EL PASO DEL TIEMPO PUEDA APARECER ALGÚN EXTRACTO NATURAL (BITALTRATOS), POR LO QUE EN ESTE CASO LE ACONSEJAMOS DECANTAR.

LA PRIMERA COSECHA DE ESTE VINO HA SIDO DE 12.137 BOTELLAS.

LE FELICITAMOS POR SER UNA DE LAS POCAS PERSONAS QUE VA A TENER LA OPORTUNIDAD DE DISFRUTAR DE ESTE VINO ÚNICO.

BOTELLA Nº

VIÑEDOS PROPIOS

RIOJA
DENOMINACION DE ORIGEN CALIFICADA

HACIENDA URBIÓN

Ctra. Nalda
26120 Albelda de Iregua (Rioja)
☎: +34 941 444 223 - Fax: +34 941 444 427
info@vinicolareal.com

PALACIO DE ALCÁNTARA 2011 T
100% tempranillo.

84

URBIÓN CUVEÈ 2010 T
90% tempranillo, 10% garnacha.

86 Colour: bright cherry. Nose: ripe fruit, sweet spices, creamy oak. Palate: flavourful, fruity, toasty, round tannins.

PALACIO DE ALCÁNTARA 2009 T
100% tempranillo.

85 Colour: cherry, garnet rim. Nose: spicy, toasty, fruit preserve. Palate: powerful, flavourful, toasty.

URBIÓN VENDIMIA 2008 TC
90% tempranillo, 10% garnacha.

88 Colour: cherry, garnet rim. Nose: ripe fruit, spicy, toasty, balsamic herbs. Palate: powerful, flavourful, toasty, round tannins.

URBIÓN 2005 TR
100% tempranillo.

88 Colour: cherry, garnet rim. Nose: ripe fruit, spicy, creamy oak, toasty, fine reductive notes. Palate: powerful, flavourful, toasty, long.

HACIENDA Y VIÑEDO MARQUÉS DEL ATRIO

Ctra. de Logroño NA-134, Km. 86,2
31587 Mendavia (Navarra)
☎: +34 941 380 057 - Fax: +34 941 380 156
info@marquesdelatrio.com
www.marquesdelatrio.com

MARQUÉS DEL ATRIO 2009 TC
tempranillo, garnacha.

88 Colour: deep cherry. Nose: toasty, creamy oak, ripe fruit. Palate: spirituous, good structure, powerful, flavourful, spicy, creamy.

MARQUÉS DEL ATRIO SINGLE VINERYARD 2007 T
tempranillo, garnacha.

89 Colour: dark-red cherry, orangey edge. Nose: ripe fruit, fruit expression, mineral, creamy oak, toasty, spicy. Palate: powerful, flavourful, spirituous, good structure, ripe fruit, creamy, spicy.

FAUSTINO RIVERO 2007 TR
tempranillo, garnacha.

88 Colour: cherry, garnet rim. Nose: ripe fruit, spicy, complex. Palate: powerful, flavourful, toasty, round tannins.

FAUSTINO RIVERO 2009 TC
tempranillo, garnacha.

85 Colour: cherry, garnet rim. Nose: ripe fruit, spicy, toasty. Palate: powerful, flavourful, toasty, spicy.

MARQUÉS DEL ATRIO 2007 TR
tempranillo, garnacha.

87 Colour: dark-red cherry, orangey edge. Nose: spicy, fine reductive notes, wet leather, aged wood nuances. Palate: spicy, toasty.

HACIENDAS DE ESPAÑA

Ctra. El Ciego, s/n
26350 Cenicero (La Rioja)
☎: +34 914 365 924
gromero@arcoinvest-group.com
www.haciendas-espana.com

MARQUÉS DE LA CONCORDIA (MARQUÉS DE LA CONCORDIA FAMILY OF WINES) 2007 TR
100% tempranillo.

87 Colour: pale ruby, brick rim edge. Nose: ripe fruit, scrubland, fine reductive notes. Palate: fresh, flavourful.

MARQUÉS DE LA CONCORDIA (MARQUÉS DE LA CONCORDIA FAMILY OF WINES) 2008 TC
100% tempranillo.

87 Colour: cherry, garnet rim. Nose: ripe fruit, spicy, toasty, fine reductive notes. Palate: flavourful, toasty, round tannins.

HACIENDA SUSAR (MARQUÉS DE LA CONCORDIA FAMILY OF WINES) 2007 T
100% tempranillo.

90 Colour: bright cherry. Nose: ripe fruit, sweet spices, creamy oak, expressive. Palate: flavourful, fruity, toasty, powerful.

HEREDAD UGARTE

Ctra. A-124, Km. 61
01309 Laguardia (Álava)
☎: +34 945 282 844 - Fax: +34 945 271 319
info@heredadugarte.com
www.egurenugarte.com

MARTÍN CENDOYA MALVASÍA 2011 B
100% malvasía.

88 Colour: bright straw. Nose: fresh, fresh fruit, white flowers, expressive. Palate: flavourful, fruity, good acidity.

TÉRMINO DE UGARTE 2011 T
90% tempranillo, 10% garnacha.

84

UGARTE 2010 TC
80% tempranillo, 20% garnacha.

87 Colour: cherry, garnet rim. Nose: medium intensity, balanced, ripe fruit. Palate: balanced, good acidity.

HEREDAD UGARTE 2009 TC
92% tempranillo, 8% garnacha.

89 Colour: cherry, garnet rim. Nose: ripe fruit, spicy, creamy oak, complex. Palate: powerful, flavourful, toasty, round tannins.

CINCUENTA UGARTE 2009 T
100% tempranillo.

87 Colour: cherry, garnet rim. Nose: ripe fruit, spicy, creamy oak. Palate: powerful, flavourful, toasty, round tannins.

ANASTASIO 2007 T
100% tempranillo.

91 Colour: bright cherry. Nose: ripe fruit, sweet spices, creamy oak, expressive, cocoa bean, dark chocolate. Palate: flavourful, fruity, toasty, round tannins, round.

CEDULA REAL 2004 TGR
90% tempranillo, 10% mazuelo.

90 Colour: pale ruby, brick rim edge. Nose: spicy, fine reductive notes, wet leather, aged wood nuances, fruit liqueur notes. Palate: spicy, fine tannins, long.

MARTÍN CENDOYA 2008 TR
80% tempranillo, 15% graciano, 5% mazuelo.

90 Colour: deep cherry. Nose: ripe fruit, spicy, nose:tic coffee, toasty. Palate: flavourful, powerful, fine bitter notes.

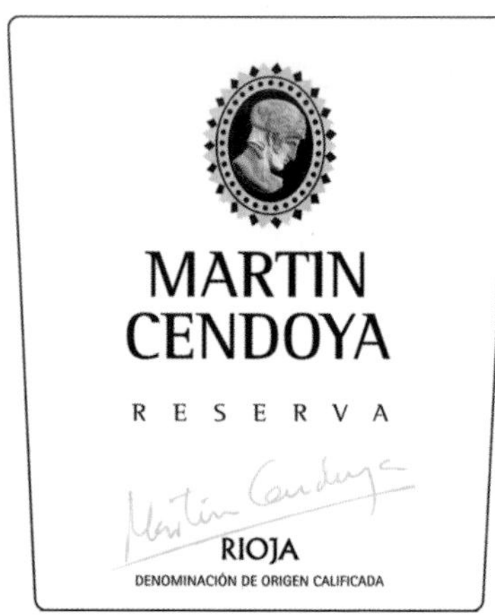

DOMINIO DE UGARTE 2008 TR
92% tempranillo, 8% graciano.

88 Colour: cherry, garnet rim. Nose: ripe fruit, spicy, toasty, fine reductive notes. Palate: powerful, flavourful, long, correct.

HERMANOS CASTILLO PÉREZ

Camino de la Estación, 15
26330 Briones (La Rioja)
☎: +34 667 730 651 - Fax: +34 941 301 006
info@bodegaszurbal.com
www.bodegaszurbal.com

ZURBAL VENDIMIA SELECCIONADA 2010 T
100% tempranillo.

89 Colour: bright cherry. Nose: ripe fruit, creamy oak, expressive, spicy. Palate: flavourful, fruity, toasty, round tannins.

ZURBAL 2009 TC
100% tempranillo.

88 Colour: cherry, garnet rim. Nose: ripe fruit, spicy, creamy oak. Palate: powerful, flavourful, toasty.

HERMANOS FRÍAS DEL VAL

Herrerías, 13
01307 Villabuena (Álava)
☎: +34 945 609 172 - Fax: +34 945 609 172
info@friasdelval.com
www.friasdelval.com

HERMANOS FRÍAS DEL VAL 2011 BFB

84

HERMANOS FRÍAS DEL VAL 2010 B

87 Colour: bright straw. Nose: candied fruit, citrus fruit. Palate: flavourful, fruity, fresh.

HERMANOS FRÍAS DEL VAL 2011 T MACERACIÓN CARBÓNICA

90 Colour: cherry, purple rim. Nose: balanced, fruit expression, violets, expressive. Palate: fruity, flavourful, good acidity.

DON PEDUZ 2011 T

90 Colour: cherry, purple rim. Nose: fresh fruit, red berry notes, floral. Palate: flavourful, fruity, good acidity, round tannins.

HERMANOS FRÍAS DEL VAL 2009 TC
tempranillo.

88 Colour: cherry, garnet rim. Nose: powerfull, ripe fruit, sweet spices. Palate: flavourful, concentrated.

HIJOS DE CRUZ VALLE SC

Santa Engracia, 52
01300 Laguardia (Álava)
☎: +34 945 600 129
bodega@cruzvalle.com
www.cruzvalle.com

CRUZ VALLE 2011 B
viura.

80

CRUZ VALLE 2011 T MACERACIÓN CARBÓNICA
tempranillo.

87 Colour: cherry, purple rim. Nose: fruit expression, balanced, violets. Palate: fruity, good finish.

CRUZ VALLE 2009 TC
tempranillo.

86 Colour: cherry, garnet rim. Nose: creamy oak, toasty, red berry notes, ripe fruit. Palate: powerful, flavourful, toasty.

JOSÉ BASOCO BASOCO

Ctra. de Samaniego, s/n

01307 Villabuena (Álava)
☎: +34 945 331 619 - Fax: +34 945 331 619
info@fincabarronte.com

FINCA BARRONTE VENDIMIA SELECCIONADA 2011 T
100% tempranillo.

89 Colour: cherry, purple rim. Nose: balanced, powerfull, red berry notes, lactic notes, fragrant herbs. Palate: fruity, easy to drink.

FINCA BARRONTE 2009 TC
85% tempranillo, 15% graciano.

90 Colour: cherry, garnet rim. Nose: medium intensity, ripe fruit, powerfull, dark chocolate. Palate: flavourful, good structure, round tannins.

FINCA BARRONTE GRACIANO 2009 T
graciano.

89 Colour: bright cherry. Nose: toasty, sweet spices, ripe fruit, balsamic herbs. Palate: flavourful, fruity, round tannins.

FINCA BARRONTE TEMPRANILLO 2009 T
100% tempranillo.

89 Colour: cherry, garnet rim. Nose: red berry notes, ripe fruit, balsamic herbs, spicy, toasty. Palate: correct, powerful, flavourful, toasty.

JUAN CARLOS SANCHA

C° de Las Barreras, s/n
Finca Fuentelacazuela
26320 Baños de Río Tobía (La Rioja)
☎: +34 941 232 160 - Fax: +34 941 232 160
juancarlossancha@yahoo.es
www.juancarlossancha.com

AD LIBITUM TEMPRANILLO BLANCO 2010 B
100% tempranillo blanco.

88 Colour: bright straw. Nose: fragrant herbs, citrus fruit, white flowers. Palate: flavourful, fruity, good acidity.

AD LIBITUM MATURANA TINTA 2010 T
100% maturana.

92 Colour: deep cherry. Nose: dark chocolate, spicy, toasty, macerated fruit, fruit expression. Palate: powerful, flavourful, varietal, good structure, powerful tannins.

PEÑA EL GATO GARNACHA 2010 T
100% garnacha.

91 Colour: bright cherry. Nose: ripe fruit, sweet spices, creamy oak. Palate: flavourful, fruity, toasty, round tannins.

LA RIOJA ALTA

Avda. de Vizcaya, 8
26200 Haro (La Rioja)
☎: +34 941 310 346 - Fax: +34 941 312 854
riojalta@riojalta.com
www.riojalta.com

VIÑA ALBERDI 2007 TC
100% tempranillo.

89 Colour: bright cherry, brick rim edge. Nose: elegant, fine reductive notes, spicy. Palate: fruity, balanced, fine bitter notes, round tannins.

VIÑA ARANA 2005 TR
95% tempranillo, 5% mazuelo.

92 Colour: bright cherry, orangey edge. Nose: elegant, ripe fruit, sweet spices, waxy notes. Palate: balanced, fine bitter notes, fine tannins.

VIÑA ARDANZA 2004 TR
80% tempranillo, 20% garnacha.

93 Colour: deep cherry, orangey edge. Nose: fruit liqueur notes, spicy, cigar, old leather, balsamic herbs. Palate: balanced, fine tannins, long, spicy.

GRAN RESERVA 904 RIOJA ALTA 2000 TGR
90% tempranillo, 10% graciano.

93 Colour: pale ruby, brick rim edge. Nose: elegant, spicy, wet leather, aged wood nuances, fruit liqueur notes, cigar. Palate: spicy, fine tannins, elegant, long.

LA RIOJA ALTA GRAN RESERVA 890 1998 TGR
95% tempranillo, 3% graciano, 2% mazuelo.

90 Colour: dark-red cherry, orangey edge. Nose: old leather, fruit preserve, spicy, reduction notes. Palate: spicy, good structure, classic aged character.

LAN

Paraje del Buicio, s/n
26360 Fuenmayor (La Rioja)
☎: +34 941 450 950 - Fax: +34 941 450 567
info@bodegaslan.com
www.bodegaslan.com

LAN 2008 TC
tempranillo.

87 Colour: cherry, garnet rim. Nose: ripe fruit, spicy, creamy oak. Palate: powerful, flavourful, toasty, correct.

CULMEN 2007 TR
tempranillo, graciano.

93 Colour: deep cherry, garnet rim. Nose: balanced, spicy, fine reductive notes. Palate: flavourful, fruity, round tannins, balanced, good acidity.

LAN D-12 2009 T
tempranillo.

91 Colour: cherry, garnet rim. Nose: ripe fruit, spicy, creamy oak, toasty, complex. Palate: powerful, flavourful, toasty, round tannins, balanced.

LAN 2009 TC
100% tempranillo.

88 Colour: cherry, garnet rim. Nose: medium intensity, ripe fruit, spicy. Palate: fruity, good structure, round tannins.

LAN A MANO 2008 T
tempranillo, graciano, mazuelo.

93 Colour: deep cherry, garnet rim. Nose: complex, ripe fruit, spicy. Palate: good structure, flavourful, balanced, spicy, ripe fruit, round tannins, good acidity.

LAN 2007 TR
90% tempranillo, 5% mazuelo, 5% graciano.

90 Colour: cherry, garnet rim. Nose: spicy, creamy oak, toasty, candied fruit. Palate: powerful, flavourful, toasty, round tannins.

VIÑA LANCIANO 2007 TR
tempranillo, mazuelo.

88 Colour: cherry, garnet rim. Nose: powerfull, ripe fruit, spicy, complex, neat. Palate: balanced, round, spicy.

LAUNA

Ctra. Vitoria-Logroño, Km. 57
01300 Laguardia (Alava)
☎: +34 946 824 108 - Fax: +34 956 824 108
info@bodegaslauna.com
www.bodegaslauna.com

OIZ 2011 B
80% viura, 20% malvasía.

85 Colour: bright straw. Nose: fresh, medium intensity, citrus fruit. Palate: fresh, light-bodied, easy to drink.

TEO'S 2009 T
100% tempranillo.

91 Colour: bright cherry. Nose: ripe fruit, sweet spices, creamy oak, dark chocolate, expressive, balanced. Palate: flavourful, fruity, toasty, round tannins, balanced.

LAUNA PLUS 2009 TC
100% tempranillo.

88 Colour: bright cherry, garnet rim. Nose: toasty, ripe fruit, medium intensity. Palate: flavourful, fruity, easy to drink.

LAUNA PLUS 2007 TR
90% tempranillo, 10% mazuelo, graciano.

88 Colour: cherry, garnet rim. Nose: spicy, creamy oak, complex, fine reductive notes. Palate: powerful, flavourful, toasty, fine tannins.

LAUNA EDICIÓN LIMITADA 2005 TR
100% tempranillo.

89 Colour: deep cherry, garnet rim. Nose: earthy notes, scrubland, spicy, fine reductive notes. Palate: correct, balanced, long, flavourful.

TEO'S 2008 T
100% tempranillo.

90 Colour: cherry, garnet rim. Nose: medium intensity, ripe fruit, warm, balanced, sweet spices. Palate: good structure, flavourful, long.

LONG WINES

Avda. del Monte, 46
28120 Algete (Madrid)
☎: +34 916 221 305 - Fax: +34 916 220 029
www.longwines.com

FINCA MÓNICA TEMPRANILLO 2009 T
100% tempranillo.

89 Colour: cherry, garnet rim. Nose: ripe fruit, spicy, creamy oak, complex, balsamic herbs. Palate: powerful, flavourful, toasty.

FINCA MÓNICA 2009 TC
100% tempranillo.

87 Colour: cherry, garnet rim. Nose: ripe fruit, spicy, creamy oak. Palate: powerful, toasty, long, correct.

LUBERRI MONJE AMESTOY

Camino de Rehoyos, s/n
01340 Elciego (Álava)
☎: +34 945 606 010 - Fax: +34 945 606 482
luberri@luberri.com
www.luberri.com

LUBERRI ZURI 2011 B
80% viura, 20% malvasía.

88 Colour: pale. Nose: faded flowers, fruit expression, fragrant herbs. Palate: fruity, fresh, full, flavourful.

LUBERRI 2011 T MACERACIÓN CARBÓNICA
95% tempranillo, 5% viura.

90 Colour: cherry, purple rim. Nose: neat, fruit expression, violets, expressive. Palate: fruity, easy to drink, balanced.

SEIS DE LUBERRI 2009 T
100% tempranillo.

92 Colour: cherry, garnet rim. Nose: spicy, creamy oak, toasty, complex, citrus fruit, red berry notes. Palate: powerful, flavourful, toasty, round tannins.

LUBERRI CEPAS VIEJAS 2006 TC
100% tempranillo.

91 Colour: cherry, garnet rim. Nose: cigar, fruit liqueur notes, spicy, toasty, expressive. Palate: balanced, flavourful, spicy, long, elegant.

MONJE AMESTOY 2006 TR
95% tempranillo, 5% cabernet sauvignon.

87 Colour: cherry, garnet rim. Nose: medium intensity, tobacco, spicy. Palate: correct, good acidity, fine bitter notes.

BIGA DE LUBERRI 2005 TC
100% tempranillo.

90 Colour: cherry, garnet rim. Nose: ripe fruit, spicy, creamy oak, toasty, complex. Palate: powerful, flavourful, toasty, round tannins.

LUIS GURPEGUI MUGA

Avda. Celso Muerza, 8
31570 San Adrián (Navarra)
☎: +34 948 670 050 - Fax: +34 948 670 259
bodegas@gurpegui.es
www.gurpegui.es

PRIMI 2011 T
tempranillo, graciano, garnacha.

85 Colour: cherry, purple rim. Nose: red berry notes, ripe fruit, scrubland. Palate: powerful, flavourful, ripe fruit.

MARQUÉS DE CÁCERES

Ctra. Logroño, s/n
26350 Cenicero (La Rioja)
☎: +34 941 454 026 - Fax: +34 941 454 400
export@marquesdecaceres.com
www.marquesdecaceres.com

MARQUÉS DE CÁCERES 2011 B
100% viura.

88 Colour: straw. Nose: expressive, fruit expression, powerfull, varietal. Palate: easy to drink, powerful.

MARQUÉS DE CÁCERES ANTEA 2011 BFB
viura, malvasía.

87 Colour: bright yellow. Nose: ripe fruit, creamy oak, citrus fruit, dried herbs. Palate: rich, flavourful, fresh, good acidity, toasty.

MC MARQUÉS DE CÁCERES 2010 T
100% tempranillo.

93 Colour: cherry, garnet rim. Nose: ripe fruit, mineral, creamy oak, nose:tic coffee, roasted coffee. Palate: elegant, powerful, flavourful, toasty.

SATINELA SEMI-DULCE 2011 B
viura, malvasía.

86 Colour: bright straw. Nose: candied fruit, citrus fruit. Palate: flavourful, fruity, fresh.

MARQUÉS DE CÁCERES RESERVA ESPECIAL 2006 TR
85% tempranillo, 15% garnacha, graciano.

91 Colour: cherry, garnet rim. Nose: ripe fruit, spicy, creamy oak, toasty, complex. Palate: powerful, flavourful, round tannins.

MARQUÉS DE CÁCERES 2011 RD
85% tempranillo, 15% garnacha, graciano.

88 Colour: rose, purple rim. Nose: fruit expression, red berry notes, fresh fruit. Palate: fruity, flavourful, fresh.

MARQUÉS DE CÁCERES 2009 TC
85% tempranillo, 15% garnacha, graciano.

90 Colour: cherry, garnet rim. Nose: red berry notes, ripe fruit, balsamic herbs, spicy, toasty. Palate: powerful, flavourful, long, toasty.

MARQUÉS DE CÁCERES 2008 TR
85% tempranillo, 15% garnacha, graciano.

92 Colour: cherry, garnet rim. Nose: medium intensity, balanced, neat, sweet spices, mineral. Palate: correct, elegant, balanced.

GAUDIUM GRAN VINO 2005 TR
95% tempranillo, 5% graciano.

93 Colour: cherry, garnet rim. Nose: spicy, creamy oak, toasty, complex, earthy notes, ripe fruit. Palate: powerful, flavourful, toasty, round tannins.

MARQUÉS DE CÁCERES 2005 TGR
85% tempranillo, 15% garnacha, graciano.

92 Colour: deep cherry. Nose: macerated fruit, fruit expression, powerfull, elegant, cocoa bean, spicy, toasty. Palate: round, full, flavourful, powerful, good structure, spicy, toasty.

MARQUÉS DE MURRIETA

Finca Ygay- Ctra. N-232 Logroño-Zaragoza, PK 403
26006 Logroño (La Rioja)
☎: +34 941 271 374 - Fax: +34 941 251 606
rrpp@marquesdemurrieta.com
www.marquesdemurrieta.com

CASTILLO YGAY 2004 TGR
93% tempranillo, 7% mazuelo.

95 Colour: cherry, garnet rim. Nose: toasty, spicy, candied fruit, wet leather. Palate: flavourful, spicy, ripe fruit, good acidity, fine tannins.

DALMAU 2007 TR
85% tempranillo, 8% cabernet sauvignon, 7% graciano.

97 Colour: cherry, garnet rim. Nose: ripe fruit, spicy, creamy oak, toasty, characterful, earthy notes. Palate: powerful, flavourful, toasty, round tannins.

MARQUÉS DE MURRIETA 2007 TR
85% tempranillo, 8% garnacha, 6% mazuelo, 1% graciano.

92 Colour: cherry, garnet rim. Nose: complex, powerfull, ripe fruit, creamy oak, sweet spices. Palate: flavourful, fine bitter notes, round, spicy, ripe fruit.

CAPELLANIA 2007 B
100% viura.

91 Colour: bright yellow. Nose: sweet spices, cocoa bean, candied fruit, citrus fruit, fruit liqueur notes. Palate: sweetness, toasty, fine bitter notes, round.

DALMAU 2009 TR
73% tempranillo, 13% cabernet sauvignon, 11% graciano.

96 Colour: cherry, garnet rim. Nose: spicy, complex, toasty, ripe fruit, fruit expression. Palate: powerful, flavourful, toasty, round tannins.

MARQUÉS DE MURRIETA 2006 TR
88% tempranillo, 7% mazuelo, 3% garnacha, 2% graciano.

91 Colour: cherry, garnet rim. Nose: candied fruit, medium intensity, nose:tic coffee. Palate: flavourful, powerful, good acidity, fine bitter notes.

CASTILLO YGAY 2001 TGR
93% tempranillo, 7% mazuelo.

97 Colour: pale ruby, brick rim edge. Nose: elegant, spicy, fine reductive notes, wet leather, aged wood nuances, fruit liqueur notes. Palate: spicy, fine tannins, elegant, long.

MARQUÉS DE REINOSA

Ctra. Rincón de Soto, s/n
26560 Autol (La Rioja)
☎: +34 941 401 327 - Fax: +34 941 390 065
bodegas@marquesdereinosa.com
www.marquesdereinosa.com

MARQUÉS DE REINOSA 2009 TC
100% tempranillo.

88 Colour: cherry, garnet rim. Nose: balanced, ripe fruit, dried herbs, toasty, spicy. Palate: fruity, round tannins.

MARQUÉS DE REINOSA 2011 B
95% viura, 5% verdejo.

88 Colour: bright straw. Nose: white flowers, fresh fruit, citrus fruit. Palate: good acidity, flavourful, fruity, fresh.

MARQUÉS DE REINOSA 2011 RD
50% garnacha, 50% tempranillo.

82

MARQUÉS DE REINOSA TEMPRANILLO 2011 T
100% tempranillo.

86 Colour: cherry, purple rim. Nose: scrubland, ripe fruit, medium intensity. Palate: correct, ripe fruit, flavourful.

MARQUÉS DE ULÍA

Paraje del Buicio, s/n
26360 Fuenmayor (La Rioja)
☎: +34 941 450 950 - Fax: +34 941 450 567
info@marquesdeulia.com
www.marquesdeulia.com

MARQUÉS DE ULÍA 2005 TR

91 Colour: cherry, garnet rim. Nose: ripe fruit, spicy, creamy oak, toasty, complex. Palate: powerful, flavourful, toasty, round tannins.

MARQUÉS DE ULÍA 2008 TC
tempranillo.

90 Colour: cherry, garnet rim. Nose: ripe fruit, spicy, tobacco. Palate: powerful, flavourful, toasty, round tannins, good acidity.

LA VENDIMIA MARQUÉS DE ULÍA 2007 T
tempranillo, graciano.

88 Colour: pale ruby, brick rim edge. Nose: spicy, fine reductive notes, wet leather, aged wood nuances, fruit liqueur notes. Palate: spicy, fine tannins, long.

MARQUÉS DEL PUERTO

Ctra. de Logroño, s/n
26360 Fuenmayor (La Rioja)
☎: +34 941 450 001 - Fax: +34 941 450 051
bmp@mbrizard.com
www.bodegamarquesdelpuerto.com

MARQUÉS DEL PUERTO 2011 B
100% viura.

88 Colour: bright straw. Nose: fragrant herbs, floral, citrus fruit, fresh fruit. Palate: fresh, fruity, flavourful.

MARQUÉS DEL PUERTO 2011 RD
50% tempranillo, 50% garnacha.

87 Colour: rose, purple rim. Nose: powerfull, ripe fruit, red berry notes, floral. Palate: , powerful, fruity, fresh.

MARQUÉS DEL PUERTO 2009 TC
90% tempranillo, 10% mazuelo.

87 Colour: bright cherry. Nose: ripe fruit, sweet spices, creamy oak. Palate: flavourful, fruity, toasty, round tannins.

BENTUS 2005 TR
80% mazuelo, 20% graciano, garnacha.

86 Colour: cherry, garnet rim. Nose: spicy, creamy oak, toasty, characterful. Palate: powerful, flavourful, toasty, round tannins.

MARQUÉS DEL PUERTO 2005 TR
90% tempranillo, 10% mazuelo.

87 Colour: cherry, garnet rim. Nose: ripe fruit, spicy, creamy oak, toasty, fine reductive notes. Palate: powerful, flavourful, toasty, round tannins.

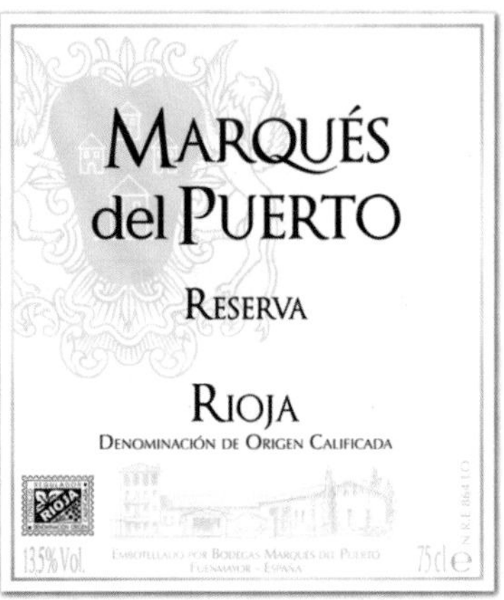

MARQUÉS DEL PUERTO 2001 TGR
92% tempranillo, 6% mazuelo, 2% graciano.

87 Colour: cherry, garnet rim. Nose: spicy, creamy oak, toasty, fruit liqueur notes. Palate: powerful, flavourful, toasty, round tannins.

ROMÁN PALADINO 1995 TGR
88% tempranillo, 7% mazuelo, 5% graciano.

90 Colour: pale ruby, brick rim edge. Nose: elegant, spicy, fine reductive notes, wet leather, aged wood nuances, fruit liqueur notes. Palate: spicy, fine tannins, elegant, long.

MARTÍNEZ LACUESTA

Paraje de Ubieta, s/n
26200 Haro (La Rioja)
☎: +34 941 310 050 - Fax: +34 941 303 748
bodega@martinezlacuesta.com
www.martinezlacuesta.com

MARTÍNEZ LACUESTA 2009 TC
85% tempranillo, 10% graciano, 5% mazuelo.

88 Colour: cherry, garnet rim. Nose: ripe fruit, spicy, toasty, medium intensity. Palate: powerful, flavourful, toasty.

MARTÍNEZ LACUESTA 2006 TR
85% tempranillo, 10% graciano, 5% mazuelo.

90 Colour: deep cherry, orangey edge. Nose: ripe fruit, sweet spices, creamy oak, fine reductive notes. Palate: flavourful, balanced, long.

MARTÍNEZ LACUESTA 2005 TGR
85% tempranillo, 10% graciano, 5% mazuelo.

87 Colour: dark-red cherry, bright ochre rim. Nose: sweet spices, toasty, waxy notes, animal reductive notes. Palate: classic aged character, spicy, smoky afterpalate:, reductive nuances.

MIGUEL ÁNGEL MURO

Avda. Gasteiz, 29
01306 Lapuebla de Labarca (Álava)
☎: +34 945 607 081 - Fax: +34 945 607 081
info@bodegasmiguelangelmuro.com
www.bodegasmuro.com

MIGUEL ÁNGEL MURO 2011 T

85 Colour: cherry, purple rim. Nose: powerfull, red berry notes, balanced. Palate: flavourful, fruity, good acidity.

AMENITAL 2009 TC

91 Colour: cherry, garnet rim. Nose: ripe fruit, creamy oak, toasty, mineral, sweet spices. Palate: powerful, flavourful, toasty, balanced.

MURO BUJANDA 2008 TC
100% tempranillo.

90 Colour: cherry, garnet rim. Nose: ripe fruit, spicy, creamy oak, complex. Palate: powerful, flavourful, round tannins.

AMENITAL 2007 TC

87 Colour: cherry, garnet rim. Nose: ripe fruit, spicy, creamy oak, toasty. Palate: powerful, flavourful, toasty, round tannins.

MURO 2006 TR

89 Colour: pale ruby, brick rim edge. Nose: ripe fruit, fine reductive notes, spicy, wild herbs. Palate: correct, powerful, flavourful, long.

AMENITAL 2005 T
80% tempranillo, 20% graciano.

90 Colour: cherry, garnet rim. Nose: ripe fruit, spicy, toasty. Palate: flavourful, toasty, spicy, good acidity.

MURO 2004 TR

89 Colour: deep cherry, garnet rim. Nose: dark chocolate, powerfull, ripe fruit. Palate: good structure, flavourful.

MIRAVINOS

Plaza de Matute 12, - 3º
28012 (Madrid)
☎: +34 609 119 248
info@miravinos.es
www.miravinos.es

CATAURO 2009 T
tempranillo.

90 Colour: very deep cherry. Nose: powerfull, ripe fruit, toasty, dark chocolate, earthy notes. Palate: flavourful, powerful, fine bitter notes, round tannins.

SONANTE 2009 T
100% tempranillo.

88 Colour: bright cherry. Nose: ripe fruit, toasty, sweet spices, wet leather. Palate: good acidity, spicy, ripe fruit, easy to drink.

MONTECILLO

Ctra. Navarrete-Fuenmayor, Km. 2
26360 Fuenmayor (La Rioja)
☎: +34 925 860 990 - Fax: +34 925 860 905
carolina.cerrato@osborne.es
www.osborne.es

VIÑA MONTY 2009 TC
100% tempranillo.

90 Colour: dark-red cherry, orangey edge. Nose: spicy, cedar wood, fruit expression. Palate: balsamic, ripe fruit, flavourful, powerful.

MONTECILLO 2008 TC
100% tempranillo.

88 Colour: cherry, garnet rim. Nose: medium intensity, ripe fruit, spicy. Palate: correct, good acidity.

VIÑA CUMBRERO 2008 TC
100% tempranillo.

87 Colour: cherry, garnet rim. Nose: medium intensity, old leather, ripe fruit. Palate: fruity, good finish.

VIÑA MONTY 2006 TR
100% tempranillo.

91 Colour: dark-red cherry, orangey edge. Nose: fine reductive notes, ripe fruit, undergrowth, sweet spices. Palate: round, flavourful, powerful, spicy, toasty, ripe fruit.

CUMBRE MONTECILLO 2006 TR
85% tempranillo, 15% graciano.

91 Colour: cherry, garnet rim. Nose: ripe fruit, spicy, creamy oak, toasty. Palate: powerful, flavourful, toasty, round tannins.

MONTECILLO 2006 TR
100% tempranillo.

88 Colour: light cherry, orangey edge. Nose: wet leather, tobacco, spicy, balsamic herbs. Palate: flavourful, long, correct.

MONTECILLO 2005 TGR
100% tempranillo.

90 Colour: dark-red cherry, brick rim edge. Nose: sweet spices, toasty, ripe fruit, old leather, fine reductive notes. Palate: powerful, flavourful, spicy, classic aged character.

NAVARRSOTILLO RIOJA ORGANIC WINES

Valle Ulzama, 2
31261 Andosilla (Navarra)
☎: +34 948 690 523 - Fax: +34 948 690 523
info@navarrsotillo.com
www.navarrsotillo.com

NOEMUS 2011 B
viura.

85 Colour: bright yellow. Nose: wild herbs, macerated fruit, slightly evolved. Palate: good acidity, fine bitter notes, fruity, spirituous.

NOEMUS 2011 RD
garnacha.

84

SEÑORÍO DE ARRIEZU 2011 T
tempranillo, garnacha.

85 Colour: cherry, purple rim. Nose: medium intensity, red berry notes. Palate: correct, easy to drink.

COMISATIO 2011 T
tempranillo.

84

NOEMUS 2011 T
tempranillo, mazuelo, garnacha.

82

SEÑORÍO DE ARRIEZU 2009 TC
tempranillo, garnacha.

86 Colour: cherry, garnet rim. Nose: ripe fruit, spicy, fine reductive notes. Palate: flavourful, long, toasty.

MAGISTER BIBENDI MAZUELO 2008 T
mazuelo.

88 Colour: deep cherry. Nose: candied fruit, scrubland. Palate: flavourful, fine bitter notes, good acidity.

SEÑORÍO DE ARRIEZU 2008 TC
tempranillo, garnacha.

88 Colour: cherry, garnet rim. Nose: spicy, creamy oak, toasty, fruit preserve. Palate: powerful, flavourful, toasty, round tannins.

MAGISTER BIBENDI 2008 TC
tempranillo, garnacha.

87 Colour: deep cherry. Nose: mineral, scrubland, spicy. Palate: spicy, ripe fruit.

MAGISTER BIBENDI GRACIANO 2008 T
graciano.

87 Colour: deep cherry, garnet rim. Nose: balanced, old leather, spicy, ripe fruit. Palate: flavourful, toasty.

MAGISTER BIBENDI GARNACHA 2008 T
garnacha.

84

MAGISTER BIBENDI 2006 TR
tempranillo, garnacha.

84

SEÑORÍO DE ARRIEZU 2005 TR
tempranillo, garnacha.

88 Colour: cherry, garnet rim. Nose: ripe fruit, spicy, toasty, tobacco. Palate: flavourful, toasty, fine tannins.

OLIVIER RIVIÈRE VINOS

Pepe Blanco, 6 1C
26140 Lardero (La Rioja)
☎: +34 690 733 541 - Fax: +34 941 452 476
olive_riviere@yahoo.fr

BASQUEVANAS 2010 B BARRICA
100% albillo.

92 Colour: bright golden. Nose: spicy, candied fruit, citrus fruit. Palate: flavourful, fine bitter notes, good acidity, round.

JEQUITIBÁ 2010 B
viura, malvasía, garnacha blanca.

91 Colour: bright straw. Nose: fresh, fresh fruit, white flowers. Palate: flavourful, fruity, good acidity, balanced.

RAYOS UVA 2011 T
50% tempranillo, 50% graciano.

90 Colour: cherry, purple rim. Nose: fresh fruit, red berry notes, floral, earthy notes, scrubland. Palate: flavourful, fruity, good acidity, round tannins.

ALTO REDONDO 2010 T
garnacha.

95 Colour: cherry, garnet rim. Nose: ripe fruit, fruit expression, grassy, sweet spices, balsamic herbs. Palate: flavourful, fruity, fresh, fine tannins, long.

GANKO 2010 T
100% garnacha.

94 Colour: deep cherry. Nose: red berry notes, fruit expression, grassy. Palate: flavourful, good acidity, fine bitter notes, fine tannins.

GABACHO 2010 T
graciano.

90 Colour: very deep cherry. Nose: creamy oak, overripe fruit, balsamic herbs. Palate: flavourful, fruity, good acidity.

GANKO 2009 T
tempranillo, garnacha, mazuelo, graciano.

94 Colour: cherry, garnet rim. Nose: characterful, elegant, red berry notes, balsamic herbs, grassy, sweet spices, mineral. Palate: flavourful, fruity, fresh, spicy, fine bitter notes.

EL QUEMADO 2009 T

92 Colour: cherry, garnet rim. Nose: ripe fruit, spicy, creamy oak, toasty, complex. Palate: powerful, flavourful, toasty, grainy tannins.

VIÑAS DEL CADASTRO 2009 T

90 Colour: bright cherry. Nose: sweet spices, creamy oak, fruit expression. Palate: flavourful, fruity, toasty, round tannins.

PAGO DE LARREA

Ctra. Elciego-Cenicero, Km. 1,2
01340 Elciego (Álava)
☎: +34 945 606 063 - Fax: +34 945 606 697
bodega@pagodelarrea.com
www.pagodelarrea.com

CAECUS VERDERÓN 2011 BFB
95% viura, 5% malvasía.

88 Colour: bright yellow. Nose: sweet spices, medium intensity, fresh fruit. Palate: good acidity, fruity, good finish.

CAECUS 2011 T
90% tempranillo, 10% garnacha.

86 Colour: cherry, garnet rim. Nose: fruit expression, varietal, violet drops. Palate: sweetness, spirituous, powerful, flavourful.

CAECUS 2009 TC
100% tempranillo.

87 Colour: cherry, garnet rim. Nose: ripe fruit, spicy, creamy oak, toasty. Palate: powerful, flavourful, toasty, spicy.

8 DE CAECUS 2008 T
100% tempranillo.

90 Colour: cherry, garnet rim. Nose: spicy, creamy oak, toasty, fruit expression. Palate: powerful, flavourful, toasty, round tannins.

CAECUS 2007 TR
100% tempranillo.

87 Colour: cherry, garnet rim. Nose: spicy, creamy oak, toasty, candied fruit. Palate: powerful, flavourful, toasty, round tannins.

PAGOS DE LEZA

Ctra. A-124 Logroño Vitoria
01309 Leza (Álava)
☎: +34 945 621 212 - Fax: +34 945 621 222
pagosdeleza@pagosdeleza.com
www.pagosdeleza.com

ANGEL SANTAMARÍA VENDIMIA SELECCIONADA 2011 BFB

88 Colour: bright yellow. Nose: powerfull, ripe fruit, sweet spices, creamy oak, fragrant herbs. Palate: rich, flavourful, fresh, good acidity.

ANGEL SANTAMARÍA VENDIMIA SELECCIONADA 2011 B JOVEN
viura, malvasía.

87 Colour: bright straw. Nose: floral, dried herbs, fresh fruit. Palate: fresh, fruity, long, good acidity.

ANGEL SANTAMARÍA VENDIMIA SELECCIONADA 2009 TC

89 Colour: cherry, garnet rim. Nose: ripe fruit, spicy, creamy oak, toasty. Palate: powerful, flavourful, toasty, roasted-coffee afterpalate:.

EDITOR 2009 TC
tempranillo.

87 Colour: cherry, garnet rim. Nose: ripe fruit, creamy oak, toasty, sweet spices. Palate: powerful, flavourful, spicy.

ANGEL SANTAMARÍA VENDIMIA SELECCIONADA 2005 TR

90 Colour: pale ruby, brick rim edge. Nose: elegant, spicy, fine reductive notes, aged wood nuances, toasty. Palate: spicy, elegant, long, flavourful, good structure.

PAGOS DEL REY

Ctra. N-232, PK 422,7
26360 Fuenmayor (La Rioja)
☎: +34 941 450 818 - Fax: +34 941 450 818
pdr@pagosdelrey.com
www.pagosdelrey.com

CASTILLO DE ALBAI 2011 B
100% viura.

88 Colour: bright straw, greenish rim. Nose: medium intensity, fresh, citrus fruit, wild herbs. Palate: fruity, fresh.

ARNEGUI 2011 B
100% viura.

84

CASTILLO DE ALBAI 2011 RD
garnacha.

85 Colour: rose, bright. Nose: fresh, red berry notes, dried flowers. Palate: fresh, fruity, easy to drink, good finish.

ARNEGUI 2001 RD
100% tempranillo.

87 Colour: rose, purple rim. Nose: powerfull, ripe fruit, red berry notes, floral, expressive. Palate: fleshy, powerful, fruity, fresh.

ARNEGUI 2011 T
100% tempranillo.

86 Colour: deep cherry. Nose: ripe fruit, balsamic herbs. Palate: flavourful, fine bitter notes, good acidity.

ARNEGUI 2010 TC
100% tempranillo.

89 Colour: cherry, garnet rim. Nose: medium intensity, ripe fruit, sweet spices. Palate: flavourful, fruity, easy to drink, good acidity.

CASTILLO DE ALBAI 2010 T
100% tempranillo.

88 Colour: bright cherry. Nose: ripe fruit, sweet spices, creamy oak. Palate: flavourful, fruity, toasty, round tannins.

CASTILLO DE ALBAI 2010 TC
100% tempranillo.

88 Colour: cherry, garnet rim. Nose: spicy, medium intensity, ripe fruit. Palate: correct, fine bitter notes, round tannins.

CASTILLO DE ALBAI 2009 TR
100% tempranillo.

87 Colour: cherry, garnet rim. Nose: medium intensity, ripe fruit, spicy. Palate: balanced, long, good acidity.

ARNEGUI 2009 TR
100% tempranillo.

87 Colour: cherry, garnet rim. Nose: spicy, creamy oak, toasty, overripe fruit. Palate: powerful, flavourful, toasty, round tannins.

PAISAJES Y VIÑEDOS

Pza. Ibarra, 1
26330 Briones (La Rioja)
☎: +34 941 322 301 - Fax: +34 941 322 302
comunicacio@vilaviniteca.es

PAISAJES VALSALADO 2009 T
tempranillo, garnacha, graciano, mazuelo.

92 Colour: bright cherry. Nose: ripe fruit, sweet spices, creamy oak, balsamic herbs, scrubland. Palate: flavourful, fruity, toasty, round tannins.

PAISAJES VIII LA PASADA 2009 T
tempranillo.

92 Colour: cherry, garnet rim. Nose: spicy, creamy oak, toasty, characterful, scrubland. Palate: powerful, flavourful, toasty, round tannins.

PAISAJES CECIAS 2009 T
garnacha.

90 Colour: very deep cherry. Nose: sweet spices, fruit preserve, scrubland. Palate: flavourful, ripe fruit, fine bitter notes, good acidity.

PASCUAL LARRIETA

Camino Santa Lucía, 5
01307 Samaniego (Álava)
☎: +34 945 609 059 - Fax: +34 945 609 306
info@pascuallarrieta.com
www.pascuallarrieta.com

PASCUAL LARRIETA 2011 T MACERACIÓN CARBÓNICA
85% tempranillo, 15% viura.

89 Colour: cherry, purple rim. Nose: balanced, red berry notes, neat. Palate: fruity, full, long.

PASCUAL LARRIETA 2009 TC
tempranillo.

88 Colour: cherry, garnet rim. Nose: ripe fruit, spicy, creamy oak, toasty. Palate: powerful, flavourful, toasty, round tannins.

PASCUAL LARRIETA 2008 TC
tempranillo.

86 Colour: cherry, garnet rim. Nose: warm, medium intensity, ripe fruit, toasty. Palate: fruity, good finish.

PASCUAL LARRIETA 2006 TR
tempranillo.

88 Colour: bright cherry, brick rim edge. Nose: tobacco, spicy, old leather, ripe fruit. Palate: balanced, fruity, flavourful.

QUIROGA DE PABLO

Antonio Pérez, 24
26323 Azofra (La Rioja)
☎: +34 606 042 478 - Fax: +34 941 379 334
info@bodegasquiroga.es
www.bodegasquiroga.es

HEREDAD DE JUDIMA 2009 TC
tempranillo.

90 Colour: cherry, garnet rim. Nose: powerfull, creamy oak, new oak, ripe fruit. Palate: long, spicy, powerful, flavourful.

HEREDAD DE JUDIMA 2007 TR
100% tempranillo.

90 Colour: cherry, garnet rim. Nose: ripe fruit, spicy, toasty, balsamic herbs. Palate: powerful, flavourful, toasty, round tannins.

R. LÓPEZ DE HEREDIA VIÑA TONDONIA

Avda. Vizcaya, 3
26200 Haro (La Rioja)
☎: +34 941 310 244 - Fax: +34 941 310 788
bodega@lopezdeheredia.com
www.tondonia.com

VIÑA TONDONIA 1993 B RESERVA

92 Colour: bright golden. Nose: ripe fruit, dry nuts, powerfull, toasty, aged wood nuances, sweet spices, expressive. Palate: flavourful, fruity, spicy, toasty, long, elegant.

VIÑA TONDONIA 2001 TR

90 Colour: pale ruby, brick rim edge. Nose: spicy, fine reductive notes, aged wood nuances, fruit liqueur notes, varnish. Palate: spicy, fine tannins, elegant, long.

RIOJA VEGA

Ctra. Logroño-Mendavia, Km. 92
31230 Viana (Navarra)
☎: +34 948 646 263 - Fax: +34 948 645 612
info@riojavega.com
www.riojavega.com

RIOJA VEGA EDICIÓN LIMITADA 2009 TC
90% tempranillo, 10% graciano.

90 Colour: cherry, garnet rim. Nose: balanced, complex, expressive, ripe fruit. Palate: fruity, easy to drink, good acidity.

RIOJA VEGA 2007 TR
85% tempranillo, 10% graciano, 5% mazuelo.

89 Colour: cherry, garnet rim. Nose: spicy, creamy oak, toasty. Palate: powerful, flavourful, toasty, round tannins.

RIOJA VEGA 130 ANIVERSARIO 2006 TR
75% tempranillo, 20% graciano, 5% mazuelo.

90 Colour: cherry, garnet rim. Nose: spicy, smoky, old leather, cigar, balsamic herbs. Palate: flavourful, long, correct.

RODRÍGUEZ SANZO

Manuel Azaña, 9
47014 (Valladolid)
☎: +34 983 150 150 - Fax: +34 983 150 151
comunicacion@valsanzo.com
www.rodriguezsanzo.com

LACRIMUS REX GARNACHA & GRACIANO 2010 T
75% garnacha, 25% graciano.

89 Colour: cherry, garnet rim. Nose: candied fruit, red berry notes, sweet spices, nose:tic coffee. Palate: flavourful, fruity, fresh, good acidity.

LACRIMUS 2009 TC
85% tempranillo, 15% graciano.

90 Colour: deep cherry. Nose: sweet spices, ripe fruit, earthy notes, spicy. Palate: fine bitter notes, long, sweet tannins, balanced.

LA SENOBA 2008 T
tempranillo.

92 Colour: cherry, garnet rim. Nose: ripe fruit, spicy, creamy oak, toasty, fruit expression, characterful. Palate: powerful, flavourful, toasty, round tannins.

SEÑORÍO DE ARANA

La Cadena, 20
01330 Labastida (Álava)
☎: +34 945 331 150 - Fax: +34 945 331 150
info@senoriodearana.com
www.senoriodearana.com

VIÑA DEL OJA 2011 T
100% tempranillo.

86 Colour: cherry, garnet rim. Nose: macerated fruit, powerfull, earthy notes, undergrowth. Palate: spirituous, warm, powerful, flavourful, ripe fruit.

VIÑA DEL OJA 2008 TC
90% tempranillo, 10% mazuelo.

85 Colour: cherry, garnet rim. Nose: warm, ripe fruit, spicy. Palate: correct, good finish.

VIÑA DEL OJA 2004 TR
90% tempranillo, 5% mazuelo, 5% graciano.

89 Colour: pale ruby, brick rim edge. Nose: spicy, fine reductive notes, wet leather, aged wood nuances, fruit liqueur notes. Palate: spicy, elegant, long.

SEÑORÍO DE SAN VICENTE

Los Remedios, 27
26338 San Vicente de la Sonsierra (La Rioja)
☎: +34 941 334 080 - Fax: +34 941 334 371
info@eguren.com
www.eguren.com

SAN VICENTE 2009 T
100% tempranillo.

95 Colour: very deep cherry. Nose: ripe fruit, dry nuts, red berry notes, toasty, sweet spices. Palate: spicy, ripe fruit, good acidity, fine bitter notes, round tannins.

SAN VICENTE 2008 T
100% tempranillo.

96 Colour: cherry, garnet rim. Nose: ripe fruit, spicy, creamy oak, toasty, characterful. Palate: powerful, flavourful, toasty, round tannins, good acidity, round.

SEÑORIO DE VILLARRICA

Camino Sto Domingo nº 27
26340 San Asensio (La Rioja)
☎: +34 941 457 171 - Fax: 349 414 571 72
bodega@villarrica.es
www.villarrica.es

SEÑORÍO DE VILLARRICA 2011 B
viura, malvasía.

84

SEÑORÍO DE VILLARRICA ROSE 2011 RD
viura, garnacha.

85 Colour: rose, purple rim. Nose: powerfull, ripe fruit, red berry notes, lactic notes. Palate: , flavourful, fresh, easy to drink.

SEÑORÍO DE VILLARRICA 2009 TC
100% tempranillo.

86 Colour: cherry, garnet rim. Nose: medium intensity, ripe fruit, balsamic herbs, spicy. Palate: flavourful, spicy, ripe fruit.

SEÑORÍO DE VILLARRICA SELECCIÓN ESPECIAL 2007 T

89 Colour: cherry, garnet rim. Nose: ripe fruit, sweet spices, creamy oak. Palate: long, spicy, flavourful, round tannins.

SEÑORÍO DE VILLARRICA 2007 TR
100% tempranillo.

87 Colour: deep cherry, orangey edge. Nose: ripe fruit, spicy, toasty. Palate: powerful, flavourful, toasty, round tannins.

V DE VILLARRICA T ROBLE
100% tempranillo.

85 Colour: bright cherry. Nose: ripe fruit, sweet spices. Palate: flavourful, fruity, toasty, ripe fruit.

SIERRA CANTABRIA

Amorebieta, 3
26338 San Vicente de la Sonsierra (La Rioja)
☎: +34 941 334 080 - Fax: +34 941 334 371
info@eguren.com
www.eguren.com

SIERRA CANTABRIA ORGANZA 2011 B
viura, malvasía, garnacha blanca.

92 Colour: bright straw. Nose: scrubland, lactic notes, ripe fruit, citrus fruit. Palate: round, good acidity, fine bitter notes.

SIERRA CANTABRIA ORGANZA 2010 B
viura, malvasía, garnacha blanca.

93 Colour: bright yellow. Nose: powerfull, sweet spices, creamy oak, fragrant herbs, mineral, fruit expression. Palate: rich, flavourful, fresh, good acidity.

SIERRA CANTABRIA 2011 RD
tempranillo, garnacha, viura.

90 Colour: brilliant rose. Nose: white flowers, red berry notes, citrus fruit. Palate: flavourful, fruity, fresh, good acidity.

MURMURÓN 2011 T
100% tempranillo.

89 Colour: cherry, purple rim. Nose: floral, fresh fruit, fruit expression. Palate: flavourful, good acidity.

SIERRA CANTABRIA COLECCIÓN PRIVADA 2010 T
100% tempranillo.

96 Colour: bright cherry. Nose: sweet spices, creamy oak, expressive, red berry notes. Palate: flavourful, fruity, toasty, round tannins.

FINCA EL BOSQUE 2010 T
100% tempranillo.

96 Colour: very deep cherry. Nose: fruit expression, raspberry, ripe fruit, toasty, creamy oak, sweet spices, mineral. Palate: flavourful, powerful, fine bitter notes, round tannins, good acidity.

SIERRA CANTABRIA COLECCIÓN PRIVADA 2009 T
100% tempranillo.

95 Colour: cherry, garnet rim. Nose: ripe fruit, spicy, creamy oak, toasty, complex, characterful, mineral. Palate: powerful, flavourful, toasty, round tannins.

FINCA EL BOSQUE 2009 T
100% tempranillo.

95 Colour: cherry, garnet rim. Nose: spicy, creamy oak, toasty, complex, earthy notes, ripe fruit, raspberry. Palate: powerful, flavourful, toasty, round tannins.

AMANCIO 2009 T
100% tempranillo.

94 Colour: cherry, garnet rim. Nose: ripe fruit, spicy, creamy oak, dark chocolatc. Palate: powerful, flavourful, toasty, round tannins, good acidity.

AMANCIO 2008 T
100% tempranillo.

96 Colour: cherry, garnet rim. Nose: spicy, characterful, fruit expression, red berry notes, new oak. Palate: powerful, flavourful, toasty, round tannins.

SIERRA CANTABRIA CUVÈE ESPECIAL 2008 T
100% tempranillo.

92 Colour: deep cherry. Nose: ripe fruit, fruit expression, creamy oak. Palate: flavourful, powerful, spicy, ripe fruit, roasted-coffee afterpalate:.

SIERRA CANTABRIA 2008 TC
tempranillo.

91 Colour: cherry, garnet rim. Nose: creamy oak, toasty, characterful, fruit expression. Palate: powerful, flavourful, toasty, long.

SIERRA CANTABRIA 2004 TGR
100% tempranillo.

94 Colour: deep cherry. Nose: elegant, spicy, toasty, ripe fruit. Palate: flavourful, spicy, fine bitter notes.

SOC. COOP. SAN ESTEBAN P.

Ctra. Agoncillo s/n
26143 Murillo de Río Leza (La Rioja)
☎: +34 941 432 031 - Fax: +34 941 432 422
export@bodegassanesteban.com
www.bodegassanesteban.com

TIERRAS DE MURILLO VIURA 2011 B
100% viura.

88 Colour: bright straw. Nose: fresh fruit, neat, fragrant herbs. Palate: fruity, correct, easy to drink.

TIERRAS DE MURILLO 2011 RD
100% tempranillo.

87 Colour: light cherry. Nose: ripe fruit, raspberry. Palate: flavourful, ripe fruit, good acidity.

TIERRAS DE MURILLO TEMPRANILLO 2011 T
100% tempranillo.

87 Colour: bright cherry, purple rim. Nose: medium intensity, varietal, ripe fruit. Palate: fruity, flavourful, good finish.

TIERRAS DE MURILLO 2009 TC
100% tempranillo.

88 Colour: bright cherry. Nose: spicy, creamy oak, ripe fruit, fruit preserve. Palate: flavourful, round tannins, easy to drink.

SOLANA DE RAMÍREZ

Arana, 24
26339 Abalos (La Rioja)
☎: +34 941 308 049 - Fax: +34 941 308 049
consultas@solanaderamirez.com
www.valsarte.com

SOLANA DE RAMÍREZ 2011 B
90% viura, 10% otras.

87 Colour: bright straw. Nose: fresh fruit, fragrant herbs. Palate: correct, good acidity, fresh, easy to drink.

SOLANA DE RAMÍREZ MADURADO EN BODEGA 2011 T
85% tempranillo, 15% graciano.

88 Colour: cherry, purple rim. Nose: powerfull, ripe fruit, scrubland. Palate: flavourful, fine bitter notes, ripe fruit.

SOLANA DE RAMÍREZ 2011 T
90% tempranillo, 5% garnacha, 5% viura.

87 Colour: cherry, purple rim. Nose: characterful, ripe fruit, spicy. Palate: flavourful, fine bitter notes, good acidity.

VALSARTE VENDIMIA SELECCIONADA 2008 T
60% tempranillo, 40% otras.

88 Colour: cherry, garnet rim. Nose: spicy, creamy oak, toasty. Palate: powerful, flavourful, toasty, round tannins.

VALSARTE 2008 TC
100% tempranillo.

84

SOLANA DE RAMÍREZ 2007 TC
100% tempranillo.

80

VALSARTE 2004 TR
85% tempranillo, 10% graciano, 5% otras.

88 Colour: bright cherry, orangey edge. Nose: toasty, smoky, tobacco. Palate: flavourful, good acidity, balanced.

VALSARTE 2001 TGR
90% tempranillo, 5% graciano, 5% otras.

88 Colour: pale ruby, brick rim edge. Nose: elegant, spicy, fine reductive notes, wet leather, aged wood nuances, fruit liqueur notes. Palate: spicy, fine tannins, elegant, long.

SOTO DE TORRES

Camino Los Arenales, s/n
01330 Labastida (Álava)
☎: +34 938 177 400 - Fax: +34 938 177 444
mailadmin@torres.es
www.torres.es

IBÉRICOS 2010 TC
100% tempranillo.

88 Colour: cherry, garnet rim. Nose: cocoa bean, ripe fruit. Palate: correct, good acidity, good finish.

TIERRA ANTIGUA

Urb. Monje Vigilia, 7
26120 Albelda de Iregua (La Rioja)
☎: +34 941 444 223 - Fax: +34 941 444 427
info@tierrantigua.com
www.tierrantigua.com

SARMIENTO 2008 T
90% tempranillo, 5% garnacha, 5% graciano.

89 Colour: cherry, garnet rim. Nose: ripe fruit, sweet spices, balsamic herbs, creamy oak, earthy notes. Palate: flavourful, long, spicy, balanced, round tannins.

TIERRA ANTIGUA 2005 TR
85% tempranillo, 15% graciano, garnacha.

92 Colour: cherry, garnet rim. Nose: ripe fruit, spicy, creamy oak, toasty, complex, mineral. Palate: powerful, flavourful, toasty, round tannins, balanced.

TOBELOS BODEGAS Y VIÑEDOS

Ctra. N 124, Km. 45
26290 Briñas (La Rioja)
☎: +34 941 305 630 - Fax: +34 941 313 028
tobelos@tobelos.com
www.tobelos.com

TOBELOS GARNACHA 2009 T
100% garnacha.

87 Colour: dark-red cherry. Nose: spicy, aged wood nuances, roasted coffee, creamy oak, ripe fruit. Palate: spirituous, powerful, flavourful, ripe fruit, classic aged character.

TAHÓN DE TOBELOS 2008 TR
100% tempranillo.

91 Colour: cherry, garnet rim. Nose: ripe fruit, spicy, creamy oak, toasty, characterful. Palate: powerful, flavourful, toasty, round tannins.

TOBELOS TEMPRANILLO 2008 T
100% tempranillo.

90 Colour: cherry, garnet rim. Nose: ripe fruit, spicy, creamy oak, toasty, complex. Palate: powerful, flavourful, toasty, round tannins.

TORRE DE OÑA

Finca San Martín
01309 Páganos (Álava)
☎: +34 945 621 154 - Fax: +34 945 621 154
info@torredeona.com
www.torredeona.com

FINCA SAN MARTÍN 2009 T
90% tempranillo, 10% graciano.

90 Colour: cherry, garnet rim. Nose: sweet spices, creamy oak, ripe fruit. Palate: flavourful, powerful, fine bitter notes, good acidity.

TORRE DE OÑA 2008 TR
97% tempranillo, 3% graciano.

92 Colour: bright cherry, garnet rim. Nose: ripe fruit, cocoa bean, creamy oak. Palate: good structure, flavourful, round tannins, good acidity.

UNZU PROPIEDAD

Avda. de la Poveda, 16
01306 Lapuebla (Álava)
☎: +34 948 812 297
info@unzupropiedad.com
www.unzupropiedad.com

J Y J UNZU 2009 T
tempranillo.

88 Colour: bright cherry. Nose: sweet spices, creamy oak, expressive, red berry notes. Palate: flavourful, fruity, toasty, round tannins.

VALORIA

Ctra. de Burgos, Km. 5
26006 Logroño (La Rioja)
☎: +34 941 204 059 - Fax: +34 941 204 155
bodega@bvaloria.com
www.vina-valoria.es

VIÑA VALORIA VENDIMIA SELECCIONADA 2011 T
100% tempranillo.

88 Colour: cherry, purple rim. Nose: powerfull, red berry notes, ripe fruit, balanced. Palate: flavourful, fruity, good acidity.

VIÑA VALORIA VENDIMIA SELECCIONADA 2011 B
100% viura.

87 Colour: bright straw. Nose: neat, fresh, expressive, fresh fruit, grassy. Palate: flavourful, fruity, fresh, fruity aftespalate:, easy to drink.

VIÑA VALORIA VENDIMIA SELECCIONADA 2011 RD
60% tempranillo, 40% garnacha.

83

VIÑA VALORIA 2007 TR
80% tempranillo, 10% graciano, 10% mazuelo.

88 Colour: deep cherry. Nose: candied fruit, toasty, spicy, wet leather. Palate: spicy, ripe fruit, good acidity.

VIÑA VALORIA 2009 TC
80% tempranillo, 10% mazuelo, 10% graciano.

89 Colour: cherry, garnet rim. Nose: medium intensity, balanced, ripe fruit, sweet spices. Palate: balanced, good acidity.

VINÍCOLA RIOJANA DE ALCANADRE S.C.

San Isidro, 46
26509 Alcanadre (La Rioja)
☎: +34 941 165 036 - Fax: +34 941 165 286
jrgarcia@riojanadealcanadre.com
www.riojanadealcanadre.com

ARADON 2011 B
100% viura.

87 Colour: bright straw. Nose: dried herbs, fresh fruit, ripe fruit, floral. Palate: flavourful, fruity, fresh.

ARADON 2009 TC
90% tempranillo, 5% garnacha, 5% mazuelo.

86 Colour: cherry, garnet rim. Nose: ripe fruit, spicy, toasty. Palate: powerful, flavourful, toasty, spicy.

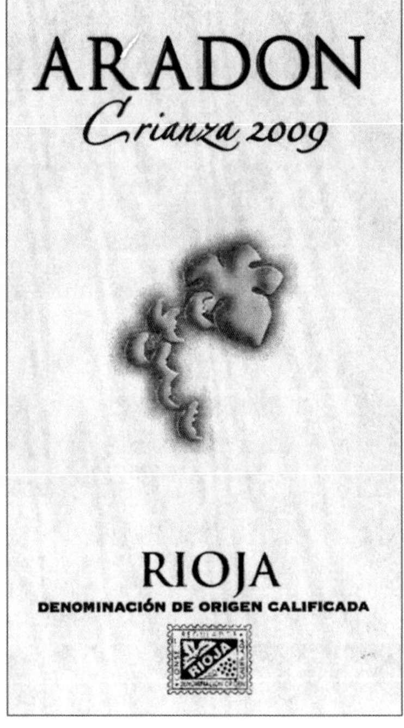

ARADON 2011 RD
100% garnacha.

85 Colour: rose, bright. Nose: fresh fruit, citrus fruit. Palate: fruity, easy to drink.

ARADON 2011 T
90% tempranillo, 10% garnacha.

84

ARADON GARNACHA VENDIMIA SELECCIONADA 2010 T
100% garnacha.

86 Colour: cherry, garnet rim. Nose: sweet spices, expressive, scrubland, overripe fruit. Palate: good structure, flavourful.

ARADON 2007 TR
90% tempranillo, 5% garnacha, 5% mazuelo.

88 Colour: cherry, garnet rim. Nose: spicy, creamy oak, toasty, ripe fruit. Palate: powerful, flavourful, toasty, round tannins.

VIÑA BUJANDA

Diputación, s/n
01320 Oyón (Alava)
☎: +34 941 450 876 - Fax: +34 941 450 875
info@bujanda.com
www.familiamartinezbujanda.com

VIÑA BUJANDA 2011 B
100% viura.

86 Colour: bright yellow. Nose: floral, fresh fruit, balanced. Palate: flavourful, fruity, correct, fine bitter notes.

VIÑA BUJANDA 2009 TC
100% tempranillo.

85 Colour: dark-red cherry. Nose: fruit preserve, wild herbs, spicy, toasty. Palate: spicy, balsamic, toasty, lacks expression.

VIÑA BUJANDA 2011 RD
100% tempranillo.

86 Colour: rose, purple rim. Nose: powerfull, ripe fruit, red berry notes, floral, expressive. Palate: fleshy, powerful, fruity, fresh.

VIÑA BUJANDA 2011 T
100% tempranillo.

86 Colour: cherry, purple rim. Nose: wild herbs, red berry notes, ripe fruit. Palate: correct, fruity, flavourful.

VIÑA BUJANDA 2006 TR
100% tempranillo.

87 Colour: cherry, garnet rim. Nose: ripe fruit, spicy, balsamic herbs. Palate: powerful, flavourful, toasty.

VIÑA EIZAGA

Camino de la Hoya s/n
01300 Laguardia (Alava)
☎: +34 675 154 279
contacto@vinoseizaga.com
www.vinoseizaga.com

VIÑA EIZAGA 2011 T
100% tempranillo.

87 Colour: deep cherry. Nose: ripe fruit, spicy, mineral. Palate: flavourful, fine bitter notes, good acidity.

VIÑA EIZAGA 2009 TC
100% tempranillo.

87 Colour: dark-red cherry, orangey edge. Nose: spicy, aged wood nuances, ripe fruit. Palate: good structure, rich, powerful, flavourful.

LAGAR DE EIZAGA 2009 TC
100% tempranillo.

87 Colour: cherry, garnet rim. Nose: toasty, spicy, ripe fruit. Palate: fine bitter notes, good acidity.

VIÑA EIZAGA 2007 TR
100% tempranillo.

88 Colour: cherry, garnet rim. Nose: ripe fruit, sweet spices, creamy oak, toasty, fine reductive notes. Palate: powerful, flavourful, long, toasty.

VIÑA IJALBA

Ctra. Pamplona, Km. 1
26006 Logroño (La Rioja)
☎: +34 941 261 100 - Fax: +34 941 261 128
vinaijalba@ijalba.com
www.ijalba.com

IJALBA MATURANA 2011 B
100% maturana blanca.

91 Colour: bright yellow. Nose: floral, fresh fruit, fragrant herbs. Palate: powerful, flavourful, fruity, fresh, sweetness, full.

ALOQUE 2011 RD JOVEN
50% tempranillo, 50% garnacha.

87 Colour: rose, purple rim. Nose: powerfull, ripe fruit, red berry notes, floral, expressive. Palate: fleshy, powerful, fruity, fresh.

LIVOR 2011 T JOVEN
100% tempranillo.

86 Colour: cherry, purple rim. Nose: ripe fruit, scrubland, spicy. Palate: powerful, flavourful, fruity.

IJALBA 2007 TR
80% tempranillo, 20% graciano.

89 Colour: cherry, garnet rim. Nose: powerfull, balanced, spicy, cigar. Palate: flavourful, ripe fruit, round tannins.

DIONISIO RUIZ IJALBA 2010 T
maturana.

90 Colour: cherry, garnet rim. Nose: red berry notes, ripe fruit, citrus fruit, fragrant herbs, spicy. Palate: powerful, flavourful, spicy.

IJALBA GRACIANO 2010 TC
graciano.

89 Colour: cherry, garnet rim. Nose: ripe fruit, spicy, creamy oak, toasty, balsamic herbs, earthy notes. Palate: powerful, flavourful, toasty.

IJALBA 2008 TC
80% tempranillo, 20% graciano.

89 Colour: deep cherry. Nose: creamy oak, spicy, scrubland. Palate: spicy, fine bitter notes, good acidity.

MÚRICE 2008 TC
90% tempranillo, 10% graciano.

88 Colour: cherry, garnet rim. Nose: spicy, grassy, ripe fruit. Palate: fruity, good acidity.

IJALBA SELECCIÓN ESPECIAL 2005 TR
50% graciano, 50% tempranillo.

91 Colour: cherry, garnet rim. Nose: spicy, ripe fruit, candied fruit, tobacco. Palate: balanced, correct, fine bitter notes.

VIÑA OLABARRI

Ctra. Anguciana, s/n
26200 Haro (La Rioja)
☎: +34 941 310 937 - Fax: +34 941 311 602
info@bodegasolabarri.com
www.bodegasolabarri.com

VIÑA OLABARRI 2009 TC
100% tempranillo.

88 Colour: dark-red cherry. Nose: complex, cocoa bean, spicy, creamy oak, toasty, fruit preserve. Palate: complex, fruity, powerful, flavourful, balsamic.

BIKANDI VENDIMIA SELECCIONADA 2008 TC
100% tempranillo.

88 Colour: cherry, garnet rim. Nose: spicy, creamy oak, toasty, ripe fruit. Palate: powerful, flavourful, toasty, round tannins.

VIÑA OLABARRI 2008 TR
90% tempranillo, 10% graciano.

87 Colour: cherry, garnet rim. Nose: ripe fruit, spicy, toasty, old leather, tobacco. Palate: powerful, flavourful, toasty.

BIKANDI VENDIMIA SELECCIONADA 2005 TR
100% tempranillo.

89 Colour: cherry, garnet rim. Nose: spicy, creamy oak, toasty, ripe fruit, wet leather. Palate: powerful, flavourful, toasty, round tannins.

VIÑA OLABARRI 2005 TGR
80% tempranillo, mazuelo, graciano.

88 Colour: cherry, garnet rim. Nose: ripe fruit, spicy, creamy oak, toasty. Palate: powerful, flavourful, toasty, round tannins.

VIÑA REAL

Ctra. Logroño - Laguardia, Km. 4,8
01300 Laguardia (Álava)
☎: +34 945 625 255 - Fax: +34 945 625 211
marketing@cvne.com
www.cvne.com

VIÑA REAL 2006 TR
90% tempranillo, 10% graciano, garnacha, mazuelo.

92 Colour: deep cherry. Nose: cocoa bean, spicy, fruit expression, expressive, old leather, tobacco. Palate: round, balanced, flavourful, good structure, spicy, creamy, long.

VIÑA REAL 2010 TC
90% tempranillo, 10% garnacha, mazuelo, graciano.

92 Colour: bright cherry, garnet rim. Nose: balanced, expressive, medium intensity, ripe fruit. Palate: flavourful, round tannins.

VIÑA REAL 2005 TGR
95% tempranillo, 5% graciano.

92 Colour: dark-red cherry. Nose: spicy, creamy oak, fine reductive notes, damp earth, undergrowth. Palate: fine tannins, powerful, flavourful, round, full, rich, elegant.

VIÑA SALCEDA

Ctra. Cenicero, Km. 3
01340 Elciego (Álava)
☎: +34 945 606 125
info@vinasalceda.com
www.vinasalceda.com

PUENTE DE SALCEDA 2009 T
tempranillo.

91 Colour: cherry, garnet rim. Nose: spicy, creamy oak, toasty, red berry notes, ripe fruit. Palate: powerful, flavourful, toasty, round tannins.

VIÑA SALCEDA 2009 TC
tempranillo, mazuelo, graciano.

89 Colour: cherry, garnet rim. Nose: spicy, creamy oak, toasty, wet leather. Palate: powerful, flavourful, toasty, round tannins.

CONDE DE LA SALCEDA 2007 TR
tempranillo.

93 Colour: cherry, garnet rim. Nose: ripe fruit, spicy, creamy oak, characterful. Palate: powerful, flavourful, toasty, powerful tannins, mineral, long.

VIÑASPRAL

Camino Del Soto s/n
01309 Elvillar (Álava)
☎: +34 628 132 151 - Fax: +34 628 132 151
info@maisulan.com
www.maisulan.com

HONORATUS AURUM 2008 B
100% viura.

91 Colour: bright golden. Nose: ripe fruit, powerfull, toasty, aged wood nuances, sweet spices. Palate: flavourful, fruity, spicy, toasty, long.

MAISULAN SELECCIÓN 2010 T
100% tempranillo.

91 Colour: cherry, garnet rim. Nose: spicy, creamy oak, toasty, characterful. Palate: powerful, flavourful, toasty, round tannins.

HONORATUS FRUCTUS VENDIMIA SELECCIONADA 2009 T
85% tempranillo, 10% graciano, 5% garnacha.

92 Colour: cherry, garnet rim. Nose: red berry notes, ripe fruit, balsamic herbs, creamy oak, toasty. Palate: powerful, flavourful, correct, elegant.

VIÑEDOS DE ALDEANUEVA S. COOP.

Avda. Juan Carlos I, 100
26559 Aldeanueva de Ebro (La Rioja)
☎: +34 941 163 039 - Fax: +34 941 163 585
va@aldeanueva.com
www.aldeanueva.com

AZABACHE 2010 RD
garnacha.

89 Colour: light cherry. Nose: floral, red berry notes, ripe fruit. Palate: flavourful, fruity, fresh.

AZABACHE TEMPRANILLO 2011 T
tempranillo.

87 Colour: cherry, purple rim. Nose: expressive, red berry notes, ripe fruit, floral. Palate: flavourful, fruity, good acidity, round tannins.

CULTO 2007 T
60% graciano, 40% tempranillo.

90 Colour: cherry, garnet rim. Nose: ripe fruit, spicy, creamy oak, toasty, characterful. Palate: powerful, flavourful, toasty, round tannins.

AZABACHE VENDIMIA SELECCIONADA 2008 TC
70% tempranillo, 20% garnacha, 10% mazuelo.

83

AZABACHE GRACIANO 2006 TR
100% graciano.

86 Colour: dark-red cherry. Nose: spicy, roasted almonds, slightly evolved, fruit preserve. Palate: round tannins, ripe fruit, toasty, spirituous.

VIÑEDOS DE ALFARO

Camino de los Agudos s/n
26559 Aldeanueva de Ebro (La Rioja)
☎: +34 941 142 389 - Fax: +34 941 142 386
info@vinedosdealfaro.com
www.vinedosdealfaro.com

REAL AGRADO 2011 B
viura.

83

REAL AGRADO 2011 RD
garnacha.

88 Colour: raspberry rose. Nose: fresh fruit, red berry notes, citrus fruit, violet drops. Palate: fresh, fruity, sweetness, flavourful.

REAL AGRADO 2011 T
60% garnacha, 40% tempranillo.

83

CONDE DEL REAL AGRADO 2008 TC
60% garnacha, 25% tempranillo, 10% mazuelo, 5% graciano.

88 Colour: cherry, garnet rim. Nose: candied fruit, spicy, toasty. Palate: fine bitter notes, spicy, ripe fruit.

CONDE DEL REAL AGRADO 2007 TC
60% garnacha, 25% tempranillo, 10% mazuelo, 5% graciano.

83

RODILES VENDIMIA SELECCIONADA 2005 T
100% graciano.

92 Colour: very deep cherry, garnet rim. Nose: dark chocolate, tobacco, fruit preserve, balsamic herbs. Palate: balanced, fine bitter notes, spicy, good acidity.

RODILES 2005 T
25% garnacha, 25% tempranillo, 25% mazuelo, 25% graciano.

87 Colour: dark-red cherry. Nose: creamy oak, toasty, ripe fruit. Palate: toasty, smoky afterpalate:, reductive nuances, spicy.

CONDE DEL REAL AGRADO 2005 TR
40% garnacha, 45% tempranillo, 5% mazuelo, 10% graciano.

87 Colour: cherry, garnet rim. Nose: spicy, tobacco, cigar, wet leather, scrubland. Palate: long, flavourful, balanced.

VIÑEDOS DE PÁGANOS

Ctra. Navaridas, s/n
01309 Páganos (Álava)
☎: +34 945 600 590 - Fax: +34 945 600 885
info@eguren.com
www.eguren.com

LA NIETA 2010 T
100% tempranillo.

96 Colour: cherry, garnet rim. Nose: spicy, complex, red berry notes, fruit expression, new oak, sweet spices, dry stone. Palate: powerful, flavourful, toasty, round tannins, good acidity.

LA NIETA 2009 T
100% tempranillo.

95 Colour: bright cherry. Nose: ripe fruit, creamy oak, expressive, mineral, toasty, cocoa bean. Palate: flavourful, fruity, toasty, round tannins, round, spicy.

EL PUNTIDO 2009 T
100% tempranillo.

95 Colour: cherry, garnet rim. Nose: ripe fruit, spicy, creamy oak, characterful. Palate: powerful, flavourful, toasty, powerful tannins, mineral.

EL PUNTIDO 2008 T
100% tempranillo.

94 Colour: cherry, garnet rim. Nose: ripe fruit, spicy, creamy oak, mineral, toasty. Palate: powerful, flavourful, toasty, round tannins, good acidity, fine bitter notes.

VIÑEDOS DEL CONTINO

Finca San Rafael, s/n
01321 Laserna (Álava)
☎: +34 945 600 201 - Fax: +34 945 621 114
laserna@contino.es
www.cvne.com

CONTINO 2010 B
70% viura, 20% garnacha blanca, 10% malvasía.

91 Colour: bright straw. Nose: white flowers, fragrant herbs, fine lees, fresh, expressive. Palate: fruity, fresh, complex, elegant.

CONTINO VIÑA DEL OLIVO 2009 T
90% tempranillo, 10% graciano.

93 Colour: cherry, garnet rim. Nose: ripe fruit, spicy, toasty, complex, fruit expression. Palate: powerful, flavourful, toasty, round tannins.

CONTINO GARNACHA 2009 T
100% garnacha.

92 Colour: cherry, garnet rim. Nose: ripe fruit, spicy, creamy oak, toasty, scrubland. Palate: powerful, flavourful, toasty, round tannins.

CONTINO GRACIANO 2009 T
100% graciano.

91 Colour: cherry, garnet rim. Nose: spicy, creamy oak, toasty, complex, ripe fruit, red berry notes. Palate: powerful, flavourful, toasty, round tannins.

CONTINO VIÑA DEL OLIVO 2008 T
88% tempranillo, 12% graciano.

93 Colour: deep cherry, garnet rim. Nose: sweet spices, cocoa bean, creamy oak, ripe fruit, complex. Palate: good structure, flavourful, round tannins, good acidity.

CONTINO 2008 TR
85% tempranillo, 10% graciano, mazuelo, garnacha.

90 Colour: cherry, garnet rim. Nose: elegant, ripe fruit, dark chocolate, spicy. Palate: flavourful, good acidity, balanced.

CONTINO GRACIANO 2007 T
100% graciano.

93 Colour: cherry, garnet rim. Nose: ripe fruit, spicy, toasty, complex, earthy notes, scrubland. Palate: powerful, flavourful, toasty, round tannins, balsamic.

CONTINO 2007 TR
85% tempranillo, 10% graciano, 5% mazuelo, garnacha.

92 Colour: dark-red cherry. Nose: powerfull, expressive, complex, spicy, fruit expression. Palate: powerful, flavourful, complex, spicy, balsamic, toasty.

CONTINO 2005 TGR
70% tempranillo, 15% garnacha, 15% graciano.

93 Colour: cherry, garnet rim. Nose: ripe fruit, spicy, creamy oak, toasty, complex, wet leather. Palate: powerful, flavourful, toasty, round tannins.

VIÑEDOS DEL TERNERO

Finca El Ternero
09200 Miranda de Ebro (Burgos)
☎: +34 941 320 021 - Fax: +34 941 302 719
ana@vinedosdelternero.com
www.vinedosdelternero.com

MIRANDA GENÉRICO 2007 T
95% tempranillo, 5% mazuelo.

89 Colour: cherry, garnet rim. Nose: ripe fruit, spicy, creamy oak, dark chocolate, cocoa bean. Palate: powerful, flavourful, toasty, round tannins.

HACIENDA TERNERO 2011 BFB
100% viura.

90 Colour: bright yellow. Nose: powerfull, ripe fruit, sweet spices, creamy oak, fragrant herbs. Palate: rich, flavourful, fresh, good acidity.

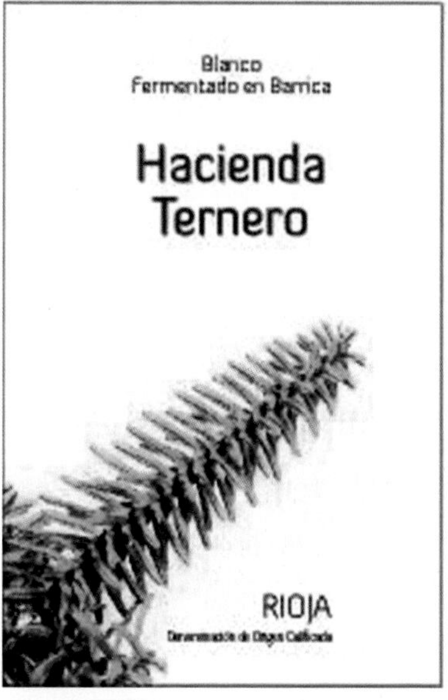

PICEA 650 2008 T
95% tempranillo, 5% mazuelo.

93 Colour: bright cherry. Nose: ripe fruit, sweet spices, creamy oak, expressive, mineral, toasty. Palate: flavourful, fruity, toasty, round tannins, balanced, elegant.

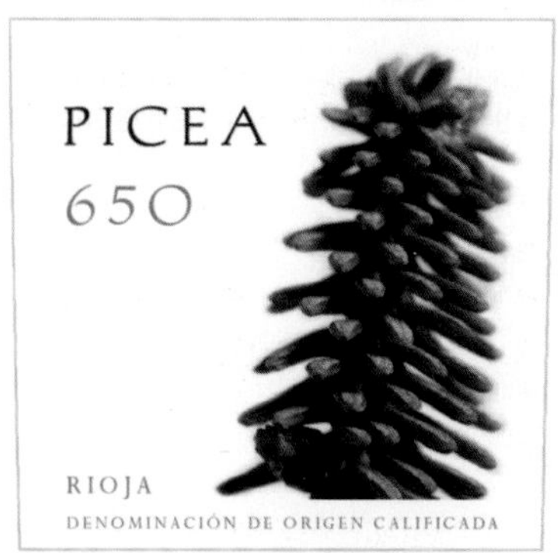

MIRANDA 2007 TC
95% tempranillo, 5% mazuelo.

90 Colour: cherry, garnet rim. Nose: ripe fruit, spicy, creamy oak, toasty, complex. Palate: powerful, flavourful, toasty, round tannins, balanced.

VIÑEDOS SINGULARES

Cuzco, 26 - 28, Nave 8
08030 (Barcelona)
☎: +34 609 168 191 - Fax: +34 934 807 076
info@vinedossingulares.com
www.vinedossingulares.com

JARDÍN ROJO 2010 T
tempranillo.

89 Colour: cherry, garnet rim. Nose: ripe fruit, spicy, creamy oak, balsamic herbs. Palate: powerful, flavourful, toasty, fresh, fruity.

VIÑEDOS Y BODEGAS DE LA MARQUESA - VALSERRANO

Herrería, 76
01307 Villabuena (Álava)
☎: +34 945 609 085 - Fax: +34 945 623 304
info@valserrano.com
www.valserrano.com

VALSERRANO 2011 BFB
95% viura, 5% malvasía.

87 Colour: bright straw. Nose: fresh fruit, smoky, spicy. Palate: fruity, fresh, creamy.

VALSERRANO 2000 B GRAN RESERVA
95% viura, 5% malvasía.

93 Colour: bright golden. Nose: ripe fruit, dry nuts, powerfull, toasty, aged wood nuances. Palate: flavourful, fruity, spicy, toasty, long.

VALSERRANO GARNACHA 2009 T
100% garnacha.

91 Colour: cherry, garnet rim. Nose: spicy, toasty, ripe fruit, sweet spices. Palate: powerful, flavourful, toasty, round tannins.

VALSERRANO 2009 TC
90% tempranillo, 10% mazuelo.

88 Colour: cherry, garnet rim. Nose: ripe fruit, spicy, toasty. Palate: powerful, flavourful, toasty, spicy.

VALSERRANO MAZUELO 2008 T
100% mazuelo.

90 Colour: cherry, garnet rim. Nose: ripe fruit, spicy, balsamic herbs, tobacco, fine reductive notes. Palate: long, powerful, flavourful, balanced.

FINCA MONTEVIEJO 2007 T
95% tempranillo, garnacha, 5% graciano.

92 Colour: cherry, garnet rim. Nose: balanced, ripe fruit, sweet spices, earthy notes. Palate: good structure, flavourful, full, long, fine bitter notes, good acidity.

VALSERRANO 2007 TR
90% tempranillo, 10% graciano.

90 Colour: cherry, garnet rim. Nose: sweet spices, creamy oak, cocoa bean, ripe fruit. Palate: good structure, flavourful, ripe fruit, long.

VALSERRANO GRACIANO 2005 T
100% graciano.

89 Colour: deep cherry, orangey edge. Nose: nose:tic coffee, creamy oak, cigar, old leather. Palate: balanced, flavourful, spicy.

VALSERRANO 2001 TGR
90% tempranillo, 10% mazuelo.

87 Colour: pale ruby, brick rim edge. Nose: fruit liqueur notes, nose:tic coffee, waxy notes, wet leather. Palate: fine bitter notes, spicy.

WINNER WINES

Avda. del Mediterráneo, 38
28007 Madrid (Madrid)
☎: +34 915 019 042 - Fax: +34 915 017 794
winnerwines@ibernoble.com
www.ibernoble.com

VIÑA SASETA 2011 T

87 Colour: cherry, purple rim. Nose: ripe fruit, red berry notes, wild herbs. Palate: correct, powerful, flavourful.

VIÑA SASETA 2008 TC

88 Colour: deep cherry. Nose: sweet spices, cocoa bean, ripe fruit. Palate: spicy, ripe fruit, fine bitter notes.

VIÑA SASETA 2005 TR
90% tempranillo, 5% graciano, 5% mazuelo.

90 Colour: cherry, garnet rim. Nose: spicy, ripe fruit, balanced. Palale: balanced, good acidity, round tannins.

DO RUEDA

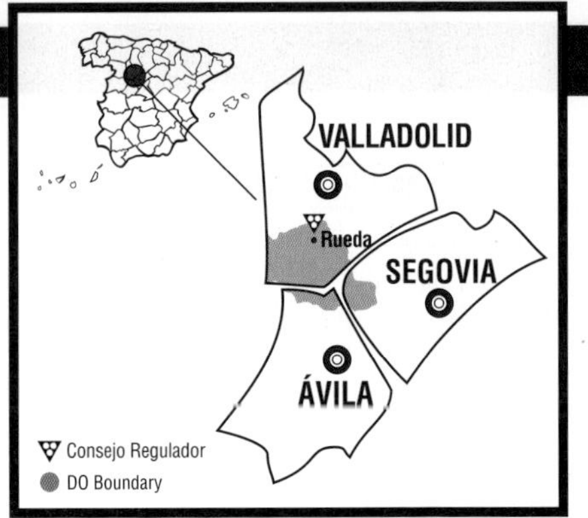

LOCATION:

In the provinces of Valladolid (53 municipal districts), Segovia (17 municipal districts) and Ávila (2 municipal districts). The vineyards are situated on the undulating terrain of a plateau and are conditioned by the influence of the river Duero that runs through the northern part of the region.

CLIMATE:

Continental in nature, with cold winters and short hot summers. Rainfall is concentrated in spring and autumn. The average altitude of the region is between 600 m and 700 m, and only in the province of Segovia does it exceed 800 m.

SOIL:

Many pebbles on the surface. The terrain is stony, poor in organic matter, with good aeration and drainage. The texture of the soil is variable although, in general, sandy limestone and limestone predominate.

GRAPE VARIETIES:

WHITE: *Verdejo* (52%), *Viura* (22%), *Sauvignon Blanc* (7%) and *Palomino Fino* (19%).
RED: *Tempranillo, Cabernet Sauvignon, Merlot* and *Garnacha.*

FIGURES:

Vineyard surface: 12,644 – **Wine-Growers:** 1,600 – **Wineries:** 58 – **2011 Harvest rating:** Excellent – **Production:** 52,165,000 litres – **Market percentages:** 84% domestic. 16% export

VINTAGE RATING PEÑÍNGUIDE

2008	2009	2010	2011
VERY GOOD	VERY GOOD	EXCELLENT	VERY GOOD

CONSEJO REGULADOR
Real, 8 - 47490 Rueda (Valladolid) - ☎: +34 983 868 248 - Fax: +34 983 868 135
@ crdo.rueda@dorueda.com - www.dorueda.com

AGRÍCOLA CASTELLANA. BODEGA CUATRO RAYAS

Ctra. Rodilana, s/n
47491 La Seca (Valladolid)
☎: +34 983 816 320 - Fax: +34 983 816 562
info@cuatrorayas.org
www.cuatrorayas.org

CUATRO RAYAS VIÑEDOS CENTENARIOS 2011 B
100% verdejo.

92 Colour: bright straw. Nose: fresh, white flowers, expressive, mineral, grassy. Palate: flavourful, fruity, good acidity, balanced.

CUATRO RAYAS VERDEJO 2011 B
100% verdejo.

90 Colour: bright straw. Nose: fresh, fresh fruit, white flowers. Palate: flavourful, fruity, good acidity, balanced.

AZUMBRE VERDEJO VIÑEDOS CENTENARIOS 2011 B
100% verdejo.

88 Colour: bright straw. Nose: fresh, white flowers, varietal, ripe fruit. Palate: flavourful, good acidity, balanced.

VISIGODO VERDEJO 2011 B
100% verdejo.

88 Colour: bright straw. Nose: white flowers, dried herbs, fruit expression. Palate: powerful, flavourful, fresh, fruity.

CUATRO RAYAS SAUVIGNON 2011 B
100% sauvignon blanc.

88 Colour: bright straw. Nose: varietal, grassy, green pepper. Palate: flavourful, powerful, fine bitter notes.

VELITERRA 2011 B
100% verdejo.

84

APOTEOSIS 2011 B
100% verdejo.

88 Colour: bright straw. Nose: white flowers, fragrant herbs, fruit expression. Palate: powerful, full, flavourful.

NAVE SUR 2011 B
100% verdejo.

88 Colour: bright straw. Nose: ripe fruit, citrus fruit, dried herbs. Palate: flavourful, fruity, fresh.

BITÁCORA VERDEJO 2011 B
100% verdejo.

86 Colour: bright straw. Nose: fresh fruit, white flowers, fragrant herbs. Palate: flavourful, fruity, balanced.

CUATRO RAYAS 2010 BFB
100% verdejo.

87 Colour: bright straw. Nose: toasty, spicy, nose:tic coffee, ripe fruit. Palate: sweetness, fine bitter notes.

VACCEOS 2011 RD
100% tempranillo.

87 Colour: brilliant rose. Nose: elegant, candied fruit, dried flowers, fragrant herbs, red berry notes. Palate: light-bodied, flavourful, good acidity, long, spicy.

VACCEOS TEMPRANILLO 2010 T ROBLE
100% tempranillo.

88 Colour: bright cherry. Nose: ripe fruit, sweet spices, creamy oak. Palate: flavourful, fruity, toasty, round tannins.

VACCEOS 2009 TC
100% tempranillo.

88 Colour: bright cherry. Nose: ripe fruit, sweet spices, varietal, characterful. Palate: flavourful, fruity, toasty, round tannins.

PÁMPANO 2011 SEMIDULCE
100% verdejo.

83

AGRÍCOLA SANZ

Ctra. Madrid - Coruña, km. 170
47490 Rueda (Valladolid)
☎: +34 983 804 132

ANTONIO SANZ 2011 B
100% verdejo.

92 Colour: bright straw. Nose: fresh, fresh fruit, white flowers, mineral. Palate: flavourful, fruity, good acidity, balanced.

ALTAENCINA GLOBAL

Cañada Real, 30 1ºA
47008 (Valladolid)
☎: +34 639 780 716 - Fax: +34 983 868 905
altaencina@altaencina.com
www.altaencina.com

QUIVIRA VERDEJO 2011 B
100% verdejo.

88 Colour: bright straw. Nose: fresh, fresh fruit, white flowers, expressive, fragrant herbs. Palate: flavourful, fruity, good acidity.

ÁLVAREZ Y DÍEZ

Juan Antonio Carmona, 12
47500 Nava del Rey (Valladolid)
☎: +34 983 850 136 - Fax: +34 983 850 761
bodegas@alvarezydiez.com
www.alvarezydiez.com

MANTEL BLANCO RUEDA VERDEJO 2011 B
verdejo.

88 Colour: bright straw. Nose: fresh, white flowers, fruit expression. Palate: flavourful, fruity, balanced.

MANTEL BLANCO SAUVIGNON BLANC 2011 B
sauvignon blanc.

88 Colour: bright straw. Nose: fresh, fresh fruit, white flowers. Palate: flavourful, fruity, good acidity, balanced.

MONTE ALINA 2011 B

85 Colour: bright straw. Nose: dried flowers, ripe fruit, dried herbs, medium intensity. Palate: easy to drink, flavourful, fresh.

MANTEL BLANCO 2008 BFB

87 Colour: bright straw. Nose: warm, spicy, toasty, candied fruit. Palate: spicy, ripe fruit, sweetness.

ÁNGEL RODRÍGUEZ VIDAL

Torcido, 1
47491 La Seca (Valladolid)
☎: +34 983 816 302 - Fax: +34 983 816 302
martinsancho@martinsancho.com

MARTÍNSANCHO VERDEJO 2011 B
100% verdejo.

90 Colour: bright straw. Nose: fresh, fresh fruit, white flowers, expressive. Palate: flavourful, fruity, good acidity, balanced.

AURA (DOMECQ BODEGAS)

Autovía del Noroeste, Km. 175
47490 Rueda (Valladolid)
☎: +34 983 868 286 - Fax: +34 983 868 168
mcarreir@domecqbodegas.com
www.domecqbodegas.com

AURA SAUVIGNON BLANC 2011 B
100% sauvignon blanc.

90 Colour: bright straw. Nose: fresh, fresh fruit, white flowers, grassy. Palate: flavourful, fruity, good acidity, balanced.

AURA VERDEJO 2011 B
75% verdejo, 25% sauvignon blanc.

88 Colour: bright yellow. Nose: ripe fruit, dried flowers, fragrant herbs. Palate: powerful, flavourful, fresh.

AVELINO VEGAS

Real del Pino, 36
40460 Santiuste (Segovia)
☎: +34 921 596 002 - Fax: +34 921 596 035
ana@avelinovegas.com
www.avelinovegas.com

MONTESPINA VERDEJO 2011 B JOVEN
verdejo.

90 Colour: bright straw. Nose: fresh, fresh fruit, white flowers, expressive, fine lees. Palate: flavourful, fruity, good acidity, balanced.

MONTESPINA SAUVIGNON 2011 B JOVEN
sauvignon blanc.

90 Colour: bright straw. Nose: fresh, white flowers, balanced, citrus fruit. Palate: flavourful, fruity, good acidity, balanced.

CIRCE 2011 B
verdejo.

90 Colour: bright straw. Nose: fresh, fresh fruit, white flowers, expressive. Palate: flavourful, fruity, good acidity, sweetness.

BELLORIVINOS

Cobalto, 37
47012 (Valladolid)
☎: +34 619 708 546
juan@bellorivinos.com

BELLORI 2011 B
100% verdejo.

90 Colour: bright straw. Nose: white flowers, fragrant herbs, ripe fruit, expressive, varietal. Palate: powerful, flavourful, long, balanced.

BELLORI 2010 BFB
100% verdejo.

94 Colour: bright yellow. Nose: powerfull, ripe fruit, creamy oak, fragrant herbs, dried flowers. Palate: rich, flavourful, fresh, good acidity, balanced.

BELONDRADE

Quinta San Diego - Camino del Puerto, s/n
47491 La Seca (Valladolid)
☎: +34 983 481 001 - Fax: +34 600 590 024
info@belondrade.com
www.belondrade.com

BELONDRADE Y LURTON 2010 BFB
verdejo.

95 Colour: bright yellow. Nose: powerfull, ripe fruit, sweet spices, creamy oak, fragrant herbs. Palate: rich, flavourful, fresh, good acidity.

BODEGA EL ALBAR LURTON

Camino Magarin, s/n
47529 Villafranca del Duero (Valladolid)
☎: +34 983 034 030 - Fax: +34 983 034 040
bodega@francoislurton.es
www.francoislurton.es

HERMANOS LURTON CUESTA DE ORO 2009 BFB
100% verdejo.

93 Colour: bright yellow. Nose: powerfull, ripe fruit, sweet spices, creamy oak, fragrant herbs, expressive. Palate: rich, flavourful, fresh, good acidity, balanced.

HERMANOS LURTON SAUVIGNON BLANC 2011 B
100% sauvignon blanc.

90 Colour: bright straw. Nose: white flowers, fresh fruit, herbaceous, fragrant herbs, elegant. Palate: fresh, fruity, flavourful, balanced.

HERMANOS LURTON VERDEJO 2011 B
100% verdejo.

88 Colour: bright straw. Nose: dried herbs, varietal, floral, fresh fruit. Palate: powerful, fresh, fruity, flavourful, easy to drink.

BODEGA EMINA MEDINA DEL CAMPO

Ctra. Medina del Campo - Olmedo, Km. 1,5
47400 Medina del Campo (Valladolid)
☎: +34 983 800 001 - Fax: +34 902 430 189
eminarueda@emina.es
www.eminarueda.es

EMINA PRESTIGIO VERDEJO 2011 B
100% verdejo.

91 Colour: bright straw. Nose: fresh, fresh fruit, white flowers, expressive, varietal, grassy. Palate: flavourful, fruity, good acidity, balanced.

MELIOR VERDEJO 2011 B
100% verdejo.

89 Colour: bright straw. Nose: grassy, dried flowers, powerfull, citrus fruit, ripe fruit. Palate: flavourful, fruity, complex.

EMINA VERDEJO 2011 B
100% verdejo.

88 Colour: bright yellow. Nose: ripe fruit, dried flowers, fragrant herbs. Palate: good acidity, powerful, flavourful.

EMINA RUEDA 2011 B
90% verdejo, 10% viura.

85 Colour: bright yellow. Nose: ripe fruit, faded flowers, dried herbs. Palate: correct, fresh, fruity.

SELECCIÓN PERSONAL CARLOS MORO EMINA VERDEJO 2009 B
100% verdejo.

93 Colour: bright yellow. Nose: powerfull, ripe fruit, fragrant herbs, pattiserie, toasty. Palate: rich, smoky afterpalate:, flavourful, fresh, good acidity.

EMINA BRUT NATURE ESP
100% verdejo.

83

EMINA ROSADO ESP
100% tempranillo.

78

EMINA SS
100% verdejo.

85 Colour: bright yellow. Nose: lees reduction notes, honeyed notes, dried herbs. Palate: powerful, flavourful, spirituous, sweetness.

BODEGA GÓTICA

Ctra. Rueda - La Seca, Km. 1,2
47490 Rueda (Valladolid)
☎: +34 629 458 235 - Fax: +34 983 868 387
mjhmonsalve@ya.com
www.bodegagotica.com

POLÍGONO 10 VERDEJO 2011 B
100% verdejo.

88 Colour: bright straw. Nose: fresh, fresh fruit, white flowers, expressive. Palate: flavourful, fruity, good acidity, balanced.

MONSALVE VERDEJO 2011 B
100% verdejo.

91 Colour: bright straw. Nose: fresh, white flowers, expressive, ripe fruit, citrus fruit. Palate: flavourful, fruity, good acidity, fine bitter notes.

TRASCAMPANAS VERDEJO 2011 B
100% verdejo.

90 Colour: bright straw. Nose: white flowers, expressive, varietal, fresh fruit, wild herbs. Palate: flavourful, fruity, good acidity, balanced.

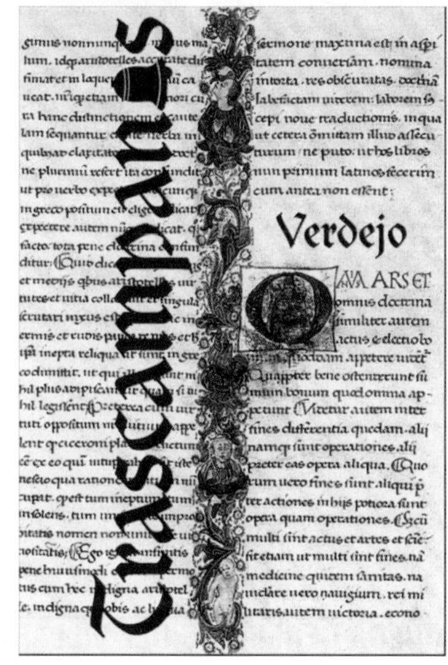

TRASCAMPANAS SAUVIGNON 2011 B
100% sauvignon blanc.

88 Colour: bright straw. Nose: expressive, ripe fruit, powerfull, fragrant herbs. Palate: flavourful, fruity, good acidity, balanced.

MOYORIDO 2011 B
100% verdejo.

87 Colour: bright straw. Nose: fresh, fresh fruit, white flowers. Palate: flavourful, fruity, good acidity, balanced.

BADAJO RUEDA 2011 B
100% verdejo.

85 Colour: bright straw. Nose: floral, ripe fruit, dried herbs. Palate: light-bodied, fresh, easy to drink.

CAMINO LA FARA VERDEJO 2011 B
100% verdejo.

86 Colour: bright straw. Nose: fresh, fresh fruit, white flowers, expressive. Palate: flavourful, fruity, balanced.

BODEGA HERMANOS DEL VILLAR

Zarcillo, s/n
47490 Rueda (Valladolid)
☎: +34 983 868 904 - Fax: +34 983 868 905
info@orodecastilla.com
www.orodecastilla.com

ORO DE CASTILLA VERDEJO 2011 B
100% verdejo.

90 Colour: bright straw. Nose: fresh, white flowers, ripe fruit. Palate: flavourful, fruity, good acidity, balanced.

ORO DE CASTILLA SAUVIGNON BLANC 2011 B
100% sauvignon blanc.

85 Colour: bright straw. Nose: fresh, fresh fruit, white flowers. Palate: flavourful, fruity, good acidity.

BODEGA LA SOTERRAÑA

Ctra. Valladolid - Madrid N-601, Km. 151
47410 Olmedo (Valladolid)
☎: +34 983 601 026 - Fax: +34 983 601 026
info@bodegaslasoterrana.com
www.bodegaslasoterrana.com

ERESMA VERDEJO 2011 B
100% verdejo.

90 Colour: bright straw. Nose: fresh, white flowers, ripe fruit, grassy. Palate: flavourful, fruity, good acidity, balanced.

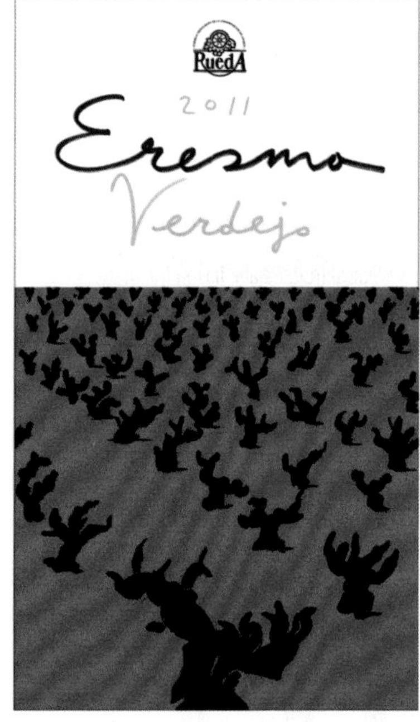

ERESMA SAUVIGNON 2011 B
100% sauvignon blanc.

89 Colour: bright straw. Nose: white flowers, fragrant herbs, citrus fruit. Palate: flavourful, fresh, fruity, easy to drink.

V&R 2011 B
100% verdejo.

88 Colour: bright straw. Nose: powerfull, varietal, ripe fruit, fruit expression, grassy. Palate: flavourful, fruity, good acidity.

77 RUEDA 2011 B
80% verdejo, 20% viura.

87 Colour: bright straw. Nose: white flowers, tropical fruit, fragrant herbs. Palate: light-bodied, fresh, fruity, easy to drink.

ERESMA 2009 BFB
100% verdejo.

90 Colour: bright straw. Nose: faded flowers, ripe fruit, fragrant herbs, sweet spices, creamy oak. Palate: flavourful, spicy, long.

BODEGA MONTE BLANCO

Ctra. Valladolid, Km. 24,5
47239 Serrada (Valladolid)
☎: +34 941 310 295 - Fax: +34 941 310 832
info@bodegas-monteblanco.es
www.bodegas-monteblanco.es

MONTE BLANCO DE RAMÓN BILBAO VERDEJO 2011 B
100% verdejo.

91 Colour: bright straw. Nose: fresh, fresh fruit, white flowers, tropical fruit. Palate: flavourful, fruity, good acidity, balanced.

BODEGA PALACIO DE BORNOS

Ctra. Madrid - Coruña, km. 170,6
47490 Rueda (Valladolid)
☎: +34 983 868 116 - Fax: +34 983 868 432
info@taninia.com
www.palaciodeborno.com

PALACIOS DE BORNOS VERDEJO 2011 B
verdejo.

90 Colour: bright straw. Nose: ripe fruit, fresh fruit, fruit expression, grassy. Palate: flavourful, fruity, good acidity.

PALACIO DE BORNOS SAUVIGNON BLANC 2011 B
sauvignon blanc.

88 Colour: bright straw. Nose: fresh, fresh fruit, white flowers. Palate: flavourful, fruity, good acidity, balanced.

PALACIO DE BORNOS SEMIDULCE 2011 B
sauvignon blanc.

85 Colour: golden. Nose: powerfull, floral, candied fruit, fragrant herbs. Palate: flavourful, sweet, fresh, fruity, long.

PALACIO DE BORNOS VERDEJO VENDIMIA SELECCIONADA 2010 BFB
verdejo.

92 Colour: bright yellow. Nose: powerfull, ripe fruit, sweet spices, creamy oak. Palate: rich, smoky afterpalate:, flavourful, fresh, good acidity.

PALACIOS DE BORNOS VERDEJO 2010 BFB
verdejo.

90 Colour: bright yellow. Nose: powerfull, ripe fruit, sweet spices, creamy oak. Palate: rich, smoky afterpalate:, flavourful, fresh, good acidity.

PALACIOS DE BORNOS LA CAPRICHOSA 2010 B
verdejo.

90 Colour: bright straw. Nose: fresh, white flowers, expressive, varietal, mineral. Palate: flavourful, fruity, good acidity, balanced.

PALACIOS DE BORNOS BR
verdejo.

85 Colour: bright straw. Nose: medium intensity, fresh fruit, dried herbs, fine lees, floral. Palate: fresh, fruity, flavourful, good acidity.

PALACIOS DE BORNOS BN
verdejo.

84

PALACIOS DE BORNOS ROSADO ESP
tempranillo.

83

PALACIOS DE BORNOS SS
verdejo.

84

BODEGA REINA DE CASTILLA

Camino de La Moya, s/n Ctra. La Seca - Serrada
47491 La Seca (Valladolid)
☎: +34 983 816 667 - Fax: +34 983 816 663
bodega@reinadecastilla.es
www.reinadecastilla.es

EL BUFÓN VERDEJO 2011 B
100% verdejo.

91 Colour: bright straw. Nose: fresh, fresh fruit, white flowers, mineral. Palate: flavourful, fruity, good acidity, balanced.

REINA DE CASTILLA SAUVIGNON BLANC 2011 B
sauvignon blanc.

91 Colour: bright straw. Nose: fresh, fresh fruit, white flowers, mineral, varietal. Palate: flavourful, fruity, good acidity, balanced.

REINA DE CASTILLA VERDEJO 2011 B
100% verdejo.

90 Colour: bright straw. Nose: fresh, white flowers, citrus fruit, fruit expression. Palate: flavourful, fruity, good acidity, balanced.

ISABELINO RUEDA 2011 B
70% verdejo, 30% viura.

87 Colour: bright yellow. Nose: ripe fruit, dried flowers, fragrant herbs. Palate: powerful, flavourful, good acidity.

EL BUFÓN VERDEJO SEMIDULCE 2011 B
100% verdejo.

87 Colour: golden. Nose: powerfull, candied fruit, fragrant herbs, dried flowers. Palate: flavourful, sweet, fresh, fruity.

VASALLO VERDEJO 2011 B
100% verdejo.

85 Colour: bright yellow. Nose: fragrant herbs, dried flowers, ripe fruit. Palate: fresh, fruity, flavourful.

ISABELINO 2011 RD
100% tempranillo.

87 Colour: rose, purple rim. Nose: powerfull, ripe fruit, red berry notes, floral. Palate: , powerful, fruity, fresh.

BODEGA VALDEHERMOSO

Pasión, 13
47001 (Valladolid)
☎: +34 651 993 680
valdehermoso@valdehermoso.com
www.valdehermoso.com

VIÑA PEREZ 2011 B
100% verdejo.

90 Colour: bright straw. Nose: white flowers, expressive, ripe fruit, varietal, balanced. Palate: flavourful, fruity, good acidity, balanced.

LAGAR DEL REY VERDEJO 2011 B
100% verdejo.

89 Colour: bright straw. Nose: fresh, fresh fruit, varietal. Palate: flavourful, fruity, good acidity, balanced.

BODEGA VIÑA VILANO S. COOP.

Ctra. de Anguix, 10
09314 Pedrosa de Duero (Burgos)
☎: +34 947 530 029 - Fax: +34 947 530 037
info@vinavilano.com
www.vinavilano.com

VIÑA VILANO VERDEJO 2011 B
100% verdejo.

89 Colour: bright yellow. Nose: ripe fruit, dried flowers, fragrant herbs, sweet spices. Palate: full, flavourful, long.

BODEGAS ABANICO

Pol. Ind Ca l'Avellanet - Susany, 6
08553 Seva (Barcelona)
☎: +34 938 125 676 - Fax: +34 938 123 213
info@exportiberia.com
www.bodegasabanico.com

FINCA REMEDIO VERDEJO 2011 B
100% verdejo.

88 Colour: bright straw. Nose: dried flowers, citrus fruit, dried herbs, varietal, fresh. Palate: powerful, flavourful, fruity, rich.

FINCA REMEDIO RUEDA 2011 B
50% viura, 50% verdejo.

86 Colour: bright straw. Nose: fresh fruit, white flowers, citrus fruit, tropical fruit. Palate: flavourful, fruity, good acidity.

BODEGAS ALTA PAVINA

Camino de Santibáñez, s/n
47328 La Parrilla (Valladolid)
☎: +34 983 681 521
bodegas@altapavina.com
www.altapavina.com

VALDRINAL DE SANTAMARÍA 2011 B

88 Colour: bright straw. Nose: ripe fruit, white flowers, fragrant herbs. Palate: powerful, flavourful, fresh, fruity.

BODEGAS BALUARTE

Calle de la Ribera 32
31592 Cintruénigo (Navarra)
☎: +34 948 811 000
info@bodegaschivite.com

BALUARTE 2011 B
verdejo.

90 Colour: bright straw. Nose: fresh, white flowers, tropical fruit. Palate: flavourful, fruity, good acidity, balanced.

BODEGAS CASTELO DE MEDINA

Ctra. CL-602, Km. 48
47465 Villaverde de Medina (Valladolid)
☎: +34 983 831 932 - Fax: +34 983 831 857
jcortega@castelodemedina.es
www.castelodemedina.es

CASTELO DE MEDINA VERDEJO VENDIMIA SELECCIONADA 2011 B
100% verdejo.

92 Colour: bright straw, greenish rim. Nose: floral, fragrant herbs, citrus fruit, ripe fruit. Palate: powerful, flavourful, fine bitter notes, balsamic.

CASTELO DE MEDINA VERDEJO 2011 B
100% verdejo.

91 Colour: bright yellow. Nose: citrus fruit, fresh fruit, fragrant herbs, floral. Palate: flavourful, fresh, fruity, elegant.

CASTELO DE MEDINA SAUVIGNON BLANC 2011 B
100% sauvignon blanc.

91 Colour: bright straw. Nose: fresh, fresh fruit, white flowers, expressive, fragrant herbs. Palate: flavourful, fruity, good acidity, balanced.

CASTELO DE LA DEHESA 2011 B
50% verdejo, 30% viura, 20% sauvignon blanc.

90 Colour: bright straw. Nose: fresh, fresh fruit, white flowers, expressive. Palate: flavourful, fruity, good acidity, balanced, easy to drink.

REAL CASTELO 2011 B
85% verdejo, 15% sauvignon blanc.

89 Colour: bright straw. Nose: fresh fruit, white flowers. Palate: flavourful, fruity, good acidity, balanced.

CASTELO ÁMBAR SEMIDULCE 2011 B
100% sauvignon blanc.

86 Colour: bright straw. Nose: fresh, fresh fruit, white flowers, varietal. Palate: flavourful, fruity, good acidity, sweetness.

CASTELO NOBLE 2009 BFB
85% verdejo, 15% sauvignon blanc.

88 Colour: bright yellow. Nose: powerfull, ripe fruit, sweet spices, creamy oak. Palate: rich, smoky afterpalate:, flavourful, good acidity.

BODEGAS COPABOCA

N-122, Km. 407
47114 Torrecilla de la Abadesa (Valladolid)
☎: +34 983 395 655 - Fax: +34 983 307 729
copaboca@copaboca.com
www.copaboca.com

COPABOCA VERTICAL 2011 B
100% verdejo.

88 Colour: bright straw. Nose: fresh, fresh fruit, white flowers, expressive. Palate: flavourful, fruity, good acidity.

GORGORITO VERDEJO 2011 B
100% verdejo.

87 Colour: bright straw. Nose: fresh, fresh fruit, white flowers. Palate: flavourful, fruity, balanced.

PERAMOR 2011 B
100% verdejo.

86 Colour: bright straw. Nose: faded flowers, grassy, ripe fruit. Palate: powerful, fruity, easy to drink.

FEROES 2011 B
100% verdejo.

82

BODEGAS DE LOS HEREDEROS DEL MARQUÉS DE RISCAL

Ctra. N-VI, km. 172,6
47490 Rueda (Valladolid)
☎: +34 983 868 029 - Fax: +34 983 868 563
marquesderiscal@marquesderiscal.com
www.marquesderiscal.com

MARQUÉS DE RISCAL LIMOUSIN 2011 B
100% verdejo.

93 Colour: bright straw. Nose: powerfull, ripe fruit, sweet spices, creamy oak. Palate: rich, smoky afterpalate:, flavourful, fresh, good acidity.

FINCA MONTICO 2011 B
100% verdejo.

93 Colour: bright yellow. Nose: dried flowers, fine lees, ripe fruit, citrus fruit, dried herbs, earthy notes. Palate: flavourful, powerful, good acidity, round.

MARQUÉS DE RISCAL RUEDA VERDEJO 2011 B
100% verdejo.

92 Colour: bright straw. Nose: fresh, fresh fruit, white flowers, expressive, fragrant herbs, mineral. Palate: flavourful, fruity, good acidity, balanced.

MARQUÉS DE RISCAL SAUVIGNON BLANC 2011 B
100% sauvignon blanc.

89 Colour: straw. Nose: candied fruit, tropical fruit, floral. Palate: fruity, fresh, light-bodied.

BODEGAS DE LOS RÍOS PRIETO

Ctra. Pesquera - Renedo, 1
47315 Pesquera de Duero (Valladolid)
☎: +34 983 880 383 - Fax: +34 983 878 032
info@bodegasdelosriosprieto.com
www.bodegasdelosriosprieto.com

PRIOS MAXIMUS VERDEJO 2011 B
verdejo.

88 Colour: straw. Nose: ripe fruit, fruit expression, tropical fruit, grassy. Palate: fine bitter notes, good acidity, balanced.

BODEGAS FÉLIX LORENZO CACHAZO

Ctra. Medina del Campo, Km. 9
47220 Pozáldez (Valladolid)
☎: +34 983 822 008 - Fax: +34 983 822 008
bodega@cachazo.com
www.cachazo.com

MANIA RUEDA VERDEJO 2011 B
100% verdejo.

91 Colour: bright straw. Nose: fresh fruit, white flowers, varietal, citrus fruit. Palate: flavourful, fruity, good acidity, balanced.

CARRASVIÑAS VERDEJO 2011 B
100% verdejo.

90 Colour: bright straw. Nose: floral, tropical fruit, fragrant herbs, medium intensity. Palate: fresh, flavourful, fruity.

CARRASVIÑAS ESPUMOSO BR
verdejo.

88 Colour: bright straw. Nose: medium intensity, fresh fruit, dried herbs, fine lees, floral. Palate: fresh, fruity, flavourful, good acidity.

GRAN CARDIEL RUEDA VERDEJO 2011 B
100% verdejo.

89 Colour: bright straw. Nose: floral, candied fruit, citrus fruit, dried herbs. Palate: fresh, fruity, easy to drink.

QUIETUS VERDEJO 2011 B
100% verdejo.

89 Colour: bright straw. Nose: fresh, fresh fruit, white flowers, expressive. Palate: flavourful, fruity, good acidity, balanced.

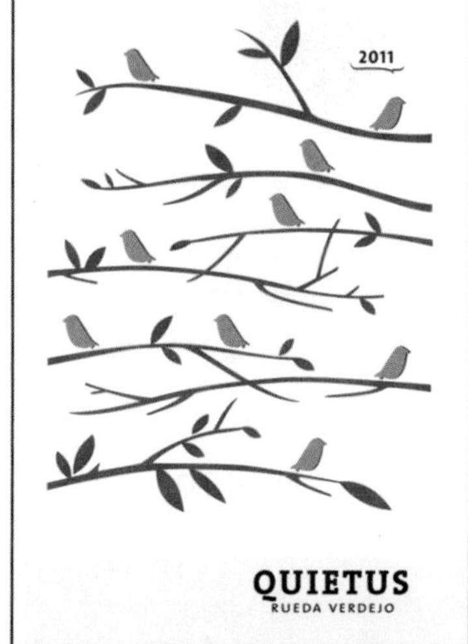

BODEGAS FÉLIX SANZ

Santísimo Cristo, 28
47490 Rueda (Valladolid)
☎: +34 983 868 044 - Fax: +34 983 868 133
pedidos@bodegasfelixsanz.es
www.bodegasfelixsanz.es

VIÑA CIMBRÓN RUEDA 2011 B
70% verdejo, 30% viura.

88 Colour: bright straw. Nose: ripe fruit, citrus fruit. Palate: flavourful, fine bitter notes, good acidity.

VIÑA CIMBRÓN SAUVIGNON 2011 B
100% sauvignon blanc.

88 Colour: bright straw. Nose: dried flowers, grassy, citrus fruit, ripe fruit. Palate: light-bodied, fresh, fruity, easy to drink.

VIÑA CIMBRÓN VERDEJO 2011 B
100% verdejo.

88 Colour: bright straw. Nose: expressive, fresh, fragrant herbs, fresh fruit. Palate: flavourful, fresh, fruity.

VIÑA CIMBRÓN 2011 RD
70% tempranillo, 30% garnacha.

88 Colour: rose, purple rim. Nose: powerfull, red berry notes, floral, varietal. Palate: , powerful, fruity, fresh.

BODEGAS FRONTAURA

Santiago, 17 - 4°
47001 (Valladolid)
☎: +34 983 360 284 - Fax: +34 983 345 546
info@bodegasfrontaura.es
www.bodegasfrontaura.es

VEGA MURILLO VERDEJO 2010 B
100% verdejo.

88 Colour: bright straw. Nose: medium intensity, candied fruit. Palate: fine bitter notes, sweetness, ripe fruit.

BODEGAS FRUTOS VILLAR

Ctra. Burgos-Portugal Km. 113,7
47270 Cigales (Valladolid)
☎: +34 983 586 868 - Fax: +34 983 580 180
bodegasfrutosvillar@bodegasfrutosvillar.com
www.bodegasfrutosvillar.com

MARÍA MOLINA VERDEJO 2011 B
verdejo.

89 Colour: bright straw. Nose: fresh, white flowers, expressive, fruit expression, citrus fruit, tropical fruit. Palate: flavourful, fruity, good acidity, balanced.

VIÑA MOREJONA 2011 B
verdejo, viura.

88 Colour: bright straw. Nose: fresh fruit, white flowers, varietal. Palate: flavourful, fruity, good acidity, balanced.

BODEGAS GARCÍA DE ARANDA

Ctra. de Soria, s/n
09400 Aranda de Duero (Burgos)
☎: +34 947 501 817 - Fax: +34 947 506 355
bodega@bodegasgarcia.com
www.bodegasgarcia.com

SEÑORÍO DE LOS BALDÍOS VERDEJO 2011 B
100% verdejo.

88 Colour: bright straw. Nose: fresh fruit, white flowers, varietal, medium intensity, grassy. Palate: flavourful, fruity, good acidity, balanced.

ORO BLANCO VERDEJO 2011 B
100% verdejo.

87 Colour: bright straw. Nose: fresh, fresh fruit, grassy, varietal. Palate: flavourful, fruity, good acidity, balanced.

ORO BLANCO 2011 B
90% verdejo, 10% viura.

86 Colour: bright straw. Nose: fresh, expressive, ripe fruit. Palate: flavourful, fruity, good acidity, balanced.

BODEGAS GARCÍAREVALO

Pza. San Juan, 4
47230 Matapozuelos (Valladolid)
☎: +34 983 832 914 - Fax: +34 983 832 986
enologo@garciarevalo.com
www.garciarevalo.com

TRES OLMOS LÍAS 2011 B
100% verdejo.

90 Colour: straw. Nose: white flowers, ripe fruit, grassy, mineral. Palate: flavourful, good acidity.

VIÑA ADAJA VERDEJO 2011 B
100% verdejo.

88 Colour: bright straw. Nose: fresh, white flowers, tropical fruit. Palate: flavourful, fruity, good acidity.

CASAMARO 2011 B
85% verdejo, 15% viura.

86 Colour: bright straw. Nose: fresh, white flowers, tropical fruit. Palate: flavourful, fruity, good acidity, balanced.

BODEGAS GARCIGRANDE

Aradillas s/n
57490 Rueda (Valladolid)
☎: +34 983 868 561 - Fax: +34 983 868 449
info@hispanobodegas.com
www.hispanobodegas.com

ANIER VENDIMIA SELECCIONADA 2011 B
100% verdejo.

92 Colour: bright straw. Nose: ripe fruit, fresh fruit, citrus fruit, grassy, mineral. Palate: flavourful, fruity, fresh.

12 LINAJES VERDEJO 2011 B
100% verdejo.

90 Colour: bright straw. Nose: fresh, fresh fruit, white flowers, expressive, tropical fruit, grassy. Palate: flavourful, fruity, good acidity, balanced.

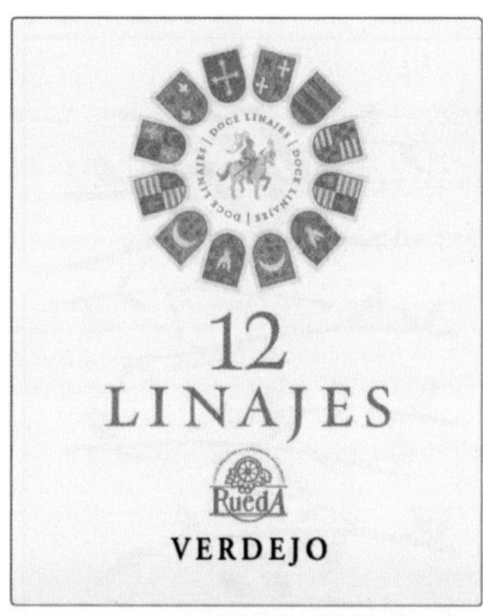

SEÑORÍO DE GARCI GRANDE VERDEJO 2011 B
100% verdejo.

91 Colour: bright straw. Nose: fresh, fresh fruit, white flowers, expressive, grassy. Palate: flavourful, fruity, good acidity, balanced.

BODEGAS IMPERIALES

Ctra. Madrid - Irun, Km. 171
09370 Gumiel de Izán (Burgos)
☎: +34 947 544 070 - Fax: +34 947 525 759
direccion@bodegasimperiales.com
www.bodegasimperiales.com

ABADÍA DE SAN QUIRCE VERDEJO 2011 B
100% verdejo.

90 Colour: bright straw. Nose: fresh, white flowers, varietal, ripe fruit. Palate: flavourful, fruity, good acidity, balanced.

BODEGAS JOSÉ PARIENTE

Ctra. Rueda - La Seca, km. 2.5
47491 La Seca (Valladolid)
☎: +34 983 816 600 - Fax: +34 983 816 620
info@josepariente.com
www.josepariente.com

JOSÉ PARIENTE SAUVIGNON BLANC 2011 B
100% sauvignon blanc.

92 Colour: bright straw. Nose: fresh, white flowers, expressive, varietal, ripe fruit. Palate: flavourful, fruity, good acidity, balanced.

APASIONADO DE JOSE PARIENTE 2011 B
100% sauvignon blanc.

90 Colour: bright straw. Nose: white flowers, candied fruit. Palate: flavourful, fine bitter notes, sweetness.

JOSÉ PARIENTE VERDEJO 2011 B
100% verdejo.

91 Colour: bright straw. Nose: fresh, white flowers, ripe fruit, citrus fruit, varietal. Palate: flavourful, fruity, good acidity, balanced.

JOSÉ PARIENTE 2010 BFB
100% verdejo.

91 Colour: bright yellow. Nose: powerfull, ripe fruit, sweet spices, creamy oak, fragrant herbs. Palate: rich, smoky afterpalate:, flavourful, fresh, good acidity.

BODEGAS MENADE

Cuatro Calles, s/n
47491 La Seca (Valladolid)
☎: +34 983 103 223 - Fax: +34 983 816 561
info@sitiosdebodega.com

MENADE VERDEJO 2011 B
100% verdejo.

90 Colour: bright straw. Nose: fresh, fresh fruit, white flowers, varietal. Palate: flavourful, fruity, good acidity, balanced.

MENADE SAUVIGNON BLANC DULCE 2011 B
100% sauvignon blanc.

90 Colour: bright straw. Nose: fresh, fresh fruit, white flowers, expressive. Palate: flavourful, fruity, good acidity, sweetness.

LA CASA DE SITIOS DE BODEGA 2011 B
verdejo.

88 Colour: bright straw. Nose: fresh, fresh fruit, white flowers, citrus fruit, tropical fruit. Palate: flavourful, fruity, good acidity, balanced.

MENADE SAUVIGNON BLANC 2011 B
100% sauvignon blanc.

87 Colour: bright straw. Nose: grassy, green pepper, fresh fruit. Palate: flavourful, fruity, fresh.

BODEGAS MOCEN

Arribas, 7-9
47490 Rueda (Valladolid)
☎: +34 983 868 533 - Fax: +34 983 868 514
info@bodegasmocen.com
www.bodegasantano.com

MOCÉN VERDEJO 2011 B
100% verdejo.

89 Colour: bright yellow. Nose: dried flowers, dried herbs, fruit expression. Palate: light-bodied, fresh, fruity.

LEGUILLÓN VERDEJO 2011 B
100% verdejo.

90 Colour: straw. Nose: ripe fruit, citrus fruit, dried herbs. Palate: powerful, good acidity, fine bitter notes.

ALTA PLATA VERDEJO 2011 B
100% verdejo.

90 Colour: bright straw. Nose: fresh fruit, white flowers, varietal. Palate: flavourful, fruity, good acidity, balanced.

BODEGAS NAIA

Camino San Martín, s/n
47491 La Seca (Valladolid)
☎: +34 628 434 933
info@bodegasnaia.com
www.bodegasnaia.com

NAIA 2011 B
100% verdejo.

93 Colour: bright straw. Nose: fresh, white flowers, varietal, ripe fruit, mineral. Palate: flavourful, fruity, good acidity, balanced.

K-NAIA 2011 B
100% verdejo.

90 Colour: bright straw. Nose: dried flowers, citrus fruit, fruit expression, fragrant herbs. Palate: fresh, fruity, light-bodied, easy to drink.

DUCADO DE ALTAN 2011 B
verdejo.

87 Colour: bright straw. Nose: fresh, fresh fruit, expressive, dried flowers. Palate: flavourful, fruity, balanced.

NAIADES 2009 BFB
100% verdejo.

94 Colour: bright straw. Nose: powerfull, varietal, ripe fruit, sweet spices, cocoa bean. Palate: flavourful, ripe fruit, spicy.

BODEGAS NIDIA

Ctra. La Seca 17
47400 Medina del Campo (Valladolid)
☎: +34 983 812 581
danieltorio@laborquo.es

NIDIA 2011 B
100% verdejo.

88 Colour: bright straw. Nose: fresh, fresh fruit, white flowers, fragrant herbs. Palate: flavourful, fruity, good acidity.

NIDIA 2008 BFB
100% verdejo.

90 Colour: bright yellow. Nose: ripe fruit, sweet spices, creamy oak, fragrant herbs. Palate: rich, flavourful, fresh, good acidity, balanced.

BODEGAS NILO

Federico García Lorca, 7
47490 Rueda (Valladolid)
☎: +34 690 068 682 - Fax: +34 983 868 366
info@bodegasnilo.com
www.bodegasnilo.com

BIANCA 2011 B
verdejo.

90 Colour: bright straw. Nose: white flowers, fruit expression, fragrant herbs, expressive. Palate: flavourful, fruity, balanced, long.

BODEGAS ORDÓÑEZ

Bartolomé Esteban Murillo, 11
29700 Vélez- Málaga (Málaga)
☎: +34 952 504 706 - Fax: +34 951 284 796
office@jorge-ordonez.es
www.grupojorgeordonez.com

NISIA 2011 B
100% verdejo.

95 Colour: bright straw. Nose: fresh, fresh fruit, white flowers, expressive, varietal, sweet spices. Palate: flavourful, fruity, good acidity, balanced.

BODEGAS PEÑAFIEL

Ctra. N-122, Km. 311
47300 Peñafiel (Valladolid)
☎: +34 983 881 622 - Fax: +34 983 881 944
bodegaspenafiel@bodegaspenafiel.com
www.bodegaspenafiel.com

ALBA MIROS 2011 B
100% verdejo.

90 Colour: bright straw. Nose: fresh, fresh fruit, white flowers. Palate: flavourful, fruity, good acidity, balanced.

BODEGAS PRADOREY

Ctra. Nacional VI, Km. 172,5
47490 Rueda (Valladolid)
☎: +34 983 444 048 - Fax: +34 983 868 564
bodega@pradorey.com
www.pradorey.com

PRADOREY SAUVIGNON BLANC 2011 B
100% sauvignon blanc.

91 Colour: bright straw. Nose: white flowers, fragrant herbs, fine lees, mineral. Palate: powerful, flavourful, complex, fruity.

PR 3 BARRICAS 2009 BFB
100% verdejo.

93 Colour: bright straw. Nose: fresh, white flowers, expressive, ripe fruit, sweet spices, creamy oak. Palate: flavourful, fruity, good acidity, balanced.

PRADOREY VERDEJO 2011 B
100% verdejo.

91 Colour: bright straw. Nose: expressive, citrus fruit, fresh fruit, fragrant herbs, mineral. Palate: good acidity, flavourful, fruity, balanced.

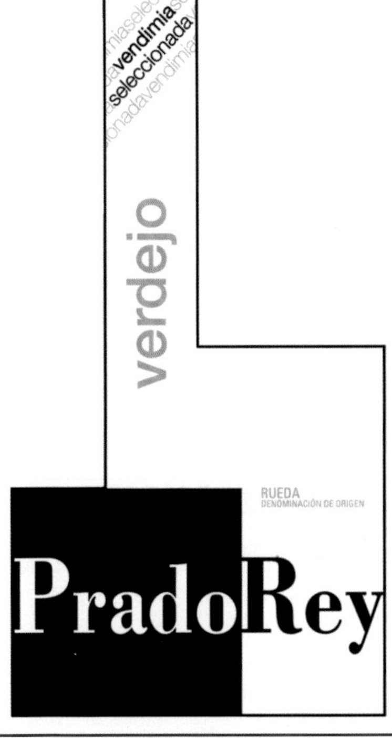

BODEGAS PROTOS

Ctra. CL 610, Medina - La Seca Km. 32,5
47491 La Seca (Valladolid)
☎: +34 983 816 608
bodega@bodegasprotos.com
www.bodegasprotos.com

PROTOS 2010 B BARRICA
100% verdejo.

92 Colour: bright golden. Nose: ripe fruit, dry nuts, powerfull, toasty, aged wood nuances, fragrant herbs. Palate: flavourful, fruity, spicy, toasty, long.

PROTOS VERDEJO 2011 B
100% verdejo.

91 Colour: bright straw. Nose: fresh fruit, white flowers, fine lees, powerfull. Palate: flavourful, fruity, good acidity, balanced.

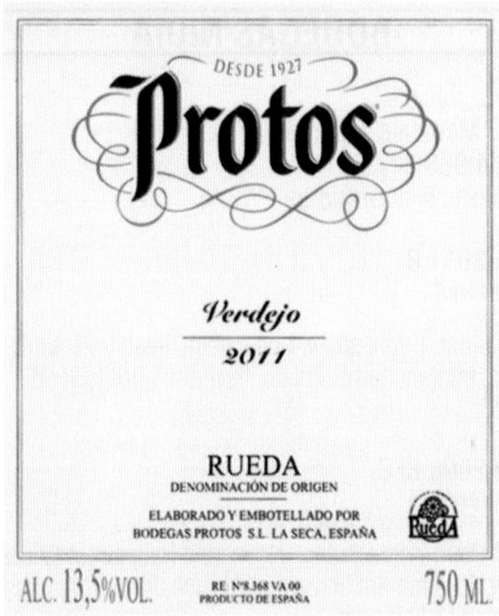

BODEGAS RUEDA PÉREZ

Boyón
47220 Pozáldez (Valladolid)
☎: +34 650 454 657 - Fax: +34 983 822 049
satruedaperez@terra.es
www.bodegasruedaperez.es

VIÑA BURÓN VERDEJO 2011 B
100% verdejo.

91 Colour: bright straw. Nose: fresh fruit, white flowers, expressive, mineral. Palate: flavourful, fruity, good acidity, balanced.

JOSÉ GALO VERDEJO SELECCIÓN 2011 B
100% verdejo.

89 Colour: bright straw. Nose: fresh, fresh fruit, white flowers, tropical fruit. Palate: flavourful, fruity, good acidity, balanced.

ZAPADORADO VERDEJO 2011 B
100% verdejo.

85 Colour: bright straw. Nose: fresh, fresh fruit, white flowers. Palate: flavourful, fruity, thin.

BODEGAS SEÑORÍO DE NAVA

Ctra. Valladolid - Soria, s/n
09318 Nava de Roa (Burgos)
☎: +34 987 209 712 - Fax: +34 947 550 003
snava@senoriodenava.es
www.senoriodenava.es

VIÑA MARIAN VERDEJO 100% 2011 B
100% verdejo.

89 Colour: bright yellow. Nose: white flowers, fresh fruit, fragrant herbs. Palate: powerful, flavourful, fruity, long.

VIÑA MARIAN VERDEJO 2011 B
100% verdejo.

87 Colour: bright straw. Nose: white flowers, ripe fruit, citrus fruit. Palate: flavourful, powerful, ripe fruit.

VAL DE LAMAS VERDEJO 100% 2011 B
100% verdejo.

86 Colour: bright straw. Nose: fresh fruit, white flowers, fragrant herbs. Palate: flavourful, fruity, good acidity, balanced.

SEÑORÍO DE NAVA VERDEJO 100% 2011 B
100% verdejo.

86 Colour: bright straw. Nose: dried flowers, grassy, ripe fruit. Palate: fresh, flavourful, correct, easy to drink.

VAL DE LAMAS RUEDA 2011 B

84

SEÑORÍO DE NAVA RUEDA 2011 B
verdejo, viura.

82

BODEGAS TAMARAL

Ctra. N-122, Km. 310,6
47300 Peñafiel (Valladolid)
☎: +34 983 878 017 - Fax: +34 983 878 089
exterior@tamaral.com
www.tamaral.com

TAMARAL VERDEJO 2011 B
100% verdejo.

88 Colour: bright straw. Nose: fresh, fresh fruit, white flowers, expressive. Palate: flavourful, fruity, good acidity,

BODEGAS TIONIO

Ctra. de Valoria, Km. 7
47315 Pesquera de Duero (Valladolid)
☎: +34 933 950 811 - Fax: +34 983 870 185
info@parxet.es
www.parxet.es

AUSTUM VERDEJO 2011 B
verdejo.

87 Colour: bright straw. Nose: fresh, fresh fruit, expressive, dried herbs, floral, citrus fruit. Palate: flavourful, fruity, good acidity.

BODEGAS VAL DE VID

Ctra. Valladolid - Medina, Km. 23,6
47231 Serrada (Valladolid)
☎: +34 983 559 914 - Fax: +34 983 559 914
esther.vega@avintec.es

VAL DE VID VERDEJO 2011 B
100% verdejo.

91 Colour: bright straw. Nose: fresh, fresh fruit, white flowers, expressive, varietal, grassy. Palate: flavourful, fruity, good acidity, balanced.

CONDESA EYLO 2011 B
100% verdejo.

90 Colour: bright straw. Nose: white flowers, citrus fruit, fruit expression, balsamic herbs, mineral. Palate: powerful, flavourful, fresh, fruity.

VAL DE VID 2011 B
70% verdejo, 30% viura.

90 Colour: bright yellow. Nose: white flowers, fragrant herbs, fresh fruit. Palate: powerful, flavourful, long, good acidity, balanced.

EYLO RUEDA 2011 B
70% verdejo, 30% viura.

89 Colour: bright straw. Nose: fresh, fresh fruit, white flowers, expressive, fragrant herbs. Palate: flavourful, fruity, good acidity.

BODEGAS VALPINCIA

Ctra. de Melida, 3,5
47300 Peñafiel (Valladolid)
☎: +34 983 878 007 - Fax: +34 983 880 620
comunicacion@bodegasvalpincia.com
www.bodegasvalpincia.com

VALPINCIA VERDEJO 2011 B
100% verdejo.

88 Colour: bright straw. Nose: candied fruit. Palate: balanced, good acidity.

VALPINCIA 2011 B
50% verdejo, 50% viura.

87 Colour: bright straw. Nose: characterful, medium intensity, expressive. Palate: flavourful, fruity, ripe fruit.

BODEGAS VERACRUZ

Juan A. Carmona, 1
47500 Nava del Rey (Valladolid)
☎: +34 670 581 157
j.benito@bodegasveracruz.com
www.bodegasveracruz.com

ERMITA VERACRUZ VERDEJO 2011 B
verdejo.

92 Colour: bright straw. Nose: fresh, fresh fruit, white flowers, varietal, mineral, dried herbs. Palate: flavourful, fruity, good acidity, balanced.

BODEGAS VERDEAL

Nueva, 8
40200 Cuéllar (Segovia)
☎: +34 921 140 125 - Fax: +34 921 142 421
info@bodegasverdeal.com
www.bodegasverdeal.com

VERDEAL 2011 B
100% verdejo.

90 Colour: bright straw. Nose: dried herbs, ripe fruit, citrus fruit. Palate: flavourful, fruity, fresh, easy to drink, varietal.

AYRE 2011 B
100% verdejo.

87 Colour: bright straw. Nose: fresh, fresh fruit, white flowers, dried herbs. Palate: flavourful, fruity, good acidity.

BODEGAS VICENTE GANDÍA

Ctra. Cheste a Godelleta, s/n
46370 Chiva (Valencia)
☎: +34 962 524 242 - Fax: +34 962 524 243
vuboldi@vicentegandia.com
www.vicentegandia.es

NEBLA VERDEJO 2011 B
100% verdejo.

90 Colour: bright straw. Nose: fresh, fresh fruit, white flowers, varietal. Palate: flavourful, fruity, good acidity, balanced.

BODEGAS VICENTE SANZ

Las Flores, 5 - Bajo
47240 Valdestillas (Valladolid)
☎: +34 983 551 197 - Fax: +34 983 551 197
bodega@bodegasvicentesanz.com
www.bodegasvicentesanz.com

VICARAL RUEDA VERDEJO 2011 B
100% verdejo.

85 Colour: bright straw. Nose: faded flowers, ripe fruit, grassy. Palate: powerful, flavourful, fruity.

BODEGAS VIORE

Camino de la Moy, s/n
47491 La Seca (Valladolid)
☎: +34 941 454 050 - Fax: +34 941 454 529
bodega@bodegasriojanas.com
www.bodegasriojanas.com

VIORE VERDEJO 2011 B
100% verdejo.

90 Colour: bright straw. Nose: fresh fruit, white flowers, neat, powerfull, varietal. Palate: flavourful, fruity, balanced, fine bitter notes, correct.

VIORE RUEDA 2011 B
verdejo, viura.

88 Colour: bright straw. Nose: candied fruit, citrus fruit, tropical fruit. Palate: fruity, flavourful.

BODEGAS Y VIÑEDOS ÁNGEL LORENZO CACHAZO

Estación, 53
47220 Pozaldez (Valladolid)
☎: +34 983 822 481 - Fax: +34 983 822 012
bodegamartivilli@jet.es
www.martivilli.com

MARTIVILLÍ VERDEJO 2011 B

91 Colour: bright straw. Nose: complex, scrubland, white flowers, ripe fruit. Palate: flavourful, fruity, fresh, fine bitter notes.

MARTIVILLÍ 2010 BFB

89 Colour: bright yellow. Nose: powerfull, ripe fruit, sweet spices, creamy oak, fragrant herbs. Palate: rich, flavourful, fresh.

MARTIVILLÍ SAUVIGNON BLANC 2011 B

88 Colour: bright straw. Nose: fresh fruit, white flowers, varietal. Palate: flavourful, fruity, good acidity, balanced.

LORENZO CACHAZO 2011 B

88 Colour: straw. Nose: white flowers, fresh fruit, ripe fruit. Palate: balanced, good acidity.

BODEGAS Y VIÑEDOS MONTEABELLÓN

Calvario, s/n
09318 Nava de Roa (Burgos)
☎: +34 947 550 000 - Fax: +34 947 550 219
info@monteabellon.com
www.monteabellon.com

MONTEABELLÓN VERDEJO 2011 B
100% verdejo.

88 Colour: bright straw. Nose: fresh fruit, white flowers, varietal, powerfull, neat, characterful. Palate: flavourful, fruity.

BODEGAS Y VIÑEDOS NEO

Ctra. N-122, Km. 274,5
09391 Castrillo de la Vega (Burgos)
☎: +34 947 514 393 - Fax: +34 947 515 445
info@bodegasconde.com
www.bodegasneo.com

PRIMER MOTIVO VERDEJO 2011 B
100% verdejo.

90 Colour: bright straw. Nose: fragrant herbs, dried flowers, fruit expression, varietal. Palate: fine bitter notes, powerful, flavourful, fruity.

BODEGAS Y VIÑEDOS SHAYA

Ctra. Aldeanueva del Codonal s/n
40642 Aldeanueva del Codonal (Segovia)
☎: +34 968 435 022
info@orowines.com
www.orowines.com

SHAYA 2011 B
100% verdejo.

92 Colour: bright straw. Nose: fresh, fresh fruit, white flowers, varietal, ripe fruit, mineral. Palate: flavourful, fruity, good acidity, balanced.

ARINDO 2011 B
100% verdejo.

88 Colour: bright straw. Nose: fresh, fresh fruit, white flowers, tropical fruit. Palate: flavourful, balanced, sweetness.

SHAYA HABIS 2010 BFB
100% verdejo.

94 Colour: bright yellow. Nose: powerfull, ripe fruit, sweet spices, creamy oak, fragrant herbs. Palate: rich, smoky afterpalate:, flavourful, fresh.

BODEGAS Y VIÑEDOS TÁBULA

Ctra. de Valbuena, km. 2
47359 Olivares de Duero (Valladolid)
☎: +34 608 219 019 - Fax: +34 983 107 300
armando@bodegastabula.es
www.bodegastabula.es

DAMANA VERDEJO 2011 B
100% verdejo.

89 Colour: bright straw. Nose: ripe fruit, fragrant herbs, citrus fruit, dried flowers. Palate: light-bodied, fruity, flavourful, easy to drink.

BUIL & GINÉ

Ctra. de Gratallops - Vilella Baixa, Km. 11,5
43737 Gratallops (Tarragona)
☎: +34 977 839 810 - Fax: +34 977 839 811
info@builgine.com
www.builgine.com

NOSIS 2010 B
verdejo.

87 Colour: bright yellow. Nose: ripe fruit, fragrant herbs, dried flowers. Palate: flavourful, fresh, fruity.

CAMPOS DE SUEÑOS

Avda. Diagonal, 590, 5º 1ª
08021 (Barcelona)
☎: +34 660 445 464
info@vinergia.com
www.vinergia.com

CAMPOS DE SUEÑOS 2011 B
100% verdejo.

90 Colour: bright straw. Nose: fresh fruit, white flowers, neat, varietal, complex, grassy. Palate: flavourful, fruity, good acidity, balanced.

COMENGE BODEGAS Y VIÑEDOS

Camino del Castillo, s/n
47316 Curiel de Duero (Valladolid)
☎: +34 983 880 363 - Fax: +34 983 880 717
admin@comenge.com
www.comenge.com

COMENGE 2011 B
100% verdejo.

90 Colour: bright straw. Nose: fresh, fresh fruit, white flowers. Palate: flavourful, fruity, good acidity, balanced.

COMERCIAL GRUPO FREIXENET

Joan Sala, 2
08770 Sant Sadurní D'Anoia (Barcelona)
☎: +34 938 917 000 - Fax: +34 938 183 095
freixenet@freixenet.es
www.freixenet.es

VALDUBON VERDEJO 2011 BFB
100% verdejo.

90 Colour: bright yellow. Nose: powerfull, ripe fruit, sweet spices, creamy oak, fragrant herbs. Palate: rich, flavourful, fresh, fruity, spicy.

FRAY GERMÁN VERDEJO 2011 B
100% verdejo.

89 Colour: bright straw. Nose: fresh, fresh fruit, white flowers, expressive. Palate: flavourful, fruity, good acidity.

ETCÉTERA 2011 B
50% verdejo, 50% viura.

87 Colour: bright straw. Nose: floral, ripe fruit, tropical fruit, dried herbs. Palate: light-bodied, fresh, fruity, easy to drink.

FRAY GERMÁN SAUVIGNON BLANC 2011 B
100% sauvignon blanc.

85 Colour: bright straw. Nose: citrus fruit, tropical fruit, grassy. Palate: fresh, fruity, flavourful.

COMPAÑÍA DE VINOS MIGUEL MARTÍN

Ctra. Burgos - Portugal, Km. 101
47290 Cubillas de Santa María (Valladolid)
☎: +34 983 250 319 - Fax: +34 983 250 329
exportacion@ciadevinos.com
www.ciadevinos.com

CASA CASTILLA 2011 B
100% verdejo.

88 Colour: bright straw. Nose: floral, citrus fruit, fragrant herbs. Palate: correct, light-bodied, fresh, fruity.

DÒMINE 2011 B
95% verdejo, 5% sauvignon blanc.

86 Colour: bright straw. Nose: warm, ripe fruit, faded flowers, dried herbs. Palate: flavourful, fruity, easy to drink.

COMPAÑÍA DE VINOS TELMO RODRÍGUEZ

El Monte
01308 Lanciego (Álava)
☎: +34 945 628 315 - Fax: +34 945 628 314
contact@telmorodriguez.com
www.telmorodriguez.com

BASA 2011 B
100% verdejo.

88 Colour: bright straw. Nose: fresh, fresh fruit, white flowers, expressive, varietal, fragrant herbs. Palate: flavourful, fruity, good acidity, balanced.

EL TRANSISTOR 2010 B
100% verdejo.

94 Colour: bright straw. Nose: ripe fruit, grassy, expressive, mineral. Palate: flavourful, powerful, fruity, fine bitter notes, good acidity, round.

CUEVAS DE CASTILLA

Ctra. Madrid - Coruña, Km. 170,6
47490 Rueda (Valladolid)
☎: +34 983 686 116 - Fax: +34 983 868 432
info@taninia.com
www.taninia.com

ESPADAÑA VERDEJO 2011 B
verdejo.

87 Colour: bright straw. Nose: fresh, fresh fruit, white flowers. Palate: flavourful, fruity, good acidity.

HUERTA DEL REY 2011 RD
tempranillo.

88 Colour: rose, purple rim. Nose: powerfull, ripe fruit, red berry notes, floral, expressive. Palate: fleshy, powerful, fruity, fresh.

SEÑORÍO DE ILLESCAS 2004 TC
tempranillo.

84

CVNE - COMPAÑÍA VINÍCOLA DEL NORTE DE ESPAÑA

Barrio de la Estación, s/n
26200 Haro (La Rioja)
☎: +34 941 304 800 - Fax: +34 941 304 815
marketing@cvne.com
www.cvne.com

MONOPOLE S. XXI 2011 B
100% verdejo.

87 Colour: bright straw. Nose: fresh, fresh fruit, white flowers, tropical fruit. Palate: flavourful, fruity, good acidity.

DE ALBERTO

Ctra. de Valdestillas, 2
47239 Serrada (Valladolid)
☎: +34 983 559 107 - Fax: +34 983 559 084
info@dealberto.com
www.dealberto.com

DE ALBERTO VERDEJO 2011 B
verdejo.

91 Colour: bright straw. Nose: fresh, fresh fruit, white flowers, expressive. Palate: flavourful, fruity, good acidity, balanced.

GUTI 2011 B
verdejo.

90 Colour: bright straw. Nose: fresh fruit, white flowers, varietal. Palate: flavourful, fruity, good acidity, balanced.

MONASTERIO DE PALAZUELOS 2011 B
70% verdejo, 30% viura.

89 Colour: bright straw. Nose: fresh, white flowers, balanced, citrus fruit. Palate: flavourful, fruity, good acidity, balanced.

MONASTERIO DE PALAZUELOS VERDEJO 2011 B
verdejo.

87 Colour: bright straw. Nose: grassy, dried flowers, citrus fruit, ripe fruit. Palate: round, flavourful, fruity.

DIEZ SIGLOS DE VERDEJO

Ctra. Valladolid Km. 24,5
47231 Serrada (Valladolid)
☎: +34 983 559 910 - Fax: +34 983 559 020
comercial1@diezsiglos.es
www.diezsiglos.es

DIEZ SIGLOS 2011 B
100% verdejo.

90 Colour: bright straw. Nose: fresh, fresh fruit, white flowers, expressive. Palate: flavourful, fruity, good acidity, balanced.

CANTO REAL 2011 B
100% verdejo.

89 Colour: straw. Nose: powerfull, varietal, ripe fruit, grassy. Palate: flavourful, powerful, fine bitter notes, good acidity.

ESTANCIA PIEDRA

Ctra. Toro a Salamanca, km. 5

49800 Toro (Zamora)
☎: +34 980 693 900 - Fax: +34 980 693 901
info@estanciapiedra.com
www.estanciapiedra.com

PIEDRA VERDEJO 2011 B
100% verdejo.

90 Colour: bright yellow. Nose: fragrant herbs, citrus fruit, ripe fruit, dried flowers, grassy. Palate: powerful, flavourful, fresh, fruity, balanced.

FINCA CASERÍO DE DUEÑAS

Ctra. Cl. 602, km. 50,2
47465 Villaverde de Medina (Valladolid)
☎: +34 915 006 000 - Fax: +34 915 006 006
pzumft@habarcelo.es
www.habarcelo.es

VIÑA MAYOR 2010 BFB
100% verdejo.

90 Colour: bright straw. Nose: fresh, fresh fruit, white flowers, lactic notes, sweet spices. Palate: flavourful, fruity, good acidity, balanced.

FINCA LAS CARABALLAS

Camino Velascálvaro, 2
47400 Medina del Campo (Valladolid)
☎: +34 689 309 515
info@lascaraballas.com
www.lascaraballas.com

FINCA LAS CARABALLAS 2011 B
100% verdejo.

91 Colour: bright straw. Nose: fresh fruit, white flowers, fragrant herbs, mineral. Palate: flavourful, fruity, good acidity, rich.

FINCA LAS CARABALLAS SEMIDULCE 2011 B
50% verdejo, 50% sauvignon blanc.

90 Colour: golden. Nose: powerfull, floral, candied fruit, fragrant herbs. Palate: flavourful, sweet, fresh, fruity, good acidity.

FINCA MONTEPEDROSO

Término La Morejona, s/n
47490 Rueda (Valladolid)
☎: +34 983 868 977 - Fax: +34 983 868 055
info@bujanda.com
www.familiamartinezbujanda.com

FINCA MONTEPEDROSO VERDEJO 2011 B
verdejo.

91 Colour: bright straw. Nose: fresh, fresh fruit, white flowers, varietal, tropical fruit. Palate: flavourful, fruity, good acidity, balanced.

FRANCISCO JAVIER SANZ CANTALAPIEDRA

San Judas, 2
47491 La Seca (Valladolid)
☎: +34 983 816 669 - Fax: +34 983 816 639
nacional@ordentercera.com
www.ordentercera.com

ORDEN TERCERA VERDEJO 2011 B JOVEN
100% verdejo.

90 Colour: bright straw. Nose: fresh, fresh fruit, white flowers, expressive. Palate: flavourful, fruity, good acidity, balanced.

GRUPO ALGAR

Carpinteros, 13
28670 Villaviciosa de Odón (Madrid)
☎: +34 916 169 122 - Fax: +34 916 166 724
vcotelo@grupoalgar.com
www.grupoalgar.com

ABILIA VERDEJO VIURA 2011 B
verdejo, viura.

86 Colour: bright straw. Nose: fresh, white flowers, expressive, ripe fruit. Palate: fruity, good acidity, balanced, sweetness.

ABILIA VERDEJO 2011 B
100% verdejo.

85 Colour: bright straw. Nose: fresh, white flowers, varietal, ripe fruit. Palate: flavourful, fruity, correct.

GRUPO YLLERA

Autovía A-6, Km. 173, 5
47490 Rueda (Valladolid)
☎: +34 983 868 097 - Fax: +34 983 868 177
grupoyllera@grupoyllera.com
www.grupoyllera.com

YLLERA VERDEJO VENDIMIA NOCTURNA 2011 B
verdejo.

90 Colour: bright straw. Nose: dried flowers, varietal, wild herbs, earthy notes, expressive. Palate: balsamic, correct, flavourful, light-bodied, fruity.

TIERRA BUENA 2011 B
100% verdejo.

89 Colour: bright straw. Nose: fragrant herbs, white flowers, candied fruit, medium intensity. Palate: good acidity, fresh, fruity, flavourful.

VIÑA CANTOSÁN VARIETAL VERDEJO 2011 B
100% verdejo.

91 Colour: bright straw. Nose: varietal, floral, fragrant herbs, citrus fruit, fresh fruit, expressive. Palate: rich, flavourful, balsamic, long, balanced.

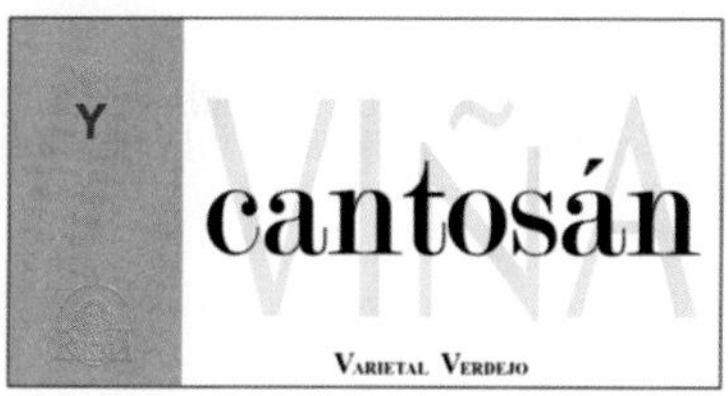

YLLERA SAUVIGNON BLANC VENDIMIA NOCTURNA 2011 B
sauvignon blanc.

89 Colour: bright straw. Nose: fresh fruit, dried flowers, fragrant herbs. Palate: flavourful, fruity, good acidity.

BRACAMONTE VERDEJO SUPERIOR 2011 B
100% verdejo.

88 Colour: bright straw. Nose: candied fruit, dried herbs, floral. Palate: fresh, fruity, light-bodied, easy to drink.

BRACAMONTE VERDEJO 2011 B
100% verdejo.

87 Colour: bright straw. Nose: fresh, fresh fruit, white flowers. Palate: fruity, good acidity, fresh, easy to drink.

CANTOSÁN BR
100% verdejo.

85 Colour: bright yellow. Nose: citrus fruit, dried flowers, fragrant herbs, fine lees. Palate: fresh, fruity, light-bodied, easy to drink.

CANTOSÁN BN
100% verdejo.

82

CANTOSÁN RESERVA ESPECIAL ESP
100% verdejo.

85 Colour: bright golden. Nose: dried flowers, lees reduction notes, ripe fruit, balsamic herbs, dry nuts. Palate: fine bitter notes, powerful, flavourful.

CANTOSÁN SS
100% verdejo.

82

HACIENDAS DE ESPAÑA

Avenida Nava del Rey, 8
47490 Rueda (Valladolid)
☎: +34 914 365 924
comunicacion@arcoinvest-group.com
www.haciendas-espana.com

HACIENDA ZORITA VEGA DE LA REINA VERDEJO (MARQUÉS DE LA CONCORDIA FAMILY OF WINES) 2011 B
100% verdejo.

91 Colour: bright straw. Nose: dried flowers, wild herbs, citrus fruit, fruit expression. Palate: powerful, flavourful, complex, long, balanced.

HACIENDA ZORITA VEGA DE LA REINA SAUVIGNON BLANC (MARQUÉS DE LA CONCORDIA FAMILY OF WINES) 2011 B
100% sauvignon blanc.

88 Colour: bright straw. Nose: dried flowers, dried herbs, herbaceous, powerfull, expressive. Palate: light-bodied, fresh, fruity, balanced.

JAVIER SANZ VITICULTOR

San Judas, 2
47491 La Seca (Valladolid)
☎: +34 983 816 669 - Fax: +34 983 816 639
nacional@jsviticultor.com
www.jsviticultor.com

VILLA NARCISA RUEDA VERDEJO 2011 B
verdejo.

90 Colour: bright straw. Nose: fresh, fresh fruit, white flowers, expressive, fragrant herbs. Palate: flavourful, fruity, good acidity, balanced.

VILLA NARCISA SAUVIGNON BLANC 2011 B
sauvignon blanc.

89 Colour: bright straw. Nose: dried flowers, grassy, fresh fruit. Palate: light-bodied, fresh, fruity, easy to drink.

LA COLECCIÓN DE VINOS

Domingo Martínez, 6- Bajo
47007 (Valladolid)
☎: +34 983 271 595 - Fax: +34 983 271 608
info@lacolecciondevinos.com
www.lacolecciondevinos.com

OTER DE CILLAS VERDEJO 2011 B
100% verdejo.

88 Colour: bright straw. Nose: fresh fruit, white flowers, neat, varietal. Palate: flavourful, fruity, good acidity, balanced.

LEGARIS

Ctra. Peñafiel - Encinas de Esgueva, km. 4,3
47316 Curiel de Duero (Valladolid)
☎: +34 983 878 088 - Fax: +34 983 881 034
info@legaris.com
www.grupocodorniu.com

LEGARIS VERDEJO 2011 B
100% verdejo.

89 Colour: bright straw. Nose: candied fruit, citrus fruit, grassy, white flowers. Palate: flavourful, fruity, fresh.

LIBERALIA ENOLÓGICA

Camino del Palo, s/n
49800 Toro (Zamora)
☎: +34 980 692 571 - Fax: +34 980 692 571
liberalia@liberalia.es
www.liberalia.es

ENEBRAL 2011 B
100% verdejo.

91 Colour: bright straw. Nose: faded flowers, fragrant herbs, citrus fruit, expressive. Palate: powerful, flavourful, good acidity, correct.

LOESS

El Monte, 7- Bajo
47195 Arroyo de la Encomienda (Valladolid)
☎: +34 983 664 898 - Fax: +34 983 406 579
loess@loess.es
www.loess.es

LOESS COLLECTION 2010 BFB
100% verdejo.

91 Colour: bright straw. Nose: fresh, white flowers, ripe fruit, sweet spices. Palate: flavourful, fruity, good acidity, balanced.

MIRAVINOS

Plaza de Matute 12, - 3º
28012 (Madrid)
☎: +34 609 119 248
info@miravinos.es
www.miravinos.es

NAIPES 2011 B
verdejo.

92 Colour: bright straw. Nose: fresh fruit, expressive, floral, varietal, mineral. Palate: flavourful, fruity, good acidity, balanced.

INFRAGANTI 2011 B
verdejo.

89 Colour: bright straw. Nose: expressive, varietal, fresh fruit, fruit expression. Palate: flavourful, fruity, good acidity, fine bitter notes.

MONTEBACO

Finca Montealto
47359 Valbuena de Duero (Valladolid)
☎: +34 983 485 128 - Fax: +34 983 485 033
montebaco@bodegasmontebaco.com
www.bodegasmontebaco.com

MONTEBACO VERDEJO SOBRE LÍAS 2011 B
verdejo.

90 Colour: bright straw. Nose: fresh fruit, white flowers, expressive, mineral, grassy, varietal. Palate: flavourful, fruity, balanced, fine bitter notes.

NUEVOS VINOS CB

Alfafara, 12
03803 Alcoy (Alicante)
☎: +34 965 549 172 - Fax: +34 965 549 173
josecanto@nuevosvinos.es
www.nuevosvinos.es

PERLA MARIS VERDEJO 2011 B
100% verdejo.

89 Colour: bright straw. Nose: fresh, white flowers, fragrant herbs, fruit expression. Palate: flavourful, fruity, good acidity.

OLID INTERNACIONAL

Juan García Hortelano, 21-7ºC
47014 (Valladolid)
☎: +34 983 132 690
olidinternacional@gmail.com
www.olidinternacional.com

983 2011 B
100% verdejo.

90 Colour: bright straw. Nose: fresh fruit, white flowers, citrus fruit, dried herbs. Palate: flavourful, fruity, good acidity, balanced.

OSBORNE RIBERA DEL DUERO

Fernán Caballero, 7
11500 El Puerto de Santa María (Cádiz)
☎: +34 925 860 990 - Fax: +34 925 860 905
carolina.cerrato@osborne.es
www.osborne.es

SEÑORIO DEL CID VERDEJO 2011 B
100% verdejo.

89 Colour: bright straw. Nose: fresh, fresh fruit, white flowers, expressive. Palate: flavourful, fruity, good acidity, balanced.

OSSIAN VIDES Y VINOS

San Marcos, 5
40447 Nieva (Segovia)
☎: +34 696 159 121 - Fax: +34 921 594 207
ossian@ossian.es
www.ossian.es

QUINTALUNA 2011 B
verdejo.

89 Colour: bright straw. Nose: ripe fruit, wild herbs, white flowers, medium intensity. Palate: flavourful, fresh, fruity.

PAGO TRASLAGARES

Autovía Noroeste km 166,4 Apdo. 507
47490 Rueda (Valladolid)
☎: +34 983 667 023
export@traslagares.com
www.traslagares.com

TRASLAGARES SAUVIGNON BLANC 2011 B
100% sauvignon blanc.

89 Colour: bright straw. Nose: fresh, fresh fruit, white flowers, expressive. Palate: flavourful, fruity, good acidity, balanced.

TRASLAGARES VERDEJO 2011 B
100% verdejo.

90 Colour: bright straw. Nose: fresh fruit, white flowers, ripe fruit. Palate: flavourful, fruity, good acidity, balanced.

PAGOS DEL REY RUEDA

Avda. Morejona, 6
47490 Rueda (Valladolid)
☎: +34 983 868 182 - Fax: +34 983 868 182
rueda@pagosdelrey.com
www.pagosdelrey.com

ANALIVIA SAUVIGNON BLANC 2011 B
100% sauvignon blanc.

91 Colour: bright straw. Nose: fresh, fresh fruit, white flowers, herbaceous. Palate: flavourful, fruity, balanced, good acidity.

BLUME SAUVIGNON BLANC 2011 B
100% sauvignon blanc.

89 Colour: bright straw. Nose: fresh, fresh fruit, white flowers, grassy. Palate: flavourful, fruity, good acidity.

BLUME RUEDA 2011 B
50% verdejo, 50% sauvignon blanc.

88 Colour: bright yellow. Nose: candied fruit, floral, dried herbs. Palate: light-bodied, fresh, fruity, flavourful.

BLUME VERDEJO 2011 B
100% verdejo.

88 Colour: bright straw. Nose: white flowers, expressive, floral, faded flowers, ripe fruit. Palate: flavourful, fruity, good acidity, balanced.

ANALIVIA VERDEJO 2011 B
100% verdejo.

87 Colour: bright straw. Nose: powerfull, candied fruit, citrus fruit. Palate: ripe fruit, fine bitter notes.

ANALIVIA RUEDA 2011 B
50% verdejo, 50% sauvignon blanc.

87 Colour: bright straw. Nose: dried herbs, candied fruit, citrus fruit. Palate: fruity, fresh.

PREDIO DE VASCARLÓN

Ctra. Rueda, s/n
47491 La Seca (Valladolid)
☎: +34 983 816 325 - Fax: +34 983 816 326
vascarlon@prediodevascarlon.com
www.prediodevascarlon.com

ATELIER VERDEJO 2011 B
100% verdejo.

90 Colour: bright straw. Nose: fresh, white flowers, varietal, ripe fruit. Palate: flavourful, fruity, good acidity, balanced, fine bitter notes.

TARDEVIENES 2011 B
50% verdejo, 50% viura.

88 Colour: bright straw. Nose: citrus fruit, fresh fruit, fragrant herbs. Palate: fresh, fruity, light-bodied, easy to drink.

RED BOTTLE INTERNATIONAL

Rosales, 6
09400 Aranda de Duero (Burgos)
☎: +34 947 515 884 - Fax: +34 947 515 886
rbi@redbottleint.com

PLUMA BLANCA 2011 B
100% verdejo.

89 Colour: bright straw. Nose: fresh, white flowers, varietal, ripe fruit, citrus fruit. Palate: flavourful, fruity, good acidity, balanced.

RODRÍGUEZ SANZO

Manuel Azaña, 9
47014 (Valladolid)
☎: +34 983 150 150 - Fax: +34 983 150 151
comunicacion@valsanzo.com
www.rodriguezsanzo.com

VIÑA SANZO VERDEJO 2011 B
100% verdejo.

91 Colour: bright straw. Nose: fresh fruit, white flowers, expressive. Palate: flavourful, fruity, good acidity, balanced.

VIÑA SANZO SOBRE LÍAS 2010 B
100% verdejo.

93 Colour: bright yellow. Nose: powerfull, sweet spices, fragrant herbs, ripe fruit, citrus fruit. Palate: rich, smoky afterpalate:, flavourful, fresh, good acidity.

TERNA BODEGAS

Cuatro Calles, s/n
47491 La Seca (Valladolid)
☎: +34 983 103 223 - Fax: +34 983 816 561
info@sitiosdebodega.com
www.sitiosdebodega.com

V3 VIÑAS VIEJAS VERDEJO 2010 BFB
100% verdejo.

94 Colour: bright straw. Nose: mineral, ripe fruit, candied fruit, sweet spices. Palate: flavourful, powerful, spicy, ripe fruit.

TERROIR 34

Castellote 26
Aranda de Duero (Burgos)
☎: +34 606 941 434
info@terroir34.com
www.terroir34.com

TERROIR 34 "SEDUCTION FROM COOL STONES" 2011 B
100% verdejo.

91 Colour: bright straw. Nose: fresh, fresh fruit, white flowers, varietal, mineral. Palate: flavourful, fruity, good acidity, balanced.

TOMÁS POSTIGO

Estación, 12
47300 Peñafiel (Valladolid)
☎: +34 983 873 019 - Fax: +34 983 880 258
administracion@tomaspostigo.es

TOMÁS POSTIGO 2010 BFB
verdejo.

91 Colour: bright yellow. Nose: powerfull, ripe fruit, fragrant herbs, spicy, cocoa bean. Palate: rich, smoky afterpalate:, flavourful, fresh, good acidity.

UNZU PROPIEDAD

Avda. de la Poveda, 16
01306 Lapuebla (Álava)
☎: +34 948 812 297
info@unzupropiedad.com
www.unzupropiedad.com

LABORES DE UNZU VERDEJO 2011 B
100% verdejo.

91 Colour: bright straw. Nose: fresh, fresh fruit, expressive, varietal. Palate: flavourful, fruity, good acidity, balanced.

UVAS FELICES

Agullers, 7
08003 Barcelona (Barcelona)
☎: +34 902 327 777
www.vilaviniteca.es

EL PERRO VERDE 2011 B
verdejo.

89 Colour: bright straw. Nose: grassy, candied fruit, ripe fruit. Palate: flavourful, fine bitter notes, good acidity.

FENOMENAL 2011 B
verdejo, viura.

88 Colour: bright yellow. Nose: floral, tropical fruit, fragrant herbs, ripe fruit. Palate: light-bodied, fresh, fruity, flavourful.

VALTRAVIESO

Finca La Revilla, s/n
47316 Piñel de Arriba (Valladolid)
☎: +34 983 484 030 - Fax: +34 983 484 037
valtravieso@valtravieso.com
www.valtravieso.com

DOMINIO D NOGARA 2011 B
100% verdejo.

90 Colour: bright yellow. Nose: white flowers, fruit expression, wild herbs, fragrant herbs. Palate: rich, powerful, flavourful.

VETUS

Ctra. Toro a Salamanca, Km. 9,5
49800 Toro (Zamora)
☎: +34 945 609 086 - Fax: +34 980 056 012
vetus@bodegasvetus.com
www.bodegasvetus.com

FLOR DE VETUS VERDEJO 2011 B
100% verdejo.

89 Colour: bright straw. Nose: white flowers, neat, ripe fruit, citrus fruit. Palate: flavourful, fruity, good acidity, balanced.

VINOS JOC - JORDI OLIVER CONTI

Mas Marti
17467 Sant Mori (Girona)
☎: +34 607 222 002
info@vinojoc.com
www.vinojoc.com

JOC RUEDA 2011 B
100% verdejo.

91 Colour: bright straw. Nose: floral, fragrant herbs, fruit expression, expressive, varietal. Palate: powerful, flavourful, fruity, balanced.

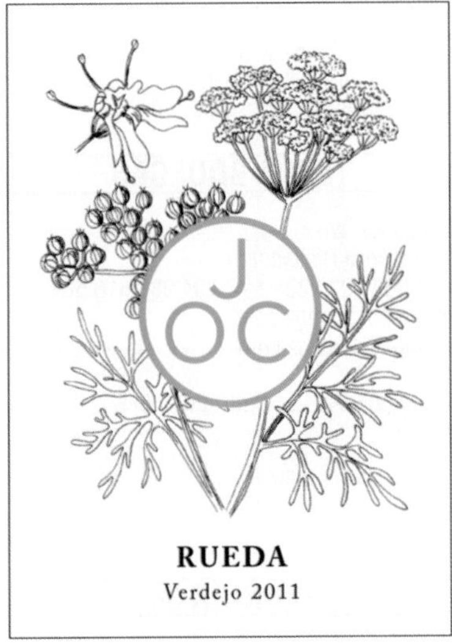

VINOS SANZ

Ctra. Madrid - La Coruña, Km. 170,5
47490 Rueda (Valladolid)
☎: +34 983 868 100 - Fax: +34 983 868 117
vinossanz@vinossanz.com
www.vinossanz.com

SANZ CLÁSICO 2011 B
70% verdejo, 30% viura.

90 Colour: bright straw. Nose: expressive, varietal, ripe fruit, dried herbs. Palate: flavourful, fruity, fresh.

SANZ SAUVIGNON BLANC 2011 B
100% sauvignon blanc.

90 Colour: bright straw. Nose: fresh, white flowers, varietal, ripe fruit, grassy. Palate: flavourful, fruity, good acidity.

FINCA LA COLINA VERDEJO CIEN X CIEN 2011 B
100% verdejo.

93 Colour: bright straw. Nose: fresh fruit, white flowers, mineral, grassy. Palate: flavourful, fruity, good acidity, balanced.

FINCA LA COLINA SAUVIGNON BLANC 2011 B
100% sauvignon blanc.

93 Colour: bright straw. Nose: ripe fruit, citrus fruit, white flowers, grassy. Palate: flavourful, good acidity, fine bitter notes.

SANZ VERDEJO 2011 B
100% verdejo.

91 Colour: bright straw. Nose: fresh, fresh fruit, white flowers, dried herbs, fine lees. Palate: flavourful, fruity, good acidity, balanced.

VINOS TERRIBLES

Paseo Marques de Zafra, 35
28028 (Madrid)
☎: +34 910 005 834
flequi@ziries.es

TERRIBLE 2011 B
100% verdejo.

88 Colour: bright yellow. Nose: citrus fruit, ripe fruit, floral, dried herbs. Palate: rich, fruity, powerful, flavourful, long.

TERRIBLE 2010 T BARRICA
100% tinto fino.

89 Colour: cherry, garnet rim. Nose: ripe fruit, balanced, neat. Palate: flavourful, fruity, good acidity, easy to drink.

VIÑA MAGNA

El Porro, 24
47239 Serrada (Valladolid)
☎: +34 962 691 090 - Fax: +34 962 690 963
direccioncomercial@vinamagna.es
www.vinamagna.es

DINASTÍA DE HELENIO 2011 B
100% verdejo.

89 Colour: bright straw. Nose: fresh, fresh fruit, white flowers, expressive. Palate: flavourful, fruity, good acidity, balanced.

OPTIMUS 2011 B
100% verdejo.

88 Colour: bright straw. Nose: fresh, white flowers, medium intensity, ripe fruit. Palate: flavourful, fruity, good acidity, balanced.

VIÑEDO VALLELADO SÁNCHEZ

Fausto Herrero, 4 3ºB
47420 Iscar (Valladolid)
☎: +34 679 797 002 - Fax: +34 983 620 504
info@campogrande.com.es
www.campogrande.com.es

CAMPO GRANDE 2011 B
100% verdejo.

87 Colour: bright straw. Nose: white flowers, candied fruit, tropical fruit, dried herbs. Palate: fresh, light-bodied, easy to drink.

VIÑEDOS DE NIEVA

Camino Real, s/n
40447 Nieva (Segovia)
☎: +34 921 594 628 - Fax: +34 921 595 409
info@vinedosdenieva.com
www.vinedosdenieva.com

BLANCO NIEVA PIE FRANCO 2011 B
100% verdejo.

93 Colour: bright straw. Nose: white flowers, citrus fruit, fruit expression, fragrant herbs, mineral. Palate: powerful, flavourful, long, balanced.

BLANCO NIEVA 2011 B
100% verdejo.

91 Colour: bright straw. Nose: fresh, fresh fruit, white flowers, expressive, mineral. Palate: flavourful, fruity, good acidity, balanced.

BLANCO NIEVA SAUVIGNON 2011 B
100% sauvignon blanc.

90 Colour: bright straw. Nose: mineral, fresh fruit, citrus fruit, grassy. Palate: flavourful, fruity, fresh, spicy.

LOS NAVALES VERDEJO 2011 B
100% verdejo.

90 Colour: bright straw. Nose: fresh, fresh fruit, white flowers, expressive, tropical fruit. Palate: flavourful, fruity, good acidity, balanced.

BLANCO NIEVA 2009 BFB
100% verdejo.

89 Colour: bright yellow. Nose: powerfull, ripe fruit, sweet spices, creamy oak, fragrant herbs. Palate: rich, smoky afterpalate:, flavourful, fresh, good acidity.

VIÑEDOS SINGULARES

Cuzco, 26 - 28, Nave 8
08030 (Barcelona)
☎: +34 609 168 191 - Fax: +34 934 807 076
info@vinedossingulares.com
www.vinedossingulares.com

AFORTUNADO 2011 B
verdejo.

89 Colour: bright straw. Nose: fresh, white flowers, ripe fruit, fragrant herbs. Palate: flavourful, fruity, good acidity, balanced.

DO SOMONTANO

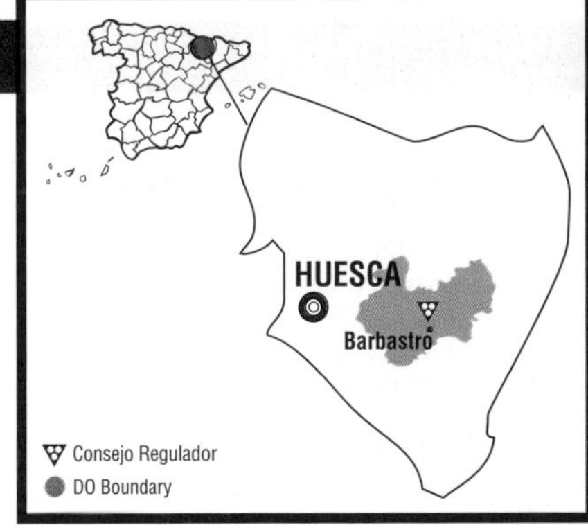

LOCATION:

In the province of Huesca, around the town of Barbastro. The region comprises 43 municipal districts, mainly centred round the region of Somontano and the rest of the neighbouring regions of Ribagorza and Monegros.

CLIMATE:

Characterised by cold winters and hot summers, with sharp contrasts in temperature at the end of spring and autumn. The average annual rainfall is 500 mm, although the rains are scarcer in the south and east

SOIL:

The soil is mainly brownish limestone, not very fertile, with a good level of limestone and good permeability.

GRAPE VARIETIES:

WHITE: *Macabeo, Garnacha Blanca, Alcañón, Chardonnay, Riesling, Sauvignon Blanc* and *Gewürztraminer.*
RED: *Tempranillo, Garnacha Tinta, Cabernet Sauvignon, Merlot, Moristel, Parraleta, Pinot Noir* and *Syrah.*

FIGURES:

Vineyard surface: 4,517 – **Wine-Growers:** 485 – **Wineries:** 33 – **2011 Harvest rating:** Very Good – **Production:** 12,260,000 litres – **Market percentages:** 69% domestic. 31% export

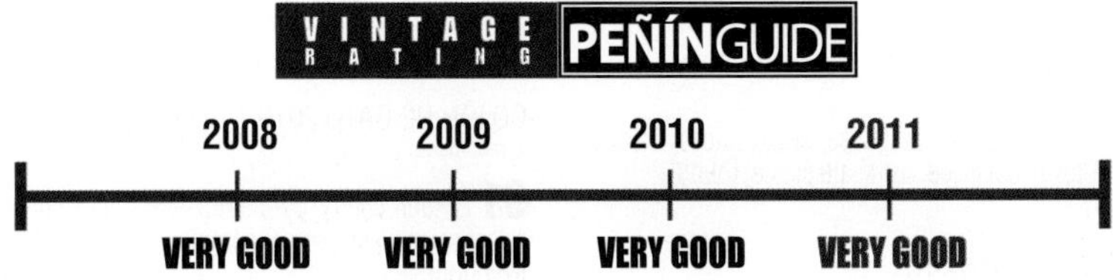

CONSEJO REGULADOR
Avda. de la Merced, 64 - 22300 Barbastro (Huesca) - ☎: +34 974 313 031 - Fax: +34 974 315 132
@ erio@dosomontano.com - www.dosomontano.com

ALDAHARA BODEGA

Ctra. Barbastro, 10
22423 Estadilla (Huesca)
☎: +34 974 305 236 - Fax: +34 974 305 236
bodega@aldahara.es
www.aldahara.es

VAL D'ALFERCHE CHARDONNAY 2011 B
100% chardonnay.

87 Colour: bright straw. Nose: floral, fresh fruit, ripe fruit, fragrant herbs. Palate: fresh, flavourful, easy to drink.

ALDAHARA SELECCIÓN 2010 B
100% chardonnay.

86 Colour: bright yellow. Nose: powerfull, ripe fruit, sweet spices, creamy oak. Palate: rich, flavourful, fresh, good acidity.

ALDAHARA 2011 RD
merlot.

85 Colour: light cherry. Nose: powerfull, ripe fruit, floral, candied fruit. Palate: fruity, flavourful, correct, unctuous.

ALDAHARA 2011 T
tempranillo, merlot, syrah.

87 Colour: cherry, purple rim. Nose: ripe fruit, scrubland. Palate: flavourful, fruity, easy to drink.

ALDAHARA TEMPRANILLO 2010 T
tempranillo.

88 Colour: light cherry, garnet rim. Nose: medium intensity, red berry notes, ripe fruit. Palate: fruity, easy to drink.

VAL D'ALFERCHE 2009 T
100% syrah.

90 Colour: cherry, garnet rim. Nose: sweet spices, floral, expressive. Palate: balanced, fruity aftestaste, round tannins, long.

VAL D'ALFERCHE 2009 TC
50% merlot, 40% cabernet sauvignon, 10% syrah.

87 Colour: cherry, garnet rim. Nose: ripe fruit, spicy, creamy oak, toasty, complex. Taste powerful, flavourful, toasty, round tannins.

BAL D'ISABENA BODEGAS

Ctra. A-1605, Km. 11,2
22587 Laguarres (Huesca)
☎: +34 605 785 178 - Fax: +34 974 310 151
info@baldisabena.com
www.baldisabena.com

COJÓN DE GATO 2011 B
gewürztraminer, chardonnay.

90 Colour: bright yellow. Nose: medium intensity, balanced, white flowers. Palate: balanced, flavourful, full, good acidity.

REIS D'ISABENA 2011 B
chardonnay, gewürztraminer.

88 Colour: bright straw. Nose: fresh, white flowers, expressive, ripe fruit. Palate: flavourful, fruity, good acidity, balanced.

IXEIA 2011 B
chardonnay.

86 Colour: bright yellow. Nose: medium intensity, floral, fresh. Palate: fruity, light-bodied, fresh, easy to drink.

IXEIA 2011 RD
garnacha, merlot.

88 Colour: rose, purple rim. Nose: floral, lactic notes, fresh fruit, red berry notes. Palate: correct, flavourful, fresh, fruity, easy to drink.

ISÁBENA 2011 T
garnacha, merlot, syrah.

86 Colour: cherry, purple rim. Nose: powerfull, fruit preserve, sweet spices. Palate: flavourful, ripe fruit, round tannins, spicy.

COJÓN DE GATO 2010 T ROBLE
syrah, merlot.

91 Colour: cherry, purple rim. Nose: dark chocolate, sweet spices, expressive, complex, ripe fruit. Palate: fruity, flavourful, full.

REIS D'ISABENAQ 2010 T
moristel.

86 Colour: cherry, garnet rim. Nose: ripe fruit, balsamic herbs, spicy. Palate: powerful, flavourful, long.

IXEIA 2010 T
cabernet sauvignon, merlot, tempranillo.

86 Colour: bright cherry. Nose: ripe fruit, sweet spices, creamy oak. Palate: flavourful, fruity, toasty.

REIS D'ISABENA 2008 T
merlot, cabernet sauvignon.

89 Colour: cherry, garnet rim. Nose: ripe fruit, spicy, creamy oak, toasty, complex. Taste powerful, flavourful, toasty, round tannins.

BLECUA

Ctra. Naval, Km. 3,7
22300 Barbastro (Huesca)
☎: +34 974 302 216 - Fax: +34 974 302 098
marketing@vinasdelvero.es
www.bodegablecua.com

BLECUA 2007 TR
garnacha, tempranillo, cabernet sauvignon.

95 Colour: deep cherry, garnet rim. Nose: complex, elegant, expressive, balsamic herbs, cocoa bean, spicy. Palate: balanced, full, flavourful.

BLECUA 2005 T
garnacha, tempranillo, merlot, cabernet sauvignon.

93 Colour: cherry, garnet rim. Nose: ripe fruit, spicy, creamy oak, complex, mineral. Palate: powerful, flavourful, toasty, round tannins.

BODEGA OTTO BESTUÉ

Ctra. A-138, Km. 0,5
22312 Enate (Huesca)
☎: +34 974 305 157 - Fax: +34 974 305 157
info@bodega-ottobestue.com
www.bodega-ottobestue.com

OTTO BESTUÉ CHARDONNAY 2011 B
chardonnay.

88 Colour: bright straw. Nose: white flowers, fruit expression, fragrant herbs. Palate: powerful, flavourful, fruity, balanced.

OTTO BESTUÉ 2011 RD
50% cabernet sauvignon, 50% tempranillo.

88 Colour: rose. Nose: red berry notes, ripe fruit, balanced. Palate: fruity, flavourful, easy to drink.

OTTO BESTUÉ FINCA SANTA SABINA 2009 TC
80% cabernet sauvignon, 20% tempranillo.

88 Colour: cherry, garnet rim. Nose: medium intensity, balanced, ripe fruit. Palate: good structure, flavourful, round tannins.

OTTO BESTUÉ FINCA RABLEROS 2009 T
50% tempranillo, 50% cabernet sauvignon.

87 Colour: cherry, garnet rim. Nose: balanced, ripe fruit, sweet spices, scrubland. Palate: good structure, spicy, round tannins.

BODEGA PIRINEOS

Ctra. Barbastro - Naval, Km. 3,5
22300 Barbastro (Huesca)
☎: +34 974 311 289 - Fax: +34 974 306 688
info@bodegapirineos.com
www.bodegapirineos.com

PIRINEOS SELECCIÓN GEWÜRZTRAMINER 2011 B
gewürztraminer.

90 Colour: bright straw. Nose: fresh, white flowers, expressive. Palate: flavourful, fruity, good acidity, balanced, full.

PIRINEOS SELECCIÓN MESACHE 2011 B
macabeo, chardonnay, gewürztraminer.

88 Colour: bright straw. Nose: fresh, fresh fruit, white flowers, expressive. Palate: flavourful, fruity, balanced.

MONTESIERRA 2011 B
macabeo, chardonnay.

86 Colour: bright yellow. Nose: ripe fruit, dried flowers, tropical fruit. Palate: powerful, flavourful, good acidity.

PIRINEOS SELECCIÓN MARBORÉ 2010 B

91 Colour: bright straw. Nose: fresh, fresh fruit, white flowers, expressive, sweet spices. Palate: flavourful, fruity, good acidity, balanced.

PIRINEOS 2011 RD
merlot, cabernet sauvignon.

90 Colour: rose, purple rim. Nose: powerfull, red berry notes, floral, expressive. Palate: , powerful, fruity, fresh, easy to drink.

MONTESIERRA 2011 RD
tempranillo, garnacha.

87 Colour: rose, purple rim. Nose: red berry notes, ripe fruit, fragrant herbs. Palate: fresh, fruity, light-bodied, easy to drink.

ALQUÉZAR 2011 RD
tempranillo, garnacha.

86 Colour: rose, purple rim. Nose: powerfull, ripe fruit, floral. Palate: , powerful, fruity, fresh.

PIRINEOS MESACHE 2011 T
garnacha, parraleta, syrah, cabernet sauvignon.

88 Colour: cherry, purple rim. Nose: medium intensity, balanced, red berry notes. Palate: flavourful, balanced, fruity.

MONTESIERRA ECOLÓGICO 2010 T
merlot, tempranillo.

87 Colour: bright cherry. Nose: ripe fruit, sweet spices, expressive, fragrant herbs. Palate: flavourful, fruity, round tannins.

PIRINEOS SELECCIÓN SYRAH GARNACHA 2008 T
syrah, garnacha.

89 Colour: bright cherry, garnet rim. Nose: balanced, sweet spices, cocoa bean, ripe fruit. Palate: spicy, long, round tannins.

PIRINEOS SELECCIÓN MERLOT CABERNET 2008 T
50% merlot, 50% cabernet sauvignon.

87 Colour: cherry, garnet rim. Nose: ripe fruit, spicy, creamy oak, toasty, complex, scrubland. Palate: powerful, toasty, round tannins.

MONTESIERRA 2007 TC
tempranillo, cabernet sauvignon, moristel.

88 Colour: cherry, garnet rim. Nose: ripe fruit, spicy, creamy oak, toasty. Palate: powerful, flavourful, toasty.

SEÑORÍO DE LAZÁN 2006 TR
tempranillo, cabernet sauvignon, moristel.

88 Colour: cherry, garnet rim. Nose: ripe fruit, spicy, creamy oak, complex, tobacco. Palate: powerful, flavourful, toasty, harsh oak tannins.

PIRINEOS SELECCIÓN MARBORÉ 2005 T
tempranillo, merlot, cabernet sauvignon, moristel, parraleta.

90 Colour: deep cherry, garnet rim. Nose: complex, ripe fruit, sweet spices. Palate: good structure, powerful, flavourful.

BODEGAS ABINASA

Ctra. N 240, Km. 180
22124 Lascellas (Huesca)
☎: +34 974 319 156 - Fax: +34 974 319 156
info@bodegasabinasa.com
www.bodegasabinasa.com

ANA 2010 T ROBLE
merlot, cabernet sauvignon.

87 Colour: bright cherry. Nose: ripe fruit, sweet spices, creamy oak, expressive. Taste flavourful, fruity, toasty, round tannins.

ANA 2007 TC
merlot, cabernet sauvignon.

85 Colour: cherry, garnet rim. Nose: spicy, fine reductive notes, wet leather, fruit liqueur notes. Palate: spicy, fine tannins, long.

ANA 2004 TR
merlot, cabernet sauvignon.

86 Colour: pale ruby, brick rim edge. Nose: spicy, fruit liqueur notes, creamy oak. Palate: powerful, flavourful, spirituous, spicy, long.

BODEGAS ALODIA

Ctra. de Colungo, s/n
22147 Adahuesca (Huesca)
☎: +34 974 318 265
info@alodia.es
www.alodia.es

ALODIA ALCAÑÓN 2011 B
100% alcañón.

85 Colour: bright straw. Nose: fresh, ripe fruit, balsamic herbs. Palate: flavourful, fruity, good acidity, balanced.

ALODIA LUXURIA B
80% chardonnay, 20% macabeo.

84

ALODIA LUXURIA RD
50% cabernet sauvignon, 50% garnacha.

80

ALODIA PARRALETA 2009 T
100% parraleta.

90 Colour: cherry, garnet rim. Nose: ripe fruit, spicy, creamy oak, earthy notes. Palate: powerful, flavourful, toasty.

ALODIA GARNACHA 2009 T
100% garnacha.

87 Colour: cherry, garnet rim. Nose: ripe fruit, spicy, creamy oak, earthy notes. Palate: powerful, flavourful, toasty.

ALODIA MORISTEL 2009 T
100% moristel.

86 Colour: bright cherry. Nose: ripe fruit, creamy oak, earthy notes. Palate: flavourful, fruity, toasty, round tannins.

ALODIA SYRAH 2009 T
100% syrah.

85 Colour: cherry, garnet rim. Nose: fruit preserve, spicy, creamy oak, earthy notes. Palate: powerful, ripe fruit, spicy.

ALODIA CRUZ DE LOS 2006 T
50% garnacha, 50% cabernet sauvignon.

89 Colour: pale ruby, brick rim edge. Nose: elegant, spicy, fine reductive notes, fruit liqueur notes. Palate: spicy, elegant, long, balanced.

BODEGAS BALLABRIGA

Ctra. de Cregenzán, Km. 3
22300 Barbastro (Huesca)
☎: +34 974 310 216 - Fax: +34 974 306 163
info@bodegasballabriga.com
www.bodegasballabriga.com

PETRET 2011 B
gewürztraminer, chardonnay.

86 Colour: bright straw. Nose: floral, ripe fruit, fragrant herbs. Palate: light-bodied, fresh, fruity, easy to drink.

PETRET 2011 RD

88 Colour: rose, purple rim. Nose: lactic notes, floral, red berry notes, fresh fruit. Palate: powerful, flavourful, easy to drink, light-bodied.

PARRALETA EMOTION 2010 T
100% parraleta.

90 Colour: cherry, garnet rim. Nose: ripe fruit, earthy notes, scrubland, spicy. Palate: ripe fruit, powerful, flavourful.

PETRET 2008 TC
50% cabernet sauvignon, 50% merlot.

91 Colour: pale ruby, brick rim edge. Nose: ripe fruit, scrubland, fine reductive notes, spicy, complex. Palate: balanced, flavourful, long, spicy.

NUNC 2007 T
merlot, syrah, garnacha, otras.

93 Colour: bright cherry, garnet rim. Nose: elegant, ripe fruit, scrubland, spicy. Palate: long, ripe fruit, complex, round tannins.

PARRALETA EMOCIÓN 2007 T
parraleta.

91 Colour: cherry, garnet rim. Nose: expressive, balanced, scrubland, cocoa bean. Palate: fruity, flavourful, good acidity.

AUCTOR SELECCIÓN FINCA ROSELLAS 2007 T
40% cabernet sauvignon, 40% merlot, 20% garnacha.

87 Colour: pale ruby, brick rim edge. Nose: spicy, fine reductive notes, wet leather, fruit liqueur notes. Palate: spicy, elegant, long.

BODEGAS ESTADA

Ctra. A-1232, Km. 6,4
22313 Castillazuelo (Huesca)
☎: +34 687 891 701
info@bodegasestada.com
www.bodegasestada.com

ESTATA 2020 VICIOUS 2011 BFB
chardonnay.

90 Colour: bright yellow. Nose: balanced, powerfull, ripe fruit, jasmine, sweet spices. Palate: flavourful, full, fruity, spicy.

ESTADA SAN CARBÁS 2011 B
chardonnay.

87 Colour: bright straw. Nose: medium intensity, ripe fruit, white flowers. Palate: flavourful, rich, good acidity.

ESTADA 2010 T ROBLE
30% tempranillo, 25% syrah, 25% cabernet sauvignon, 20% garnacha.

86 Colour: bright cherry. Nose: ripe fruit, sweet spices, toasty. Palate: flavourful, fruity, toasty, round tannins.

ESTATA 2020 ORIGEN 2010 T
15% garnacha, 15% tempranillo, 35% syrah, 35% cabernet sauvignon.

85 Colour: cherry, garnet rim. Nose: ripe fruit, balsamic herbs, sweet spices. Palate: flavourful, toasty, spicy.

ESTATA 2020 VICIOUS 2008 T
20% garnacha, 20% tempranillo, 40% syrah, 20% cabernet sauvignon.

89 Colour: cherry, garnet rim. Nose: ripe fruit, balsamic herbs, spicy, toasty. Palate: balanced, powerful, flavourful.

VILLA ESTATA 2007 T
30% cabernet sauvignon, 35% tempranillo, 35% garnacha.

89 Colour: cherry, garnet rim. Nose: ripe fruit, scrubland, spicy, creamy oak. Palate: spicy, powerful, flavourful, balanced.

BODEGAS FÁBREGAS

Cerler, s/n
22300 Barbastro (Huesca)
☎: +34 974 310 498 - Fax: +34 974 310 498
info@bodegasfabregas.com
www.bodegasfabregas.com

MINGUA 2011 B
65% garnacha blanca, 35% chardonnay.

88 Colour: bright straw. Nose: fresh, fresh fruit, white flowers, expressive. Taste flavourful, fruity, good acidity, balanced.

MINGUA GEWÜRZTRAMINER 2011 B
85% gewürztraminer, 10% chardonnay, 5% garnacha blanca.

87 Colour: bright straw. Nose: fresh, fresh fruit, white flowers, tropical fruit. Palate: flavourful, fruity, good acidity, fresh, easy to drink.

MINGUA 2011 RD
87% garnacha, 13% syrah.

85 Colour: rose, purple rim. Nose: floral, ripe fruit, balsamic herbs. Palate: balanced, light-bodied, fruity.

MINGUA 2011 T
merlot, cabernet sauvignon, garnacha.

86 Colour: cherry, garnet rim. Nose: ripe fruit, floral, balsamic herbs, fresh. Palate: powerful, correct, ripe fruit.

FÁBREGAS PURO MERLOT 2007 T
100% merlot.

88 Colour: cherry, garnet rim. Nose: medium intensity, ripe fruit, wild herbs. Palate: fruity, easy to drink, spicy.

FÁBREGAS PURO SYRAH 2007 TC
100% syrah.

87 Colour: pale ruby, brick rim edge. Nose: fruit liqueur notes, old leather, tobacco, creamy oak. Palate: powerful, flavourful, spicy, long.

MINGUA 2007 TC
60% cabernet sauvignon, 30% merlot, 10% syrah.

87 Colour: cherry, garnet rim. Nose: ripe fruit, spicy, toasty, complex. Palate: powerful, flavourful, toasty, round tannins.

VEGA FERRERA 2007 TC
50% merlot, 40% cabernet sauvignon, 10% syrah.

85 Colour: cherry, garnet rim. Nose: ripe fruit, spicy, toasty, creamy oak. Palate: powerful, flavourful, toasty.

BODEGAS IRIUS

Ctra. N-240, Km. 154,5
22300 Barbastro (Huesca)
☎: +34 974 269 900
visitairius@bodegairius.com
www.bodegairius.com

ALBAT ELIT 2011 B
80% gewürztraminer, 20% chardonnay.

87 Colour: bright straw. Nose: ripe fruit, dried flowers, balsamic herbs, expressive. Palate: powerful, flavourful, ripe fruit.

ABSUM COLECCIÓN GEWÜRZTRAMINER 2010 B ROBLE
100% gewürztraminer.

90 Colour: bright yellow. Nose: complex, expressive, white flowers, elegant, sweet spices. Palate: rich, flavourful, good acidity, balanced.

ABSUM VARIETALES 2010 B
60% chardonnay, 25% gewürztraminer, 15% pinot noir.

89 Colour: bright yellow. Nose: wild herbs, medium intensity, floral, spicy. Palate: correct, balanced, easy to drink.

ALBAT ELIT GEWÜRZTRAMINER 2010 B
100% gewürztraminer.

86 Colour: bright straw. Nose: white flowers, tropical fruit, fragrant herbs. Palate: fresh, fruity, flavourful, easy to drink.

ABSUM VARIETALES 2010 T
50% tempranillo, 35% merlot, 10% cabernet sauvignon, 5% syrah.

92 Colour: bright cherry, garnet rim. Nose: balanced, expressive, ripe fruit, sweet spices, cocoa bean, creamy oak. Palate: good structure, long, spicy.

ALBAT ELIT 2010 T ROBLE
45% tempranillo, 30% merlot, 25% cabernet sauvignon.

88 Colour: deep cherry, purple rim. Nose: toasty, nose:tic coffee, ripe fruit. Palate: powerful, good structure, round tannins.

ABSUM COLECCIÓN SYRAH 2009 T
100% syrah.

94 Colour: bright cherry. Nose: sweet spices, creamy oak, expressive, red berry notes, ripe fruit. Palate: flavourful, fruity, toasty, round tannins.

ABSUM COLECCIÓN MERLOT 2009 T
100% merlot.

91 Colour: deep cherry, purple rim. Nose: complex, expressive, creamy oak, cocoa bean, ripe fruit. Palate: good structure, round tannins.

IRIUS PREMIUM 2008 T
40% tempranillo, 20% cabernet sauvignon, 20% merlot, 20% syrah.

96 Colour: bright cherry, purple rim. Nose: complex, ripe fruit, sweet spices, elegant. Palate: spicy, long, balanced, fine bitter notes, round tannins.

IRIUS SELECCIÓN 2008 T
30% tempranillo, 30% merlot, 25% cabernet sauvignon, 15% syrah.

92 Colour: very deep cherry, garnet rim. Nose: powerfull, expressive, dark chocolate, creamy oak, sweet spices, candied fruit. Palate: full, flavourful, good structure, rich.

ALBAT ELIT 2008 TC
60% cabernet sauvignon, 20% merlot, 20% tempranillo.

89 Colour: very deep cherry, purple rim. Nose: medium intensity, balanced, ripe fruit, cocoa bean. Palate: good structure, ripe fruit.

ALBAT ELIT 2007 TR
75% tempranillo, 15% cabernet sauvignon, 10% merlot.

91 Colour: cherry, garnet rim. Nose: ripe fruit, sweet spices, dark chocolate, cocoa bean, creamy oak. Palate: powerful, flavourful, long, toasty.

BODEGAS LASIERRA

Baja, 12
22133 Bespén (Huesca)
☎: +34 974 260 365 - Fax: +34 974 260 365
info@bodegaslasierra.es
www.bodegaslasierra.es

BESPÉN CHARDONNAY MACABEO 2011 B
chardonnay, macabeo.

86 Colour: bright straw. Nose: medium intensity, balanced, floral. Palate: flavourful, rich, easy to drink.

BESPÉN 2011 RD
cabernet sauvignon.

85 Colour: light cherry. Nose: warm, ripe fruit, balsamic herbs. Palate: powerful, flavourful, fruity, correct.

BESPÉN 2011 T
merlot, tempranillo.

85 Colour: cherry, purple rim. Nose: red berry notes, ripe fruit, earthy notes, scrubland. Palate: fresh, fruity, easy to drink.

BESPÉN VENDIMIA SELECCIONADA SYRAH 2010 T
syrah.

87 Colour: cherry, garnet rim. Nose: medium intensity, balanced, ripe fruit, dark chocolate, sweet spices. Palate: correct, balanced, round tannins.

BESPÉN VENDIMIA SELECCIONADA MERLOT 2009 T
merlot.

89 Colour: cherry, garnet rim. Nose: ripe fruit, dark chocolate, sweet spices, balsamic herbs. Palate: powerful, flavourful, long, toasty.

BESPÉN 2008 TC
cabernet sauvignon.

86 Colour: cherry, garnet rim. Nose: spicy, creamy oak, toasty, fruit preserve. Palate: powerful, flavourful, toasty, round tannins.

BODEGAS LAUS

Ctra. N-240, km 154,8
22300 Barbastro (Huesca)
☎: +34 974 269 708 - Fax: +34 974 269 715
info@bodegaslaus.com
www.bodegaslaus.com

LAUS FLOR DE GEWÜRZTRAMINER 2011 B
100% gewürztraminer.

91 Colour: bright straw. Nose: white flowers, fresh fruit, fragrant herbs, expressive. Palate: fresh, fruity, flavourful, varietal, balanced.

LAUS FLOR DE CHARDONNAY 2011 B
100% chardonnay.

89 Colour: bright straw. Nose: white flowers, fresh fruit, balanced, expressive, fragrant herbs. Palate: powerful, flavourful, complex.

LAUS 700 ALT 2007 B
65% chardonnay, 35% gewürztraminer.

89 Colour: bright golden. Nose: faded flowers, balanced, honeyed notes, candied fruit. Palate: flavourful, rich, toasty, long, slightly evolved.

LAUS FLOR DE MERLOT 2011 RD
80% merlot, 15% cabernet sauvignon, 5% syrah.

87 Colour: rose, bright. Nose: balanced, medium intensity, red berry notes. Palate: fruity, flavourful.

LAUS 2009 T ROBLE
55% merlot, 40% cabernet sauvignon, 5% tempranillo.

86 Colour: bright cherry. Nose: ripe fruit, creamy oak, fine reductive notes. Palate: flavourful, fruity, toasty.

LAUS 2005 TR
100% cabernet sauvignon.

88 Colour: pale ruby, brick rim edge. Nose: elegant, spicy, fine reductive notes, fruit liqueur notes. Palate: spicy, fine tannins, long.

LAUS 700 ALT 2005 TC
40% syrah, 35% cabernet sauvignon, 25% merlot.

88 Colour: deep cherry, orangey edge. Nose: ripe fruit, expressive, spicy, creamy oak. Palate: powerful, flavourful, spicy.

BODEGAS MELER

Pico Perdiguero, 13
22300 Barbastro (Huesca)
☎: +34 974 269 907 - Fax: +34 974 269 907
info@bodegasmeler.com
www.bodegasmeler.com

MELER CHARDONNAY EDICIÓN LIMITADA 2011 B
100% chardonnay.

87 Colour: bright yellow. Nose: ripe fruit, white flowers, expressive. Palate: powerful, rich, flavourful, balanced.

MELER 95 SOBRE ALJEZ CHARDONNAY 2008 B
100% chardonnay.

91 Colour: bright yellow. Nose: powerfull, ripe fruit, sweet spices, creamy oak, fragrant herbs. Palate: rich, smoky aftertaste, flavourful, fresh.

MELER CABERNET 2011 RD
100% cabernet sauvignon.

87 Colour: rose, purple rim. Nose: powerfull, ripe fruit, red berry notes, balsamic herbs. Palate: , powerful, fruity, fresh.

MELER SYRAH EDICIÓN LIMITADA 2010 T
100% syrah.

85 Colour: cherry, garnet rim. Nose: floral, ripe fruit, scrubland. Palate: powerful, flavourful, ripe fruit.

MELER LUMBRETA 2008 T ROBLE
cabernet sauvignon, garnacha, tempranillo.

88 Colour: light cherry, garnet rim. Nose: ripe fruit, cocoa bean, dark chocolate, sweet spices. Palate: long, powerful, flavourful, toasty.

ANDRES MELER 2006 T
100% cabernet sauvignon.

92 Colour: cherry, garnet rim. Nose: spicy, creamy oak, toasty, complex, fragrant herbs. Palate: powerful, flavourful, toasty, round tannins.

MELER 2006 TC
merlot, cabernet sauvignon.

90 Colour: cherry, garnet rim. Nose: spicy, fine reductive notes, wet leather, aged wood nuances, fruit liqueur notes. Palate: spicy, fine tannins, elegant, long.

BODEGAS MONTE ODINA

Monte Odina, s/n
22415 Ilche (Huesca)
☎: +34 974 343 480 - Fax: +34 974 343 484
bodega@monteodina.com
www.monteodina.com

VICTORIA DE MONTE ODINA 2011 B
100% gewürztraminer.

87 Colour: bright straw. Nose: fresh, white flowers, expressive, tropical fruit. Palate: flavourful, fruity, good acidity, balanced.

MONTE ODINA 2009 TC
50% cabernet sauvignon, 50% merlot.

86 Colour: cherry, garnet rim. Nose: ripe fruit, spicy, creamy oak, toasty. Palate: powerful, flavourful, toasty, round tannins.

MONTE ODINA MERLOT 2007 T
merlot.

87 Colour: cherry, garnet rim. Nose: warm, powerfull, wet leather. Palate: flavourful, spicy, round tannins.

MONTE ODINA 2006 TC
50% cabernet sauvignon, 50% merlot.

85 Colour: cherry, garnet rim. Nose: ripe fruit, spicy, toasty, old leather. Palate: powerful, flavourful, toasty.

MONTE ODINA CABERNET 2008
cabernet sauvignon.

87 Colour: bright cherry, garnet rim. Nose: candied fruit, dark chocolate, sweet spices. Palate: flavourful, good structure, fruity.

BODEGAS OBERGO

Ctra. La Puebla, Km. 0,6
22439 Ubiergo (Huesca)
☎: +34 669 357 866
bodegasobergo@obergo.es
www.obergo.es

OBERGO EXPRESSION 2010 BFB
chardonnay, sauvignon blanc, otras.

89 Colour: bright yellow. Nose: powerfull, sweet spices, creamy oak, fragrant herbs, toasty. Palate: rich, smoky aftertaste, flavourful, good acidity.

LÁGRIMAS DE OBERGO 2011 RD
60% garnacha, 40% syrah.

88 Colour: rose, purple rim. Nose: powerfull, ripe fruit, red berry notes, floral, expressive. Taste fleshy, powerful, fruity, fresh.

OBERGO CARAMELOS 2011 T
100% garnacha.

89 Colour: cherry, garnet rim. Nose: ripe fruit, spicy, toasty, sweet spices. Palate: powerful, flavourful, long, toasty.

OBERGO SYRAH 2009 T
100% syrah.

92 Colour: cherry, purple rim. Nose: red berry notes, ripe fruit, sweet spices, creamy oak. Palate: powerful, flavourful, balanced.

OBERGO "FINCA LA MATA" 2009 T
40% merlot, 40% cabernet sauvignon, 20% garnacha.

90 Colour: cherry, garnet rim. Nose: ripe fruit, spicy, toasty, fine reductive notes. Palate: powerful, flavourful, toasty, round tannins.

OBERGO VARIETALES 2009 T
100% cabernet sauvignon.

90 Colour: cherry, garnet rim. Nose: ripe fruit, spicy, creamy oak, toasty. Palate: powerful, flavourful, toasty, round tannins.

BODEGAS OLVENA

Paraje El Ariño, s/n
Ctra. Nacional 123, Km. 5
22300 Barbastro (Huesca)
☎: +34 974 308 481 - Fax: +34 974 308 482
info@bodegasolvena.com
www.bodegasolvena.com

OLVENA CHARDONNAY 2011 B
chardonnay.

88 Colour: bright straw. Nose: fresh, fresh fruit, white flowers, fragrant herbs. Palate: flavourful, fruity, good acidity.

OLVENA CHARDONNAY 2010 BFB
chardonnay.

89 Colour: bright yellow. Nose: ripe fruit, dried flowers, sweet spices, creamy oak, toasty. Palate: rich, powerful, flavourful, complex, spicy.

OLVENA 2011 RD
merlot.

83 Colour: rose, purple rim. Nose: ripe fruit, floral, slightly evolved, grassy. Palate: , powerful, fruity, fresh.

OLVENA 2011 T
tempranillo, garnacha.

86 Colour: cherry, purple rim. Nose: powerfull, balsamic herbs, ripe fruit. Palate: flavourful, fruity, correct, easy to drink.

OLVENA CUATRO O EL PAGO DE LA LIBÉLULA 2008 T
tempranillo, merlot, cabernet sauvignon, syrah.

90 Colour: cherry, garnet rim. Nose: red berry notes, ripe fruit, fragrant herbs, floral, sweet spices. Palate: round tannins, fresh, fruity, spicy, long.

OLVENA HACHE 2008 T
garnacha, syrah.

87 Colour: cherry, garnet rim. Nose: creamy oak, toasty, dark chocolate, fruit preserve. Palate: balanced, fine bitter notes, rich.

OLVENA 2007 TC

86 Colour: cherry, garnet rim. Nose: fruit preserve, sweet spices, dark chocolate. Palate: flavourful, correct.

BODEGAS OSCA

La Iglesia, 1
22124 Ponzano (Huesca)
☎: +34 974 319 017 - Fax: +34 974 319 175
bodega@bodegasosca.com
www.bodegasosca.com

OSCA 2011 B
garnacha blanca, macabeo.

84

OSCA GARNACHA BLANCA 2010 B
100% garnacha blanca.

85 Colour: bright yellow. Nose: fresh fruit, balanced, medium intensity, floral. Palate: fruity, flavourful.

OSCA 2011 RD

81

OSCA 2010 T

82

MASCÚN SYRAH 2009 T
syrah.

87 Colour: cherry, garnet rim. Nose: ripe fruit, floral, scrubland, toasty. Palate: powerful, flavourful, balanced, toasty.

MASCÚN GARNACHA 2009 T
garnacha.

85 Colour: cherry, garnet rim. Nose: ripe fruit, creamy oak, toasty. Palate: powerful, flavourful, toasty.

OSCA 2008 TC
tempranillo, merlot.

88 Colour: cherry, garnet rim. Nose: ripe fruit, spicy, fine reductive notes. Palate: powerful, flavourful, toasty.

OSCA COLECCIÓN 2008 TR
merlot.

88 Colour: cherry, garnet rim. Nose: ripe fruit, spicy, creamy oak, toasty, complex. Palate: powerful, flavourful, toasty.

OSCA MORISTEL 2008 TC
moristel.

88 Colour: cherry, garnet rim. Nose: ripe fruit, old leather, spicy, creamy oak. Palate: powerful, flavourful, balanced.

OSCA GRAN EROLES 2007 TR
cabernet sauvignon, tempranillo.

88 Colour: cherry, garnet rim. Nose: ripe fruit, balsamic herbs, spicy, creamy oak. Palate: powerful, flavourful, complex, spicy.

BODEGAS RASO HUETE

Joaquín Costa, 23
22423 Estadilla (Huesca)
☎: +34 974 305 357 - Fax: +34 974 305 357
info@bodegasrasohuete.com
www.bodegasrasohuete.com

PARTIDA ARNAZAS CABERNET-MERLOT 2011 T
50% merlot, 50% cabernet sauvignon.

86 Colour: cherry, purple rim. Nose: medium intensity, ripe fruit, scrubland. Palate: fruity, flavourful.

ARNAZAS SELECCIÓN 2008 T ROBLE
34% syrah, 33% merlot, 33% tempranillo.

81

ARNAZAS CABERNET-MERLOT 2006 TC
60% cabernet sauvignon, 40% merlot.

88 Colour: pale ruby, brick rim edge. Nose: elegant, spicy, fine reductive notes, wet leather, aged wood nuances, fruit liqueur notes. Taste spicy, fine tannins, elegant, long.

TRASHUMANTE 2006 TC
55% cabernet sauvignon, 45% merlot.

87 Colour: pale ruby, brick rim edge. Nose: fruit liqueur notes, spicy, wet leather, tobacco, creamy oak. Palate: flavourful, ripe fruit, spirituous.

ARNAZAS MERLOT 2006 T ROBLE
100% merlot.

84

ARNAZAS 2004 TR
50% merlot, 50% cabernet sauvignon.

86 Colour: bright cherry, orangey edge. Nose: spicy, old leather, fruit preserve. Palate: fruity, easy to drink.

BODEGAS SERS

Pza. Mayor, 7
22417 Cofita (Huesca)
☎: +34 652 979 718
info@bodegassers.es
www.bodegassers.es

SÈRS BLANQUÉ 2011 BFB
100% chardonnay.

90 Colour: bright yellow. Nose: balanced, expressive, scrubland, floral, sweet spices. Palate: balanced, spicy.

SÈRS SINGULAR 2010 T
100% parraleta.

91 Colour: bright cherry. Nose: ripe fruit, sweet spices, creamy oak, expressive, complex. Palate: flavourful, fruity, toasty, round tannins.

SÈRS PRIMER 2010 T
100% syrah.

88 Colour: cherry, purple rim. Nose: powerfull, ripe fruit, sweet spices. Palate: spicy, round tannins, long.

SÈRS TEMPLE 2009 TC
40% merlot, 60% cabernet sauvignon.

90 Colour: bright cherry. Nose: ripe fruit, sweet spices, creamy oak, expressive. Taste flavourful, fruity, toasty, round tannins.

SÈRS 2008 TR
60% cabernet sauvignon, 30% merlot, 10% syrah.

90 Colour: bright cherry, garnet rim. Nose: complex, candied fruit, dark chocolate, creamy oak, nose:tic coffee. Palate: flavourful, balanced, long.

BODEGAS SIERRA DE GUARA

Ctra. A-1 1229, Km. 0,2
22124 Las Cellas (Huesca)
☎: +34 974 340 671 - Fax: +34 974 319 363
idrias@bodegassierradeguara.es
www.bodegassierradeguara.es

IDRIAS CHARDONNAY 2011 B
100% chardonnay.

87 Colour: bright yellow. Nose: ripe fruit, dried flowers, balsamic herbs, fresh. Palate: powerful, flavourful, ripe fruit.

IDRIAS CHARDONNAY 2007 BFB
100% chardonnay.

90 Colour: bright yellow. Nose: ripe fruit, sweet spices, creamy oak, fragrant herbs. Palate: rich, smoky aftertaste, flavourful, fresh, good acidity.

IDRIAS MERLOT 2011 RD
100% merlot.

88 Colour: rose, purple rim. Nose: red berry notes, floral, fragrant herbs, expressive. Palate: fresh, fruity, flavourful, easy to drink.

IDRIAS TEMPRANILLO 2011 T
100% tempranillo.

85 Colour: cherry, purple rim. Nose: ripe fruit, balsamic herbs, medium intensity. Palate: powerful, flavourful, ripe fruit.

IDRIAS ABIEGO 2009 T
50% merlot, 50% cabernet sauvignon.

90 Colour: bright cherry. Nose: ripe fruit, sweet spices, creamy oak, balsamic herbs. Palate: flavourful, fruity, toasty, round tannins.

IDRIAS SEVIL 2008 T
50% merlot, 50% cabernet sauvignon.

88 Colour: cherry, garnet rim. Nose: ripe fruit, spicy, creamy oak, toasty. Palate: powerful, flavourful, toasty, balanced.

IDRIAS SEVIL 2007 T
50% merlot, 50% cabernet sauvignon.

89 Colour: bright cherry, garnet rim. Nose: spicy, tobacco, ripe fruit. Palate: fruity, flavourful, long.

BODEGAS VILLA D'ORTA

Ctra. Alquezar s/n
22313 Huerta de Vero (Huesca)
☎: +34 695 991 967 - Fax: +34 974 302 072
villadorta@hotmail.com
www.villadorta.com

VILLA D'ORTA 2008 TC
tempranillo, merlot, cabernet sauvignon.

82

CHESA

Autovía A-22, km. 57
22300 Barbastro (Huesca)
☎: +34 649 870 637 - Fax: +34 974 313 552
bodegaschesa@hotmail.com
www.bodegaschesa.com

CHESA GEWÜRZTRAMINER 2011 B
100% gewürztraminer.

86 Colour: bright straw. Nose: white flowers, fragrant herbs, tropical fruit. Palate: powerful, fresh, fruity, easy to drink.

CHESA MERLOT CABERNET 2010 T
65% merlot, 35% cabernet sauvignon.

87 Colour: cherry, purple rim. Nose: floral, red berry notes, ripe fruit, balsamic herbs. Palate: balanced, flavourful, fruity, spicy.

CHESA 2009 T ROBLE
65% merlot, 35% cabernet sauvignon.

90 Colour: bright cherry. Nose: ripe fruit, sweet spices, creamy oak, expressive. Taste flavourful, fruity, toasty, round tannins.

DALCAMP

Constitución, 4
22415 Monesma de San Juan (Huesca)
☎: +34 973 760 018 - Fax: +34 973 760 523
rdalfo@mixmail.com
www.castillodemonesma.com

CASTILLO DE MONESMA 2011 RD
70% garnacha, 30% tempranillo.

85 Colour: light cherry. Nose: powerfull, ripe fruit, scrubland. Palate: fruity, flavourful.

CASTILLO DE MONESMA 2009 TC
80% cabernet sauvignon, 20% merlot.

89 Colour: cherry, garnet rim. Nose: ripe fruit, balsamic herbs, spicy, creamy oak. Palate: flavourful, powerful, toasty.

CASTILLO DE MONESMA 2009 T ROBLE
80% cabernet sauvignon, 20% merlot.

86 Colour: bright cherry. Nose: ripe fruit, creamy oak, spicy, medium intensity. Palate: flavourful, fruity, toasty, round tannins.

CASTILLO DE MONESMA 2007 TR
90% cabernet sauvignon, 10% merlot.

90 Colour: cherry, garnet rim. Nose: ripe fruit, spicy, creamy oak, toasty, complex. Taste powerful, flavourful, toasty, round tannins.

DE BEROZ

Pol. Valle del Cinca - Calle B- 26-24
22300 Barbastro (Huesca)
☎: +34 974 269 921 - Fax: +34 974 269 921
bodega@deberoz.com
www.deberoz.com

DE BEROZ ESENCIA DE BLANCOS 2011 B
90% chardonnay, 10% gewürztraminer.

90 Colour: bright straw. Nose: fruit expression, ripe fruit, white flowers, balsamic herbs. Palate: powerful, flavourful, balanced.

DE BEROZ ESENCIA DE TINTOS 2011 RD
40% cabernet sauvignon, 30% merlot, 20% garnacha, 10% tempranillo.

88 Colour: rose, purple rim. Nose: red berry notes, expressive, fresh, fragrant herbs. Palate: , powerful, fruity, fresh, easy to drink.

DE BEROZ ESENCIA DE GEWÜRZ 2011 B
100% gewürztraminer.

88 Colour: bright yellow. Nose: expressive, jasmine, ripe fruit, powerfull. Palate: flavourful, correct, ripe fruit, long.

DE BEROZ NUESTRO ROBLE 2010 T
cabernet sauvignon, merlot, tempranillo, moristel.

87 Colour: cherry, purple rim. Nose: medium intensity, balanced, fragrant herbs, spicy. Palate: flavourful, ripe fruit.

DE BEROZ CRIANZA ESPECIAL 2007 T
cabernet sauvignon, merlot, syrah.

90 Colour: bright cherry, garnet rim. Nose: complex, cocoa bean, toasty, wild herbs, ripe fruit. Palate: flavourful, fruity.

DE BEROZ RESERVA FAMILIA 2006 T
cabernet sauvignon, merlot, syrah, tempranillo.

91 Colour: bright cherry, garnet rim. Nose: spicy, ripe fruit, balanced, powerfull. Palate: flavourful, good acidity, balanced.

LAR DE BEROZ 2006 T
cabernet sauvignon, syrah, garnacha, parraleta.

91 Colour: deep cherry, garnet rim. Nose: toasty, sweet spices, warm, ripe fruit. Palate: good structure, round tannins.

ENATE

Avda. de las Artes, 1
22314 Salas Bajas (Huesca)
☎: +34 974 302 580 - Fax: +34 974 300 046
bodega@enate.es
www.enate.es

ENATE CHARDONNAY 20 ANIVERSARIO 2009 BFB
100% chardonnay.

93 Colour: bright yellow. Nose: ripe fruit, honeyed notes, sweet spices, creamy oak. Palate: spicy, powerful, toasty, long, flavourful, roasted-coffee aftertaste.

ENATE CHARDONNAY-234 2011 B
100% chardonnay.

90 Colour: bright straw. Nose: fresh, white flowers, expressive, balanced. Palate: flavourful, fruity, good acidity, balanced.

ENATE GEWÜRZTRAMINER 2011 B
100% gewürztraminer.

89 Colour: bright yellow. Nose: expressive, white flowers, varietal, ripe fruit. Palate: rich, flavourful.

ENATE CHARDONNAY 2009 BFB
100% chardonnay.

92 Colour: bright yellow. Nose: powerfull, ripe fruit, sweet spices, creamy oak, fragrant herbs. Palate: rich, flavourful, roasted-coffee aftertaste.

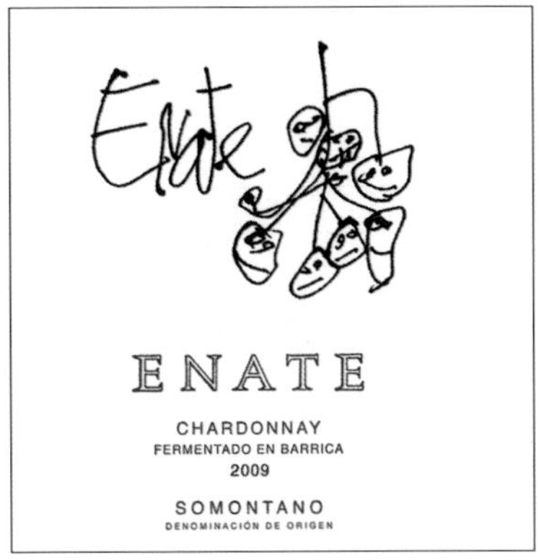

ENATE 2011 RD
100% cabernet sauvignon.

89 Colour: rose, bright. Nose: fresh, red berry notes, ripe fruit, fragrant herbs. Palate: fruity, good structure.

ENATE 20 ANIVERSARIO CABERNET SAUVIGNON SYRAH 2009 T
cabernet sauvignon, syrah.

89 Colour: cherry, garnet rim. Nose: ripe fruit, spicy, creamy oak, balsamic herbs, mineral. Palate: powerful, flavourful, toasty.

ENATE CABERNET SAUVIGNON MERLOT 2009 T
50% cabernet sauvignon, 50% merlot.

88 Colour: cherry, garnet rim. Nose: medium intensity, cocoa bean, creamy oak, ripe fruit. Palate: flavourful, long.

ENATE MERLOT-MERLOT 2008 T
100% merlot.

92 Colour: cherry, garnet rim. Nose: spicy, creamy oak, toasty, complex, candied fruit. Palate: powerful, flavourful, toasty, round tannins.

ENATE SYRAH-SHIRAZ 2007 T
100% syrah.

92 Colour: bright cherry, garnet rim. Nose: expressive, creamy oak, dark chocolate, ripe fruit. Palate: flavourful, full.

ENATE RESERVA ESPECIAL 2006 TR
65% cabernet sauvignon, 35% merlot.

94 Colour: cherry, garnet rim. Nose: ripe fruit, cocoa bean, spicy, dark chocolate, toasty, elegant. Palate: powerful, flavourful, spicy, balanced.

ENATE VARIETALES 2006 T
40% merlot, 40% cabernet sauvignon, 20% syrah.

91 Colour: cherry, garnet rim. Nose: balanced, scrubland, ripe fruit, dark chocolate. Palate: flavourful, powerful, long, full.

ENATE 2006 TC
70% tempranillo, 30% cabernet sauvignon.

88 Colour: cherry, garnet rim. Nose: ripe fruit, spicy, creamy oak, toasty. Palate: powerful, flavourful, toasty, round tannins, fine bitter notes.

ENATE UNO 2005 T
60% cabernet sauvignon, 20% merlot, 20% syrah.

93 Colour: deep cherry, garnet rim. Nose: expressive, cocoa bean, ripe fruit, powerfull, scrubland. Palate: full, complex, good structure, round tannins.

ENATE 2005 TR
100% cabernet sauvignon.

92 Colour: cherry, garnet rim. Nose: balanced, powerfull, ripe fruit, spicy, warm, mineral. Palate: flavourful, balanced, fine bitter notes.

VINSOM

Ctra. Berbegal, Km. 2,5
22300 Barbastro (Huesca)
☎: +34 974 269 188 - Fax: +34 974 269 188
info@lafirmadevinos.com
www.docelunas.es

12 LUNAS 2011 B
90% chardonnay, 10% gewürztraminer.

90 Colour: bright straw. Nose: white flowers, fruit expression, ripe fruit, expressive. Palate: powerful, flavourful, full, long, balanced.

12 LUNAS 2011 RD
100% syrah.

89 Colour: rose, bright. Nose: fresh, red berry notes, rose petals. Palate: flavourful, long, ripe fruit, full.

12 LUNAS 2008 T
55% tempranillo, 20% syrah, 20% cabernet sauvignon, 5% garnacha.

91 Colour: cherry, garnet rim. Nose: ripe fruit, sweet spices, creamy oak, toasty. Palate: powerful, flavourful, balanced, complex.

VIÑAS DEL VERO

Ctra. Naval, Km. 3,7
22300 Barbastro (Huesca)
☎: +34 974 302 216 - Fax: +34 974 302 098
marketing@vinasdelvero.es
www.vinasdelvero.es

VIÑAS DEL VERO CHARDONNAY COLECCIÓN 2011 B
100% chardonnay.

92 Colour: bright yellow, greenish rim. Nose: elegant, balanced, medium intensity, floral. Palate: fruity, full, fine bitter notes.

VIÑAS DEL VERO GEWÜRZTRAMINER COLECCIÓN 2011 B
100% gewürztraminer.

90 Colour: bright straw. Nose: fresh, fresh fruit, white flowers, expressive, varietal. Palate: flavourful, fruity, good acidity, balanced, easy to drink.

VIÑAS DEL VERO RIESLING COLECCIÓN 2011 B
100% riesling.

88 Colour: bright yellow. Nose: medium intensity, fresh fruit, wild herbs, floral. Palate: flavourful, easy to drink, correct.

VIÑAS DEL VERO CLARIÓN 2010 B

91 Colour: bright yellow. Nose: medium intensity, fresh fruit, wild herbs, faded flowers. Palate: flavourful, fruity, fine bitter notes.

VIÑAS DEL VERO CLARIÓN MAGNUM 2008 B

92 Colour: bright yellow, greenish rim. Nose: elegant, ripe fruit, floral, sweet spices, fragrant herbs. Palate: flavourful, fine bitter notes, balanced.

VIÑAS DEL VERO 2011 RD
tempranillo, cabernet sauvignon.

89 Colour: rose, purple rim. Nose: powerfull, ripe fruit, red berry notes, floral, expressive. Taste fleshy, powerful, fruity, fresh.

VIÑAS DEL VERO LA MIRANDA DE SECASTILLA 2009 T
garnacha, parraleta, syrah.

90 Colour: bright cherry, purple rim. Nose: elegant, medium intensity, red berry notes, ripe fruit, scrubland. Palate: ripe fruit, powerful.

VIÑAS DEL VERO SECASTILLA 2008 T
garnacha.

92 Colour: bright cherry, garnet rim. Nose: elegant, cocoa bean, creamy oak, nose:tic coffee, ripe fruit. Palate: flavourful, balanced.

VIÑAS DEL VERO MERLOT COLECCIÓN 2007 T
100% merlot.

91 Colour: bright cherry, garnet rim. Nose: medium intensity, ripe fruit, balanced, complex. Palate: flavourful, ripe fruit, good acidity.

VIÑAS DEL VERO SYRAH COLECCIÓN 2007 T
100% syrah.

89 Colour: cherry, purple rim. Nose: toasty, spicy, ripe fruit, powerfull. Palate: flavourful, powerful, full, toasty, round tannins.

VIÑAS DEL VERO CABERNET SAUVIGNON COLECCIÓN 2007 T
100% cabernet sauvignon.

88 Colour: bright cherry. Nose: scrubland, ripe fruit, fruit preserve, spicy. Palate: flavourful, fruity, long.

VIÑAS DEL VERO GRAN VOS 2005 TR

90 Colour: cherry, garnet rim. Nose: complex, spicy, fine reductive notes. Palate: flavourful, full, ripe fruit, long, spicy.

VIÑEDOS DE HOZ

Mayor, 17
22312 Hoz de Barbastro (Huesca)
☎: +34 619 686 765
info@vinosdehoz.com
www.vinosdehoz.com

HOZ 2010 T ROBLE
garnacha, cabernet sauvignon, syrah.

88 Colour: deep cherry, garnet rim. Nose: balanced, dark chocolate, creamy oak, ripe fruit. Palate: good structure, full, flavourful, long.

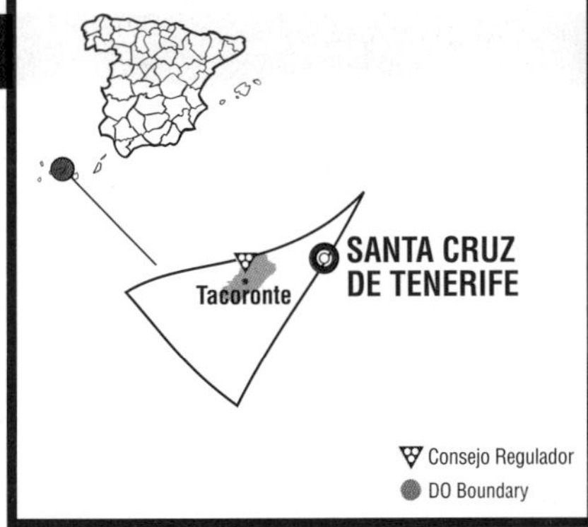

DO TACORONTE-ACENTEJO

LOCATION:

Situated in the north of Tenerife, stretching for 23 km and is composed of 9 municipal districts: Tegueste, Tacoronte, El Sauzal, La Matanza de Acentejo, La Victoria de Acentejo, Santa Úrsula, La Laguna, Santa Cruz de Tenerife and El Rosario.

CLIMATE:

Typically Atlantic, affected by the orientation of the island and the relief which give rise to a great variety of microclimates. The temperatures are in general mild, thanks to the influence of the trade winds, which provide high levels of humidity, around 60%, although the rains are scarce.

SOIL:

The soil is volcanic, reddish, and is made up of organic matter and trace elements. The vines are cultivated both in the valleys next to the sea and higher up at altitudes of up to 1,000 m.

GRAPE VARIETIES:

WHITE: PREFERRED: *Güal, Malvasía, Listán Blanco* and *Marmajuelo.*
AUTHORIZED: *Pedro Ximénez, Moscatel, Verdello, Vijariego, Forastera Blanca, Albillo, Sabro, Bastardo Blanco, Breval, Burra Blanca* and *Torrontés.*
RED: PREFERRED: *Listán Negra* and *Negramoll.*
AUTHORIZED: *Tintilla, Moscatel Negro, Castellana Negra, Cabernet Sauvignon, Merlot, Pinot Noir, Ruby Cabernet, Syrah, Tempranillo, Bastardo Negro, Listán Prieto, Vijariego Negro* and *Malvasía Rosada.*

SUB-REGIONS:

Anaga (covering the municipal areas of La Laguna, Santa Cruz de Tenerife and Tegueste) which falls within the limits of the Anaga Rural Park.

FIGURES:

Vineyard surface: 1,134 – **Wine-Growers:** 1,839 – **Wineries:** 50 – **2011 Harvest rating:** Good – **Production:** 650,000 litres – **Market percentages:** --% domestic. --% export

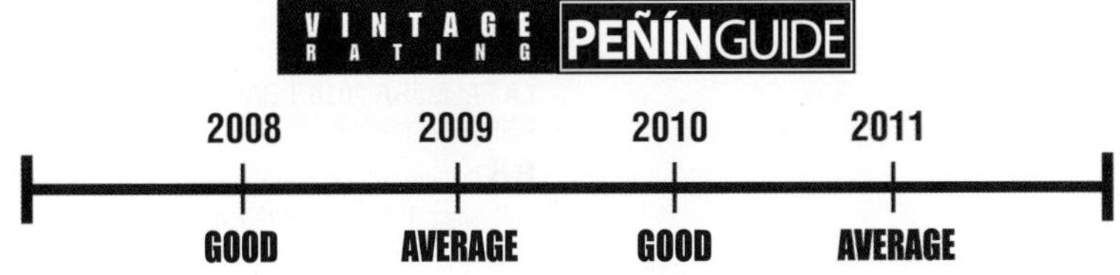

CONSEJO REGULADOR
Ctra. General del Norte, 97 - 38350 Tacoronte (Santa Cruz de Tenerife) - ☎: +34 922 560 107 - Fax: +34 922 561 155
@ consejo@tacovin.com - www.tacovin.com

BODEGA DOMÍNGUEZ CUARTA GENERACIÓN

Calvario, 79
38350 Tacoronte (Santa CruzTenerife)
☎: +34 922 572 435 - Fax: +34 922 572 435
administracion@bodegadominguez.es
www.bodegadominguez.com

DOMÍNGUEZ MALVASÍA CLÁSICO 2010 B
malvasía.

91 Colour: old gold. Nose: complex, elegant, candied fruit, faded flowers, sweet spices. Palate: rich, flavourful, balanced.

DOMÍNGUEZ BLANCO DE UVA TINTA 2010 B
85% negramoll, 15% malvasía.

83

DOMÍNGUEZ CLÁSICO 2011 T
listán negro, negramoll, tintilla.

86 Colour: cherry, purple rim. Nose: red berry notes, balanced, sweet spices. Palate: balanced, good acidity, fine bitter notes.

DOMÍNGUEZ SELECCIÓN NEGRAMOLL 2008 T
negramoll.

86 Colour: cherry, garnet rim. Nose: spicy, ripe fruit, nose:tic coffee. Palate: flavourful, ripe fruit, good acidity.

BODEGA EL LOMO

Ctra. El Lomo, 18
38280 Tegueste (Santa Cruz de Tenerife)
☎: +34 922 545 254 - Fax: +34 922 546 453
oficina@bodegaellomo.com
www.bodegaellomo.com

EL LOMO 2011 B
listán blanco, gual.

82

EL LOMO 2011 T
listán negro, negramoll, listán blanco.

83

BODEGA EL MOCANERO

Ctra. General, 347
38350 Tacoronte (Santa Cruz de Tenerife)
☎: +34 922 560 762 - Fax: +34 922 564 452
elmocanerosl@hotmail.com

EL MOCANERO 2011 T MACERACIÓN CARBÓNICA
100% listán negro.

84

EL MOCANERO 2011 T
90% listán negro, 10% negramoll.

84

EL MOCANERO NEGRAMOLL 2011 T
100% negramoll.

83

BODEGA INSERCASA

Finca El Fresal - Camino Juan Fernandez, Valle Guerra
38270 La Laguna (Santa Cruz de Tenerife)
☎: +34 680 446 868 - Fax: +34 922 270 626
info@vinobronce.com
www.vinobronce.com

BRONCE VENDIMIA SELECCIONADA 2011 T BARRICA

87 Colour: bright cherry, purple rim. Nose: red berry notes, sweet spices, balanced. Palate: balanced, fine bitter notes, good acidity.

BODEGA LA PALMERA

Camino La Herrera, 83
38350 El Sauzal (Santa Cruz de Tenerife)
☎: +34 922 573 485 - Fax: +34 922 652 566
info@bodegalapalmera.com
www.bodegalapalmera.com

LA PALMERA 2011 T
listán negro, castellana.

85 Colour: cherry, purple rim. Nose: wild herbs, fresh, medium intensity. Palate: fruity, flavourful, good acidity.

LA PALMERA 2010 T BARRICA
listán negro, castellana.

86 Colour: bright cherry, garnet rim. Nose: neat, ripe fruit, spicy. Palate: flavourful, fruity, good acidity.

BODEGAS CRATER

San Nicolás, 122
38360 El Sauzal (Santa Cruz de Tenerife)
☎: +34 922 573 272 - Fax: +34 922 573 272
crater@bodegasbutens.com
www.craterbodegas.com

MAGMA DE CRÁTER 2008 TC
80% negramoll, 20% syrah.

93 Colour: cherry, garnet rim. Nose: mineral, complex, expressive, ripe fruit, neat, powerfull, elegant. Palate: good structure, spicy, long.

CRÁTER 2008 TC
70% listán negro, 30% negramoll.

92 Colour: deep cherry, garnet rim. Nose: complex, balanced, ripe fruit, creamy oak, sweet spices, fragrant herbs. Palate: full, flavourful, good structure, round tannins.

BODEGAS INSULARES TENERIFE

Vereda del Medio, 48
38350 Tacoronte (Santa Cruz de Tenerife)
☎: +34 922 570 617 - Fax: +34 922 570 043
bitsa@bodegasinsularestenerife.es
www.bodegasinsularestenerife.es

HUMBOLDT MALVASÍA 2008 B
100% malvasía.

94 Colour: bright yellow. Nose: expressive, complex, candied fruit, floral, honeyed notes, sweet spices, pattiserie. Palate: good structure, flavourful, good acidity, rich.

HUMBOLDT VENDIMIA TARDÍA 2005 B
100% listán blanco.

92 Colour: old gold, amber rim. Nose: complex, expressive, acetaldehyde, candied fruit. Palate: creamy, balanced, long.

VIÑA NORTE 2011 T
95% listán negro, 5% negramoll.

89 Colour: cherry, purple rim. Nose: red berry notes, violets, balanced, expressive. Palate: fruity, flavourful, good acidity, balanced.

VIÑA NORTE 2011 T MACERACIÓN CARBÓNICA
95% listán negro, 5% negramoll.

88 Colour: cherry, purple rim. Nose: fresh, fruit expression, red berry notes. Palate: flavourful, fruity, easy to drink.

VIÑA NORTE 2011 T BARRICA
90% listán negro, 10% negramoll.

87 Colour: deep cherry, purple rim. Nose: ripe fruit, scrubland, sweet spices. Palate: flavourful, spicy, long.

VIÑA NORTE 2007 TC
90% listán negro, 10% otras.

89 Colour: cherry, garnet rim. Nose: balanced, neat, ripe fruit, spicy, nose:tic coffee. Palate: balanced, fine bitter notes.

HUMBOLDT VERDELLO 2005 BLANCO DULCE
100% verdello.

94 Colour: bright yellow. Nose: candied fruit, faded flowers, caramel, sweet spices, petrol notes. Palate: rich, flavourful, good acidity.

HUMBOLDT 1997 BLANCO DULCE
100% listán blanco.

95 Colour: light mahogany. Nose: petrol notes, candied fruit, balanced, elegant, honeyed notes. Palate: rich, powerful, flavourful, full, long.

HUMBOLDT 2001 TINTO DULCE
100% listán negro.

95 Colour: deep cherry, garnet rim. Nose: complex, balanced, expressive, spicy, nose:tic coffee, fruit liqueur notes. Palate: balanced, rich, good structure, sweet tannins, full.

BODEGAS VIÑÁTIGO

Cabo Verde, s/n
38440 La Guancha (Santa Cruz de Tenerife)
☎: +34 922 828 768 - Fax: +34 922 829 936
vinatigo@vinatigo.com
www.vinatigo.com

CEPAS DE LAS HESPÉRIDES 2009 T
baboso negro, tintilla, vijariego negro, negramoll, listán negro.

86 Colour: cherry, garnet rim. Nose: ripe fruit, toasty, spicy. Palate: flavourful, fine bitter notes, spicy, ripe fruit.

CÁNDIDO HERNÁNDEZ PÍO

Los Tomillos s/n
38530 Candelaria (Santa Cruz de Tenerife)
☎: +34 922 513 288 - Fax: +34 922 511 631
almacenlahidalga@telefonica.net

VIÑA RIQUELAS 2011 T
negramoll, listán negro, vidueño.

83

BALCÓN CANARIO 2011 T
negramoll, listán negro, vidueño.

82

BALCÓN CANARIO 2006 TC
negramoll, lado
listán negro, tintilla, vidueño.

85 Colour: light cherry, orangey edge. Nose: balanced, ripe fruit, old leather. Palate: fruity, flavourful, balanced, good acidity.

CARBAJALES

Barranco de San Juan, s/n
38350 Tacoronte (Santa Cruz de Tenerife)
☎: +34 922 275 763 - Fax: +34 922 275 763
loscarbajales@gmail.com
www.carbajales.es

CARBAJALES 2011 T BARRICA

85 Colour: cherry, garnet rim. Nose: medium intensity, balsamic herbs, fresh fruit. Palate: fruity, fresh, correct, good acidity.

EL GRANILETE

El Torreon, s/n
38350 Tacoronte (Santa Cruz de Tenerife)
☎: +34 922 211 414 - Fax: +34 922 209 945
jgescuela@terra.es

EL GRANILETE 2011 T
70% listán negro, 20% tempranillo, 10% tintilla.

83

FINCA LA HORNACA

Camino Hacienda el Pino, 42
38350 Tacoronte (Santa Cruz de Tenerife)
☎: +34 922 560 676
info@hoyadelnavio.com
www.hoyadelnavio.com

HOYA DEL NAVÍO 2010 T
50% listán negro, 50% negramoll.

88 Colour: bright cherry, purple rim. Nose: dark chocolate, sweet spices, balsamic herbs, expressive, candied fruit. Palate: flavourful, long.

HACIENDA DE ACENTEJO

Pérez Díaz, 44
38380 La Victoria de Acentejo (Santa Cruz de Tenerife)
☎: +34 922 581 003 - Fax: +34 922 581 831
almac.gutierrez@gmail.com

HACIENDA ACENTEJO 2011 B
100% listán blanco.

82

HACIENDA ACENTEJO 2011 T BARRICA
90% listán negro, 5% negramoll, 5% otras.

87 Colour: cherry, purple rim. Nose: powerfull, red berry notes, ripe fruit, spicy. Palate: flavourful, fruity, good structure, good acidity.

HACIENDA ACENTEJO 2011 T
90% listán negro, 10% negramoll.

85 Colour: cherry, purple rim. Nose: powerfull, ripe fruit, scrubland, grassy. Palate: flavourful, good structure, long.

MARBA

Ctra. del Socorro, 253 - Portezuelo
38280 Tegueste (Santa Cruz de Tenerife)
☎: +34 639 065 015 - Fax: +34 922 638 400
marba@bodegasmarba.es
www.bodegasmarba.es

MARBA AFRUTADO 2011 B

88 Colour: bright straw. Nose: floral, fresh, citrus fruit. Palate: fruity, flavourful, good finish, correct, fresh.

MARBA BLANCO BARRICA 2011 B

87 Colour: bright straw. Nose: balanced, spicy, ripe fruit, tropical fruit. Palate: flavourful, fruity, balanced, good acidity.

MARBA 2011 B

84

MARBA 2008 B BARRICA

88 Colour: bright golden. Nose: candied fruit, toasty, sweet spices. Palate: fine bitter notes, spicy, good acidity.

MARBA 2011 RD

87 Colour: rose, purple rim. Nose: balanced, expressive, red berry notes, ripe fruit, rose petals. Palate: balanced, flavourful.

MARBA 2011 T MACERACIÓN CARBÓNICA

86 Colour: cherry, purple rim. Nose: grassy, powerfull, fresh fruit. Palate: fruity, flavourful, good acidity.

MARBA 2011 T BARRICA

85 Colour: bright cherry, purple rim. Nose: toasty, spicy, balsamic herbs. Palate: fruity, easy to drink, spicy, toasty.

MONJE

Camino Cruz de Leandro, 36
38359 El Sauzal (Santa Cruz de Tenerife)
☎: +34 922 585 027 - Fax: +34 922 585 027
monje@bodegasmonje.com
www.bodegasmonje.com

HOLLERA MONJE 2011 T MACERACIÓN CARBÓNICA
100% listán negro.

85 Colour: cherry, purple rim. Nose: medium intensity, red berry notes, dried herbs. Palate: correct, good acidity, good finish.

PRESAS OCAMPO

Los Alamos de San Juan, 5
38350 Tacoronte (Santa Cruz de Tenerife)
☎: +34 922 571 689 - Fax: +34 922 561 700
administracion@presasocampo.com
www.presasocampo.com

PRESAS OCAMPO 2011 T MACERACIÓN CARBÓNICA

87 Colour: cherry, purple rim. Nose: fresh, medium intensity, red berry notes, violets. Palate: fruity, flavourful, fresh, balanced.

ALYSIUS 2011 T
listán negro, syrah.

84

PRESAS OCAMPO 2011 T
listán negro, negramoll.

83

TROPICAL MAR

Ctra. Los Angeles, 69
38360 Sauzal (Santa Cruz de Tenerife)
☎: +34 922 575 184
info@dongustavo.eu

DON GUSTAVO 2011 B

84

DON GUSTAVO 2011 RD

82

DON GUSTAVO 2011 T

81

VIÑA EL MATO

Calvario, 270
38350 Tacoronte (Santa Cruz de Tenerife)
☎: +34 625 148 774 - Fax: +34 922 561 752
josesarabia@hotmail.com

VIÑA EL MATÓ 2011 T
listán negro, negramoll, listán blanco.

83

VIÑA EL MATÓ 2011 T MACERACIÓN CARBÓNICA
listán negro, negramoll.

80

VIÑA ESTEVEZ

Pérez Díaz, 80
38380 La Victoria (Santa Cruz de Tenerife)
☎: +34 922 580 779
elena.vinaestevez@gmail.com

VIÑA ESTÉVEZ 2011 T
listán negro, baboso negro, vijariego blanco.

87 Colour: cherry, purple rim. Nose: balanced, medium intensity, red berry notes, spicy. Palate: flavourful, fruity, good structure, good acidity.

DO TARRAGONA

TARRAGONA

Consejo Regulador

DO Boundary

LOCATION:

The region is situated in the province of Tarragona. It comprises two different wine-growing regions: El Camp and Ribera d'Ebre, with a total of 72 municipal areas.

CLIMATE:

Mediterranean in the region of El Camp, with an average annual rainfall of 500 mm. The region of the Ribera has a rather harsh climate with cold winters and hot summers; it also has the lowest rainfall in the region (385 mm per year).

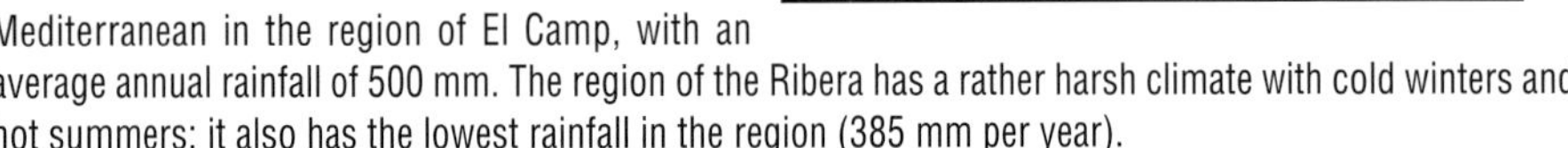

SOIL:

El Camp is characterized by its calcareous, light terrain, and the Ribera has calcareous terrain and also some alluvial terrain.

GRAPE VARIETIES:

WHITE: *Chardonnay, Macabeo, Xarel·lo, Garnacha Blanca, Parellada, Moscatel de Alejandría, Moscatel de Frontignan, Sauvignon Blanc, Malvasía.*
RED: *Samsó (Cariñena), Garnacha, Ull de Llebre (Tempranillo), Cabernet Sauvignon, Merlot, Monastrell, Pinot Noir, Syrah.*

SUB-REGIONS:

El Camp and Ribera d'Ebre
(See specific characteristics in previous sections).

FIGURES:

Vineyard surface: 6.250 – **Wine-Growers:** 2.061 – **Wineries:** 33 – **2011 Harvest rating:** Very Good – **Production:** 4,000,000 litres – **Market percentages:** 50% domestic. 50% export

CONSEJO REGULADOR
Avda. Catalunya, 50 - 43002 Tarragona - ☎: +34 977 217 931 - Fax: +34 977 229 102
@ dotarragona@ctmail.net

AGRÍCOLA I CAIXA AGRÀRIA I SECCIÓ DE CREDIT DE BRAFIM S.C.C.L.

Major, 50
43812 Brafim (Tarragona)
☎: +34 977 620 061 - Fax: +34 977 620 061
oficina@agricolabrafim.com
www.agricolabrafim.com

PUIG RODÓ XAREL.LO 2011 B

86 Colour: bright straw. Nose: fresh, fresh fruit, fragrant herbs, citrus fruit. Palate: flavourful, fruity, good acidity, balanced.

PUIG RODÓ MACABEU 2011 B
macabeo.

85 Colour: bright straw. Nose: expressive, citrus fruit, fragrant herbs. Palate: correct, easy to drink, good finish.

PUIG RODÓ 2011 RD

86 Colour: light cherry. Nose: fresh, red berry notes, fragrant herbs, citrus fruit. Palate: flavourful, easy to drink.

PUIG RODÓ NEGRA 2011 T
ull de llebre, merlot.

85 Colour: cherry, purple rim. Nose: ripe fruit, warm, scrubland. Palate: correct, balanced.

PUIG RODÓ NEGRA 2008 T ROBLE
ull de llebre, merlot.

85 Colour: cherry, garnet rim. Nose: toasty, spicy, tobacco, balanced. Palate: light-bodied, easy to drink.

AGRÍCOLA I S.C. MONTBRIÓ DEL CAMP

Avda. Sant Jordi, 19-21
43340 Montbrió del Camp (Tarragona)
☎: +34 977 826 039 - Fax: +34 977 826 576
montebrione@retemail.es
www.montebrione.com

MOSCATELL MONTEBRIONE BLANCO DULCE

90 Colour: bright yellow. Nose: balanced, expressive, candied fruit, pattiserie, white flowers. Palate: flavourful, fruity.

AGRÍCOLA SANT VICENÇ

Sant Antoni, 29
43748 Ginestar (Ribera d'Ebre) (Tarragona)
☎: +34 977 409 039 - Fax: +34 977 409 006
www.vinsiolisuner.com

SUÑER S/C RD
merlot.

84

SUÑER 2008 T
merlot.

87 Colour: cherry, garnet rim. Nose: ripe fruit, toasty, complex, dark chocolate. Palate: powerful, flavourful, toasty, round tannins, balsamic.

AGRÍCOLA Y SECCIÓ DE CRÉDIT DE RODONYA

St. Sebastia, 3
43812 Rodonya (Tarragona)
☎: +34 977 608 010
crodonya@telefonica.net

SOLIXENT S/C B

82

MIGJORN S/C RD

87 Colour: rose, bright. Nose: fresh, red berry notes, neat, rose petals. Palate: fruity, easy to drink, good finish.

SUMOI CAPVESPRE S/C T

90 Colour: light cherry. Nose: overripe fruit, powerfull, expressive, sweet spices, caramel. Palate: good structure, flavourful, long.

CAPVESPRE S/C T

88 Colour: cherry, purple rim. Nose: ripe fruit, scrubland, medium intensity, mineral. Palate: correct, flavourful, long.

IOMUS CRYO 2009 ESP

86 Colour: rose, bright. Nose: balanced, floral, fruit expression. Palate: fruity, fine bitter notes, balsamic.

IOMUS ANCESTRAL 2009 ESP

86 Colour: rose, bright. Nose: medium intensity, balanced, rose petals. Palate: correct, good acidity, fine bitter notes.

IOMUS BLANC DE NOIRES 2009 ESP

86 Colour: bright straw. Nose: medium intensity, candied fruit, pattiserie. Palate: correct, fine bitter notes, good finish.

IOMUS CLAS 2009 ESP

85 Colour: rose. Nose: slightly evolved, medium intensity, ripe fruit. Palate: flavourful, fine bitter notes.

BODEGAS J. M. BACH I FILLS

Camí Vell de Cambrils 180
43480 Vilaseca (Tarragona)
☎: +34 977 353 099 - Fax: +34 977 353 154
closbarenys@closbarenys.com
www.closbarenys.com

CLOS BARENYS MARIANA RESERVA ESPECIAL DE FAMILIA MAGNUM 2007 T
100% cabernet sauvignon.

90 Colour: cherry, garnet rim. Nose: balanced, expressive, sweet spices, scrubland. Palate: good structure, flavourful, balsamic, ripe fruit, long.

CASTELL D'OR

Mare Rafols, 3- 1º 4º
08720 Vilafranca del Penedès (Barcelona)
☎: +34 938 905 446 - Fax: +34 938 905 446
castelldor@castelldor.com
www.castelldor.com

FLAMA ROJA 2011 B
50% macabeo, 50% xarel.lo.

83

FLAMA ROJA 2011 RD
100% tempranillo.

84

FLAMA ROJA 2009 T
85% tempranillo, 15% garnacha.

85 Colour: cherry, garnet rim. Nose: ripe fruit, wild herbs, spicy. Palate: fruity, correct, easy to drink.

FLAMA ROJA 2006 TR
tempranillo, merlot.

83

CELLER DPEGNA

Mas DPegna. Pol. 2 parcela 5
43747 Miravet (Tarragona)
☎: +34 607 981 525
info@dpegna.com
www.dpegna.com

DAURAT 2011 B
100% macabeo.

83

DPEGNA 2010 T
100% syrah.

86 Colour: cherry, garnet rim. Nose: neat, ripe fruit, toasty. Palate: flavourful, fruity, correct, easy to drink.

CELLER MAS BELLA

Sant Roc, 8 - Masmolets
43813 Valls (Tarragona)
☎: +34 600 269 786 - Fax: +34 977 613 092
cellermasbella@gmail.com

BELLA 2011 B
75% macabeo, 25% parellada.

86 Colour: bright straw. Nose: fresh, wild herbs, citrus fruit. Palate: easy to drink, fresh, good acidity.

BELLA 2010 B
75% macabeo, 25% parellada.

85 Colour: bright straw. Nose: medium intensity, floral, neat, closed. Palate: fruity, fresh, good acidity, good finish.

BELLA 2011 RD
100% ull de llebre.

87 Colour: light cherry, bright. Nose: citrus fruit, fragrant herbs, medium intensity, red berry notes. Palate: fruity, good acidity, fine bitter notes.

BELLA 2010 T
100% ull de llebre.

86 Colour: deep cherry, garnet rim. Nose: powerfull, ripe fruit, spicy, old leather. Palate: correct, easy to drink.

CELLER MAS LA BOELLA

Autovía Reus - Tarragona (T-11), km. 12
43110 La Canonja (Tarragona)
☎: +34 977 771 515 - Fax: +34 977 774 993
celler@laboella.com
www.cellerlaboella.com

MAS LA BOELLA ROURE 2010 T
40% monastrell, 37% cabernet sauvignon, 23% merlot.

86 Colour: cherry, garnet rim. Nose: powerfull, fruit preserve, sweet spices. Palate: fruity, flavourful, good finish.

CELLER PEDROLA

Creu, 5
43747 Miravet (Tarragona)
☎: +34 650 093 906
pedrola97@yahoo.es

CAMÍ DE SIRGA 2011 B
sauvignon blanc, macabeo.

85 Colour: bright yellow. Nose: ripe fruit, faded flowers. Palate: flavourful, fruity, long.

CAMÍ DE SIRGA 2011 T
syrah, merlot.

88 Colour: bright cherry, purple rim. Nose: powerfull, balanced, ripe fruit, spicy, scrubland, dark chocolate. Palate: flavourful, fine bitter notes, round tannins.

CELLERS UNIÓ

Joan Oliver, 16-24
43206 Reus (Tarragona)
☎: +34 977 330 055 - Fax: +34 977 330 070
info@cellersunio.com
www.cellersunio.com

ROUREDA BLANC DE BLANCS 2011 B
50% macabeo, 40% xarel.lo, 10% moscatel.

86 Colour: bright straw. Nose: balanced, fresh, ripe fruit, white flowers. Palate: flavourful, fruity, fine bitter notes.

ROUREDA MERLOT 2011 RD
100% merlot.

86 Colour: light cherry, bright. Nose: medium intensity, red berry notes, floral. Palate: fruity, flavourful, good acidity.

ROUREDA CABERNET SAUVIGNON 2011 T
100% cabernet sauvignon.

86 Colour: cherry, garnet rim. Nose: powerfull, warm, scrubland, ripe fruit. Palate: flavourful, ripe fruit, long.

ROUREDA 2008 TC
40% garnacha, 40% ull de llebre, 20% cabernet sauvignon.

85 Colour: bright cherry, garnet rim. Nose: fruit preserve, toasty, creamy oak. Palate: powerful, ripe fruit, long.

ROUREDA 2008 TR
50% ull de llebre, 25% mazuelo, 25% cabernet sauvignon.

84

DE MULLER

Camí Pedra Estela, 34
43205 Reus (Tarragona)
☎: +34 977 757 473 - Fax: +34 977 771 129
lab@demuller.es
www.demuller.es

DE MULLER CHARDONNAY 2011 BFB
100% chardonnay.

91 Colour: bright golden. Nose: balanced, expressive, faded flowers, citrus fruit, honeyed notes. Palate: fine bitter notes, balanced, good acidity, ripe fruit.

DE MULLER MUSCAT 2011 B
moscatel de alejandría.

87 Colour: bright straw. Nose: expressive, varietal, white flowers, jasmine. Palate: flavourful, fruity, good acidity, balanced.

SOLIMAR 2011 B
35% moscatel de alejandría, 50% macabeo, 15% sauvignon blanc.

86 Colour: bright straw. Nose: medium intensity, white flowers, fresh fruit. Palate: flavourful, fruity, easy to drink.

SOLIMAR 2011 RD
70% tempranillo, 15% syrah, 15% cabernet sauvignon.

87 Colour: rose, purple rim. Nose: powerfull, ripe fruit, red berry notes, floral, expressive. Palate: fleshy, powerful, fruity, fresh.

DE MULLER SYRAH 2011 T
100% syrah.

89 Colour: cherry, garnet rim. Nose: powerfull, balanced, ripe fruit, sweet spices. Palate: balanced, fine bitter notes, long.

DE MULLER MERLOT 2009 T BARRICA
100% merlot.

88 Colour: cherry, garnet rim. Nose: balanced, ripe fruit, expressive, dried herbs, sweet spices. Palate: ripe fruit, balanced.

SOLIMAR 2009 TC
60% cabernet sauvignon, 40% merlot.

87 Colour: dark-red cherry, orangey edge. Nose: ripe fruit, spicy, powerfull, balsamic herbs. Palate: toasty, round tannins, good structure.

DE MULLER CABERNET SAUVIGNON 2009 TC
100% cabernet sauvignon.

84

PORPORES DE MULLER 2007 TR
cabernet sauvignon, merlot, tempranillo.

88 Colour: dark-red cherry, orangey edge. Nose: powerfull, ripe fruit, wild herbs. Palate: ripe fruit, long, spicy.

VINO DE MISA DULCE SUPERIOR
60% garnacha blanca, 40% macabeo.

90 Colour: old gold. Nose: fruit liqueur notes, honeyed notes, sweet spices, aged wood nuances, spicy. Palate: long, rich, powerful, flavourful, balanced.

DE MULLER AVREO SECO AÑEJO
70% garnacha, 30% garnacha blanca.

91 Colour: mahogany. Nose: roasted almonds, balanced, acetaldehyde. Palate: good structure, flavourful, fine bitter notes.

DE MULLER AVREO SEMIDULCE AÑEJO
garnacha, garnacha blanca.

91 Colour: light mahogany. Nose: spicy, fruit liqueur notes, fruit liqueur notes, toasty, nose:tic coffee. Palate: powerful, sweet.

MAS DE VALLS 2010 BN
55% macabeo, 35% chardonnay, 10% parellada.

88 Colour: bright yellow. Nose: ripe fruit, faded flowers, dry nuts. Palate: balanced, good acidity, fine bitter notes.

RESERVA REINA VIOLANT 2008 ESP
50% chardonnay, 50% pinot noir.

89 Colour: bright yellow. Nose: complex, candied fruit, spicy, faded flowers, fine lees. Palate: balanced, flavourful.

PAJARETE SOLERA 1851 RANCIO
moscatel de alejandría, garnacha, garnacha blanca.

93 Colour: iodine, amber rim. Nose: powerfull, complex, elegant, dry nuts, toasty. Palate: rich, fine bitter notes, fine solera notes, long, spicy.

DE MULLER GARNACHA SOLERA 1926 SOLERA
100% garnacha.

94 Colour: iodine, amber rim. Nose: powerfull, complex, elegant, dry nuts, toasty. Palate: rich, fine bitter notes, fine solera notes, long, spicy.

DE MULLER RANCIO SECO VINO DE LICOR
garnacha, cariñena.

91 Colour: light mahogany. Nose: balanced, expressive, roasted almonds, sweet spices, acetaldehyde. Palate: good structure, flavourful, complex.

DE MULLER MOSCATEL AÑEJO VINO DE LICOR
moscatel de alejandría.

90 Colour: light mahogany. Nose: powerfull, varietal, fruit liqueur notes, honeyed notes. Palate: fine bitter notes, good acidity, spirituous.

MAS DEL BOTÓ

Bon Recer, 13
43007 (Tarragona)
☎: +34 630 982 747 - Fax: +34 977 236 396
pep@masdelboto.cat
www.masdelboto.cat

MAS DEL BOTÓ 2010 T
47% garnacha, 33% cabernet sauvignon, 20% samsó.

86 Colour: cherry, garnet rim. Nose: powerfull, warm, ripe fruit, dried herbs. Palate: flavourful, easy to drink, good finish.

GANAGOT 2008 T
60% garnacha, 40% samsó.

89 Colour: bright cherry, garnet rim. Nose: balanced, expressive, wild herbs, spicy, dark chocolate. Palate: full, round tannins, good acidity.

GANAGOT 2007 T
60% garnacha, 25% cabernet sauvignon, 15% samsó.

88 Colour: cherry, garnet rim. Nose: creamy oak, dark chocolate, fruit preserve. Palate: good structure, flavourful, balanced, fine bitter notes.

GANAGOT 2006 T
85% garnacha, 10% samsó, 5% cabernet sauvignon.

87 Colour: cherry, garnet rim. Nose: fruit preserve, creamy oak, dark chocolate. Palate: flavourful, round tannins, fine bitter notes.

GANAGOT 2005 T
85% garnacha, 10% samsó, 5% cabernet sauvignon.

88 Colour: cherry, garnet rim. Nose: toasty, wild herbs, warm, ripe fruit. Palate: good structure, round tannins.

MAS DELS FRARES (FACULTAT D'ENOLOGIA DE TARRAGONA)

Ctra. TV-7211, Km. 7,2
43120 Constantí (Tarragona)
☎: +34 977 520 197 - Fax: +34 977 522 156
fincafe@urv.cat

URV NOSE:TIC 2011 B
60% moscatel, 10% sauvignon blanc, 30% parellada.

84

URV 2011 B
50% xarel.lo, 50% chardonnay.

84

URV 2011 T
85% tempranillo, 15% merlot.

83

URV 2008 TC
50% cabernet sauvignon, 20% merlot, 20% tempranillo, 10% garnacha.

86 Colour: cherry, garnet rim. Nose: spicy, ripe fruit, toasty. Palate: fruity, flavourful, good finish.

URV 2007 TR
50% cabernet sauvignon, 50% merlot.

87 Colour: cherry, garnet rim. Nose: scrubland, ripe fruit, cocoa bean, balanced. Palate: fine bitter notes, correct.

URV BLANC DE BLANCS 2009 BR
40% macabeo, 30% xarel.lo, 20% parellada, 10% chardonnay.

86 Colour: bright yellow. Nose: faded flowers, slightly evolved. Palate: flavourful, fruity, good finish, good acidity.

MAS VICENÇ

Mas Vicenç, s/n
43811 Cabra de Camp (Tarragona)
☎: +34 977 630 024
masvicens@masvicens.com
www.masvicens.com

EL VI DEL VENT 2011 B
moscatel grano menudo.

88 Colour: bright straw. Nose: white flowers, varietal, expressive, jasmine. Palate: rich, flavourful, balanced.

EL TERRAT 2011 B
macabeo, moscatel.

87 Colour: bright straw. Nose: fresh, fresh fruit, white flowers, expressive. Palate: flavourful, fruity, good acidity, balanced.

DENT DE LLEÓ 2011 B
chardonnay.

86 Colour: bright yellow. Nose: powerfull, sweet spices, roasted coffee. Palate: rich, flavourful, toasty.

NIT DE LLUNA 2010 TC
ull de llebre, syrah.

87 Colour: cherry, garnet rim. Nose: ripe fruit, spicy, creamy oak, toasty, warm. Palate: powerful, flavourful, toasty, round tannins.

ROMBES D'ARLEQUI 2009 TC
ull de llebre, cabernet sauvignon, cariñena.

89 Colour: bright cherry. Nose: ripe fruit, sweet spices, creamy oak, expressive. Palate: flavourful, fruity, toasty, round tannins, balsamic.

VINÍCOLA DE NULLES S.C.C.L.

Estació, s/n
43887 Nulles (Tarragona)
☎: +34 977 602 622 - Fax: +34 977 602 622
botiga@vinicoladenulles.com
www.vinicoladenulles.com

ADERNATS 2011 BFB
100% xarel.lo.

89 Colour: bright yellow. Nose: balanced, sweet spices, floral, ripe fruit. Palate: flavourful, fruity, good acidity.

ADERNATS SEDUCCIÓ 2011 B
46% moscatel, 29% xarel.lo, 14% chardonnay, 11% macabeo.

87 Colour: bright yellow. Nose: ripe fruit, white flowers, powerfull. Palate: flavourful, fruity, ripe fruit, long.

ADERNATS BLANC 2011 B
50% macabeo, 26% xarel.lo, 23% parellada, 1% chardonnay.

86 Colour: bright straw. Nose: medium intensity, white flowers, dried herbs. Palate: correct, fine bitter notes, good finish.

ADERNATS ROSAT 2011 RD
57% tempranillo, 25% merlot, 18% cabernet sauvignon.

89 Colour: rose, purple rim. Nose: powerfull, ripe fruit, red berry notes, floral, expressive. Palate: fleshy, powerful, fruity, fresh.

ADERNATS NEGRE JOVE 2011 T
60% tempranillo, 35% merlot, 5% cabernet sauvignon.

84

ADERNATS ANGELUS 2010 T
50% tempranillo, 36% cabernet sauvignon, 14% merlot.

83

ADERNATS 2008 TC
50% ull de llebre, 25% cabernet sauvignon, 25% merlot.

88 Colour: cherry, garnet rim. Nose: powerfull, fruit preserve, dark chocolate, sweet spices. Palate: flavourful, good structure, round tannins, good acidity.

VINOS PADRÓ

Avda. Catalunya, 64-70
43812 Brafim (Tarragona)
☎: +34 977 620 012 - Fax: +34 977 620 486
info@vinspadro.com
www.vinspadro.com

IPSIS BLANCO FLOR 2011 B
xarel.lo, macabeo, moscatel.

87 Colour: bright straw. Nose: white flowers, fragrant herbs. Palate: flavourful, fruity, balanced.

IPSIS CHARDONNAY 2011 B
chardonnay.

87 Colour: bright yellow. Nose: ripe fruit, sweet spices, dried flowers. Palate: rich, smoky afterpalate:, flavourful, fresh, good acidity.

IPSIS TEMPRANILLO MERLOT 2011 T
tempranillo, merlot.

87 Colour: deep cherry, purple rim. Nose: ripe fruit, powerfull, wild herbs. Palate: powerful, full, long.

CRINEL 2011 T
tempranillo, merlot.

86 Colour: bright cherry, purple rim. Nose: balanced, medium intensity, ripe fruit. Palate: flavourful, correct, good finish.

IPSIS 2009 TC
tempranillo, merlot.

90 Colour: bright cherry, purple rim. Nose: sweet spices, toasty, ripe fruit. Palate: ripe fruit, long, round tannins.

CRINEL 2009 TC
tempranillo, garnacha.

88 Colour: cherry, garnet rim. Nose: ripe fruit, spicy, creamy oak, toasty. Palate: powerful, flavourful, toasty, round tannins.

IPSIS TEMPRANILLO SELECCIÓ 2009 TC
tempranillo.

87 Colour: deep cherry, garnet rim. Nose: medium intensity, ripe fruit, spicy. Palate: flavourful, fruity, good finish.

VINS ECOLÒGICS HELGA HARBIG CEREZO

Plaça St. Joan, 3
43513 Rasquera (Tarragona)
☎: +34 977 404 711
biopaumera@gmail.com

ERIKA DE PAUMERA 2011 RD
garnacha, cabernet sauvignon.

81

ADRIÀ DE PAUMERA 2010 T ROBLE
garnacha, cabernet sauvignon.

88 Colour: bright cherry. Nose: toasty, ripe fruit, fruit preserve, scrubland. Palate: flavourful, fruity, toasty, full.

VINYA JANINE

Anselm Clavé, 1
43812 Rodonyá (Tarragona)
☎: +34 977 628 305 - Fax: +34 977 628 305
vjanine@tinet.org
www.vinyajanine.com

VINYA JANINE XAREL.LO 2011 B
100% xarel.lo.

85 Colour: bright straw. Nose: fresh, medium intensity, dried flowers. Palate: correct, good acidity, easy to drink.

BLANC MARÍ 2011 B
xarel.lo vermell.

84

VINYA JANINE MERLOT 2011 RD
100% merlot.

84

SYH 2011 T
100% syrah.

87 Colour: cherry, purple rim. Nose: red berry notes, ripe fruit, balanced, powerfull. Palate: balanced, fine bitter notes, round tannins, spicy.

VINYES DEL TERRER

Camí del Terrer, s/n
43480 Vila-Seca (Tarragona)
☎: +34 977 269 229 - Fax: +34 977 269 229
info@terrer.net
www.terrer.net

NUS DEL TERRER 2010 T
65% cabernet sauvignon, 35% garnacha.

93 Colour: cherry, garnet rim. Nose: ripe fruit, spicy, creamy oak, toasty, complex, fruit expression, red berry notes. Palate: powerful, flavourful, toasty, round tannins, round.

TERRER D'AUBERT 2010 T
95% cabernet sauvignon, 5% garnacha.

92 Colour: cherry, garnet rim. Nose: spicy, creamy oak, toasty, characterful. Palate: powerful, flavourful, toasty, round tannins.

NUS DEL TERRER 2009 T
55% cabernet sauvignon, 45% garnacha.

93 Colour: cherry, garnet rim. Nose: ripe fruit, spicy, creamy oak, toasty, complex, cigar. Palate: powerful, flavourful, toasty, round tannins.

DO TERRA ALTA

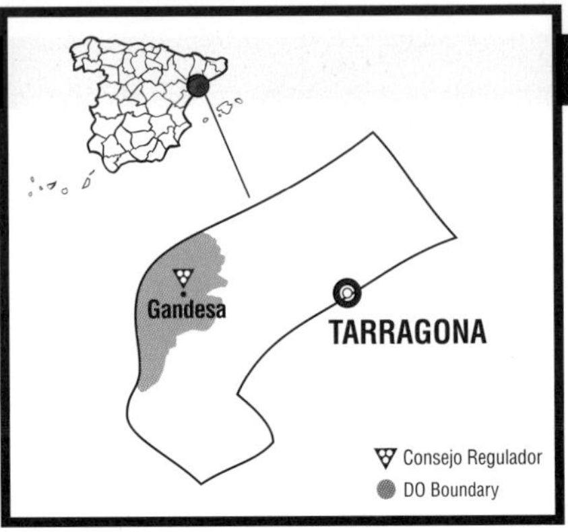

LOCATION:

In the southeast of Catalonia, in the province of Tarragona. It covers the municipal districts of Arnes, Batea, Bot, Caseres, Corbera d Ebre, La Fatarella, Gandesa, Horta de Sant Joan, Pinell de Brai, La Pobla de Massaluca, Prat de Comte and Vilalba dels Arcs.

CLIMATE:

Mediterranean, with continental influences. It is characterized by its hot, dry summers and very cold winters, especially in the higher regions in the east. The average annual rainfall is 400 mm. Another vital aspect is the wind: the 'Cierzo' and the 'Garbi' (Ábrego) winds.

SOIL:

The vineyards are located on an extensive plateau at an altitude of slightly over 400 m. The soil is calcareous and the texture mainly clayey, poor in organic matter and with many pebbles.

GRAPE VARIETIES:

WHITE: *Chardonnay, Garnacha Blanca, Parellada, Macabeo, Moscatel, Sauvignon Blanc, Chenin, Pedro Ximénez.* Experimental: *Viognier.*
RED: *Cabernet Sauvigon, Cariñena, Garnacha Tinta, Garnacha Peluda, Syrah, Tempranillo, Merlot, Samsó, Cabernet Franc.* Experimental: *Petit Verdot, Marselane, Caladoc.*

FIGURES:

Vineyard surface: 5,895 – **Wine-Growers:** 1,460 – **Wineries:** 48 – **2011 Harvest rating:** Good – **Production:** 13,981,423 litres – **Market percentages:** 30% domestic. 70% export

CONSEJO REGULADOR
Avinguda Catalunya, 31 - 43780 Gandesa (Tarragona) - ☎: +34 977 421 278 - Fax: +34 977 421 623
@ info@doterraalta.com - www.doterraalta.com

AGRÍCOLA CORBERA D'EBRE

Ponent, 21
43784 Corbera d'Ebre (Tarragona)
☎: +34 977 420 432
coop@corbera.tinet.org
www.agricolacorberadebre.com

NAKENS 2011 B
parellada, moscatel de alejandría.

87 Colour: bright straw. Nose: fresh, fresh fruit, white flowers, expressive. Palate: flavourful, fruity, good acidity, balanced.

MIRMIL-LÓ PARELLADA 2011 B
parellada.

83

VALL EXCELS 2010 BFB
garnacha blanca.

78

MIRMIL-LÓ ROSAT 2011 RD
garnacha.

84

MIRMIL-LÓ NEGRE 2011 T
garnacha, cariñena, tempranillo, syrah.

84

VALL EXCELS 2009 TC
garnacha, tempranillo.

84

AGRÍCOLA I S.C. TERRA ALTA S.C.C.L.(CATERRA)

Glorieta, s/n
43783 La Pobla de Massaluca (Tarragona)
☎: +34 977 439 765 - Fax: +34 977 439 765
catapoma@caterra.es
www.caterra.es

HEREUS CATERRA 2011 T
garnacha, cariñena, syrah.

84

FONT CALENTA NEGRE 2011 T
garnacha, cariñena.

83

AGRÍCOLA SANT JOSEP

Estació, 2
43785 Bot (Tarragona)
☎: +34 977 428 035 - Fax: +34 977 428 192
info@coopbot.com
www.coopbot.com

CLOT D'ENCÍS 2011 B
80% garnacha blanca, 20% sauvignon blanc, chardonnay, chenin blanc, moscatel.

86 Colour: bright straw. Nose: fresh, fresh fruit, white flowers. Palate: flavourful, fruity, good acidity, balanced.

BRAU DE BOT 2011 B
80% sauvignon blanc, chardonnay, chenin blanc, moscatel, 20% garnacha blanca.

84

LLÀGRIMES DE TARDOR 2010 BFB
100% garnacha blanca.

92 Colour: bright yellow. Nose: powerfull, ripe fruit, sweet spices, creamy oak, fragrant herbs. Palate: rich, smoky afterpalate:, flavourful, fresh, good acidity.

CLOT D'ENCIS 2011 RD
50% garnacha, 50% syrah.

84

CLOT D'ENCÍS 2011 T
70% garnacha, 10% cabernet sauvignon, 10% syrah, 10% cariñena.

86 Colour: bright cherry. Nose: ripe fruit, sweet spices, expressive. Palate: flavourful, fruity, round tannins.

BRAU DE BOT 2011 T
51% garnacha, 23% cariñena, 20% tempranillo, 6% syrah.

83

LLÀGRIMES DE TARDOR 2008 TC
45% garnacha, 10% samsó, 15% cabernet sauvignon, 15% merlot, 15% syrah.

89 Colour: cherry, garnet rim. Nose: ripe fruit, spicy, creamy oak, toasty, balsamic herbs. Palate: powerful, flavourful, toasty.

LLÀGRIMES DE TARDOR SELECCIÓ 2006 TC
30% cariñena, 23% cabernet sauvignon, 23% syrah, 14% merlot, 10% garnacha.

91 Colour: cherry, garnet rim. Nose: ripe fruit, spicy, creamy oak, toasty. Palate: powerful, flavourful, toasty, round tannins.

LLÀGRIMES DE TARDOR MISTELA BLANCA 2010
100% garnacha blanca.

89 Colour: golden. Nose: powerfull, floral, honeyed notes, candied fruit, fragrant herbs. Palate: flavourful, sweet, fresh, fruity, good acidity, long.

LLÀGRIMES DE TARDOR MISTELA NEGRA 2011 VINO DE LICOR
100% garnacha.

90 Colour: cherry, garnet rim. Nose: fruit liqueur notes, sweet spices, creamy oak, dark chocolate. Palate: rich, powerful, flavourful, balanced.

ALGRAMAR

Major, 12
43782 Vilalba dels Arcs (Tarragona)
☎: +34 628 818 759
algramar@algramar.com
www.algramar.com

VALL NOVENES BLANC 2011 B
chenin blanc, sauvignon blanc.

87 Colour: bright straw. Nose: faded flowers, ripe fruit, citrus fruit. Palate: flavourful, good acidity, fine bitter notes.

ALTAVINS VITICULTORS

Tarragona, 42
43786 Batea (Tarragona)
☎: +34 977 430 596 - Fax: +34 977 430 371
altavins@altavins.com
www.altavins.com

ILERCAVONIA 2011 B

87 Colour: bright straw. Nose: ripe fruit, powerfull, characterful. Palate: flavourful, powerful.

ALMODÍ PETIT BLANC 2011 B

84

ALMODÍ PETIT NEGREG 2011 T

85 Colour: cherry, garnet rim. Nose: scrubland, fruit preserve, overripe fruit. Palate: powerful, sweetness, fine bitter notes.

ALMODÍ 2010 T ROBLE

86 Colour: cherry, garnet rim. Nose: ripe fruit, fruit preserve, roasted coffee. Palate: flavourful, long, balsamic.

TEMPUS 2009 T ROBLE

87 Colour: deep cherry, garnet rim. Nose: powerfull, ripe fruit, dark chocolate, warm, fruit preserve. Palate: good structure, concentrated, round tannins.

DOMUS PENSI 2006 TC

87 Colour: cherry, garnet rim. Nose: ripe fruit, spicy, creamy oak, toasty. Palate: powerful, flavourful, toasty, round tannins.

ANDREU ROCA VAQUE

Avda. Terra Alta, 67
43786 Batea (Tarragona)
☎: +34 610 254 964 - Fax: +34 977 705 773
roca.andreu@gmail.com

VALL DE VINYES 2011 B
macabeo, garnacha blanca, chardonnay.

85 Colour: bright straw. Nose: white flowers, expressive, ripe fruit. Palate: flavourful, fruity, good acidity.

VALL DE VINYES 2011 T
garnacha, syrah.

85 Colour: deep cherry. Nose: powerfull, ripe fruit, red berry notes, scrubland. Palate: powerful, sweetness.

VALL DE VINYES 2005 T BARRICA

89 Colour: cherry, garnet rim. Nose: ripe fruit, spicy, creamy oak, toasty, complex. Palate: powerful, flavourful, toasty, round tannins.

BODEGAS ABANICO

Pol. Ind Ca l'Avellanet - Susany, 6
08553 Seva (Barcelona)
☎: +34 938 125 676 - Fax: +34 938 123 213
info@exportiberia.com
www.bodegasabanico.com

LAS COLINAS DEL EBRO 2011 B
100% garnacha blanca.

87 Colour: bright straw. Nose: fresh, fresh fruit, white flowers, expressive. Palate: flavourful, fruity, good acidity, balanced.

LAS COLINAS DEL EBRO 2011 T
60% garnacha, 40% syrah.

87 Colour: light cherry, garnet rim. Nose: red berry notes, ripe fruit, floral, balsamic herbs. Palate: flavourful, fresh, fruity, easy to drink.

LAS COLINAS DEL EBRO SELECCIÓN 2008 T
60% merlot, 25% syrah, 15% garnacha.

88 Colour: cherry, garnet rim. Nose: spicy, creamy oak, toasty, characterful, ripe fruit. Palate: powerful, flavourful, toasty, round tannins.

BODEGAS PINORD

Doctor Pasteur, 6
08720 Vilafranca del Penedès (Barcelona)
☎: +34 938 903 066 - Fax: +34 938 170 979
pinord@pinord.es
www.pinord.es

PINORD DIORAMA GARNACHA BLANCA 2011 B
garnacha blanca.

88 Colour: bright straw. Nose: complex, balanced, expressive, neat. Palate: fine bitter notes, good acidity.

PINORD DIORAMA GARNACHA NEGRA 2010 T
garnacha.

88 Colour: cherry, garnet rim. Nose: medium intensity, expressive, red berry notes, ripe fruit, wild herbs. Palate: flavourful, fruity.

CELLER BÁRBARA FORÉS

Santa Anna, 28
43780 Gandesa (Tarragona)
☎: +34 977 420 160 - Fax: +34 977 421 399
info@cellerbarbarafores.com
www.cellerbarbarafores.com

BÁRBARA FORÉS 2011 B
97% garnacha blanca, 3% viognier.

89 Colour: bright straw. Nose: fresh, fresh fruit, white flowers, grassy. Palate: flavourful, fruity, good acidity, balanced.

QUINTÀ BÁRBARA FORÉS 2011 BFB
100% garnacha blanca.

89 Colour: yellow. Nose: ripe fruit, powerfull, sweet spices, creamy oak, floral. Palate: balanced, rich, flavourful.

VI DOLÇ NATURAL BÁRBARA FORÉS 2009 B
garnacha blanca.

93 Colour: bright golden. Nose: candied fruit, acetaldehyde, expressive, balanced. Palate: flavourful, rich, balanced.

BÁRBARA FORÉS 2011 RD
46% garnacha, 43% syrah, 11% cariñena.

87 Colour: rose, purple rim. Nose: powerfull, ripe fruit, red berry notes, floral, expressive. Palate: fleshy, powerful, fruity, fresh.

EL TEMPLARI BÁRBARA FORÉS 2010 T
55% garnacha, 45% morenillo.

92 Colour: deep cherry. Nose: ripe fruit, red berry notes, earthy notes. Palate: ripe fruit, good acidity, balanced.

BÁRBARA FORÉS NEGRE 2010 T
59% garnacha, 16% syrah, 15% cariñena, 10% merlot.

88 Colour: bright cherry. Nose: ripe fruit, sweet spices, creamy oak. Palate: flavourful, fruity, toasty.

COMA D'EN POU BÀRBARA FORÉS 2008 T
45% garnacha, 30% syrah, 25% cabernet sauvignon.

91 Colour: cherry, garnet rim. Nose: ripe fruit, spicy, creamy oak, complex, wild herbs. Palate: powerful, flavourful, round tannins.

CELLER BATEA

Moli, 30
43786 Batea (Tarragona)
☎: +34 977 430 056 - Fax: +34 977 430 589
cellerbatea@cellerbatea.com
www.cellerbatea.com

PRIMICIA CHARDONNAY 2011 B
chardonnay.

88 Colour: bright straw. Nose: fresh, fresh fruit, white flowers, expressive. Palate: flavourful, fruity, good acidity, balanced.

VALL MAJOR 2011 B
garnacha blanca.

87 Colour: bright straw. Nose: fresh, white flowers, ripe fruit. Palate: flavourful, fruity, good acidity, balanced.

EQUINOX B

91 Colour: golden. Nose: powerfull, floral, honeyed notes, candied fruit, fragrant herbs. Palate: flavourful, sweet, fresh, fruity, good acidity, long.

EQUINOX "GARNATXA BLANCA" B ROBLE

87 Colour: light mahogany. Nose: spicy, nose:tic coffee, roasted almonds. Palate: powerful, sweet.

VALL MAJOR 2011 RD
garnacha, syrah.

85 Colour: rose, purple rim. Nose: powerfull, ripe fruit, red berry notes, floral, expressive. Palate: fleshy, powerful, fruity, fresh.

VALL MAJOR NEGRE 2011 T
garnacha, syrah.

87 Colour: cherry, purple rim. Nose: scrubland, ripe fruit, earthy notes. Palate: powerful, flavourful, correct.

PRIMICIA GARNACHA SYRAH 2009 T
garnacha, syrah.

87 Colour: cherry, garnet rim. Nose: powerfull, ripe fruit, fruit liqueur notes, earthy notes. Palate: powerful, spicy, ripe fruit.

L'AUBE "SELECCIO DE VINYES VELLES" 2008 TC
merlot, garnacha, cabernet sauvignon.

88 Colour: deep cherry, very deep cherry. Nose: powerfull, wild herbs, ripe fruit, fruit preserve. Palate: good structure, concentrated.

TIPICITAT 2008 T
garnacha, samsó.

88 Colour: bright cherry. Nose: ripe fruit, sweet spices, creamy oak, expressive, mineral. Palate: flavourful, fruity, toasty, round tannins.

VIVERTELL 2008 TC
garnacha, syrah, cabernet sauvignon, tempranillo.

86 Colour: deep cherry. Nose: powerfull, fruit preserve, overripe fruit, warm. Palate: fine bitter notes, toasty, concentrated.

EQUINOX S/C MISTELA
garnacha.

90 Colour: black cherry. Nose: toasty, fruit preserve. Palate: flavourful, long, concentrated, powerful, sweet, fruity.

CELLER COMA D'EN BONET

Camí de Les Comes d'En Bonet s/n
43780 Gandesa (Tarragona)
☎: +34 977 055 014 - Fax: +34 977 234 665
dardell@dardell.es
www.dardell.es

PROHOM 2011 B
garnacha, viognier.

88 Colour: bright straw. Nose: fresh, fresh fruit, white flowers. Palate: flavourful, fruity, good acidity.

DARDELL GARNACHA & VIOGNIER 2011 B
garnacha, viognier.

87 Colour: bright straw. Nose: fresh, fresh fruit, white flowers, medium intensity. Palate: flavourful, fruity, good acidity.

DARDELL GARNACHA Y SYRAH 2011 T
garnacha, syrah.

83

PROHOM 2010 T
syrah, merlot.

84

DARDELL 10 MESES BARRICA 2009 T BARRICA
garnacha, syrah, cabernet sauvignon.

86 Colour: cherry, garnet rim. Nose: ripe fruit, spicy, creamy oak, toasty. Palate: powerful, flavourful, toasty, round tannins.

CELLER COOPERATIU GANDESA

Avda. Catalunya, 28
43780 Gandesa (Tarragona)
☎: +34 977 420 017 - Fax: +34 977 420 403
perefiguereo@coopgandesa.com
www.coopgandesa.com

GANDESOLA 2011 B
85% garnacha blanca, 15% macabeo.

87 Colour: bright straw. Nose: fresh, fresh fruit, white flowers. Palate: flavourful, fruity, good acidity, balanced.

ANTIC CASTELL 2010 B ROBLE
100% garnacha blanca.

83

GANDESOLA 2011 RD
100% garnacha.

82

GANDESOLA 2011 T
85% garnacha, 15% tempranillo.

86 Colour: cherry, purple rim. Nose: ripe fruit, medium intensity, scrubland. Palate: flavourful, fruity, good finish.

ANTIC CASTELL NEGRE 2009 T
70% garnacha, 20% cariñena, 10% syrah.

84

GANDESOLA 2008 TC
40% garnacha, 40% cariñena, 20% syrah.

84

VARVALL NEGRE 2006 TC
33% garnacha, 33% cariñena, 18% syrah, 16% cabernet sauvignon.

87 Colour: deep cherry, orangey edge. Nose: balanced, ripe fruit, spicy. Palate: fruity, flavourful.

GANDESA MISTELA TINTA 2007 MISTELA
100% garnacha.

87 Colour: cherry, garnet rim. Nose: powerfull, floral, candied fruit, fruit liqueur notes. Palate: flavourful, sweet, fresh, fruity, good acidity, long.

GANDESA VI RANCI RANCIO
100% garnacha blanca.

90 Colour: iodine, amber rim. Nose: powerfull, complex, elegant, dry nuts, toasty. Palate: rich, fine bitter notes, fine solera notes, long, spicy.

GANDESA MISTELA BLANCA 2009 VINO DE LICOR
100% garnacha blanca.

82

VI DE LICOR 1919 VINO DE LICOR
100% garnacha blanca.

89 Colour: light mahogany. Nose: candied fruit, honeyed notes, acetaldehyde, varnish, nose:tic coffee. Palate: flavourful, fine bitter notes, balanced.

CELLER JORDI MIRÓ

Sant Marc, 96
43784 Corbera d'Ebre (Tarragona)
☎: +34 650 010 639
jordi@ennak.com
www.jordimirodiego.blogsopt.com

JORDI MIRÓ MP 2011 B
garnacha blanca.

84

JORDI MIRÓ MC 2011 T
garnacha, syrah.

87 Colour: cherry, purple rim. Nose: fruit preserve, balsamic herbs. Palate: ripe fruit, sweetness, fruity.

ENNAK 2011 T
garnacha, merlot, ull de llebre, cabernet sauvignon.

85 Colour: cherry, garnet rim. Nose: powerfull, characterful, warm, overripe fruit. Palate: powerful, fine bitter notes, round tannins.

ENNAK 2010 TC
garnacha, tempranillo, merlot, cabernet sauvignon.

91 Colour: cherry, garnet rim. Nose: ripe fruit, spicy, creamy oak, toasty, complex, earthy notes. Palate: powerful, flavourful, toasty, round tannins.

CELLER LA BOLLIDORA

Tacons, 8
43782 Vilalba dels Arcs (Tarragona)
☎: +34 600 484 900
laboratori@cellerlabollidora.com
www.cellerlabollidora.com

CALITJA 2011 B
garnacha blanca.

85 Colour: coppery red. Nose: medium intensity, candied fruit. Palate: flavourful, sweetness, ripe fruit.

FLOR DE GARNATXA 2007 BFB
garnacha blanca.

88 Colour: bright yellow. Nose: powerfull, ripe fruit, sweet spices, creamy oak, fragrant herbs. Palate: rich, smoky afterpalate:, flavourful, fresh, good acidity.

PLAN B 2008 T
garnacha, morenillo, syrah.

81

PUNTO G 2007 T
carignan, garnacha, syrah.

87 Colour: very deep cherry. Nose: powerfull, overripe fruit, fruit liqueur notes, spicy. Palate: powerful, fine bitter notes, warm.

CELLER M.V. BALART

Buenos Aires, 4
43780 Gandesa (Tarragona)
☎: +34 600 484 900
cellermvbalart@gmail.com

BORRETES 2004 TC
carignan.

84

CELLER MARIOL/CASA MARIOL

Rosselló, 442
08025 (Barcelona)
☎: +34 934 367 628 - Fax: +34 934 500 281
celler@cellermariol.es
www.casamariol.com

CASA MARIOL CUPATGE DINÀMIC CHARDONNAY 2011 B
chardonnay.

85 Colour: bright straw. Nose: medium intensity, white flowers, ripe fruit. Palate: fruity, good finish.

CASA MARIOL CABERNET SAUVIGNON 2010 TC
100% cabernet sauvignon.

88 Colour: cherry, garnet rim. Nose: ripe fruit, spicy, creamy oak, toasty, complex. Palate: powerful, flavourful, toasty, round tannins.

CASA MARIOL ULL DE LLEBRE (TEMPRANILLO) 2010 TC
100% ull de llebre.

88 Colour: bright cherry. Nose: ripe fruit, sweet spices, creamy oak. Palate: flavourful, fruity, toasty, round tannins.

CASA MARIOL MERLOT 2008 TR
100% merlot.

89 Colour: cherry, garnet rim. Nose: spicy, balanced, powerfull. Palate: balanced, ripe fruit, long.

CASA MARIOL SYRAH 2008 TR
100% syrah.

86 Colour: cherry, garnet rim. Nose: medium intensity, ripe fruit, sweet spices. Palate: good structure, flavourful.

CELLER MENESCAL

Joan Amades, 2
43785 Bot (Tarragona)
☎: +34 977 428 095 - Fax: +34 977 428 261
info@cellermenescal.com
www.cellermenescal.com

MAS DEL MENESCAL 2011 T
90% garnacha, 10% syrah.

87 Colour: deep cherry, purple rim. Nose: red berry notes, ripe fruit, balanced, expressive. Palate: correct, flavourful, fruity.

AVUS DOLÇ 2010 T
garnacha.

88 Colour: pale ruby, brick rim edge. Nose: fruit liqueur notes, fruit preserve, warm. Palate: powerful, sweet, good acidity, warm.

CELLER PIÑOL

Avda. Aragón, 9
43786 Batea (Tarragona)
☎: +34 977 430 505 - Fax: +34 977 430 498
info@cellerpinol.com
www.vinospinol.com

PORTAL N. SRA. PORTAL 2011 B
80% garnacha blanca, 10% sauvignon blanc, 10% viognier.

91 Colour: bright straw. Nose: fresh, fresh fruit, white flowers. Palate: flavourful, fruity, good acidity, balanced.

RAIG DE RAIM 2011 B
80% garnacha blanca, 20% macabeo.

88 Colour: bright straw. Nose: fresh, white flowers. Palate: flavourful, fruity, good acidity, balanced.

L'AVI ARRUFÍ 2010 BFB
garnacha blanca.

92 Colour: bright yellow. Nose: powerfull, ripe fruit, sweet spices, creamy oak. Palate: rich, smoky afterpalate:, flavourful, fresh, good acidity.

RAIG DE RAIM 2011 T
50% garnacha, 15% cariñena, 15% merlot, 20% syrah.

89 Colour: bright cherry. Nose: ripe fruit, sweet spices, creamy oak. Palate: flavourful, fruity, toasty, round tannins.

PORTAL N. SRA. PORTAL 2010 T ROBLE
50% garnacha, 20% cariñena, 15% merlot, 15% syrah.

90 Colour: cherry, garnet rim. Nose: ripe fruit, spicy, creamy oak, toasty, complex. Palate: powerful, flavourful, toasty, round tannins.

FINCA MORENILLO 2010 T
100% morenillo.

90 Colour: bright cherry. Nose: expressive, overripe fruit, spicy. Palate: fine bitter notes, good acidity, long.

SA NATURA 2009 T
60% cariñena, 20% syrah, 20% tempranillo.

89 Colour: deep cherry, garnet rim. Nose: balanced, ripe fruit, dark chocolate, wild herbs. Palate: fruity, spicy, round tannins.

L'AVI ARRUFÍ 2008 T
60% cariñena, 30% garnacha, 10% syrah.

92 Colour: bright cherry. Nose: ripe fruit, sweet spices, creamy oak, toasty. Palate: flavourful, fruity, toasty, round tannins.

MATHER TERESINA SELECCIÓN DE VIÑAS VIEJAS 2008 T
50% garnacha, 30% cariñena, 20% morenillo.

91 Colour: cherry, garnet rim. Nose: spicy, creamy oak, toasty, complex. Palate: powerful, flavourful, toasty, round tannins.

JOSEFINA PIÑOL VENDIMIA TARDÍA 2010 TINTO DULCE
100% garnacha.

91 Colour: cherry, garnet rim. Nose: red berry notes, fruit liqueur notes, spicy, dark chocolate, creamy oak. Palate: powerful, flavourful, spirituous, long.

CELLER TERN

Ctra. Vilalba, s/n
43786 Batea (Tarragona)
☎: +34 654 529 64 - Fax: +34 977 430 433
ternobradordevi@gmail.com
www.ternobradordevi.com

TERN 2011 B
garnacha blanca.

90 Colour: bright yellow. Nose: powerfull, ripe fruit, sweet spices, fragrant herbs. Palate: rich, smoky afterpalate:, flavourful, fresh, good acidity.

CELLER VINS FRISACH

Avda. Catalunya 26
43784 Corbera D'Ebre (Tarragona)
☎: +34 696 023 617 - Fax: +34 977 421 215
celler-frisach@celler-frisach.com
www.celler-frisach.com

FRISACH SELECCIÓ 2011 B
100% garnacha blanca.

83

FRISACH CUPATGE 2011 T
64% garnacha, 36% samsó.

83

CELLERS TARRONÉ

Calvari, 22
43786 Batea (Tarragona)
☎: +34 977 430 109 - Fax: +34 977 430 183
inma@cellerstarrone.com
www.cellerstarrone.com

MERIAN 2011 B
100% garnacha blanca.

88 Colour: bright straw. Nose: fresh, fresh fruit, white flowers, expressive. Palate: flavourful, fruity, good acidity, balanced.

MERIAN DULCE NATURAL 2011 T
100% garnacha.

90 Colour: cherry, garnet rim. Nose: fruit preserve, fruit liqueur notes, sweet spices. Palate: powerful, flavourful, sweet.

MERIAN 2011 T
garnacha, cabernet sauvignon, syrah, merlot.

84

TORREMADRINA ROBLE 2009 T
garnacha, cabernet sauvignon, merlot, ull de llebre.

86 Colour: cherry, garnet rim. Nose: fruit preserve, scrubland. Palate: good structure, flavourful.

TORREMADRINA 2007 TC
garnacha, cabernet sauvignon, syrah, merlot.

88 Colour: bright cherry. Nose: ripe fruit, sweet spices, creamy oak. Palate: flavourful, fruity, toasty, round tannins.

TORREMADRINA SELECCIÓN 2005 TC
garnacha, cabernet sauvignon, syrah, merlot.

89 Colour: cherry, garnet rim. Nose: balanced, ripe fruit, creamy oak, spicy. Palate: flavourful, concentrated, round tannins.

CELLERS UNIÓ

Joan Oliver, 16-24
43206 Reus (Tarragona)
☎: +34 977 330 055 - Fax: +34 977 330 070
info@cellersunio.com
www.cellersunio.com

GRAN COPOS GARNACHA BLANCA 2011 B
100% garnacha blanca.

87 Colour: bright straw. Nose: fresh, white flowers, candied fruit. Palate: flavourful, fruity, good acidity, balanced.

CLOS DEL PINELL 2011 B
100% garnacha blanca.

86 Colour: bright straw. Nose: medium intensity, citrus fruit, floral. Palate: fruity, correct, flavourful.

COPOS NATURE 2011 B
50% garnacha blanca, 50% macabeo.

84

CLOS DEL PINELL 2011 RD
100% syrah.

81

COPOS NATURE 2011 T
40% cabernet sauvignon, 20% cariñena, 40% tempranillo.

87 Colour: cherry, purple rim. Nose: expressive, red berry notes, overripe fruit. Palate: flavourful, fruity, good acidity, round tannins.

CLOS DEL PINELL GARNATXA 2011 T
100% garnacha.

85 Colour: deep cherry. Nose: ripe fruit, powerfull, earthy notes. Palate: ripe fruit, spicy.

CLOS DEL PINELL 2008 TC
50% garnacha, 45% cariñena, 5% morenillo.

85 Colour: very deep cherry. Nose: fruit preserve, sweet spices. Palate: flavourful, ripe fruit, round tannins.

REINA ELIONOR 2007 TR
40% garnacha, 40% tempranillo, 20% cabernet sauvignon.

86 Colour: deep cherry. Nose: powerfull, ripe fruit, spicy, toasty. Palate: flavourful, fine bitter notes, good acidity, spicy.

GRAN COPOS 2006 TR
40% garnacha, 30% cariñena, 20% cabernet sauvignon, 10% syrah.

86 Colour: cherry, garnet rim. Nose: ripe fruit, spicy, toasty. Palate: powerful, toasty, round tannins, good finish.

COCA I FITÓ

Avda. 11 de Setembre s/n
43736 El Masroig (Tarragona)
☎: +34 619 776 948 - Fax: +34 935 457 092
info@cocaifito.cat
www.cocaifito.com

JASPI BLANC 2011 B
70% garnacha blanca, 30% macabeo.

87 Colour: bright straw. Nose: fresh, fresh fruit, white flowers, expressive. Palate: flavourful, fruity, good acidity, balanced.

ECOVITRES

La Verge, 6
43782 Vilalba dels Arcs (Tarragona)
☎: +34 977 438 196
info@ecovitres.com
www.ecovitres.com

ASPIRALL 2011 T
100% garnacha.

83

GRAN GOTANYA 2008 TC
garnacha, morenillo, syrah, merlot.

87 Colour: deep cherry, garnet rim. Nose: toasty, scrubland. Palate: flavourful, fruity.

CATXAP 2008 T
garnacha, merlot, cabernet sauvignon.

83

EDETÀRIA

Finca El Mas
43780 Gandesa (Tarragona)
☎: 977 421 534 - Fax: 977 421 534
info@edetaria.com
www.edetaria.com

VÍA TERRA 2011 B
100% garnacha blanca.

90 Colour: bright straw. Nose: fresh, fresh fruit, white flowers, complex, characterful. Palate: flavourful, fruity, good acidity, balanced.

EDETANA 2011 B
70% garnacha blanca, 30% viognier.

89 Colour: bright yellow. Nose: dried flowers, citrus fruit, scrubland, mineral. Palate: correct, powerful, flavourful, good acidity.

EDETÀRIA 2010 B
85% garnacha blanca, 15% macabeo.

92 Colour: bright yellow. Nose: citrus fruit, candied fruit, balsamic herbs, mineral, dark chocolate, cocoa bean, sweet spices, toasty. Palate: rich, flavourful, fruity, fresh, good acidity, balanced.

EDETANA MAGNUM 2010 B
70% garnacha blanca, 30% viognier.

91 Colour: bright straw. Nose: white flowers, fresh fruit, fragrant herbs, sweet spices, creamy oak. Palate: powerful, flavourful, fresh, fruity, spicy, balanced.

EDETÀRIA 2008 B
85% garnacha blanca, 15% macabeo.

94 Colour: bright yellow. Nose: smoky, dry nuts, fragrant herbs, dry stone, sweet spices, creamy oak. Palate: round, rich, flavourful, long, spicy, balanced.

VÍA TERRA 2011 T
100% garnacha.

88 Colour: cherry, garnet rim. Nose: powerfull, ripe fruit, earthy notes, scrubland. Palate: flavourful, fine bitter notes, ripe fruit.

EDETÀRIA DOLÇ 2009 T
70% garnacha, 30% cariñena.

90 Colour: bright cherry. Nose: ripe fruit, sweet spices, creamy oak, dark chocolate, cocoa bean. Palate: flavourful, fruity, toasty, round tannins.

EDETANA 2009 T
60% garnacha, 30% garnacha peluda, 10% cariñena.

89 Colour: cherry, garnet rim. Nose: powerfull, ripe fruit, creamy oak, cocoa bean. Palate: powerful, good acidity, balanced.

EDETÀRIA 2008 T
60% garnacha peluda, 30% syrah, 5% cariñena, cabernet sauvignon.

91 Colour: cherry, garnet rim. Nose: ripe fruit, spicy, toasty, nose:tic coffee, earthy notes. Palate: powerful, flavourful, toasty, long, balanced.

EDETÀRIA DOLÇ 2007 T
70% garnacha, 30% cabernet sauvignon.

91 Colour: cherry, garnet rim. Nose: ripe fruit, spicy, toasty, balsamic herbs, earthy notes. Palate: powerful, flavourful, toasty, round tannins, balanced.

HERÈNCIA ALTÉS

Joan Miró, 2
43786 Batea (Tarragona)
☎: +34 938 125 676 - Fax: +34 938 123 213
rdehaan@exportiberia.com
www.herenciaaltes.com

HERENCIA ALTÉS BENUFET 2011 B
garnacha blanca.

89 Colour: bright straw. Nose: fresh fruit, white flowers, expressive, fragrant herbs. Palate: flavourful, fruity, fine bitter notes, long, balanced.

HERENCIA ALTÉS GARNATXA BLANCA 2011 B
100% garnacha blanca.

87 Colour: bright straw. Nose: fresh fruit, white flowers, citrus fruit. Palate: flavourful, fruity, good acidity, balsamic.

HERENCIA ALTÉS GARNATXA NEGRA 2011 T
100% garnacha.

86 Colour: cherry, garnet rim. Nose: red berry notes, ripe fruit, balsamic herbs, medium intensity. Palate: fresh, fruity, light-bodied.

HERENCIA ALTÉS L'ESTEL 2010 T
80% garnacha, 20% syrah.

87 Colour: cherry, garnet rim. Nose: ripe fruit, fruit preserve, balsamic herbs, spicy, creamy oak. Palate: powerful, flavourful, long, spicy.

JOSEP VICENS VALLESPÍ

Aragó, 20
43780 Gandesa (Tarragona)
☎: +34 686 135 921 - Fax: +34 977 421 080
josepvicens.celler@gmail.com
www.vinsjosepvicens.com

VINYES DEL GRAU 2011 B
garnacha blanca.

87 Colour: bright straw. Nose: fresh, fresh fruit, white flowers, expressive. Palate: flavourful, fruity, good acidity, balanced.

VINYES DEL GRAU 2011 B
sauvignon blanc.

84

VINYES DEL GRAU 2011 RD
garnacha.

85 Colour: rose, purple rim. Nose: powerfull, ripe fruit, red berry notes, floral, expressive. Palate: fleshy, powerful, fruity, fresh.

VINYES DEL GRAU SYRAH 2011 T
100% syrah.

87 Colour: cherry, garnet rim. Nose: ripe fruit, overripe fruit, spicy. Palate: flavourful, powerful, sweetness.

VINYES DEL GRAU NEGRO 2011 T
60% garnacha, 20% syrah, 15% samsó, 5% cabernet sauvignon.

84

VINYES DEL GRAU SYRAH 2008 TC
syrah.

88 Colour: deep cherry, garnet rim. Nose: ripe fruit, sweet spices, cocoa bean. Palate: powerful, warm, round tannins.

VINYES DEL GRAU 2006 TC
garnacha, cariñena, syrah.

87 Colour: cherry, garnet rim. Nose: balanced, powerfull, ripe fruit. Palate: good structure, flavourful, round tannins.

LA VINICOLA DE GANDESA

Camí de Calvari, s/n
43780 Gandesa (Tarragona)
☎: +34 977 420 650 - Fax: +34 977 401 107
eliasgil@eliasgil.com

PUIG VENTÓS 2010 T
tempranillo, syrah.

88 Colour: cherry, garnet rim. Nose: ripe fruit, spicy, creamy oak, toasty, complex. Palate: powerful, flavourful, toasty, round tannins.

LAFOU CELLER

Can Figueras, Plaza Catalunya, 34
43786 Batea (Tarragona)
☎: +34 938 743 511 - Fax: +34 938 737 204
info@lafou.net
www.lafou.net

LAFOU 2008 T
75% garnacha, 15% syrah, 10% cabernet sauvignon.

91 Colour: cherry, garnet rim. Nose: spicy, creamy oak, toasty, characterful, overripe fruit. Palate: powerful, flavourful, toasty, round tannins.

SERRA DE CAVALLS

Bonaire, 1
43594 El Pinell de Brai (Tarragona)
☎: +34 977 426 049
sat@serradecavalls.com
www.serradecavalls.com

SERRA DE CAVALLS 2011 BFB
garnacha blanca.

88 Colour: bright straw. Nose: sweet spices, creamy oak, ripe fruit, citrus fruit. Palate: flavourful, powerful, fine bitter notes.

SERRA DE CAVALLS 2011 B
garnacha blanca.

87 Colour: bright straw. Nose: fresh, white flowers, candied fruit. Palate: flavourful, fruity, good acidity, balanced.

SERRA DE CAVALLS 2011 T
merlot, cabernet sauvignon, garnacha.

84

SERRA DE CAVALLS 1938 2010 T FERMENTADO EN BARRICA
merlot, cabernet sauvignon, syrah.

84

SOMDINOU

Avda. Catalunya, 28
43780 Gandesa (Tarragona)
☎: +34 977 420 017 - Fax: +34 977 420 403
joanmariariera@hotmail.com
www.somdinou.cat

SOMDINOU BLANC JOVE 2011 B
90% garnacha blanca, 10% macabeo.

88 Colour: bright straw. Nose: fresh, fresh fruit, white flowers, dried herbs. Palate: flavourful, fruity, good acidity, balanced.

SOMDINOU 19 2008 B
100% garnacha blanca.

88 Colour: bright yellow. Nose: ripe fruit, sweet spices, creamy oak, fragrant herbs. Palate: rich, smoky afterpalate:, flavourful, fresh, good acidity.

SOMDINOU NEGRE JOVE 2011 T
cariñena.

88 Colour: cherry, purple rim. Nose: red berry notes, ripe fruit, balsamic herbs, mineral. Palate: powerful, flavourful, fruity, complex.

PURESA 2007 T
100% cariñena.

91 Colour: cherry, garnet rim. Nose: spicy, creamy oak, toasty. Palate: powerful, flavourful, toasty, round tannins.

SOMDINOU 19 2006 T
40% garnacha, 25% garnacha gris, 35% samsó.

86 Colour: cherry, garnet rim. Nose: ripe fruit, spicy, creamy oak, toasty. Palate: powerful, flavourful, toasty, round tannins.

VINS ALGARS

Algars, 68
43786 Batea (Tarragona)
☎: +34 617 478 152
vinsalgars@vinsalgars.com
www.vinsalgars.com

DE NICANOR 2011 T
40% garnacha, 30% merlot, 15% marselan, 15% syrah.

86 Colour: deep cherry. Nose: powerfull, fruit liqueur notes, fruit preserve. Palate: powerful, fine bitter notes, good acidity.

VINS DEL TROS

Major, 13
43782 Vilalba dels Arcs (Tarragona)
☎: +34 605 096 447
info@vinsdeltros.com
www.vinsdeltros.com

AY DE MÍ 2010 T
80% garnacha, 20% syrah.

86 Colour: cherry, garnet rim. Nose: fruit preserve, creamy oak, sweet spices. Palate: flavourful, round tannins.

VINS SAT LA BOTERA

Sant Roc, 26
43786 Batea (Tarragona)
☎: +34 977 430 009 - Fax: +34 977 430 801
labotera@labotera.com
www.labotera.com

VILA-CLOSA CHARDONNAY 2011 BFB
100% chardonnay.

88 Colour: bright yellow. Nose: powerfull, ripe fruit, sweet spices, creamy oak, fragrant herbs. Palate: rich, smoky afterpalate:, flavourful, fresh, good acidity.

VILA-CLOSA 2011 B
100% garnacha blanca.

87 Colour: bright yellow. Nose: dried flowers, ripe fruit, medium intensity, neat. Palate: fruity, flavourful.

L'ARNOT 2011 B
garnacha blanca, macabeo.

85 Colour: yellow. Nose: faded flowers, ripe fruit. Palate: flavourful, easy to drink, fine bitter notes.

L'ARNOT 2011 RD
100% merlot.

84

L'ARNOT 2011 T
garnacha, syrah.

86 Colour: cherry, purple rim. Nose: fresh fruit, red berry notes, floral. Palate: flavourful, fruity, good acidity.

VILA-CLOSA 2011 T
garnacha, samsó, syrah, merlot.

84

BRUNA DOLÇ 2010 T
garnacha, syrah.

91 Colour: deep cherry. Nose: fruit preserve, fruit liqueur notes, powerfull. Palate: long, creamy, pruney.

MUDÈFER 2009 T
garnacha, samsó.

83

VINYA D'IRTO

Plaça Comerç , 5
43780 Gandesa (Tarragona)

VINYA D'IRTO 2011 B
70% garnacha blanca, 20% macabeo, 10% viognier.

88 Colour: bright straw. Nose: fresh fruit, dried herbs, floral, expressive. Palate: flavourful, fruity, good acidity, balanced.

VINYA D'IRTO 2011 T
70% garnacha, 30% syrah.

89 Colour: cherry, garnet rim. Nose: ripe fruit, wild herbs, mineral, floral, balanced. Palate: powerful, flavourful, fresh, fruity.

XAVIER CLUA COMA

Ctra. Gandesa - Vilalba, km. 9
43782 Vilalba dels Arcs (Tarragona)
☎: +34 977 263 069 - Fax: +34 977 439 003
rosa@cellerclua.com
www.cellerclua.com

IL.LUSIÓ DE CLUA 2011 B
100% garnacha blanca.

85 Colour: bright yellow. Nose: fresh, citrus fruit, ripe fruit, balanced. Palate: correct, fine bitter notes, fruity.

MAS D'EN POL 2011 B
garnacha blanca, chardonnay, sauvignon blanc, moscatel.

84

MAS D'EN POL 2011 T
garnacha, syrah, merlot, cabernet sauvignon.

85 Colour: cherry, purple rim. Nose: red berry notes, floral. Palate: flavourful, fruity, good acidity, round tannins.

CLUA MIL.LENNIUM 2008 TC
garnacha, cabernet sauvignon, syrah, merlot.

88 Colour: bright cherry. Nose: sweet spices, creamy oak, ripe fruit. Palate: flavourful, fruity, toasty, round tannins.

CLUA MIL.LENNIUM 2007 TC
garnacha, cabernet sauvignon, syrah, merlot.

88 Colour: cherry, garnet rim. Nose: ripe fruit, spicy, creamy oak, toasty, dark chocolate. Palate: powerful, flavourful, toasty, round tannins.

MAS D'EN POL 2007 T BARRICA
garnacha, syrah, merlot, cabernet sauvignon.

87 Colour: bright cherry. Nose: ripe fruit, sweet spices, creamy oak. Palate: flavourful, toasty, round tannins.

DO TIERRA DE LEÓN

LOCATION

In the south of the province of León with the vineyard almost exclusively around the municipality of Valencia de Don Juan in a sort of triangle with the rivers Cea and Esla taking the other two corners. It includes also 19 municipal districts of the province of Valladolid.

CLIMATE:

The climate of the river valleys would follow a milder Atlantic continental pattern, but the high plateau of that part of León where most of the vines are planted turns the conditions into cooler ones. There is a marked temperature differential all through the year, winters are harsh and summers mild, there is always the risk of spring frosts and rainfall (500 mm average) happens mainly during the autumn months.

SOIL:

They are of great quality for vine growing purposes and have good drainage. Most of the vines are planted on alluvial terraces with varying percentages of clay and limestone and a rocky subsoil.

GRAPE VARIETIES:

WHITE: *Albarín, Verdejo, Godello, Palomino, Malvasía.*
RED: *Prieto picudo, Mencía, Garnacha* and *Tempranillo.*

FIGURES:

Vineyard surface: 1,325 – **Wine-Growers:** 376 – **Wineries:** 32 – **2011 Harvest rating:** Very Good – **Production:** -- – **Market percentages:** --% domestic. --% export

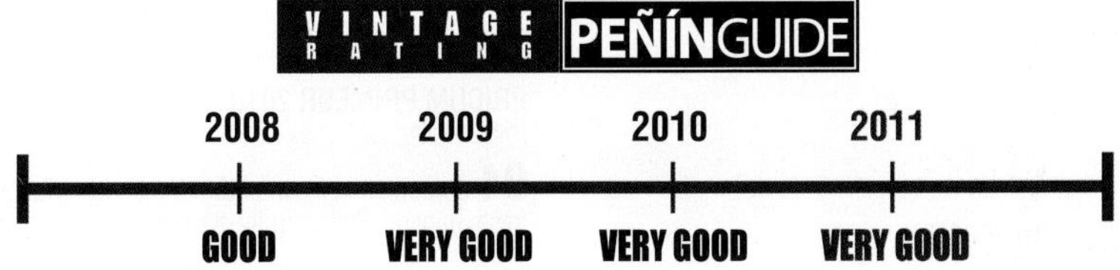

CONSEJO REGULADOR
Alonso Castrillo, 29. - 24200 Valencia de Don Juan (León) - ☎: +34 987 751 089 - Fax: +34 987 750 012
@ vinotierradeleon@yahoo.es / directortecnico@dotierradeleon.es - www.dotierradeleon.es

BODEGAS FRANCISCO GONZÁLEZ

La Fragua, s/n
24324 Villeza (León)
☎: +34 987 263 710 - Fax: +34 987 263 710
info@villeza.com
www.villeza.es

LÁGRIMA DE VILLEZA 2011 B
albarín.

87 Colour: bright straw. Nose: fresh, fresh fruit, white flowers, varietal. Palate: flavourful, fruity, good acidity, balanced.

LÁGRIMA DE VILLEZA 2011 RD
prieto picudo.

85 Colour: onion pink. Nose: fine reductive notes, short, fruit expression. Palate: sweetness, flavourful.

TINTO VILLEZA 6 MESES 2009 T
50% prieto picudo, 50% mencía.

88 Colour: deep cherry. Nose: earthy notes, fruit expression, varietal. Palate: mineral, flavourful, fresh.

TINTO VILLEZA 12 MESES 2008 TC
prieto picudo.

88 Colour: cherry, garnet rim. Nose: powerfull, ripe fruit, creamy oak, dark chocolate. Palate: flavourful, fine bitter notes, good acidity.

BODEGAS JULIO CRESPO

Finca Villazán - Ctra. Sahagún, km. 6
24326 Joara, Sahagún (León)
☎: +34 987 130 010 - Fax: +34 987 130 010
info@bodegasjuliocrespo.com
www.bodegasjuliocrespo.com

LA RENTERA 2007 T ROBLE

82

PREMEDITACIÓN 2006 T

86 Colour: cherry, garnet rim. Nose: powerfull, ripe fruit, aged wood nuances, sweet spices, dark chocolate. Palate: flavourful, sweetness.

BODEGAS MARCOS MIÑAMBRES

Camino de Pobladura, s/n
24234 Villamañán (León)
☎: +34 987 767 038
satvined@picos.com

LOS SILVARES 2005 TR
prieto picudo.

88 Colour: dark-red cherry. Nose: fruit expression, varietal, earthy notes. Palate: fruity, flavourful, balanced.

BODEGAS MARGÓN

Avda de Valencia de Don Juan, s/n
24209 Pajares de los Oteros (León)
☎: +34 987 750 800 - Fax: +34 987 750 481
comercial@bodegasmargon.com
www.bodegasmargon.com

PRICUM ALBARÍN 2010 B BARRICA
albarín.

90 Colour: bright yellow. Nose: powerfull, sweet spices, creamy oak, ripe fruit, citrus fruit. Palate: rich, smoky afterpalate:, flavourful, fresh, good acidity.

PRICUM ALDEBARÁN VENDIMIA TARDÍA 2008 B
100% verdejo.

95 Colour: bright yellow. Nose: ripe fruit, citrus fruit, dried flowers, fragrant herbs, expressive, complex. Palate: elegant, unctuous, fresh, fruity, flavourful, balanced.

PRICUM 2011 RD
prieto picudo.

90 Colour: onion pink. Nose: elegant, candied fruit, dried flowers, red berry notes. Palate: light-bodied, flavourful, good acidity, long, spicy.

PRICUM PRIMEUR 2010 T
prieto picudo.

94 Colour: cherry, garnet rim. Nose: powerfull, varietal, fresh, mineral. Palate: fruity, flavourful, mineral.

PRICUM PARAJE DEL SANTO 2009 T
100% prieto picudo.

91 Colour: cherry, garnet rim. Nose: ripe fruit, spicy, creamy oak, toasty, complex. Palate: powerful, flavourful, toasty, round tannins.

VALDEMUZ 2009 T
100% prieto picudo.

90 Colour: bright cherry. Nose: ripe fruit, sweet spices, creamy oak. Palate: flavourful, fruity, toasty, round tannins.

PRICUM PRIETO PICUDO 2009 T
100% prieto picudo.

90 Colour: cherry, garnet rim. Nose: ripe fruit, red berry notes, creamy oak, spicy. Palate: flavourful, powerful, spicy, ripe fruit.

PRICUM PARAJE DEL SANTO 2008 T
prieto picudo.

92 Colour: cherry, garnet rim. Nose: ripe fruit, spicy, creamy oak, toasty, complex. Palate: powerful, flavourful, toasty, round tannins.

PRICUM PRIETO PICUDO 2008 T
prieto picudo.

91 Colour: cherry, garnet rim. Nose: sweet spices, creamy oak, candied fruit, balsamic herbs, scrubland. Palate: flavourful, fruity, spicy, ripe fruit.

PRICUM VALDEMUZ 2008 T
prieto picudo.

91 Colour: cherry, garnet rim. Nose: ripe fruit, spicy, creamy oak, toasty, mineral. Palate: powerful, flavourful, toasty, round tannins.

BODEGAS VINOS DE LEÓN

La Vega, s/n
24009 Armunia (León)
☎: +34 987 209 712 - Fax: +34 987 209 800
info@bodegasvinosdeleon.es
www.bodegasvinosdeleon.es

VALJUNCO 2011 RD
100% prieto picudo.

84

VALJUNCO 2011 T
100% prieto picudo.

85 Colour: cherry, garnet rim. Nose: floral, ripe fruit, scrubland. Palate: light-bodied, fresh, fruity, easy to drink.

VALJUNCO 2008 TC
100% prieto picudo.

88 Colour: cherry, garnet rim. Nose: fruit preserve, spicy, creamy oak, toasty. Palate: flavourful, spicy, long.

DON SUERO 2008 TC
100% prieto picudo.

88 Colour: cherry, garnet rim. Nose: fruit preserve, sweet spices, dark chocolate, toasty. Palate: powerful, flavourful, toasty.

DON SUERO 2004 TR
100% prieto picudo.

88 Colour: dark-red cherry. Nose: spicy, ripe fruit. Palate: flavourful, spicy, balanced.

BODEGAS Y VIÑEDOS CASIS

Las Bodegas, s/n
24325 Gordaliza del Pino (León)
☎: +34 987 699 618
anacasis@gmail.com
www.bodegascasis.com

CASIS GODELLO 2011 B
godello, albarín.

86 Colour: bright straw. Nose: white flowers, ripe fruit. Palate: flavourful, fruity, fine bitter notes.

CASIS PRIETO PICUDO 2011 RD
prieto picudo.

83

CASIS PRIETO PICUDO 2011 T
prieto picudo.

86 Colour: cherry, purple rim. Nose: varietal, ripe fruit, red berry notes. Palate: flavourful, fruity, fresh.

CASIS PRIETO PICUDO 2010 T
prieto picudo.

88 Colour: dark-red cherry. Nose: earthy notes, lacks fruit. Palate: sweetness, good acidity, flavourful, fruity.

CASIS MENCÍA 2009 T
mencía.

89 Colour: dark-red cherry. Nose: fruit expression, varietal, toasty. Palate: flavourful, fresh, good acidity.

COOP. VINÍCOLA COMARCAL VALDEVIMBRE

Ctra. de León, s/n
24230 Valdevimbre (León)
☎: +34 987 304 195 - Fax: +34 987 304 195
valdevim@hotmail.com
www.vinicoval.com

ABADÍA DE BALDEREDO 2011 B
verdejo.

85 Colour: bright straw. Nose: ripe fruit, citrus fruit, white flowers, dried flowers. Palate: flavourful, good acidity.

ABADÍA DE BALDEREDO 2011 RD
prieto picudo.

85 Colour: rose. Nose: fruit expression, medium intensity, fresh fruit. Palate: flavourful, fine bitter notes.

ABADÍA DE BALDEREDO 2011 T
prieto picudo.

86 Colour: dark-red cherry. Nose: fruit expression, earthy notes, wild herbs. Palate: fruity, flavourful.

ABADÍA DE BALDEREDO 2007 TC
prieto picudo.

86 Colour: dark-red cherry. Nose: fruit expression, toasty, wild herbs, earthy notes. Palate: oaky, fruity, fresh.

GORDONZELLO

Alto de Santa Marina, s/n
24294 Gordoncillo (León)
☎: +34 987 758 030 - Fax: +34 987 757 201
info@gordonzello.com
www.gordonzello.com

PEREGRINO ALBARÍN 2011 B
100% albarín.

88 Colour: bright straw. Nose: white flowers, fresh fruit, expressive, fragrant herbs. Palate: powerful, flavourful, balanced, easy to drink.

PEREGRINO ALBARÍN 2011 BFB
100% albarín.

88 Colour: bright yellow. Nose: powerfull, ripe fruit, sweet spices, creamy oak. Palate: rich, smoky afterpalate:, flavourful, fresh, good acidity.

PEREGRINO VERDEJO 2011 B
100% verdejo.

87 Colour: bright yellow. Nose: white flowers, tropical fruit, fragrant herbs. Palate: flavourful, fruity, fresh, easy to drink.

PEREGRINO CUVÈE 2010 BFB
100% albarín.

81 Colour: bright yellow. Nose: acetaldehyde, overripe fruit, dried herbs, varnish, toasty. Palate: light-bodied, fruity, fresh.

PEREGRINO 2011 RD
100% prieto picudo.

89 Colour: rose, purple rim. Nose: lactic notes, floral, red berry notes, citrus fruit. Palate: fine bitter notes, flavourful, fruity.

GURDOS 2011 RD
100% prieto picudo.

87 Colour: rose, purple rim. Nose: floral, lactic notes, red berry notes, ripe fruit. Palate: long, powerful, flavourful, fruity.

PEREGRINO 2011 T
100% prieto picudo.

87 Colour: cherry, purple rim. Nose: lactic notes, red berry notes, ripe fruit, floral, earthy notes. Palate: powerful, flavourful, fruity.

PEREGRINO 2009 T ROBLE
100% prieto picudo.

87 Colour: cherry, garnet rim. Nose: ripe fruit, fruit liqueur notes, earthy notes, sweet spices. Palate: powerful, flavourful, spicy, easy to drink.

PEREGRINO 2009 TC
100% prieto picudo.

85 Colour: cherry, garnet rim. Nose: earthy notes, scrubland, ripe fruit, creamy oak. Palate: powerful, flavourful, spicy, toasty.

PEREGRINO 14 2008 TC
100% prieto picudo.

89 Colour: cherry, garnet rim. Nose: ripe fruit, spicy, creamy oak, toasty, mineral. Palate: powerful, flavourful, toasty, round tannins.

PEREGRINO 2006 TR
100% prieto picudo.

88 Colour: pale ruby, brick rim edge. Nose: spicy, fine reductive notes, wet leather, earthy notes, acetaldehyde. Palate: spicy, fine tannins, elegant, long.

LEYENDA DEL PÁRAMO

Ctra. de León s/n, Paraje El Cueto
24230 Valdevimbre (León)
☎: +34 626 194 347
info@leyendadelparamo.com
www.leyendadelparamo.com

MITTEL 2011 B
100% albarín.

90 Colour: straw. Nose: fruit expression, fresh, varietal, expressive, balanced. Palate: fruity, varietal, good acidity, sweetness, balanced.

MITTEL 2011 RD
100% prieto picudo.

88 Colour: raspberry rose. Nose: powerfull, raspberry, ripe fruit. Palate: fruity, flavourful, varietal.

EL MÉDICO 2010 T ROBLE
100% prieto picudo.

94 Colour: cherry, garnet rim. Nose: red berry notes, ripe fruit, mineral, sweet spices, cocoa bean, dark chocolate, balsamic herbs, scrubland. Palate: powerful, flavourful, complex, long, toasty. Personality.

EL MÚSICO 2009 T
100% prieto picudo.

91 Colour: cherry, garnet rim. Nose: powerfull, ripe fruit, red berry notes, toasty, new oak. Palate: flavourful, powerful, spicy, ripe fruit.

LOS PALOMARES

Los Palomares, 6
24230 Valdevimbre (León)
☎: +34 987 304 218 - Fax: +34 987 304 193
lospalomares@bodegalospalomares.com
www.bodegalospalomares.com

3 PALOMARES 2011 B
verdejo.

89 Colour: straw. Nose: fruit expression, varietal, fresh. Palate: powerful, flavourful, varietal.

3 PALOMARES 2011 RD

87 Colour: light cherry. Nose: ripe fruit, fresh fruit, red berry notes, citrus fruit. Palate: flavourful, fruity, fresh.

3 PALOMARES 2010 T
prieto picudo.

85 Colour: cherry, garnet rim. Nose: ripe fruit, candied fruit, warm. Palate: powerful, flavourful.

3 PALOMARES 2009 TC

89 Colour: cherry, garnet rim. Nose: ripe fruit, spicy, creamy oak, toasty, characterful, mineral. Palate: powerful, flavourful, toasty, round tannins.

SDAD. COOP. VINOS DE LA RIBERA DEL CEA

Avda. Panduro y Villafañe, 15
24220 Valderas (León)
☎: +34 987 762 191 - Fax: +34 987 762 191
info@riberacea.e.telefonica.net

VIÑA TRASDERREY 2011 RD

86 Colour: rose, purple rim. Nose: ripe fruit, red berry notes, expressive. Palate: , powerful, fruity, fresh.

VIÑA TRASDERREY 2010 T

87 Colour: dark-red cherry. Nose: fine reductive notes, fruit expression, varietal. Palate: fruity, grainy tannins.

VIÑA TRASDERREY 2007 TC

83

TAMPESTA

La Socollada, s/n
24230 Valdevimbre (León)
☎: +34 987 351 025 - Fax: +34 987 351 025
bodegas@tampesta.com
www.tampesta.com

MANEKI 2010 B
100% albarín.

88 Colour: straw. Nose: new oak, fine lees, fresh fruit. Palate: varietal, flavourful, fruity.

TAMPESTA 2011 RD
prieto picudo.

90 Colour: onion pink. Nose: elegant, candied fruit, dried flowers, red berry notes. Palate: light-bodied, flavourful, good acidity, long, spicy.

GOLÁN SOBRE LÍAS 2011 RD
100% prieto picudo.

87 Colour: rose, purple rim. Nose: ripe fruit, lactic notes. Palate: flavourful, fruity, fresh.

TAMPESTA IMELDA 2010 T
100% prieto picudo.

89 Colour: bright cherry. Nose: ripe fruit, sweet spices, creamy oak, varietal. Palate: flavourful, fruity, toasty, round tannins.

TAMPESTA 2010 T ROBLE
85% prieto picudo, 15% tempranillo.

86 Colour: cherry, garnet rim. Nose: ripe fruit, candied fruit, dried herbs. Palate: spicy, ripe fruit, fine bitter notes.

TAMPESTA GOLÁN 2009 T
prieto picudo.

90 Colour: dark-red cherry. Nose: fruit expression, creamy oak, varietal. Palate: flavourful, creamy, toasty, harsh oak tannins.

TAMPESTA FINCA DE LOS VIENTOS 2009 T
100% prieto picudo.

88 Colour: cherry, garnet rim. Nose: spicy, dark chocolate, ripe fruit. Palate: flavourful, fine bitter notes, good acidity.

VIÑEDOS Y BODEGA PARDEVALLES

Ctra. de León, s/n
24230 Valdevimbre (León)
☎: +34 987 304 222 - Fax: +34 987 304 222
info@pardevalles.es
www.pardevalles.com

PARDEVALLES ALBARÍN 2011 B
100% albarín.

89 Colour: straw. Nose: ripe fruit, wild herbs, tropical fruit. Palate: flavourful, fruity, mineral.

PARDEVALLES 2011 RD
100% prieto picudo.

88 Colour: rose, bright. Nose: powerfull, fruit expression, earthy notes, mineral, varietal. Palate: powerful, fruity, flavourful, varietal.

PARDEVALLES GAMONAL 2009 T
100% prieto picudo.

91 Colour: cherry, garnet rim. Nose: powerfull, expressive, sweet spices, dark chocolate, mineral. Palate: flavourful, powerful, fine bitter notes, good acidity.

PARDEVALLES CARROLEÓN 2008 T
100% prieto picudo.

91 Colour: bright cherry. Nose: sweet spices, creamy oak, ripe fruit. Palate: flavourful, fruity, toasty, round tannins.

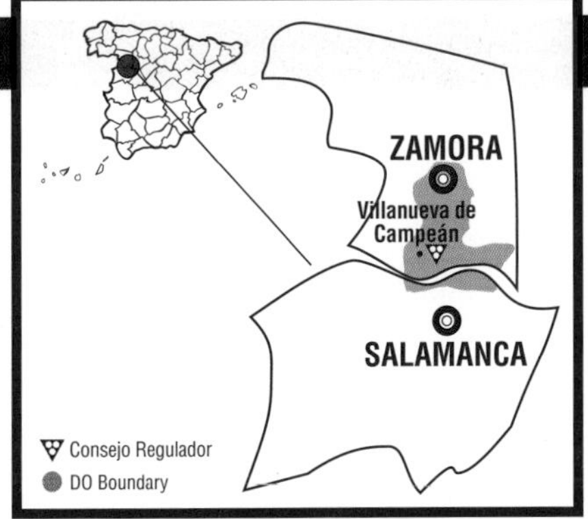

DO TIERRA DEL VINO DE ZAMORA

LOCATION:

In the southeast part of Zamora, on the Duero river banks. This region comprises 46 municipal districts in the province Zamora and 10 in neighbouring Salamanca. Average altitude is 750 meters.

CLIMATE:

Extreme temperatures as correspond to a dry continental pattern, with very hot summers and cold winters. It does not rain much and average annual rainfall hardly reaches 400 mm.

SOIL:

The character of the territory derives from the river Duero tributaries, so it is predominantly alluvial and clay in the lower strata that might not allow great drainage, though they vary a lot depending on the altitude. There are also some sandy patches on the plain land and stony ones on the hill side.

GRAPE VARIETIES:

WHITE: *Malvasía, Moscatel de grano menudo* and *Verdejo* (preferential); *Albillo, Palomino* and *Godello* (authorized).
RED: *Tempranillo* (main), *Cabernet Sauvignon* and *Garnacha.*

FIGURES:

Vineyard surface: 696 – **Wine-Growers:** 205 – **Wineries:** 9 – **2011 Harvest rating:** N/A – **Production:** 660,851 litres – **Market percentages:** 60% domestic. 40% export

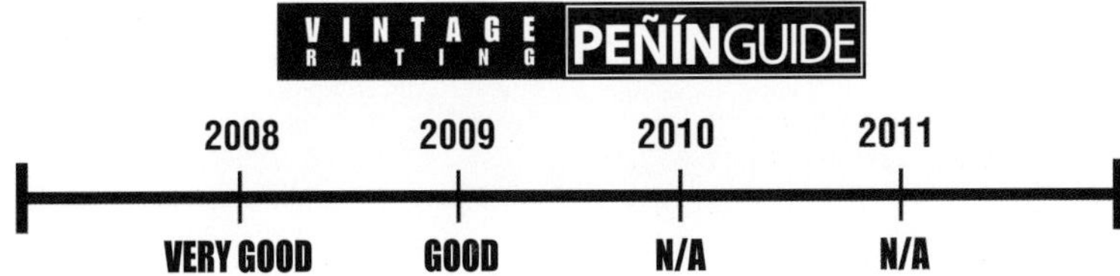

CONSEJO REGULADOR
Plaza Mayor, 1 - 49708 Villanueva de Campeán (Zamora) - ☎: +34 980 560 055 - Fax: +34 980 560 055
@ info@tierradelvino.net - www.tierradelvino.net

VIÑAS DEL CÉNIT

Ctra. de Circunvalación, s/n
49708 Villanueva de Campeán (Zamora)
☎: +34 980 569 346 - Fax: +34 980 569 328
info@bodegascenit.com
www.bodegascenit.com

VIA CENIT 2010 T
100% tempranillo.

94 Colour: cherry, garnet rim. Nose: spicy, creamy oak, toasty, complex, mineral, fruit expression, red berry notes. Palate: powerful, flavourful, toasty, round tannins.

CENIT 2008 T
100% tempranillo.

95 Colour: cherry, garnet rim. Nose: powerfull, varietal, ripe fruit, fruit expression, creamy oak, toasty. Palate: flavourful, powerful, good acidity, round tannins.

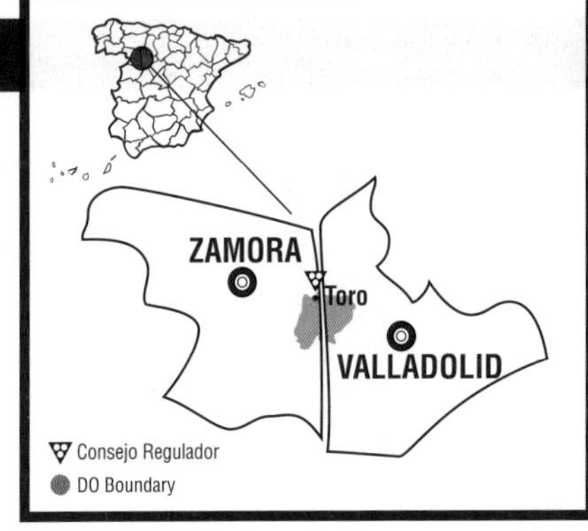

DO TORO

LOCATION:

Comprising 12 municipal districts of the province of Zamora (Argujillo, Boveda de Toro, Morales de Toro, El Pego, Peleagonzalo, El Piñero, San Miguel de la Ribera, Sanzoles, Toro, Valdefinjas, Venialbo and Villanueva del Puente) and three in the province of Valladolid (San Román de la Hornija, Villafranca de Duero and the vineyards of Villaester de Arriba and Villaester de Abajo in the municipal district of Pedrosa del Rey), which practically corresponds to the agricultural region of Bajo Duero. The production area is to the south of the course of the Duero, which crosses the region from east to west.

CLIMATE:

Extreme continental, with Atlantic influences and quite arid, with an average annual rainfall of between 350 mm and 400 mm. The winters are harsh (which means extremely low temperatures and long periods of frosts) and the summers short, although not excessively hot, with significant contrasts in day-night temperatures.

SOIL:

The geography of the DO is characterised by a gently-undulating terrain. The vineyards are situated at an altitude of 620 m to 750 m and the soil is mainly brownish-grey limestone. However, the stony alluvial soil is better.

GRAPE VARIETIES:

WHITE: *Malvasía* and *Verdejo.*
RED: *Tinta de Toro* (majority) and *Garnacha.*

FIGURES:

Vineyard surface: 5,716 – **Wine-Growers:** 1,321 – **Wineries:** 51 – **2011 Harvest rating:** Excellent – **Production:** 13,360,414 litres – **Market percentages:** 67% domestic. 33% export

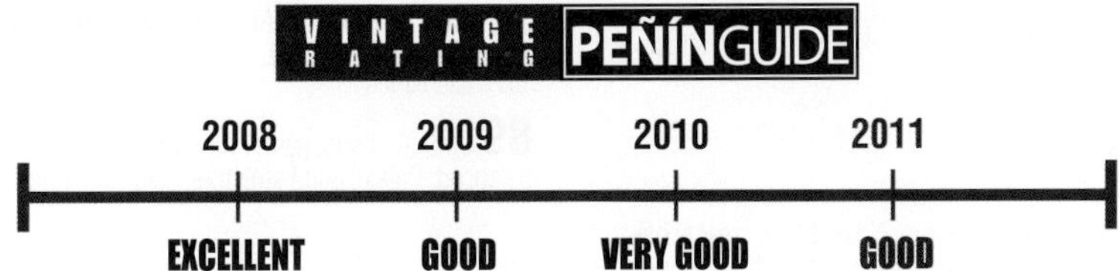

CONSEJO REGULADOR
De la Concepción, 3 - Palacio de los Condes de Requena - 49800 Toro (Zamora) - ☎:+34 980 690 335 - Fax: +34 980 693 201
@ consejo@dotoro.es - www.dotoro.es

ÁLVAREZ Y DÍEZ

Juan Antonio Carmona, 12
47500 Nava del Rey (Valladolid)
☎: +34 983 850 136 - Fax: +34 983 850 761
bodegas@alvarezydiez.com
www.alvarezydiez.com

VALMORO 2007 T
tinta de Toro.

89 Colour: cherry, garnet rim. Nose: balanced, sweet spices, creamy oak, fruit preserve. Palate: flavourful, good structure, fruity.

BODEGA BURDIGALA (F. LURTON & M. ROLLAND)

Camino Magarín, s/n
47529 Villafranca del Duero (Valladolid)
☎: +34 983 034 030 - Fax: +34 983 034 040
bodega@burdigala.es
www.francoislurton.com

CAMPESINO 2009 T
100% tinta de Toro.

92 Colour: cherry, garnet rim. Nose: spicy, creamy oak, toasty. Palate: powerful, flavourful, toasty, round tannins.

CAMPO ALEGRE 2009 T
100% tinta de Toro.

91 Colour: cherry, garnet rim. Nose: balanced, complex, ripe fruit, sweet spices, creamy oak. Palate: good structure, powerful, full.

CAMPO ELISEO 2006 T
100% tinta de Toro.

92 Colour: cherry, garnet rim. Nose: spicy, creamy oak, toasty, complex, overripe fruit. Palate: powerful, flavourful, toasty, round tannins.

BODEGA CYAN

Ctra. Valdefinjas - Venialbo, Km. 9,2, Finca La Calera
49800 Toro (Zamora)
☎: +34 980 568 029 - Fax: +34 980 568 036
cyan@matarromera.es
www.bodegacyan.es

CYAN 12 MESES 2005 T
100% tinta de Toro.

85 Colour: pale ruby, brick rim edge. Nose: fruit liqueur notes, wet leather, tobacco, spicy. Palate: spicy, flavourful, ripe fruit, slightly evolved.

SELECCIÓN PERSONAL CARLOS MORO CYAN 2004 T RESERVA ESPECIAL
100% tinta de Toro.

89 Colour: cherry, garnet rim. Nose: ripe fruit, spicy, balanced. Palate: good structure, balanced, ripe fruit, long.

BODEGA ELÍAS MORA

Juan Mora, s/n
47530 San Román de Hornija (Valladolid)
☎: +34 983 784 029 - Fax: +34 983 784 190
info@bodegaseliasmora.com
www.bodegaseliasmora.com

VIÑAS ELÍAS MORA 2010 T ROBLE
tinta de Toro.

90 Colour: cherry, garnet rim. Nose: ripe fruit, spicy, creamy oak, toasty, earthy notes. Palate: powerful, flavourful, toasty.

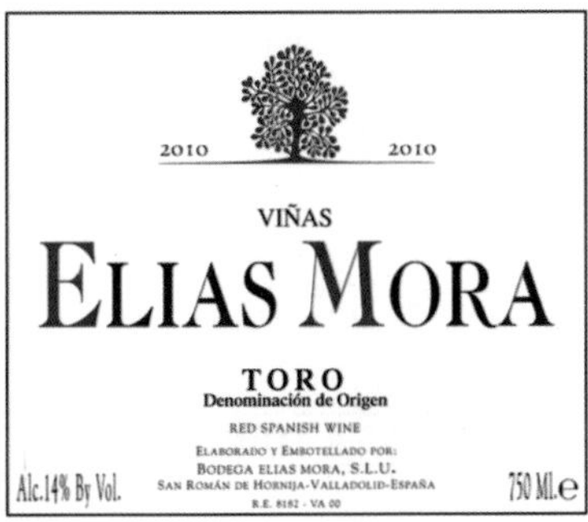

ELÍAS MORA 2009 TC
100% tinta de Toro.

91 Colour: cherry, garnet rim. Nose: ripe fruit, cocoa bean, creamy oak, complex. Palate: balanced, round tannins, long.

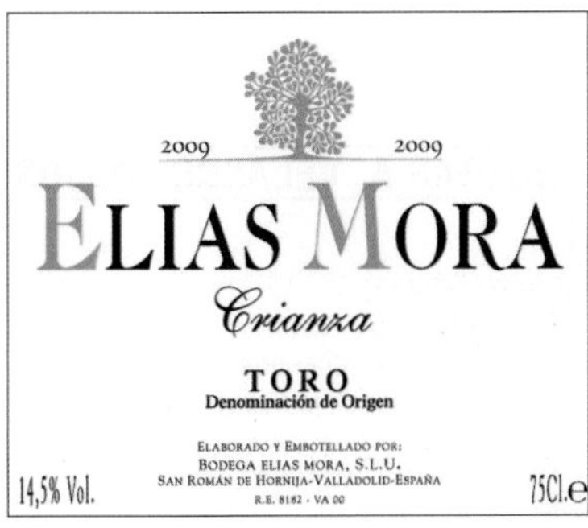

2V PREMIUM 2008 T
tinta de Toro.

91 Colour: cherry, garnet rim. Nose: spicy, creamy oak, toasty, complex, ripe fruit. Palate: powerful, flavourful, toasty, round tannins.

BODEGA FLORENCIO SALGADO NARROS

Ctra. Toro - Salamanca, Km. 3,20
49800 Toro (Zamora)
☎: +34 649 761 324
bodega.salgadonarros@yahoo.com

PICO ROYO 2011 B
malvasía.

87 Colour: bright straw. Nose: medium intensity, fresh fruit, floral. Palate: flavourful, fruity, easy to drink.

PICO ROYO 2011 T

84

PICO ROYO 2008 T

82

BODEGA NUMANTHIA

Real, s/n
49882 Valdefinjas (Zamora)
☎: +34 980 699 147 - Fax: +34 980 699 164
www.numanthia.com

TERMANTHIA 2010 T
100% tinta de Toro.

97 Colour: bright cherry. Nose: ripe fruit, sweet spices, creamy oak, expressive, fruit expression, red berry notes, mineral. Palate: flavourful, fruity, toasty, round tannins, long, mineral.

TERMES 2010 T
tinta de Toro.

94 Colour: cherry, purple rim. Nose: fresh fruit, red berry notes, floral, lactic notes. Palate: flavourful, fruity, good acidity, round tannins.

NUMANTHIA 2010 T
tinta de Toro.

96 Colour: very deep cherry. Nose: ripe fruit, red berry notes, fruit expression, sweet spices, dark chocolate. Palate: flavourful, concentrated, powerful, fine bitter notes, good acidity, round, mineral.

BODEGA PAGO DE CUBAS

Ctra. Toro Valdefinjas, Km. 6,9
49882 Valdefinjas (Zamora)
☎: +34 626 410 524 - Fax: +34 980 059 965

ASTERISCO 2010 T
100% tinta de Toro.

85 Colour: cherry, garnet rim. Nose: ripe fruit, spicy, creamy oak, toasty. Palate: powerful, flavourful, toasty, harsh oak tannins.

INCRÉDULO 2009 T
100% tinta de Toro.

90 Colour: cherry, garnet rim. Nose: ripe fruit, spicy, creamy oak, toasty, complex. Palate: powerful, flavourful, toasty, round tannins.

INCRÉDULO 2008 T
100% tinta de Toro.

88 Colour: cherry, garnet rim. Nose: ripe fruit, spicy, creamy oak, toasty. Palate: powerful, flavourful, toasty, round tannins.

BODEGA TOROENO

Judería, 25 Bajo
49800 Toro (Zamora)
☎: 003 366 373 1644
toroeno@hotmail.fr

NOSE:NA 2010 T
100% tempranillo.

88 Colour: bright cherry. Nose: ripe fruit, sweet spices, creamy oak, expressive. Palate: flavourful, fruity, toasty, round tannins.

BODEGAS A. VELASCO E HIJOS

Corredera, 23
49800 Toro (Zamora)
☎: +34 980 692 455
admon@bodegasvelascoehijos.com
www.bodegasvelascoehijos.com

PEÑA REJAS 2010 T ROBLE
tinta de Toro.

87 Colour: bright cherry. Nose: ripe fruit, sweet spices, creamy oak, expressive. Palate: flavourful, fruity, toasty, balanced.

GARABITAS SELECCIÓN VIÑAS VIEJAS 2009 T
tinta de Toro.

88 Colour: cherry, garnet rim. Nose: ripe fruit, creamy oak, varnish, dark chocolate. Palate: flavourful, powerful, round tannins.

PEÑA REJAS 2009 TC
tinta de Toro.

87 Colour: cherry, garnet rim. Nose: ripe fruit, spicy, creamy oak, toasty. Palate: powerful, flavourful, toasty, round tannins.

BODEGAS ABANICO

Pol. Ind Ca l'Avellanet - Susany, 6
08553 Seva (Barcelona)
☎: +34 938 125 676 - Fax: +34 938 123 213
info@exportiberia.com
www.bodegasabanico.com

ETERNUM VITI 2009 T
100% tinta de Toro.

91 Colour: cherry, garnet rim. Nose: ripe fruit, spicy, creamy oak, toasty, earthy notes. Palate: powerful, flavourful, toasty, balanced.

LOS COLMILLOS 2009 T
100% tinta de Toro.

90 Colour: bright cherry. Nose: ripe fruit, sweet spices, creamy oak, balsamic herbs, earthy notes. Palate: flavourful, fruity, toasty, round tannins.

BODEGAS CAMPIÑA

Ctra. Toro-Veniablo, Km. 6,9
49882 Valdefinjas (Zamora)
☎: +34 980 568 125 - Fax: +34 980 059 965
info@bodegascampina.com
www.bodegascampina.com

CAMPIÑA 2011 T
100% tinta de Toro.

85 Colour: very deep cherry, purple rim. Nose: sweet spices, ripe fruit. Palate: flavourful, ripe fruit, grainy tannins.

CAMPIÑA VIÑAS CENTENARIAS 2009 T
100% tinta de Toro.

85 Colour: cherry, garnet rim. Nose: ripe fruit, spicy, creamy oak. Palate: powerful, flavourful, spicy.

CAMPIÑA 2008 TC
100% tinta de Toro.

87 Colour: cherry, garnet rim. Nose: ripe fruit, mineral, spicy, toasty. Palate: spicy, long, flavourful, toasty.

BODEGAS CARMEN RODRÍGUEZ

Ctra. Salamanca, ZA 605, Km. 1,6
49800 Toro (Zamora)
☎: +34 980 568 005
info@carodorum.com
www.carodorum.com

CARODORUM SELECCIÓN 2009 TC
tinta de Toro.

92 Colour: black cherry, garnet rim. Nose: ripe fruit, scrubland, earthy notes, sweet spices. Palate: flavourful, long, round, balanced.

CARODORUM 2009 TC
tinta de Toro.

89 Colour: cherry, garnet rim. Nose: ripe fruit, spicy, toasty, varnish, woody, mineral. Palate: powerful, flavourful, toasty, harsh oak tannins.

CARODORUM ISSOS 2009 TC
tinta de Toro.

88 Colour: cherry, garnet rim. Nose: ripe fruit, spicy, creamy oak, toasty, balsamic herbs. Palate: powerful,

BODEGAS COVITORO

Ctra. de Tordesillas, 13
49800 Toro (Zamora)
☎: +34 980 690 347 - Fax: +34 980 690 143
covitoro@covitoro.com
www.covitoro.com

CERMEÑO 2011 B
malvasía.

85 Colour: bright straw. Nose: white flowers, dried herbs, ripe fruit. Palate: flavourful, fruity, balanced.

CERMEÑO 2011 RD
100% tinta de Toro.

85 Colour: rose, purple rim. Nose: red berry notes, ripe fruit, powerfull. Palate: good structure, flavourful.

CERMEÑO VENDIMIA SELECCIONADA 2011 T
100% tinta de Toro.

88 Colour: cherry, purple rim. Nose: powerfull, ripe fruit, red berry notes. Palate: flavourful, ripe fruit.

MARQUÉS DE LA VILLA 2011 T ROBLE
100% tinta de Toro.

86 Colour: deep cherry. Nose: medium intensity, ripe fruit. Palate: sweetness, spicy.

GRAN CERMEÑO 2008 TC
100% tinta de Toro.

89 Colour: cherry, garnet rim. Nose: ripe fruit, creamy oak, toasty. Palate: powerful, flavourful, toasty, round tannins, balanced.

CAÑUS VERUS VIÑAS VIEJAS 2008 T
100% tinta de Toro.

88 Colour: cherry, garnet rim. Nose: creamy oak, sweet spices, toasty. Palate: flavourful, long, spicy, round tannins.

MARQUÉS DE LA VILLA 2008 TC
100% tinta de Toro.

87 Colour: cherry, garnet rim. Nose: spicy, creamy oak, overripe fruit. Palate: powerful, flavourful, round tannins.

MARQUÉS DE LA VILLA 2005 TR
100% tinta de Toro.

89 Colour: pale ruby, brick rim edge. Nose: spicy, fine reductive notes, wet leather, aged wood nuances, fruit liqueur notes. Palate: spicy, fine tannins, elegant, long.

BODEGAS FARIÑA

Camino del Palo, s/n
49800 Toro (Zamora)
☎: +34 980 577 673 - Fax: +34 980 577 720
comercial@bodegasfarina.com
www.bodegasfarina.com

COLEGIATA 2011 RD
100% tinta de Toro.

90 Colour: rose, purple rim. Nose: powerfull, ripe fruit, red berry notes, floral. Palate: , powerful, fruity, fresh.

COLEGIATA 2011 T
100% tinta de Toro.

90 Colour: cherry, purple rim. Nose: fresh fruit, red berry notes, floral. Palate: flavourful, fruity, good acidity, round tannins.

GRAN COLEGIATA VINO DE LÁGRIMA 2010 T ROBLE
100% tinta de Toro.

88 Colour: cherry, garnet rim. Nose: ripe fruit, cocoa bean, dark chocolate, sweet spices, creamy oak. Palate: powerful, flavourful, long, toasty.

GRAN COLEGIATA CAMPUS 2008 TC
100% tinta de Toro.

93 Colour: cherry, garnet rim. Nose: ripe fruit, spicy, creamy oak, toasty, complex, balanced. Palate: powerful, flavourful, toasty, round tannins, round.

GRAN COLEGIATA ROBLE FRANCÉS 2008 TC
100% tinta de Toro.

90 Colour: cherry, garnet rim. Nose: balanced, expressive, spicy, powerfull, ripe fruit. Palate: good structure, fruity.

BODEGAS FRANCISCO CASAS

Paseo de San Cosme, 6
28600 Navalcarnero (Madrid)
☎: +34 918 110 207 - Fax: +34 918 110 798
f.casas@bodegascasas.com
www.bodegascasas.com

CAMPARRÓN SELECCION 2011 T
100% tinta de Toro.

88 Colour: cherry, purple rim. Nose: red berry notes, floral, ripe fruit. Palate: flavourful, fruity, good acidity, round tannins.

CAMPARRÓN NOVUM 2011 T
100% tinta de Toro.

87 Colour: cherry, purple rim. Nose: expressive, fresh fruit, red berry notes, floral. Palate: flavourful, fruity, good acidity, round tannins.

CAMPARRÓN 2009 TC
100% tinta de Toro.

88 Colour: cherry, garnet rim. Nose: spicy, creamy oak, toasty, ripe fruit. Palate: powerful, flavourful, toasty, round tannins.

ABBA 2008 T
100% tinta de Toro.

88 Colour: cherry, garnet rim. Nose: balanced, ripe fruit, dark chocolate. Palate: good structure, flavourful.

CAMPARRÓN 2007 TR
100% tinta de Toro.

87 Colour: cherry, garnet rim. Nose: fruit liqueur notes, sweet spices, creamy oak, toasty. Palate: flavourful, spicy, round tannins.

BODEGAS FRONTAURA

Santiago, 17 - 4º
47001 (Valladolid)
☎: +34 983 360 284 - Fax: +34 983 345 546
info@bodegasfrontaura.es
www.bodegasfrontaura.es

FRONTAURA 2010 B
100% verdejo.

88 Colour: bright straw. Nose: ripe fruit, citrus fruit, spicy, candied fruit. Palate: fruity, powerful, sweetness.

VEGA MURILLO 2011 T
100% tinta de Toro.

88 Colour: cherry, purple rim. Nose: red berry notes, ripe fruit, violets. Palate: fruity, flavourful, long.

DOMINIO DE VALDELACASA 2009 T
100% tinta de Toro.

90 Colour: cherry, garnet rim. Nose: red berry notes, ripe fruit, mineral, sweet spices, creamy oak. Palate: powerful, flavourful, toasty.

APONTE 2006 T
100% tinta de Toro.

93 Colour: cherry, garnet rim. Nose: complex, ripe fruit, sweet spices, expressive. Palate: good structure, flavourful, round tannins, long.

FRONTAURA 2006 TC
100% tinta de Toro.

90 Colour: cherry, garnet rim. Nose: earthy notes, spicy, creamy oak, ripe fruit, fine reductive notes. Palate: flavourful, long, round tannins.

FRONTAURA 2005 TR
100% tinta de Toro.

92 Colour: cherry, garnet rim. Nose: balanced, complex, sweet spices, ripe fruit. Palate: good structure, flavourful, complex.

BODEGAS GIL LUNA

Ctra. Toro - Salamanca, Km. 2
49800 Toro (Zamora)
☎: +34 980 698 509 - Fax: +34 980 698 294
pbgiluna@giluna.com
www.giluna.com

TRES LUNAS VERDEJO 2011 B
100% verdejo.

91 Colour: bright straw. Nose: fresh, fresh fruit, white flowers, expressive, tropical fruit. Palate: flavourful, fruity, good acidity, balanced.

TRES LUNAS ECOLÓGICO 2009 T
95% tinta de Toro, 5% garnacha.

86 Colour: deep cherry. Nose: dark chocolate, nose:tic coffee, fruit preserve. Palate: sweetness, fine bitter notes.

TRES LUNAS 2008 T
95% tinta de Toro, 5% garnacha.

91 Colour: cherry, garnet rim. Nose: ripe fruit, spicy, creamy oak, toasty, complex. Palate: powerful, flavourful, toasty, round tannins.

GIL LUNA 2005 T
95% tinta de Toro, 5% garnacha.

88 Colour: cherry, garnet rim. Nose: spicy, toasty, fruit liqueur notes, new oak. Palate: powerful, flavourful, toasty, round tannins.

BODEGAS ITURRIA

Avda. Torrecilla De La Abadesa 2.2e
47100 Tordesillas (Valladolid)
☎: +34 600 523 070
contact@bodegas-iturria.com

TINTO ITURRIA 2010 T
90% tinta de Toro, 10% garnacha.

87 Colour: bright cherry. Nose: ripe fruit, sweet spices, creamy oak, wild herbs. Palate: flavourful, fruity, toasty.

TINTO ITURRIA 2009 T
90% tinta de Toro, 10% garnacha.

91 Colour: cherry, garnet rim. Nose: spicy, creamy oak, toasty, complex, fragrant herbs. Palate: powerful, flavourful, toasty, round tannins.

VALDOSAN 2009 T
tinta de Toro.

88 Colour: cherry, garnet rim. Nose: spicy, creamy oak, toasty, ripe fruit. Palate: powerful, flavourful, toasty, round tannins.

BODEGAS LIBA Y DELEITE

Paseo De Zorrilla, 77 – 3º Dcha.
47007 (Valladolid)
☎: +34 983 355 543 - Fax: +34 983 340 824
acontia@acontia.es
www.acontia.es

ACONTIA '06 ROBLE ESPAÑOL 2011 T
85% tinta de Toro, 15% garnacha.

89 Colour: dark-red cherry, garnet rim. Nose: ripe fruit, mineral, sweet spices, creamy oak. Palate: powerful, flavourful, long, toasty.

ACONTIA '12 ROBLE ESPAÑOL 2009 T
85% tinta de Toro, 15% garnacha.

90 Colour: cherry, garnet rim. Nose: ripe fruit, spicy, toasty, scrubland. Palate: flavourful, spicy, balanced.

BODEGAS MATARREDONDA

Ctra. Toro - Valdefinjas, km. 2,5
49800 Toro (Zamora)
☎: +34 687 965 280 - Fax: +34 980 059 981
libranza@vinolibranza.com
www.vinolibranza.com

JUAN ROJO 2006 T
100% tinta de Toro.

90 Colour: cherry, garnet rim. Nose: ripe fruit, macerated fruit, dark chocolate, sweet spices. Palate: full, powerful, round tannins.

LIBRANZA 2006 T
100% tinta de Toro.

87 Colour: cherry, garnet rim. Nose: sweet spices, fruit preserve, warm. Palate: powerful, good finish.

BODEGAS MONTE LA REINA

Ctra. Toro - Zamora, Km. 436,7
49881 Toro (Zamora)
☎: +34 980 082 011 - Fax: +34 980 082 012
bodega@montelareina.es
www.montelareina.es

CASTILLO DE MONTE LA REINA 2011 B
100% verdejo.

86 Colour: bright yellow. Nose: powerfull, ripe fruit, sweet spices, dried herbs. Palate: rich, flavourful, good acidity.

CASTILLO DE MONTE LA REINA 2010 T ROBLE
100% tempranillo.

87 Colour: cherry, purple rim. Nose: ripe fruit, sweet spices. Palate: balanced, long, ripe fruit, astringent.

TORCANTO 2011 B
100% verdejo.

85 Colour: bright yellow. Nose: ripe fruit, dried flowers, fragrant herbs. Palate: powerful, flavourful, fruity.

TORCANTO 2011 T
100% tinta de Toro.

83

TERTIUS 2010 T ROBLE
100% tempranillo.

84

CASTILLO DE MONTE LA REINA 2008 T FERMENTADO EN BARRICA
100% tempranillo.

89 Colour: cherry, garnet rim. Nose: ripe fruit, balsamic herbs, earthy notes, spicy, creamy oak. Palate: powerful, flavourful, toasty.

INARAJA 2006 T
100% tempranillo.

91 Colour: dark-red cherry, garnet rim. Nose: ripe fruit, creamy oak, sweet spices, earthy notes. Palate: concentrated, powerful, flavourful, balanced.

CASTILLO DE MONTE LA REINA VENDIMIA SELECCIONADA 2005 T
100% tempranillo.

90 Colour: cherry, garnet rim. Nose: spicy, creamy oak, toasty. Palate: powerful, flavourful, toasty, round tannins.

BODEGAS REJADORADA

Rejadorada, 11
49800 Toro (Zamora)
☎: +34 980 693 089 - Fax: +34 980 693 089
rejadorada@rejadorada.com
www.rejadorada.com

BRAVO DE REJADORADA 2009 T
100% tinta de Toro.

90 Colour: bright cherry. Nose: ripe fruit, sweet spices, creamy oak, toasty. Palate: flavourful, fruity, toasty, round tannins.

NOVELLUM REJADORADA 2008 TC
100% tinta de Toro.

90 Colour: cherry, garnet rim. Nose: ripe fruit, spicy, creamy oak, toasty. Palate: powerful, flavourful, toasty, round tannins.

SANGO DE REJADORADA 2008 TR
100% tinta de Toro.

88 Colour: cherry, garnet rim. Nose: powerfull, complex, balanced, dark chocolate, sweet spices. Palate: good structure, balanced.

REJADORADA ROBLE 2010 T ROBLE
100% tinta de Toro.

88 Colour: bright cherry. Nose: ripe fruit, sweet spices, expressive, toasty. Palate: flavourful, fruity, toasty, balanced.

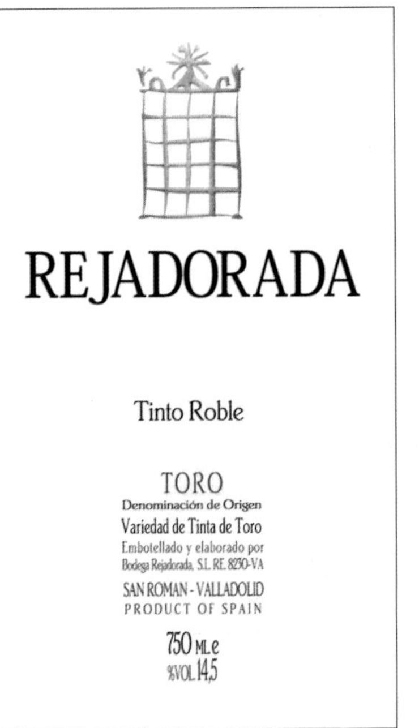

QUEBRANTARREJAS 2010 T
100% tinta de Toro.

88 Colour: black cherry. Nose: ripe fruit, creamy oak, spicy, balsamic herbs. Palate: flavourful, fruity, toasty, long.

VALDELAZARZA 2009 TC
100% tinta de Toro.

86 Colour: cherry, garnet rim. Nose: warm, ripe fruit, scrubland, creamy oak. Palate: spicy, long, flavourful.

BODEGAS SIETECERROS

Finca Villaester
47540 Villaester de Arriba (Valladolid)
☎: +34 983 784 083 - Fax: +34 983 784 142
sietecerros@bodegasietecerros.com
www.bodegasietecerros.com

VALDELAZARZA 2010 T
100% tinta de Toro.

84

VALDELAZARZA 2010 T ROBLE
tinta de Toro.

84

VALDELAZARZA 2005 TR
100% tinta de Toro.

86 Colour: cherry, garnet rim. Nose: ripe fruit, spicy, roasted coffee, wet leather, cigar. Palate: powerful, flavourful, toasty.

BODEGAS SOBREÑO

Ctra. N-122, Km. 423
49800 Toro (Zamora)
☎: +34 980 693 417 - Fax: +34 980 693 416
sobreno@sobreno.com
www.sobreno.com

FINCA SOBREÑO 2010 T ROBLE
100% tinta de Toro.

87 Colour: bright cherry. Nose: ripe fruit, sweet spices, creamy oak. Palate: flavourful, fruity, toasty, round tannins.

FINCA SOBREÑO ECOLÓGICO 2010 T
100% tinta de Toro.

85 Colour: cherry, purple rim. Nose: fruit preserve, sweet spices. Palate: fruity, flavourful, good finish.

FINCA SOBREÑO CRIANZA 2009 TC
100% tinta de Toro.

84

FINCA SOBREÑO SELECCIÓN ESPECIAL 2008 TR
100% tinta de Toro.

88 Colour: cherry, garnet rim. Nose: dark chocolate, creamy oak, candied fruit, warm. Palate: balanced, fine bitter notes.

FINCA SOBREÑO RESERVA FAMILIAR 2005 TR
100% tinta de Toro.

88 Colour: light cherry, orangey edge. Nose: ripe fruit, spicy, slightly evolved, wet leather, cigar. Palate: flavourful, spicy, spirituous.

BODEGAS TORREDUERO

Pol. Ind. Norte - Parcela 5
49800 Toro (Zamora)
☎: +34 941 454 050 - Fax: +34 941 454 529
bodega@bodegasriojanas.com
www.bodegasriojanas.com

PEÑAMONTE 2011 B
100% verdejo.

84

PEÑAMONTE 2011 RD
85% tinta de Toro, 15% garnacha.

85 Colour: rose, purple rim. Nose: ripe fruit, lactic notes, floral, medium intensity. Palate: correct, powerful, flavourful.

PEÑAMONTE 2011 T
100% tinta de Toro.

85 Colour: cherry, purple rim. Nose: ripe fruit, dried flowers, balsamic herbs, medium intensity. Palate: powerful, flavourful, fresh, fruity.

PEÑAMONTE 2010 T BARRICA
100% tinta de Toro.

85 Colour: cherry, purple rim. Nose: red berry notes, ripe fruit, spicy, creamy oak. Palate: powerful, flavourful, spicy, toasty.

MARQUÉS DE PEÑAMONTE COLECCIÓN PRIVADA 2009 T
100% tinta de Toro.

90 Colour: cherry, garnet rim. Nose: ripe fruit, spicy, creamy oak, toasty, complex. Palate: powerful, flavourful, toasty, balanced.

PEÑAMONTE 2008 TC
100% tinta de Toro.

89 Colour: cherry, garnet rim. Nose: creamy oak, sweet spices, cocoa bean, ripe fruit. Palate: balanced, long, spicy.

MARQUÉS DE PEÑAMONTE 2006 TR
100% tinta de Toro.

87 Colour: deep cherry. Nose: toasty, nose:tic coffee, ripe fruit. Palate: spicy, ripe fruit.

BODEGAS VEGA SAUCO

Avda. Comuneros, 108
49810 Morales de Toro (Zamora)
☎: +34 980 698 294 - Fax: +34 980 698 294
vegasauco@vegasauco.com
www.vegasauco.com

VEGA SAÚCO EL BEYBI 2010 T ROBLE
100% tinta de Toro.

85 Colour: deep cherry. Nose: ripe fruit, medium intensity, spicy. Palate: flavourful, fine bitter notes, good acidity.

VEGA SAÚCO "TO" 2008 T
100% tinta de Toro.

85 Colour: cherry, garnet rim. Nose: ripe fruit, slightly evolved, spicy, toasty. Palate: powerful, flavourful, spicy, long.

ADOREMUS 2005 TR
100% tinta de Toro.

91 Colour: cherry, garnet rim. Nose: dark chocolate, tobacco, ripe fruit. Palate: good structure, flavourful, spicy, round tannins, long.

ADOREMUS 2004 TR
100% tinta de Toro.

90 Colour: cherry, garnet rim. Nose: fruit preserve, cigar, old leather, aged wood nuances. Palate: spicy, flavourful, spirituous, long.

WENCES 25 ANIVERSARIO 2004 T
80% tinta de Toro, 20% otras.

89 Colour: pale ruby, brick rim edge. Nose: elegant, spicy, wet leather, aged wood nuances, fruit liqueur notes. Palate: spicy, fine tannins, elegant, long.

ADOREMUS 2001 TGR
100% tinta de Toro.

86 Colour: pale ruby, brick rim edge. Nose: fruit liqueur notes, cigar, wet leather, smoky, earthy notes, medium intensity. Palate: spirituous, flavourful, slightly evolved.

ADOREMUS 1998 TGR
100% tinta de Toro.

91 Colour: pale ruby, brick rim edge. Nose: elegant, fine reductive notes, wet leather, aged wood nuances, fruit liqueur notes. Palate: spicy, fine tannins, elegant, long.

BODEGAS Y VIÑEDOS ANZIL

Ctra. Camino El Pego s/n, Ctra. Toro a Villabuena del Puente, km. 9,400
49800 Toro (Zamora)
☎: +34 915 006 000 - Fax: +34 915 006 006
www.bodegasanzil.es

VIÑA MAYOR TORO 2010 T
100% tempranillo.

90 Colour: cherry, garnet rim. Nose: spicy, creamy oak, toasty. Palate: powerful, flavourful, toasty, round tannins.

FINCA ANZIL VENDIMIA SELECCIONADA 2009 T
100% tempranillo.

88 Colour: cherry, garnet rim. Nose: ripe fruit, spicy, creamy oak, toasty. Palate: powerful, flavourful, toasty, round tannins.

BODEGAS Y VIÑEDOS MAURODOS

Ctra. N-122, Km. 412 - Villaester
47112 Pedrosa del Rey (Valladolid)
☎: +34 983 784 118 - Fax: +34 983 784 018
comunicacion@bodegasmauro.com
www.bodegasanroman.com

PRIMA 2010 TC
90% tinta de Toro, 10% garnacha.

88 Colour: bright cherry. Nose: ripe fruit, sweet spices, creamy oak. Palate: flavourful, fruity, toasty, round tannins.

SAN ROMÁN 2009 T
100% tinta de Toro.

94 Colour: cherry, garnet rim. Nose: spicy, creamy oak, toasty, complex, red berry notes, dark chocolate. Palate: powerful, flavourful, toasty, round tannins.

BODEGAS Y VIÑEDOS PINTIA

Ctra. de Morales, s/n
47530 San Román de Hornija (Valladolid)
☎: +34 983 680 147 - Fax: +34 983 680 263
rhernan-perez@vega-sicilia.com
www.bodegaspintia.com

PINTIA 2009 T
100% tinta de Toro.

95 Colour: cherry, garnet rim. Nose: powerfull, ripe fruit, cocoa bean, expressive. Palate: good structure, full, fine tannins, spicy.

BODEGUEROS QUINTA ESENCIA

Eras, 37
47520 Castronuño (Valladolid)
☎: +34 605 887 100 - Fax: +34 983 866 391
ferrin@bodeguerosquintaesencia.com
www.bodeguerosquintaesencia.com

SOFROS 2010 T
100% tinta de Toro.

91 Colour: cherry, garnet rim. Nose: spicy, creamy oak, toasty, mineral, ripe fruit. Palate: powerful, flavourful, toasty, round tannins.

CAÑADA DEL PINO

Pol. Ind. 6 - Parcela 83
49810 Morales de Toro (Zamora)
☎: +34 676 701 918 - Fax: +34 980 698 318
fincayerro@terra.es

FINCA YERRO 2011 T

88 Colour: cherry, purple rim. Nose: fresh fruit, red berry notes, floral. Palate: flavourful, fruity, good acidity, round tannins.

PIÉLAGO 2009 T

89 Colour: cherry, garnet rim. Nose: ripe fruit, spicy, creamy oak, toasty. Palate: powerful, flavourful, toasty, long.

FINCA YERRO 2008 T ROBLE

88 Colour: deep cherry. Nose: powerfull, toasty, sweet spices, dark chocolate. Palate: spicy, ripe fruit.

CEPAS Y BODEGAS

Paseo de Zorrilla, 77 - 3º D
47001 Valladolid (Valladolid)
☎: +34 983 355 543 - Fax: +34 983 340 824
info@cepasybodegas.com
www.cepasybodegas.com

VIÑALCASTA 2011 T ROBLE
tinta de Toro.

84

VIÑALCASTA 2009 TC
100% tinta de Toro.

87 Colour: cherry, garnet rim. Nose: fruit preserve, fragrant herbs, cigar, citrus fruit, spicy. Palate: powerful, flavourful, spicy.

COMPAÑÍA DE VINOS TELMO RODRÍGUEZ

El Monte
01308 Lanciego (Álava)
☎: +34 945 628 315 - Fax: +34 945 628 314
contact@telmorodriguez.com
www.telmorodriguez.com

PAGO LA JARA 2008 T
100% tinta de Toro.

93 Colour: very deep cherry. Nose: powerfull, varietal, characterful, ripe fruit, toasty, earthy notes. Palate: good acidity, fine bitter notes, round, powerful, round tannins.

CORAL DUERO

Ascensión, s/n
49154 El Pego (Zamora)
☎: +34 980 606 333 - Fax: +34 980 606 333
rompesedas@rompesedas.com
www.rompesedas.com

ROMPESEDAS FINCA LAS PARVAS 2006 T
100% tinta de Toro.

93 Colour: cherry, garnet rim. Nose: ripe fruit, spicy, creamy oak, complex. Palate: powerful, flavourful, round tannins, full.

ROMPESEDAS 2006 T
100% tinta de Toro.

90 Colour: bright cherry. Nose: ripe fruit, sweet spices, creamy oak. Palate: flavourful, fruity, toasty, round tannins.

DOMAINES MAGREZ ESPAGNE

Pza. de la Trinidad, 5
49800 Toro (Zamora)
☎: +34 980 698 172 - Fax: +34 980 698 172
ventas@vocarraje.es
www.bernard-magrez.com

PACIENCIA 2008 T
100% tinta de Toro.

93 Colour: cherry, garnet rim. Nose: spicy, creamy oak, toasty, complex, fragrant herbs, mineral. Palate: powerful, flavourful, toasty, round tannins.

DOMINIO DEL BENDITO

Pza. Santo Domingo, 8
49800 Toro (Zamora)
☎: +34 980 693 306 - Fax: +34 980 694 991
info@bodegadominiodelbendito.es

DOMINIO DEL BENDITO EL PRIMER PASO 2010 T ROBLE

90 Colour: bright cherry. Nose: sweet spices, creamy oak, ripe fruit. Palate: flavourful, fruity, toasty, round tannins.

EL TITÁN DEL BENDITO 2009 T

94 Colour: bright cherry. Nose: ripe fruit, sweet spices, creamy oak, expressive, toasty, mineral. Palate: flavourful, fruity, toasty, balanced.

DOMINIO DEL BENDITO LAS SABIAS 16 MESES 2008 T

92 Colour: cherry, garnet rim. Nose: spicy, creamy oak, toasty, characterful, ripe fruit. Palate: powerful, flavourful, toasty, round tannins.

ESTANCIA PIEDRA

Ctra. Toro a Salamanca, km. 5

49800 Toro (Zamora)
☎: +34 980 693 900 - Fax: +34 980 693 901
info@estanciapiedra.com
www.estanciapiedra.com

PIEDRA AZUL 2011 T
100% tinta de Toro.

90 Colour: cherry, purple rim. Nose: expressive, fresh fruit, red berry notes, floral, lactic notes, mineral. Palate: flavourful, fruity, good acidity, balanced.

PIEDRA ROJA 2009 TC
100% tinta de Toro.

92 Colour: cherry, garnet rim. Nose: ripe fruit, creamy oak, toasty, sweet spices, earthy notes. Palate: powerful, flavourful, toasty, long.

PIEDRA PAREDINAS 2007 T
100% tinta de Toro.

93 Colour: dark-red cherry, garnet rim. Nose: ripe fruit, earthy notes, spicy, creamy oak, toasty. Palate: long, powerful, flavourful, spicy.

LA GARONA 2007 T
75% tinta de Toro, 25% garnacha.

89 Colour: cherry, garnet rim. Nose: ripe fruit, spicy, balsamic herbs, fine reductive notes. Palate: powerful, flavourful, round tannins, long, spicy.

PIEDRA PLATINO SELECCIÓN 2006 TR
100% tinta de Toro.

92 Colour: pale ruby, brick rim edge. Nose: elegant, spicy, fine reductive notes, aged wood nuances, ripe fruit. Palate: spicy, fine tannins, elegant, long, balanced.

FRUTOS VILLAR

Eras de Santa Catalina, s/n
49800 Toro (Zamora)
☎: +34 983 586 868 - Fax: +34 983 580 180
bodegasfrutosvillar@bodegasfrutosvillar.com
www.bodegasfrutosvillar.com

MURUVE 2011 T
tinta de Toro.

87 Colour: cherry, purple rim. Nose: faded flowers, ripe fruit. Palate: powerful, fine bitter notes, ripe fruit.

MURUVE ÉLITE 2009 T
100% tinta de Toro.

89 Colour: deep cherry. Nose: powerfull, ripe fruit, sweet spices, scrubland. Palate: flavourful, spicy, ripe fruit.

MURUVE 2010 T ROBLE
tinta de Toro.

87 Colour: bright cherry. Nose: sweet spices, creamy oak, overripe fruit. Palate: flavourful, fruity, toasty, round tannins.

MURUVE 2009 TC
100% tinta de Toro.

89 Colour: cherry, garnet rim. Nose: medium intensity, balanced, ripe fruit, sweet spices. Palate: balanced, round tannins.

MURUVE 2008 TR
tinta de Toro.

90 Colour: cherry, garnet rim. Nose: balanced, powerfull, ripe fruit, dark chocolate, sweet spices. Palate: balanced, fine bitter notes.

GRUPO YLLERA

Autovía A-6, Km. 173, 5
47490 Rueda (Valladolid)
☎: +34 983 868 097 - Fax: +34 983 868 177
grupoyllera@grupoyllera.com
www.grupoyllera.com

GARCILASO 2004 TC
100% tempranillo.

87 Colour: cherry, garnet rim. Nose: ripe fruit, spicy, creamy oak, balsamic herbs, fine reductive notes. Palate: powerful, flavourful, toasty, round tannins.

HACIENDA TERRA DURO

Campanas, 4, 1° A
47001 (Valladolid)
☎: +34 983 362 591 - Fax: +34 983 357 663
manueldenicolas@gmail.com
www.terraduro.com

TERRA D'URO FINCA LA RANA 2010 T
tinta de Toro.

90 Colour: bright cherry. Nose: ripe fruit, sweet spices, creamy oak, fragrant herbs. Palate: flavourful, fruity, toasty, round tannins.

URO 2009 T
tinta de Toro.

91 Colour: deep cherry. Nose: earthy notes, overripe fruit, toasty, dark chocolate. Palate: powerful, fine bitter notes, spicy.

TERRA D'URO SELECCIÓN 2009 T
tinta de Toro.

90 Colour: cherry, garnet rim. Nose: earthy notes, fruit preserve, spicy, toasty. Palate: powerful, flavourful, long, spicy.

TERRA D'URO SELECCIÓN 2008 T
tinta de Toro.

92 Colour: cherry, garnet rim. Nose: ripe fruit, earthy notes, spicy, creamy oak. Palate: flavourful, powerful, spicy, long, balanced.

URO 2008 T
tinta de Toro.

91 Colour: cherry, garnet rim. Nose: ripe fruit, spicy, creamy oak, toasty, complex. Palate: powerful, flavourful, toasty, round tannins.

LIBERALIA ENOLÓGICA

Camino del Palo, s/n
49800 Toro (Zamora)
☎: +34 980 692 571 - Fax: +34 980 692 571
liberalia@liberalia.es
www.liberalia.es

LIBERALIA CERO 2011 T FERMENTADO EN BARRICA
100% tinta de Toro.

89 Colour: bright cherry. Nose: sweet spices, creamy oak, ripe fruit. Palate: flavourful, fruity, toasty, round tannins.

LIBERALIA TRES 2011 T ROBLE
100% tinta de Toro.

88 Colour: cherry, purple rim. Nose: fresh fruit, red berry notes, floral. Palate: flavourful, fruity, good acidity, round tannins.

LIBERALIA CUATRO 2008 TC
100% tinta de Toro.

91 Colour: cherry, garnet rim. Nose: ripe fruit, spicy, creamy oak, toasty, characterful, varietal. Palate: powerful, flavourful, toasty, round tannins.

LIBERALIA CABEZA DE CUBA 2007 TC
100% tinta de Toro.

90 Colour: cherry, garnet rim. Nose: ripe fruit, spicy, creamy oak, cocoa bean, fine reductive notes. Palate: powerful, flavourful, long, toasty.

LIBERALIA CINCO 2006 TR
100% tinta de Toro.

92 Colour: deep cherry. Nose: characterful, dark chocolate, spicy. Palate: spicy, ripe fruit, round tannins.

LIBER 2005 TGR
100% tinta de Toro.

91 Colour: cherry, garnet rim. Nose: spicy, creamy oak, toasty, ripe fruit. Palate: powerful, toasty, round tannins.

LONG WINES

Avda. del Monte, 46
28120 Algete (Madrid)
☎: +34 916 221 305 - Fax: +34 916 220 029
www.longwines.com

EL BOS 2010 T ROBLE
100% tinta de Toro.

85 Colour: deep cherry, purple rim. Nose: ripe fruit, macerated fruit, sweet spices. Palate: flavourful, fruity.

MARQUÉS DE OLIVARA

Eras de Santa Catalina, s/n
49800 Toro (Zamora)
☎: +34 980 693 425 - Fax: +34 980 693 409
marquesdeolivara@marquesdeolivara.com
www.marquesdeolivara.com

VIÑAS DE OLIVARA 2011 T
100% tinta de Toro.

86 Colour: cherry, purple rim. Nose: ripe fruit, powerfull, balanced. Palate: flavourful, concentrated.

MARQUÉS DE OLIVARA VENDIMIA SELECCIONADA 2009 T
100% tinta de Toro.

90 Colour: cherry, garnet rim. Nose: complex, balanced, ripe fruit, creamy oak. Palate: full, flavourful, long.

MARQUÉS DE OLIVARA 2008 TC
100% tinta de Toro.

87 Colour: cherry, garnet rim. Nose: ripe fruit, spicy, creamy oak, toasty. Palate: powerful, flavourful, toasty.

PAGOS DEL REY

Avda. de los Comuneros, 90
49810 Morales de Toro (Zamora)
☎: +34 980 698 023 - Fax: +34 980 698 020
toro@pagosdelrey.com
www.pagosdelrey.com

BAJOZ MALVASÍA 2011 B
100% malvasía.

84

FINCA LA MEDA 2011 B
100% malvasía.

83

BAJOZ 2011 RD
100% tinta de Toro.

85 Colour: rose, bright. Nose: balanced, medium intensity, fresh. Palate: fruity, fresh, easy to drink.

FINCA LA MEDA 2011 RD
100% tinta de Toro.

84

GRAN BAJOZ DE AUTOR 2011 T
100% tinta de Toro.

91 Colour: cherry, purple rim. Nose: red berry notes, ripe fruit, spicy, creamy oak, dark chocolate, cocoa bean.

FINCA LA MEDA ALTA EXPRESIÓN 2011 T
100% tinta de Toro.

90 Colour: deep cherry, purple rim. Nose: powerfull, candied fruit, creamy oak, sweet spices, macerated fruit. Palate: long, spicy.

BAJOZ 01 2011 T
100% tinta de Toro.

88 Colour: cherry, purple rim. Nose: red berry notes, ripe fruit, balsamic herbs, mineral. Palate: correct, fresh, fruity, flavourful.

FINCA LA MEDA 2011 T ROBLE
100% tinta de Toro.

87 Colour: cherry, purple rim. Nose: toasty, sweet spices. Palate: good structure, flavourful, spicy.

FINCA LA MEDA 2011 T
100% tinta de Toro.

85 Colour: cherry, purple rim. Nose: red berry notes, floral, ripe fruit. Palate: flavourful, fruity, correct, easy to drink.

CAÑO 2011 T
50% tinta de Toro, 50% garnacha.

85 Colour: cherry, purple rim. Nose: candied fruit, balanced, neat. Palate: flavourful, fruity.

BAJOZ 2011 T
100% tinta de Toro.

84

FINCA LA MEDA 2010 TC
100% tinta de Toro.

90 Colour: cherry, purple rim. Nose: ripe fruit, medium intensity, sweet spices. Palate: flavourful, fruity, good finish.

BAJOZ 2010 TC
100% tinta de Toro.

88 Colour: cherry, garnet rim. Nose: ripe fruit, spicy, creamy oak, toasty. Palate: powerful, flavourful, toasty.

CAÑO TEMPRANILLO 2010 T
100% tempranillo.

87 Colour: cherry, garnet rim. Nose: powerfull, ripe fruit, scrubland. Palate: flavourful, ripe fruit.

PALACIO DE VILLACHICA

Ctra. Nacional 122, Km. 433
49800 Toro (Zamora)
☎: +34 609 144 711 - Fax: +34 983 381 356
admin@palaciodevillachica.com
www.palaciodevillachica.com

PALACIO DE VILLACHICA 2011 T
100% tinta de Toro.

87 Colour: cherry, purple rim. Nose: powerfull, ripc fruit, red berry notes. Palate: flavourful, fine bitter notes.

PALACIO DE VILLACHICA 2010 T ROBLE
100% tinta de Toro.

86 Colour: cherry, purple rim. Nose: medium intensity, spicy, ripe fruit. Palate: flavourful, correct.

PALACIO DE VILLACHICA SELECCIÓN 2008 T
100% tinta de Toro.

88 Colour: cherry, garnet rim. Nose: ripe fruit, spicy, creamy oak, toasty. Palate: powerful, flavourful, toasty, round tannins.

QUINOLA SUÁREZ

Paseo de Zorrilla, 11- 4 izq.
47007 Valladolid (Valladolid)
☎: +34 625 227 321
garagewine@quinola.es
www.quinola.es

QUINOLA GARAGE WINE 2009 T ROBLE
100% tinta de Toro.

93 Colour: cherry, garnet rim. Nose: ripe fruit, spicy, creamy oak, toasty, complex, mineral, powerfull. Palate: powerful, flavourful, toasty, round tannins.

QUINTA DE LA QUIETUD

Camino de Bardales, s/n
49800 Toro (Zamora)
☎: +34 980 568 019
info@quintaquietud.com
www.quintaquietud.com

CORRAL DE CAMPANAS 2010 T
100% tinta de Toro.

88 Colour: very deep cherry. Nose: powerfull, fruit preserve, overripe fruit. Palate: powerful, ripe fruit, round tannins.

QUINTA QUIETUD 2007 T
100% tinta de Toro.

94 Colour: cherry, garnet rim. Nose: ripe fruit, spicy, creamy oak, toasty, complex, earthy notes, varietal. Palate: powerful, flavourful, toasty, round tannins.

RODRÍGUEZ SANZO

Manuel Azaña, 9
47014 (Valladolid)
☎: +34 983 150 150 - Fax: +34 983 150 151
comunicacion@valsanzo.com
www.rodriguezsanzo.com

TERRAS DE JAVIER RODRÍGUEZ 2009 T
100% tinta de Toro.

93 Colour: bright cherry. Nose: ripe fruit, sweet spices, creamy oak, dark chocolate. Palate: flavourful, fruity, toasty, round tannins.

DAMALISCO 2009 TC
tinta de Toro.

92 Colour: cherry, garnet rim. Nose: ripe fruit, spicy, creamy oak, toasty, complex, earthy notes. Palate: powerful, flavourful, toasty, round tannins.

TESO LA MONJA

Paraje Valdebuey- Ctra. ZA-611, Km. 6,3
49882 Valdefinjas (Zamora)
☎: +34 980 568 143 - Fax: +34 980 508 144
info@eguren.com
www.eguren.com

VICTORINO 2010 T
100% tinta de Toro.

96 Colour: cherry, garnet rim. Nose: ripe fruit, spicy, creamy oak, toasty, complex, fruit expression, red berry notes, earthy notes. Palate: powerful, flavourful, toasty, round tannins.

ALABASTER 2010 T
100% tinta de Toro.

96 Colour: cherry, garnet rim. Nose: ripe fruit, spicy, creamy oak, toasty, complex, earthy notes. Palate: powerful, flavourful, toasty, round tannins, round, fine bitter notes, good acidity.

ALMIREZ 2010 T
100% tinta de Toro.

94 Colour: bright cherry. Nose: ripe fruit, sweet spices, creamy oak, red berry notes. Palate: flavourful, fruity, toasty, round tannins.

ROMANICO 2010 T
100% tinta de Toro.

91 Colour: cherry, purple rim. Nose: fruit expression, ripe fruit, spicy. Palate: flavourful, good acidity, ripe fruit.

VICTORINO 2009 T
100% tinta de Toro.

97 Colour: cherry, garnet rim. Nose: spicy, creamy oak, toasty, characterful, varietal, powerfull. Palate: powerful, flavourful, toasty, round tannins, good acidity, round.

ALABASTER 2009 T
100% tinta de Toro.

95 Colour: cherry, garnet rim. Nose: ripe fruit, spicy, creamy oak, toasty, complex, nose:tic coffee, dark chocolate. Palate: powerful, flavourful, toasty, round tannins, round.

TESO LA MONJA 2008 T
tinta de Toro.

97 Colour: cherry, garnet rim. Nose: ripe fruit, toasty, expressive, characterful, sweet spices, cocoa bean, earthy notes. Palate: powerful, toasty, round, long, fine tannins, elegant.

TORESANAS

Ctra. Tordesillas, s/n
49800 Toro (Zamora)
☎: +34 983 868 116 - Fax: +34 983 868 432
info@taninia.com
www.toresanas.com

AMANT NOVILLO 2011 T
tinta de Toro.

88 Colour: deep cherry. Nose: powerfull, warm, ripe fruit, toasty. Palate: powerful, fine bitter notes, good acidity.

AMANT 2010 T ROBLE
tinta de Toro.

87 Colour: cherry, garnet rim. Nose: red berry notes, ripe fruit, spicy, creamy oak. Palate: flavourful, fruity, long, toasty.

OROT 2005 TC
tinta de Toro.

88 Colour: bright cherry, garnet rim. Nose: cocoa bean, sweet spices, ripe fruit. Palate: balanced, long, round tannins.

VALBUSENDA

Ctra. Toro - Peleagonzalo s/n
49800 Toro (Zamora)
☎: +34 980 699 560 - Fax: +34 980 699 566
bodega@valbusenda.com
www.valbusenda.com

VALBUSENDA CEPAS VIEJAS 2008 T
100% tinta de Toro.

90 Colour: cherry, garnet rim. Nose: spicy, creamy oak, toasty, fruit expression. Palate: powerful, flavourful, toasty, round tannins.

VALBUSENDA 2007 TC
100% tinta de Toro.

88 Colour: bright cherry. Nose: ripe fruit, creamy oak, nose:tic coffee. Palate: flavourful, good acidity, fine bitter notes.

VETUS

Ctra. Toro a Salamanca, Km. 9,5
49800 Toro (Zamora)
☎: +34 945 609 086 - Fax: +34 980 056 012
vetus@bodegasvetus.com
www.bodegasvetus.com

CELSUS 2010 T
100% tinta de Toro.

94 Colour: very deep cherry. Nose: ripe fruit, fruit expression, creamy oak, sweet spices, cocoa bean. Palate: round, powerful, good acidity, fine bitter notes, round tannins.

FLOR DE VETUS 2010 T
100% tinta de Toro.

91 Colour: bright cherry. Nose: sweet spices, creamy oak, red berry notes. Palate: flavourful, fruity, toasty, round tannins.

VINOS Y VIÑEDOS DE LA CASA MAGUILA

Ctra. El Piñero s/n - Pol. Ind. 1 - parc. 715
49153 Venialbo (Zamora)
☎: +34 616 262 549
administracion@casamaguila.com
www.casamaguila.com

CACHITO MÍO 2011 T
100% tinta de Toro.

91 Colour: bright cherry. Nose: ripe fruit, sweet spices, creamy oak, balsamic herbs. Palate: flavourful, fruity, toasty, round tannins.

VIÑAGUAREÑA

Ctra. Toro a Salamanca, Km. 12,5
49800 Toro (Zamora)
☎: +34 980 568 013 - Fax: +34 980 568 134
info@vinotoro.com
www.vinotoro.com

IDUNA 2010 B
100% verdejo.

87 Colour: bright yellow. Nose: toasty, sweet spices, candied fruit. Palate: rich, flavourful, ripe fruit, toasty.

MUNIA 2010 T ROBLE
100% tinta de Toro.

86 Colour: bright cherry. Nose: ripe fruit, sweet spices, creamy oak, expressive. Palate: flavourful, fruity, toasty, round tannins.

MUNIA 2009 TC
100% tinta de Toro.

90 Colour: cherry, garnet rim. Nose: spicy, creamy oak, toasty, complex, ripe fruit. Palate: powerful, flavourful, toasty, round tannins.

PICTOR 2008 T ROBLE
100% tinta de Toro.

91 Colour: bright cherry. Nose: sweet spices, creamy oak, expressive, ripe fruit, red berry notes, fragrant herbs. Palate: flavourful, fruity, toasty, round tannins.

MUNIA ESPECIAL 2008 T ROBLE
100% tinta de Toro.

90 Colour: bright cherry. Nose: sweet spices, creamy oak. Palate: flavourful, fruity, toasty, round tannins.

VIÑEDOS ALONSO DEL YERRO

Finca Santa Marta - Ctra. Roa-Anguix, Km. 1,8
09300 Roa (Burgos)
☎: +34 913 160 121 - Fax: +34 913 160 121
mariadelyerro@vay.es
www.alonsodelyerro.com

PAYDOS 2009 T
100% tinta de Toro.

90 Colour: cherry, garnet rim. Nose: ripe fruit, earthy notes, fruit preserve, spicy, toasty. Palate: powerful, flavourful, complex, toasty.

VIÑEDOS DE VILLAESTER

49800 Toro (Zamora)
☎: +34 948 645 008 - Fax: +34 948 645 166
info@familiabelasco.com
www.familiabelasco.com

TAURUS 2007 TC
100% tinta de Toro.

88 Colour: cherry, garnet rim. Nose: spicy, creamy oak, toasty, expressive. Palate: powerful, flavourful, toasty, round tannins.

TAURUS 2007 T ROBLE
100% tinta de Toro.

87 Colour: cherry, garnet rim. Nose: overripe fruit, powerfull, toasty, spicy. Palate: ripe fruit, correct.

VILLAESTER 2004 T
100% tinta de Toro.

91 Colour: pale ruby, brick rim edge. Nose: elegant, spicy, fine reductive notes, wet leather, aged wood nuances, fruit liqueur notes. Palate: spicy, fine tannins, elegant, long, balanced.

VOCARRAJE

Ctra. San Román, s/n
49810 Moral de Toro (Zamora)
☎: +34 630 084 080 - Fax: +34 980 698 172
info@vocarraje.es
www.vocarraje.es

ABDÓN SEGOVIA 2011 T ROBLE
100% tinta de Toro.

87 Colour: cherry, purple rim. Nose: powerfull, ripe fruit, warm, dark chocolate. Palate: ripe fruit, spicy.

ABDÓN SEGOVIA 2009 TC
100% tinta de Toro.

91 Colour: cherry, garnet rim. Nose: spicy, creamy oak, toasty, varietal. Palate: powerful, flavourful, toasty, round tannins.

DO UCLÉS

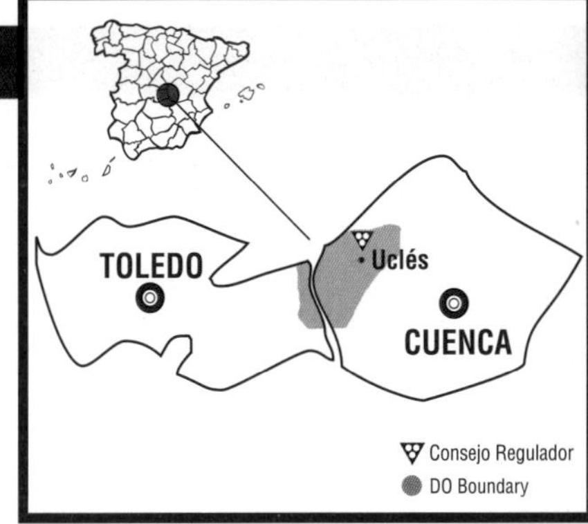

LOCATION:

Midway between Cuenca (to the west) and Toledo (to the northwest), this DO is made up of 25 towns from the first province and three from the second. However, the majority of vineyards are situated in Tarancón and the neighbouring towns of Cuenca, as far as Huete - where La Alcarria starts - the largest stretch of border in the DO.

CLIMATE:

The Altamira sierra forms gentle undulations that rise from an average of 600 metres in La Mancha, reaching 1,200 metres. These ups and downs produce variations in the continental climate, which is less extreme, milder and has a Mediterranean touch. As such, rain is scarce, more akin to a semi-dry climate.

SOIL:

Despite spreading over two provinces with different soil components, the communal soils are deep and not very productive, of a sandy and consistent texture, becoming more clayey as you move towards the banks of the rivers Riansares and Bendija.

GRAPE VARIETIES:

RED: *Tempranillo, Merlot, Cabernet Sauvignon, Garnacha* and *Syrah.*
WHITE: *Verdejo, Moscatel de Grano Menudo, Chardonnay, Sauvignon Blanc* and *Viura (macabeo).*

FIGURES:

Vineyard surface: 1,700 – **Wine-Growers:** 122 – **Wineries:** 5 – **2011 Harvest rating:** Very Good – **Production:** 1,677,563 litres – **Market percentages:** 25% domestic. 75% export

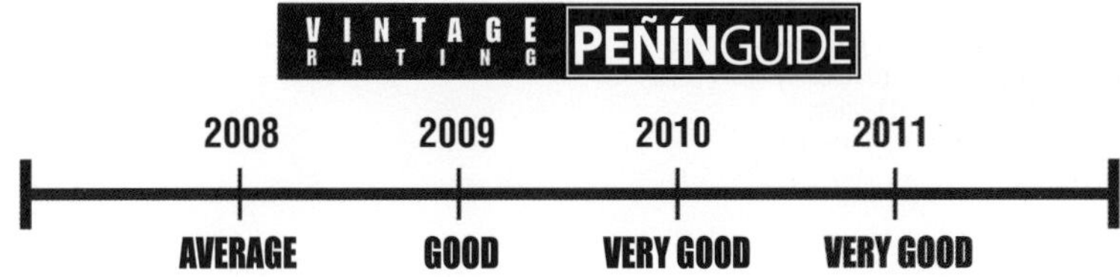

CONSEJO REGULADOR
Avda. Miguel Cervantes, 93 - 16400 Tarancón (Cuenca) - ☎: +34 969 135 056 - Fax: +34 969 135 421
@ gerente@vinosdeucles.com - www.vinosdeucles.com

COOPERATIVA NUESTRA SEÑORA DE LA SOLEDAD

Ctra. Tarancón, s/n
16411 Fuente de Pedro Naharro (Cuenca)
☎: +34 969 125 039 - Fax: +34 969 125 907
info@bodegasoledad.com
www.bodegasoledad.com

SOLMAYOR CHARDONNAY 2011 B
chardonnay.

84

SOLMAYOR SAUVIGNON BLANC 2011 B
sauvignon blanc.

82

SOLMAYOR 2011 T
tempranillo.

85 Colour: cherry, purple rim. Nose: red berry notes, ripe fruit, scrubland. Palate: powerful, flavourful, fruity, easy to drink.

SOLMAYOR 2010 T ROBLE
tempranillo.

84

FONTANA

Extramuros, s/n
16411 Fuente de Pedro Naharro (Cuenca)
☎: +34 969 125 433 - Fax: +34 969 125 387
gemag@bodegasfontana.com
www.bodegasfontana.com

ESENCIA DE FONTANA 2010 TC
90% tempranillo, 10% merlot.

91 Colour: bright cherry, garnet rim. Nose: medium intensity, ripe fruit, balsamic herbs, creamy oak. Palate: good structure, full, long, round tannins.

LA VID Y LA ESPIGA

San Antón, 30
16415 Villamayor de Santiago (Cuenca)
☎: +34 969 139 069 - Fax: +34 969 139 069
export@vidyespiga.es
www.vidyespiga.es

CAÑADA REAL 2011 B
sauvignon blanc, verdejo.

84

CAÑADA REAL 2011 RD
tempranillo.

85 Colour: rose, bright. Nose: red berry notes, ripe fruit, rose petals. Palate: flavourful, fruity.

CAÑADA REAL 2011 T
tempranillo.

84

CAÑADA REAL 2009 TC
tempranillo.

86 Colour: cherry, garnet rim. Nose: ripe fruit, spicy, toasty. Palate: powerful, flavourful, toasty, round tannins.

CAÑADA REAL TINTO ROBLE 2010

84

LOCATION:

In thewest of the province of Valencia. It comprises the municipal districts of Camporrobles, Caudete de las Fuentes, Fuenterrobles, Requena, Siete Aguas, Sinarcas, Utiel, Venta del Moro and Villagordc de Cabriel.

CLIMATE:

Continental,with Mediterranean influences, coldwinters and slightly milder summers than in other regions of the province. Rainfall is quite scarcewith an annual average of 400 mm.

SOIL:

Mainly brownish-grey, almost red limestone, poor in organic matter andwith good permeability. The horizon of the vineyards are broken by the silhouette of the odd tree planted in the middle of the vineyards,which, bordered bywoods, offer a very attractive landscape.

GRAPE VARIETIES:

RED: *Bobal, Tempranillo, Garnacha, Cabernet Sauvignon, Merlot, Syrah, Pinot Noir, Garnacha Tintorera, Petit Verdot* and *Cabernet Franc.*
WHITE: *Tardana, Macabeo, Merseguera, Chardonnay, Sauvignon Blanc, Parellada, Xarel.lo, Verdejo, Moscatel de Grano Menudo, Viognier* and *Albariño.*

FIGURES:

Vineyard surface: 37,000 – **Wine-Growers:** 6,500 – **Wineries:** 110 – **2011 Harvest rating:** Excellent – **Production:** 29,108,264 litres – **Market percentages:** 44% domestic. 56% export

CONSEJO REGULADOR
Sevilla, 12. Apdo. 61 - 46300 Utiel (Valencia) - ☎: +34 962 171 062 - Fax: +34 962 172 185
@ info@utielrequena.org - www.utielrequena.org

BODEGA Y VIÑEDOS CARRES

Francho, 1
46352 Casas de Eufema (Valencia)
☎: +34 675 515 729
torrescarpiojl@gmail.com
www.bodegacarres.com

EL OLIVASTRO 2009 T
100% bobal.

90 Colour: cherry, garnet rim. Nose: ripe fruit, scrubland, earthy notes, spicy, toasty. Palate: powerful, flavourful, long, toasty.

BODEGAS ARANLEÓN

Ctra. Caudete, 3, Los Marcos
46310 Venta del Moro (Valencia)
☎: +34 963 631 640 - Fax: +34 962 185 150
vinos@aranleon.com
www.aranleon.com

ARANLEÓN SÓLO 2011 B
60% chardonnay, 40% sauvignon blanc.

90 Colour: bright straw. Nose: fresh, fresh fruit, white flowers, expressive. Palate: flavourful, fruity, good acidity, balanced.

ARANLEÓN SÓLO 2009 T
40% bobal, 40% tempranillo, 20% syrah.

87 Colour: cherry, garnet rim. Nose: powerfull, ripe fruit, creamy oak, sweet spices. Palate: flavourful, spicy, ripe fruit.

ARANLEÓN HELIX 2007 T ROBLE
tempranillo.

90 Colour: bright cherry. Nose: creamy oak, ripe fruit, cocoa bean. Palate: flavourful, fruity, toasty, round tannins.

BODEGAS COVILOR

Antonio Bartual, 21
46313 Cuevas de Utiel (Valencia)
☎: +34 962 182 053 - Fax: +34 962 182 055
oficina@bodegascovilor.com
www.bodegascovilor.com

ALTO CUEVAS MACABEO 2011 B
100% macabeo.

85 Colour: pale. Nose: white flowers, fresh fruit, lactic notes, fresh. Palate: light-bodied, fresh, flavourful, easy to drink.

ALTO CUEVAS 2011 RD
100% bobal.

85 Colour: brilliant rose. Nose: powerfull, varietal, ripe fruit, floral. Palate: flavourful, fruity, fresh.

SUCESIÓN BOBAL 2011 T
bobal.

88 Colour: cherry, purple rim. Nose: red berry notes, raspberry, floral, creamy oak. Palate: fresh, fruity, flavourful, spicy.

ALTO CUEVAS BOBAL TEMPRANILLO 2011 T
bobal, tempranillo.

87 Colour: deep cherry. Nose: powerfull, ripe fruit, grassy. Palate: flavourful, good acidity.

ALTO CUEVAS TEMPRANILLO 2011 T
tempranillo.

84

BODEGAS COVIÑAS

Avda. Rafael Duyos, s/n
46340 Requena (Valencia)
☎: +34 962 300 680 - Fax: +34 962 302 651
covinas@covinas.com
www.covinas.com

AL VENT SAUVIGNON BLANC 2011 B
100% sauvignon blanc.

90 Colour: bright straw. Nose: fresh, fresh fruit, white flowers, expressive. Palate: flavourful, fruity, good acidity, balanced.

AULA MACABEO BLANCO DE LÁGRIMA 2011 B
100% macabeo.

85 Colour: bright straw. Nose: fresh, fresh fruit, white flowers, expressive. Palate: flavourful, fruity, good acidity, balanced.

VIÑA ENTERIZO BOBAL 2011 RD
100% bobal.

87 Colour: rose, purple rim. Nose: powerfull, ripe fruit, red berry notes, floral. Palate: , powerful, fruity, fresh, easy to drink.

AL VENT BOBAL 2011 RD
100% bobal.

86 Colour: rose, purple rim. Nose: ripe fruit, red berry notes, floral. Palate: , powerful, fruity, fresh.

AULA SYRAH 2009 TC
100% syrah.

88 Colour: deep cherry. Nose: powerfull, ripe fruit, creamy oak, spicy. Palate: powerful, fine bitter notes, round tannins.

AULA CABERNET SAUVIGNON 2009 T
cabernet sauvignon.

86 Colour: deep cherry. Nose: ripe fruit, toasty, spicy. Palate: flavourful, fine bitter notes, spirituous.

MONTE MAYOR 2009 TC
tempranillo, bobal.

85 Colour: bright cherry. Nose: sweet spices, creamy oak. Palate: flavourful, fruity, toasty, round tannins.

AULA MERLOT 2008 TC
100% merlot.

90 Colour: cherry, garnet rim. Nose: sweet spices, dark chocolate, ripe fruit. Palate: flavourful, spicy.

MONTE MAYOR 2008 TR
tempranillo, merlot, cabernet sauvignon, syrah, garnacha.

87 Colour: deep cherry. Nose: ripe fruit, creamy oak, dark chocolate. Palate: flavourful, spicy.

ENTERIZO 2008 TR
garnacha.

86 Colour: cherry, garnet rim. Nose: ripe fruit, spicy, creamy oak, toasty, complex. Palate: powerful, flavourful, toasty, round tannins.

MONTE MAYOR 2006 TGR
garnacha, bobal.

88 Colour: light cherry, orangey edge. Nose: spicy, wet leather, aged wood nuances, fruit liqueur notes. Palate: spicy, fine tannins, long.

ENTERIZO 2006 TGR
garnacha.

86 Colour: pale ruby, brick rim edge. Nose: elegant, spicy, wet leather, aged wood nuances, fruit liqueur notes. Palate: spicy, fine tannins, long.

BODEGAS HISPANO SUIZAS

Ctra. N-322, Km. 451,7 El Pontón
46357 Requena (Valencia)
☎: +34 661 894 200
info@bodegashispanosuizas.com
www.bodegashispanosuizas.com

IMPROMPTU 2011 B
sauvignon blanc.

93 Colour: bright straw. Nose: fresh, fresh fruit, white flowers, varietal. Palate: flavourful, fruity, good acidity, balanced.

BASSUS PINOT NOIR 2010 T
pinot noir.

92 Colour: cherry, garnet rim. Nose: ripe fruit, sweet spices, nose:tic coffee, tobacco. Palate: powerful, flavourful, spicy, toasty.

BASSUS PREMIUM 2009 T
bobal, cabernet sauvignon, merlot, syrah.

92 Colour: deep cherry, garnet rim. Nose: fruit liqueur notes, spicy, nose:tic coffee, dark chocolate. Palate: fine bitter notes, good acidity, spirituous.

QUOD SUPERIUS 2008 T
bobal, cabernet sauvignon, merlot, syrah.

93 Colour: cherry, garnet rim. Nose: ripe fruit, spicy, creamy oak, toasty, complex, mineral. Palate: powerful, flavourful, toasty, round tannins.

BODEGAS IRANZO

Ctra. de Madrid, 60
46315 Caudete de las Fuentes (Valencia)
☎: +34 962 319 282 - Fax: +34 962 319 282
comercial@bodegasiranzo.com
www.bodegasiranzo.com

CAÑADA HONDA 2011 T
tempranillo, cabernet sauvignon.

81

BODEGAS IRANZO TEMPRANILLO SELECCIÓN 2010 T
tempranillo.

84

FINCA CAÑADA HONDA 2010 TC
cabernet sauvignon, tempranillo.

84

FINCA CAÑADA HONDA 2010 T BARRICA
tempranillo, cabernet sauvignon.

80

BODEGAS MURVIEDRO

Ampliación Pol. El Romeral, s/n
46340 Requena (Valencia)
☎: +34 962 329 003 - Fax: +34 962 329 002
murviedro@murviedro.es
www.murviedro.es

CUEVA DE LA ESPERA 2011 B
80% chardonnay, 20% pinot noir.

90 Colour: bright straw. Nose: fresh, fresh fruit, white flowers, characterful. Palate: flavourful, fruity, good acidity, balanced.

MURVIEDRO COLECCIÓN SAUVIGNON BLANC 2011 B
sauvignon blanc.

88 Colour: bright straw. Nose: expressive, ripe fruit, grassy. Palate: flavourful, fruity, fresh.

COROLILLA VERDEJO 2011 B
100% verdejo.

85 Colour: bright straw. Nose: fresh fruit, citrus fruit, white flowers. Palate: flavourful, fruity, fresh.

MURVIEDRO COLECCIÓN TEMPRANILLO 2011 T
tempranillo.

86 Colour: deep cherry. Nose: ripe fruit, grassy, red berry notes. Palate: flavourful, fine bitter notes, long.

CUEVA DE LA CULPA 2009 T
60% bobal, 40% merlot.

91 Colour: cherry, garnet rim. Nose: ripe fruit, sweet spices, creamy oak. Palate: flavourful, powerful, good acidity, round tannins.

COROLILLA 2009 TC
100% bobal.

89 Colour: cherry, garnet rim. Nose: red berry notes, ripe fruit, creamy oak, sweet spices. Palate: powerful, flavourful, toasty, balanced.

COROLILLA 2007 TR
100% bobal.

89 Colour: cherry, garnet rim. Nose: ripe fruit, sweet spices, cocoa bean, toasty. Palate: powerful, flavourful, long, toasty.

BODEGAS PALMERA

Corral Charco de Agut, 19, 23
46300 Utiel (Valencia)
☎: +34 626 706 394
klauslauerbach@hotmail.com
www.bodegas-palmera.com

VIÑA CABRIEL SUPERIOR 2010 T
44% tempranillo, 36% cabernet sauvignon, 20% merlot.

88 Colour: cherry, garnet rim. Nose: ripe fruit, balsamic herbs, sweet spices. Palate: powerful, flavourful, spicy, long.

BOBAL Y TEMPRANILLO SUPERIOR 2010 T
33% bobal, 55% tempranillo, 12% merlot.

88 Colour: bright cherry. Nose: ripe fruit, creamy oak, spicy. Palate: flavourful, fruity, toasty, round tannins.

CAPRICHO 2010 T
60% cabernet sauvignon, 17% merlot, 13% tempranillo.

87 Colour: cherry, garnet rim. Nose: ripe fruit, spicy, creamy oak, toasty. Palate: powerful, flavourful, toasty.

L'ANGELET 2008 TC
55% tempranillo, 27% cabernet sauvignon, 18% merlot.

90 Colour: pale ruby, brick rim edge. Nose: earthy notes, balsamic herbs, ripe fruit, fine reductive notes, spicy. Palate: balanced, powerful, flavourful.

BODEGAS SIERRA NORTE

Pol. Ind. El Romeral. Transporte- Parc. C2
46340 Requena (Valencia)
☎: +34 962 323 099 - Fax: +34 962 323 048
info@bodegasierranorte.com
www.bodegasierranorte.com

FUENTESECA 2011 B
macabeo, sauvignon blanc.

88 Colour: bright straw. Nose: fresh, fresh fruit, white flowers. Palate: flavourful, fruity, good acidity, balanced.

CERRO BERCIAL 2010 B
chardonnay, sauvignon blanc, macabeo.

90 Colour: bright straw. Nose: creamy oak, spicy, ripe fruit. Palate: ripe fruit, spicy, creamy.

PASION DE BOBAL 2011 RD
bobal.

90 Colour: rose, purple rim. Nose: powerfull, ripe fruit, red berry notes, floral, expressive, elegant. Palate: , powerful, fruity, fresh, balanced.

FUENTESECA 2011 RD
bobal, cabernet sauvignon.

88 Colour: rose, purple rim. Nose: powerfull, ripe fruit, red berry notes, floral. Palate: , powerful, fruity, fresh, easy to drink.

CERRO BERCIAL 2011 RD
bobal.

86 Colour: rose, purple rim. Nose: floral, ripe fruit, fragrant herbs. Palate: light-bodied, flavourful, fresh, fruity.

FUENTESECA 2011 T
bobal, cabernet sauvignon.

86 Colour: cherry, purple rim. Nose: fresh fruit, red berry notes, floral, balsamic herbs. Palate: flavourful, fruity, round tannins.

PASION DE BOBAL 2010 T
bobal.

91 Colour: cherry, garnet rim. Nose: red berry notes, ripe fruit, balsamic herbs, sweet spices, creamy oak. Palate: powerful, flavourful, fruity, spicy.

TEMPERAMENTO DE BOBAL 2010 T
bobal.

90 Colour: cherry, garnet rim. Nose: red berry notes, ripe fruit, spicy, toasty. Palate: powerful, flavourful, harsh oak tannins.

CERRO BERCIAL 2009 T BARRICA
tempranillo, bobal.

91 Colour: bright cherry. Nose: ripe fruit, sweet spices, cocoa bean. Palate: flavourful, powerful, ripe fruit, fine bitter notes.

FUENTESECA 2009 TC
tempranillo.

88 Colour: cherry, garnet rim. Nose: ripe fruit, spicy, creamy oak, toasty. Palate: powerful, flavourful, toasty.

CERRO BERCIAL PARCELA "LADERA LOS CANTOS" 2006 T
bobal, cabernet sauvignon.

91 Colour: cherry, garnet rim. Nose: dry stone, ripe fruit, fine reductive notes, spicy. Palate: good acidity, powerful, flavourful, spicy.

CERRO BERCIAL 2006 TC
tempranillo, bobal.

87 Colour: deep cherry. Nose: spicy, ripe fruit, toasty, earthy notes. Palate: flavourful, spicy, ripe fruit.

CERRO BERCIAL 2004 TR
tempranillo, bobal, cabernet sauvignon.

90 Colour: cherry, garnet rim. Nose: ripe fruit, spicy, creamy oak, toasty, complex. Palate: powerful, flavourful, toasty, round tannins.

BODEGAS UTIELANAS

San Fernando, 18
46300 Utiel (Valencia)
☎: +34 962 171 157 - Fax: +34 962 170 801
info@bodegasutielanas.com
www.bodegasutielanas.com

VEGA INFANTE 2011 B
macabeo.

88 Colour: bright straw. Nose: fresh, fresh fruit, white flowers, expressive. Palate: flavourful, fruity, good acidity, balanced.

VEGA INFANTE 2010 BFB

86 Colour: bright golden. Nose: ripe fruit, powerfull, toasty, sweet spices. Palate: flavourful, fruity, spicy, toasty.

VEGA INFANTE 2011 RD

85 Colour: rose, purple rim. Nose: ripe fruit, red berry notes, floral. Palate: , powerful, fruity, fresh.

VEGA INFANTE MADURADO EN BARRICA 2011 T
bobal, tempranillo.

91 Colour: cherry, purple rim. Nose: red berry notes, fragrant herbs, sweet spices, creamy oak. Palate: powerful, flavourful, spicy.

VEGA INFANTE 2011 T
bobal.

85 Colour: cherry, purple rim. Nose: fresh fruit, red berry notes, balsamic herbs. Palate: flavourful, fruity, good acidity.

VEGA INFANTE 2008 TC

87 Colour: bright cherry. Nose: ripe fruit, sweet spices, wet leather. Palate: flavourful, good acidity, fine bitter notes.

VEGA INFANTE 2004 TR

88 Colour: pale ruby, brick rim edge. Nose: elegant, spicy, fine reductive notes, wet leather, aged wood nuances. Palate: spicy, fine tannins, elegant, long.

BODEGAS VICENTE GANDÍA

Ctra. Cheste a Godelleta, s/n
46370 Chiva (Valencia)
☎: +34 962 524 242 - Fax: +34 962 524 243
vuboldi@vicentegandia.com
www.vicentegandia.es

FINCA DEL MAR CHARDONNAY 2011 B
100% chardonnay.

88 Colour: bright straw. Nose: fresh, fresh fruit, white flowers, expressive. Palate: flavourful, fruity, good acidity, balanced.

HOYA DE CADENAS 2011 B
50% chardonnay, 30% sauvignon blanc, 20% macabeo.

85 Colour: bright straw. Nose: floral, tropical fruit, fragrant herbs. Palate: light-bodied, fresh, fruity.

HOYA DE CADENAS CHARDONNAY 2011 B
100% chardonnay.

85 Colour: bright straw. Nose: white flowers, ripe fruit, powerfull. Palate: flavourful, fruity, easy to drink.

HOYA DE CADENAS 2011 RD
100% bobal.

85 Colour: rose, purple rim. Nose: floral, lactic notes, red berry notes. Palate: flavourful, fresh, fruity, light-bodied, easy to drink.

HOYA DE CADENAS MERLOT 2011 T
100% merlot.

87 Colour: cherry, purple rim. Nose: red berry notes, ripe fruit, scrubland. Palate: powerful, flavourful, balsamic.

HOYA DE CADENAS SHIRAZ 2011 T
100% syrah.

86 Colour: deep cherry. Nose: red berry notes, fruit expression, spicy. Palate: flavourful, fruity, fresh.

FINCA DEL MAR TEMPRANILLO 2011 T
100% tempranillo.

85 Colour: bright cherry. Nose: ripe fruit, sweet spices, creamy oak. Palate: flavourful, fruity, toasty.

FINCA DEL MAR CABERNET SAUVIGNON 2011 T
100% cabernet sauvignon.

84

HOYA DE CADENAS CABERNET SAUVIGNON 2011 T
100% cabernet sauvignon.

83

FINCA DEL MAR MERLOT 2010 T
100% merlot.

78

BO - BOBAL ÚNICO 2009 T
bobal.

88 Colour: cherry, garnet rim. Nose: ripe fruit, spicy, creamy oak, toasty, balsamic herbs. Palate: powerful, flavourful, toasty, harsh oak tannins.

MARQUÉS DE CHIVÉ 2009 TC
100% tempranillo.

82

HOYA DE CADENAS RESERVA PRIVADA 2008 TR
85% tempranillo, 15% cabernet sauvignon.

85 Colour: pale ruby, brick rim edge. Nose: spicy, fine reductive notes, wet leather, aged wood nuances, fruit liqueur notes. Palate: spicy, long, correct.

MARQUÉS DE CHIVÉ 2008 TR
100% tempranillo.

83

CEREMONIA 2007 TR
60% tempranillo, 30% cabernet sauvignon, 10% bobal.

88 Colour: cherry, garnet rim. Nose: spicy, creamy oak, toasty, ripe fruit. Palate: powerful, flavourful, toasty, round tannins.

HOYA DE CADENAS TEMPRANILLO 2007 TR
100% tempranillo.

82

GENERACIÓN 1 2006 T
70% bobal, 15% cabernet sauvignon, 15% syrah.

90 Colour: cherry, garnet rim. Nose: ripe fruit, fruit liqueur notes, balsamic herbs, old leather, tobacco, spicy. Palate: powerful, flavourful, long, spicy.

BODEGAS Y VIÑEDOS DE UTIEL

Finca El Renegado, s/n
46315 Caudete de las Fuentes (Valencia)
☎: +34 962 174 029 - Fax: +34 962 171 432
gestion@bodegasdeutiel.com
www.nodus.es

ACTUM COLECCIÓN MACABEO CHARDONNAY 2011 B
macabeo, chardonnay.

87 Colour: bright straw. Nose: white flowers, fragrant herbs, medium intensity, fresh fruit. Palate: light-bodied, fresh, fruity, easy to drink.

NODUS CHARDONNAY 2011 B
chardonnay.

86 Colour: bright straw. Nose: fresh, fresh fruit, white flowers, expressive, sweet spices. Palate: flavourful, fruity, good acidity.

CAPELLANA 2011 B
macabeo.

84

NODUS BOBAL 2010 T
100% bobal.

83

ACTUM COLECCIÓN SYRAH TEMPRANILLO 2010 T
syrah, tempranillo.

82

CAPELLANA 2010 T
tempranillo.

81

NODUS TINTO DE AUTOR 2009 TC
merlot, cabernet sauvignon, syrah, bobal.

89 Colour: cherry, garnet rim. Nose: ripe fruit, sweet spices, dark chocolate. Palate: flavourful, fine bitter notes, good acidity.

CAPELLANA TINTO DE AUTOR 2009 TC
cabernet sauvignon, tempranillo.

89 Colour: cherry, garnet rim. Nose: ripe fruit, spicy, toasty. Palate: flavourful, fine bitter notes, good acidity.

ACTUM VARIETAL 2009 T
merlot, cabernet sauvignon.

87 Colour: light cherry. Nose: ripe fruit, spicy, toasty. Palate: flavourful, spicy.

NODUS RESERVA DE FAMILIA 2008 T
tempranillo, cabernet sauvignon, syrah.

88 Colour: cherry, garnet rim. Nose: ripe fruit, spicy, creamy oak, toasty. Palate: powerful, flavourful, toasty, round tannins.

CERROGALLINA

Travesía Industria, 5
46352 Campo Arcis (Valencia)
☎: +34 676 897 251 - Fax: +34 962 338 135
info@cerrogallina.com
www.cerrogallina.com

CERROGALLINA 2009 T
100% bobal.

93 Colour: cherry, garnet rim. Nose: mineral, red berry notes, ripe fruit, cocoa bean, sweet spices, creamy oak. Palate: powerful, flavourful, complex, balanced.

CHOZAS CARRASCAL

Vereda San Antonio Pol. Ind. Catastral, 16 Parcelas 136-138
46340 San Antonio de Requena (Valencia)
☎: +34 963 410 395 - Fax: +34 963 168 067
chozas@chozascarrascal.es
www.chozascarrascal.es

LAS DOSCES 2011 B
80% macabeo, 20% sauvignon blanc.

90 Colour: bright straw. Nose: fresh, fresh fruit, white flowers, expressive. Palate: flavourful, fruity, good acidity, balanced.

LAS DOSCES 2011 T
bobal, tempranillo, syrah.

90 Colour: cherry, purple rim. Nose: expressive, fresh fruit, red berry notes, floral, creamy oak, sweet spices. Palate: flavourful, fruity, good acidity, round tannins.

LAS OCHO 2008 T
bobal, monastrell, garnacha, tempranillo, cabernet franc, syrah, merlot.

92 Colour: cherry, garnet rim. Nose: ripe fruit, spicy, creamy oak, toasty, earthy notes. Palate: powerful, flavourful, toasty, round tannins.

EL CF DE CHOZAS CARRASCAL 2010 T
cabernet franc.

94 Colour: cherry, garnet rim. Nose: mineral, earthy notes, balsamic herbs, toasty. Palate: flavourful, complex, fine tannins. Personality.

JUANPEDRÓS 2009 T

90 Colour: deep cherry. Nose: candied fruit, spicy, toasty. Palate: ripe fruit, spicy, fine bitter notes, round tannins.

DOMINIO DE LA VEGA

Ctra. Madrid - Valencia, Km. 270,6
46390 San Antonio. (Valencia)
☎: +34 962 320 570 - Fax: +34 962 320 330
info@dominiodelavega.com
www.dominiodelavega.com

SAUVIGNON BLANC DOMINIO DE LA VEGA 2011 BFB
100% sauvignon blanc.

88 Colour: bright yellow. Nose: powerfull, creamy oak, fragrant herbs, white flowers, citrus fruit. Palate: rich, flavourful, fresh, good acidity.

DOMINIO DE LA VEGA ICE WINE 2011 B
sauvignon blanc, chardonnay, macabeo.

88 Colour: golden. Nose: powerfull, floral, honeyed notes, candied fruit, fragrant herbs, citrus fruit. Palate: flavourful, sweet, fresh, fruity, good acidity, long.

DOMINIO DE LA VEGA 2010 T ROBLE
cabernet sauvignon, syrah, bobal.

84

DOMINIO DE LA VEGA BOBAL 2010 T
100% bobal.

84

DOMINIO DE LA VEGA 2008 TC
bobal, cabernet sauvignon, syrah.

87 Colour: deep cherry. Nose: ripe fruit, toasty, dark chocolate. Palate: flavourful, powerful, good acidity, fine bitter notes.

DOMINIO DE LA VEGA 2005 TR
bobal, cabernet sauvignon, syrah.

85 Colour: pale ruby, brick rim edge. Nose: toasty, dark chocolate, candied fruit, fine reductive notes. Palate: spicy, fine bitter notes.

ARTE MAYOR III 2005/2006/2007 T
bobal.

91 Colour: cherry, garnet rim. Nose: spicy, creamy oak, candied fruit. Palate: powerful, flavourful, toasty, round tannins.

EMILIO CLEMENTE

Camino de San Blas, s/n
46340 Requena (Valencia)
☎: +34 963 173 584 - Fax: +34 963 173 726
info@eclemente.es
www.eclemente.es

FLORANTE 2010 B
25% tardana, 75% macabeo.

88 Colour: bright straw. Nose: white flowers, citrus fruit, fresh fruit, spicy. Palate: powerful, flavourful, elegant, balanced.

FLORANTE 2010 BFB
54% chardonnay, 20% sauvignon blanc, 20% macabeo, 6% tardana.

88 Colour: bright yellow. Nose: powerfull, ripe fruit, sweet spices, creamy oak. Palate: rich, smoky afterpalate:, flavourful, fresh, good acidity.

PEÑAS NEGRAS MADURADO 2010 T
50% merlot, 50% cabernet sauvignon.

83

PEÑAS NEGRAS 2010 T
66% bobal, 34% merlot.

78

EXCELENCIA 2009 T
52% cabernet sauvignon, 48% merlot.

88 Colour: cherry, garnet rim. Nose: ripe fruit, spicy, creamy oak, toasty. Palate: powerful, flavourful, toasty, round tannins.

EMILIO CLEMENTE 2005 TC
50% tempranillo, 25% merlot, 15% cabernet sauvignon, 10% bobal.

87 Colour: cherry, garnet rim. Nose: spicy, creamy oak, toasty, ripe fruit. Palate: powerful, flavourful, toasty, round tannins.

FINCA CASA LO ALTO

Ctra. Caudete - Los Isidros
46310 Venta del Moro (Valencia)
☎: +34 962 139 381
info@casa-lo-alto.es
www.casa-lo-alto.es

FINCA CASA LO ALTO 2010 TC
tempranillo, garnacha, cabernet sauvignon, syrah.

78

FINCA CASA LO ALTO 2009 TR
syrah, garnacha, cabernet sauvignon.

86 Colour: cherry, garnet rim. Nose: ripe fruit, spicy, toasty. Palate: powerful, flavourful, toasty, round tannins.

FINCA CASA LO ALTO 2008 TR
syrah, garnacha, cabernet sauvignon.

87 Colour: cherry, garnet rim. Nose: medium intensity, ripe fruit, sweet spices. Palate: flavourful, powerful, spicy.

FINCA SAN BLAS

Partida de San Blas, s/n
46340 Requena (Valencia)
☎: +34 963 375 617 - Fax: +34 963 370 707
info@fincasanblas.com
www.fincasanblas.com

FINCA SAN BLAS 2010 B
merseguera, chenin blanc, chardonnay.

85 Colour: bright straw. Nose: dried herbs, faded flowers, spicy, aged wood nuances. Palate: powerful, flavourful, slightly evolved.

LOMALTA M&S 2011 T
merlot, syrah.

87 Colour: deep cherry. Nose: powerfull, ripe fruit, red berry notes, spicy. Palate: flavourful, fine bitter notes, spicy.

FINCA SAN BLAS 2005 T
merlot, tempranillo.

86 Colour: cherry, garnet rim. Nose: ripe fruit, spicy, creamy oak, toasty, complex. Palate: powerful, flavourful, toasty, round tannins.

LATORRE AGROVINÍCOLA

Ctra. Requena, 2
46310 Venta del Moro (Valencia)
☎: +34 962 185 028 - Fax: +34 962 185 422
vinos@latorreagrovinicola.com
www.latorreagrovinicola.com

PARREÑO 2011 B
viura, verdejo.

78

PARREÑO 2011 RD
bobal.

84

PARREÑO 2011 T
tempranillo, cabernet sauvignon.

84

DUQUE DE ARCAS 2007 TC
tempranillo, bobal, cabernet sauvignon.

80

MAS DE BAZÁN

Ctra. Villar de Olmos, Km. 2
46340 Requena (Valencia)
☎: +34 986 555 562
export@agrodebazan.es
www.agrodebazansa.es

MAS DE BAZAN 2011 RD
100% bobal.

85 Colour: rose, purple rim. Nose: powerfull, ripe fruit, red berry notes, floral, lactic notes. Palate: , powerful, fruity, fresh.

PRIMUM BOBAL

Constitución, 50 pta. 6
46340 Requena (Valencia)
☎: +34 625 464 377
vinos@primumbobal.com
www.primumbobal.com

PRIMUM BOBAL 2011 T
100% bobal.

90 Colour: cherry, purple rim. Nose: expressive, fresh fruit, red berry notes, floral. Palate: flavourful, fruity, good acidity, round tannins.

TORRE ORIA

Ctra. Pontón - Utiel, Km. 3
46390 Derramador - Requena (Valencia)
☎: +34 962 320 289 - Fax: +34 962 320 311
info.torreoria@torreoria.es
www.torreoria.com

MARQUÉS DE REQUENA 2007 TC
tempranillo.

88 Colour: bright cherry. Nose: ripe fruit, sweet spices, nose:tic coffee. Palate: flavourful, fruity, toasty, round tannins.

MARQUÉS DE REQUENA 2006 TR
tempranillo.

90 Colour: cherry, garnet rim. Nose: ripe fruit, spicy, creamy oak, toasty. Palate: powerful, flavourful, toasty, round tannins.

UNIÓN VINÍCOLA DEL ESTE

Pl. Ind. El Romeral- Construcción, 74
46340 Requena (Valencia)
☎: +34 962 323 343 - Fax: +34 962 349 413
cava@uveste.es
www.uveste.es

BESO DE RECHENNA 2009 T

90 Colour: cherry, garnet rim. Nose: ripe fruit, spicy, creamy oak, toasty, wild herbs. Palate: powerful, flavourful, toasty, round tannins.

VALSAN 1831

Ctra. Cheste - Godelleta, Km. 1
46370 Chiva (Valencia)
☎: +34 962 510 861 - Fax: +34 962 511 361
cherubino@cherubino.es
www.cherubino.es

BOBAL DE SANJUAN 2011 RD
bobal.

87 Colour: brilliant rose. Nose: fresh fruit, red berry notes, floral. Palate: flavourful, easy to drink, ripe fruit.

MARQUÉS DE CARO 2011 RD
bobal.

85 Colour: rose, purple rim. Nose: ripe fruit, wild herbs, medium intensity. Palate: light-bodied, fresh, fruity.

BOBAL DE SANJUAN 2011 T
bobal.

87 Colour: deep cherry. Nose: powerfull, characterful, ripe fruit. Palate: flavourful, ripe fruit, spicy.

VERA DE ESTENAS

Junto N-III, km. 266 - Paraje La Cabeuzela
46300 Utiel (Valencia)
☎: +34 962 171 141 - Fax: +34 962 174 352
estenas@estenas.es
www.estenas.es

VIÑA LIDÓN 2011 BFB
100% chardonnay.

91 Colour: bright yellow. Nose: powerfull, ripe fruit, sweet spices, creamy oak, fragrant herbs. Palate: rich, flavourful, fresh, good acidity.

VERA DE ESTENAS 2011 B
95% macabeo, 5% chardonnay.

89 Colour: bright straw. Nose: white flowers, ripe fruit, citrus fruit. Palate: flavourful, fruity, fresh.

VERA DE ESTENAS BOBAL 2011 RD
100% bobal.

89 Colour: rose, purple rim. Nose: powerfull, red berry notes, expressive, balsamic herbs. Palate: , fruity, fresh, flavourful, balanced.

VERA DE ESTENAS 2011 T BARRICA
60% bobal, 25% cabernet sauvignon, 15% tempranillo, 15% merlot.

89 Colour: cherry, purple rim. Nose: red berry notes, balsamic herbs, sweet spices. Palate: powerful, flavourful, spicy, long.

MARTÍNEZ BERMELL MERLOT 2010 T FERMENTADO EN BARRICA
100 % merlot.

86 Colour: cherry, garnet rim. Nose: ripe fruit, fragrant herbs, spicy. Palate: powerful, flavourful, long.

VERA DE ESTENAS 2009 TC
60% bobal, 25% cabernet sauvignon, 15% tempranillo, 15% merlot.

90 Colour: cherry, garnet rim. Nose: ripe fruit, toasty, spicy. Palate: powerful, flavourful, toasty, round tannins.

CASA DON ÁNGEL BOBAL 2007 T
100% bobal.

93 Colour: cherry, garnet rim. Nose: ripe fruit, fragrant herbs, sweet spices, toasty, earthy notes. Palate: long, balanced, powerful, flavourful, spicy.

VERA DE ESTENAS 2007 TR
bobal, cabernet sauvignon, tempranillo, merlot.

87 Colour: cherry, garnet rim. Nose: ripe fruit, scrubland, spicy. Palate: powerful, flavourful, long, spicy.

VINOS PASIEGO

Avda. Virgen de Tejeda, 28
46320 Sinarcas (Valencia)
☎: +34 962 306 175 - Fax: +34 962 306 175
bodega@vinospasiego.com
www.vinospasiego.com

PASIEGO LAS SUERTES 2010 B
60% chardonnay, 40% sauvignon blanc.

90 Colour: bright straw. Nose: fresh, fresh fruit, white flowers, expressive, creamy oak, sweet spices. Palate: flavourful, fruity, good acidity, balanced.

PASIEGO LA BLASCA 2008 TC
39% cabernet sauvignon, 27% tempranillo, 31% merlot, 3% bobal.

88 Colour: cherry, garnet rim. Nose: ripe fruit, spicy, creamy oak, fine reductive notes, earthy notes. Palate: powerful, flavourful, toasty.

PASIEGO DE AUTOR 2005 TC
47% cabernet sauvignon, 33% bobal, 20% tempranillo.

91 Colour: cherry, garnet rim. Nose: spicy, creamy oak, toasty, dark chocolate, ripe fruit. Palate: powerful, flavourful, toasty, round tannins.

VIÑA CASTARO

Ctra. N-III, Km. 271
46390 San Antonio Requena (Valencia)
☎: +34 630 973 065 - Fax: +34 962 320 533
info@castaro.com
www.castaro.com

VIÑA CASTARO 2005 TR
cabernet sauvignon, tempranillo.

87 Colour: cherry, garnet rim. Nose: ripe fruit, spicy, creamy oak, toasty. Palate: powerful, flavourful, toasty.

VIÑA CASTARO SELECCIÓN 2005 TR
cabernet sauvignon.

87 Colour: deep cherry, orangey edge. Nose: ripe fruit, scrubland, spicy, creamy oak. Palate: balanced, flavourful, powerful.

VIÑEDOS LA MADROÑERA

Traginers, 9
46014 Valencia (Valencia)
☎: +34 963 992 400 - Fax: +34 963 992 451
pguzman@grupoguzman.com
www.constantia.es

DULCE DE CONSTANTIA 2009 T
merlot, cabernet sauvignon.

90 Colour: cherry, garnet rim. Nose: ripe fruit, fruit liqueur notes, toasty, nose:tic coffee, acetaldehyde. Palate: powerful, flavourful, spirituous, toasty.

CONSTANTIA 2007 TC
bobal, tempranillo, merlot, cabernet sauvignon.

85 Colour: cherry, garnet rim. Nose: ripe fruit, fruit preserve, mineral, toasty. Palate: powerful, flavourful, correct.

VIÑEDOS Y BODEGAS VEGALFARO

Ctra. Pontón - Utiel, Km. 3
46430 El Derramador - Requena (Valencia)
☎: +34 962 320 680 - Fax: +34 962 321 126
info@vegalfaro.com
www.vegalfaro.com

VEGALFARO CHARDONNAY 2011 B
75% chardonnay, 25% sauvignon blanc.

89 Colour: bright straw. Nose: fresh, fresh fruit, white flowers, expressive. Palate: flavourful, fruity, balanced, easy to drink.

VEGALFARO 2011 RD
50% bobal, 50% merlot.

86 Colour: coppery red. Nose: expressive, ripe fruit, balsamic herbs. Palate: flavourful, good acidity.

REBEL.LIA 2011 T
tempranillo, garnacha tintorera, bobal.

87 Colour: cherry, purple rim. Nose: medium intensity, ripe fruit, sweet spices. Palate: powerful, flavourful, long.

DO VALDEORRAS

Vilamartí
OURENSE
Consejo Regulador
DO Boundary

LOCATION:

The DO Valdeorras is situated in the northeast of the province of Orense. It comprises the municipal areas of Larouco, Petín, O Bolo, A Rua, Vilamartín, O Barco, Rubiá and Carballeda de Valdeorras.

CLIMATE:

Continental, with Atlantic influences. The average annual temperature is 11°C and the average annual rainfall ranges between 850 mm and 1,000 mm.

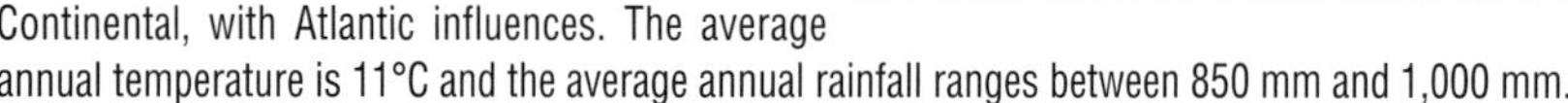

SOIL:

Quite varied. There are three types: the first type which is settled on shallow slate with many stones and a medium texture; the second type on deeper granite with a lot of sand and finally the type that lies on sediments and terraces, where there are usually a lot of pebbles.

GRAPE VARIETIES:

WHITE: *Godello, Dona Blanca, Palomino, Loureira, Treixadura, Dona Branca, Albariño, Torrontes* and *Lado.*
RED: *Mencía, Merenzao, Grao Negro*, *Garnacha, Tempranillo (Araúxa), Brancellao, Sousón, Caíño Tinto, Espadeiro, Ferrón, Gran Negro, Garnacha Tintureira* and *Mouratón.*

FIGURES:

Vineyard surface: 1,158 – **Wine-Growers:** 1,502 – **Wineries:** 46 – **2011 Harvest rating:** N/A – **Production:** 5,115,750 litres – **Market percentages:** 95% domestic. 5% export

VINTAGE RATING PEÑÍNGUIDE

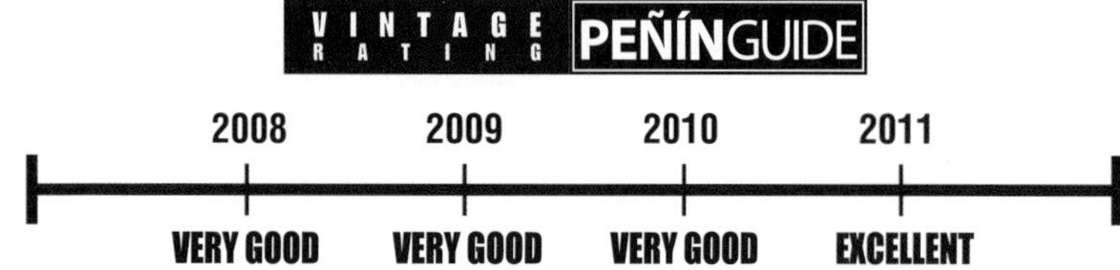

CONSEJO REGULADOR
Ctra. Nacional 120, km. 463 - 32340 Vilamartín de Valdeorras (Ourense) - ☎: +34 988 300 295 - Fax: +34 988 336 887
@ consello@dovaldeorras.com - www.dovaldeorras.com

A TAPADA S.A.T.

Finca A Tapada
32310 Rubiá (Ourense)
☎: +34 988 324 197 - Fax: +34 988 324 197

GUITIÁN GODELLO SOBRE LÍAS 2011 B
godello.

93 Colour: bright straw. Nose: fresh, fresh fruit, white flowers, fine lees, mineral, burnt matches. Palate: flavourful, fruity, good acidity, balanced.

GUITIÁN GODELLO 2011 B

91 Colour: bright straw. Nose: fruit expression, fragrant herbs, ripe fruit. Palate: flavourful, fruity, fresh, fine bitter notes.

GUITIÁN GODELLO 2010 BFB
godello.

94 Colour: bright yellow. Nose: ripe fruit, sweet spices, cocoa bean, creamy oak. Palate: spicy, ripe fruit, long, mineral.

ADEGA A COROA

A Coroa, s/n
32350 A Rúa (Ourense)
☎: +34 988 310 648 - Fax: +34 988 311 439
acoroa@acoroa.com
www.acoroa.com

A COROA 2011 B
100% godello.

89 Colour: bright straw. Nose: fresh, fresh fruit, white flowers, fragrant herbs. Palate: flavourful, fruity, good acidity, balanced.

A COROA "LÍAS" 2010 B
100% godello.

90 Colour: bright straw. Nose: lactic notes, ripe fruit, citrus fruit, scrubland, sweet spices. Palate: flavourful, sweetness, concentrated.

ADEGA ALAN

San Roque, 36
32350 A Rúa (Ourense)
☎: +34 988 311 457 - Fax: +34 988 311 457
alandeval@alandeval.com
www.alandeval.com

ALAN DE VAL GODELLO 2011 B
godello.

87 Colour: bright straw. Nose: fresh, white flowers, expressive, grassy. Palate: flavourful, fruity, easy to drink.

ALAN DE VAL MENCÍA 2011 T
mencía.

87 Colour: cherry, purple rim. Nose: fresh fruit, red berry notes, floral, balsamic herbs. Palate: flavourful, fruity, good acidity.

ALAN DE VAL PEDRAZAIS MENCÍA 2010 T BARRICA
mencía.

89 Colour: cherry, garnet rim. Nose: ripe fruit, spicy, toasty, dry stone. Palate: powerful, flavourful, toasty.

ALAN DE VAL ESCADA GARNACHA 2009 T
garnacha tintorera.

86 Colour: cherry, garnet rim. Nose: ripe fruit, spicy, complex, earthy notes, balsamic herbs. Palate: powerful, flavourful, balanced.

ADEGA DA PINGUELA

Camino del Disco, 17 Petín
32350 A Rúa (Ourense)
☎: +34 654 704 753
adega@adegadapinguela.com
www.adegadapinguela.com

MEMORIA DE VENTURA GODELLO 2011 B
100% godello.

88 Colour: bright straw. Nose: ripe fruit, citrus fruit, grassy. Palate: flavourful, fruity, fresh.

MEMORIA DE VENTURA MENCÍA 2011 T
100% mencía.

94 Colour: cherry, purple rim. Nose: expressive, fresh fruit, red berry notes, floral, mineral, balsamic herbs. Palate: flavourful, fruity, good acidity, round tannins.

MEMORIA DE VENTURA GARNACHA 2011 T
100% garnacha tintorera.

91 Colour: very deep cherry. Nose: powerfull, ripe fruit, raspberry, spicy, cocoa bean. Palate: powerful, concentrated, complex.

ADEGA MELILLAS E FILLOS

A Coroa, 22
32350 A Rúa (Ourense)
☎: +34 988 310 510
info@adegamelillas.com
www.adegamelillas.com

LAGAR DO CIGUR 2011 B
godello.

87 Colour: bright yellow. Nose: powerfull, ripe fruit, mineral, burnt matches. Palate: flavourful, sweetness.

LAGAR DO CIGUR 2011 T
mencía, alicante.

90 Colour: cherry, purple rim. Nose: ripe fruit, red berry notes, scrubland. Palate: flavourful, powerful, fine bitter notes, good acidity.

LAGAR DO CIGUR 2008 T
mencía, alicante, tempranillo, merenzao.

87 Colour: bright cherry. Nose: sweet spices, creamy oak, fruit preserve. Palate: flavourful, toasty, round tannins, sweetness.

ADEGA O CASAL

Malladín, s/n
32310 Rubiá (Ourense)
☎: +34 689 675 800
casalnovo@casalnovo.es
www.casalnovo.es

CASAL NOVO GODELLO 2011 B
100% godello.

89 Colour: bright straw. Nose: white flowers, ripe fruit, citrus fruit, grassy. Palate: flavourful, powerful, fruity, good acidity.

CASAL NOVO MENCÍA 2011 T
100% mencía.

90 Colour: cherry, purple rim. Nose: fresh fruit, red berry notes, floral, ripe fruit. Palate: flavourful, fruity, good acidity, round tannins.

ADEGA O CEPADO

O Patal, 11
32310 Rubia de Valdeorras (Ourense)
☎: +34 666 186 128
info@cepado.com
www.cepado.com

CEPADO GODELLO 2011 B
godello.

90 Colour: bright straw. Nose: fresh, fresh fruit, white flowers, dried herbs. Palate: flavourful, fruity, good acidity, balanced.

CEPADO MENCÍA 2011 T
100% mencía.

89 Colour: cherry, purple rim. Nose: red berry notes, mineral, damp earth, balsamic herbs. Palate: fresh, fruity, flavourful.

ADEGA QUINTA DA PEZA

Ctra. Nacional 120, km.467
32350 A Rua de Valdeorras (Ourense)
☎: +34 988 311 537 - Fax: +34 981 232 642
quintadapeza@gmail.com
www.quintadapeza.es

QUINTA DA PEZA GODELLO 2011 B
godello.

90 Colour: bright yellow. Nose: ripe fruit, citrus fruit, white flowers, balsamic herbs, fragrant herbs. Palate: flavourful, rich, fruity.

QUINTA DA PEZA ORO MENCÍA BARRICA 2010 TC
mencía.

88 Colour: bright cherry. Nose: sweet spices, creamy oak, fruit expression. Palate: flavourful, fruity, toasty, round tannins.

ADEGAS O RIBOUZO S.A.T.

Valencia do Sil
32349 Valdeorras (Ourense)
☎: +34 626 323 945
ribouzo@yahoo.es
www.adegasribouzo.com

GODELLO RIBOUZO 2011 B
godello.

88 Colour: bright yellow. Nose: ripe fruit, citrus fruit, scrubland. Palate: correct, powerful, flavourful.

MISTURA RIBOUZO 2011 T
negreda, garnacha, mencía.

87 Colour: cherry, purple rim. Nose: expressive, fresh fruit, red berry notes, floral. Palate: flavourful, fruity, good acidity, balanced.

MENCÍA RIBOUZO 2011 T
100% mencía.

86 Colour: cherry, purple rim. Nose: red berry notes, balsamic herbs, floral, medium intensity. Palate: fresh, fruity, powerful, flavourful.

AVELINA S.A.T.

Estrada e Arcos, 6 Córgomo
32316 Vilamartín de Valdeorras (Ourense)
☎: +34 687 819 099
adegavelinasat@yahoo.com
www.adegaavelina.es

CASAL DE FURCOS ROCIO GODELLO 2011 B
100% godello.

86 Colour: bright straw. Nose: fresh fruit, white flowers, grassy. Palate: flavourful, fruity, good acidity.

CASAL DE FURCOS ROCIO MENCÍA 2011 T
100% mencía.

84

BODEGA COOP. SANTA MARÍA DE LOS REMEDIOS

Langullo, 11
32358 Larouco (Ourense)
☎: +34 988 348 043 - Fax: +34 988 348 043
bodegaslarouco@terra.es
www.bodegas-larouco.com

ARUME 2011 B
100% godello.

86 Colour: bright straw. Nose: fresh, fresh fruit, white flowers, dried herbs. Palate: flavourful, fruity, good acidity.

MEDULIO 2011 T
100% mencía.

88 Colour: cherry, purple rim. Nose: red berry notes, fragrant herbs, floral, balsamic herbs. Palate: flavourful, fruity, good acidity.

BODEGA COOPERATIVA JESÚS NAZARENO

Florencio Delgado Gurriarán, 62
32300 O Barco de Valdeorras (Ourense)
☎: +34 988 320 262 - Fax: +34 988 320 242
coopbarco@infonegocio.com
www.vinosbarco.com

VIÑA ABAD GODELLO 2011 B
100% godello.

88 Colour: bright straw. Nose: ripe fruit, fruit expression, citrus fruit, white flowers. Palate: flavourful, good acidity, balanced.

VALDOURO 2009 T
mencía, garnacha.

86 Colour: cherry, garnet rim. Nose: ripe fruit, spicy, creamy oak, balsamic herbs, fine reductive notes. Palate: powerful, flavourful, toasty.

BODEGA ELADIO SANTALLA PARADELO

Conde Fenosa, 36
32300 O Barco de Valdeorras (Ourense)
☎: +34 686 240 374
eladio@bodegaseladiosantalla.com
www.bodegaseladiosantalla.com

HACIENDA UCEDIÑOS 2011 B
godello.

92 Colour: bright straw. Nose: fresh, white flowers, grassy, ripe fruit. Palate: flavourful, fruity, good acidity, balanced.

HACIENDA UCEDIÑOS 2010 T
mencía.

89 Colour: deep cherry. Nose: ripe fruit, red berry notes, creamy oak, spicy. Palate: spicy, ripe fruit, fine bitter notes.

BODEGA ROANDI

O Lagar s/n Entoma
32313 O Barco (Ourense)
☎: +34 646 127 384 - Fax: +34 988 347 107
bodega@roandi.es
www.bodegaroandi.com

ALENTO SOBRE LÍAS 2011 B
100% godello.

89 Colour: bright straw. Nose: white flowers, ripe fruit, fragrant herbs, mineral. Palate: flavourful, rich, fruity, complex.

DONA DELFINA 2011 B
100% godello.

88 Colour: bright straw. Nose: ripe fruit, citrus fruit, grassy, balsamic herbs. Palate: flavourful, powerful, fine bitter notes, good acidity.

FLAVIA 2010 T
85% mencía, 15% sousón, tempranillo, albarello.

89 Colour: cherry, purple rim. Nose: characterful, ripe fruit, fruit expression, mineral. Palate: powerful, flavourful, spicy, ripe fruit.

BANCALES MORAL BARRICA 2009 T
85% mencía, 15% sousón, albarello, tempranillo.

87 Colour: bright cherry, garnet rim. Nose: ripe fruit, sweet spices, expressive, mineral. Palate: flavourful, fruity, toasty.

BODEGAS ABANICO

Pol. Ind Ca l'Avellanet - Susany, 6
08553 Seva (Barcelona)
☎: +34 938 125 676 - Fax: +34 938 123 213
info@exportiberia.com
www.bodegasabanico.com

TEMPESTAD 2011 B
100% godello.

91 Colour: bright yellow. Nose: citrus fruit, wild herbs, balsamic herbs, ripe fruit, mineral, balanced. Palate: powerful, flavourful, long, good acidity, balanced.

BOCA DO MONTE 2011 B
70% palomino, 30% godello.

89 Colour: bright straw. Nose: fresh, fresh fruit, white flowers, dried herbs. Palate: flavourful, fruity, light-bodied, easy to drink.

BODEGAS AVANTHIA

Bartolomé Esteban Murillo, 11
29700 Vélez- Málaga (Málaga)
☎: +34 952 504 706 - Fax: +34 951 284 796
office@jorge-ordonez.es
www.jorge-ordonez.es

AVANTHIA GODELLO 2011 B
100% godello.

92 Colour: bright straw. Nose: ripe fruit, floral, dried herbs. Palate: flavourful, fruity, good acidity, balanced.

AVANTHIA ROSE 2011 RD
100% mencía.

89 Colour: rose, purple rim. Nose: ripe fruit, red berry notes, floral, lactic notes, expressive. Palate: , powerful, fruity, fresh, easy to drink, sweetness.

AVANTHIA MENCÍA 2009 T
100% mencía.

91 Colour: bright cherry, garnet rim. Nose: ripe fruit, sweet spices, balsamic herbs, mineral, nose:tic coffee. Palate: flavourful, fruity, toasty, round tannins.

BODEGAS GODEVAL

Avda. de Galicia, 20
32300 El Barco de Valdeorras (Ourense)
☎: +34 988 108 282 - Fax: +34 988 325 309
godeval@godeval.com
www.godeval.com

GODEVAL CEPAS VELLAS 2011 B

92 Colour: bright straw. Nose: fresh, white flowers, expressive, ripe fruit, scrubland. Palate: flavourful, fruity, good acidity, balanced.

GODEVAL 2011 B

88 Colour: bright straw. Nose: expressive, varietal, ripe fruit, citrus fruit. Palate: flavourful, fruity, fresh.

BODEGAS RUCHEL

Ctra. de Cernego, s/n
32340 Vilamartín de Valdeorras (Ourense)
☎: +34 986 253 345 - Fax: +34 986 253 345
info@vinosruchel.com
www.vinosruchel.com

RUCHEL GODELLO 2011 B
100% godello.

88 Colour: bright straw. Nose: fresh, fresh fruit, white flowers, expressive. Palate: flavourful, fruity, good acidity, balanced.

GRAN RUCHEL GODELLO 2006 B
100% godello.

84

RUCHEL MENCÍA 2011 T
mencía.

90 Colour: cherry, purple rim. Nose: expressive, fresh fruit, red berry notes, floral, mineral. Palate: flavourful, fruity, good acidity, balanced.

DON AMADEO MENCÍA 2008 T
85% mencía, 15% tempranillo.

84

BODEGAS SAMPAYOLO

Ctra. de Barxela, s/n
32358 Petín de Valdeorras (Ourense)
☎: +34 679 157 977
info@sampayolo.com
www.sampayolo.com

SAMPAYOLO GODELLO 2011 B
100% godello.

89 Colour: bright straw. Nose: fresh, fresh fruit, white flowers, characterful. Palate: flavourful, fruity, good acidity, balanced.

SAMPAYOLO GODELLO 2010 B BARRICA
100% godello.

90 Colour: bright yellow. Nose: powerfull, ripe fruit, sweet spices, creamy oak, fragrant herbs. Palate: rich, flavourful, fresh, good acidity.

SAMPAYOLO MENCÍA 2011 T
100% mencía.

88 Colour: cherry, purple rim. Nose: red berry notes, floral, fragrant herbs, sweet spices. Palate: correct, powerful, flavourful.

GARNACHA VELLA DA CHAIRA DO RAMIRIÑO 2009 T
100% garnacha.

88 Colour: bright cherry. Nose: ripe fruit, sweet spices, creamy oak, expressive, roasted coffee. Palate: flavourful, fruity, toasty, round tannins.

BODEGAS VALDESIL

Ctra. a San Vicente OU 807, km. 3
32348 Vilamartín de Valdeorras (Ourense)
☎: +34 988 337 900 - Fax: +34 988 337 901
valdesil@valdesil.com
www.valdesil.com

VALDESIL GODELLO SOBRE LÍAS 2011 B
godello.

93 Colour: bright yellow. Nose: white flowers, balsamic herbs, fragrant herbs, mineral, expressive. Palate: powerful, flavourful, elegant.

MONTENOVO GODELLO 2011 B
godello.

88 Colour: bright straw. Nose: fresh, white flowers, characterful, ripe fruit, citrus fruit. Palate: flavourful, good acidity, balanced.

PEDROUZOS MAGNUM 2010 B
godello.

96 Colour: bright yellow. Nose: balsamic herbs, scrubland, ripe fruit, citrus fruit, fruit expression, mineral. Palate: fine bitter notes, good acidity, fruity, long, mineral.

PEZAS DA PORTELA 2010 BFB
godello.

93 Colour: bright straw. Nose: powerfull, characterful, varietal, ripe fruit, fruit expression. Palate: flavourful, good acidity, fine bitter notes, elegant.

VALDERROA 2011 T
mencía.

92 Colour: cherry, purple rim. Nose: floral, red berry notes, expressive, scrubland. Palate: flavourful, fruity, good acidity, round tannins.

VALDERROA CARBALLO 2009 T
mencía.

92 Colour: bright cherry. Nose: medium intensity, balsamic herbs, scrubland, ripe fruit, earthy notes. Palate: flavourful, fine bitter notes, good acidity, balsamic.

CARBALLAL

Ctra. de Carballal, km 2,2
32356 Petín de Valdeorras (Ourense)
☎: +34 988 311 281 - Fax: +34 988 311 281
bodegascarballal@hotmail.com

EREBO GODELLO 2011 B
godello.

91 Colour: bright yellow. Nose: fresh fruit, white flowers, wild herbs. Palate: rich, flavourful, fruity, balanced.

EREBO MENCÍA 2011 T
mencía.

88 Colour: cherry, purple rim. Nose: red berry notes, ripe fruit, mineral, medium intensity. Palate: powerful, flavourful, fruity.

COMPAÑÍA DE VINOS TELMO RODRÍGUEZ

El Monte
01308 Lanciego (Álava)
☎: +34 945 628 315 - Fax: +34 945 628 314
contact@telmorodriguez.com
www.telmorodriguez.com

GABA DO XIL GODELLO 2011 B
godello.

92 Colour: bright straw. Nose: expressive, fresh, ripe fruit, white flowers. Palate: flavourful, fruity, ripe fruit, long.

AS CABORCAS 2010 T
mencía, merenzao, garnacha, godello.

95 Colour: bright cherry. Nose: fruit expression, red berry notes, scrubland, balsamic herbs. Palate: flavourful, ripe fruit, spicy, long.

GABA DO XIL MENCÍA 2010 T
100% mencía.

90 Colour: bright cherry. Nose: red berry notes, scrubland, balsamic herbs. Palate: flavourful, fruity, fresh.

GUITIAN Y BLANCO (BODEGAS D'BERNA)

Córgomo
32340 Villamartín de Valdeorras (Ourense)
☎: +34 988 324 557 - Fax: +34 988 324 557
info@bodegasdberna.com
www.bodegasdberna.com

D'BERNA GODELLO 2011 B
100% godello.

91 Colour: bright straw. Nose: fresh fruit, white flowers, expressive, grassy. Palate: flavourful, fruity, good acidity, balanced.

D'BERNA MENCÍA 2011 T
100% mencía.

88 Colour: cherry, purple rim. Nose: red berry notes, scrubland, mineral, expressive. Palate: light-bodied, fresh, fruity, flavourful, balanced.

JOAQUÍN REBOLLEDO

San Roque, 11
32350 A Rúa (Ourense)
☎: +34 988 372 307 - Fax: +34 988 371 427
info@joaquinrebolledo.com
www.joaquinrebolledo.com

JOAQUÍN REBOLLEDO GODELLO 2011 B
godello.

92 Colour: bright straw. Nose: white flowers, citrus fruit, fresh fruit, dried herbs, mineral. Palate: powerful, flavourful, good acidity, balanced.

JOAQUÍN REBOLLEDO MENCÍA 2011 T
mencía.

94 Colour: cherry, purple rim. Nose: expressive, fresh fruit, red berry notes, floral, balsamic herbs, mineral. Palate: flavourful, fruity, good acidity, round tannins.

JOAQUÍN REBOLLEDO 2010 T BARRICA
mencía, tempranillo, otras.

93 Colour: cherry, garnet rim. Nose: red berry notes, dry stone, earthy notes, fragrant herbs, spicy, expressive. Palate: balanced, flavourful, fruity, complex.

LADERA SAGRADA

Penas Forcadas, 15 Of. 6
32300 Barco de Valdeorras (Ourense)
☎: +34 988 347 062 - Fax: +34 988 347 290
laderasagrada@gmail.com

CASTELO DO PAPA 2011 B
100% godello.

88 Colour: bright straw. Nose: fresh, fresh fruit, white flowers, expressive. Palate: flavourful, fruity, correct.

CASTELO DO PAPA MENCÍA 2010 T
100% mencía.

88 Colour: deep cherry. Nose: expressive, ripe fruit, scrubland, balsamic herbs. Palate: flavourful, balsamic, fine bitter notes.

MANUEL CORZO RODRÍGUEZ

Chandoiro, s/n
32372 O Bolo (Ourense)
☎: +34 629 893 649
manuelcorzorodriguez@hotmail.com

VIÑA CORZO GODELLO 2011 B
100% godello.

90 Colour: bright straw. Nose: fresh, fresh fruit, white flowers, expressive. Palate: flavourful, fruity, good acidity, balanced.

VIÑA CORZO MENCÍA 2011 T
100% mencía.

86 Colour: bright cherry. Nose: ripe fruit, sweet spices, expressive. Palate: flavourful, fruity, toasty, round tannins.

MARÍA TERESA NÚÑEZ VEGA

Barxela, s/n
32356 Petín (Ourense)
☎: +34 988 311 251 - Fax: +34 988 311 251
biocaarroyo@yahoo.es
www.bioca.es

BIOCA GODELLO 2011 B
godello.

88 Colour: bright yellow. Nose: fresh fruit, tropical fruit, balsamic herbs. Palate: rich, flavourful, fruity.

BIOCA MENCÍA 2011 T

88 Colour: cherry, purple rim. Nose: red berry notes, ripe fruit, sulphur notes, powerfull. Palate: flavourful, ripe fruit, spicy.

MENCÍAS DE DOS

Cuatro Calles, s/n
47491 La Seca (Valladolid)
☎: +34 983 103 223 - Fax: +34 983 816 561
info@sitiosdebodega.com
www.sitiosdebodega.com

OLLO DE GALO 2011 B
100% godello.

89 Colour: bright straw. Nose: citrus fruit, fresh fruit, floral, fragrant herbs. Palate: light-bodied, fresh, fruity, flavourful.

RAFAEL PALACIOS

Avda. de Somoza, 81
32350 A Rúa de Valdeorras (Ourense)
☎: +34 988 310 162 - Fax: +34 988 310 643
bodega@rafaelpalacios.com
www.rafaelpalacios.com

AS SORTES 2011 B
100% godello.

95 Colour: bright straw. Nose: powerfull, ripe fruit, fragrant herbs, grassy. Palate: rich, flavourful, fresh, good acidity.

LOURO DO BOLO 2011 B
88% godello, 12% treixadura.

93 Colour: bright straw. Nose: fresh, white flowers, varietal, ripe fruit. Palate: flavourful, fruity, good acidity, balanced.

SANTA MARTA BODEGAS

Córgomo, s/n
32348 Villamartín de Ourense (Ourense)
☎: +34 988 324 559 - Fax: +34 988 324 559
info@vinaredo.com
www.vinaredo.com

VIÑAREDO GODELLO 2011 B
100% godello.

92 Colour: bright straw. Nose: powerfull, varietal, ripe fruit, citrus fruit. Palate: flavourful, powerful, good acidity, fine bitter notes.

VIÑAREDO GODELLO BARRICA 2010 B
100% godello.

89 Colour: bright yellow. Nose: sweet spices, cocoa bean, ripe fruit, citrus fruit, creamy oak. Palate: spicy, ripe fruit, fine bitter notes, long.

VIÑAREDO MENCÍA 2011 T
100% mencía.

84

VIÑAREDO SOUSÓN 2009 T BARRICA
100% sausón.

90 Colour: cherry, purple rim. Nose: floral, rose petals, violet drops, sweet spices. Palate: flavourful, fruity, good acidity, round tannins.

VIÑAREDO MENCÍA BARRICA 2009 T
100% mencía.

82

VINIGALICIA

Ctra. Antigua Santiago, km. 3
27500 Chantada (Lugo)
☎: +34 982 454 005 - Fax: +34 982 454 094
vinigalicia@vinigalicia.es
www.vinigalicia.es

VERDES CASTROS 2011 B
godello.

88 Colour: bright straw. Nose: white flowers, citrus fruit, fruit expression, wild herbs. Palate: fresh, fruity, light-bodied, flavourful.

VERDES CASTROS 2011 T
100% mencía.

89 Colour: cherry, purple rim. Nose: expressive, red berry notes, floral, scrubland, spicy. Palate: flavourful, fruity, good acidity.

VIÑA SOMOZA BODEGAS Y VIÑEDOS

Avda. Somoza, s/n
32350 A Rúa (Ourense)
☎: +34 988 310 918 - Fax: +34 988 310 918
bodega@vinosomoza.com
www.vinosomoza.com

VIÑA SOMOZA GODELLO SOBRE LIAS 2011 B
100% godello.

91 Colour: bright straw. Nose: fresh, white flowers, expressive, citrus fruit, mineral, grassy. Palate: flavourful, fruity, good acidity, balanced.

VIÑA SOMOZA GODELLO SELECCIÓN 2010 B ROBLE
100% godello.

92 Colour: bright golden. Nose: ripe fruit, powerfull, toasty, aged wood nuances, expressive. Palate: flavourful, fruity, spicy, toasty, long.

VIRXEN DE GALIR

Las Escuelas, s/n Estoma
32336 O Barco de Valdeorras (Ourense)
☎: +34 988 335 600 - Fax: +34 988 335 592
bodega@virxendegalir.es
www.virxendegalir.es

PAGOS DEL GALIR GODELLO 2011 B
godello.

93 Colour: bright yellow. Nose: white flowers, balsamic herbs, fragrant herbs, fresh fruit, expressive. Palate: flavourful, fruity, rich, balanced, complex. Personality.

VÍA NOVA GODELLO 2011 B
godello.

90 Colour: bright straw. Nose: fresh, fresh fruit, ripe fruit. Palate: flavourful, fruity, good acidity, balanced.

G DEL GALIR, LÍAS 2010 B
100% godello.

88 Colour: bright yellow. Nose: powerfull, ripe fruit, sweet spices, creamy oak. Palate: rich, smoky afterpalate:, flavourful, fresh, good acidity.

VÍA NOVA MENCÍA 2011 T
mencía.

90 Colour: cherry, purple rim. Nose: fresh fruit, red berry notes, floral, characterful, scrubland. Palate: flavourful, fruity, good acidity, round tannins.

PAGOS DEL GALIR MENCÍA 2010 T ROBLE
mencía.

85 Colour: bright cherry. Nose: ripe fruit, sweet spices, creamy oak, dry stone. Palate: flavourful, fruity, toasty, round tannins.

PAGOS DEL GALIR ROSA RIVERO 2009 TC
mencía.

85 Colour: cherry, garnet rim. Nose: sweet spices, ripe fruit, sulphur notes. Palate: flavourful, fine bitter notes, good acidity.

DO VALDEPEÑAS

LOCATION:

On the southern border of the southern plateau, in the province of Ciudad Real. It comprises the municipal districts of Alcubillas, Moral de Calatrava, San Carlos del Valle, Santa Cruz de Mudela, Torrenueva and Valdepeñas and part of Alhambra, Granátula de Calatrava, Montiel and Torre de Juan Abad.

CLIMATE:

Continental in nature, with cold winters, very hot summers and little rainfall, which is usually around 250 and 400 mm per year.

SOIL:

Mainly brownish-red and brownish-grey limestone soil with a high lime content and quite poor in organic matter.

GRAPE VARIETIES:

WHITE: *Airén, Macabeo, Chardonnay, Sauvignon Blanc, Moscatel de Grano Menudo* and *Verdejo.*
RED: *Cencibel (Tempranillo), Garnacha, Cabernet Sauvignon, Merlot, Syrah* and *Petit Verdot.*

FIGURES:

Vineyard surface: 24,365 – **Wine-Growers:** 2,942 – **Wineries:** 42 – **2011 Harvest rating:** Excellent – **Production:** 57,480,337 litres – **Market percentages:** 58% domestic. 42% export

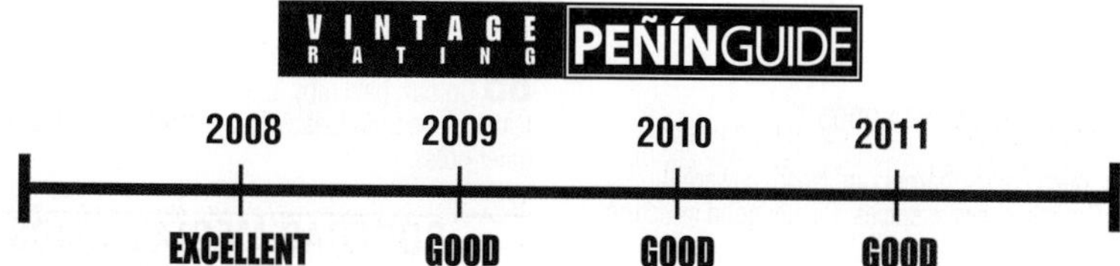

CONSEJO REGULADOR
Constitución, 23 - 13300 Valdepeñas (Ciudad Real) - ☎: +34 926 322 788 - Fax: +34 926 321 054
@ consejo@dovaldepenas.es - www.dovaldepenas.es

BODEGA HACIENDA LA PRINCESA

Ctra. San Carlos del Valle, km. 8 -
Apdo. Correos 281
13300 Valdepeñas (Ciudad Real)
☎: +34 638 335 185
haciendalaprincesa@telefonica.net
www.haciendalaprincesa.com

HACIENDA LA PRINCESA DEBIR PRINCESA 2011 BFB
100% chardonnay.

84

HACIENDA LA PRINCESA DEBIR CECILIA 2011 B
100% airén.

83

BODEGAS FERNANDO CASTRO

Paseo Castelar, 70
13730 Santa Cruz de Mudela (Ciudad Real)
☎: +34 926 342 168 - Fax: +34 926 349 029
fernando@bodegasfernandocastro.com
www.bodegasfernandocastro.com

RAÍCES 2007 TC

82

RAÍCES SELECCIÓN 2006 TR

87 Colour: deep cherry, purple rim. Nose: powerfull, roasted coffee, sweet spices, ripe fruit. Palate: correct, long, ripe fruit.

RAÍCES SYRAH SELECCIÓN 2006 T
syrah.

84

CASTILLO SANTA BÁRBARA 2005 T

87 Colour: deep cherry, garnet rim. Nose: powerfull, toasty, dark chocolate, sweet spices. Palate: good structure, flavourful, ripe fruit.

BODEGAS JUAN RAMÍREZ

Torrecilla, 138
13300 Valdepeñas (Ciudad Real)
☎: +34 926 322 021 - Fax: +34 926 320 495
info@bodegasjuanramirez.com
www.bodegasjuanramirez.com

ALBA DE LOS INFANTES 2006 TC
100% tempranillo.

84

ALBA DE LOS INFANTES 2005 TR
100% tempranillo.

84

BODEGAS MARÍN PERONA

Castellanos, 99
13300 Valdepeñas (Ciudad Real)
☎: +34 926 313 192 - Fax: +34 926 313 347
bodegas@merxi.com
www.tejeruelas.com

VIÑA ALDANTE 2011 B
100% airén.

84

VIÑA ALDANTE 2011 T
100% tempranillo.

82

VIÑA ALDANTE 2008 TC
100% tempranillo.

83

CALAR VIEJO 2007 TC
100% tempranillo.

84

MARÍN PERONA 2005 TR
100% tempranillo.

85 Colour: pale ruby, brick rim edge. Nose: candied fruit, fruit liqueur notes, dark chocolate, toasty. Palate: powerful, flavourful, long.

MARÍN PERONA 2000 TGR
100% tempranillo.

85 Colour: pale ruby, brick rim edge. Nose: cigar, old leather, ripe fruit, toasty. Palate: powerful, spicy, long, fine bitter notes.

BODEGAS MEGÍA E HIJOS - CORCOVO-

Magdalena, 33
13300 Valdepeñas (Ciudad Real)
☎: +34 926 347 828 - Fax: +34 926 347 829
jamegia@corcovo.com
www.corcovo.com

CORCOVO VERDEJO 2011 B
100% verdejo.

86 Colour: bright yellow. Nose: ripe fruit, tropical fruit, balanced, floral. Palate: flavourful, ripe fruit.

CORCOVO AIREN 2011 B
100% airén.

85 Colour: yellow. Nose: medium intensity, dried herbs. Palate: flavourful, ripe fruit, correct, easy to drink.

CORCOVO VERDEJO 24 BARRICAS 2010 B ROBLE
100% verdejo.

88 Colour: bright yellow. Nose: ripe fruit, citrus fruit, sweet spices. Palate: fruity, flavourful, rich, spicy, easy to drink.

CORCOVO SYRAH 2011 T
100% syrah.

88 Colour: cherry, purple rim. Nose: fruit expression, violets, balanced, varietal. Palate: flavourful, fruity, easy to drink, long.

CORCOVO TEMPRANILLO 2011 T
100% tempranillo.

87 Colour: cherry, purple rim. Nose: expressive, fresh fruit, red berry notes, floral, lactic notes. Palate: flavourful, fruity, good acidity.

CORCOVO SYRAH 24 BARRICAS 2010 T ROBLE
100% syrah.

88 Colour: very deep cherry, purple rim. Nose: red berry notes, ripe fruit, sweet spices. Palate: flavourful, fruity, easy to drink, spicy.

CORCOVO TEMPRANILLO 2010 T ROBLE
100% tempranillo.

85 Colour: cherry, garnet rim. Nose: ripe fruit, spicy, roasted coffee. Palate: correct, flavourful, toasty.

CORCOVO 2009 TC
100% tempranillo.

86 Colour: cherry, garnet rim. Nose: dark chocolate, sweet spices, candied fruit. Palate: powerful, flavourful, ripe fruit.

CORCOVO 2007 TR
100% tempranillo.

86 Colour: cherry, garnet rim. Nose: ripe fruit, sweet spices, fine reductive notes, medium intensity. Palate: flavourful, good structure, long.

BODEGAS MUREDA

Ctra. N-IV, Km. 184,1
13300 Valdepeñas (Ciudad Real)
☎: +34 926 318 058 - Fax: +34 926 318 058
administracion@mureda.es
www.mureda.es

MUREDA CUVÉE BRUT 2008 ESP
airén, macabeo, sauvignon blanc.

85 Colour: bright straw. Nose: ripe fruit, lees reduction notes, dry nuts, faded flowers, pattiserie. Palate: fresh, fruity, flavourful, fine bead.

MUREDA CUVÉE BRUT ROSÉ 2008 ESP
garnacha.

82

MUREDA GRAN CUVÉE 2007 ESP RESERVA
airén, macabeo, chardonnay.

86 Colour: bright golden. Nose: dried flowers, fragrant herbs, fine lees, balanced. Palate: good acidity, powerful, flavourful, easy to drink.

BODEGAS NAVARRO LÓPEZ

Autovía Madrid - Cádiz, Km. 193
13300 Valdepeñas (Ciudad Real)
☎: +34 902 193 431 - Fax: +34 902 193 432
marketing@navarrolopez.com;jopilal@terra.es;
www.navarrolopez.com

DON AURELIO MACABEO VERDEJO 2011 B
50% macabeo, 50% verdejo.

85 Colour: bright straw. Nose: fresh fruit, white flowers, expressive, citrus fruit. Palate: flavourful, fruity, fine bitter notes.

DON AURELIO 2011 RD
100% tempranillo.

87 Colour: brilliant rose, bright. Nose: fresh, balanced, red berry notes, medium intensity, dried flowers. Palate: fruity, fresh, easy to drink.

DON AURELIO GARNACHA 2011 T
100% garnacha.

87 Colour: cherry, purple rim. Nose: red berry notes, floral, ripe fruit. Palate: flavourful, fruity, good acidity, round tannins.

DON AURELIO TEMPRANILLO 2011 T
100% tempranillo.

85 Colour: cherry, purple rim. Nose: raspberry, overripe fruit, floral. Palate: light-bodied, fresh, fruity, easy to drink.

DON AURELIO 2010 T BARRICA
100% tempranillo.

85 Colour: bright cherry, purple rim. Nose: balanced, ripe fruit, sweet spices. Palate: flavourful, spicy, easy to drink.

DON AURELIO 2009 TC
100% tempranillo.

87 Colour: cherry, garnet rim. Nose: red berry notes, medium intensity, sweet spices. Palate: powerful, flavourful, balanced, long.

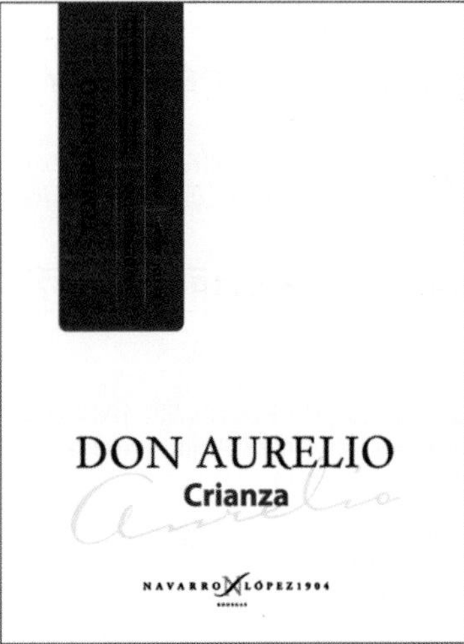

DON AURELIO 2007 TR
100% tempranillo.

85 Colour: cherry, garnet rim. Nose: spicy, fine reductive notes, sweet spices. Palate: spicy, fine tannins, long.

DON AURELIO 2006 TGR
100% tempranillo.

86 Colour: deep cherry, orangey edge. Nose: spicy, fine reductive notes, aged wood nuances, fruit liqueur notes. Palate: spicy, fine tannins, long.

CANUTO BODEGAS DE VALDEPEÑAS

Caldereros, 33
13300 Valdepeñas (Ciudad Real)
☎: +34 926 322 009 - Fax: +34 926 322 009
cabovasa@cabovasa.com
www.cabovasa.com

MONTECLARO AIRÉN B
100% airén.

80

MONTECLARO 2009 T
100% tempranillo.

83

MONTECLARO 2007 TC
100% tempranillo.

84

FÉLIX SOLÍS

Autovía del Sur, Km. 199
13300 Valdepeñas (Ciudad Real)
☎: +34 926 322 400 - Fax: +34 926 322 417
fsa@felixsolisavantis.com
www.felixsolisavantis.com

ALBALI ARIUM VERDEJO 2011 B
100% verdejo.

86 Colour: bright yellow. Nose: ripe fruit, balanced, white flowers. Palate: flavourful, fruity, long, easy to drink.

VIÑA ALBALI VERDEJO 2011 B
100% verdejo.

83

VIÑA ALBALI 2011 RD
100% tempranillo.

86 Colour: rose, purple rim. Nose: ripe fruit, red berry notes, lactic notes. Palate: , powerful, fruity, fresh, easy to drink.

ALBALI ARIUM 2011 RD
100% tempranillo.

86 Colour: rose, purple rim. Nose: powerfull, ripe fruit, red berry notes, expressive, lactic notes. Palate: , powerful, fruity, fresh.

ALBALI ARIUM TEMPRANILLO 2011 T
tempranillo.

87 Colour: cherry, purple rim. Nose: red berry notes, floral, ripe fruit, lactic notes. Palate: fruity, easy to drink, fresh.

VIÑA ALBALI TEMPRANILLO 2011 T
100% tempranillo.

85 Colour: deep cherry. Nose: ripe fruit, medium intensity, wild herbs. Palate: flavourful, ripe fruit, long.

ALBALI ARIUM 2008 TC
100% tempranillo.

86 Colour: cherry, garnet rim. Nose: ripe fruit, sweet spices, toasty, fine reductive notes. Palate: correct, powerful, flavourful.

VIÑA ALBALI 2008 TC
100% tempranillo.

84

ALBALI ARIUM 2007 TR
100% tempranillo.

87 Colour: very deep cherry. Nose: balanced, ripe fruit, fine reductive notes, spicy. Palate: good structure, spicy, balanced.

VIÑA ALBALI 2007 TR
100% tempranillo.

86 Colour: cherry, garnet rim. Nose: medium intensity, old leather, spicy. Palate: flavourful, fruity.

ALBALI ARIUM 2006 TGR
100% tempranillo.

88 Colour: pale ruby, brick rim edge. Nose: spicy, tobacco, dark chocolate, sweet spices, expressive. Palate: flavourful, spicy, long, good structure.

LOS MOLINOS 2006 TGR
100% tempranillo.

87 Colour: light cherry, orangey edge. Nose: spicy, wet leather, aged wood nuances. Palate: spicy, long, correct.

VIÑA ALBALI 2006 TGR
100% tempranillo.

85 Colour: cherry, garnet rim. Nose: medium intensity, fine reductive notes, spicy. Palate: flavourful, correct.

VIÑA ALBALI SELECCIÓN PRIVADA 2005 TGR
100% tempranillo.

88 Colour: deep cherry, garnet rim. Nose: fine reductive notes, tobacco, ripe fruit. Palate: balanced, ripe fruit, flavourful.

VIÑA ALBALI GRAN RESERVA DE LA FAMILIA 2004 TGR
85% tempranillo, 15% cabernet sauvignon.

88 Colour: deep cherry, orangey edge. Nose: balanced, expressive, spicy, tobacco. Palate: balanced, ripe fruit, spicy.

GRUPO DE BODEGAS VINARTIS

Ctra. A-IV, Km. 200,5
13300 Valdepeñas (Ciudad Real)
☎: +34 926 347 860 - Fax: +34 926 322 742
ricardo.donado@jgc.es
www.grupodebodegasvinartis.com

SEÑORÍO DE LOS LLANOS S/C T
100% tempranillo.

80

SEÑORÍO DE LOS LLANOS 2009 TC
100% tempranillo.

84

PATA NEGRA 2009 T ROBLE
100% tempranillo.

83

SEÑORÍO DE LOS LLANOS 2008 TR
100% tempranillo.

85 Colour: light cherry, orangey edge. Nose: toasty, spicy, fine reductive notes, fruit preserve. Palate: powerful, flavourful, long.

SEÑORÍO DE LOS LLANOS 2006 TGR
100% tempranillo.

84

PATA NEGRA 2006 TR
100% tempranillo.

83

PATA NEGRA 2005 TGR
100% tempranillo.

86 Colour: deep cherry, orangey edge. Nose: fruit liqueur notes, toasty, spicy, fine reductive notes. Palate: flavourful, correct, long.

LA INVENCIBLE VINOS Y ACEITES

Torrecilla, 130
13300 Valdepeñas (Ciudad Real)
☎: +34 926 321 700 - Fax: +34 926 311 080
lainvencible@lainvencible.eu
www.lainvencible.eu

VALDEAZOR 2011 B
airén.

82

VALDEAZOR 2011 T
tempranillo.

85 Colour: cherry, purple rim. Nose: red berry notes, fruit liqueur notes, scrubland. Palate: flavourful, fruity, easy to drink.

SANCTI PAULI

Paseo Estación, 47
13300 Valdepeñas (Ciudad Real)
☎: +34 926 316 938 - Fax: +34 926 316 007
sanctipauli@gmail.com

SANCTI PAULI 2007 TC
100% tempranillo.

86 Colour: deep cherry, orangey edge. Nose: fruit preserve, candied fruit, old leather, dark chocolate. Palate: powerful, flavourful, slightly overripe.

LOCATION:

In the province of Valencia. It comprises 66 municipal districts in 4 different sub-regions: Alto Turia, Moscatel de Valencia, Valentino and Clariano.

CLIMATE:

Mediterranean, marked by strong storms and downpours in summer and autumn. The average annual temperature is 15°C and the average annual rainfall is 500 mm.

SOIL:

Mostly brownish-grey with limestone content; there are no drainage problems.

GRAPE VARIETIES:

WHITE: *Macabeo, Malvasía, Merseguera, Moscatel de Alejandría, Moscatel de Grano Menudo, Pedro Ximénez, Plantafina, Plantanova, Tortosí, Verdil, Chardonnay, Semillon Blanc, Sauvignon Blanc, Verdejo, Riesling, Viognier* and *Gewüztraminer.*
RED: *Garnacha, Monastrell, Tempranillo, Tintorera, Forcallat Tinta, Bobal, Cabernet Cauvignon, Merlot, Pinot Noir, Syrah, Graciano, Malbec, Mandó, Marselan, Mencía, Merlot, Mazuelo* and *Petit Verdot.*

SUB-REGIONS:

There are four in total: **Alto Turia,** the highest sub-region (700 to 800 m above sea level) comprising 6 municipal districts; **Valentino** (23 municipal districts), in the centre of the province; the altitude varies between 250 m and 650 m; **Moscatel de Valencia** (9 municipal districts), also in the central region where the historical wine from the region is produced; and **Clariano** (33 municipal districts), to the south, at an altitude of between 400 m and 650 m.

FIGURES:

Vineyard surface: 13,080 – **Wine-Growers:** 10,800 – **Wineries:** 90 – **2011 Harvest rating:** Excellent – **Production:** 71,620,000 litres – **Market percentages:** 26% domestic. 74% export

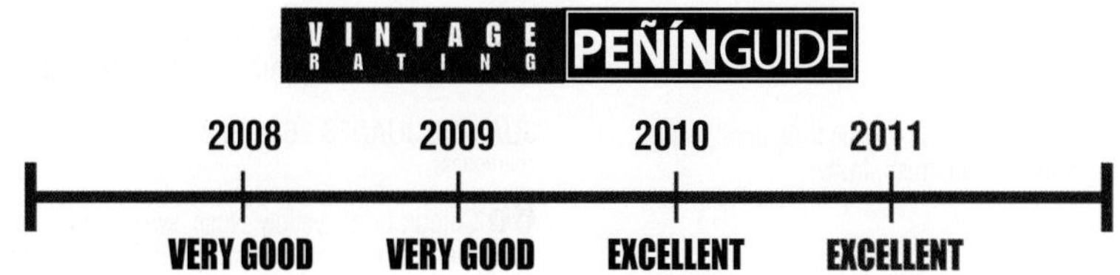

CONSEJO REGULADOR
Quart, 22 - 46001 Valencia - ☎: +34 963 910 096 - Fax: +34 963 910 029
@ info@vinovalencia.org - www.vinovalencia.org

BODEGA CHESTE AGRARIA ANECOOP BODEGAS

La Estación, 5
46380 Cheste (Valencia)
☎: +34 962 511 671 - Fax: +34 962 511 732
bodega@chesteagraria.com
www.reymos.es

AMATISTA BLANCO 2011 ESP
100% moscatel.

87 Colour: bright yellow. Nose: fresh fruit, white flowers, tropical fruit. Palate: good acidity, sweetness, fresh, fruity.

AMATISTA ROSADO 2011 ESP
95% moscatel, 5% garnacha.

80

REYMOS SELECCIÓN 2011 ESP
100% moscatel.

80

REYMOS 2011 ESP
100% moscatel.

76

SOL DE REYMOS 2009 MISTELA
100% moscatel.

80

BODEGA J. BELDA

Avda. Conde Salvatierra, 54
46635 Fontanars dels Alforins (Valencia)
☎: +34 962 222 278 - Fax: +34 962 222 245
info@danielbelda.com
www.danielbelda.com

DANIEL BELDA VERDIL 2011 B
verdil.

87 Colour: bright straw. Nose: expressive, tropical fruit, fresh fruit. Palate: flavourful, fine bitter notes, fruity, fresh.

TENDENCIA 2011 B
50% moscatel, 50% verdil.

87 Colour: bright yellow. Nose: ripe fruit, floral, wild herbs. Palate: light-bodied, fresh, fruity.

DANIEL BELDA CHARDONNAY 2011 B
chardonnay.

87 Colour: bright golden. Nose: ripe fruit, dry nuts, powerfull, toasty, aged wood nuances. Palate: flavourful, fruity, spicy, toasty, long.

DANIEL BELDA PINOT NOIR 2010 T
pinot noir.

88 Colour: cherry, garnet rim. Nose: ripe fruit, sweet spices, powerfull, red berry notes. Palate: powerful, good structure, concentrated.

CA'BELDA 2007 T FERMENTADO EN BARRICA
monastrell, garnacha tintorera.

91 Colour: cherry, garnet rim. Nose: toasty, spicy, nose:tic coffee, ripe fruit. Palate: powerful, spicy, ripe fruit.

DANIEL BELDA MERLOT 2007 TR
merlot.

87 Colour: cherry, garnet rim. Nose: ripe fruit, spicy, creamy oak, toasty. Palate: powerful, flavourful, toasty.

DANIEL BELDA SHIRAZ 2007 TR
syrah.

87 Colour: cherry, garnet rim. Nose: spicy, creamy oak, toasty. Palate: powerful, flavourful, toasty, round tannins.

MIGJORN 2007 T
cabernet sauvignon, merlot, garnacha tintorera.

85 Colour: cherry, garnet rim. Nose: ripe fruit, earthy notes, spicy, creamy oak. Palate: long, spicy, balsamic, correct.

BODEGA LA VIÑA

Portal de Valencia, 52
46630 La Font de la Figuera (Valencia)
☎: +34 962 290 078 - Fax: +34 962 232 039
info@vinosdelavina.com
www.vinosdelavina.com

ICONO CHARDONNAY 2011 B
chardonnay.

88 Colour: bright straw. Nose: fresh, white flowers, ripe fruit. Palate: flavourful, fruity, good acidity, balanced.

JUAN DE JUANES 2011 BFB
chardonnay.

86 Colour: bright yellow. Nose: sweet spices, creamy oak, ripe fruit. Palate: rich, flavourful, fresh, good acidity, thin.

ICONO SYRAH 2011 T
syrah.

90 Colour: cherry, purple rim. Nose: fresh fruit, red berry notes, ripe fruit, rose petals. Palate: flavourful, fruity, good acidity, round tannins.

ICONO MERLOT 2011 T
merlot.

89 Colour: cherry, purple rim. Nose: fresh fruit, red berry notes, floral. Palate: flavourful, fruity, good acidity, round tannins.

ICONO CABERNET SAUVIGNON 2011 T
cabernet sauvignon.

86 Colour: cherry, purple rim. Nose: red berry notes, ripe fruit, earthy notes, wild herbs. Palate: flavourful, fruity, concentrated.

CASA L'ANGEL CABERNET 2011 T
tempranillo, cabernet sauvignon.

86 Colour: deep cherry. Nose: grassy, fruit preserve, spicy, nose:tic coffee. Palate: powerful, spicy, ripe fruit.

CASA L'ANGEL ORGANIC 2011 T
tempranillo, syrah.

86 Colour: cherry, purple rim. Nose: expressive, ripe fruit, scrubland. Palate: flavourful, powerful, fine bitter notes.

VENTA DEL PUERTO 12 2009 T
tempranillo, cabernet sauvignon, merlot, syrah.

90 Colour: cherry, garnet rim. Nose: spicy, creamy oak, roasted coffee, overripe fruit. Palate: powerful, flavourful, toasty, round tannins.

JUAN DE JUANES 2009 T
syrah, merlot, cabernet sauvignon, cabernet franc.

90 Colour: cherry, garnet rim. Nose: ripe fruit, spicy, creamy oak, toasty, complex. Palate: powerful, flavourful, toasty, round tannins.

CASA L'ANGEL CEPAS VIEJAS 2009 T
tempranillo, cabernet sauvignon.

87 Colour: cherry, garnet rim. Nose: ripe fruit, fruit liqueur notes, earthy notes, creamy oak. Palate: flavourful, concentrated, spicy, harsh oak tannins.

VENTA DEL PUERTO 18 VENDIMIA SELECCIONADA 2008 T BARRICA
tempranillo, cabernet sauvignon, merlot, syrah.

88 Colour: cherry, garnet rim. Nose: ripe fruit, cocoa bean, spicy, new oak. Palate: long, powerful, flavourful, toasty.

BODEGAS ARANLEÓN

Ctra. Caudete, 3, Los Marcos
46310 Venta del Moro (Valencia)
☎: +34 963 631 640 - Fax: +34 962 185 150
vinos@aranleon.com
www.aranleon.com

EL ÁRBOL DE ARANLEÓN 2008 TC
30% monastrell, 30% tempranillo, 20% cabernet sauvignon, 10% merlot, 10% syrah.

92 Colour: cherry, garnet rim. Nose: spicy, creamy oak, toasty, characterful, ripe fruit. Palate: powerful, flavourful, toasty, round tannins.

BODEGAS 40 GRADOS NORTE

46635 Fontanars dels Alforins (Valencia)
☎: +34 615 167 040
amartin@40gradosnorte.com
www.40gradosnorte.com

SO DE SYRAH 2011 T JOVEN
syrah.

85 Colour: cherry, purple rim. Nose: red berry notes, warm, violets, medium intensity. Palate: fresh, fruity, light-bodied, easy to drink.

MAR DE SO 2009 T
syrah, bobal, tempranillo.

85 Colour: cherry, garnet rim. Nose: ripe fruit, fruit preserve, sweet spices. Palate: powerful, flavourful, toasty.

COTA 830 2008 T
bobal, tempranillo, cabernet sauvignon.

88 Colour: cherry, garnet rim. Nose: ripe fruit, spicy, creamy oak, premature reduction notes. Palate: powerful, flavourful, toasty.

BODEGAS ARRAEZ

Arcediano Ros, 35
46630 Fuente La Higuera (Valencia)
☎: +34 962 290 031 - Fax: +34 962 290 339
info@bodegasarraez.com
www.antonioarraez.com

A2 VERDIL 2011 B
verdil.

88 Colour: bright straw. Nose: fresh, fresh fruit, white flowers. Palate: flavourful, fruity, good acidity, balanced.

EDUARDO BERMEJO 2011 B
malvasía, macabeo.

86 Colour: bright straw. Nose: fresh, fresh fruit, white flowers, expressive. Palate: flavourful, fruity, good acidity, balanced.

MALA VIDA 2010 T ROBLE
cabernet sauvignon, syrah, tempranillo, monastrell.

91 Colour: bright cherry. Nose: ripe fruit, sweet spices, creamy oak, characterful. Palate: flavourful, fruity, toasty, round tannins.

EDUARDO BERMEJO 2010 T
tempranillo, monastrell.

88 Colour: bright cherry. Nose: ripe fruit, sweet spices, creamy oak. Palate: flavourful, fruity, toasty, round tannins.

LAGARES 2009 TC
cabernet sauvignon.

90 Colour: bright cherry. Nose: ripe fruit, sweet spices, creamy oak, complex, characterful. Palate: flavourful, fruity, toasty, round tannins.

A2 MONASTRELL 2009 T ROBLE
monastrell.

86 Colour: bright cherry. Nose: ripe fruit, sweet spices, creamy oak, expressive. Palate: flavourful, fruity, toasty.

A2 SYRAH 2009 T ROBLE
syrah.

86 Colour: cherry, garnet rim. Nose: scrubland, toasty, dark chocolate, nose:tic coffee. Palate: powerful, concentrated, roasted-coffee afterpalate:.

LAGARES 2007 TR
cabernet sauvignon, syrah, monastrell.

85 Colour: cherry, garnet rim. Nose: ripe fruit, spicy, creamy oak, nose:tic coffee. Palate: powerful, flavourful, toasty, round tannins.

BODEGAS EL ANGOSTO

Ctra. Fontanars CV-660, km. 24
46870 Ontinyent (Valencia)
☎: +34 962 380 638 - Fax: +34 962 911 349
info@bodegaelangosto.com
www.bodegaelangosto.com

ALMENDROS 2011 B
33% chardonnay, 33% sauvignon blanc, 33% riesling.

93 Colour: bright yellow. Nose: powerfull, ripe fruit, sweet spices, creamy oak, fragrant herbs, complex. Palate: rich, smoky afterpalate:, flavourful, fresh, good acidity. Personality.

ANGOSTO BLANCO 2011 B
sauvignon blanc, moscatel grano menudo, chardonnay, riesling.

91 Colour: bright straw. Nose: fresh fruit, white flowers, fresh, complex, fine lees. Palate: flavourful, fruity, good acidity, balanced.

LA TRIBU 2011 T
garnacha tintorera, syrah, monastrell.

91 Colour: cherry, purple rim. Nose: expressive, fresh fruit, red berry notes, floral. Palate: flavourful, fruity, good acidity, round tannins.

ALMENDROS 2010 T
garnacha tintorera, syrah, marselan.

93 Colour: dark-red cherry, bright cherry. Nose: red berry notes, ripe fruit, mineral, creamy oak, expressive. Palate: powerful, flavourful, elegant, long, spicy.

ANGOSTO TINTO 2010 T
garnacha tintorera, syrah, cabernet franc.

92 Colour: bright cherry. Nose: ripe fruit, sweet spices, creamy oak. Palate: flavourful, fruity, toasty, round tannins.

JEFE DE LA TRIBU 2010 T
50% touriga, 50% marselan.

90 Colour: bright cherry. Nose: ripe fruit, sweet spices, creamy oak, nose:tic coffee, roasted coffee, mineral. Palate: flavourful, toasty, round tannins.

BODEGAS EL VILLAR S.C.V.

Avda. del Agricultor, 1- P.I. San Vicente
46170 Villar de Arzobispo (Valencia)
☎: +34 962 720 050 - Fax: +34 961 646 060
coopvillar@elvillar.com
www.elvillar.com

LADERAS 2011 B

86 Colour: bright straw. Nose: fresh fruit, citrus fruit, grassy. Palate: flavourful, good acidity.

XIMO 2010 B
semillón.

82

LADERAS TEMPRANILLO BOBAL 2011 RD
tempranillo, bobal.

84

LADERAS TEMPRANILLO 2011 T
tempranillo.

85 Colour: cherry, purple rim. Nose: red berry notes, scrubland, spicy. Palate: light-bodied, fresh, fruity, balsamic.

VIÑA VILLAR 2008 TC

87 Colour: cherry, garnet rim. Nose: toasty, dark chocolate, fruit preserve. Palate: powerful, sweetness, concentrated.

TAPIAS 2007 TC

84

BODEGAS ENGUERA

Ctra. CV - 590, Km. 51,5
46810 Enguera (Valencia)
☎: +34 962 224 318 - Fax: +34 961 364 167
oficina@bodegasenguera.com
www.bodegasenguera.com

BLANC D'ENGUERA 2011 B
verdil, sauvignon blanc, chardonnay, viognier.

90 Colour: bright yellow. Nose: ripe fruit, sweet spices, creamy oak, fragrant herbs. Palate: rich, smoky afterpalate:, flavourful, fresh, good acidity.

VERDIL DE GEL 2011 B
verdil.

84

MEGALA 2009 T
monastrell, syrah.

91 Colour: cherry, garnet rim. Nose: red berry notes, ripe fruit, sweet spices, creamy oak. Palate: flavourful, balanced, toasty, long.

PARADIGMA 2008 T
monastrell.

93 Colour: deep cherry. Nose: candied fruit, raspberry, grassy, expressive, scrubland, balsamic herbs, toasty. Palate: spicy, ripe fruit, easy to drink, long.

SUEÑO DE MEGALA 2007 T
monastrell, merlot, tempranillo.

91 Colour: cherry, garnet rim. Nose: ripe fruit, toasty, complex, new oak, sweet spices, scrubland. Palate: powerful, flavourful, toasty, round tannins.

BODEGAS LOS FRAILES

Casa Los Frailes, s/n
46635 Fontanaresdels Alforins (Valencia)
☎: +34 962 222 220 - Fax: +34 963 363 153
info@bodegaslosfrailes.com
www.bodegaslosfrailes.com

BLANC DE TRILOGÍA 2011 B
70% sauvignon blanc, 10% moscatel, 20% verdil.

90 Colour: bright yellow. Nose: sweet spices, creamy oak, fragrant herbs, white flowers. Palate: rich, flavourful, fresh, good acidity, elegant.

EFE MONASTRELL ROSADO 2011 RD
100% monastrell.

84

LOS FRAILES 2011 T
100% monastrell.

88 Colour: cherry, purple rim. Nose: fresh fruit, red berry notes, floral, expressive. Palate: flavourful, fruity, easy to drink.

LA DANZA DE LA MOMA 2009 T BARRICA
50% monastrell, 50% marselan.

92 Colour: cherry, garnet rim. Nose: ripe fruit, spicy, creamy oak, scrubland. Palate: powerful, flavourful, toasty, round tannins.

EFE BARRICA 2009 T BARRICA
80% monastrell, 20% cabernet sauvignon.

89 Colour: bright cherry. Nose: ripe fruit, sweet spices, creamy oak, expressive. Palate: flavourful, fruity, toasty, round tannins.

BILOGÍA 2008 T
50% monastrell, 50% tempranillo.

90 Colour: cherry, garnet rim. Nose: powerfull, warm, fruit preserve, toasty, creamy oak. Palate: powerful, flavourful, sweetness, spicy.

BODEGAS LOS PINOS

Casa Los Pinos, s/n
46635 Fontanars dels Alforins (Valencia)
☎: +34 962 222 090 - Fax: +34 600 584 397
bodegaslospinos@bodegaslospinos.com
www.bodegaslospinos.com

BROTE 2011 BFB
verdil, viognier.

87 Colour: bright straw. Nose: white flowers, fragrant herbs, candied fruit. Palate: correct, flavourful, fruity, spicy.

DOMINIO LOS PINOS SALVATGE 2011 B
moscatel grano menudo, verdil, sauvignon blanc.

84

DOMINIO LOS PINOS 2011 T BARRICA
cabernet sauvignon, syrah, tempranillo.

88 Colour: cherry, purple rim. Nose: warm, red berry notes, sweet spices. Palate: powerful, flavourful, spicy, easy to drink.

LOS PINOS 0 % 2011 T
garnacha, monastrell, syrah.

87 Colour: deep cherry. Nose: ripe fruit, fruit preserve, powerfull. Palate: powerful, concentrated.

DOMINIO LOS PINOS 2010 TC
merlot, monastrell, cabernet sauvignon.

91 Colour: cherry, garnet rim. Nose: spicy, creamy oak, toasty, characterful. Palate: powerful, flavourful, toasty, round tannins.

BROTE 2009 TC
monastrell, garnacha, merlot.

89 Colour: cherry, garnet rim. Nose: red berry notes, ripe fruit, sweet spices, dark chocolate. Palate: powerful, flavourful, fruity, toasty, balanced.

BODEGAS MURVIEDRO

Ampliación Pol. El Romeral, s/n
46340 Requena (Valencia)
☎: +34 962 329 003 - Fax: +34 962 329 002
murviedro@murviedro.es
www.murviedro.es

ALBA DE MURVIEDRO 2011 B
60% sauvignon blanc, 40% moscatel.

90 Colour: bright yellow. Nose: white flowers, tropical fruit, fragrant herbs, expressive. Palate: full, flavourful, easy to drink.

ESTRELLA 10 B
100% moscatel de alejandría.

88 Colour: bright straw. Nose: fresh fruit, citrus fruit. Palate: flavourful, fruity, fresh.

ROSA DE MURVIEDRO 2011 RD
100% cabernet sauvignon.

88 Colour: rose, purple rim. Nose: powerfull, ripe fruit, red berry notes, floral, expressive. Palate: fleshy, powerful, fruity, fresh.

MURVIEDRO COLECCIÓN CABERNET SAUVIGNON 2011 RD
cabernet sauvignon.

87 Colour: brilliant rose. Nose: ripe fruit, red berry notes, balsamic herbs. Palate: flavourful, fruity, fresh.

ESTRELLA FRIZZANTE RD
40% tempranillo, 25% bobal, 35% moscatel.

83

MURVIEDRO COLECCIÓN PETIT VERDOT 2011 T
petit verdot.

90 Colour: cherry, purple rim. Nose: ripe fruit, balsamic herbs, spicy. Palate: flavourful, good acidity, fine bitter notes.

MURVIEDRO COLECCIÓN SYRAH 2011 T
syrah.

89 Colour: cherry, purple rim. Nose: expressive, red berry notes, violets, ripe fruit. Palate: flavourful, fruity, warm.

MURVIEDRO 2009 TC
50% tempranillo, 30% monastrell, 20% syrah.

90 Colour: cherry, garnet rim. Nose: ripe fruit, spicy, creamy oak, toasty, balanced. Palate: powerful, flavourful, toasty, round tannins.

MURVIEDRO EXPRESIÓN 2009 TC
55% monastrell, 45% garnacha.

89 Colour: cherry, garnet rim. Nose: ripe fruit, spicy, toasty, aged wood nuances, new oak. Palate: powerful, flavourful, toasty, spicy.

CUEVA DEL PECADO 2008 T
60% tempranillo, 40% cabernet sauvignon.

93 Colour: cherry, garnet rim. Nose: ripe fruit, spicy, creamy oak, toasty. Palate: powerful, flavourful, toasty, round tannins.

MURVIEDRO 2008 TR
40% tempranillo, 40% monastrell, 20% cabernet sauvignon.

88 Colour: cherry, garnet rim. Nose: ripe fruit, spicy, creamy oak, toasty, nose:tic coffee. Palate: powerful, flavourful, toasty, round tannins.

BODEGAS ONTINIUM

Avda. Almansa, 17
46870 Ontinyent (Valencia)
☎: +34 962 380 849 - Fax: +34 962 384 419
info@coopontinyent.com
www.coopontinyent.com

ONTINIUM 2011 B
macabeo, merseguera.

83

ONTINIUM SYRAH 2011 T
100% syrah.

88 Colour: cherry, purple rim. Nose: red berry notes, ripe fruit, dried flowers, scrubland. Palate: flavourful, fruity, easy to drink.

ONTINIUM TEMPRANILLO 2011 T
100% tempranillo.

86 Colour: cherry, purple rim. Nose: red berry notes, ripe fruit, balsamic herbs. Palate: flavourful, fruity, good acidity.

BODEGAS POLO MONLEÓN

Ctra. Valencia - Ademuz, Km. 86
46178 Titaguas (Valencia)
☎: +34 961 634 148
info@hoyadelcastillo.com
www.hoyadelcastillo.com

HOYA DEL CASTILLO ALTO TURIA 2011 B
merseguera, macabeo.

89 Colour: bright straw. Nose: fresh, fresh fruit, white flowers, expressive, grassy. Palate: flavourful, fruity, good acidity.

BODEGAS SÁNCHEZ ZAHONERO

Ricardo Serrano, 13
46392 Siete Aguas (Valencia)
☎: +34 962 340 052
bodega@sanchezzahonero.com
www.sanchezzahonero.com

BRESSOL 2011 B
100% merseguera.

88 Colour: bright straw. Nose: expressive, earthy notes, ripe fruit, balsamic herbs. Palate: flavourful, fruity, good acidity.

BRESSOL 2011 T
100% merlot.

88 Colour: cherry, garnet rim. Nose: red berry notes, ripe fruit, balsamic herbs, spicy, creamy oak. Palate: flavourful, spicy, balsamic.

LÉSSÈNCIA 2009 T
tempranillo, syrah.

88 Colour: dark-red cherry. Nose: powerfull, characterful, candied fruit, fruit preserve, toasty, dark chocolate. Palate: powerful, fine bitter notes, round tannins.

CAPRICHO 2009 T
tempranillo, syrah, garnacha.

86 Colour: deep cherry. Nose: candied fruit, scrubland, toasty. Palate: spicy, fine bitter notes.

BODEGAS SIERRA NORTE

Pol. Ind. El Romeral. Transporte- Parc. C2
46340 Requena (Valencia)
☎: +34 962 323 099 - Fax: +34 962 323 048
info@bodegasierranorte.com
www.bodegasierranorte.com

MARILUNA 2011 B
macabeo, chardonnay, sauvignon blanc.

82

MARILUNA 2010 T
bobal, tempranillo, monastrell.

90 Colour: bright cherry. Nose: expressive, red berry notes, raspberry, sweet spices. Palate: flavourful, fruity, round tannins, balanced.

BODEGAS UTIELANAS

San Fernando, 18
46300 Utiel (Valencia)
☎: +34 962 171 157 - Fax: +34 962 170 801
info@bodegasutielanas.com
www.bodegasutielanas.com

SUEÑOS DEL MEDITERRÁNEO 2011 T
100% bobal.

87 Colour: cherry, purple rim. Nose: red berry notes, floral, lactic notes, expressive. Palate: powerful, flavourful, fruity.

DULCE TENTACIÓN 2011 T
100% bobal.

84

BODEGAS VEGAMAR

Garcesa, s/n
46175 Calles (Valencia)
☎: +34 962 109 813
info@bodegasvegamar.com
www.bodegasvegamar.com

TITO REY 2011 B

89 Colour: bright straw. Nose: fresh, white flowers, fine lees, ripe fruit. Palate: flavourful, fruity, good acidity, balanced.

VIÑA COSTOSA 2011 B
macabeo, sauvignon blanc.

85 Colour: bright straw. Nose: fresh, fresh fruit, white flowers, tropical fruit. Palate: flavourful, fruity, good acidity, balanced.

VIÑAS DE CALLES 2011 B
100% macabeo.

83

VEGAMAR 2007 TR
tempranillo, cabernet sauvignon.

85 Colour: deep cherry. Nose: medium intensity, spicy, fruit liqueur notes, toasty. Palate: flavourful, fine bitter notes, ripe fruit.

VIÑA CARRASSES 2007 TC
tempranillo, merlot, cabernet sauvignon.

84

VEGAMAR 2006 TR
tempranillo, cabernet sauvignon.

87 Colour: cherry, garnet rim. Nose: ripe fruit, creamy oak. Palate: powerful, flavourful, toasty, round tannins.

VEGAMAR SYRAH 2006 TC
syrah.

82

BODEGAS VICENTE GANDÍA

Ctra. Cheste a Godelleta, s/n
46370 Chiva (Valencia)
☎: +34 962 524 242 - Fax: +34 962 524 243
vuboldi@vicentegandia.com
www.vicentegandia.es

EL MIRACLE 120 2011 B
60% chardonnay, 40% sauvignon blanc.

88 Colour: bright straw. Nose: fresh, fresh fruit, white flowers, expressive, cocoa bean, fine lees. Palate: flavourful, fruity, good acidity, balanced.

FUSTA NOVA BLANC 2011 B
45% chardonnay, 35% sauvignon blanc, 20% moscatel de alejandría.

86 Colour: bright straw. Nose: fresh, white flowers, dried herbs. Palate: flavourful, fruity, good acidity.

CASTILLO DE LIRIA 2011 B
80% viura, 20% sauvignon blanc.

81

CASTILLO DE LIRIA SEMI DULCE 2011 B
80% viura, 20% sauvignon blanc.

80

FUSTA NOVA MOSCATEL B
100% moscatel de alejandría.

85 Colour: golden. Nose: powerfull, floral, honeyed notes, candied fruit, fragrant herbs. Palate: flavourful, sweet, fresh, fruity, good acidity, long.

CASTILLO DE LIRIA 2011 RD
100% bobal.

86 Colour: rose, purple rim. Nose: floral, red berry notes, fresh fruit, lactic notes. Palate: light-bodied, fresh, fruity, easy to drink.

CASTILLO DE LIRIA 2011 T
80% bobal, 20% syrah.

82

EL MIRACLE BY MARISCAL 2010 T
100% garnacha tintorera.

87 Colour: bright cherry. Nose: ripe fruit, sweet spices, expressive, scrubland. Palate: flavourful, fruity, toasty, round tannins.

EL MIRACLE 120 ANIVERSARIO 2010 T
65% tempranillo, 35% syrah.

83

CASTILLO DE LIRIA 2009 TC
85% tempranillo, 15% syrah.

83

CASTILLO DE LIRIA 2008 TR
100% tempranillo.

84

CASTILLO DE LIRIA MOSCATEL
100% moscatel de alejandría.

85 Colour: bright straw. Nose: powerfull, fruit liqueur notes, honeyed notes. Palate: sweet, good acidity.

BODEGAS Y DESTILERÍAS VIDAL

Pol. Ind. El Mijares, c/Valencia, 16
12550 Almazora (Castellón)
☎: +34 964 503 300 - Fax: +34 964 560 604
jordan@bodegasvidal.com
www.bodegasvidal.com

UVA D'OR MOSCATEL MISTELA
moscatel.

90 Colour: golden. Nose: powerfull, floral, honeyed notes, candied fruit, fragrant herbs, citrus fruit. Palate: flavourful, sweet, fresh, fruity, good acidity, long. Personality.

BODEGAS Y VIÑEDOS DE UTIEL

Finca El Renegado, s/n
46315 Caudete de las Fuentes (Valencia)
☎: +34 962 174 029 - Fax: +34 962 171 432
gestion@bodegasdeutiel.com
www.nodus.es

ADOLFO DE LAS HERAS TINTO DE AUTOR 2009 T
bobal.

86 Colour: cherry, garnet rim. Nose: ripe fruit, spicy, creamy oak, toasty, earthy notes. Palate: powerful, flavourful, toasty, round tannins.

BODEGUES I VINYES LA CASA DE LAS VIDES

Corral el Galtero, s/n
46890 Agullent (Valencia)
☎: +34 962 135 003 - Fax: +34 962 135 494
bodega@lacasadelasvides.com
www.lacasadelasvides.com

VALLBLANCA 2011 B
verdil, gewürztraminer.

84

ROSA ROSAE 2011 RD
garnacha, cabernet sauvignon.

80

ABC 2011 T
tempranillo, petit verdot, garnacha, merlot.

88 Colour: cherry, purple rim. Nose: powerfull, ripe fruit, red berry notes. Palate: flavourful, fruity, fresh.

CUP DE CUP 2010 T
tempranillo, syrah, garnacha.

85 Colour: bright cherry. Nose: ripe fruit, sweet spices, creamy oak, expressive. Palate: flavourful, fruity, toasty.

ACVLIVS 2008 T
monastrell, tempranillo, syrah.

88 Colour: cherry, garnet rim. Nose: toasty, dark chocolate, ripe fruit. Palate: powerful, flavourful, fine bitter notes.

CELLER DEL ROURE

Ctra. de Les Alcusses, Km. 11,1
46640 Moixent (Valencia)
☎: +34 962 295 020 - Fax: +34 962 295 142
info@cellerdelroure.es

CULLEROT 2011 B
30% verdil, 30% pedro ximénez, 20% macabeo, 20% chardonnay.

89 Colour: bright straw. Nose: fresh, fresh fruit, white flowers, expressive, fragrant herbs. Palate: flavourful, fruity, good acidity.

SETZE GALLETS 16 2011 T
30% garnacha tintorera, 30% monastrell, 15% mandó, 25% merlot.

91 Colour: bright cherry. Nose: ripe fruit, sweet spices, creamy oak. Palate: flavourful, fruity, toasty, round tannins.

MADURESA 2008 T
25% mandó, 25% syrah, 15% petit verdot, 15% garnacha tintorera, 10% monastrell, 10% cabernet sauvignon.

93 Colour: cherry, garnet rim. Nose: earthy notes, red berry notes, ripe fruit, creamy oak. Palate: powerful, flavourful, complex, fine tannins.

LES ALCUSSES 2008 T
60% monastrell, 10% garnacha tintorera, 10% cabernet sauvignon, 15% merlot, 5% syrah.

91 Colour: bright cherry. Nose: ripe fruit, sweet spices, creamy oak. Palate: flavourful, fruity, toasty, round tannins.

COOP. V. SAN PEDRO APÓSTOL. MOIXENT

Pza. de la Hispanidad, 4
46640 Moixent (Valencia)
☎: +34 962 260 020 - Fax: +34 962 260 560
info@closdelavall.com
www.closdelavall.com

CLOS DE LA VALL 2009 T

84

CLOS DE LA VALL 2011 B

88 Colour: bright straw. Nose: fresh, fresh fruit, white flowers, citrus fruit. Palate: flavourful, fruity, good acidity, balanced.

CLOS DE LA VALL PX 2010 BFB
pedro ximénez.

90 Colour: bright golden. Nose: ripe fruit, dry nuts, powerfull, toasty, sweet spices. Palate: flavourful, fruity, spicy, toasty, long.

CLOS DE LA VALL 2008 TC

89 Colour: cherry, garnet rim. Nose: ripe fruit, spicy, creamy oak, toasty, complex. Palate: powerful, flavourful, toasty, round tannins.

CLOS DE LA VALL 2007 TC

86 Colour: cherry, garnet rim. Nose: ripe fruit, spicy, toasty, creamy oak. Palate: powerful, flavourful, spicy.

CLOS DE LA VALL 2006 TR
monastrell, cabernet sauvignon, tempranillo.

87 Colour: pale ruby, brick rim edge. Nose: spicy, fine reductive notes, aged wood nuances, ripe fruit. Palate: fine tannins, long.

HERETAT DE TAVERNERS

Ctra. Fontanars - Moixent, Km. 1,8
46635 Fontanars dels Alforins (Valencia)
☎: +34 962 132 437 - Fax: +34 962 222 298
info@heretatdetaverners.com
www.heretatdetaverners.com

HERETAT DE TAVERNERS REIXIU 2011 BC

90 Colour: bright yellow. Nose: powerfull, ripe fruit, sweet spices, creamy oak, white flowers. Palate: rich, flavourful, fresh, good acidity.

HERETAT DE TAVERNERS BEN VIU SC T

88 Colour: very deep cherry. Nose: powerfull, warm, toasty, spicy, fruit liqueur notes. Palate: powerful, fine bitter notes, long.

HERETAT DE TAVERNERS GRACIANO 2008 TR

91 Colour: cherry, garnet rim. Nose: earthy notes, scrubland, toasty, dark chocolate. Palate: powerful, fine bitter notes, good acidity.

HERETAT DE TAVERNERS MALLAURA 2008 TR

89 Colour: cherry, garnet rim. Nose: powerfull, complex, sweet spices. Palate: powerful, good acidity, fine bitter notes.

HERETAT DE TAVERNERS EL VERN 2008 TC

87 Colour: pale ruby, brick rim edge. Nose: elegant, spicy, fine reductive notes, fruit liqueur notes. Palate: spicy, fine tannins, elegant, long.

PUNT DOLÇ T

91 Colour: cherry, purple rim. Nose: expressive, red berry notes, ripe fruit, spicy, toasty. Palate: flavourful, fruity, good acidity, sweetness, toasty.

LA BARONÍA DE TURIS

Ctra. Godelleta, 22
46389 Turis (Valencia)
☎: +34 962 526 011 - Fax: +34 962 527 282
baronia@baroniadeturis.es
www.baroniadeturis.es

LA LUNA DE MAR 2011 B
moscatel.

88 Colour: bright straw. Nose: fresh, fresh fruit, white flowers. Palate: flavourful, fruity, good acidity, balanced.

PLAZA MARQUÉS 2011 B
malvasía.

85 Colour: bright straw. Nose: fresh, white flowers. Palate: flavourful, fruity, good acidity, balanced.

LA LUNA DE MAR 2009 T
merlot, garnacha tintorera, cabernet sauvignon, syrah.

88 Colour: cherry, garnet rim. Nose: earthy notes, ripe fruit, sweet spices, creamy oak. Palate: round tannins, flavourful, long, spicy.

1920 2009 T
merlot, syrah, garnacha tintorera, cabernet sauvignon.

88 Colour: cherry, garnet rim. Nose: ripe fruit, spicy, creamy oak, toasty. Palate: powerful, flavourful, toasty, round tannins, warm.

DONA DOLÇA MISTELA
moscatel.

82

PAGO CASA GRAN

Ctra. Mogente Fontanares, km. 9,5
46640 Mogente (Valencia)
☎: +34 962 261 004 - Fax: +34 962 261 004
comercial@pagocasagran.com
www.pagocasagran.com

CASA BENASAL 2011 B
gewürztraminer, moscatel.

89 Colour: bright straw. Nose: fresh, fresh fruit, white flowers, fragrant herbs. Palate: flavourful, fruity, good acidity, correct.

FALCATA BIO 2011 RD
monastrell, syrah.

86 Colour: rose, purple rim. Nose: powerfull, ripe fruit, red berry notes, floral. Palate: , powerful, fruity, flavourful.

FALCATA BIO 2011 T
syrah, monastrell, merlot.

87 Colour: cherry, purple rim. Nose: ripe fruit, scrubland, floral, earthy notes. Palate: fresh, fruity, easy to drink.

CASA BENASAL 2010 T
syrah, monastrell, petit verdot.

88 Colour: cherry, garnet rim. Nose: ripe fruit, spicy, creamy oak, toasty, earthy notes, wild herbs. Palate: powerful, flavourful, toasty, round tannins.

CASA BENASAL ELEGANT 2009 T
garnacha tintorera, syrah, monastrell.

89 Colour: cherry, garnet rim. Nose: ripe fruit, spicy, toasty, mineral. Palate: toasty, round tannins, balanced, flavourful.

CASA BENASAL CRUX 2008 T
garnacha tintorera, monastrell, syrah.

90 Colour: cherry, garnet rim. Nose: creamy oak, toasty, dark chocolate, sweet spices, overripe fruit. Palate: powerful, flavourful, toasty, round tannins, balanced.

FALCATA ARENAL 2007 T
garnacha tintorera, monastrell.

91 Colour: cherry, garnet rim. Nose: balsamic herbs, mineral, ripe fruit, spicy. Palate: flavourful, spicy, long, good acidity, round tannins.

FALCATA CASA GRAN 2007 T
garnacha tintorera, monastrell, syrah.

89 Colour: cherry, garnet rim. Nose: ripe fruit, scrubland, spicy, creamy oak. Palate: flavourful, complex, long, spicy.

RAFAEL CAMBRA

Naus Artesanals, 14
46635 Fontanars dels Alforins (Valencia)
☎: +34 626 309 327 - Fax: +34 962 383 855
rafael@rafaelcambra.es
www.rafaelcambra.es

EL BON HOMME 2011 T
50% cabernet sauvignon, 50% monastrell.

91 Colour: cherry, purple rim. Nose: ripe fruit, red berry notes, fragrant herbs. Palate: flavourful, fruity, fine bitter notes, round.

RAFAEL CAMBRA DOS 2010 T
cabernet sauvignon, cabernet franc.

91 Colour: bright cherry. Nose: sweet spices, creamy oak, ripe fruit. Palate: flavourful, fruity, toasty, round tannins.

MINIMUM 2009 T

94 Colour: cherry, garnet rim. Nose: spicy, creamy oak, toasty, ripe fruit, characterful. Palate: powerful, flavourful, toasty, round tannins.

RAFAEL CAMBRA UNO 2009 T
monastrell.

91 Colour: cherry, garnet rim. Nose: ripe fruit, spicy, creamy oak, toasty, mineral. Palate: powerful, flavourful, toasty, round tannins.

THE TAPAS WINE COLLECTION

Casas de la Hoya, s/n
30520 Jumilla (Murcia)
☎: +34 968 437 137 - Fax: +34 968 437 200
export@thetapaswinecollection.com
www.thetapaswinecollection.com

THE TAPAS WINE COLLECTION 2010 B

82

THE TAPAS WINE COLLECTION 2009 T

88 Colour: bright cherry. Nose: sweet spices, creamy oak, fruit expression. Palate: flavourful, fruity, toasty, round tannins.

VALSAN 1831

Ctra. Cheste - Godelleta, Km. 1
46370 Chiva (Valencia)
☎: +34 962 510 861 - Fax: +34 962 511 361
cherubino@cherubino.es
www.cherubino.es

LES DUNES 2011 B
macabeo, moscatel.

89 Colour: bright straw. Nose: fresh, fresh fruit, white flowers. Palate: flavourful, fruity, good acidity, balanced.

MARQUÉS DE CARO 2011 B
macabeo, moscatel.

86 Colour: bright yellow. Nose: white flowers, fresh fruit, fragrant herbs. Palate: light-bodied, fresh, fruity.

MARQUÉS DE CARO MOSCATEL B
moscatel.

86 Colour: bright straw. Nose: fruit liqueur notes, honeyed notes, powerfull. Palate: powerful, confected, spirituous.

LES DUNES 2011 RD
bobal.

88 Colour: rose, purple rim. Nose: powerfull, ripe fruit, red berry notes, floral, expressive. Palate: fleshy, powerful, fruity, fresh.

MARQUÉS DE CARO TEMPRANILLO 2011 T
tempranillo.

89 Colour: cherry, purple rim. Nose: fresh fruit, red berry notes, floral, varietal. Palate: flavourful, fruity, good acidity, round tannins.

LES DUNES 2011 T
tempranillo.

88 Colour: cherry, purple rim. Nose: varietal, ripe fruit, red berry notes. Palate: flavourful, fruity, fresh.

MARQUÉS DE CARO 2009 TC
bobal, tempranillo, syrah.

85 Colour: cherry, garnet rim. Nose: ripe fruit, spicy, creamy oak, toasty. Palate: powerful, flavourful, toasty.

MARQUÉS DE CARO 2008 TR
tempranillo, cabernet sauvignon.

84

CUVA VELLA MOSCATEL
moscatel.

93 Colour: light mahogany. Nose: powerfull, candied fruit, fruit liqueur notes, dry nuts, honeyed notes, nose:tic coffee, dark chocolate. Palate: powerful, sweet, spirituous.

VIÑAS DEL PORTILLO

P.I. El Llano F2 P4 Apdo. 130
46360 Buñol (Valencia)
☎: +34 962 504 827 - Fax: +34 962 500 937
vinasdelportillo@vinasdelportillo.es

ALTURIA 2011 B
malvasía, moscatel de alejandría.

90 Colour: bright straw. Nose: fresh, fresh fruit, white flowers, fragrant herbs. Palate: flavourful, fruity, good acidity, balanced. Personality.

COSTA DE ORO 2011 T
tempranillo, monastrell.

85 Colour: deep cherry. Nose: medium intensity, ripe fruit. Palate: fruity, light-bodied, easy to drink.

COSTA DE ORO 2008 TC
tempranillo, monastrell, merlot.

84

VIÑEDOS Y BODEGAS VEGALFARO

Ctra. Pontón - Utiel, Km. 3
46430 El Derramador - Requena (Valencia)
☎: +34 962 320 680 - Fax: +34 962 321 126
info@vegalfaro.com
www.vegalfaro.com

PASAMONTE 2011 B
88% sauvignon blanc, 12% garnacha blanca.

88 Colour: bright straw. Nose: fresh, fresh fruit, white flowers, expressive. Palate: flavourful, fruity, good acidity, balanced.

PASAMONTE 2010 T
100% garnacha tintorera.

90 Colour: bright cherry. Nose: ripe fruit, sweet spices, creamy oak, expressive. Palate: flavourful, fruity, toasty, round tannins.

VEGALFARO 2009 TC
tempranillo, merlot, bobal.

89 Colour: cherry, garnet rim. Nose: ripe fruit, spicy, creamy oak, toasty. Palate: powerful, flavourful, toasty, round tannins.

ZAGROMONTE - BODEGAS TORREVELLISCA

Ctra. L'Ombria, Km. 1
46635 Fontanars dels Alforins (Valencia)
☎: +34 962 222 261 - Fax: +34 962 222 257
info@bodegas-torrevellisca.es
www.bodegas-torrevellisca.com

PALACIO DE TORREVELLISCA 2011 B
verdil, macabeo, verdejo.

82

EMBRUJO 2011 B
malvasía.

82

PALACIO DE TORREVELLISCA 2011 T
tempranillo, syrah.

81

EMBRUJO NEGRO 2011 T
monastrell, syrah.

79

AURUM DE ZAGROMONTE 2009 TC
merlot, cabernet sauvignon.

86 Colour: cherry, garnet rim. Nose: ripe fruit, balsamic herbs, sweet spices, roasted coffee. Palate: correct, powerful, flavourful.

ARGENTUM 2009 TC
tempranillo, cabernet sauvignon.

84

BRUNDISIUM 2008 TC
tempranillo, cabernet sauvignon, cabernet franc.

86 Colour: cherry, garnet rim. Nose: ripe fruit, fruit preserve, fine reductive notes, spicy. Palate: powerful, flavourful, long, spicy.

DO VALLE DE GÜÍMAR

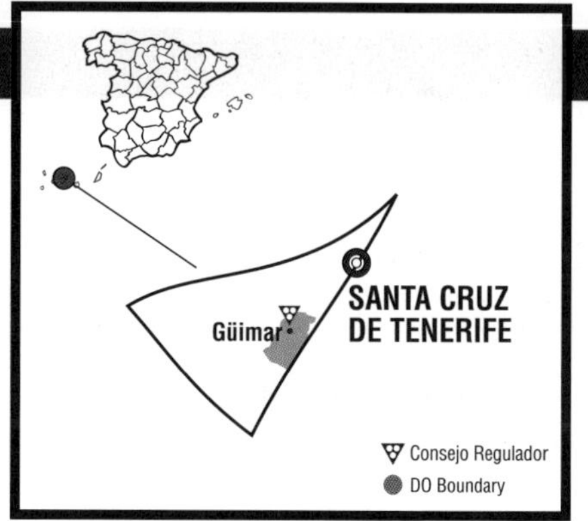

LOCATION:

On the island of Tenerife. It practically constitutes a prolongation of the Valle de la Orotava region to the southeast, forming a valley open to the sea, with the Las Dehesas region situated in the mountains and surrounded by pine forests where the vines grow in an almost Alpine environment. It covers the municipal districts of Arafo, Candelaria and Güímar.

CLIMATE:

Although the influence of the trade winds is more marked than in Abona, the significant difference in altitude in a much reduced space must be pointed out, which gives rise to different microclimates, and pronounced contrasts in day-night temperatures, which delays the harvest until 1st November.

SOIL:

Volcanic at high altitudes, there is a black tongue of lava crossing the area where the vines are cultivated on a hostile terrain with wooden frames to raise the long vine shoots.

GRAPE VARIETIES:

WHITE: *Gual, Listán Blanco, Malvasía, Moscatel, Verdello* and *Vijariego.*
RED: *Bastardo Negro, Listán Negro* (15% of total), *Malvasía Tinta, Moscatel Negro, Negramoll, Vijariego Negro, Cabernet Sauvignon, Merlot, Pinot Noir, Ruby Cabernet, Syrah* and *Tempranillo.*

FIGURES:

Vineyard surface: 560 – **Wine-Growers:** 548 – **Wineries:** 16 – **2011 Harvest rating:** N/A – **Production:** 150,250 litres – **Market percentages:** 100% domestic

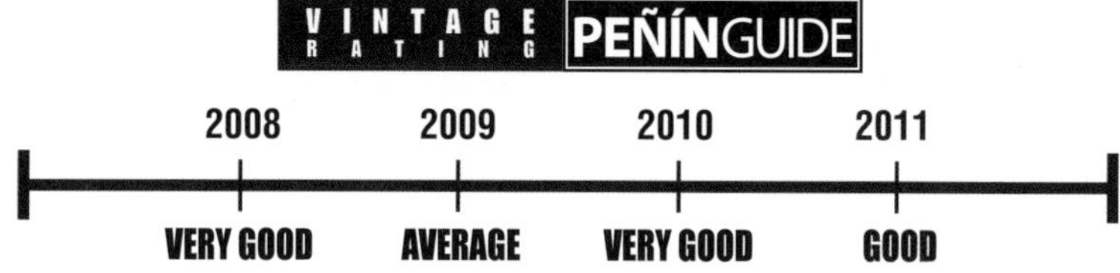

CONSEJO REGULADOR
Tafetana, 14 - 38500 Güímar (Santa Cruz de Tenerife) - ☎: +34 922 514 709 - Fax: +34 922 514 485
@ consejo@vinosvalleguimar.com - www.vinosvalleguimar.com

BODEGA COMARCAL VALLE DE GÜIMAR

Subida a Los Loros, Km. 4
38550 Arafo (Santa Cruz de Tenerife)
☎: +34 922 510 437 - Fax: +34 922 510 437
info@bodegacomarcalguimar.com
www.bodegacomarcalguimar.com

BRUMAS DE AYOSA 2011 B
listán blanco.

85 Colour: bright straw. Nose: medium intensity, white flowers, citrus fruit. Palate: fresh, easy to drink.

PICO CHO MARCIAL 2011 B
listán blanco.

82

BRUMAS DE AYOSA AFRUTADO B
listán blanco, moscatel de alejandría.

86 Colour: bright straw. Nose: medium intensity, fresh fruit, floral. Palate: flavourful, fruity, good finish, sweetness, balanced.

BRUMAS DE AYOSA 2011 T
listán negro.

83

PICO CHO MARCIAL 2011 T
listán negro.

79

BRUMAS DE AYOSA MALVASÍA 2011 BLANCO DULCE
malvasía.

86 Colour: bright straw. Nose: white flowers, ripe fruit, balanced. Palate: correct, easy to drink.

BRUMAS DE AYOSA 2011 ESP
listán blanco.

80

BRUMAS DE AYOSA AFRUTADO 2011 ESP
listán blanco.

80

BRUMAS DE AYOSA 2007 ESP RESERVA
listán blanco.

80

BODEGA CONTIEMPO

Chinguaro, 26-B - San Francisco Javier
38500 Güímar (Santa Cruz de Tenerife)
☎: +34 922 512 552
bodega@vinocontiempo.com
www.vinocontiempo.com

CONTIEMPO VIDUEÑOS SECO 2011 B
marmajuelo, verdejo, gual.

88 Colour: bright straw. Nose: medium intensity, balanced, wild herbs, fresh fruit, citrus fruit. Palate: flavourful, fine bitter notes, good acidity.

CONTIEMPO MOSCATEL AFRUTADO 2011 B
100% moscatel.

88 Colour: bright straw. Nose: white flowers, medium intensity, fresh fruit. Palate: easy to drink, correct, sweetness, good acidity.

CONTIEMPO MALVASÍA SECO 2010 B
malvasía.

86 Colour: bright straw. Nose: faded flowers, powerfull, neat. Palate: flavourful, fruity, good acidity, balanced.

CONTIEMPO MALVASÍA 2008 B
100% malvasía.

87 Colour: bright yellow. Nose: toasty, spicy, candied fruit, faded flowers. Palate: flavourful, ripe fruit, long.

CONTIEMPO 2011 RD
listán negro, merlot.

84

CONTIEMPO TINTO DE POSTRE 2011 T
100% baboso negro.

86 Colour: deep cherry, garnet rim. Nose: powerfull, pattiserie, ripe fruit, slightly evolved. Palate: fruity, good finish.

CONTIEMPO MALVASÍA DULCE 2011 BLANCO DULCE
100% malvasía.

86 Colour: yellow. Nose: floral, citrus fruit, medium intensity. Palate: flavourful, fruity, balanced.

BODEGA PICO ARGUAMA

Lomo la Arena, 9
38530 Igueste Candelaria (Santa Cruz de Tenerife)
☎: +34 922 501 110

PICO ARGUAMA 2011 T

80

CÁNDIDO HERNÁNDEZ PÍO

Los Tomillos s/n
38530 Candelaria (Santa Cruz de Tenerife)
☎: +34 922 513 288 - Fax: +34 922 511 631
almacenlahidalga@telefonica.net

CALIUS 2011 B
marmajuelo, malvasía, verdejo, vijariego blanco.

86 Colour: bright straw. Nose: balanced, expressive, fresh fruit, white flowers. Palate: fruity, flavourful, good acidity.

CALIUS 2011 T
vijariego negro, merlot.

85 Colour: cherry, purple rim. Nose: wild herbs, fresh fruit. Palate: fresh, fruity.

CALIUS 2008 TR
vijariego negro, merlot, tintilla.

87 Colour: cherry, garnet rim. Nose: ripe fruit, spicy, balanced. Palate: flavourful, ripe fruit, round tannins.

EL BORUJO

Ctra. a la Cumbre, Km. 4,2
38550 Arafo (Santa Cruz de Tenerife)
☎: +34 636 824 919
el_borujo@hotmail.com
www.elborujo.es

EL BORUJO 2011 B
50% listán blanco, 20% albillo, 20% moscatel, 10% marmajuelo.

89 Colour: bright straw. Nose: balanced, expressive, white flowers, fresh fruit. Palate: flavourful, fruity, good acidity, balanced.

EL BORUJO 2011 B
70% listán blanco, 30% moscatel.

85 Colour: bright straw. Nose: medium intensity, white flowers, faded flowers. Palate: fruity, good finish.

FERRERA

Calvo Sotelo, 44
38550 Arafo (Santa Cruz de Tenerife)
☎: +34 649 487 835 - Fax: +34 922 237 359
carmengloria@bodegaferrera.com

MOMENTO DE FERRERA 2011 BFB
70% malvasía, 30% albillo.

89 Colour: bright straw. Nose: white flowers, fresh fruit, powerfull, expressive, sweet spices. Palate: balanced, fine bitter notes, good acidity, flavourful.

FERRERA AFRUTADO 2011 B
50% listán blanco, 50% moscatel.

84

FERRERA 2011 B
60% albillo, 30% listán blanco, 10% moscatel.

81

FERRERA 2011 T
50% syrah, 20% castellana, ruby, cabernet sauvignon, merlot, listán negro.

87 Colour: cherry, purple rim. Nose: red berry notes, ripe fruit, sweet spices, balsamic herbs. Palate: flavourful, good structure, fruity, good acidity.

LOS PELADOS

Hoya Cartaya, 32 - Chacona
38500 Güimar (Santa Cruz de Tenerife)
☎: +34 922 512 786 - Fax: +34 922 514 485
bodegaslospelados@hotmail.com

LOS PELADOS 2011 B

82.

SAT VIÑA LAS CAÑAS

Barranco Badajoz, s/n
38500 Güimar (Santa Cruz de Tenerife)
☎: +34 637 592 759 - Fax: +34 922 512 716
vegalascanas@hotmail.com

GRAN VIRTUD LISTÁN BLANCO 2011 B

88 Colour: bright straw. Nose: balanced, fresh, fresh fruit, citrus fruit. Palate: fresh, fruity, flavourful, good acidity, fine bitter notes.

VEGA LAS CAÑAS AFRUTADO 2011 B

85 Colour: bright straw. Nose: medium intensity, wild herbs, fresh fruit, floral. Palate: correct, balanced.

VEGA LAS CAÑAS 2011 B

84

GRAN VIRTUD 2010 BFB

91 Colour: bright straw. Nose: ripe fruit, sweet spices, creamy oak, jasmine. Palate: fruity, flavourful, good acidity, fine bitter notes.

AMOR ALMA & ORIGEN 2011 RD

83

GRAN VIRTUD 2010 T FERMENTADO EN BARRICA

90 Colour: cherry, purple rim. Nose: ripe fruit, dark chocolate, medium intensity, wild herbs. Palate: rich, fruity, round tannins.

VIÑA HERZAS

38004 Santa Cruz de Tenerife
☎: +34 922 511 405 - Fax: +34 922 290 064
morraherza@yahoo.es

VIÑAS HERZAS 2011 B
listán blanco, gual, moscatel.

85 Colour: bright straw. Nose: medium intensity, fresh, dried herbs. Palate: fruity, fresh, correct.

VIÑAS HERZAS 2011 T
tempranillo, merlot, cabernet sauvignon, listán negro.

79

DO VALLE DE LA OROTAVA

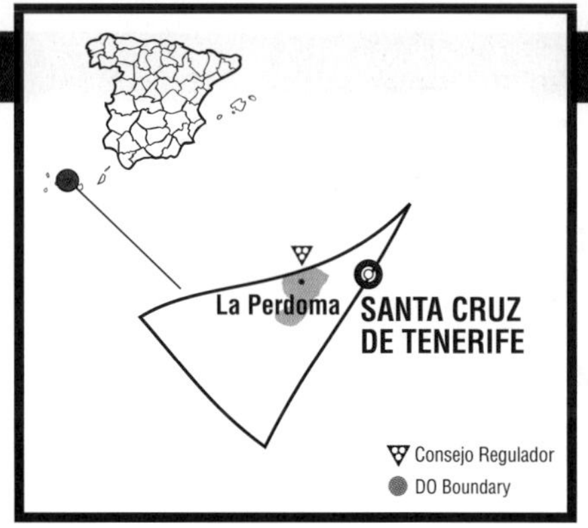

LOCATION:

In the north of the island of Tenerife. It borders to the west with the DO Ycoden-Daute-Isora and to the east with the DO Tacoronte-Acentejo. It extends from the sea to the foot of the Teide, and comprises the municipal districts of La Orotava, Los Realejos and El Puerto de la Cruz.

CLIMATE:

As with the other regions on the islands, the weather is conditioned by the trade winds, which in this region result in wines with a moderate alcohol content and a truly Atlantic character. The influence of the Atlantic is also very important, in that it moderates the temperature of the costal areas and provides a lot of humidity. Lastly, the rainfall is rather low, but is generally more abundant on the north face and at higher altitudes.

SOIL:

Light, permeable, rich in mineral nutrients and with a slightly acidic pH due to the volcanic nature of the island. The vineyards are at an altitude of between 250 mm and 700 m.

GRAPE VARIETIES:

WHITE:
MAIN: *Güal, Malvasía, Verdello, Vijariego, Albillo, Forastera Blanca* o *Doradilla, Sabro, Breval* and *Burrablanca.*
AUTHORIZED: *Bastardo Blanco, Forastera Blanca* (*Gomera*), *Listán Blanco, Marmajuelo, Moscatel, Pedro Ximénez* and *Torrontés.*
RED:
MAIN: *Listán Negro, Malvasía Rosada, Negramoll, Castellana Negra, Mulata, Tintilla, Cabernet Sauvignon, Listán Prieto, Merlot, Pinot Noir, Ruby Cabernet, Syrah* and *Tempranillo.*
AUTHORIZED: *Bastardo Negro, Moscatel Negra, Tintilla* and *Vijariego Negra.*

FIGURES:

Vineyard surface: 600 – **Wine-Growers:** 763 – **Wineries:** 20 – **2011 Harvest rating:** N/A – **Production:** 381,213 litres – **Market percentages:** 92% domestic. 8% export

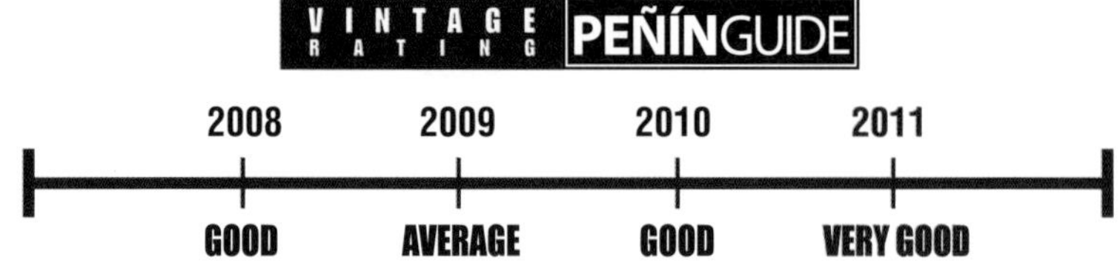

CONSEJO REGULADOR
Parque Recreativo El Bosquito, nº1 - Urb. La Marzagana II - La Perdona - 38315 La Orotava (Santa Cruz de Tenerife)
☎: +34 922 309 923 - Fax: +34 922 309 924
@ do-valleorotava@terra.es - www.dovalleorotava.com

BODEGA SECADERO

Trinidad, 4
38410 Los Realejos (Santa Cruz de Tenerife)
☎: +34 665 807 966
pab_estevez@hotmail.com
www.bodegasecadero.com

CUPRUM 2011 B
75% listán blanco, 25% malvasía.

79

CUPRUM 2011 T BARRICA
75% tintilla, 25% listán negro.

86 Colour: cherry, purple rim, bright cherry. Nose: grassy, fresh, expressive. Palate: light-bodied, fruity.

CUPRUM 2011 T
listán negro.

84

BODEGA TAJINASTE

El Ratiño, 5
38315 La Orotava (Santa Cruz de Tenerife)
☎: +34 696 030 347 - Fax: +34 922 308 720
bodega@tajinaste.net
www.tajinaste.net

TAJINASTE 2011 B
100% listán blanco.

85 Colour: bright straw. Nose: fresh fruit, floral, medium intensity. Palate: easy to drink, fresh, correct.

TAJINASTE AFRUTADO 2011 B
100% listán blanco.

83

TAJINASTE 2011 RD
100% listán negro.

84

TAJINASTE TRADICIONAL 2011 T
100% listán negro.

86 Colour: cherry, purple rim. Nose: medium intensity, fresh, red berry notes. Palate: fruity, easy to drink, short.

TAJINASTE 2011 T MACERACIÓN CARBÓNICA
100% listán negro.

84

CAN 2010 T
listán negro, vijariego negro.

90 Colour: deep cherry, garnet rim. Nose: balanced, ripe fruit, cocoa bean, creamy oak, sweet spices. Palate: good structure, flavourful, long.

TAJINASTE 2010 T BARRICA
100% listán negro.

87 Colour: cherry, garnet rim. Nose: balanced, red berry notes, scrubland, spicy. Palate: fruity, flavourful, good acidity, balanced.

TAJINASTE VENDIMIA SELECCIONADA 2010 T
100% listán negro.

86 Colour: cherry, garnet rim. Nose: balanced, neat, spicy, balsamic herbs. Palate: fruity, good finish.

BODEGAS EL PENITENTE

Camino La Habanera, 286
38300 La Orotava (Santa Cruz de Tenerife)
☎: +34 922 309 024 - Fax: +34 922 309 024
bodegas@elpenitentesl.es
www.bodegaselpenitentesl.es

ARAUTAVA 2011 B
listán blanco.

86 Colour: bright straw. Nose: fresh fruit, medium intensity, floral. Palate: easy to drink, good acidity, fresh.

ARAUTAVA 2011 T FERMENTADO EN BARRICA
100% listán negro.

88 Colour: bright cherry, purple rim. Nose: balanced, expressive, red berry notes, ripe fruit, dark chocolate. Palate: good structure, fruity, good acidity.

ARAUTAVA 2011 T
100% listán negro.

86 Colour: cherry, purple rim. Nose: medium intensity, fresh, wild herbs, red berry notes. Palate: fruity, flavourful, easy to drink.

ARAUTAVA DULCE 2009 T
100% listán negro.

89 Colour: deep cherry, purple rim. Nose: powerfull, candied fruit, fruit liqueur notes, varnish, sweet spices. Palate: balanced, long, rich.

LA SUERTITA

Real de la Cruz Santa, 35-A
38413 Los Realejos (Santa Cruz de Tenerife)
☎: +34 669 408 761
bodegalasuertita@yahoo.es
www.lasuertita.com

LA SUERTITA AFRUTADO 2011 B
100% listán blanco.

84

LA SUERTITA 2011 B
100% listán blanco.

82

LA SUERTITA 2010 B BARRICA
100% listán blanco.

88 Colour: bright yellow. Nose: sweet spices, candied fruit, faded flowers. Palate: balanced, fine bitter notes, good acidity.

LOS GÜINES

Pista Los Guines, s/n - El Horno
38410 Los Realejos (Santa Cruz de Tenerife)
☎: +34 922 343 320 - Fax: +34 922 353 855
www.bodegalosguines.com

LOS GÜINES 2011 B

85 Colour: bright yellow. Nose: medium intensity, ripe fruit, floral, dried herbs. Palate: easy to drink, fresh, flavourful.

LOS GÜINES 2011 T

76

PROPIEDAD VITÍCOLA SUERTES DEL MARQUÉS

Tomás Zerolo, 15
38300 La Orotava (Santa Cruz de Tenerife)
☎: +34 922 501 300 - Fax: +34 922 503 462
ventas@suertesdelmarques.com
www.suertesdelmarques.com

SUERTES DEL MARQUÉS VIDONIA 2011 B
100% listán blanco.

89 Colour: bright straw. Nose: white flowers, ripe fruit, dried flowers, dried herbs. Palate: flavourful, fruity, good acidity, balanced.

SUERTES DEL MARQUÉS 2011 B BARRICA
75% listán blanco, 25% vidueño.

87 Colour: bright yellow. Nose: toasty, spicy, candied fruit, aromatic coffee. Palate: fruity, toasty.

SUERTES DEL MARQUÉS LOS PASITOS 2011 T
90% baboso negro, 10% listán negro.

88 Colour: cherry, purple rim. Nose: fresh fruit, red berry notes, floral, balsamic herbs. Palate: flavourful, fruity, good acidity, light-bodied, easy to drink.

SUERTES DEL MARQUÉS CANDIO 2010 T
100% listán negro.

90 Colour: cherry, garnet rim. Nose: complex, balanced, spicy, balsamic herbs, ripe fruit. Palate: fruity, good structure, long, good acidity.

SUERTES DEL MARQUÉS LA SOLANA 2010 T
100% listán negro.

88 Colour: cherry, garnet rim. Nose: powerfull, balanced, sweet spices, cocoa bean. Palate: fruity, flavourful, easy to drink.

SUERTES DEL MARQUÉS EL ESQUILÓN 2010 T
70% listán negro, 30% tintilla.

88 Colour: cherry, garnet rim. Nose: balanced, expressive, sweet spices, ripe fruit, balsamic herbs. Palate: fruity, good acidity, balanced.

7 FUENTES 2010 T
90% listán negro, 10% tintilla.

86 Colour: cherry, garnet rim. Nose: scrubland, wild herbs, balanced. Palate: fruity, easy to drink.

SUERTES DEL MARQUÉS EL CIRUELO 2011
100% listán negro.

90 Colour: light cherry. Nose: floral, fragrant herbs, ripe fruit, varnish, sweet spices, expressive. Palate: fresh, fruity, light-bodied, flavourful, balanced.

DO VINOS DE MADRID

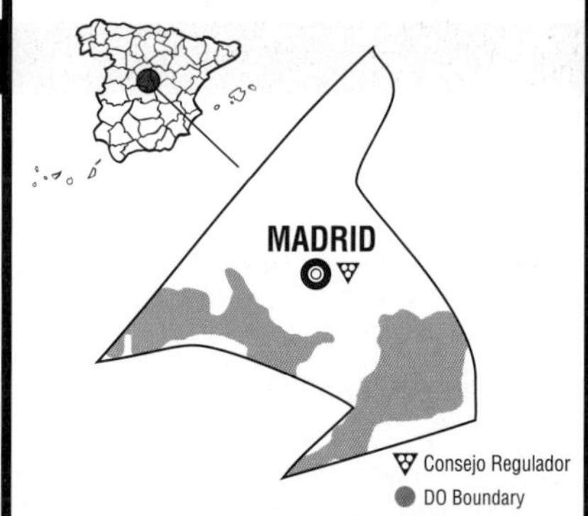

LOCATION:

In the south of the province of Madrid, it covers three distinct sub-regions: Arganda, Navalcarnero and San Martín de Valdeiglesias.

CLIMATE:

Extreme continental, with cold winters and hot summers. The average annual rainfall ranges from 461 mm in Arganda to 658 mm in San Martín.

SOIL:

Rather unfertile soil and granite subsoil in the sub-region of San Martín de Valdeiglesias; in Navalcarnero the soil is brownish-grey, poor, with a subsoil of coarse sand and clay; in the sub-region of Arganda the soil is brownish-grey, with an acidic pH and granite subsoil.

GRAPE VARIETIES:

WHITE: *Malvar*, *Airén*, *Albillo, Parellada, Macabeo, Torrontés* and *Moscatel de Grano Menudo.*
RED: *Tinto Fino* (Tempranillo), *Garnacha*, *Merlot, Cabernet Sauvignon* and *Syrah*.

SUB-REGIONS:

San Martín. It comprises 9 municipal districts and has more than 3,821 Ha of vineyards, with mainly the Garnacha (red) and Albillo (white) varieties.
Navalcarnero. It comprises 19 municipal districts with a total of about 2,107 Ha. The most typical wines are reds and rosés based on the Garnacha variety.
Arganda. With 5,830 Ha and 26 municipal districts, it is the largest sub-region of the DO. The main varieties are the white Malvar and the red Tempranillo or Tinto Fino.

FIGURES:

Vineyard surface: 8,390 – **Wine-Growers:** 2,891 – **Wineries:** 44 – **2011 Harvest rating:** Very Good – **Production:** 17,856,924 litres – **Market percentages:** 76% domestic. 24% export

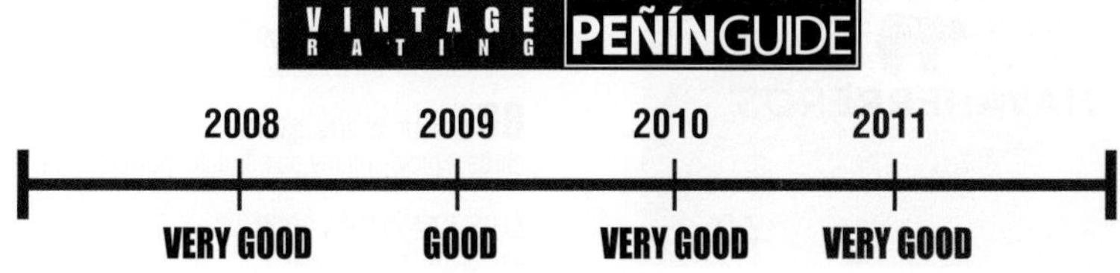

CONSEJO REGULADOR
Ronda de Atocha, 7 - 28012 Madrid - ☎: +34 915 348 511 / +34 915 347 240 - +34 Fax: 915 538 574
@ aprovim@vinosdemadrid.es - www.vinosdemadrid.es

BERNABELEVA

Ctra. Avila Toledo (N-403), Km. 81,600
28680 San Martín de Valdeiglesias (Madrid)
☎: +34 915 091 909
bodega@bernabeleva.com
www.bernabeleva.com

CANTOCUERDAS MOSCATEL DE BERNABELEVA 2010 B
100% moscatel.

94 Colour: bright golden. Nose: floral, jasmine, fragrant herbs, citrus fruit, candied fruit. Palate: flavourful, fresh, fruity, complex, good acidity, elegant.

CANTOCUERDAS ALBILLO 2010 B
100% albillo.

93 Colour: bright yellow. Nose: powerfull, ripe fruit, sweet spices, fragrant herbs, faded flowers, mineral. Palate: rich, smoky afterpalate:, flavourful, fresh, balanced, long.

NAVAHERREROS BLANCO DE BERNABELEVA 2010 B
60% albillo, 40% macabeo.

92 Colour: bright yellow. Nose: citrus fruit, ripe fruit, mineral, dried flowers, wild herbs, expressive. Palate: powerful, flavourful, rich, long, balanced.

BERNABELEVA VIÑA BONITA 2010 T
garnacha.

94 Colour: cherry, purple rim. Nose: expressive, red berry notes, floral, sweet spices, creamy oak, mineral, fragrant herbs. Palate: flavourful, fruity, fresh.

NAVAHERREROS 2010 T
100% garnacha.

93 Colour: bright cherry. Nose: sweet spices, creamy oak, red berry notes, ripe fruit, dark chocolate, fragrant herbs. Palate: flavourful, fruity, toasty, round tannins.

BERNABELEVA "CARRIL DEL REY" 2010 T
100% garnacha.

93 Colour: bright cherry. Nose: red berry notes, ripe fruit, scrubland, mineral, spicy, toasty, balanced. Palate: powerful, flavourful, long, good acidity.

BERNABELEVA "ARROYO DE TÓRTOLAS" 2010 T
100% garnacha.

93 Colour: bright cherry. Nose: ripe fruit, scrubland, floral, dry stone, cocoa bean, dark chocolate, spicy, expressive. Palate: long, flavourful, spicy, complex, balanced.

BODEGA ECOLÓGICA LUIS SAAVEDRA

Ctra. de Escalona, 5
28650 Cenicientos (Madrid)
☎: +34 962 912 4622 - Fax: +34 914 606 053
info@bodegasaavedra.com
www.bodegasaavedra.com

CORUCHO ALBILLO MOSCATEL 2011 B
95% albillo, 5% moscatel grano menudo.

84

CORUCHO 2010 T ROBLE
100% garnacha.

86 Colour: deep cherry. Nose: powerfull, warm, candied fruit. Palate: flavourful, fine bitter notes, spicy, round tannins.

CORUCHO 2009 TC
100% garnacha.

88 Colour: deep cherry. Nose: fruit liqueur notes, fruit expression, varietal, toasty, spicy. Palate: powerful, fine bitter notes, warm.

CORUCHO KOSHER 2009 T ROBLE
100% garnacha.

86 Colour: deep cherry. Nose: warm, fruit expression, fruit liqueur notes. Palate: flavourful, fine bitter notes, good acidity.

LUIS SAAVEDRA 2009 T
95% garnacha, 5% tinto fino.

86 Colour: cherry, garnet rim. Nose: ripe fruit, fragrant herbs, spicy, creamy oak. Palate: powerful, flavourful, fruity.

LUIS SAAVEDRA 2008 TC
90% garnacha, 10% syrah.

89 Colour: deep cherry. Nose: fruit preserve, toasty, spicy, characterful. Palate: flavourful, powerful, fine bitter notes, round tannins.

BODEGA MARAÑONES

Hilero, 7 - Nave 9
28696 Pelayos de la Presa (Madrid)
☎: +34 918 647 702
fernandogarcia@bodegamaranones.com
www.bodegamaranones.com

PICARANA 2011 B
100% albillo.

93 Colour: bright yellow. Nose: mineral, earthy notes, citrus fruit, ripe fruit, dried flowers, dry nuts. Palate: powerful, rich, flavourful, spicy, long, balanced, elegant.

PIESDESCALZOS 2011 B
100% albillo.

92 Colour: bright yellow. Nose: ripe fruit, sweet spices, fragrant herbs, dried flowers, earthy notes. Palate: rich, flavourful, fresh, good acidity, fine bitter notes.

PEÑA CABALLERA 2010 T
garnacha.

94 Colour: cherry, garnet rim. Nose: spicy, creamy oak, toasty, fragrant herbs, dry stone, fruit liqueur notes. Palate: powerful, flavourful, toasty, round tannins, elegant.

MARAÑONES 2010 T
garnacha.

93 Colour: light cherry. Nose: red berry notes, ripe fruit, fragrant herbs, floral, violets, sweet spices, creamy oak, expressive. Palate: balanced, elegant, flavourful, fresh, fruity. Personality.

TREINTA MIL MARAVEDÍES 2010 T
garnacha, syrah.

92 Colour: bright cherry. Nose: ripe fruit, sweet spices, creamy oak, cocoa bean, caramel. Palate: flavourful, fruity, toasty, fresh, balanced.

LABROS 2010 T
100% garnacha.

91 Colour: bright cherry. Nose: candied fruit, wild herbs, spicy, mineral, earthy notes, expressive. Palate: balanced, flavourful, fresh, fruity, spicy.

BODEGAS CASTEJÓN

Ronda de Watres, 29
28500 Arganda del Rey (Madrid)
☎: +34 918 710 264 - Fax: +34 918 713 343
castejon@bodegascastejon.com
www.bodegascastejon.com

VIÑA REY 2011 B
malvar, viura.

85 Colour: pale. Nose: candied fruit, citrus fruit, white flowers. Palate: flavourful, good acidity.

VIÑA REY 2011 RD
tempranillo.

83

VIÑA REY TEMPRANILLO 2011 T
tempranillo.

81

VIÑA REY "70 BARRICAS" 2010 T
tempranillo.

85 Colour: cherry, garnet rim. Nose: ripe fruit, spicy, creamy oak. Palate: powerful, flavourful, toasty.

TISOL 2010 T
tempranillo.

81

VIÑARDUL 2008 TC
tempranillo.

84

VIÑARDUL 2006 TR
tempranillo.

88 Colour: deep cherry. Nose: creamy oak, nose:tic coffee, dark chocolate. Palate: long, ripe fruit, fine bitter notes.

VIÑARDUL 2001 TGR
tempranillo.

88 Colour: pale ruby, brick rim edge. Nose: spicy, fine reductive notes, wet leather, aged wood nuances, fruit liqueur notes. Palate: spicy, fine tannins, long.

BODEGAS EL REGAJAL

Antigua Ctra. Andalucía, Km. 50,5
28300 Aranjuez (Madrid)
☎: +34 913 078 903 - Fax: +34 913 576 312
isabel@elregajal.es

EL REGAJAL SELECCIÓN ESPECIAL 2010 T
tempranillo, merlot, syrah, cabernet sauvignon.

92 Colour: deep cherry. Nose: fruit expression, overripe fruit, creamy oak, spicy, toasty. Palate: ripe fruit, flavourful, powerful, fine bitter notes, good acidity.

LAS RETAMAS DEL REGAJAL 2010 T
tempranillo, merlot, syrah, cabernet sauvignon.

91 Colour: deep cherry. Nose: ripe fruit, scrubland, toasty, spicy. Palate: flavourful, powerful, fine bitter notes, good acidity.

BODEGAS NUEVA VALVERDE

Domingo de Silos, 6 - bajo
28036 (Madrid)
☎: +34 915 640 191
info@bodegasnuevavalverde.com
www.bodegasnuevavalverde.com

TEJONERAS ALTA SELECCIÓN 2008 T
syrah, cabernet sauvignon, merlot, garnacha.

88 Colour: bright cherry. Nose: sweet spices, creamy oak, ripe fruit. Palate: flavourful, fruity, toasty, round tannins.

750 2006 T
merlot, cabernet sauvignon, syrah, garnacha.

88 Colour: cherry, garnet rim. Nose: ripe fruit, creamy oak. Palate: powerful, flavourful, toasty, round tannins.

BODEGAS ORUSCO

Alcalá, 54
28511 Valdilecha (Madrid)
☎: +34 918 738 006 - Fax: +34 918 738 336
esther@bodegasorusco.com
www.bodegasorusco.com

VIÑA MAÍN 2011 T
85% tempranillo, 15% syrah.

84

MAÍN TEMPRANILLO 2010 T
tempranillo.

83

ARMONIUM 2008 T
70% merlot, 30% cabernet sauvignon.

90 Colour: bright cherry. Nose: ripe fruit, sweet spices, creamy oak, fragrant herbs. Palate: flavourful, fruity, toasty, round tannins, balanced.

MAÍN 2007 TR
100% tempranillo.

84

BODEGAS PABLO MORATE

Avda. Generalísimo, 34
28391 Valdelaguna (Madrid)
☎: +34 918 937 172 - Fax: +34 918 937 172
bodegasmorate@bodegasmorate.com
www.bodegasmorate.com

ARATE 2011 B
macabeo, malvar.

84

VIÑA CHOZO 2011 B
macabeo, malvar.

83

SEÑORÍO DE MORATE GRAN SELECCIÓN 2010 T
tempranillo, syrah.

86 Colour: cherry, purple rim. Nose: red berry notes, floral, fruit preserve. Palate: flavourful, fruity, good acidity.

SEÑORÍO DE MORATE SELECCIÓN 2010 T ROBLE
tempranillo, syrah.

83

SEÑORÍO DE MORATE GRAN SELECCIÓN 2008 TC
tempranillo, syrah.

86 Colour: bright cherry. Nose: toasty, fruit liqueur notes, fruit preserve, spicy. Palate: flavourful, fine bitter notes, warm, round tannins.

SEÑORÍO DE MORATE GRAN SELECCIÓN 2006 TR
tempranillo.

87 Colour: deep cherry. Nose: fruit preserve, spicy, toasty. Palate: fine bitter notes, good acidity, spicy, ripe fruit.

SEÑORÍO DE MORATE SELECCIÓN 2004 TGR
tempranillo, syrah.

87 Colour: pale ruby, brick rim edge. Nose: fruit liqueur notes, fruit liqueur notes, scrubland, spicy. Palate: powerful, flavourful, long.

BODEGAS Y VIÑEDOS PEDRO GARCÍA

Soledad, 10
28380 Colmenar de Oreja (Madrid)
☎: +34 918 943 278 - Fax: +34 918 942 589
byv_pedrogarcia@telefonica.net

PEDRO GARCÍA MALVAR 2011 BFB
malvar, viura.

89 Colour: bright yellow. Nose: powerfull, ripe fruit, sweet spices, creamy oak, fragrant herbs. Palate: rich, smoky afterpalate:, flavourful, fresh, good acidity.

PEDRO GARCÍA MALVAR 2011 B
100% malvar.

84

FEMME SEMIDULCE 2011 B
100% malvar.

84

FEMME SEMIDULCE 2011 RD
100% garnacha.

85 Colour: brilliant rose. Nose: powerfull, red berry notes, ripe fruit. Palate: flavourful, ripe fruit, long, sweet.

LA ROMERA 2010 T JOVEN
merlot, tempranillo, syrah.

86 Colour: bright cherry. Nose: ripe fruit, sweet spices, dark chocolate, cocoa bean. Palate: flavourful, toasty, correct.

SIP 2008 T
syrah, tempranillo.

89 Colour: bright cherry. Nose: ripe fruit, sweet spices, creamy oak. Palate: flavourful, fruity, toasty, round tannins.

ISLA DE SAN PEDRO 2008 TC
syrah, tempranillo.

85 Colour: very deep cherry. Nose: powerfull, ripe fruit, toasty, dark chocolate. Palate: flavourful, powerful, good acidity.

COMANDO G

Villamanin, 27 - 4º E
28011 (Madrid)
☎: +34 696 366 555
daniel@jimenezlandi.com

LA BRUJA AVERÍA 2011 T
100% garnacha.

94 Colour: deep cherry. Nose: fresh fruit, red berry notes, balsamic herbs, scrubland. Palate: good acidity, fine bitter notes, ripe fruit, long.

LAS UMBRÍAS 2010 T
100% garnacha.

93 Colour: bright cherry. Nose: medium intensity, elegant, balanced, red berry notes. Palate: flavourful, fine bitter notes, ripe fruit.

COMERCIAL GRUPO FREIXENET

Joan Sala, 2
08770 Sant Sadurní D'Anoia (Barcelona)
☎: +34 938 917 000 - Fax: +34 938 183 095
freixenet@freixenet.es
www.freixenet.es

HEREDAD TORRESANO 2008 TC
100% tinto fino.

87 Colour: cherry, garnet rim. Nose: ripe fruit, spicy, creamy oak, toasty. Palate: powerful, flavourful, toasty, round tannins.

HEREDAD TORRESANO 2008 T ROBLE
100% tempranillo.

86 Colour: bright cherry. Nose: ripe fruit, spicy, balsamic herbs, creamy oak, cocoa bean, dark chocolate. Palate: flavourful, fruity, toasty, balanced.

LA CUEVA DEL TORRESANO 2007 TC
100% tinto fino.

88 Colour: dark-red cherry, orangey edge. Nose: ripe fruit, balsamic herbs, spicy, aged wood nuances, fine reductive notes. Palate: long, powerful, flavourful, spicy.

FIGUEROA

Convento, 19
28380 Colmenar de Oreja (Madrid)
☎: +34 918 944 859 - Fax: +34 918 944 859
bodegasjesusfigueroa@hotmail.com

FIGUEROA 2011 B
malvar, macabeo, moscatel grano menudo.

86 Colour: bright straw. Nose: fresh, fresh fruit, white flowers. Palate: flavourful, fruity, good acidity, balanced.

FIGUEROA SEMIDULCE 2011 B
macabeo, malvar.

85 Colour: bright straw. Nose: candied fruit, citrus fruit. Palate: flavourful, fine bitter notes, good acidity.

FIGUEROA 2010 T ROBLE
80% tempranillo, 20% merlot.

87 Colour: cherry, garnet rim. Nose: powerfull, ripe fruit, creamy oak, sweet spices. Palate: ripe fruit, spicy, long.

FIGUEROA SYRAH 2010 T
100% syrah.

84

FIGUEROA 2010 T
tempranillo.

84

FIGUEROA 2009 TC
100% tempranillo.

88 Colour: deep cherry. Nose: powerfull, ripe fruit, toasty, creamy oak, sweet spices. Palate: flavourful, powerful, good acidity.

FIGUEROA 2006 TR
100% tempranillo.

84

JESÚS DÍAZ

Convento, 38
28380 Colmenar de Oreja (Madrid)
☎: +34 918 943 378 - Fax: +34 918 944 890
bodegasjdiaz@interbook.net
www.bodegasjesusdiaz.com

CONVENTO SAN BERNARDINO 2011 B
100% malvar.

85 Colour: bright straw. Nose: fresh, white flowers, honeyed notes. Palate: flavourful, fruity, good acidity.

JESÚS DÍAZ 2011 B
malvar.

84

JESÚS DÍAZ 2011 RD
tempranillo.

79

LA CASA DE MONROY

José Moya, 12
45940 Valmojado (Toledo)
☎: +34 918 170 102
info@bodegasmonroy.es
www.bodegasmonroy.es

LA CASA DE MONROY SELECCIÓN VIÑAS VIEJAS 2010 T
95% garnacha, 5% syrah.

90 Colour: cherry, garnet rim. Nose: earthy notes, wild herbs, ripe fruit, fruit liqueur notes, spicy, toasty. Palate: powerful, flavourful, spicy, long.

LA CASA DE MONROY "EL REPISO" 2009 TC
70% tempranillo, 20% cabernet sauvignon, 10% garnacha.

90 Colour: cherry, garnet rim. Nose: ripe fruit, spicy, creamy oak, wild herbs, balsamic herbs. Palate: powerful, flavourful, toasty, round tannins.

LA CASA DE MONROY SELECCIÓN VIÑAS VIEJAS 2008 T
90% garnacha, 5% garnacha tintorera, 5% syrah.

91 Colour: ruby red, orangey edge. Nose: fruit liqueur notes, scrubland, spicy, earthy notes, balanced. Palate: powerful, flavourful, long, balsamic, spicy.

LAS MORADAS DE SAN MARTÍN

Ctra. M-541, Km. 4,7. Pago de Los Castillejos Apdo. Correos 25
28680 San Martín de Valdeiglesias (Madrid)
☎: +34 691 676 570 - Fax: +34 915 417 590
bodega@lasmoradasdesanmartin.es
www.lasmoradasdesanmartin.es

LAS MORADAS DE SAN MARTÍN LAS LUCES 2007 T
100% garnacha.

91 Colour: cherry, garnet rim. Nose: toasty, dark chocolate, fruit liqueur notes, mineral. Palate: fine bitter notes, good acidity, spicy, warm.

LAS MORADAS DE SAN MARTÍN INITIO 2007 T
92% garnacha, 8% cabernet sauvignon, syrah.

89 Colour: cherry, garnet rim. Nose: ripe fruit, spicy, creamy oak. Palate: powerful, flavourful, toasty, round tannins.

PAGOS DE FAMILIA MARQUÉS DE GRIÑÓN

Finca Casa de Vacas - Ctra. CM-4015, Km. 23
45692 Malpica de Tajo (Toledo)
☎: +34 925 597 222 - Fax: +34 925 789 416
service@hotmail.com
www.pagosdefamilia.com

EL RINCÓN 2007 T
95% syrah, 5% garnacha.

90 Colour: cherry, garnet rim. Nose: ripe fruit, spicy, creamy oak, toasty, complex. Palate: powerful, flavourful, toasty, round tannins.

RICARDO BENITO

Las Eras, 5
28600 Navalcarnero (Madrid)
☎: +34 918 110 097 - Fax: +34 918 112 663
bodega@ricardobenito.com
www.ricardobenito.com

TAPÓN DE ORO 2011 B
malvar, moscatel.

87 Colour: bright straw. Nose: powerfull, expressive, citrus fruit, honeyed notes. Palate: flavourful, ripe fruit, easy to drink.

MADRILEÑO DE RICARDO BENITO 2009 T
tempranillo.

85 Colour: cherry, garnet rim. Nose: ripe fruit, spicy, creamy oak, toasty, fine reductive notes. Palate: powerful, flavourful, toasty.

ASIDO 2008 T
tinto fino, merlot, cabernet sauvignon.

90 Colour: deep cherry. Nose: ripe fruit, toasty, dark chocolate. Palate: powerful, fine bitter notes, good acidity.

DIVIDIVO 2008 T

89 Colour: deep cherry, garnet rim. Nose: powerfull, warm, fruit liqueur notes, toasty, spicy. Palate: powerful, flavourful, fine bitter notes.

DIVO 2007 T

93 Colour: cherry, garnet rim. Nose: ripe fruit, spicy, creamy oak, toasty, characterful. Palate: powerful, flavourful, toasty, round tannins.

TAPÓN DE ORO 2007 T
tempranillo, garnacha.

89 Colour: cherry, garnet rim. Nose: spicy, creamy oak, toasty, characterful, ripe fruit. Palate: powerful, flavourful, toasty, round tannins.

DUÁN 2007 T

87 Colour: cherry, garnet rim. Nose: spicy, creamy oak, toasty, characterful, fruit liqueur notes. Palate: powerful, flavourful, toasty, round tannins.

S.A.T. 1431 SAN ESTEBAN PROTOMÁRTIR

Pza. de los Caños, 30-46
28650 Cenicientos (Madrid)
☎: +34 918 642 487 - Fax: +34 918 642 487
sanesteban@918642487.e.telefonica.net

PIEDRA ESCRITA 2011 RD
garnacha, tempranillo.

80

PIEDRA ESCRITA 2011 T
garnacha, tempranillo.

84

SEÑORÍO DE VAL AZUL

Urb. Valgrande, 37
28370 Chinchón (Madrid)
☎: +34 616 005 565 - Fax: +34 915 445 520
evaayuso@arrakis.es
www.senoriodevalazul.es

FABIO 2008 T
36% syrah, 47% cabernet sauvignon, 10% merlot, 7% tempranillo.

87 Colour: cherry, garnet rim. Nose: ripe fruit, toasty, dark chocolate, sweet spices. Palate: powerful, flavourful, toasty.

VAL AZUL 2008 T
60% cabernet sauvignon, 15% syrah, 25% merlot, 5% tempranillo.

84

VAL AZUL 2007 T
syrah, cabernet sauvignon, merlot, tempranillo.

85 Colour: cherry, garnet rim. Nose: ripe fruit, spicy, creamy oak, wet leather. Palate: powerful, flavourful, toasty.

FABIO 2007 T
syrah, cabernet sauvignon, tempranillo.

84

SOLERA BODEGAS

Arco, 14
28380 Colmenar de Oreja (Madrid)
☎: +34 918 943 407 - Fax: +34 918 943 407
info@solerabodegas.com
www.solerabodegas.com

JULIO HERRERO 2010 B
malvar.

83

MOURIZ VENDIMIA 2009 T
tempranillo.

86 Colour: deep cherry. Nose: powerfull, candied fruit, spicy, creamy oak. Palate: powerful, fine bitter notes, ripe fruit.

MOURIZ 2008 T BARRICA
tempranillo.

87 Colour: cherry, garnet rim. Nose: ripe fruit, spicy, creamy oak, balsamic herbs. Palate: powerful, flavourful, spicy.

TAGONIUS

Ctra. Ambite, Km. 4,4
28550 Tielmes (Madrid)
☎: +34 918 737 505 - Fax: +34 918 746 161
director@tagonius.com
www.tagonius.com

TAGONIUS 2010 T ROBLE
merlot, tempranillo, syrah, cabernet sauvignon.

89 Colour: bright cherry. Nose: ripe fruit, sweet spices, creamy oak, balsamic herbs, earthy notes. Palate: flavourful, fruity, toasty.

TAGONIUS SYRAH 2008 T
syrah.

89 Colour: cherry, garnet rim. Nose: floral, ripe fruit, fragrant herbs, spicy, creamy oak. Palate: fresh, flavourful, long, spicy, round tannins.

TAGONIUS 2008 TC
cabernet sauvignon, merlot, tempranillo, syrah.

87 Colour: cherry, garnet rim. Nose: ripe fruit, toasty, balsamic herbs, fine reductive notes, waxy notes. Palate: powerful, flavourful, toasty, round tannins.

TAGONIUS MERLOT 2006 T
merlot.

90 Colour: pale ruby, brick rim edge. Nose: fruit liqueur notes, fruit liqueur notes, fragrant herbs, old leather, cigar, tobacco. Palate: spicy, balsamic, powerful, flavourful, long, balanced.

TAGONIUS MARIAGE 2005 T
tempranillo, merlot.

90 Colour: ruby red, orangey edge. Nose: ripe fruit, fruit liqueur notes, scrubland, fine reductive notes. Palate: long, balsamic, spicy, spirituous, round.

TAGONIUS 2004 TR
merlot, tempranillo, syrah, cabernet sauvignon.

91 Colour: pale ruby, brick rim edge. Nose: spicy, fine reductive notes, wet leather, aged wood nuances, fruit liqueur notes, toasty. Palate: fine tannins, long, spicy, balsamic.

UVAS FELICES

Agullers, 7
08003 Barcelona (Barcelona)
☎: +34 902 327 777
www.vilaviniteca.es

EL HOMBRE BALA 2010 T
100% garnacha.

94 Colour: deep cherry. Nose: spicy, ripe fruit, fruit expression, balsamic herbs, scrubland. Palate: fine bitter notes, round tannins, good acidity.

VALLE DEL SOL S.A.T. 4478

Ctra. de Cadalso de los Vidrios, Km. 0,3
28600 Navalcarnero (Madrid)
☎: +34 918 101 075 - Fax: +34 918 110 926
valledelsol@bodegasvalledelsol.com

LOS CASTINES 2011 RD
garnacha.

85 Colour: rose, purple rim. Nose: powerfull, ripe fruit, red berry notes, floral, lactic notes. Palate: , powerful, fresh, flavourful.

VALDECEPA 2011 RD JOVEN
garnacha.

84

ANTÏNOS 2011 T ROBLE
cabernet sauvignon.

87 Colour: bright cherry. Nose: sweet spices, creamy oak, balsamic herbs, ripe fruit. Palate: fruity, toasty, powerful.

LOS CASTINES 2011 T

87 Colour: cherry, purple rim. Nose: fresh fruit, red berry notes, floral. Palate: flavourful, fruity, good acidity, round tannins.

VALDECEPA 2011 T JOVEN
tempranillo, garnacha, syrah.

86 Colour: cherry, purple rim. Nose: powerfull, ripe fruit, red berry notes. Palate: flavourful, fruity, good acidity.

ANTÏNOS 2010 T ROBLE

87 Colour: deep cherry. Nose: spicy, toasty, ripe fruit. Palate: flavourful, powerful, spicy.

VINÍCOLA DE ARGANDA SOCIEDAD COOPERATIVA MADRILEÑA

Camino de San Martín de la Vega, 16
28500 Arganda del Rey (Madrid)
☎: +34 918 710 201 - Fax: +34 918 710 201
vinicola@cvarganda.e.telefonica.net
www.vinicoladearganda.com

PAGO VILCHES 2011 B
100% malvar.

83

BALADÍ 2010 BFB
100% malvar.

84

PAGO VILCHES 2011 RD
100% tempranillo.

82

VIÑA RENDERO S.C. T
100% tempranillo.

80

VIÑA RENDERO SELECCIÓN ESPECIAL 2010 T ROBLE
100% tempranillo.

88 Colour: bright cherry. Nose: ripe fruit, sweet spices, creamy oak. Palate: flavourful, fruity, toasty, round tannins.

PAGO VILCHES 2010 T
100% tempranillo.

84

PERUCO 2007 TR
100% tempranillo.

89 Colour: cherry, garnet rim. Nose: spicy, creamy oak, toasty, candied fruit, characterful. Palate: powerful, flavourful, toasty, round tannins.

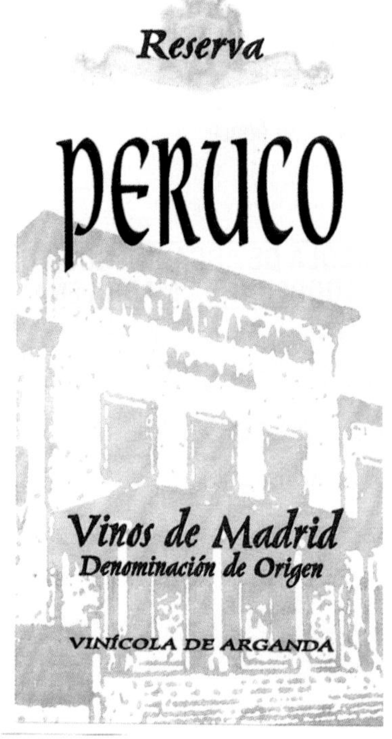

VIÑA RENDERO 2007 TC
100% tempranillo.

84

VINOS JEROMÍN

San José, 8
28590 Villarejo de Salvanés (Madrid)
☎: +34 918 742 030 - Fax: +34 918 744 139
comercial@vinosjeromin.com
www.vinosjeromin.com

PUERTA DEL SOL MALVAR 2011 BFB
malvar.

85 Colour: bright yellow. Nose: powerfull, ripe fruit, sweet spices, creamy oak. Palate: rich, flavourful, fresh.

PUERTA DE ALCALÁ 2011 B
malvar.

85 Colour: bright straw. Nose: fresh, fresh fruit, white flowers. Palate: flavourful, fruity, good acidity, balanced.

PUERTA DEL SOL MALVAR 2011 B
malvar.

85 Colour: bright straw. Nose: fresh, fresh fruit, white flowers, dried herbs. Palate: flavourful, fruity, good acidity, correct.

GREGO MOSCATEL SECO 2011 B
moscatel grano menudo.

84

PUERTA CERRADA 2011 B
malvar, airén.

83

PUERTA CERRADA 2011 RD
tempranillo, garnacha, malvar.

84

PUERTA DE ALCALÁ 2011 RD
tempranillo, garnacha.

84

PUERTA DEL SOL 2 2011 T JOVEN
tempranillo, syrah, merlot.

86 Colour: cherry, garnet rim. Nose: ripe fruit, balsamic herbs, medium intensity. Palate: powerful, flavourful, balsamic, easy to drink.

PUERTA DE ALCALÁ 2011 T
tempranillo, syrah.

85 Colour: cherry, purple rim. Nose: red berry notes, floral, wild herbs. Palate: flavourful, balsamic, correct.

GREGO GARNACHA CENTENARIAS 2010 T ROBLE
garnacha.

85 Colour: cherry, garnet rim. Nose: characterful, ripe fruit, toasty, spicy. Palate: flavourful, powerful, fine bitter notes.

PUERTA DEL SOL TEMPRANILLO 2010 TC
tempranillo.

84

GREGO 2009 TC
tempranillo, syrah, garnacha.

90 Colour: bright cherry. Nose: sweet spices, creamy oak, ripe fruit. Palate: flavourful, fruity, toasty, round tannins.

PUERTA DE ALCALÁ 2009 TC
tempranillo.

90 Colour: cherry, garnet rim. Nose: sweet spices, toasty, ripe fruit, scrubland. Palate: flavourful, powerful, fine bitter notes.

PUERTA DEL SOL VARIETALES 2009 TC
cabernet sauvignon, merlot.

88 Colour: bright cherry. Nose: sweet spices, creamy oak, overripe fruit. Palate: flavourful, fruity, toasty, round tannins.

GREGO 2009 T ROBLE
tempranillo, syrah.

87 Colour: very deep cherry. Nose: fruit preserve, warm, toasty, spicy, dark chocolate. Palate: flavourful, powerful, fine bitter notes, round tannins.

FÉLIX MARTÍNEZ CEPAS VIEJAS 2008 TR
90% tempranillo, 10% otras.

90 Colour: bright cherry. Nose: ripe fruit, sweet spices, creamy oak, expressive. Palate: flavourful, fruity, toasty, round tannins, balanced.

DOS DE MAYO EDICIÓN LIMITADA 2008 TC
tempranillo.

88 Colour: cherry, garnet rim. Nose: ripe fruit, spicy, creamy oak, toasty. Palate: powerful, flavourful, toasty, round tannins.

MANU VINO DE AUTOR 2007 TC
tempranillo, syrah, garnacha, cabernet sauvignon, merlot.

90 Colour: cherry, garnet rim. Nose: spicy, creamy oak, toasty, characterful, ripe fruit. Palate: powerful, flavourful, toasty, round tannins.

DO YCODEN-DAUTE-ISORA

La Guancha
SANTA CRUZ DE TENERIFE
Consejo Regulador
DO Boundary

LOCATION:

Occupying the northeast of the island of Tenerife and comprising the municipal districts of San Juan de La Rambla, La Guancha, Icod de los Vinos, Los Silos, El Tanque, Garachico, Buenavista del Norte, Santiago del Teide and Guía de Isora.

CLIMATE:

Mediterranean, characterised by the multitude of microclimates depending on the altitude and other geographical conditions. The trade winds provide the humidity necessary for the development of the vines. The average annual temperature is 19°C and the average annual rainfall is around 540 mm.

SOIL:

Volcanic ash and rock on the higher grounds, and clayey lower down. The vines are cultivated at very different heights, ranging from 50 to 1,400 m.

GRAPE VARIETIES:

WHITE: *Bermejuela* (or *Marmajuelo*), *Güal, Malvasía, Moscatel, Pedro Ximénez, Verdello, Vijariego, Albillo, Bastardo Blanco, Forastera Blanca, Listán Blanco* (majority), *Sabro* and *Torrontés.*
RED: *Tintilla, Listán Negro* (majority), *Malvasía Rosada, Negramoll Castellana, Bastardo Negra, Moscatel Negra* and *Vijariego Negra.*

FIGURES:

Vineyard surface: 262 – **Wine-Growers:** 576 – **Wineries:** 18 – **2011 Harvest rating:** Very Good – **Production:** 296,000 litres – **Market percentages:** 96% domestic. 4% export

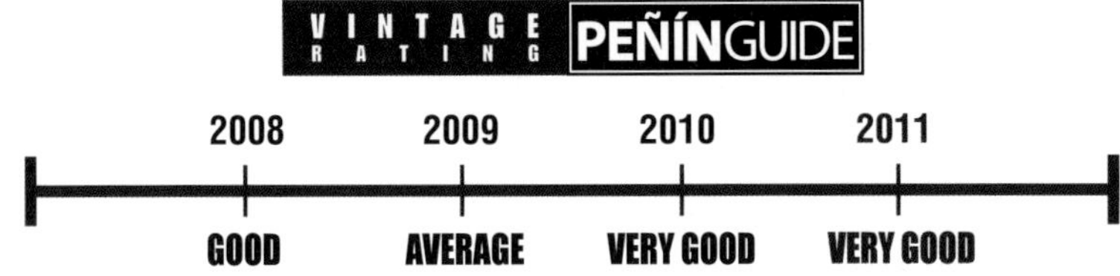

CONSEJO REGULADOR
La Palmita, 10 - 38440 La Guancha (Sta. Cruz de Tenerife) - ☎: +34 922 130 246 - Fax: +34 922 828 159
@ ycoden@ycoden.com / promocion@ycoden.com - www.ycoden.com

BODEGA COMARCAL DE ICOD

Camino Cuevas del Rey, 1
38430 Icod de los Vinos (Santa Cruz de Tenerife)
☎: +34 922 122 395 - Fax: +34 922 814 688
icod@bodegasinsularestenerife.es
www.bodegasinsularestenerife.es

TÁGARA 2011 B
listán blanco.

88 Colour: bright straw. Nose: fresh fruit, fragrant herbs, citrus fruit, medium intensity. Palate: flavourful, fruity, fresh, fine bitter notes.

TÁGARA AFRUTADO 2011 B
listán blanco.

86 Colour: bright straw. Nose: medium intensity, fresh, fresh fruit, floral. Palate: correct, good acidity.

TÁGARA MALVASÍA MARMAJUELO 2010 B
marmajuelo, malvasía.

86 Colour: bright straw. Nose: medium intensity, fresh, floral. Palate: flavourful, powerful, ripe fruit.

EL ANCÓN 2011 T
listán negro.

89 Colour: cherry, purple rim. Nose: red berry notes, ripe fruit, powerfull, expressive, balanced. Palate: good structure, fruity, flavourful, good acidity.

EL ANCÓN 2011 T BARRICA
listán negro, tintilla.

88 Colour: bright cherry, purple rim. Nose: sweet spices, red berry notes, balanced. Palate: good structure, ripe fruit.

EL ANCÓN 2011 T
tintilla.

88 Colour: cherry, purple rim. Nose: expressive, fragrant herbs, ripe fruit. Palate: flavourful, fruity, good acidity, spicy.

MIRADERO 2011 BLANCO AFRUTADO
listán blanco.

86 Colour: bright straw. Nose: medium intensity, dried herbs. Palate: correct, flavourful, fruity, good finish, sweetness.

BODEGA VIÑA ENGRACIA

Paseo La Centinela, 53
38430 Icod de los Vinos (Santa Cruz de Tenerife)
☎: +34 922 810 857 - Fax: +34 922 860 895
vinosengracia@hotmail.com

VIÑA ENGRACIA 2011 B

85 Colour: bright straw, greenish rim. Nose: dried herbs, faded flowers, citrus fruit. Palate: fruity, correct, easy to drink.

VIÑA ENGRACIA 2011 T

76

BODEGA VIÑA ZANATA

El Sol, 3
38440 La Guancha (Santa Cruz de Tenerife)
☎: +34 922 828 166 - Fax: +34 922 828 166
zanata@zanata.net
www.zanata.net

VIÑA ZANATA 2011 B
listán blanco.

84

VIÑA ZANATA MALVASÍA SECO 2011 B
malvasía.

84

VIÑA ZANATA MARMAJUELO 2011 B
marmajuelo.

81

VIÑA ZANATA 2011 RD
listán negro.

74

VIÑA ZANATA TARA TINTILLA 2009 T
tintilla.

85 Colour: cherry, garnet rim. Nose: powerfull, wild herbs. Palate: correct, fruity, fine bitter notes.

VIÑA ZANATA MALVASÍA 2009 BLANCO DULCE
malvasía.

88 Colour: old gold. Nose: balanced, candied fruit, pattiserie, sweet spices. Palate: rich, flavourful, fruity, balanced.

BODEGAS ACEVIÑO

La Patita, 63
38430 Icod de los Vinos (Santa Cruz de Tenerife)
☎: +34 922 810 237 - Fax: +34 922 810 237
bodegasacevino@yahoo.es

ACEVIÑO 2011 B

86 Colour: bright straw. Nose: balanced, medium intensity, white flowers. Palate: flavourful, fruity, good finish.

ACEVIÑO SEMISECO 2011 B

84

ACEVIÑO 2011 B

83

ACEVIÑO AFRUTADO 2011 B

82

ACEVIÑO 2011 T

81

ACEVIÑO 2011 T BARRICA

78

BODEGAS VIÑAMONTE

Avda. Villanueva, 34
38440 La Guancha (Santa Cruz de Tenerife)
☎: +34 922 130 037 - Fax: +34 922 130 037
bodegasvmonte@hotmail.com

VIÑAMONTE DULCE 2011 B
80% listán blanco, 20% otras.

85 Colour: bright straw. Nose: medium intensity, fresh, balanced, dried flowers. Palate: flavourful, fruity, good finish.

VIÑAMONTE AFRUTADO 2011 B
100% listán blanco.

82

VIÑAMONTE DULCE 2010 B
80% listán blanco, 20% otras.

87 Colour: bright yellow. Nose: candied fruit, balanced, complex, faded flowers. Palate: ripe fruit, balanced.

VIÑAMONTE 2011 T
100% listán negro.

80

VIÑAMONTE DULCE 2010 T
70% listán negro, 30% otras.

86 Colour: bright cherry, garnet rim. Nose: grassy, powerfull, toasty. Palate: fruity, flavourful, balanced, spicy.

BODEGAS VIÑÁTIGO

Cabo Verde, s/n
38440 La Guancha (Santa Cruz de Tenerife)
☎: +34 922 828 768 - Fax: +34 922 829 936
vinatigo@vinatigo.com
www.vinatigo.com

VIÑÁTIGO MARMAJUELO 2011 B
100% marmajuelo.

89 Colour: bright yellow. Nose: fresh fruit, white flowers, citrus fruit, fragrant herbs. Palate: fresh, flavourful, long, good acidity.

VIÑÁTIGO MALVASÍA 2011 B
100% malvasía.

86 Colour: bright straw. Nose: wild herbs, fresh, medium intensity. Palate: flavourful, fruity, sweetness.

VIÑÁTIGO GUAL 2010 B
100% gual.

89 Colour: bright straw. Nose: white flowers, fresh fruit, citrus fruit, expressive, neat. Palate: balanced, good acidity, fruity.

VIÑÁTIGO VIJARIEGO 2008 BFB
100% vijariego blanco.

85 Colour: bright yellow. Nose: medium intensity, spicy, candied fruit, citrus fruit. Palate: powerful, flavourful, spicy.

VIÑÁTIGO MALVASÍA CLÁSICO 2007 B
100% malvasía.

88 Colour: bright yellow. Nose: medium intensity, balanced, ripe fruit, floral, complex. Palate: rich, full, flavourful.

VIÑÁTIGO BABOSO 2010 T
100% baboso negro.

86 Colour: cherry, garnet rim. Nose: ripe fruit, spicy, balsamic herbs. Palate: fruity, flavourful, good acidity.

VIÑÁTIGO TINTILLA 2008 T ROBLE
100% tintilla.

87 Colour: bright cherry, orangey edge. Nose: ripe fruit, spicy, toasty. Palate: balanced, spicy, ripe fruit, good acidity, fine bitter notes.

C.B. LUIS, ANTONIO Y JAVIER LÓPEZ DE AYALA

El Majuelos, 2
38450 Garachico (Santa Cruz de Tenerife)
☎: +34 922 133 079 - Fax: +34 922 830 066
jlopezaz38@hotmail.es

HACIENDA SAN JUAN 2011 B
100% malvasía.

84

HACIENDA SAN JUAN 2011 BN
100% malvasía.

79

CUEVA DEL REY

Camino Cuevas del Rey, 8
38430 Icod de los Vinos (Santa Cruz de Tenerife)
☎: +34 670 243 354 - Fax: +34 922 121 414

CUEVA DEL REY 2011 B
listán blanco.

83

CUEVA DEL REY 2011 RD
listán negro.

80

TINOCA

Camino Las Suertes, 18
38430 Icod de los Vinos (Santa Cruz de Tenerife)
☎: +34 658 992 743 - Fax: +34 922 335 002
vinotinoca@gmail.com
www.vinotinoca.com

TINOCA MALVASÍA 2009 BLANCO DULCE

89 Colour: bright yellow. Nose: candied fruit, jasmine, expressive, sweet spices. Palate: flavourful, balanced, rich.

VIÑA SPINOLA

Camino Esparragal, s/n
38470 Los Silos (Santa Cruz de Tenerife)
☎: +34 922 840 977 - Fax: +34 922 840 977

VIÑA SPINOLA 2011 B

74

VIÑA SPINOLA MALVASÍA SECO 2010 B

83

VIÑA SPINOLA MALVASÍA SECO 2009 B

82

VIÑA SPINOLA MALVASÍA SECO 2008 B

87 Colour: old gold, amber rim. Nose: candied fruit, toasty, neat. Palate: fruity, flavourful, balanced.

VIÑA SPINOLA MALVASÍA SECO 2004 B

87 Colour: bright golden. Nose: wild herbs, candied fruit, balanced, spicy. Palate: light-bodied, good acidity.

VIÑA SPINOLA MALVASÍA SECO 2003 B

87 Colour: bright golden. Nose: medium intensity, balanced, wild herbs. Palate: flavourful, spicy, good acidity.

VIÑA SPINOLA MALVASÍA SECO 2002 B

85 Colour: bright golden. Nose: candied fruit, spicy, faded flowers. Palate: powerful, flavourful, sweetness.

VIÑA SPINOLA 2011 RD

81

DO YECLA

LOCATION:

In the northeast of the province of Murcia, within the plateau region, and comprising a single municipal district, Yecla.

CLIMATE:

Continental, with a slight Mediterranean influence, with hot summers and cold winters, and little rainfall, which is usually around 300 mm per annum.

SOIL:

Fundamentally deep limestone, with good permeability. The vineyards are on undulating terrain at a height of between 400 m and 800 m above sea level.

GRAPE VARIETIES:

WHITE: *Merseguera, Airén, Macabeo, Malvasía, Chardonnay.*
RED: *Monastrell* (majority 85% of total), *Garnacha Tinta, Cabernet Sauvignon, Cencibel* (*Tempranillo*), *Merlot, Tintorera, Syrah.*

SUB-REGIONS:

Yecla Campo Arriba, with Monastrell as the most common variety and alcohol contents of up to 14°, and **Yecla Campo Abajo,** whose grapes produce a lower alcohol content (around 12° for reds and 11.5° for whites).

FIGURES:

Vineyard surface: 5,900 – **Wine-Growers:** 501 – **Wineries:** 8 – **2011 Harvest rating:** Excellent – **Production:** 7,101,000 litres – **Market percentages:** 12% domestic. 88% export

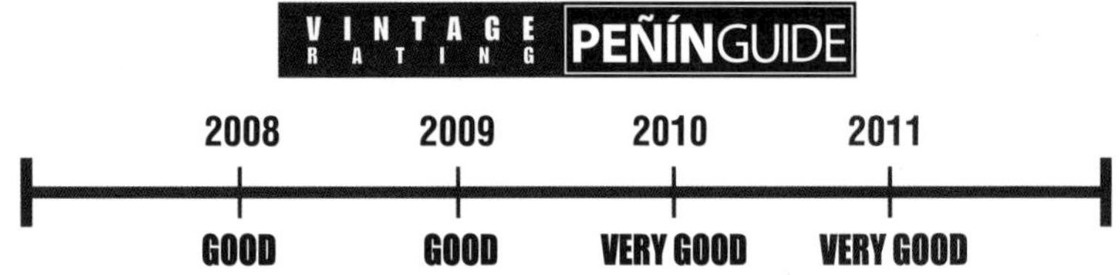

CONSEJO REGULADOR
Centro de Desarrollo Local - Poeta Francisco A. Jiménez, s/n - P.I. Urbayecla II - 30510 Yecla (Murcia)
☎: +34 968 792 352 - Fax: +34 968 792 352
@ indo@yeclavino.com - www.yeclavino.com

BODEGAS CASTAÑO

Ctra. Fuenteálamo, 3 - Apdo. 120
30510 Yecla (Murcia)
☎: +34 968 791 115 - Fax: +34 968 791 900
info@bodegascastano.com
www.bodegascastano.com

CASTAÑO MACABEO CHARDONNAY 2011 B
chardonnay, macabeo.

87 Colour: bright straw. Nose: citrus fruit, ripe fruit, faded flowers. Palate: fine bitter notes, flavourful, warm.

CASTAÑO MONASTRELL 2011 RD JOVEN
monastrell.

83

CASTAÑO MONASTRELL 2011 T
100% monastrell.

89 Colour: cherry, purple rim. Nose: fresh fruit, red berry notes, floral, grassy. Palate: flavourful, fruity, good acidity, round tannins.

CASA CISCA 2010 T
100% monastrell.

96 Colour: cherry, garnet rim. Nose: spicy, creamy oak, toasty, complex, expressive, ripe fruit, lactic notes. Palate: powerful, flavourful, toasty, round tannins.

HÉCULA 2010 T
100% monastrell.

88 Colour: cherry, garnet rim. Nose: overripe fruit, varietal, spicy. Palate: powerful, concentrated, spicy.

CASTAÑO COLECCIÓN 2009 T
75% monastrell, 25% cabernet sauvignon.

92 Colour: cherry, garnet rim. Nose: ripe fruit, spicy, creamy oak, toasty, complex. Taste powerful, flavourful, toasty, round tannins.

CASTAÑO MONASTRELL DULCE 2009 T
100% monastrell.

90 Colour: cherry, garnet rim. Nose: spicy, toasty, ripe fruit, dried fruit, dark chocolate. Palate: powerful, flavourful, complex.

POZUELO 2009 TC
60% monastrell, 20% cabernet sauvignon, 10% syrah, 10% garnacha tintorera.

88 Colour: cherry, garnet rim. Nose: spicy, creamy oak, toasty, red berry notes. Palate: powerful, flavourful, toasty, long.

POZUELO 2008 TR

90 Colour: cherry, garnet rim. Nose: ripe fruit, mineral, balsamic herbs, dark chocolate, cocoa bean, creamy oak. Palate: spicy, long, flavourful, toasty.

VIÑA AL LADO DE LA CASA 2008 T

89 Colour: cherry, garnet rim. Nose: ripe fruit, earthy notes, balsamic herbs, spicy. Palate: powerful, flavourful, long, toasty.

VIÑA DETRÁS DE LA CASA SYRAH 2007 T
syrah.

94 Colour: cherry, garnet rim. Nose: expressive, earthy notes, ripe fruit, spicy. Palate: powerful, flavourful, complex, balanced, long, toasty.

VIÑA DETRÁS DE LA CASA CABERNET SAUVIGNON-TINTORERA 2007 TC

93 Colour: cherry, garnet rim. Nose: ripe fruit, expressive, balsamic herbs, earthy notes, creamy oak. Palate: powerful, flavourful, long, toasty.

BODEGAS LA PURÍSIMA

Ctra. de Pinoso, 3
30510 Yecla (Murcia)
☎: +34 968 751 257 - Fax: +34 968 795 116
info@bodegaslapurisima.com
www.bodegaslapurisima.com

ESTÍO MACABEO 2011 B
80% macabeo, 20% sauvignon blanc.

83

ESTÍO 2011 RD
70% monastrell, 20% syrah, 10% tempranillo.

85 Colour: rose, purple rim. Nose: ripe fruit, red berry notes, floral. Palate: , powerful, fruity, fresh.

VALCORSO SYRAH 2011 T
100% syrah.

89 Colour: cherry, purple rim. Nose: raspberry, red berry notes, floral. Palate: powerful, fresh, fruity, flavourful.

VALCORSO ECOLÓGICO 2011 T
70% monastrell, 30% syrah.

86 Colour: cherry, purple rim. Nose: red berry notes, floral, ripe fruit. Palate: flavourful, fruity, good acidity, round tannins.

ESTÍO 2011 T
60% monastrell, 10% cabernet sauvignon, 20% syrah, 10% merlot.

85 Colour: cherry, purple rim. Nose: expressive, floral, ripe fruit, red berry notes. Palate: flavourful, fruity, good acidity.

VALCORSO MONASTRELL 2010 T BARRICA
100% monastrell.

87 Colour: bright cherry. Nose: ripe fruit, sweet spices, creamy oak, expressive. Taste flavourful, fruity, toasty, round tannins.

ESTÍO MONASTRELL ECOLÓGICO 2010 T BARRICA
70% monastrell, 30% syrah.

84

IV EXPRESIÓN 2008 T
80% monastrell, 15% syrah, 5% garnacha tintorera.

86 Colour: cherry, garnet rim. Nose: ripe fruit, scrubland, fruit liqueur notes, fine reductive notes. Palate: balanced, flavourful, long.

TRAPÍO 2008 T
100% monastrell.

85 Colour: pale ruby, brick rim edge. Nose: fine reductive notes, wet leather, fruit liqueur notes, creamy oak. Palate: spicy, fine tannins, elegant, long.

IGLESIA VIEJA 2006 TC
70% monastrell, 20% syrah, 10% tempranillo.

83

IGLESIA VIEJA 2004 TR
80% monastrell, 20% cabernet sauvignon.

85 Colour: deep cherry, orangey edge. Nose: ripe fruit, spicy, toasty, old leather. Palate: powerful, flavourful, toasty, round tannins.

BODEGAS SEÑORÍO DE BARAHONDA

Ctra. de Pinoso, km. 3
30510 Yecla (Murcia)
☎: +34 968 718 696 - Fax: +34 968 790 928
info@barahonda.com
www.barahonda.com

BARAHONDA 2011 B
macabeo.

85 Colour: bright straw. Nose: white flowers, ripe fruit, wild herbs. Palate: fresh, fruity, flavourful.

BARAHONDA 2011 RD
monastrell.

82

BARAHONDA MONASTRELL 2011 T
monastrell.

87 Colour: cherry, purple rim. Nose: red berry notes, ripe fruit, floral, fresh. Palate: correct, fruity, flavourful.

CARRO 2011 T
monastrell, syrah, merlot, tempranillo.

85 Colour: cherry, purple rim. Nose: ripe fruit, red berry notes, scrubland. Palate: flavourful, powerful, concentrated.

59H 35' 03" 2010 T

91 Colour: bright cherry. Nose: ripe fruit, sweet spices, creamy oak. Palate: flavourful, fruity, toasty, round tannins.

BARAHONDA BARRICA 2010 T BARRICA
monastrell, syrah.

87 Colour: bright cherry. Nose: ripe fruit, sweet spices, creamy oak, expressive. Palate: flavourful, fruity, toasty.

NIREA 2010 T

87 Colour: cherry, garnet rim. Nose: spicy, overripe fruit, fruit liqueur notes. Palate: flavourful, spicy, good finish.

HEREDAD CANDELA MONASTRELL 2010 T
monastrell.

86 Colour: cherry, garnet rim. Nose: ripe fruit, sweet spices, scrubland. Palate: flavourful, fine bitter notes, good acidity.

BARAHONDA 2009 TC
monastrell, syrah.

88 Colour: cherry, garnet rim. Nose: ripe fruit, spicy, creamy oak, toasty, complex. Taste powerful, flavourful, toasty, round tannins.

ZONA ZEPA 2008 T

90 Colour: cherry, garnet rim. Nose: spicy, creamy oak, toasty, ripe fruit. Palate: powerful, flavourful, toasty, round tannins.

CUEVA NEGRA 2008 T
70% monastrell, 15% syrah, 15% garnacha.

85 Colour: deep cherry. Nose: powerfull, overripe fruit, fruit liqueur notes, roasted coffee, dark chocolate. Palate: powerful, sweetness, fine bitter notes.

BELLUM EL REMATE 2006 T

87 Colour: deep cherry. Nose: sweet spices, dark chocolate, candied fruit. Palate: powerful, flavourful, concentrated.

DANIEL ALBA BODEGAS

Avda. Córdoba, 25
30510 Yecla (Murcia)
☎: +34 628 687 673
info@danielalbabodegas.com
www.danielalbabodegas.com

LA MÁQUINA MONASTRELL 2009 T
85% monastrell, 8% syrah, 7% garnacha tintorera.

89 Colour: cherry, garnet rim. Nose: red berry notes, overripe fruit, spicy, roasted coffee. Palate: powerful, flavourful, long.

LONG WINES

Avda. del Monte, 46
28120 Algete (Madrid)
☎: +34 916 221 305 - Fax: +34 916 220 029
www.longwines.com

CASA DEL CANTO 2009 T ROBLE
monastrell, syrah, cabernet sauvignon.

89 Colour: cherry, garnet rim. Nose: red berry notes, sweet spices, creamy oak, expressive. Palate: powerful, flavourful, complex.

CASA DEL CANTO 2007 TR
monastrell, cabernet sauvignon, syrah.

89 Colour: cherry, garnet rim. Nose: ripe fruit, spicy, creamy oak, toasty. Palate: powerful, flavourful, toasty, round tannins.

TRENZA WINES

Avda. Matías Saenz Tejada, s/n. Edif. Fuengirola Center - Local 1
29640 Fuengirola (Málaga)
☎: +34 615 343 320 - Fax: +34 952 588 467
david@vinnico.com
www.trenzawines.com

LA NYMPHINA 2011 T
100% monastrell.

90 Colour: bright cherry. Nose: ripe fruit, sweet spices, scrubland. Palate: flavourful, fruity, toasty, round tannins.

TRENZA Z-STRAND 2009 T
85% syrah, 10% cabernet sauvignon, 5% monastrell.

89 Colour: cherry, garnet rim. Nose: spicy, toasty, complex, overripe fruit. Palate: powerful, flavourful, toasty, round tannins.

TRENZA FAMILY COLLECTION 2009 T
58% monastrell, 24% cabernet sauvignon, 12% syrah, 6% garnacha tintorera.

93 Colour: cherry, garnet rim. Nose: ripe fruit, spicy, creamy oak, toasty, complex. Taste powerful, flavourful, toasty, round tannins.

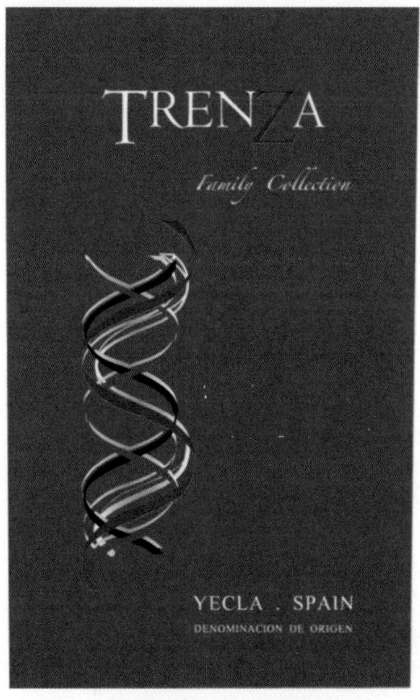

VINNICO EXPORT

Muela, 16
03730 Jávea (Alicante)
☎: +34 965 791 967 - Fax: +34 966 461 471
info@vinnico.com
www.vinnico.com

PAU 2011 B
50% macabeo, 50% sauvignon blanc.

84

PAU 2011 T
100% monastrell.

87 Colour: cherry, purple rim. Nose: red berry notes, ripe fruit, fresh. Palate: powerful, flavourful, fruity.

FLOR DEL MONTGÓ ORGANIC MONASTRELL 2011 T
100% monastrell.

87 Colour: cherry, purple rim. Nose: red berry notes, ripe fruit, wild herbs. Palate: powerful, fruity, flavourful.

FINCA ROSAL 2010 T
100% monastrell.

87 Colour: cherry, garnet rim. Nose: ripe fruit, spicy, toasty. Palate: powerful, flavourful, toasty, round tannins.

MONTGÓ 2010 T
70% monastrell, 20% syrah, 10% cabernet sauvignon.

85 Colour: cherry, garnet rim. Nose: red berry notes, ripe fruit, toasty, spicy. Palate: correct, flavourful, powerful.

MONTGÓ BARREL SELECT 2008 T
54% monastrell, 27% cabernet sauvignon, 12% syrah, 7% garnacha tintorera.

87 Colour: cherry, garnet rim. Nose: ripe fruit, spicy, creamy oak, characterful. Palate: powerful, flavourful, toasty, round tannins.

The "Vinos de Pago" are linked to a single winery, and it is a status given to that winery on the grounds of unique micro-climatic features and proven evidence of consistent high quality over the years, with the goal to produce wines of sheer singularity. So far, only 14 "Vinos de Pago" labels have been granted for different autonomous regions (Aragón, La Mancha, Comunidad Valenciana and Navarra). The "Vinos de Pago" category has the same status as a DO. This "pago" should not be confused with the other "pago" term used in the wine realm, which refers to a plot, a smaller vineyard within a bigger property. The "Pagos de España" association was formed in 2000 when a group of small producers of single estate wines got together to defend the singularity of their wines. In 2003, the association became Grandes Pagos de España, responding to the request of many colleagues in other parts of the country who wished to make the single-growth concept better known, and to seek excellence through the direct relationship between wines and their places of origin.

PAGO AYLÉS: Situated in the municipality of Mezalocha (Zaragoza), within the limits of the Cariñena appellation. The production area is located within the Ebro basin, principally around the depression produced by the River Huerva. The soils consist of limestone, marl and composites. The climate is temperate continental with low average annual rainfall figures of 350 to 550mm. The varieties authorized for the production of red and rosé wines are: garnacha, merlot, tempranillo and cabernet sauvignon.

PAGO CALZADILLA: Located in the Mayor river valley, in the part of the Alcarria region that belongs to the province of Cuenca, it enjoys altitude levels ranging between 845 and 1005 meters. The vines are mostly planted on limestone soils with pronounced slopes (with up to a 40% incline), so terraces and slant plots have become the most common feature, following the altitude gradients. The grape varieties planted are tempranillo, cabernet-sauvignon, garnacha and syrah.

PAGO CAMPO DE LA GUARDIA: The vineyards are in the town of La Guardia, to the northeast of the province of Toledo, on a high plateau known as Mesa de Ocaña. Soils are deep and with varying degrees of loam, clay and sand. The climate follows a continental pattern, with hot and dry summers and particularly dry and cold winters. The presence of the Tajo River to the north and the Montes de Toledo to the south promote lower rainfall levels than in neighbouring areas, and thus more concentration of nose:s and phenolic compounds.

PAGO CASA DEL BLANCO: Its vineyards are located at an altitude of 617 metres in Campo de Calatrava, in the town of Manzanares, right in the centre of the province of Ciudad Real, and therefore with a mediterranean/continental climate. Soils have varying degrees of loam and sand, and are abundant in lithium, surely due to the ancient volcanic character of the region.

PAGO DEHESA DEL CARRIZAL: Property of Marcial Gómez Sequeira, Dehesa del Carrizal is located in the town of Retuerta de Bullaque, to the north of Ciudad Real. It enjoys a continental climate and high altitude (900 metres). The winemaker, Ignacio de Miguel, uses primarily foreign (French) varieties such as *cabernet sauvignon*.

PAGO DOMINIO DE VALDEPUSA: Located in the town of Malpica de Tajo (Toledo), its owner, Carlos Falcó (Marqués de Griñón) pioneered the introduction in Spain of foreign grape varieties such as *cabernet sauvignon* and *chardonnay* as well as the wire training techniques for warm climates designed by Richard Smart. Using long-cycled grape varieties, its wines are meaty, succulent, and with elegant tannins.

PAGO EL TERRERAZO: El Terrerazo, property of Bodegas Mustiguilo, is the first "Vinos de Pago" label granted within the autonomous region of Valencia. It comprises 62 hectares at an altitude of 800 meters between Utiel and Sinarcas where an excellent clone of *bobal* – that yields small and loose berries– is grown. It enjoys a mediterranean-continental climate and the vineyard gets the influence of humid winds blowing from the sea, which is just 80 kilometres away from the property. Soils are characterized limestone and clay in nature, with abundant sand and stones.

PAGO FINCA ÉLEZ: It became the first of all Vino de Pago designations of origin. Its owner is Manuel Manzaneque, and it is located at an altitude of 1000 metres in El Bonillo, in the province of Albacete. The winery became renown by its splendid *chardonnay*, but today also make a single-varietal *syrah* and some other red renderings.

PAGO FLORENTINO: Located in the municipality of Malagón (Ciudad Real), between natural lagoons to the south and the Sierra de Malagón to the north, at an altitude of some 630-670 metres. Soils are mainly siliceous with limestone and stones on the surface and a subsoil of slate and limestone. The climate is milder and dryer than that of neighbouring towns.

PAGO GUIJOSO: Finca El Guijoso is property of Bodegas Sánchez Muliterno, located in El Bonillo, between the provinces of Albacete and Ciudad Real. Surrounded by bitch and juniper woods, the vines are planted on stone (guijo in Spanish, from which it takes its name) soils at an altitude of 1000 metres. Wines are all made from French varieties, and have a clear French lean also in terms of style.

PAGO LOS BALAGUESES: The "Pago de los Balagueses" is located to the south west of the Utiel-Requena wine region, just 20 kilometres away from Requena. At approximately 700 metres over the sea level, it enjoys a continental type of climate with mediterranean influence and an average annual rainfall of around 450 mm. The vines are planted on low hills –a feature that favours water drainage– surrounded by pines, almond and olive trees, thus giving shape to a unique landscape.

PAGO DE OTAZU: Its vineyards are located in Navarra, between two mountain ranges (Sierra del Perdón and Sierra de Echauri), and is probably the most northerly of all Spanish wine regions. It is a cool area with Atlantic climate and a high day-night temperature contrast. Soils in that part of the country, near the city of Pamplona, are limestone-based with abundant clay and stones, therefore with good drainage that allows vines to sink their roots deeper into the soil.

PAGO PRADO DE IRACHE: Its vineyard is located in the municipality of Ayegui (Navarra) at an altitude of 450 metres. Climate is continental with strong Atlantic influence and soils are mainly of a loamy nature.

PAGO SEÑORÍO DE ARÍNZANO: Located in the city of Estella, in Navarra, to the northeast of Spain, the vineyard is in a valley near the Pyrenees and crossed by the Ega river, which moderates the temperatures. Climate has here a strong Atlantic influence with high day-night temperature contrast. Soils are complex in nature, with varying levels of loam, marl, clay and highly degraded limestone rock.

PAGO AYLÉS

FINCA AYLÉS

Finca Aylés. Ctra. A-1101, Km. 24
50152 Mezalocha (Zaragoza)
☎: +34 976 140 473 - Fax: +34 976 140 268
info@pagoayles.com
www.pagoayles.com

"L" DE AYLÉS 2011 RD
garnacha, cabernet sauvignon.

87 Colour: brilliant rose. Nose: ripe fruit, fruit expression, powerfull. Palate: flavourful, powerful, sweetness.

"A" DE AYLÉS 2011 T
garnacha, merlot, cabernet sauvignon, tempranillo.

88 Colour: deep cherry. Nose: ripe fruit, overripe fruit, sweet spices. Palate: powerful, flavourful, fine bitter notes, good acidity.

"Y" DE AYLÉS 2010 T
tempranillo, merlot, garnacha, cabernet sauvignon.

93 Colour: cherry, garnet rim. Nose: ripe fruit, spicy, creamy oak, complex, scrubland, new oak. Palate: powerful, flavourful, toasty, round tannins.

"A" DE AYLÉS 2010 T
tempranillo, merlot, garnacha, cabernet sauvignon.

90 Colour: bright cherry. Nose: ripe fruit, sweet spices, creamy oak, cocoa bean, dark chocolate. Palate: flavourful, fruity, toasty, round tannins.

PAGO CALZADILLA

PAGO CALZADILLA

Ctra. Huete a Cuenca, Km. 3
16500 Huete (Cuenca)
☎: +34 969 143 020 - Fax: +34 969 147 047
info@pagodecalzadilla.com
www.pagodecalzadilla.net

OPTA CALZADILLA 2008 T
tempranillo, garnacha, syrah.

88 Colour: cherry, garnet rim. Nose: balanced, creamy oak, ripe fruit, nose:tic coffee. Palate: balanced, flavourful, spicy.

CALZADILLA CLASSIC 2007 T
tempranillo, cabernet sauvignon, garnacha, syrah.

90 Colour: cherry, garnet rim. Nose: balanced, ripe fruit, cocoa bean, creamy oak. Palate: good structure, flavourful, good acidity.

CALZADILLA ALLEGRO 2007 T
syrah.

90 Colour: cherry, purple rim. Nose: balanced, sweet spices, creamy oak. Palate: ripe fruit, round tannins.

GRAN CALZADILLA 2006 T
70% tempranillo, 30% cabernet sauvignon.

91 Colour: bright cherry, garnet rim. Nose: complex, sweet spices, creamy oak, cocoa bean. Palate: balanced, fine bitter notes, good acidity..

PAGO CAMPO DE LA GUARDIA

BODEGAS MARTÚE LA GUARDIA

Campo de la Guardia, s/n
45760 La Guardia (Toledo)
☎: +34 925 123 333 - Fax: +34 925 123 332
bodegasenlaguardia@martue.com
www.martue.com

MARTÚE CHARDONNAY 2011 B
100% chardonnay.

87 Colour: bright yellow. Nose: ripe fruit, dried herbs, dried flowers, sweet spices, toasty. Palate: rich, powerful, flavourful, spicy.

MARTÚE 2009 TC
33% cabernet sauvignon, 22% merlot, 21% tempranillo, 13% petit verdot, 11% syrah.

88 Colour: cherry, garnet rim. Nose: ripe fruit, spicy, creamy oak, balsamic herbs. Palate: powerful, flavourful, spicy.

MARTÚE ESPECIAL 2008 TR
50% merlot, 27% cabernet sauvignon, 21% syrah, 2% malbec.

89 Colour: cherry, garnet rim. Nose: ripe fruit, creamy oak, toasty, cocoa bean, dark chocolate. Palate: powerful, flavourful, toasty, balanced.

MARTÚE SYRAH 2008 T
100% syrah.

88 Colour: cherry, garnet rim. Nose: ripe fruit, fruit preserve, earthy notes, fragrant herbs. Palate: long, powerful, flavourful, spicy.

PAGO CASA DEL BLANCO

PAGO CASA DEL BLANCO

Ctra. Manzanares a Moral , Km. 23,2
13200 Manzanares (Ciudad Real)
☎: +34 917 480 606 - Fax: +34 913 290 266
antonio@pagocasadelblanco.com
www.pagocasadelblanco.com

QUIXOTE MERLOT TEMPRANILLO PETIT VERDOT 2007 T
tempranillo, petit verdot, merlot.

89 Colour: cherry, garnet rim. Nose: ripe fruit, spicy, creamy oak, toasty, balsamic herbs. Palate: powerful, toasty, round tannins, long, flavourful.

QUIXOTE PETIT VERDOT 2007 T
petit verdot.

88 Colour: cherry, garnet rim. Nose: ripe fruit, medium intensity, scrubland. Palate: fine bitter notes, flavourful, spicy.

QUIXOTE CABERNET SAUVIGNON SYRAH 2007 T
cabernet sauvignon, syrah.

87 Colour: cherry, garnet rim. Nose: ripe fruit, scrubland, earthy notes, spicy. Palate: powerful, flavourful, round tannins.

QUIXOTE MALBEC CABERNET FRANC 2007 T
malbec, cabernet franc.

87 Colour: cherry, garnet rim. Nose: medium intensity, ripe fruit, scrubland. Palate: balanced, spicy, flavourful.

PAGO DEHESA DEL CARRIZAL

DEHESA DEL CARRIZAL

Ctra. de Retuerta a Navas de Estena, Km. 5
13194 Retuerta del Bullaque (Ciudad Real)
☎: +34 925 421 773 - Fax: +34 926 867 093
bodega@dehesadelcarrizal.com
www.dehesadelcarrizal.com

DEHESA DEL CARRIZAL CHARDONNAY 2010 B
chardonnay.

89 Colour: bright yellow. Nose: dried flowers, fragrant herbs, mineral, creamy oak, ripe fruit. Palate: balanced, flavourful, round tannins.

DEHESA DEL CARRIZAL SYRAH 2008 T
syrah.

92 Colour: cherry, garnet rim. Nose: ripe fruit, balsamic herbs, earthy notes, spicy, creamy oak. Palate: full, flavourful, toasty.

DEHESA DEL CARRIZAL MV ROJO 2008 T
cabernet sauvignon, merlot, petit verdot, tempranillo, syrah.

88 Colour: cherry, garnet rim. Nose: ripe fruit, balsamic herbs, earthy notes, spicy, toasty. Palate: flavourful, complex, long, toasty.

DEHESA DEL CARRIZAL CABERNET SAUVIGNON 2007 T
cabernet sauvignon.

91 Colour: cherry, garnet rim. Nose: ripe fruit, scrubland, varietal, sweet spices. Palate: spicy, powerful, flavourful, complex.

DEHESA DEL CARRIZAL COLECCIÓN PRIVADA 2007 T
cabernet sauvignon, syrah, merlot, petit verdot.

90 Colour: cherry, garnet rim. Nose: ripe fruit, spicy, creamy oak, toasty, complex. Palate: powerful, flavourful, toasty, round tannins.

PAGO DOMINIO DE VALDEPUSA

PAGOS DE FAMILIA MARQUÉS DE GRIÑÓN

Finca Casa de Vacas - Ctra. CM-4015, Km. 23
45692 Malpica de Tajo (Toledo)
☎: +34 925 597 222 - Fax: +34 925 789 416
service@hotmail.com
www.pagosdefamilia.com

CALIZA 2008 T
70% syrah, 30% petit verdot.

90 Colour: deep cherry, garnet rim. Nose: fruit preserve, dark chocolate, fruit liqueur notes, tobacco. Palate: balanced, fine bitter notes, round tannins.

MARQUÉS DE GRIÑÓN EMERITVS 2007 TR
63% cabernet sauvignon, 32% petit verdot, 5% syrah.

93 Colour: cherry, garnet rim. Nose: spicy, creamy oak, toasty, characterful, ripe fruit, mineral. Palate: powerful, flavourful, toasty, round tannins.

SVMMA VARIETALIS 2007 T
45% cabernet sauvignon, 42% syrah, 13% petit verdot.

92 Colour: cherry, garnet rim. Nose: expressive, creamy oak, ripe fruit, cocoa bean, wild herbs. Palate: good structure, complex, full.

MARQUÉS DE GRIÑÓN CABERNET SAUVIGNON 2007 T
100% cabernet sauvignon.

91 Colour: bright cherry, garnet rim. Nose: elegant, ripe fruit, scrubland, varietal. Palate: full, spicy, ripe fruit.

MARQUÉS DE GRIÑÓN PETIT VERDOT 2007 T
100% petit verdot.

91 Colour: bright cherry, garnet rim. Nose: complex, wild herbs, balanced. Palate: flavourful, ripe fruit, round tannins.

MARQUÉS DE GRIÑÓN SYRAH 2007 T
100% syrah.

89 Colour: bright cherry, garnet rim. Nose: old leather, tobacco, balanced, fruit preserve. Palate: full, spicy, long.

PAGO EL TERRERAZO

MUSTIGUILLO VIÑEDOS Y BODEGA

Ctra. N-330, km 196,5 El Terrerazo
46300 Utiel (Valencia)
☎: +34 962 168 260 - Fax: +34 962 168 259
info@bodegamustiguillo.com
www.bodegamustiguillo.com

FINCA TERRERAZO 2010 T
100% bobal.

95 Colour: bright cherry. Nose: ripe fruit, expressive, mineral, cocoa bean. Palate: flavourful, fruity, toasty, round tannins.

PAGO FINCA ÉLEZ

VIÑEDOS Y BODEGA MANUEL MANZANEQUE

Ctra. Ossa de Montiel a El Bonillo, Km. 11,500
02610 El Bonillo (Albacete)
☎: +34 967 585 003 - Fax: +34 967 370 649
info@manuelmanzaneque.com
www.manuelmanzaneque.com

MANUEL MANZANEQUE CHARDONNAY 2008 BFB
chardonnay.

90 Colour: bright yellow. Nose: powerfull, ripe fruit, sweet spices, creamy oak, fragrant herbs. Palate: rich, flavourful, fresh, good acidity.

MANUEL MANZANEQUE ESCENA 2007 T
90% tempranillo, 10% cabernet sauvignon.

93 Colour: cherry, garnet rim. Nose: ripe fruit, spicy, toasty, fine reductive notes, balsamic herbs. Palate: powerful, flavourful, toasty, round tannins.

MANUEL MANZANEQUE NUESTRA SELECCIÓN 2007 T
70% tempranillo, 20% cabernet sauvignon, 10% merlot.

91 Colour: cherry, garnet rim. Nose: ripe fruit, spicy, creamy oak, toasty, complex, balsamic herbs. Palate: powerful, flavourful, toasty, round tannins, elegant.

MANUEL MANZANEQUE SYRAH 2007 T
syrah.

90 Colour: cherry, garnet rim. Nose: ripe fruit, violets, earthy notes, spicy, creamy oak. Palate: powerful, flavourful, balanced, round tannins.

MANUEL MANZANEQUE FINCA ÉLEZ 2007 TC
50% cabernet sauvignon, 40% tempranillo, 10% merlot.

88 Colour: cherry, garnet rim. Nose: ripe fruit, spicy, creamy oak, toasty, balsamic herbs. Palate: powerful, flavourful, toasty, round tannins

PAGO FLORENTINO

BODEGAS Y VIÑEDOS LA SOLANA

Ctra. Porzuna - Camino Cristo del Humilladero, km. 3
13420 Malagón (Ciudad Real)
☎: +34 983 681 146 - Fax: +34 983 681 147
bodega@pagoflorentino.com
www.pagoflorentino.com

PAGO FLORENTINO 2009 TR
100% cencibel.

89 Colour: bright cherry. Nose: sweet spices, creamy oak, roasted coffee. Palate: flavourful, fruity, toasty, round tannins.

PAGO GUIJOSO

BODEGAS Y VIÑEDOS SÁNCHEZ MULITERNO

Tesifonte Gallego, 5
02002 (Albacete)
☎: +34 967 193 222 - Fax: +34 967 193 292
bodegas@sanchez-muliterno.com
www.sanchez-muliterno.com

DIVINUS 2008 BFB
100% chardonnay.

87 Colour: bright yellow. Nose: powerfull, ripe fruit, sweet spices, creamy oak, fragrant herbs. Palate: rich, flavourful, fresh, good acidity.

VEGA GUIJOSO 2009 T
63% merlot, 30% syrah, 7% cabernet sauvignon.

88 Colour: cherry, garnet rim. Nose: ripe fruit, spicy, creamy oak, balsamic herbs. Palate: powerful, flavourful, toasty, long.

MAGNIFICUS 2006 T
100% syrah.

91 Colour: dark-red cherry, orangey edge. Nose: ripe fruit, mineral, cocoa bean, sweet spices, creamy oak, fine reductive notes. Palate: balanced, powerful, flavourful, long, round tannins.

VIÑA CONSOLACIÓN 2004 TR
100% cabernet sauvignon.

88 Colour: deep cherry. Nose: balanced, ripe fruit, tobacco, dark chocolate, spicy. Palate: good structure, complex, flavourful.

PAGO LOS BALAGUESES

VIÑEDOS Y BODEGAS VEGALFARO

Ctra. Pontón - Utiel, Km. 3
46430 El Derramador - Requena (Valencia)
☎: +34 962 320 680 - Fax: +34 962 321 126
info@vegalfaro.com
www.vegalfaro.com

PAGO DE LOS BALAGUESES SYRAH 2009 TC
syrah.

93 Colour: cherry, garnet rim. Nose: spicy, creamy oak, toasty, characterful, earthy notes, ripe fruit. Palate: flavourful, toasty, round tannins.

PAGO PRADO DE IRACHE

IRACHE

Monasterio de Irache, 1
31240 Ayegui (Navarra)
☎: +34 948 551 932 - Fax: +34 948 554 954
irache@irache.com
www.irache.com

PRADO IRACHE VINO DE PAGO 2006 T
tempranillo, cabernet sauvignon, merlot.

90 Colour: bright cherry, orangey edge. Nose: red berry notes, ripe fruit, fragrant herbs, mineral. Palate: good acidity, flavourful, fleshy, mineral, long.

PAGO DE OTAZU

BODEGA OTAZU

Señorío de Otazu, s/n
31174 Etxauri (Navarra)
☎: +34 948 329 200 - Fax: +34 948 329 353
otazu@otazu.com
www.otazu.com

SEÑORÍO DE OTAZU 2007 T
cabernet sauvignon, tempranillo, merlot.

94 Colour: cherry, garnet rim. Nose: ripe fruit, spicy, creamy oak, toasty, complex, characterful, mineral. Palate: powerful, flavourful, toasty, round tannins.

SEÑORIO DE OTAZU VITRAL 2007 TC
95% cabernet sauvignon, 5% tempranillo.

93 Colour: cherry, garnet rim. Nose: spicy, creamy oak, toasty, complex, ripe fruit, overripe fruit, dark chocolate. Palate: powerful, flavourful, toasty, sweet tannins.

SEÑORÍO DE OTAZU ALTAR 2006 T
90% cabernet sauvignon, 10% tempranillo.

95 Colour: cherry, garnet rim. Nose: spicy, creamy oak, toasty, complex, mineral, earthy notes, ripe fruit. Palate: powerful, flavourful, toasty, round tannins

PAGO SEÑORÍO DE ARÍNZANO

SEÑORÍO DE ARÍNZANO

Crta. NA-132, km. 3,1
31292 Aberin (Navarra)
☎: +34 948 555 258
info@arinzano.com
www.bodegaschivite.com

ARÍNZANO LA CASONA 2008 T

93 Colour: bright cherry. Nose: sweet spices, creamy oak, powerfull, red berry notes, fruit expression. Palate: flavourful, fruity, toasty, round tannins, round.

ARÍNZANO 2004 T

95 Colour: cherry, garnet rim. Nose: ripe fruit, spicy, creamy oak, toasty, complex, elegant, balanced, mineral. Palate: powerful, flavourful, toasty, round tannins, long.

VINOS DE CALIDAD

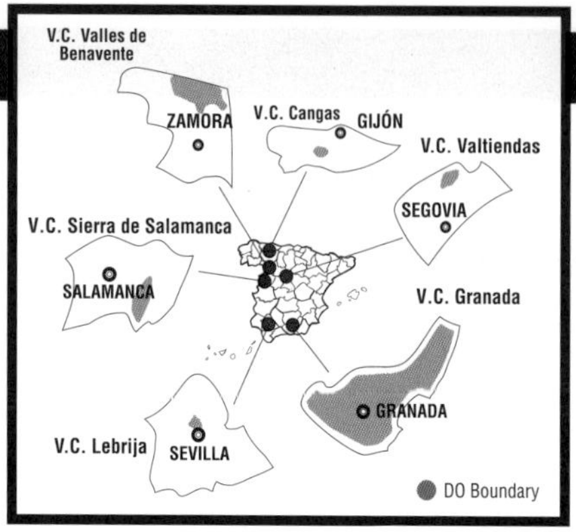

So far, there are only six wine regions that have achieved the status "Vino de Calidad" ("Quality Wine Produced in Specified Regions"): Cangas, Lebrija, Valtiendas, Granada, Sierra de Salamanca and Valles de Benavente, regions that are allowed to label their wines with the VCPRD seal. This quality seal works as a sort of "training" session for the DO category, although it is still quite unknown for the average consumer.

VINO DE CALIDAD DE CANGAS

Located to the south-eastern part of the province of Asturias, bordering with León, Cangas del Narcea has unique climatic conditions, completely different to the rest of the municipalities of Asturias; therefore, its wines have sheer singularity. With lower rainfall levels and more sunshine hours than the rest the province, vines are planted on slate, siliceous and sandy soils. The main varieties are albarín blanco and albillo (white), along with *garnacha tintorera*, *mencía* and *verdejo negro* (red).

VINO DE CALIDAD DE GRANADA

Wines that come from anywhere within the provincial limits of Granada, it includes nearly 20 wineries and a hundred growers. It enjoys a mediterranean climate with Atlantic influence. Characterized by a rugged topography, the vineyards occupy mostly the highest areas, with an average altitude of around 1200 meters, a feature that provides this territory with an ample day-night temperature differential. The region is promoting white grape varieties such as *vijiriega*, *moscatel* and *pedro ximénez*, as well as red (*tempranillo*, *garnacha*, *monastrell*) and even some French ones, widely planted in the province. Soil structure, although diverse, is based mainly on clay and slate.

VINO DE CALIDAD DE LEBRIJA

Recognized by the Junta de Andalucía on March the 11th 2009. The production area includes the towns of Lebrija and El Cuervo, in the province of Sevilla.
The wines ascribed to the "Vino de Calidad de Lebrija" designation of quality will be made solely from the following grape varieties:
– **White varieties:** *moscatel de Alejandría*, *palomino*, *palomino fino*, *sauvignon blanc* and that traditionally known as *vidueño* (*montúo de pilas*, *mollar cano*, *moscatel morisco*, *perruno*).
– **Red varieties:** *cabernet sauvignon*, *syrah*, *tempranillo*, *merlot* and *tintilla de Rota*.
Types of wines: white, red, generosos (fortified) and generosos de licor, naturally sweet and mistelas.

VINO DE CALIDAD SIERRA DE SALAMANCA

The "Vino de Calidad" status was ratified to Sierra de Salamanca by the Junta de Castilla y León (Castilla y León autonomous government) in June 2010, becoming the third one to be granted within the region. Sierra de Salamanca lies in the south of the province of Salamanca, and includes 26 towns, all within the same province. Vines are planted mostly on terraces at the top of the hills and on clay soils based on limestone. Authorized varieties are *viura*, *moscatel de grano menudo* and *palomino* (white), as well as *rufete*, *garnacha* and *tempranillo* (red).

VINO DE CALIDAD DE LOS VALLES DE BENAVENTE

Recognized by the Junta de Castilla y León in September 2000, the VCPRD comprises nowadays more than 50 municipalities and three wineries in Benavente, Santibáñez de Vidriales and San Pedro de Ceque. The production areas within the region are five (Valle Vidriales, Valle del Tera, Valle Valverde, La Vega and Tierra de Campos) around the city of Benavente, the core of the region. Four rivers (Tera, Esla, Órbigo and Valderadey, all of them tributary to the Duero river) give the region its natural borders.

VINO DE CALIDAD VALTIENDAS

An area to the north of the province of Segovia relatively known thanks to the brand name Duratón, also the name of the river that crosses a region that has mainly *tempranillo* planted, a grape variety known there also as *tinta del país*. The wines are fruitier and more acidic than those from Ribera del Duero, thanks to an altitude of some 900 metres and clay soils with plenty of stones.

CANGAS

BODEGAS OBANCA

Obanca, 12
33800 Cangas del Narcea (Asturias)
☎: +34 626 956 571 - Fax: +34 985 811 539
informacion@obanca.com
www.obanca.com

CASTRO DE LIMÉS OROCANTABRICO 2011 BFB
albarín.

91 Colour: bright yellow. Nose: powerfull, ripe fruit, sweet spices, creamy oak, fragrant herbs. Palate: rich, flavourful, fresh, good acidity.

OBANCA 2011 T JOVEN
mencía, carrasquín, albarín tinto, verdejo negro.

88 Colour: cherry, garnet rim. Nose: red berry notes, floral, balsamic herbs, dry stone, expressive. Palate: fresh, fruity, flavourful, easy to drink, balanced.

LLUMES 2010 T
verdejo negro.

91 Colour: bright cherry. Nose: creamy oak, spicy, red berry notes, ripe fruit, balsamic herbs, mineral. Palate: flavourful, fruity, toasty, round tannins, elegant.

DOMINIO DEL UROGALLO

Pol. Obanca, C. Empresas, nave 2
33819 Cangas de Narcea (Asturias)
☎: +34 626 568 238
info@dominiodelurogallo.com
www.dominiodelurogallo.com

PESICO 2010 B
100% albarín.

92 Colour: bright straw. Nose: dried flowers, ripe fruit, fragrant herbs, dry stone. Palate: fresh, fruity, light-bodied, good acidity, balanced.

PESICO 2010 T
60% carrasquín, 20% verdejo negro, 10% albarín tinto, 10% mencía.

90 Colour: cherry, garnet rim. Nose: ripe fruit, creamy oak, toasty, balsamic herbs, mineral. Palate: powerful, flavourful, toasty, round tannins, balanced.

GRANADA

BODEGA ANCHURÓN

Cortijo de Anchurón, s/n
18181 Darro (Granada)
☎: +34 958 277 764 - Fax: +34 958 277 764
info@anchuron.es
www.anchuron.es

ANCHURÓN 2011 B
90% sauvignon blanc, 10% chardonnay.

85 Colour: bright straw. Nose: faded flowers, dried herbs, ripe fruit. Palate: light-bodied, fresh, fruity.

ANCHURÓN MERLOT 2011 T
100% merlot.

85 Colour: dark-red cherry, garnet rim. Nose: powerfull, dried fruit, fruit liqueur notes, pattiserie. Palate: correct, balanced.

ANCHURÓN 2010 TC
40% cabernet sauvignon, 30% syrah, 30% tempranillo.

88 Colour: cherry, garnet rim. Nose: ripe fruit, spicy, creamy oak, toasty, complex. Palate: powerful, flavourful, toasty, round tannins.

ANCHURÓN 2009 T
50% syrah, 50% cabernet sauvignon.

88 Colour: cherry, garnet rim. Nose: ripe fruit, spicy, toasty, balsamic herbs, earthy notes. Palate: powerful, flavourful, toasty, round tannins.

ANCHURÓN 2009 T
50% merlot, 50% tempranillo.

85 Colour: cherry, garnet rim. Nose: fruit preserve, scrubland, earthy notes, spicy. Palate: powerful, flavourful, spicy.

BODEGAS AL ZAGAL

Paraje Las Cañaillas, s/n
18518 Cogollos de Guadix (Granada)
☎: +34 958 105 605
bodegas@bodegasalzagal.es
www.bodegasalzagal.es

REY ZAGAL 2009 T
80% tempranillo, 20% merlot.

84

REY ZAGAL 12 MESES 2008 T
50% tempranillo, 50% merlot.

82

BODEGAS SEÑORÍO DE NEVADA

Ctra. de Cónchar, s/n
18659 Villamena (Granada)
☎: +34 958 777 092 - Fax: +34 958 777 062
info@senoriodenevada.es
www.bodegassenoriodenevada.es

SEÑORÍO DE NEVADA 2011 RD
syrah, tempranillo, cabernet sauvignon.

88 Colour: rose, purple rim. Nose: powerfull, ripe fruit, red berry notes, floral, lactic notes. Palate: , powerful, fruity, fresh.

SEÑORÍO DE NEVADA CLUB DE LA BARRICA 2009 T
100% syrah.

88 Colour: cherry, garnet rim. Nose: ripe fruit, spicy, creamy oak, toasty, earthy notes. Palate: powerful, flavourful, toasty, round tannins.

SEÑORÍO DE NEVADA CABERNET / MERLOT 2007 T
cabernet sauvignon, merlot.

88 Colour: cherry, garnet rim. Nose: ripe fruit, spicy, creamy oak, toasty, complex. Palate: powerful, flavourful, toasty, round tannins.

SEÑORÍO DE NEVADA SELECCIÓN 2007 T
cabernet sauvignon, merlot, syrah.

87 Colour: cherry, garnet rim. Nose: ripe fruit, earthy notes, spicy, wet leather. Palate: long, spicy, toasty, flavourful.

SEÑORÍO DE NEVADA SYRAH-MERLOT 2007 T
syrah, merlot.

86 Colour: cherry, garnet rim. Nose: ripe fruit, floral, scrubland, spicy, creamy oak. Palate: powerful, flavourful, spicy.

BODEGAS FONTEDEI

Doctor Horcajadas, 10
18570 Deifontes (Granada)
☎: +34 958 407 957 - Fax: +34 958 407 957
bodegasfontedei@gmail.com
www.bodegasfontedei.com

AL BAYDA 2011 B
sauvignon blanc, chardonnay.

87 Colour: bright straw. Nose: fresh, fresh fruit, white flowers, expressive, earthy notes. Palate: flavourful, fruity, good acidity, balanced.

AYNADAMAR 2011 T
tempranillo, garnacha.

81

DOMINIO BUENAVISTA

Ctra. de Almería, s/n
18480 Ugíjar (Granada)
☎: +34 958 767 254 - Fax: +34 958 990 226
info@dominiobuenavista.com
www.dominiobuenavista.com

VELETA VIJIRIEGA 2011 B
90% vijariego blanco, 10% chardonnay.

86 Colour: bright straw. Nose: citrus fruit, ripe fruit, white flowers, fragrant herbs. Palate: powerful, flavourful, fresh, fruity.

VELETA CHARDONNAY 2011 B
90% chardonnay, 10% vijariego blanco.

85 Colour: bright yellow. Nose: ripe fruit, dried herbs, faded flowers. Palate: fine bitter notes, powerful, flavourful.

VELETA TEMPRANILLO ROSÉ 2011 RD
100% tempranillo.

82

VELETA TEMPRANILLO 2011 T
90% tempranillo, 10% merlot.

85 Colour: cherry, purple rim. Nose: fresh fruit, red berry notes, floral, medium intensity. Palate: flavourful, fruity, good acidity.

VELETA NOLADOS 2009 T
40% cabernet sauvignon, 40% cabernet franc, 20% tempranillo.

90 Colour: cherry, garnet rim. Nose: ripe fruit, spicy, creamy oak, toasty, balsamic herbs, earthy notes. Palate: powerful, flavourful, toasty, spicy.

VELETA TEMPRANILLO 2009 T
100% tempranillo.

88 Colour: cherry, garnet rim. Nose: ripe fruit, scrubland, earthy notes, spicy. Palate: long, rich, flavourful.

VELETA CABERNET SAUVIGNON 2009 T
90% cabernet sauvignon, 10% merlot.

87 Colour: cherry, garnet rim. Nose: ripe fruit, scrubland, balsamic herbs, spicy, creamy oak. Palate: powerful, flavourful, spicy, balsamic.

LOS BARRANCOS

Ctra. Cádiar - Albuñol, km. 9,4
18449 Lobras (Granada)
☎: +34 958 343 218 - Fax: +34 958 343 412
cesarortega@gmail.com
www.losbarrancos.es

CORRAL DE CASTRO 2009 T
tempranillo, cabernet sauvignon.

87 Colour: cherry, garnet rim. Nose: ripe fruit, earthy notes, balsamic herbs, spicy. Palate: flavourful, correct, harsh oak tannins.

MARQUÉS DE CASA PARDIÑAS C.B.

Finca San Torcuato
18540 Huélago (Granada)
☎: +34 630 901 094 - Fax: +34 958 252 297
info@spiracp.es
www.marquesdecasapardiñas.com

SPIRA VENDIMIA SELECCIONADA 2010 T
60% tempranillo, 35% cabernet sauvignon, 5% merlot.

90 Colour: bright cherry. Nose: ripe fruit, sweet spices, creamy oak, expressive. Palate: flavourful, fruity, toasty, round tannins.

NESTARES RINCÓN VINOS Y BODEGAS

Finca Juan de Reyes, s/n Contraviesa Alpujarra
18430 Torvizcon (Granada)
☎: +34 655 959 500 - Fax: +34 958 272 125
info@alpujarride.com
www.alpujarride.com

NESTARES RINCÓN 1.0 2011 T
tempranillo, syrah, merlot.

90 Colour: cherry, garnet rim. Nose: red berry notes, floral, balsamic herbs, earthy notes. Palate: good acidity, powerful, flavourful, long.

PAGO DE ALMARAES

Ctra. Fonelas, s/n - Camino de los Almaraes
18518 Benalua (Granada)
☎: +34 958 348 752 - Fax: +34 958 333 444
bodegapagodealmaraes@hotmail.es

MENCAL 2011 B
moscatel, chardonnay, sauvignon blanc, torrontés.

86 Colour: bright straw. Nose: white flowers, fresh fruit, fragrant herbs. Palate: light-bodied, fresh, fruity, easy to drink.

ALMARAES 2009 T
35% merlot, 31% tempranillo, 20% cabernet sauvignon, 14% syrah.

89 Colour: cherry, garnet rim. Nose: red berry notes, ripe fruit, balsamic herbs, creamy oak. Palate: powerful, flavourful, long.

SIERRA DE SALAMANCA

CÁMBRICO

Paraje El Guijarral
37658 Villanueva del Conde (Salamanca)
☎: +34 923 281 006 - Fax: +34 923 213 605
alberto@cambrico.com
www.cambrico.com

VIÑAS DEL CÁMBRICO 2010 T
52% tempranillo, 41% rufete, 7% garnacha.

91 Colour: cherry, garnet rim. Nose: red berry notes, expressive, mineral, sweet spices, creamy oak.

575 UVAS DE CÁMBRICO 2008 T
64% tempranillo, 32% rufete, 4% garnacha.

89 Colour: cherry, garnet rim. Nose: ripe fruit, mineral, spicy, toasty. Palate: powerful, flavourful, long, toasty.

VINOS LA ZORRA

San Pedro, s/n
37610 Mogarraz (Salamanca)
☎: +34 923 418 042
estanverdes@vinoslazorra.es
www.vinoslazorra.es

LA VIEJA ZORRA 20 BARRICAS SELECCIÓN ESPECIAL 2010 T
52% rufete, 43% tempranillo, 5% garnacha.

93 Colour: bright cherry. Nose: sweet spices, creamy oak, expressive, scrubland, ripe fruit. Palate: flavourful, fruity, toasty, round tannins.

LA ZORRA 2010 T
80% rufete, 20% tempranillo.

90 Colour: cherry, purple rim. Nose: fresh fruit, red berry notes, floral, sweet spices. Palate: flavourful, fruity, good acidity, round tannins.

VALLES DE BENAVENTE

BODEGAS OTERO

Avda. El Ferial, 22
49600 Benavente (Zamora)
☎: +34 980 631 600 - Fax: +34 980 631 722
info@bodegasotero.es
www.bodegasotero.es

VALLEOSCURO PRIETO PICUDO 2011 RD
100% prieto picudo.

87 Colour: rose, purple rim. Nose: floral, lactic notes, red berry notes, ripe fruit. Palate: fresh, fruity, light-bodied.

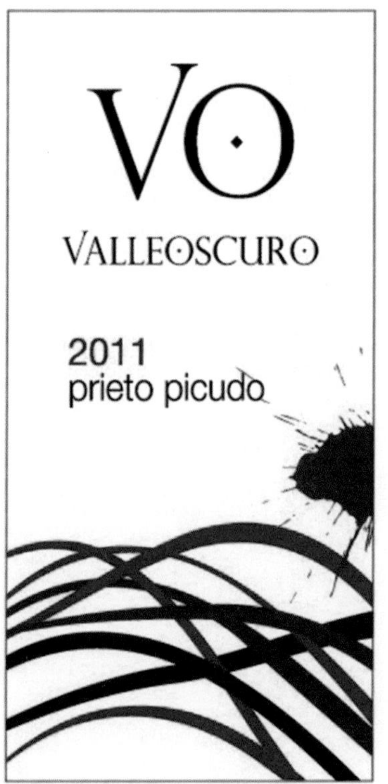

VALLEOSCURO 2011 B
verdejo.

86 Colour: bright straw. Nose: fresh, white flowers, candied fruit. Palate: flavourful, fruity, good acidity.

VALLEOSCURO 2011 RD
prieto picudo, tempranillo.

88 Colour: rose, purple rim. Nose: floral, red berry notes, lactic notes. Palate: light-bodied, fresh, fruity, easy to drink.

VALLEOSCURO PRIETO PICUDO TEMPRANILLO 2010 T
prieto picudo, tempranillo.

89 Colour: cherry, garnet rim. Nose: balanced, medium intensity, red berry notes, balsamic herbs. Palate: fruity, flavourful, good acidity.

OTERO 2008 TC
prieto picudo.

86 Colour: cherry, garnet rim. Nose: balanced, ripe fruit, old leather, tobacco, fragrant herbs. Palate: flavourful, fine bitter notes, correct.

OTERO 2006 TR
prieto picudo.

86 Colour: cherry, garnet rim. Nose: ripe fruit, spicy, creamy oak, toasty. Palate: spicy, long, flavourful, correct.

VALTIENDAS

BODEGA PAGO EL ALMENDRO

Paseo Ezequiel González, 25
40002 (Segovia)
☎: +34 921 461 545

VIVENCIAS 2010 T
100% tempranillo.

86 Colour: bright cherry. Nose: sweet spices, creamy oak, balsamic herbs, candied fruit, fruit preserve. Palate: flavourful, fruity, toasty, round tannins.

BODEGA VIÑA SANCHA

Coto de Cárdaba, s/n
40314 Valtiendas (Segovia)
☎: +34 947 500 428 - Fax: +34 947 502 866
info@fincacardaba.com
www.fincacardaba.com

VIÑA SANCHA FINCA CÁRDABA 2011 RD
100% tempranillo.

86 Colour: brilliant rose. Nose: floral, ripe fruit, balsamic herbs, closed. Palate: flavourful, light-bodied, fresh, fruity, easy to drink

BODEGAS VAGAL

La Fuente, 19
40314 Valtiendas (Segovia)
☎: +34 921 527 331 - Fax: +34 921 527 332
jose.vagal@gmail.com
www.vagal.com

VAGAL CUVÉE JOANA 2010 T

87 Colour: cherry, garnet rim. Nose: balanced, warm, ripe fruit. Palate: flavourful, ripe fruit, spicy.

VAGAL SELECCIÓN 2009 T

92 Colour: cherry, garnet rim. Nose: ripe fruit, spicy, toasty, earthy notes, balsamic herbs. Palate: powerful, flavourful, toasty, round tannins.

VAGAL PAGO ARDALEJOS 2009 T
tinta del país.

91 Colour: cherry, garnet rim. Nose: red berry notes, ripe fruit, sweet spices, creamy oak. Palate: powerful, flavourful, balanced, long, toasty.

BODEGAS ZARRAGUILLA

Iglesia, 14
40237 Sacramenia (Segovia)
☎: +34 678 610 090 - Fax: +34 921 527 270
informacion@bodegaszarraguilla.es
www.bodegaszarraguilla.es

SEGOVIANO 2011 T
tempranillo.

87 Colour: cherry, purple rim. Nose: red berry notes, floral, balsamic herbs. Palate: flavourful, fruity, good acidity, round tannins.

VENNUR 2009 TC
tempranillo.

88 Colour: cherry, garnet rim. Nose: ripe fruit, creamy oak, toasty. Palate: powerful, flavourful, long, spicy.

ZARRAGUILLA 2009 T
tempranillo, syrah.

85 Colour: cherry, garnet rim. Nose: ripe fruit, spicy, toasty, scrubland. Palate: powerful, flavourful, toasty.

RESERVA DE MARTÍN 2008 T
tempranillo.

90 Colour: bright cherry. Nose: ripe fruit, sweet spices, creamy oak, fresh. Palate: flavourful, fruity, toasty, round tannins.

ZETA 37 2007 T
tempranillo.

88 Colour: cherry, garnet rim. Nose: ripe fruit, spicy, creamy oak, toasty, earthy notes. Palate: powerful, flavourful, toasty.

The number of "Vino de la Tierra" categories granted so far, 45, means the status is growing in importance, given that growers are only required to specify geographical origin, grape variety and alcohol content. For some, it means an easy way forward for their more experimental projects, difficult to be contemplated by the stern regulations of the designations of origin, as it is the case of vast autonomous regions such as La Mancha, Castilla y León or Extremadura. For the great majority, it is a category able to fostering vineyards with high quality potential, a broader varietal catalogue and therefore the opportunity to come up with truly singular wines, a sort of sideway entrance to the DO status.

The different "Vino de la Tierra" designations have been listed in alphabetical order.

In theory, the "Vino de la Tierra" status is one step below that of the DO, and it is the Spanish equivalent to the French "Vins de Pays", which pioneered worldwide this sort of category. In Spain, however, it has some unique characteristics. For example, the fact that the designation "Vino de la Tierra" is not always the ultimate goal, but it is rather used as a springboard to achieve the highly desired DO category. In addition, as it has happened in other countries, many producers have opted for this type of association with less stringent regulations that allow them greater freedom to produce wine. Therefore, in this section there is a bit of everything: from great wines to more simple and ordinary examples, a broad catalogue that works as a sort of testing (and tasting!) field for singularity as well as for new flavours and styles derived from the use of local, autochthonous varieties.

The new Spanish Ley del Vino (Wine Law) maintains the former status of "Vino de la Tierra", but establishes an intermediate step between this and the DO one. They are the so-called 'Vinos de Calidad con Indicación Geográfica' (Quality Wines with Geographical Indication), under which the region in question must remain for a minimum of five years.

In the light of the tasting carried out for this section, there is a steady improvement in the quality of these wines, as well as fewer misgivings on the part of the wineries about the idea of joining these associations.

VT 3 RIBERAS

Granted by the administration at the end of 2008 for the wines produced and within the "3 Riberas" geographical indication. The different typologies are: rosé, white, red and noble wines.

VT ABANILLA

This small wine region comprises the municipalities of Abanilla and Fortuna –in the eastern part of the province of Murcia– and some 1500 hectares, although most of its production is sold to the neighbouring DO Alicante. The region enjoys a hot, dry climate, limestone soils and low rainfall, features all that account for good quality prospects, although there are some differences to be found between the northern and the southern areas within it, given the different altitudes. The grape varieties allowed in the region for red winemaking are: *bonicaire*, *cabernet sauvignon*, *forcallat tinta*, *garnacha tintorera*, *merlot*, *petit verdot*, *crujidera* and *syrah*. For white wines, we find *chardonnay*, *malvasía*, *moravia dulce*, *moscatel de grano menudo* and *sauvignon blanc*.

VT ALTIPLANO DE SIERRA NEVADA

With the goal to free Granada's geographical indication exclusively for the "Vino de Calidad" category, in 2009 the VT Norte de Granada changed its name to VT Altiplano de Sierra Nevada. The new geographical indication comprises 43 municipalities in the north of the province of Granada. The authorized grape varieties for white wine production in the region are *chardonnay, baladí verdejo, airen, torrontés, palomino, pedro ximénez, macabeo and sauvignon blanc*; also *tempranillo, monastrell, garnacha tinta, cabernet franc, cabernet sauvignon, pinot noir, merlot*, and *syrah* for red wines.

VT BAILÉN

Bailén wine region comprises 350 hectares in some municipal districts within the province of Jaén but fairly close to La Mancha. Wines are made mainly from the grape variety known as "*molinera de Bailén*", that cannot be found anywhere else in the world, but also from other red grape varieties such as *garnacha tinta, tempranillo* and *cabernet sauvignon*, as well as the white *pedro ximénez*.

VT BAJO ARAGÓN

The most "mediterranean" region within Aragón autonomous community, it borders three different provinces (Tarragona, Castellón and Teruel) and is divided in four areas: Campo de Belchite, Bajo Martín, Bajo Aragón and Matarraña. Soils are mainly clay and limestone in nature, very rich in minerals with high potash content. The climate is suitable for the right maturation of the grapes, with the added cooling effect of the 'Cierzo' (northerly wind), together with the day-night temperature contrast, just the perfect combination for the vines. The main varieties are *garnacha* (both red and white), although foreign grapes like *syrah, cabernet sauvignon, merlot* and *chardonnay* are also present, as well as *tempranillo* and *cariñena*.
www.vinodelatierradelbajoaragon.com

VT BARBANZA E IRIA

The last geographical indication to be granted to the autonomous region of Galicia back in 2007, Barbanza e Iria is located within the Ribera de la Ría de Arosa wine region, in the north of the province of Pontevedra. They make both red an white wines from with varieties such as *albariño, caíño blanco, godello, loureiro blanco* (also known as *marqués*), *treixadura* and *torrontés* (white); and *brancellao, caíño tinto, espadeiro, loureiro tinto, mencía* and *susón* (red).

VT BETANZOS

Betanzos, in the province of La Coruña, became the second VT designation to be granted in Galicia. The vineyards is planted with local white varieties like *blanco legítimo, Agudelo* (*godello*) and *jerez*, as well as red grapes like *garnacha, mencía* and *tempranillo*.

VT CÁDIZ

Located in the south of the province of Cádiz, a vast region with a long history of wine production, the "Vinos de la Tierra de Cádiz" comprises 15 municipalities still under the regulations of the DO regarding grape production, but not winemaking. The authorised white varieties are: *garrido, palomino, chardonnay, moscatel, mantúa, perruno, macabeo, sauvignon blanc* y *pedro ximénez*; as well as the red *tempranillo, syrah, cabernet sauvignon, garnacha tinta, monastrel, merlot, tintilla de rota, petit verdot* and *cabernet franc*.

VT CAMPO DE CARTAGENA

Campo de Cartagena is a flatland region close to the Mediterranean Sea and surrounded by mountains of a moderate height. The vineyard surface ascribed to the VT is just 8 hectares. The climate is mediterranean bordering on an arid, desert type, with very hot summers, mild temperatures for the rest of the year, and low and occasional rainfall. The main varieties in the region are *bonicaire, forcallat tinta, petit verdot, tempranillo, garnacha tintorera, crujidera, merlot, syrah* and *cabernet sauvignon* (red); and *chardonnay, malvasía, moravia dulce, moscatel de grano menudo* and *sauvignon blanc* (white).

VT CASTELLÓ

Located in the eastern part of Spain, on the Mediterranean coast, the geographical indication Vinos de la Tierra de Castelló is divided in two different areas: Alto Palancia –Alto Mijares, Sant Mateu and Les Useres–, and Vilafamés. The climatic conditions in this wine region are good to grow varieties such as *tempranillo, monastrell, garnacha, garnacha tintorera, cabernet sauvignon, merlot* and *syrah* (red),

along with *macabeo* and *merseguera* (white).
www.vinosdecastellon.com

VT CASTILLA Y LEÓN
Another one of the regional 'macro-designations' for the wines produced in up to 317 municipalities within the autonomous region of Castilla y León. A continental climate with little rainfall, together with diverse soil patterns, are the most distinctive features of a region that can be divided into the Duero basin (part of the Spanish central high plateau) and the mountainous perimeter that surrounds it.
www.asovintcal.com

VT CASTILLA
Castilla-La Mancha, a region that has the largest vineyard surface in the planet (600.000 hectares, equivalent to 6% of the world's total vineyard surface, and to half of Spain's) has been using this Vino de la Tierra label since 1999 (the year the status was granted) for wines produced outside its designations of origin. The main grape varieties are *airén, albillo, chardonnay, macabeo* (*viura*), *malvar, sauvignon blanc, merseguera, moscatel de grano menudo, pardillo* (marisancho), *Pedro Ximénez* and *torrontés* (white);and *bobal, cabernet sauvignon, garnacha tinta, merlot, monastrell, petit verdot, syrah, tempranillo, cencibel* (*jacivera*), *colour:aíllo, frasco, garnacha tintorera, moravia agria, moravia dulce* (*crujidera*), *negral* (tinto basto) and *tinto velasco* (red).

VT CÓRDOBA
It includes the wines produced in the province of Córdoba, with the exception of those bottled within the DO Montilla-Moriles label. All in all, we are talking of some 300 hectares and red and rosé wines made from *cabernet sauvignon, merlot, syrah, tempranillo, pinot noir* and *tintilla de Rota* grape varieties.

VT COSTA DE CANTABRIA
Wines produced in the Costa de Cantabria wine region as well as some inland valleys up to an altitude of 600 meters. The grape varieties used for white winemaking are *godello, albillo, chardonnay, malvasía, ondarribi zuri, picapoll blanco* and *verdejo blanco*; and just two for red wines: *ondarribi beltza* and *verdejo negro*. The region comprises some 8 hectares of vineyards.

VT CUMBRES DE GUADALFEO
Formerly known as "Vino de la Tierra de Contraviesa-Alpujarra", this geographical indication is used for wines made in the wine region located in the western part of the Alpujarras, in a border territory between two provinces (Granada and Almería), two rivers (Guadalfeo and Andarax), and very close to the Mediterranean Sea. The grape varieties used for white wine production are *montúa, chardonnay, sauvignon blanc, moscatel, jaén blanca, Pedro Ximénez, vijirego* y *perruno*; for red wines, they have *garnacha tinta, tempranillo, cabernet sauvignon, cabernet franc, merlot, pinot noir* and *syrah*.

VT DESIERTO DE ALMERÍA
Granted in the summer of 2003, the wine region comprises a diverse territory in the north of the province of Almería that includes the Tabernas Dessert as well as parts of the Sierra de Alhamilla, Sierra de Cabrera and the Cabo de Gata Natural Park. Harsh, climatic desert conditions follow a regular pattern of hot days and cooler nights that influence heavily the character of the resulting wines. The vineyard's average altitude is 525 meters. The varieties planted are *chardonnay, moscatel, macabeo* and *sauvignon blanc* (white); as well as *tempranillo, cabernet sauvignon, monastrell, merlot, syrah* and *garnacha tinta* (red).
www.vinosdealmeria.es/zonas-viticolas/desierto-de-almeria

VT EIVISSA
The production area includes the entire island of Ibiza (Eivissa), with the vineyards located in small valleys amongst the mountains –which are never higher than 500 meters– on clay-reddish soil covered by a thin limestone crust. Low rainfall levels and hot, humid summers are the most interesting climatic features. The authorized red varieties are *monastrell,*

tempranillo, *cabernet sauvignon*, *merlot* and *syrah*; *macabeo*, *parellada*, *malvasía*, *chardonnay* and *moscatel* make up the white-grape catalogue.

VT EXTREMADURA
It comprises all the municipalitics within the provinces of Cáceres and Badajoz, made up of six different wine regions. In December 1990, the regional government approved the regulations submitted by the Comisión Interprofesional de Vinos de la Tierra de Extremadura, and approved its creation. The varieties used for the production of white wines are *alarije*, *borba*, *cayetana blanca*, *chardonnay*, *chelva*, *malvar*, *viura*, *parellada*, *Pedro Ximénez* and *verdejo*; for red wines, they have *bobal*, *mazuela*, *monastrell*, *tempranillo*, *garnacha*, *graciano*, *merlot*, *syrah* and *cabernet sauvignon*.

VT FORMENTERA
This geographical indication comprises the wines produced in the island of Formentera. The dry, subtropical mediterranean climate, characterised by abundant sunshine hours and summers with high temperatures and humidity levels but little rainfall, evidently requires grape varieties well adapted to this type of weather. Red varieties are *monastrell*, *fogoneu*, *tempranillo*, *cabernet sauvignon* and *merlot*; *malvasía*, *premsal blanco*, *chardonnay* and *viognier* make up its white-grape catalogue.

VT GÁLVEZ
Gálvez wine region, located in the province of Toledo, comprises nine municipalities: Cuerva, Gálvez, Guadamur, Menasalvas, Mazambraz, Polán, Pulgar, San Martín de Montalbán and Totanes. The authorized grape varieties are *tempranillo* and *garnacha tinta*.

VT ILLA DE MENORCA
The island of Menorca, a Biosphere Reserve, has a singular topography of gentle slopes; marl soils with a complex substratum of limestone, sandstone and slate, a mediterranean climate and northerly winter winds are the most significant features from a viticultural point of view. The wines produces in the island should be made exclusively from white grape varieties like *chardonnay*, *macabeo*, *malvasía*, *moscatel*, *parellada* or *moll*; as for the red renderings, *cabernet sauvignon*, *merlot*, *monastrell*, *tempranillo* and *syrah* get clearly the upper hand.

VT LADERAS DE GENIL
Formerly known (up to 2009) as VT Granada Suroeste, the label includes some 53 municipalities in the province of Granada. The region enjoys a unique microclimate very suitable for grape growing, given its low rainfall and the softening effect of the Mediterranean Sea. The white grape varieties used for wine production are *vijiriego*, *macabeo*, *Pedro Ximénez*, *palomino*, *moscatel de Alejandría*, *chardonnay* and *sauvignon blanc*; as well as the red *garnacha tinta*, *perruna*, *tempranillo*, *cabernet sauvignon*, *merlot*, *syrah* and *pinot noir*, predominantly.

VT LAUJAR-ALPUJARRA
This wine region is located at an altitude of 800 to 1500 meters between the Sierra de Gádor and the Sierra Nevada Natural Park. It has some 800 hectares of vines grown on terraces. Soils are chalk soils poor in organic matter, rocky and with little depth. The climate is moderately continental, given the sea influence and its high night-day temperature differential. The predominant grape varieties are *jaén blanco*, *macabeo*, *vijiriego*, *Pedro Ximénez*, *chardonay* and *moscatel de grano menudo* (white); and *cabernet sauvignon*, *merlot*, monastrell, *tempranillo*, *garnachas tinta* and *syrah* (red).
www.vinosdealmeria.es/bodegas/vino-de-la-tierra-laujar-alpujarra

VT LIÉBANA
VT Liébana includes the municipalities of Potes, Pesagüero, Cabezón de Liébana, Camaleño, Castro Cillorigo y Vega de Liébana, all of them within the area of Liébana, located in the southwest of the Cantabria bordering

with Asturias, León and Palencia. The authorized varieties are *mencía, tempranillo, garnacha, garciano, merlot, syrah, pinot noir, albarín negro* and *cabernet sauvignon* (red); and *palomino, godello, verdejo, albillo, chardonnay* and *albarín blanco* (white).

VT LOS PALACIOS
Los Palacios is located in the south-western part of the province of Sevilla, by the lower area of the Guadalquivir river valley. The wines included in this VT are white wines made from *airén, chardonnay, colombard* and *sauvignon blanc*.

VT MALLORCA
The production area of VT Mallorca includes all the municipalities within the island, which has predominantly limestone soils with abundant clay and sandstone, and a mediterranean climate with mild temperatures all-year-round. Red varieties present in the island are *callet, manto negro, cabernet sauvignon, fogoneu, merlot, monastrell, syrah, tempranillo* and *pinot noir*, along with the white *prensal* (*moll*), *chardonnay, macabeo, malvasía, moscatel de Alejandría, moscatel de grano menudo, parellada, riesling* and *sauvignon blanc*.

VT NORTE DE ALMERÍA
The Vinos de la Tierra Norte de Almería label comprises four municipalities in the Norte de Almería area, right in the north of the province. They produce white, red and rosé wines from grape varieties such as *airén, chardonnay, macabeo* and *sauvignon blanc* (white); as well as *cabernet sauvignon, merlot, monastrell, tempranillo* and *syrah* for red winemaking and *tempranillo* and *monastrell* for rosé.

VT POZOHONDO
The regulations for VT Pozoblanco were approved by the autonomous government of Castilla-La Mancha in the year 2000. It comprises the municipalities of Alcadozo, Peñas de San Pedro and Pozohondo, all of them in the province of Albacete.

VT RIBERA DEL ANDARAX
The Ribera del Andarax wine region is located in the middle area of the Andarax river valley at an altitude of 700 to 900 meters. Soils are varied in structure, with abundant slate, clay and sand. It enjoys an extreme mediterranean climate, with low occasional rainfall and high average temperatures. The grape varieties present in the region are predominantly *macabeo, chardonnay* and *sauvignon blanc* (white); and *cabernet sauvignon, merlot, syrah, garnacha, tempranillo, monastrell* and *pinot noir* (red).
www.vinosdealmeria.es/zonas-viticolas/ribera-de-andarax

VT RIBERA DEL GÁLLEGO-CINCO VILLAS
Ribera del Gállego-Cinco Villas wine region is located in the territory along the Gállego river valley until it almost reaches the city of Zaragoza. Although small, its vineyards are shared between the provinces of Huesca and Zaragoza. Soils are mostly gravel in structure, which affords good drainage. The grape varieties used for wine production are *garnacha, tempranillo, carbernet sauvignon* and *merlot* (red), and mostly *macabeo* for white wines.
www.vinosdelatierradearagon.es

VT RIBERA DEL JILOCA
Ribera del Jiloca, located in the south-eastern part of Aragón along the Jiloca river valley, is a wine region with a great winemaking potential, given its geo-climatic conditions. Vines are mostly planted on slate terraces perched on the slopes of the Sistema Ibérico mountain range, at high altitude, something that affords wines of great quality and singularity. Vines are planted mostly on alluvial limestone terraces of ancient river beds. *Garnacha* is the predominant grape, followed by *macabeo*. A dry climate, abundant sunlight hours and cold winters are the features that account for the excellent quality of the local grapes.
www.vinosdelatierradearagon.es/empresas/ribera_del_jiloca.php

VT RIBERA DEL QUEILES

Up to sixteen municipalities from two different provinces (seven from Navarra and nine from Zaragoza) are part of the VT Ribera del Queiles. Wines are exclusively red, made from *cabernet sauvignon, graciano, garnacha tinta, merlot, tempranillo* and *syrah*. It has a regulating and controlling body (Comité Regulador de Control y Certificación) and so far just one winery.
www.vinosdelatierradearagon.es

VT SERRA DE TRAMUNTANA-COSTA NORD

Currently, this VT comprises 41,14 hectares an up to eighteen municipal districts in the island of Mallorca, between the cape of Formentor and the southwest coast of Andratx, with mainly brownish-grey and limestone soils. Single-variety wines from *malvasía, moscatel, moll, parellada, macabeo, chardonnay* and *sauvignon blanc* (white), as well as *cabernet sauvignon, merlot, syrah, monastrell, tempranillo, callet* and *manto negro* (red) stand out.

VT SIERRA DE ALCARAZ

The Sierra del Alcaraz wine region comprises the municipal districts of Alcaraz, El Ballestero, El Bonillo, Povedilla, Robledo, and Viveros, located in the western part of the province of Albacete, bordering with Ciudad Real. The VT status was granted by the autonomous government of Castilla-La Mancha in the year 2000. The red varieties planted in the region are *cabernet sauvignon, merlot, bobal, monastrell, garnacha tinta* and *garnacha tintorera*; along with white *moravia dulce, chardonnay, chelva, eva, alarije, malvar, borba, parellada, cayetana blanca* and *Pedro Ximénez*.

VT SIERRA DE LAS ESTANCIAS Y LOS FILABRES

Located in the namesake mountain region in the province of Almería, this VT was approved along with its regulations in 2008. The grape varieties planted in the region are *airén, chardonnay, macabeo, sauvignon blanc* and *moscatel de grano menudo* –also known as morisco–, all of them white; and red *cabernet sauvignon, merlot, monastrell, tempranillo, syrah, garnacha tinta, pinot noir* and *petit verdot*.

VT SIERRA NORTE DE SEVILLA

This region, located in the north of the province of Sevilla at the foothills of Sierra Morena, has a landscape of gentle hills and altitudes that range from 250 to almost 1000 metres. The climate in the region is mediterranean, with hot, dry summers, mild winters and a fairly high average rainfall. Since 1998, grape varieties such as *tempranillo, garnacha tinta, cabernet sauvignon, cabernet franc, merlot, pinot noir, petit verdot* and *syrah* (red); and *chardonnay, Pedro Ximénez, colombard, sauvignon blanc, palomino* and *moscatel de Alejandría* (white) have been planted in the region.

VT SIERRA SUR DE JAÉN

In this VT there are some 400 hectares planted with vines, although a minor percentage are table grapes. The label includes wines made in the Sierra Sur de Jaén wine region. White wines are made from *jaén blanca* and *chardonnay*, and red from *garnacha tinta, tempranillo, cabernet sauvignon, merlot, syrah* and *pinot noir*.

VT TORREPEROGIL

This geographical indication in the province of Jaén, whose regulations were approved in 2006, comprises 300 hectares in the area of La Loma, right in the centre of the province. The climate is mediterranean with continental influence, with cold winters and dry and hot summers. The wines are made mainly from *garnacha tinta, syrah, cabernet sauvignon* and *tempranillo* (red); and *jaén blanco* and *Pedro Ximénez* (white).

VT VALDEJALÓN

Established in 1998, it comprises 36 municipal districts in the mid- and lower-Jalón river valley. The vines are planted on alluvial, brownish-grey limestone soils, with low annual average rainfall of some 350 mm. They grape varieties planted are white (*macabeo, garnacha blanca, moscatel* and *airén*) and red

(*garnacha*, *tempranillo*, *cabernet sauvignon*, *syrah*, *monastrell* and *merlot*).
www.vinodelatierravaldejalon.com

VT VALLE DEL CINCA
Located in the southeast of the province of Huesca, almost bordering with Catalunya, Valle del Cinca is a traditional wine region that enjoys favourable climatic and soil conditions for vine growing: soils are mainly limestone and clay, and the average annual rainfall barely reaches 300 mm (irrigation is usually required). Grape varieties predominantly planted in the region are *macabeo* and *chardonnay* (white), along with *garnacha tinta*, *tempranillo*, *cabernet sauvignon* and *merlot* (red).
www.vinosdelatierradearagon.es

VT VALLE DEL MIÑO-OURENSE
This wine region is located in the north of the province of Ourense, along the Miño river valley. The authorized grape varieties are *treixadura*, *torrontés*, *godello*, *albariño*, *loureira* and *palomino* –also known as *xerez*– for white wines, and *mencía*, *brancellao*, *mouratón*, *sousón*, *caíño* and *garnacha* for reds.

VT VALLES DE SADACIA
A designation created to include the wines made from the grape variety known as *moscatel riojana*, which was practically lost with the phylloxera bug and has been recuperated to produce both "vino de licor" and normal white *moscatel*. Depending on winemaking, the latter may either be dry, semi-dry or sweet. The vineyards that belong to this VT are mainly located in the south-western part of the region, in the Sadacia and Cidacos river valleys, overall a very suitable territory for vine growing purposes.

VT VILLAVICIOSA DE CÓRDOBA
One of the most recent geographical indications granted by the autonomous government of Andalucía back in 2008, it includes white and sweet wines made in the Villaviciosa wine region. The authorized varieties are *baladí verdejo*, *moscatel de Alejandría*, *palomino fino*, *palomino*, *Pedro Ximénez*, *airén*, *calagraño Jaén*, *torrontés* and *verdejo*.

ALTIPLANO DE SIERRA NEVADA

BODEGA JABALCÓN

Ctra. de Granada, Km. 3
18800 Baza (Granada)
☎: +34 958 063 887 - Fax: +34 958 063 887
info@bodegasjabalcon.com
www.bodegasjabalcon.com

JABALCÓN BENZALEMA 2011 B

83

JABALCÓN 2010 T
tempranillo, cabernet sauvignon, garnacha.

87 Colour: cherry, garnet rim. Nose: ripe fruit, earthy notes, fragrant herbs. Palate: light-bodied, flavourful, long, spicy.

JABALCÓN CERROJO 2007 T
tempranillo, cabernet sauvignon, garnacha.

85 Colour: cherry, garnet rim. Nose: fruit preserve, spicy, roasted coffee. Palate: ripe fruit, toasty, light-bodied.

BODEGAS MUÑANA

Finca Peñas Prietas - Ctra. Graena a La Peza
18517 Cortes y Graena (Granada)
☎: +34 958 670 715 - Fax: +34 958 670 715
bodegasmunana@gmail.com
www.bodegasmunana.com

MUÑANA 3 CEPAS 2009 T
syrah, cabernet sauvignon, merlot.

90 Colour: cherry, garnet rim. Nose: red berry notes, ripe fruit, mineral, balsamic herbs, spicy. Palate: light-bodied, flavourful, long, round.

MUÑANA Ñ 2009 T
tempranillo, cabernet sauvignon, monastrell.

89 Colour: light cherry, garnet rim. Nose: ripe fruit, earthy notes, scrubland. Palate: long, flavourful, balanced, spicy.

MUÑANA PETIT VERDOT 2009 T
petit verdot.

87 Colour: cherry, garnet rim. Nose: ripe fruit, balsamic herbs, spicy, toasty. Palate: flavourful, spicy, long, toasty.

DOMINGO Y QUILES

Calvo Sotelo, 3
18840 Galera (Granada)
☎: +34 958 739 227
info@bodegasdq.es
www.bodegasdq.es

BARBATA 2011 B
100% macabeo.

82

VIÑA GALIRA 2009 T ROBLE
tempranillo, cabernet sauvignon.

84

VIÑA GALIRA 2008 T
tempranillo, cabernet sauvignon.

89 Colour: bright cherry. Nose: ripe fruit, sweet spices, creamy oak, expressive. Palate: flavourful, fruity, toasty, round tannins.

IRVING

Finca el Duque Ctra. de Huéscar a Santiago de la Espada. km 13,500
18830 Huéscar (Granada)
☎: +34 653 527 560 - Fax: +34 917 150 632
pedidos@irving.es
www.irving.es

IRVING COLECCIÓN FAMILIAR 2008 T
50% tempranillo, 35% cabernet sauvignon, 7,5% merlot, 7,5% syrah.

84

MARQUÉS DE CASA PARDIÑAS C.B.

Finca San Torcuato
18540 Huélago (Granada)
☎: +34 630 901 094 - Fax: +34 958 252 297
info@spiracp.es
www.marquesdecasapardiñas.com

SPIRA VENDIMIA SELECCIONADA 2011 T
80% tempranillo, 20% cabernet sauvignon.

91 Colour: cherry, garnet rim. Nose: red berry notes, ripe fruit, balsamic herbs, scrubland, roasted coffee. Palate: fine bitter notes, flavourful, long, balsamic, toasty.

SPIRA 2008 TC
60% tempranillo, 35% cabernet sauvignon, 5% merlot.

88 Colour: light cherry, orangey edge. Nose: earthy notes, ripe fruit, balsamic herbs. Palate: powerful, flavourful, toasty.

MÉNDEZ MOYA

Ctra. El Pocico, Km. 9,5
18512 Dólar (Granada)
☎: +34 629 123 399 - Fax: +34 958 698 018
jose@mendezmoya.com
www.mendezmoya.com

MENDEZ MOYA 2008 T
100% cabernet sauvignon.

86 Colour: cherry, garnet rim. Nose: earthy notes, acetaldehyde, fruit preserve, wild herbs, spicy. Palate: powerful, flavourful, reductive nuances.

PAGO DE ALMARAES

Ctra. Fonelas, s/n - Camino de los Almaraes
18518 Benalua (Granada)
☎: +34 958 348 752 - Fax: +34 958 333 444
bodegapagodealmaraes@hotmail.es

ALMARAES MEMENTO 2008 T
cabernet sauvignon, tempranillo, syrah, merlot, cabernet franc.

88 Colour: cherry, garnet rim. Nose: earthy notes, ripe fruit, scrubland, spicy, toasty. Palate: powerful, flavourful, complex.

BAJO ARAGÓN

AMPRIUS LAGAR

Los –Enebros, 74 – 2ª planta
44002 (Teruel)
☎: +34 978 623 077
pedrocasas@ampriuslagar.es
www.ampriuslagar.es

LAGAR D'AMPRIUS CHARDONNAY 2011 B
chardonnay.

90 Colour: bright straw. Nose: white flowers, candied fruit, wild herbs. Palate: flavourful, fruity, good acidity.

LAGAR D'AMPRIUS GARNACHA 2010 T
garnacha.

89 Colour: bright cherry. Nose: sweet spices, creamy oak, fruit liqueur notes, balsamic herbs. Palate: flavourful, fruity, toasty, long.

LAGAR D'AMPRIUS GARNACHA SYRAH 2010 T
35% garnacha, 65% syrah.

87 Colour: bright cherry. Nose: ripe fruit, sweet spices, creamy oak, grassy. Palate: flavourful, fruity, toasty, round tannins.

BODEGA COOP. NTRA. SRA. DEL OLIVAR

Avda. José Antonio s/n
50131 Lecera (Zaragoza)
☎: +34 976 835 016 - Fax: +34 976 835 016
valssira@bodegasvalssira.es
www.bodegasvalssira.es

VALSSIRA 2011 T
100% garnacha.

87 Colour: bright cherry, cherry, garnet rim. Nose: balanced, fruit expression, wild herbs. Palate: flavourful, fruity, easy to drink.

VALSSIRA 2011 T FERMENTADO EN BARRICA
100% garnacha.

84

VALSSIRA 12 2007 T
100% garnacha.

88 Colour: cherry, garnet rim. Nose: ripe fruit, creamy oak, toasty, fine reductive notes. Palate: flavourful, toasty, round tannins.

VALSSIRA 24 MESES BARRICA 2005 T
100% garnacha.

84

BODEGAS CRIAL LLEDÓ

Arrabal de la Fuente, 23
44624 Lledó (Teruel)
☎: +34 978 891 909 - Fax: +34 978 891 995
crial@bodegascrial.com

CRIAL 2011 B
86% macabeo, 14% garnacha.

87 Colour: bright straw. Nose: fresh fruit, white flowers, dried herbs. Palate: flavourful, fruity, good acidity.

CRIAL 2011 RD
100% garnacha.

84

CRIAL 2011 T
50% garnacha, 50% syrah.

87 Colour: cherry, purple rim. Nose: red berry notes, ripe fruit, floral, violets. Palate: correct, light-bodied, fresh, fruity.

CRIAL LLEDÓ 2007 TC
cabernet sauvignon.

86 Colour: cherry, garnet rim. Nose: ripe fruit, spicy, toasty, balsamic herbs. Palate: powerful, flavourful, toasty, long.

CELLER D'ALGARS

Cooperativa, 9
44622 Arenys De Lledó (Teruel)
☎: +34 978 853 147 - Fax: +34 978 853 147
info@cellerdalgars.com
www.enigmma.es

MUSAS 2011 B
40% garnacha blanca, 40% chenin blanc, 20% macabeo.

88 Colour: bright straw. Nose: faded flowers, fruit expression, fresh fruit. Palate: good acidity, flavourful.

DOGMA 2009 T
70% garnacha, 20% syrah, 10% cabernet sauvignon.

88 Colour: bright cherry. Nose: ripe fruit, sweet spices, nose:tic coffee, dark chocolate, scrubland. Palate: flavourful, fruity, toasty, round tannins.

VIRTUTIS CAUSA 2007 T
50% syrah, 35% garnacha, 15% cabernet sauvignon.

91 Colour: cherry, garnet rim. Nose: ripe fruit, spicy, creamy oak, toasty, expressive, mineral. Palate: powerful, flavourful, toasty, round tannins.

COOPERATIVA DEL CAMPO SAN PEDRO

Avda. Reino de Aragón, 10
44623 Cretas (Teruel)
☎: +34 978 850 309 - Fax: +34 978 850 309
coop.cretas@telefonica.net
www.cooperativasanpedro.es

BELVÍ 2011 B
100% garnacha blanca.

83

BELVÍ 2011 RD
100% garnacha.

84

EMPERLE 2011 T
garnacha, tempranillo, syrah.

82

BELVÍ 2009 T
garnacha, tempranillo, syrah.

83

DOMINIO MAESTRAZGO

Royal III, B12
44550 Alcorisa (Teruel)
☎: +34 978 840 642 - Fax: +34 978 840 642
bodega@dominiomaestrazgo.com
www.dominiomaestrazgo.com

SANTOLEA 2011 T
85% garnacha, 15% tempranillo.

86 Colour: cherry, garnet rim. Nose: ripe fruit, spicy, creamy oak, toasty, balsamic herbs. Palate: powerful, flavourful, toasty.

DOMINIO MAESTRAZGO 2010 T ROBLE
65% garnacha, 20% tempranillo, 15% syrah.

91 Colour: cherry, garnet rim. Nose: red berry notes, ripe fruit, scrubland, spicy, creamy oak. Palate: long, powerful, flavourful, spicy.

DOMINIO MAESTRAZGO SYRAH 2010 T BARRICA
100% syrah.

85 Colour: cherry, garnet rim. Nose: spicy, creamy oak, fruit preserve. Palate: powerful, flavourful, toasty.

REX DEUS 2005 T ROBLE
85% garnacha, 10% syrah, 5% cabernet sauvignon.

90 Colour: bright cherry. Nose: ripe fruit, creamy oak, earthy notes, spicy, toasty, dry stone. Palate: flavourful, fruity, toasty, balanced.

EVOHE BODEGAS

Ignacio de Ara, 3
50002 Zaragoza (Zaragoza)
☎: +34 976 461 056 - Fax: +34 976 461 558
nosotros@evohegarnacha.com
www.evohegarnacha.com

EVOHÉ GARNACHA 2011 T
100% garnacha.

90 Colour: cherry, purple rim. Nose: floral, red berry notes, scrubland, earthy notes. Palate: full, powerful, flavourful, long, balsamic.

GRUPO MAGALIA

Avda. de Aragón 110
50710 Maella (Zaragoza)
☎: +34 976 638 004 - Fax: +34 976 639 215
gerencia@magalia.org
www.magalia.org

MAGALIA 2011 B
garnacha blanca.

83

MAGALIA 2011 T
garnacha.

85 Colour: light cherry, garnet rim. Nose: ripe fruit, fruit preserve, balsamic herbs. Palate: light-bodied, fresh, fruity.

MAGALIA SELECCIÓN 2010 T
garnacha, syrah.

88 Colour: cherry, garnet rim. Nose: ripe fruit, earthy notes, balsamic herbs, creamy oak. Palate: powerful, flavourful, toasty.

MONTANER

Avda. Aragón 85
50710 Maella (Zaragoza)
☎: +34 976 638 384 - Fax: +34 976 638 384
vinosmontaner@telefonica.net

BARONO GARNACHA BLANCA 2011 B
garnacha blanca.

83

FINCA MAS NOU BARONO 2011 T
garnacha, syrah, cabernet sauvignon.

88 Colour: cherry, purple rim. Nose: candied fruit, ripe fruit, balsamic herbs. Palate: light-bodied, fresh, fruity, flavourful.

BARONO 2010 T
garnacha, syrah, cabernet sauvignon.

89 Colour: light cherry, garnet rim. Nose: red berry notes, ripe fruit, sweet spices, creamy oak. Palate: powerful, flavourful, full.

BARONO 2 ANGEL & JAVIER 2009 T
garnacha, syrah, cabernet sauvignon.

88 Colour: cherry, garnet rim. Nose: ripe fruit, floral, sweet spices, toasty. Palate: flavourful, fruity, toasty, long.

VENTA D'AUBERT

Ctra. Valderrobres a Arnes, Km. 28
44623 Cretas (Teruel)
☎: +34 978 769 021 - Fax: +34 978 769 031
ventadaubert@gmx.net
www.ventadaubert.com

VENTA D'AUBERT 2011 B
chardonnay, garnacha blanca, viognier.

91 Colour: bright golden. Nose: floral, ripe fruit, fragrant herbs, mineral, spicy. Palate: powerful, flavourful, long, spicy, balanced.

VENTA D'AUBERT VIOGNIER 2011 B
viognier.

90 Colour: bright straw. Nose: white flowers, fragrant herbs, citrus fruit, fruit expression, mineral. Palate: flavourful, fresh, balanced.

VENTA D'AUBERT CABERNET SAUVIGNON 2007 T
cabernet sauvignon.

89 Colour: cherry, garnet rim. Nose: ripe fruit, spicy, toasty, earthy notes, balsamic herbs. Palate: powerful, flavourful, toasty, round tannins.

VENTA D'AUBERT SYRAH 2006 T
syrah.

90 Colour: cherry, garnet rim. Nose: ripe fruit, spicy, creamy oak, toasty, complex. Palate: powerful, flavourful, toasty, round tannins.

VENTA D'AUBERT 2005 T
cabernet sauvignon, merlot, cabernet franc.

88 Colour: pale ruby, brick rim edge. Nose: spicy, fine reductive notes, wet leather, aged wood nuances, scrubland. Palate: spicy, fine tannins, elegant, long.

DIONUS 2005 TR

86 Colour: pale ruby, brick rim edge. Nose: spicy, aged wood nuances, fruit liqueur notes, balsamic herbs, toasty. Palate: spicy, fine tannins, long, balanced.

CÁDIZ

BODEGAS BARBADILLO

Luis de Eguilaz, 11
11540 Sanlúcar de Barrameda (Cádiz)
☎: +34 956 385 500 - Fax: +34 956 385 501
barbadillo@barbadillo.com
www.barbadillo.com

CASTILLO DE SAN DIEGO 2011 B
palomino.

85 Colour: bright golden. Nose: dried flowers, candied fruit, medium intensity. Palate: fresh, fruity, easy to drink.

MAESTRANTE 2011 B
palomino.

85 Colour: golden. Nose: powerfull, floral, candied fruit, fragrant herbs. Palate: flavourful, sweet, fresh, fruity, easy to drink.

GIBALBÍN 2010 T
tempranillo, syrah, merlot, cabernet sauvignon.

87 Colour: cherry, garnet rim. Nose: red berry notes, ripe fruit, floral, wild herbs. Palate: flavourful, fruity, warm, easy to drink.

GIBALBÍN 2009 T ROBLE
tempranillo, merlot, tintilla de rota.

84

CORTIJO DE JARA

Cortijo de Jara, Ctra. de Gibalbin, Km. 5
11407 Jerez de la Frontera (Cádiz)
☎: +34 956 338 163 - Fax: +34 956 338 163
puerta.nueva@terra.es
www.cortijodejara.com

CORTIJO DE JARA 2009 T ROBLE
tempranillo, merlot, syrah.

84

FINCA MONCLOA

Manuel María González, 12
11403 Jerez de la Frontera (Cádiz)
☎: +34 956 357 000 - Fax: +34 956 357 043
nacional@gonzalezbyass.com
www.gonzalezbyass.com

FINCA MONCLOA 09 BARRICAS 2009 T
52,2% cabernet sauvignon, 28,3% syrah, 13% petit verdot, 6,5% tintilla de rota.

90 Colour: cherry, garnet rim. Nose: red berry notes, scrubland, mineral, toasty. Palate: balanced, flavourful, spicy, toasty.

FINCA MONCLOA 2009 T
51,9% syrah, 45,9% cabernet sauvignon, 1,6% tintilla de rota, petit verdot.

88 Colour: cherry, garnet rim. Nose: ripe fruit, earthy notes, spicy, toasty. Palate: long, powerful, flavourful, toasty.

HUERTA DE ALBALÁ

Ctra. CA - 6105, Km. 4
11630 Arcos de la Frontera (Cádiz)
☎: +34 956 101 300 - Fax: +34 856 023 053
bodega@huertadealbala.com
www.huertadealbala.com

BARBAZUL 2010 T
syrah, merlot, cabernet sauvignon.

88 Colour: bright cherry. Nose: sweet spices, creamy oak, expressive, candied fruit. Palate: flavourful, fruity, toasty, round tannins, fine bitter notes.

CASTELLÓ

BODEGAS CASTILLO DE LA DUQUESA

Calle Mar, 116
12181 Benlloch (Castellón)
☎: +34 693 299 449 - Fax: +34 964 339 958
info@banus.eu
www.banus.eu

BANÚS 2011 B
100% verdejo.

87 Colour: bright straw. Nose: fresh, fresh fruit, citrus fruit, expressive, floral. Palate: flavourful, fruity, good acidity, balanced.

BANÚS 2011 RD
garnacha, cabernet sauvignon, monastrell.

84

ILDVM TEMPRANILLO 2011 T
100% tempranillo.

87 Colour: cherry, purple rim. Nose: expressive, red berry notes, floral, spicy. Palate: flavourful, fruity, good acidity, round, balanced.

ILDVM CABERNET SAUVIGNON 2011 T
100% cabernet sauvignon.

86 Colour: cherry, purple rim. Nose: red berry notes, floral, fragrant herbs. Palate: flavourful, fruity, balsamic, spicy.

ILDVM SYRAH 2011 T
100% syrah.

85 Colour: cherry, purple rim. Nose: red berry notes, floral, sweet spices, creamy oak. Palate: flavourful, fruity, good acidity, round tannins.

BANÚS 2011 T
garnacha, cabernet sauvignon.

83

BODEGAS Y VIÑEDOS BARÓN D'ALBA

Partida Vilar la Call, 10
12118 Les Useres (Castellón)
☎: +34 608 032 884 - Fax: +34 964 313 455
barondalba@gmail.com
www.barondalba.com

CLOS D'ESGARRACORDES 2011 B
macabeo.

84

CLOS D' ESGARRACORDES 2011 RD
50% tempranillo, 50% garnacha.

80

CLOS D'ESGARRACORDES 2008 T BARRICA
60% tempranillo, 30% merlot, 10% monastrell.

88 Colour: pale ruby, brick rim edge. Nose: ripe fruit, balsamic herbs, aged wood nuances, spicy, toasty. Palate: fresh, flavourful, balsamic, spicy.

CLOS D'ESGARRACORDES 2007 TC
cabernet sauvignon, tempranillo, merlot, syrah.

87 Colour: cherry, garnet rim. Nose: fruit preserve, dark chocolate, balanced, scrubland, warm. Palate: balanced, fine bitter notes, round tannins.

FINCA TORREGIL

Santo Tomás, 18
12560 Benicassim (Castellón)
☎: +34 669 476 586 - Fax: +34 669 476 586
rgil@lumensoft.net
www.banus.eu

ALVARO GIL SYRAH 2011 T
syrah.

86 Colour: cherry, purple rim. Nose: ripe fruit, balsamic herbs, spicy, toasty. Palate: fresh, fruity, flavourful, correct.

ALVARO GIL MERLOT 2011 T
merlot.

84

CASTILLA

AGRÍCOLA CASA DE LA VIÑA

Ctra. de la Solana Vva de los Infantes, Km. 15,2
13248 Alhambra (Ciudad Real)
☎: +34 926 696 044
bodega@bodegascasadelavina.com
www.bodegascasadelavina.com

CASA DE LA VIÑA CHARDONNAY 2011 B
chardonnay.

83

CASA DE LA VIÑA EDICIÓN LIMITADA 2009 T
tempranillo, syrah.

88 Colour: cherry, garnet rim. Nose: red berry notes, ripe fruit, cocoa bean, sweet spices. Palate: powerful, flavourful, toasty, long.

CASA DE LA VIÑA TEMPRANILLO 2011 T
tempranillo.

86 Colour: cherry, purple rim. Nose: floral, lactic notes, red berry notes, ripe fruit. Palate: powerful, flavourful, easy to drink, warm.

CASA DE LA VIÑA TEMPRANILLO 2008 T BARRICA
tempranillo.

87 Colour: cherry, garnet rim. Nose: red berry notes, ripe fruit, balsamic herbs, sweet spices. Palate: fine bitter notes, flavourful, long.

ALTOLANDÓN

Ctra. N-330, km. 242
16330 Landete (Cuenca)
☎: +34 962 300 662 - Fax: +34 962 300 662
altolandon@altolandon.com
www.altolandon.com

L AME MALBEC 2008 T
100% malbec.

89 Colour: cherry, garnet rim. Nose: ripe fruit, floral, fragrant herbs, spicy, creamy oak. Palate: flavourful, complex, long, balsamic.

ARÚSPIDE

Ciriaco Cruz, 2
13300 Valdepeñas (Ciudad Real)
☎: +34 926 347 075
info@aruspide.com
www.aruspide.com

ÁGORA VIOGNIER 2011 B
100% viognier.

86 Colour: bright yellow. Nose: floral, ripe fruit, tropical fruit, fresh. Palate: powerful, flavourful, fruity.

ÁGORA LÁGRIMA 2011 B
85% airén, 15% verdejo.

85 Colour: bright straw. Nose: dried flowers, candied fruit, fresh. Palate: light-bodied, fresh, fruity, sweetness.

EL LINZE 2010 B
100% viognier.

87 Colour: bright yellow. Nose: ripe fruit, dried herbs, faded flowers, creamy oak. Palate: correct, flavourful, fruity.

AUTOR DE ARÚSPIDE CHARDONNAY 2009 B
100% chardonnay.

86 Colour: bright yellow. Nose: powerfull, ripe fruit, sweet spices, jasmine. Palate: rich, flavourful, fresh, good acidity.

PURA SAVIA 2011 T
100% tempranillo.

87 Colour: cherry, purple rim. Nose: red berry notes, ripe fruit, sweet spices, creamy oak. Palate: powerful, flavourful, fruity, easy to drink.

ÁGORA 2011 T MACERACIÓN CARBÓNICA
100% tempranillo.

87 Colour: cherry, purple rim. Nose: expressive, fresh fruit, red berry notes, floral. Palate: flavourful, fruity, good acidity.

ÁGORA MALBEC 2011 T
100% malbec.

85 Colour: cherry, purple rim. Nose: ripe fruit, floral, fragrant herbs, spicy. Palate: light-bodied, fresh, fruity.

EL LINZE 2008 T
85% syrah, 15% tinto velasco.

89 Colour: deep cherry, garnet rim. Nose: raspberry, red berry notes, spicy, creamy oak, violets. Palate: powerful, flavourful, fruity, toasty.

AUTOR DE ARÚSPIDE TEMPRANILLO 2007 T
100% tempranillo.

89 Colour: cherry, garnet rim. Nose: ripe fruit, creamy oak, sweet spices, dark chocolate. Palate: powerful, flavourful, toasty, harsh oak tannins.

ÁGORA 2007 T ROBLE
100% tempranillo.

84

BODEGA ABAXTERRA

CMM 3200, Km. 27,500
13343 Villamanrique (Ciudad Real)
☎: +34 635 295 098 - Fax: +34 916 925 426
info@bodegas-abaxterra.com
www.bodegas-abaxterra.com

ABAXTERRA 2011 RD
tempranillo.

88 Colour: raspberry rose. Nose: dried flowers, fragrant herbs, red berry notes, ripe fruit. Palate: light-bodied, flavourful, good acidity, long.

2 TIERRAS 2011 T
tempranillo.

85 Colour: cherry, purple rim. Nose: expressive, fresh fruit, red berry notes, floral. Palate: flavourful, fruity, good acidity, round tannins.

ABAXTERRA 2010 T
70% tempranillo, 30% syrah.

90 Colour: cherry, garnet rim. Nose: ripe fruit, sweet spices, creamy oak. Palate: powerful, flavourful, long, toasty.

BODEGA DEHESA DE LUNA

CM-3106, km. 16
02630 La Roda (Albacete)
☎: +34 967 548 508 - Fax: +34 967 548 022
contacto@dehesadeluna.com
www.dehesadeluna.com

DEHESA DE LUNA TEMPRANILLO 2010 T
100% tempranillo.

90 Colour: deep cherry. Nose: creamy oak, sweet spices, ripe fruit, mineral. Palate: flavourful, powerful, complex, good acidity.

DEHESA DE LUNA 2010 T
tempranillo, syrah, cabernet sauvignon, merlot.

88 Colour: cherry, garnet rim. Nose: creamy oak, toasty, complex, red berry notes, earthy notes. Palate: powerful, flavourful, toasty, round tannins.

BODEGA FINCA EL RETAMAR

Ctra. CM-4022, km. 2,5
45100 Sonseca (Toledo)
☎: +34 687 765 400 - Fax: +34 925 380 950
info@fincaelretamar.com
www.peces-barba.com

ROSADO BARBAROSA 2011 RD

78

BODEGA GARCÍA DE LA ROSA (AGROCONGOSTO)

Pol. La Carbonera, Podadores, 12
45350 Noblejas (Toledo)
☎: +34 925 140 605 - Fax: +34 925 140 605
carlosgarciarosa@bodegagarciadelarosa.es
www.bodegagarciadelarosa.es

GARCÍA DE LA ROSA 2011 B
100% macabeo.

83

GARCÍA DE LA ROSA 2010 T ROBLE
tempranillo.

90 Colour: cherry, purple rim. Nose: lactic notes, ripe fruit, sweet spices, creamy oak. Palate: balanced, powerful, flavourful, toasty.

NÓBRIGA 2010 T
tempranillo, syrah.

89 Colour: cherry, garnet rim. Nose: ripe fruit, earthy notes, balsamic herbs, spicy, creamy oak. Palate: powerful, flavourful, full.

CASTILLO PALOMARES T
tempranillo.

82

MISTELA GARCÍA DE LA ROSA 2011 MISTELA
moscatel grano menudo.

86 Colour: old gold, amber rim. Nose: honeyed notes, sweet spices, grapey, ripe fruit. Palate: powerful, flavourful, rich.

BODEGA HACIENDA LA PRINCESA

Ctra. San Carlos del Valle, km. 8 - Apdo. Correos 281
13300 Valdepeñas (Ciudad Real)
☎: +34 638 335 185
haciendalaprincesa@telefonica.net
www.haciendalaprincesa.com

HACIENDA LA PRINCESA DEBIR GALA 2008 T
100% tempranillo.

86 Colour: cherry, garnet rim. Nose: ripe fruit, spicy, creamy oak. Palate: powerful, flavourful, toasty, balanced.

HACIENDA LA PRINCESA DEBIR SUCUNZA 2008 TC
50% merlot, 50% tempranillo.

85 Colour: cherry, garnet rim. Nose: ripe fruit, spicy, creamy oak. Palate: powerful, flavourful, toasty.

HACIENDA LA PRINCESA DEBIR JAKUE 2008 T BARRICA
100% cencibel.

85 Colour: cherry, garnet rim. Nose: ripe fruit, creamy oak, old leather. Palate: flavourful, toasty, correct.

BODEGA INIESTA

Ctra. Fuentealbilla - Villamalea, km. 1,5
02260 Fuentealbilla (Albacete)
☎: +34 967 090 650 - Fax: +34 967 090 651
info@bodegainiesta.com
www.bodegainiesta.com

DULCE CORAZÓN 2011 B
moscatel.

88 Colour: golden. Nose: powerfull, candied fruit, fragrant herbs, white flowers. Palate: flavourful, sweet, fresh, fruity, good acidity, long.

CORAZÓN LOCO 2011 B
sauvignon blanc, verdejo.

87 Colour: bright straw. Nose: fresh, white flowers, tropical fruit. Palate: flavourful, fruity, good acidity, balanced.

CORAZÓN LOCO 2011 RD
bobal.

88 Colour: rose, purple rim. Nose: powerfull, ripe fruit, red berry notes, floral, expressive, lactic notes. Palate: , powerful, fruity, fresh.

CORAZÓN LOCO 2010 T
tempranillo.

88 Colour: cherry, garnet rim. Nose: red berry notes, balsamic herbs, earthy notes, fresh, characterful. Palate: light-bodied, fresh, fruity, easy to drink.

BODEGA LOS ALJIBES

Finca Los Aljibes
02520 Chinchilla de Montearagón (Albacete)
☎: +34 918 843 472 - Fax: +34 918 844 324
info@fincalosaljibes.com
www.fincalosaljibes.com

VIÑA ALJIBES 2011 B
80% sauvignon blanc, 20% chardonnay.

87 Colour: bright yellow. Nose: citrus fruit, ripe fruit, floral, dried herbs. Palate: fine bitter notes, fresh, fruity.

VIÑA ALJIBES 2011 RD
100% syrah.

86 Colour: rose, purple rim. Nose: powerfull, ripe fruit, red berry notes, floral. Palate: , powerful, fruity, sweetness.

VIÑA ALJIBES 2009 T
38% petit verdot, 38% cabernet sauvignon, 24% tempranillo.

84

ALJIBES PETIT VERDOT 2008 T
100% petit verdot.

88 Colour: black cherry, garnet rim. Nose: ripe fruit, floral, sweet spices, creamy oak. Palate: powerful, spicy, toasty.

SELECTUS 2007 T
syrah, cabernet franc, merlot, cabernet sauvignon.

91 Colour: cherry, garnet rim. Nose: ripe fruit, balsamic herbs, cocoa bean, earthy notes. Palate: powerful, spicy, long, balanced.

ALJIBES CABERNET FRANC 2007 T
100% cabernet franc.

90 Colour: cherry, garnet rim. Nose: red berry notes, ripe fruit, balsamic herbs, mineral, sweet spices. Palate: balanced, powerful, flavourful, long.

ALJIBES 2007 T
35% merlot, 30% cabernet franc, 35% cabernet sauvignon.

89 Colour: cherry, garnet rim. Nose: floral, red berry notes, balsamic herbs, spicy, expressive. Palate: balanced, powerful, flavourful, long, toasty.

ALJIBES SYRAH 2005 T
100% syrah.

89 Colour: light cherry, garnet rim. Nose: floral, red berry notes, ripe fruit, scrubland, spicy, toasty. Palate: powerful, complex, flavourful, long.

BODEGA PALAREA

Virgen del Pilar, 53 - Bajo
02006 (Albacete)
☎: +34 967 619 619 - Fax: +34 967 619 620
fincamanzanares@vinospalarea.com
www.vinospalarea.com

PALAREA 2007 T
merlot, cabernet sauvignon, syrah.

88 Colour: cherry, garnet rim. Nose: ripe fruit, balsamic herbs, spicy, fine reductive notes. Palate: powerful, flavourful, round tannins.

PALAREA MERLOT 2006 T
merlot.

85 Colour: cherry, garnet rim. Nose: warm, ripe fruit, fruit liqueur notes, spicy, toasty, fine reductive notes. Palate: powerful, flavourful, warm.

PALAREA EXPRESSION 2005 T
merlot, cabernet sauvignon, syrah.

87 Colour: cherry, garnet rim. Nose: ripe fruit, fruit preserve, fragrant herbs, spicy. Palate: warm, flavourful, long.

PALAREA TRONCO 2005 T
merlot, cabernet sauvignon, syrah.

85 Colour: cherry, garnet rim. Nose: earthy notes, fruit preserve, spicy, waxy notes, cigar. Palate: long, flavourful, slightly evolved.

PALAREA 2004 T
merlot, cabernet sauvignon, syrah.

88 Colour: pale ruby, brick rim edge. Nose: spicy, wet leather, aged wood nuances, fruit liqueur notes. Palate: spicy, fine tannins, long.

BODEGA ROMAILA

Ctra. Almonacid de Toledo a Nambroca s/n
45420 Almoncid de Toledo (Toledo)
☎: +34 915 416 561
crojo@romaila.es
www.romaila.es

OH! DE ROMAILA 2011 T
graciano, cabernet sauvignon, syrah, tempranillo, petit verdot.

85 Colour: dark-red cherry. Nose: powerfull, ripe fruit. Palate: fruity, sweetness, powerful, flavourful.

FINCA ROMAILA 2009 T
syrah, graciano, cabernet sauvignon, tempranillo.

88 Colour: cherry, purple rim. Nose: ripe fruit, balsamic herbs, spicy, toasty. Palate: powerful, flavourful, long, balanced.

FINCA ROMAILA 2008 T
syrah, graciano, cabernet sauvignon, tempranillo.

89 Colour: deep cherry. Nose: spicy, creamy oak, toasty, overripe fruit. Palate: powerful, flavourful, toasty, round tannins.

BODEGA SC. "UNION CAMPESINA INIESTENSE"

San Idefonso, 1
16235 Iniesta (Cuenca)
☎: +34 967 490 120 - Fax: +34 967 490 777
comercial@cooperativauci.com
www.cooperativauci.com

SEÑORÍO DE INIESTA SAUVIGNON BLANC 2011 B
sauvignon blanc.

84

SEÑORÍO DE INIESTA BOBAL 2011 RD
bobal.

87 Colour: rose, purple rim. Nose: red berry notes, candied fruit, floral. Palate: long, ripe fruit, flavourful.

UNIÓN CAMPESINA 2011 RD
bobal.

84

SEÑORÍO DE INIESTA 2011 T ROBLE
tempranillo, syrah.

85 Colour: cherry, garnet rim. Nose: ripe fruit, spicy, roasted coffee. Palate: powerful, flavourful, toasty.

SEÑORÍO DE INIESTA TEMPRANILLO 2011 T
tempranillo.

84

INIESTENSE 2011 T JOVEN
syrah.

84

BODEGA TIKALO

Finca Guadianeja - Ctra. de Catellar de Santiago a Torre de Juan Abad, Km. 28,800
13343 Villamanrique (Ciudad Real)
☎: +34 926 694 091
info@bodegatikalo.com
www.bodegatikalo.com

KIOS 2005 T
tempranillo.

86 Colour: cherry, garnet rim. Nose: medium intensity, ripe fruit, warm, sweet spices. Palate: round tannins, long, balanced.

KIOS ÉLITE 2004 T
tempranillo.

89 Colour: cherry, garnet rim. Nose: ripe fruit, creamy oak, fine reductive notes, dark chocolate. Palate: powerful, flavourful, complex, toasty.

KIOS CABERNET SAUVIGNON 2004 T
cabernet sauvignon.

88 Colour: bright cherry, orangey edge. Nose: balanced, candied fruit, spicy. Palate: flavourful, balanced, correct.

BODEGA Y VIÑEDO TINEDO

Ctra. CM 3102, Km. 30
13630 Socuéllamos (Ciudad Real)
☎: +34 926 118 999
info@tinedo.com
www.tinedo.com

CALA N 1 2009 T
tempranillo, syrah, cabernet sauvignon.

88 Colour: bright cherry. Nose: ripe fruit, sweet spices, creamy oak. Palate: flavourful, fruity, toasty.

CALA N 2 2009 T
tempranillo, cabernet sauvignon.

87 Colour: cherry, garnet rim. Nose: red berry notes, ripe fruit, balsamic herbs, sweet spices. Palate: harsh oak tannins, powerful, flavourful.

BODEGAS ABANICO

Pol. Ind Ca l'Avellanet - Susany, 6
08553 Seva (Barcelona)
☎: +34 938 125 676 - Fax: +34 938 123 213
info@exportiberia.com
www.bodegasabanico.com

SINFONÍA TEMPRANILLO 2011 T
100% tempranillo.

88 Colour: cherry, garnet rim. Nose: ripe fruit, balsamic herbs, floral, powerfull, expressive. Palate: powerful, flavourful, fruity, spicy, long.

BODEGAS BARREDA

Ramalazo, 2
45880 Corral de Almaguer (Toledo)
☎: +34 925 207 223 - Fax: +34 925 207 223
nacional@bodegas-barreda.com
www.bodegas-barreda.com

TORRE DE BARREDA SYRAH 2010 T
100% syrah.

87 Colour: cherry, purple rim. Nose: floral, red berry notes, fresh fruit, lactic notes. Palate: light-bodied, fresh, fruity, easy to drink.

TORRE DE BARREDA TEMPRANILLO 2010 T
100% tempranillo.

85 Colour: cherry, garnet rim. Nose: red berry notes, ripe fruit, warm, wild herbs. Palate: flavourful, fruity, light-bodied.

TORRE DE BARREDA PAÑOFINO 2008 T
100% tempranillo.

91 Colour: cherry, garnet rim. Nose: red berry notes, ripe fruit, fragrant herbs, mineral, creamy oak, toasty. Palate: balanced.

TORRE DE BARREDA AMIGOS 2008 T
65% tempranillo, 25% syrah, 10% cabernet sauvignon.

89 Colour: cherry, garnet rim. Nose: red berry notes, balsamic herbs, dark chocolate, creamy oak. Palate: powerful, flavourful, long, round tannins.

BODEGAS CASAQUEMADA

Ctra. Ruidera, Km. 5,5
13710 Argamasilla de Alba (Ciudad Real)
☎: +34 628 621 187 - Fax: +34 926 511 515
casaquemada@casaquemada.es
www.casaquemada.es

ALBA DE CASA QUEMADA 2008 T
100% syrah.

91 Colour: cherry, garnet rim. Nose: fruit liqueur notes, fragrant herbs, violets, earthy notes, spicy, toasty. Palate: powerful, flavourful, spicy, long.

BRINCHO KOSHER 2007 T
100% tempranillo.

88 Colour: cherry, garnet rim. Nose: ripe fruit, balsamic herbs, sweet spices, toasty. Palate: spicy, long, toasty, balanced.

HACIENDA CASAQUEMADA 2007 T
100% tempranillo.

88 Colour: cherry, garnet rim. Nose: ripe fruit, spicy, toasty, balsamic herbs, mineral. Palate: powerful, flavourful, toasty, round tannins.

ANEA DE CASAQUEMADA 2005 T
100% syrah.

90 Colour: cherry, garnet rim. Nose: ripe fruit, spicy, creamy oak, balsamic herbs. Palate: powerful, flavourful, toasty, balanced.

BODEGAS EGUREN

Avda. del Cantábrico, s/n
01013 Vitoria (Álava)
☎: +34 945 282 844 - Fax: +34 945 271 319
info@heredadugarte.com
www.egurenwines.com

KAME 2011 B
macabeo.

87 Colour: bright straw. Nose: white flowers, fragrant herbs, ripe fruit. Palate: light-bodied, fresh, long, warm.

MERCEDES EGUREN SAUVIGNON BLANC 2011 B
sauvignon blanc.

85 Colour: bright yellow. Nose: dried flowers, ripe fruit, grassy. Palate: balanced, flavourful, long.

REINARES 2011 B
viura.

84

REINARES 2011 RD
tempranillo.

84

MERCEDES EGUREN CABERNET SAUVIGNON 2011 RD
cabernet sauvignon.

81

REINARES TEMPRANILLO 2011 T
tempranillo.

83

CONDADO DE EGUREN TEMPRANILLO 2010 T
tempranillo.

87 Colour: bright cherry. Nose: ripe fruit, creamy oak, spicy. Palate: flavourful, toasty, harsh oak tannins.

PAZOS DE EGUREN TEMPRANILLO 2010 T

87 Colour: cherry, purple rim. Nose: lactic notes, red berry notes, fresh, expressive. Palate: powerful, flavourful, fresh, fruity.

MERCEDES EGUREN SHIRAZ TEMPRANILLO 2010 T
syrah, tempranillo.

87 Colour: cherry, purple rim. Nose: red berry notes, ripe fruit, sweet spices, toasty. Palate: powerful, flavourful, fruity, round tannins.

MERCEDES EGUREN CABERNET SAUVIGNON 2010 T
cabernet sauvignon.

85 Colour: cherry, garnet rim. Nose: ripe fruit, floral, scrubland, creamy oak. Palate: flavourful, toasty, harsh oak tannins.

KAME 2009 T
syrah, tempranillo, cabernet sauvignon.

88 Colour: bright cherry. Nose: ripe fruit, sweet spices, creamy oak, expressive. Palate: flavourful, fruity, toasty, round tannins.

BODEGAS ERCAVIO

Camino de los Molinos, s/n
45312 Cabañas de Yepes (Toledo)
☎: +34 925 122 281 - Fax: +34 925 137 033
masquevinos@fer.es
www.bodegasercavio.com

LA MALVAR DE ERCAVIO 2011 B
100% malvar.

90 Colour: bright straw. Nose: fresh, fragrant herbs, balanced, medium intensity, citrus fruit. Palate: good structure, spicy, long.

ERCAVIO 2011 B
airén.

89 Colour: bright straw, greenish rim. Nose: balanced, expressive, tropical fruit. Palate: balanced, fine bitter notes, flavourful, ripe fruit.

ERCAVIO 2011 RD
100% tempranillo.

88 Colour: rose, purple rim. Nose: powerfull, ripe fruit, red berry notes, floral. Palate: , powerful, fruity, fresh, easy to drink.

ERCAVIO TEMPRANILLO 2011 T
100% tempranillo.

89 Colour: cherry, purple rim. Nose: balanced, ripe fruit, neat, varietal. Palate: flavourful, correct, easy to drink, good finish.

LA MESETA 2010 T
50% tempranillo, 50% syrah.

91 Colour: deep cherry, garnet rim. Nose: balanced, expressive, ripe fruit. Palate: complex, balanced, flavourful, round tannins.

LA BUENA VID 2009 T
80% tempranillo, 20% graciano.

91 Colour: bright cherry. Nose: creamy oak, medium intensity, red berry notes, ripe fruit, fresh. Palate: flavourful, fruity, toasty, round tannins.

EL SEÑORITO DE ERCAVIO 2009 T
100% tempranillo.

90 Colour: cherry, garnet rim. Nose: powerfull, characterful, ripe fruit, raspberry, spicy, toasty. Palate: flavourful, fine bitter notes, round tannins.

ERCAVIO TEMPRANILLO 2010 T ROBLE

89 Colour: bright cherry, garnet rim. Nose: expressive, balanced, creamy oak. Palate: flavourful, good structure, spicy.

ERCAVIO SELECCIÓN LIMITADA 2009 T
90% tempranillo, 10% merlot.

88 Colour: cherry, garnet rim. Nose: powerfull, fruit expression, toasty, woody, ripe fruit, fruit preserve. Palate: flavourful, powerful, concentrated.

LA PLAZUELA 2007 T

92 Colour: cherry, garnet rim. Nose: ripe fruit, spicy, creamy oak, complex. Palate: powerful, flavourful, toasty, round tannins.

BODEGAS FINCA LA ESTACADA

Ctra. N-400, Km. 103
16400 Tarancón (Cuenca)
☎: +34 969 327 099 - Fax: +34 969 327 199
enologia@fincalaestacada.com
www.fincalaestacada.com

SECUA CRIANZA EN LÍAS 2010 B
viognier, sauvignon blanc.

92 Colour: bright yellow. Nose: powerfull, ripe fruit, sweet spices, creamy oak, fragrant herbs. Palate: rich, flavourful, good acidity, long. Personality.

SECUA DULCE 2010 B
chardonnay.

83

FINCA LA ESTACADA 12 MESES BARRICA 2009 T BARRICA
tempranillo.

86 Colour: cherry, garnet rim. Nose: ripe fruit, dark chocolate, nose:tic coffee, toasty. Palate: powerful, flavourful, long, spicy.

SECUA CABERNET-SYRAH 2008 T
cabernet sauvignon, syrah.

90 Colour: cherry, garnet rim. Nose: ripe fruit, spicy, creamy oak, toasty, complex, earthy notes. Palate: powerful, flavourful, toasty, round tannins.

FINCA LA ESTACADA SELECCIÓN VARIETALES 2007 T BARRICA
tempranillo, cabernet sauvignon, merlot, syrah.

88 Colour: black cherry, garnet rim. Nose: earthy notes, ripe fruit, cocoa bean, spicy, toasty. Palate: powerful, flavourful, toasty.

FINCA LA ESTACADA ROSADO DE AGUJA 2011 SEMIDULCE
tempranillo.

82

BODEGAS HACIENDA ALBAE

Ctra. de Argamasilla de Alba a Cinco Casas, km. 25.500 CM
13710 Argamasilla de Alba (Ciudad Real)
☎: +34 917 756 330 - Fax: +34 913 132 135
ctorres@haciendaalbae.com
www.haciendaalbae.com

ALBAE ESENCIA CHARDONNAY 2011 B
chardonnay.

86 Colour: bright straw. Nose: white flowers, ripe fruit, fragrant herbs. Palate: flavourful, fruity, good acidity.

HACIENDA ALBAE CHARDONNAY 2010 B
chardonnay.

88 Colour: bright yellow. Nose: ripe fruit, sweet spices, creamy oak. Palate: rich, flavourful, fresh, good acidity.

ALBAE ESENCIA 3 MESES 2009 T
70% syrah, 30% merlot.

85 Colour: cherry, garnet rim. Nose: ripe fruit, sweet spices, creamy oak. Palate: powerful, flavourful, spicy.

ALBAE ESENCIA 4 MESES 2009 T
60% tempranillo, 40% cabernet sauvignon.

83

HACIENDA ALBAE 2007 T BARRICA
90% tempranillo, 10% syrah.

89 Colour: cherry, garnet rim. Nose: balanced, ripe fruit, neat, spicy, balsamic herbs. Palate: flavourful, ripe fruit, good acidity.

HACIENDA ALBAE SELECCIÓN 60/40 2007 T
60% cabernet sauvignon, 40% merlot.

87 Colour: cherry, garnet rim. Nose: ripe fruit, spicy, creamy oak, balsamic herbs. Palate: powerful, flavourful, toasty.

BODEGAS HERMANOS RUBIO

Ctra. de Villamuelas, s/n
45740 Villasequilla (Toledo)
☎: +34 925 310 284 - Fax: +34 925 325 133
info@bhrubio.com
www.bhrubio.com

VIÑA ALAMBRADA 2011 B
airén.

84

VIÑA ALAMBRADA 2007 TC
tempranillo.

83

BODEGAS JUAN RAMÍREZ

Torrecilla, 138
13300 Valdepeñas (Ciudad Real)
☎: +34 926 322 021 - Fax: +34 926 320 495
info@bodegasjuanramirez.com
www.bodegasjuanramirez.com

AMPELO SYRAH 2010 T ROBLE
syrah.

84

AMPELO TEMPRANILLO 2010 T ROBLE
tempranillo.

83

BODEGAS LÓPEZ PANACH

Finca El Calaverón, s/n
02600 Villarrobledo (Albacete)
☎: +34 967 573 140 - Fax: +34 967 573 297
bodegas@lopezpanach.com
www.lopezpanach.com

LÓPEZ PANACH TEMPRANILLO T-9 2006 T
tempranillo.

85 Colour: cherry, garnet rim. Nose: ripe fruit, spicy, creamy oak, toasty, complex. Palate: powerful, flavourful, toasty, round tannins.

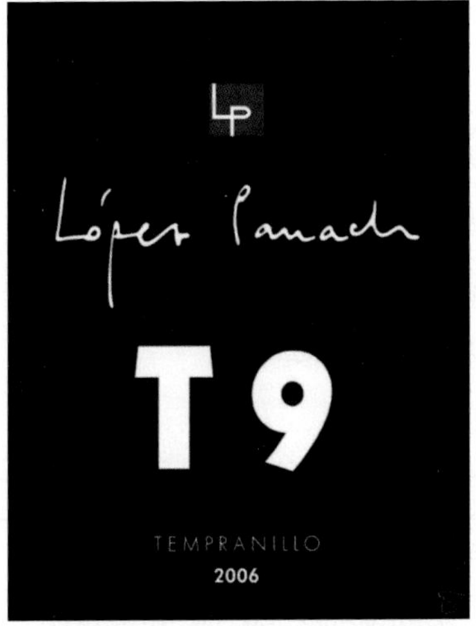

BODEGAS MANO A MANO

Ctra. CM-412, Km. 100
13248 Alhambra (Ciudad Real)
☎: +34 619 349 394 - Fax: +34 926 691 162
info@bodegamanoamano.com
www.bodegamanoamano.com

MANO A MANO 2011 T
tempranillo.

89 Colour: cherry, purple rim. Nose: ripe fruit, sweet spices, nose:tic coffee, creamy oak, roasted coffee. Palate: powerful, flavourful, toasty, grainy tannins.

VENTA LA OSSA TNT 2010 T
75% touriga nacional, 25% tempranillo.

93 Colour: cherry, garnet rim. Nose: ripe fruit, nose:tic coffee, creamy oak, scrubland, balsamic herbs. Palate: flavourful, full, long, toasty.

VENTA LA OSSA 2010 TC
100% tempranillo.

92 Colour: cherry, garnet rim. Nose: ripe fruit, dark chocolate, sweet spices, creamy oak. Palate: powerful, flavourful, complex, long.

VENTA LA OSSA SYRAH 2009 T
100% syrah.

94 Colour: cherry, garnet rim. Nose: ripe fruit, floral, sweet spices, creamy oak. Palate: round, flavourful, fruity, full, complex, balanced.

BODEGAS MÁXIMO

Camino Viejo de Logroño, 26
01320 Oyón (Álava)
☎: +34 945 622 216 - Fax: +34 945 622 315
maximo@bodegasmaximo.com
www.bodegasmaximo.com

MÁXIMO VIURA 2011 B
100% viura.

82

MÁXIMO TEMPRANILLO 2011 RD
100% tempranillo.

86 Colour: raspberry rose. Nose: faded flowers, red berry notes, ripe fruit. Palate: flavourful, fresh, fruity, light-bodied, easy to drink.

MÁXIMO TEMPRANILLO 2010 T
100% tempranillo.

84

MÁXIMO MERLOT 2010 T
100% merlot.

80

BODEGAS MIGUEL ANGEL AGUADO

Cantalejos, 2
45165 San Martín de Montalbán (Toledo)
☎: +34 925 417 206
info@bodegasmiguelaguado.com
www.bodegasmiguelaguado.com

SAN MARTINEÑO 2011 B
100% macabeo.

84

PASIÓN DE CASTILLO DE MONTALBAN 2011 RD
100% garnacha.

82

SAN MARTINEÑO 2011 RD
100% garnacha.

85 Colour: rose, purple rim. Nose: lactic notes, red berry notes, candied fruit. Palate: flavourful, fresh, fruity, easy to drink.

SAN MARTINEÑO GARNACHA SEMI 2011 RD
100% garnacha.

81

SAN MARTINEÑO 2011 T JOVEN
100% garnacha.

86 Colour: cherry, garnet rim. Nose: jasmine, ripe fruit, wild herbs. Palate: powerful, flavourful, balsamic.

SAN MARTINEÑO 2011 T JOVEN
100% tempranillo.

82

SAN MARTINEÑO 2008 TC
60% cabernet sauvignon, 40% garnacha.

85 Colour: cherry, garnet rim. Nose: ripe fruit, sweet spices, creamy oak. Palate: flavourful, toasty, long.

SAN MARTINEÑO 2008 TC
100% tempranillo.

83

PASIÓN DE CASTILLO DE MONTALBAN ESP
macabeo.

86 Colour: bright straw. Nose: medium intensity, dried herbs, fine lees, floral. Palate: fresh, fruity, flavourful.

BODEGAS MONTALVO WILMOT

Ctra. Ruidera, km. 10,2 Finca Los Cerrillos
13710 Argamasilla de Alba (Ciudad Real)
☎: +34 926 699 069 - Fax: +34 926 699 069
silvia@montalvowilmot.com
www.montalvowilmot.com

MONTALVO WILMOT COLECCIÓN 2010 B
100% verdejo.

81

MONTALVO WILMOT SYRAH 2010 T ROBLE
100% syrah.

90 Colour: cherry, garnet rim. Nose: ripe fruit, sweet spices, creamy oak, toasty, floral, lactic notes. Palate: powerful, flavourful, toasty.

MONTALVO WILMOT TEMPRANILLO-CABERNET 2010 T ROBLE
75% tempranillo, 25% cabernet sauvignon.

88 Colour: cherry, garnet rim. Nose: ripe fruit, balsamic herbs, dark chocolate, toasty. Palate: flavourful, toasty, balanced.

MONTALVO WILMOT COLECCIÓN PRIVADA 2008 T ROBLE
75% tempranillo, 25% cabernet sauvignon.

88 Colour: cherry, garnet rim. Nose: ripe fruit, wild herbs, floral, spicy, toasty. Palate: powerful, flavourful, mineral.

MONTALVO WILMOT CABERNET DE FAMILIA 2006 T
100% cabernet sauvignon.

89 Colour: light cherry, orangey edge. Nose: ripe fruit, balsamic herbs, spicy, creamy oak, fine reductive notes. Palate: flavourful, long, balanced.

BODEGAS MUREDA

Ctra. N-IV, Km. 184,1
13300 Valdepeñas (Ciudad Real)
☎: +34 926 318 058 - Fax: +34 926 318 058
administracion@mureda.es
www.mureda.es

MUREDA CHARDONNAY 2011 B
chardonnay.

86 Colour: bright straw. Nose: faded flowers, ripe fruit, fragrant herbs. Palate: light-bodied, fresh, easy to drink.

MUREDA SAUVIGNON BLANC 2011 B
sauvignon blanc.

84

MUREDA SYRAH 2011 T
syrah.

91 Colour: cherry, purple rim. Nose: expressive, fresh fruit, red berry notes, floral. Palate: flavourful, fruity, good acidity, round tannins.

MUREDA CABERNET SAUVIGNON 2011 T
cabernet sauvignon.

86 Colour: cherry, purple rim. Nose: red berry notes, ripe fruit, balsamic herbs, warm. Palate: powerful, flavourful, correct.

MUREDA 100 2009 T
tempranillo.

88 Colour: bright cherry. Nose: ripe fruit, sweet spices, creamy oak, expressive. Palate: flavourful, fruity, toasty, round tannins.

BODEGAS NAVARRO LÓPEZ

Autovía Madrid - Cádiz, Km. 193
13300 Valdepeñas (Ciudad Real)
☎: +34 902 193 431 - Fax: +34 902 193 432
marketing@navarrolopez.com;jopilal@terra.es;
www.navarrolopez.com

PREMIUM 1904 2010 T
tempranillo, cabernet sauvignon.

88 Colour: cherry, purple rim. Nose: red berry notes, candied fruit, spicy, creamy oak, balsamic herbs. Palate: powerful, flavourful, toasty, long.

BODEGAS RÍO NEGRO

Ctra. CM 1001, Km. 37,400
19230 Cogolludo (Guadalajara)
☎: +34 639 301 817 - Fax: +34 913 026 750
info@fincarionegro.es
www.fincarionegro.com

FINCA RÍO NEGRO 2009 T
80% tempranillo, 20% syrah.

92 Colour: cherry, garnet rim. Nose: balsamic herbs, floral, red berry notes, ripe fruit, sweet spices, creamy oak. Palate: powerful, flavourful, fruity, toasty, balanced.

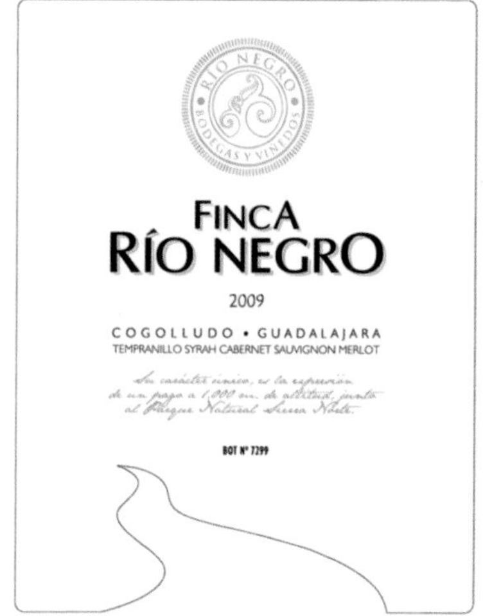

BODEGAS ROMERO DE ÁVILA SALCEDO

Avda. Constitución, 4
13200 La Solana (Ciudad Real)
☎: +34 926 631 426
comercial@bodegasromerodeavila.com
www.bodegasromerodeavila.com

TESTIGO 20 MONTHS IN BARRELS 2008 T ROBLE
tempranillo, cabernet sauvignon, syrah.

88 Colour: cherry, garnet rim. Nose: ripe fruit, balsamic herbs, spicy, fine reductive notes. Palate: powerful, flavourful, toasty.

BODEGAS TIERRAS DE ORGAZ

Orgaz, 12
45460 Manzaneque (Toledo)
☎: +34 666 417 377
jcserrano@btor.es
www.bodegastierrasdeorgaz.com

BUCAMEL 2008 T
100% tempranillo.

88 Colour: cherry, garnet rim. Nose: ripe fruit, creamy oak, toasty, sweet spices. Palate: powerful, flavourful, toasty, long.

BODEGAS VERUM

Juan Antonio López Ramírez, 4
13700 Tomelloso (Ciudad Real)
☎: +34 926 511 404 - Fax: +34 926 515 047
administracion@bodegasverum.com
www.bodegasverum.com

VERUM 2011 B
30% sauvignon blanc, 70% gewürztraminer.

87 Colour: pale. Nose: fresh fruit, tropical fruit, white flowers, fragrant herbs. Palate: easy to drink, light-bodied, fruity.

VERUM TERRA 2011 B
100% airén.

85 Colour: bright straw. Nose: ripe fruit, candied fruit, white flowers. Palate: flavourful, fruity, easy to drink.

VERUM 2011 RD
50% tempranillo, 50% cabernet franc.

86 Colour: brilliant rose. Nose: floral, red berry notes, ripe fruit, fragrant herbs. Palate: fresh, fruity, flavourful, easy to drink.

VERUM 2010 T
60% cabernet sauvignon, 20% tempranillo, 20% cabernet sauvignon.

87 Colour: cherry, garnet rim. Nose: ripe fruit, spicy, creamy oak, scrubland. Palate: powerful, flavourful, toasty.

VERUM 2009 T
50% merlot, 40% cabernet sauvignon, 10% tempranillo.

90 Colour: cherry, garnet rim. Nose: red berry notes, ripe fruit, sweet spices, toasty, dark chocolate, expressive. Palate: powerful, flavourful, balanced, round tannins.

VERUM 2009 T ROBLE
50% cabernet sauvignon, 40% tempranillo, 10% merlot.

88 Colour: cherry, garnet rim. Nose: scrubland, spicy, cocoa bean, creamy oak. Palate: powerful, flavourful, long, toasty.

BODEGAS VILLAVID, DULCE NOMBRE DE JESÚS SOC. COOP. DE C-LM

Niño Jesús, 25
16280 Villarta (Cuenca)
☎: +34 962 189 006 - Fax: +34 962 189 125
info@villavid.com
www.villavid.com

WOMAN SOUL OF VILLAVID 2010 B
verdejo, macabeo.

82

BOBAL DESIRE OF VILLAVID 2011 RD
bobal.

85 Colour: rose, purple rim. Nose: lactic notes, red berry notes, candied fruit. Palate: flavourful, fruity, fresh, easy to drink.

VILLAVID 2011 T
100% tempranillo.

86 Colour: cherry, garnet rim. Nose: red berry notes, ripe fruit, balsamic herbs, medium intensity. Palate: fresh, fruity, light-bodied, easy to drink.

SECRET BUBBLES OF VILLAVID ROSADO 2011 ESP
bobal.

87 Colour: brilliant rose. Nose: floral, lactic notes, raspberry, red berry notes. Palate: powerful, flavourful, fruity, easy to drink.

BODEGAS Y VIÑEDOS ALCARREÑOS

Cº Viejo de las Navas, s/n
19162 Pioz (Guadalajara)
☎: +34 949 820 812 - Fax: +34 949 310 985
bovial@bovial.es
www.bovial.es

BOVIAL CAMINO BLANCO 2011 B
sauvignon blanc.

85 Colour: bright straw. Nose: ripe fruit, dried flowers, fragrant herbs. Palate: fruity, balanced, easy to drink.

BOVIAL CAMINO ROSADO 2011 RD
tempranillo.

84

CASTILLO DE PIOZ 2009 T
tempranillo, syrah.

88 Colour: cherry, garnet rim. Nose: ripe fruit, spicy, creamy oak, toasty, smoky. Palate: powerful, flavourful, toasty.

BOVIAL MONTE ALCARRIA 2009 T
tempranillo.

86 Colour: bright cherry. Nose: ripe fruit, sweet spices, creamy oak, balsamic herbs. Palate: flavourful, fruity, toasty, oaky.

BODEGAS Y VIÑEDOS CASTIBLANQUE

Isaac Peral, 19
13610 Campo de Criptana (Ciudad Real)
☎: +34 926 589 147 - Fax: +34 926 589 148
info@bodegascastiblanque.com
www.bodegascastiblanque.com

ILEX AIRÉN 2011 B
100% airén.

83

BALDOR TRADICIÓN CHARDONNAY 2010 BFB
100% chardonnay.

87 Colour: bright yellow. Nose: dried flowers, ripe fruit, sweet spices, creamy oak. Palate: powerful, flavourful, toasty.

ILEX 2011 RD
100% syrah.

85 Colour: rose, purple rim. Nose: red berry notes, dried flowers, lactic notes. Palate: easy to drink, light-bodied, fruity.

ILEX 2010 T
80% syrah, 10% tempranillo, 10% garnacha.

85 Colour: cherry, garnet rim. Nose: red berry notes, ripe fruit, slightly evolved. Palate: fresh, fruity, flavourful, easy to drink.

ILEX COUPAGE 2009 T
50% syrah, 30% tempranillo, 10% cabernet sauvignon, 10% garnacha.

87 Colour: cherry, garnet rim. Nose: toasty, ripe fruit, sweet spices. Palate: flavourful, fruity, balanced, good acidity.

BALDOR TRADICIÓN SYRAH 2009 T
100% syrah.

86 Colour: cherry, garnet rim. Nose: ripe fruit, fruit preserve, floral, sweet spices. Palate: powerful, flavourful, long.

BALDOR OLD VINES 2009 T
100% cabernet sauvignon.

84

BODEGAS Y VIÑEDOS PINUAGA

Ctra. N-301- Km. 95,5
45880 Corral de Almaguer (Toledo)
☎: +34 914 577 117 - Fax: +34 914 577 117
info@bodegaspinuaga.com
www.bodegaspinuaga.com

PINUAGA NATURE 3 MESES BARRICA 2010 T
100% tempranillo.

86 Colour: bright cherry. Nose: ripe fruit, sweet spices, creamy oak. Palate: flavourful, fruity, toasty, round tannins.

PINUAGA LA SENDA 2010 T
80% merlot, 20% tempranillo.

84

PINUAGA 200 CEPAS 2008 T
100% tempranillo.

88 Colour: cherry, garnet rim. Nose: ripe fruit, floral, fragrant herbs, creamy oak, earthy notes. Palate: flavourful, balanced, toasty.

BODEGAS Y VIÑEDOS SÁNCHEZ MULITERNO

Tesifonte Gallego, 5
02002 (Albacete)
☎: +34 967 193 222 - Fax: +34 967 193 292
bodegas@sanchez-muliterno.com
www.sanchez-muliterno.com

FINCA LA SABINA 2010 T
100% tempranillo.

88 Colour: bright cherry. Nose: ripe fruit, sweet spices, creamy oak. Palate: flavourful, fruity, toasty, round tannins.

BODEGAS Y VIÑEDOS TAVERA

Ctra. Valmojado - Toledo, Km. 22
45182 Arcicóllar (Toledo)
☎: +34 666 294 012
info@bodegastavera.com
www.bodegastavera.com

CENDAL CHARDONNAY 2011 B
chardonnay.

84

NEREO GARNACHA 2011 RD
100% garnacha.

84

NEREO SYRAH TEMPRANILLO 2010 T
tempranillo, syrah.

83

TAVERA VENDIMIA SELECCIONADA 2008 T
tempranillo, syrah.

86 Colour: cherry, garnet rim. Nose: ripe fruit, toasty, sweet spices. Palate: powerful, flavourful, toasty.

NEREO TEMPRANILLO SYRAH GARNACHA 2008 T
tempranillo, syrah, garnacha.

86 Colour: cherry, garnet rim. Nose: ripe fruit, spicy, toasty, new oak. Palate: powerful, flavourful, toasty.

BODEGAS YUNTERO

Pol. Ind. Ctra. Alcázar, s/n
13200 Manzanares (Ciudad Real)
☎: +34 926 610 309 - Fax: +34 926 610 516
yuntero@yuntero.com
www.yuntero.com

LAZARILLO 2011 B
airén.

83

LAZARILLO 2011 T JOVEN
tempranillo.

84

BODEGAS ZIRIES

Menasalbas, 18
45120 San Pablo de los Montes (Toledo)
☎: +34 679 443 792
flequi@ziries.es
www.lobecasope.com

NAVALEGUA 2011 T BARRICA
garnacha.

87 Colour: cherry, purple rim. Nose: medium intensity, ripe fruit, sweet spices. Palate: ripe fruit, balanced.

ZIRIES 2010 T
100% garnacha.

88 Colour: cherry, garnet rim. Nose: dark chocolate, fruit preserve, sweet spices, fruit liqueur notes. Palate: balanced, fine bitter notes.

CAMINO ALTO

Polillo, 4
45860 Villacañas (Toledo)
☎: +34 925 200 878
julioraboso@bodegascaminoalto.com
www.bodegascaminoalto.com

CAMINO ALTO 2011 RD
100% cabernet sauvignon.

84

CAMINO ALTO 2009 T
100% cabernet sauvignon.

88 Colour: cherry, garnet rim. Nose: ripe fruit, earthy notes, scrubland, spicy, creamy oak. Palate: powerful, flavourful, long, toasty.

CAPILLA DEL FRAILE

Finca Capilla del Fraile, s/n
45654 San Bartolomé de las Abiertas (Toledo)
☎: +34 925 599 329
info@capilladelfraile.com
www.capilladelfraile.com

VIÑALTO 2010 T
syrah, petit verdot.

85 Colour: bright cherry. Nose: ripe fruit, sweet spices, roasted coffee. Palate: flavourful, fruity, toasty.

CAPILLA DEL FRAILE 2006 T
60% syrah, 40% petit verdot.

88 Colour: cherry, garnet rim. Nose: balanced, ripe fruit, sweet spices. Palate: good structure, flavourful, fine bitter notes, round tannins.

CASA CARRIL CRUZADO

Ctra. Iniesta-Villagarcía del Llano, km. 13
16236 Villagarcía del Llano (Cuenca)
☎: +34 967 571 154 - Fax: +34 967 571 155
bodega@carrilcruzado.com
www.carrilcruzado.com

CASA CARRIL CRUZADO 2011 T
cabernet sauvignon, syrah, tempranillo, merlot, petit verdot.

82

MEMENTO OLD VINES 2010 T
tempranillo, syrah, petit verdot.

87 Colour: dark-red cherry, garnet rim. Nose: ripe fruit, balsamic herbs, cocoa bean, sweet spices. Palate: powerful, flavourful, toasty.

2010
memento
Old Vines
PRODUCT OF SPAIN
Vino de la Tierra de Castilla
CARRIL CRUZADO
14% Alc/Vol.

CASA GUALDA

Tapias, 8
16708 Pozoamargo (Cuenca)
☎: +34 969 387 173 - Fax: +34 969 387 202
info@casagualda.com
www.casagualda.com

CASA GUALDA SINGULAR 2011 T
tempranillo, bobal, syrah.

85 Colour: bright cherry, purple rim. Nose: medium intensity, dried herbs, ripe fruit. Palate: flavourful, fruity.

CASA GUALDA NATURA 2011 T
tempranillo, syrah.

85 Colour: cherry, purple rim. Nose: floral, grassy, ripe fruit, balanced, creamy oak. Palate: flavourful, fruity, spicy.

CASA GUALDA NATURA 2011 T ROBLE

85 Colour: cherry, purple rim. Nose: powerfull, ripe fruit, dried herbs. Palate: flavourful, easy to drink, ripe fruit.

VALTOJO SINGULAR 2011 T
tempranillo, bobal, syrah.

84

VALTOJO PRESIDENT SELECTION 2009 T
tempranillo, cabernet sauvignon, syrah.

86 Colour: bright cherry, garnet rim. Nose: medium intensity, toasty, cocoa bean, ripe fruit. Palate: flavourful, easy to drink, ripe fruit.

CASA GUALDA PLUS ULTRA 2007 T

84

CASA ROJO

Sánchez Picazo, 53
30332 Balsapintada (Murcia)
☎: +34 968 151 520 - Fax: +34 968 151 690
marketing@casarojo.com
www.casarojo.com

NATURE ORGANIC BLANC 2011 B
100% airén.

85

MUSSO CHARDONNAY 2011 B
100% chardonnay.

84

MUSSO SAUVIGNON BLANC 2011 B
100% sauvignon blanc.

84

SEXY CHARDONNAY 2011 B
100% chardonnay.

84

SEXY GARNACHA 2011 RD
100% garnacha.

85 Colour: light cherry. Nose: candied fruit, floral, fragrant herbs. Palate: fresh, fruity, sweetness.

MUSSO TEMPRANILLO 2011 T
100% tempranillo.

83

SEXY TEMPRANILLO 2011 T
100% tempranillo.

82

MUSSO CABERNET SAUVIGNON 2010 T
100% cabernet sauvignon.

85 Colour: cherry, garnet rim. Nose: scrubland, creamy oak, red berry notes, ripe fruit. Palate: spicy, flavourful.

MUSSO MERLOT 2010 T
100% merlot.

84

PIEDRAS ROJAS 2010 TC
100% tempranillo.

82

NATURE ORGANIC RED 2009 T
100% tempranillo.

86 Colour: bright cherry. Nose: ripe fruit, sweet spices, creamy oak. Palate: flavourful, fruity, toasty, easy to drink.

MUSSO SYRAH 2009 T
100% syrah.

83

CASALOBOS

Ctra. Porzuna CM-412, Km. 6,5
13196 Picón (Ciudad Real)
☎: +34 926 600 002
bodega@casalobos.es
www.casalobos.es

CASALOBOS 2007 T
syrah, cabernet sauvignon, petit verdot, tempranillo.

90 Colour: cherry, garnet rim. Nose: ripe fruit, scrubland, earthy notes, spicy, creamy oak. Palate: flavourful, long, fine bitter notes, round tannins.

COOPERATIVA NUESTRA SEÑORA DE LA ESTRELLA

Elías Fernández, 10
16290 El Herrumbar (Cuenca)
☎: +34 962 313 029 - Fax: +34 962 313 232
laestrella@ucaman.es

ANTARES VERDEJO 2011 B
100% verdejo.

83

COSECHEROS Y CRIADORES

Diputación, s/n
01320 Oyón (Álava)
☎: +34 945 601 944 - Fax: +34 945 601 412
nacional@cosecherosycriadores.com
www.familiamartinezbujanda.com

INFINITUS GEWÜRZTRAMINER 2011 B
gewürztraminer.

89 Colour: bright straw. Nose: white flowers, fragrant herbs, tropical fruit. Palate: light-bodied, fresh, fruity, flavourful, easy to drink.

INFINITUS MOSCATEL 2011 B
moscatel.

87 Colour: bright yellow. Nose: white flowers, ripe fruit, fragrant herbs, tropical fruit. Palate: sweetness, ripe fruit, fruity.

INFINITUS VIURA CHARDONNAY 2011 B
viura, chardonnay.

80

INFINITUS TEMPRANILLO CABERNET FRANC 2011 RD
cabernet franc, tempranillo.

84

INFINITUS TEMPRANILLO 2011 T
tempranillo.

88 Colour: cherry, purple rim. Nose: red berry notes, raspberry, ripe fruit, floral, expressive. Palate: flavourful, fresh, fruity.

INFINITUS CABERNET SAUVIGNON 2011 T
cabernet sauvignon.

87 Colour: cherry, purple rim. Nose: red berry notes, ripe fruit, wild herbs. Palate: powerful, flavourful, fruity, correct.

INFINITUS SYRAH 2011 T
syrah.

87 Colour: cherry, purple rim. Nose: red berry notes, ripe fruit, floral. Palate: light-bodied, fresh, fruity, easy to drink.

INFINITUS MERLOT 2011 T
merlot.

86 Colour: cherry, purple rim. Nose: ripe fruit, balsamic herbs, floral. Palate: fresh, fruity, easy to drink.

INFINITUS MALBEC 2011 T
malbec.

86 Colour: cherry, purple rim. Nose: red berry notes, fruit liqueur notes, floral, scrubland. Palate: light-bodied, fruity, easy to drink.

INFINITUS TEMPRANILLO CABERNET SAUVIGNON 2010 T
cabernet sauvignon, tempranillo.

85 Colour: cherry, garnet rim. Nose: ripe fruit, spicy, toasty, balsamic herbs. Palate: warm, powerful, flavourful, toasty.

DEHESA DE LOS LLANOS

Ctra. Peñas de San Pedro, Km. 5,5
02006 (Albacete)
☎: +34 967 243 100 - Fax: +34 967 243 093
info@dehesadelosllanos.es
www.dehesadelosllanos.com

MAZACRUZ 2011 B
sauvignon blanc, verdejo.

88 Colour: bright yellow. Nose: white flowers, fragrant herbs, tropical fruit, ripe fruit. Palate: powerful, flavourful, long.

MAZACRUZ CIMA 2010 B
verdejo.

88 Colour: bright golden. Nose: ripe fruit, sweet spices, creamy oak, floral, slightly evolved. Palate: rich, flavourful, ripe fruit.

MAZACRUZ 2010 T
petit verdot, tempranillo, syrah, cabernet sauvignon.

87 Colour: cherry, garnet rim. Nose: ripe fruit, scrubland, earthy notes, spicy, toasty. Palate: fresh, flavourful, ripe fruit.

MAZACRUZ CIMA 2008 T
cabernet sauvignon, syrah, merlot, petit verdot.

90 Colour: cherry, garnet rim. Nose: ripe fruit, balsamic herbs, earthy notes, creamy oak. Palate: balanced, powerful, flavourful, complex.

DEHESA Y VIÑEDOS DE NAVAMARÍN

Ctra. Comarcal 313, Km. 1
02160 Lezuza (Albacete)
☎: +34 967 376 005 - Fax: +34 967 376 003
pedrojnavarro@aldonzavinos.com
www.aldonzavinos.com

ALDONZA ALBO 2011 B
sauvignon blanc, macabeo.

86 Colour: bright yellow. Nose: ripe fruit, white flowers, wild herbs. Palate: light-bodied, fresh, fruity.

ALDONZA SELECCIÓN 2007 TR
cabernet sauvignon, tempranillo, merlot, syrah.

84

ALDONZA NAVAMARÍN 2007 T
cabernet sauvignon, merlot, syrah, tempranillo.

84

ALDONZA PISCES 2007 T
tempranillo, merlot, cabernet sauvignon, syrah.

82

DIONISOS

Unión, 82
13300 Valdepeñas (Ciudad Real)
☎: +34 926 313 248 - Fax: +34 926 322 813
dionisos@labodegadelasestrellas.com
www.labodegadelasestrellas.com

VINUM VITAE 2006 TC
100% tempranillo.

89 Colour: dark-red cherry, orangey edge. Nose: ripe fruit, earthy notes, old leather, spicy. Palate: long, toasty, balanced, flavourful.

EGO PRIMUS 2006 TC
70% tempranillo, 15% cabernet sauvignon, 15% syrah.

88 Colour: deep cherry, orangey edge. Nose: fruit preserve, sweet spices, creamy oak, old leather. Palate: powerful, flavourful, long, spicy.

PAGOS DEL CONUCO 2006 T
100% tempranillo.

87 Colour: deep cherry, orangey edge. Nose: ripe fruit, fragrant herbs, sweet spices, fine reductive notes. Palate: powerful, flavourful, long, spicy.

DOMINIO DE EGUREN

Camino de San Pedro, s/n
01309 Páganos (Álava)
☎: +34 945 600 117 - Fax: +34 945 600 590
info@eguren.com
www.eguren.com

CÓDICE 2010 T
100% tempranillo.

90 Colour: cherry, purple rim. Nose: floral, red berry notes, lactic notes, expressive, roasted coffee. Palate: powerful, flavourful, fresh, fruity.

DOMINIO DE PUNCTUM ORGANIC & BIODYNAMIC WINES

Finca Fabian, s/n - Aptdo. 71
16660 Las Pedroñeras (Cuenca)
☎: +34 912 959 997 - Fax: +34 912 959 998
export@dominiodepunctum.com
www.dominiodepunctum.com

LOBETIA CHARDONNAY 2011 B
100% chardonnay.

88 Colour: bright yellow. Nose: tropical fruit, ripe fruit, floral, lactic notes, fragrant herbs. Palate: light-bodied, fresh, fruity, flavourful.

PUNCTUM CHARDONNAY SELECCIÓN 2011 B
100% chardonnay.

87 Colour: bright yellow. Nose: floral, ripe fruit, tropical fruit, lactic notes. Palate: fresh, fruity, light-bodied, flavourful, easy to drink.

PUNCTUM VIOGNIER 2011 B
100% viognier.

87 Colour: bright straw. Nose: white flowers, ripe fruit, fragrant herbs. Palate: light-bodied, fresh, fruity, flavourful, easy to drink.

PUNCTUM SAUVIGNON BLANC 2011 B
100% sauvignon blanc.

83

PUNCTUM SYRAH 2011 T
100% syrah.

87 Colour: cherry, purple rim. Nose: floral, red berry notes, balsamic herbs, medium intensity. Palate: powerful, flavourful, correct, easy to drink.

PUNCTUM TEMPRANILLO PETIT VERDOT 2011 T
70% tempranillo, 30% petit verdot.

84

LOBETIA TEMPRANILLO 2011 T
100% tempranillo.

84

VIENTO ALISEO CABERNET SAUVIGNON GRACIANO 2010 T ROBLE
70% cabernet sauvignon, 30% graciano.

86 Colour: cherry, garnet rim. Nose: earthy notes, scrubland, ripe fruit, creamy oak. Palate: powerful, flavourful, toasty.

LOBETIA TEMPRANILLO PETIT VERDOT 2010 T ROBLE
70% tempranillo, 30% petit verdot.

84

EL PROGRESO SOCIEDAD COOP. CLM

Avda. de la Virgen, 89
13670 Villarubia de los Ojos (Ciudad Real)
☎: +34 926 896 088 - Fax: +34 926 896 135
administracion@bodegaselprogreso.com
www.bodegaselprogreso.com

MI CHUPITO 2011 B
100% airén.

80

ENCOMIENDA DE CERVERA

Arzobispo Cañizares, 1
13270 Almagro (Ciudad Real)
☎: +34 926 102 099 - Fax: +34 926 222 297
info@ecervera.com
www.encomiendadecervera.com

VULCANUS CABERNET SAUVIGNON 2010 TC
100% cabernet sauvignon.

87 Colour: cherry, purple rim. Nose: ripe fruit, spicy, roasted coffee, balsamic herbs. Palate: powerful, flavourful, toasty.

MAAR DE CERVERA SYRAH 2010 TC
syrah.

86 Colour: bright cherry, garnet rim. Nose: creamy oak, sweet spices, cocoa bean. Palate: good structure, round tannins.

POKER DE TEMPRANILLOS 2009 TC
tempranillo.

89 Colour: cherry, garnet rim. Nose: ripe fruit, sweet spices. Palate: flavourful, round tannins, good structure.

FÉLIX SOLÍS

Autovía del Sur, Km. 199
13300 Valdepeñas (Ciudad Real)
☎: +34 926 322 400 - Fax: +34 926 322 417
fsa@felixsolisavantis.com
www.felixsolisavantis.com

ORQUESTA CHARDONNAY 2011 B
chardonnay.

85 Colour: bright yellow. Nose: white flowers, ripe fruit, fragrant herbs. Palate: powerful, flavourful, fresh, fruity.

CONSIGNA CHARDONNAY 2011 B
100% chardonnay.

84

CONSIGNA 2011 RD
100% tempranillo.

83

ORQUESTA TEMPRANILLO 2011 T
tempranillo.

85 Colour: cherry, purple rim. Nose: fresh fruit, red berry notes, floral, balsamic herbs. Palate: flavourful, fruity, good acidity.

CONSIGNA TEMPRANILLO 2011 T
100% tempranillo.

85 Colour: cherry, purple rim. Nose: expressive, fresh fruit, red berry notes, floral. Palate: flavourful, fruity, good acidity.

CONSIGNA MERLOT 2011 T
100% merlot.

85 Colour: cherry, purple rim. Nose: floral, ripe fruit, balsamic herbs. Palate: light-bodied, fresh, fruity.

ORQUESTA MERLOT 2011 T
merlot.

85 Colour: cherry, purple rim. Nose: ripe fruit, fragrant herbs, floral. Palate: powerful, flavourful, balsamic.

CONSIGNA SHIRAZ 2011 T
100% syrah.

84

CONSIGNA CABERNET SAUVIGNON 2011 T
100% cabernet sauvignon.

84

ORQUESTA CABERNET SAUVIGNON 2011 T
cabernet sauvignon.

84

FINCA CASA ALARCÓN

Ctra. Montealegre, km 4,5
02660 Caudete (Albacete)
☎: +34 965 929 193 - Fax: +34 965 229 405
beatriz.andres@anara.es
www.casalarcon.com

CASA ALARCÓN VIOGNIER 2011 B
100% viognier.

84

CASA ALARCÓN 2011 RD
syrah, petit verdot.

83

NEA 2009 T
100% petit verdot.

84

BLAU 2008 T
monastrell, merlot.

87 Colour: cherry, garnet rim. Nose: ripe fruit, spicy, creamy oak, toasty. Palate: powerful, flavourful, toasty.

TRIA ROBLE AMERICANO 2008 T
syrah, petit verdot, merlot.

86 Colour: cherry, garnet rim. Nose: ripe fruit, balsamic herbs, sweet spices, creamy oak. Palate: spicy, ripe fruit, flavourful.

TRÍA ROBLE FRANCÉS 2007 T
syrah, petit verdot, merlot.

87 Colour: bright cherry. Nose: ripe fruit, sweet spices, creamy oak, expressive. Palate: flavourful, fruity, toasty, round tannins.

FINCA CONSTANCIA

Camino del Bravo, s/n
45543 Otero (Toledo)
☎: +34 914 903 700 - Fax: +34 916 612 124
lslara@gonzalezbyass.es
www.gonzalezbyass.es

FINCA CONSTANCIA TEMPRANILLO P23 2010 T
tempranillo.

89 Colour: cherry, garnet rim. Nose: red berry notes, floral, sweet spices, creamy oak. Palate: flavourful, fruity, balanced, long, toasty.

ALTOS DE LA FINCA 2009 T
petit verdot, syrah.

90 Colour: black cherry, garnet rim. Nose: overripe fruit, scrubland, fine reductive notes, toasty. Palate: long, flavourful, harsh oak tannins.

FINCA CONSTANCIA 2009 T
syrah, cabernet sauvignon, cabernet franc, petit verdot, tempranillo, graciano.

87 Colour: cherry, garnet rim. Nose: red berry notes, candied fruit, sweet spices. Palate: powerful, flavourful, harsh oak tannins.

FINCA EL REFUGIO

Ctra. CM 3102, km. 14,6
13630 Socuéllamos (Ciudad Real)
☎: +34 913 562 746
info@fincaelrefugio.es
www.fincaelrefugio.es

LEGADO FINCA EL REFUGIO VERDEJO 2011 B
100% verdejo.

85 Colour: bright yellow. Nose: ripe fruit, faded flowers, herbaceous. Palate: flavourful, correct, balsamic.

LEGADO SYRAH ROSÉ 2011 RD
100% syrah.

84

LEGADO FINCA EL REFUGIO 3 MESES 2010 T ROBLE
100% tempranillo.

87 Colour: cherry, garnet rim. Nose: ripe fruit, earthy notes, spicy, creamy oak. Palate: powerful, flavourful, spicy.

LEGADO FINCA EL REFUGIO 14 MESES 2009 T ROBLE
cabernet sauvignon, merlot.

86 Colour: bright cherry. Nose: ripe fruit, sweet spices, creamy oak, balsamic herbs. Palate: flavourful, fruity, toasty.

LEGADO FINCA EL REFUGIO 15 MESES 2009 T
100% petit verdot.

86 Colour: cherry, garnet rim. Nose: ripe fruit, balsamic herbs, creamy oak. Palate: fine bitter notes, powerful, flavourful.

LEGADO FINCA EL REFUGIO 14 MESES 2007 T
cabernet sauvignon, merlot.

84

FINCA EL REGAJO

Lope de Vega, 24
02651 Fuenteálamo (Albacete)
☎: +34 699 311 950
www.fincadelregajo.es

PUERTO PINAR VIOGNIER 2009 B
viognier.

85 Colour: bright yellow. Nose: dried flowers, ripe fruit, spicy, toasty. Palate: flavourful, fresh, spicy, easy to drink.

MACEDONIO 2009 T ROBLE
monastrell, petit verdot.

83

MACEDONIO SELECCIÓN 2008 T
petit verdot.

87 Colour: cherry, garnet rim. Nose: ripe fruit, toasty, earthy notes, balsamic herbs. Palate: powerful, flavourful, toasty, balanced.

FINCA LA VALONA VIÑEDOS Y BODEGAS

D. Victoriano González, 39
16220 Quintanar del Rey (Cuenca)
☎: +34 967 496 600 - Fax: +34 967 495 495
info@fincalavalona.com
www.fincalavalona.com

LA VALONA SELECCIÓN 2007 T
100% tempranillo.

90 Colour: cherry, garnet rim. Nose: ripe fruit, wild herbs. Palate: flavourful, full, long.

LA VALONA 4 MESES EN BARRICA 2007 T
100% tempranillo.

89 Colour: cherry, garnet rim. Nose: ripe fruit, spicy, creamy oak. Palate: powerful, flavourful, toasty, long.

LA VALONA 12 MESES EN BARRICA 2007 T
100% tempranillo.

87 Colour: cherry, garnet rim. Nose: ripe fruit, balsamic herbs, spicy, creamy oak. Palate: spicy, long, harsh oak tannins.

FINCA LORANQUE

Finca Loranque, s/n
45593 Bargas (Toledo)
☎: +34 925 590 316 - Fax: +34 925 512 450
fincaloranque@fincaloranque.com
www.fincaloranque.com

LACRUZ TEMPRANILLO SYRAH 2010 T
70% tempranillo, 30% syrah.

86 Colour: cherry, garnet rim. Nose: ripe fruit, earthy notes, warm, sweet spices. Palate: powerful, flavourful, spicy.

LORANQUE EL GRANDE 2007 T
syrah.

87 Colour: cherry, garnet rim. Nose: ripe fruit, fruit preserve, spicy, fine reductive notes. Palate: balanced, powerful, flavourful.

LACRUZ CABERNET SAUVIGNON 2006 T
100% cabernet sauvignon.

87 Colour: deep cherry, orangey edge. Nose: ripe fruit, balsamic herbs, spicy, tobacco. Palate: long, warm, toasty, harsh oak tannins.

LACRUZ SYRAH 2006 T
100% syrah.

85 Colour: pale ruby, brick rim edge. Nose: spicy, fine reductive notes, aged wood nuances, fruit preserve. Palate: spicy, long, round tannins.

FINCA LOS ALIJARES

Avda. de la Paz, 5
45180 Camarena (Toledo)
☎: +34 918 174 364 - Fax: +34 918 174 364
gerencia@fincalosalijares.com
www.fincalosalijares.com

FINCA LOS ALIJARES VIOGNIER 2011 B
100% viognier.

85 Colour: bright yellow. Nose: honeyed notes, ripe fruit, dried flowers. Palate: powerful, flavourful, fruity, easy to drink.

FINCA LOS ALIJARES PETIT VERDOT SYRAH 2011 T
petit verdot.

87 Colour: cherry, garnet rim. Nose: ripe fruit, candied fruit, balsamic herbs, toasty. Palate: fresh, flavourful, balsamic, spicy.

FINCA LOS ALIJARES GRACIANO 2009 TC
100% graciano.

88 Colour: cherry, garnet rim. Nose: ripe fruit, spicy, creamy oak, toasty. Palate: powerful, flavourful, toasty.

FINCA LOS ALIJARES GRACIANO AUTOR 2009 T
graciano.

87 Colour: bright cherry. Nose: ripe fruit, sweet spices, creamy oak. Palate: flavourful, fruity, toasty.

FINCA LOS ALIJARES SYRAH GRACIANO 2009 TC
syrah, graciano.

86 Colour: cherry, garnet rim. Nose: fruit preserve, scrubland, sweet spices, toasty. Palate: powerful, flavourful, spicy.

FINCA LOS JUANES

Almendro, 2
45870 Lillo (Toledo)
☎: +34 657 015 600
sanchezbrunete5@gmail.com

SÁNCHEZ-BRUNETE COLECCIÓN PARTICULAR 2007 T
syrah, merlot, cabernet sauvignon.

85 Colour: cherry, garnet rim. Nose: ripe fruit, spicy, scrubland, wet leather, cigar. Palate: powerful, flavourful, spirituous.

SÁNCHEZ-BRUNETE COLECCIÓN PARTICULAR 2005 T
syrah, merlot, cabernet sauvignon.

83

FONTANA

Extramuros, s/n
16411 Fuente de Pedro Naharro (Cuenca)
☎: +34 969 125 433 - Fax: +34 969 125 387
gemag@bodegasfontana.com
www.bodegasfontana.com

GRAN FONTAL VENDIMIA SELECCIONADA 2007 TR
100% tempranillo.

90 Colour: cherry, garnet rim. Nose: balanced, expressive, fruit expression, sweet spices. Palate: balanced, fruity, spicy.

QUERCUS 2007 TC
100% tempranillo.

91 Colour: bright cherry, garnet rim. Nose: complex, elegant, spicy, ripe fruit, dark chocolate. Palate: fruity, rich, round tannins, long.

QUERCUS EDICIÓN ESPECIAL JESÚS MATEO 2006 T
100% tempranillo.

87 Colour: deep cherry, garnet rim. Nose: tobacco, wet leather, powerfull, spicy. Palate: powerful, ripe fruit, long.

DUETO DE FONTANA 2004 TC
50% merlot, 50% cabernet sauvignon.

90 Colour: cherry, garnet rim. Nose: ripe fruit, tobacco, spicy. Palate: fine bitter notes, good structure, ripe fruit, round tannins.

OSBORNE MALPICA DE TAJO

Ctra. Malpica - Pueblanueva, km 6
45692 Malpica de Tajo (Toledo)
☎: +34 925 860 990 - Fax: +34 925 860 905
carolina.cerrato@osborne.es
www.osborne.es

SOLAZ 2011 B
viura, verdejo.

84

SOLAZ 2011 RD
syrah, mencía.

85 Colour: light cherry. Nose: candied fruit, ripe fruit, floral. Palate: sweetness, flavourful, fruity, easy to drink.

SOLAZ CABERNET SELECCIÓN FAMILIAR 2009 T
syrah, tempranillo.

86 Colour: cherry, garnet rim. Nose: red berry notes, ripe fruit, balsamic herbs, medium intensity. Palate: flavourful, fruity, toasty.

SOLAZ TEMPRANILLO CABERNET SAUVIGNON 2009 T
tempranillo, cabernet sauvignon.

84

PAGO DE GUZQUE

Marqués de Molins, 7- 7º
02001 (Albacete)
☎: +34 967 219 076 - Fax: +34 967 214 709
info@pagodeguzque.com
www.pagodeguzque.com

GRACIANO DE GUZQUE 2006 T
graciano.

86 Colour: pale ruby, brick rim edge. Nose: spicy, fine reductive notes, wet leather, aged wood nuances, damp earth. Palate: spicy, long, flavourful.

PAGO DE MONTAL

Paraje Mainetes
02651 Fuenteálamo (Albacete)
☎: +34 938 743 511 - Fax: +34 938 737 204
info@pagodemontal.com
www.pagodemontal.com

MONTAL MACABEO AIRÉN 2010 B
70% macabeo, 30% airén.

84

MONTAL MONASTRELL-SYRAH 2010 T
85% monastrell, 15% syrah.

87 Colour: cherry, garnet rim. Nose: ripe fruit, scrubland, spicy, creamy oak. Palate: powerful, flavourful, correct.

MONTAL GARNACHA 2009 T
100% garnacha.

87 Colour: bright cherry, purple rim. Nose: powerfull, scrubland, ripe fruit. Palate: correct, balanced, ripe fruit.

PAGO DE VALLEGARCÍA

Claudio Coello, 35 Bajo C
28001 Madrid (Madrid)
☎: +34 925 421 407 - Fax: +34 925 421 822
comercial@vallegarcia.com
www.vallegarcia.com

VALLEGARCÍA VIOGNIER 2010 BFB
100% viognier.

94 Colour: bright yellow. Nose: powerfull, ripe fruit, sweet spices, fragrant herbs, mineral. Palate: rich, smoky afterpalate:, flavourful, fresh, good acidity.

PETIT HIPPERIA 2010 T
38% merlot, 37% cabernet sauvignon, 16% petit verdot, 5% syrah, 4% cabernet franc.

91 Colour: cherry, purple rim. Nose: earthy notes, spicy, balsamic herbs, ripe fruit. Palate: elegant, full, flavourful, long.

VALLEGARCÍA SYRAH 2008 T
100% syrah.

92 Colour: bright cherry. Nose: ripe fruit, sweet spices, creamy oak. Palate: flavourful, fruity, toasty, round tannins.

HIPPERIA 2008 T
47% merlot, 46% cabernet sauvignon, 5% petit verdot, 2% cabernet franc.

92 Colour: cherry, garnet rim. Nose: ripe fruit, spicy, creamy oak, toasty, complex, mineral. Palate: powerful, flavourful, toasty, round tannins, balanced.

PAGO DEL VICARIO

Ctra. Ciudad Real - Porzuna, (CM-412) Km. 16
13196 (Ciudad Real)
☎: +34 926 666 027 - Fax: +34 670 099 520
info@pagodelvicario.com
www.pagodelvicario.com

PAGO DEL VICARIO BLANCO DE TEMPRANILLO 2011 B
tempranillo.

87 Colour: bright straw. Nose: dried flowers, faded flowers, fragrant herbs, ripe fruit. Palate: powerful, flavourful, correct.

PAGO DEL VICARIO PETIT VERDOT 2011 RD
petit verdot.

86 Colour: rose, purple rim. Nose: powerfull, ripe fruit, red berry notes, floral, lactic notes. Palate: , powerful, fruity, flavourful.

PAGO DEL VICARIO MERLOT DULCE 2010 T
merlot.

83

PAGO DEL VICARIO PENTA 2008 T
tempranillo, syrah, cabernet sauvignon, merlot, petit verdot.

87 Colour: cherry, garnet rim. Nose: spicy, scrubland, earthy notes. Palate: flavourful, fruity, easy to drink, good finish.

PAGO DEL VICARIO 50-50 2007 T
tempranillo, cabernet sauvignon.

87 Colour: cherry, garnet rim. Nose: powerfull, fruit preserve, slightly evolved. Palate: fine bitter notes, flavourful, round tannins.

PAGO DEL VICARIO MONAGÓS 2007 T
syrah, graciano.

87 Colour: cherry, garnet rim. Nose: toasty, nose:tic coffee, spicy. Palate: flavourful, fruity, fine bitter notes.

PAGO DEL VICARIO AGIOS 2007 T
tempranillo.

85 Colour: bright cherry. Nose: toasty, dark chocolate, sweet spices, fruit preserve, old leather. Palate: powerful, round tannins, correct, fine bitter notes.

QUINTA DE AVES

Ctra. CR-P-5222, Km. 11,200
13350 Moral de Calatrava (Ciudad Real)
☎: +34 915 716 514 - Fax: +34 915 711 151
qda@grupomaresa.com
www.quintadeaves.es

QUINTA DE AVES ALAUDA 2011 B
75% sauvignon blanc, 25% moscatel grano menudo.

86 Colour: bright yellow. Nose: ripe fruit, citrus fruit, white flowers, fragrant herbs. Palate: light-bodied, fresh, fruity.

QUINTA DE AVES AIRÉN 2011 B
100% airén.

85 Colour: bright straw. Nose: fresh, fresh fruit, white flowers. Palate: flavourful, fruity, good acidity.

QUINTA DE AVES NOCTUA 2009 T BARRICA
50% tempranillo, 21% merlot, 21% syrah, 8% graciano.

88 Colour: bright cherry. Nose: ripe fruit, creamy oak, expressive, fragrant herbs. Palate: flavourful, fruity, toasty.

SELEENTE WINERY & VINEYARDS

Ctra. Toledo - Talavera, Km. 56,500
45685 Montearagón (Toledo)
☎: +34 628 935 890 - Fax: +34 925 865 435
info@seleente.com
www.seleente.com

SELEENTE COLECCIÓN PRIVADA 2010 T
cabernet sauvignon, merlot, petit verdot.

86 Colour: deep cherry, purple rim. Nose: nose:tic coffee, toasty, sweet spices. Palate: fruity, good finish.

SELEENTE VINTAGE 2008 T
cabernet sauvignon, syrah, merlot, petit verdot.

87 Colour: cherry, garnet rim. Nose: balanced, red berry notes, ripe fruit, warm, sweet spices. Palate: flavourful, fruity, good finish.

SELEENTE 2007 T
cabernet sauvignon, merlot, tempranillo, syrah, petit verdot.

86 Colour: cherry, garnet rim. Nose: overripe fruit, balsamic herbs, sweet spices. Palate: fine bitter notes, flavourful, toasty.

VINNICO EXPORT

Muela, 16
03730 Jávea (Alicante)
☎: +34 965 791 967 - Fax: +34 966 461 471
info@vinnico.com
www.vinnico.com

EL PASO 2011 B
80% viura, 20% verdejo.

87 Colour: bright straw. Nose: fresh, fresh fruit, white flowers, expressive. Palate: flavourful, fruity, good acidity, balanced.

LA NIÑA DE COLUMBUS 2011 B
sauvignon blanc.

84

ALMEZ ORGANIC MONASTRELL SHIRAZ 2011 T
85% monastrell, 15% syrah.

90 Colour: cherry, purple rim. Nose: red berry notes, floral, ripe fruit. Palate: flavourful, fruity, good acidity, round tannins.

EL PASO TEMPRANILLO SHIRAZ 2011 T
85% tempranillo, 15% syrah.

89 Colour: cherry, purple rim. Nose: medium intensity, scrubland, ripe fruit, sweet spices. Palate: fruity, good acidity, balanced.

DOS PUNTOS TEMPRANILLO 2011 T
90% tempranillo, 10% syrah.

88 Colour: cherry, purple rim. Nose: ripe fruit, floral, balsamic herbs, spicy, toasty. Palate: long, flavourful, balanced.

VANESA 2011 T
100% monastrell.

88 Colour: cherry, purple rim. Nose: red berry notes, floral, wild herbs. Palate: fresh, fruity, easy to drink, flavourful.

CAPA TEMPRANILLO 2011 T
90% tempranillo, 10% syrah.

86 Colour: cherry, purple rim. Nose: red berry notes, ripe fruit, sweet spices, toasty. Palate: powerful, flavourful, harsh oak tannins.

LA NIÑA DE COLUMBUS SHIRAZ 2011 T
100% syrah.

86 Colour: cherry, purple rim. Nose: red berry notes, floral, balsamic herbs. Palate: light-bodied, fresh, fruity, flavourful, easy to drink.

CEPUNTO ORO T
tempranillo, cabernet sauvignon.

84

VINOS COLOMAN

Goya, 17
13620 Pedro Muñoz (Ciudad Real)
☎: +34 926 586 410 - Fax: +34 926 586 656
coloman@satcoloman.com
www.satcoloman.com

PEDROTEÑO AIRÉN 2011 B
100% airén.

80

PEDROTEÑO 2011 T
100% tempranillo.

84

VINOS Y BODEGAS

Ctra. de las Mesas, Km. 1
13630 Socuéllanos (Ciudad Real)
☎: +34 926 531 067 - Fax: +34 926 532 249
export@vinosybodegas.com
www.vinosybodegas.com

AMELASIO 2011 B
100% sauvignon blanc.

85 Colour: coppery red. Nose: ripe fruit, faded flowers, fragrant herbs. Palate: light-bodied, fresh, fruity, flavourful.

TEMPLUM 2010 T
tempranillo, merlot, syrah, cabernet sauvignon.

84

IMPERIUM VINI 2010 T
tempranillo, merlot, syrah, cabernet sauvignon.

83

AMELASIO 2010 T
tempranillo, merlot, syrah, cabernet sauvignon.

82

MIRADOR DE CASTILLA 6 MESES 2009 T
50% tempranillo, 30% cabernet sauvignon, 20% syrah.

84

MIRADOR DE CASTILLA 12 MESES 2008 T
50% tempranillo, 30% cabernet sauvignon, 20% syrah.

85 Colour: deep cherry, orangey edge. Nose: ripe fruit, spicy, fine reductive notes, creamy oak. Palate: long, flavourful.

VIÑEDOS BALMORAL

Mayor, 32 - 1º
02001 (Albacete)
☎: +34 967 508 382 - Fax: +34 967 235 301
info@vinedosbalmoral.com
www.edone.es

MARAVIDES 2010 T

90 Colour: bright cherry. Nose: ripe fruit, sweet spices, creamy oak, roasted coffee. Palate: flavourful, fruity, toasty, round tannins.

EDONÉ 2009 ESP
chardonnay, macabeo.

83

VIÑEDOS MEJORANTES

Ctra. de Villafranca, Km. 2
45860 Villacañas (Toledo)
☎: +34 925 201 036 - Fax: +34 925 200 023
portillejo@portillejo.com
www.portillejo.es

VALDEPORT 2008 T ROBLE
70% cabernet sauvignon, 15% merlot, 10% tempranillo, 5% petit verdot.

84

VIÑEDOS Y BODEGAS EL CASTILLO

Ctra. Ossa de Montiel, Km. 1,8
02600 Villarrobledo (Albacete)
☎: +34 967 573 230 - Fax: +34 967 573 048
info@bodegaselcastillo.com
www.bodegaselcastillo.com

ARGUM 2011 B
sauvignon blanc.

86 Colour: bright straw. Nose: fresh fruit, white flowers, varietal. Palate: flavourful, fruity, good acidity, balanced.

ARGUM 2011 B
sauvignon blanc.

85 Colour: bright straw. Nose: fresh, white flowers, candied fruit, balanced. Palate: flavourful, fruity, good acidity, sweetness.

ARGUM 2011 T
tempranillo, cabernet sauvignon.

85 Colour: deep cherry. Nose: ripe fruit, fruit expression, balsamic herbs. Palate: flavourful, powerful, fine bitter notes.

ARGUM SYRAH 2010 T
syrah.

88 Colour: cherry, purple rim. Nose: fresh fruit, red berry notes, floral, powerfull. Palate: flavourful, fruity, good acidity, round tannins.

TIERRAS DE ARGUM 2009 T
tempranillo, cabernet sauvignon, merlot.

88 Colour: cherry, garnet rim. Nose: spicy, creamy oak, toasty, powerfull. Palate: powerful, flavourful, toasty, round tannins.

ARGUM 2008 T ROBLE
tempranillo, cabernet sauvignon, merlot.

84

ROBLE PARRA 2008 T
100% tempranillo.

90 Colour: deep cherry. Nose: powerfull, expressive, characterful, ripe fruit, toasty, new oak. Palate: flavourful, powerful, concentrated, fine bitter notes.

VIÑEDOS Y BODEGAS MUÑOZ

Ctra. Villarrubia, 11
45350 Noblejas (Toledo)
☎: +34 925 140 070 - Fax: +34 925 141 334
info@bodegasmunoz.com
www.bodegasmunoz.com

FINCA MUÑOZ CEPAS VIEJAS 2008 T
100% tempranillo.

90 Colour: cherry, garnet rim. Nose: ripe fruit, spicy, toasty, fine reductive notes, acetaldehyde. Palate: powerful, flavourful, toasty, ripe fruit.

FINCA MUÑOZ BARREL AGED 2008 T ROBLE

87 Colour: cherry, garnet rim. Nose: balsamic herbs, spicy, creamy oak, ripe fruit. Palate: spicy, powerful, flavourful.

VITIVINOS ANUNCIACIÓN SC DE CLM

Camino de Cabezuelas, s/n
02270 Villamalea (Albacete)
☎: +34 967 483 114 - Fax: +34 967 483 964
info@vitivinos.com
www.vitivinos.com

LLANOS DEL MARQUÉS BOBAL 2010 T
100% bobal.

86 Colour: cherry, garnet rim. Nose: floral, ripe fruit, fruit preserve, scrubland. Palate: light-bodied, fresh, fruity.

LLANOS DEL MARQUÉS BOBAL ECOLÓGICO 2010 T
100% bobal.

84

LLANOS DEL MARQUÉS TEMPRANILLO 2010 T
tempranillo.

83

CASTILLA-CAMPO DE CALATRAVA

AMANCIO MENCHERO MÁRQUEZ

Legión, 27
13260 Bolaños de Calatrava (Ciudad Real)
☎: +34 926 870 076 - Fax: +34 926 871 558
amanciomenchero@hotmail.com

CUBA 38 2011 T
100% cencibel.

84

CASTILLA Y LEÓN

ABADÍA RETUERTA

Ctra. N-122 Soria, km. 332,5
47340 Sardón de Duero (Valladolid)
☎: +34 983 680 314 - Fax: +34 983 680 286
elena.revilla@abadia-retuerta.es
www.abadia-retuerta.com

ABADÍA RETUERTA LE DOMAINE 2010 B
80% sauvignon blanc, 20% verdejo.

92 Colour: bright yellow. Nose: ripe fruit, sweet spices, creamy oak, fragrant herbs, expressive. Palate: rich, flavourful, fresh, balanced.

ABADÍA RETUERTA PAGO NEGRALADA 2009 T BARRICA
100% tempranillo.

95 Colour: dark-red cherry, garnet rim. Nose: ripe fruit, sweet spices, creamy oak, balanced. Palate: long, spicy, powerful, flavourful, round.

ABADÍA RETUERTA PAGO VALDEBELLÓN 2009 T BARRICA
100% cabernet sauvignon.

95 Colour: cherry, garnet rim. Nose: ripe fruit, earthy notes, fragrant herbs, spicy, toasty, balanced. Palate: powerful, flavourful, balsamic, spicy, round tannins. Personality.

PAGO LA GARDUÑA SYRAH 2009 T
100% syrah.

93 Colour: cherry, garnet rim. Nose: ripe fruit, violets, dark chocolate, sweet spices, creamy oak. Palate: powerful, flavourful, long, toasty, round tannins.

ABADÍA RETUERTA SELECCIÓN ESPECIAL 2009 T
75% tempranillo, 15% cabernet sauvignon, 10% syrah.

92 Colour: bright cherry. Nose: sweet spices, creamy oak, expressive, red berry notes, ripe fruit, balanced, mineral. Palate: flavourful, fruity, toasty, round tannins, long.

AGRÍCOLA CASTELLANA. BODEGA CUATRO RAYAS

Ctra. Rodilana, s/n
47491 La Seca (Valladolid)
☎: +34 983 816 320 - Fax: +34 983 816 562
info@cuatrorayas.org
www.cuatrorayas.org

DOLCE BIANCO VERDEJO 2011 SEMIDULCE
100% verdejo.

86 Colour: bright golden. Nose: candied fruit, citrus fruit, tropical fruit, floral, fresh. Palate: fresh, fruity, sweetness, easy to drink.

ALTOS DE SAN ESTEBAN

Ildefonso Sánchez del Río, 4 - 3ºB
33001 Oviedo (Asturias)
☎: +34 660 145 313
mamarques@telecable.es

ALTOS DE SAN ESTEBAN VIÑAS DE MONTE 2009 TC
85% mencía, 12% cabernet sauvignon, 3% merlot.

90 Colour: cherry, garnet rim. Nose: ripe fruit, spicy, complex, earthy notes, scrubland. Palate: powerful, flavourful, toasty, round tannins.

ALTOS DE SAN ESTEBAN 2009 TC
35% mencía, 33% cabernet sauvignon, 32% merlot.

88 Colour: cherry, garnet rim. Nose: ripe fruit, earthy notes, scrubland, powerfull. Palate: spicy, balsamic, flavourful, balanced.

ALTOS DE SAN ESTEBAN LA MENDAÑONA 2008 TC
100% mencía.

92 Colour: cherry, garnet rim. Nose: red berry notes, ripe fruit, wild herbs, earthy notes, mineral, expressive. Palate: balanced, powerful, flavourful, spicy.

ARRIAGA Y MIMÉNDEZ COMPAÑÍA DE VINOS

Capitán Cortés, 6. Piso 4º Puerta 3
26003 Logroño (La Rioja)
☎: +34 687 421 306 - Fax: +34 941 287 072
administracion@arriagaymimendez.com
www.arriagaymimendez.com

MITERNA CORTE DOS 2007 T BARRICA
100% prieto picudo.

89 Colour: cherry, garnet rim. Nose: mineral, ripe fruit, wild herbs, spicy, scrubland. Palate: powerful, flavourful, long, toasty.

MITERNA CORTE UNO 2006 T BARRICA
100% prieto picudo.

91 Colour: cherry, garnet rim. Nose: earthy notes, cigar, old leather, aged wood nuances, ripe fruit, balsamic herbs. Palate: elegant, powerful, flavourful, long, balanced.

BEATRIZ HERRANZ

Cuesta de las descargas, 11 bis
28005 Madrid (Madrid)
☎: 655 890 949

BARCO DEL CORNETA 2010 B
100% verdejo.

90 Colour: bright straw. Nose: powerfull, ripe fruit, citrus fruit, sweet spices, grassy. Palate: flavourful, good acidity, spicy.

BELONDRADE

Quinta San Diego - Camino del Puerto, s/n
47491 La Seca (Valladolid)
☎: +34 983 481 001 - Fax: +34 600 590 024
info@belondrade.com
www.belondrade.com

QUINTA APOLONIA BELONDRADE 2011 B
100% verdejo.

91 Colour: bright straw. Nose: fresh, fresh fruit, white flowers, varietal. Palate: flavourful, fruity, good acidity.

QUINTA CLARISA BELONDRADE 2011 RD
100% tempranillo.

87 Colour: light cherry. Nose: candied fruit, overripe fruit. Palate: fine bitter notes, good acidity, ripe fruit.

BODEGA ALISTE

Pza. de España, 4
49520 Figueruela de Abajo (Zamora)
☎: +34 676 986 570 - Fax: +34 944 231 816
javier@hacedordevino.com
www.vinosdealiste.com

GEIJO 2011 BFB
90% viura, 5% chardonnay, 5% verdejo.

88 Colour: bright yellow. Nose: ripe fruit, sweet spices, creamy oak, fragrant herbs. Palate: rich, flavourful, good acidity.

ALISTE 2011 T ROBLE
95% tempranillo, 5% syrah.

88 Colour: bright cherry. Nose: ripe fruit, creamy oak, expressive, earthy notes. Palate: flavourful, fruity, toasty, balanced.

MARINA DE ALISTE 2010 T
90% tempranillo, 10% syrah.

90 Colour: cherry, garnet rim. Nose: spicy, creamy oak, ripe fruit, earthy notes. Palate: powerful, flavourful, long, spicy.

BODEGA DON JUAN DEL AGUILA

Real de Abajo, 100
05110 El Barraco (Ávila)
☎: +34 920 281 032
bodegadonjuandelaguila@gmail.com
www.donjuandelaguila.es

GAZNATA 2011 RD
garnacha.

82

GAZNATA 2010 T
garnacha.

87 Colour: cherry, garnet rim. Nose: red berry notes, ripe fruit, scrubland, mineral. Palate: flavourful, balsamic, long.

GAZNATA CONCRETE 2010 T
garnacha.

84

GAZNATA FINCA MARIANO 2009 T
garnacha.

93 Colour: light cherry, garnet rim. Nose: fruit liqueur notes, scrubland, mineral, dry stone, spicy, creamy oak. Palate: balanced, flavourful, complex, spicy, long, round.

GAZNATA GREDOS 2009 T
garnacha.

84

BODEGA EL ALBAR LURTON

Camino Magarin, s/n
47529 Villafranca del Duero (Valladolid)
☎: +34 983 034 030 - Fax: +34 983 034 040
bodega@francoislurton.es
www.francoislurton.es

EL ALBAR LURTON EXCELENCIA 2008 T
100% tempranillo.

92 Colour: cherry, garnet rim. Nose: ripe fruit, expressive, sweet spices, toasty. Palate: spicy, powerful, flavourful.

EL ALBAR LURTON BARRICAS 2008 T
100% tinta de Toro.

90 Colour: cherry, garnet rim. Nose: mineral, ripe fruit, sweet spices, creamy oak. Palate: flavourful, toasty, ripe fruit, long.

BODEGA EMINA MEDINA DEL CAMPO

Ctra. Medina del Campo - Olmedo, Km. 1,5
47400 Medina del Campo (Valladolid)
☎: +34 983 800 001 - Fax: +34 902 430 189
eminarueda@emina.es
www.eminarueda.es

HEREDAD DE EMINA CHARDONNAY 2011 B
100% chardonnay.

88 Colour: bright yellow. Nose: floral, citrus fruit, ripe fruit, fragrant herbs. Palate: powerful, flavourful, long, balanced.

HEREDAD DE EMINA GEWÜRZTRAMINER 2011 B
100% gewürztraminer.

85 Colour: bright yellow. Nose: white flowers, tropical fruit, overripe fruit. Palate: flavourful, full, ripe fruit.

BODEGA FINCA FUENTEGALANA

Ctra. M-501, Alcorcón - Plasencia, km. 65
05429 Navahondilla (Ávila)
☎: +34 646 843 231
info@fuentegalana.com
www.fuentegalana.com

TOROS DE GUISANDO SYRAH 2009 T
syrah.

87 Colour: cherry, garnet rim. Nose: ripe fruit, spicy, creamy oak, toasty. Palate: powerful, flavourful, toasty, harsh oak tannins.

TOROS DE GUISANDO 2009 T
merlot, syrah, tempranillo.

87 Colour: cherry, garnet rim. Nose: ripe fruit, fragrant herbs, spicy, creamy oak. Palate: powerful, flavourful, harsh oak tannins.

TOROS DE GUISANDO SYRAH 2008 T
syrah.

88 Colour: cherry, garnet rim. Nose: ripe fruit, spicy, creamy oak, toasty, floral. Palate: powerful, flavourful, toasty, balanced.

BODEGA GÓTICA

Ctra. Rueda - La Seca, Km. 1,2
47490 Rueda (Valladolid)
☎: +34 629 458 235 - Fax: +34 983 868 387
mjhmonsalve@ya.com
www.bodegagotica.com

CÍMBALO 2010 T ROBLE
100% tempranillo.

88 Colour: bright cherry. Nose: ripe fruit, sweet spices, creamy oak, expressive. Palate: flavourful, fruity, toasty, round tannins.

BODEGA PAGO DE CALLEJO

Avda. Aranda, 3
09441 Sotillo de la Ribera (Burgos)
☎: +34 947 532 312 - Fax: +34 947 532 304
callejo@bodegasfelixcallejo.com
www.noecallejo.blogspot.com

FINCA VALDELROBLE 2009 T
60% tempranillo, 30% merlot, 10% syrah.

89 Colour: cherry, garnet rim. Nose: ripe fruit, fragrant herbs, spicy, creamy oak, mineral. Palate: powerful, flavourful, toasty.

BODEGA Y VIÑEDOS GARMENDIA

Finca Santa Rosalia, s/n
34260 Vizmalo (Burgos)
☎: +34 947 166 171 - Fax: +34 947 166 147
maria@bodegasgarmendia.com
www.bodegasgarmendia.com

GARMENDIA 2011 B
verdejo, viura.

90 Colour: bright straw. Nose: fresh, fresh fruit, white flowers, fragrant herbs. Palate: flavourful, fruity, good acidity, balanced.

BODEGAS ABABOL

Tomás Bayón, 56
47491 La Seca (Valladolid)
☎: +34 635 504 720 - Fax: +34 983 034 995
labodega@bodegasababol.com
www.bodegasababol.com

ABABOL SOBRE LÍAS 2010 B
verdejo.

87 Colour: bright yellow. Nose: fine lees, fragrant herbs, ripe fruit. Palate: powerful, flavourful, long, spicy.

GRAN ABABOL 2008 BFB
verdejo.

88 Colour: bright golden. Nose: fragrant herbs, ripe fruit, sweet spices, roasted coffee. Palate: powerful, full, flavourful, long, rich.

ABABOL 2010 T
tempranillo.

82

BODEGAS ALDEASOÑA

Ctra. Peñafiel - San Idelfonso, s/n
40235 Aldeasoña (Segovia)
☎: +34 983 878 052 - Fax: +34 983 873 052
bodega@bodegaconvento.com

ALDEASOÑA 2006 T
100% aragones.

90 Colour: cherry, garnet rim. Nose: ripe fruit, expressive, sweet spices, dark chocolate, creamy oak. Palate: powerful, flavourful, toasty.

BODEGAS ALTA PAVINA

Camino de Santibáñez, s/n
47328 La Parrilla (Valladolid)
☎: +34 983 681 521
bodegas@altapavina.com
www.altapavina.com

ALTA PAVINA PINOT NOIR CITIUS 2009 TC
100% pinot noir.

88 Colour: bright cherry, garnet rim. Nose: ripe fruit, complex, balanced, spicy. Palate: good structure, flavourful, rich.

ALTA PAVINA PAGO LA PAVINA 2009 T
80% pinot noir, 20% tempranillo.

86 Colour: cherry, garnet rim. Nose: medium intensity, ripe fruit, wild herbs, spicy. Palate: fruity, balanced.

BODEGAS CANOPY

Avda. Barber, 71
45004 (Toledo)
☎: +34 619 244 878 - Fax: +34 925 283 681
achacon@bodegascanopy.com

K OS 2008 T
garnacha.

93 Colour: very deep cherry. Nose: powerfull, ripe fruit, mineral, earthy notes, toasty, smoky. Palate: mineral, powerful, good acidity, fine bitter notes, round tannins.

BODEGAS CASTELO DE MEDINA

Ctra. CL-602, Km. 48
47465 Villaverde de Medina (Valladolid)
☎: +34 983 831 932 - Fax: +34 983 831 857
jcortega@castelodemedina.es
www.castelodemedina.es

VALPASO 2011 B
100% chardonnay.

86 Colour: bright yellow. Nose: ripe fruit, dried flowers, citrus fruit, balsamic herbs. Palate: fresh, fruity, fine bitter notes.

VIÑA CASTELO 2011 RD
garnacha.

87 Colour: rose, purple rim. Nose: powerfull, ripe fruit, red berry notes, floral, medium intensity. Palate: , powerful, fruity, fresh.

VEGA BUSIEL 2009 T
80% syrah, 20% tempranillo.

83

SYTÉ 2008 T
60% syrah, 40% tempranillo.

91 Colour: cherry, garnet rim. Nose: ripe fruit, spicy, creamy oak, toasty, complex, balanced. Palate: powerful, flavourful, toasty, round tannins, good acidity.

BODEGAS CASTILLO DE LA DUQUESA

Calle Mar, 116
12181 Benlloch (Castellón)
☎: +34 693 299 449 - Fax: +34 964 339 958
info@banus.eu
www.banus.eu

MATIZALES 2008 T
tempranillo, tinta de Toro.

84

FLOR DE F.A.C.V.S 2005 T
tempranillo, tinta de Toro.

89 Colour: cherry, garnet rim. Nose: ripe fruit, spicy, creamy oak, old leather, tobacco, waxy notes. Palate: powerful, flavourful, spicy.

BODEGAS COPABOCA

N-122, Km. 407
47114 Torrecilla de la Abadesa (Valladolid)
☎: +34 983 395 655 - Fax: +34 983 307 729
copaboca@copaboca.com
www.copaboca.com

ALVA MATER VERDEJO 2011 B
100% verdejo.

85 Colour: bright straw. Nose: white flowers, candied fruit, tropical fruit. Palate: light-bodied, fresh, fruity, easy to drink.

ABREBOCAS DE DOMINGO 2011 B
85% verdejo, 15% sauvignon blanc.

85 Colour: bright straw. Nose: dried flowers, tropical fruit, ripe fruit, grassy. Palate: fresh, fruity, flavourful.

LIÚ & LIÙ 2011 B
34% verdejo, 33% macabeo, 33% sauvignon blanc.

84

ALVA MATER 2011 RD
100% tempranillo.

83

ALVA MATER 2011 T
100% tempranillo.

85 Colour: cherry, garnet rim. Nose: ripe fruit, balsamic herbs, medium intensity. Palate: light-bodied, fresh, fruity, easy to drink.

BODEGAS FRUTOS VILLAR

Ctra. Burgos-Portugal Km. 113,7
47270 Cigales (Valladolid)
☎: +34 983 586 868 - Fax: +34 983 580 180
bodegasfrutosvillar@bodegasfrutosvillar.com
www.bodegasfrutosvillar.com

DON FRUTOS VERDEJO 2011 B
100% verdejo.

87 Colour: bright straw. Nose: white flowers, fragrant herbs, tropical fruit. Palate: light-bodied, fresh, fruity, easy to drink.

BODEGAS GARCÍA NIÑO

Avda. Julio, s/n
09410 Arandilla (Burgos)
☎: +34 916 192 294 - Fax: +34 916 126 072
fernando@bodegasgarcianino.es
www.altorredondo.es

PAGO DE COSTALAO 24 MESES 2009 TC
100% tempranillo.

90 Colour: cherry, garnet rim. Nose: ripe fruit, dark chocolate, sweet spices, toasty, mineral. Palate: powerful, flavourful, toasty, balanced.

ALTORREDONDO 14 MESES 2009 T
100% tempranillo.

88 Colour: very deep cherry, purple rim. Nose: medium intensity, ripe fruit, balanced, spicy. Palate: flavourful, good structure, round tannins.

BODEGAS GODELIA

Antigua Ctra. N-VI, Km. 403,5
24547 Pieros (Cacabelos) (León)
☎: +34 987 546 279 - Fax: +34 987 548 026
info@godelia.es
www.godelia.es

LIBAMUS 2010 T
100% mencía.

91 Colour: cherry, garnet rim. Nose: red berry notes, ripe fruit, dark chocolate, cocoa bean, sweet spices, creamy oak. Palate: powerful, flavourful, fruity, full.

BODEGAS LEDA

Mayor, 48
47320 Tudela de Duero (Valladolid)
☎: +34 983 520 682 - Fax: +34 983 520 682
info@bodegasleda.com
www.bodegasleda.com

MÁS DE LEDA 2009 TC
100% tempranillo.

92 Colour: cherry, garnet rim. Nose: ripe fruit, balsamic herbs, spicy, cocoa bean. Palate: powerful, flavourful, balanced, toasty.

BODEGAS MAURO

Cervantes, 12
47320 Tudela de Duero (Valladolid)
☎: +34 983 521 972 - Fax: +34 983 521 439
comunicacion@bodegasmauro.com
www.bodegasmauro.com

MAURO 2010 TC
tempranillo, syrah.

90 Colour: cherry, purple rim. Nose: ripe fruit, floral, earthy notes, sweet spices, toasty. Palate: powerful, flavourful, complex, balanced, toasty.

TERREUS 2009 TC
100% tempranillo.

92 Colour: cherry, garnet rim. Nose: fruit preserve, mineral, spicy, toasty, creamy oak. Palate: powerful, flavourful, full, complex, long, toasty.

MAURO VENDIMIA SELECCIONADA 2007 T
100% tempranillo.

91 Colour: cherry, garnet rim. Nose: ripe fruit, spicy, creamy oak, fine reductive notes, mineral. Palate: powerful, flavourful, full, toasty.

BODEGAS MENADE

Cuatro Calles, s/n
47491 La Seca (Valladolid)
☎: +34 983 103 223 - Fax: +34 983 816 561
info@sitiosdebodega.com

DUO ROSE ESP

88 Colour: raspberry rose. Nose: floral, red berry notes, fragrant herbs, expressive. Palate: powerful, fruity, flavourful, fine bead.

DUO BLANC ESP

86 Colour: bright yellow. Nose: white flowers, ripe fruit, sweet spices, lees reduction notes. Palate: powerful, flavourful, fruity, correct.

BODEGAS MONTE LA REINA

Ctra. Toro - Zamora, Km. 436,7
49881 Toro (Zamora)
☎: +34 980 082 011 - Fax: +34 980 082 012
bodega@montelareina.es
www.montelareina.es

VIZORRO 2011 B
100% verdejo.

84

VIZORRO 2011 RD
100% tempranillo.

83

VIZORRO TEMPRANILLO 2011 T
100% tempranillo.

84

BODEGAS SANTA RUFINA

Pago Fuente La Teja. Pol. Ind. 3 - Parcela 102
47290 Cubillas de Santa Marta (Valladolid)
☎: +34 983 585 202 - Fax: +34 983 585 202
info@bodegassantarufina.com
www.bodegassantarufina.com

BOSQUE REAL VERDEJO 2011 B
100% verdejo.

86 Colour: bright straw. Nose: floral, citrus fruit, wild herbs. Palate: light-bodied, fresh, fruity, easy to drink.

BOSQUE REAL CABERNET 2009 T
100% cabernet sauvignon.

84

BODEGAS TRITÓN

Pol.1 Parc. 146/148 Paraje Cantagrillos
49708 Villanueva de Campeán (Zamora)
☎: +34 968 435 022 - Fax: +34 968 716 051
info@orowines.com
www.orowines.com

TRIDENTE MENCÍA 2011 T
100% mencía.

88 Colour: very deep cherry. Nose: characterful, ripe fruit, toasty. Palate: round tannins, ripe fruit, spicy.

TRIDENTE TEMPRANILLO 2010 T
100% tempranillo.

92 Colour: cherry, garnet rim. Nose: ripe fruit, dark chocolate, sweet spices, creamy oak, mineral. Palate: powerful, flavourful, long, balanced, toasty.

TRIDENTE ENTRESUELOS 2010 T
100% tempranillo.

90 Colour: bright cherry. Nose: ripe fruit, sweet spices, creamy oak, balanced. Palate: flavourful, fruity, toasty, round tannins.

BODEGAS VALDEÁGUILA

Avda. de la Paz, 26
37658 Garcibuey (Salamanca)
☎: +34 923 437 168 - Fax: +34 923 437 168
info@valdeaguila.com
www.valdeaguila.com

VIÑA SALAMANCA RUFETE-TEMPRANILLO 2011 RD
rufete, tempranillo.

85 Colour: rose, purple rim. Nose: fruit liqueur notes, candied fruit, balsamic herbs. Palate: powerful, flavourful, light-bodied.

VIÑA SALAMANCA RUFETE-TEMPRANILLO 2010 T
rufete, tempranillo.

86 Colour: cherry, purple rim. Nose: red berry notes, ripe fruit, floral, powerfull, mineral. Palate: powerful, flavourful, long.

ALAGÓN 2008 T ROBLE
rufete, tempranillo.

88 Colour: cherry, garnet rim. Nose: macerated fruit, sweet spices, creamy oak, earthy notes. Palate: balanced, flavourful, toasty, long.

BODEGAS VINUM TERRAE

Lugar de Axis - Simes, s/n
36968 Meaño (Pontevedra)
☎: +34 986 747 566 - Fax: +34 986 747 621
pepa.formoso@vinumterrae.com
www.vinumterrae.com

YOU & ME RED EXPERIENCE 2011 T
100% tempranillo.

89 Colour: cherry, purple rim. Nose: expressive, fresh fruit, red berry notes, floral, lactic notes. Palate: flavourful, fruity, good acidity, easy to drink.

BODEGAS Y VIÑEDOS EL CODONAL

Pza. de la Constitución, 3
40462 Aldeanueva del Codonal (Segovia)
☎: +34 921 582 063
pedro.gomez@bodegaselcodonal.com
www.bodegaselcodonal.com

CODONAL VINUM NOBILE 2010 B
verdejo.

90 Colour: bright yellow. Nose: powerfull, ripe fruit, sweet spices, fragrant herbs. Palate: rich, flavourful, fresh, good acidity.

BODEGAS Y VIÑEDOS LA MEJORADA

Monasterio de La Mejorada
47410 Olmedo (Valladolid)
☎: +34 606 707 041 - Fax: +34 983 483 061
contacto@lamejorada.es
www.lamejorada.es

LA MEJORADA LAS CERCAS 2009 T ROBLE
tempranillo, syrah.

92 Colour: bright cherry. Nose: ripe fruit, sweet spices, creamy oak, scrubland. Palate: flavourful, fruity, toasty, round tannins, balanced.

LA MEJORADA LAS NORIAS 2009 T ROBLE
tempranillo.

91 Colour: bright cherry. Nose: ripe fruit, sweet spices, creamy oak. Palate: flavourful, fruity, toasty, round tannins, balanced.

VILLALAR ORO 2009 T ROBLE
100% tempranillo.

89 Colour: bright cherry. Nose: ripe fruit, spicy, dark chocolate, toasty. Palate: flavourful, fruity, toasty, round tannins, good finish.

VILLALAR 2009 T ROBLE
65% cabernet sauvignon, 35% tempranillo.

87 Colour: cherry, garnet rim. Nose: red berry notes, raspberry, fragrant herbs, sweet spices, creamy oak. Palate: light-bodied, fresh, fruity, flavourful.

BODEGAS Y VIÑEDOS MENTO

Calvario, 13
47320 Tudela de Duero (Valladolid)
☎: +34 983 521 233
info@bodegasmento.com
www.bodegasmento.com

MENTO 2009 T ROBLE
100% tempranillo.

87 Colour: bright cherry. Nose: ripe fruit, sweet spices, creamy oak. Palate: flavourful, fruity, toasty, long.

MENTO 2008 T ROBLE
100% tempranillo.

86 Colour: cherry, garnet rim. Nose: ripe fruit, sweet spices, dark chocolate, fine reductive notes. Palate: correct, flavourful, harsh oak tannins.

MENTO 2007 T ROBLE
100% tempranillo.

86 Colour: light cherry, garnet rim. Nose: fruit preserve, scrubland, tobacco, wet leather. Palate: flavourful, spicy, harsh oak tannins.

MENTO VENDIMIA SELECCIONADA 2006 T ROBLE
100% tempranillo.

90 Colour: cherry, garnet rim. Nose: ripe fruit, dark chocolate, cocoa bean, creamy oak, tobacco. Palate: powerful, flavourful, spicy, long.

MENTO 2006 T ROBLE
100% tempranillo.

87 Colour: cherry, garnet rim. Nose: ripe fruit, scrubland, spicy, earthy notes, fine reductive notes. Palate: balanced, flavourful, round tannins.

BODEGAS Y VIÑEDOS VALHONDO

Estrada, 10
05001 (Ávila)
☎: +34 920 256 559 - Fax: +34 920 256 559
info@teolegido.com
www.vetone.es

VETONÉ 2008 TC
tempranillo, syrah, cabernet sauvignon.

87 Colour: cherry, garnet rim. Nose: tobacco, old leather, ripe fruit, medium intensity. Palate: fruity, easy to drink, correct.

CASTO PEQUEÑO

Calvario, s/n
24220 Valderas (León)
☎: +34 987 762 426 - Fax: +34 987 763 147
bodega@castopequeno.com
www.castopequeno.com

QUINTA HINOJAL 2011 B
100% verdejo.

83

QUINTA HINOJAL 2011 RD
100% tempranillo.

83

QUINTA HINOJAL 2008 T
100% tempranillo.

86 Colour: cherry, garnet rim. Nose: ripe fruit, spicy, creamy oak, toasty. Palate: powerful, flavourful, toasty.

CLUNIA

Camino Torre, 1
09410 Coruña del Conde (Burgos)
☎: +34 607 185 951 - Fax: +34 948 818 574
pavez@principedeviana.com

CLUNIA SYRAH 2010 T
100% syrah.

92 Colour: cherry, purple rim. Nose: ripe fruit, violets, mineral, complex, expressive. Palate: flavourful, full, spicy, long, balanced.

CLUNIA TEMPRANILLO 2010 T
100% tempranillo.

91 Colour: cherry, garnet rim. Nose: complex, expressive, ripe fruit, earthy notes, sweet spices. Palate: powerful, flavourful, spicy, balanced.

COMANDO G

Villamanin, 27 - 4º E
28011 (Madrid)
☎: +34 696 366 555
daniel@jimenezlandi.com

RUMBO AL NORTE 2010 T
100% garnacha.

94 Colour: deep cherry. Nose: mineral, candied fruit, red berry notes, floral, scrubland, balsamic herbs, spicy. Palate: flavourful, spicy.

COMPAÑÍA DE VINOS MIGUEL MARTÍN

Ctra. Burgos - Portugal, Km. 101
47290 Cubillas de Santa María (Valladolid)
☎: +34 983 250 319 - Fax: +34 983 250 329
exportacion@ciadevinos.com
www.ciadevinos.com

MARTÍN VERÁSTEGUI P.X. S/C B
100% pedro ximénez.

88 Colour: golden. Nose: powerfull, honeyed notes, candied fruit, fragrant herbs, cocoa bean, dark chocolate. Palate: flavourful, sweet, fresh, fruity, long.

RETOLA VERDEJO 2011 B
100% verdejo.

84

MARTÍN VERÁSTEGUI 2008 BFB
100% verdejo.

88 Colour: bright yellow. Nose: ripe fruit, faded flowers, fragrant herbs, sweet spices. Palate: rich, flavourful, toasty.

RETOLA 2011 RD
100% tempranillo.

84

RETOLA TEMPRANILLO 2011 T
100% tempranillo.

85 Colour: cherry, purple rim. Nose: ripe fruit, balsamic herbs, fruit liqueur notes. Palate: flavourful, fruity, good acidity.

RETOLA 6 MESES 2010 T BARRICA
100% tempranillo.

84

RETOLA 12 MESES 2008 T BARRICA
100% tempranillo.

87 Colour: bright cherry. Nose: ripe fruit, creamy oak, expressive. Palate: flavourful, fruity, toasty, balanced.

MARTÍN VERÁSTEGUI VENDIMIA SELECCIONADA 2006 T
75% tempranillo, 25% garnacha.

89 Colour: bright cherry. Nose: ripe fruit, sweet spices, creamy oak, toasty. Palate: flavourful, fruity, toasty, round tannins.

COMPAÑÍA DE VINOS TELMO RODRÍGUEZ

El Monte
01308 Lanciego (Álava)
☎: +34 945 628 315 - Fax: +34 945 628 314
contact@telmorodriguez.com
www.telmorodriguez.com

PEGASO "GRANITO" 2009 T
100% garnacha.

93 Colour: bright cherry. Nose: mineral, red berry notes, spicy, floral. Palate: flavourful, warm, elegant, fine tannins.

PEGASO "BARRANCOS DE PIZARRA" 2009 T
100% garnacha.

93 Colour: deep cherry. Nose: spicy, ripe fruit, fruit expression, earthy notes. Palate: ripe fruit, long, fruity, elegant.

DANIEL EL TRAVIESO

Cuesta de las Descargas, 11 bis
28005 (Madrid)
☎: +34 696 366 555
daniel@jimenezlandi.com

LAS UVAS DE LA IRA 2010 B
100% albillo.

93 Colour: bright yellow. Nose: powerfull, warm, candied fruit, honeyed notes, fragrant herbs, sweet spices. Palate: flavourful, sweetness, fine bitter notes, good acidity.

EL REVENTÓN 2010 T
100% garnacha.

96 Colour: light cherry. Nose: fragrant herbs, floral, earthy notes, mineral, expressive, red berry notes, ripe fruit. Palate: balanced, fresh, fruity, long, elegant. Personality.

DANIEL V. RAMOS (ZERBEROS FINCA)

Real de Abajo, 100
05110 El Barraco (Ávila)
☎: +34 687 410 952
dvrcru@gmail.com
winesdanielramosvinos.blogspot.com

ZERBEROS DELTIEMBLO 2010 T
garnacha.

93 Colour: light cherry, garnet rim. Nose: red berry notes, fruit liqueur notes, mineral, creamy oak, spicy, fragrant herbs. Palate: flavourful, powerful, balanced, long, balsamic.

ZERBEROS ARENA 2009 T ROBLE
garnacha.

93 Colour: cherry, garnet rim. Nose: ripe fruit, balsamic herbs, mineral, sweet spices, creamy oak, expressive. Palate: powerful, flavourful, full, complex, long, spicy, elegant.

ZERBEROS A + P 2009 T ROBLE
garnacha.

92 Colour: light cherry, orangey edge. Nose: red berry notes, ripe fruit, balsamic herbs, mineral, dry stone, spicy. Palate: light-bodied, balanced, flavourful, complex.

ZERBEROS EL BERRACO 2008 T
garnacha.

88 Colour: cherry, garnet rim. Nose: fruit liqueur notes, mineral, dry stone, spicy, scrubland. Palate: complex, flavourful, long.

DEHESA DE CADOZOS

Pº Pintor Rosales, 72 Bajo
28008 (Madrid)
☎: +34 914 550 252 - Fax: +34 915 448 142
nmaranon@cadozos.com
www.cadozos.com

CADOZOS PINOT NOIR 2008 T
100% pinot noir.

89 Colour: cherry, garnet rim. Nose: fruit liqueur notes, fragrant herbs, sweet spices, creamy oak. Palate: spicy, flavourful, toasty.

CADOZOS 2007 T
80% tinto fino, 20% pinot noir.

90 Colour: cherry, garnet rim. Nose: earthy notes, ripe fruit, scrubland, spicy, creamy oak. Palate: balanced, powerful, flavourful, harsh oak tannins.

DOMINIO DE DOSTARES

P.I. Bierzo Alto, Los Barredos, 4
24318 San Román de Bembibre (León)
☎: +34 987 514 550 - Fax: +34 987 514 570
info@dominiodetares.com
www.dominiodostares.com

TOMBÚ 2011 RD
100% prieto picudo.

88 Colour: rose, purple rim. Nose: floral, ripe fruit, candied fruit. Palate: powerful, flavourful, fresh, fruity, easy to drink.

CUMAL 2010 T
100% prieto picudo.

93 Colour: cherry, garnet rim. Nose: ripe fruit, spicy, dark chocolate, creamy oak, mineral. Palate: powerful, flavourful, long, toasty.

ESTAY 2010 T
100% prieto picudo.

87 Colour: cherry, garnet rim. Nose: ripe fruit, balsamic herbs, spicy, cocoa bean, creamy oak. Palate: powerful, flavourful, toasty.

LEIONE 2008 T
100% prieto picudo.

91 Colour: black cherry, garnet rim. Nose: ripe fruit, cocoa bean, dark chocolate, spicy, creamy oak. Palate: powerful, flavourful, toasty.

ERMITA DEL CONDE

Camino de la Torre, 1
09410 Coruña del Conde (Burgos)
☎: +34 682 207 160 - Fax: +34 913 193 279
bodega@ermitadelconde.com
www.ermitadelconde.com

PAGO DEL CONDE 2009 T
tinto fino.

93 Colour: cherry, garnet rim. Nose: ripe fruit, cocoa bean, dark chocolate, sweet spices, mineral. Palate: powerful, flavourful, complex, toasty, long.

ERMITA DEL CONDE 2009 T
100% tinto fino.

91 Colour: cherry, garnet rim. Nose: ripe fruit, mineral, spicy, creamy oak. Palate: powerful, flavourful, spicy, long.

FINCA CÁRDABA

Coto de Cárdaba, s/n
40314 Valtiendas (Segovia)
☎: +34 921 527 470 - Fax: +34 921 527 470
info@fincacardaba.com
www.fincacardaba.com

FINCA CÁRDABA 2006 T
100% tempranillo.

87 Colour: dark-red cherry, orangey edge. Nose: fruit preserve, wet leather, cigar, toasty. Palate: powerful, flavourful, spicy.

FINCA CÁRDABA SELECCIÓN 2005 T
100% tempranillo.

90 Colour: dark-red cherry, orangey edge. Nose: ripe fruit, balsamic herbs, old leather, tobacco, spicy. Palate: powerful, flavourful, spicy.

FINCA LA RINCONADA

Castronuño
47520 Castronuño (Valladolid)
☎: +34 914 901 871 - Fax: +34 916 620 430
info@barcolobo.com
www.fincalarinconada.es

BARCOLOBO VERDEJO 2011 BFB
100% verdejo.

87 Colour: bright yellow. Nose: ripe fruit, floral, citrus fruit, fragrant herbs, sweet spices, toasty. Palate: rich, flavourful, long, toasty.

BARCOLOBO BARRICA 2011 T
95% tempranillo, 3% syrah, 2% cabernet sauvignon.

89 Colour: bright cherry. Nose: ripe fruit, sweet spices, creamy oak, expressive. Palate: flavourful, fruity, toasty, round tannins, balanced.

BARCOLOBO 12 MESES BARRICA 2009 T
75% tempranillo, 20% syrah, 5% cabernet sauvignon.

90 Colour: cherry, garnet rim. Nose: red berry notes, ripe fruit, floral, sweet spices, creamy oak. Palate: balanced, elegant, powerful, flavourful, toasty.

FINCA TORREMILANOS BODEGAS PEÑALBA LÓPEZ

Finca Torremilanos, s/n
09400 Aranda de Duero (Burgos)
☎: +34 947 510 377 - Fax: +34 947 512 856
torremilanos@torremilanos.com
www.torremilanos.com

PEÑALBA-LÓPEZ 2011 B
40% blanca del pais, 40% sauvignon blanc, 10% viura, 10% chardonnay.

89 Colour: bright yellow. Nose: powerfull, ripe fruit, sweet spices, creamy oak, dried herbs. Palate: rich, smoky afterpalate:, flavourful, fresh.

PEÑALBA-LÓPEZ PINOT NOIR 2009 T
100% pinot noir.

90 Colour: cherry, garnet rim. Nose: ripe fruit, spicy, creamy oak, toasty, complex, scrubland. Palate: powerful, flavourful, toasty, round tannins.

PEÑALBA-LÓPEZ GARNACHA 2009
100% garnacha.

85 Colour: cherry, garnet rim. Nose: fruit preserve, earthy notes, scrubland. Palate: powerful, flavourful, spicy.

FORTUNA WINES

Sanjurjo Badia, 22 - 3B
36207 Vigo (Pontevedra)
☎: +34 691 561 471
info@fortunawines.es
www.fortunawines.es

ALAIA VERDEJO 2011 B
100% verdejo.

85 Colour: bright yellow. Nose: ripe fruit, dried flowers, tropical fruit. Palate: fresh, fruity, flavourful.

DEHESA DE RUBIALES ALAIA 2010 T
50% prieto picudo, 35% tempranillo, 15% merlot.

85 Colour: cherry, garnet rim. Nose: balanced, warm, fragrant herbs, medium intensity. Palate: flavourful, correct.

ALAIA CABERNET SAUVIGNON 2009 T ROBLE
100% cabernet sauvignon.

88 Colour: bright cherry, garnet rim. Nose: medium intensity, ripe fruit, closed, balsamic herbs. Palate: balanced, ripe fruit, long.

GARNACHA ALTO ALBERCHE

Camino del Pimpollar, s/n
05100 Navaluenga (Ávila)
☎: +34 616 416 542
info@altoalberche.es
www.altoalberche.es

7 NAVAS 2011 T
100% garnacha.

91 Colour: cherry, purple rim. Nose: expressive, red berry notes, floral, fragrant herbs, mineral. Palate: flavourful, fruity, good acidity, round tannins.

7 NAVAS DULCE NATURAL 2010 T
100% garnacha.

92 Colour: cherry, garnet rim. Nose: acetaldehyde, dried fruit, wild herbs, dried flowers, dark chocolate, toasty. Palate: balanced, sweet, powerful, flavourful, spicy.

7 NAVAS FINCA CATALINO 2009 T
100% garnacha.

94 Colour: cherry, garnet rim. Nose: ripe fruit, scrubland, earthy notes, spicy, expressive. Palate: fresh, flavourful, complex, spicy, long, balanced.

GARNACHAS ÚNICAS C.B.

Los Pinillas, 1 Bajo B
28032 (Madrid)
☎: +34 615 163 719
carlos@maldivinas.es
www.maldivinas.es

LA MOVIDA 2010 T
100% garnacha.

92 Colour: cherry, garnet rim. Nose: floral, fruit preserve, balsamic herbs, sweet spices, creamy oak, mineral. Palate: spirituous, powerful, flavourful, long.

LA MOVIDA LADERAS 2010 T
100% garnacha.

88 Colour: cherry, garnet rim. Nose: fruit preserve, overripe fruit, mineral, spicy, creamy oak. Palate: correct, flavourful, ripe fruit.

GORDONZELLO

Alto de Santa Marina, s/n
24294 Gordoncillo (León)
☎: +34 987 758 030 - Fax: +34 987 757 201
info@gordonzello.com
www.gordonzello.com

CANDIDUS 2011 B
100% verdejo.

84

GRUPO YLLERA

Autovía A-6, Km. 173, 5
47490 Rueda (Valladolid)
☎: +34 983 868 097 - Fax: +34 983 868 177
grupoyllera@grupoyllera.com
www.grupoyllera.com

CUVI 2010 T ROBLE
tempranillo.

84

YLLERA 25 ANIVERSARIO 2005 T
tempranillo.

90 Colour: dark-red cherry, garnet rim. Nose: ripe fruit, wild herbs, toasty, spicy, creamy oak, mineral. Palate: fine tannins, flavourful, spicy.

YLLERA VENDIMIA SELECCIONADA 2004 TR
100% tempranillo.

88 Colour: cherry, garnet rim. Nose: ripe fruit, spicy, creamy oak, toasty, complex. Palate: powerful, flavourful, toasty, round tannins, balanced.

YLLERA ROBLE FRANCÉS Y AMERICANO 2009 TC
tempranillo.

89 Colour: cherry, garnet rim. Nose: ripe fruit, spicy, creamy oak, toasty. Palate: powerful, flavourful, toasty, correct.

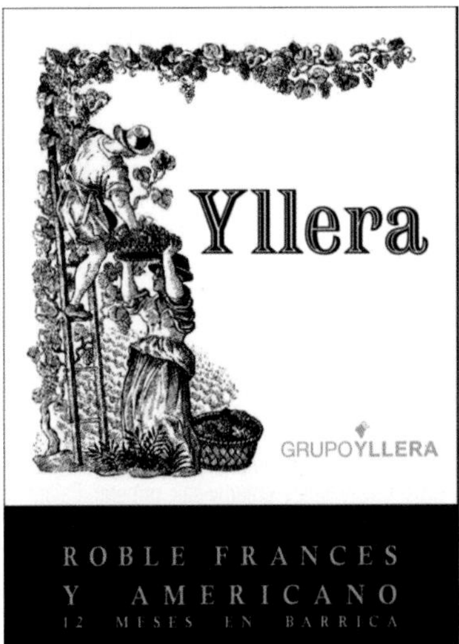

YLLERA 5.5 ROSÉ FRIZZANTE ESP
tempranillo, verdejo.

86 Colour: rose, purple rim. Nose: lactic notes, floral, candied fruit, dried herbs. Palate: light-bodied, fresh, fruity, sweet, flavourful.

YLLERA 5.5 VERDEJO FRIZZANTE ESP
verdejo.

85 Colour: bright straw. Nose: dried flowers, fresh fruit, fragrant herbs, medium intensity. Palate: sweet, fresh, fruity, easy to drink.

YLLERA DOMINUS GRAN SELECCIÓN VIÑEDOS VIEJOS 2005 T
100% tempranillo.

90 Colour: ruby red, garnet rim. Nose: ripe fruit, balsamic herbs, earthy notes, spicy, creamy oak, fine reductive notes. Palate: long, spicy, flavourful, round tannins.

HACIENDAS DE ESPAÑA

Hacienda Zorita, Ctra. Ledesma, Km. 12
37115 Valverdón (Salamanca)
☎: +34 914 365 924
comunicacion@arcoinvest-group.com
www.haciendas-espana.com

HACIENDA ZORITA NATURAL RESERVE (MARQUÉS DE LA CONCORDIA FAMILY OF WINES) 2009
100% syrah.

90 Colour: cherry, garnet rim. Nose: red berry notes, ripe fruit, violets, sweet spices, creamy oak. Palate: flavourful, fresh, fruity, complex, balanced.

HEREDAD DE URUEÑA

Ctra. Toro a Medina de Rioseco, km 21,300
47862 Urueña (Valladolid)
☎: +34 915 610 920 - Fax: +34 915 634 131
direccion@heredaduruena.com
www.heredaduruena.com

FORUM ETIQUETA NEGRA 2010 T
tinta de Toro, tinta del país.

92 Colour: cherry, garnet rim. Nose: ripe fruit, earthy notes, creamy oak, dark chocolate, toasty. Palate: powerful, flavourful, long, balanced.

SANTOS SYRAH 2010 T
syrah.

91 Colour: cherry, garnet rim. Nose: floral, ripe fruit, toasty, sweet spices. Palate: balanced, powerful, flavourful, long, toasty.

SANTOS MERLOT 2010 T
merlot, cabernet sauvignon.

90 Colour: cherry, garnet rim. Nose: ripe fruit, spicy, creamy oak, toasty, complex. Palate: powerful, flavourful, toasty, round tannins.

LEYENDA DEL PÁRAMO

Ctra. de León s/n, Paraje El Cueto
24230 Valdevimbre (León)
☎: +34 626 194 347
info@leyendadelparamo.com
www.leyendadelparamo.com

FLOR DEL PÁRAMO 2011 B
100% albarín.

90 Colour: bright straw. Nose: fresh, fresh fruit, white flowers, citrus fruit. Palate: flavourful, fruity, good acidity, balanced, elegant.

FLOR DEL PÁRAMO 2011 RD
100% prieto picudo.

88 Colour: rose, purple rim. Nose: powerfull, ripe fruit, red berry notes, floral, lactic notes. Palate: , powerful, fruity, fresh, easy to drink.

FLOR DEL PÁRAMO 2011 T
100% prieto picudo.

89 Colour: cherry, purple rim. Nose: expressive, fresh fruit, red berry notes, floral, dry stone. Palate: flavourful, fruity, good acidity, balanced.

FLOR DEL PÁRAMO 2010 T
100% prieto picudo.

88 Colour: cherry, garnet rim. Nose: red berry notes, floral, balsamic herbs, mineral. Palate: powerful, flavourful, fruity.

LOS PALOMARES

Los Palomares, 6
24230 Valdevimbre (León)
☎: +34 987 304 218 - Fax: +34 987 304 193
lospalomares@bodegalospalomares.com
www.bodegalospalomares.com

IMPRESIONES 2011 B
100% verdejo.

85 Colour: bright straw. Nose: fresh fruit, ripe fruit, fruit expression, grassy. Palate: flavourful, fruity, sweetness.

OSSIAN VIDES Y VINOS

San Marcos, 5
40447 Nieva (Segovia)
☎: +34 696 159 121 - Fax: +34 921 594 207
ossian@ossian.es
www.ossian.es

OSSIAN 2009 BFB
100% verdejo.

94 Colour: bright yellow. Nose: powerfull, ripe fruit, sweet spices, creamy oak, fragrant herbs. Palate: rich, smoky afterpalate:, flavourful, fresh, good acidity.

PEÑALBA LA VERDE BODEGAS VIZAR

Ctra. N 122, Km. 341,5
47329 Villabáñez (Valladolid)
☎: +34 983 682 690 - Fax: +34 983 682 125
info@bodegasvizar.es
www.bodegasvizar.es

ELBO 2011 T
100% tempranillo.

88 Colour: cherry, purple rim. Nose: expressive, fresh fruit, red berry notes, floral, lactic notes. Palate: flavourful, fruity, good acidity, round tannins.

VIZAR SELECCIÓN ESPECIAL 2009 T
tempranillo, syrah.

92 Colour: deep cherry, purple rim. Nose: elegant, complex, ripe fruit, sweet spices. Palate: fruity, complex, good structure, round tannins.

VIZAR SYRAH 2009 T
100% syrah.

92 Colour: bright cherry, purple rim. Nose: complex, elegant, sweet spices, violets. Palate: good structure, fine tannins, fruity.

VIZAR 5 MESES 2009 T
tempranillo, merlot.

87 Colour: cherry, purple rim. Nose: toasty, ripe fruit, powerfull, spicy. Palate: fruity, flavourful, harsh oak tannins.

VIZAR 12 MESES 2007 T
tempranillo, cabernet sauvignon.

89 Colour: deep cherry, purple rim. Nose: sweet spices, ripe fruit, creamy oak. Palate: balanced, fine bitter notes.

QUINTA SARDONIA

Casa, s/n - Granja Sardón
47340 Sardón de Duero (Valladolid)
☎: +34 650 498 353 - Fax: +34 983 032 884
jbougnaud@quintasardonia.com
www.quintasardonia.es

QUINTA SARDONIA QS 2008 T
57,7% tinto fino, 29,5% cabernet sauvignon, 4,5% syrah, 4% merlot, 4,3% otras.

93 Colour: cherry, garnet rim. Nose: ripe fruit, balsamic herbs, earthy notes, spicy, creamy oak. Palate: powerful, flavourful, long, toasty, balanced.

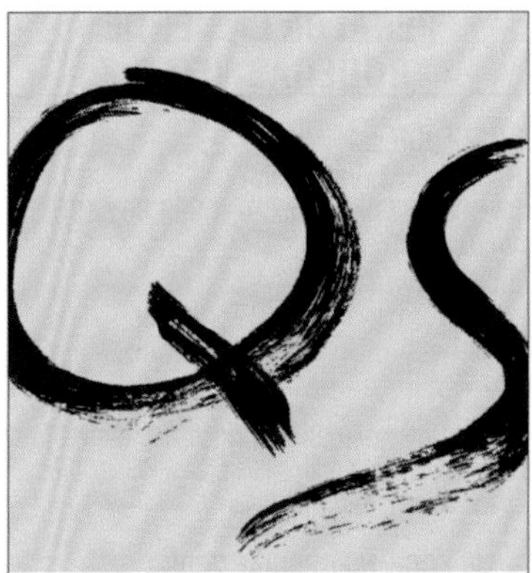

RODRÍGUEZ SANZO

Manuel Azaña, 9
47014 (Valladolid)
☎: +34 983 150 150 - Fax: +34 983 150 151
comunicacion@valsanzo.com
www.rodriguezsanzo.com

SANZO VERDEJO FRIZZANTE 2011 B
100% verdejo.

90 Colour: bright straw. Nose: fresh fruit, white flowers, expressive, fragrant herbs. Palate: flavourful, fruity, good acidity, fine bead.

SANZO TEMPRANILLO FRIZZANTE 2011 RD
tempranillo.

87 Colour: rose, purple rim. Nose: floral, rose petals, red berry notes, ripe fruit. Palate: light-bodied, fresh, fruity, flavourful.

RUBEN DIAZ Y JOSE BRAGADO VITICULTORES

Nueva, 26
05260 Cebreros (Ávila)
☎: +34 654 975 456 - Fax: +34 918 631 346
ruben.cerberux10@gmail.com

CERRO DE LA ESTRELLA 2009 T
garnacha.

94 Colour: light cherry, garnet rim. Nose: ripe fruit, scrubland, mineral, spicy, creamy oak. Palate: powerful, flavourful, long, mineral.

AIRUN 2008 T
garnacha.

88 Colour: cherry, garnet rim. Nose: fruit liqueur notes, ripe fruit, scrubland, spicy, earthy notes. Palate: powerful, flavourful, long, complex.

SELECCIÓN CÉSAR MUÑOZ

Acera de Recoletos, 14
47004 (Valladolid)
☎: +34 666 548 751
info@cesarmunoz.es
www.cesarmunoz.es

CIENFUEGOS 2009 BFB
albarín, verdejo, godello.

86 Colour: bright yellow. Nose: powerfull, ripe fruit, sweet spices, creamy oak, fragrant herbs. Palate: rich, flavourful, good acidity.

TERNA BODEGAS

Cuatro Calles, s/n
47491 La Seca (Valladolid)
☎: +34 983 103 223 - Fax: +34 983 816 561
info@sitiosdebodega.com
www.sitiosdebodega.com

E TERNA PRIETO PICUDO 2009 T
100% prieto picudo.

91 Colour: cherry, garnet rim. Nose: red berry notes, ripe fruit, balsamic herbs, spicy, mineral. Palate: powerful, flavourful, complex, long, toasty.

DOMINIO DE MORFEO "CEPAS VIEJAS" 2009 T
tempranillo, garnacha.

88 Colour: cherry, garnet rim. Nose: floral, red berry notes, sweet spices, creamy oak. Palate: flavourful, fruity, long, toasty.

E TERNA GARNACHA 2007 T
100% garnacha.

89 Colour: light cherry, garnet rim. Nose: floral, ripe fruit, earthy notes, spicy, toasty. Palate: round tannins, powerful, flavourful, complex.

VINOS DE ARGANZA

Río Ancares, 2
24560 Toral de los Vados (León)
☎: +34 987 544 831 - Fax: +34 987 563 532
admon@vinosdearganza.com
www.vinosdearganza.com

LAGAR DE ROBLA 2008 T
mencía.

90 Colour: cherry, garnet rim. Nose: ripe fruit, spicy, creamy oak, toasty, complex, expressive. Palate: powerful, flavourful, toasty, fine tannins, elegant.

VINOS MALAPARTE

Avda. Camilo José Cela, 2
40200 Cuéllar (Segovia)
☎: +34 921 105 204
info@vinosmalaparte.es
www.vinosmalaparte.es

MALAPARTE 2009 T
tinta del país.

91 Colour: bright cherry. Nose: ripe fruit, sweet spices, creamy oak, expressive. Palate: flavourful, fruity, toasty, round tannins.

VIÑA ALBARES

Camino Real, s/n
24310 Albares de la Ribera (León)
☎: +34 987 519 147 - Fax: +34 987 519 152
info@vinaalbareswine.com
www.vinaalbareswine.com

V A GEWÜRZTRAMINER 2011 B
gewürztraminer.

88 Colour: golden. Nose: powerfull, floral, honeyed notes, candied fruit, fragrant herbs. Palate: flavourful, sweet, fresh, fruity, good acidity, long.

V A CHARDONNAY - GEWÜRZTRAMINER 2011 B
chardonnay, gewürztraminer.

87 Colour: bright straw. Nose: white flowers, fragrant herbs, ripe fruit, citrus fruit. Palate: fresh, fruity, flavourful, fine bitter notes, balanced.

V A ROSADO 2011 RD
syrah, merlot.

87 Colour: rose, purple rim. Nose: floral, fragrant herbs, red berry notes. Palate: light-bodied, fresh, flavourful, fine bitter notes.

QUINTA DEL OBISPO 2010 T
mencía, tempranillo, merlot, cabernet sauvignon.

86 Colour: bright cherry, garnet rim. Nose: medium intensity, balsamic herbs, ripe fruit. Palate: flavourful, fruity, easy to drink.

QUINTA DEL OBISPO 2009 T ROBLE
mencía.

88 Colour: bright cherry. Nose: ripe fruit, expressive, spicy, fragrant herbs. Palate: fruity, toasty, round tannins, good structure.

ALBARES EDICIÓN LIMITADA 2007 T BARRICA
mencía.

87 Colour: cherry, garnet rim. Nose: ripe fruit, spicy, creamy oak, toasty, dark chocolate, cocoa bean. Palate: powerful, flavourful, toasty.

VIÑAS DEL CÉNIT

Ctra. de Circunvalación, s/n
49708 Villanueva de Campeán (Zamora)
☎: +34 980 569 346 - Fax: +34 980 569 328
info@bodegascenit.com
www.bodegascenit.com

VENTA MAZARRÓN 2010 T
100% tempranillo.

92 Colour: very deep cherry. Nose: powerfull, nose:tic coffee, spicy, ripe fruit. Palate: powerful, spicy, ripe fruit, roasted-coffee afterpalate:.

ALEO 2010 T ROBLE
100% tempranillo.

90 Colour: bright cherry. Nose: ripe fruit, sweet spices, creamy oak, cocoa bean, dark chocolate. Palate: flavourful, fruity, toasty, round tannins.

VIÑEDOS DE VILLAESTER

49800 Toro (Zamora)
☎: +34 948 645 008 - Fax: +34 948 645 166
info@familiabelasco.com
www.familiabelasco.com

AVUTARDA 2010 T
tempranillo, cabernet sauvignon.

88 Colour: cherry, garnet rim. Nose: red berry notes, ripe fruit, sweet spices, toasty. Palate: long, flavourful, correct.

CÓRDOBA

BODEGAS JESÚS NAZARENO

Avda. Cañete de las Torres, 33
14850 Baena (Córdoba)
☎: +34 957 670 225 - Fax: +34 957 690 873
bjn@bjn1963.com
www.bjn1963.com

CASTILLO DE BAENA S/C T ROBLE
tempranillo, syrah.

82

NAVISA

Ctra. Montalbán, s/n
14550 Montilla (Córdoba)
☎: +34 957 650 450 - Fax: +34 957 651 747
abaena@navisa.es
www.navisa.es

VALPINA 2008 T
tempranillo, syrah, cabernet sauvignon.

84

COSTA DE CANTABRIA

SEÑORÍO DEL PAS

Bº San Martín s/n
39638 Villafufre (Cantabria)
☎: +34 630 543 351
info@senoriodelpas.es
www.senoriodelpas.es

SEÑORÍO DEL PAS 2011 B
90% godello, 10% gewürztraminer.

88 Colour: bright straw. Nose: fresh fruit, white flowers, dried herbs, tropical fruit. Palate: flavourful, fruity, easy to drink.

CUMBRES DE GUADALFEO

BODEGA GARCÍA DE VERDEVIQUE

Los García de Verdevique
18439 Castaras (Granada)
☎: +34 958 957 025
info@bodegasgarciadeverdevique.com
www.bodegasgarciadeverdevique.com

LOS GARCÍA DE VERDEVIQUE 2007 T BARRICA
tempranillo, cabernet sauvignon, syrah.

90 Colour: cherry, garnet rim. Nose: ripe fruit, earthy notes, mineral, balsamic herbs, sweet spices. Palate: correct, powerful, flavourful, spicy.

LOS GARCÍA DE VERDEVIQUE 2006 T
tempranillo, cabernet sauvignon, syrah.

89 Colour: cherry, garnet rim. Nose: ripe fruit, fruit preserve, earthy notes, sweet spices, creamy oak. Palate: powerful, flavourful, spirituous, long.

GARCÍA DE VERDEVIQUE 2008 ESP
100% verijadiego.

76

DOMINIO BUENAVISTA

Ctra. de Almería, s/n
18480 Ugíjar (Granada)
☎: +34 958 767 254 - Fax: +34 958 990 226
info@dominiobuenavista.com
www.dominiobuenavista.com

VELETA SWEET MELODIES DULCE NATURAL 2011 B
viognier.

84

SIERRA SOL 2010 T
tempranillo.

84

DON MIGUEL 2009 T
merlot.

84

EIVISSA

CAN RICH DE BUSCATELL

Camí de Sa Vorera, s/n
07820 San Antonio (Illes Balears)
☎: +34 971 803 377 - Fax: +34 971 803 377
info@bodegascanrich.com
www.bodegascanrich.com

CAN RICH 2011 B
50% chardonnay, 50% malvasía.

90 Colour: bright yellow. Nose: fresh, white flowers, expressive. Palate: flavourful, fruity, good acidity, balanced, fine bitter notes.

CAN RICH ERESO 2011 BFB
100% chardonnay.

87 Colour: bright yellow. Nose: medium intensity, ripe fruit, spicy. Palate: flavourful, correct.

CAN RICH BRUT NATURE 2010 B
100% malvasía.

86 Colour: bright straw. Nose: candied fruit, white flowers, citrus fruit. Palate: flavourful, fruity, correct. Personality.

CAN RICH 2011 RD
60% syrah, 40% tempranillo.

83

BES CAN RICH 2011 RD
100% syrah.

80

CAN RICH BRUT NATURE 2010 RD
100% syrah.

85 Colour: raspberry rose. Nose: balanced, pattiserie, floral. Palate: flavourful, good finish, correct.

CAN RICH VI NEGRE 2009 T
40% tempranillo, 40% cabernet sauvignon, 20% merlot.

87 Colour: cherry, garnet rim. Nose: medium intensity, ripe fruit, sweet spices. Palate: flavourful, correct, easy to drink.

LAUSOS CABERNET SAUVIGNON 2007 T
100% cabernet sauvignon.

92 Colour: bright cherry. Nose: expressive, balanced, varietal, balsamic herbs, ripe fruit. Palate: full, good structure, spicy.

CAN RICH SELECCIÓN 2007 T
60% cabernet sauvignon, 30% merlot, 10% tempranillo.

88 Colour: cherry, garnet rim. Nose: medium intensity, spicy, ripe fruit, scrubland. Palate: spicy, ripe fruit.

CAN RICH DULCE VINO DE LICOR
100% malvasía.

84

SA COVA

Sa Cova
07816 Sant Mateu D'Albarca (Illes Ballears)
☎: +34 971 187 046 - Fax: +34 971 187 046
sacova-ibiza@telefonica.net
www.sacovaibiza.com

SA COVA 2011 RD
100% monastrell.

86 Colour: coppery red. Nose: medium intensity, candied fruit, faded flowers, citrus fruit. Palate: correct, fresh.

SA COVA 9 2008 T
monastrell, syrah.

88 Colour: cherry, garnet rim. Nose: balanced, scrubland, ripe fruit, warm. Palate: good structure, round tannins.

SA COVA PRIVAT 2005 T
syrah, tempranillo.

89 Colour: cherry, garnet rim. Nose: powerfull, dark chocolate, creamy oak, candied fruit. Palate: good structure, full, ripe fruit.

TOTEM WINES

Post Box 654 San Mateo, s/n (a las afueras)
07830 San José (Illes Balears)
☎: +34 654 507 809
laurentfresard@yahoo.fr
www.totemwines.com

IBIZKUS S/C RD

86 Colour: coppery red. Nose: medium intensity, faded flowers, fresh fruit. Palate: flavourful, fruity, good finish.

IBIZKUS 2009 T
monastrell.

89 Colour: bright cherry. Nose: balanced, scrubland, ripe fruit. Palate: fruity, elegant, spicy, good acidity.

TÓTEM 2008 T
monastrell.

90 Colour: bright cherry, garnet rim. Nose: medium intensity, ripe fruit, sweet spices. Palate: good structure, flavourful, spicy.

VINOS CAN MAYMÓ

Casa Can Maymó
07816 Sant Mateu d'Albarca (Illes Balears)
☎: +34 971 805 100 - Fax: +34 971 805 100
info@bodegascanmaymo.com

CAN MAYMÓ 2011 B
60% malvasía, 40% moscatel.

86 Colour: bright straw. Nose: medium intensity, white flowers, fresh. Palate: correct, easy to drink, good acidity.

CAN MAYMÓ 2011 RD
100% syrah.

88 Colour: light cherry, bright. Nose: balanced, medium intensity, red berry notes, fresh fruit. Palate: fresh, fruity, easy to drink.

CAN MAYMÓ TRADICIÓN 2010 T
40% syrah, 30% tempranillo, 30% merlot.

86 Colour: light cherry, purple rim. Nose: balanced, wild herbs, ripe fruit. Palate: ripe fruit, good finish.

CAN MAYMÓ 2010 T BARRICA
60% tempranillo, 20% merlot, 20% syrah.

86 Colour: cherry, purple rim. Nose: scrubland, neat, spicy. Palate: correct, good acidity, easy to drink.

CAN MAYMÓ MERLOT 2009 T
100% merlot.

89 Colour: bright cherry. Nose: ripe fruit, expressive, scrubland. Palate: flavourful, fruity, round tannins.

EXTREMADURA

BODEGA DE MIRABEL

Buenavista, 31
10220 Pago de San Clemente (Cáceres)
☎: +34 927 323 154 - Fax: +34 927 323 154
bodegademirabel@hotmail.com

MIRABEL 2009 T
75% tempranillo, 25% cabernet sauvignon.

91 Colour: cherry, garnet rim. Nose: ripe fruit, spicy, creamy oak, scrubland. Palate: powerful, flavourful, long, balanced.

TRIBEL DE MIRABEL 2009 T
60% cabernet sauvignon, 40% syrah.

89 Colour: cherry, garnet rim. Nose: ripe fruit, fruit preserve, scrubland, creamy oak. Palate: flavourful, spicy, long, balsamic.

BODEGA MARQUÉS DE VALDUEZA

Autovía de Extremadura A-5 Km. 360
06800 Mérida (Badajoz)
☎: +34 913 191 508 - Fax: +34 913 088 450
contact@marquesdevaldueza.com
www.marquesdevaldueza.com

VALDUEZA 2009 T
53% syrah, 29% cabernet sauvignon, 18% merlot.

91 Colour: deep cherry, purple rim. Nose: scrubland, powerfull, ripe fruit. Palate: fruity, long, spicy, round tannins.

MARQUÉS DE VALDUEZA ETIQUETA ROJA 2009 T
58% cabernet sauvignon, 42% syrah.

90 Colour: deep cherry, purple rim. Nose: medium intensity, ripe fruit, sweet spices, wild herbs. Palate: fruity, good structure, ripe fruit.

MARQUÉS DE VALDUEZA VENDIMIA TARDÍA 2009 T
cabernet sauvignon, merlot.

87 Colour: bright cherry, garnet rim. Nose: balanced, candied fruit, dried fruit, sweet spices. Palate: rich, flavourful, balanced.

MARQUÉS DE VALDUEZA 2008 T
cabernet sauvignon, merlot, syrah.

94 Colour: cherry, garnet rim. Nose: red berry notes, ripe fruit, wild herbs, spicy. Palate: flavourful, spicy, sweet tannins.

MARQUÉS DE VALDUEZA 2007 T
47% syrah, 38% cabernet sauvignon, 21% merlot.

93 Colour: cherry, garnet rim. Nose: balanced, medium intensity, spicy, cocoa bean, mineral. Palate: good structure, fruity, flavourful, round tannins.

BODEGA SAN MARCOS

Ctra. Aceuchal, s/n
06200 Almendralejo (Badajoz)
☎: +34 924 670 410 - Fax: +34 924 665 505
ventas@bodegasanmarcos.com
www.campobarro.com

CAMPOBRAVO 2011 B
50% moscatel, 50% cayetana blanca.

85 Colour: bright straw. Nose: medium intensity, white flowers, fresh fruit, balanced. Palate: fruity, easy to drink, good finish.

CAMPOBRAVO SYRAH 2011 RD
100% syrah.

85 Colour: light cherry. Nose: medium intensity, faded flowers, dried herbs, rose petals. Palate: flavourful, correct, easy to drink.

BODEGAS CAÑALVA

Coto, 54
10136 Cañamero (Cáceres)
☎: +34 927 369 405 - Fax: +34 927 369 405
info@bodegascanalva.com
www.bodegascañalva.com

CAÑALVA CABERNET SAUVIGNON MERLOT 2010 T
75% cabernet sauvignon, 25% merlot.

86 Colour: bright cherry, purple rim. Nose: powerfull, wild herbs, ripe fruit. Palate: flavourful, fruity, full.

CAÑALVA COUPAGE ESPECIAL 2009 TC
25% cabernet sauvignon, 25% merlot, 25% syrah, 25% tempranillo.

88 Colour: bright cherry, garnet rim. Nose: fruit expression, ripe fruit, lactic notes. Palate: good structure, full, long, round tannins.

CAÑALVA TINTO FINO 2008 T
tempranillo.

84

LUZ S/C SEMIDULCE
80% macabeo, 20% moscatel de alejandría.

84

BODEGAS CARLOS PLAZA

Sol s/n
06196 Cortegana (Badajoz)
☎: +34 924 687 932 - Fax: +34 924 667 569
export@bodegascarlosplaza.com
www.bodegascarlosplaza.com

CARLOS PLAZA 2011 T
90% tempranillo, 10% syrah.

89 Colour: bright cherry, purple rim. Nose: balanced, ripe fruit, red berry notes, powerfull. Palate: good structure, fruity, flavourful.

LA LLAVE ROJA BY CARLOS PLAZA 2011 T
90% tempranillo, 10% syrah.

89 Colour: bright cherry. Nose: ripe fruit, sweet spices, creamy oak. Palate: flavourful, fruity, toasty, round tannins.

CARLOS PLAZA 2009 T
70% tempranillo, 15% merlot, 15% syrah.

85 Colour: bright cherry. Nose: ripe fruit, expressive, scrubland. Palate: flavourful, fruity, toasty, round tannins.

BODEGAS DE AGUILAR

P.I. N-430 La Radio, 10
06760 Navalvillar de Pela (Badajoz)
☎: +34 924 861 257 - Fax: +34 924 861 257
bodegasaguilar@gmail.com
www.bodegasdeaguilar.es

AGUILAR 12 MESES 2006 T
85% cabernet sauvignon, 15% graciano.

83

BODEGAS DE OCCIDENTE

Granados, 1
06200 Almendralejo (Badajoz)
☎: +34 662 952 801
info@bodegasdeoccidente.es
www.bodegasdeoccidente.es

GRAN BUCHE 2009 T
tempranillo.

90 Colour: cherry, garnet rim. Nose: ripe fruit, spicy, creamy oak, complex. Palate: powerful, flavourful, round tannins, spicy.

BODEGAS HABLA

Ctra. A-V, km. 259
10200 Trujillo (Cáceres)
☎: +34 927 659 180 - Fax: +34 927 659 180
habla@bodegashabla.com
www.bodegashabla.com

HABLA DEL SILENCIO 2010 T
cabernet sauvignon, syrah, tempranillo.

88 Colour: deep cherry, garnet rim. Nose: scrubland, ripe fruit, fruit preserve, spicy. Palate: powerful, flavourful, ripe fruit.

BODEGAS RUIZ TORRES

Ctra. EX 116, km.33,8
10136 Cañamero (Cáceres)
☎: +34 927 369 027 - Fax: +34 927 369 302
info@ruiztorres.com
www.ruiztorres.com

TRAMPAL 2011 B
100% macabeo.

83

RUIZ TORRES 2008 T
100% syrah.

89 Colour: bright cherry, garnet rim. Nose: balanced, expressive, spicy, creamy oak, ripe fruit. Palate: good structure, flavourful, full, round tannins.

RUIZ TORRES 2008 T
100% cabernet sauvignon.

86 Colour: cherry, garnet rim. Nose: medium intensity, ripe fruit, spicy, scrubland. Palate: correct, ripe fruit, spicy.

TRAMPAL 2008 TC
60% tempranillo, 40% garnacha.

81

EX DE EXTREMADURA 2011 BN
chardonnay, macabeo.

78

BODEGAS SANI

La Zarza, s/n
06200 Almendralejo (Badaloz)
☎: +34 924 677 917 - Fax: +34 924 670 421
sani@bodegassani.com
www.bodegassani.com

SALUD DE SANI PRIMAVERA 2011 B
100% chardonnay.

84

FLAMENCO DE SANI 2011 B
100% macabeo.

83

CELOSO DE SANI 2011 RD
50% tempranillo, 50% syrah.

84

SALUD DE SANI PRIMAVERA 2011 RD
100% tempranillo.

83

BODEGAS TORIBIO VIÑA PUEBLA

Luis Chamizo, 12-21
06310 Puebla de Sancho Pérez (Badajoz)
☎: +34 924 551 449 - Fax: +34 924 551 449
info@bodegastoribio.com
www.bodegastoribio.com

VIÑA PUEBLA GOLOSINA 2011 RD
garnacha.

87 Colour: rose, purple rim. Nose: powerfull, ripe fruit, red berry notes, floral. Palate: , powerful, fruity, fresh.

TORIBIO ECOLÓGICO 2010 T
tempranillo.

89 Colour: deep cherry. Nose: spicy, candied fruit, scrubland. Palate: flavourful, powerful, concentrated.

VIÑA PUEBLA GOLOSINA EVA 2011
80% eva, 10% verdejo, 10% macabeo.

85 Colour: bright straw. Nose: white flowers, citrus fruit, ripe fruit, fragrant herbs. Palate: light-bodied, fresh, flavourful, easy to drink.

BODEGAS VIÑA EXTREMEÑA

Lago de Alange, s/n
06200 Almendralejo (Badajoz)
☎: +34 924 670 158 - Fax: +34 924 670 159
info@vinexsa.com
www.vinexsa.com

TENTUDIA PREMIUM 2009 T
50% cabernet sauvignon, 50% syrah.

87 Colour: cherry, garnet rim. Nose: powerfull, dark chocolate, sweet spices. Palate: good structure, full, round tannins.

TORRE DE SANDE 2009 T
100% syrah.

86 Colour: cherry, purple rim. Nose: medium intensity, fruit expression, violets. Palate: ripe fruit, easy to drink, correct, spicy.

MONASTERIO DE TENTUDIA 2008 T
100% tempranillo.

85 Colour: light cherry, garnet rim. Nose: toasty, spicy, candied fruit. Palate: correct, easy to drink, ripe fruit.

CORTE REAL 2007 T
50% tempranillo, 50% cabernet sauvignon.

85 Colour: cherry, garnet rim. Nose: fruit preserve, scrubland, spicy. Palate: flavourful, rich, full.

CORTE REAL PLATINUM 2006 T
50% merlot, 50% cabernet sauvignon.

87 Colour: cherry, garnet rim. Nose: scrubland, varietal, characterful, fine reductive notes. Palate: correct, easy to drink, balanced.

TERRA MAGNA 2006 T
50% cabernet sauvignon, 50% merlot.

86 Colour: cherry, garnet rim. Nose: ripe fruit, spicy, old leather. Palate: powerful, flavourful, toasty, round tannins.

BODEGAS Y VIÑEDOS ÁNGEL SÁNCHEZ REDONDO

Circunvalación sur(Ex 304) Urbanización Haza del obispo (500m) Finca Pago de los Ángeles
10600 Plasencia (Cáceres)
☎: +34 927 116 250 - Fax: +34 927 418 102
info@vinaplacentina.com
www.vinaplacentina.es

VIÑA PLACENTINA ETIQUETA ROJA 2009 T ROBLE
cabernet sauvignon, merlot.

86 Colour: bright cherry, purple rim. Nose: sweet spices, cocoa bean, ripe fruit. Palate: flavourful, ripe fruit, spicy.

VIÑA PLACENTINA ETIQUETA NEGRA 2007 T
cabernet sauvignon.

85 Colour: cherry, garnet rim. Nose: candied fruit, creamy oak, cocoa bean, toasty. Palate: flavourful, long, sweet tannins, toasty.

VIÑA PLACENTINA PAGO DE LOS ÁNGELES 2005 T
cabernet sauvignon.

86 Colour: bright cherry, orangey edge. Nose: spicy, tobacco, old leather, fruit liqueur notes. Palate: flavourful, powerful, rich, good structure.

LUIS GURPEGUI MUGA

Avda. Celso Muerza, 8
31560 San Adrián (Navarra)
☎: +34 948 670 050 - Fax: +34 948 670 259
bodegas@gurpegui.es
www.gurpegui.es

PINTORESCO 2011 T
tempranillo.

86 Colour: cherry, purple rim. Nose: medium intensity, ripe fruit, wild herbs. Palate: correct, flavourful, fruity.

EL HAYEDO CARREFOUR 2010 T
tempranillo, garnacha.

85 Colour: cherry, purple rim. Nose: medium intensity, ripe fruit. Palate: fruity, easy to drink, fruity aftespalate:.

MARCELINO DÍAZ

Mecánica, s/n
06200 Almendralejo (Badajoz)
☎: +34 924 677 548 - Fax: +34 924 660 977
bodega@madiaz.com
www.madiaz.com

THEODOSIUS 2008 TC
tempranillo, graciano.

85 Colour: cherry, garnet rim. Nose: powerfull, fruit preserve, toasty, spicy. Palate: ripe fruit, correct.

PAGO DE LAS ENCOMIENDAS, VIÑEDOS Y BODEGA

Finca Las Encomiendas s/n
06220 Villafranca de los Barros (Badajoz)
☎: +34 924 118 280
pagodelasencomiendas@pagodelasencomiendas.es
www.pagodelasencomiendas.es

UNADIR 2011 B
cayetana blanca.

86 Colour: bright straw. Nose: fresh, citrus fruit, floral. Palate: flavourful, ripe fruit, long, good acidity, balanced.

UNADIR 2011 RD
tempranillo, petit verdot.

87 Colour: light cherry, bright. Nose: red berry notes, ripe fruit, balanced, powerfull. Palate: flavourful, fruity, long.

UNADIR 2010 T ROBLE
tempranillo, syrah.

88 Colour: deep cherry, purple rim. Nose: powerfull, warm, candied fruit, creamy oak. Palate: flavourful, good structure, round tannins.

XENTIA 2009 T
30% petit verdot, 40% tempranillo, 20% syrah, 10% graciano.

90 Colour: bright cherry, purple rim. Nose: powerfull, characterful, ripe fruit, creamy oak, sweet spices, complex. Palate: good structure, full, long, spicy.

SOCIEDAD COOPERATIVA VIRGEN DE LA ESTRELLA

Mérida, 1
06230 Los Santos de Maimona (Badajoz)
☎: +34 924 544 094 - Fax: +34 924 572 490
gerente@maimona.com
www.maimona.com

DULCE EVA 2011 B
eva, beba de los santos.

84

SOLO EVA 2011 B
eva, beba de los santos.

81

FORMENTERA

CAP DE BARBARIA

Elisenda de Pinos, 1 Casa A
08034 (Barcelona)
☎: +34 609 855 556
info@capdebarbaria.com
www.capdebarbaria.com

CAP DE BARBARIA 2009 T
35% cabernet sauvignon, 35% merlot, 25% monastrell, 5% fogoneu.

93 Colour: cherry, garnet rim. Nose: complex, expressive, spicy, scrubland, mineral. Palate: good structure, long, round tannins, ripe fruit.

TERRAMOLL

Ctra. de La Mola, Km. 15,5
07872 El Pilar de la Mola (Illes Balears)
☎: +34 971 327 257 - Fax: +34 971 327 293
info@terramoll.es
www.terramoll.es

TERRAMOLL PRIMUS 2011 BFB
viognier.

89 Colour: bright straw. Nose: fresh, medium intensity, white flowers, tropical fruit. Palate: spicy, toasty, ripe fruit.

SAVINA 2011 B
viognier, malvasía, moscatel, garnacha blanca.

88 Colour: bright straw. Nose: balanced, floral, ripe fruit, fragrant herbs. Palate: fruity, correct, good acidity, easy to drink.

ROSA DE MAR 2011 RD
merlot, cabernet sauvignon, monastrell.

87 Colour: rose, purple rim. Nose: ripe fruit, red berry notes, floral, expressive, citrus fruit. Palate: , powerful, fruity, fresh.

TERRAMOLL ES MONESTIR 2009 TC
100% monastrell.

91 Colour: bright cherry. Nose: elegant, complex, balanced, ripe fruit, sweet spices. Palate: flavourful, good structure, round tannins.

TERRAMOLL PRIMUS 2006 TC
merlot, monastrell.

90 Colour: bright cherry, garnet rim. Nose: balanced, ripe fruit, sweet spices. Palate: fruity, flavourful, good acidity.

ILLA DE MENORCA

HORT

Cami de Sant Patrici, s/n
07750 Ferreries (Illes Balears)
☎: +34 971 373 702 - Fax: +34 971 155 193
info@santpatrici.com
www.santpatrici.com

HORT MERLOT 2009 T
merlot.

90 Colour: bright cherry. Nose: ripe fruit, sweet spices, creamy oak, expressive. Palate: flavourful, fruity, toasty, round tannins.

HORT CUPATGE 2008 T
cabernet sauvignon, merlot.

87 Colour: cherry, garnet rim. Nose: toasty, scrubland, spicy. Palate: balanced, fruity, easy to drink.

VINYA SA CUDIA

Cos de Gracia, 7
07702 Mahón (Illes Balears)
☎: +34 686 361 445 - Fax: +34 971 353 607
info@vinyasacudia.com
www.vinyasacudia.com

VINYA SA CUDÍA 2011 B
100% malvasía.

85 Colour: bright yellow. Nose: medium intensity, ripe fruit. Palate: easy to drink, correct, fruity.

VINYES BINITORD DE MENORCA

Camino Lloc de Monges
07769 Ciutadella de Menorca (Illes Balears)
☎: +34 654 909 714
info@binitord.com
www.binitord.com

BINITORD BLANC 2011 B
chardonnay, merlot, macabeo.

89 Colour: bright straw. Nose: powerfull, ripe fruit, floral. Palate: ripe fruit, balanced, fine bitter notes.

BINITORD ROSAT 2011 RD
tempranillo, syrah.

85 Colour: rose, bright. Nose: candied fruit, faded flowers. Palate: ripe fruit, flavourful.

BINITORD NEGRE 2010 T
cabernet sauvignon, syrah, tempranillo, merlot.

87 Colour: cherry, purple rim. Nose: medium intensity, scrubland, sweet spices, red berry notes. Palate: light-bodied, fruity.

BINITORD NEGRE 2009 T
cabernet sauvignon, merlot.

87 Colour: bright cherry. Nose: medium intensity, ripe fruit, spicy, scrubland. Palate: ripe fruit, balanced.

BINITORD ROURE 2009 T
tempranillo, cabernet sauvignon, syrah.

86 Colour: bright cherry. Nose: ripe fruit, sweet spices, creamy oak. Palate: flavourful, fruity, toasty, round tannins.

BINITORD ROURE 2008 T
tempranillo, cabernet sauvignon, merlot, syrah.

88 Colour: bright cherry, garnet rim. Nose: toasty, sweet spices. Palate: fruity, easy to drink, good acidity, balanced.

LAUJAR-ALPUJARRA

BODEGA ECOLÓGICA EL CORTIJO DE LA VIEJA

Paraje de la Vieja, s/n Ctra. A-348 Km. 75
04480 Alcolea (Almería)
☎: +34 950 343 919 - Fax: +34 950 343 919
comercial@iniza.net
www.iniza.net

INIZA MACABEO 2011 B
macabeo, sauvignon blanc, moscatel, viognier.

82

INIZA 2011 T MACERACIÓN CARBÓNICA
garnacha, tempranillo.

90 Colour: cherry, purple rim. Nose: expressive, fresh fruit, red berry notes, floral, lactic notes. Palate: flavourful, fruity, good acidity, round tannins.

VINO DE LA TIERRA LAUJAR-ALPUJARRA
iniza
MACERACIÓN CARBÓNICA
Vino de uva de agricultura ecológica.
14,5% vol
75 cl

INIZA 2010 T
tempranillo, syrah, merlot, cabernet sauvignon.

84

INIZA CABERNET SAUVIGNON 2009 T
100% cabernet sauvignon.

88 Colour: black cherry, cherry, garnet rim. Nose: floral, scrubland, ripe fruit, earthy notes, creamy oak. Palate: powerful, flavourful, long.

INIZA 4 CEPAS 2009 T
tempranillo, syrah, merlot, petit verdot.

85 Colour: cherry, garnet rim. Nose: ripe fruit, spicy, creamy oak, toasty, earthy notes. Palate: powerful, flavourful, toasty.

LIÉBANA

BODEGA RÍO SANTO

Cillorigo de Liébana
39584 Esanos (Cantabria)
☎: +34 652 286 474
info@riosanto.es
www.riosanto.es

LUSIA 2010 T ROBLE
85% mencía, 15% tempranillo.

91 Colour: cherry, purple rim. Nose: mineral, red berry notes, ripe fruit, floral, sweet spices, creamy oak. Palate: powerful, flavourful, long, toasty.

MALLORCA

4 KILOS VINÍCOLA

1ª Volta, 168 Puigverd
07200 Felanitx (Illes Balears)
☎: +34 660 226 641 - Fax: +34 971 580 523
fgrimalt@4kilos.com
www.4kilos.com

4 KILOS 2010 T
callet, cabernet sauvignon, merlot.

94 Colour: cherry, garnet rim. Nose: spicy, creamy oak, toasty, mineral, earthy notes, characterful, fruit expression. Palate: powerful, flavourful, toasty, round tannins.

GRIMALT CABALLERO 2010 T
100% callet.

94 Colour: bright cherry. Nose: fruit expression, balsamic herbs, scrubland, earthy notes. Palate: flavourful, good acidity, long, mineral.

12 VOLTS 2010 T
syrah, merlot, cabernet sauvignon, callet, fogoneu.

93 Colour: bright cherry. Nose: expressive, dark chocolate, ripe fruit. Palate: flavourful, fruity, toasty, round tannins.

ÁN NEGRA VITICULTORS

3ª Volta, 18 - Apdo. 130
07200 Faianitx (Illes Ballears)
☎: +34 971 584 481 - Fax: +34 971 584 482
info@annegra.com
www.animanegra.com

QUÍBIA 2011 B
50% callet, 50% prensal.

89 Colour: bright straw. Nose: ripe fruit, faded flowers, dried herbs, earthy notes, mineral. Palate: fresh, fruity, flavourful, correct.

ÀN 2010 T
95% callet, 5% manto negro, fogoneu.

93 Colour: cherry, garnet rim. Nose: elegant, ripe fruit, sweet spices. Palate: good structure, fine tannins, complex, fruity.

AN/2 2010 T
65% callet, 20% manto negro, fogoneu, 15% syrah.

88 Colour: cherry, garnet rim. Nose: balanced, ripe fruit, wild herbs. Palate: good structure, flavourful, good acidity, fine bitter notes.

BINIGRAU

Fiol, 33
07143 Biniali (Illes Balears)
☎: +34 971 512 023 - Fax: +34 971 886 495
info@binigrau.es
www.binigrau.es

NOU NAT 2011 B
prensal, chardonnay.

92 Colour: bright yellow. Nose: white flowers, fresh fruit, expressive, sweet spices. Palate: ripe fruit, fruity, flavourful, fine bitter notes, good acidity.

E BINIGRAU 2011 RD
manto negro, merlot.

88 Colour: light cherry, bright. Nose: fragrant herbs, red berry notes, ripe fruit, characterful. Palate: ripe fruit, correct.

E NEGRE DE BINIGRAU 2010 T
manto negro, merlot.

92 Colour: cherry, purple rim. Nose: elegant, complex, warm, ripe fruit, sweet spices. Palate: fruity, full, balanced, good acidity.

OBAC DE BINIGRAU 2010 TC

91 Colour: cherry, garnet rim. Nose: expressive, ripe fruit, sweet spices, new oak, toasty. Palate: mineral, long, spicy, ripe fruit.

BINIGRAU SELECCIÓ 2008 T
manto negro, callet, merlot.

94 Colour: bright cherry. Nose: complex, elegant, expressive, creamy oak, ripe fruit. Palate: flavourful, good structure, balanced, good acidity.

OBAC DE BINIGRAU 2009 TC
manto negro, callet, merlot, cabernet sauvignon, syrah.

90 Colour: bright cherry. Nose: fresh, balsamic herbs, scrubland, dark chocolate, spicy. Palate: ripe fruit, round tannins, balanced.

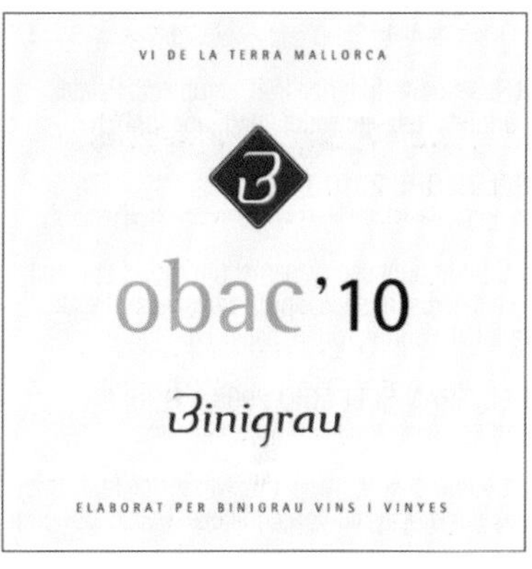

VI DE LA TERRA MALLORCA
obac'10
Binigrau
ELABORAT PER BINIGRAU VINS I VINYES

BINIGRAU DOLÇ 2009 T
manto negro, merlot.

87 Colour: bright cherry. Nose: balanced, expressive, candied fruit, sweet spices. Palate: fruity, easy to drink.

BODEGAS ÁNGEL

Ctra. Sta María - Sencelles, km. 4,8
07320 Santa María del Camí (Illes Balears)
☎: +34 971 621 638 - Fax: +34 971 621 638
info@bodegasangel.com
www.bodegasangel.com

ÁNGEL BLANC DE BLANCA 2011 B
prensal, chardonnay.

89 Colour: bright yellow. Nose: medium intensity, neat, floral, dried herbs. Palate: correct, easy to drink, fine bitter notes.

ÁNGEL VIOGNIER 2011 BFB
100% viognier.

88 Colour: bright yellow. Nose: ripe fruit, white flowers, balanced. Palate: flavourful, toasty, ripe fruit, spicy.

ÁNGEL CHARDONNAY 2011 B
chardonnay.

87 Colour: bright yellow. Nose: ripe fruit, floral, medium intensity. Palate: flavourful, rich, ripe fruit.

ÁNGEL MANT BLANC 2011 B
manto negro.

86 Colour: bright straw, bright golden. Nose: ripe fruit, floral, citrus fruit. Palate: flavourful, fruity, balanced.

ÁNGEL LAU ROSA 2011 RD
manto negro, merlot.

85 Nose: powerfull, ripe fruit, scrubland. Palate: flavourful, correct, powerful, long, ripe fruit.

ÁNGEL NEGRE 2010 T ROBLE
manto negro, merlot, cabernet sauvignon, callet, syrah.

92 Colour: light cherry, garnet rim. Nose: ripe fruit, balsamic herbs, mineral, spicy, creamy oak. Palate: powerful, flavourful, round, balanced.

ÁNGEL GRAN SELECCIÓ 2009 T ROBLE
cabernet sauvignon, merlot, callet, manto negro.

91 Colour: cherry, garnet rim. Nose: ripe fruit, spicy, creamy oak, toasty, complex, mineral. Palate: powerful, flavourful, toasty, round tannins, elegant.

BODEGAS CA'N VIDALET

Ctra. Alcudia - Pollença Ma 2201, Km. 4,85
07460 Pollença (Illes Balears)
☎: +34 971 531 719 - Fax: +34 971 535 395
info@canvidalet.com
www.canvidalet.com

CA'N VIDALET BLANC DE BLANCS 2011 B
60% chardonnay, 30% sauvignon blanc, 10% prensal.

85 Colour: bright straw. Nose: fresh, medium intensity, white flowers. Palate: fruity, correct.

CA'N VIDALET BLANC DE NEGRES 2011 RD
70% merlot, 20% cabernet sauvignon, 10% syrah.

86 Colour: raspberry rose. Nose: scrubland, fresh. Palate: correct, ripe fruit, balanced.

CA'N VIDALET TERRA FUSCA 2009 T
100% syrah.

91 Colour: bright cherry. Nose: ripe fruit, sweet spices, creamy oak, expressive, medium intensity, floral. Palate: flavourful, fruity, toasty, round tannins.

CA'N VIDALET SO DEL XIPRER-GRAN SELECCIÓN 2008 T
20% merlot, 80% cabernet sauvignon.

92 Colour: bright cherry, garnet rim. Nose: cocoa bean, creamy oak, red berry notes, ripe fruit, mineral. Palate: full, fruity, elegant.

BODEGAS RIBAS

Muntanya, 2
07330 Consell (Illes Balears)
☎: +34 971 622 673 - Fax: +34 971 622 746
info@bodegaribas.com
www.bodegaribas.com

RIBAS DE CABRERA 2010 T
50% manto negro, 35% syrah, 10% merlot, 5% cabernet sauvignon.

91 Colour: bright cherry, garnet rim. Nose: toasty, sweet spices, creamy oak, candied fruit, violets. Palate: complex, good structure, round tannins.

SIÓ 2010 T
40% manto negro, 25% cabernet sauvignon, 15% syrah, 20% merlot.

91 Colour: bright cherry, purple rim. Nose: ripe fruit, sweet spices, creamy oak, complex. Palate: flavourful, fruity, easy to drink.

BODEGAS SON PUIG

Finca Son Puig, s/n
07194 Puigpunyent Mallorca (Illes Balears)
☎: +34 971 614 184 - Fax: +34 971 614 184
info@sonpuig.com
www.sonpuig.com

SONPUIG 2010 BFB
62% chardonnay, 33% prensal, 5% sauvignon blanc.

86 Colour: bright yellow. Nose: candied fruit, sweet spices, powerfull. Palate: fruity, flavourful, spicy.

SONPUIG BLANC D'ESTIU 2010 B
31% chardonnay, 64% prensal, 5% sauvignon blanc.

86 Colour: bright yellow. Nose: fresh, fragrant herbs, balanced. Palate: fresh, easy to drink.

SONPUIG ESTIU 2010 T
15% cabernet sauvignon, 28% merlot, 31% tempranillo, 26% callet.

85 Colour: cherry, garnet rim. Nose: candied fruit, spicy, old leather. Palate: correct, light-bodied, easy to drink.

SONPUIG 2009 T
63% cabernet sauvignon, 30% merlot, 7% callet.

87 Colour: bright cherry. Nose: medium intensity, spicy, ripe fruit, balsamic herbs. Palate: ripe fruit, good acidity.

GRAN SONPUIG 2006 T
62% merlot, 8% cabernet sauvignon, 30% tempranillo.

89 Colour: cherry, garnet rim. Nose: balanced, spicy, ripe fruit, scrubland. Palate: fruity, easy to drink.

COMERCIAL GRUPO FREIXENET

Joan Sala, 2
08770 Sant Sadurní D'Anoia (Barcelona)
☎: +34 938 917 000 - Fax: +34 938 183 095
freixenet@freixenet.es
www.freixenet.es

SUSANA SEMPRE 2010 B
chardonnay, prensal, manto negro.

89 Colour: bright golden. Nose: ripe fruit, floral, sweet spices, expressive. Palate: good acidity, powerful, flavourful, long.

SUSANA SEMPRE 2010 T ROBLE
manto negro, cabernet sauvignon, merlot.

88 Colour: cherry, garnet rim. Nose: ripe fruit, scrubland, spicy, creamy oak. Palate: balanced, flavourful, spicy.

SUSANA SEMPRE MAIOR NEGRE 2009 T
cabernet sauvignon, merlot, manto negro.

90 Colour: bright cherry. Nose: ripe fruit, creamy oak, expressive, balsamic herbs. Palate: flavourful, fruity, toasty, round tannins.

FINCA SON BORDILS

Ctra. Inca - Sineu, Km. 4,1
07300 Inca (Illes Balears)
☎: +34 971 182 200 - Fax: +34 971 182 202
info@sonbordils.es
www.sonbordils.es

FINCA SON BORDILS CHARDONNAY 2011 BFB
100% chardonnay.

91 Colour: bright yellow. Nose: powerfull, ripe fruit, creamy oak, fragrant herbs. Palate: rich, flavourful, fresh, good acidity.

SON BORDILS BLANC DE RAÏM BLANC 2011 B
90,7% prensal, 9,3% chardonnay.

90 Colour: bright straw. Nose: fresh fruit, white flowers, dried herbs, balanced. Palate: flavourful, fruity, balanced.

SON BORDILS BLANC DOLC 2011 B
70% pansa blanca, 30% moscatel grano menudo.

90 Colour: bright yellow. Nose: floral, citrus fruit, ripe fruit, fragrant herbs, fresh. Palate: fine bitter notes, good acidity, powerful, flavourful, sweet.

SON BORDILS MUSCAT 2011 B
100% moscatel grano menudo.

89 Colour: bright straw. Nose: white flowers, fresh fruit, fragrant herbs. Palate: fine bitter notes, fresh, fruity, flavourful.

SON BORDILS ROSAT DE MONASTRELL 2011 RD
100% monastrell.

90 Colour: rose, purple rim. Nose: powerfull, ripe fruit, red berry notes, floral, expressive. Palate: , powerful, fruity, fresh, easy to drink, balanced.

FINCA SON BORDILS MERLOT 2006 T
93,1% merlot, 3,7% manto negro, 2,4% cabernet sauvignon, callet, monastrell.

90 Colour: cherry, garnet rim. Nose: ripe fruit, spicy, creamy oak, fragrant herbs. Palate: powerful, flavourful, toasty, round tannins.

FINCA SON BORDILS CABERNET SAUVIGNON 2006 T
99,2% cabernet sauvignon, callet.

88 Colour: cherry, garnet rim. Nose: ripe fruit, spicy, creamy oak, toasty, earthy notes, scrubland. Palate: flavourful, toasty, round tannins.

FINCA SON BORDILS SYRAH 2006 T
95% syrah, 5% cabernet sauvignon.

88 Colour: deep cherry, orangey edge. Nose: dried flowers, fruit liqueur notes, fine reductive notes, spicy, damp earth. Palate: fresh, flavourful, long, round tannins.

BISBALS DE SON BORRDILS 2006 T
64,5% merlot, 20% manto negro, 10,9% cabernet sauvignon, 4,5% cabernet sauvignon, callet.

87 Colour: pale ruby, brick rim edge. Nose: spicy, fine reductive notes, wet leather, aged wood nuances, fruit liqueur notes. Palate: spicy, long, spirituous.

JAUME DE PUNTIRÓ

Pza. Nova, 23
07320 Santa María del Camí (Illes Balears)
☎: +34 971 620 023 - Fax: +34 971 620 023
pere@vinsjaumedepuntiro.com
www.vinsjaumedepuntiro.com

PORPRAT 2009 T
merlot.

87 Colour: cherry, garnet rim. Nose: fruit expression, balanced, scrubland, sweet spices. Palate: flavourful, spicy, long.

JOSÉ L. FERRER

Conquistador, 103
07350 Binissalem (Illes Balears)
☎: +34 971 511 050 - Fax: +34 971 870 084
info@vinosferrer.com
www.vinosferrer.com

JOSÉ L. FERRER DUES MOLL CHARDONNAY MOLL 2011 B
50% moll, 50% chardonnay.

86 Colour: bright yellow. Nose: balanced, scrubland, white flowers, ripe fruit. Palate: balanced, fine bitter notes.

JOSÉ L. FERRER DUES SYRAH CALLET 2009 T
50% syrah, 50% callet.

89 Colour: bright cherry, purple rim. Nose: expressive, red berry notes, ripe fruit, creamy oak, sweet spices. Palate: good structure, fruity, easy to drink.

JOSÉ L. FERRER DUES MANTONEGRO CABERNET 2009 T
50% cabernet sauvignon, 50% manto negro.

88 Colour: cherry, garnet rim. Nose: ripe fruit, spicy, complex, scrubland. Palate: powerful, flavourful, toasty, round tannins.

SON CAMPANER

Pou Bauza 19ª, Pol Ind. Binissalem
07350 Binissalem (Mallorca)
☎: +34 971 870 004
info@soncampaner.es
www.soncampaner.es

SON CAMPANER BLANC DE BLANCS 2011 B
macabeo, prensal.

89 Colour: bright straw. Nose: fresh, fresh fruit, white flowers, expressive. Palate: flavourful, fruity, good acidity, balanced.

SON CAMPANER BLANC DE NEGRES 2011 RD
manto negro.

84

SON CAMPANER MERLOT 2010 T
merlot.

90 Colour: cherry, garnet rim. Nose: ripe fruit, sweet spices, earthy notes, fragrant herbs. Palate: spicy, flavourful, long, toasty.

SON CAMPANER ATHOS 2010 T
cabernet sauvignon, merlot, tempranillo.

89 Colour: cherry, garnet rim. Nose: earthy notes, balsamic herbs, ripe fruit, sweet spices. Palate: powerful, flavourful, long, spicy.

SON CAMPANER TERRA ROSSA 2010 T
manto negro, tempranillo, syrah, cabernet sauvignon, merlot.

87 Colour: bright cherry. Nose: ripe fruit, sweet spices, creamy oak, roasted coffee. Palate: flavourful, fruity, toasty.

SON PRIM PETIT

Ctra. Inca - Sencelles, Km. 4,9
07140 Sencelles (Mallorca)
☎: +34 971 872 758
correo@sonprim.com
www.sonprim.com

SON PRIM BLANC DE MERLOT 2011 B
merlot.

80

SON PRIM ROSSAT 2011 RD
manto negro, cabernet sauvignon.

89 Colour: onion pink. Nose: elegant, candied fruit, dried flowers, fragrant herbs, red berry notes. Palate: light-bodied, flavourful, good acidity, long, spicy.

SON PRIM CABERNET 2009 T
cabernet sauvignon.

92 Colour: cherry, garnet rim. Nose: earthy notes, dry stone, ripe fruit, balsamic herbs, spicy, creamy oak. Palate: long, flavourful, elegant, round tannins.

SON PRIM CUP 2009 T BARRICA
manto negro, cabernet sauvignon, merlot.

92 Colour: bright cherry. Nose: sweet spices, mineral, red berry notes, ripe fruit. Palate: flavourful, fruity, toasty, round tannins, balanced.

SON PRIM SYRAH 2009 T
syrah.

91 Colour: bright cherry. Nose: ripe fruit, sweet spices, creamy oak, balsamic herbs, violets. Palate: flavourful, fruity, toasty, round tannins.

SON PRIM MERLOT 2009 T
merlot.

90 Colour: cherry, garnet rim. Nose: ripe fruit, spicy, toasty, fragrant herbs. Palate: powerful, flavourful, toasty, balanced.

SON VIVES

Font de la Vila, 2
07191 Banyalbufar (Illes Ballears)
☎: +34 609 601 904 - Fax: +34 971 718 065
toni@darder.com
www.sonvives.com

JUXTA MARE MALVASÍA 2010 B
malvasía.

87 Colour: bright yellow. Nose: balanced, white flowers, ripe fruit. Palate: rich, long, easy to drink.

FUSIÓ DE BLANCS 2010 B
malvasía, chardonnay.

87 Colour: bright yellow. Nose: ripe fruit, candied fruit, balanced, expressive, white flowers. Palate: rich, flavourful.

NEGRE 2008 T BARRICA
cabernet sauvignon, merlot, syrah, manto negro.

88 Colour: bright cherry, orangey edge. Nose: powerfull, spicy, ripe fruit, warm. Palate: flavourful, ripe fruit, long.

N SELECCIO 2007

90 Colour: bright cherry, orangey edge. Nose: spicy, toasty, ripe fruit, complex. Palate: powerful, correct, balanced.

VINS NADAL

Ramón Llull, 2
07350 Binissalem (Illes Balears)
☎: +34 971 511 058 - Fax: +34 971 870 150
albaflor@vinsnadal.com
www.vinsnadal.com

COUPAGE 110 VINS NADAL 2009 T BARRICA
39% manto negro, 22% cabernet sauvignon, 31% merlot, 8% syrah.

88 Colour: cherry, garnet rim. Nose: medium intensity, red berry notes, ripe fruit, sweet spices. Palate: fruity, good acidity, spicy.

MERLOT 110 VINS NADAL 2009 T BARRICA
100% merlot.

87 Colour: bright cherry, garnet rim. Nose: creamy oak, toasty, cocoa bean. Palate: fruity, spicy, correct.

VINYES MORTITX

Ctra. Pollensa Lluc, Km. 10,9
07315 Escorca (Illes Balears)
☎: +34 971 182 339 - Fax: +34 971 182 340
info@vinyesmortitx.com
www.vinyesmortitx.com

MORTITX BLANC 2011 B
88% malvasía, 7,5% chardonnay, 3,5% moscatel, 1% riesling.

87 Colour: bright straw. Nose: fresh, fresh fruit, white flowers, expressive. Palate: flavourful, fruity, good acidity, balanced.

L'ERGULL DE MORTITX 2010 BFB
malvasía, moscatel, chardonnay, riesling.

85 Colour: yellow. Nose: toasty, creamy oak, candied fruit. Palate: rich, flavourful, good acidity.

MORTITX NEGRE 2010 T
cabernet sauvignon, merlot, syrah, tempranillo, monastrell.

88 Colour: bright cherry, purple rim. Nose: balsamic herbs, red berry notes, ripe fruit, balanced. Palate: ripe fruit, spicy, good finish.

RODAL PLA DE MORTITX 2008 T
syrah, tempranillo, cabernet sauvignon.

89 Colour: bright cherry. Nose: medium intensity, ripe fruit, sweet spices. Palate: balanced, good acidity, fruity.

MORTITX SYRAH 2008 T
syrah.

88 Colour: bright cherry, purple rim. Nose: toasty, creamy oak, ripe fruit. Palate: fruity, spicy, easy to drink.

L'U DE MORTITX 2007 TC
64% syrah, 24% merlot, 12% cabernet sauvignon.

91 Colour: cherry, purple rim. Nose: medium intensity, creamy oak, cocoa bean, ripe fruit. Palate: fruity, flavourful, good acidity.

RIBERA DEL ANDARAX

FINCA ÁNFORA

Paraje Barranco del Obispo, s/n.
04729 Enix (Almería)
☎: +34 950 520 336 - Fax: +34 950 341 614
info@vegaenix.com
www.vegaenix.com

VEGA ENIX JUVENAL 2011 RD
57% merlot, 29% cabernet sauvignon, 14% garnacha.

85 Colour: light cherry. Nose: floral, fragrant herbs, red berry notes, ripe fruit. Palate: correct, fruity, flavourful.

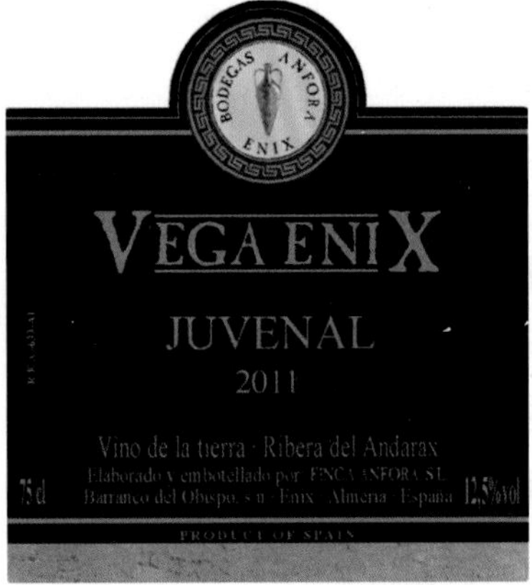

VEGA ENIX CALIDÓN 2008 T
57% cabernet sauvignon, 27% merlot, 13% syrah, 2% garnacha, 1% monastrell.

88 Colour: cherry, garnet rim. Nose: ripe fruit, spicy, earthy notes, scrubland. Palate: powerful, flavourful, toasty, long, spicy.

VEGA ENIX CALIDÓN 2007 T
59% monastrell, 23% garnacha, 7% syrah, 6% merlot, 5% cabernet sauvignon.

89 Colour: dark-red cherry, orangey edge. Nose: ripe fruit, scrubland, earthy notes, spicy, toasty. Palate: long, spicy, flavourful, round tannins.

VEGA ENIX XOLAIR 2006 T
100% merlot.

91 Colour: pale ruby, brick rim edge. Nose: ripe fruit, scrubland, spicy, creamy oak, fine reductive notes. Palate: flavourful, long, spicy, balanced.

VEGA ENIX LAURENTI 2006 T
100% cabernet sauvignon.

90 Colour: pale ruby, brick rim edge. Nose: ripe fruit, aged wood nuances, spicy, creamy oak, earthy notes. Palate: powerful, flavourful, long, spicy.

VEGA ENIX DAMARIS 2006 T
100% syrah.

90 Colour: cherry, garnet rim. Nose: ripe fruit, creamy oak, sweet spices, balsamic herbs. Palate: powerful, flavourful, toasty, round tannins.

PAGOS DE INDALIA

Paseo de los Baños, 2
04458 Padules (Almería)
☎: +34 950 510 728
juanma@pagosdeindalia.com
www.pagosdeindalia.com

FLOR DE INDALIA 2011 B
vermentino, chardonnay, macabeo.

88 Colour: bright yellow. Nose: floral, ripe fruit, fragrant herbs, complex. Palate: flavourful, balanced, ripe fruit.

INDALIA 2010 T
tempranillo, cabernet franc, cabernet sauvignon.

91 Colour: cherry, garnet rim. Nose: earthy notes, balsamic herbs, floral, red berry notes, ripe fruit, spicy, creamy oak. Palate: powerful, flavourful, balanced, round tannins.

RIBERA DEL GÁLLEGO CINCO VILLAS

BODEGA PEGALAZ

Ctra. A-1202, Km. 7 Desvío Ermita Santa Quiteria
22806 Santa Eulalia de Gállego (Zaragoza)
www.pegalaz.com

FIRÉ 2009 B

92 Colour: bright yellow. Nose: powerfull, ripe fruit, sweet spices, creamy oak, fragrant herbs. Palate: rich, smoky afterpalate:, flavourful, fresh, good acidity.

FIRÉ 2007 T
cabernet sauvignon, merlot, tempranillo.

93 Colour: cherry, garnet rim. Nose: spicy, creamy oak, complex, fresh, red berry notes, ripe fruit. Palate: powerful, flavourful, toasty, round tannins.

BODEGAS EJEANAS

Avda. Cosculluela, 23
50600 Ejea de los Caballeros (Zaragoza)
☎: +34 976 663 770 - Fax: +34 976 663 770
info@bodegasejeanas.com
www.bodegasejeanas.com

UN UVA NOCTURNA 2011 B
chardonnay, verdejo, moscatel.

87 Colour: bright straw. Nose: fresh, white flowers, expressive, ripe fruit. Palate: flavourful, fruity, good acidity, balanced.

VEGA DE LUCHÁN MOSCATEL 2009 B
85% moscatel, 15% verdejo.

87 Colour: golden. Nose: powerfull, floral, honeyed notes, candied fruit, fragrant herbs. Palate: flavourful, fresh, fruity.

UN UVA NOCTURNA TEMPRANILLO 2011 T
100% tempranillo.

88 Colour: cherry, purple rim. Nose: red berry notes, floral, lactic notes, fresh fruit. Palate: light-bodied, fresh, fruity, flavourful.

UN UVA NOCTURNA MERLOT 2010 T
100% merlot.

88 Colour: cherry, garnet rim. Nose: ripe fruit, fragrant herbs, fresh, creamy oak. Palate: fresh, fruity, flavourful, long.

UN UVA NOCTURNA GARNACHA PLUS 2007 T
100% garnacha.

86 Colour: cherry, garnet rim. Nose: ripe fruit, spicy, creamy oak, toasty, complex. Palate: powerful, flavourful, toasty, round tannins.

VEGA DE LUCHÁN CABERNET SAUVIGNON 2006 T
80% tempranillo, 20% cabernet sauvignon.

88 Colour: light cherry, orangey edge. Nose: ripe fruit, scrubland, creamy oak, fine reductive notes. Palate: flavourful, powerful, long.

VEGA DE LUCHÁN TEMPRANILLO CABERNET 2005 TC
80% tempranillo, 20% cabernet sauvignon.

87 Colour: cherry, garnet rim. Nose: ripe fruit, spicy, creamy oak, toasty, complex, earthy notes. Palate: powerful, flavourful, toasty, round tannins.

EDRA

Ctra A - 132, km 26
22800 Ayerbe (Huesca)
☎: +34 679 420 455 - Fax: +34 974 380 829
edra@bodega-edra.com
www.bodega-edra.com

EDRA 2011 T
parraleta.

88 Colour: deep cherry, purple rim. Nose: powerfull, candied fruit, scrubland. Palate: fruity, flavourful, round tannins.

EDRA GRULLAS DE PASO 2008 T
tempranillo, garnacha, merlot, cabernet sauvignon.

89 Colour: bright cherry, garnet rim. Nose: medium intensity, balanced, ripe fruit, earthy notes. Palate: good structure, flavourful, full, round tannins.

EDRA XTRA SYRAH 2007 T
syrah.

89 Colour: cherry, garnet rim. Nose: medium intensity, ripe fruit, sweet spices. Palate: good structure, fruity, round tannins.

EDRA MERLOT SYRAH 2006 T
syrah, merlot.

89 Colour: bright cherry, garnet rim. Nose: expressive, red berry notes, ripe fruit, creamy oak. Palate: good structure, good acidity.

EVOHE BODEGAS

Ignacio de Ara, 3
50002 Zaragoza (Zaragoza)
☎: +34 976 461 056 - Fax: +34 976 461 558
nosotros@evohegarnacha.com
www.evohegarnacha.com

EVOHÉ TEMPRANILLO 2011 T
100% tempranillo.

86 Colour: cherry, purple rim. Nose: floral, red berry notes, balsamic herbs, fruit liqueur notes. Palate: powerful, flavourful, fruity.

RIBERA DEL JILOCA

VINAE MURERI

Ctra. Murero-Atea - Finca La Moratilla
50366 Murero (Zaragoza)
☎: +34 976 808 033
info@vinaemureri.com
www.vinaemureri.com

XILOCA 2010 T
80% garnacha, 20% tempranillo.

88 Colour: bright cherry. Nose: ripe fruit, floral, red berry notes, sweet spices. Palate: flavourful, fruity, easy to drink.

MURET ORO 2009 T
100% garnacha.

89 Colour: cherry, garnet rim. Nose: mineral, ripe fruit, fruit liqueur notes, dark chocolate, spicy, toasty. Palate: flavourful, complex, toasty.

MURET VIDADILLO 2009 T
80% vidadilo, bobal.

89 Colour: cherry, garnet rim. Nose: ripe fruit, spicy, cocoa bean, creamy oak. Palate: balanced, flavourful, long.

MURET AZUL 2008 T
100% garnacha.

87 Colour: cherry, garnet rim. Nose: candied fruit, ripe fruit, sweet spices, creamy oak. Palate: powerful, flavourful, correct.

MURERO ÉLITE 2005 T
100% garnacha.

92 Colour: cherry, garnet rim. Nose: mineral, ripe fruit, sweet spices, cocoa bean, toasty. Palate: spicy, powerful, flavourful, toasty, balanced.

MURERO 2005 T
100% garnacha.

88 Colour: pale ruby, brick rim edge. Nose: elegant, spicy, fine reductive notes, wet leather, aged wood nuances, fruit liqueur notes. Palate: spicy, fine tannins, long.

RIBERA DEL QUEILES

BODEGA DEL JARDÍN

San Juan, 14
31520 Cascante (Navarra)
☎: +34 948 850 055 - Fax: +34 948 850 097
info@bodegadeljardin.es
www.bodegadeljardin.es

3PULSO 24 MESES 2008 T
tempranillo, garnacha.

89 Colour: cherry, garnet rim. Nose: ripe fruit, spicy, creamy oak, toasty, complex. Palate: powerful, flavourful, toasty.

2PULSO 12 MESES 2008 T
tempranillo, otras.

88 Colour: cherry, garnet rim. Nose: ripe fruit, warm, mineral, spicy, toasty. Palate: powerful, flavourful, long, toasty.

1PULSO 8 MESES 2008 T
tempranillo, garnacha.

86 Colour: cherry, garnet rim. Nose: red berry notes, ripe fruit, balsamic herbs, sweet spices. Palate: powerful, flavourful, warm.

GUELBENZU

Paraje La Lombana
50513 Vierlas (Zaragoza)
☎: +34 948 202 200 - Fax: +34 948 202 200
info@taninia.com
www.guelbenzu.com

GUELBENZU VIERLAS 2010 T
syrah.

84

GUELBENZU AZUL 2009 T
tempranillo.

87 Colour: cherry, purple rim. Nose: medium intensity, ripe fruit, spicy. Palate: correct, balanced.

GUELBENZU EVO 2007 T
cabernet sauvignon.

87 Colour: cherry, garnet rim. Nose: ripe fruit, wild herbs, toasty. Palate: powerful, flavourful, toasty, balanced.

GUELBENZU LOMBANA 2006 T
graciano.

87 Colour: cherry, garnet rim. Nose: spicy, fine reductive notes, wet leather, aged wood nuances. Palate: spicy, fine tannins, elegant, long.

GUELBENZU LAUTUS 2005 T

89 Colour: cherry, garnet rim. Nose: ripe fruit, balsamic herbs, old leather, creamy oak. Palate: spicy, flavourful, balanced.

SIERRA DE LAS ESTANCIAS Y DE LOS FILABRES

FINCA ONEGAR

Paraje Onegar, s/n Purchena
04870 Macael (Almería)
☎: +34 950 126 008 - Fax: +34 950 445 545
info@fincaonegar.com
www.fincaonegar.com

ONEGAR TEMPRANILLO CUVÉE 2009 T
100% tempranillo.

88 Colour: cherry, garnet rim. Nose: ripe fruit, spicy, creamy oak, aged wood nuances. Palate: powerful, flavourful, toasty, balanced.

ONEGAR TEMPRANILLO 2009 T
100% tempranillo.

87 Colour: deep cherry, garnet rim. Nose: toasty, fruit preserve, powerfull, slightly evolved. Palate: good structure, flavourful, fine bitter notes, round tannins.

ONEGAR EXPRESIÓN 2008 T
80% tempranillo, 15% petit verdot, 5% cabernet sauvignon.

89 Colour: cherry, garnet rim. Nose: ripe fruit, spicy, toasty, balsamic herbs, earthy notes. Palate: powerful, flavourful, toasty, round tannins, good acidity, balanced.

SIERRA NORTE DE SEVILLA

COLONIAS DE GALEÓN

Plazuela, 39
41370 Cazalla de la Sierra (Sevilla)
☎: +34 955 710 092 - Fax: +34 955 710 093
info@coloniasdegaleon.com
www.coloniasdegaleon.com

OCNOS 2010 BFB
80% chardonnay, 20% viognier.

84

PETIT OCNOS SOBRE LÍAS 2010 B
100% chardonnay.

84

COLONIAS DE GALEÓN 2011 T MACERACIÓN CARBÓNICA
50% cabernet franc, 30% tempranillo, 20% syrah.

85 Colour: light cherry, garnet rim. Nose: candied fruit, floral, balsamic herbs, fresh. Palate: powerful, flavourful, fruity, sweetness.

COLONIAS DE GALEÓN 2009 T ROBLE
40% cabernet franc, 30% tempranillo, 15% syrah, 15% merlot.

84

SILENTE SELECCIÓN 2007 T ROBLE
50% cabernet franc, 30% merlot, 10% tempranillo, 10% syrah.

89 Colour: bright cherry. Nose: sweet spices, creamy oak, ripe fruit, fruit preserve, scrubland. Palate: flavourful, fruity, toasty, balanced.

VALDEJALÓN

LATIDOS DE VINO (EPILENSE DE VINOS Y VIÑEDOS)

La Quimera del oro 30 3ºD
50019 (Zaragoza)
☎: +34 669 148 771
fmora@latidosdevino.com
www.latidosdevino.com

LATIDOS DE VINO "PLACER" 2011 B
100% moscatel.

88 Colour: bright golden. Nose: candied fruit, fruit liqueur notes, fragrant herbs, floral, neat. Palate: powerful, flavourful, full, sweetness.

LATIDOS DE VINO "DESEO" 2011 B
80% macabeo, 20% garnacha blanca.

82

LATIDOS DE VINO "BESO" 2011 RD
garnacha.

86 Colour: rose, purple rim. Nose: floral, lactic notes, red berry notes, ripe fruit. Palate: powerful, flavourful, easy to drink, fresh, fruity.

LATIDOS DE VINO "PASIÓN" 2011 T
garnacha.

87 Colour: cherry, purple rim. Nose: medium intensity, fruit preserve, cocoa bean. Palate: flavourful, ripe fruit, balanced.

LATIDOS DE VINO "AMOR" 2008 T BARRICA
90% garnacha, 10% syrah.

89 Colour: bright cherry, garnet rim. Nose: balanced, creamy oak, sweet spices, balsamic herbs, ripe fruit. Palate: flavourful, good structure.

VALLE DEL CINCA

BODEGAS VALONGA

Monte Valonga, s/n
22533 Belver de Cinca (Huesca)
☎: +34 974 435 127 - Fax: +34 974 339 101
bodegas@valonga.com
www.valonga.com

VALONGA 2011 RD
tempranillo, cabernet sauvignon.

85 Colour: light cherry. Nose: ripe fruit, dried flowers, fragrant herbs. Palate: fruity, flavourful, warm.

BUSARDO SELECCIÓN T ROBLE
garnacha, syrah, tempranillo.

88 Colour: cherry, garnet rim. Nose: ripe fruit, fruit preserve, balsamic herbs, spicy, creamy oak, earthy notes. Palate: fine bitter notes.

BUSARDO TEMPRANILLO T
tempranillo.

87 Colour: bright cherry. Nose: sweet spices, creamy oak, ripe fruit. Palate: flavourful, fruity, toasty, round tannins.

BUSARDO SYRAH T

87 Colour: bright cherry. Nose: ripe fruit, creamy oak, wild herbs. Palate: flavourful, fruity, toasty.

VIÑEDOS DE ESPAÑA

CASA CORREDOR - SELECCIÓN MARE NOSTRUM BODEGAS

Casas de Corredor s/n (Autovía Madrid/Alicante, salida 168, La Encina
02660 Caudete (Alicante)
☎: +34 966 842 064
jdminano@casacorredor.es
www.casacorredor.es

SENSUM MACABEO 2011 B
100% macabeo.

85 Colour: bright straw. Nose: fresh, fresh fruit, white flowers. Palate: flavourful, fruity, good acidity.

CASA CORREDOR TEMPRANILLO 2010 T
100% tempranillo.

84

CASA CORREDOR CABERNET TEMPRANILLO MERLOT 2009 T ROBLE
tempranillo, merlot, cabernet sauvignon.

86 Colour: bright cherry. Nose: ripe fruit, sweet spices, creamy oak, balsamic herbs. Palate: flavourful, fruity, toasty.

CASA CORREDOR SYRAH 2008 T
100% syrah.

82

CASA CORREDOR CABERNET 2007 T
100% cabernet sauvignon.

85 Colour: cherry, garnet rim. Nose: warm, ripe fruit, scrubland, fine reductive notes. Palate: powerful, flavourful, toasty.

SENSUM CABERNET 2006 T
100% cabernet sauvignon.

88 Colour: deep cherry, orangey edge. Nose: scrubland, spicy.

Just outside the "Vino de Calidad" status, we find the "Vino de Mesa" ("Table Wine") category, which are those not included in any of the other categories (not even in the "Vino de la Tierra" one, regarded as "Vino de Mesa" by the Ley del Vino ("Wine Law"). The present editions of our Guide has up to 41 table wines rated as excellent, something which is quite telling, and force us to a change of mind in regard to the popular prejudice against this category, traditionally related –almost exclusively– to bulk, cheap wines.

In this section we include wines made in geographical areas that do not belong to any designation of origin (DO as such) or association of Vino de la Tierra, although most of them come indeed from wines regions with some vine growing and winemaking tradition.

We do not pretend to come up with a comprehensive account of the usually overlooked vinos de mesa (table wines), but to enumerate here some Spanish wines that were bottled with no geographic label whatsoever.

The wineries are listed alphabetically within their Autonomous regions. The reader will discover some singular wines of –in some cases– excellent quality that could be of interest to those on the look out for novelties or alternative products to bring onto their tables.

ANDALUCÍA

BODEGA JOAQUÍN FERNÁNDEZ

Finca Los Frutales Paraje de los Frontones
29400 Ronda (Málaga)
☎: +34 665 899 200 - Fax: +34 951 166 043
info@bodegajf.es
www.bodegajf.com

BLANCO DE TINTA 2011 B
80% merlot, 20% garnacha.

85 Colour: bright straw. Nose: medium intensity, dried flowers. Palate: flavourful, easy to drink, correct.

BODEGA KIENINGER

Los Frontones, 67
29400 Ronda (Málaga)
☎: +34 952 879 554
martin@bodegakieninger.com
www.bodegakieninger.com

7 VIN 2010 T
50% blaufraenkisch, 50% zweigelt.

91 Colour: cherry, garnet rim. Nose: balanced, expressive, ripe fruit, spicy, complex. Palate: long, spicy, fruity, good acidity.

BODEGAS DEL NÉVALO

Tomás Carretero, 42
14300 Villaviciosa de Córdoba (Córdoba)
☎: +34 957 050 387
info@bodegasdelnevalo.com
www.bodegasdelnevalo.com

BLANCO NÉVALO B
airén, pedro ximénez, palomino.

90 Colour: iodine, amber rim. Nose: powerfull, complex, elegant, dry nuts, toasty. Palate: rich, fine bitter notes, fine solera notes, long, spicy.

BLANCO MARAVILLA B
airén, pedro ximénez, palomino.

86 Colour: bright yellow. Nose: lees reduction notes, floral, candied fruit. Palate: fine bitter notes, spicy, long.

BLANCO JOVEN B
airén, pedro ximénez, palomino.

83

BODEGAS BENTOMIZ

Finca Almendro - Pago Cuesta Rábano
29752 Sayalonga (Málaga)
☎: +34 658 845 285
info.bodegasbentomiz@gmail.com
www.bodegasbentomiz.com

ARIYANAS DAVID 2010 T
100% merlot.

88 Colour: cherry, garnet rim. Nose: expressive, overripe fruit, balanced. Palate: fruity, flavourful, sweetness.

BODEGAS FONTEDEI

Doctor Horcajadas, 10
18570 Deifontes (Granada)
☎: +34 958 407 957 - Fax: +34 958 407 957
bodegasfontedei@gmail.com
www.bodegasfontedei.com

FONTEDEI 2009 T ROBLE
tempranillo, garnacha.

81

FONTEDEI SM 2009 T
syrah, merlot.

79

FINCA PRADO NEGRO 2009 T
tempranillo, cabernet sauvignon, garnacha.

77

BODEGAS MÁLAGA VIRGEN

Autovía A-92, Málaga-Sevilla, Km. 132
29520 Fuente de Piedra (Málaga)
☎: +34 952 319 454 - Fax: +34 952 359 819
didier.bricout@bodegasmalagavirgen.com
www.bodegasmalagavirgen.com

MOSCATEL NARANJA B

85 Colour: bright yellow. Nose: balanced, expressive, citrus fruit, floral. Palate: rich, ripe fruit, correct.

EQUIPO NAVAZOS

Cartuja, 1 - módulo 6
11401 Jerez de la Frontera (Cádiz)
equipo@navazos.com
www.equiponavazos.com

NAVAZOS NIEPOORT 2011 B
100% palomino.

93 Colour: bright yellow. Nose: elegant, faded flowers, flor yeasts, fine lees. Palate: balanced, fine bitter notes, complex. Personality.

NESTARES RINCÓN VINOS Y BODEGAS

Finca Juan de Reyes, s/n Contraviesa Alpujarra
18430 Torvizcon (Granada)
☎: +34 655 959 500 - Fax: +34 958 272 125
info@alpujarride.com
www.alpujarride.com

NESTARES RINCÓN IN 3.0 2008 T
tempranillo, syrah, merlot.

88 Colour: cherry, garnet rim. Nose: ripe fruit, fruit preserve, mineral, creamy oak. Palate: powerful, flavourful, toasty.

PAGO DEL MARENOSTRUM

Ctra. A-348, Km. 85-86
04460 Fondón (Almería)
☎: +34 926 666 027 - Fax: +34 670 099 520
info@pagodelvicario.com

1500 H PINOT NOIR 2007 T
100% pinot noir.

90 Colour: deep cherry, garnet rim. Nose: balanced, elegant, spicy, tobacco. Palate: powerful, good structure, fine bitter notes.

1500 H 2007 T
merlot, tempranillo, cabernet sauvignon, pinot noir.

88 Colour: very deep cherry. Nose: powerfull, warm, fruit preserve. Palate: long, spicy, ripe fruit, round tannins.

PRÍNCIPE ALFONSO DE HOHENLOHE

Estación de Parchite, 104
29400 Ronda (Málaga)
☎: +34 914 365 900
gromero@arcoinvest-group.com
www.haciendas-espana.com

ÁNDALUS PETIT VERDOT (MARQUÉS DE LA CONCORDIA FAMILY OF WINES) 2006 T
petit verdot.

90 Colour: cherry, garnet rim. Nose: ripe fruit, spicy, toasty, scrubland, aged wood nuances. Palate: powerful, flavourful, toasty, fine bitter notes.

SEDELLA VINOS

Término Las Viñuelas, s/n
29715 Sedella (Málaga)
☎: +34 687 463 082 - Fax: +34 967 140 723
info@sedellavinos.com
www.sedellavinos.com

SEDELLA 2009 T
romé, garnacha.

91 Colour: cherry, garnet rim. Nose: ripe fruit, scrubland, earthy notes, spicy, creamy oak. Palate: powerful, flavourful, long, round tannins.

ARAGÓN

DALCAMP

Constitución, 4
22415 Monesma de San Juan (Huesca)
☎: +34 973 760 018 - Fax: +34 973 760 523
rdalfo@mixmail.com
www.castillodemonesma.com

MONTE NERI CHARDONNAY S/C B
100% chardonnay.

82

MONTE NERI GEWÜRZTRAMINER B
100% gewürztraminer.

83

MONTE NERI 1999 T
80% cabernet sauvignon, 20% merlot.

88 Colour: pale ruby, brick rim edge. Nose: spicy, fine reductive notes, wet leather, aged wood nuances, fruit liqueur notes, fruit liqueur notes. Palate: spicy, fine tannins, elegant, long.

EDRA

Ctra A - 132, km 26
22800 Ayerbe (Huesca)
☎: +34 679 420 455 - Fax: +34 974 380 829
edra@bodega-edra.com
www.bodega-edra.com

EDRA BLANCOLUZ 2011 B
viognier.

87 Colour: bright yellow. Nose: ripe fruit, dried flowers, fragrant herbs. Palate: powerful, flavourful, correct.

EVOHE BODEGAS

Ignacio de Ara, 3
50002 Zaragoza (Zaragoza)
☎: +34 976 461 056 - Fax: +34 976 461 558
nosotros@evohegarnacha.com
www.evohegarnacha.com

EVOHÉ MAZUELA 2011 T
100% mazuelo.

84

GRANDES VINOS Y VIÑEDOS

Ctra. Valencia Km 45,700
50400 Cariñena (Zaragoza)
☎: +34 976 621 261 - Fax: +34 976 621 253
info@grandesvinos.com
www.grandesvinos.com

MOSCATEL CORONA DE ARAGÓN B
moscatel de alejandría.

84

GARNACCIO VINO DE LICOR
garnacha.

83

MAS DE TORUBIO

Plaza del Carmen, 4
44623 Cretas (Teruel)
☎: +34 669 214 845 - Fax: +34 978 850 324
masdetorubio@hotmail.com

XADO 2011 B
100% garnacha blanca.

85 Colour: bright straw. Nose: fresh, fresh fruit, dried herbs, floral. Palate: flavourful, fruity, good acidity.

MAS DE TORUBIO 2011 T
70% garnacha, 30% merlot.

84

XADO 2011 T ROBLE
60% garnacha, 40% cabernet sauvignon.

84

VIÑAS DE ALADREN

Via Universitas, 15 11°C
50009 (Zaragoza)
☎: +34 637 809 441
info@vdaladren.com
www.viñasdealadren.com

SOLANILLO 2011 T
cabernet sauvignon, merlot, syrah.

86 Colour: cherry, purple rim. Nose: sweet spices, creamy oak, fruit preserve. Palate: flavourful, fruity, toasty, round tannins.

ASTURIAS

BODEGAS OBANCA

Obanca, 12
33800 Cangas del Narcea (Asturias)
☎: +34 626 956 571 - Fax: +34 985 811 539
informacion@obanca.com
www.obanca.com

LA DESCARGA 2011 B
albarín, albillo.

90 Colour: bright straw. Nose: white flowers, fragrant herbs, mineral, fresh fruit, elegant. Palate: rich, fruity, flavourful, long.

DESCARGA 2011 T
verdejo negro, carrasquín, mencía, albarín tinto.

90 Colour: cherry, garnet rim. Nose: red berry notes, ripe fruit, sweet spices, fragrant herbs, creamy oak. Palate: long, flavourful, fresh, fruity, spicy.

CASTRO DE LIMÉS 2009 T
100% carrasquín.

93 Colour: cherry, garnet rim. Nose: ripe fruit, mineral, dark chocolate, creamy oak, toasty, balsamic herbs. Palate: powerful, flavourful, long, balanced, good acidity.

LA DESCARGA 2009 T
albarín tinto, verdejo negro, carrasquín, mencía.

90 Colour: cherry, garnet rim. Nose: ripe fruit, creamy oak, toasty, sweet spices, scrubland. Palate: powerful, flavourful, round tannins, spicy.

CANARIAS

JUAN JESÚS PÉREZ Y ADRIÁN

Bajada al Puerto de Santo Domingo
38787 Garafia (Santa Cruz de Tenerife)
☎: +34 618 309 374
tagalguen@hotmail.com

PRAXIS VINO DE PASAS B
malvasía, listán blanco, gual, marmajuelo.

90 Colour: light mahogany. Nose: powerfull, floral, honeyed notes, candied fruit, fragrant herbs. Palate: flavourful, sweet, fresh, fruity, good acidity, long, roasted-coffee afterpalate:.

CASTILLA Y LEÓN

BODEGAS ARZUAGA NAVARRO

Ctra. N-122, Km. 325
47350 Quintanilla de Onésimo (Valladolid)
☎: +34 983 681 146 - Fax: +34 983 681 147
bodeg@arzuaganavarro.com
www.arzuaganavarro.com

FAN D. ORO 2010 BFB
100% chardonnay.

88 Colour: bright yellow. Nose: powerfull, ripe fruit, sweet spices, fragrant herbs, honeyed notes, toasty. Palate: smoky afterpalate:, flavourful, good acidity.

BODEGA ELÍAS MORA

Juan Mora, s/n
47530 San Román de Hornija (Valladolid)
☎: +34 983 784 029 - Fax: +34 983 784 190
info@bodegaseliasmora.com
www.bodegaseliasmora.com

DULCE BENAVIDES S/C
tinta de Toro uvas pasas.

89 Colour: cherry, garnet rim. Nose: scrubland, expressive, candied fruit. Palate: balanced, sweet, fruity, good acidity. Personality.

BODEGAS COPABOCA

N-122, Km. 407
47114 Torrecilla de la Abadesa (Valladolid)
☎: +34 983 395 655 - Fax: +34 983 307 729
copaboca@copaboca.com
www.copaboca.com

SECRET MOMENT FRIZZANTE MOSTO PARCIALMENTE FERMENTADO B
100% verdejo.

84

BODEGAS MARCOS MIÑAMBRES

Camino de Pobladura, s/n
24234 Villamañán (León)
☎: +34 987 767 038
satvined@picos.com

M. MIÑAMBRES ALBARÍN 2011 B
albarín.

87 Colour: bright straw. Nose: fresh, fresh fruit, white flowers, varietal. Palate: flavourful, fruity, good acidity, balanced.

DANIEL V. RAMOS (ZERBEROS FINCA)

Real de Abajo, 100
05110 El Barraco (Ávila)
☎: +34 687 410 952
dvrcru@gmail.com
winesdanielramosvinos.blogspot.com

ZERBEROS VINO PRECIOSO 2010 B
albillo.

90 Colour: bright golden. Nose: faded flowers, dry stone, earthy notes, ripe fruit. Palate: flavourful, spicy, long, balanced.

ZERBEROS VIENTO ZEPHYROS 2009 B ROBLE
albillo, sauvignon blanc.

91 Colour: bright yellow. Nose: ripe fruit, dried herbs, spicy, creamy oak, mineral. Palate: spicy, long, good acidity, elegant.

LIBERALIA ENOLÓGICA

Camino del Palo, s/n
49800 Toro (Zamora)
☎: +34 980 692 571 - Fax: +34 980 692 571
liberalia@liberalia.es
www.liberalia.es

ARIANE 2010 ESP FERMENTADO EN BARRICA
verdejo, moscatel.

88 Colour: bright golden. Nose: ripe fruit, dried flowers, fragrant herbs, sweet spices, toasty. Palate: balanced, flavourful, powerful.

ARIANE 2010 ESP
92% verdejo, 8% moscatel.

85 Colour: bright yellow. Nose: fine lees, floral, ripe fruit, candied fruit, dried herbs. Palate: fine bead, light-bodied, fruity.

PÉREZ CARAMÉS

Peña Picón, s/n
24500 Villafranca del Bierzo (León)
☎: +34 987 540 197 - Fax: +34 987 540 314
enoturismo@perezcarames.com
www.perezcarames.com

CASAR DE SANTA INÉS 2010 T
68% merlot, 30% pinot noir, 2% tempranillo.

83

RUDELES

Trasterrera, 10
42345 Peñalba de San Esteban (Soria)
☎: +34 618 644 633 - Fax: +34 975 350 582
jmartin@rudeles.com
www.rudeles.com

VALDEBONITA 2011 B
albillo.

85 Colour: bright straw. Nose: candied fruit, white flowers, scrubland. Palate: flavourful, ripe fruit, fine bitter notes.

SEÑORÍO DE VALDESNEROS

Avda. La Paz, 4
34230 Torquemada (Palencia)
☎: +34 979 800 545 - Fax: +34 979 800 545
sv@bodegasvaldesneros.com
www.bodegasvaldesneros.com

AMANTIA 2010 TC
tempranillo.

87 Colour: pale ruby, brick rim edge. Nose: fruit liqueur notes, sweet spices, creamy oak, dry nuts. Palate: powerful, flavourful, spicy, spirituous.

CASTILLA-LA MANCHA

BODEGAS ISLA

Nuestra Señora de la Paz, 9
13210 Villarta San Juan (Ciudad Real)
☎: +34 926 640 004 - Fax: +34 926 640 004
b.isla@terra.es
www.bodegasisla.com

ALTO GRANDE T

75

BODEGAS TORRES FILOSO

Ctra. San Clemente, Km. 3
02600 Villarrobledo (Albacete)
☎: +34 967 144 426 - Fax: +34 967 146 419
bodega@torresfiloso.com
www.torresfiloso.com

AD PATER 2010 T
tempranillo, cabernet sauvignon, syrah.

82

JUAN JOSÉ 2009 T
tempranillo, cabernet sauvignon.

83

ARBOLES DE CASTILLEJO T
cabernet sauvignon, syrah.

81

BODEGAS Y VIÑEDOS CASTIBLANQUE

Isaac Peral, 19
13610 Campo de Criptana (Ciudad Real)
☎: +34 926 589 147 - Fax: +34 926 589 148
info@bodegascastiblanque.com
www.bodegascastiblanque.com

SOLAMENTE 2011 B
60% airén, 40% verdejo.

84

SOLAMENTE 2011 RD
100% syrah.

86 Colour: rose, purple rim. Nose: powerfull, ripe fruit, red berry notes, floral, lactic notes. Palate: , powerful, fruity, fresh.

SOLAMENTE 2011 T
50% tempranillo, 50% syrah.

84

LAGAR DE ENSANCHA T
60% tempranillo, 25% garnacha, 15% syrah.

85 Colour: cherry, purple rim. Nose: fresh fruit, red berry notes, floral, balsamic herbs. Palate: flavourful, fruity, good acidity.

EL PROGRESO SOCIEDAD COOP. CLM

Avda. de la Virgen, 89
13670 Villarubia de los Ojos (Ciudad Real)
☎: +34 926 896 088 - Fax: +34 926 896 135
administracion@bodegaselprogreso.com
www.bodegaselprogreso.com

VIÑA XETAR MOSTO PARCIALMENTE FERMENTADO 2011 T
100% tempranillo.

84

VINOS COLOMAN

Goya, 17
13620 Pedro Muñoz (Ciudad Real)
☎: +34 926 586 410 - Fax: +34 926 586 656
coloman@satcoloman.com
www.satcoloman.com

MANCHEGAL 2011 T
tempranillo.

81

MANCHEGAL ROSADO AGUJA 2011 RD
100% tempranillo.

85 Colour: raspberry rose. Nose: floral, candied fruit, fresh, medium intensity. Palate: light-bodied, fresh, flavourful, sweet.

CATALUNYA

AVINYÓ CAVAS

Masia Can Fontanals
08793 Avinyonet del Penedès (Barcelona)
☎: +34 938 970 055 - Fax: +34 938 970 691
avinyo@avinyo.com
www.avinyo.com

ESTEVE VÍA BLANC DE NOIRS 2011 B
merlot blanc.

88 Colour: bright straw. Nose: fresh, fresh fruit, white flowers, expressive. Palate: flavourful, fruity, good acidity, balanced.

PETILLANT BLANC 2011 B
moscatel de frontignan, macabeo, xarel.lo.

86 Colour: bright straw. Nose: fresh fruit, white flowers, fragrant herbs. Palate: fresh, correct, fine bitter notes.

ESTEVE VÍA ROSA TRANQUILO 2011 RD
merlot.

84

ESTEVE VÍA NEGRE D'ANYADA T
merlot, cabernet sauvignon.

84

CARRIEL DELS VILARS

Mas Can Carriel Els Vilars
17753 Espolla (Girona)
☎: +34 972 563 335
carrieldelsvilars@hotmail.com

CARRIEL DELS VILARS 2010 B
45% macabeo, 30% xarel.lo, 20% parellada, 5% chardonnay.

84

CARRIEL DELS VILARS 2011 T
50% garnacha, 30% syrah, 15% cabernet sauvignon, 5% samsó.

90 Colour: cherry, garnet rim. Nose: fruit preserve, scrubland, damp earth, mineral, petrol notes, wet leather. Palate: fresh, fruity, flavourful, round tannins.

CARRIEL DELS VILARS 2007 T
40% garnacha, 35% syrah, 20% cabernet sauvignon, 5% samsó.

88 Colour: bright cherry, orangey edge. Nose: fruit preserve, scrubland, dry stone, earthy notes, cigar, wet leather, waxy notes, aged wood nuances. Palate: flavourful, good acidity, long, spicy.

ESCUMÒS D'ANYADA 2009 ESP
macabeo, xarel.lo, parellada, garnacha blanca.

90 Colour: bright golden. Nose: dry nuts, fragrant herbs, lees reduction notes, pattiserie, citrus fruit. Palate: powerful, flavourful, good acidity, fine bitter notes.

ESCUMÒS RESERVA ANYADA 2001 ESP
macabeo, xarel.lo, parellada, garnacha blanca.

93 Colour: bright golden. Nose: dry nuts, complex, lees reduction notes, aged wood nuances, faded flowers, toasty. Palate: powerful, flavourful, good acidity, fine bead, fine bitter notes. Personality.

MISTELA DE CHARDONNAY 2011 MISTELA ROBLE
100% chardonnay.

88 Colour: old gold, amber rim. Nose: ripe fruit, pattiserie, varnish, fragrant herbs, expressive. Palate: spirituous, spicy, ripe fruit, flavourful.

CAVAS DEL AMPURDÁN

Pza. del Carme, 1
17491 Perelada (Girona)
☎: +34 972 538 011 - Fax: +34 972 538 277
perelada@castilloperelada.com
www.blancpescador.com

CRESTA AZUL S/C B
50% moscatel, 30% macabeo, 10% xarel.lo, 10% parellada.

84

BLANC PESCADOR VINO DE AGUJA S/C B
50% macabeo, 25% parellada, 25% xarel.lo.

82

CRESTA ROSA VINO DE AGUJA S/C RD
40% tempranillo, 40% cariñena, 20% garnacha.

83

BLANC PESCADOR PREMIUM S/C BLANCO DE AGUJA
67% xarel.lo, 33% chardonnay.

86 Colour: bright yellow. Nose: ripe fruit, dry nuts, faded flowers, expressive. Palate: flavourful, ripe fruit.

CRESTA ROSA PREMIUM S/C ROSADO DE AGUJA
85% pinot noir, 15% syrah.

86 Colour: rose, purple rim. Nose: balanced, red berry notes, ripe fruit, rose petals. Palate: flavourful, fruity, easy to drink, good acidity.

PESCADOR ROSÉ ROSADO DE AGUJA
60% trepat, 20% garnacha, 20% merlot.

84

CELLER RAMÓN SADURNI

Can Sadurní
08799 Olerdola (Barcelona)
☎: +34 666 771 308
auladelvi@hotmail.com

RR SADURNÍ 2011 B
xarel.lo.

85 Colour: bright straw. Nose: medium intensity, dried flowers, dried herbs, ripe fruit. Palate: good finish, easy to drink.

RR SADURNÍ 2011 RD
merlot.

84

RR SADURNÍ 2007 TR
merlot, cabernet sauvignon.

85 Colour: cherry, garnet rim. Nose: spicy, creamy oak, toasty, fruit preserve. Palate: powerful, flavourful, spicy.

CELLER SORT DEL CASTELL

Ctra. Reus - El Morell, km. 7,8
43760 El Morell (Tarragona)
☎: +34 977 840 655 - Fax: +34 977 842 146
vermut@vermutyzaguirre.com
www.vermutyzaguirre.com

ALTARIS VINO DE MISA DULCE NATURAL

82

ECCOCIWINE

GIV 6701, km. 4
17462 San Martí Vell (Girona)
☎: +34 616 863 209
info@eccociwine.com
www.eccociwine.com

ECCOCI BLANCO 2010 B
viognier, roussanne, petit manseng.

87 Colour: bright straw. Nose: ripe fruit, faded flowers, earthy notes, fragrant herbs. Palate: flavourful, correct, ripe fruit, good acidity.

ECCOCI 2011 RD
petit verdot.

87 Colour: onion pink. Nose: ripe fruit, faded flowers, dried herbs, mineral, citrus fruit. Palate: balsamic, fruity, light-bodied.

ECCOMI TINTO SUPER PREMIUM 2009 TC
merlot, cabernet franc, marselan.

92 Colour: cherry, garnet rim. Nose: red berry notes, ripe fruit, balsamic herbs, mineral, creamy oak. Palate: long, rich, flavourful, toasty, elegant.

ECCOCI TINTO PREMIUM 2009 T
merlot, cabernet franc, marselan.

90 Colour: cherry, garnet rim. Nose: ripe fruit, scrubland, earthy notes, fine reductive notes, spicy. Palate: flavourful, balsamic, balanced.

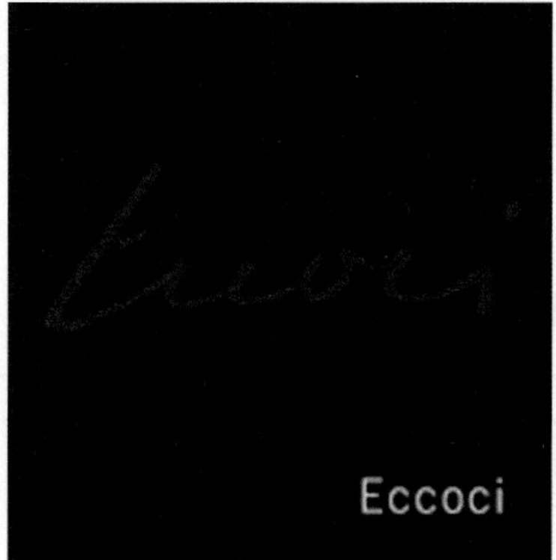

JOAN SARDÀ

Ctra. Vilafranca a St. Jaume dels Domenys, Km. 8,1
08732 Castellvi de la Marca (Barcelona)
☎: +34 937 720 900 - Fax: +34 937 721 495
joansarda@joansarda.com
www.joansarda.com

BLANC DE SALOBRE BLANCO DULCE
garnacha, moscatel, macabeo, pedro ximénez.

88 Colour: coppery red. Nose: woody, varnish, sweet spices, creamy oak, dry nuts, ripe fruit. Palate: powerful, flavourful, spicy, long.

KAIROS

Dels Nostris, 26-A
08185 Lliça de Vall (Barcelona)
☎: +34 938 436 061 - Fax: +34 938 439 671
kairos@vinodegaraje.com
www.kairosvino.com

KAIROS 2011 T
100% tempranillo.

90 Colour: cherry, garnet rim. Nose: earthy notes, mineral, floral, ripe fruit, spicy. Palate: powerful, flavourful, balanced, long.

LAVINYETA

Ctra. de Mollet de Peralada a Masarac, s/n
17752 Mollet de Peralada (Girona)
☎: +34 647 748 809 - Fax: +34 972 505 323
celler@lavinyeta.es
www.lavinyeta.es

SERENO 2009 SOLERA
100% garnacha roja.

80

LOXAREL

Can Mayol, s/n
08735 Vilobí del Penedès (Barcelona)
☎: +34 938 978 001 - Fax: +34 938 978 111
loxarel@loxarel.com
www.loxarel.com

LXV 2011 B
100% xarel.lo vermell.

88 Colour: coppery red. Nose: faded flowers, ripe fruit, fragrant herbs. Palate: fine bitter notes, powerful, flavourful, fruity.

MAS COMTAL

Mas Comtal, 1
08793 Avinyonet del Penedès (Barcelona)
☎: +34 938 970 052 - Fax: +34 938 970 591
mascomtal@mascomtal.com
www.mascomtal.com

GRAN ANGULAR - IN.M 100% 2010 B
Incroccio manzoni.

92 Colour: bright straw. Nose: fresh, white flowers, fragrant herbs, mineral. Palate: flavourful, fruity, good acidity, balanced. Personality.

GRAN ANGULAR INCROCIO MANZONI CHARDONNAY 2010 B
80% Incroccio manzoni, 20% chardonnay.

90 Colour: bright yellow. Nose: fine lees, citrus fruit, dried herbs, floral, mineral. Palate: good acidity, balanced, flavourful, long, complex.

PIZZICATO FRIZZANT DE MUSCAT 2011 RD
muscato de Hamburgo.

87 Colour: onion pink. Nose: candied fruit, dried flowers, fragrant herbs, red berry notes. Palate: light-bodied, flavourful, good acidity.

LYRIC LICOROSO
merlot.

92 Colour: light mahogany. Nose: varnish, caramel, spicy, dark chocolate, candied fruit, dry nuts. Palate: powerful, flavourful, long, spicy, balanced

OLIVER CONTI

Puignau, s/n
17550 Capmany (Girona)
☎: +34 972 193 161 - Fax: +34 972 193 040
dolors@oliverconti.com
www.oliverconti.com

OLIVER CONTI MARTA B
100% gewürztraminer.

87 Colour: bright yellow. Nose: candied fruit, honeyed notes, floral, sweet spices. Palate: rich, light-bodied, fruity.

PARDAS

Finca Can Comas, s/n
08775 Torrelavit (Barcelona)
☎: +34 938 995 005
pardas@cancomas.com
www.pardas.net

PARDAS SUMOLL ROSAT 2011 RD
100% sumoll.

89 Colour: rose, purple rim. Nose: powerfull, ripe fruit, red berry notes, floral, expressive. Palate: fleshy, powerful, fruity, fresh.

VINS DE TALLER

Nou, 5
17469 Siurana d'Empordà (Girona)
☎: +34 972 525 578 - Fax: +34 934 816 434
info@vinsdetaller.com
www.vinsdetaller.com

VINS DE TALLER VRM 2010 BFB
viognier, roussanne, marsanne, cortese.

90 Colour: bright yellow. Nose: ripe fruit, fine lees, earthy notes, fragrant herbs, sweet spices. Palate: rich, flavourful, long, toasty.

VINS DE TALLER GRIS 2011 RD
marselan, merlot.

89 Colour: light cherry. Nose: ripe fruit, wild herbs, mineral, balsamic herbs, lactic notes. Palate: powerful, flavourful, fresh, fruity.

VINS DE TALLER MM 2009 TC
merlot, marcelan.

90 Colour: cherry, garnet rim. Nose: fruit preserve, dry stone, earthy notes, spicy, cocoa bean, expressive. Palate: powerful, flavourful, complex, long.

COMUNIDAD VALENCIANA

BODEGA MAS L'ALTET

Mas L'Altet Partida de la Creu, s/n
03838 Alfafara (Alicante)
☎: +34 609 759 708
nina@bodegamaslaltet.com
www.bodegamaslaltet.com

AVI DE MAS L'ALTET 2010 T
58% syrah, 25% cabernet sauvignon, 13% garnacha, 4% merlot.

90 Colour: deep cherry, purple rim. Nose: powerfull, ripe fruit, fruit preserve, scrubland, spicy. Palate: concentrated, fruity.

AVI DE MAS L'ALTET 2009 T
65% syrah, 26% cabernet sauvignon, 5% merlot, 4% garnacha.

91 Colour: cherry, garnet rim. Nose: balanced, ripe fruit, cocoa bean, spicy, wild herbs. Palate: ripe fruit, long, round tannins.

LUKA 2008 T
65% syrah, 26% cabernet sauvignon, 5% merlot, 4% garnacha.

91 Colour: cherry, garnet rim. Nose: spicy, creamy oak, toasty, characterful, mineral. Palate: powerful, flavourful, toasty, round tannins.

BODEGA VICENTE FLORS

Pda. Pou D'encalbo, s/n
12118 Les Useres (Castellón)
☎: +34 671 618 851
bodega@bodegaflors.com
www.bodegaflors.com

FLOR DE CLOTÀS 2009 T
tempranillo, cabernet sauvignon.

87 Colour: cherry, garnet rim. Nose: ripe fruit, scrubland, sweet spices. Palate: correct, warm, flavourful.

CLOTÀS 2008 T
tempranillo.

88 Colour: cherry, garnet rim. Nose: ripe fruit, spicy, creamy oak, complex. Palate: powerful, flavourful, toasty, round tannins.

CELLER LA MUNTANYA

Compositor Paco Esteve, 13
03830 Muro de l'Alcoi (Alicante)
☎: +34 607 902 235 - Fax: +34 965 531 248
info@cellerlamuntanya.com
www.cellerlamuntanya.com

LLIURE ALBIR 2010 B
50% malvasía, 35% garnacha blanca, 15% verdil.

92 Colour: bright yellow. Nose: powerfull, ripe fruit, sweet spices, creamy oak, fragrant herbs, dry nuts. Palate: rich, smoky afterpalate:, flavourful, fresh, good acidity, long.

ALBIR 2010 B
50% malvasía, 25% merseguera, 15% macabeo, 10% verdil.

88 Colour: bright straw. Nose: mineral, citrus fruit, ripe fruit, balsamic herbs, creamy oak. Palate: spicy, flavourful, long.

CELLER LA MUNTANYA DOLÇ NATURAL 2009 B
100% malvasía.

92 Colour: golden. Nose: powerfull, honeyed notes, candied fruit, fragrant herbs, citrus fruit. Palate: flavourful, sweet, fresh, fruity, good acidity, long.

MINIFUNDI 2010 T
50% monastrell, 25% giró, 25% garnacha tintorera.

89 Colour: bright cherry. Nose: ripe fruit, spicy, wild herbs. Palate: flavourful, fruity, toasty, round tannins.

CELLER LA MUNTANYA NEGRE 2009 T
65% monastrell, 10% giró, 10% garnacha tintorera, 8% bobal, 7% bonicaire.

92 Colour: bright cherry, garnet rim. Nose: elegant, balanced, scrubland, spicy, mineral, dark chocolate. Palate: good structure, flavourful, round tannins.

PAQUITO EL CHOCOLATERO 2009 T
50% monastrell, 25% giró, 25% garnacha tintorera.

87 Colour: cherry, garnet rim. Nose: powerfull, warm, ripe fruit, spicy. Palate: flavourful, correct, ripe fruit, good finish.

ALMOROIG 2007 T
69% monastrell, 16% giró, 15% garnacha tintorera.

91 Colour: deep cherry, garnet rim. Nose: scrubland, balanced, complex, expressive. Palate: good structure, flavourful, balanced, fine bitter notes.

BRUNO MURCIANO & DAVID SAMPEDRO GIL

8 Avenida Banda De Musica El Angel
46315 Caudete de las Fuentes (Valencia)
☎: +34 962 319 096
bru.murciano@yahoo.es

LA MALKERIDA 100% BOBAL 2011 T
100% bobal.

90 Colour: cherry, purple rim. Nose: expressive, red berry notes, floral, balsamic herbs, mineral. Palate: flavourful, fruity, good acidity, round tannins.

EL SUEÑO DE BRUNO 2010 T
100% bobal.

88 Colour: cherry, garnet rim. Nose: ripe fruit, balsamic herbs, spicy, creamy oak. Palate: powerful, flavourful, correct, toasty.

MAS DE LA REAL DE SELLA

Avda. País Valencia 8, Bajo
03570 Villajoyosa (Alicante)
☎: +34 699 308 250 - Fax: +34 965 890 819
info@masdelarealdesella.es
www.masdelarealdesella.es

MAS DE SELLA VINO DE AUTOR 2008 T
cabernet sauvignon, cabernet franc, garnacha tintorera, syrah, marselan.

90 Colour: cherry, garnet rim. Nose: ripe fruit, spicy, creamy oak, toasty, complex, earthy notes. Palate: powerful, flavourful, toasty, round tannins.

MUSTIGUILLO VIÑEDOS Y BODEGA

Ctra. N-330, km 196,5 El Terrerazo
46300 Utiel (Valencia)
☎: +34 962 168 260 - Fax: +34 962 168 259
info@bodegamustiguillo.com
www.bodegamustiguillo.com

MESTIZAJE 2010 B
63% merseguera, 30% viognier, 7% malvasía.

93 Colour: bright straw. Nose: expressive, characterful, lactic notes, white flowers, ripe fruit. Palate: flavourful, fine bitter notes, long, ripe fruit.

MESTIZAJE 2011 T

91 Colour: cherry, purple rim. Nose: expressive, fresh fruit, red berry notes, floral, mineral, lactic notes. Palate: flavourful, fruity, good acidity, round tannins.

TRESGE WINERY

Ctra. de Picaña, 18 Puerta 10
46200 Paiporta (Valencia)
☎: +34 961 182 737
info@3gwineconsulting.com
www.3gwineconsulting.com

GRATIAS ROSÉ 2010 RD
100% bobal.

86 Colour: rose, bright. Nose: fruit preserve, dried herbs, floral. Palate: powerful, rich, flavourful.

GRATIAS MÁXIMAS 2009 T
100% bobal.

85 Colour: cherry, garnet rim. Nose: fruit liqueur notes, scrubland, earthy notes, spicy. Palate: powerful, flavourful, long.

VERA DE ESTENAS

Junto N-III, km. 266 - Paraje La Cabeuzela
46300 Utiel (Valencia)
☎: +34 962 171 141 - Fax: +34 962 174 352
estenas@estenas.es
www.estenas.es

CASA DON ÁNGEL MALBEC 7-8 T
malbec.

92 Colour: cherry, garnet rim. Nose: spicy, creamy oak, ripe fruit. Palate: powerful, flavourful, toasty, round tannins.

VINS DEL COMTAT

Turballos, 1 - 3
03820 Cocentaina (Alicante)
☎: +34 965 593 194 - Fax: +34 965 593 590
info@vinsdelcomtat.com
www.vinsdelcomtat.com

VIOGNIER DE VINS DEL COMTAT 2011 B
100% viognier.

87 Colour: bright straw. Nose: powerfull, fresh fruit, citrus fruit, white flowers. Palate: flavourful, fruity, fresh, ripe fruit.

VIÑEDO Y BODEGA HERETAT DE CESILIA

Paraje Alcaydias, 4
03660 Novelda (Alicante)
☎: +34 965 605 385 - Fax: +34 965 604 763
administracion@heretatdecesilia.com
www.heretatdecesilia.com

AZAL 2011 B
33% sauvignon blanc, 33% macabeo, 33% albariño.

85 Colour: bright straw. Nose: fresh, white flowers, ripe fruit, dried herbs. Palate: flavourful, fruity, good acidity.

AD GAUDE HERETAT 2009 BC
85% albariño, 15% loureiro.

88 Colour: bright yellow. Nose: powerfull, ripe fruit, sweet spices, creamy oak, fragrant herbs. Palate: rich, flavourful, fresh, good acidity.

AD 2011 T
75% syrah, 15% cabernet sauvignon, 10% petit verdot.

87 Colour: cherry, purple rim. Nose: red berry notes, floral, balsamic herbs. Palate: flavourful, fruity, good acidity.

AD GAUDE 2006 T
70% monastrell, 15% syrah, 15% petit verdot.

91 Colour: very deep cherry. Nose: spicy, ripe fruit, nose:tic coffee. Palate: flavourful, powerful, fine bitter notes, good acidity.

CARDENAL ÁLVAREZ 2007 TINTO
60% monastrell, 20% cabernet sauvignon, 20% petit verdot.

92 Colour: dark mahogany. Nose: dry nuts, acetaldehyde, dark chocolate, sweet spices, roasted coffee, dried fruit. Palate: powerful, flavourful, complex, long, toasty, sweet.

VIÑEDOS CULTURALES

Plaza Constitución, 8 - 1º
03380 Bigastro (Alicante)
☎: +34 966 770 353 - Fax: +34 966 770 353
vinedosculturales@gmail.com
http://vinedosculturales.blogspot.com.es/

PARQUE NATURAL "EL CARRO" 2011 B
100% moscatel de alejandría.

93 Colour: bright straw. Nose: fresh, fresh fruit, white flowers, expressive. Palate: flavourful, fruity, good acidity, balanced.

PARQUE NATURAL "LA VIÑA DE SIMÓN" 2011 B
100% merseguera.

92 Colour: bright straw. Nose: spicy, candied fruit, ripe fruit, citrus fruit, violet drops, faded flowers. Palate: flavourful, sweetness, fine bitter notes.

VIÑEDOS Y BODEGAS MAYO CASANOVA

San Antonio, 90
12192 Vilafamés (Castellón)
☎: +34 964 329 312 - Fax: +34 964 329 312
mail@mayocasanova.com
www.mayocasanova.com

MAGNANIMVS VINO DE AUTOR 2009 T
cabernet sauvignon, merlot, syrah.

86 Colour: bright cherry. Nose: ripe fruit, sweet spices, creamy oak, roasted coffee. Palate: flavourful, fruity, toasty.

EXTREMADURA

SANTA MARTA VIRGEN

Cooperativa, s/n
06150 Santa Marta de los Barros (Badajoz)
☎: +34 924 690 218 - Fax: +34 924 690 043
info@bodegasantamarta.com
www.bodegasantamarta.com

CALAMÓN 2011 B
pardina.

83

CALAMÓN 2011 RD

84

GALICIA

COTO DE GOMARIZ

Barrio de Gomariz
32429 Leiro (Ourense)
☎: +34 671 641 982 - Fax: +34 988 488 174
gomariz@cotodegomariz.com
www.cotodegomariz.com

VX CUVÉE PRIMO 2007 T
sousón, caiño longo, caiño da Terra, carabuñeira, mencía.

93 Colour: very deep cherry. Nose: mineral, earthy notes, red berry notes, fruit expression, creamy oak, sweet spices. Palate: flavourful, powerful, ripe fruit, long, mineral.

ENVINATE

Gran Vía, 2 1ºC
27600 Sarría (Lugo)
☎: +34 682 207 160
asesoria.envinate@gmail.com

TINTA AMARELA 2011 T
100% Trincadeira preta.

93 Colour: bright cherry, purple rim. Nose: red berry notes, ripe fruit, expressive, balsamic herbs, toasty. Palate: full, flavourful, round tannins, balanced.

PUZZLE 2010 T
tempranillo, garnacha, listán negro, touriga.

93 Colour: dark-red cherry, garnet rim. Nose: fruit preserve, sweet spices, balsamic herbs, dark chocolate. Palate: rich, round tannins, long, toasty.

DAS LOUSAS MENCÍA 2010 T
mencía.

91 Colour: cherry, purple rim. Nose: red berry notes, medium intensity, dry stone, spicy. Palate: fruity, flavourful, complex, long, spicy.

PEDRO MANUEL RODRÍGUEZ PÉREZ

Sanmil, 43 - Santa Cruz de Brosmos
27425 Sober (Lugo)
☎: +34 982 152 508 - Fax: +34 982 402 000
adegasguimaro@gmail.com

GBG 2011 B
80% godello, 15% treixadura, 5% dona blanca.

91 Colour: bright yellow. Nose: ripe fruit, faded flowers, sweet spices, dried herbs, earthy notes. Palate: rich, powerful, flavourful, long.

ILLES BALEARS

VINS TONI GELABERT

Camí dels Horts de Llodrá Km. 1,3
07500 Manacor (Illes Balears)
☎: +34 610 789 531
info@vinstonigelabert.com
www.vinstonigelabert.com

TORRE DES CANONGE BLANC 2010 B
giró.

90 Colour: bright yellow. Nose: balanced, expressive, candied fruit, dried herbs, sweet spices. Palate: fruity, rich, toasty.

MADRID

VALQUEJIGOSO

Ctra, Villamanta - Méntrida, s/n
28610 Villamanta (Madrid)
☎: +34 650 492 390
aureliogarcia@valquejigoso.com
www.valquejigoso.com

VALQUEJIGOSO V2 2007 T
cabernet sauvignon, syrah, petit verdot, cabernet franc, merlot, negral.

94 Colour: very deep cherry. Nose: powerfull, ripe fruit, toasty, dark chocolate, mineral, earthy notes. Palate: flavourful, powerful, fine bitter notes, good acidity, round tannins.

MURCIA

CASA ROJO

Sánchez Picazo, 53
30332 Balsapintada (Murcia)
☎: +34 968 151 520 - Fax: +34 968 151 690
marketing@casarojo.com
www.casarojo.com

L'AURA 2011 B
chardonnay.

85 Colour: golden. Nose: powerfull, floral, candied fruit, fragrant herbs, tropical fruit. Palate: flavourful, sweet, fresh, fruity.

L'AURA 2011 RD
100% syrah.

84

AUTOR DE CASA ROJO 2005 TR
50% cabernet sauvignon, 30% syrah, 20% petit verdot.

85 Colour: pale ruby, brick rim edge. Nose: spicy, fine reductive notes, wet leather, aged wood nuances, fruit liqueur notes, varnish. Palate: spicy, long, flavourful, powerful.

NAVARRA

LA CALANDRIA. PURA GARNACHA

Camino de Aspra, s/n
31521 Murchante (Navarra)
☎: +34 630 904 327
luis@lacalandria.org
www.lacalandria.org

TIERGA 2010 T
100% garnacha.

92 Colour: cherry, purple rim. Nose: ripe fruit, wild herbs, creamy oak, dry stone. Palate: full, flavourful, fruity aftespalate:, long.

SPARKLING WINES-TRADITIONAL METHOD

All the wines included in this section are made by the so-called traditional method of a second fermentation in the bottle, the same one used in Cava –and Champagne– production, but in areas outside those ascribed to Cava or any other Spanish DO. They represent a tiny part of all the sparkling wines made in Spain and their figures and quality are understandably far away from those of Cava.

BODEGAS BARBADILLO

Luis de Eguilaz, 11
11540 Sanlúcar de Barrameda (Cádiz)
☎: +34 956 385 500 - Fax: +34 956 385 501
barbadillo@barbadillo.com
www.barbadillo.com

BARBADILLO BETA BR
palomino, chardonnay.

86 Colour: bright yellow. Nose: fine lees, dried flowers, candied fruit, fragrant herbs. Palate: light-bodied, fresh, fruity, easy to drink.

DOMINIO BUENAVISTA

Ctra. de Almería, s/n
18480 Ugíjar (Granada)
☎: +34 958 767 254 - Fax: +34 958 990 226
info@dominiobuenavista.com
www.dominiobuenavista.com

VELETA ROSADO BLANC DE NOIR S/C ESP
70% tempranillo, 30% garnacha.

83

VELETA BLANCO S/C ESP
80% vijariego blanco, 20% chardonnay.

78

LOBBAN WINES

Creueta, 24
08784 St. Jaume Sesoliveres (Barcelona)
☎: +34 667 551 695
info@lapamelita.com
www.lapamelita.com

LA ROSITA 2009 ROSADO ESPUMOSO
95% garnacha, 5% syrah.

81

LA PAMELITA 2006 TINTO ESPUMOSO
95% syrah, 5% garnacha.

80

PRADA A TOPE

La Iglesia, s/n
24546 Canedo (León)
☎: +34 987 563 366 - Fax: +34 987 567 000
info@pradaatope.es
www.pradaatope.es

XAMPRADA EXTRA BRUT 2007 RD
mencía, godello.

80

XAMPRADA 2007 ESP
godello, chardonnay.

83

XAMPRADA EXTRA BRUT 2009 EXTRA BRUT
godello, chardonnay.

81

XAMPRADA ROSADO 2007 SC
mencía, godello.

82

VIÑEDOS Y BODEGAS LA MAGDALENA

Ctra. La Roda, s/n
16611 Casas de Haro (Cuenca)
☎: +34 969 380 722 - Fax: +34 969 380 722
vinos@vegamoragona.com
www.vegamoragona.com

VEGA MORAGONA 2011 RD
bobal.

84

VEGA MORAGONA 2011 BN
macabeo, moscatel.

84

VEGA MORAGONA 2011 SS
macabeo, moscatel.

82

GLOSSARY and INDEXES

TERMINOLOGY RELATED TO COLOUR

AMBER. The first step in the oxidative ageing of sherry generoso wines, brandies, whiskies and rum, somewhere between yellow and coppery red.
BEADS. The slow rising string of bubbles in a sparkling wine.
BRICK RED. An orangey hue, similar to that of a brick, used to describe reds aged in bottle for more than 10 years or in barrel for longer than six.
BRILLIANT. Related to a young and neat wine.
CANDY CHERRY. This is used to define a colour lighter than a red but darker than a rosé.
CLEAN. Utterly clean, immaculate.
CLOUDY. Lacking clarity.
COPPERY. A reddish nuance that can be appreciated in whites aged in wood for a long period, generally amontillados and some palo cortados.
CHERRY. Commonly used to express red colour. It can take all sort of degrees from 'light' all the way to 'very dark' or almost 'black cherry'.
DARK. This often refers to a tone slightly lighter than 'deep' and synonymous to "medium-intensity".
DEEP. A red with a very dark colour, which hardly lets us see the bottom of the glass.
DULL. A wine lacking in liveliness, usually with an ochre hue.
GARNET RED. A common nuance in medium to light reds. If the wine is an intense cherry red it could have a garnet rim only if it comes from cooler regions; if it is more luminous and open than the violet rim of a dark wine, it generally would be a young wine.
GOLDEN. Gold in colour with yellow –predominantly– to reddish tones.
GLIMMER. A vague brilliance.
IODINE. A tone similar to iodine tincture stains (old gold and brownish) displayed by rancio and generoso wines have after their long oxidative ageing.
LIVELY. A reflection of the youth of a wine through bright, brilliant colours.
MAHOGANY. Describes the second stage of ageing in brandies, rum and generoso sherry (fortified) wines. A hue between brown and yellow displayed by wines when long aged.
OCHRE. Yellow-orangey hue, the last colour phase of a table wine, generally found in wines with a long oxidative ageing; it is a sign of their decline.
OILY. A wine that appears dense to the eye, usually sweet and with high alcohol content.
OLD GOLD. Gold colour with the brownish tones found in amontillados and a bit lighter than the mahogany nuance predominant in oloroso sherry.
ONION SKIN. A touch lighter than salmon colour.
OPAQUE. A wine with such depth of colour we cannot see the bottom of the glass. Generally found in very old pedro ximénez and therefore akin to caramelised notes.
OPEN. Very pale, not at all intense.
ORANGEY EDGE. Intermediate phase between a deep red and brick red found towards the rim in red wines of a medium age. It generally appears sooner in wines with higher alcohol content and it is also typical of wines made from pinot noir.
RASPBERRY. Sort of pinkish colour with a bluish rim, it is the optimal colour for rosé wines since it denotes freshness, youth and a good acidity.
RIM. Also known as 'edge', it refers to the lighter colour the wine displays at the edge of the oval when we hold the glass at 45°, as opposed to the 'core' or main body of colour right in the centre. If it is a young red, it will show normally violet or raspberry nuances; when slightly older, it will be a deeper red or garnet, and if has been in the bottle for more than five years it might be anything from ruby to tawny through brick red and orangey.
RUBY. Slightly orangey hue with a yellow nuance found in old wines that have lost part of their original cherry colour.
SALMON. A tone slightly redder than pink found in rosé wines with less acidity and more alcohol.
STEELY. Pale colour with metallic reflections (reminiscent of those from steel) found in some whites.
STRAW-COLOURED. This term should be understood as straw yellow, the colour found in the majority of young white wines, halfway between yellow and green. It can also be described as "lemony".

TERMINOLOGY RELATED TO AROMA

ACETONE. Very close notes to those of nail varnish, typical of very old eau de vie.
ALCOHOL. It is not a pejorative term for an excess of alcohol –in which case we would refer to it as burning–, but just a predominant, non-aggressive note.

ALDEHYDE. A sensory note of oxidized, slightly rancid alcohol, typical of old wines with high alcohol content that have undergone oxidative ageing.

ANIMAL. Not a positive note, generally the result of long storage in bottle, also referred to as 'wet dog' or 'wet hide' and normally associated with a lack of hygiene. If it is found in younger vintages, then it could be a symptom of "brett" (see brett).

ATTIC. An aroma associated with that of old dry wood and dust typical of attics, mainly found in fortified wines aged in wood and in very old wines aged for a long period in old barrels which happen to have also been bottled for more than ten years.

BALSAMIC. A trait usually associated to wood-aged wines in hot regions, where high temperatures accelerate their evolution. It also refers to the aroma of dry herbs such as eucalyptus and bay leaf, as well as incense and tar.

BLACK FRUIT. It refers to the sort of toasted aromas of very ripe grapes, those almost 'burnt skin' notes found in reds that have undergone a long vatting period in contact with the skins.

"BRETT". This is the abbreviation for a new term (brettanomyces) to describe an old problem: the aroma of stables, henhouse, and wet new leather generally found along with reductive off-odours in wines that have been in the bottle for more than ten years. These aromas were considered part of the sensory complexity of old wines and therefore tolerated. Nowadays, due to better olfactory research and more hygienic working conditions in the wineries, they are easily detected and considered more a defect. In addition, today brett is often found in younger wines as this particular bacteria or yeast usually develops better in wines with higher ph levels. The increase in the ph of wines is quite common these days due to global warming, riper grapes and the use of fertilizers over the past thirty-five years.

BROOM. An aroma reminiscent of Mediterranean shrubs, only a bit dryer.

CANDIED FRUIT. This is a sweet nuance, somewhere between toasted and jammy, which is found in whites with a long oxidative ageing and in some sweet white wines.

CAROB. Anybody who has chewed or smelt one of those beans cannot would easily recall its typical blend of sweetness and toasted notes, as well as the slightly rustic nuance. It is usually found in old brandy aged in soleras of pedro ximénez and in deep, concentrated wines made from very ripe grapes.

CEDAR. The somewhat perfumed aroma of cedar, a soft wood commonly found in Morocco.

CHARACTERFUL. Used to express the singularity of a wine above the rest. It may refer to winemaking, terroir or the peculiarities of its ageing.

CITRUS. An aroma reminiscent of lemon, orange and grapefruit.

CLASSIC RIOJA. A note named after the more traditional and popular style of Rioja, with predominantly woody notes (normally from very old wood) along with a typical character of sweet spices and occasionally candle wax nuances instead of fruit, given the oxidative character provided by long ageing periods.

CLEAR. A wine with no defects, neither in the nose nor in the palate.

CLOSED. A term to describe a faint or not properly developed nose. Almost always found in concentrated wines from a good vintage, which evolve very slowly in the bottle, but it can also be found in wines recently bottled.

COCOA. Delicate, slightly toasted aroma found in wines aged in wood for a moderately long time that have evolved very well in the bottle.

COMPLEX. A wine abundant in aromas and flavours related either to grape variety, soil or ageing, although none of those features is particularly prominent.

CREAMY. Aroma of finely toasted oak (usually French) with notes of caramelised vanilla.

DATES. A sweet aroma with hints of dates and a raisiny nuance.

EARTHY. An aroma somewhere between clay and dust typical of red wines made from ripe grapes and with high alcohol content. It can also refer in some wines to a mineral nuance.

ELEGANT. A harmonious combination of fine, somewhat restrained aromatic notes related to perfumed wood, and a light, pleasantly balanced richness or complexity (see complex).

ETHEREAL. This is used to describe spirits, fortified wines and wines with a certain intensity of alcohol in their oxidative evolution; the strength of the alcohol reveals the rancid-type aromas. It has a lot to do with age.

EVOLUTION NOTES. Generally used to describe wines aged prematurely by either oxygen or heat, e.g., a wine that has been left in a glass for several hours.

FINE. A synonym for elegant.

FINE LEES. This is an aroma between herbaceous and slightly toasty that is produced by the contact of the wine with the lees (dead yeasts cells) after the fermentation has taken place, a process called autolysis that helps to make the wine more complex and to give it a richer aroma.
FLOR. This is a pungent, saline aroma typically found in sherry wines, particularly fino, manzanilla and, to a lesser degree, amontillado. It is caused by a film-forming yeast known as 'flor' in Spanish (literally flower), which transfers to the wine its singular smell and flavour.
FLORAL. Reminiscent of the petals of certain flowers –such as roses and jasmine–noticeable in certain northern withes or in quality reds after a bottle-ageing spell that also delivers some spicy notes.
FRAGRANT HERBS. An aroma similar to soaps and perfumes made from lavender, rosemary, lemon, orange blossom or jasmine. It is found in white wines that undergo pre-fermentative cold skin maceration.
FRESH. A wine with lively aroma and hardly any alcohol expression.
FRESH FRUIT. These are fruity notes produced by a slow grape-ripening cycle typical of mild climates.
FRUIT EXPRESSION. Related to different flavours and aromas reminiscent of various fruits and fine herbs.
FRUITY. Fruit notes with a fine herbal character and even hints of green grass.
HERBACEOUS. A vague note of vine shoots, scrub and geranium leaf caused by an incomplete maturation of the grape skin.
INTENSE. A powerful aroma that can be immediately referred to as such when first nosing the wine.
IODINE. This refers to iodine tincture, a combination of the sweetish smell of alcohol, toasted notes, liniment and varnish or lacquer.
JAM. Typical notes of very ripe black fruit slightly caramelised by a slow oxidative ageing in oak barrels. Very similar to forest fruit jam (prunes, blackberries, blueberries, redcurrants, cherries…). Found in red wines –generally from southern regions– with a high concentration of fruit notes giving that they are made resorting to long vatting periods, which provide longer contact with the skins.
MACERATION. These are aromas similar to those produced during fermentation and that –logically– found in young wines.
MEDITERRANEAN. An aroma where various prominent notes (sweetness, alcohol, burning and raisiny notes, caramel…) produced by grapes grown in hot regions blend in to characterize the wines.
MINERAL NOTES. Used to describe wines that have a subtle nose with plenty of notes reminiscent of flint, slate, hot stones or dry sand.
MUSK. A term to describe the sweet and grapey notes typical of highly aromatic varieties such as moscatel, riesling and gewürztraminer.
ROASTED COFFEE. (See terms of taste).
SUBDUED FRUIT. It generally refers to aromas produced by a fast ripening of the grapes typical of warm climates.
NUTS. Notes generally found in white wines with oxidative ageing; the oxygen in the air gives rise to aromas and flavours reminiscent of nuts (bitter almond, hazelnut, walnut…). When ageing spells are longer and –most importantly– take place in older casks, there will appear notes that are closer to fruits like figs, dates and raisins.
ORANGE PEEL. Typical fruity aroma found in certain white wines with, above all, a vibrant spicy character.
ORGANIC NOTES. A way to define the fermentative aromas –essentially related to yeast– and typical of young white wines and also fortified generoso wines from the sherry region.
OVERRIPE FRUIT. An aroma typical of young wines that are already slightly oxidized and reminiscent of grape bunches with some signs of rot –noble or not–, or simply bruised or recently pressed grapes.
OXIDATIVE EVOLUTION. Notes related to the tendency of a wine to age by the action of oxygen that passes through the pores of the cask or barrel (micro-oxidation), or during racking.
PATISSERIE. An aroma between sweet and toasted with hints of caramelised sugar and vanilla typical of freshly baked cakes. It is found in wines –generally sweet– that have been aged in oak for a long time and it is caused by both oxidative evolution and the aromatic elements (mainly vanillin) found in oak.
PEAT. A slightly burnt aroma that occurs when the notes of ripe grapes blend in with the toasted aromas of new oak in wines with a high alcohol content.
PHENOLIC. A short and derivative way to describe polyphenols (a combination of the tannins and anthocyanins, vegetal elements of the grape), it describes aromas of grape skins macerated for a long time that yield notes somewhere between ink and a pressed bunch of grapes.
PORT. This is the sweet aroma of wine made from somewhat raisiny or overripe grapes and reminiscent of the vintage Ports made with a short oxidative ageing.

PUNGENT. A prominent aromatic note produced by the combination of alcohol, wood and flor notes and typical of –particularly– fino sherry wines.

RANCIO. This is not a defect but a note better known as "sherryfied" and brought about by oxidative ageing.

RED FRUIT. An aromatic note that refers to forest red fruits (blackberries, redcurrants, mulberries) as well as slightly unripe cherries and plums.

REDUCTION. A wine aroma caused by the lack of oxygen during long bottle ageing, which gives rise to notes like tobacco, old leather, vanilla, cinnamon, cocoa, attic, dust, etc.

REDUCTION OFF-ODOURS. This is a negative set of aromas, halfway between boiled cabbage and boiled eggs, produced by the lees in wines that have not been properly aerated or racked.

REDUCTIVE TANK OFF-ODOURS. A smell between metal and boiled fruit typical of wines stored in large vats at high temperatures. The sulphur added –probably in excess– combines with the wine and reduces its freshness and the expression of fruit notes. This phenomenon is largely found in the production of bulk wines.

RIPE GRAPE SKIN. The aroma that a very ripe grape gives off when squeezed, similar to that of ink or of ripe grape bunches just pressed.

SALINE. This is the note acquired by a fino that has aged in soleras under flor yeast.

SEASONED WOOD. It refers to notes that may appear in wines aged in barrel for a long period –more than four or five years– which have lost the fine toasted aromas and flavours of new oak.

SHRUB. An aroma typically herbal found in Mediterranean regions, a mixture of rosemary, thyme and other typically semi-arid herbs. It refers to the dry, herbaceous note found generally in white and red wines from warmer regions.

SOLERA. An aroma close to the damp, seasoned, aged aroma of an old bodega for oloroso wines.

SPICY. It refers to the most common household spices (pepper, cloves, cinnamon) that appear in wines that undergo long and slow oxidative ageing in oak casks or barrels.

SPIRITUOUS. Both a flavour and an olfactory feature related to high alcohol content but without burning sensations. It is an almost 'intellectual' term to define alcohol, since that product is nothing else but the "spirit of wine".

STEWED FRUIT. Notes of stewed or 'cooked' fruit appear in wines made from well-ripened –not overripe– grapes and are similar to those of jam.

TAR. The pitchy, petrolly aromas of very toasted wood, associated with concentrated red wines with lots of colour, structure and alcohol.

TERROIR. An aromatic note determined by the soil and climate and therefore with various nuances: mountain herbs, minerals, stones, etc.

TOASTED SUGAR. Sweet caramelised aromas.

TOFFEE. A note typical of the milk coffee creams (lactic and toasted nuances mixed together) and present in some crianza red wines.

TROPICAL NOTES. The sweet white fruit aromas present in white wines made from grapes that have ripened very quickly and lack acidity.

TRUFFLE. Similar note to that of a mixture of damp earth and mushrooms.

UNDERGROWTH. This is the aromatic nuance between damp earth, grass and fallen leaves found in well-assembled, wood-aged reds that have a certain fruity expression and good phenolic concentration.

VANILLA. A typical trait of wines –also fortified– aged in oak, thanks to the vanillin, an element contained in that type of wood.

VARIETAL EXPRESSION. This is the taste and aroma of the variety or varieties used to make the wine.

VARNISH. A typical smell found in very old or fortified wines due to the oxidation of the alcohol after a long wood-ageing period. The varnished-wood note is similar to the aroma of eau de vie or spirits aged in wood.

VARNISHED WOOD. A sharp note typical of wines aged in wood for a long period, during which the alcohol oxidises and gives off an aroma of acetone, wood or nail varnish.

VISCOUS. The sweet taste and aromatic expression of wines with high alcohol content.

VOLATILE. A note characteristic of wines with high volatile acidity, i.e., just the first sign of them turning into vinegar. It is typical of poorly stabilized young wines or aged wines either with a high alcohol content or that have taken on this note during the slow oxidative wood-ageing phase, although we should remember it is a positive trait in the case of generoso wines.

WINE PRESS. The aroma of the vegetal parts of the grape aft er fermentation, vaguely reminiscent of pomace brandy, grapeskins and ink.

WITHERED FLOWERS. This is a sort of 'toasty' nuance typical of good champagnes made with a high percentage of pinot noir and some cavas which have aged perfectly in the bottle and on their lees for a long time.

WOODY. It describes an excess of notes of wood in a wine. The reason could be either a too long ageing period or the wine's lack of structure.

YEASTY. The dry aroma of bread yeast that can be perceived in young cavas or champagnes, or wines that have just been bottled.

TERMINOLOGY RELATED TO THE PALATE

ALCOHOL. A gentle, even sweet note of fine spirits; it is not a defect.

ALCOHOLIC EDGES. A slight excess of alcohol perceived on the tongue, but which does not affect the overall appreciation of the wine.

AMPLE. A term used to describe richness. It is a sensation generally experienced on the attack.

BITTER. A slight, non-aggressive note of bitterness, often found in some sherry wines (finos, amontillados) and the white wines from Rueda; it should not be regarded as a negative feature, quite on the contrary, it helps to counterbalance soft or slightly sweet notes.

CARAMELISED. A very sweet and toasted note typical of some unctuous wines aged in oloroso or pedro ximénez casks.

DENSE. This is related to the body of the wine, a thick sensation on the palate.

FATNESS. "Gordo" (fat) is the adjective used in Jerez to describe a wine with good body; it is the antonym of "fino" (light).

FLABBY. Used to describe a wine low in acidity that lacks freshness.

FLAVOURFUL. A pronounced and pleasant sensation on the palate produced by the combination of various sweet nuances.

FULL. A term used to describe volume, richness, some sweetness and round tannins; that is, a wine with a fleshy character and an almost fat palate.

LIGHT. The opposite of meaty, dense or concentrated; i.e., a wino with littlo body.

LONG. This refers to the persistence of the flavour after the wine has been swallowed.

MEATY. A wine that has body, structure and which can almost literally be "chewed".

NOTES OF WOOD. Well-defined notes somewhere between woody and resin generally found in wines matured in younger casks.

OILY. This is the supple, pleasantly fat sensation produced by glycerine. It is more prominent in older wines –thanks to the decrease in acidity– or in certain varieties such as riesling, gewürztraminer, chardonnay, albariño and godello.

OXIDATIVE AGEING. It refers to the influence of the air in the evolution of wine. Depending on the level of oxygen in the air, oxidation will take place in wine to a greater or lesser extent. Oxidative ageing happens when the air comes in contact with the wine either during racking –which ages the wine faster– or through the pores of the wood.

PASTY. This is not a pejorative term, simply a very sweet and dense taste.

ROASTED COFFEE. The sweet and toasted note of caramelised sugar typically found in wines aged in oak barrels –generally burnt inside–, or else the taste of very ripe (sometimes even overripe) grapes.

ROUGH TANNINS. Just unripe tannins either from the wood or the grape skins.

ROUND. This is an expression commonly used to describe a wine without edges, supple, with volume and body.

SWEETENED. Related to sweetness, only with an artificial nuance.

SWEETNESS. A slightly sweet note that stands out in a wine with an overall dry or tannic character.

SOFT TANNINS. Both alcohol and adequately ripened grapes help to balance out the natural bitter character of the tannins. They are also referred to as fat or oily tannins.

TANNIC. This is term derived from tannin, a substance generally found in the skin of the grape and in the wood that yields a somewhat harsh, vegetal note. In wines, it displays a slightly harsh, sometimes even grainy texture.

UNCTUOUS. This refers to the fat, pleasant note found in sweet wines along with their somewhat sticky sweetness.

VELVETY. A smooth, pleasant note on the palate typical of great wines where the tannins and the alcohol have softened down during ageing.

VIGOROUS. A wine with high alcohol content.

WARM. The term speaks of alcohol in a more positive way.

WELL-BALANCED. A term that helps to define a good wine: none of the elements that are part of it (alcohol, acidity, dry extract, oak) is more prominent than the other, just pure balance.

C

D

W

X

Z

A

B

G

H

I

K

L

M

S

T